Contents

COMPLETE ADVANCED LEVEL MATHEMATICS

Statistics

Fiona McGill • Stewart McLennan • Jane Migliorini

STANLEY THORNES

First published in 2000 by
Stanley Thornes (Publishers) Ltd
Delta Place
27 Bath Road
Cheltenham
Glos GL53 7TH

A catalogue record for this book is available from the British Library.

ISBN 0 7487 3560 7

00 01 02 03 04 / 10 9 8 7 6 5 4 3 2

The publishers are grateful to the following for permission to use copyright material:
Robert Adams, letter to *The Times*, p1
ICI, photograph, p2

All other photographs, including cover, from STP Archive

Every effort has been made to contact copyright holders. The author and publishers apologise to anyone whose rights have been overlooked and will be happy to rectify any errors or omissions at the earliest opportunity.

Typeset by The Alden Group, Oxford
Printed and bound in Italy by STIGE, Turin

About the Authors

- **Fiona McGill** is Head of Mathematics in a Northamptonshire school. Fiona has extensive teaching and writing experience and was formerly an Assistant Examiner. She has previously developed published materials for Advanced Level.
- **Stewart McLennan** is Head of Mathematics in a Northamptonshire school. Stewart has a wide range of teaching and examining experience. He was formerly a Mathematics advisory teacher, an Assistant Examiner for Advanced Level and an External Moderator for coursework.
- **Jane Migliorini** teaches Mathematics in a Somerset school. Jane's previous teaching experience has involved her in the introduction of Statistics at GCSE. She has also previously developed resource support material for Advanced Level.

Examination Papers

We are grateful to the following awarding bodies for permission to reproduce questions from their past examination papers:

- Assessment and Qualifications Alliance (AQA), including Northern Examinations and Assessment Board (NEAB) and Associated Examining Board (AEB).
- The Edexcel Foundation, including University of London Examinations and Assessment Council (ULEAC).
- Oxford, Cambridge and RSA (OCR), including University of Cambridge Local Examinations Syndicate (UCLES), Oxford & Cambridge Schools Examination Board (OCSEB) and Mathematics in Education and Industry (MEI).
- Northern Ireland Council for the Curriculum, Examinations and Assessment (NICCEA).
- Welsh Joint Education Committee (WJEC).

All answers and worked solutions provided for examination questions are the responsibility of the authors.

Introduction

Complete Advanced Level Mathematics is an exciting new series of mathematics books, Teacher Resource Files and other support materials from **Stanley Thornes** for those studying at Advanced Level. It has been developed following an extensive period of research and consultation with a wide number of teachers, students and others. All the authors are experienced and practising teachers and, in some cases, Advanced Level Mathematics Examiners. Chapters have been trialled in schools and colleges. All the requirements for complete success in Advanced Level Mathematics are provided by this series.

This book covers all the requirements for **Statistics** from all the latest Advanced Level specifications and course requirements for AS and A-Level Mathematics, the new Subject Criteria and Subject Specifications. It will provide you with:

● Material that builds on work done at GCSE level, where appropriate.
● Comprehensive coverage and clear explanations of all Statistics topics and skills.
● Numerous exercises and worked examples with questions and clear diagrams.
● Precise and comprehensive teaching text with clear progression.
● Margin notes that provide supporting commentary on key topics, formulas and other aspects of the work.
● In text highlighted 'hints' to assist with important areas, such as specific calculations in worked examples and key formulas.
● A comprehensive list of formulas that students need to know, with chapter references, and a full index.

Chapters in this book contain a number of **key features**:

● **What you need to know** sections covering prerequisite knowledge for a chapter.
● **Review** sections with practice questions on what you need to know.
● **Worked Examples** and supporting commentary.
● **Technique** and **Contextual Exercises** to give thorough practice in all Statistics concept areas and skills.
● **Consolidation A** and **B Exercises**, which include actual examination questions, to build on the work in a chapter and provide practice in a variety of question types.
● **Applications and Activities** as a support to coursework.
● A **Summary** of all the key concepts covered.

Companion volumes for *Pure Mathematics* (0 7487 3558 5) and *Mechanics* (0 7487 3559 3) and a *Statistics Teacher Resource File* (0 7487 3563 1) are also available in this series.

1 Principles of Statistics

What is statistics?

Statistics and probability affect many areas of our everyday lives. For example calculating the number of beds required in your local hospital, or predicting the result of local or general elections. Daily, we are bombarded with statistics and data in many different forms. Statistics is a powerful science dealing with the collection and interpretation of quantitative data. Probability theory is a vital tool which is used to analyse data and classify a variety of population and sample data.

You are already familiar with several aspects of statistics, for example carrying out a survey, drawing bar charts and working out probabilities. These are some of the topics that you covered in GCSE mathematics.

Vital statistics

From Mr Robert Adams

Sir, There are roughly three million people in Wales. It may be estimated that 100 of them have no legs, and another 1,000 of them have only one leg. The remaining 2,998,900 persons have two legs. This makes a total in Wales of 5,998,800 legs, shared amongst all the inhabitants – an average of 1.9996 legs each. Thus, nearly everyone in Wales (99.96 per cent) has more than the average number of legs (letters, April 10, 11, 15, 17).

Yours faithfully,
ROBERT ADAMS (Fellow, Royal Statistical Society),
1 Rhyd-y-Penau Road, Cardiff.

Published in The Times

1.1 Mathematical Modelling

Mathematical modelling is a key aspect of working in statistics. Here is an example:

A company decides to launch a new type of fizzy drink. Initially they will have to find answers to many questions, such as:

● To whom will the drink appeal?

● In what type/size of container should it be sold?

● Is the taste acceptable?

● Will people be able to distinguish between its flavour and that of a rival product?

● How much are people prepared to pay for the product?

Here the problem is being **defined**.

The next stage is to **collect the data** necessary to answer these questions.

● A sample of people will be interviewed and asked what type of drink they buy, what flavours they like, and so on.

● Taste tests will be held, where people will be asked to rate a range of flavoured drinks.

● Possible bottle designs and shapes will be shown to a group of people and their views recorded.

The data must then be **analysed** using mathematical techniques. All the information, or data, will be used to try to answer the initial questions. For example:

- What proportion of the people who were interviewed preferred the new product?

- Do people like the colour of the packaging?

... and so forth.

Once the analysis has been carried out the results must be **interpreted**.

- Have the surveys and tests adequately answered the initial questions?

- Are there new questions that need to be answered?

- Has enough information been gathered to successfully launch the new drink?

Finally it is important to go back and review the outcome in relation to the original problem and decide if further analysis is required.

These steps can be shown in a flow chart which illustrates the cyclical nature of the modelling process.

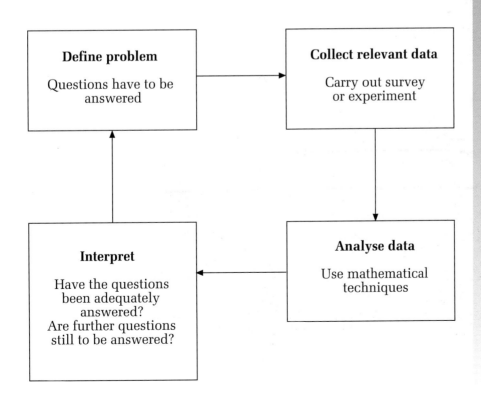

There are many situations where statistical modelling is used. Medical research is one of these.

Example

A doctor believes that eating porridge offers some protection against a heart attack. Suggest a mathematical model to test this hypothesis.

Solution

- **Define the problem:** Do people who eat porridge suffer fewer heart attacks than those who don't eat porridge?

- **Collect data:** The doctor chooses two distinct samples from the population. One sample consists of people who have not suffered a heart attack and another a group of people who have suffered heart attacks. The doctor then records the number of people in each group who eat porridge.

- **Analyse data:** Having collected the data the doctor carries out various mathematical calculations to determine whether the results are significant.

- **Interpret:** The doctor must consider whether valid conclusions based on the calculations can be drawn, or whether there are other factors that have influenced the results. The doctor will have to decide if it is necessary to gather further data to confirm the hypothesis.

The techniques listed above are those that you will carry out throughout your course and which will become more familiar to you as you work through many of the exercises, questions and activities in this book.

1.1 Mathematical Modelling Exercise

Contextual

1 You want to find out if red is the most popular car colour. What data do you need to collect? How would you go about collecting the data?

2 Describe how you would plan a holiday using the mathematical modelling process.

3 Think of a project you have carried out (possibly for GCSE maths), and explain how the modelling process can be applied to that task.

4 A student tells you that the 'Interpret' stage can be missed out. How would you convince him that he is wrong?

Applications and Activities

1 Suggest how to use mathematical modelling to investigate:

a   a day trip to London
b   a school theatre trip
c   comparison of two local supermarkets.

2 Carry out one, or more, of the activities in Question 1 using your models.

Summary

- The four stages in the modelling process are:

  1. defining the problem
  2. collecting the data
  3. analysing the data
  4. interpreting the data.

- You should be able to use the modelling process to analyse a real situation.

2 Collection of Data

What you need to know

● How to draw tally charts.

Review

1 For the following data sets, draw up a tally chart.

a Marks obtained by 30 pupils in a test:

6	3	5	6	0	1	8	5	6	7
4	4	3	1	0	2	2	7	9	7
5	4	6	6	8	0	8	8	10	6

b Number of chairs in each of 20 rooms of various houses:

| 8 | 2 | 4 | 2 | 2 | 2 | 3 | 8 | 5 | 4 |
| 7 | 6 | 3 | 5 | 7 | 2 | 7 | 1 | 3 | 5 |

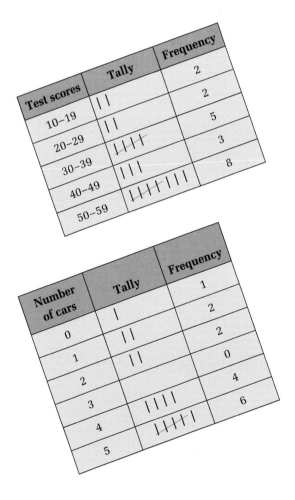

Test scores	Tally	Frequency
10–19	| |	2
20–29	| |	2
30–39	||||	5
40–49	|||	3
50–59	|||| |||	8

Number of cars	Tally	Frequency
0	|	1
1	||	2
2	||	2
3		0
4	||||	4
5	|||| |	6

2.1 Types of Data

Data is by definition a series of observations, measurements or facts but we must appreciate the importance of distinguishing between these different types of data if they are to be correctly analysed.

To illustrate the different types of data let us use the example of one individual's answers to a school questionnaire.

shoe size 5
height 150.5 cm
eye colour brown

In this example there are three different **variates**. The variates are not all of the same **type**. Shoe size and height are numerical variates and eye colour is a non-numerical variate. When a variate is numerical, the data is **quantitative** and when it is non-numerical, the data is **qualitative.** For qualitative variates such as eye colour, we use **non-numerical descriptors** to record different observations.

A variate is something we observe or measure.

Red and blue are examples of non-numerical descriptors.

Example 1

State whether each of the following variates is quantitative or qualitative:

a   weight
b   type of car
c   distance travelled each day
d   town of birth.

Solution
a   Weight is a quantitative variate and could be measured in kilograms.
b   Type of car is a qualitative variate, for example saloon, hatchback or estate.
c   Distance travelled each day is a quantitative variate and could be measured in kilometres or miles.
d   Town of birth is a qualitative variate, for example Bath or Chester.

Look at the numerical data in the school questionnaire again. There are two different types of quantitative data.

shoe size 5
height 150.5 cm

Shoe size, which can be either a whole number or a half size, is called **discrete** data, whereas height which can take any value within a certain range is called **continuous** data.

Example 2

State whether each of the following quantitative variates is discrete or continuous:

a   time taken to run 100 m
b   daily attendance at a cinema
c   temperature on a particular day
d   cost in £ and p
e   weight of a new-born baby
f   height of St Paul's Cathedral
g   pulse rate
h   blood pressure.

Solution

a   Time taken to run 100 m is continuous.
b   Daily attendance at a cinema is discrete.
c   Temperature on a particular day is continuous.
d   Cost in £ and p is discrete.
e   Weight is continuous.
f   Height of St Paul's Cathedral is continuous.
g   Pulse rate is discrete.
h   Blood pressure is continuous.

Sources of data

Data can be acquired in two main ways:

● by using records already in existence

● by carrying out original research.

Data already collected for some other purpose is known as **secondary data** and data acquired by original research is known as **primary data**.

When you are using different types of data, consider the advantages and disadvantages, such as accuracy, and if the information is up to date.

A great deal of data is constantly being collected for research and analysis. Examples of such data can readily be found in government publications and national and trade press publications.

2.1 Types of Data
Exercise

Technique

1 Classify each variate as qualitative or quantitative. If the variate is qualitative suggest possible non-numerical descriptors. If it is quantitative, state whether the variate is discrete or continuous.

   a colour of hair
   b gender
   c year of birth
   d daily rainfall
   e favourite colour
   f examination grade
   g test result as a percentage.

2 Which of the following variates are discrete and which are continuous:

   a height of a sunflower
   b number of fish in a pond
   c length of a cycle ride
   d weight of an egg
   e number of people at a rugby match
   f score on a dice?

3 Explain the difference between qualitative and quantitative data and give an example of each type.

4 Explain briefly why weight is a quantitative and continuous variate whereas money spent on a shopping trip is a quantitative and discrete variate.

5 What do you think are the main advantages and disadvantages associated with the use of:

   a primary data
   b secondary data?

2.2 Sampling

Before we look at sampling as a topic we must first define some terms.

A **population** is a collection of individuals or items.
A **census** is a collection of data relating to a whole population.
A **sample** is a selection of individuals from a given population.
A **sampling unit** is an individual member of a sample.
A **sampling frame** consists of all the items in the population.

Let us look at these definitions in context. Say we wanted to find out opinions of students of a particular school on a certain topic.

In this case, the **population** is the whole school.

A **census** would be the school's admission records.
A **sample** could be a particular class, chosen to fill in a questionnaire on a special topic.
A **sampling unit** is an individual student in that class.
The **sampling frame** is the list of all students in the school.

Example 1

Suggest a possible sampling frame from which samples could be taken to study the following:

a   voting patterns in Norfolk in April 1997
b   couples married in Birmingham in 1998
c   runners taking part in the 1998 London marathon.

Solution
a   the 1997–98 electoral register of voters in Norfolk
b   the Registrar's list of marriages in 1998 in Birmingham
c   the entry list of participants in the 1998 marathon.

Why sample?
There are various reasons why a statistician might decide to take a sample of the population. These reasons include:

● **Cost**
It is very expensive to examine every item in a population both in terms of time and money and therefore we must decide whether the degree of accuracy of the research justifies the cost. A sample, if taken correctly, can be used to answer questions relating to the whole population. By taking a sample the quality of the information collected about each sampling unit is often better than if a whole population census is taken, since more time and money can be spent on each element of a sample than on an element in the whole population.

Florence Nightingale became a Fellow of the Royal Statistical Society in 1858 and an honorary member of the American Statistical Association in 1874. She was an innovator in the collection, tabulation, interpretation and graphical display of descriptive statistics and used the data as a tool to improve hospitals.

- **Utility**

  For some populations the sampling units are destroyed in the process of sampling, for example in testing the life span of batteries. This is known as **destructive** sampling. Clearly in this case, sampling is essential since there is no point in knowing all about the population if it no longer exists.

- **Accessibility**

  Often information about certain of the sampling units in the sampling frame is difficult to obtain. For example, historical records might be incomplete, or scientific readings for a particular experiment might not have been fully recorded. In such cases, we may have to take a sample of the population because some of the data are missing.

Sampling methods

If we decide to take a sample, it is important that it is a *representative sample* of the population.

A sample can be either

- random or

- non-random

Random samples

In choosing a random sample each member of a population has an equal chance of being selected. This can be done by numbering each member of the population. Numbers can then be selected randomly either by using tables of random numbers or by generating random numbers on a computer or a calculator.

Simple random sampling

When a number is selected which has already been included in the sample we have to decide whether or not to include this member twice. If each member of the population can only appear once in the sample this is known as sampling without replacement. However, if we decide that any member of the population can be included in the sample more than once this is known as sampling with replacement.

It is worth noting that sampling without replacement is more accurate than sampling with replacement.

- **Advantage**
  1. Simplicity

- **Disadvantages**
  1. Limited application for very large populations as a large amount of time is needed to select and then meet the sample chosen.

2. If a unit in the sample is unavailable it cannot be replaced by another unit with the same basic characteristics; the interviewer must call back.

Example 2

a Explain clearly how to obtain a simple random sample of 20 people from a population of 100.

b What is the main advantage and disadvantage associated with this kind of sample?

Solution

a 1. Allocate a two-digit number to each member of the population, starting at 00 and ending at 99.

2. If using tables, select a random starting point and read off 20 numbers (either horizontally or vertically).

3. Pick out the elements of the population that correspond to the numbers you have chosen and this will be your sample.

b The main advantage of simple random sampling is that it is truly random and free from bias. Its main disadvantage is that it is not suitable for a very large population as it is very time consuming.

Systematic sampling

Systematic sampling might be more appropriate when choosing a random sample from a large population. Usually the population is arranged in some order, for example alphabetical, and one member is chosen at random, then every nth, say every fifth, member on the list is chosen.

● **Advantage**

1. Convenient and produces a random sample.

● **Disadvantage**

1. Problems can occur, such as, if research was being done on money spent on heating and we chose to consider every fourth house in a street without considering the difference between terraced and detached houses. Mid-terrace houses have two outside walls whereas detached houses have four and this factor could affect the amount of heating required.

Stratified sampling

Stratified sampling is an important sampling method which is useful when a population is split into different groups that could have contrasting opinions on the subject being researched.

Examples of such groups include age, income and gender and these are known as **strata** (singular **stratum**). A random sample is taken from each stratum, usually in proportion to its size. The resulting sample is representative of the whole population.

Strata of a population are sub-groups whose members have more in common with each other than they have with the population as a whole.

- **Advantages**
    1. More accurate than non-stratified methods in terms of sampling error.
    2. If a unit in the sample is unavailable it can usually be replaced with another unit from the same stratum.
- **Disadvantage**
    1. More difficult to organise.

Example 3

In a report on conditions in the workplace, it was decided to conduct a survey in three factories, A, B and C, in a particular area, employing 180, 126 and 144 workers respectively. Describe how you would obtain a stratified sample of 30 workers.

Solution

First we need to calculate what percentage of the total number of workers each factory employs.

a $\frac{180}{450} \times 100 = 40\%$ **b** $\frac{126}{450} \times 100 = 28\%$ **c** $\frac{144}{450} \times 100 = 32\%$

So, of the 30 workers, 40% must be from factory A, 28% from B and 32% from C.

That is, $0.4 \times 30 = 12$, so 12 workers from factory A
            $0.28 \times 30 = 8.4$, so 8 workers from factory B
            $0.32 \times 30 = 9.6$, so 10 workers from factory C

The workers are then randomly chosen from each factory.

Non-random samples
Quota sampling

Quota sampling is a type of stratified sampling where units in a particular stratum are chosen in a non-random way. As with stratified sampling, the population is first divided into strata, for example age, gender, income, but, once the number from each group to be interviewed has been chosen, the actual choice of sampling units is the decision of the interviewer. The interviewer is given a series of quotas, for example one quota might be 40 women and men aged between 20 and 30.

This method involves an element of accessibility as the interviewer will certainly only interview people available at a particular time and at a particular place and therefore a large percentage of the population will have no chance of being selected. This factor could certainly lead to bias being introduced.

An example of quota sampling can be found in market research investigations, for example Timeshare surveys.

- **Advantages**
    1. Cheap to administer.
    2. If no sampling frame exists, this is a sensible practical method.
    3. Any sample member can be replaced with another member having the same characteristics.

- **Disadvantages**
    1. Can lead to an unrepresentative result and numbers of people within each stratum must be known if any sense is to be made of the data collected.
    2. Difficult to rely on any statistical result obtained as the sample is so completely non-random.

Cluster sampling

Cluster sampling involves taking a random sample of large units in the population, for example local education authorities. Then, from these chosen units further samples of individuals, for example schools, are taken.

- **Advantages**
    1. Reduces fieldwork costs as less travelling is required.
    2. Can be used even when there is no satisfactory sampling frame for the whole population.

- **Disadvantage**
    1. Risk of obtaining an unrepresentative sample, particularly if there is wide variation between the clusters.

Example 4

For the following situations, state a suitable method of sampling and describe why it would be most appropriate.

a   In a local sports club, the manager has decided to install a new coffee bar and wishes to know the views of the members of the club.

b   A local council is researching the leisure facilities in the town and wishes to ensure that it is catering for all ages of the community.

Solution

a   In this case a systematic sample would be ideal as there is a sampling frame by way of a membership list already in existence. Therefore the method would be relatively quick and easy. This method uses randomisation and would give a good indication as to general opinion on the coffee bar.

b   In this situation it is important that the needs of different ages are addressed and therefore it is necessary to divide the population into strata. Quota sampling would be an appropriate method as it involves splitting the population into strata. It also would take care of the problem of non-response as interviewers could choose the correct number from each quota and not have to worry about interviewing a specific individual whom it might be difficult to contact.

2.2 Sampling
Exercise

Technique

1 Use an example to explain the difference between a population and a sample.

2 Explain briefly what is meant by 'taking a sample of the population'. Describe the main reasons why a sample is taken.

3 Describe how you would use random numbers to select a random sample of 15 members from a population of 258 members.

4 A school has 20 classes of 30 children each, up to Year 11, and there are also 150 students in Years 12 and 13. There are equal numbers of boys and girls throughout the school. Explain how you would obtain a stratified sample of size 60. The sample sizes should be proportional to the sizes of the strata.

5 For each of the following, state the most appropriate method of sampling giving reasons for your choice:

   a the opinion of people in the UK on a particular brand of cereal;
   b local residents' views on a night club in the town;
   c students' opinion of sports facilities in a co-educational school with a 1 : 3 split of boys and girls;
   d students' views on canteen food in a school.

Contextual

1 It is decided to obtain the views of the students of a college on the possibility of providing a college magazine. A sample of 20 is to be consulted. The college consists of 600 students, 150 in Year 7, 100 in each of Years 8, 9, and 10, and 50 in each of Years 11, 12, and 13. Describe briefly how you would take such a sample by:

   a random sampling
   b stratified random sampling
   c quota sampling.

2 A sample of 150 members is required from a population comprising 5000 members. The population is known to fall into three main groups made up of 1500 in the first group, 3000 in the second group and 500 in the third group. Explain clearly how you would take a stratified sample of the required size.

2.3 Collecting the Data

A survey can be carried out either by taking a census or a sample from the population. A **census** involves the entire population whereas, as we have seen already, sampling only involves a proportion of the population.

Information can be collected by several different methods for instance:

- direct observation

- personal surveys

- postal surveys

- telephone surveys.

Direct observation has the main advantage of reducing the chance of incorrect data collection but obviously it is not always feasible. It would be used, for example in cases such as data on traffic flow in a particular street at a particular time, but it would not be appropriate if we were collecting data on the type of confectionery and magazines a teenager spent his or her money on in a month.

Personal surveys are the most popular way of collecting information and are used a great deal in market research. Interviewers ask questions of individuals based on a questionnaire. The main advantages of this method are that it is quick and high response rates are achievable. The main disadvantage is that the interviewer may introduce bias into the research.

Telephone surveys are personal surveys over the phone.

Postal surveys can use systematic sampling, simple random sampling or stratified sampling to select individuals who are then sent a questionnaire. The main advantages of this method are that the introduction of bias is limited and that the costs are generally low. However, the disadvantages include low response rates, misinterpreted questions resulting in void questionnaires and the length of time involved in sending questionnaires and waiting for the response.

Before starting any data collection it is essential that a small scale replica of the actual survey is carried out. This is known as a **pilot survey** and can save a lot of time and money by highlighting possible problems associated with the suggested survey.

A pilot survey is very useful in giving an estimate of the non-response rate and also gives a guide to the adequacy of the sampling frame chosen.

Questionnaires

When designing a questionnaire it is important to make sure that the language can be understood by the whole population and that the style of the questionnaire is such that it is totally impartial.

A few points are worth remembering:

1. The questions should be simple and unambiguous. Avoid long questions that could 'lose' the respondent.
2. Loaded questions that communicate the researcher's personal view must not be used.
3. Questions that are likely to cause personal embarrassment or that are irrelevant should be avoided.
4. Questionnaires are analysed later and it is much easier to do this if the majority of the questions are of a closed nature, that is with a set number of responses involving a tick or cross, or circling a choice.

Example

For a questionnaire about what type of confectionery teenagers like, the following questions were suggested. In each case state whether the question is suitable and if not suggest an alternative.

a   How old are you?

b   How much money do you spend on sweets and/or chocolate each week? Please circle:

Less than £1   £1–£3   More than £3

c   How often do you buy sweets and chocolate?

d   Do you like ready-salted crisps?   Yes   No

Solution

a   This question is not really suitable as it has not stated whether age is required in full years, or years and months.

Better version
How old are you?   ____ years ____ months

b   This is a suitable question.

c   We need to give options in this question.

Better version
How often do you buy sweets and chocolate? Please circle:

Never   Occasionally   Once or twice a week   Every day

d   This is a suitable question.

2.3 Collecting the Data
Exercise

Technique

1 Explain the main differences between a census and a sample survey and give an example of the use of each.

2 For each of the following, state an appropriate method of data collection:

   a   the number of cyclists using a particular road for going to work;
   b   the preferred shampoo in households;
   c   the customers' general opinion of the new store layout of a particular supermarket.

3 Discuss the main advantages of personal surveys over postal surveys.

4 What are the major benefits of undertaking a pilot survey, in advance, of a large postal survey researching household preferences in coffee.

5 In a piece of research on questionnaires, the following examples were extracted as poorly designed questions. State why each is unsuitable.

   a   How many people are there in your family?
   b   Age: Young   Middle-aged   Old
       Please circle
   c   Do you feel the killing of young helpless badgers by savage dogs is cruel?
   d   What do you think of the library facilities in your area ?

Contextual

1 A local fast food store wishes to cater for the requirements of its customers. The manager wishes to know a little about the age structure of the customers, together with how often they visit and what types of food they prefer. The manager is also interested in their opinion of the provision of a salad bar as a new promotion. Design a simple questionnaire that could be used by the manager.

Consolidation

Exercise A

1 Which of the following are quantitative and which are qualitative:

a	favourite food	**b**	hand span
c	speed of a car	**d**	colour of eyes?

2 Which of the following are continuous and which are discrete:

a clothes size
b time to boil an egg
c number of faxes received in an office in a day
d length of cotton required in making a skirt?

3 Why is it inappropriate to take a complete census if we are testing the life-spans of light bulbs? What would be a more suitable course of action?

4 Describe clearly how you could obtain a simple random sample of 30 items from a population of 500. What is the main disadvantage of this type of sampling?

5 When designing questionnaires it is important that they are 'accessible' to the whole population. What advice would you give someone with regard to the writing of questions.

6 Comment on the following suggestions for obtaining a random sample. If a better method is appropriate describe how it could be undertaken.

a A random sample of all adults in a particular town is required. The suggested method is to stand outside the largest supermarket in the town and stop every fifth person who leaves.

b A random sample of pupils in a particular school is required. The suggested method is to put a blank sheet on the school notice board and ask pupils to sign up. A selection of the volunteers will be interviewed.

7 **a** Explain what you understand by:

  i a population   **iii** a sampling frame

  ii a sampling unit   **iv** a sample.

b Give one advantage and one disadvantage of using:

  i a stratified sample

  ii a systematic sample.

c Studying at a sixth form college are 600 male students and 400 female students. One third of the male students and 40% of the female students are studying modular mathematics. The college principal requires a sample of 100 students to complete a questionnaire. Explain how you would advise the principal to obtain a suitable sample. Show any relevant calculations.

(ULEAC)

8 A library wishes to investigate whether there is a problem with damage to its books and a sample of the books is to be checked.

a Give one advantage and one disadvantage of taking a sample as opposed to a census.

b Suggest a possible sampling frame.

c Describe the sampling unit.

The librarian was told to take the top two shelves of children's books as the sample.

d State, giving a reason, whether or not you feel this would be a sensible procedure.

9 On a particular day there are 2125 books on the shelves in the fiction section of a library. Describe how random numbers could be used to select a random sample of size 20 from the 2125 books.

(AEB)

10 **a** Briefly describe 'quota sampling'.

b A 'free' paper is meant to be delivered to every house of 234 houses in a particular estate. The dispatch manager wishes to check that the casual labour employed to deliver the newspapers is correctly delivering them. Instead of checking every house, she wishes to check just a sample from the estate. Describe briefly how she can use a set of random number tables or a random number generator to select a simple random sample of 30 houses.

(NICCEA)

Exercise B

1 Write down three examples of discrete data and three examples of continuous data, making a clear distinction of the difference between each category.

2 A project on fish keeping was undertaken and different pieces of data were collected. Classify each of the following as qualitative or quantitative:

a   species of fish   b   volume of tank

c   weight of gravel   d   life span of different species.

3 State three main reasons why a statistician might decide to take a sample in preference to a complete census.

4 It is stated that 'Quota sampling is a special kind of stratified sampling.' What is the main difference between the two methods?

5 What is a pilot survey and how is it most effectively used?

6 a   Give two reasons for considering the use of:
     i   cluster sampling
     ii   quota sampling.

   b   Give two advantages and two disadvantages associated with stratified sampling.

     A class contains 35 children and the teacher wishes to take a simple random sample of 10 children from the class.

   c   Write down the procedure the teacher might use if the sample is to be taken using random numbers.

(ULEAC)

7 The committee of a squash club is discussing whether or not to incorporate a sauna as part of the club's facilities. It is decided to ask a sample of members for their view.

   a   Suggest a suitable sampling frame.

   b   Explain the difference between a sample and a census, using this example to illustrate your answer.

   c   State why you think the committee might have decided to take a sample in this case rather than a census.

(ULEAC)

8 The principal of a school wants some information on the number of pupils who were absent each day in the school year 1994/5. He records the number who were absent on each of 40 Fridays.

a Why is this sampling procedure unlikely to be representative?

b Suggest a better procedure to obtain a random sample of 40 days.

(NICCEA)

9 The *Guardian* newspaper commissioned the market research firm ICM to conduct an opinion poll, publishing the results on 17 February 1995 with the following statement.

'ICM interviewed a quota sample of 1427 adults, aged 18-plus, in 103 randomly selected parliamentary constituencies country-wide.'

a Describe a suitable random process for selecting 103 constituencies, clearly identifying the sampling frame you would use. There are 651 parliamentary constituencies.

b Making reference to the above quotation, explain the meaning of a *quota sample.*

(NEAB)

10 In each of the following cases, give two reasons to explain why the sampling procedure is not satisfactory.

a The population is housewives in the Greater Belfast area. To get a random sample, an interviewer questions women he meets near Belfast City Hall on a Monday morning after 9 a.m.

b The population is all animal feed suppliers in Northern Ireland. A researcher first listed all those in the *Yellow Pages*. This gives a list of 36 firms. They are assigned a number, from 1 to 36. Then an ordinary dice is rolled six times and the score determines which firm is chosen. This is repeated to get the random sample.

c The population is all voters in Northern Ireland. To get a random sample a researcher takes the Northern Ireland telephone directory, drops the book until it falls open at a page, then with his eyes closed sticks a pin in it. The number closest to the pin is the one rung. This is repeated to get a sample of voters.

(NICCEA)

Applications and Activities

1 | *Leaves*

An activity to compare the estimates of the mean of a population derived from different sampling methods.

Make a collection of 50 leaves, 10 from each of five different types of trees. From this population:

a take a simple random sample of five leaves by numbering every element in the population using digits 00 to 49; then generate random numbers and find the mean length of your sample;

b take a systematic sample of five leaves from your population and find the mean length of your sample;

c take a stratified sample of five leaves and find the mean length of your sample;

d take a quota sample of five leaves ensuring that each variety is represented and find the mean length of your sample;

e using all 50 leaves amongst your group measure them and find the mean length of the whole population;

f compare the mean lengths you obtain from the different methods and comment on your results.

Note that this activity could be completed using different populations. For example, a population of pencils could be investigated and the mean length calculated. A population of books from your school library, making sure that strata of fiction and non-fiction are considered, could be another area of research and the amount of times a book has been stamped could be investigated.

2 |

Design a questionnaire for one of the following:

a A school wants to know the opinions of students concerning canteen food.

b A coffee company wants to know purchasers' opinions on one of its brands.

c Town planners want to know local residents' views on traffic problems.

Carry out a pilot study to assess the viability of your questionnaire.

To find the mean, add all the data items and divide by the number of items.

Summary

- **Quantitative** variates are those that have numerical values.

- **Qualitative** variates are non-numerical values.

- **Continuous** variates can take any value within a certain range.

- **Discrete** variates can only take particular values.

- A **census** is a collection of data relating to an entire population.

- A **population** is a collection of individuals or items.

- A **sample** is a selection of individuals from a given population.

- A **sampling unit** is an individual member of a sample.

- A **sampling frame** consists of all the items in the population.

- **Simple random sampling** is a method of sampling in which every member of the population has an equal chance of being selected. Each element is given a number, random numbers are generated and the corresponding elements constitute the sample.

- **Systematic random sampling** consists of taking every nth member of the population from the sampling frame list, starting at a randomly chosen member.

- **Stratified sampling** is a method in which the population is divided up into distinguishable groups known as strata and a random sample is taken from each.

- **Quota sampling** is a form of stratified sampling in which the selection of members in each stratum is non-random. The choice of elements in a sample is chosen by an interviewer.

- **Cluster sampling** involves taking a random sample of large units in the population and then taking sample of individuals from these large units.

- The **reasons for sampling** are to reduce cost or time, and sampling is essential in cases of destructive sampling and necessary in cases where data is incomplete.

- The **methods of data collection** are direct observation, personal or telephone surveys and postal surveys.

3 Data Analysis I

What you need to know

- How to find one amount as a percentage of another.

- How to calculate a percentage increase or decrease.

- How to square numbers using a calculator.

Review

1 Calculate the first amount as a percentage of the second amount:

a	16, 25	**f**	16.4, 23.5
b	27, 45	**g**	1.64, 5.82
c	27, 20	**h**	$1\frac{1}{2}$, $2\frac{3}{4}$
d	240, 250	**i**	$3\frac{1}{4}$, $6\frac{3}{4}$
e	1800, 1500	**j**	3575, 2445

2 Calculate the percentage increase or decrease of the second number from the first:

a	25, 40	**f**	5.3, 4.5
b	600, 450	**g**	24.95, 30
c	800, 700	**h**	$9\frac{1}{2}$, 8
d	350, 375	**i**	$15\frac{3}{4}$, $12\frac{1}{2}$
e	9500, 16 250	**j**	0.119, 0.021

3 Square, using a calculator, the result of the following:

a $32 + 16$ **f** $12\frac{1}{2} - 5\frac{3}{4}$

b $48 - 25$ **g** $9\frac{1}{4} - 11\frac{1}{2}$

c $18 - 22$ **h** $\dfrac{59 - 77}{3}$

d $23.5 - 29.8$ **i** $\dfrac{63 - 85}{11}$

e $4.59 - 13.771$ **j** $\dfrac{1.96 - 2.42}{0.34}$

3.1 Tables

Population of the United Kingdom   **Title**

Thousands   **Units**

	1961	1971	1981	1991	1994	2001	2031
England	43 561	46 412	46 821	48 208	48 707	50 023	52 435
Wales	2 635	2 740	2 813	2 891	2 913	2 966	2 977
Scotland	5 184	5 236	5 180	5 107	5 132	5 143	4 998
Northern Ireland	1 427	1 540	1 538	1 601	1 642	1 667	1 831
United Kingdom	52 807	55 928	56 352	57 808	58 395	59 800	62 241

Headings (column headings row)

Totals (United Kingdom row)

Source: Social Trends 26   **Source**

A clear, well presented table is one of the simplest ways of displaying numerical information.

For the information contained in the table to be easily read it is important to have certain features; these features have been indicated in the table above.

Title	Printed clearly and precisely indicating what the information is about.
Units	Units used in the table
Headings	All columns and rows are labelled.
Totals	All the relevant totals are given.
Source	The source of the information is given.

It is essential that information can be extracted quickly and accurately. The value highlighted in the table indicates that the population of Wales in 1981 was 2813 thousands, or 2 813 000.

3.1 Tables
Exercise

Contextual

1 From the table on page 26 answer the following questions:

a What was the percentage increase in the total population of the United Kingdom from 1961 to 1994?

b In 1994 what percentage of the United Kingdom population lived in Wales?

c Between which years was the greatest yearly percentage rise in population of the United Kingdom, and what was that rise?

d Which country has a different population trend from the other three? Describe this trend.

e In which year does England's population form the greatest percentage of the United Kingdom's total population?

2 **Labour force of Great Britain: by age**

Thousands

Year	Age					
	16–24	25–44	45–59	60–64	65 and over	All aged over 16
1991	5684	14 256	7311	1102	462	28 815
1992	5224	14 192	7596	1069	501	28 582
1993	4941	14 258	7742	1070	443	28 454
1994	4710	14 301	7922	1051	437	28 421
1996	4404	14 609	8227	1049	429	28 717

Source: Social Trends 26

a Which age range has consistently shown an increase in the size of its labour force?

b Before 1996, in which year did the largest fall in numbers of the labour force occur?

c Before 1996, in which year did the largest percentage fall occur?

d In 1996 which age group had the largest percentage fall in numbers compared with 1994?

e Describe, in detail, the changes in the labour force between 1991 and 1996.

3.2 Bar Charts

Simple bar charts

Example

Using the table of the population of the United Kingdom on page 26, the population of England from 1961 to 1991 is:

Thousands

Year	1961	1971	1981	1991
England	43 561	46 412	46 821	48 208

Display this information diagrammatically.

Solution

To display this information diagrammatically a bar chart can be used, since the years are discrete and a comparison between the years is the main feature to be illustrated.

Population of England from 1961 to 1991

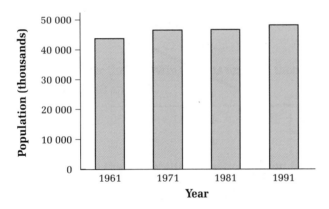

To enable the bar chart to be easily read the following must be included:

● a clearly printed title

● axes that are clearly labelled with given units.

Features of this bar chart are:

● Each bar is of the same width and centred on the year.

● The values on the vertical scale are written on the lines, not in the gaps.

● The **height** of each bar represents the population for that year.

● The bars are blocked in to emphasise the differences and are separated by a gap (which is not necessary in every bar chart).

From the corresponding figures it appears that the population of England is rising slowly with time, but by adjusting the vertical scale so that it does not start at zero, differences between the yearly totals can be accentuated. Care must be taken when reading bar charts. Always read the axes and scales carefully to make sure they are not misleading.

Population of England from 1961 to 1991

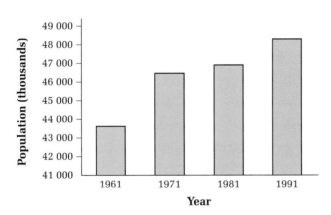

Note the different vertical scale – the difference between years looks much greater than in the previous bar chart, which illustrates the same data.

Composite bar charts

A composite bar chart shows the components that actually make up the bar. Composite bar charts can also be used to show population trends. In this case the bar can also show how the population totals for each year is subdivided.

Population of the United Kingdom from 1961 to 1991

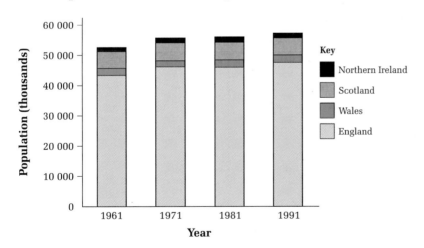

The height of each bar represents the total population of the four countries, with each division within the bar representing the population of the individual country. A key is given to show the section of each bar that represents each country. From the chart it is possible to see a gradual rise in the total population, due mainly to a rise in the population of England.

Comparative bar charts

Comparative bar charts are useful in comparing amounts that occur at the same time, and make it possible to see the trend related to each individual total.

Four bars are constructed for each year to represent the populations of each country. The bars are blocked in using different patterns and a key given to identify the country. It is important to keep the bars in the same order each year.

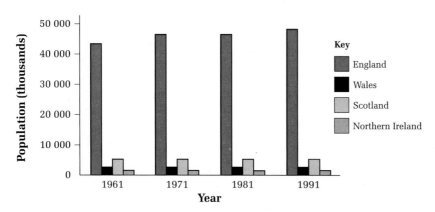

From the chart it is possible to see that the population of England is gradually increasing while the other countries seem to have relatively stable populations. The chart also shows how much greater the population of England is, in comparison to the other three countries.

3.2 Bar Charts
Exercise

Contextual

Labour force of Great Britain: by age

Thousands

Year	Age					All aged over 16
	16–24	25–44	45–59	60–64	65 and over	
1991	5684	14 256	7311	1102	462	28 815
1992	5224	14 192	7596	1069	501	28 582
1993	4941	14 258	7742	1070	443	28 454
1994	4710	14 301	7922	1051	437	28 421
1996	4404	14 609	8227	1049	429	28 717

Source: Social Trends 26

Using the figures from the table construct bar charts to show:

1 The changes in the labour force of those aged 65 and over, from 1991 to 1996 inclusive.

2 The changes in the labour force of those aged under 25, from 1991 to 1996 inclusive.

3 How the total labour force of under 45s changed from 1991 to 1996 inclusive.

4 How the total labour force of those aged 45 and over changed from 1991 to 1996 inclusive.

5 Use your charts to compare and contrast the change in the labour force of those aged 65 and over and under 25s.

6 Use your charts to compare and contrast the changes in the labour force of over and under 45s.

3.3 Pie Charts

The most effective way to show how the individual parts of a total compare to each other, is to use a pie chart. In a pie chart a circle is divided up so that each section is proportional to the size of that part of the total. To do this, the angles at the centre of the circle must be calculated. This is done by taking each amount and dividing by the total, then multiplying by $360°$, the number of degrees in a circle.

Example

Draw a pie chart to show the population distribution of the United Kingdom in 1994.

Solution

The population in 1994 was:

Thousands

England	Wales	Scotland	Northern Ireland	Total
48 707	2913	5132	1642	58 395

England

$$\text{angle} = \frac{\text{population of England}}{\text{total population}} \times 360° = \frac{48\,707}{58\,395} \times 360° = 300°$$

Wales

$$\text{angle} = \frac{\text{population of Wales}}{\text{total population}} \times 360° = \frac{2913}{58\,395} \times 360° = 18°$$

Scotland

$$\text{angle} = \frac{\text{population of Scotland}}{\text{total population}} \times 360° = \frac{5132}{58\,395} \times 360° = 32°$$

Northern Ireland

$$\text{angle} = \frac{\text{population of N. Ireland}}{\text{total population}} \times 360° = \frac{1642}{58\,395} \times 360° = 10°$$

The angles have been corrected to the nearest degree and in this case the total angle is $360°$. To construct the pie chart draw a circle and measure the angles from the centre.

The size of each sector relative to the others is clear, but there is no indication as to the actual population of each country.

In some cases the total might not be exactly $360°$ due to rounding errors.

The distribution of the population of the United Kingdom 1994

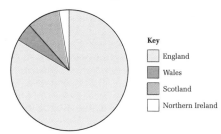

Key
☐ England
▨ Wales
▧ Scotland
☐ Northern Ireland

3.3 Pie Charts
Exercise

Technique

1 Find the angles, correct to the nearest degree, required to draw a pie chart to represent the following amounts:

   a   10, 10, 20, 20, 30

   b   46, 58, 76

   c   110, 120, 150, 160, 180

   d   234, 243, 256, 296, 325, 446

   e   173, 224, 346, 446, 479, 537, 593

   f   3.5, 4.2, 5.5, 6.3

   g   2.75, 3.50, 6.25

   h $3\frac{1}{2}$, $2\frac{1}{4}$, $1\frac{3}{4}$, $1\frac{1}{2}$, $\frac{3}{4}$

   i $5\frac{1}{4}$, $6\frac{3}{4}$, $6\frac{3}{4}$, $9\frac{1}{2}$, $12\frac{3}{4}$, $16\frac{1}{2}$

   j   1 h 10 min, 2 h 30 min, 3 h 20 min, 5 h 15 min, 5 h 40 min

2 Accurately draw the pie charts for question **1**.

Contextual

1 In 1996 a company exported goods to four countries. Use the data in the table to draw a pie chart to illustrate the company's trading.

USA	France	Germany	Japan
£13 288 000	£8 376 000	£5 640 000	£2 096 000

2 The following table represents how students in Year 12 travel to school.

Bus	Walk	Car	Bicycle
45	37	23	15

   a   Construct a pie chart to illustrate these figures.

   b   Year 13 carried out a similar survey and found that the angle for the 55 students who travelled by bus was 120°. How many students are in Year 13?

3 A government department conducted a traffic census at a roundabout with five exits, to monitor the number of vehicles using each exit. The results were:

Exit	A	B	C	D	E
Number of vehicles	66	94	27	38	15

a   Construct a pie chart to illustrate these figures.

b   A similar survey at a second roundabout with four exits, found that the number of vehicles using Exit A was 72. When constructing the pie chart of the results, the angle for Exit A was calculated at 108°. Use this information to calculate the number of vehicles using this roundabout.

4 A survey into family structures recorded the number of children in each family. The results were:

Number of children	0	1	2	3	4	5+
Families	12	32	43	27	11	5

a   Calculate the angles required to represent these figures in a pie chart.

b   Accurately construct the pie chart for these figures.

c   In another survey it was found that the number of families that had only one child was 24 which was represented by an angle of 60°. How many families were in this survey?

5 In an English GCSE exam the grades awarded to the students of a particular school were:

Grade	A	B	C	D	E	F	G
Boys	32	41	30	25	18	10	4
Girls	36	53	38	17	7	4	3

Draw accurate pie charts to represent the results for the boys and girls. Comment on the differences between the two sets of results.

3.4 Line Graphs

The advantage of drawing a line graph is that a connection between one variable and another becomes clear. If the values of the two variables are related then a line graph can be used to estimate missing values or to predict future trends.

The axes for the graph are drawn so that there are equal intervals between the values which change by the same amount each time. Select a simple scale, increasing in 10s, 20s, 100s and so on, for each axis, to make reading the scales easier. Make sure the scales chosen use as much of the space available as possible.

It is also important to give the graph a title, label the axes and indicate any units that are used.

Example

Draw a line graph to show the change in the number of homeless families in Britain between 1982 and 1994.

Homeless families in Britain, 1982 to 1994

Thousands

Year	1982	1983	1984	1985	1986	1987	1988	1989	1990	1991	1992	1993	1994
Families	10.5	11.1	13.7	17.3	22.7	26.8	32.3	40.5	49.1	64.3	67.6	58.0	52

Source: Social Trends 26

Solution

Homeless families in Britain 1982 to 1994

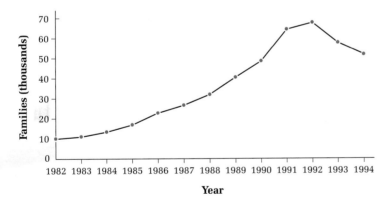

There is a clearly printed title to the graph and each axis is labelled. The horizontal axis is divided into years and the number printed on the line, not in the space. The vertical axis is divided into tens. The points are plotted and marked on the graph, and a straight line is drawn through them. In this example a continuous line is drawn, as the data are continuous; when the data are discrete a dotted line is used.

From the graph it can be seen that a general rise in the number of homeless families was taking place between 1982 and 1992, with the steepest increase happening between 1990 and 1991.

3.4 Line Graphs
Exercise

Contextual

The following table shows the price index of certain items in relationship to 1990, that is the price in 1990 is equal to 100% and all the other years are given as a percentage of the price in 1990.

	1971	1981	1986	1991	1994
Housing	68	81	93	100	104
Motor vehicles	48	62	83	91	101
Food	87	91	95	100	104
Recreation	31	58	76	99	112
Catering	56	58	73	93	96
Household goods	59	68	85	98	111
Alcohol	73	93	98	96	95
Clothing and footwear	52	67	92	100	114
Fuel light and power	86	94	103	108	107
Tobacco	136	121	101	98	86

Source: Social Trends 26

1 Housing, food, clothing and footwear, household goods and fuel, light and power can be classed as essential items. Using the same scales, draw five line graphs to show the variation in the cost of each of these items and comment on any similarities or differences.

2 Motor vehicles, recreation, catering, alcohol and tobacco can be classed as non-essential items. Using the same scales, draw five line graphs to show the variation in the cost of these items and comment on any similarities or differences.

3 From your answers to questions ① and ②, comment on any similarities or differences between the changes in cost of essential and non-essential items.

3.5 Stem and Leaf Diagrams

It is often useful to organise data in ascending or descending order, as this can give some indication of the spread of the numbers and the values of the averages. To be able to do this quickly is an advantage and for this a stem and leaf diagram can be used. Such a diagram is also a quick alternative to a bar chart and has the advantage of retaining all of the information.

Example 1

The heights of 30 boys (to the nearest centimetre) were as follows:

159	155	164	171	166	162	173	167	164	161
159	162	158	155	147	161	147	143	170	141
167	164	179	174	147	164	172	152	159	161

Construct a stem and leaf diagram for this data.

Solution

To arrange the heights in order the first two digits of each height are used for the stem, ranging from 140 (14) to 170 (17). The heights are then placed in the correct row in the diagram according to the first two figures and then just the last number is written down.

17	1	3	0	9	4	2				
16	4	6	2	7	4	1	2	1	7	4	4	1
15	9	5	9	8	5	2	9			
14	7	7	3	1	7					

The highlighted box is the number 167, made up of the 16 from the stem and the 7 from the leaf.

The heights are now rearranged in order, first checking there are still 30 heights.

Stem and leaf diagram showing the heights of 30 boys

17	0	1	2	3	4	9				
16	1	1	1	2	2	4	4	4	4	6	7	7
15	2	5	5	8	9	9	9			
14	1	3	7	7	7					

Key: 14|1 means 141 cm

Include a key to explain what the numbers represent.

From the table some important information can be gained.

- The **mode, the height that appears most often**, is 164 cm (highlighted on the stem and leaf diagram).

- The **median, the height that is in the middle when the heights are in numerical order**, is 161.5 cm. The vertical line between 161 and 162 divides the heights into two groups of 15 boys, so the median is half way between 161 and 162.

- The **range, the difference between the tallest and shortest** boy is 179 − 141 cm, which is 38 cm.

- Most of the heights (16 of them) are between 158 cm and 167 cm.

Example 2

A second sample was taken of the heights of 30 girls. The results were:

158	149	157	165	161	166	150	160	164	156
158	170	158	158	171	169	152	155	162	164
163	168	148	154	170	154	164	163	159	163

Construct a stem and leaf diagram for this data.

Solution

17	0	1	0								
16	5	1	6	0	4	9	2	4	3	8	4	3	3
15	8	7	0	6	8	8	8	2	5	4	4	9
14	9	8									

Put the heights in order:

Stem and leaf diagram showing the heights of 30 girls

17	0	0	1								
16	0	1	2	3	3	3	4	4	4	5	6	8	9
15	0	2	4	4	5	6	7	8	8	8	8	9
14	8	9									

Key: 14|8 means 148 cm

For the girls:

- The **mode** is 158 cm.

- The **median** is midway between 160 cm and 161 cm, making it 160.5 cm.

- The **range** is 171 − 148 cm, which gives 23 cm.

A stem and leaf diagram can then be used to compare the results from Examples 1 and 2.

Stem and leaf diagram showing the heights of 30 girls and 30 boys

```
            Girls           |   |        Boys
              1  0  0 | 17 | 0  1  2  3  4  9
9 8 6 5 4 4 4 3 3 3 2 1 0 | 16 | 1  1  1  2  2  4  4  4  4  6  7  7
    9 8 8 8 8 7 6 5 4 4 2 0 | 15 | 2  5  5  8  9  9  9
                      9  8 | 14 | 1  3  7  7  7
```

Key: 14|1 means 141 cm

Two-way and five-way stem and leaf diagrams

When the results are closely grouped together it may be easier to see any patterns by dividing them into groups using a **two-way** or **five-way** stem and leaf diagram.

Example 3

Draw a two-way stem and leaf diagram for the heights of the students from the previous examples.

Solution

A two-way stem and leaf diagram has a stem numbered, 14, 14, 15, 15, 16, 16, 17, 17, and each group has a width of five values, 140–144, 145–149, 150–154, 155–159, and so on.

Redrawing the stem and leaf diagram gives:

```
         Girls          |    |       Boys
                        | 17 | 9
                1  0  0 | 17 | 0  1  2  3  4
             9  8  6  5 | 16 | 6  7  7
4 4 4 3 3 3 2 1 0 | 16 | 1  1  1  2  2  4  4  4  4
  9 8 8 8 8 7 6 5 | 15 | 5  5  8  9  9  9
          4  4  2  0 | 15 | 2
                9  8 | 14 | 7  7  7
                    | 14 | 1  3
```

Key: 14|1 means 141 cm

Example 4

Draw a five-way stem and leaf diagram of the heights of the students in the previous examples.

Solution

The stem is numbered 14, 14, 14, 14, 14, 15, 15, 15, 15, 15, 16, 16, 16, 16, 16, 17, 17, 17, 17, 17, and each group has a width of two values: 140–141, 142–143, 144–145, 146–147, and so on.

Redrawing the stem-and-leaf diagram gives:

Girls					stem	Boys			
					17	9			
					17				
					17	4			
					17	2	3		
		1	0	0	17	0	1		
			9	8	16				
				6	16	6	7	7	
	5	4	4	4	16	4	4	4	4
	3	3	3	2	16	2	2		
			1	0	16	1	1	1	
9	8	8	8	8	15	8	9	9	9
			7	6	15				
	5		4	4	15	5	5		
				2	15	2			
				0	15				
			9	8	14				
					14	7	7	7	
					14				
					14	3			
					14	1			

Key: 14|1 means 141 cm

For a sample of this size and this type of distribution, a two-way stem and leaf diagram describes the information most appropriately.

Example 5

The lengths of 20 nails were measured to the nearest 0.1 cm. Present these measurements in a two-way stem and leaf diagram.

5.0	3.4	3.3	4.8	5.2	4.5	4.1	3.8	4.4	4.3
4.0	4.4	4.9	4.7	4.7	3.5	4.6	5.1	3.8	4.4

Solution

5						
5	0	1	2			
4	5	6	7	7	8	9
4	0	1	3	4	4	4
3	5	8	8			
3	3	4				

Key: 3|4 means 3.4 cm

3.5 Stem and Leaf Diagrams
Exercise

Contextual

1 The following stem and leaf diagram represents the scores of students in a test.

5	0							
4	0	2	2	6				
3	1	2	2	3	5	7		
2	1	1	4	6	7	9	9	9
1	3	4	6	7	9			
0	8	9						

Key: 0|8 means 8 marks

a How many students sat the test?

b What are the lowest and highest scores achieved? From this, what is the range of marks?

c What is the mode of the marks?

d What is the median of the marks?

2 In a biology experiment the lengths of some eels were measured, to the nearest centimetre:

35	33	32	29	32	36	37	36	32	31
26	29	22	27	34	29	23	31	25	28
35	23	21	32	33	24	25	30	22	40
28	36	32	29	24	37	26	21	29	24
36	25	29	31	26	33	40	38	30	34
39	35	27	25	22	39	28			

Present these measurements in a stem and leaf diagram.

a How many eels were caught?

b What is the range of lengths?

c What is the modal length?

d What is the median length?

3 A driving examiner timed how long it took to complete each driving test she examined. The time was measured to the nearest minute.

37	47	42	36	30	34	32	34	46	36
34	42	24	31	55	34	31	30	45	56
36	30	34	24	40	30	46	39	42	40
24	24	40	34	24	42	39	46	62	30
37	31	41	56	43	32	32	41	36	42
46	34	38	33	42	43	41	46	41	30

Present the information in a stem and leaf diagram.

a What is the range of times taken to complete the tests?

b What is the median length of time taken?

4 In a biology experiment the lengths of 25 worms were measured, to the nearest 0.1 cm:

9.5	8.1	5.1	6.6	9.3	9.1	6.5	5.0	6.9	7.6
9.3	8.3	6.0	6.2	7.4	7.7	7.8	7.9	7.0	7.8
5.4	9.8	6.3	7.5	8.4					

Present these measurements in a stem and leaf diagram.

a What is the range of lengths?

b What is the median length?

3.6 Scatter Diagrams

Scatter diagrams are so called because they show the extent of scattering of points plotted on a grid. The closer the points are to a straight line then the more closely the two variables are connected, or **correlated**. This is known as linear correlation. Two variables can have a very close relationship which is not linear.

Example

The shoe sizes of 20 boys were recorded together with their heights. The results were:

Shoe size	$5\frac{1}{2}$	6	$6\frac{1}{2}$	$7\frac{1}{2}$	6	$6\frac{1}{2}$	5	7	$7\frac{1}{2}$	5
Height (cm)	158	159	157	165	161	162	159	160	164	156

Shoe size	$8\frac{1}{2}$	7	6	$5\frac{1}{2}$	9	$8\frac{1}{2}$	8	7	$9\frac{1}{2}$	10
Height (cm)	165	162	156	155	172	170	167	164	179	174

Draw a scatter diagram using shoe size as the x-value and height as the y-value.

Solution

The diagram shows that the general trend is that as the heights of the boys increase so do their shoe sizes; a fairly predictable result. This is a **positive correlation.**

Negative correlation

No correlation

Negative correlation is where as one variable increases the other variable decreases, and **no correlation** exists when the points are scattered across the graph with no pattern to their distribution.

3.6 Scatter Diagrams
Exercise

Contextual

1 The following table sets out the number of passengers and the amount of cargo that 20 leading airports handle in a year.

Airport	Passengers (000)	Cargo (000 tonnes)
O'Hare International, Chicago	64 441	846.4
Dallas International, Texas	51 944	430.0
Los Angeles International	46 965	1090.0
Heathrow Airport, London	44 968	754.8
Tokyo International (Haneda)	42 639	489.7
Hartsfield International, Atlanta	42 033	464.0
San Francisco International	31 789	438.2
Frankfurt International	30 085	1053.9
JFK International, New York	27 761	1203.3
Miami International	26 484	941.3
Orly Airport, Paris	25 009	275.3
Charles De Gaulle, Paris	24 770	612.2
Newark International, New York	24 287	523.1
Osaka International, Japan	23 457	434.9
Logan International, Boston	22 989	316.2
Metropolitan, Detroit	22 841	156.4
Hong Kong International	22 061	956.9
Honolulu International	21 290	338.2
Kimpo International, S Korea	21 231	959.7
Gatwick, London	19 841	190.2

By drawing a scatter diagram of the number of passengers against the weight of cargo handled, find out if there is any correlation between the two.

2 In the following table the number of gold medals won by the most successful countries in the Olympic games are listed. The table shows the number of gold medals won in the Summer and Winter Olympics. By drawing a scatter diagram determine whether there is any connection between the number of gold medals won in summer and winter.

Country	Summer	Winter
USA	789	53
USSR/Unified	442	88
Germany	186	45
UK	177	7
France	161	16
Sweden	133	39
GDR	154	39
Italy	153	25
Finland	98	36
Japan	90	3
Poland	48	1
Canada	45	19
Netherlands	45	14
Switzerland	42	27
Belgium	35	1
S Korea	31	6

3 The following table gives the annual size of cinema audiences and the number of television licences in the UK. By drawing a scatter diagram representing the figures, comment on any correlation between the size of the cinema audiences and the number of television licences.

Year	Cinema audiences (000)	TV licences (000)
1950	9501	304
1955	8783	558
1960	7896	942
1965	7638	1264
1970	5401	1309
1975	4004	1637
1980	4861	1708
1985	4753	1686
1990	4409	1724
1995	4662	1950

3.7 Histograms

Histograms are often confused with bar charts as they are similar in appearance. The important differences are:

● The horizontal scale on a bar chart usually represents a category, whereas the horizontal scale on a histogram represents a continuous variable, or a discrete variable with many possible values.

● The height of a bar in a bar chart represents the frequency of the variable, whereas in a histogram it is the area of the block that is proportional to the frequency.

Ungrouped data

For ungrouped data, single numbers are used to sort the results into a frequency table, such as in Example 1.

Example 1

The ages, in years, of a group of 50 children aged under 11 were:

6	9	5	5	7	1	2	2	4	3
5	7	6	0	9	8	6	4	5	3
8	1	4	4	7	10	5	9	4	4
3	6	2	8	4	7	2	8	3	3
5	7	4	5	1	6	5	4	3	2

Arrange the data in a frequency table.

Solution

Age (years)	0	1	2	3	4	5	6	7	8	9	10
Frequency	1	3	5	6	9	8	5	5	4	3	1

When a variable, in this case the age of the children, occurs more than once, we have what is called a **frequency distribution**. The **frequency** is the number of times each age occurs. The frequency distribution can be arranged systematically in a table or shown on a graph, such as a histogram.

Example 2

Draw a histogram of the ages of the children in Example 1.

Solution

To draw the histogram the x-axis is numbered from 0 to 11, with the numbers being placed on the lines – not in the gaps. The ages, measured in years, represent a gap of one year, as the age 0 contains all the children from 0 to under 1, the age 1 contains all the children from 1 to under 2 and so on, with the last age, 10, containing those children from 10 to under 11. The area of each block must represent the frequency for that block. Using 'area = height × width' we see that, for this example, the widths are equal so the height of each bar is proportional to frequency. The first block width begins at 0 and is one unit wide. The rest of the blocks are drawn in a similar way. With this method no gaps should appear between the blocks unless the frequency is zero.

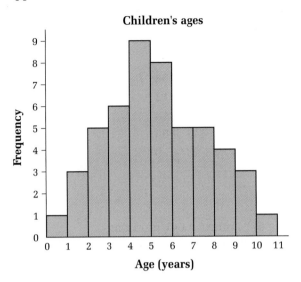

Children's ages

Grouped data – equal groups

Data is grouped when results are too widely spread to analyse as individual items. The size of the group selected is called the **class interval**. When selecting the interval, or width, of the groups it is important to consider the number of groups and the resulting class interval. Too few groups result in large blocks which are difficult to interpret, while too many groups do not simplify the data enough. Usually a class interval that gives between five and eight groups is the most appropriate size to take. A rule of thumb to calculate the class interval is:

$$\text{class interval} = \frac{\text{largest value} - \text{smallest value}}{\text{number of groups}}$$

This result can be used as a guide. Remember to keep the values of the class intervals as simple as possible.

The class intervals can be written in a number of different ways and care must be taken to ensure that no gaps appear between the groups. If the ages of individuals have been measured in complete years, the following groups are the same:

Grouping 1	Grouping 2	Grouping 3	Grouping 4
0–4	0–5	$0 \leq x < 5$	−5
5–9	5–10	$5 \leq x < 10$	−10
10–14	10–15	$10 \leq x < 15$	−15

The groups cover the same ages and have the same mid-values: 2.5, 7.5, 12.5 and so on. If Groupings 2 and 4 are used then a decision as to which group 5, 10, 15 and so on appear in has to be made: this is not necessary with Groupings 1 and 3.

Example 3

The scores of 50 students in a test were:

12	10	34	36	32	3	45	67	41	38
26	33	19	50	45	37	58	34	56	13
8	27	44	61	66	40	22	36	45	64
37	21	31	35	48	57	54	32	44	63
67	26	35	39	24	17	11	14	9	9

Display the data in a grouped frequency table.

Solution

As the smallest value is 3 and the largest value 67 (a range of 64), grouping the figures with an equal class interval of 10 would give a frequency table with seven groups. The first group includes all numbers from 0 but less than 10, and so on.

Group	0–9	10–19	20–29	30–39	40–49	50–59	60–69
Frequency	4	7	6	14	8	5	6

As the class intervals are equal the widths of the bars are equal, so their heights are proportional to the frequency of the group. The x-axis starts at 0 and graduates in steps of 10 up to 70, the numbers being written on the line; not in the spaces. It is important to remember not to use the class interval on the x-axis, as the axis should be a continuous scale. The width of each bar is from the lowest value of the group to the lowest value of the next group and the height of each bar is equal to the frequency when class intervals are equal.

Grouped data – unequal groups

With results that are widely spread it might be necessary to have group widths that vary. In this case the **frequency density** must be calculated, to find the height of each bar relative to the width of the bar, so that the *area* of the bar is proportional to the frequency.

The frequency density is calculated thus:

$$\text{frequency density} = \frac{\text{group frequency}}{\text{group width}}$$

Example 4

The ages, in years, of a sample of 50 people were taken. The results were:

3	69	13	8	21	18	7	11	51	32
22	16	4	2	17	28	35	61	51	12
15	19	26	55	47	28	12	34	26	18
53	51	13	2	34	1	8	45	67	54
22	21	16	34	57	7	17	23	14	43

Construct a grouped frequency table.

Solution

From the raw figures it can be seen that there are more people of a younger age, so it seems sensible to have narrow group intervals in the lower age range and wider intervals in the older age range. Any value that is on a boundary is placed in the higher group.

Group age (years)	Frequency	Group interval	Frequency density (frequency ÷ interval)
−5	5	5	$5 \div 5 = 1$
−10	4	5	$4 \div 5 = 0.8$
−15	6	5	$6 \div 5 = 1.2$
−25	13	10	$13 \div 10 = 1.3$
−35	8	10	$8 \div 10 = 0.8$
−45	2	10	$2 \div 10 = 0.2$
−60	9	15	$9 \div 15 = 0.6$
−70	3	10	$3 \div 10 = 0.3$

With this arrangement of group intervals there are eight groups. Even though the frequencies of the groups from 25 onwards appear to be significantly larger than the other groups, it must be remembered that they have a larger group interval.

The frequency density is calculated by dividing the frequency by the group interval. When this calculation is carried out it re-emphasises the fact that the frequencies of the groups give very similar results, so no group dominates the distribution.

It is important when drawing the histogram to label the vertical axis as *frequency density*. **A true histogram should always be labelled as showing the frequency density but as in the previous examples equal class intervals have now become accepted as being histograms.**

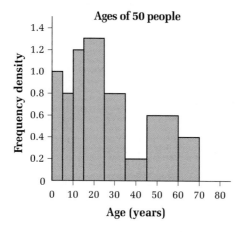

Frequency polygons and curves

A **frequency polygon** is a line graph used in place of, or superimposed on, a histogram. A frequency polygon joins together the midpoints of the tops of the columns of a histogram with straight lines. A frequency curve joins the same points but in a smooth curve.

3.7 Histograms
Exercise

Contextual

1 Twenty seeds were sown in each of 100 trays and the number of seeds that germinated was recorded.

Number of seeds	20	19	18	17	16	15	14	13
Number of trays	13	21	27	16	9	7	5	2

Draw a histogram to display this information.

2 The distance travelled by 150 commuters to work was measured to the nearest five miles.

Distance travelled	5	10	15	20	25	30	35	40
Number of commuters	12	23	45	32	21	9	5	3

Draw a histogram to display the information and then superimpose a frequency polygon.

3 The number of days between incidents of pollution in an inland waterway were recorded.

Time interval	Frequency
$0 < x \leq 10$	19
$10 < x \leq 20$	24
$20 < x \leq 30$	29
$30 < x \leq 40$	21
$40 < x \leq 50$	12
$50 < x \leq 60$	5

Draw a histogram to represent the information.

4 A group of students measured the time it took for snails to cover a distance of 20 cm. The time was measured to the nearest second.

Time interval	Frequency
60–69	5
70–79	9
80–89	12
90–99	14
100–109	11
110–119	10
120–129	6
130–139	3

Draw a histogram to represent the information.

5 The time intervals between successive trains arriving at an underground station were recorded.

Time interval	$0 < x \leq 2$	$2 < x \leq 4$	$4 < x \leq 8$	$8 < x \leq 12$	$12 < x \leq 18$	$18 < x \leq 24$
Frequency	12	25	18	16	6	3

Draw a frequency polygon to represent the information.

6 The volumes of 150 cans of lemonade were measured to the nearest millilitre, and are grouped in the table below.

Volume	333–337	338–339	340–341	342–343	344–347	348–352
Frequency	15	34	49	24	18	10

Draw a histogram to represent the information.

Consolidation

Exercise A

1   **a**   From the sixth form of 75 students, 30 cycled to school, 20 came by bus, 9 came by car and 16 walked. A pie chart was drawn to represent this distribution. Calculate the angle of each sector and draw the pie chart.

     b   A second pie chart was drawn to compare the following year's distribution. The number of students had increased. Twenty-one students travelled by bus and the angle for that sector was now 70°. Calculate the number of students in this year.

2   The table below shows, for each of the years 1989 to 1995, the average unemployment rate (%) and the number of crimes (millions) committed, in a particular country.

Year	1989	1990	1991	1992	1993	1994	1995
Unemployment rate	18.1	17.3	19.4	16.8	13.5	11.1	12.3
Number of crimes	1.70	1.82	2.21	2.24	2.57	2.71	2.96

Plot a scatter diagram on graph paper, showing unemployment rate on the horizontal axis and number of crimes on the vertical axis. Comment on the correlation between the figures.

3   The reasons that adults moved house in 1995 were:

Reason	Death	Partnership split	Children leaving home	Whole household move	Other changes
Percentage	7	9	13	60	11

     a   Calculate the angles required to draw a pie chart representing this information.

     b   Draw a pie chart to represent this information.

4   This table gives a grouped frequency distribution of the heights of girls, at the start of Year 7.

Draw a histogram to represent the data, showing your calculations for the height of each column.

Height (cm)	Frequency
$110 < x \le 120$	13
$120 < x \le 130$	18
$130 < x \le 135$	34
$135 < x \le 140$	27
$140 < x \le 150$	17
$150 < x \le 160$	11

5 A test was set to a group of students and marked out of 70. The minimum mark for a grade A is 48, and the minimum mark for a grade B is 36. Marks of 35 or less are given Grade C. The results can be represented by the following stem and leaf diagram.

Marks out of 70

1	1	5						
2	2	8						
3	2	5	7	9	9			
4	0	3	3	5	5	6	6	8
5	1	3	3	9				
6	0	4	9					

Key: a mark of 39 is shown as 3|9

a How many students sat the test?

b Draw a suitable diagram illustrating the percentage of students in the various grades.

c Grouping the data with classes 10 to 19, 20 to 29, . . . , 60 to 69, determine the frequencies for these classes and illustrate this grouped frequency distribution with a suitable diagram.

(*UCLES*)

6 The population, to the nearest million, of the United Kingdom from 1901 to 1994 is given in the following table. Draw a line graph to illustrate these figures, extending the scales to be able to make predictions for the year 2031.

Year	1901	1911	1921	1931	1941	1951	1961	1971	1981	1991	1994
Population	38	42	44	46	48	51	53	56	56	58	58

a From the graph, estimate the population of the United Kingdom in 2001 and 2031.

b From the graph, state the years between which the largest rise occurs, explaining your answer.

7 The following data show the annual income per head, x, (in US$) and the infant mortality, y, (per thousand live births) for a sample of 11 countries.

Country	A	B	C	D	E	F	G	H	I	J	K
x	130	5950	560	2010	1870	170	390	580	820	6620	3800
y	150	43	121	53	41	169	143	59	75	20	39

Draw a scattergram of the data. Describe any relationship between infant mortality and income per head suggested by the scattergram.

(*AEB*)

8 The following data give the percentage of the population of a number of European countries who live in urban areas. The countries are divided into those who are members of the European Community and others.

Community	Percentage
Austria	56
Belgium	97
Denmark	85
Finland	63
France	73
Germany	87
Greece	65
Ireland	58
Italy	67
Netherlands	89
Portugal	36
Spain	76
Sweden	83
UK	90

Others	Percentage
Albania	37
Bosnia	49
Croatia	64
Estonia	73
Latvia	73
Lithuania	72
Macedonia	60
Norway	73
Slovenia	64
Switzerland	61
Yugoslavia	57

a Display this information for all the countries using a two-way stem and leaf diagram.

b Comment on the overall pattern of population distribution.

c Construct separate stem and leaf diagrams for the two groups, and compare their population distribution.

9 The following table gives the data related to General Elections before 1995.

Date	3/5/79	6/6/83	11/6/87	10/4/92
Turnout (percentage)	76.1	72.7	75.3	76.3
Votes per party (%)				
Conservative	43.9	42.4	42.3	41.8
Labour	36.9	27.6	30.8	35.2
Liberal Democrats	13.8	13.7	12.8	17.0
Social Democratic Party		11.6	9.7	
Plaid Cymru	0.4	0.4	0.4	0.4
SNP	1.6	1.1	1.3	1.9
N. Ireland Parties	2.2	2.5	2.2	2.1
Green Party	0.1	0.2	0.3	0.6
Others	1.1	0.5	0.2	1.1
Total (thousands)	31 221	30 671	32 530	33 275

a From the turnout percentage and total figures, calculate the total possible number of people eligible to vote in each election. Do the answers indicate a change in the total number of voters?

b Using your answers from **a**, calculate the percentage of all people who were eligible to vote, who voted either for the Conservative party or for the Labour party, in each election.

c Display the results of the three largest parties in each election, using a comparative bar chart and comment on the results.

d For 1992, display the results of all the parties using a pie chart.

10 In a survey the ages of 100 cars were measured to the completed number of years. The results were:

6	0	1	11	22	2	0	7	5	3
8	12	18	8	4	3	5	5	1	0
9	15	4	6	11	4	6	3	9	16
8	8	9	0	2	1	14	11	2	7
10	3	2	4	1	7	15	22	1	3
13	8	5	9	11	3	6	9	18	0
4	7	2	5	4	5	14	9	4	6
1	2	7	6	10	8	2	4	7	1
12	6	6	3	4	14	3	7	9	16
7	23	13	1	7	4	2	17	3	4

a From the results construct a frequency table to find the frequency for each age.

b From the frequency table in **a** illustrate the results.

c Using the groups, 0–1, 2–3, 4–5, 6–7, 8–9, 10–12, 13–15, 16–20 and 21–25, construct a grouped frequency chart of these results.

d From the frequency chart in **c** construct a histogram showing clearly the calculations used to find the frequency density.

e Comment on any differences between the diagrams in **b** and **d**.

Exercise B

1 **a** A survey was carried out of 160 office workers on how they travelled to work. It was found that 45 travelled to work by train, 38 by bus, 56 by car and the rest walked. A pie chart was drawn to represent this distribution. Calculate the angle of each sector and draw the pie chart.

b A similar survey was carried out in another office. The number of staff who travelled by car was 40. The angle for that sector was now 96°. Calculate the number of workers in the second office.

2 The table below shows, for each of the years 1989 to 1995, the average unemployment rate (%) and the number of crimes (millions) committed, in a particular country.

Year	1989	1990	1991	1992	1993	1994	1995
Unemployment rate	8.4	7.7	8.5	7.4	6.8	6.1	5.9
Number of crimes	0.97	0.93	1.06	0.91	0.85	0.77	0.74

Plot a scatter diagram on graph paper, showing unemployment rate on the horizontal axis and number of crimes on the vertical axis. Comment on the correlation between the figures.

3 The reasons that adults moved house in 1996 were:

Reason	Death	Partnership split	Children leaving home	Whole household move	Other changes
Percentage	5	16	19	49	11

a Calculate the angles required to draw a pie chart representing this information.

b Draw a pie chart to represent this information.

4 The following table gives a grouped frequency distribution of the heights of boys, at the start of Year 7.

Draw a histogram to represent the data, showing your calculations for the height of each section.

Height (cm)	Frequency
$115 < x \leq 120$	17
$120 < x \leq 125$	28
$125 < x \leq 135$	25
$135 < x \leq 145$	19
$145 < x \leq 160$	8
$160 < x \leq 175$	3

5 A test was set to a group of students and marked out of 40. The minimum mark for a grade A is 32, and the minimum mark for a grade B is 24. Marks of 23 or less are given Grade C. The results can be represented by the following stem and leaf diagram.

Marks out of 40

1	0	4	4	4					
1	5	6	8	9	9				
2	0	0	1	2	3	3	3	3	4	4
2	5	6	6	8	9	9	9		
3	0	0	1	2	3	3			
3	5	6	8						

Key: a mark of 38 is shown as 3|8

a How many students sat the test?

b Draw a suitable diagram illustrating the percentage of students in the various grades.

c Grouping the data with classes 10 to 14, 15 to 19, ..., 35 to 39, determine the frequencies for these classes and illustrate this grouped frequency distribution with a suitable diagram.

6 The percentage of men, over the age of 16, who are in the labour market is given in the following table. Draw a line graph to illustrate these figures, extending the scales to be able to make predictions for the year 2006.

a From the graph, estimate the percentages of men in the labour market in 2001 and 2006.

b From the graph, state the years between which the largest fall occurs, explaining your answer.

Year	Percentage
1984	79.9
1986	75.2
1991	74.9
1992	73.9
1993	72.9
1994	72.6
1996	72.2

7 The following data show the average hours usually worked per week by men, x, and their mortality rate from circulatory disease, y, (per 100 000 population) for a sample of 11 countries.

Draw a scattergram of the data. Describe any relationship between hours worked and mortality rate suggested by the scattergram.

Country	x	y
A	45.4	450
B	38.8	379
C	39.8	443
D	40.6	255
E	39.9	473
F	41.4	395
G	41.6	504
H	39.7	376
I	40.6	413
J	39.6	370
K	42.7	447

8 The following data give the life expectancy of men and women in a number of European countries. The countries are divided into those who are members of the European Community and others.

Community	Men	Women
Austria	74	80
Belgium	74	81
Denmark	73	79
Finland	73	80
France	74	81
Germany	74	80
Greece	76	81
Ireland	73	79
Italy	75	81
Netherlands	75	81
Portugal	72	79
Spain	75	81
Sweden	76	82
UK	74	79

Others	Men	Women
Albania	70	76
Bosnia	70	76
Croatia	68	76
Estonia	64	75
Latvia	63	75
Lithuania	65	76
Macedonia	70	76
Norway	74	81
Slovenia	69	78
Switzerland	75	82
Yugoslavia	70	75

a Display the information for the life expectancy of men in Europe, using a five-way stem and leaf diagram.

b Display the information for the life expectancy of women in Europe, using a five-way stem and leaf diagram.

c Compare the life expectancy of men and women.

9 The following table gives the data related to by-elections before 1996.

Date	5/79 to 6/83	6/83 to 6/87	6/87 to 4/92	4/92 to 9/95
Number of by-elections	20	31	24	14
Turnout (percentage)	61.2	62.4	57.6	52.8
Votes per party (%)				
Conservative	23.8	16.0	23.8	18.2
Labour	25.7	14.9	38.9	36.2
Liberal Democrats	9.0	15.0	19.1	29.0
Social Democratic Party	14.2	5.6	3.2	
Plaid Cymru	0.5	0.3	2.3	0.6
SNP	1.7		4.8	6.5
N. Ireland Parties	23.3	47.4	3.7	5.4
Green Party	0.3		1.8	0.1
Others	1.6	0.8	2.5	4.0
Total (thousands)	715	1979	877	494

a From the turnout percentage and total figures, calculate the total possible number of people eligible to vote in each election.

b Using your answers from **a**, calculate the percentage of all people eligible to vote, who voted either for the Conservative party or for the Labour party, in each election.

c Display the results of the Conservative, Labour and Liberal Democrat parties in each election, using a comparative bar chart and comment on the results.

d For 1983 to 1987, display the results of all the parties using a pie chart. Why might the Northern Ireland parties have achieved such a high percentage?

10 The fuel consumption of each of 100 cars was measured to the completed number of miles per gallon. The results were:

24	37	41	49	44	21	29	17	11	28
34	17	20	41	43	36	37	36	34	34
42	52	29	32	49	40	35	25	50	20
12	30	30	37	21	25	12	19	43	11
27	25	23	25	28	19	39	33	47	38
33	11	48	56	36	27	44	37	41	39
19	48	44	14	37	37	21	43	39	43
38	29	27	50	13	33	53	24	45	48
49	28	55	42	18	49	25	18	13	56
21	35	21	13	20	53	37	42	17	35

a From the results construct a frequency chart to find the frequency for each number of miles per gallon.

b From the frequency chart in **a** illustrate the results.

c Using the groups 10–14, 15–19, 20–24, 25–29, and so on, construct a grouped frequency chart of these results.

d From the frequency chart in **c** construct a histogram.

e Comment on any differences between the diagrams in **b** and **d**.

Applications and Activities

1 From Activity 2, Chapter 2, collect the information and display it in either a leaflet or a poster.

2 Write an illustrated article discussing whether there is any evidence to suggest a difference between the living standards of people in the south of the country and those in the north.

Summary

● **Tables** are used to display numerical information.

● **Bar charts** and **pie charts** are used to illustrate data and help to show patterns in the data.

● **Stem and leaf diagrams**, including two-way and five-way stem and leaf diagrams, are used to organise data in ascending or descending order.

● A **scatter diagram** shows two related variables, for example height and shoe size, as single points on a graph, and shows if there is any correlation between them.

● A **histogram** is similar to a bar chart but in a histogram the area of each block is proportional to the frequency, and the height of each block is equal to the frequency density, where:

$$\text{frequency density} = \frac{\text{group frequency}}{\text{group interval}}$$

4 Data Analysis II

What you need to know

● How to use the Σ symbol for summation.

● How to draw smooth, accurate curves.

Review

1 Calculate Σx, Σx^2, $\Sigma(x^2 - x)$, and $(\Sigma x^2 - \Sigma x)$ for the following figures:

a   1, 3, 5, 7, 9
b   2, 2, 2, 3, 3, 3, 3, 4, 4, 4, 5, 5, 6
c   12, 13, 14, 14, 15, 15, 15, 16
d   0.2, 0.3, 0.3, 0.3, 0.4, 0.4, 0.5, 0.5, 0.5, 0.5
e   2.54, 3.67, 3.74, 3.88, 4.21, 4.43, 5.09
f   −7, −5, −2, −1, 0, 1, 1, 3, 3, 5
g $1\frac{1}{2}$, $1\frac{1}{4}$, $2\frac{1}{2}$, $2\frac{3}{4}$, 2, 2
h $8\frac{1}{2}$, $6\frac{1}{4}$, $7\frac{1}{4}$, $9\frac{3}{4}$, $6\frac{1}{2}$, $6\frac{1}{4}$, $7\frac{1}{2}$

2 Draw curves for the following points and use them to find the value of x when $y = 10$, 20 and 35:

a

x	0	1	2	3	4	5	6
y	0	1	4	9	16	25	36

b

x	0	1	2	3	4	5	6
y	0	1	4	11	26	57	100

c

x	0	1	2	3	4	5	6
y	0	3	7	12	18	25	33

d

x	0	1	2	3	4	5	6
y	0	3	9	18	30	45	63

4.1 Averages

The word average is often mistakenly used to refer only to the arithmetic mean. There are in fact three averages that are commonly used to indicate a central value which is representative of a distribution.

- The **mean**, or the arithmetic mean, is calculated by adding all the values together to find the total and then dividing this total by the number of items or the total frequency.

- The **mode** is the item that has the greatest frequency.

- The **median** is the value that is exactly in the middle of a distribution, providing that the distribution is arranged in descending or ascending numerical order.

Example

Find the mean, mode and median of the following numbers:

10, 15, 12, 16, 13, 13, 16, 11, 13, 18, 17

Solution

The mean is $\dfrac{\Sigma x}{n}$, where Σ means the sum of all the values, and n is the number of items.

$$\frac{\Sigma x}{n} = \frac{10 + 15 + 12 + 16 + 13 + 13 + 16 + 11 + 13 + 18 + 17}{11}$$

$$= \frac{154}{11} = 14$$

The mode is 13.

There are three 13s.

Arrange the numbers in order to find the median.

10, 11, 12, 13, 13, **13**, 15, 16, 16, 17, 18

The median is 13.

The numbers are in ascending order, and there are five numbers above and five numbers below the underlined 13.

If there is an even number of values the mean of the two middle values is taken as the median. For example, the median of

15, 16, 18, 20, 22, 24

is midway between 18 and 20; it is 19.

When required to calculate an average for a group of figures it is important to select the most appropriate one rather than calculate all three averages. The mean is usually the best type of average, but in data sets where there is an extreme observation, known as an **outlier**, the mean is not a true representative of the whole population. In such cases the median is a better measure of the central value of the data set as it is not distorted by the outlier. The mode is used in cases where data is qualitative rather than quantitative, for example favourite colours.

4.1 Averages
Exercise

Technique

Find the mean, mode and median of the following figures:

1   13, 15, 15, 16, 17

2   25, 31, 35, 36, 36, 40

3 $-5, -3, -1, -1, -1, 0, 0, 1, 4, 5$

4   2, 3, 3, 3, 4, 4, 4, 4, 5, 5, 5, 5, 5, 6, 6, 6, 6, 7, 7, 8

5   21, 26, 33, 36, 41, 47, 52, 54, 47, 43, 38, 34, 22, 33, 47, 49, 35

6   1, 5, -3, -1, 4, 7, -2, -2, 0, 1, -1, 0, -2, 5, 3, -4

7   15, 19, 26, 55, 47, 28, 12, 34, 26, 18, 43, 51, 13, 2, 34, 1, 8, 45, 67, 54

8 $\frac{1}{2}$, $6\frac{1}{4}$, $4\frac{3}{4}$, $2\frac{1}{2}$, $\frac{1}{4}$, $5\frac{3}{4}$, $4\frac{1}{2}$, $4\frac{1}{4}$, 3

9   6.8, 7.4, 6.5, 3.2, 5.6, 9.7, 8.8, 7.4, 5.8, 7.5, 6.3, 7.3, 8.5

10   0.67, 0.7, 0.685, 0.85, 0.699, 0.73, 0.6, 0.573, 0.6, 0.72, 0.7, 0.703, 0.7

Contextual

1   The following stem and leaf diagram represents the scores of students in a test.

5	0							
4	0	2	2	6				
3	1	2	2	3	5	7		
2	1	1	4	6	7	9	9	9
1	3	4	6	7	9			
0	8	9						

Key: 4|2 means 42

   a   Write down the value of the median and the mode.

   b   Calculate the mean score of the students.

   c   What would be the most appropriate average to use to represent the score of the students and why?

2 In a biology experiment the lengths of 25 worms, measured to the nearest 0.1 cm, were:

9.5	8.1	5.1	6.6	9.3	9.1	6.5	5.0	6.9	7.6
9.3	8.3	6.0	6.2	7.4	7.7	7.8	7.9	7.0	7.8
5.4	9.8	6.3	7.5	8.4					

a Find the modal length of the sample of worms.
b Find the median length of the sample of worms.
c Find the mean length of the worms.

3 A driving examiner timed how long it took to complete each driving test she examined. The times, measured to the nearest minute, were:

37	47	42	36	30	34	32	34	46	36	34	42
24	31	55	34	31	30	45	56	36	30	34	24
40	30	46	39	42	40	24	24	40	34	24	42
39	46	62	30	37	31	41	56	43	32	32	41
36	42	46	34	38	33	42	43	41	46	41	30

a Find the modal time taken.
b Find the median time taken.
c Find the mean time taken for each test.
d Comment on your results.

4.2 Averages of Frequency Distributions

The **mean** of a frequency distribution is denoted by $\bar{x}$ (x bar), and

$$\bar{x} = \frac{\Sigma fx}{\Sigma f}$$

Σfx is the sum of all the individual values of the variable, x, multiplied by their frequencies. Σf is the sum of all the frequencies.

The **mode** is the value that has the highest frequency.

The **median** is found by adding the frequencies of each value, arranged in order, until a total greater than half the total frequency is reached. The value at that point is the median.

Example

The number of children per family in a survey of 60 families is shown in the table:

Children	0	1	2	3	4	5	6
Frequency	5	16	22	8	5	3	1

Find the mean, mode and median for these figures.

Solution

Children (x)	Frequency (f)	Number of children (fx)
0	5	$0 \times 5 = 0$
1	16	$1 \times 16 = 16$
2	22	$2 \times 22 = 44$
3	8	$3 \times 8 = 24$
4	5	$4 \times 5 = 20$
5	3	$5 \times 3 = 15$
6	1	$6 \times 1 = 6$
	$\Sigma f = 60$	$\Sigma fx = 125$

$$\text{mean} = \frac{\Sigma fx}{\Sigma f} = \frac{125}{60} = 2.08 \text{ children}$$

$$\text{mode} = 2 \text{ children}$$

Total frequency $= 60$

The midpoint is between the 30th and the 31st value.

Starting at the top of the frequency column add the frequencies until the total is greater than 31. This occurs in the row where $x = 2$.

The median is therefore 2 children per family.

The highest frequency is for two children (22).

4.2 Averages of Frequency Distributions

Exercise

Contextual

1 Twenty seeds were sown in each of 100 trays and the number of seeds that germinated was recorded.

Number of seeds germinating per tray	20	19	18	17	16	15	14	13
Number of trays	13	21	27	16	9	7	5	2

Work out:

a   the mean   **b**   the median   **c**   the mode

for the number of seeds that germinate per tray. Which would be the best average to quote to accurately reflect the success rate?

2 The distances travelled to work by 150 commuters were measured to the nearest five miles.

Distance travelled	5	10	15	20	25	30	35	40
Number of commuters	12	23	45	32	21	9	5	3

Work out:

a   the mean   **b**   the median   **c**   the mode

for the rounded distances that the commuters travelled.

3 The weights, measured to the nearest kilogram, of 75 Year 12 students were recorded.

Weight	66	67	68	69	70	71	72	73	74	75
Frequency	5	3	4	8	15	12	12	9	4	3

Work out:

a the mean   **b**   the median   **c**   the mode

for the weights of the students.

4 A survey recorded the number of minutes difference between the arrival time of trains and the timetable times. The results were recorded to the nearest five minutes and were:

Difference	−10 min	−5 min	0 min	5 min	10 min	15 min	20 min	25 min	30 min
Frequency	7	15	48	23	11	9	7	7	3

Work out

a the mean **b** the median **c** the mode

for the arrival times of the trains.

5 The scores awarded to an ice-skater in a competition were:

Judge	1	2	3	4	5	6	7	8	9	10
Section 1	5.8	5.7	5.4	5.5	5.6	5.3	5.6	5.5	5.4	5.6
Section 2	5.8	5.4	5.5	5.6	5.2	5.2	5.3	5.4	5.5	5.2
Section 3	5.6	5.5	5.6	5.6	5.4	5.6	5.5	5.1	5.1	5.2

a Form a frequency chart for each section of the scores.
b Work out:
  i the mean
  ii the median
  iii the mode
  for each of the sections.

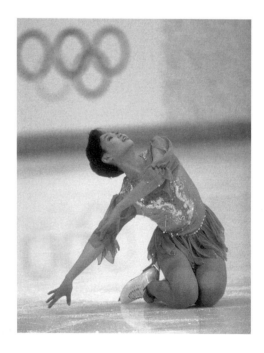

4.3 Averages of Grouped Frequency Distributions

Since we do not know all the exact values in a grouped frequency distribution, we **estimate** the mean value, using the **midpoint** of each group for the variable. The mean is then found as for a frequency distribution by calculating

$$\bar{x} = \frac{\Sigma fx}{\Sigma f}$$

This gives an estimate of the mean, because we have assumed the items in each group are evenly spread, so that the midpoint of each group is the mean of that group.

The individual value that represents the mode cannot be found for grouped data, therefore the **modal group** is quoted, being the group with the largest frequency.

A cumulative frequency curve is used to find the median of grouped data.

Remember the work on grouped data visited in the section on histograms.

This will be covered later.

Example 1

Taking the ages of 50 people, as in the example on page 49, find an estimate for the mean, the modal group and the median.

Solution

Group age (years)	Midpoint of group (x)	Frequency (f)	$f \times x$ frequency × midpoint
−5	2.5	5	$2.5 \times 5 = 12.5$
−10	7.5	4	$7.5 \times 4 = 30$
−15	12.5	6	$12.5 \times 6 = 75$
−25	20	13	$20 \times 13 = 260$
−35	30	8	$30 \times 8 = 240$
−45	40	2	$40 \times 2 = 80$
−60	52.5	9	$52.5 \times 9 = 472.5$
−70	65	3	$65 \times 3 = 195$
		$\Sigma f = 50$	$\Sigma fx = 1365$

$$\text{mean} = \frac{\Sigma fx}{\Sigma f} = \frac{1365}{50} = 27.3 \text{ years}$$

$$\text{modal group} = 15 \text{ to } 25$$

This group has the highest frequency.

69

An estimate for the median can be found by taking the mean age of the 25th and 26th persons. The group that contains the median is the group 15 to 25 with a frequency of 13. Up to the lower limit of this group there is a combined frequency of 15 found by adding the frequencies of the groups less than 15. A further 10.5 people are required to get to the median point of 25.5 people. 10.5 people, out of the group of 13, are approximately 0.8 of the group, and 0.8 is equivalent to 8 years. Therefore the median is the lower group value plus 8 years. This is $15 + 8 = 23$ years.

0.8 of the group width of 10 years = 8 years

Another method is to draw a cumulative frequency curve.

See Section 4.4.

Assumed mean and coding

The use of an assumed mean or the use of coding can simplify the calculation of the mean.

Using an assumed mean

Example 2

Find the mean age of the 60 people aged between 0 and 35 whose ages are given in this grouped frequency table.

Age (years)	Midpoint	Frequency (f)	Midpoint −17.5 (x)	fx
0–5	2.5	5	−15	−75
5–10	7.5	8	−10	−80
10–15	12.5	12	−5	−60
15–20	17.5	18	0	0
20–25	22.5	9	5	45
25–30	27.5	6	10	60
30–35	32.5	2	15	30
		$\Sigma f = 60$		$\Sigma fx = -80$

Solution

The midpoint of the middle group in the table is 17.5 and we will take this value as the assumed mean. To find how much this assumed mean differs from the true mean carry out the following calculation:

- Subtract 17.5 from the midpoint of each group and multiply by the frequency f to give the fx column.

- The total of the fx column (Σfx) divided by the total frequency (Σf) gives the difference between the assumed mean and the true mean.

$$\text{mean} = \text{assumed mean} + \frac{\Sigma fx}{\Sigma f} = 17.5 + \frac{(-80)}{60}$$

$$= 17.5 - 1.333$$

$$= 16.17$$

Coding

With **coding** a similar form of simplifying the data is used. In the above example all the midpoints are divisible by 2.5. When this division is done the resulting values become $1, 3, 5, \ldots$, and these values are then used to calculate Σfx. The result of $\dfrac{\Sigma fx}{\Sigma f}$ is then multiplied by 2.5 to get the true mean.

For example, using the figures of the previous example,

Age (years)	Midpoint	Frequency (f)	Midpoint ÷ 2.5 (x)	fx
0–5	2.5	5	1	5
5–10	7.5	8	3	24
10–15	12.5	12	5	60
15–20	17.5	18	7	126
20–25	22.5	9	9	81
25–30	27.5	6	11	66
30–35	32.5	2	13	26
		$\Sigma f = 60$		$\Sigma fx = 388$

$$\text{Mean} = \frac{\Sigma fx}{\Sigma f} \times 2.5$$

$$= \frac{388}{60} \times 2.5$$

$$= 16.17$$

Weighted mean

In the last year the cost of food increased by 8%, the cost of housing by 4% and the cost of petrol by 5%, but the cost of heating fell by 5%. If an average percentage change in the combined cost of these items is required, then all the changes could be added together and then divided by 4 to give a mean value.

The percentage changes are 108%, 104%, 105% and 95% respectively.

$$\text{Total} = 108 + 104 + 105 + 95$$

$$= 412$$

$$\text{Mean} = 412 \div 4 = 103$$

This gives a mean rise of 3%.

However, people do not spend equal amounts on each of these items. A rise of 4% in the cost of housing could prove more expensive than a 5% rise in the cost of petrol because people may spend more on rent and mortgages than they do on petrol. To allow for this each item can be given a **weight, which is proportional to how much is actually spent by people on each of these items.** The weights act as a frequency in the calculation of the mean change.

Example 3

From government spending surveys it is known that spending on food, housing, petrol and heating is in the ratio $8:4:1:3$. Using the percentage changes given above calculate a weighted mean change in price of all the items combined.

Solution

Item	Weight	% Change	Weight ×% Change
Food	8	108	864
Housing	4	104	416
Petrol	1	105	105
Heating	3	95	285
Totals	16		1670

$$\text{Weight mean} = 1670 \div 16$$
$$= 104.375$$

which represents a mean rise of 4.38% to two decimal places.

Indexes

An index is a weighted mean that is used to indicate the change in a group of items over a fixed period of time. An example of this is the index of the cost of living. This measures the percentage change, usually on a monthly basis, in the cost of the items on which people spend most of their money. The value of an item at the starting date for the calculation is called the base value, and is equated to 100%. All later values are calculated from this point as percentages of the original value. In the index of the cost of living, the items on which people spend their money are grouped into a number of categories such as, Food, Housing, Heating, Transport, Leisure etc. Each category is then given a weight depending on how much people in general spend on each category. To make the calculations easier the total weight is usually a round number such as 100 or 1000. The larger the total weight the more accurate the proportion between each category can be adjusted. The percentage change in each category is calculated in relation to the base value. The index is then calculated as a weighted mean.

4.3 Averages of Grouped Frequency Distributions

Exercise

Contextual

1 A tyre company researched the life expectancy of one type of their cycle tyres. The results were:

Distance (1000 km)	$10 < x \leq 20$	$20 < x \leq 30$	$30 < x \leq 40$	$40 < x \leq 50$	$50 < x \leq 60$	$60 < x \leq 70$
Number of tyres	30	69	93	57	36	15

a What is the modal group?
b What is the estimated mean distance?
c Calculate an estimate for the median.

2 The speeds of bicycles passing a particular point were recorded, to the nearest mile per hour, and were:

Speed	4–6	7–9	10–12	13–15	16–18
Frequency	8	24	62	43	13

a What is the modal group?
b What is the estimated mean speed?

3 The volumes of 150 cans of lemonade were measured, to the nearest millilitre, and are grouped in the table below.

Volume	333–337	338–339	340–341	341–342	343–347	348–352
Frequency	15	34	49	24	18	10

a What is the modal group?
b What is the estimated mean volume of the cans?
c What is an estimate of the median?

4 The scores in a darts match were recorded as follows:

Scores	0–20	20–40	40–60	60–80	80–100	100–140	140–180
Frequency	9	16	28	13	37	29	18

a What is the modal group?
b What is the estimated mean score?
c What is an estimate of the median?

5 In a GCSE mathematics exam there are three papers which contribute 50%, 30% and 20% respectively to the student's final grade. Using a weighted mean calculate the final mark for a student who scores 65% in the first paper, 84% in the second paper and 70% in the third paper.

4.4 Cumulative Frequency Graphs

An estimate of the median of grouped data can be made from a cumulative frequency table or graph. The previous example (see p. 69), of 50 people aged from 0 to 70, will be used to demonstrate how to draw up a cumulative frequency table.

Group age (years)	Frequency	Cumulative frequency (total number of people under stated age)
0–5	5	Under 5 years old = 5
5–10	4	Under 10 years old = 9 (5 under 5 yr + 4 under 10 yr)
10–15	6	Under 15 years old = 15 (9 under 10 yr + 6 under 15 yr)
15–25	13	Under 25 years old = 28 (15 under 15 yr + 13 under 25 yr)
25–35	8	Under 35 years old = 36 (28 under 25 yr + 8 under 35 yr)
35–45	2	Under 45 years old = 38 (36 under 35 yr + 2 under 45 yr)
45–60	9	Under 60 years old = 47 (38 under 45 yr + 9 under 60 yr)
60–70	3	Under 70 years old = 50 (47 under 60 yr + 3 under 70 yr)

The cumulative frequency is found by adding the frequency of the present group to the total of all the frequencies of lower groups.

Each point is plotted on a graph, so that the x-coordinate is the *highest possible value* in the group and the y-coordinate is the value of the cumulative frequency; so the first point is $(5, 5)$, the second $(10, 9)$ and so on. In the case where the length of an object is measured to the nearest centimetre and the results grouped as 0–4, 5–9, 10–14, 15–19, . . . , the highest values of the group would be 4.5, 9.5, 14.5, 19.5, ...

Cumulative frequency curve of the ages of 50 people

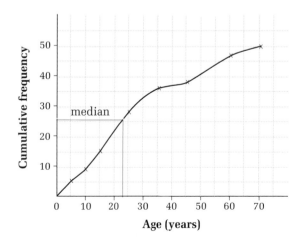

To estimate the median, the midpoint of the cumulative frequency is found, which is $\frac{1}{2}(n+1)$, where n is the total frequency. In this case the midpoint is $\frac{1}{2}(50+1) = 25.5$.

A horizontal line is drawn from the value 25.5 on the vertical scale until it meets the curve. The x-coordinate at this point represents the median. So in this case, the median is 23 years.

> **The median is the $\frac{1}{2}(n+1)$th value.**

> **When n is large, the median is the $\frac{1}{2}n$th value.**

Advantages and disadvantages of the different averages

	Advantages	Disadvantages
Mean	Can be calculated exactly, with ease All data are used in the calculation Can be developed for further statistical analysis.	Can be unduly influenced by extreme values, whether large or small, known as outliers.
Median	Easy to understand Is not influenced by outliers.	It cannot be easily developed for further statistical analysis Cannot be used for non-numerical data.
Mode	Simply understood Can be used for non-numeric data.	Is not used in further analysis of data.

4.4 Cumulative Frequency Graphs

Exercise

Technique

Copy and complete the following tables.

1

Age (years)	Frequency	Cumulative frequency	Maximum value of group
0–4	6	6	5
5–9	19	25	10
10–14	21	46	
15–19	24		
20–24	16		
25–29	4		

2

Length (cm)	Frequency	Cumulative frequency	Maximum value of group
10–15	2	2	15
15–20	7	9	20
20–25	19		
25–30	33		
30–40	27		
40–50	24		
50–60	22		
60–80	16		

3

Length (m)	Frequency	Cumulative frequency	Maximum value of group
20–24	18		24.5
25–29	28		29.5
30–34	32		
35–39	22		
40–44	17		
45–49	13		
50–54	9		
55–59	6		
60–64	5		

4

Time (s)	Frequency	Cumulative frequency	Maximum value of group
$0 \leq t < 5$	4		
$5 \leq t < 10$	11		
$10 \leq t < 15$	32		
$15 \leq t < 20$	46		
$20 \leq t < 25$	44		
$25 \leq t < 30$	29		
$30 \leq t < 35$	17		
$35 \leq t < 40$	11		
$40 \leq t < 45$	6		

5

Earnings (£)	Percentage	Cumulative percentage	Maximum value of group
<4 000	5.5		
−6 000	7.1		
−8 000	9.3		
−10 000	15.9		
−12 000	11.2		
−15 000	14.6		
−20 000	18.9		
−25 000	9.4		
−30 000	4.1		
−50 000	2.3		
−100 000	1.7		

6 From the cumulative frequency charts in questions $\boxed{1}$ to $\boxed{5}$, draw the cumulative frequency curves.

7 From the cumulative frequency curves in question $\boxed{6}$ find estimates for the medians.

Contextual

1 The times taken, to the nearest minute, for an examiner to mark a complete examination paper were recorded and the results were grouped in the table below.

Time taken	10–14	15–19	20–24	25–29	30–35
Number of papers	8	22	34	30	26

a   Calculate an estimate of the mean time taken.
b   Construct a cumulative frequency table for this distribution and draw
    a cumulative frequency curve.
c   Use your curve to estimate the median.

2 The ages, in years, of 240 teenagers were recorded and grouped as follows:

Age	$13 < x \leq 15$	$15 < x \leq 16$	$16 < x \leq 17$	$17 < x \leq 20$
Number of teenagers	48	84	90	18

a   Calculate an estimate of the mean age.
b   Construct a cumulative frequency table for this distribution and draw
    a cumulative frequency curve.
c   Use your curve to estimate the median age.

3 The weights of 250 students, to the nearest kilogram, were recorded and
    grouped in the following table:

Weight	$50 < x \leq 55$	$55 < x \leq 60$	$60 < x \leq 65$	$65 < x \leq 70$	$70 < x \leq 75$	$75 < x \leq 80$
Number of students	32	40	62	51	36	29

a   Calculate an estimate of the mean weight.
b   Construct a cumulative frequency table for this distribution and draw
    a cumulative frequency curve.
c   Use your curve to estimate the median weight.
d   Which average best reflects this distribution, and why?

4 The scores in a darts match were recorded as follows:

Scores	0–20	20–40	40–60	60–80	80–100	100–140	140–180
Frequency	9	16	28	13	37	29	18

Construct a cumulative frequency graph and use it to find the median
score. Compare this with the answer to Exercise 4.3, question **4**c.

5 The running times of 180 CDs were recorded as:

Time (min)	35–39	40–43	44–45	46–47	48–50	51–55	56–60
Frequency	4	15	46	49	36	21	9

Construct a cumulative frequency curve for the running times of the CDs
and use it to find the median time.

4.5 Measurements of Dispersion

Measurements of dispersion give information on the spread of the data.

The range

The **range** is the difference between the highest and lowest value of a set of data, and consists of a single value. The larger the value of the range the wider spread is the data. Care should be taken with this measurement, as it is very crude.

Refer to Chapter 3, Section 3.5 for the calculation of the range.

Interquartile range

The **interquartile range** is a measure of spread used particularly in data sets where there is an extreme observation known as an outlier. It is often used in conjunction with the median. The median, Q_2, is the midpoint of the distribution; it splits the distribution into two halves. There are two more points, which together with the median, split the distribution into quarters. These two points are the **lower and upper quartiles**.

The lower quartile, Q_1, is found by dividing the total frequency by 4 and finding the corresponding value that relates to that position. Similarly the upper quartile, Q_3, is found by dividing the total frequency by 4, multiplying by 3, and finding the value that relates to that position.

The interquartile range (IQR) is the difference in value between the upper and lower quartile.

$$IQR = Q_3 - Q_1$$

The interquartile range measures the spread of the middle 50% of the distribution, as is shown on the cumulative frequency graph.
All the methods employed in finding the median for different types of distributions can be used to find the quartiles.

Cumulative frequency curve of the ages of 50 people

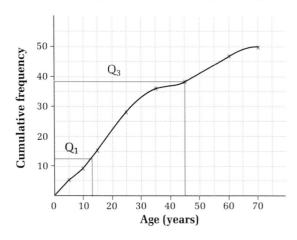

The lower quartile's position is found by (total frequency $+ 1) \times \frac{1}{4} = \frac{51}{4}$, which is the 12.75th value. Thus the lower quartile is 13 years.

The upper quartile's position is found by (total frequency $+ 1) \times \frac{3}{4} = 51 \times \frac{3}{4}$, which is the 38.25th value. Thus the upper quartile is 45 years.

Therefore the interquartile range is $45 - 13 = 32$ years.

> $Q_1 = \frac{1}{4}(n+1)$th value
>
> $Q_3 = \frac{3}{4}(n+1)$th value

For large values of n it is accurate enough to use:

> $Q_1 = \frac{1}{4}n$th value
>
> $Q_3 = \frac{3}{4}n$th value

Percentiles

With large samples it is sometimes useful to be able to divide the distribution into smaller sections than quartiles. In this situation the use of percentiles could be more appropriate. Percentiles divide the distribution into 100 sections where each section represents 1% of the total frequency.

Example 1

From the cumulative frequency graph on the previous page, find the age range which represents:

a   the youngest 40%   **b**   the oldest 10% of the population.

Solution

a   40% of the total frequency $= 0.4 \times 50 = 20$

Using the cumulative frequency graph, go to 20 on the vertical axis then across to the curve, as with the method for quartiles, and read off the age. This gives the age as 18. So the youngest 40% of the population are between 0 and 18 years of age.

b   10% of the population $= 0.1 \times 50 = 5$

Using the cumulative frequency graph, start at the maximum value on the vertical axis and subtract 5, which gives 45. As before, go across from 45 to the curve and read off the age. This gives the age as 57. So the oldest 10% of the population are between 57 and 70 years of age.

The method for calculating a percentile within a distribution is:

$$\frac{\text{Percentile}}{100} \times n \qquad \text{where } n \text{ is the total frequency}$$

4.5 Measurements of Dispersion

Exercise

Technique

Using the cumulative frequency curves from Exercise 4.4 (Technique) find an estimate for Q_1, Q_3 and the interquartile range. Find also, the range of values representing the lowest 10% and the highest 15% of each distribution. The groups and frequencies are:

1

Age (years)	0–4	5–9	10–14	15–19	20–24	25–30
Frequency	6	19	21	24	16	4

2

Length (cm)	10–15	15–20	20–25	25–30	30–40	40–50	50–60	60–80
Frequency	2	7	19	33	27	24	22	16

3

Length (m)	20–24	25–29	30–34	35–39	40–44	45–49	50–54	55–59	60–64
Frequency	18	28	32	22	17	13	9	6	5

4

Time	Frequency
$0 \leq t < 5$	4
$5 \leq t < 10$	11
$10 \leq t < 15$	32
$15 \leq t < 20$	46
$20 \leq t < 25$	44
$25 \leq t < 30$	29
$30 \leq t < 35$	17
$35 \leq t < 40$	11
$40 \leq t < 45$	6

5

Earnings (£)	Percentage
<4 000	5.5
−6 000	7.1
−8 000	9.3
−10 000	15.9
−12 000	11.2
−15 000	14.6
−20 000	18.9
−25 000	9.4
−30 000	4.1
−50 000	2.3
−100 000	1.7

4.6 Box and Whisker Diagrams (Box Plots)

A **box plot** shows all the information concerning range, interquartile range and median in diagrammatic form. The box shows the interquartile range and the position of the median. The whiskers indicate the range.

The box plot for the previous data on the ages of 50 people is:

See page 49.

This type of diagram is useful in helping to describe a distribution, especially the information gained from a cumulative frequency curve.

It is important to have a scale indicating the values of each measurement.

Skewed data

When data is symmetrically distributed so that the mean, mode and median have the same value and the graph of the frequencies is bell-shaped, the data is said to be **normally distributed**. The graph of a normal distribution with the corresponding box plot is shown here.

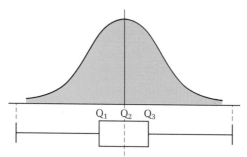

In this case, $Q_2 - Q_1 = Q_3 - Q_2$.

If the data has more lower values and tapers towards the higher values the distribution is **positively skewed.**

The graph of a positively skewed distribution with the corresponding box plot is shown here.

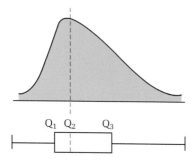

In this case the mode < median < mean, and $Q_2 - Q_1 < Q_3 - Q_2$.

If the data has a greater number of higher values than lower values the distribution is **negatively skewed**. The graph of a negatively skewed distribution with the corresponding box plot is shown here.

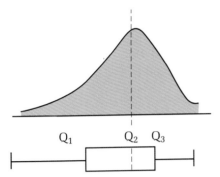

In this case the mode > median > mean and $Q_2 - Q_1 > Q_3 - Q_2$.

4.6 Box and Whisker Diagrams

Exercise

Technique

For each of the distributions in Exercise 4.4 (Technique) construct box plots and comment on any the skewness of the data. The groups and frequencies are:

1

Age (years)	0–4	5–9	10–14	15–19	20–24	25–30
Frequency	6	19	21	24	16	4

2

Length (cm)	10–15	15–20	20–25	25–30	30–40	40–50	50–60	60–80
Frequency	2	7	19	33	27	24	22	16

3

Length (m)	20–24	25–29	30–34	35–39	40–44	45–49	50–54	55–59	60–64
Frequency	18	28	32	22	17	13	9	6	5

4

Time (s)	Frequency
$0 \leq t < 5$	4
$5 \leq t < 10$	11
$10 \leq t < 15$	32
$15 \leq t < 20$	46
$20 \leq t < 25$	44
$25 \leq t < 30$	29
$30 \leq t < 35$	17
$35 \leq t < 40$	11
$40 \leq t < 45$	6

5

Earnings (£)	Percentage
<4 000	5.5
−6 000	7.1
−8 000	9.3
−10 000	15.9
−12 000	11.2
−15 000	14.6
−20 000	18.9
−25 000	9.4
−30 000	4.1
−50 000	2.3
−100 000	1.7

Contextual

For each of the questions in Exercise 4.4 (Contextual), the frequency charts of which are given below, find an estimate for the upper quartile, the lower quartile and the inter-quartile range, then construct box plots to display this information. Comment on any skewness of the data.

1

Time taken	10–14	15–19	20–24	25–29	30–35
Number of papers	8	22	34	30	26

2

Age	$13 < x \le 15$	$15 < x \le 16$	$16 < x \le 17$	$17 < x \le 20$
Number of teenagers	48	84	90	18

3

Weight (kg)	Number of students
$50 < x \le 55$	32
$55 < x \le 60$	40
$60 < x \le 65$	62
$65 < x \le 70$	51
$70 < x \le 75$	36
$75 < x \le 80$	29

4

Score	0–20	20–40	40–60	60–80	80–100	100–140	140–180
Frequency	9	16	28	13	37	29	18

5

Time (min)	35–39	40–43	44–45	46–47	48–50	51–55	56–60
Frequency	4	15	46	49	36	21	9

4.7 Standard Deviation I

Standard deviation measures the spread of a distribution from the mean. The smaller the value of the standard deviation the more closely grouped is the data. The standard deviation can be misleading if there are outliers.

The standard deviation is an important measurement of spread as it can be used to measure exactly the percentage of a population within desired limits.

One of the most notable developments of the use of standard deviation and its relationship to the normal distribution was by psychologists, from the middle of the 19th century, in the study of human behaviour. The popular belief was that human intelligence could not alter after the age of seven and could be measured by testing. Tests were devised to measure people's Intelligence Quotient (IQ), and by using the normal distribution and the standard deviation of the test scores all individuals could be exactly placed in the overall population. These tests were then used to select on the grounds of people's intelligence.

It is important to understand the different symbols that are used when dealing with the mean and standard deviation of populations and samples.

● In a **population** the **standard deviation** is given the symbol σ.

● The **mean** is given the symbol μ.

● In a **sample** the **standard deviation** is given the letter s.

● The **mean** is given the symbol $\bar{x}$. [Read as x bar.]

σ is the lower case Greek letter *sigma*. μ is the lower case Greek letter *mu*.

Consider the difference between each data item and the mean. Those values which are less than the mean will have a negative difference, while those values greater than the mean will have a positive difference.

If the differences are summed the answer will always equal zero.

However, if we square the differences all the values will be positive.

The mean of the squared differences from the mean can now be calculated. This gives us a value known as the **variance**, which is a measure of the spread of the data.

Statisticians more usually work with the square root of the variance which is the **standard deviation**.

The method for calculating the standard deviation can be summarised as:

1. The difference between each variable and the mean is squared.
2. The mean of these squares is calculated.
3. The standard deviation is the square root of the mean of the squares.

The formula for calculating the variance of the population is:

$$\sigma^2 = \frac{\Sigma(x - \mu)^2}{n}$$

where σ is the standard deviation, x is the variable, μ is the mean and n is the number of data items.

The standard deviation is:

$$\sigma = \sqrt{\frac{\Sigma(x - \mu)^2}{n}}$$

The formulas are the same for a sample, except that s and $\bar{x}$ are used.

$$s^2 = \frac{\Sigma(x - \bar{x})^2}{n}$$

In a normal distribution approximately 68% of the population are within one standard deviation either side of the mean. Approximately 95% of the population are within two standard deviations either side of the mean. Any member of the population outside this range may require further investigation as it could be an **outlier**.

Example 1 (single values)

Find the standard deviation of the following:

| 45 | 47 | 49 | 50 | 52 | 54 | 55 | 59 | 60 | 64 |

Solution

$$\text{Mean} = \frac{\Sigma x}{n} = \frac{535}{10} = 53.5$$

$$s^2 = \frac{\Sigma(x - \bar{x})^2}{n}$$

$$= \tfrac{1}{10}[(45 - 53.5)^2 + (47 - 53.5)^2 + (49 - 53.5)^2 + (50 - 53.5)^2$$

$$+ (52 - 53.5)^2 + (54 - 53.5)^2 + (55 - 53.5)^2 + (59 - 53.5)^2$$

$$+ (60 - 53.5)^2 + (64 - 53.5)^2]$$

$$= \tfrac{1}{10}[(-8.5)^2 + (-6.5)^2 + (-4.5)^2 + (-3.5)^2 + (-1.5)^2 + (0.5)^2$$

$$+ (1.5)^2 + (5.5)^2 + (6.5)^2 + (10.5)^2]$$

$$= \tfrac{1}{10}(72.25 + 42.25 + 20.25 + 12.25 + 2.25 + 0.25 + 2.25$$

$$+ 30.25 + 42.25 + 110.25)$$

$$= \tfrac{1}{10}(334.5) = 33.45$$

So $s = \sqrt{33.45} = 5.78$ (2 d.p.)

To calculate the standard deviation of a frequency distribution the formula becomes

$$s^2 = \frac{\Sigma f(x - \bar{x})^2}{\Sigma f} \quad \text{or} \quad s = \sqrt{\frac{\Sigma f(x - \bar{x})^2}{\Sigma f}}$$

Example 2 (frequency distribution)

Find the standard deviation of the following distribution of the number of children per family:

Children	0	1	2	3	4	5	6
Frequency	5	16	22	8	5	3	1

Solution

From the example on p.66 the mean, $\bar{x} = 2.08$ to two decimal places.

Children (x)	Frequency (f)	$x - \bar{x}$	$(x - \bar{x})^2$	$f(x - \bar{x})^2$
0	5	−2.08	4.33	21.63
1	16	−1.08	1.17	18.72
2	22	−0.08	0.0064	0.14
3	8	0.92	0.85	6.77
4	5	1.92	3.69	18.45
5	3	2.92	8.53	25.58
6	1	3.92	15.37	15.37
$\Sigma f = 60$				$\Sigma f(x - \bar{x})^2 = 106.66$

$$s^2 = \frac{\Sigma f(x - \bar{x})^2}{\Sigma f}$$
$$= \frac{106.66}{60}$$
$$= 1.7777$$
$$s = \sqrt{1.7777}$$
$$= 1.33 \ (2 \text{ d.p.})$$

4.7 Standard Deviation I
Exercise

Technique

1 Work out the mean and standard deviation of the following figures.

a   1, 3, 4, 6, 7, 9, 12

b   3, 7, 11, 15, 17, 22, 25, 34

c   0, 3, 5, 6, 9, 10, 12, 14, 15, 17, 19, 20

d   42, 44, 47, 48, 51, 52, 54, 57, 58, 60

e   3.2, 3.4, 3.5, 3.5, 3.7, 3.8, 3.9, 3.9, 4.0, 4.1, 4.1, 4.2, 4.4, 4.5

f   0.4, 0.2, 0.1, 0.4, 0.7, 0.4, 0.6, 0.8, 0.3, 0.4, 0.4, 0.5, 0.6, 0.1, 0.4

g   0.12, 0.14, 0.14, 0.12, 0.15, 0.17, 0.14, 0.12, 0.13, 0.14, 0.10

h $1\frac{1}{4}$, $2\frac{1}{4}$, $4\frac{3}{4}$, $3\frac{1}{2}$, 4, 2, $3\frac{3}{4}$, $2\frac{1}{2}$, $\frac{3}{4}$, $1\frac{3}{4}$, $3\frac{1}{4}$

i $-5, -3, -4, -1, 0, 2, -3, 1, -2, 0, -2, -3, -1, 0, 3, -1$

j $1\frac{1}{2}$, $3\frac{1}{4}$, $2\frac{1}{2}$, $2\frac{3}{4}$, $1\frac{1}{2}$, $-2\frac{1}{4}$, $-3\frac{1}{2}$, $-\frac{1}{2}$

2 Work out the mean and standard deviation of the following distributions:

a

Number	1	2	3	4	5	6
Frequency	5	7	9	8	6	5

b

Number	12	14	16	18	20	22	24	26
Frequency	6	10	22	28	25	16	11	2

c

Number	2.0	2.5	3.0	3.5	4.0	4.5	5.0	5.5	6.0
Frequency	9	12	17	18	35	38	23	12	6

d

Number	0.1	0.2	0.3	0.4	0.5	0.6	0.7	0.8	0.9
Frequency	112	83	65	47	38	21	16	11	7

e

Number	$\frac{1}{4}$	$\frac{1}{2}$	$\frac{3}{4}$	1	$1\frac{1}{4}$	$1\frac{1}{2}$	$1\frac{3}{4}$	2	$2\frac{1}{4}$	$2\frac{1}{2}$	$2\frac{3}{4}$	3
Frequency	25	39	49	67	51	42	24	13	9	6	4	3

4.8 Standard Deviation II

Example 1

Find an estimate for the standard deviation of the following distribution:

Age (years)	0–5	5–10	10–15	15–20	20–25	25–30	30–35
Frequency	5	8	12	18	9	6	2

Solution

In Example 2, Section 4.3, the mean, $\bar{x}$, was calculated as 16.17 years. We use the midpoint of each interval as the variable x for that interval. This leads to the following table:

Age (years)	Midpoint (x)	Frequency (f)	$(x - \bar{x})$	$f(x - \bar{x})^2$
0–5	2.5	5	−13.67	934.4
5–10	7.5	8	−8.67	601.35
10–15	12.5	12	−3.67	161.63
15–20	17.5	18	1.33	31.84
20–25	22.5	9	6.33	360.62
25–30	27.5	6	11.33	770.21
30–35	32.5	2	16.33	533.34
		$\Sigma f = 60$		$\Sigma f(x - \bar{x})^2 = 3393.33$

$$s^2 = \frac{\Sigma f(x - \bar{x})^2}{\Sigma f}$$

$$= \frac{3393.33}{60}$$

$$= 56.56$$

$$s = \sqrt{56.56}$$

$$= 7.52 \ (2 \ \text{d.p.})$$

A shorter working formula can be used to calculate the standard deviation. It is:

$$s^2 = \frac{\Sigma f x^2}{\Sigma f} - \bar{x}^2$$

Example 2

Using the figures from Example 1, on p.89, use the shorter formula to find the standard deviation.

Solution

Age (years)	Midpoint (x)	Frequency (f)	x^2	fx^2
0–5	2.5	5	6.25	31.25
5–10	7.5	8	56.25	450.00
10–15	12.5	12	156.25	1875.00
15–20	17.5	18	306.25	5512.50
20–25	22.5	9	506.25	4556.25
25–30	27.5	6	756.25	4537.50
30–35	32.5	2	1056.25	2112.50
		$\Sigma f = 60$		$\Sigma fx^2 = 19\,075.00$

$$s^2 = \frac{\Sigma fx^2}{\Sigma f} - \bar{x}^2$$

$$= \frac{19\,075}{60} - 16.17^2$$

$$= 317.917 - 261.47$$

$$= 56.45$$

$$s = \sqrt{56.45}$$

$$= 7.51 \ (2 \text{ d.p.})$$

There is a small difference between the values obtained using the two methods which is due to accumulation of rounding errors during the calculations.

This formula tends to lead to rounding errors, particularly when $\bar{x}$ is large. In such cases the other formula will give a more accurate answer.

4.8 Standard Deviation II
Exercise

Technique

Calculate an estimate of the mean and standard deviation of the following grouped data:

1

Age (years)	0–4	5–9	10–14	15–19	20–24	25–29
Frequency	8	11	13	19	7	2

2

Age (years)	Frequency
$15 < x \leq 20$	16
$20 < x \leq 25$	24
$25 < x \leq 30$	28
$30 < x \leq 40$	25
$40 < x \leq 50$	19
$50 < x \leq 65$	11
$65 < x \leq 80$	2

3

Length (cm)	Frequency
$1.0 < x \leq 1.5$	4
$1.5 < x \leq 2.0$	8
$2.0 < x \leq 2.5$	14
$2.5 < x \leq 3.0$	26
$3.0 < x \leq 4.0$	32
$4.0 < x \leq 5.0$	28
$5.0 < x \leq 6.0$	14
$6.0 < x \leq 8.0$	8
$8.0 < x \leq 10.0$	6

4

Time (s)	0–1	1–2	2–4	4–6	6–10	10–15	15–20	20–30	30–35
Frequency	86	65	43	28	17	9	7	5	4

5

Velocity ($m\,s^{-1}$)	0–5	5–10	10–15	15–20	20–30	30–50	50–80
Frequency	11	17	24	23	15	12	8

Contextual

1 In a test students were timed to find how long they took to answer a question, the times being taken to the nearest minute, up to a maximum of 20 minutes. The results were:

Time (min)	12	13	14	15	16	17	18	19
Students	2	11	17	21	27	15	5	2

Calculate an estimate of the mean and standard deviation of the times taken by the students.

2 On a random sample of 1000 claims Acne Insurance plc recorded the total amount, to the nearest pound, that was paid out. The grouped table shows the results.

Claim (£)	50–74	75–99	100–149	150–199	200–299	300–399	400–599	600–999
Claimants	57	266	208	193	95	81	55	45

   a Estimate, by means of a cumulative frequency graph, the median, quartiles and interquartile range of the distribution.

   b Calculate estimates for the mean and standard deviation of the distribution.

3 A class of physics students measured the time it took for different objects to roll down a rough plane. The time was measured to the nearest second.

Time interval	0–9	10–19	20–29	30–39	40–49	50–59	60–69	70–79
Frequency	10	14	16	18	16	15	8	3

Calculate estimates for the mean and standard deviation of the time taken.

4 The difference, in minutes, between the estimated journey time for buses on a particular route and the actual time taken was recorded as follows:

Time difference (min)	−10 to −5	−5 to 0	0 to 5	5 to 10	10 to 15	15 to 20
Frequency	9	35	48	23	11	8

Calculate estimates for the mean and standard deviation of the difference in journey times.

5 In trying to assess the level of difficulty of a test the following results were studied:

Score	0–20	20–30	30–40	40–50	50–60	60–70	70–80	80–90	90–100
Frequency	28	61	111	132	93	56	34	20	15

The test was supposed to have a mean of 50 and a standard deviation of 10. By calculating estimates of the mean and standard deviation from this sample assess whether the test fulfils its criteria.

Consolidation

Exercise A

1 The weights of 7 boys and 13 girls were measured. It was found that the mean weight of the boys was 58.1 kg and that of the girls was 62.7 kg. What was the mean weight of the whole group?

2 The average weekly incomes, in £s, of 14 selected occupations in the United Kingdom were:

161, 181, 227, 274, 340, 435, 585, 165, 263, 401, 764, 188, 329, 503

a Find the median, upper and lower quartiles.
b On graph paper, draw a box plot to represent these incomes.
c Calculate the mean weekly income and the standard deviation.

3 The times taken by competitors in a race were recorded to the nearest minute and grouped as below.

Time (min)	160–169	170–174	175–179	180–189	190–204
Number of competitors	16	12	20	30	12

Draw a histogram to represent this information and state the modal group.

4 Lightning Match Company's quality control department randomly sampled boxes to check the average contents. The results were:

Number of matches	63	64	65	66	67	68	69
Number of boxes	24	35	58	39	28	26	10

a Display this information graphically.
b Find the mode, the median and the mean.
c The average contents are stated on the box. Which figure should be quoted, and why?

5 The times, to the nearest minute, taken by a group of students to complete a fun run were recorded and grouped in the table below.

Time (min)	80–84	85–89	90–94	95–99	100–104
Number of students	12	38	45	32	23

Construct a cumulative frequency table for this distribution and draw a cumulative frequency curve. Use your curve to estimate:
a the median of students' times

b the interquartile range

c the percentage of students who took less than 86 minutes to complete the course.

A further group of 30 students completed the course but were outside the time allowed. If these students are taken into account, use your cumulative frequency curve to estimate the median time.

6 The table gives the ages, in years, of the population in an area of the United Kingdom.

Age	0–4	5–14	15–44	45–64	65–79	80 and over
Number (thousands)	260	543	1727	756	577	135

When a histogram was drawn to represent the population figures the 5–14 age group was represented by a bar of width 1 cm and height 5.4 cm.

a Find the widths and height, in centimetres, to one decimal place, of the bars representing the other age groups.

b Draw a histogram representing this distribution.

c Taking the midpoint of the last group to be 90 years, calculate an estimate for the mean age of the population in this region.

d Calculate the standard deviation of the distribution.

(ULEAC)

7 The following data shows the time taken, to the nearest minute, of the first 50 games in a chess tournament.

```
29  18  74  36  21  93  58  72  45  98  19  33  46  37  29
58  65  81  40  86  71  44  23  47  50  15  38  17  78  26
75  34  58  95  62  27  39  53  36  28  54  44  27  53  40
85  37  53  90  76
```

a Construct a stem and leaf diagram to represent these data.

b Find the median and quartiles of these times.

c Construct a box plot for these data.

d Form a grouped frequency table with equal groups 10–19, 20–29, and so on, and use this to calculate an estimate of the mean.

e Use the grouped figures to calculate an estimate for the standard deviation.

8 X is the set of numbers $\{1, 2, 3, 4, 5\}$ and Y is the set $\{6, 7, 8, 9\}$.

a Showing all working and without using any calculator facilities other than $+$, $-$, $\times$, and $\div$, calculate the mean M_x and the standard deviation S_x for set X.

b Find, using any aids, the mean M_y and the standard deviation S_y for the set Y.

c Write down the 20 numbers obtained by adding each number in set X to each number in set Y, and show this set, Z, in a frequency table.

d Find the mean M_z for the set Z and show that the standard deviation S_z is about 1.8.

e State the percentage of set Z which is within one standard deviation of its mean.

f State a relationship between M_x, M_y, M_z and a relationship between S_x, S_y, S_z.

(*OCSEB*)

9 A random sample of 70 buses were monitored for lateness, arriving at one of their destinations. The times, to the nearest minute, are shown in the table.

	Minutes late (0|2 means 2)														Totals
0	1	1	1	2	2	3	3	3	4	4	4	5	5		13
0	6	6	6	6	6	7	7	8	8	8	8	9	9	9	
1	0	0	1	1	1	2	2	3	3	4	5	5	5		
1	6	6	7	7	7	7	8	8	9	9					10
2	0	0	1	2	2	2	3	4							
2	5	7	8												
3	2	2	5												3
3	8														1
4	1	3													2
4	6	8													2
5	0														1

a Write down the values needed to complete the stem and leaf diagram.

b Find the median and quartiles of these times.

c Find the 35th percentile.

d On graph paper construct a box plot for these data, showing clearly your scale.

A random sample of buses arriving at the same destination on another route, had a minimum value of 9 minutes late and a maximum value of 33 minutes. The quartiles were 15, 21 and 29 minutes.

e On the same graph paper and using the same scale, construct a box plot for these data.

f Compare and contrast the bus journeys based on these data.

10 The heights of a group of 20 students were recorded to the nearest centimetre as follows:

162	160	157	164	175	153	157	159	161	164
161	159	158	164	161	159	160	160	161	159

a **i** Find the mean and standard deviation of the group.
    ii An outlier is defined as a value that is more than two standard deviations away from the mean. In this group, give the boundaries for outliers and identify the single outlier.

b If this one value is eliminated from the group, leaving only 19 values:
    i will the mean be greater or less than that of the whole group;
    ii will the standard deviation be greater or less than that of the group as a whole?

c It is now required that the mean is found. One way is to start again, with no reference to previous work, to find the mean of the 19 values. Alternatively, the mean can be found from the previous value using the formula:

$$m_2 = \frac{am_1 - x}{19}$$

where m_1 is the mean of the 20 values already found, x is the value of the outlier and m_2 is the mean of the 19 values.
    i State the value of a in the formula.
    ii Using this formula, find the mean of the 19 values.

(MEI)

Exercise B

1 The heights of 13 boys and 12 girls were measured. It was found that the mean height of the boys was 1.69 m and that of the girls was 1.62 m. What was the mean height of the whole group?

2 The average weekly incomes, in £s, of 18 selected occupations in the United Kingdom were:

244,   146,   278,   396,   435,   641,   577,   122,   294,
357,   802,   730,   286,   484,   169,   559,   208,   498

a Find the median, upper and lower quartiles.
b On graph paper, draw a box plot to represent these incomes.
c Calculate the mean weekly income and the standard deviation.

3 The times taken by competitors in a marathon race were recorded to the nearest minute and grouped as below.

Time (min)	200–219	220–229	230–249	250–269	270–300
Number of competitors	36	65	158	84	45

Draw a histogram to represent this information, and obtain the modal group.

4 Lite Snaks Crisp Company's quality control department regularly samples packets of crisps to gauge the average contents. During one production run the results were:

Number of crisps	18	19	20	21	22	23	24
Number of boxes	11	15	61	47	34	22	10

a Display this information graphically.
b Find the mode, the median and the mean.
c The company would like to advertise the average number of crisps in a packet. Which figure should be quoted and why? (Assuming there are no legal restrictions on which value is given.)

5 The time, to the nearest minute, taken by participants on an outward bound course to complete an obstacle course were recorded and grouped in the table below.

Time (min)	5–7	8–10	11–13	14–16	17–19
Number of students	4	13	37	28	18

Construct a cumulative frequency table for this distribution and draw a cumulative frequency curve. Use your curve to estimate:

a the median of participants' times
b the interquartile range
c the percentage of participants who took more than 15 minutes to complete the course.

Twenty other participants completed the course but took longer than 20 minutes. If they are taken into account use your cumulative frequency curve to estimate the median time.

6 The table gives the ages, in years, of the population in a particular region of the United Kingdom.

Age	0–9	10–14	15–29	30–49	50–69	70 and over
Number (thousands)	531	657	1452	1899	740	463

When a histogram was drawn to represent the population figures the 10–14 age group was represented by a bar of width 1 cm and height 6.6 cm.

a Find the widths and height, in centimetres to one decimal place, of the bars representing the other age groups.
b Draw a histogram representing this distribution.
c Taking the midpoint of the last group to be 85 years, calculate an estimate for the mean age of the population in this region.
d Calculate the standard deviation of the distribution.

7 Biology students measured the lengths of a sample of 70 grasses, to the nearest centimetre. The results were:

64	36	91	16	53	77	32	28	72	90	42	25	68	15
23	50	34	82	16	98	42	85	63	58	61	30	89	22
34	37	63	58	88	83	64	41	59	86	13	45	67	59
52	41	84	66	74	59	58	40	73	64	11	14	82	56
43	85	67	42	91	24	76	40	55	83	24	76	54	36

a Construct a stem and leaf diagram to represent these data.

b Find the median and quartiles of these lengths.

c Construct a box plot for these data.

d Form a grouped frequency table with equal groups 10–19, 20–29, and so on, and use this to calculate an estimate of the mean.

e Use the grouped figures to calculate an estimate for the standard deviation.

8 X is the set of numbers $\{2, 4, 6, 8\}$ and Y is the set $\{1, 3, 5, 7, 9\}$.

a Showing all working and without using any calculator facilities other than $+$, $-$, $\times$ and $\div$, calculate the mean M_x and the standard deviation S_x for set X.

b Find, using any aids, the mean M_y and the standard deviation S_y for the set Y.

c Write down the numbers obtained by adding each number in set X to each number in set Y, and show this set, Z, in a frequency table.

d Find the mean M_z for the set Z and the standard deviation S_z.

e State the percentage of set Z which is within one standard deviation of its mean.

f State a relationship between M_x, M_y, M_z and a relationship between S_x, S_y, S_z.

9 Summarised below is the data relating to the number of minutes, to the nearest minute, that a random sample of 65 trains from Darlingborough were late arriving at a main line station.

														Totals
0	2	3	3	3	4	4	4	4	5	5	5	5	5	5	14
0	6	6	6	7	7	8	8	8	9					9
1	0	0	0	2	2	3	3	4	4	4	5			
1	2	6	7	7	8	8	8	9	9					
2	1	2	2	3	3	3	3	4						
2	6													
3	3	4	4	5										4
3	6	8												2
4	1	3												2
4	7	7	9											3
5	2	4												2

Key: 0|2 means 2 min late

a Write down the values needed to complete the stem and leaf diagram.
b Find the median and quartiles of these times.
c Find the 67th percentile.
d On graph paper construct a box plot for these data, showing clearly your scale.

A random sample of trains arriving at the same main line station from Shefton had a minimum value of 15 minutes late and a maximum value of 30 minutes. The quartiles were 18, 22 and 27 minutes.

e On the same graph paper and using the same scale, construct a box plot for these data.
f Compare and contrast the train journeys from Darlingborough and Shefton based on these data.

(*ULEAC*)

10 The heights of a group of 20 students were recorded to the nearest centimetre as follows:

| 77 | 64 | 68 | 71 | 73 | 75 | 74 | 61 | 64 | 68 |
| 63 | 51 | 76 | 64 | 67 | 76 | 63 | 67 | 66 | 76 |

a **i** Find the mean and standard deviation of the group.
  ii An outlier is defined as a value that is more than two standard deviations away from the mean. In this group, give the boundaries for outliers and identify the single outlier.
b If this one value is eliminated from the group, leaving only 19 values:
  i will the mean be greater or less than that of the whole group,
  ii will the standard deviation be greater or less than that of the group as a whole?
c It is now required that this mean be found. One way is to start again, with no reference to previous work, to find the mean of the 19 values. Alternatively, the mean can be found from the previous value using the formula:

$$m_2 = \frac{am_1 - x}{19}$$

where m_1 is the mean of the 20 values already found, x is the value of the outlier and m_2 is the mean of the 19 values.
  i State the value of a in the formula.
  ii Using this formula, find the mean of the 19 values.

Applications and Activities

1 Using the information from Chapter 3, Activity 2, develop your discussion to include measurements in support or otherwise of your argument for the North/South divide.

2 Define, by description and measurement, the average Year 12 student.

Summary

- The three averages are:

  1. the *mean*, $\bar{x}$, which is $\dfrac{\Sigma fx}{\Sigma f}$;
  2. the *mode*, which is the value with the highest frequency;
  3. the *median*, which is the middle value if values are in numerical order.

- For grouped data, the mean can be estimated using the midpoint of the group as the value.

- For grouped data, the median can be estimated by drawing a cumulative frequency curve.

- A cumulative frequency curve can also be used to find the upper and lower quartiles and, from those, the interquartile range.

- With larger samples the distribution can be divided into smaller sections using percentiles.

- A box and whisker diagram (box plot) is used to illustrate the range, quartiles and median.

- The standard deviation of a distribution is calculated either by using the formula

$$s^2 = \frac{\Sigma f(x - \bar{x})^2}{\Sigma f},$$

where s is the standard deviation, f is the frequency, x is the variable, $\bar{x}$ is the mean and Σf is the total frequency,

or the formula

$$s^2 = \frac{\Sigma fx^2}{\Sigma f} - \bar{x}^2$$

5 Probability

What you need to know

- An event is the outcome from an experiment or trial.

- Probability is measured on a scale from 0 to 1.

- The probability of an event occurring $= \dfrac{\text{number of successful outcomes}}{\text{total number of outcomes}}$

Review

1 When two teams play each other at hockey how many outcomes are there?

2 What is the probability that:

   a   tomorrow is Tuesday
   b   it will rain tomorrow?

3 If the probability that Joe is late is $\frac{1}{3}$, what is the probability that he will be on time?

4 An ordinary dice is thrown. What is the probability that the number thrown is:

   a   less than 3
   b   more than 7
   c   a factor of 6?

5.1 Calculating Probabilities

There are several methods of finding probabilities; for example, theoretically, experimentally and subjectively.

Theoretical probability is when we can calculate probabilities using previous knowledge.

For example we know that a fair dice has six sides, all of which are equally likely to land face up when the dice is thrown. The probability of throwing a five with a fair dice is one out of six or $\frac{1}{6}$.

Experimental, or **empirical**, probability is when we actually have to carry out a large number of trials to determine the probability of any particular outcome. To find the probability that a slice of bread will land butter-side up when dropped, we would have to drop a large number of slices of buttered bread and record the number that landed butter-side up. By recording the relative frequency of 'successes' we could find the probability of any one slice landing butter-side up.

For some events, the outcomes are not equally likely, and it is not possible to repeat the experiment a large number of times. In such cases we have to form a **subjective** probability. To find the probability that it will rain on St Swithin's day we would have to look at the weather records for many years. On the basis of that information we could estimate the probability that it might rain on the next St Swithin's day.

Superstitution says that if it rains on St Swithin's day (15 July) it will rain for the next 40 days.

Probability notation

If we consider a sixth form with 100 students, of whom 20 are studying maths, 15 are studying chemistry and eight are studying both maths and chemistry, we can illustrate this information in a **Venn diagram**.

All those students studying mathematics belong to the set M. (A **set** is the name for a group of objects that are linked in some way.) In a Venn diagram each set is represented by a circle. The numbers inside the circles, or parts of circles, give the number of objects (people) in that particular set.

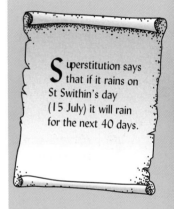
John Venn (1834–1923) Inventor of the Venn diagram. Venn published the *Logic of Chance* in 1866.

As there are eight students studying both maths and chemistry the number 8 is written in the part of the diagram that represents both maths and chemistry. The total number in the M circle must be 20, as there are 20 students altogether studying maths. Similarly the total number in the C circle must be 15. Note that each student is only represented once, even though they are taking both maths and chemistry.

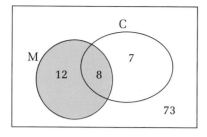

If we choose a sixth form student at random, the probability that the student studies maths is written $P(M)$, where

$$P(M) = \frac{20}{100} = \frac{1}{5}$$

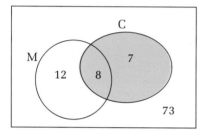

Similarly the probability that a randomly chosen student studies chemistry is

$$P(C) = \frac{15}{100} = \frac{3}{20}$$

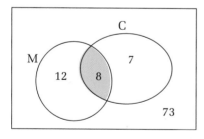

The shaded region on the Venn diagram above shows the probability that the student studies *both* maths *and* chemistry. The shaded region is written as $M \cap C$, and is read as M **intersection** C. The probability that a student studies both maths and chemistry is written $P(M \cap C)$, where

$$P(M \cap C) = \frac{8}{100} = \frac{2}{25}$$

The 73 outside the circles represents the students who take neither maths nor chemistry.

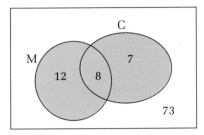

The probability that the student studies *either* maths *or* chemistry is shown by the shading in the above diagram. The shaded region is written as M ∪ C, and is read as M **union** C. The probability that a student studies either maths or chemistry is

$$P(M \cup C) = \frac{(12+8+7)}{100} = \frac{27}{100}$$

We can also find the probability that a student *does not* study maths from the Venn diagram. The notation $P(M')$ is used to stand for the probability of *not* M. An alternative notation is $P(\bar{M})$.

Thus $P(M') = \frac{(7+73)}{100} = \frac{80}{100} = \frac{4}{5}$

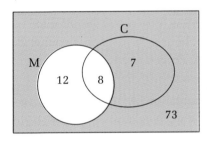

All students must either study maths or not study maths.

It is important to realise that

$$P(M') = 1 - P(M)$$

This is known as **complementary** probability.

$P(M' \cap C)$ is the probability that a student does *not* study maths but *does* study chemistry.

$$P(M' \cap C) = \frac{7}{100}$$

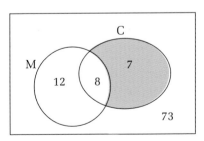

The shaded area of the diagram shows that there are seven students who do not study maths but do study chemistry.

5.1 Calculating Probablities
Exercise

Contextual

1 Draw a Venn diagram to show the following information. In a group of 30 students, 15 play chess, 10 play snooker and 6 play both. Use your diagram to find:

a the probability that a student chosen at random from the group plays snooker;

b the probability that the student plays both chess and snooker;

c the probability that the student plays neither chess nor snooker.

2 You may find it helpful to use a Venn diagram to answer this question. In a class of 25 students five are left-handed. There are 13 girls in the class, of whom three are left-handed. If a student is chosen at random calculate the probability that:

a the student is right-handed

b the student is a left-handed male

c the student is a right-handed female.

3 In a road of 30 houses, three have double glazing and cavity wall insulation. Eleven houses have neither double glazing nor cavity wall insulation, and 17 altogether have double glazing. What is the probability that a house chosen at random has:

a cavity wall insulation but not double glazing

b either cavity wall insulation or double glazing?

4 In a junior school class of 28 pupils, seven are in both a sports team and the school band. There are 16 pupils involved in sports teams and ten in the school band. Find the probability that a pupil chosen at random:

a is only in the school band

b is in either a sports team or the school band

c is in neither a sports team nor the school band.

5 In a road of 30 houses, 25 are known to have a video recorder. Eight of these houses also have a mobile phone. One house has neither a video recorder nor a mobile phone. If one house is chosen at random what is the probability that:

a it has a mobile phone

b it has either a video recorder or a mobile phone?

6 A group of 60 people were asked whether they had watched Channel 5 or Sky TV during the past week. Thirty-five said they watched Channel 5, 20 watched Sky TV and 14 watched neither channel. What is the probability that a person chosen at random watched:

a both channels

b Channel 5 but not Sky TV

c either Channel 5 or Sky TV?

5.2 Addition Rule for Probability

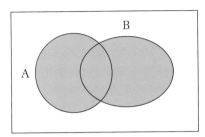

The diagram shows two events A and B. The shaded area represents $P(A \cup B)$, that is the probability of A *or* B occurring. This can be found by adding the probability of A to the probability of B and subtracting the probability of both A and B.

The probability of A or B occurring means A occurs, or B occurs, or both occur.

This gives us the important result

$$P(\mathbf{A} \cup \mathbf{B}) = P(\mathbf{A}) + P(\mathbf{B}) - P(\mathbf{A} \cap \mathbf{B})$$

$P(A \cap B)$ is subtracted as the members of the intersection are already included in $P(A)$ and $P(B)$.

Using the example in the last section,

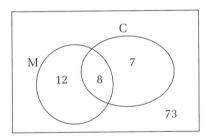

$P(M) = \frac{1}{5}$, $P(C) = \frac{3}{20}$, and $P(M \cap C) = \frac{2}{25}$,

so $P(M \cup C) = \frac{1}{5} + \frac{3}{20} - \frac{2}{25}$

$= \frac{27}{100}$

Notice this is the same as the answer obtained on p. 104.

Mutually exclusive events

A card is chosen from a pack of 52 playing cards. If that card is a spade then it cannot be a red card.

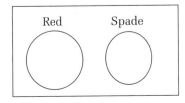

Events such as this, where two outcomes cannot occur at the same time are said to be **mutually exclusive** and we have:

$$P(A \cup B) = P(A) + P(B)$$

If A and B are mutually exclusive $P(A \cap B) = 0$.

If $P(A \cup B) = 1$ then the events A and B are said to **exhaustive.** This means that there are only two possible outcomes; A and B. For example, if a playing card is chosen at random it can either be red or black:

$P(\text{red card}) = \frac{1}{2}, \; P(\text{black card}) = \frac{1}{2}$

$P(\text{red} \cup \text{black}) = \frac{1}{2} + \frac{1}{2}$

$\qquad\qquad\qquad = 1$

Example 1

A card is drawn at random from an ordinary pack of 52 playing cards. Find the probability that the card is:

a a spade or a diamond
b a spade or an ace.

Solution

a If S is the event 'a spade is drawn' and D is the event 'a diamond is drawn' then S and D are mutually exclusive as a card cannot be both a spade and a diamond.

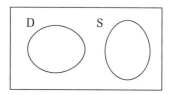

$P(S \cup D) = P(S) + P(D)$

$\qquad\qquad = \frac{1}{4} + \frac{1}{4} = \frac{1}{2}$

b

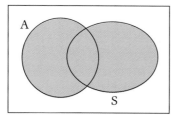

A card can be both a spade and an ace. Therefore,

$P(S \cup A) = P(S) + P(A) - P(S \cap A)$

$\qquad\qquad = \frac{1}{4} + \frac{1}{13} - \frac{1}{52}$

$\qquad\qquad = \frac{4}{13}$

Example 2

An octahedral (eight-sided) dice is thrown. Work out the probability that the number thrown is:

a an even number
b a multiple of 3
c a multiple of 4
d either an even number or a multiple of 3
e either an odd number or a multiple of 4.

Solution

The possible outcomes are 1, 2, 3, 4, 5, 6, 7, 8.

a $P(\text{an even number}) = \frac{4}{8} = \frac{1}{2}$
b $P(\text{a multiple of 3}) = \frac{2}{8} = \frac{1}{4}$
c $P(\text{a multiple of 4}) = \frac{2}{8} = \frac{1}{4}$
d $P(\text{either an even number or a multiple of 3}) =$

$P(\text{even number}) + P(\text{multiple of 3}) - P(\text{even number and multiple of 3})$

$$= \frac{1}{2} + \frac{1}{4} - \frac{1}{8}$$

$$= \frac{5}{8}$$

e $P(\text{either an odd number or a multiple of 4})$

These events are mutually exclusive as a number cannot be both odd and a multiple of 4.

So the required probability $= \frac{1}{2} + \frac{1}{4}$

$$= \frac{3}{4}$$

5.2 Addition Rule for Probability

Exercise

Contextual

1 A card is drawn at random from a pack of 52 playing cards. Work out the probability that:

   a   the card is either a heart or a queen

   b   the card is either a heart or a diamond

   c   the card is either a red card or a ten.

2 A ten-sided dice, numbered 1 to 10, is thrown. Calculate the probability that:

   a   the number scored is a prime number

   b   the number scored is either a prime number or a multiple of 4

   c   the number scored is either a multiple of 4 or a multiple of 3.

3 If E and F are two events such that $P(E) = \frac{1}{4}$, $P(F) = \frac{1}{2}$, and $P(E \cap F) = \frac{1}{8}$, find:

   a $P(E \cup F)$ **b** $P(E \cup F)'$

4 For each of the following pairs of events, X and Y, say whether or not they are: **i** mutually exclusive **ii** exhaustive.

   a   A student is chosen at random from a tutor group. Event X: student is right-handed, event Y: student is left-handed.

   b   A fair dice is thrown. Event X: dice shows a multiple of 3, event Y: dice shows a prime number.

   c   A card is dealt from a pack of playing cards. Event X: the card is a spade, event Y: the card is a King.

5 A twelve-sided dice is thrown. Work out the probability that the number thrown is:

   a   an even number

   b   a multiple of 3

   c   either an even number or a multiple of 3

   d   either an odd number or a multiple of 6.

6 If $P(A) = 0.2$, $P(B) = 0.5$ and $P(A \cap B) = 0.1$, find:

   a $P(A \cup B)$ **b** $P(A \cup B)'$ **c** $P(A' \cup B)$

7 Two events K and L are such that $P(K) = 0.2$, $P(L) = 0.1$ and $P(K \cup L) = 0.3$. Are K and L mutually exclusive? Explain your answer clearly.

5.3 Product Rule for Independent Events

C is the event 'result of spinning a fair coin' and D is the event 'number obtained when a fair dice is rolled'. These events are unconnected. Obtaining a head on the coin will not influence the outcome on the dice. Such events are said to be **independent**.

When events are independent

$$P(C \cap D) = P(C) \times P(D)$$

This result can be shown by using a **probability space diagram** (or **possibility space diagram**). This diagram is formed by recording all the possible outcomes in a table.

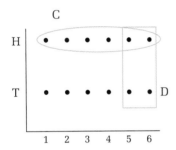

Let C be the event 'a head is obtained' and let D be the event 'a number greater than 4' occurs. These events can be indicated by drawing a loop around the relevant outcomes. From the diagram you can see that

$$P(C) = \tfrac{6}{12} = \tfrac{1}{2}, \ P(D) = \tfrac{4}{12} = \tfrac{1}{3} \text{ and } P(C \cap D) = \tfrac{2}{12} = \tfrac{1}{6}$$

Using the product rule gives

$$P(C \cap D) = P(C) \times P(D)$$
$$= \tfrac{1}{2} \times \tfrac{1}{3}$$
$$= \tfrac{1}{6}$$

which is the same as the result obtained directly from the diagram.

Example 1

A coin is thrown and a card is drawn from a pack of eight cards numbered 1 to 8. By drawing a probability space diagram, find:

a the probability that a head and a 4 are obtained;
b the probability that the outcome is a tail and a card greater than 5.

Solution

a

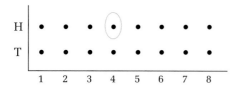

$P(\text{head and a 4}) = \frac{1}{16}$

b

$P(\text{tail and a card greater than 5}) = \frac{3}{16}$

In both cases the events are independent. It is therefore possible to calculate these answers using the product rule.

a $P(\text{head}) = \frac{1}{2}$ and $P(4) = \frac{1}{8}$
$\therefore P(\text{head and a four}) = \frac{1}{2} \times \frac{1}{8}$
$= \frac{1}{16}$

b $P(\text{tail}) = \frac{1}{2}$ and $P(\text{a card greater than 5}) = \frac{3}{8}$
$\therefore P(\text{tail and a card greater than 5}) = \frac{1}{2} \times \frac{3}{8}$
$= \frac{3}{16}$

Example 2

Two events F and G are independent. $P(F) = 0.4$ and $P(G) = 0.25$. Calculate:

a $P(F \cap G)$ **b** $P(F \cup G)$

Solution

As F and G are independent events the product rule can be used.

a $P(F \cap G) = 0.4 \times 0.25$
$= 0.1$

b $P(F \cup G) = 0.4 + 0.25 - 0.1$
$= 0.55$

Remember that $P(F \cup G)$
$P(F) + P(G) - P(F \cap G)$

5.3 Product Rule for Independent Events

Exercise

Contextual

1 Draw a probability space diagram to represent the scores when two dice are thrown. Find the probability of:

   a   obtaining a score of 7   **b**   throwing a double

   c   scoring less than 4.

2 D and E are two independent events such that $P(D) = 0.3$ and $P(E) = 0.4$. Find:

   a $P(D \cap E)$ **b** $P(D \cup E)$

3 Three events, A, B and C, are such that A and B are mutually exclusive and $P(A) = 0.3$, $P(C) = 0.4$, $P(A \cup B) = 0.5$ and $P(B \cup C) = 0.54$.

   a   Calculate $P(B)$ and $P(B \cap C)$.

   b   Determine whether or not B and C are independent.

(WJEC)

4 A bag contains four blue counters and six yellow counters. One counter is taken from the bag, its colour is noted and it is then replaced. A second counter is then taken from the bag and its colour is noted before it is replaced. What is the probability that the first counter is blue and the second counter is yellow? If a third counter is then taken from the bag, what is the probability that the first counter is yellow, the second counter is blue and the third counter is blue?

5 A coin is thrown four times.

   a   What is the probability that it lands 'heads' each time?

   b   What is the probability that it lands 'heads' only once?

6 Repeat question 4, but this time the counters are not replaced after they have been taken from the bag.

5.4 Conditional Probability

Let us return to the group of students at the beginning of the chapter.

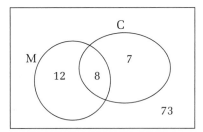

If you know that a particular student studies chemistry, how does this affect the probability that they study maths? Altogether 15 students study chemistry, of whom eight also study maths. Therefore the probability that a student studies maths *given* that they study chemistry, is

$$\frac{\text{number of students in } M \cap C}{\text{number of students in } C} = \frac{8}{15}$$

This is known as **conditional probability** and is written $P(M|C)$. It is read as 'the probability of M given C'.

If we divide top and bottom of this fraction by the total number of students we obtain

$$P(M|C) = \frac{8/100}{15/100} = \frac{P(M \cap C)}{P(C)}$$

So $\boxed{P(M|C) = \dfrac{P(M \cap C)}{P(C)}}$ ◀ Learn this important result.

It is possible to rearrange this formula by multiplying both sides by $P(C)$. This gives

$$P(M \cap C) = P(M|C) \times P(C)$$

Example 1

D and E are two events are such that $P(D) = 0.3$, $P(E) = 0.5$ and $P(D|E) = 0.25$. Find:

a $P(D \cap E)$
b $P(D \cup E)$
c $P(D|E')$

Solution

a $P(D \cap E) = P(D|E) \times P(E)$
$\qquad = 0.25 \times 0.5$
$\qquad = 0.125$

b $P(D \cup E) = P(D) + P(E) - P(D \cap E)$
$\qquad = 0.3 + 0.5 - 0.125$
$\qquad = 0.675$

c

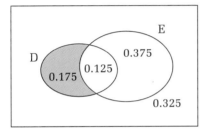

$$P(D|E') = \frac{P(D \cap E')}{P(E')}$$

$$= \frac{0.175}{0.5}$$

$$= 0.35$$

From the Venn diagram, $P(D \cap E') = 0.175$ and $P(E') = 0.175 + 0.325$ $= 0.5$.

Example 2

A card is chosen at random from a set of twenty-five cards numbered from 1 to 25. What is the probability that the card chosen is a multiple of 4, given that it is greater than 15?

Solution

$$P(\text{multiple of } 4 | \text{greater than } 15) = \frac{P(\text{multiple of } 4 \cap \text{greater than } 15)}{P(\text{greater than } 15)}$$

Three numbers are multiples of 4 and greater than 15, namely 16, 20 and 24.

Thus $P(\text{multiple of } 4 \cap \text{greater than } 15) = \frac{3}{25}$
and $P(\text{greater than } 15) = \frac{10}{25}$

Now $P(\text{multiple of } 4 | \text{greater than } 15) = \frac{3/25}{10/25}$
$\qquad\qquad\qquad\qquad\qquad\qquad = \frac{3}{10}$

115

5.4 Conditional Probability
Exercise

Contextual

1 Two events R and S have probabilities $P(R) = 0.3$, $P(S) = 0.2$ and $P(R \cap S) = 0.1$. Calculate:

    a $P(R \cup S)$ **b** $P(R|S)$

2 When an eight-sided dice is thrown, an odd number occurs. What is the probability that it is a prime number?

3 The events A and B are such that $P(A) = \frac{3}{5}$, $P(B) = \frac{1}{4}$, $P(A \cup B) = \frac{11}{20}$. Find:

    a $P(A \cap B)$ **b** $P(B|A)$

4 Two cards are drawn, one at a time, from a pack of 52 playing cards, and are not replaced. Find the probability that the second card is an ace given that:

    a   the first card was an ace   **b**   the first card was not an ace.

5 A box contains eight milk chocolates and seven plain chocolates. Jane chooses a chocolate at random, and eats it. She then chooses another chocolate. Find the probability that:

    a   the first chocolate is a milk chocolate;

    b   the first chocolate is a milk chocolate and the second is a plain chocolate;

    c   the two chocolates are different (one plain and one milk).

6 R and S are two events such that $P(R) = \frac{2}{5}$, $P(R|S) = \frac{1}{3}$, $P(S|R) = \frac{1}{2}$. Find $P(R \cup S)$ and state, with reasons, whether R and S are mutually exclusive.

7 A box contains five silver coins and seven gold coins. One coin is taken out of the box, and is put to one side. A second coin is then taken from the box. Find the probability that:

    a   the first coin is silver   **b**   both coins are silver

    c   the second coin is gold given that the first coin was silver.

8 In a school sixth form 12% of the students are left-handed, 15% of the students wear glasses, and 3% are both left-handed and wear glasses.

    a   Given that a student wears glasses, find the probability that that student is left-handed.

    b   What is the probability that a left-handed student also wears glasses?

9 In a group of 50 people, 25 own a cat, 15 own a dog and five own both a cat and a dog. If a person is chosen at random find the probability that they:

    a   own a dog or a cat

    b   own either a cat or a dog but not both

    c   own a cat given that they own a dog.

5.5 Probability Tree Diagrams

Tree diagrams are very useful in solving probability problems, either where one event is repeated, or where more than one event occurs.

Example 1

The probability that Jeffrey is late for college on any one day is 0.15 and is independent of whether he was late on the previous day. Find the probability that Jeffrey is:

a late on Monday and Tuesday
b arrives on time on one of these days.

Solution

Monday	Tuesday	Outcome	Probability
	late	l, l	$0.15 \times 0.15 = 0.0225$

late
0.15
0.85
on time

late 0.15
on time 0.85
late 0.15
on time 0.85

		Outcome	Probability
	late	l, l	$0.15 \times 0.15 = 0.0225$
	on time	l, ot	$0.15 \times 0.85 = 0.1275$
	late	ot, l	$0.85 \times 0.15 = 0.1275$
	on time	ot, ot	$0.85 \times 0.85 = 0.7225$

a From the tree diagram you can read off the probability that Jeffrey is late on Monday and Tuesday, which is 0.0225.

b The outcome that Jeffrey arrives on time on one of these days means either **i** he is on time on Monday and is late on Tuesday, or **ii** he is late on Monday but arrives on time on Tuesday. The probability can be found by adding together the probabilities of outcomes **i** and **ii**. This gives $0.1275 + 0.1275 = 0.255$

Example 2

Research shows that if it rains on any one day in the town of Non, then the probability that it rains the next day is 30%. If it is fair one day then the probability that it rains the next day is 15%. If it is fair on Wednesday, what is the probability that it rains on Friday?

Solution

A probability of 30% is the same as a probability of 0.3. Similarly a probability of 15% can be written as 0.15. If it is fair on Wednesday, the probability that it rains on Thursday is 0.15 and the probability that it is fair must be 0.85. If it does rain on Thursday, then the probability that it rains on Friday will be 0.3, and the probability that it is fair will be 0.7.

Wednesday	Thursday	Friday	Outcome	Probability
		rain	r, r	$0.15 \times 0.3 = 0.045$
	rain (0.3)			
	(0.15) (0.7)	fair	r, f	$0.15 \times 0.7 = 0.105$
fair		rain	f, r	$0.85 \times 0.15 = 0.1275$
	(0.85) (0.15)			
	fair			
	(0.85)	fair	f, f	$0.85 \times 0.85 = 0.7225$

Note that the sum of the probabilities in the final column is 1.

You can see from the tree diagram that there are two outcomes that give rain on Friday 'rain, rain' and 'fair, rain'. In order to find the probability that it rained on Friday you must add the probabilities of the two required outcomes.

$$P(\text{rain, rain}) + P(\text{fair, rain}) = (0.15 \times 0.3) + (0.85 \times 0.15)$$
$$= 0.045 + 0.1275$$
$$= 0.1725$$

Remember!
To find the probabilities you must **multiply** along the branches, and **add** between the branches

Example 3

A box contains eight blue pens and four red pens. Abdul chooses two pens.

a What is the probability that both pens are red?

b What is the probability that he chooses one pen of each colour?

Solution

We can think of this as Abdul choosing one pen, which is not replaced before he chooses a second pen. This means that when he chooses the second pen he is choosing from only 11 pens.

1st pen	2nd pen	Outcome	Probability
blue (8/12)	blue (7/11)	b, b	$\frac{8}{12} \times \frac{7}{11} = \frac{14}{33}$
	red (4/11)	b, r	$\frac{8}{12} \times \frac{4}{11} = \frac{8}{33}$
red (4/12)	blue (8/11)	r, b	$\frac{4}{12} \times \frac{8}{11} = \frac{8}{33}$
	red (3/11)	r, r	$\frac{4}{12} \times \frac{3}{11} = \frac{3}{33}$

a From the tree diagram there is only one outcome that gives two red pens:

$$P(\text{red, red}) = \frac{3}{33}$$

$$= \frac{1}{11}$$

b You can see from the tree diagram that there are two outcomes that give 'a pen of each colour' – blue, red and red, blue.

In order to find the probability that the pens are of different colours you must add the probabilities of the two required outcomes.

$$P(\text{blue, red}) + P(\text{red, blue}) = \frac{8}{33} + \frac{8}{33}$$

$$= \frac{16}{33}$$

5.5 Probability Tree Diagrams
Exercise

Contextual

1 A bag contains three green balls and five yellow balls. One ball is chosen and its colour noted before being replaced in the bag. A second ball is selected and its colour is also noted. By drawing a probability tree work out:

   a the probability that two green balls are chosen;
   b the probability that the two balls are of different colours.

2 The experiment is repeated, but this time the first ball is *not replaced* before the second ball is chosen. Find the probability that both balls are yellow.

3 In a sixth form of 100 students 12 are left-handed. If two students are chosen at random what is the probability that:

   a both are left-handed
   b neither are left-handed?

Extend your probability tree diagram to show the possible outcomes if three students are chosen.

4 At an activity holiday centre children choose either painting or drama as their activity on the first morning and horse-riding, football or swimming as their activity on the first afternoon. Past records show that in one morning 60% choose painting, and in the afternoon 45% choose horse-riding and 30% choose football, and that the afternoon choices are made independently of the morning choices.

   a Draw a tree diagram to illustrate the probabilities of the various choices for a child selected at random.
   b Use your tree diagram to find the probabilities that a child selected at random chooses:
      i drama in the morning and swimming in the afternoon;
      ii neither drama nor horse-riding.

(OCSEB)

5 The probability of a person catching a disease, when they have been exposed to it, is 0.3% if they have been vaccinated against the disease, and 0.9% if they have not been vaccinated. If 75% of the population have been vaccinated against the disease, what is the probability that someone, chosen at random, has been vaccinated and catches the disease?

6 The probability that a biased coin lands 'heads' is 0.6. This coin is thrown twice. Draw a probability tree diagram to show the possible outcomes. Find the probability that exactly one head is obtained. Extend your tree diagram to show the possible outcomes if the coin is thrown a third time. Find the probability that you will only obtain one head.

Consolidation

Exercise A

1 From a pack of 52 playing cards two cards are drawn without replacement. Giving your answers as fractions in their simplest forms, calculate the probability that:

a both are spades

b neither card is red

c one card is red and the other is black.

2 Two events K and L are such that $P(K) = 0.2$, $P(K' \cap L) = 0.22$ and $P(K \cap L) = 0.18$. Find:

a $P(K \cap L')$ **b** $P(K|L)$

3 Two school football teams play each other twice in a season. The probability that team A wins is $\frac{1}{2}$, and the probability that team B wins is $\frac{2}{5}$. By drawing a tree diagram, find the probability that:

a both matches are drawn

b teams A and B each win one match.

4 **a** An ordinary six-sided dice is thrown once. A is the event: Score is 1 or 2 and B is the event: Score is 3 or 4

    i Explain why A and B are mutually exclusive, but not exhaustive.

    ii Describe a third event, C, such that A and C are exhaustive, but not mutually exclusive.

b An employee wants to go home early at the end of the working day. To do so, permission must be sought from the supervisor. Either Angela or Bill is the supervisor on duty. Angela is on duty for three-fifths of the time. Angela gives permission with probability 0.1 and Bill with probability 0.05.

    i Find the probability that the employee is given permission to go home early.

    ii If the employee is given permission to go home early, what is the probability that Angela is on duty?

(NICCEA)

5 In a group of 60 students, 30 study either chemistry or physics. If 20 study chemistry and 17 study physics, what is the probability that a student chosen at random studies:

a both physics and chemistry

b neither physics nor chemistry

c chemistry but not physics?

6 Two unbiased six-sided dice are thrown together. Calculate the probability that:

    a   the scores on each dice are at least 4

    b   the scores on the two dice differ by 2.

7 Two events A and B are such that $P(A) = 0.5$, $P(B) = 0.4$ and $P(A|B) = 0.25$. Determine:

    a $P(A \cap B)$

    b $P(A \cup B)$

    c $P(A' \cap B')$

        A third event C is such that A and C are independent, $P(A \cap C) = 0.15$ and $P(B \cup C) = 0.7$.

    d   Find $P(C)$.

    e   Show that B and C are mutually exclusive.

                                                            (WJEC)

8 At a firing range the probability of Alex hitting a target is 0.6 and the probability of Ben hitting the same target is p. Given that, when both aim together at the target, the probability that only Ben hits is 0.22, find:

    a   the value of p

    b   the probability that neither Alex nor Ben hits the target.

                                                            (UCLES)

9 A domino is chosen at random from a standard set of 28 dominoes. Find the probability that:

    a   at least one of the numbers on the domino is 6;

    b   the domino is a double;

    c   the sum of the numbers is a multiple of 3.

10 There are two children in a family. What is the conditional probability that both are boys, given that at least one is a boy? (Assume that boys and girls are equally likely.)

Exercise B

1 A set of cards consists of three blue cards, four red cards, four yellow cards and five green cards. If a card is drawn and then replaced, and another card is drawn find the probability that:

    a   both cards are blue

    b   neither card is red

    c   one card is yellow and the other is green.

2 A test for a certain disease has a probability of 0.8 of detecting the disease when it is present, and a probability of 0.1 of falsely detecting the disease when it is not present. The disease is actually present in 5% of the population. If a person is tested at random and gives a positive result, what is the probability that they really have the disease?

3 Two events A and B are such that $P(A) = \frac{1}{4}$, $P(B) = \frac{1}{2}$ and $P(A \cap B) = \frac{1}{8}$. Find:

a $P(A \cup B)$ b $P(A \cup B')$

c $P(A|B)$

4 Two friends play chess with each other twice a week. The probability that Tom wins is 0.3 and the probability that Jake wins is 0.4. By drawing a tree diagram, find the probability that in one particular week:

a both games are drawn

b Tom and Jake each win one game.

5 Three events A, B, C are such that $P(B) = \frac{1}{4}$, $P(C) = \frac{1}{3}$, $P(A \cup B) = \frac{3}{5}$ and $P(A \cup C) = \frac{2}{3}$. Events A and B are independent and events B and C are mutually exclusive.

a Find $P(A)$.

b Determine whether or not A and C are independent.

c Show that $P(B \cup C|A) = \frac{15}{28}$.

(WJEC)

6 In a group of 50 students, 18 take history and 26 take English. If 14 students take neither history nor English find the probability that a student chosen at random takes:

a both history and English

b history but not English

c either history or English.

7 A safety system has three major components A, B, and C, all of which are subject to failure and need to be replaced by a service engineer from time to time. The components are such that each will only fit into its correct socket. A service engineer has a box of twenty assorted components, five of which are replacements for A, nine for B and six for C. When a component is required the engineer makes a random selection from the box *without replacement*. Find the probability that the engineer selects:

a a replacement for component B at the first selection;

b no replacement for component A in the first two selections;

c at least one replacement for component A in the first two selections.

(ULEAC)

8 A dice is thrown twice. Find the probability of obtaining a four on the first throw and an odd number on the second throw. Find also the probability of obtaining a number less than three on both throws.

9 Computer chips are difficult to manufacture, and need to be checked for faults before they can be used. A test procedure has two stages, and in each stage the probability of a faulty chip failing is 0.9. Any chip that fails the first stage is immediately rejected and does not go through the second stage of the test. Chips with no faults always pass both stages of the test. The probability of any randomly chosen chip being faulty is 0.4. This information is illustrated in the following tree diagram.

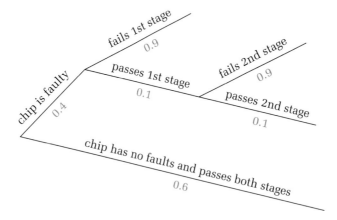

a   Find the probability that a randomly chosen chip is faulty and passes both stages of the test.

b   Find the probability that a randomly chosen chip passes both stages of the test.

c   Find the conditional probability that a randomly chosen chip is faulty, given that it passes both stages of the test.

(*UCLES*)

10 The probability of the occurrence of each of three events, A, B, and C is 0.2, 0.3 and 0.4 respectively.

a   Given that A, B and C are mutually exclusive, find the probability that none of them occurs.

b   Given that A, B and C are independent, find the probability that exactly one of them occurs.

(*UCLES*)

Applications and Activities

1 Compare an experimental probability with its theoretical value. For example, throw two dice 100 times and record the score obtained by adding both numbers together. Use these results to calculate the probability of throwing doubles, on any one throw. Compare your result with the calculated theoretical value.

2 Estimate the probability that a person chosen at random is left-handed. Count the number of left-handers in a sample of, say, 100 students. Try two different samples, for example boys and girls, to see if you obtain the same probability.

3 Calculate the probability of a car being red, given that it has a registration year letter N.

Summary

- The probability of events A and B both occurring $= P(A \cap B)$.

- The probability of event A or event B, or both events occurring $= P(A \cup B)$.

- The probability of event A not occurring $= P(A')$.

- The sum of the probability of A occurring and the probability of A not occurring is equal to 1.

$$P(A) + P(A') = 1 \qquad \text{so} \qquad P(A') = 1 - P(A)$$

- For events A and B to be exhaustive, $P(A \cup B) = 1$

- The addition rule for probability is

$$P(A \cup B) = P(A) + P(B) - P(A \cap B)$$

- For mutually exclusive events

$$P(A \cup B) = P(A) + P(B) \qquad \text{and} \qquad P(A \cap B) = 0$$

- The product rule for independent events is

$$P(A \cap B) = P(A) \times P(B)$$

- Conditional probability, $P(A|B)$, is the probability that event A occurs given that event B has already occurred:

$$P(A|B) = \frac{P(A \cap B)}{P(B)}$$

6 Permutations and Combinations

What you need to know

● How to multiply and cancel fractions.

Review

Work out the following, giving each answer in its simplest form:

1 $\dfrac{5}{6} \times \dfrac{4}{5}$

2 $\dfrac{12}{13} \times \dfrac{26}{29} \times \dfrac{18}{24}$

Do not use a calculator.

3 $\dfrac{56}{58} \times \dfrac{98}{105} \times \dfrac{25}{64}$

6.1 Permutations

A school plans to introduce an identity card for staff and students to increase security. Each card will have a unique code which consists of three letters and three digits, for example ABC123.

If there are no restrictions on which letters and digits are used, the total number of different codes is 17 576 000. This can be calculated as follows. There are 26 possibilities for the first letter, 26 possibilities for the second letter, 26 possibilities for the third letter and 10 possible values for each of the three digits. The total number of arrangements is:

As there are 26 letters in the alphabet.

$$26 \times 26 \times 26 \times 10 \times 10 \times 10 = 26^3 \times 10^3 = 17\,576\,000$$

Clearly this is far more than the total number of codes required. To reduce the possible number of codes it is decided that each digit can be used only once in the numerical part. The number of ways of choosing the three digits for the code can be found as follows.

There are 10 ways of choosing the first digit, but only nine ways of choosing the second digit, as one has already been used, and eight ways of choosing the third digit. The total number of possible arrangements is:

$$10 \times 9 \times 8 = 720$$

To further reduce the number of codes, the letters are restricted to A, B, C, D and E and each letter can be used only once. There are five possible choices for the first letter, four choices for the second letter and three choices for the third letter, giving $5 \times 4 \times 3 = 60$ possible arrangements for the letters. So the total number of codes is now:

$$60 \times 720 = 43\,200$$

Suppose all five letters were to be used in the code we could arrange them in:

$$5 \times 4 \times 3 \times 2 \times 1 = 120 \text{ ways}$$

If there were 10 letters then the number of ways in which they could be arranged is:

$$10 \times 9 \times 8 \times 7 \times 6 \times 5 \times 4 \times 3 \times 2 \times 1$$

This is very long to write out so we use a shorter form, 10!, read as 'ten factorial'. Look on your calculator to find the $\boxed{x!}$ button.
Use it to check that $5! = 120$.

The general result is:

$$n! = n(n-1)(n-2)\ldots 1$$

Example 1

a Evaluate:

   i   10!   **ii** $\dfrac{10!}{8!}$ **iii** $\dfrac{6!\,2!}{4!}$

b Express in factorial notation:

   i $6 \times 5 \times 4$ **ii** $14 \times 13 \times 12 \times 11 \times 10$

Solution

a **i** Using the factorial function on your calculator,

$$10! = 3\,628\,800$$

    ii Using the factorial function on your calculator,

$$\frac{10!}{8!} = \frac{3\,628\,800}{40\,320} = 90$$

or $\dfrac{10\times9\times8\times7\times6\times5\times4\times3\times2\times1}{8\times7\times6\times5\times3\times2\times1} = 10 \times 9 = 90$

    iii Using the factorial function on your calculator,

$$\frac{6!\,2!}{4!} = \frac{720\times2}{24} = 60$$

or $\dfrac{6\times5\times4\times3\times2\times1\times2\times1}{4\times3\times2\times1} = 6 \times 5 \times 2 \times 1 = 60$

b **i** $6 \times 5 \times 4 = 6 \times 5 \times 4 \times \dfrac{3\times2\times1}{3\times2\times1} = \dfrac{6!}{3!}$

    ii $14 \times 13 \times 12 \times 11 \times 10 = 14 \times 13 \times 12 \times 11 \times 10 \times \dfrac{9\times8\times\ldots\times1}{9\times8\times\ldots\times1}$

$$= \frac{14!}{9!}$$

The three letters A, B and C can be arranged in 3!, or 6, different ways:

    ABC   ACB   BAC   BCA   CAB   CBA

These arrangements are called **permutations**. A permutation is an arrangement of objects *in a particular order*.

We only want to use three letters in our code, so the problem is: *in how many ways can we arrange three letters chosen from five?*

We have already worked this out as $5 \times 4 \times 3 = 60$.
How can this be written in factorial notation?

$$5 \times 4 \times 3 = 5 \times 4 \times 3 \times \frac{2 \times 1}{2 \times 1} = \frac{5!}{2!}$$

The number of permutations of three letters chosen from five is $\frac{5!}{(5-3)!}$.

Since $2! = (5-3)!$

> **The number of permutations of *r* objects chosen from *n* unlike objects is**
>
> $$^nP_r = \frac{n!}{(n-r)!}$$

Example 2

For a class photograph the eight tallest students have to stand in the back row. There are six boys and two girls in the back row. How many different ways can they be arranged if:

a it does not matter who they stand next to
b the girls do not stand next to each other?

Solution

a There are eight people who can be arranged in 8! ways, that is 40 320 ways.

b Find the number of ways the girls *can* stand together and subtract this from the total number of arrangements.

The six boys can stand in 6! different ways, for example,

B_1 B_2 B_3 B_4 B_5 B_6
B_1 B_2 B_3 B_4 B_6 B_5
B_1 B_2 B_3 B_5 B_6 B_4 and so on

The two girls can stand together in 2! ways. There are seven places where the two girls can stand – at either end of the row or in any one of the five gaps between the boys, for example

G_1 G_2 B_1 B_2 B_3 B_4 B_5 B_6

The number of permutations where the two girls are standing together is

$6! \times 2! \times 7 = 10\,080$

so the number of permutations where the two girls are *not* together is

$40\,320 - 10\,080 = 30\,240$

6! is the number of different ways the boys can stand in a row.
2! is the number of different ways the girls can stand together.
7 is the number of places where the two girls can stand.

Example 3

a In how many different ways can the letters in SHOE be arranged?

b In how many ways can the letters of SHOES be arranged?

Solution

a SHOE has four different letters which can be arranged in 4! different ways, that is 24 different ways.

b SHOES has five letters, including two Ss. If all letters were different there would be 5! permutations. It is not possible to distinguish between the two letters S so $EHOS_1S_2$ is the same arrangement as $EHOS_2S_1$. As there are 2! ways of arranging two objects it is necessary to divide the total number of arrangements of five objects by the number of ways of arranging two objects.

This gives $\frac{5!}{2!} = 60$ different permutations of the letters in the word SHOES.

> **The number of ways of arranging n objects of which p are alike is**
>
> $$\frac{n!}{p!}$$

This result can be extended where more than one object, or letter is repeated.

$\dfrac{n!}{p!q!r!\ldots}$ gives the number of ways of arranging n objects, of which p are alike, q are alike, and r are alike and so on.

Example 4

In how many ways can the letters of the word MATHEMATICS be arranged?

Solution

$n = 11$ (there are 11 letters altogether) $q = 2$ (there are two letter As)

$p = 2$ (there are two letter Ms) $r = 2$ (there are two letter Ts)

The number of arrangements of the letters in the word MATHEMATICS is

$$\frac{11!}{2!2!2!} = 4\,989\,600$$

Example 5

Six people are having dinner at a round table, in how many different ways can they be seated?

Solution

Starting from one particular chair there are 6! ways in which the six people could sit around the table. If everyone moved one place clockwise, we would still have the same arrangement of people, relative to one another. Moving everyone one place clockwise a second time would still leave the order unchanged, relative to each other. People could move clockwise six times and still be sitting in the same arrangement.

The number of different arrangements of six people round a circular table is

$$\frac{6!}{6} = \frac{6 \times 5 \times 4 \times 3 \times 2 \times 1}{6} = 5 \times 4 \times 3 \times 2 \times 1 = 5!$$

The general result is:

> **n objects can be arranged in a circle in $(n - 1)!$ ways**

Example 6

Five different coloured beads are threaded on a wire to make a bracelet. How many different bracelets can be made?

Solution

This is similar to the previous example, which might lead us to conclude that there are $(5 - 1)!$ arrangements. This does not take into account the fact that the wire bracelet could be turned over, and two arrangements which at first seem different, are actually the same. Hence, our $(5 - 1)!$ arrangements must be divided by two, giving

$$\tfrac{1}{2}(5 - 1)! = 12 \text{ different arrangements}$$

The general result is:

> **n different objects can be arranged on a circular wire in $\frac{(n-1)!}{2}$ ways**

This can also be written as $\dfrac{n!}{n \times 2}$

6.1 Permutations
Exercise

Technique

1 Evaluate:

a $\dfrac{12!}{8!}$ b $\dfrac{14!}{7!4!}$ c $\dfrac{24!}{16!6!}$

2 Write the following in factorial notation:

a $8 \times 7 \times 6$ b $18 \times 17 \times 16 \times 15$ c 12×11

3 Evaluate:

a $^4P_2$ b $^8P_3$ c $^{13}P_6$

4 Without using a calculator, evaluate:

a $\dfrac{8!}{5!2!}$ b $\dfrac{10!}{6!3!}$ c $\dfrac{9!}{(3!)^2}$

Contextual

1 In how many ways can eight different ornaments be arranged on a mantelpiece?

2 How many arrangements are there of the letters in the words:

a HOME b SCHOOL c STATISTICS?

3 Six volumes of an encyclopaedia are placed on a shelf. In how many different ways can they be arranged? Two of the volumes are bound in red. In how many ways can the books now be arranged if the two red volumes are *not* next to each other?

4 A disc jockey has 14 records to choose from. If he plays nine during a programme, how many different permutations are there?

5 How many different arrangements can be made with the letters in the word ALGEBRA? In how many of these arrangements are the letters L and R next to each other?

6 Calculate how many different numbers can be formed by taking one, two or three digits from the digits 8, 5, 2. How many of these numbers will be odd and greater than 250? Each digit can be used only once in each number.

7 There are eight competitors in the final of a 400 m race. The first three competitors to complete the course will all receive medals. Calculate the number of different possible groups of medal winners.

8 Find the number of different three-letter arrangements that can be made from the letters of the word PERMUTATION.

9 In how many different ways can eight people sit at a round table?

10 One blue, one red, one yellow, one green, one black and one white bead are to be used to make a bracelet. In how many different ways can the beads be arranged?

6.2 Combinations

In the last section we looked at permutations of different numbers of objects. The order in which the objects are arranged is important, for example ABC is a different permutation to BCA.

Suppose there are 18 students in a class, and three are to be selected as representatives to the School Council. All that matters is the number of ways in which three students can be selected from 18. The order in which they are chosen is not important.

An arrangement where the *order is not important* is called a **combination**. So while ABC and BCA are different permutations they are the same combination of letters.

Three students could be chosen, in order, from a total of 18 in $\frac{18!}{15!}$ ways. However, each of these choices can be arranged in 3! ways (ABC, ACB, BAC, BCA, CAB, CBA), so the number of combinations of three items chosen from 18 is

$$\frac{18!}{15!\,3!} = 816$$

$$^{18}P_3 = \frac{18!}{(18-3)!}$$

> **The number of combinations (or selections) of r objects chosen from n unlike objects is**
>
> $$^{n}C_r = \frac{n!}{(n-r)!\,r!}$$

$^{n}C_r$ is sometimes written
$$\binom{n}{r}$$

Your calculator may have the functions $\boxed{^{n}C_r}$ and $\boxed{^{n}P_r}$. Learn how to use these to work out permutations and combinations.

Example 1

a   A quiz team of four is chosen from a group of 15 students. In how many ways could the team be chosen?

b   If there are eight girls and seven boys in the group, in how many ways could the team be chosen so that there are two boys and two girls in the team?

c   In how many ways could the team be chosen if there are to be more girls than boys in the team?

Solution

a $^{15}C_4 = \dfrac{15!}{11!\,4!} = 1365$

   Therefore the team can be chosen in 1365 ways.

b Two girls can be chosen in $^{8}C_2$ ways, and the two boys can be chosen in $^{7}C_2$ ways. For each of the $^{8}C_2$ ways of selecting the girls there are $^{7}C_2$ ways of selecting the boys. In total there are $^{8}C_2 \times {}^{7}C_2$ ways of selecting the team.

> Order of selecting students is not important.

$$^{8}C_2 \times {}^{7}C_2 = \frac{8!}{6!\,2!} \times \frac{7!}{5!\,2!}$$

$$= 28 \times 21$$

$$= 588$$

So there are 588 ways of choosing a team consisting of two boys and two girls.

c If there are to be more girls than boys in the team then the team will either have four girls and no boys, or three girls and one boy.
Four girls can be chosen in $^{8}C_4$ ways

$$^{8}C_4 = \frac{8!}{4!\,4!}$$

$$= 70$$

Three girls and one boy can be chosen in $^{8}C_3 \times {}^{7}C_1$ ways

$$^{8}C_3 \times {}^{7}C_1 = \frac{8!}{5!\,3!} \times \frac{7!}{6!\,1!}$$

$$= 56 \times 7$$

$$= 392$$

Therefore the number of ways of choosing the team if there are more girls than boys is

$$70 + 392 = 462 \text{ ways}$$

6.2 Combinations
Exercise

Contextual

1 In how many ways can a tennis team of six be chosen from a squad of eight players?

2 A school committee consists of six boys and four girls. A social sub-committee consisting of four students is to be formed.

    a   Work out how many ways the sub-committee can be formed.

    b   If the sub-committee is to include at least two boys find the number of possible combinations.

3 Fourteen people each spin a £1 coin. How many ways are there of obtaining exactly five heads?

4 Find the number of selections of four letters that can be made from the letters in the word INTEGRAL. How many of these selections do not contain a vowel?

5 Judith is planning a small garden. She has found six bushes that she would like, but only has room to plant four of them. She has also seen 10 border plants, but there is only space for eight of them. How many different ways can she plant her garden?

6 From 10 teachers at a school, three are to be chosen to serve on the parent–teacher committee.

    a   In how many ways can this be done?

    Paul says that he will not serve on the committee if John is chosen.

    b   With this restriction, in how many ways can the choice of teachers be made?

                                                                    (OCSEB)

7 Find the number of different selections of three letters that can be made from the letters a, b, c, d, e, f, g, h. How many of these selections have no vowels?

8 A quiz team of five is to be chosen from seven men and six women. In how many ways can the team be chosen if:

   a   there is no restriction on the number of men and women;

   b   there are three men and two women in the team;

   c   there are three women and two men in the team;

   d   there are more men than women in the team?

9 How many different selections can be made from the four letters *w, x, y, z*?

Remember, any number of letters may be selected.

10 An art gallery has a total of 11 paintings by a particular artist; of these, five are oil paintings and six are watercolour paintings. The art gallery is asked to provide a special exhibition of this artist's work but is restricted to showing only five of the paintings. Calculate the number ways in which the five paintings can be selected for the exhibition if:

   a   there are no restrictions;

   b   one particular painting must be included;

   c   there must be exactly three watercolour paintings;

   d   there must be more watercolour paintings than oil paintings.

(*UCLES*)

Consolidation

Exercise A

1 Calculate the number of arrangements of seven different books on a library shelf. If three of these books are to remain together how many arrangements are there now?

2 A chess club has 10 members of whom six are men and four are women. A team of four members is selected to play in a match.

    a Find the number of different ways of selecting the team if:
        i all the players are to be of the same sex,
        ii there must be an equal number of men and women.
    b Given that the six men include two brothers, find the total number of ways in which the team can be selected if one of the brothers, but not both, must be included.

(UCLES)

3 Calculate the number of arrangements of eight ornaments on a shelf. If three of these ornaments form a set and are to be kept together, how many arrangements are there now?

4 **a** An examination paper has five questions on it and candidates must answer any three of them. In how many ways can a candidate choose which questions to answer? (Note that the order in which the questions are answered is not important.)

For each of the following examination papers determine the number of ways a candidate may choose the required number of questions. Continue to ignore the order in which questions are attempted. *Show your working clearly.*

    b The paper has two sections, A and B. A has six questions from which candidates must answer any four; B has five questions from which candidates must answer any three.
    c The paper has five questions and the candidate must answer at least three questions.
    d The paper has three sections, A, B, and C, each with two questions. Candidates must answer four questions in total, including at least one from each section.

(OCSEB)

5 A meeting involves representatives from four schools, each school sending a Deputy Head, another member of staff and a sixth form student. In how many ways can the 12 people be seated at a circular table? If the three people from each school sit together, in how many different ways can they now sit?

6 In a school cross-country competition there are 14 runners. The first three will receive certificates. Calculate the number of different possible groups of certificate winners.

7 A committee of four is to be chosen from five men and three women. Find the number of ways of choosing the committee if:

a there are no restrictions

b the committee must contain at least one man and one woman.

8 Calculate the number of permutations of the nine letters of the word PATAGONIA when:

a there are no restrictions

b the three As all come together.

9 a How many four-digit numbers can be made from the six digits 2, 3, 4, 5, 7, 9 if no digit can be used more than once?

b How many of these numbers are less than 5000?

c How many of the numbers are even?

10 A concert pianist agrees to take part in a charity concert. She offers a choice of 10 works, of which five were composed by Chopin, three by Liszt and two by Schumann. The concert committee is to select four of these works. Calculate the number of ways these four works can be selected if

a there are no restrictions

b there are two works by Chopin, one by Liszt and one by Schumann

c there must be at least one work by each composer

d the selection contains works by exactly two of the three composers.

(*UCLES*)

Exercise B

1 Calculate the number of arrangements of nine different books on a library shelf. If four of the books are by the same author and are to stay together, how many arrangements are possible?

2 A committee of three is to be chosen from four men and five women. Calculate the total number of ways in which the committee can be chosen and show that in 30 of these the committee consists of two men and one woman.

(*OCSEB*)

3 A football player owns six pairs of boots. How many different ways are there of selecting:

  a   four boots from the 12
  b   two right boots and two left boots
  c   two pairs of boots?

4 A child has a box of 12 different coloured pencils.

  a   In how many ways can the pencils be arranged in a line?
  b   In how many ways can the child choose four colours to complete a drawing?

5 How many odd numbers greater than 400 000 can be made from the digits 3, 4, 5, 6, 7, 8:

  a   if repetitions are not allowed
  b   if repetitions are allowed?

6 How many circular rings can be formed from eight differently coloured beads?

7 Find the total number of permutations of all the nine letters of the word ISOSCELES. Find the number of these permutations that:

  a   start and finish with E,
  b   have the letters S, S, S together
  c   have no two of the letters C, L, S, S, S consecutive.

(UCLES)

8 Find the number of ways a committee of five can be chosen from six men and six women if:

  a   it must contain two men and three women
  b   it must contain at least one man
  c   there are more women than men on the committee.

9 A set of five fiction books is to be put on the same shelf as a set of three non-fiction books. In how many ways can the books be arranged if:

  a   the fiction and non-fiction books are not to be mixed
  b   the three non-fiction books are all separated?

10 Find the number of permutations of the letters in the word MATHEMATICS.

Applications and Activities

1 Ten children start playing musical chairs. How many different combinations of seating arrangements are there in total before the winner is found? Illustrate your answer.

Summary

- A **permutation** is an arrangements of objects in a particular order.

- A **combination** is a selection of objects where order is not important.

- The number of permutations of r objects chosen from n unlike objects is

$$^{n}P_{r} = \frac{n!}{(n-r)!}$$

- The number of arrangements of n objects in a circle is $(n-1)!$

- The number of arrangements of n objects on a circular ring is

$$\frac{(n-1)!}{2}$$

- The number of arrangements of n objects of which p are alike is

$$\frac{n!}{p!}$$

- The number of arrangements of n objects of which p are alike, q are alike and r are alike is

$$\frac{n!}{p!q!r!}$$

- The number of combinations of r objects chosen from n unlike objects is

$$^{n}C_{r} = \frac{n!}{(n-r)!r!}$$

7 Discrete Probability Distributions

What you need to know

● How to find the mean of a set of data.

● How to find the standard deviation of a set of data.

Review

1 Calculate the mean of the following.

  a 12, 18, 17, 16, 19, 18, 13, 20, 16
  b 2, 3, 3, 5, 5, 8, 8, 9
  c 0.7, 0.6, 0.8, 0.9, 0.7

2 Calculate the standard deviation of the following:

  a 24, 25, 29, 31, 32, 28, 27, 28
  b 15, 20, 47, 43, 16, 13, 21, 35, 68, 27, 25, 67
  c 0.05, 0.01, 0.3, 0.57, 0.27, 0.38, 0.49, 0.44, 0.07

7.1 Discrete Probability Distributions

Before looking at probability distributions we need to know:

1. What is a **discrete random variable**?
2. What is a **discrete probability distribution**?

A **random variable** is a numerical variate whose value depends on chance. For example, when throwing a dice the number obtained is a random variable. If the random variable can only have certain distinct values, for example 1, 2, 3, 4, 5 or 6, then it is a **discrete** random variable.

Example 1

A fair dice is thrown and the number on the dice is the random variable X. What is $P(X = 2)$?

Solution

There are six possible outcomes, all equally likely, so the probability that we get a 2 is $\frac{1}{6}$.

$$P(X = 2) = \frac{1}{6}$$

This table lists all the possible values of the random variable X, and their probabilities.

x	1	2	3	4	5	6
$P(X = x)$	$\frac{1}{6}$	$\frac{1}{6}$	$\frac{1}{6}$	$\frac{1}{6}$	$\frac{1}{6}$	$\frac{1}{6}$

Note that capital letters are used to denote random variables.

This is a simple example of a **probability distribution table** because it fully describes all the possible outcomes together with the probability of each happening. For it to be a probability distribution, all the probabilities must sum to one.

Example 2

Two unbiased spinners, one numbered 1, 2, 3, 4 and the other numbered 1, 2, 3 are spun. X (the random variable) is the sum of the two results.

a   Tabulate the distribution of X.
b   Find $P(X > 5)$.
c   State the mode.
d   The experiment is repeated 60 times. Give the expected frequency distribution of X.

The expected frequency distribution is a table of how many times you would expect to get each sum.

Solution

a To begin with we must first list all possible outcomes.

$$(1, 1) \quad (1, 2) \quad (1, 3)$$
$$(2, 1) \quad (2, 2) \quad (2, 3)$$
$$(3, 1) \quad (3, 2) \quad (3, 3)$$
$$(4, 1) \quad (4, 2) \quad (4, 3)$$

There are 12 possible outcomes, all equally likely.

$X = 1$	never occurs	$P(X = 1) = 0$
$X = 2$	$(1, 1)$	$P(X = 2) = \frac{1}{12}$
$X = 3$	$(1, 2)\ (2, 1)$	$P(X = 3) = \frac{2}{12}$
$X = 4$	$(1, 3)\ (3, 1)\ (2, 2)$	$P(X = 4) = \frac{3}{12}$
$X = 5$	$(2, 3)\ (3, 2)\ (4, 1)$	$P(X = 5) = \frac{3}{12}$
$X = 6$	$(3, 3)\ (4, 2)$	$P(X = 6) = \frac{2}{12}$
$X = 7$	$(4, 3)$	$P(X = 7) = \frac{1}{12}$

So the probability distribution of X is

x	2	3	4	5	6	7
$P(X = x)$	$\frac{1}{12}$	$\frac{2}{12}$	$\frac{3}{12}$	$\frac{3}{12}$	$\frac{2}{12}$	$\frac{1}{12}$

> Always check you have calculated your probabilities correctly by making sure they sum to 1.

b $P(X > 5) = P(X = 6) + P(X = 7)$

$$= \tfrac{2}{12} + \tfrac{1}{12}$$
$$= \tfrac{3}{12}$$
$$= \tfrac{1}{4}$$

c The mode is the value with the highest probability. In this example there are two modes, 4 and 5. We say that the distribution is **bi-modal**.

> Bi-modal distributions are those with two modes.

d If we repeat the experiment 60 times, we can expect $\frac{1}{12}$, that is 5, of the outcomes to be a score of 2; $\frac{2}{12}$, that is 10, of the outcomes to be a score of 3, and so on. So in order to calculate the expected frequencies, we must multiply each of the probabilities by 60.

Since $P(X = 4) = \frac{3}{12}$, the expected frequency of a score of 4 is

$$60 \times \tfrac{3}{12} = 15$$

The complete frequency distribution is:

x	2	3	4	5	6	7
Expected frequency	5	10	15	15	10	5

Probability distribution functions

Sometimes it is possible to describe a probability distribution by writing it as a **function**, for example

$$P(X = x) = \frac{x}{6}, \text{ for } x = 1, 2, 3$$

This is a shorthand way of writing:

$$P(X = 1) = \frac{1}{6}, \quad P(X = 2) = \frac{2}{6}, \quad P(X = 3) = \frac{3}{6}$$

We can check that it is a probability distribution by finding the sum of the probabilities. It should be 1.

The probability that the random variable, X, has a particular value, x, is $\frac{x}{6}$.

Example 3

For the following probability distribution function, find the value of a.

$$P(Y = y) = ay, \text{ for } y = 1, 2, 3, 4$$

Solution

First, we need to draw up a probability distribution table.

When $y = 1$, $P(Y = 1) = a \times 1 = a$

When $y = 2$, $P(Y = 2) = a \times 2 = 2a$ and so on.

The complete table is

y	1	2	3	4
$P(Y = y)$	a	$2a$	$3a$	$4a$

and since the sum of the probabilities is 1:

$$a + 2a + 3a + 4a = 1$$
$$10a = 1$$
$$a = \frac{1}{10}$$

Therefore the probability distribution function is $P(Y = y) = \frac{y}{10}$, for $y = 1, 2, 3, 4$.

Diagrams of probability distributions

It is also possible to describe a probability distribution of a discrete random variable using a diagram. For example, the following distribution,

x	1	2	2	4
$P(X = x)$	0.1	0.4	0.3	0.2

could be shown as:

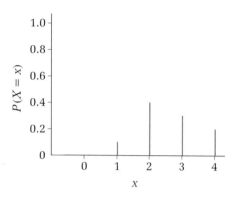

Note that individual lines are drawn as it is a discrete distribution.

Example 4

Draw a suitable diagram to illustrate the following probability distribution.

x	0	1	2	3	4
$P(X = x)$	0.3	0.1	0.1	0.2	0.3

Solution

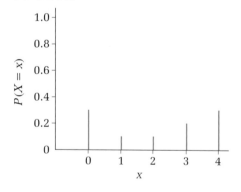

7.1 Discrete Probability Distributions

Exercise

Contextual

1 Two ordinary dice are thrown. Write down all 36 possible outcomes.

   a Given that X is the sum of the two results:
      i make a table of the probability distribution
      ii find $P(X > 4)$
      iii state the mode.
   b If the experiment is repeated 70 times, give the expected frequency distribution of X.

2 A bag contains eight blue discs and seven orange ones. Two discs are removed without replacement.

   a Given that X is the number of orange discs taken out, draw up a probability distribution table, showing all the values of X together with the probability of each happening.
   b Draw a simple diagram illustrating the probability distribution.

3 The random variable Y is the number of tails obtained when three fair coins are tossed.

   a Write out the probability distribution of Y. (You might need to draw a tree diagram to help you.)
   b Find the probability that more tails are obtained than heads.

4 In my purse, I have two 50p coins, three 20p coins and one 10p coin.

   a I take out one coin at random. Given that X represents the value of the coin removed, write down the probability distribution of its value.
   b If I take out two coins at random (the first coin not being replaced before I take out the second coin) and Y represents the total value of the two coins, what would the probability distribution of Y look like? (You might need to draw a tree diagram to help you.)

5 Four cards are drawn from a normal pack of 52 cards without replacement.

   a Draw a probability distribution table for the number of red cards chosen.
   b Find the probability that the number of red cards chosen is less than two.

6 The probability distribution of a discrete random variable X is given by

$P(X = x) = kx$, where k is a constant for $x = 1, 2, 3, 4, 5$.

a Find the value of k.   **b** Find $P(X \leq 3)$.

$P(X \leq 3)$ can be written as $F(3)$. In general $F(r) = P(X = 0) + P(X = 1) + \ldots + P(X = $

7 A discrete random variable Z has the following probability distribution:

z	1	2	3
$P(Z = z)$	m	$4m$	$2m$

where m is a constant.

a Find the value of m **b** Find $P(Z \geq 2)$.

8 A discrete random variable X has the following probability distribution:

x	1	2	3	4	5
$P(X = x)$	$\frac{1}{16}$	$\frac{1}{8}$	b	$2b$	$\frac{1}{4}$

where b is a constant. Find the value of b.

9 The following probability distribution is that of a particular experiment:

x	1	2	3	4
$P(X = x)$	0.4	0.1	0.2	0.3

Given that the experiment was carried out 240 times, write out the expected frequency distribution of X.

10 The discrete random variables A and B are independent and have the following distributions:

a	1	2
$P(A = a)$	$\frac{3}{4}$	$\frac{1}{4}$

b	1	2	3
$P(B = b)$	$\frac{1}{5}$	$\frac{3}{5}$	$\frac{1}{5}$

The random variable C is the product of one observation from A and one observation from B.

a Show that $P(C = 2) = \frac{10}{20}$.

b Find the probability distribution for C.

7.2 The Mean

Sometimes we want to compare two or more frequency distributions, for example whether the cost of living is higher in France or the UK. When making a comparison it is useful to be able to refer to a measure that represents the whole distribution. A typical such measure is called a **measure of central tendency** or an average. One particular measure of central tendency is the **arithmetic mean** or **expected value.**

Average – care needs to be taken with this word as it is often mistakenly used to refer only to the arithmetic mean.

Example 1

A fair dice is thrown 60 times and the results are recorded in a frequency distribution table.

Score, x	1	2	3	4	5	6
Frequency, f	9	11	12	8	13	7
fx	9	22	36	32	65	42

Find the mean score.

This is a frequency distribution table resulting from a *practical* experiment (see Chapter 2).

Solution

To calculate the mean score, we multiply each score by its frequency, sum these values and then divide by the total frequency, as in the following formula.

$$\bar{x} = \frac{\Sigma fx}{\Sigma f}$$

$$= \frac{1}{60}[(1 \times 9) + (2 \times 11) + (3 \times 12) + (4 \times 8) + (5 \times 13) + (6 \times 7)]$$

$$= \frac{206}{60}$$

$$= 3.43 \ (2 \ \text{d.p.})$$

This value of 3.43 is the *mean value* calculated from the *frequency distribution*.

Σfx is the sum of the scores $\times$ the frequencies. Σf is the sum of the frequencies.

Example 2

Calculate the expected value of the score, X, when a dice is thrown 60 times.

Solution

First we need to draw a probability distribution table:

x	1	2	3	4	5	6
$P(X = x)$	$\frac{1}{6}$	$\frac{1}{6}$	$\frac{1}{6}$	$\frac{1}{6}$	$\frac{1}{6}$	$\frac{1}{6}$

This time we are considering outcomes theoretically.

The **expected value** of X can be calculated from a *probability distribution* in the same way as the *mean* value is calculated from a *frequency distribution.* So to calculate the expected value of X:

● multiply each value of X by its corresponding probability

● add these values

● divide by the total probability.

$$\text{expected value} = [(1 \times \tfrac{1}{6}) + (2 \times \tfrac{1}{6}) + (3 \times \tfrac{1}{6}) + (4 \times \tfrac{1}{6})$$
$$+ (5 \times \tfrac{1}{6}) + (6 \times \tfrac{1}{6})] \div 1$$
$$= \tfrac{21}{6}$$
$$= 3.5$$

So, generally for any probability distribution of the form:

x	x_1	x_2	x_3	x_4	x_5
$P(X = x)$	p_1	p_2	p_3	p_4	p_5

the mean, or expected value, $E(X)$ is:

$$E(X) = \Sigma x P(X = x)$$

$E(X)$ is the notation used for expectation and this is read 'the expected value of X'.

Since the probabilities of a probability distribution sum to 1 to find the expected value we simply multiply each random variable with its associated probability and then add.

$\Sigma x P(X = x)$ is the sum of each possible score multiplied by its theoretical probability.

Example 3

Here is the probability distribution from Example 2 in Section 7.1. Calculate the mean of this distribution.

x	2	3	4	5	6	7
$P(X = x)$	$\tfrac{1}{12}$	$\tfrac{2}{12}$	$\tfrac{3}{12}$	$\tfrac{3}{12}$	$\tfrac{2}{12}$	$\tfrac{1}{12}$

Solution

The mean is

$$E(X) = (2 \times \tfrac{1}{12}) + (3 \times \tfrac{2}{12}) + (4 \times \tfrac{3}{12}) + (5 \times \tfrac{3}{12}) + (6 \times \tfrac{2}{12}) + (7 \times \tfrac{1}{12})$$
$$= (2 + 6 + 12 + 15 + 12 + 7) \times \tfrac{1}{12}$$
$$= \tfrac{54}{12}$$
$$= 4.5$$

Remember that the terms mean, expected value and expectation are interchangeable.

Example 4

A discrete random variable Z has the following probability distribution:

z	1	2	t
$P(Z = z)$	0.1	0.2	0.7

Find the value of t if $E(Z) = 4$.

$E(Z) = \Sigma z P(Z = z)$

Solution

Since $E(Z) = 4$, we know that

$$(1 \times 0.1) + (2 \times 0.2) + (t \times 0.7) = 4$$

$$0.1 + 0.4 + 0.7t = 4$$

$$0.5 + 0.7t = 4$$

$$0.7t = 3.5$$

$$t = 5$$

Example 5

A discrete random variable can only take the values 2 and 3, and has expectation 2.6. Find the probabilities $P(X = 2)$ and $P(X = 3)$.

Solution

Let $P(X = 2) = a$

Since the probabilities sum to 1, we know that

$$P(X = 3) = 1 - a$$

x	2	3
$P(X = x)$	a	$1 - a$

We also know that $E(X) = 2.6$, so:

$$2a + 3(1 - a) = 2.6$$

$$2a + 3 - 3a = 2.6$$

$$3 - a = 2.6$$

$$a = 0.4$$

To find $E(X)$ multiply each value of X by its corresponding probability.

So $P(X = 2) = 0.4$ and $P(X = 3) = 0.6$

Expectation of a function of X

If $f(X)$ is a function of the discrete random variable X, $E(f(X))$ can be calculated as follows:

$$E(f(X)) = \Sigma f(x) P(X = x)$$

Example 6

A random variable X can take the values 1, 2 and 3. The probability distribution of X is given in the following table:

x	1	2	3
P(X = x)	0.1	0.5	0.4

a   Find $E(X)$.

b   Find $E(2X + 1)$.

Solution

a $E(X) = (1 \times 0.1) + (2 \times 0.5) + (3 \times 0.4)$

$= 0.1 + 1.0 + 1.2$

$= 2.3$

b   To find $E(2X + 1)$, draw up a probability distribution table:

x	1	2	3
f(X) = 2X + 1	3	5	7
P(X = x)	0.1	0.5	0.4

Now calculate $E(2X + 1)$.

$E(2X + 1) = (3 \times 0.1) + (5 \times 0.5) + (7 \times 0.4)$

$= 0.3 + 2.5 + 2.8$

$= 5.6$

Work out the value of $2E(X) + 1$ for the random variable X in Example 6.

$E(X) = 2.3$

so $2E(X) + 1 = (2 \times 2.3) + 1$

$= 4.6 + 1$

$= 5.6$

This is the same as $E(2X + 1)$, so:

$E(2X + 1) = 2E(X) + 1$

In fact, this is a very useful result when calculating expectation of functions. In general:

$$E(aX + b) = aE(X) + b$$

This is an extension of the results: $E(aX) = aE(X)$ and $E(c) = c$ (the expected value of a constant is itself), which can be proved using the original definition of $E(f(X))$.

We can extend the expectation of a function to include the expectation of the sum of two functions of a random variable.

$$E[f(X) + g(X)] = E[f(X)] + E[g(X)]$$

This can be proved using the original definition of $E(f(X))$.

$$E(aX) = \Sigma axP(X = x)$$
$$= a\Sigma xP(X = x)$$
$$= aE(X)$$
$$E(c) = \Sigma cP(X = x)$$
$$= c\Sigma P(X = x)$$
$$= c$$

$$E[f(X) + g(X)]$$
$$= \Sigma[f(x) + g(x)]P(X = x)$$
$$= \Sigma f(x)P(X = x)$$
$$+ \Sigma g(x)P(X = x)$$
$$= E(f(X)) + E(g(X))$$

Example 7

A random variable has the following probability distribution:

x	1	2	3	4
$P(X = x)$	0.6	0.1	0.2	0.1

Calculate $E(3X + 4)$.

Solution

First calculate $E(X)$.

$$E(X) = (1 \times 0.6) + (2 \times 0.1) + (3 \times 0.2) + (4 \times 0.1)$$
$$= 0.6 + 0.2 + 0.6 + 0.4$$
$$= 1.8$$

Then use the property $E(aX + b) = aE(X) + b$

$$E(3X + 4) = 3E(X) + 4$$
$$= (3 \times 1.8) + 4$$
$$= 5.4 + 4$$
$$= 9.4$$

7.2 The Mean
Exercise
Technique

1 Find the mean of the following probability distributions of X:

a

x	0	1	2
$P(X = x)$	$\frac{1}{6}$	$\frac{1}{2}$	$\frac{1}{3}$

b

x	-1	0	1	2
$P(X = x)$	$\frac{1}{8}$	$\frac{1}{4}$	$\frac{1}{2}$	$\frac{1}{8}$

2 A discrete random variable Y has a probability distribution as follows:

y	1	2	m	10	15
$P(Y = y)$	0.2	0.1	0.3	0.3	0.1

Find the value of m when:

a $E(Y) = 6.4$ **b** $E(Y) = 7.6$

3 The discrete random variable X has a probability distribution given by $P(X = x) = x/10$ for $x = 1, 2, 3, 4$. Find:

a $E(X)$
b $E(X^2)$
c $E(X^2 + 2X - 3)$.
d Verify that $E(X^2 + 2X - 3) = E(X^2) + 2E(X) - 3$.

Contextual

1 Two dice are thrown. Calculate the mean of the random variable X, the sum of the two results.

2 In my purse, I have two 50p coins, three 20p coins and one 10p coin.

a I take out one coin at random. Given that X represents the value of this coin, find the mean of X.
b I now take out two coins at random (the first coin is not replaced before I take out the second coin) and Y represents the total value of the two coins. Find the mean of Y.

3 A bag contains five marbles: three red and two blue. Marbles are removed one at a time (without replacement) until the first blue marble is removed. Given that X is the number of marbles removed, find the mean of X.

7.3 The Variance

For a discrete random variable X whose mean $E(X) = \mu$ (pronounced 'mew'), the **variance**, written $\text{Var}(X)$ is, by definition

$$\text{Var}(X) = E[(X - \mu)^2]$$

When we looked at frequency distributions in Chapter 4, we found that the formula for the variance

$$s^2 = \frac{\Sigma f(x - \bar{x}^2)}{\Sigma f} \text{ simplified to } s^2 = \frac{\Sigma fx^2}{\Sigma f} - \bar{x}^2.$$

In the same way, when calculating the $\text{Var}(X)$ it is sometimes quicker to use the alternative definition:

$$\text{Var}(X) = E(X^2) - \mu^2 \quad \blacktriangleleft \mu = E(X) \text{ and } \mu^2 = [E(X)]^2$$

It is also important to remember from Chapter 4 that

$$\text{Var}(X) = (\textbf{standard deviation})^2$$

So, in order to find the standard deviation of a probability distribution, first find the variance and then find its square root.

$$\text{Var}(X) = E[(X - \mu)^2]$$
$$= E(X^2 - 2\mu X + \mu^2)$$
$$= E(X^2) - 2\mu E(X) + E(\mu^2)$$
$$= E(X^2) - 2\mu^2 + \mu^2$$
$$= E(X^2) - \mu^2$$

Example 1

Find the variance and the standard deviation of the following distribution:

x	2	3	4	5	6	7
x^2	4	9	16	25	36	49
$P(X = x)$	$\frac{1}{12}$	$\frac{2}{12}$	$\frac{3}{12}$	$\frac{3}{12}$	$\frac{2}{12}$	$\frac{1}{12}$

Solution

In Section 7.2, Example 3, we calculated that $E(X) = 4.5$. To find the variance we must also find $E(X^2)$.

$$E(X^2) = \left(4 \times \tfrac{1}{12}\right) + \left(9 \times \tfrac{2}{12}\right) + \left(16 \times \tfrac{3}{12}\right) + \left(25 \times \tfrac{3}{12}\right) + \left(36 \times \tfrac{2}{12}\right) + \left(49 \times \tfrac{1}{12}\right)$$

$$= (4 + 18 + 48 + 75 + 72 + 49) \times \tfrac{1}{12}$$

$$= \tfrac{266}{12}$$

$$\text{Var}(X) = E(X^2) - \mu^2$$
$$= \tfrac{266}{12} - (4.5)^2$$
$$= 1.91\dot{6}\ldots$$

Standard deviation $= \sqrt{1.91\dot{6}} = 1.38$ (2 d.p.)

Example 2

A four-sided dice is thrown. Find the mean and variance of the score.

Solution

If X denotes the score, the probability distribution is:

x	1	2	3	4
x^2	1	4	9	16
$P(X = x)$	$\frac{1}{4}$	$\frac{1}{4}$	$\frac{1}{4}$	$\frac{1}{4}$

$$E(X) = (1 \times \tfrac{1}{4}) + (2 \times \tfrac{1}{4}) + (3 \times \tfrac{1}{4}) + (4 \times \tfrac{1}{4})$$
$$= 10 \times \tfrac{1}{4}$$
$$= \tfrac{10}{4}$$
$$= 2.5$$

$$E(X^2) = (1 \times \tfrac{1}{4}) + (4 \times \tfrac{1}{4}) + (9 \times \tfrac{1}{4}) + (16 \times \tfrac{1}{4})$$
$$= 30 \times \tfrac{1}{4}$$
$$= \tfrac{30}{4}$$
$$= 7.5$$

$$\text{Var}(X) = E(X^2) - E(X)^2$$
$$= 7.5 - 2.5^2$$
$$= 7.5 - 6.25$$
$$= 1.25$$

Example 3

If a random variable X has the following probability distribution

x	1	2	3	4
$P(X = x)$	0.4	0.2	0.3	0.1

Find:

a $\text{Var}(X)$

b $\text{Var}(2X)$

c $\text{Var}(4)$

d $\text{Var}(2X + 4)$

Solution

$$E(X) = (1 \times 0.4) + (2 \times 0.2) + (3 \times 0.3) + (4 \times 0.1)$$

$$= 2.1$$

$$E(X^2) = (1 \times 0.4) + (4 \times 0.2) + (9 \times 0.3) + (16 \times 0.1)$$

$$= 5.5$$

a $\text{Var}(X) = E(X^2) - [E(X)]^2$

$$= 5.5 - 2.1^2$$

$$= 1.09$$

b $\text{Var}(2X) = E[(2X)^2] - [E(2X)]^2$

$$= E(4X^2) - [2E(X)]^2$$

$$= 4E(X^2) - (2 \times 2.1)^2$$

$$= (4 \times 5.5) - 4.2^2$$

$$= 4.36$$

Remember that $E(aX) = aE(X)$.

c $\text{Var}(4) = E(4^2) - [E(4)]^2$

$$= E(16) - 16$$

$$= 16 - 16$$

$$= 0$$

Remember that $E(c) = c$.

d $\text{Var}(2X + 4) = E[(2X + 4)^2] - [E(2X + 4)]^2$

$$= E(4X^2 + 16X + 16) - [2E(X) + 4]^2$$

$$= E(4X^2) + E(16X) + E(16) - [(2 \times 2.1) + 4]^2$$

$$= 4E(X^2) + 16E(X) + 16 - 67.24$$

$$= (4 \times 5.5) + (16 \times 2.1) + 16 - 67.24$$

$$= 71.6 - 67.24$$

$$= 4.36$$

Remember that $E(aX + b) = aE(X) + b$.

We can use the above example to highlight certain rules.

Firstly, from **a** note that $\text{Var}(X) = 1.09$ and $\text{Var}(2X) = 4.36$.

If we multiply 1.09 by 4 that gives 4.36, so:

$$\mathbf{Var(2X) = 4Var(X)}$$

Let us consider a different example, say $\text{Var}(3X)$, to see if there is a pattern.

$$\begin{aligned}
\text{Var}(3X) &= E[(3X)^2] - [E(3X)]^2 \\
&= E(9X^2) - [3E(X)]^2 \\
&= 9E(X^2) - [3 \times 2.1]^2 \\
&= (9 \times 5.5) - 39.69 \\
&= 9.81
\end{aligned}$$

Comparing this with $\text{Var}(X)$, 1.09 multiplied by 9 gives 9.81, so:

$$\mathbf{Var(3X) = 9Var(X)}$$

We can see a pattern evolving.

$$\mathbf{Var(aX) = a^2 Var(X)}$$

Secondly, from **c**, $\text{Var}(4) = 0$. We could try this for any value of X but would soon discover that for any constant c,

$$\mathbf{Var(c) = 0}$$

since if a number is itself it will have no variance.

Finally, from **b** and **d**, we can see that the solutions are the same: $\text{Var}(2X) = 4.36$ and $\text{Var}(2X + 4) = 4.36$. This is due to the fact that the $\text{Var}(c) = 0$. From this we can write a general rule:

$$\mathbf{Var(aX + c) = a^2 Var(X)}$$

$\text{Var}(aX)$

$$\begin{aligned}
&= E[(aX)^2] - [E(aX)]^2 \\
&= E(a^2 X^2) - [aE(X)]^2 \\
&= a^2 E(X^2) - a^2[E(X)]^2 \\
&= a^2\{E(X^2) - [E(X)]^2\} \\
&= a^2 \text{Var}(X)
\end{aligned}$$

$$\begin{aligned}
\text{Var}(c) &= E(c^2) - [E(c)]^2 \\
&= c^2 - c^2 \\
&= 0
\end{aligned}$$

7.3 The Variance
Exercise

Technique

1 Find $\text{Var}(X)$ for the following probability distributions:

a

x	0	2	3	5
$P(X = x)$	0.15	0.34	0.31	0.2

b

x	-2	0	2
$P(X = x)$	$\frac{1}{8}$	$\frac{5}{8}$	$\frac{1}{4}$

2 A discrete random variable X has the following probability distribution:

x	1	2	5	10	15
$P(X = x)$	0.2	0.1	0.3	0.3	0.1

Find:

a $E(X)$ **b** $\text{Var}(X)$

c Verify that $\text{Var}(3X) = 9\text{Var}(X)$.

3 A discrete random variable Z has the following probability distribution:

z	1	2	3
$P(Z = z)$	0.3	0.2	0.5

Show that $\text{Var}(3Z + 6) = 9\text{Var}(Z)$.

4 Two four-sided dice are thrown. Y is the discrete random variable that denotes the sum of the scores. Find:

a $E(Y)$ **b** $\text{Var}(Y)$

c $\text{Var}(3Y)$ **d** $\text{Var}(3Y + 2)$

5 A fair coin is tossed three times and the discrete random variable W represents the number of heads recorded. Find:

a the distribution of W **b** $E(W)$

c $\text{Var}(W)$ **d** $\text{Var}(2W + 3)$

6 A discrete random variable X has the following probability distribution:

x	3	4	5
$p(X = x)$	$2t$	t	$3t$

where t is a constant. Find:

a the value of t **b** $E(X)$

c $\text{Var}(X)$

7.4 Linear Combination of Discrete Random Variables

To understand the effect of combining random variables we will use the following experiment of removing marbles from a bag, both with and without replacement.

I have a bag containing five red marbles and three green marbles. I remove one marble from the bag, note down its colour and *replace* it. I then remove another marble and note down its colour also. If the random variable X denotes the number of red marbles taken out, the probability distribution of X is:

x	0	1	2
$P(X = x)$	$\frac{9}{64}$	$\frac{30}{64}$	$\frac{25}{64}$

$$E(X) = (1 \times \tfrac{30}{64}) + (2 \times \tfrac{25}{64})$$
$$= \tfrac{5}{4}$$
$$E(X^2) = (1^2 \times \tfrac{30}{64}) + (2^2 \times \tfrac{25}{64})$$
$$= (1 \times \tfrac{30}{64}) + (4 \times \tfrac{25}{64})$$
$$= \tfrac{130}{64}$$
$$\text{Var}(X) = E(X^2) - E(X)^2$$
$$= \tfrac{130}{64} - (\tfrac{5}{4})^2$$
$$= \tfrac{15}{32}$$

I could consider the same experiment but choose the random variables Y_1 and Y_2 to represent the outcomes of each event. $Y = 1$ if a red marble is picked; $Y = 0$ if a green marble is picked. So $X = Y_1 + Y_2$.

The probability distribution of Y_1 will be:

y	0	1
$P(Y_1 = y)$	$\frac{3}{8}$	$\frac{5}{8}$

Y_1 and Y_2 are independent events since the probability of getting a red or green second marble is not affected by the colour of the first marble taken out of the bag.

Using the probability distribution we can calculate

$$E(Y_1) = (0 \times \tfrac{3}{8}) + (1 \times \tfrac{5}{8}) = \tfrac{5}{8}$$

The probability tree diagram is

First marble | Second marble

	R RR 25/64
	G RG 15/64
	R GR 15/64
	G GG 9/64

If the first and second marbles are both red, $Y_1 = 1$, $Y_2 = 1$ and $X = 2$. If the first marble is red and the second green, $Y_1 = 1$ and $Y_2 = 0$; or if the first marble is green and the second red, $Y_1 = 0$ and $Y_2 = 1$. In both cases, $X = 1$. If both marbles are green, $Y_1 = 0$, $Y_2 = 0$ and $X = 0$.

and similarly, $E(Y_2) = \frac{5}{8}$

so $\qquad E(Y_1) + E(Y_2) = \frac{5}{8} + \frac{5}{8} = \frac{5}{4}$

and $\qquad\qquad E(X) = E(Y_1 + Y_2) = \frac{5}{4}$

So, in fact

$$E(Y_1 + Y_2) = E(Y_1) + E(Y_2)$$

Let us now look at the variance:

$$E(Y_1) = \frac{5}{8}$$
$$E(Y_1^2) = \left(0 \times \frac{3}{8}\right) + \left(1^2 \times \frac{5}{8}\right)$$
$$= \frac{5}{8}$$
$$\text{Var}(Y_1) = E(Y_1^2) - E(Y_1)^2$$
$$= \frac{5}{8} - \frac{25}{64}$$
$$= \frac{15}{64}$$

and therefore $\text{Var}(Y_2) = \frac{15}{64}$

$$\text{Var}(X) = \text{Var}(Y_1 + Y_2) = \frac{15}{32}, \text{ as calculated on p. 160}$$
$$\text{and Var}(Y_1) + \text{Var}(Y_2) = \frac{15}{64} + \frac{15}{64}$$
$$= \frac{15}{32}$$

So for *independent* events

$$\mathbf{Var(Y_1 + Y_2) = Var(Y_1) + Var(Y_2)}$$

If I repeat the experiment, but this time I remove two marbles from the bag *without replacement* then the probability distribution of X, the number of red marbles is:

x	0	1	2
$P(X = x)$	$\frac{3}{28}$	$\frac{15}{28}$	$\frac{5}{14}$

$$E(X) = \left(1 \times \frac{15}{28}\right) + \left(2 \times \frac{5}{14}\right)$$
$$= \frac{5}{4}$$
$$E(X^2) = \left(1 \times \frac{15}{28}\right) + \left(4 \times \frac{5}{14}\right)$$
$$= \frac{55}{28}$$
$$\text{Var}(X) = E(X^2) - E(X)^2$$
$$= \frac{55}{28} - \left(\frac{5}{4}\right)^2$$
$$= \frac{45}{112}$$

The probability tree diagram is

First marble   Second marble

$\frac{5}{8}$ R
$\frac{4}{7}$ R RR 20/56
$\frac{3}{7}$ G RG 15/56

$\frac{3}{8}$ G
$\frac{5}{7}$ R GR 15/56
$\frac{2}{7}$ G GG 6/56

If the random variables Y_1 and Y_2 represent first and second outcomes as before, then X, which is the number of red marbles is

$$X = Y_1 + Y_2$$

The probability distribution of Y_1 will remain the same as before. This time Y_1 and Y_2 are not independent since the probability of getting a red or green second marble changes depending on which colour marble was taken out first time.

However, the probability distributions of Y_1 and Y_2 will be the same. The reason being that Y_2 could have been taken out first and then Y_1. Due to this symmetry the probability distributions of Y_1 and Y_2 are the same.

So $\qquad\qquad E(Y_1) = (0 \times \frac{3}{8}) + (1 \times \frac{5}{8}) = \frac{5}{8}$

and $\qquad\qquad E(Y_2) = \frac{5}{8}$

therefore, $\quad E(Y_1) + E(Y_2) = \frac{5}{8} + \frac{5}{8} = \frac{5}{4}$

also, $\qquad\qquad E(X) = E(Y_1 + Y_2) = \frac{5}{4}$

So, for *any* events,

$$E(Y_1 + Y_2) = E(Y_1) + E(Y_2)$$

Let us next look at the variance:

$$\mathrm{Var}(Y_1) = \frac{15}{64}$$

and $\mathrm{Var}(Y_2) = \frac{15}{64}$ as calculated earlier

$$\mathrm{Var}(X) = \mathrm{Var}(Y_1 + Y_2) = \frac{45}{112}$$

$$\mathrm{Var}(Y_1) + \mathrm{Var}(Y_2) = \frac{15}{64} + \frac{15}{64} = \frac{15}{32}$$

In this case, $\mathrm{Var}(Y_1 + Y_2)$ is not the same as $\mathrm{Var}(Y_1) + \mathrm{Var}(Y_2)$.

So, generally

$$E(X \pm Y) = E(X) \pm E(Y) \text{ for any two events}$$

but $\mathbf{Var}(X \pm Y) = \mathbf{Var}(X) + \mathbf{Var}(Y)$ only for independent events.

We always add variances:

$\mathrm{Var}(X - Y)$

$= \mathrm{Var}(X + (-1)Y)$

$= \mathrm{Var}(X) + \mathrm{Var}(-1)Y$

$= \mathrm{Var}(X) + (-1)^2 \mathrm{Var}($

$= \mathrm{Var}(X) + \mathrm{Var}(Y)$

* Remember

$\mathrm{Var}(aX) = a^2 \mathrm{Var}(X)$

Example 1

A random variable X has mean 3 and variance 8, and the random variable Y has mean 4 and variance 7. X and Y are independent of each other. Find:

a $E(X + Y)$ **b** $\text{Var}(X + Y)$

c $E(2X - 3Y)$ **d** $\text{Var}(4X - Y + 1)$

Solution

a $$E(X + Y) = E(X) + E(Y)$$

$$= 3 + 4$$

$$= 7$$

b $$\text{Var}(X + Y) = \text{Var}(X) + \text{Var}(Y)$$

$$= 8 + 7$$

$$= 15$$

X and Y are independent.

c $$E(2X - 3Y) = E(2X) - E(3Y)$$

$$= 2E(X) - 3E(Y)$$

$$= (2 \times 3) - (3 \times 4)$$

$$= -6$$

$E(aX) = aE(X)$

d $$\text{Var}(4X - Y + 1) = \text{Var}(4X) + \text{Var}(Y) + \text{Var}(1)$$

$$= 16\text{Var}(X) + \text{Var}(Y) + \text{Var}(1)$$

$$= 16\text{Var}(X) + \text{Var}(Y)$$

$$= (16 \times 8) + 7$$

$$= 135$$

$\text{Var}(X - Y) = \text{Var}(X) + \text{Var}(Y)$

$\text{Var}(aX) = a^2\text{Var}(X)$

$\text{Var}(c) = 0$

7.4 Linear Combination of Discrete Random Variables

Exercise

Technique

1 The random variable A has mean 2 and variance 6, and the random variable B has mean 1.5 and variance 8. A and B are independent of each other. Find:

  a $E(A+B)$ **b** $\text{Var}(A+B)$

  c $E(5A+2B)$ **d** $\text{Var}(3A-2B+2)$

2 The random variable W has mean 1 and variance 3, and the random variable Z has mean 2 and variance 5. W and Z are *not* independent. With the information given find, where possible:

  a $E(W-Z)$ **b** $\text{Var}(W-Z)$

  c $E(2W-1)$ **d** $E(3W+Z+4)$

3 Independent random variables X and Y have the following probability distributions:

x	0	1	2
$P(X=x)$	0.2	0.3	0.5

y	0	1	2	3	4
$P(Y=y)$	0.2	0.1	0.3	0.25	0.15

  a   Find $E(X)$ and $E(Y)$.   **b**   Find $\text{Var}(X)$ and $\text{Var}(Y)$.

By constructing the probability distribution for the random variable $X+Y$, show that:

  c $E(X+Y)=E(X)+E(Y)$ **d** $\text{Var}(X+Y)=\text{Var}(X)+\text{Var}(Y)$

4 The discrete random variable X has the following probability distribution:

x	0	1
$P(X=x)$	0.4	0.6

The discrete random variable Y has the following probability distribution:

y	2	3
$P(Y=y)$	0.3	0.7

X and Y are independent random variables. Find:

  a $E(X)$ and $E(Y)$ **b** $\text{Var}(X)$ and $\text{Var}(Y)$

  c $E(3X+Y-1)$ **d** $\text{Var}(5X+3Y+2)$

5 A pair of unbiased cubical dice are thrown. If R_1 and R_2 represent the individual scores on each die and S denotes the sum of the scores:

  a   construct the probability distributions for R_1 and R_2

  b   construct the probability distribution for S

  c   find the mean of S **d**   find the variance of S.

Consolidation

Exercise A

1 On a local committee three people are to be elected from 15 members, nine of whom are women and six men. X is the random variable 'the number of women on the committee'.

   a Construct a probability distribution for X.
   b Find $E(X)$.
   c Find $\text{Var}(X)$.

2 Two four-sided dice are thrown. Y is the random variable 'the product of the two results'.

   a Construct a probability distribution for Y.
   b Find $P(Y < 4)$.
   c State the mode.
   d If the experiment is repeated 100 times, give the expected frequencies.

3 From a bag containing five purple and seven green marbles, two marbles are taken out *without* replacement. If X is the random variable 'the number of green marbles removed', find $E(2X + 3)$ and $\text{Var}(2X + 3)$.

4 A discrete random variable X can take any one of five possible values and has the following probability distribution:

x	0	2	5	8	n
Probability $P(X = x)$	0.1	0.25	0.2	$2p$	p

Calculate:

   a the value of p
   b the value of n, given that $E(X) = 5.7$
   c $E(X^2)$ and the variance of X.

(UCLES)

5 A computer is programmed to produce a sequence of integers, R, in the range 0 to 5 inclusive, with probabilities as shown below.

r	0	1	2	3	4	5
$P(R = r)$	k	$\frac{1}{30}$	$\frac{2}{30}$	$\frac{3}{30}$	$\frac{4}{30}$	$\frac{5}{30}$

   a Show that $k = \frac{1}{2}$.
   b Calculate the mean and variance of R.

(UCLES)

6 A newsagent sells phone cards valued at £1, £2, £4, £10 or £20. The value, in pounds, of a phone card sold may be regarded as a random variable, X, with the following probability distribution.

x	1	2	4	10	20
$P(X = x)$	0.20	0.40	0.22	0.11	0.07

a Find the mean and standard deviation of X.

b What is the probability that the value of the next phone card sold is less than £4? (*AEB*)

7 The distribution of the number of muffins, X, bought by a customer at a particular shop, is given in the following table:

X	1	2	3	4	5	6	>6
Prob	$\frac{1}{12}$	$\frac{2}{12}$	$\frac{3}{12}$	a	$\frac{2}{12}$	$\frac{1}{12}$	0

a Find the value of a.

b By symmetry, or otherwise, state the expected value of X.

c Evaluate the variance of X.

Initially the shopkeeper charges 40p for each muffin, which costs 10p to produce.

d Using the answer to **b**, or otherwise, find the expected profit made per customer buying muffins. (*OCSEB*)

8 The discrete random variable X has probability function

$$P(X = x) = \begin{cases} \dfrac{kx}{(x^2 + 1)} & \text{for } x = 2, 3 \\ \dfrac{2kx}{(x^2 - 1)} & \text{for } x = 4, 5 \\ 0 & \text{otherwise} \end{cases}$$

a Show that the value of k is $\frac{20}{33}$.

b Find the probability that X is less than 3 or greater than 4. (*ULEAC*)

9 The discrete random variables A and B are independent and have the following probability distributions:

a	1	2	3
$P(A = a)$	$\frac{1}{4}$	$\frac{1}{2}$	$\frac{1}{4}$

b	1	2
$P(B = b)$	$\frac{1}{3}$	$\frac{2}{3}$

The random variable Q is the product of one observation from A and one observation from B.

a Show that $P(Q = 2) = \frac{1}{3}$.

b Find the probability distribution for Q.

c Hence, or otherwise, show that $E(Q) = \frac{10}{3}$.

d Find Var(Q).

(*ULEAC*)

10 At a stall in a charity fair, a card is selected at random from a set of 13 different cards and placed face down. The player has up to three guesses to say which card it is. Let X be the number of guesses made. (For example, if the player guesses incorrectly at the first attempt and correctly at the second attempt, then $X = 2$.)

a Write down the values of $P(X = 1)$ and $P(X = 2)$, and show that $P(X = 3) = \frac{11}{13}$.

b Find $E(X)$ and $\text{Var}(X)$.

If a player guesses correctly at the first attempt he wins 50p; a correct guess at the second attempt wins 25p; a correct guess at the third attempt wins 15p; otherwise he wins nothing. Let Y pence be the amount won.

c Write down the probability distribution for Y, and use it to find the expected amount won.

Players pay 10p to play the game, and the stall hopes to attract about 200 players during the day;

d Approximately what profit is the stall likely to make? *(MEI)*

Exercise B

1 Two ordinary dice are thrown. Given that Z is the random variable 'the difference of the two results', construct a probability distribution for Z and use it to find the mean and standard deviation of the probability distribution.

2 The random variable T has the probability distribution shown in the table below:

t	2	4	6
$P(T = t)$	0.3	0.6	0.1

a Find $E(3T + 2)$. **b** Find $\text{Var}(5T + 3)$.

3 The random variable X has mean 3 and standard deviation 2, and the random variable Y has mean 1.7 and standard deviation 3. X and Y are independent random variables. Find:

a $E(X + Y)$ **b** $\text{Var}(X + Y)$
c $E(2X + Y - 1)$ **d** $\text{Var}(2X - 2Y + 4)$

4 A variable X has the probability distribution shown in the table below.

X	2	4	6	8
Probability	$7k$	$5k$	$3k$	k

Given that X can only take the values 2, 4, 6 and 8, calculate:

a the value of k **b** the variance of X.

(UCLES)

5 Two fair dice are thrown and their scores added to form the random variable Z. Copy and complete the following table showing the probability distribution for Z:

z	2	3	4	...	11	12
$P(Z = z)$	$\frac{1}{36}$	$\frac{2}{36}$		...	$\frac{2}{36}$	$\frac{1}{36}$

a Using symmetry, or otherwise, find the expected value of Z.
b Calculate the variance of Z.

(*OCSEB*)

6 A curiously shaped six-faced dice produces a score, X, for which the probability distribution is given in the following table:

r	1	2	3	4	5	6
$P(X = r)$	k	$\frac{k}{2}$	$\frac{k}{3}$	$\frac{k}{4}$	$\frac{k}{5}$	$\frac{k}{6}$

Show that the constant k is $\frac{20}{49}$. Find the mean and variance of X. The dice is thrown twice. Show that the probability of obtaining equal scores is approximately $\frac{1}{4}$.

(*MEI*)

7 The Weighton Corner Shop Bakery produces fresh cream gateaux, making a profit of £3 on each one sold but losing £1 on each one unsold at the end of the day. Experience has shown that the daily demand for such gateaux can be modelled by a random variable X with probability distribution as shown below:

x	0	1	2	3	4	5	6	7	8
$P(X = x)$	0.05	0.05	0.10	0.20	0.15	0.15	0.15	0.10	0.05

a Show that the expected demand for gateaux on a given day is 4.2.
b The random variable Y represents the daily profit when eight gateaux are produced.
  i Express Y in terms of X.
  ii Find the expected daily profit when eight gateaux are produced.
c The bakery is considering a reduction in the number of gateaux produced from eight per day to six per day. Assuming the same model for demand, show that the expected daily profit is £10 when the bakery produces six gateaux per day.
d Give a reason for:
  i supporting the change to six gateaux per day,
  ii not supporting the change to six gateaux per day.

(*NEAB*)

8 The discrete random variable X has probability function:

$$P(X = x) = \begin{cases} kx & \text{for } x = 1, 2, \ldots, 5 \\ 0 & \text{otherwise} \end{cases}$$

a Show that $k = \frac{1}{15}$.

Find the value of:

b $E(X + 3)$ 　　　　　　　　　　　　　**c** $\text{Var}(2X - 4)$

(ULEAC)

9 An unbiased cubical dice has three faces numbered '1', two faces numbered '2' and one face numbered '3'. The random variable X is the number showing on the top face of the dice when it is thrown. Show that $E(X) = \frac{5}{3}$ and find $\text{Var}(X)$.

(UCLES)

10 A competition consists of matching inventors and inventions from a list of four inventors and four inventions. The inventors are Bell, Cockerell, Marconi and Nobel, and their respective inventions are the telephone, the hovercraft, radio and dynamite. Suppose I guess which person invented which item and define X as the random variable which represents the number of correct matchings. For example $X = 1$ might arise from the matchings:

Bell invented dynamite	*wrong*
Cockerell invented the hovercraft	*correct*
Marconi invented the telephone	*wrong*
Nobel invented radio	*wrong*

a Find the total number of possible matchings. Hence show that $P(X = 4) = \frac{1}{24}$.

b Explain why $P(X = 3) = 0$.

c Find $P(X = 2)$ and $P(X = 1)$. Hence show that $P(X = 0) = \frac{3}{8}$.

Copy and complete the table to show the probability distribution for X:

r	0	1	2	3	4
$P(X = r)$	$\frac{3}{8}$			0	$\frac{1}{24}$

d Find the mean and variance of the number of correct matchings.

e Two friends both enter the competition by guessing the matchings. Find the probability that they guess the same number of correct matchings.

(MEI)

Applications and Activities

1 Design three biased dice, each with a mean score of 4. Tabulate the probability distribution for each dice showing supporting calculations.

Summary

- A **discrete random variable** is a numerical variable whose value depends to some extent on chance.

- A **discrete probability distribution** is a list of all possible outcomes together with the probability of each happening.

- The expectation or expected value of a random variable X is

    $$E(X) = \Sigma x P(X = x)$$

- The expectation or expected value of a function or combination of functions is

    $$E(f(X)) = \Sigma f(x) P(X = x)$$

    $$E[f(X)) + g(X)] = E[f(X)] + E[g(X)]$$

- The general rules for the expected value are

    $$E(aX + b) = aE(X) + b$$

    $$E(X \pm Y) = E(X) \pm E(Y) \text{ for any two events.}$$

- The variance of X is Var(X), where

    $$\mathbf{Var}(X) = E[(X - \mu)^2]$$

    $$\mathbf{Var}(X) = E(X^2) - E(X)^2$$

- The general rules of variance are

    $$\mathbf{Var}(aX + c) = a^2 \mathbf{Var}(X)$$

    $$\mathbf{Var}(X \pm Y) = \mathbf{Var}(X) + \mathbf{Var}(Y) \text{ for independent events.}$$

8 Binomial, Geometric and Poisson Distributions

What you need to know

- How to use ^nC_r notation.

- How to find $E(X)$ of a given probability distribution.

- How to find $\text{Var}(X)$ of a given probability distribution.

Review

1 Evaluate (without the use of a calculator):

   a $^6C_2$ **b** $^{10}C_1$ **c** $^{12}C_4$

   d $^8C_7$ **e** $^5C_3$ **f** $^8C_0$

2

x	0	1	2	3
$P(X = x)$	0.25	0.1	0.3	0.35

Find the $E(X)$ and $\text{Var}(X)$ for the given probability distribution.

3

y	1	2	3	4
$P(Y = y)$	$\frac{1}{4}$	$\frac{1}{8}$	$\frac{1}{2}$	$\frac{1}{8}$

Find the $E(Y)$ and $\text{Var}(Y)$ for the given probability distribution.

8.1 Binomial Theorem

Binomial expressions

A **binomial expression** is one of the form $(x + y)^n$ and you might have already considered these in pure mathematics.

For example,

$$(x + y)^2 = (x + y)(x + y) = x^2 + 2xy + y^2$$

$$(x + y)^3 = (x^2 + 2xy + y^2)(x + y) = x^3 + 3x^2y + 3xy^2 + y^3$$

Calculating these expressions by multiplying out the terms is very lengthy and there is another method.

Let us consider again $(x + y)^3 = (x + y)(x + y)(x + y)$

In the result obtained earlier every resulting term is 'cubic' since we have picked one term out of each of the brackets. We can also see that every *type* of cubic term is represented, that is x^3, $3x^2y$, $3xy^2$ and y^3.

x^3 is made up of xxx

$3x^2y$ is made up of $xxy + yxx + xyx$

$3xy^2$ is made up of $xyy + yxy + yyx$

y^3 is made up of yyy

So there is a systematic way of expanding these expressions. First we write down each type of cubic term possible, starting with x^3y^0, then reduce the power of x by one each time and raise the power of y by one each time until we reach x^0y^3. Then calculate the coefficients of each term.

Remember that $x^0 = 1$.

Remembering the work on arrangements:

xxy can be arranged $^3C_2 = \dfrac{3!}{2!1!} = 3$ ways

yyx can be arranged $^3C_1 = \dfrac{3!}{2!1!} = 3$ ways

Generally, the coefficient of the term
$$x^ry^{n-r} \text{ is } {}^nC_r = \frac{n!}{r!(n-r)!}$$

Some calculators have a $\boxed{{}^nC_r}$ button that can evaluate this directly.

Example 1

Write down the binomial expansion of $(x + y)^4$.

Solution

First write down every quartic term possible:

$$x^4 \qquad x^3 y \qquad x^2 y^2 \qquad xy^3 \qquad y^4$$

Now, work out the coefficients of each term.

$$x^4 \text{ can be arranged } {}^4C_4 = \frac{4!}{4!\,0!} = 1 \text{ way}$$

$$x^3 y \text{ can be arranged } {}^4C_3 = \frac{4!}{3!\,1!} = 4 \text{ ways}$$

$$x^2 y^2 \text{ can be arranged } {}^4C_2 = \frac{4!}{2!\,2!} = 6 \text{ ways}$$

$$xy^3 \text{ can be arranged } {}^4C_1 = \frac{4!}{1!\,3!} = 4 \text{ ways}$$

$$y^4 \text{ can be arranged } {}^4C_0 = \frac{4!}{0!\,4!} = 1 \text{ way}$$

So, the binomial expansion of $(x + y)^4$ is:

$$(x + y)^4 = x^4 + 4x^3 y + 6x^2 y^2 + 4xy^3 + y^4$$

Note: decrease the power of x each time and increase the power of y.

Remember that by convention, $0! = 1$.

Example 2

Find the x^6 term in the expansion of $(x + y)^9$.

Solution

The term will be of the form $Ax^6 y^3$.

To find A remember the coefficient will be ${}^9C_6 = \frac{9!}{6!\,3!} = 84$.

So, the term is $84x^6 y^3$.

173

8.1 Binomial Theorem
Exercise

Technique

1 Expand the binomial expression $(x + y)^5$.

2 Expand the binomial expression $(a + b)^7$.

3 In the expansion of $(p + q)^{12}$ find the terms in

    a p^6 **b** p^8 **c** p^{10}

4 Find the coefficient of the term x^4y^4 in the expansion of $(x + y)^8$.

5 The term $Bx^{14}y^c$ arises in the expansion of $(x + y)^{18}$.

    a Calculate c.   **b** Calculate the coefficient B.

6 Find the coefficients of the following terms in the expansion of $(x + y)^6$.

    a x^4y^2 **b** y^6 **c** x^3y^3

7 Find the term in x^2y^5 of $\left(\dfrac{2x}{3} + \dfrac{y}{3}\right)^7$.

8 Find the term in a^2b^2 in the binomial expansion of $\left(\dfrac{a}{2} + \dfrac{b}{2}\right)^4$.

9 Find the term in t^5 in the binomial expansion of $\left(\dfrac{2}{3} + \dfrac{t}{3}\right)^8$.

10 Write down the p^r term in the expansion of $(p + q)^n$.

8.2 The Binomial Distribution

Binomial distributions are used to model situations where there are just two possible outcomes, **success** and **failure**.

Together with this property, the following conditions *also* need to be fulfilled.

● There must be a *fixed number of trials* (called *n*).

● The *probability of success* (called *p*) must be the *same* for each trial.

● The trials must be *independent*.

Examples where a binomial model could be used

Trial	Success	Failure
Spinning a coin	heads	tails
Throwing a dice	score 6	score not 6

Example 1

An unbiased dice is thrown three times and the random variable X denotes the number of sixes obtained. How can we describe the probability distribution of X?

Solution

There are a *fixed number of trials*, that is three, each consisting of throwing the dice once.

Each trial has *two outcomes* since we are looking at the number of sixes obtained. If a six is obtained this is a *success*, and any other outcome is a *failure*.

The trials are *independent*.

The *probability of getting a success*, that is a six, is *constant* for each trial at $\frac{1}{6}$.

The above experiment satisfies the conditions for modelling by a binomial distribution but what does the probability distribution of a binomial distribution look like?

We can evaluate the probabilities by drawing a tree diagram.

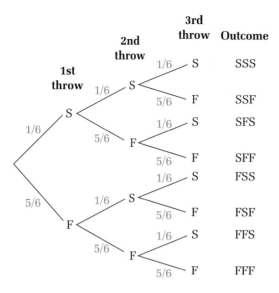

If X represents the number of successes then:

SSS is equivalent to $P(X = 3)$

$P(X = 3) = \frac{1}{6} \times \frac{1}{6} \times \frac{1}{6}$ or $\left(\frac{1}{6}\right)^3$

and

FFF is equivalent to $P(X = 0)$

$P(X = 0) = \frac{5}{6} \times \frac{5}{6} \times \frac{5}{6}$ or $\left(\frac{5}{6}\right)^3$

What about $P(X = 2)$? The tree diagram shows that this occurs with SSF, SFS and FSS. So, add these probabilities together.

$P(\text{SSF}) = \frac{1}{6} \times \frac{1}{6} \times \frac{5}{6} = \left(\frac{1}{6}\right)^2 \left(\frac{5}{6}\right)$

$P(\text{SFS}) = \frac{1}{6} \times \frac{5}{6} \times \frac{1}{6} = \left(\frac{1}{6}\right)^2 \left(\frac{5}{6}\right)$

$P(\text{FSS}) = \frac{5}{6} \times \frac{1}{6} \times \frac{1}{6} = \left(\frac{1}{6}\right)^2 \left(\frac{5}{6}\right)$

So

$P(X = 2) = 3 \times \left(\frac{1}{6}\right)^2 \left(\frac{5}{6}\right)$

All of these outcomes, SSF, SFS and FSS, are equivalent. We could have simply calculated the probability of two successes and one failure and multiplied the probability by the number of possible arrangements of that situation.

Two successes and one failure yields $^3C_2$ or $\dfrac{3!}{2!\,1!} = 3$ different arrangements.

So,

$$P(X = 2) = 3 \times \left(\tfrac{1}{6}\right)^2 \left(\tfrac{5}{6}\right)$$

Now, obviously for this case it was just as quick to calculate the probabilities by either method, but if you were throwing the dice 15 times, the short cut method would be invaluable.

Finally, $P(X = 1)$, in other words one success and two failures.

$$P(\text{one success and two failures}) = \tfrac{1}{6} \times \tfrac{5}{6} \times \tfrac{5}{6}$$

$$= \left(\tfrac{1}{6}\right)\left(\tfrac{5}{6}\right)^2$$

As for $P(X = 2)$ there will be three arrangements (since $^3C_2 = 3$).

$$P(X = 1) = 3 \times \left(\tfrac{1}{6}\right)\left(\tfrac{5}{6}\right)^2$$

So, the probability distribution is:

x	0	1	2	3
$P(X = x)$	$\left(\tfrac{5}{6}\right)^3$	$3\left(\tfrac{1}{6}\right)\left(\tfrac{5}{6}\right)^2$	$3\left(\tfrac{1}{6}\right)^2\left(\tfrac{5}{6}\right)$	$\left(\tfrac{1}{6}\right)^3$

Check it is a probability distribution by finding if the probabilities sum to 1.

The dice experiment is an example of a situation that can be modelled by a binomial distribution. The probabilities of the distribution can be calculated because the probabilities are terms in the binomial expansion with $p = \tfrac{1}{6}$ and $q = \tfrac{5}{6}$ (where q is the probability of failure, that is $q = 1 - p$).

So generally, the probability that the number of successes, X, in n trials is r is given by

$$P(X = r) = {}^nC_r\, p^r (1 - p)^{n-r}$$

The dice example is just one of a whole family of binomial distributions and so when defining a binomial distribution it is important to fully describe it by giving the number of trials n, and the probability of success p. These values are known as the **parameters** of the distribution. A binomial distribution is written as

$$X \sim B(n, p)$$

and is read 'X is distributed binomially with number of trials n and probability of success p'. For the dice example just considered $X \sim B\left(3, \tfrac{1}{6}\right)$.

Since the probability of two successes and one failure is $\tfrac{1}{6} \times \tfrac{1}{6} \times \tfrac{5}{6}$.

Remember:
$(q + p)^3 = q^3 + 3q^2p + 3qp^2 + p^3$ and compare this with the probability distribution table.

Where $^nC_r = \dfrac{n!}{r!(n-r)!}$

Example 2

A four-sided dice is thrown five times. If X denotes the number of threes obtained, describe the distribution of X and find $P(X = 2)$.

Solution

X has a binomial distribution, with $n = 5$ and $p = \frac{1}{4}$.

$$X \sim B\left(5, \tfrac{1}{4}\right)$$

$$P(X = 2) = {}^5C_2 \times \tfrac{1}{4}^2 \times \tfrac{3}{4}^3$$

$$= \frac{5!}{3!\,2!} \times \tfrac{1}{16} \times \tfrac{27}{64}$$

$$= \frac{5 \times 4}{2} \times \tfrac{1}{16} \times \tfrac{27}{64}$$

$$= \tfrac{135}{512}$$

$$= 0.2637 \ (4 \text{ d.p.})$$

Substitute $n = 5$, $r = 2$
$p = \frac{1}{4}$ in the formula
$P(X = r) = {}^nC_r\,p^r(1 - p)$

Example 3

In a biology examination 45% of students pass. If a class of 20 students takes the exam, find the probability that:

a exactly 15 students pass   **b** at least two students pass

c more than 16 students pass.

Solution

If X is the number of students who pass, then $X \sim B(20, 0.45)$.

a $P(X = 15) = {}^{20}C_{15}(0.45)^{15}(0.55)^5$

$$= \frac{20!}{5!15!}(0.45)^{15}(0.55)^5$$

$$= 0.0049$$

$X \sim B(20, 0.45)$ means
there are 20 trials and
the probability of
success is 0.45.

b $P(X \geq 2) = 1 - P(X \leq 1)$

$$= 1 - [P(X = 0) + P(X = 1)]$$

$$= 1 - [(0.55)^{20} + 20 \times (0.45) \times (0.55)^{19}]$$

$$= 1 - 0.0001$$

$$= 0.9999$$

c $P(X > 16) = P(X = 17) + P(X = 18) + P(X = 19) + P(X = 20)$

$$= {}^{20}C_{17}(0.45)^{17}(0.55)^3 + {}^{20}C_{18}(0.45)^{18}(0.55)^2$$

$$+ {}^{20}C_{19}(0.45)^{19}(0.55) + {}^{20}C_{20}(0.45)^{20}$$

$$= [1140 \times (0.45)^{17} \times (0.55)^3] + [190 \times (0.45)^{18} \times (0.55)^2]$$

$$+ [20 \times (0.45)^{19} \times (0.55)] + [1 \times (0.45)^{20}]$$

$$= 0.0003$$

8.2 The Binomial Distribution
Exercise

Technique

1 Describe the distribution $B(12, 0.72)$ and find $P(X = 4)$.

2 If $X \sim B(24, 0.63)$, find:

   a $P(X = 16)$ **b** $P(X = 5)$

3 If $X \sim B(10, 0.9)$, find:

   a $P(X = 6)$ **b** $P(X > 8)$ **c** $P(X \geq 2)$

4 If $X \sim B(15, 0.35)$, find:

   a $P(X = 8)$ **b** $P(X < 3)$ **c** $P(X > 13)$

5 In a particular town approximately 75% of people pass their driving test first time. If a group of 35 people takes the exam, find the probability that:

   a exactly 13 pass   **b** more than 32 pass.

6 The throwing of coins can be modelled using a binomial distribution. I throw a coin 10 times and want to find the probability of getting six heads.

   a State a suitable distribution to model this situation.
   b Find the probability of getting six heads.

8.3 Cumulative Binomial Probability Tables

Cumulative probability is similar to cumulative frequency. If X is a discrete random variable, the corresponding cumulative probabilities are obtained by summing up all the probabilities up to a particular value as can be seen in the following example.

Example 1

Find the cumulative probability for the random variable X where X is the score on an unbiased dice.

x	1	2	3	4	5	6
$P(X = x)$	$\frac{1}{6}$	$\frac{1}{6}$	$\frac{1}{6}$	$\frac{1}{6}$	$\frac{1}{6}$	$\frac{1}{6}$

Solution

$P(X \leq 1) = \frac{1}{6}$ $P(X \leq 2) = \frac{2}{6}$ $P(X \leq 3) = \frac{3}{6}$

$P(X \leq 4) = \frac{4}{6}$ $P(X \leq 5) = \frac{5}{6}$ $P(X \leq 6) = 1$

For certain common binomial distributions the cumulative probability tables have already been worked out. In Example 3, on p. 178, where $X \sim B(20, 0.45)$, we might have been asked to find the probability that at least half the class fail, that is to evaluate $P(X \leq 10)$. Rather than doing a lengthy calculation this value can be read from the relevant table.

Binomial Cumulative Distribution Function
The tabulated value is $P(X \leq x)$, where X has a binomial distribution with index n and parameter p.

$p =$	0.05	0.10	0.15	0.20	0.25	0.30	0.35	0.40	0.45	0.50
$n = 20, x = 0$	0.3585	0.1216	0.0388	0.0115	0.0032	0.0008	0.0002	0.0000	0.0000	0.0000
1	0.7358	0.3917	0.1756	0.0692	0.0243	0.0076	0.0021	0.0005	0.0001	0.0000
2	0.9245	0.6769	0.4049	0.2061	0.0913	0.0355	0.0121	0.0036	0.0009	0.0002
3	0.9841	0.8670	0.6477	0.4114	0.2252	0.1071	0.0444	0.0160	0.0049	0.0013
4	0.9974	0.9568	0.8298	0.6296	0.4148	0.2375	0.1182	0.0510	0.0189	0.0059
5	0.9997	0.9887	0.9327	0.8042	0.6172	0.4164	0.2454	0.1256	0.0553	0.0207
6	1.0000	0.9976	0.9781	0.9133	0.7858	0.6080	0.4166	0.2500	0.1299	0.0577
7	1.0000	0.9996	0.9941	0.9679	0.8982	0.7723	0.6010	0.4159	0.2520	0.1316
8	1.0000	0.9999	0.9987	0.9900	0.9591	0.8867	0.7624	0.5956	0.4143	0.2517
9	1.0000	1.0000	0.9998	0.9974	0.9861	0.9520	0.8782	0.7553	0.5914	0.4119
10	1.0000	1.0000	1.0000	0.9994	0.9961	0.9829	0.9468	0.8725	0.7507	0.5881
11	1.0000	1.0000	1.0000	0.9999	0.9991	0.9949	0.9804	0.9435	0.8692	0.7483
12	1.0000	1.0000	1.0000	1.0000	0.9998	0.9987	0.9940	0.9790	0.9420	0.8684
13	1.0000	1.0000	1.0000	1.0000	1.0000	0.9997	0.9985	0.9935	0.9786	0.9423
14	1.0000	1.0000	1.0000	1.0000	1.0000	1.0000	0.9997	0.9984	0.9936	0.9793
15	1.0000	1.0000	1.0000	1.0000	1.0000	1.0000	1.0000	0.9997	0.9985	0.9941
16	1.0000	1.0000	1.0000	1.0000	1.0000	1.0000	1.0000	1.0000	0.9997	0.9987
17	1.0000	1.0000	1.0000	1.0000	1.0000	1.0000	1.0000	1.0000	1.0000	0.9998
18	1.0000	1.0000	1.0000	1.0000	1.0000	1.0000	1.0000	1.0000	1.0000	1.0000

From the table, $P(X \leq 10) = 0.7507$.

It is also possible to use the table to evaluate $P(X > 16)$ in the same example, since $P(X > 16) = 1 - P(X \leq 16)$, and again we could have simply read off $P(X \leq 16)$ from the table and then subtracted this from 1.

Secondly, the table can also be useful if you want to calculate a specific probability like $P(X = 15)$ since

$$P(X = 15) = P(X \leq 15) - P(X \leq 14)$$

Using the table we can simply read off these values and subtract.

Since the binomial is a discrete distribution, $P(X > 16)$ is equivalent to $P(X \geq 17)$.

Example 2

For the binomial distribution where $n = 20$ and $p = 0.45$, and using the table extract opposite, find:

a $P(X \leq 5)$ b $P(X > 8)$ c $P(X = 12)$

Solution

a $P(X \leq 5) = 0.0553$

b $P(X > 8) = 1 - P(X \leq 8)$

$$= 1 - 0.4143$$

$$= 0.5857$$

c $P(X = 12) = P(X \leq 12) - P(X \leq 11)$

$$= 0.9420 - 0.8692$$

$$= 0.0728$$

Although these tables save time it is important to remember that, when probabilities are very small, tables only give values to four decimal places and therefore some accuracy will be lost. You must also remember that the cumulative probability tables are only calculated for certain binomial distributions and some will still have to be calculated using the formula.

Example 3

Use cumulative binomial probability tables for the distribution $X \sim B(10, 0.2)$ to find:

a $P(X = 5)$ **b** $P(X \leq 6)$ **c** $P(X \geq 8)$

Solution

Binomial Cumulative Distribution Function
The tabulated value is $P(X \leq x)$, where X has a binomial distribution with index n and parameter p.

$p =$	0.05	0.10	0.15	0.20	0.25
$n = 10, x = 0$	0.5987	0.3487	0.1969	0.1074	0.0563
1	0.9139	0.7361	0.5443	0.3758	0.2440
2	0.9885	0.9298	0.8202	0.6778	0.5256
3	0.9990	0.9872	0.9500	0.8791	0.7759
4	0.9999	0.9984	0.9901	0.9672	0.9219
5	1.0000	0.9999	0.9986	0.9936	0.9803
6	1.0000	1.0000	0.9999	0.9991	0.9965
7	1.0000	1.0000	1.0000	0.9999	0.9996
8	1.0000	1.0000	1.0000	1.0000	1.0000
9	1.0000	1.0000	1.0000	1.0000	1.0000

a $P(X = 5) = P(X \leq 5) - P(X \leq 4)$

$$= 0.9936 - 0.9672$$

$$= 0.0264$$

b $P(X \leq 6) = 0.9991$

c $P(X \geq 8) = 1 - P(X \leq 7)$

$$= 1 - 0.9999$$

$$= 0.0001$$

In general use tables for given binomial distributions to:

1. calculate $P(X \leq r)$ for any value of r: simply read off the required value
2. calculate $P(X = r)$ for any value of r: find $P(X \leq r) - P(X \leq r - 1)$
3. calculate $P(X \geq r)$ for any value of r: find $1 - P(X \leq r - 1)$.

8.3 Cumulative Binomial Probability Tables

Exercise

Technique

Use cumulative probability tables.

1 If $X \sim B(5, 0.2)$, find:

  a $P(X \leq 4)$ **b** $P(X = 2)$ **c** $P(X \geq 3)$

2 If $Y \sim B(10, 0.4)$, find:

  a $P(Y < 3)$ **b** $P(Y = 7)$ **c** $P(Y \geq 9)$

3 If $W \sim B(10, 0.25)$, find:

  a $P(W \leq 5)$ **b** $P(W = 2)$ **c** $P(3 \leq W \leq 6)$

Contextual

1 Four unbiased dice are thrown. Find the probability that there are:

  a   exactly two sixes   **b**   at least two sixes.

2 Six coins are tossed. Find the probability that there are:

  a   not more than four heads   **b**   at least two heads.

3 Market research has shown that in a certain town only 55% of people use the local library regularly. Find the probability that in a sample of 10 people chosen at random:

  a   exactly four people use the library regularly;
  b   more than six people use the library regularly.

4 For a particular strain of seed only one in five germinates. If I plant 20 of these seeds what is the probability of exactly five germinating?

5 In the United Kingdom, only 14% of women aged between 16 and 19 cycle, whereas 37% of men aged between 16 and 19 cycle. Given these percentages find:

a the probability that in a random sample of eight women aged 16–19 at least two are cyclists;

b the probability that in a random sample of eight men aged 16–19 at least two are cyclists.

6 Murphy's law states that if you drop a piece of toast it is more likely than not to land butter side down. In fact it is considered that 90% of the time the toast will land butter side down. What is the probability that, if I drop 10 pieces of toast, fewer than seven will land butter side down?

7 In a local election 35% of people support the Future Party. A random sample of 14 voters is taken. What is the probability that it contains:

a no supporters of the Future Party

b at least two supporters of the Future Party?

8.4 Mean and Variance of a Binomial Distribution

The mean and variance are defining characteristics of a probability distribution in the same way as they are for a data set. We shall now evaluate the mean and variance of the probability distribution of scoring sixes when a dice is thrown three times (see Section 8.2).

Example 1

Calculate the mean and variance of the following distribution:

x	0	1	2	3
$P(X=x)$	$\frac{125}{216}$	$\frac{25}{72}$	$\frac{5}{72}$	$\frac{1}{216}$

Solution

This distribution is $B\left(3,\frac{1}{6}\right)$ and we can work out both its mean and variance from the original definitions of $E(X)$ and $\mathrm{Var}(X)$.

$$E(X) = \left(1 \times \tfrac{25}{72}\right) + \left(2 \times \tfrac{5}{72}\right) + \left(3 \times \tfrac{1}{216}\right)$$

$$= \tfrac{1}{2}$$

$$E(X^2) = \left(1 \times \tfrac{25}{72}\right) + \left(4 \times \tfrac{5}{72}\right) + \left(9 \times \tfrac{1}{216}\right)$$

$$= \tfrac{2}{3}$$

$$\mathrm{Var}(X) = \tfrac{2}{3} - \left(\tfrac{1}{2}\right)^2$$

$$= \tfrac{5}{12}$$

$$E(X) = \Sigma x P(X=x)$$

$$\mathrm{Var}(X) = E(X^2) - E(X)^2$$

The above method is one way of calculating the mean and variance of a binomial distribution. However by looking at the nature of a binomial we can work out general formulas for calculating both the mean and variance of any binomial distribution.

Consider a general random variable $X \sim B(n,p)$ and the random variables:

- Y_1, the result of the first trial. $Y_1 = 1$ if the first trial is a success and $Y_1 = 0$ if the first trial is a failure.

- Y_2, the result of the second trial. $Y_2 = 1$ if the second trial is a success and $Y_2 = 0$ if the second trial is a failure

  and so on . . .

The distribution of Y_1 is:

Y_1	0	1
Probability	q	p

185

$$E(Y_1) = (0 \times q) + (1 \times p) = p$$

$$E(Y_1^2) = (0 \times q) + (1 \times p) = p$$

So

$$\text{Var}(Y_1) = p - p^2 = p(1-p)$$

Since $Y_2, Y_3, \ldots, Y_n$ are of the same nature as Y_1 they will have the same distribution and therefore the same expectation and variance.

The random variable X is the total number of successes in n trials and therefore

$$X = Y_1 + Y_2 + \cdots + Y_n$$

In Chapter 7 we looked at linear combinations of discrete random variables and discovered the property that $E(X + Y) = E(X) + E(Y)$. In the same way,

$$E(X) = E(Y_1 + Y_2 + \cdots + Y_n)$$

$$= E(Y_1) + E(Y_2) + \cdots + E(Y_n)$$

$$= p + p + \cdots + p$$

$$= np$$

Since for every success will result in a 1 and X denotes the total number of successes.

We also discovered that for variance, as long as X and Y are independent, $\text{Var}(X + Y) = \text{Var}(X) + \text{Var}(Y)$. Therefore,

$$\text{Var}(X) = \text{Var}(Y_1 + Y_2 + \cdots + Y_n)$$

$$= \text{Var}(Y_1) + \text{Var}(Y_2) + \cdots + \text{Var}(Y_n)$$

$$= p(1-p) + p(1-p) + \cdots + p(1-p)$$

$$= np(1-p)$$

Since each trial is independent and therefore each Y is independent.

So generally,

If $X \sim B(n, p)$ then $E(X) = np$ and $\text{Var}(X) = np(1-p)$

Returning to Example 1, we can test our formulas.

$$X \sim B\left(3, \tfrac{1}{6}\right)$$

So

$$E(X) = np = 3 \times \tfrac{1}{6} = \tfrac{1}{2}$$

and

$$\text{Var}(X) = np(1-p) = \left(3 \times \tfrac{1}{6}\right) \times \tfrac{5}{6} = \tfrac{5}{12} \text{ as calculated earlier.}$$

Example 2

If $X \sim B\left(8, \frac{1}{3}\right)$, calculate the mean and variance of the distribution.

Solution

$$E(X) = np = 8 \times \tfrac{1}{3} = \tfrac{8}{3}$$

$$\mathrm{Var}(X) = np(1-p) = \left(8 \times \tfrac{1}{3}\right) \times \tfrac{2}{3} = \tfrac{16}{9}$$

Remember, if asked to calculate the standard deviation, that $\mathrm{Var}(X) = \text{s.d.}^2$

Example 3

At the local swimming club, the expected number of people that can swim a mile is 4.5 and the variance is 3.15. Find the probability that at least three people can swim a mile.

Solution

$$E(X) = np = 4.5$$

$$\mathrm{Var}(X) = np(1-p) = 3.15$$

Replace $np = 4.5$ in the variance to get

$$\mathrm{Var}(X) = 4.5(1-p) = 3.15$$

So,

$$1 - p = 0.7$$

Hence

$$p = 0.3$$

Substitute this value of p in $E(X) = np$ to give:

$$E(X) = 0.3n = 4.5$$

So

$$0.3n = 4.5$$

$$n = 15$$

Remember that expected value is the same as the mean.

Dividing 3.15 by 4.5.

Dividing 4.5 by 0.3.

So the distribution is $B(15, 0.3)$
We must now calculate the probability that at least three people can swim a mile, that is $P(X \geq 3)$.

$$P(X \geq 3) = 1 - P(X \leq 2)$$

$$= 1 - [0.7^{15} + {}^{15}C_1 0.3 \times 0.7^{14} + {}^{15}C_2 0.3^2 \times 0.7^{13}]$$

$$= 1 - 0.1268$$

$$= 0.8732$$

Example 4

Market research has shown that one household in every five uses washing powder rather than washing liquid in the washing machine. A random sample of 20 households was asked what they used.

a What is the expectation of the number of households that use washing powder?

b What is the probability that exactly three households use washing powder?

c How large a sample would be needed for the probability of it containing at least one household that uses washing powder to be greater that 99.9%?

Solution

For this question $n = 20$, $p = \frac{1}{5}$ and $q = \frac{4}{5}$.

Let the random variable X denote the number of households that use washing powder.

a $E(X) = np$

$$= 20 \times \tfrac{1}{5}$$

$$= 4 \text{ households}$$

b $P(X = 3) = {}^{20}C_3 \left(\tfrac{1}{5}\right)^3 \left(\tfrac{4}{5}\right)^{17}$

$$= 0.2054$$

c   Let the sample size be n households. The probability that at least one household uses the washing powder is:

$$P(X \geq 1) = 1 - P(X = 0)$$

$$= 1 - \left(\tfrac{4}{5}\right)^n$$

Now, we want

$$1 - \left(\tfrac{4}{5}\right)^n > 0.999$$

$$\left(\tfrac{4}{5}\right)^n < 0.001$$

Solve

$$\left(\tfrac{4}{5}\right)^n = 0.001$$

$$n \log \left(\tfrac{4}{5}\right) = \log 0.001$$

$$n = \frac{\log 0.001}{\log \tfrac{4}{5}}$$

$$n = 30.96$$

We will need a sample of 31 in order that there is a 99.9% chance of the sample containing at least one household that uses washing powder.

We could use appropria
tables here with $n = 20$
and $p = 0.2$:
$P(X = 3)$
$= P(X \leq 3) - P(X \leq 2)$

Remember to swap the
inequality sign round
when dividing by -1.

Take log of both sides
$\log a^n = n \log a$

8.4 Mean and Variance of a Binomial Distribution

Exercise

Contextual

1 Find the mean and variance of the binomial distribution, $B\left(6, \frac{1}{4}\right)$.

2 Find the mean and variance of the binomial distribution, $B(12, 0.6)$.

3 A coin is tossed 40 times. Find the mean and standard deviation of the number of heads.

4 Of the pupils in a particular school, 35% come to school by bus. In a random sample of 20 pupils, find the expected number of pupils that come to school by bus and the standard deviation.

5 X is a random variable such that $X \sim B(n, p)$. Given that the mean of the distribution is 8 and $p = 0.4$, find:

   a n **b** the standard deviation of X.

6 For a random variable X with a binomial distribution $B(n, p)$, $E(X) = 0.8$ and $\text{Var}(X) = 0.72$. Find the values of n and p and hence calculate $P(X = 5)$.

7 In a local youth group the expected number of people who can play a musical instrument is 4 and the variance is 3.2. Find the probability that:

   a four people can play a musical instrument
   b fewer than six people can play a musical instrument.

8 The successful sale of hats in a local shop can be modelled binomially and the probability of selling a hat (if the customer enters the shop) is 0.3. Find the probability that the shopkeeper will have at least two sales in the next ten customers that visit his shop. Calculate the least number of customers needed in order that the probability of the shopkeeper getting at least one sale is greater than 99%.

8.5 Fitting a Binomial Distribution to Data

If you are given a sample of values from a population that is thought to have a binomial distribution, $B(n, p)$ where p is unknown, you can test to see whether this is so by calculating what the expected frequencies would be under the supposed binomial distribution.

To do this you need to follow these steps:

Step ① Calculate the *sample mean* and use this as an estimate for the population mean (np).

Step ② Having calculated $E(X) = np$, rearrange to calculate the unknown p.

Step ③ Calculate the *theoretical probabilities* under this binomial distribution with p now known.

Step ④ Use the theoretical probabilities to work out *expected frequencies*, by multiplying each probability by the total number in the sample.

Step ⑤ *Compare* expected frequencies with actual frequencies to see how well the binomial distribution fits.

Example

Bottles of vinegar are packed in cases of six for the supermarket. After a journey, 100 boxes were inspected and the number of broken bottles was counted. The following results were obtained:

Number of broken bottles in a case	0	1	2	3	4	5	6
Number of cases	60	31	8	0	0	1	0

The above distribution is thought to be binomial. Find a binomial distribution and comment on how well you think it fits the data.

Solution

$$\text{Sample mean} = \frac{(1 \times 31) + (2 \times 8) + (5 \times 1)}{100}$$

◀ ① Calculate sample mean.

Use the figures in the table.

$$= 0.52$$

Mean number of broken bottles per case.

So,

$$6p = 0.52$$ ◀ ② Calculate p.

There are six trials (six bottles per case).

$$p = 0.0867$$

Under the binomial distribution $B(6, 0.0867)$ calculate the theoretical probabilities, for example

$$P(X = 1) = {}^6C_1(0.0867)(0.9133)^5 \quad \blacktriangleleft \text{ ③ Calculate the theoretical}$$
$$\text{probabilites.}$$
$$= 6 \times 0.0867 \times 0.6354$$

$$= 0.3306 \text{ (4 d.p.)}$$

Number of broken bottles in a case, x	0	1	2	3	4	5	6
Probability, $P(X = x)$	0.5803	0.3306	0.0784	0.0099	0.0007	0	0

From theoretical probabilities work out expected frequencies, for example the expected number of cases having one broken bottle is

$$0.3306 \times 100 = 33.1 \quad \blacktriangleleft \text{ ④ Calculate expected frequencies.}$$

There are 100 cases.

Number of broken bottles in a case	0	1	2	3	4	5	6
Expected frequency	58.0	33.1	7.8	1.0	0	0	0

Comparing expected frequencies with actual frequencies we can see that they are quite close and therefore the binomial distribution fits the data well. $\blacktriangleleft$ ⑤ Compare expected frequencies with actual frequencies.

One table could be used to incorporate both the theoretical probabilities and the expected frequencies.

8.5 Fitting a Binomial Distribution to Data

Exercise

Contextual

1 A biased dice is thrown twice and the number of sixes is recorded. The experiment is repeated 100 times and the results noted as shown.

Number of 6s	0	1	2
Frequency	46	30	24

    a   Calculate the sample mean number of sixes thrown.

    b   Using the sample mean, calculate p, the probability of getting a six.

    c   Calculate the theoretical probabilities of obtaining 0, 1 or 2 sixes under the binomial distribution with p known.

    d   Calculate the expected frequencies under the same binomial distribution.

    e   Does the binomial distribution fit the data well?

2 A local bus runs four times a day. A record is kept of the number of times the bus arrives late at its final destination each day. Over a period of 60 days the following results were noted.

Number of times the bus is late	0	1	2	3	4
Number of days	16	22	16	6	0

    a   Calculate the mean value of X.

    b   If $X \sim B(4, p)$, estimate p.

    c   Calculate both the theoretical probabilities and the expected frequencies under the binomial distribution described in **b**.

    d   Comment on how well the model fits.

3 Fit a theoretical binomial distribution to the following frequency distribution, given that $n = 3$.

x	0	1	2	3
f	37	80	50	13

8.6 Geometric Distribution

When playing a board game in which you need to throw a six to start, it often seems to take you longer to throw a six than it takes your opponents. Are you simply unlucky if it takes you five throws to obtain that six?

Defining X as the random variable 'number of throws *up to* and *including* the first six', the probability of throwing a six on your first throw will be

$$P(X = 1) = \frac{1}{6} = 0.1667 \ (4 \text{ d.p.})$$

The probability of throwing the first six on your second throw will be

$$P(X = 2) = P \text{ (not 6 on 1st throw, 6 on 2nd throw)} = \frac{5}{6} \times \frac{1}{6} = 0.1389$$

Similarly

$$P(X = 3) = P \text{ (not 6 on 1st, not 6 on 2nd, 6 on 3rd throw)}$$

$$= \frac{5}{6} \times \frac{5}{6} \times \frac{1}{6} = \left(\frac{5}{6}\right)^2 \times \frac{1}{6} = 0.1157$$

$$P(X = 4) = \frac{5}{6} \times \frac{5}{6} \times \frac{5}{6} \times \frac{1}{6} = \left(\frac{5}{6}\right)^3 \times \frac{1}{6} = 0.0965$$

$$P(X = 5) = \frac{5}{6} \times \frac{5}{6} \times \frac{5}{6} \times \frac{5}{6} \times \frac{1}{6} = \left(\frac{5}{6}\right)^4 \times \frac{1}{6} = 0.0804$$

From these results we can see that

$$P(X = r) = \left(\frac{5}{6}\right)^{r-1} \times \frac{1}{6}$$

Putting these results into a table gives:

x	1	2	3	4	5	r
$P(X = x)$	$\frac{1}{6}$	$\left(\frac{5}{6}\right)\left(\frac{1}{6}\right)$	$\left(\frac{5}{6}\right)^2\left(\frac{1}{6}\right)$	$\left(\frac{5}{6}\right)^3\left(\frac{1}{6}\right)$	$\left(\frac{5}{6}\right)^4\left(\frac{1}{6}\right)$	$\left(\frac{5}{6}\right)^{r-1}\left(\frac{1}{6}\right)$

X is said to have a **geometric distribution**, where $X \sim G\left(\frac{1}{6}\right)$

Geometric distributions are used to model situations where there are just two possible outcomes, success and failure, and where trials are carried out until success is obtained, after which no further trials take place.

This distribution has some similarities with the binomial distribution. Both distributions have just two outcomes, the probability for success must be the same for each trial, and the trials must be independent. The difference is that the number of trials must be fixed for a binomial distribution whereas in the geometric distribution there can be any number of trials.

The geometric distribution is defined as $X \sim G(p)$ where p is the probability of success.

The probability that the number of successes, X, is r is given by

$$P(X = r) = q^{r-1}p$$

where $q = 1 - p$

If there are no successes in the first r trials then $P(X > r) = q^r$

$P(X \leq r)$ means the probability that success occurs in the first r trials, which is the same as 1−(the probability that there are no successes in the first r trials).

This can be written as

$$P(X \leq r) = 1 - P(X > r)$$
$$= 1 - q^r$$

Example 1

Jo decides to enter a weekly lottery where the organisers claim there is a 1 in 40 chance of her winning a prize. X is the random variable representing the number of times Jo enters the lottery up to and including her first win.

a Explain which type of distribution would be appropriate to model X.
b Calculate
    i $P(X = 10)$ **ii** $P(X \leq 50)$ **iii** $P(X > 15)$
c Calculate the minimum number of times that Jo would need to take part in the lottery to be 90% certain of winning a prize.

Solution

a The geometric distribution would be most appropriate, as X is a discrete random variable with only two outcomes, success and failure, and the trials end when the first success is achieved.

b **i** $p = \dfrac{1}{40} = 0.025$ $q = 1 - 0.025 = 0.975$

        $p(X = 10) = q^9 p = 0.975^9 \times 0.025 = 0.0199$ (4 d.p.)

  ii $P(X \leq 50) = 1 - 0.975^{50}$
                   $= 0.7180$

  iii $P(X > 15) = 0.975^{15}$
                   $= 0.6840$

c

but

therefore

$$P(X \le n) = 0.9$$

$$P(X \le n) = 1 - 0.975^n$$

$$1 - 0.975^n = 0.9$$

$$1 - 0.9 = 0.975^n$$

$$0.1 = 0.975^n$$

$$\ln 0.1 = n \ln 0.975$$

$$\frac{\ln 0.1}{\ln 0.975} = n$$

$$n = 90.947$$

thus the minimum number of entries is 91.

If a geometric distribution is given as

x	1	2	3	4	5	r
$P(X = x)$	p	qp	q^2p	q^3p	q^4p	$q^{r-1}p$

then the mean can be found as follows

$$E(X) = 1p + 2qp + 3q^2p + 4q^3p + \ldots$$

$$= p(1 + 2q + 3q^2 + 4q^3 + \ldots)$$

$$= p(1 - q)^{-2}$$

$$= p \times p^{-2}$$

$$= \frac{1}{p}$$

Using
$$1 + 2q + 3q^2 + 4q^3 + \ldots = (1 - q)^{-2}$$

We can also calculate the variance of this distribution

$$E(X^2) = p(1 + 2^2q + 3^2q^2 + 4^2q^3 + \ldots + r^2q^{r-1} + \ldots)$$

$$= p(1 + q)(1 - q)^{-3}$$

$$= p(1 + q)(p^{-3})$$

$$= \frac{1 + q}{p^2}$$

$$Var(X) = \frac{1 + q}{p^2} - \frac{1}{p^2} = \frac{q}{p^2}$$

It can be shown that
$$1 + 2^2q + 3^2q^2 + 4^2q^3 + \ldots = (1 + q)(1 - q)^{-3}$$

$$E(X) = \frac{1}{p} \qquad Var(X) = \frac{q}{p^2}$$

Example 2

A coin is biased so that the probability of throwing a tail is 0.72.

Find the expected number of throws that would be required to throw a head.

Solution

The probability of throwing a head is $1 - 0.72 = 0.28$, so $p = 0.28$.

$$E(X) = \frac{1}{p} = \frac{1}{0.28} = 3.57$$

thus number of throws required to throw a head is 4.

8.6 Geometric Distribution
Exercise

Contextual

1 Laura is playing indoor hockey and the probability that she scores when she shoots at goal is distributed geometrically, with $p = 0.3$. What is the probability that she scores first with her fourth shot? What is the probability that she takes more than ten shots before she scores?

2 The chance of Matthew hitting a double to finish a game of darts is distributed as $G(0.2)$. How many attempts should Matthew expect to take to hit a double? What is the probability he will take no more than three attempts?

3 Two golfers are practising their putting. One golfer usually takes five attempts to successfully putt from a range of 5 m, while the second golfer usually puts the ball on the fourth attempt. Find the probability that they will both putt the ball on their sixth attempt.

4 A school is holding a competition where the chance of success is claimed to be 1 in 50. The cost of entry is 50p and the prize money is £5. You are only allowed to win one prize.

   a What is the probability of a student winning and making a profit?
   b What is the least number of attempts a student must make in order to be 50% certain of winning?

5 If $X \sim G(0.3)$ find the mean and variance of the distribution.

6 A game at a school fete consists of choosing a matchbox from a display of 150 sealed matchboxes, of which ten contain a £1 coin. You cannot continue to play after choosing a winning box.

   a What is the probability of choosing a winning box on your first attempt?
   b How many attempts would you expect to take to choose a winning box?
   c How may attempts would you need to make to be 75% certain of winning?
   d If it cost 20p for each attempt in part **c**, how much would you have won or lost?

8.7 The Poisson Distribution as an Approximation for the Binomial Distribution

Poisson distributions are used in two main ways:

● as a distribution in their own right used to model specific situations

● as an approximation for binomial distributions when n is so large and p so small that working out the binomial value exactly would take a great deal of time, whereas using an approximation to the value is much quicker and only loses a relatively small degree of accuracy.

In order to examine this approximation of the binomial distribution consider a situation that could be modelled by a $B\left(80\,000, \frac{1}{50\,000}\right)$. An example where this might occur is in the modelling of a particular rare disease amongst a population of size 80 000. This model could only be used if it was assumed that trials were independent, that is that the disease was not infectious.

If you are asked to calculate the probability of four or more people catching this rare disease, calculate each of the probabilities of 0, 1, 2 and 3 cases and then subtract this sum of probabilities from 1.

So, for $X \sim B\left(80\,000, \frac{1}{50\,000}\right)$

$$n = 80\,000$$

$$p = \frac{1}{50\,000}$$

$$q = \frac{49\,999}{50\,000}$$

$$E(X) = np = 1.6$$

$$P(X = 0) = {}^{80\,000}C_0 \left(\frac{49\,999}{50\,000}\right)^{80\,000} = 0.2019$$

$$P(X = 1) = {}^{80\,000}C_1 \left(\frac{49\,999}{50\,000}\right)^{79\,999} \left(\frac{1}{50\,000}\right) = 0.3230$$

$$P(X = 2) = {}^{80\,000}C_2 \left(\frac{49\,999}{50\,000}\right)^{79\,998} \left(\frac{1}{50\,000}\right)^2 = 0.2584$$

$$P(X = 3) = {}^{80\,000}C_3 \left(\frac{49\,999}{50\,000}\right)^{79\,997} \left(\frac{1}{50\,000}\right)^3 = 0.1378$$

which means that

$$P(X \geq 4) = 1 - [0.2019 + 0.3230 + 0.2584 + 0.1378]$$

$$= 0.0789 \text{ (4 d.p.)}$$

Remember that
$$P(X \geq r) = 1 - P(X \leq r - 1)$$

How could these binomial terms be approximated? Let us start by looking at the last term.

$$P(X = 3) = {}^{80\,000}C_3 \left(\frac{49\,999}{50\,000}\right)^{79\,997} \left(\frac{1}{50\,000}\right)^3$$

If we write this expression out in full we get

$$P(X = 3) = \frac{80\,000!}{79\,997! \times 3!} \times \left(\frac{49\,999}{50\,000}\right)^{79\,997} \left(\frac{1}{50\,000}\right)^3$$

$$= \frac{80\,000 \times 79\,999 \times 79\,998 \times (49\,999)^{79\,997}}{3 \times 2 \times 1 \times (50\,000)^3 \times (50\,000)^{79\,997}}$$

From the definition of ${}^nC$

$${}^nC_r = \frac{n!}{r!(n-r)!}$$

Since n is so large one way to approximate is to simplify the previous expressions without losing too much accuracy. Writing 79 999 as 80 000 and 79 998 as 80 000 and 49 999 as 50 000 but leaving powers as they are gives:

$$P(X = 3) = \frac{80\,000 \times 80\,000 \times 80\,000 \times (50\,000)^{79\,997}}{3 \times 2 \times 1 \times (50\,000)^3 \times (50\,000)^{79\,997}}$$

$$= \frac{1}{3!} \times \left(\frac{80\,000}{50\,000}\right)^3$$

$$= \frac{1.6^3}{3!}$$

This approximation is possible because n is lar and p is small.

Doing the same with the other terms gives:

$$P(X = 0) = 1$$

$$P(X = 1) = \left(\frac{80\,000}{50\,000}\right) = 1.6$$

$$P(X = 2) = \frac{1}{2!} \times \left(\frac{80\,000}{50\,000}\right)^2 = \frac{(1.6)^2}{2!}$$

For this to be a probability distribution, probabilities must sum to 1. One way to ensure this is to divide each term by the total of all probabilities. The sum of the terms we have just created in the above example

$$1 + 1.6 + \frac{1.6^2}{2!} + \frac{1.6^3}{3!}$$

is of the same structure as the series known as the **exponential series,** where each consecutive term is raised to a further power and divided by that power factorial.

$$e^x = 1 + \frac{x}{1!} + \frac{x^2}{2!} + \frac{x^3}{3!} + \cdots + \frac{x^r}{r!} + \cdots$$

This is done in very muc the same way as if you want a group of number to add to 1. Find the sum of the numbers and then divide each value by tha total. For example, $3 + 4 + 5 = 12$, and $\frac{3}{12} + \frac{4}{12} + \frac{5}{12} = 1$.

Putting $x = 1.6$, the series $e^{1.6}$ is the sum of the probabilities. Since $e^{1.6}$ is the sum of all the terms, we divide each term by $e^{1.6}$, and then the resulting values will sum to 1 and thus be suitable to be a probability distribution that can be used to model the rare disease in the population.

Notice that 1.6 is the *mean* of the binomial distribution as calculated earlier.

So, the resulting distribution is of the form:

$$P(X = 0) = \frac{1}{e^{1.6}}$$

$$P(X = 1) = \frac{1.6}{e^{1.6}}$$

$$P(X = 2) = \frac{1.6^2}{2!e^{1.6}}, \text{ and so on.}$$

However, dividing by $e^{1.6}$ is exactly the same as multiplying by $e^{-1.6}$, since $e^{-1.6} = \frac{1}{e^{1.6}}$. Therefore we usually write out the probabilities as shown in the following table:

Number of casualties	0	1	2	3
Probability	$e^{-1.6}$	$e^{-1.6} \times 1.6$	$e^{-1.6} \times \frac{(1.6)^2}{2!}$	$e^{-1.6} \times \frac{(1.6)^3}{3!}$

In general, the probability of the discrete random variable X denoting the number of occurrences of the disease is calculated by:

$$\boldsymbol{P(X = r) = e^{-1.6} \times \frac{(1.6)^r}{r!}}$$

This resulting distribution is known as the **Poisson distribution**.

Comparing the results,

$P(X \geq 4) = 0.078\,811\,59$ using the binomial distribution

$P(X \geq 4) = 0.078\,813\,487$ using the Poisson approximation

So, by looking at the two results, for large n and small p the approximation is a good one. Generalising further, the Poisson distribution is a good approximation to the binomial distribution.

If $X \sim B(n, p)$ and

- n is large
- p is small

then X can be approximated by $Po(\lambda)$ where $\lambda = np$, the **mean** of the binomial distribution, and the formula for evaluating the probabilities is

Po means Poisson distribution.

$$P(X = r) = e^{-\lambda} \times \frac{\lambda^r}{r!}$$

Example

On a particular production line, the probability that an item is defective is 0.01. Using a suitable approximation, find the probability that, in a batch of 200 items:

a   there are no defective items
b   there are exactly five defective items.

Compare your answers with the exact values using the binomial distribution.

Solution

Let X = number of defective items, then $X \sim B(200, 0.01)$. Since n is large and p is small, X is approximately $\sim Po(0.01 \times 200)$, that is $X \sim Po(2)$.

a $P(X = 0) \approx e^{-2}$

Remember that $0! = 1$.

$\qquad = 0.135$ (3 d.p.)

b $P(X = 5) \approx e^{-2}(2)^5/5!$

$\qquad = 0.036$ (3 d.p.)

Using the binomial distribution

a $P(X = 0) = (0.99)^{200} = 0.134$ (3 d.p.)

b $P(X = 5) = {}^{200}C_5(0.01)^5(0.99)^{195} = 0.036$ (3 d.p.)

8.7 The Poisson Distribution as an Approximation for the Binomial Distribution

Exercise

Contextual

1 Find the probability that $X = 2$ for each of the following binomial distributions:

a $B(50, 0.1)$ **b** $B(150, 0.01)$ **c** $B(2000, 0.0025)$

Now, using suitable Poisson approximations, find the probability that $X = 2$.

2 If $X \sim B(200, 0.007)$ use

a the binomial distribution
b a suitable Poisson approximation

to evaluate:

i $P(X = 0)$ **ii** $P(X = 2)$ **iii** $P(X < 3)$

3 In a manufacturing plant, the proportion of defective articles is 1.5%. Using a suitable approximation find the probability that in a batch of 500 articles there are:

a no defective articles   **b** exactly eight defective articles
c fewer then three defective articles.

4 Nectarines are shipped out in boxes of 180 to supermarkets and on average 2% of the fruit arrives bruised or rotten and therefore unsaleable. Find the probability that in a single shipment there are exactly 10 pieces of fruit that are unsaleable using:

a the binomial distribution $B(180, 0.02)$
b a suitable Poisson approximation to the binomial distribution.

5 The probability that a particular make of battery is faulty is 0.003. Batteries are packed in boxes of 250. Find the probability that in a certain box there are:

a no faulty batteries   **b** at least three faulty batteries.

6 A particular rare blood condition is found in 0.5% of the population. A local hospital tests 400 people at random. What is the probability that they will find seven people with this particular condition?

8.8 The Poisson Distribution

As was stated earlier, the Poisson distribution can be used as a distribution in its own right. By looking at the distribution as an approximation to the binomial we have discovered that the Poisson distribution has just one **parameter**, λ, and that, like the binomial distribution, different values of the parameter λ lead to different Poisson distributions.

Poisson distributions are used to model situations where the random variable X is the number of occurrences of a particular event over a given period of time (or space). Together with this property, the following conditions must also be fulfilled:

- events are *independent* of each other

- events occur *singly*

- events occur at a *constant rate* (in other words for a given time interval the mean number of occurrences is proportional to the length of the interval).

A parameter is a characteristic constant a distribution that in its completely defines the distribution. In the case the Poisson distribution the parameter is the mean.

Examples where a Poisson model could be used

- telephone calls made to a switchboard in a given minute

- road accidents on a particular motorway in one day

- flaws in a metre of fabric

A specific time or distance interval is required.

Generally, the probability that the number of occurrences, X, over a given period of time is equal to r is:

$$P(X = r) = e^{-\lambda} \times \frac{\lambda^r}{r!}$$

where λ is the *average* or *mean* number of events that occur in that set interval. We say that X has a Poisson distribution with parameter λ, and it is written

$$X \sim \text{Po}(\lambda)$$

Example 1

The number of telephone calls made to a switchboard during an afternoon can be modelled by a Poisson distribution with a mean of eight calls per five-minute period. Find the probability that in the next five minutes:

a no calls are made
b five calls are made
c at least three calls are made
d fewer than four calls are made.

Solution

X = the number of calls made in a five-minute period

$\lambda = 8$

So, $X \sim \text{Po}(8)$

a $P(X = 0) = e^{-8} = 0.0003$

b $P(X = 5) = e^{-8} \times \dfrac{(8)^5}{5!} = 0.0916$

c $P(X \geq 3) = 1 - [P(X = 0) + P(X = 1) + P(X = 2)]$

$= 1 - [e^{-8}(1 + 8 + 32)]$

$= 0.9862$

d $P(X < 4) = P(X = 0) + P(X = 1) + P(X = 2) + P(X = 3)$

$= e^{-8}(1 + 8 + 32 + 85.3)$

$= 0.0424$

Remember
$x^0 = 1$
$0! = 1$

$P(X = 0) = e^{-8}$
$P(X = 1) = e^{-8} \times 8$
$P(X = 2) = e^{-8} \times \dfrac{8^2}{2!}$

$P(X = 3) = e^{-8} \times \dfrac{8^3}{3!}$

Cumulative Poisson probability tables

It should be noted that as for binomial distributions, there are cumulative Poisson probability tables for certain Poisson distributions.

So using the tables for Example 1 with $\lambda = 8$ to find:

Poisson Cumulative Distribution Function
The tabulated value is $P(X \leq r)$, where $X \sim \text{Po}(\lambda)$.

$\lambda =$	7.5	8.0	8.5
$r = 0$	0.0006	0.0003	0.0002
1	0.0047	0.0030	0.0019
2	0.0203	0.0138	0.0093
3	0.0591	0.0424	0.0301
4	0.1321	0.0996	0.0744
5	0.2414	0.1912	0.1496
6	0.3782	0.3134	0.2562
7	0.5246	0.4530	0.3856
8	0.6620	0.5925	0.5231
9	0.7764	0.7166	0.6530
10	0.8622	0.8159	0.7634
11	0.9208	0.8881	0.8487
12	0.9573	0.9362	0.9091
13	0.9784	0.9658	0.9486
14	0.9897	0.9827	0.9726
15	0.9954	0.9918	0.9862
16	0.9980	0.9963	0.9934
17	0.9992	0.9984	0.9970
18	0.9997	0.9993	0.9987
19	0.9999	0.9997	0.9995
20	1.0000	0.9999	0.9998
21	1.0000	1.0000	0.9999
22	1.0000	1.0000	1.0000

c $P(X \geq 3)$

Read off $P(X \leq 2) = 0.0138$ and then subtract from 1 to give 0.9862.

d $P(X < 4)$

Read off $P(X \leq 3) = 0.0424$

We could also have used the tables in **b**:

$$P(X = 5) = P(X \leq 5) - P(X \leq 4)$$

$$= 0.1912 - 0.0996$$

$$= 0.0916, \text{ as calculated earlier.}$$

Example 2

In a local sports shop the number of customers buying a pair of SUPER-T trainers on any particular day can be modelled by a Poisson distribution with mean 1.5. Find the probabilities that:

a   on a particular day no customer buys a pair of SUPER-T trainers
b   on a particular day exactly four customers buy a pair of SUPER-T trainers
c   in five days more than six customers buy a pair of SUPER-T trainers.

Solution

$X =$ the number of customers who buy a pair of SUPER-T trainers

$\lambda = 1.5$

So $X \sim \text{Po}(1.5)$

a $P(X = 0) = e^{-1.5} = 0.2231$

b $P(X = 4) = P(X \leq 4) - P(X \leq 3)$

Or simply reading off from the tables $\lambda = 1.5$

$$= 0.9814 - 0.9344$$

$$= 0.047$$

c   We are looking at a five-day period, in other words the time interval has changed and therefore must be modelled by a different Poisson distribution.
For a five day period, $\lambda = (5 \times 1.5) = 7.5$

$$X \sim \text{Po}(7.5)$$

$$P(X > 6) = 1 - P(X \leq 6)$$

$$= 1 - 0.3782$$

$$= 0.6218$$

Using the tables with $\lambda = 7.5$

Example 3

On average in a particular day, of 50 breakdowns attended on a stretch of road, 3% of cars require a new battery.

a   State the distribution of X, the number of breakdowns requiring a new battery.
b   Using a suitable approximation find the probability that the number of batteries required on a particular day is more than two.
c   Determine the minimum number of batteries required at the beginning of the day in order that there is at least a 95% chance of being able to meet the need for that day.

Solution

a   If X = the number of breakdowns requiring a new battery then, $X \sim B(50, 0.03)$.
b   A Poisson approximation is suitable since n is large and p is small. So,

$$X \sim \text{Po}(np), \text{ that is } X \sim \text{Po}(1.5)$$

$$P(X > 2) = 1 - P(X \leq 2)$$

$$= 1 - 0.8088$$

$$= 0.1912$$

Using the tables with $\lambda = 1.5$

c $P(X \leq 3) = 0.9344$

$P(X \leq 4) = 0.9814$

The question has asked us to determine the minimum number of batteries required in order that the probability that the demand is met is at least 0.95, therefore four batteries are needed.

8.8 The Poisson Distribution
Exercise

Technique

1 If $X \sim \text{Po}(3.0)$, find:

    a $P(X = 0)$ **b** $P(X > 2)$

    c $P(X \leq 8)$ **d** $P(2 \leq X \leq 6)$

2 The random variable $Y \sim \text{Po}(1.0)$. Find:

    a $P(Y = 7)$ **b** $P(Y = 4)$

    c $P(Y \leq 5)$ **d** $P(Y \geq 3)$

3 If $X \sim \text{Po}(5.5)$, find:

    a $P(X \leq 7)$ **b** $P(X \leq 0)$

    c $P(X \leq 11)$ **d** $P(X \leq 3)$

4 The random variable X has a Poisson distribution with mean 4.5. Find $P(X > 6)$.

5 Find the values of a, b, c and d given that $X \sim \text{Po}(2.5)$:

    a $P(X \leq a) = 0.8912$ **b** $P(X < b) = 0.5438$

    c $P(X \leq c) = 0.9997$ **d** $P(X > d) = 0.0420$

Contextual

1 The number of letters arriving at a particular address each day can be modelled by a Poisson distribution with a mean of seven letters per day. Find the probability that tomorrow:

    a   no letters will arrive

    b   four letters will arrive

    c   at least two letters will arrive

    d   fewer than five letters will arrive.

2 An insurance company receives on average four claims a week in a certain town. Assuming that the number of claims follow a Poisson distribution, find the probability that the insurance company receives:

    a   no claims in a given week

    b   more than three claims in a given fortnight.

3 The number of swimming accidents per week on a particular stretch of coastline is a Poisson variable with parameter 3.

    a Find the probability that in any one week chosen at random exactly two swimming accidents occur.

    b Find the probability that in any four-week period there are fewer than four swimming accidents.

4 A shop sells a particular make of computer at a rate of five per week on average. The number sold in a week has a Poisson distribution.

    a Find the probability that the shop sells at least three in a week.

    b Find the smallest number of computers that can be in stock at the beginning of the week in order to have at least 95% chance of being able to meet the demands of the week.

5 An average of four flaws per 150 m of material is produced in a particular factory. Assuming that flaws occur randomly, find the probability that:

    a in a particular 150 m length of material there will be more than three flaws

    b in a particular 300 m length of material there will be exactly five flaws.

6 In a particular document there are on average eight typing errors a page. Find the probability that:

    a on a certain page there are fewer than four typing errors

    b on a half page section there are six typing errors.

7 A particular radio show receives requests at a rate of six per hour, the number of requests being modelled by a Poisson distribution.

    a Find the probability that the show receives at least five requests in a given hour.

    b Find the smallest number of request spots needed in order to have at least 99% chance of being able to allow everyone to speak on the show.

8.9 Mean and Variance of a Poisson Distribution

In order to define the mean and variance of a Poisson distribution we need to return to the original probability distribution.

x	0	1	2	3	$\cdots$
$P(X = x)$	$e^{-\lambda}$	$e^{-\lambda} \times \lambda$	$e^{-\lambda} \times \dfrac{\lambda^2}{2!}$	$e^{-\lambda} \times \dfrac{\lambda^3}{3!}$	$\cdots$

Now,

$$E(X) = \Sigma x P(X = x)$$

So, for a Poisson distribution

$$E(X) = 0 \times e^{-\lambda} + (1 \times e^{-\lambda} \times \lambda) + \left(2 \times e^{-\lambda} \times \frac{\lambda^2}{2!}\right) + \left(3 \times e^{-\lambda} \times \frac{\lambda^3}{3!}\right) + \cdots$$

which can be rewritten as

$$E(X) = \lambda e^{-\lambda}\left(1 + \lambda + \frac{\lambda^2}{2!} + \frac{\lambda^3}{3!} + \cdots\right)$$

Taking $\lambda e^{-\lambda}$ out as a common factor.

and by definition

$$e^{\lambda} = \left(1 + \lambda + \frac{\lambda^2}{2!} + \frac{\lambda^3}{3!} + \cdots\right)$$

So

$$E(X) = \lambda e^{-\lambda} \times e^{\lambda}$$

$$= \lambda$$

$e^{-\lambda} \times e^{\lambda} = e^{-\lambda+\lambda} = e^0 =$

$$\boxed{E(X) = \lambda}$$

In order to find the variance of the Poisson distribution we must first find $E(X^2)$ since

$$\text{Var}(X) = E(X^2) - E(X)^2$$

So

$$E(X^2) = \Sigma x^2 P(X = x)$$

$$= e^{-\lambda}\left(0 + \lambda + \frac{4\lambda^2}{2!} + \frac{9\lambda^3}{3!} + \cdots\right)$$

Taking $e^{-\lambda}$ out as a common factor.

$$= \lambda e^{-\lambda}\left(1 + 2\lambda + \frac{3\lambda^2}{2!} + \cdots\right)$$

Taking λ out as a comm factor and cancelling fractions.

$$= \lambda e^{-\lambda}\left[\left(1 + \lambda + \frac{\lambda^2}{2!} + \cdots\right) + \left(\lambda + \frac{2\lambda^2}{2!} + \cdots\right)\right]$$

$$= \lambda e^{-\lambda}\left[e^{\lambda} + \left(\lambda + \frac{2\lambda^2}{2!} + \cdots\right)\right]$$

Splitting up the terms.

$$= \lambda e^{-\lambda}\left[e^{\lambda} + \lambda\left(1 + \lambda + \frac{\lambda^2}{2!} + \cdots\right)\right]$$

From the definition of e^{λ}

$$= \lambda e^{-\lambda}(e^{\lambda} + \lambda e^{\lambda})$$

$e^{\lambda} = \left(1 + \lambda + \dfrac{\lambda^2}{2!} + \dfrac{\lambda^3}{3!} + \cdots\right.$

$$= \lambda e^{-\lambda}e^{\lambda} + \lambda^2 e^{-\lambda}e^{\lambda}$$

$e^{-\lambda} \times e^{\lambda} = e^{-\lambda+\lambda}$

$$= \lambda + \lambda^2$$

$$= e^0 = 1$$

Therefore

$$\mathrm{Var}(X) = \mathrm{E}(X^2) - \mathrm{E}(X)^2$$

$$= (\lambda + \lambda^2) - \lambda^2$$

$$= \lambda$$

$\mathrm{Var}(X) = \lambda$

Example 1

The number of letters received each day over a period of 200 days was recorded as shown in the table below.

Number of letters, x	0	1	2	3	4	5
Frequency, f	110	66	20	4	0	0

Calculate the mean and variance of the number of letters received each day. Explain how the values you have obtained support the view that these data could be modelled by a Poisson distribution.

Solution

$$\mathrm{mean} = \frac{(1 \times 66) + (2 \times 20) + (3 \times 4)}{200}$$

$$= \frac{118}{200}$$

$$= 0.59$$

$$\mathrm{variance} = \frac{182}{200} - (0.59)^2$$

$$= 0.56$$

Remember that

$$\bar{x} = \frac{\Sigma x}{n}$$

Remember that

$$\mathrm{variance} = \frac{\Sigma f x^2}{n} - \bar{x}^2$$

The mean and variance are approximately equal, and this indicates that the data could be modelled by a Poisson distribution.

Fitting a Poisson distribution to data

As with the binomial distribution it is possible to test whether or not a given sample has a Poisson distribution. You must calculate the mean, λ in this case, and use it to calculate the theoretical probabilities and from these the expected frequencies for a Poisson distribution with the same mean as that of the sample.

Use the following steps:

Step ①   Calculate the *mean* of the sample and use this as the parameter λ of the Poisson distribution.

Step ②   Calculate the *theoretical probabilities* under this Poisson distribution with λ now known.

Step ③   Use the theoretical probabilities to work out *expected frequencies* by multiplying each probability by the total number in the sample.

Step ④   *Compare* expected frequencies with actual frequencies to see how well the Poisson distribution fits.

Example 2

The number of phone calls received by a household each day over a period of 300 days was recorded and the results were as follows:

Number of calls	0	1	2	3	4	5	6
Number of days	121	110	50	16	3	0	0

The above distribution is thought to have a Poisson distribution. Fit a Poisson distribution and comment on how suitable it is.

Solution

$$\text{Sample mean} = \frac{(1 \times 110) + (2 \times 50) + (3 \times 16) + (4 \times 3)}{300}$$

◀ ① Calculate sample mean.

$$= \frac{270}{300}$$

$$= 0.9$$

Hence $\lambda = 0.9$

Using Poisson cumulative probability tables we can work out the theoretical probabilities under $X \sim \text{Po}(0.9)$ ◀ ② Calculate theoretical probabilities.

x	0	1	2	3	4	5	6
$P(X = x)$	0.4066	0.3659	0.1647	0.0494	0.0111	0.002	0.0003

Using the theoretical probabilities we can calculate the expected frequencies by multiplying each probability by 300, the size of our sample.   ◀ ③ Calculate expected frequencies.

Number of calls	0	1	2	3	4	5	6
Expected frequency	121.97	109.77	49.40	14.82	3.33	0.6	0.09

Comparing expected frequencies with actual frequencies we can see that they are very close and therefore the Poisson distribution is an excellent fit.   ◀ ④ Compare expected and actual frequencies.

8.9 Mean and Variance of a Poisson Distribution

Exercise

Technique

1 Calculate the mean and variance of the following frequency table. Could these data be modelled by a Poisson distribution? If so suggest a suitable value for λ.

x	0	1	2	3	4
f	68	24	11	5	2

2 The number of phone calls received in an office each hour over a period of 100 hours was recorded and the results were as follows:

x	0	1	2	3	4	5
f	30	34	23	10	3	0

Would a Poisson distribution be a suitable model?

3 Given that both the mean and variance of the following data is approximately 0.2, suggest possible values for a and b if the total frequency is 20.

x	0	1	2	3
f	a	b	1	0

Contextual

1 The following table gives the number of cycling accidents a day on a particular stretch of road over the past 90 weeks.

Number of cycling accidents	0	1	2	3	4	5	6
Number of weeks	45	34	5	5	1	0	0

a Find the mean number of accidents.
b For a Poisson distribution with the mean found in **a**, calculate the theoretical probabilities of 0, 1, 2, 3, 4, 5 and 6 accidents.
c Calculate the expected frequencies.
d Comment on how well this model fits.

2 Fit a theoretical Poisson distribution to the following probability distribution. Draw a table showing the theoretical probabilities and expected frequencies.

x	0	1	2	3	4	5
f	58	33	4	3	0	0

3 The following table is a record of the number of goals scored in 40 matches.

Number of goals	0	1	2	3	4	5	6
Number of matches	18	12	7	2	1	0	0

a Calculate the mean and variance of this distribution.
b Using the mean as the parameter for a Poisson distribution, calculate theoretical probabilities.
c Calculate expected frequencies under this Poisson model.
d State whether or not it is a good model and give a reason for your answer.

8.10 The Sum of Two or More Poisson Distributions

Suppose you had two independent Poisson distributions, for example $X \sim \text{Po}(\lambda)$ and $Y \sim \text{Po}(\psi)$. You know from the work you have done so far that their probability distributions look like the following:

For $X \sim \text{Po}(\lambda)$:

x	0	1	2	$\cdots$
$P(X = x)$	$e^{-\lambda}$	$e^{-\lambda} \times \lambda$	$e^{-\lambda} \times \dfrac{\lambda^2}{2!}$	$\cdots$

For $Y \sim \text{Po}(\psi)$:

y	0	1	2	$\cdots$
$P(Y = y)$	$e^{-\psi}$	$e^{-\psi} \times \psi$	$e^{-\psi} \times \dfrac{\psi^2}{2!}$	$\cdots$

What would the distribution of $X + Y$ look like?

$$P(X + Y = 0) = P(X = 0) \times P(Y = 0)$$

$$= e^{-\lambda} \times e^{-\psi}$$

$$= e^{-(\lambda + \psi)}$$

$$P(X + Y = 1) = P(X = 0) \times P(Y = 1) + P(X = 1) \times P(Y = 0)$$

$$= e^{-\lambda} \times e^{-\psi}\psi + e^{-\lambda}\lambda \times e^{-\psi}$$

$$= e^{-(\lambda + \psi)}\psi + e^{-(\lambda + \psi)}\lambda$$

$$= e^{-(\lambda + \psi)}(\lambda + \psi)$$

$$P(X + Y = 2) = P(X = 0) \times P(Y = 2) + P(X = 1) \times P(Y = 1)$$

$$+ P(X = 2) \times P(Y = 0)$$

$$= e^{-\lambda} \times \frac{\psi^2}{2!}e^{-\psi} + e^{-\lambda}\lambda \times e^{-\psi}\psi + e^{-\lambda}\frac{\lambda^2}{2!}e^{-\psi}$$

$$= e^{-(\lambda + \psi)}\frac{\psi^2}{2!} + e^{-(\lambda + \psi)}\lambda\psi + e^{-(\lambda + \psi)}\frac{\lambda^2}{2!}$$

$$= \frac{e^{-(\lambda + \psi)}}{2!}(\psi^2 + 2\psi\lambda + \lambda^2)$$

$$= \frac{e^{-(\lambda + \psi)}}{2!}(\lambda + \psi)^2$$

Note that you have to multiply $\psi\lambda$ by 2 in order to take out the factor $\frac{1}{2!}$

and so on.

Tabulating we get

$x + y$	0	1	2	...
$P(X + Y = x + y)$	$e^{-(\lambda + \psi)}$	$e^{-(\lambda + \psi)}(\lambda + \psi)$	$e^{-(\lambda + \psi)}\dfrac{(\lambda + \psi)^2}{2!}$	...

In other words, if X and Y are independent random variables and $X \sim Po(\lambda)$ and $Y \sim Po(\psi)$ then

$$X + Y \sim Po(\lambda + \psi)$$

Example 1

If $X \sim Po(2)$ and $Y \sim Po(3.5)$ are both independent of each other, find:

a $P(X + Y = 4)$ **b** $P(X + Y \geq 2)$

Solution

Since both random variables are independent, $X + Y \sim Po(5.5)$

a $P(X + Y = 4) = 0.3575 - 0.2017$

                   $= 0.1558$

Using appropriate table $(\lambda = 5.5)$

b $P(X + Y \geq 2) = 1 - P(X \leq 1)$

                     $= 1 - 0.0266$

                     $= 0.9734$

Example 2

In an office a secretary receives internal calls at an average rate of three in a two-minute period and independently receives external calls at an average rate of four in a two-minute period. Calculate the probability that there will be at least four calls in the next two minutes.

Solution

Internal calls in a two-minute period can be modelled by $X \sim Po(3)$ and external calls in a two-minute period can be modelled by $Y \sim Po(4)$. Therefore, since both random variables are independent, the total number of calls in a two-minute period can be modelled by $X + Y \sim Po(7)$.

So,

$$P(X \geq 4) = 1 - P(X \leq 3)$$

$$= 1 - 0.0818$$

$$= 0.9182$$

The probability that there will be at least four calls in the next two minutes is 0.9182.

8.10 The Sum of Two or More Poisson Distributions
Exercise

Contextual

1 In a given office hourly internal telephone calls made can be modelled by a Poisson distribution with mean 2 and external calls made by a Poisson distribution with mean 4. The number of internal and external calls made are independent of each other.

   a What is the distribution of the total number of calls in an hour?

   b During a given hour, find the probability that more than five calls are made.

2 On a local stretch of road during a recent traffic survey one morning, it was discovered that the mean rate for cars travelling towards the town centre was five in any two-minute period and the mean rate for cars travelling away from the town centre was three in any two-minute period. Find the probability that:

   a at least two cars will pass in the next two-minute period

   b no cars will pass in the next minute

   c 10 cars will pass in the next two minutes.

3 At the school tuck shop, crisps and chocolate bars are the big sellers. During morning break, crisps sell at a rate of five bags per minute and bars of chocolate at a rate of four per minute. Assuming sales are independent and can be modelled using a Poisson distribution, calculate the probability that:

   a in a given minute exactly three bags of crisps are sold

   b in a given two-minute period fewer than six bars of chocolate are sold

   c in a given minute nine items of tuck are sold.

Consolidation

Exercise A

1 Market research has shown that the cereal 'Readies' is eaten by 45% of the population. Find the probability that in a sample of 10 people chosen at random:

a exactly eight people eat 'Readies'

b fewer than six people eat 'Readies'.

2 If $X \sim \text{Po}(4.5)$:

a state the mean and standard deviation of the distribution

b find $P(X \geq 6)$.

c If $P(X < a) = 0.5321$, find a.

3 In the autumn of 1992 the Department of Transport carried out roadside checks on the lighting of randomly chosen commercial vehicles. The investigation showed that 35% of all commercial vehicles had some fault with their lighting. For a random sample of 15 commercial vehicles, find the probability that:

a fewer than five vehicles have faulty lights

b between three and eight vehicles inclusive have faulty lights

c exactly six vehicles have faulty lights.

(NEAB)

4 Lisa is playing an arcade game. The game involves using a mechanical crane to grab a prize within a 30-second time interval. If Lisa is successful she wins the prize, otherwise she loses. She pays 20p for each game and she keeps playing until she wins. From past experience Lisa estimates that she has a 60% chance of winning at each attempt.

a Calculate the probability that it costs her exactly £1.40 to win the prize. Give your answer correct to three significant figures.

The value of the prize is £2.50

b Calculate the probability that Lisa will pay more to win the prize than its value. Give your answer correct to three significant figures.

c Given that Lisa has already failed to win her first nine games, find the conditional probability that it will take more than 16 games in total for her to win the prize.

Next to the machine on which Lisa is playing is an identical machine. After she has lost her first nine games she is joined by her friend, Kevin, who starts to play on the neighbouring machine. You may assume that he also has a 60% chance of winning at each attempt.

d Find the probability that Kevin takes more than seven games to win the prize on the machine he is playing.

(OCSEB)

5 Breakdowns occur on a particular machine at a rate of 2.5 per month. Assuming that the number of breakdowns can be modelled by a Poisson distribution, find the probability that:

a exactly three occur in a particular month

b more than 10 occur in a three-month period

c exactly three occur in each of two successive months.

(ULEAC)

6 On a particular day in June, the probability of there being rain at Benone is p. The random variable X is the number of days, in one particular week in June, on which there was rain at Benone.

a State an assumption about the weather which is necessary if X is to be modelled by the binomial distribution.

b If the variance of X is 1.68, find the two possible values of p, showing your working.

c Taking $p = 0.4$, calculate the probability that during a seven-day holiday at Benone in June, there will be no rain.

(OCSEB)

7 A Royal Automobile Association patrolman starts a 12-hour shift with a supply of spare parts, which includes two emergency fan belts. Past experience suggests that on average, 7% of breakdowns require a replacement fan belt. In the first hour the patrolman attends four breakdowns. Calculate the probability that:

a none of the four breakdowns requires a fan belt

b exactly two of the four breakdowns require a fan belt.

In a typical 12-hour shift the patrolman attends a total of 30 breakdowns.

c What is the expected number of replacement fan belts needed in a typical 12-hour shift?

d Using the Poisson distribution, or otherwise, find the probability that the number of fan belts needed in the shift is more than two.

e Determine the minimum number of fan belts required at the start of the shift if the patrolman is to have at least a 95% chance of being able to meet the need.

(MEI)

8 The weekly number of detached dwellings sold by an estate agent may be modelled by a Poisson distribution with mean 2.75 and, independently, the weekly number of other dwellings sold may be modelled by a Poisson distribution with mean 3.25. Determine the probability that the estate agent sells:

a exactly four detached dwellings in a week

b between 10 and 15, inclusive, detached dwellings over a four-week period

c fewer than five dwellings in a week.

(NEAB)

9 A bag contains a large number of beads of which 45% are yellow. A random sample of 20 beads is taken from the bag. Use the binomial distribution to calculate the probability that the sample contains:

a fewer than 12 yellow beads   b exactly 12 yellow beads.

(ULEAC)

10 An insurance company has 40 000 clients covered for 'severe industrial accident'. Such accidents are estimated to affect 1 in 200 000 of the population in any year, and they are assumed to occur independently of one another. Let X be the number of claims for severe industrial accident received by the company in a randomly chosen year.

a State the distribution of X, and explain why an appropriate Poisson distribution would give a good approximation.

b Find the probability that the number of claims received by the company in a year is:

i 0   ii 1   iii 2 or more.

A second insurance company offers cover on the same terms for severe industrial accident, and it receives an average of 1.25 claims per year.

c Estimate the number of clients insured for severe industrial accident with the second company.

d The two companies merge. Find the probability that the number of claims received in a year by the merged company is

i 0   ii 2.

(MEI)

Exercise B

1 Given that $X \sim B(10, 0.25)$:

a find $P(X \geq 6)$ b state the value of the mean of the distribution.

2 A local furniture shop sells both new and second-hand armchairs. The probability that a randomly chosen sale is a new armchair is 0.3 and the probability of an old armchair being sold is 0.6. Assuming sales are independent and randomly distributed throughout a week. Find the probability that in a week in which 20 armchairs are sold

a at most five new armchairs are sold

b fewer than four old armchairs are sold.

3 Jonathan decided to play in a weekly lottery game. He is prepared to play indefinitely. The lottery organisers claim that a participant in the lottery has a 1 in 57 chance of winning a prize.

Let X be the random variable representing the number of games he plays up to and including his first win.

a Explain why a geometric distribution may be an appropriate model for this random variable distribution.

b Calculate

   i $P(X \leq 12)$ **ii** $P(13 \leq X < 70)$

c Determine the minimum number of games Jonathan will need to play to be at least 95% certain of having won at least one prize by that time.

(OCSEB)

4 Suppose that, for eggs bought in a supermarket, the probability of any egg having a double yolk is 0.005, independently of other eggs bought. Use an appropriate Poisson distribution to find the probability that, of 150 eggs bought in a supermarket, exactly two will have a double yolk.

(UCLES)

5 a The probability that a fisherman has a successful day's fishing is 0.6. Given that he fishes for six days every week, find the probability that in any week he has:

   i exactly four successful days,   **ii** at least two successful days.

The fisherman fishes for six days every week for many weeks. Estimate the mean and the standard deviation of the number of successful days per week over this period.

b In practising the high jump a certain athlete has five attempts at a particular height. The probability that she succeeds at any one attempt is p. Find an expression, in terms of p, for the probability that she succeeds:

   i exactly four times   **ii** exactly twice.

The probability that she succeeds exactly four times is twice the probability that she succeeds exactly twice. Find the value of p.

(UCLES)

6 An insurance company employs agents who use their cars to travel a large number of miles each year. The company observes that the number of accidents involving each agent can be modelled by a Poisson distribution with mean 0.2 per year.

a What is the probability that a particular agent is involved in:

   i two or fewer accidents in a particular year

   ii exactly three accidents in a particular year?

Recently 20 agents were issued with mobile phones. The company observes that, for the six of these 20 agents who used mobile phones while driving, the number of accidents can be modelled by a Poisson distribution with mean 0.7 per year. The accident rate for the other 14 agents has a Poisson distribution with mean 0.2 per year.

b Deduce that for these 20 agents their total number of accidents in a particular year may be modelled by a Poisson distribution with mean 7.

c Determine the probability that these 20 agents are involved in a total of more than six accidents in a particular year.

(AEB)

7 An archer fires arrows at a target and for each arrow, independently of all other, the probability that it hits the bull's-eye is $\frac{1}{8}$.

  a Given that the archer fires five arrows, find the probability that fewer than two arrows hit the bull's-eye.

  b The archer fires five arrows, collects them from the target and fires all five again. Find the probability that on both occasions fewer than two hit the bull's-eye.

  (ULEAC)

8 An angler goes fishing at the same spot every Saturday morning. From long experience he reckons that the number of fish he catches per hour can be modelled by the Poisson distribution with mean 3.2. One particular Saturday he fishes for two hours.

  a Find the following probabilities, giving you answers correct to four decimal places:

  i he catches exactly three fish in the first hour

  ii he catches three or more fish in the second hour

  iii he catches six or more fish in the two hours.

  b Find the probability that he catches exactly three fish in the first hour and three or more fish in the second hour.

  (MEI)

9 A biologist is studying the behaviour of sheep in a large field. The field is divided into a number of equal sized squares and the average number of sheep per square is 2.5. The sheep are randomly spread throughout the field.

  a Suggest a suitable model for the number of sheep in a square and give a suitable value for any parameter or parameters required.

  b Calculate the probability that a randomly selected square contains:

  i no sheep　　　　**ii** more than four sheep.

  c A sheep dog has been sent into the field to round up the sheep. Explain why the model may no longer be applicable.

  (ULEAC)

10 The daily demand X for a certain video in a shop has a Poisson distribution with mean 3.

  a The shop has four copies of the video available for daily hire and Y denotes the number of copies hired out daily by the shop.

  i Show that the probability distribution of Y is given by

y	0	1	2	3	4
$P(Y = y)$	0.0498	0.1494	0.2240	0.2240	0.3528

  where the probabilities in the table are recorded correct to four decimal places.

  ii Find, showing your method, the mean and variance of Y. Record your answers correct to two decimal places.

  b Find, giving a brief explanation of your method, the least number of copies of the video that the shop should stock in order that the probability of meeting the demand should exceed 0.95.

  (WJEC)

Applications and Activities

1 Carry out a taste testing experiment to determine whether people can tell the difference between two items of food that are similar, such as:

Chocolate versus Carob (or artificial chocolate)
Butter versus Margarine
Brand name versus Supermarket own brand

Are your results similar to those given by the binomial distribution?

2 Using a suitable time interval, count the number of cars passing a particular point on a road. Ensure your time interval gives no more than seven cars. Would a Poisson distribution be an appropriate model for this data?

Summary

- In a binomial distribution:
  - there are only two possible outcomes
  - the fixed number of trials is denoted n
  - the probability of success, denoted p, is the same for each trial
  - the trials are independent.

- A binomial distribution of the random variable X is written as $X \sim B(n, p)$.

- The probability that the number of successes, X, in n trials is r is given by

$$P(X = r) = {}^nC_r\, p^r (1 - p)^{n-r}$$

where ${}^nC_r = \dfrac{n!}{r!(n-r)!}$

- Cumulative binomial probability tables are used to find:
  - $P(X \leq r)$ for any value of r by reading off the required value
  - $P(X = r)$ for any value of r by finding $P(X \leq r) - P(X \leq r - 1)$
  - $P(X \geq r)$ for any value of r by calculating $1 - P(X \leq r - 1)$.

- If $X \sim B(n, p)$ then the mean $E(X) = np$ and the variance $\text{Var}(X) = np(1 - p)$.

- To fit a binomial distribution to a sample:
  - calculate the sample mean and use it as an estimate of the population mean (np);
  - use your value of np to find p;
  - use p to calculate the theoretical probabilities for the sample;
  - use the theoretical probabilities to work out the expected frequencies by multiplying each probability by the total number in the sample;
  - compare the expected and actual frequencies to see how well the binomial distribution fits.

● In a geometric distribution:

  – there are only two possible outcomes;
  – the number of trials is limited by the first success;
  – the probability of success, denoted by p, is the same for each trial;
  – the trials are independent.

● $X \sim G(p)$ means that the random variable X is geometrically distributed with probability of success p.

● $P(X = r) = q^{(r-1)}p$

● $p(X \leq r) = 1 - q^r$

● If $X \sim G(p)$ then

  the mean $\quad E(X) = \frac{1}{p}$ and

  the variance $\text{Var}(X) = \frac{q}{p^2}$

● A Poisson distribution can be used as an approximation for the binomial distribution.

● $X \sim \text{Po}(\lambda)$ means that the random variable X is Poisson distributed with mean λ.

● If $X \sim B(n, p)$ and n is large and p is small then the distribution of X can be approximated by $\text{Po}(\lambda)$.

● In a Poisson distribution:

  – events are independent of each other
  – events occur singly
  – events occur at a constant rate.

● In a Poisson distribution the probability that the number of successes X is r is given by

$$P(X = r) = e^{-\lambda} \times \frac{\lambda^r}{r!}$$

● Cumulative Poisson probability tables are used to find:

  – $P(X \leq r)$ for any value of r by reading off the required value
  – $P(X = r)$ for any value of r by finding $P(X \leq r) - P(X \leq r - 1)$
  – $P(X \geq r)$ for any value of r by calculating $1 - P(X \leq r - 1)$.

● If $X \sim \text{Po}(\lambda)$ then the mean $E(X) = \lambda$ and the variance $\text{Var}(X) = \lambda$.

● To fit a Poisson distribution to a sample:

  – calculate the mean of the sample and use this value as the parameter λ of the Poisson distribution;
  – calculate the theoretical probabilities using λ;
  – use the theoretical probabilities to work out expected frequencies by multiplying each probability by the total number in the sample;
  – compare the expected and actual frequencies to see how well the Poisson distribution fits.

9 Continuous Probability Distributions

What you need to know

- The definition of a random variable.

- The difference between a discrete random variable and a continuous random variable.

- How to integrate simple functions.

Review

1 State whether each of the following random variables is discrete or continuous:

   a   the number of students who drive to college each day

   b   the length of time a student spends in the library each week

   c   the number of 6s obtained when three dice are thrown.

2 Integrate the following functions with respect to x:

   a $4x^3$

   b $2x^4 + 3x^3$

   c $x^2 - 4x + 5$

9.1 Probability Density Functions

In Chapter 7 we considered discrete probability distributions: now we are going to look at continuous probability distributions.

You will remember that discrete probability distributions can be applied to many real situations, such as throwing a dice, where the random variables are 1, 2, 3, 4, 5, 6. Continuous probability distributions sometimes seem to be less 'real' but *continuous random variables* are theoretical representations of continuous variables such as time or height.

A continuous random variable is defined by its **probability density function** which is written as $f(x)$. This function is defined over the range $(-\infty, \infty)$.

From negative infinity to infinity.

A commuter wants to calculate the probability of her train being late. She notes the number of minutes the train is late each weekday for six weeks, and records the results in a grouped frequency table.

Minutes late	0–2	2–4	4–6	6–8	8–10
Frequency	12	8	5	2	3

In order to work out the probability that the train is less than two minutes late the commuter uses the relative frequency, $\frac{12}{30} = 0.4$

The train is between 0 and 2 minutes late on 12 days out of the 30 days surveyed.

The probabilities can be shown in a probability distribution table.

Minutes late	0–2	2–4	4–6	6–8	8–10
Probability	0.4	0.267	0.167	0.067	0.1
Relative probability density	0.2	0.133	0.0833	0.0333	0.05

Relative probability density is found by dividing the probability by the group width, in this case 2.

This information can be plotted on a histogram, as shown.

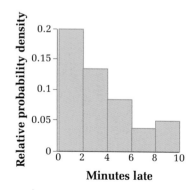

Remember: the total area of the columns is equal to one, since the probabilities must sum to one.

These probabilities could be plotted as a line graph.

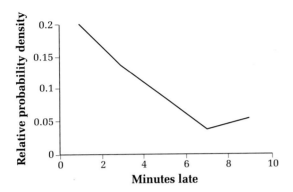

The area under the line must be equal to one, as this graph is showing the same information as the histogram.

It is possible to use a straight line graph to *model* the data. One possible line is shown here.

The equation of this line is

$$y = 0.2 - 0.02x$$

and the area under the line equals one.

The probability density function gives a 'smooth' version of the relative frequency histogram.

The probability distribution function is defined as

$$f(x) = 0.2 - 0.02x, \text{ valid for } 0 \leq x \leq 10, f(x) = 0 \text{ otherwise}$$

where X is the random variable 'number of minutes that the train is late'.

The area under the curve, which equals one, can be found by integrating the function $f(x)$.

$$\int f(x)\, dx = \int_0^{10} (0.2 - 0.02x)\, dx$$

Suppose the commuter wants to calculate the probability that her train is less than three minutes late. She needs to find the area under the curve between 0 and 3.

$$P(0 \le X \le 3) = \int_0^3 (0.2 - 0.02x)\, dx$$

$$= \left[0.2x - 0.01x^2 \right]_0^3$$

$$= 0.6 - 0.09$$

$$= 0.51$$

Therefore the probability that the train will be less than three minutes late is 0.51.

If the commuter wants to find the probability that the train is between two and five minutes late she must calculate the area under the graph between 2 and 5.

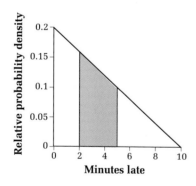

$$P(2 \le X \le 5) = \int_2^5 (0.2 - 0.02x)\, dx$$

$$= \left[0.2x - 0.01x^2 \right]_2^5$$

$$= (1 - 0.25) - (0.4 - 0.04)$$

$$= 0.75 - 0.36$$

$$= 0.39$$

If we try to calculate the probability that the train is **exactly** three minutes late, we find that

$$\int_3^3 (0.2 - 0.02x)\, dx = 0$$

For a continuous probability distribution we must calculate the probability that X lies within a particular range. This result can be expressed generally as:

> If X is a continuous random variable with $f(x) \geq 0$ for all x, and $\int_a^b f(x)\, dx = 1$, then $P(-\infty \leq X \leq \infty) = \int_{-\infty}^{\infty} f(x)\, dx$.

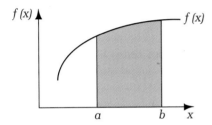

The function f is known as the **probability density function** (or **p.d.f.** for short) of the variable X. It describes mathematically how the unit of probability is distributed over the range. $f(x)$ does not itself represent the probability; it is only when we integrate between two limits that we obtain a probability. $P(X = k) = 0$, where k is a constant, because probability is measured by means of area and the line $x = k$ has no thickness and therefore its area is zero. As probability is defined as the area between two limits and the probability of $X = k$ is zero then

$$P(k \leq X \leq l) = P(k < X \leq l) = P(k \leq X < l) = P(k < X < l).$$

Unlike discrete distributions we do not need to worry about inequalities.

Example 1

A continuous random variable X has probability density function

$$f(x) = \tfrac{1}{4}(4 - x), \text{ for } 1 \leq x \leq 3$$

a   Sketch the graph of $f(x)$ and verify that it satisfies the conditions to be a probability density function.
b   Find $P(X < 2)$
c   Find $P(1.5 \leq X < 2.6)$

Solution

a $f(x)$

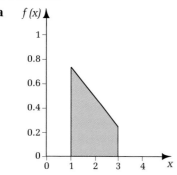

$$\int_1^3 \tfrac{1}{4}(4-x)\,dx = \tfrac{1}{4}\left[4x - \frac{x^2}{2}\right]_1^3$$

$$= \tfrac{1}{4}\left[(12 - \tfrac{9}{2}) - (4 - \tfrac{1}{2})\right]$$

$$= \tfrac{1}{4}\left[\tfrac{15}{2} - \tfrac{7}{2}\right]$$

$$= 1$$

The area under the graph between 1 and 3 is one, which satisfies the condition for a probability density function.

b $P(X < 2) = \int_1^2 \tfrac{1}{4}(4-x)\,dx$

$$= \tfrac{1}{4}\left[4x - \frac{x^2}{2}\right]_1^2$$

$$= \tfrac{1}{4}\left[(8 - 2) - (4 - \tfrac{1}{2})\right]$$

$$= \tfrac{1}{4}\left[6 - 3\tfrac{1}{2}\right]$$

$$= 0.625$$

c $P(1.5 < X < 2.6) = \tfrac{1}{4}\int_{1.5}^{2.6}(4-x)\,dx$

$$= \tfrac{1}{4}\left[4x - \frac{x^2}{2}\right]_{1.5}^{2.6}$$

$$= \tfrac{1}{4}\left[(10.4 - 3.38) - (6 - 1.125)\right]$$

$$= \tfrac{1}{4}\left[7.02 - 4.875\right]$$

$$= 0.536 \ (3 \ \text{s.f.})$$

Example 2

A continuous random variable has probability density function

$$f(x) = kx^3, \text{ for } 0 \le x \le 4$$

Find:

a   the value of k b $P(1 \le X \le 3)$ c $P(X > 2)$

Solution

a The area under the curve between 0 and 4 must equal one, therefore

$$\int_0^4 kx^3 \, dx = 1$$

$$k\left[\frac{x^4}{4}\right]_0^4 = 1$$

$$64k = 1$$

$$k = \tfrac{1}{64}$$

b $P(1 \leq X \leq 3) = \tfrac{1}{64}\int_1^3 x^3 \, dx$

$$= \tfrac{1}{64}\left[\frac{x^4}{4}\right]_1^3$$

$$= \tfrac{1}{64}\left[\tfrac{81}{4} - \tfrac{1}{4}\right]$$

$$= 0.3125$$

c $P(X > 2) = \tfrac{1}{64}\int_2^4 x^3 \, dx$

$$= \tfrac{1}{64}\left[\frac{x^4}{4}\right]_2^4$$

$$= \tfrac{1}{64}[64 - 4]$$

$$= 0.9375$$

Example 3

The continuous random variable X has probability density function

$$f(x) = \begin{cases} k(x+1) & 0 \leq x \leq 2 \\ 2k & 2 \leq x \leq 3 \\ 0 & \text{otherwise} \end{cases}$$

a Find the value of the constant k.
b Sketch the probability density function.
c Find $P(1.5 < X < 2.5)$.
d Find $P(X > 1.8)$.

Solution

a The total area under the function must equal one, hence

$$\int_0^2 k(x+1) \, dx + \int_2^3 2k \, dx = 1$$

$$k\left[\frac{x^2}{2} + x\right]_0^2 + 2k\left[x\right]_2^3 = 1$$

$$k[4 - 0] + 2k[3 - 2] = 1$$

$$4k + 2k = 1$$

$$6k = 1$$

$$k = \tfrac{1}{6}$$

Therefore the probability density function is

$$f(x) = \begin{cases} \frac{1}{6}(x + 1) & 0 \le x \le 2 \\ \frac{1}{3} & 2 \le x \le 3 \\ 0 & \text{otherwise} \end{cases}$$

b

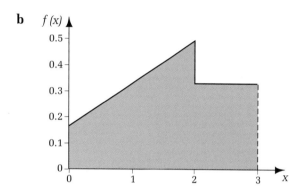

c   It is necessary to find the area in two parts. First we find the area
under the curve between 1.5 and 2, then the area between 2 and 2.5.

$$P(1.5 < X < 2.5) = \tfrac{1}{6}\int_{1.5}^{2}(x + 1)\,dx + \int_{2}^{2.5}\tfrac{1}{3}\,dx$$

$$= \tfrac{1}{6}\left[\frac{x^2}{2} + x\right]_{1.5}^{2} + \tfrac{1}{3}\left[x\right]_{2}^{2.5}$$

$$= \tfrac{1}{6}[(2 + 2) - (1.125 + 1.5)] + \tfrac{1}{3}[2.5 - 2]$$

$$= \tfrac{1}{6}[1.375] + \tfrac{1}{3}[0.5]$$

$$= 0.396 \text{ (3 s.f.)}$$

f(x) changes at $x = 2$.

d   Again, we have to find the area in two parts.

$$P(X > 1.8) = \tfrac{1}{6}\int_{1.8}^{2}(x + 1)\,dx + \int_{2}^{3}\tfrac{1}{3}\,dx$$

$$= \tfrac{1}{6}\left[\frac{x^2}{2} + x\right]_{1.8}^{2} + \tfrac{1}{3}\left[x\right]_{2}^{3}$$

$$= \tfrac{1}{6}[(2 + 2) - (1.62 + 1.8)] + \tfrac{1}{3}[3 - 2]$$

$$= \tfrac{1}{6}[0.58] + \tfrac{1}{3}[1]$$

$$= 0.43$$

9.1 Probability Density Functions

Exercise

Technique

1 X is a continuous random variable with probability density function
$f(x) = \frac{1}{4}(3 - x)$, for $0 \le x \le 2$.

   a Sketch the graph of $f(x)$ and verify that it satisfies the conditions for a probability density function.

   b Find $P(X < 1.5)$.

   c Find $P(0.2 \le X \le 1.8)$.

2 A continuous random variable has probability density function $f(x)$ where
$f(x) = \frac{3}{26}x^2$, for $1 \le x \le 3$.

   a Find $P(X < 2.5)$.   **b** Find $P(X \ge 2.5)$.

   c Find $P(1.6 \le X \le 2)$.

3 The continuous random variable X has probability density function
$f(x) = kx^2$, for $0 \le x \le 3$.

   a Find the value of the constant k.

   b Sketch the function $f(x)$.

   c Find $P(X \le 2.3)$.

   d Find $P(0.3 \le X \le 1.5)$.

4 The continuous random variable X has probability density function
$f(x) = k(x^2 - 2x)$, for $2 \le x \le 5$.

   a Find the value of k.

   b Sketch the probability density function.

   c Find $P(X > 3.5)$.

   d Find $P(2.1 < X < 2.8)$.

5 A continuous random variable X has probability density function $f(x)$, where

$$f(x) = \begin{cases} \frac{1}{4} & 0 \le x < 1 \\ \frac{3}{8}(3 - x) & 1 \le x \le 3 \\ 0 & \text{otherwise} \end{cases}$$

   a Sketch the probability density function.

   b Find $P(0.5 \le X \le 1.5)$.

   c Find $P(X > 2)$.

9.2 Cumulative Distribution Function

In the previous section we calculated the probability that the commuter's train would be less than three minutes late by finding the area under the graph of the probability density function between 0 and 3. Using a similar method it is possible to work out the probability that the train will be less than a minute late, less than two minutes late, less than four minutes late and so on.

Time late	Probability
less than 0 minutes	0
less than 1 minute	0.19
less than 2 minutes	0.36
less than 3 minutes	0.51
less than 4 minutes	0.64
less than 5 minutes	0.75
less than 6 minutes	0.84
less than 7 minutes	0.91
less than 8 minutes	0.96
less than 9 minutes	0.99
less than 10 minutes	1

Any values could have been used – whole numbers were chosen t simplify the calculations.

Look at the values in the probability column. You should notice that the probabilities are increasing. The probability that the train will be less than 0 minutes late is 0 because in the original problem we recorded an early arrival as being on time. The probability that the train will be less than 10 minutes late is 1 because we know from the original problem that the train was never more than 10 minutes overdue.

This table reminds us of the cumulative frequency tables constructed from frequency distributions in Chapter 8.

The **cumulative distribution function** (or simply the distribution function) is denoted by $F(x)$. For the example given the cumulative distribution function is

$$F(x) = 0 \qquad \text{for } x \le 0$$

$$F(x) = \int_0^x f(x)\,dx \quad \text{for } 0 \le x \le 10$$

$$F(x) = 1 \qquad \text{for } x \ge 10$$

This means that for values of x less than, or equal to the smallest value for which the probability density function is non-zero, the probability is 0, that is, this outcome cannot happen.

For values of x for which the probability density function is non-zero the cumulative probability is found by integrating between the smallest possible value (in this example 0) and the particular value required.

For values of x greater than, or equal to, the largest possible value the probability is 1, that is all outcomes have been covered by the time the maximum value is reached.

Example 1

Find the cumulative distribution function for the random variable X, 'number of minutes that a train is late', where $f(x) = 0.2 - 0.02x$, for $0 \leq x \leq 10$.

Solution

As no trains are assumed to arrive early the cumulative distribution function $F(x)$ will be such that

$$F(x) = 0 \text{ for all } x \leq 0$$

$$F(x) = P(X \leq x_0)$$

$$= \int_0^{x_0} (0.2 - 0.02x)\, dx$$

$$= \left[0.2x - 0.01x^2 \right]_0^{x_0}$$

$$= 0.2x_0 - 0.01x_0^2$$

Substituting $x = 10$, $F(x) = 1$, which is what it should be as the whole one unit of probability is to the left of $x = 10$.

Taking all these results together gives the cumulative distribution function.

$$F(x) = 0 \qquad \text{for } x \leq 0$$

$$F(x) = 0.2x - 0.01x^2 \quad \text{for } 0 \leq x \leq 10$$

$$F(x) = 1 \qquad \text{for } x \geq 10$$

It is important to realise that $0 \leq F(x) \leq 1$.

From the example above we see that the cumulative distribution function (or c.d.f. for short) is found by integrating the probability density function.

$$F(x) = \int_a^b f(x)\, dx, \text{ where } a \leq x \leq b$$

233

Example 2

If X is a continuous random variable with probability density function $f(x) = \frac{1}{8}x$, where $0 \leq x \leq 4$, find the cumulative distribution function $F(x)$.

Solution

For $x \leq 0$, $F(x) = 0$

For $0 \leq x \leq 4$ $F(x) = \int_0^{x_0} \frac{1}{8}x\,dx$

$$= \frac{1}{8}\left[\frac{x^2}{2}\right]_0^{x_0}$$

$$= \frac{x_0^2}{16}$$

For $x \geq 4$, $F(x) = 1$

Therefore the cumulative distribution function is

$$F(x) = 0 \quad \text{for } 0 \leq x$$

$$F(x) = \frac{x^2}{16} \quad \text{for } 0 \leq x \leq 4$$

$$F(x) = 1 \quad \text{for } x \geq 4$$

From Pure Mathematics we know that integration and differentiation are inverse processes. This allows us to work out the probability density function when the cumulative distribution function is given, by

$$f(x) = \frac{d}{dx}F(x)$$

Example 3

The random variable X has a cumulative distribution function given by

$$F(x) = 0 \quad 0 \leq x$$

$$F(x) = \frac{x^3}{27} \quad 0 \leq x \leq 3$$

$$F(x) = 1 \quad x \geq 3$$

a   Find the probability density function.
b   Sketch the function $y = f(x)$.

Solution

a $f(x) = \dfrac{d}{dx} F(x)$

$\qquad = \dfrac{d}{dx}\left(\dfrac{x^3}{27}\right)$

$\qquad = \dfrac{3x^2}{27}$

$\qquad = \dfrac{x^2}{9}$

Therefore the probability density function is

$f(x) = \dfrac{x^2}{9} \quad 0 \le x \le 3$

$f(x) = 0 \quad \text{otherwise}$

b

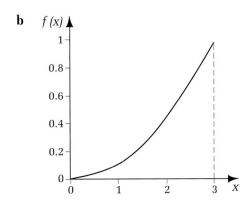

There is one value that is particularly important in the cumulative distribution function. In Chapter 4 the median was defined as the middle value, with exactly half the data lying below that value and half lying above that value. In the context of a probability density function the median will be that point below which the area is 0.5 and above which the area is also 0.5. In other words, **the median divides the area under the curve into halves**.

If the median is m then $\displaystyle\int_a^m f(x)\,dx = 0.5$, which means $F(m) = 0.5$.

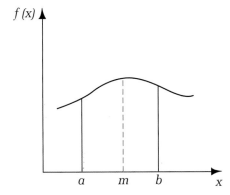

You can find the lower quartile of a continuous random variable by solving the equation $F(q_1) = 0.25$.
To find the upper quartile, solve the equation $F(q_3) = 0.75$

Example 4

X is a continuous random variable with probability density function $f(x) = \frac{1}{4}(4 - x)$, for $1 \leq x \leq 3$. Find:

a   the cumulative distribution function

b   the median m.

Solution

a $F(x) = 0$ for all $x \leq 1$, and $F(x) = 1$ for all $x \geq 3$. For $1 \leq x \leq 3$

$$F(x) = \int_{1}^{x_0} \frac{1}{4}(4 - x)\, dx$$

$$= \frac{1}{4}\left[4x - \frac{x^2}{2}\right]_{1}^{x_0}$$

$$= \frac{1}{4}\left[\left(4x_0 - \frac{x_0^2}{2}\right) - \left(4 - \frac{1}{2}\right)\right]$$

$$= \frac{1}{4}\left[4x_0 - \frac{x_0^2}{2} - \frac{7}{2}\right]$$

$$= -\frac{1}{8}\left(x_0^2 - 8x_0 + 7\right)$$

The cumulative distribution function is therefore

$$F(x) = 0 \qquad\qquad\qquad x \leq 1$$
$$F(x) = -\frac{1}{8}(x^2 - 8x + 7) \quad 1 \leq x \leq 3$$
$$F(x) = 1 \qquad\qquad\qquad x \geq 3$$

b   At the median m, $F(m) = 0.5$ so

$$-\frac{1}{8}(m^2 - 8m + 7) = 0.5$$

$$(m^2 - 8m + 7) = -4$$

$$m^2 - 8m + 11 = 0$$

Using the quadratic formula gives

$$m = \frac{8 \pm \sqrt{20}}{2}$$

$$m = 1.764 \text{ or } 6.236$$

As $1 \leq m \leq 3$, m cannot be greater than 3, so the median is 1.764.

Multiply both sides by −

9.2 Cumulative Distribution Functions

Exercise

Technique

In questions $\boxed{1}$–$\boxed{3}$, for each of the probability density functions of the continuous random variable X, find the cumulative density function and also the median.

$\boxed{1}$ $f(x) = \frac{1}{4}(3 - x)$, for $0 \leq x \leq 2$

$\boxed{2}$ $f(x) = \frac{3}{26}x^2$, for $1 \leq x \leq 3$

$\boxed{3}$ $f(x) = \frac{1}{9}x^2$, for $0 \leq x \leq 3$

$\boxed{4}$ A continuous random variable X has cumulative distribution function

$$F(x) = \begin{cases} 0 & x \leq 0 \\ \frac{1}{40}x^2 + \frac{3}{20}x & 0 \leq x \leq 4 \\ 1 & x \geq 4 \end{cases}$$

Find and sketch the probability density function.

$\boxed{5}$ The continuous random variable X has cumulative distribution function $F(x)$ where

$$F(x) = \begin{cases} 0 & x \leq 1 \\ \frac{1}{3}k(x^3 - 1) & 1 \leq x \leq 2 \\ 1 & 2 \leq x \end{cases}$$

Find the value of k.

9.3 Expectation and Variance

In Chapter 7 the expected value of a discrete random variable was calculated by multiplying each outcome by its probability and then adding these values together. The expected value of a continuous random variable can be calculated by applying a similar method.

In a continuous distribution the probability is represented by the area under the graph of the function between two values, that is

$$P(a \leq X \leq b) = \int_a^b f(x)\,dx$$

If this probability is multiplied by the corresponding outcomes, and added together, we obtain

$$E(X) = \int_a^b xf(x)\,dx$$

Similarly we can derive the formula for variance from the corresponding discrete probability result giving

$$\mathbf{Var}(X) = \int_a^b x^2 f(x)\,dx - \mu^2 \qquad \text{where } \mu \text{ denotes } E(X)$$

The expected value of a probability function is also known as the mean.

Note the parallel with the discrete probability distribution – the Σ is replaced with $\int$.

Example 1

A continuous random variable X has probability density function $f(x) = kx^2$, for $0 \leq x \leq 2$. Find:

a the value of the constant k
b the expected value of X
c the variance of X.

Solution

a $\displaystyle\int_0^2 kx^2\,dx = 1$

$$k\left[\frac{x^3}{3}\right]_0^2 = 1$$

$$\frac{8}{3} = \frac{1}{k}$$

$$k = \frac{3}{8}$$

So

$$f(x) = \tfrac{3}{8}x^2 \quad 0 \leq x \leq 2$$
$$f(x) = 0 \qquad \text{otherwise}$$

b $\mu = E(X) = \int_0^2 x\left(\frac{3}{8}x^2\right) dx$

$= \frac{3}{8} \int_0^2 x^3 \, dx$

$= \frac{3}{8} \left[\frac{x^4}{4}\right]_0^2$

$= \frac{3}{8}\left[\frac{16}{4}\right]$

$= \frac{3}{2}$

c $\text{Var}(X) = \int_0^2 x^2\left(\frac{3}{8}x^2\right) dx - \mu^2$

$= \frac{3}{8} \int_0^2 x^4 \, dx - \left(\frac{3}{2}\right)^2$

$= \frac{3}{8} \left[\frac{x^5}{5}\right]_0^2 - \left(\frac{9}{4}\right)$

$= \frac{3}{8}\left[\frac{32}{5}\right] - \frac{9}{4}$

$= \frac{12}{5} - \frac{9}{4}$

$= \frac{3}{20}$

For both discrete and continuous probability distributions the mean must lie in the interval between the smallest and the largest values that the random variable can take. However, in a discrete distribution the mean is often at a point that is not one of the values that the random variable can take.

It is a good idea to sketch the probability density function to check for symmetry before calculating the mean. If the function is symmetrical then the mean can be read off from the diagram without having to carry out a calculation.

Example 2

The continuous random variable X has probability density function $f(x) = \frac{3}{4}(3 - x)(x - 5)$ for $3 \leq x \leq 5$. Find the mean, and the standard deviation of X.

Solution

First sketch the probability density function.

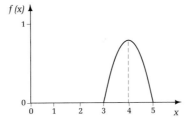

From the sketch we can see that the function is symmetrical about the line $x = 4$. By inspection therefore, we can state that the mean, or expected value, is 4. To find the standard deviation we first calculate the variance.

$\text{Var}(X) = \int_3^5 x^2 \times \frac{3}{4}(3 - x)(x - 5) \, dx - \mu^2$

$= \frac{3}{4} \int_3^5 x^2(-x^2 + 8x - 15) \, dx - \mu^2$

$= \frac{3}{4} \int_3^5 (-x^4 + 8x^3 - 15x^2) \, dx - 4^2$ Substitute $\mu = 4$.

$= \frac{3}{4} \left[-\frac{1}{5}x^5 + \frac{8}{4}x^4 - \frac{15}{3}x^3\right]_3^5 - 16$

$= \frac{3}{4}\left[\frac{108}{5}\right] - 16$

$= \frac{1}{5}$

standard deviation $= \sqrt{\frac{1}{5}} = 0.447 \ (3 \text{ s.f.})$

The **mode** is the value of the random variable X where $f(x)$ has its greatest value. The mode can occur at a stationary point on the function and this value can be found by calculating the value of x for which $f'(x) = 0$.

The function $f(x)$ should always be sketched.

Example 3

Find the mode of the functions

a $f(x) = \dfrac{3}{4}(3 - x)(x - 5)$ where $3 \le x \le 5$

b $f(x) = \dfrac{3}{8}x^2$ where $0 \le x \le 2$

Solution

a

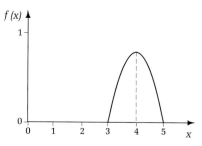

From the sketch we can see that this curve has a stationary point

$$f(x) = \frac{3}{4}(3 - x)(x - 5)$$

$$= \frac{3}{4}(-x^2 + 8x - 15)$$

$$f'(x) = \frac{3}{4}(-2x + 8)$$

when $f'(x) = 0$

$$\frac{3}{4}(-2x + 8) = 0$$

$$2x = 8$$

$$x = 4$$

The mode of this distribution is 4

b

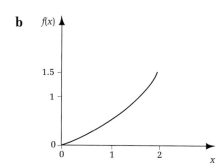

From the sketch we can see that the maximum value of $f(x)$ does not occur at a stationary point. The maximum value of $f(x)$ occurs when $x = 2$, so the mode of this distribution is 2.

9.3 Expectation and Variance
Exercise
Technique

Find the expected value and the variance for the continuous random variables in questions $\boxed{1}$–$\boxed{5}$, which come from Exercise 9.1.

$\boxed{1}$ $f(x) = \frac{1}{4}(3 - x)$, for $0 \leq x \leq 2$

$\boxed{2}$ $f(x) = \frac{3}{26}x^2$, for $1 \leq x \leq 3$

$\boxed{3}$ $f(x) = kx^2$, for $0 \leq x \leq 3$, given that $k = \frac{1}{9}$

$\boxed{4}$ $f(x) = k(x^2 - 2x)$, for $2 \leq x \leq 5$, given that $k = \frac{1}{18}$

$\boxed{5}$
$$f(x) = \begin{cases} \frac{1}{4} & 0 \leq x < 1 \\ \frac{3}{8}(3 - x) & 1 \leq x \leq 3 \\ 0 & \text{otherwise} \end{cases}$$

$\boxed{6}$ The continuous random variable, X, is defined as $f(x) = cx(16 - x^2)$, for $0 \leq x \leq 4$. Find:

  a the value of c **b** $E(X)$ **c** $\text{Var}(X)$.

$\boxed{7}$ A continuous random variable has probability density function

$$f(x) = \begin{cases} kx^3 & 0 \leq x \leq 1 \\ k & 1 \leq x \leq 2 \\ 0 & \text{otherwise} \end{cases}$$

Work out the value of k and sketch the function. Calculate the expected value and the variance of X.

9.4 Linear Combination of Random Variables

You have already considered the linear combination of discrete random variables and found some useful results. These results apply equally to continuous random variables.

If X and Y are discrete or continuous random variables, and a and b are constants then

$$E(aX) = aE(X)$$

$$E(aX + b) = aE(X) + b$$

$$\mathrm{Var}(aX) = a^2 \, \mathrm{Var}(X)$$

$$\mathrm{Var}(aX + b) = a^2 \, \mathrm{Var}(X)$$

$$E(aX \pm bY) = aE(X) \pm bE(Y)$$

$$\mathrm{Var}(aX \pm bY) = a^2 \, \mathrm{Var}(X) + b^2 \, \mathrm{Var}(Y)$$

if X and Y are independent

Example 1

The random variable X has probability density function $f(x) = \frac{1}{2}x$, where $0 \leq x \leq 2$. Find:

a   the expected value of X **b**   the variance of X

c $E(2X + 3)$ **d** $\mathrm{Var}(2X + 3)$

Solution

a $E(X) = \displaystyle\int_0^2 x \tfrac{1}{2} x \, \mathrm{d}x$

$\qquad\quad = \tfrac{1}{2} \left[\dfrac{x^3}{3} \right]_0^2$

$\qquad\quad = \tfrac{4}{3}$

b　$\text{Var}(X) = \int_0^2 x^2 \frac{1}{2}x \, dx - [E(X)]^2$

$$= \frac{1}{2}\left[\frac{x^4}{4}\right]_0^2 - \left(\frac{4}{3}\right)^2$$

$$= 2 - \frac{16}{9}$$

$$= \frac{2}{9}$$

c　$E(2X + 3) = 2E(X) + 3$

$$= 2 \times \frac{4}{3} + 3$$

$$= 5\frac{2}{3}$$

d　$\text{Var}(2X + 3) = 2^2 \, \text{Var}(X)$

$$= 4 \times \frac{2}{9}$$

$$= \frac{8}{9}$$

Example 2

Two random variables L and M are known to be independent. The probability density function of random variable L is given as $f(l) = 3l^2$ for $0 \leq l \leq 1$ and the probability density function of variable M is $f(m) = 4m^3$ for $0 \leq m \leq 1$. Find:

a　the mean and variance of L　　　**d**　$\text{Var}(3M)$

b　the mean and variance of M　　　**e**　$E(2L + 3M)$

c　$E(4L - 1)$　　　　　　　　　　　**f**　$\text{Var}(3L - M)$

Solution

a　$\mu_l = \int_0^1 l 3l^2 \, dl$

$$= \left[\frac{3l^4}{4}\right]_0^1$$

$$= \frac{3}{4}$$

$$\sigma_l^2 = \int_0^1 l^2 3l^2 \, dl - \mu^2$$

$$= \left[\frac{3l^5}{5}\right]_0^1 - \left(\frac{3}{4}\right)^2$$

$$= \frac{3}{5} - \frac{9}{16}$$

$$= \frac{3}{80}$$

243

b $\mu_m = \displaystyle\int_0^1 m4m^3 \, dm$

$= \displaystyle\int_0^1 4m^4 \, dm$

$= \left[\dfrac{4m^5}{5}\right]_0^1$

$= \frac{4}{5}$

$\sigma_m^2 = \displaystyle\int_0^1 m^2 4m^3 \, dm - \mu^2$

$= \left[\dfrac{4m^6}{6}\right]_0^1 - \left(\frac{4}{5}\right)^2$

$= \frac{4}{6} - \frac{16}{25}$

$= \frac{2}{75}$

c $E(4L - 1) = 4E(L) - 1$

$= 4 \times \frac{3}{4} - 1$

$= 2$

d $\mathrm{Var}(3M) = 3^2 \, \mathrm{Var}(M)$

$= 9 \times \frac{2}{75}$

$= \frac{6}{25}$

e $E(2L + 3M) = 2E(L) + 3E(M)$

$= 2 \times \frac{3}{4} + 3 \times \frac{4}{5}$

$= 3\frac{9}{10}$

f $\mathrm{Var}(3L - M) = 3^2 \, \mathrm{Var}(L) + \mathrm{Var}(M)$

$= 9 \times \frac{3}{80} + \frac{2}{75}$

$= 0.364 \ (3 \text{ s.f.})$

9.4 Linear Combination of Random Variables

Exercise

Technique

1 A continuous random variable X is defined as $f(x) = \frac{1}{4}x^3$ for $0 \le x \le 2$.
Find:

a $E(X)$ **b** $E(2X)$ **c** $E(4X+1)$
d $\text{Var}(X)$ **e** $\text{Var}(3X)$

2 The probability density function of a continuous random variable is
$f(x) = \frac{5}{8}(1-x^4)$ for $-1 \le x \le 1$. Calculate:

a $E(X)$ **b** $E(3X+2)$ **c** $E(5X-3)$
d $\text{Var}(X)$ **e** $\text{Var}(2X-1)$

3 If X is a continuous random variable such that $f(x) = 4x^3$ for $0 \le x \le 1$,
and Y is also a continuous random variable such that $f(y) = \frac{3}{8}(y^2+1)$ for
$-1 \le y \le 1$, find:

a $E(X)$ **b** $E(2X+Y)$ **c** $E(3X-2Y)$
d $\text{Var}(X-Y)$ **e** $\text{Var}(2X+Y)$

4 A continuous random variable has probability density function
$f(x) = 10cx^2$ for $0 \le x \le 0.6$, and $f(x) = 9c(1-x)$ for $0.6 \le x \le 1$. Find:

a the value of c, and sketch the function
b $E(3X-4)$ **d** $\text{Var}(2X+3)$
c $E(2X+2)$ **e** $\text{Var}(4X-5)$

9.5 Uniform Distribution

The uniform distribution is a special continuous distribution function which is also known as the **rectangular distribution**.

The arrival times of trains are recorded to the nearest minute. The rounding error is the difference between the exact arrival time and the recorded time. This error will be in the range 0.5 minutes. All values in this range are equally likely. The probability distribution will look like this.

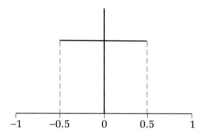

As all values are equally likely and the total area under the curve (the area of the rectangle) must be 1, the height of this rectangle will also be 1.

The probability density function is given as

$$f(x) = 1 \text{ where } -0.5 \leq x \leq 0.5$$

In general, the **uniform**, or **rectangular distribution**, is defined by

$$f(x) = \frac{1}{b-a}, \text{ where } a \leq x \leq b$$

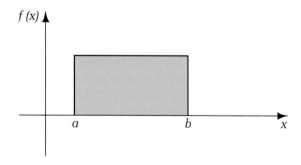

If X is a continuous random variable with a uniform, or rectangular, distribution we write this as

$$X \sim R(a, b)$$

where a and b are the constants representing the minimum and maximum values of the random variable.

Example 1

If $X \sim R(2, 5)$ write down the probability density function of X.
Find:

a $E(X)$ **b** $Var(X)$

Solution

$$f(x) = \frac{1}{(5-2)} = \tfrac{1}{3} \text{ for } 2 \leq x \leq 5$$

a If we sketch the probability density function it is clear that the function has symmetry. It is possible to state that the mean of X is 3.5.

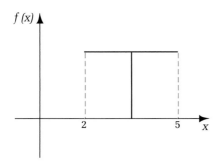

b $Var(X) = \displaystyle\int_{2}^{5} x^2 \tfrac{1}{3} dx - \mu^2$

$$= \tfrac{1}{3} \left[\frac{x^3}{3} \right]_{2}^{5} - (3.5)^2$$

$$= \tfrac{1}{3} \left[\left(\tfrac{125}{3} \right) - \left(\tfrac{8}{3} \right) \right] - 12.25$$

$$= 13 - 12.25$$

$$= 0.75$$

Let us now consider the general function

$$f(x) = \frac{1}{b-a} \text{ for } a \leq x \leq b$$

$$E(X) = \int_{a}^{b} x \frac{1}{b-a} \, dx$$

$$= \frac{1}{b-a} \left[\frac{x^2}{2} \right]_{a}^{b}$$

$$= \frac{1}{b-a} \left(\frac{b^2}{2} - \frac{a^2}{2} \right)$$

$$= \frac{1}{b-a} \left(\frac{b^2 - a^2}{2} \right)$$

$$= \frac{1}{b-a} \left(\frac{(b-a)(b+a)}{2} \right)$$

$$= \tfrac{1}{2}(b+a)$$

$$\text{Var}(X) = \int_a^b x^2 \frac{1}{b-a} \, dx - [E(X)]^2$$

$$= \frac{1}{b-a} \left[\frac{x^3}{3} \right]_a^b - [E(X)]^2$$

Remember

$$E(X) = \frac{b+a}{2}$$

$$= \frac{1}{b-a} \left(\frac{b^3}{3} - \frac{a^3}{3} \right) - [E(X)]^2$$

$$= \frac{1}{b-a} \left(\frac{(b^3 - a^3)}{3} \right) - \left(\frac{b+a}{2} \right)^2$$

$$= \frac{1}{b-a} \left(\frac{(b-a)(b^2 + ab + a^2)}{3} \right) - \left(\frac{b^2 + 2ab + a^2}{4} \right)$$

$$= \frac{b^2 + ab + a^2}{3} - \frac{b^2 + 2ab + a^2}{4}$$

$$= \frac{1}{12} [4(b^2 + ab + a^2) - 3(b^2 + 2ab + a^2)]$$

$$= \frac{1}{12} (4b^2 + 4ab + 4a^2 - 3b^2 - 6ab - 3a^2)$$

$$= \frac{1}{12} (b^2 - 2ab + a^2)$$

$$= \frac{1}{12} (b-a)^2$$

These calculations give us two very useful results for continuous uniform, or rectangular, distributions.

$$\mu = E(X) = \tfrac{1}{2}(a+b)$$

$$\text{Var}(X) = \tfrac{1}{12}(b-a)^2$$

Example 2

The continuous random variable K has a rectangular distribution such that $K \sim R(-2, 3)$. Give the probability density function for K. Find:

a   the mean of K **b**   the variance of K **c** $P(-1 < K < 1.5)$.

Solution

If $K \sim R(-2, 3)$ then $f(k) = \frac{1}{5}$, where $-2 \leq k \leq 3$.

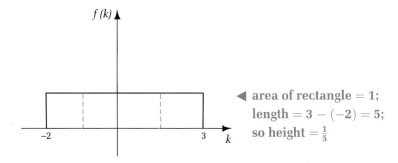

◀ area of rectangle $= 1$;
length $= 3 - (-2) = 5$;
so height $= \frac{1}{5}$

a   mean of $K = \frac{1}{2}(-2+3) = \frac{1}{2}$

b   variance of $K = \frac{1}{12}[3-(-2)]^2$

$$= \frac{1}{12}(5)^2$$

$$= \frac{25}{12}$$

c

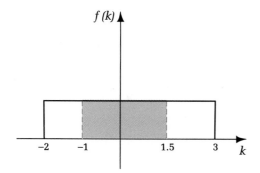

$P(-1 < K < 1.5) = $ area of the shaded rectangle

$$= \text{length} \times \text{height}$$

$$= [1.5 - (-1)] \times \frac{1}{5}$$

$$= 2.5 \times \frac{1}{5}$$

$$= 0.5$$

9.5 The Uniform Distribution
Exercise

Technique

1 X is a uniformly distributed continuous random variable, such that $X \sim R(0, 2)$. Find:

   a the probability density function of X
   b the mean and variance of the function
   c $P(0.5 \leq x \leq 1.25)$.

2 The continuous random variable Y has a rectangular distribution such that $Y \sim R(1.2, 2.4)$. Give the probability density function for Y. Find:

   a $E(Y)$ **b** $\text{Var}(Y)$ **c** $P(1.8 \leq y \leq 2.1)$.

3 M is a uniformly distributed continuous random variable such that $M \sim R(-1.3, 2.5)$. Find:

   a the probability density function of M
   b the mean of M
   c the variance of $2M$
   d $P(0 \leq m \leq 1)$.

4 Bags of sugar are weighed to the nearest 5 g. If W is the random variable 'the rounding error made when weighing the bags', describe the distribution of W. Find the mean and the variance of W.

5 The continuous random variable L has a uniform distribution such that $L \sim R(2.4, 4.8)$. Find:

   a the probability density function of L
   b $E(X)$ and $\text{Var}(X)$
   c $P(X \leq 3)$
   d $P(2.4 \leq X \leq 4.5)$.

Consolidation

Exercise A

1 The continuous random variable X has probability density function f given by

$$f(x) = kx(4 - x^2) \quad \text{for } 0 \leq x \leq 2,$$

$$f(x) = 0 \qquad \qquad \text{otherwise.}$$

a Show that $k = \frac{1}{4}$.

b Calculate the mean value of X.

(WJEC)

2 A continuous random variable X has probability density function $f(x) = \frac{1}{8}x$, for $0 \leq x \leq 4$, and a continuous random variable Y has probability density function $f(y) = 2(1 - y)$, for $0 < y < 1$. Find:

a $E(X)$ and $\text{Var}(X)$

b $E(Y)$ and $\text{Var}(Y)$

c $E(3X - 2Y)$

d $\text{Var}(2X + Y)$

3 The random variable T has probability density function given by,

$$f(t) = k(t - 2), \quad \text{for } 2 \leq t \leq 4,$$

$$f(t) = 0 \qquad \qquad \text{otherwise,}$$

where k is a constant.

a Find, in terms of k, the cumulative distribution function. Hence, or otherwise, find the value of k.

b Show that $P(T > 3) = \frac{3}{4}$.

c Find $E(T)$ and $\text{Var}(T)$.

(UCLES)

4 The time, T hours, taken for Mr Mulligan to travel to work can be adequately modelled by the probability distribution below.

$$f(t) = \begin{cases} 0 & t < 0 \\ 30t^4(1 - t) & 0 \leq t < 1 \\ 0 & 1 \leq t \end{cases}$$

a Find the mean time, in minutes, taken for the journey.

b Verify that the median time is approximately 44 minutes.

(NICCEA)

5 The random variable T represents the operational lifetime, in hundreds of hours, of a battery operated calculator. The probability density function of T is $f(t) = \frac{3}{250}(10t - t^2)$, for $5 \leq t \leq 10$, and $f(t) = 0$ otherwise.

a Find the cumulative distribution function of T.

b Calculate the probability that the operational lifetime of such a calculator will be between 600 and 800 hours.

(ULEAC)

6 A commuter travels into town by train and then has to catch a bus from the station to the office. The time, X minutes, that the commuter has to wait for the bus can be modelled by the probability density function

$$f(x) = \begin{cases} k & 0 \leq x \leq 4, \\ \frac{1}{2}k(6 - x) & 4 < x \leq 6, \\ 0 & \text{otherwise,} \end{cases}$$

where k is a constant.

a Sketch the graph of $f(x)$.

b Show that $k = 0.2$.

c Determine, for all x, the distribution function $F(x)$.

d Using $F(x)$, or your sketch, or otherwise, show that the probability that the commuter has to wait longer than $5\frac{1}{2}$ minutes for a bus is 0.0125.

(NEAB)

7 The continuous random variable L has probability density function $f(l) = l$ when $0 < l < 1$ and $f(l) = 2 - l$, when $1 < l < 2$. The continuous random variable K has probability density function $f(k) = \frac{1}{18}(6 - k)$ for $0 < k < 6$. Find:

a $E(L)$ and $\text{Var}(L)$ b $E(K)$ and $\text{Var}(K)$

c $E(L + 3K)$ d $\text{Var}(2L - 2K)$.

8 The continuous random variable X has probability density function $f(x) = \frac{3}{1024}x(x - 8)^2$, for $0 \leq x \leq 8$. A sketch of $f(x)$ is shown in the diagram. Find $E(X)$ and show that $\text{Var}(X) = 2.56$.

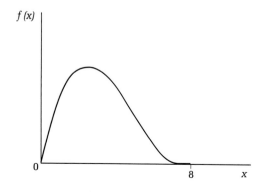

(OCSEB)

9 A gardener is attempting to light a bonfire. The time, in minutes, for which a taper will stay alight on a calm day is modelled by the random variable T. The cumulative distribution function of T is given by

$$F(t) = P(T \leq t) = \begin{cases} 0 & t < 0, \\ \frac{1}{2}t^3 - \frac{3}{16}t^4 & 0 \leq t \leq 2 \\ 1 & t > 2. \end{cases}$$

a   Find $P(T \leq 1)$.
b   Verify that the median m of T satisfies $1.22 < t < 1.23$
c   Find the probability density function $f(t)$ of T.
d   Sketch the probability density function.

(*ULEAC*)

10 The random variable, X, has a rectangular distribution with probability density function $f(x) = 0.5$, for $0 < x < 2$ and $f(x) = 0$ otherwise. What is the probability that X lies between 1 and 1.7?

(*AEB*)

Exercise B

1 A continuous random variable X has probability density function f given by $f(x) = \frac{2}{9}x$, for $0 \leq x \leq 3$, $f(x) = 0$, otherwise. Find the mean and the variance of X.

(*WJEC*)

2 A continuous random variable X has probability density function $f(x) = kx$ where $0 < x < 2$, and a continuous random variable Y has probability density function $f(y) = \frac{1}{4}y^3$ where $0 < y < 2$. Find:

a   the value of k and hence $E(X)$ and $\mathrm{Var}(X)$
b $E(Y)$ and $\mathrm{Var}(Y)$
c $E(2X - Y)$
d $\mathrm{Var}(3X - 2Y)$.

3 The continuous random variable X has cumulative distribution function F given by

$$F(x) = \begin{cases} 0 & \text{for } x \leq 0 \\ \sqrt{x} & \text{for } 0 < x < 1 \\ 1 & \text{for } x \geq 1 \end{cases}$$

Find the median of X. The probability density function of X is f. Write down an expression for $f(x)$, valid for $0 < x < 1$. Hence:

a   show that $E(X) = \frac{1}{3}$ b   find $\mathrm{Var}(X)$.

(*UCLES*)

4 The life-time, X years, of a fluorescent tube has a probability density function f given by $f(x) = k/x^3$ for $1 \leq x \leq 9$ and $f(x) = 0$, otherwise.

    a   Show that $k = 2.025$.

    b   Find the mean life-time of a tube.

    c   Determine, correct to three decimal places, the standard deviation of X.

    d   Calculate the probability that a tube lasts longer than five years.

(WJEC)

5 Every weekday Siobhan, a commuter, waits for a Rail-link bus to go from Belfast City Hall to Belfast Central Station. Buses arrive every 7 minutes. She tries to time her arrival at the bus stop with the scheduled arrival of the bus. This does not always work out, so the time, X, she has to wait, is a random variable, with linear probability density function as shown in Figure 1 below.

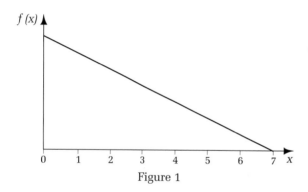

Figure 1

    a   Prove that the probability density function is defined by:

$$f(x) = \tfrac{2}{7} - \tfrac{2}{49}x \quad 0 \leqslant x \leqslant 7$$
$$ = 0 \qquad \text{otherwise}$$

    b   Find the probability that (on a particular day) she waits more than 5 minutes.

    c   Show that her expected waiting time is $2\tfrac{1}{3}$ minutes.

    d   Calculate the variance of the time that she waits.

    e   Comment on the suitability of this model.

(NICCEA)

6 The random variable X has probability density function $f(x) = a(x - x^3)$, for $0 \leq x \leq 1$, and $f(x) = 0$, otherwise.

    a   Show that $a = 4$.   **b**   Find $E(X)$.   **c**   Find $\text{Var}(X)$.

(ULEAC)

7 A continuous random variable X had probability density function $f(x) = 0.1x - 0.3$ for $4 < x < 6$ and $f(x) = 0.3$ for $6 < x < 8$. A continuous random variable Y has probability density function $f(y) = 3y^2$ for $0 < y < 1$. Find:

a $E(X)$ and $\text{Var}(X)$

b $E(Y)$ and $\text{Var}(Y)$

c $E(4X + 2Y)$

d $\text{Var}(X + Y)$.

8 The probability density function f of a continuous random variable X is given by $f(x) = k(\alpha - x)$, for $0 \le x \le \alpha$, and $f(x) = 0$, otherwise, where k and α are constants.

a Show that $k = 2/\alpha^2$.

b Show that the mean of X is $\alpha/3$.

c Find, in terms of α, the variance of X.

(*NEAB*)

9 The weekly demand for petrol, in thousands of litres, at a garage is a random variable X, with probability density function

$$f(x) = \tfrac{3}{4}x^2(2 - x) \quad 0 \le x \le 2$$
$$f(x) = 0 \qquad\qquad \text{otherwise.}$$

The storage tanks at the garage can only be filled at the beginning of each week and are always filled to their total capacity of 1900 litres.

a Find the probability that in any week the storage tanks will run dry.

b Calculate, in litres, the mean and the standard deviation of the weekly demand for petrol.

(*ULEAC*)

10 The lifetime, in tens of hours, of a certain delicate electrical component is modelled by the random variable X with probability density function

$$f(x) = k(9 - x) \quad 0 \le x \le 9$$
$$f(x) = 0 \qquad\qquad \text{otherwise}$$

where k is a positive constant.

a Show that $k = \frac{2}{81}$.

b Find the mean lifetime of a component.

c Show that the standard deviation of lifetimes is 21.2 hours.

d Find the probability that the component lasts at most 50 hours.

(*ULEAC*)

Applications and Activites

1 Research the trapezium rule and examine how it may be applied to aspects of this chapter.

2 Research the work of Gauss and its relevance to continuous data.

Summary

- If X is a continuous random variable then

  - $$\int_{-\infty}^{\infty} f(x)\,dx = 1$$
  - $$\mu = E(X) = \int_{-\infty}^{\infty} xf(x)\,dx$$

  - $$\sigma^2 = \text{Var}(X) = \int_{-\infty}^{\infty} x^2 f(x)\,dx - \mu^2$$

- If $F(x)$ is the cumulative distribution function then

  - $0 \le F(x) \le 1$

  - $$F(x) = \int_{-\infty}^{\infty} f(x)\,dx$$

  - $$f(x) = \frac{d}{dx} F(x)$$

  - the median m is such that $F(m) = 0.5$

- For discrete or continuous random variables the general rules for expectation (E) and variance (Var) are:

  $$E(aX) = aE(X)$$

  $$E(aX + b) = aE(X) + b$$

  $$\text{Var}(aX) = a^2 \text{Var}(X)$$

  $$\text{Var}(aX + b) = a^2 \text{Var}(X)$$

  $$E(aX \pm bY) = aE(X) \pm bE(Y)$$

  $$\text{Var}(aX \pm bY) = a^2 \text{Var}(X) + b^2 \text{Var}(Y)$$
  $$\text{if } X \text{ and } Y \text{ are independent}$$

- If $X \sim R(a, b)$ then

  $$E(X) = \tfrac{1}{2}(a + b) \qquad\qquad \text{Var}(X) = \tfrac{1}{12}(b - a)^2$$

10 The Normal Distribution

What you need to know

- The definition of a continuous random variable.

- The properties of a binomial distribution.

- The properties of a Poisson distribution.

Review

State whether each of the following could be modelled by a binomial or Poisson distribution.

1 The number of cars passing the front of an office block every fifteen minutes.

2 The number of sixes obtained when a dice is thrown seven times.

3 The number of multiple-choice questions a student answers correctly on a paper with 20 such questions.

4 The number of times a student arrives late in any one week.

5 The number of telephone calls to the school office every 30 minutes.

10.1 The Normal Distribution

A large number of 1 kg bags of sugar are weighed to check how accurately they have been filled, and the results are shown in the histogram below.

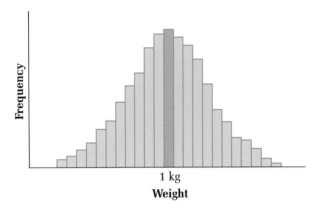

Weight
1 kg

This histogram is similar to the histograms you might obtain for a variety of different types of data, such as heights of sixth form students. The most important features of this histogram are:

●   it is (almost) symmetrical about the mean

●   there are more values close to the mean than further away from the mean.

If a smooth curve is drawn thorough the tops of the columns this will give a distribution which is roughly 'bell'-shaped.

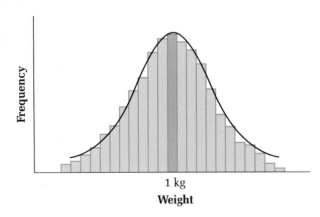

Weight
1 kg

Such a distribution can be modelled by the **normal distribution**.

For a continuous random variable X, with mean μ and standard deviation σ, the normal distribution curve has probability density function

$$f(x) = \frac{1}{\sigma\sqrt{2\pi}}e^{-(x-\mu)^2/2\sigma^2}, \text{ for } -\infty < x < \infty$$

The Normal Distribution, originally called the 'Error Law', arose from the work of 18th century mathematicians and astronomers when calculating the orbits of stars and planets. They found that they had to take into account the effect of observational error. This law describes how values that the mathematicians and astronomers observed were clustered around their average and gave the watchers estimates of the chances of an error of a given size.

This function is extremely complex and is beyond the scope of this book. However, the normal distribution is an extremely important distribution in the study and interpretation of statistics.

As the values of μ and σ vary, so the shape of the curve will change, although it will always retain its characteristic bell shape.

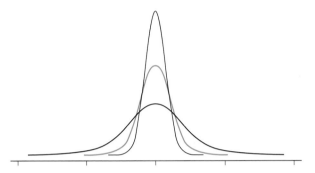

In each example the area under the curve is equal to one. This follows the results of the previous chapter. The 'peak' occurs at the mean, μ, and the value of the standard deviation, σ, determines how spread out the curve will be.

It is true, however, that for all these different normal curves almost all the values lie within ± 3 standard deviations of the mean, approximately 95% of all values lie within ± 2 standard deviations of the mean, and approximately two-thirds of all values lie within ± 1 standard deviation of the mean.

If a continuous random variable, X, has a normal distribution it is written

$$X \sim N(\mu, \sigma^2)$$

The distribution is defined by its mean, μ, and variance, σ^2.

As a normal distribution curve is a continuous distribution the probability that X lies between a and b can be calculated by finding the area under the curve between the values a and b. $P(a < X < b)$ equals the area shown.

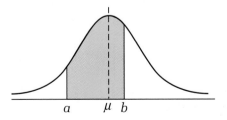

The area under the normal distribution curve can be calculated using numerical methods. These are the values given in normal distribution tables. The tables give the area under the **standard normal curve**.

Karl Freidrich Gauss (1777–1855)
A German mathematician, regarded with Newton and Archimedes, as one of the greatest mathematicians of all time. As well as his work on the normal distribution, he made discoveries in number theory, complex numbers, algebra, electricity and magnetism.

Lambert Adolphe Jacque Quetelet (1796–1874)
A Belgian statistician and astronomer, Quetelet applied the 'law', that is the Normal Distribution or 'Error Law' which takes into account the effect of observational error, to every aspect of his work in Social Science, including marriage, crime and even measurements of the human body. He drew conclusions from the supposed constancy of his data and came up with the abstract notion of the 'average man'. He is also credited, along with Dandelin, for the discovery of the relationship between a conic section and tangent spheres in its circular cone.

The **standard normal curve** is the special normal distribution where $\mu = 0$ and $\sigma = 1$ and is written

$$Z \sim N(0, 1^2)$$

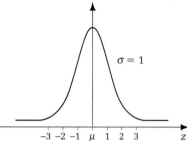

All normal distributions can be mapped onto the standard normal curve by the process known as **standardising**.

In order to use the standard normal tables it is necessary to convert a distribution to a standard normal distribution. This is done by calculating the value of z using:

$$z = \frac{X - \mu}{\sigma}$$

z is the number of standard deviation unit from the mean.

The standard normal tables give the cumulative area under the curve.

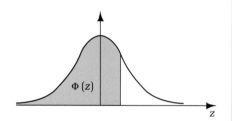

Cumulative probability is written

$$\Phi(z) = P(Z < z)$$

Φ is the Greek letter ph

Normal Distribution Function
The tabulated value is $\Phi(z) = P(Z \leq z)$, where Z
is the standardised normal random variable, $N(0, 1)$

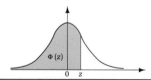

z	0.00	0.01	0.02	0.03	0.04	0.05	0.06	0.07	0.08	0.09
1.0	0.84134	0.84375	0.84614	0.84849	0.85083	0.85314	0.85543	0.85769	0.85993	0.86214
1.1	0.86433	0.86650	0.86864	0.87076	0.87286	0.87493	0.87698	0.87900	0.88100	0.88298
1.2	0.88493	0.88686	0.88877	0.89065	0.89251	0.89435	0.89617	0.89796	0.89973	0.90147
1.3	0.90320	0.90490	0.90658	0.90824	0.90988	0.91149	0.91309	0.91466	0.91621	0.91774
1.4	0.91924	0.92073	0.92220	0.92364	0.92507	0.92647	0.92785	0.92922	0.93056	0.93189
1.5	0.93319	0.93448	0.93574	0.93699	0.93822	0.93943	0.94062	0.94179	0.94295	0.94408
1.6	0.94520	0.94630	0.94738	0.94845	0.94950	0.95053	0.95154	0.95254	0.95352	0.95449
1.7	0.95543	0.95637	0.95728	0.95818	0.95907	0.95994	0.96080	0.96164	0.96246	0.96327
1.8	0.96407	0.96485	0.96562	0.96638	0.96712	0.96784	0.96856	0.96926	0.96995	0.97062
1.9	0.97128	0.97193	0.97257	0.97320	0.97381	0.97441	0.97500	0.97558	0.97615	0.97670
2.0	0.97725	0.97778	0.97831	0.97882	0.97932	0.97982	0.98030	0.98077	0.98124	0.98169

From the extract of the tables you can see that when $z = 1.6$, $\Phi(z) = 0.945\,20$. This means that the area under the normal curve to the left of 1.6 is 0.945 20, or $P(z < 1.6) = 0.945\,20$.

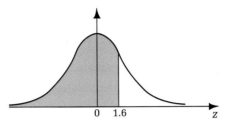

It is a good idea to sketch the normal curve to help you to answer each question as you can see clearly the area you are trying to calculate.

Example 1

Find the area under the standard normal curve:

a   between 1 and 2 standard deviations from the mean
b   between 0.5 and 1.5 standard deviations from the mean.

Solution

a   The area to the left of
$z = 2$ is 0.977 25,
and the area to the left of
$z = 1$ is 0.841 34.

Therefore the area between
$z = 1$ and $z = 2$ is

$\Phi(2) - \Phi(1)$

$= 0.977\,25 - 0.841\,34$

$= 0.135\,91$

b   shaded area

$= $ (area up to $z = 1.5$)

$\quad - $ (area up to $z = 0.5$)

$= \Phi(1.5) - \Phi(0.5)$

$= 0.993\,19 - 0.691\,46$

$= 0.241\,73$

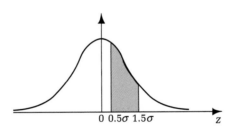

From this diagram we can see that to find the area under the normal curve for $z > 1.5$ we have to find the area under the curve for $z < 1.5$ and subtract this value from 1.

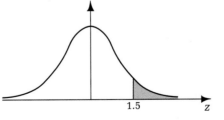

shaded area $= 1 - \Phi(1.5)$

$= 1 - 0.993\,19$

$= 0.006\,81$

Remember that the total area under the curve equals 1.

Example 2

Find the area under the curve which is more than:

a   1 standard deviation above the mean
b   2.4 standard deviations above the mean.

Solution

First draw a sketch to show the area required.

a

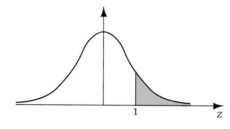

$$\text{shaded area} = 1 - \Phi(1)$$

$$= 1 - 0.841\,34$$

$$= 0.158\,66$$

b

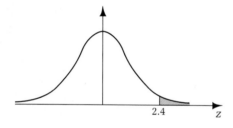

$$z > 2.4 = 1 - \Phi(2.4)$$

$$= 1 - 0.991\,80$$

$$= 0.0082$$

You will have noticed that the normal tables only give values of $\Phi(z)$ for $z \geq 0$. It is straightforward to work out values for $z < 0$ if you remember that the normal curve is symmetrical about the mean, or $z = 0$.

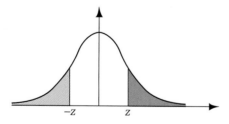

From the diagrams, it can be seen that $\Phi(-z)$ has the same area as $1 - \Phi(z)$. This result allows us to calculate the area under any section of the curve.

Example 3

Find the area under the normal curve that is less than:

a 1 standard deviation below the mean
b 1.75 standard deviations below the mean.

Solution

a

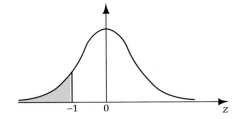

$$\Phi(-1) = 1 - \Phi(1)$$

$$= 1 - 0.841\,34$$

$$= 0.158\,66$$

b

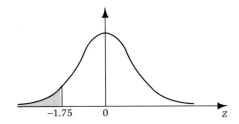

$$\Phi(-1.75) = 1 - \Phi(1.75)$$

$$= 1 - 0.959\,94$$

$$= 0.040\,06$$

The normal curve represents a continuous random variable, and in the previous chapter we found that the area under a continuous distribution curve gives the probability of that random variable lying between any two values.

Example 4

Using normal distribution tables, find:

a $P(Z < 0.75)$ **b** $P(Z > 1.25)$
c $P(Z < -1.4)$ **d** $P(Z > -2)$

Solution

a

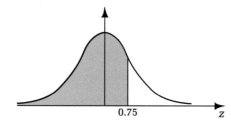

$$P(Z < 0.75) = \Phi(0.75)$$
$$= 0.773\,37$$

b

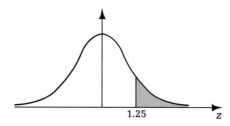

$$P(Z > 1.25) = 1 - \Phi(1.25)$$
$$= 1 - 0.894\,35$$
$$= 0.105\,65$$

c

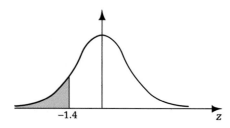

$$P(Z < -1.4) = 1 - \Phi(1.4)$$
$$= 1 - 0.919\,24$$
$$= 0.080\,76$$

d

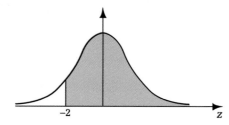

$$P(Z > -2) = P(Z < 2)$$
$$= \Phi(2)$$
$$= 0.977\,25$$

Example 5

Z is a random variable such that $Z \sim N(0, 1^2)$. Find:

a $P(Z < 0.5)$ **b** $P(0.5 < Z < 2.5)$

c $P(-1.5 < Z < 1.65)$ **d** $P(-2.3 < Z < -0.46)$

Solution

a

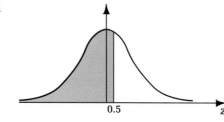

$$P(Z < 0.5) = \Phi(0.5)$$
$$= 0.691\,46$$

b

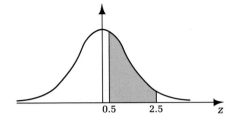

$$P(0.5 < Z < 2.5) = \Phi(2.5) - \Phi(0.5)$$

$$= 0.993\,79 - 0.691\,46$$

$$= 0.302\,33$$

c

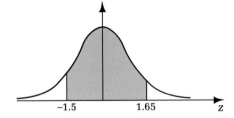

$$P(-1.5 < Z < 1.65) = \Phi(1.65) - \Phi(-1.5)$$

$$= \Phi(1.65) - [1 - \Phi(1.5)]$$

$$= 0.950\,53 - (1 - 0.933\,19)$$

$$= 0.950\,53 - 0.066\,81$$

$$= 0.883\,72$$

d

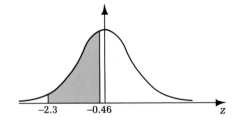

$$P(-2.3 < Z < -0.46) = \Phi(-0.46) - \Phi(-2.3)$$

$$= [1 - \Phi(0.46)] - [1 - \Phi(2.3)]$$

$$= (1 - 0.677\,24) - (1 - 0.989\,28)$$

$$= 0.322\,76 - 0.010\,72$$

$$= 0.312\,04$$

10.1 The Normal Distribution
Exercise

Technique

If $Z \sim N(0, 1^2)$, find the following, by first sketching the required area.

1 $P(Z > 1.23)$

2 $P(Z < 0.92)$

3 $P(Z < -1.37)$

4 $P(Z > 2.04)$

5 $P(0 < Z < 1.86)$

6 $P(0.14 < Z < 0.98)$

7 $P(-1.63 < Z < 0.04)$

8 $P(-2.22 < Z < -0.37)$

9 $P(-1.07 < Z < 2.66)$

10 $P(0.37 < Z < 1.71)$

For the following values of $\Phi(z)$ find the corresponding value of z.

11 $\Phi(z) = 0.5$

12 $\Phi(z) = 0.989\,28$

13 $\Phi(z) = 0.848\,49$

14 $\Phi(z) = 0.997\,74$

15 $\Phi(z) = 0.975$

10.2 Standardising Normal Distributions

The exact amount of fizzy drink in two-litre bottles is normally distributed with mean 2 litres and standard deviation 0.05 litres. How can we find the proportion of bottles containing more than 2.1 litres?

If C is the random variable, 'capacity of one bottle', then $C \sim N(2, 0.05^2)$.

$\mu = 2, \sigma^2 = 0.05^2$

We need to find the probability that C is greater than 2.1, that is $P(C > 2.1)$.

In order to use the standard normal tables, it is necessary to standardise this distribution.

$$Z = \frac{X - 2}{0.05}$$

This gives

$$P(C > 2.1) = P\left(Z > \frac{2.1 - 2}{0.05}\right)$$

$$= P(Z > 2)$$

$$= 1 - \Phi(2)$$

$$= 1 - 0.977\,25$$

$$= 0.022\,75$$

Remember that the formula for standardising is
$$z = \frac{X - \mu}{\sigma}$$

The probability that a bottle, chosen at random, contains more than 2.1 litres is 0.022 75, therefore the proportion of bottles that might be expected to contain more than 2.1 litres is 2.275%.

Example 1

The random variable $X \sim N(12, 2^2)$. Find:

a $P(X < 15)$ b $P(X > 10)$

c $P(9 < X < 13)$ d $P(11.5 < X < 14.3)$

Solution

A sketch will help by showing the area required.

a

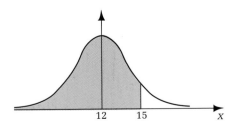

First, the distribution must be standardised

$$z = \frac{X - 12}{2}$$

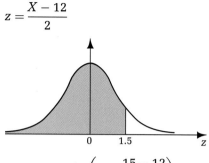

$$P(X < 15) = P\left(Z < \frac{15 - 12}{2}\right)$$

$$= P(Z < 1.5)$$

$$= \Phi(1.5)$$

$$= 0.933\,19$$

b

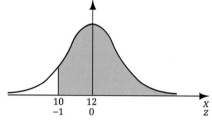

$$P(X > 10) = P\left(Z > \frac{10 - 12}{2}\right)$$

$$= P(Z > -1)$$

$$= 1 - \Phi(-1)$$

$$= \Phi(1)$$

$$= 0.841\,34$$

c

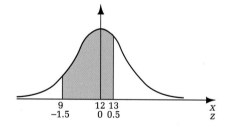

$$P(9 < X < 13) = P\left(\frac{9 - 12}{2} < Z < \frac{13 - 12}{2}\right)$$

$$= P(-1.5 < Z < 0.5)$$

$$= \Phi(0.5) - [1 - \Phi(1.5)]$$

$$= 0.691\,46 - (1 - 0.933\,19)$$

$$= 0.691\,46 - 0.066\,81$$

$$= 0.624\,65$$

d

$$P(11.5 < X < 1.43) = P\left(\frac{11.5 - 12}{2} < Z < \frac{14.3 - 12}{2}\right)$$

$$= P(-0.25 < Z < 1.15)$$

$$= \Phi(1.15) - \Phi(-0.25)$$

$$= \Phi(1.15) - [1 - \Phi(0.25)]$$

$$= 0.874\,93 - (1 - 0.598\,71)$$

$$= 0.874\,93 - 0.401\,29$$

$$= 0.473\,64$$

Example 2

The random variable $Y \sim N(8, 5^2)$.

Find: **a** the value of d where $P(Y < d) = 0.959\,07$

     b the value of d where $P(Y > d) = 0.329\,97$

Solution

a

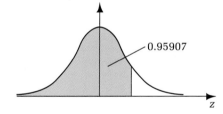

If $\Phi(z) = 0.95907$

$$z = 1.74$$

$$P(Y < d) = P\left(z < \frac{d - 8}{5}\right)$$

$$z = \frac{d - 8}{5}$$

$$1.74 = \frac{d - 8}{5}$$

$$d - 8 = 8.7$$

$$d = 16.7$$

b

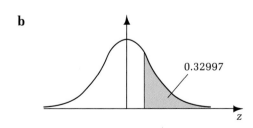

$$\Phi(z) = 1 - 0.329\,97$$

$$= 0.670\,003$$

$$z = 0.44$$

$$P(Y > d) = P\left(z > \frac{d - 8}{5}\right)$$

$$z = \frac{d - 8}{5}$$

$$0.44 = \frac{d - 8}{5}$$

$$d - 8 = 2.2$$

$$d = 10.2$$

10.2 Standardising Normal Distributions

Exercise

Technique

1 If $X \sim N(45, 12^2)$, find:

   a $P(X < 54)$ **d** $P(X < 39.96)$

   b $P(X > 42)$ **e** $P(43.56 < X < 47.4)$

   c $P(X > 48.6)$ **f** $P(38.16 < X < 44.52)$

2 If $X \sim N(150, 22^2)$, find:

   a $P(X < 164.08)$ **d** $P(X < 148.24)$

   b $P(X > 157.04)$ **e** $P(146.7 < X < 157.7)$

   c $P(X > 140.1)$ **f** $P(141.2 < X < 196.2)$

3 If $Y \sim N(89, 6^2)$, find:

   a $P(Y < 92)$ **d** $P(Y < 91.22)$

   b $P(Y > 80)$ **e** $P(89.6 < Y < 93.5)$

   c $P(Y > 87.5)$ **f** $P(81.62 < Y < 86.42)$

4 $Y \sim N(16, 2^2)$. Find the value of a in the following:

   a $P(Y < a) = 0.983\,00$ **b** $P(Y < a) = 0.807\,85$

   c $P(Y > a) = 0.149\,17$ **d** $P(Y > a) = 0.440\,38$

5 $Y \sim N(200, 12^2)$. Find the value of c in the following:

   a $P(Y < c) = 0.725\,75$ **b** $P(Y < c) = 0.988\,09$

   c $P(Y > c) = 0.004\,94$ **d** $P(Y > c) = 0.329\,97$

Contextual

1 The lengths of a particular species of worm are normally distributed with mean 21 cm and standard deviation 1.5 cm. Find the probability that a worm selected at random is:

   a   less than 23.4 cm long

   b   more than 19.8 cm long

   c   between 18 cm and 24 cm long.

2 The length of time patients have to wait in Dr Booth's waiting room is known to be normally distributed with mean 14 minutes, and standard deviation 4 minutes. Find the probability that I will have to wait more than 20 minutes to see the doctor. What proportion of patients wait less than 10 minutes?

3 Packets of breakfast cereal are said to contain 550 g. The manufacturer knows that the weights are normally distributed with mean 551.2 g, and standard deviation 15 g. What proportion of packets will contain more than the stated weight?

4 A biologist has studied a particular tropical insect and she has discovered that its lifespan is normally distributed. The mean lifespan of this insect is 72 days, and the standard deviation of its lifespan is eight days. Find the probability that the next insect studied lives:

    a fewer than 70 days   **b** more than 76 days
    c between 68 and 78 days.

5 The heights of the girls at a particular college are normally distributed with mean 166 cm and standard deviation 4 cm. Find the probability that if a student is chosen at random her height will be:

    a less than 165 cm   **b** more than 170 cm
    c between 163 cm and 168 cm.

6 $X \sim N(40, \sigma^2)$ and $P(X > 50) = 0.119$. Find the value of σ.

7 $X \sim N(\mu, 5^2)$ and $P(X < 30.7) = 0.909\,88$. Find the value of μ.

8 The lengths of metal bolts are normally distributed with mean μ cm and standard deviation 7 cm. If 2.5% of the bolts measure more than 68 cm, find the value of μ.

10.3 Linear Combination of Independent Normal Variables

In Chapter 9 the linear combination of continuous random variables was considered. When two independent normal variables are combined in a linear function the new function is itself normally distributed.

Breakfast cereals are packaged in boxes with a mean weight of 500 g and standard deviation 10 g. It is known that the weights are normally distributed. Ten of these packets fit inside a large carton. The weights of the cartons are also normally distributed with mean weight 700 g and standard deviation 15 g. What is the probability that a full carton will weight between 5.6 kg and 5.8 kg?

X is the random variable 'weight of one cereal packet'.
C is the random variable 'weight of one empty carton'.
T is the random variable 'total weight of one carton containing 10 packets of cereal'.

Let $X \sim N(500, 10^2)$ and $C \sim N(700, 15^2)$ and $T = X_1 + X_2 + X_3 + \cdots + X_{10} + C$

The random variables X and C are independent.

$$E(T) = 10E(X) + E(C)$$
$$= 10 \times 500 + 700$$
$$= 5000 + 700$$
$$= 5700 \text{ g}$$
$$\text{Var}(T) = 10\,\text{Var}(X) + \text{Var}(C)$$
$$= 10 \times 10^2 + 15^2$$
$$= 1000 + 225$$
$$= 1225$$

Therefore $T \sim N(5700, 1225)$

This can also be written as $T \sim N(5700, 35^2)$

The probability that a full carton weighs between 5.6 kg and 5.8 kg can be found as follows:

$$P(5600 < X < 5800) = P\left(\frac{5600 - 5700}{\sqrt{1225}} < Z < \frac{5800 - 5700}{\sqrt{1225}}\right)$$
$$= P(-2.86 < Z < 2.86)$$
$$= \Phi(2.86) - \Phi(-2.86)$$
$$= 0.997\,88 - 0.002\,12$$
$$= 0.995\,76$$

Values of Z are rounded to two decimal places.

The general result can be written as

> If X_1 and X_2 are independent random variables that are normally distributed as $X_1 \sim N(\mu_1, \sigma_1^2)$ and $X_2 \sim N(\mu_2, \sigma_2^2)$, then
>
> $$X_1 \pm X_2 \sim N(\mu_1 \pm \mu_2, \sigma_1^2 + \sigma_2^2)$$

Example 1

If $X \sim N(35, 0.5^2)$ and $Y \sim N(25, 0.2^2)$, find the distribution of W where:

a $\quad W = X + Y$ $\qquad\qquad$ **b** $\quad W = X - Y$

Solution

a $\quad E(W) = E(X) + E(Y)$

$\qquad\qquad = 35 + 25$

$\qquad\qquad = 60$

$\quad \text{Var}(W) = \text{Var}(X) + \text{Var}(Y)$

$\qquad\qquad = 0.5^2 + 0.2^2$

$\qquad\qquad = 0.29$

$\qquad W \sim N(60, 0.29)$

b $\quad E(W) = E(X) - E(Y)$

$\qquad\qquad = 35 - 25$

$\qquad\qquad = 10$

$\quad \text{Var}(W) = \text{Var}(X) + \text{Var}(Y)$

$\qquad\qquad = 0.5^2 + 0.2^2$

$\qquad\qquad = 0.29$

$\qquad W \sim N(10, 0.29)$

In the problem about cereal boxes, the standardised value was rounded off to two decimal places so that normal tables could be used. For most purposes the value obtained by rounding off will be sufficiently accurate. Sometimes it is necessary to use more than two decimal places. In such circumstances the process used is known as **interpolation**.

If $z = 1.275$, then as 1.275 lies between 1.27 and 1.28, $\Phi(z)$ will lie between $\Phi(1.27) = 0.897\,96$ and $\Phi(1.28) = 0.899\,73$.

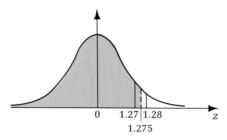

Therefore

$$\Phi(1.275) = 0.897\,96 + \tfrac{5}{10}(0.899\,73 - 0.897\,96)$$

$$= 0.897\,96 + 0.000\,885$$

$$= 0.898\,85 \ (5 \text{ d.p.})$$

Similarly to find $\Phi(0.3265)$

$$\Phi(0.32) = 0.625\,52 \text{ and } \Phi(0.33) = 0.629\,30$$

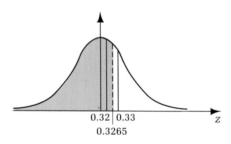

Therefore

$$\Phi(0.3265) = 0.625\,52 + \tfrac{65}{100}(0.629\,30 - 0.625\,52)$$

$$= 0.625\,52 + 0.002\,457$$

$$= 0.627\,98 \ (5 \text{ d.p.})$$

(Some calculators can work out these values directly.)

1.275 is $\tfrac{5}{10}$ of the difference between 1.27 and 1.28 so we must add $\tfrac{5}{10}$ of the difference between $\Phi(1.27)$ and $\Phi(1.28)$.

0.3265 is $\tfrac{65}{100}$ of the difference between 0.32 and 0.33.

Check to see if your calculator has this facility.

Example 2

If $A \sim N(100, 5^2)$ and $B \sim N(75, 4^2)$, find:

a $P((A + B) < 174)$ b $P(173 < (A + B) < 176)$

c $P((A - B) > 26)$ d $P((A - B) < 22)$

Solution

a $(A + B) \sim N(100 + 75, 5^2 + 4^2)$

$(A + B) \sim N(175, 41)$

$$P((A + B) < 174) = P\left(Z < \frac{174 - 175}{\sqrt{41}}\right)$$

$$= P(Z < -0.1562)$$

$$= 1 - \Phi(0.1562)$$

Rounding z to four decimal places is sufficient.
Use interpolation to find the value of $\Phi(0.1562)$.

From tables $\Phi(0.15) = 0.559\,62$ and $\Phi(0.16) = 0.563\,56$

$$\Phi(0.1562) = 0.559\,62 + \tfrac{62}{100}(0.563\,56 - 0.559\,62)$$

$$= 0.559\,62 + 0.002\,442\,8$$

$$= 0.562\,06$$

$$P((A + B) < 174) = 1 - \Phi(0.1562)$$

$$= 1 - 0.562\,06$$

$$= 0.437\,94$$

b

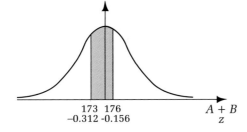

$$P(173 < (A + B) < 176) = P\left(\frac{173 - 175}{\sqrt{41}} < Z < \frac{176 - 175}{\sqrt{41}}\right)$$

$$= P(-0.3123 < Z < 0.1562)$$

$$= \Phi(0.1562) - \Phi(-0.3123)$$

$$= 0.562\,06 - (1 - \Phi(0.3123))$$

$$= 0.562\,06 - (1 - 0.622\,59)$$

$$= 0.562\,06 - 0.377\,41$$

$$= 0.184\,65$$

c $(A - B) \sim N(100 - 75, 5^2 + 4^2)$

$(A - B) \sim N(25, 41)$

$$P((A - B) > 26) = P\left(Z > \frac{26 - 25}{\sqrt{41}}\right)$$

$$= P(Z > 0.1562)$$

$$= 1 - \Phi(0.1562)$$

Using interpolation as in **a**,

$$= 1 - 0.562\,06$$

$$= 0.437\,94$$

d

$$P((A - B) < 22) = P\left(Z < \frac{22 - 25}{\sqrt{41}}\right)$$

$$= P(Z < -0.4685)$$

$$= \Phi(-0.4685)$$

$$= 1 - \Phi(0.4685)$$

$$= 1 - 0.680\,29$$

$$= 0.319\,71$$

10.3 Linear Combination of Independent Normal Variables

Exercise

Technique

1 If $C \sim N(55, 2^2)$ and $D \sim N(48, 1.5^2)$ find the probability that:

a $C + D > 104.5$ **b** $C + D < 99.8$

c $C - D > 8.2$ **d** $C - D < 7.1$

2 If $A \sim N(140, 10^2)$ and $B \sim N(105, 5^2)$ find the probability that:

a $A + B > 250$ **b** $A + B < 235$

c $A - B < 34$ **d** $A - B > 37$

3 If $X \sim N(30, 3^2)$ and $Y \sim N(20, 2^2)$ find the following probabilities:

a $P((X + Y) < 51)$ **b** $P((X + Y) > 48)$

c $P((X - Y) < 9.5)$ **d** $P((X - Y) > 10.4)$

Contextual

1 The weights of eggs are normally distributed with a mean weight of 57 g and standard deviation 3 g. Six of these eggs are packed in a box whose weight is normally distributed with mean 21 g and standard deviation 2 g. What are the mean and variance of the weight of a box containing six eggs? Find the probability that the total weight of a box of six eggs will be:

a less than 360 g

b more than 370 g.

2 The time it takes Moray to walk to the bus stop is normally distributed with mean 12 minutes and standard deviation 3 minutes. His bus journey to school is a normal variable with mean 24 minutes and standard deviation 5 minutes. Find the mean and the variance for the total time taken for Moray to travel to school. What is the probability that on Monday it will take him less than 40 minutes for the total journey?

3 The mean lifespan of a battery is 230 hours with standard deviation 22 hours, and the lifespan is known to be normally distributed. If my torch requires two of these batteries, what is the probability that the torch will work for more than 500 hours?

4 The weight of a bottle of red wine is normally distributed with mean 1.2 kg and standard deviation 200 g. Cartons that can hold six bottles have a mean weight of 190 g and standard deviation of 20 g. The weight of the cartons is normally distributed. What are the mean weight and standard deviation of a carton containing six bottles of wine? Find the probability that a carton of six bottles will weigh more than 7.4 kg.

5 The heights of the girls in a sixth form are normally distributed with mean 166 cm and standard deviation 6 cm. The heights of the boys are similarly distributed with mean 172 cm and standard deviation 8 cm. If a boy and girl are chosen at random, what is the probability that:

a   the girl is taller than the boy
b   the boy is at least 4 cm taller than the girl?

6 Thornes Fancy Cakes are packed in boxes of four. The weight of each cake is normally distributed with mean 30 g and standard deviation 5 g. The packets are also normally distributed with mean 16 g and standard deviation 4 g. Find the mean and variance of the weight of a packet of four cakes. What is the probability that a packet of four cakes has a weight of less than 130 g?

10.4 Normal Distribution as an Approximation to a Binomial Distribution

Consider the experiment of throwing a coin and recording the number of heads obtained. This can be modelled using a binomial distribution with $p = 0.5$ and $n =$ number of trials. When $n = 10$ the following distribution is obtained.

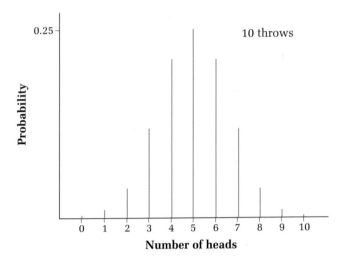

When $n = 20$ the following distribution is obtained.

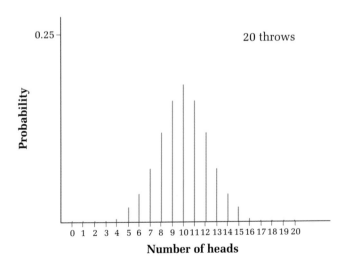

When $n = 30$ the following distribution is obtained.

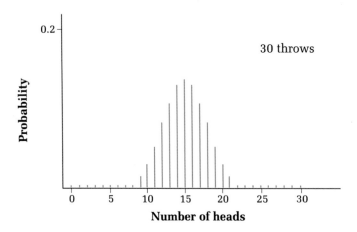

When $n = 50$ the following distribution is obtained.

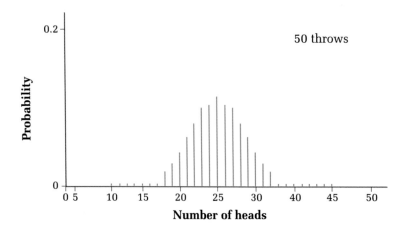

As the number of trials increases the distribution takes on the bell-shape of a normal distribution. This occurs quite quickly when $p = 0.5$ as we know that the binomial distribution is symmetrical for this value of p. However, when $p \neq 0.5$ it can be shown that as the number of trials increases the distribution will also tend to the bell-shape of the normal distribution.

This result is extremely helpful as it enable us to calculate binomial probabilities for large values of n, which would be very tedious using the binomial distribution.

Before we can rewrite a binomial distribution as a normal distribution there is one problem we must solve. You will recall that the binomial is a discrete distribution, whereas the normal distribution is a continuous distribution.

Thinking back to the coin throwing experiment, if we want to find the probability of at most five heads then we must find $P(X \leq 5)$.

In a continuous distribution $X \leq 5$ will equate to $X < 5.5$, so

$$P(X \leq 5) \rightarrow P(X < 5.5)$$

Similarly

$$P(X < 5) \rightarrow P(X < 4.5)$$

These results, together with other examples give:

Discrete variables		Continuous variables
$P(X \leq 5)$	$\rightarrow$	$P(X < 5.5)$
$P(X < 5)$	$\rightarrow$	$P(X < 4.5)$
$P(X \geq 5)$	$\rightarrow$	$P(X > 4.5)$
$P(X > 5)$	$\rightarrow$	$P(X > 5.5)$
$P(X = 5)$	$\rightarrow$	$P(4.5 < X < 5.5)$

This is known as the **continuity correction**, and must be used whenever a discrete distribution is approximated by a continuous distribution.

Remember in a continuous distribution probabilities lie within a *range*.

Example 1

When a coin is thrown 40 times, what is the probability that it will land head up fewer than 15 times?

Solution

If X is the random variable 'the number of times the coin lands head up', then

$$X \sim B(40, 0.5)$$

$$P(X < 15) = P(X \leq 14) = {}^{40}C_{14}(0.5)^{14}(0.5)^{26} + {}^{40}C_{13}(0.5)^{13}(0.5)^{27} + \cdots$$

This is quite time consuming to work out so an alternative method would be helpful.

If we use a normal distribution to represent the variable X then $X \sim N(\mu, \sigma^2)$.

$$\mu = E(X) = np, \text{ and } \sigma^2 = \text{Var}(X) = npq, \text{ where } q = 1 - p$$

See Chapter 8, Section 8.4 for the mean and variance of a binomial distribution.

This gives $X \sim N(np, npq)$, where $n = 40$ and $p = 0.5$.

So

$$X \sim N(20, 10)$$

$P(X < 15)$ transforms to $P(X < 14.5)$, or

$$P(X < 15) \rightarrow P(X < 14.5)$$

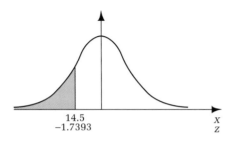

$$P(X < 14.5) = P\left(Z < \frac{14.5 - 20}{\sqrt{10}}\right)$$

$$= P(Z < -1.7393)$$

$$= \Phi(-1.7393)$$

$$= 1 - \Phi(1.7393)$$

$$= 1 - 0.959\,01$$

$$= 0.040\,99$$

Example 2

A fair tetrahedral dice is thrown 100 times. What is the probability of it landing on 3 between 23 and 30 times inclusively?

Solution

Let X be the random variable, 'number of times dice lands on 3'.

$X \sim B(n, p)$, where $n = 100$ and $p = 0.25$

As n is large we can use the normal approximation

$X \sim N(np, npq)$, where $np = 25$ and $npq = 18.75$

so,

$$X \sim N(25, 18.75)$$

$$P(23 \leq X \leq 30) \rightarrow P(22.5 < X < 30.5)$$

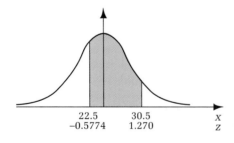

$$P(22.5 < X < 30.5) = P\left(\frac{22.5 - 25}{\sqrt{18.75}} < Z < \frac{30.5 - 25}{\sqrt{18.75}}\right)$$

$$= P(-0.5774 < Z < 1.2702)$$

$$= \Phi(1.2702) - \Phi(-0.5774)$$

$$= 0.897\,99 - 0.281\,83$$

$$= 0.616\,16$$

10.4 Normal Distribution as an Approximation to a Binomial Distribution

Exercise

Technique

1 If $X \sim B(60, 0.5)$ apply the continuity correction to (but do not work out):

a $P(X \leq 10)$ **b** $P(X > 37)$ **c** $P(20 < X \leq 30)$

2 $Y \sim B(85, 0.4)$. If this variable is approximated by a normal distribution give the transformations for:

a $P(Y \geq 35)$ **b** $P(Y < 42)$
c $P(30 \leq Y \leq 37)$ **d** $P(Y = 40)$

3 $X \sim B(75, 0.6)$. Using a normal approximation find:

a $P(X \leq 40)$ **b** $P(X > 30)$ **c** $P(35 \leq X < 42)$

4 $Y \sim B(1000, 0.3)$. Using a normal approximation, find:

a $P(Y < 280)$ **b** $P(Y \geq 320)$ **c** $P(280 \leq Y \leq 310)$
d $P(292 < Y < 306)$ **e** $P(Y = 305)$

Contextual

1 A twenty-pence coin is thrown 40 times and the number of tails is recorded. What is the probability that the number of tails is:

a less than 16   **b** more than, or equal to, 23
c between 18 and 25 inclusive?

2 It is known that a particular variety of lettuce seed has a probability of 0.85 of successfully producing a lettuce. Find the probability that if 200 such seeds are sown the number of lettuces produced will be:

a more than 175   **b** less than 160
c between 167 and 172, inclusive.

3 A four-sided dice is thrown 150 times and the number it lands on is recorded. Find the probability that it lands on a 1:

a at least 45 times   **b** 30 or fewer times.

10.5 Normal Distribution as an Approximation to a Poisson Distribution

As the mean and variance of a Poisson distribution increase, so the distribution becomes symmetrical about the mean. It will gradually begin to resemble the distinctive bell-shape of the normal distribution. Just as it was helpful to approximate a binomial distribution to a normal distribution so we can use a similar approximation for a Poisson distribution.

If $X \sim \text{Po}(\lambda)$ then $E(X)$ and $\text{Var}(X) = \lambda$.

For large values of λ we can say that

$$X \sim N(\lambda, \lambda)$$

As a Poisson distribution is a discrete distribution we must remember to apply the continuity correction when using the normal approximation.

Example 1

If $X \sim \text{Po}(45)$, find the value of:

a $P(X < 50)$ **b** $P(X = 43)$

Solution

Using the normal approximation, $X \sim N(45, 45)$.

a $P(X < 50) \rightarrow P(X < 49.5)$

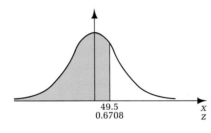

$$P(X < 49.5) = P\left(Z < \frac{49.5 - 45}{\sqrt{45}}\right)$$

$$= P(Z < 0.6708)$$

$$= \Phi(0.6708)$$

$$= 0.748\,82$$

b $P(X = 43) \rightarrow P(42.5 < X < 43.5)$

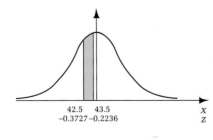

$$P(42.5 < X < 43.5)$$

$$= P\left(\frac{42.5 - 45}{\sqrt{45}} < Z < \frac{43.5 - 45}{\sqrt{45}}\right)$$

$$= P(-0.3727 < Z < -0.2236)$$

$$= \Phi(-0.2236) - \Phi(-0.3727)$$

$$= 0.411\,54 - 0.354\,69$$

$$= 0.056\,85$$

10.5 Normal Distribution as an Approximation to a Poisson Distribution

Exercise

Technique

1 If $X \sim \text{Po}(28)$ find:

    a $P(X < 25)$ **b** $P(X \geq 30)$ **c** $P(X = 24)$

2 The number of vehicles passing the school entrance every ten minutes is recorded and is found to follow a Poisson distribution with mean 35. Using a normal approximation, find the probability that in any one ten-minute period the number of vehicles passing is:

    a   more than 40   **b**   less than 30   **c**   between 32 and 42.

3 The number of telephone calls to the school office in one hour has a Poisson distribution with mean of 65. Find the probability that during a one-hour period on Tuesday the number of calls will be:

    a   more than 70   **b**   exactly 70.

4 The number of light bulbs which need changing in school each month follows a Poisson distribution with $\lambda = 25$. What is the probability that in any one month more than 30 bulbs need to be changed?

5 The number of accidents on a stretch of motorway occurs at the rate of five every month. What is the probability that over a 12-month period the number of accidents is less than 50?

Consolidation

Exercise A

1 X is a random variable with the distribution $N(150, 55.5)$. Find the probability that X is greater than 132.25.

2 The mass, in grams, of a grade A Spanish navel orange sold on a market stall is a normally distributed random variable with mean 295 g and variance 160 g^2. Find to three decimal places:

a the probability that a single grade A Spanish navel orange chosen at random has a mass less than 275 g;

b the probability that a random sample of seven of these grade A oranges has a total mass exceeding 2 kg.

(NEAB)

3 The distribution of the masses of adult husky dogs may be modelled by the normal distribution with mean 37 kg and standard deviation 5 kg.

a Calculate the probability that an adult husky has a mass greater than 30 kg.

b Calculate the probability that a randomly chosen team of six huskies has a total mass lying between 198 kg and 240 kg, giving your answer to three decimal places.

(NEAB)

4 Round pegs are to be fitted into round holes drilled into a board. The diameters of the holes are normally distributed with mean 2.10 cm and standard deviation 0.15 cm. The diameters of the pegs are normally distributed with mean 1.90 cm and standard deviation 0.10 cm. Find the probability that a randomly selected peg will be too large to fit into a randomly selected hole.

(ULEAC)

5 The heights of female students at a large university are normally distributed with a mean of 168 cm and a standard deviation of 8 cm. One of these students is chosen at random. Find the probability that her height is:

a greater than 172 cm

b between 160 cm and 170 cm

c Given that 70% of all these female students have heights greater than H cm, find the value of H, correct to one decimal place.

(UCLES)

6 A health food co-operative markets free-range eggs. Eggs weighing less than 48 g are graded small, those weighing more than 59 g are graded large and the rest are graded medium. The weight of an egg from a particular supplier is normally distributed with mean 52 g and standard deviation 4 g. Find:

a the proportion of eggs graded small

b the proportion of eggs graded medium

c the median weight of the eggs graded large.

(AEB)

7 Someone is employed to clean all the cars at a Renault garage. The times taken to clean particular models of car follow normal distributions. For a Renault 5 the mean time is 15 minutes and the standard deviation 4 minutes. For a Renault Laguna, the mean is 24 minutes and the standard deviation 6 minutes. During one part of the day, there are two Renault 5s to clean, and one Laguna. What is the probability that the time to clean the Laguna will be greater than the total time to clean the other two cars?

(NICCEA)

8 A fair coin is tossed 90 times. Use an appropriate normal distribution to estimate the probability that the number of heads obtained lies between 45 and 55 inclusive.

9 Equal numbers of sweets coloured red, yellow, green, and brown are produced in large quantities. The sweets are thoroughly mixed and dispensed at random by machine into packets.

a Find the probability of a packet of 20 sweets containing at least six red sweets.

b Use a distributional approximation to calculate, correct to two decimal places, the probability of a packet of 60 sweets containing fewer than 20 yellow sweets.

(WJEC)

10 Jam is packed into tins of advertised weight 1 kg. The weight of a randomly selected tin of jam is normally distributed about a target weight with standard deviation of 12 g.

a If the target weight is 1 kg, find the probability that a randomly chosen tin weighs:

   i less than 985 g

   ii between 970 g and 1015 g.

b If not more than one tin in 100 is to weigh less than the advertised weight, find the minimum target weight required to meet this condition.

c The target weight is fixed at 1 kg. The resulting tins are packed in boxes of six and the weight of the box is normally distributed with mean weight 250 g and standard deviation 10 g. Find the probability that a randomly chosen box of six tins will weigh less than 6.2 kg.

(ULEAC)

Exercise B

1 It is given that $X \sim N(12, 9)$. Find $P(10 < X < 13)$.

2 The random variable X has a normal distribution with mean 6 and standard deviation 4.5.

    a Calculate $P(X > 0)$
    b The distribution of X is proposed as a model for the length of time, measured in hours, for which a certain drug remains effective after being given to a randomly chosen patient. Comment on the suitability of this model with reference to your answer in **a**.

(UCLES)

3 Some children are measuring leaves. The lengths of leaves from a particular bush are normally distributed with a mean of 2.1 cm and a standard deviation of 0.25 cm.

    a Find the probability of obtaining a leaf from the bush which is shorter than 2.4 cm.
    b Show that the probability of the total length of five randomly chosen leaves from the bush being less than 12 cm is 0.996, to three decimal places.
    c The lengths of leaves from a certain tree are normally distributed with a mean of 5.5 cm and a standard deviation of 0.4 cm. Find the probability that the total length of five randomly chosen leaves from the bush is more then twice the length of a single randomly chosen leaf from the tree.

(ULEAC)

4 The lifetimes of Econ light bulbs are normally distributed with mean 1000 h and standard deviation 25 h.

    a Find, to three decimal places, the probability that an Econ light bulb will have a lifetime between 975 h and 1020 h.
    b Calculate, to three decimal places, the probability that the sum of the lifetimes of eight Econ light bulbs will exceed 7930 h. Indicate clearly the stage in your calculation when an assumption concerning independence is essential.

c The lifetimes of Enersave light bulbs are normally distributed with mean 7900 h and standard deviation 50 h. Calculate, to three decimal places, the probability that an Enersave light bulb will last at least 8 times as long as an Econ light bulb.

(NEAB)

5 The lengths of dinner knives of a particular brand are normally distributed with mean 21.94 cm and standard deviation 0.05 cm. Knives longer than 22.00 cm are called 'long'.

a A knife is selected at random from a day's production. Calculate the probability that it will be long, giving the answer to four decimal places.

b The knives are packed in boxes of 10. A box is chosen at random. Stating any necessary assumption, show that the probability of the box containing fewer than two long knives is 0.677, correct to three decimal places.

c A shop has 40 of the boxes in stock. Using a normal approximation, estimate the probability that more than 30 boxes will contain fewer than two long knives.

(UCLES)

6 A train is scheduled to arrive at its destination at 10.15, but the actual times of arrival are normally distributed about a mean of 10.18 with a standard deviation of 3.7 minutes.

a Find, correct to three decimal places, the probability that the train is:
  i late
  ii arrives before 10.22
  iii late and arrives before 10.22.

b Certain arrival times are classified as exceptionally late and the probability of a train being exceptionally late on a particular day is 0.015. Calculate, to the nearest minute, the time of arrival after which a train is classified as exceptionally late.

(WJEC)

7 When I try to send a fax, the probability that I can successfully send it is 0.85.

a I try to send eight faxes. Use a binomial model to find the probability that I can successfully send at least seven of the faxes.

b I try to send 50 faxes. Use a normal approximation to the binomial model to find the probability that I can successfully send at least 45 of the faxes.

(UCLES)

8 The speeds of vehicles passing a point on the roadside are normally distributed with a mean of 72 km h^{-1} and a standard deviation of 15 km h^{-1}. Find the probability that the speed of a vehicle, selected at random:

a is less than 45 km h^{-1}

b lies between 48 km h^{-1} and 84 km h^{-1}.

The number of vehicles passing in one hour is 245. Estimate the number of these which exceed the speed limit of 90 km h^{-1}.

(UCLES)

9 Containers of fromage frais are dispatched in groups of six. Each container is filled by a machine which delivers a normally distributed quantity of fromage frais. The mass delivered has mean 60 g and the variance is 0.36 g^2.

a Describe fully the distribution of the total mass of fromage frais in the containers of a group of six.

b The total mass of plastic and metal-backed foil for each group of six containers is also normally distributed with mean 45 g and variance 0.64 g^2. Find the probability that a group of six full and sealed containers, selected at random, weighs less than 400 g.

(NICCEA)

10 The weight of fruit delivered into an empty can is normally distributed with mean 250 g and standard deviation 1.2 g. The weight of an empty can is independently normally distributed with mean 25 g and standard deviation 0.5 g. Find:

a the mean

b the standard deviation

of the weights of filled cans.

(ULEAC)

Applications and Activities

1 Play a game of Boules. Measure the distances of the boules from the jack. What type of distribution do these distances suggest?

2 Ask people to estimate the size of an angle. Record the difference between their estimate and the actual angle. Do these differences follow a particular distribution?

Summary

- If a continuous random variable, X, has a normal distribution with mean μ and variance σ^2 this is written

  $$X \sim N(\mu, \sigma^2)$$

- The standard normal distribution is written

  $$Z \sim N(0, 1)$$

- If $X \sim N(\mu, \sigma^2)$, then the transformed random variable

  $$Z = \frac{X - \mu}{\sigma}$$

  has a standard normal distribution.

- A random variable $X \sim B(n, p)$ can be approximated by $Y \sim N(np, npq)$, where $q = 1 - p$, for large values of n.

- A random variable $X \sim Po(\lambda)$ can be approximated by $Y \sim N(\lambda, \lambda)$ for large values of λ.

- The continuity correction must be used when approximating a discrete distribution to a continuous distribution.

11 Correlation and Regression

What you need to know

- How to find the mean of a set of data.

- How to find the variance of a set of data.

Review

1 Calculate the mean of the following:

   a   24, 28, 29, 31, 36, 35, 41, 48

   b   2.8, 3.1, 4.2, 4.8, 4.7, 5.2, 4.9, 6.2, 7.1

   c   0.07, 0.012, 0.23, 0.36, 0.69, 0.58, 0.27

2 Calculate the variance of the following:

   a   12, 15, 19, 18, 15, 17, 18, 16, 14, 16, 12, 20

   b   6.8, 6.9, 5.7, 10.2, 10.6, 10.5, 11.2, 11.6

   c   0.05, 0.08, 0.135, 0.25, 0.69, 0.24, 0.1

11.1 Scatter Diagrams

Scatter diagrams are used for comparing two sets of data to see whether or not they are 'connected' or **correlated**. In Chapter 3, section 3.6, the two variables, height and shoe size, were plotted against each other and resulted in the following diagram:

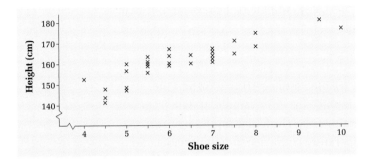

This is an example of **positive correlation**, since as one variable increases so does the other.

Negative correlation is where one variable increases as the other variable decreases. An example is shown below, where the number of winter coats sold is plotted against temperature in degrees Celsius.

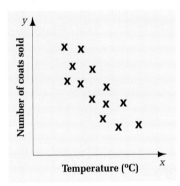

There is **no correlation** if the points are scattered across the graph with no apparent pattern to their distribution. An example of two variables with no correlation is height and IQ (intelligence quotient).

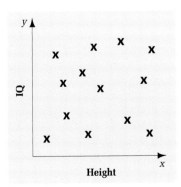

When plotting scatter diagrams you should always ask yourself the following questions:

- What scale should I use?

- Which axis should I plot a particular variable on?

Scale is important. If the scale is incorrectly chosen this can result in a misinterpretation of the data. The scales should be decided in such a way that the range on the *x*-axis and the range on the *y*-axis are represented by approximately equal lengths.

It is usual to plot the **dependent** variable on the vertical axis and the **independent** variable on the horizontal axis. For example, if data from a science experiment on the temperature of a particular liquid every 30 seconds after boiling is used, temperature is the dependent variable and time the independent variable.

However in some cases, the variables are interchangeable, for example German marks and French marks, since there is no definitive dependent and independent variable.

Example 1

For each of the following pairs of variables, state which is the dependent and which the independent variable:

a temperature (°C) and number of ice creams sold
b petrol consumption and miles driven
c age of child and weekly pocket money
d English and mathematics results

Solution

a Temperature is the independent variable and the number of ice creams the dependent one.
b Miles driven is the independent variable and the petrol consumption the dependent one.
c Age of child is the independent variable and weekly pocket money the dependent one.
d English and mathematics results are interchangeable.

Line of best fit

If a relationship or correlation between two data sets is discovered you might be asked to use the data to make predictions. For example, as in the case of height and shoe size you might be asked to predict the shoe size of someone of a particular height, not recorded in the data sample. In this case it would be necessary to draw a '**line of best fit**', that is a line that follows the trend of the data collected.

A simple method that yields an approximate line of best fit is:

Step ① Calculate both the mean of x, $\bar{x}$, and the mean of y, $\bar{y}$.

Step ② Plot the point $(\bar{x}, \bar{y})$.

Step ③ Draw a straight line which passes through $(\bar{x}, \bar{y})$ and which has an approximately equal number of points above and below the line.

Note: use the point $(\bar{x}, \bar{y})$ as the pivot about which you move your ruler until you have approximately equal numbers of points on each side of the line.

Example 2

For the following data set of the weights and heights of 30 boys:

Weight (kg)	60	61	63	66	59	62	58	60	62	60
Height (cm)	158	159	157	165	161	162	159	160	164	156

Weight (kg)	57	61	57	58	56	61	59	58	65	58
Height (cm)	159	162	158	155	147	161	147	143	170	141

Weight (kg)	65	63	64	66	60	63	65	59	60	63
Height (cm)	167	164	179	174	147	164	172	152	159	161

a plot a scatter diagram of the data

b draw a line of best fit

c use your line to predict the weight of a boy of height 160 cm.

Solution

a

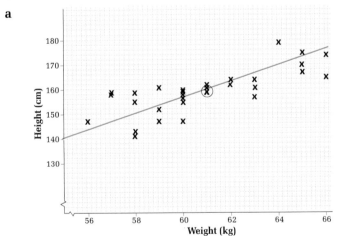

b Calculating the mean of x and y gives

$\bar{x} = 61.0$

$\bar{y} = 159.4$ ◀ ① Calculate means.

The line of best fit must pass through this point with roughly equal numbers of points above and below the line. ◀ ② Plot the point $(\bar{x}, \bar{y})$.

◀ ③ Draw the best fit line through $(\bar{x}, \bar{y})$.

c The weight of a boy of height 160 cm is approximately 61 kg.

When using a line of best fit to predict values, take care to use it correctly. In Example 2 use the line of best fit to give predictions in the height range 140 cm to 180 cm. Do not use the line to predict anything below 130 cm or above 185 cm, since no data have been collected in these regions.

11.1 Scatter Diagrams
Exercise
Contextual

1 For each of the following, where possible, state which is the independent and which is the dependent variable:

   a   wheat yield (tonnes) and rainfall (mm)

   b   French mark (percentage) and German mark (percentage)

   c   number of years smoking and lung damage (graded on a scale 0 to 100).

2 For the following diagram, describe the type of correlation between the variables and suggest an example it could illustrate.

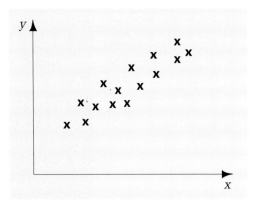

3 Draw a scatter diagram for the following data choosing appropriate scales and comment on whether there appears to be any correlation.

Handspan and foot length of 10 pupils.

Handspan (cm)	17	19.5	14	16.5	18	20	16	18	17.5	16
Foot length (cm)	19	20	15.5	17	19	22	16	17.5	19	17

4 Draw a scatter diagram to illustrate the results of 18 pupils in a recent geography and history exam.

Geography (%)	68	90	42	50	86	84	78	80	49	50	78	84	95	68	65	71	75	80
History (%)	60	85	40	41	65	89	65	78	39	80	47	79	90	70	60	55	60	70

Comment on any correlation. What can be said generally about the marks in the two exams?

5 Draw a scatter diagram of the following:

X	16	19	21	17	20	19	21	12	15	22
Y	55	56	58	57	58	58	59	47	50	63

a Calculate $\bar{x}$ and $\bar{y}$.
b Use your answer to **a** to draw a line of best fit.

6 Draw a scatter diagram for the following data, the results for nine batches experimenting on the effect of temperature on yield.

Temperature (°C) x	110	120	130	140	150	160	170	180	190
Yield (tonnes) y	78	86	97	106	115	124	133	143	152

a Draw a line of best fit.
b Use your line to estimate the yield at a temperature of 169°C.

11.2 Correlation

In this section we aim to find a numerical value, known as the **product moment correlation** coefficient, which will describe how correlated a set of data values are. So far in this chapter we have had a general look at correlation. Consider the following diagram:

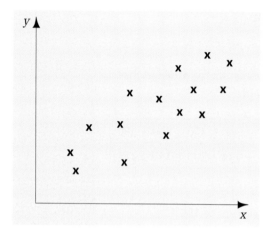

Would you say that this data has a poor, good, excellent or perfect positive correlation? As you will see we all have our own perception of how good a correlation is. What we need is a *measure* of how well correlated a pair of data sets is.

If we look at the diagram again we can divide it into four quadrants, centre $(\bar{x}, \bar{y})$.

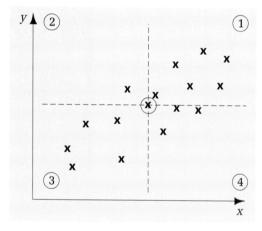

Since there is a positive correlation most points are lying in the first and third quadrant. If the correlation had been negative most points would have been in the second and fourth quadrants.

If we treat the quadrant lines as our new axes, the coordinates of the points now are all of the form $(x - \bar{x}, y - \bar{y})$. Now, let us consider $(x - \bar{x})$ and $(y - \bar{y})$ in each quadrant.

	$(x - \bar{x})$	$(y - \bar{y})$	$(x - \bar{x})(y - \bar{y})$
Quadrant 1	+	+	+
Quadrant 2	−	+	−
Quadrant 3	−	−	+
Quadrant 4	+	−	−

In the first and third quadrants $(x - \bar{x})(y - \bar{y})$ is positive for every point and in the second and fourth quadrants $(x - \bar{x})(y - \bar{y})$ is negative for every point. So if we have a positive correlation, as shown here, the majority of the points lie in the first and third quadrants and the sum of these terms, $\Sigma(x - \bar{x})(y - \bar{y})$ will be positive and large.

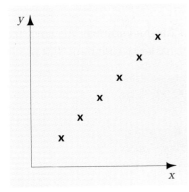

For negative correlation, the majority of the points lie in the second and fourth quadrants and therefore the sum of the terms $\Sigma(x - \bar{x})(y - \bar{y})$ will be negative and large.

For no correlation, or very weak correlation, the points are scattered randomly in all four quadrants. The values of $(x - \bar{x})(y - \bar{y})$ will be both positive and negative and will mostly cancel each other out. The sum of the values $\Sigma(x - \bar{x})(y - \bar{y})$ will be very small.

It appears that the sum $\Sigma(x - \bar{x})(y - \bar{y})$ could be used to measure how strong a correlation is. The actual sum itself is not very useful since it does not take into account:

- the number of data items
- the units of x and y and hence the spread of the data.

However, this measure is a good starting point.

$$S_{xy} = \sum (x - \bar{x})(y - \bar{y})$$

Covariance

The **covariance** is similar to the variance of a data set. The variance considers how each value x varies from the mean, $\bar{x}$, while the covariance looks at how each (x, y) pair varies from $(\bar{x}, \bar{y})$. The covariance uses the sum $\Sigma(x - \bar{x})(y - \bar{y})$ but takes into account the number of data items, n.

$$\text{covariance} = s_{xy} = \frac{1}{n}\Sigma(x - \bar{x})(y - \bar{y})$$

where n is the number of data items

In the same way as for the variance, the covariance can be written in a shorter form that is easier to calculate (but more prone to rounding errors):

$$s_{xy} = \frac{1}{n}\Sigma xy - \bar{x}\bar{y}$$

or $\quad S_{xy} = \Sigma xy - n(\bar{x}\bar{y})$

From these formulas you can see that

$$S_{xy} = ns_{xy}$$

Example

Find the covariance of the following data:

x	6	5	8	7	3
y	8	7	7	9	5

Solution

$n = 5$

$\Sigma x = 6 + 5 + 8 + 7 + 3 = 29 \qquad \bar{x} = \dfrac{\Sigma x}{n} = 5.8$

$\Sigma y = 8 + 7 + 7 + 9 + 5 = 36 \qquad \bar{y} = \dfrac{\Sigma y}{n} = 7.2$

$\Sigma xy = (6 \times 8) + (5 \times 7) + (8 \times 7) + (7 \times 9) + (3 \times 5) = 217$

Using the shorter formula:

$\text{covariance} = s_{xy}$

$\qquad = \dfrac{1}{n}\Sigma xy - \bar{x}\bar{y}$

$\qquad = \frac{1}{5} \times 217 - (5.8 \times 7.2)$

$\qquad = 1.64$

11.2 Correlation
Exercise

Technique

1 Calculate the covariance for each of the following sets of data:

a $\Sigma x = 46.4$ $\Sigma y = 50$ $\Sigma xy = 212.4$ $n = 10$
b $\Sigma x = 61.9$ $\Sigma y = 154$ $\Sigma xy = 1391.06$ $n = 7$

2 Calculate the covariance for the following data and comment on the correlation.

a

x	2	4	6	8	10	12	14	16	18	20
y	3	8	2	5	10	10	16	9	13	16

b

x	5	10	15	20	25	30
y	64	50	46	42	37	29

c

x	0	0.5	1.0	1.5	2.0	2.5	3.0	3.5
y	0.6	0.45	0.8	0.85	1.4	1.65	2.4	2.85

11.3 Pearson's Product Moment Correlation Coefficient

Although the covariance took into account the number of data items, it did not take into account the units of x and y and hence the spread of the data. **The Pearson's product moment correlation coefficient (PMCC)** takes this into account by *standardising* the values of $(x - \bar{x})$ and $(y - \bar{y})$. This is done in a similar way as standardising the normal distribution as shown in Chapter 10. In this case we need to divide by both standard deviations since the data is bivariate (involves two variables).

The resulting standardised measure denoted by r is:

$$r = \frac{\frac{1}{n}\Sigma(x - \bar{x})(y - \bar{y})}{\sqrt{\left[\frac{1}{n}\Sigma(x - \bar{x})^2\right]\left[\frac{1}{n}\Sigma(y - \bar{y})^2\right]}}$$

$$= \frac{\Sigma(x - \bar{x})(y - \bar{y})}{\sqrt{\Sigma(x - \bar{x})^2\Sigma(y - \bar{y})^2}}$$

The two standard deviations are $\sqrt{\frac{1}{n}\Sigma(x - \bar{x})^2}$ and $\sqrt{\frac{1}{n}\Sigma(y - \bar{y})^2}$

after cancelling $\frac{1}{n}$ throughout

As with the covariance which is usually denoted as s_{xy}, s_x^2 and s_y^2 are used to denote the variances of x and y respectively and s_x and s_y the respective standard deviations. So,

Note: sometimes s_x^2 is written as s_{xx}.

$$r = \frac{s_{xy}}{s_x s_y}$$

The 'working' formula we usually use in calculating the Pearson's product moment correlation coefficient is:

$$r = \frac{\frac{\Sigma xy}{n} - \bar{x}\bar{y}}{\sqrt{\left(\frac{\Sigma x^2}{n} - \bar{x}^2\right)\left(\frac{\Sigma y^2}{n} - \bar{y}^2\right)}}$$

Interpretation

r is used as a standardised measure of *linear correlation*. Since it is standardised it can be shown that it always lies between $+1$ and -1 and hence gives a good measure of how strong a correlation is.

Karl Pearson (1857–1936)
An English biologist a[nd] mathematician who[se] wrote 'The Grammar [of] Science' (1892) whic[h] stimulated a generati[on] of young scientists. H[e] applied statistical measurement to the Darwinian theory of evolution by natura[l] selection. Later in hi[s] life, his energy was a prime factor in the establishment of statistical laboratorie[s] throughout the USA a[nd] Europe.

For perfect positive correlation, $r = +1$.

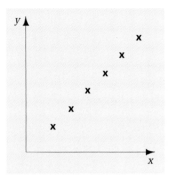

For perfect negative correlation, $r = -1$

For little or no linear correlation r is close to 0.

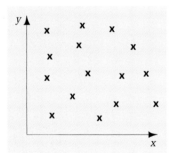

Care must be taken in interpretation of Pearson's product moment correlation coefficient to remember that it is only a measure of *linear* correlation. A value close to 0 will only detect a lack of linear correlation but that is not to say that perhaps the two variables are correlated in a different way. This is one of the main reasons that it is so important always to draw a scatter diagram as well as calculating a correlation coefficient when trying to interpret the relationship between two variables.

Cause and effect

Another factor to remember is that even when there is a good correlation between two variables we cannot automatically conclude that the changes in x are causing the changes in y.

Say for example our two variables were:

- x_i, number of radio licences taken out in a particular year
- y_i, number of people certified insane in a particular year

The value of r, the product moment correlation coefficient, is found to be both large and positive for data taken over the last 20 years. From this we could conclude that an increase in usage of radios causes an increase in the number certified insane, but clearly this is a nonsense correlation. In such cases variables may change over the years for possibly related reasons but certainly not by mutual cause and effect.

Example

Calculate the Pearson's product moment correlation coefficient for the following:

x	85	50	75	56	65
y	70	66	68	40	50

Solution

When calculating such correlation coefficients, it is best to draw up a table.

x	y	x^2	y^2	xy
85	70	7225	4900	5950
50	66	2500	4356	3300
75	68	5625	4624	5100
56	40	3136	1600	2240
65	50	4225	2500	3250
$\Sigma x = 331$	$\Sigma y = 294$	$\Sigma x^2 = 22\,711$	$\Sigma y^2 = 17\,980$	$\Sigma xy = 19\,840$

$$\bar{x} = \tfrac{331}{5} = 66.2$$

$$s_x = \sqrt{\tfrac{22\,711}{5} - 66.2^2} = 12.6396$$

$$\bar{y} = \tfrac{294}{5} = 58.8$$

$$s_y = \sqrt{\tfrac{17\,980}{5} - 58.8^2} = 11.7712$$

$$\text{covariance} = \tfrac{19\,840}{5} - (66.2 \times 58.8)$$

$$= 75.44$$

Pearson's product moment correlation coefficient

$$= \frac{75.44}{12.6396 \times 11.7712} = 0.5070$$

11.3 Pearson's Product Moment Correlation Coefficient

Exercise

Technique

1 Calculate the Pearson's product moment correlation coefficient for the following sets of data:

a $\Sigma x = 71.3$ $\Sigma y = 56$ $\Sigma xy = 573.4$
    $\Sigma x^2 = 703.53$ $\Sigma y^2 = 476$ $n = 8$

b $\Sigma x = 372$ $\Sigma y = 278$ $\Sigma xy = 14\,242$
    $\Sigma x^2 = 21\,258$ $\Sigma y^2 = 12\,467$ $n = 7$

2 For the following data, plot a scatter diagram and calculate:

a the covariance

b Pearson's product moment correlation coefficient.

x	2	2.6	3.1	3.6	4.1	4.8	5.2	5.6
y	3.6	3.9	4.2	3.8	4.7	5.2	6	6.4

3 Calculate Pearson's product correlation coefficient for the following:

x	6	8	10	12	14	16	18	20	22
y	4.1	8.6	3.2	10.4	12	8.7	9.4	13.1	16

4 For the following data calculate:
a the covariance
b Pearson's product moment correlation coefficient.

x	16	20	23	25	40	46
y	1	3	2	4	5	6

5 The following marks were obtained by 10 pupils in the same class.

English	68	43	94	89	75	71	84	90	47	52
Maths	94	86	73	41	60	92	60	71	50	63

a Plot a scatter diagram to illustrate the data.
b Calculate the covariance of the data.
c Calculate Pearson's product moment correlation coefficient.
d Comment on your results.

11.4 Spearman's Rank Correlation Coefficient

In some situations it is simply the order or rank that is important, for example judges at a dance competition might rank the dances in order rather than awarding marks for each dance.

To see if there is any correlation between the judge's verdicts we can use the formula for Pearson's product moment correlation coefficient, using the rankings as our data.

Example 1

Eight dances are performed at a local dance competition. After seeing all the dances, two judges rank the dances in order so the dance each judge likes best has rank 1.

Dance	A	B	C	D	E	F	G	H
Judge 1	1	7	2	3	5	4	6	8
Judge 2	4	3	6	7	1	8	5	2

Calculate the rank correlation coefficient for these data.

Solution

Judge 1, x	Judge 2, y	x^2	y^2	xy
1	4	1	16	4
7	3	49	9	21
2	6	4	36	12
3	7	9	49	21
5	1	25	1	5
4	8	16	64	32
6	5	36	25	30
8	2	64	4	16
$\Sigma x = 36$	$\Sigma y = 36$	$\Sigma x^2 = 204$	$\Sigma y^2 = 204$	$\Sigma xy = 141$

$n = 8 \qquad \bar{x} = 4.5 \qquad \bar{y} = 4.5$

Using Pearson's product moment correlation coefficient formula:

$$r = \frac{\dfrac{\sum xy}{n} - \bar{x}\bar{y}}{\sqrt{\left[\dfrac{\sum x^2}{n} - \bar{x}^2\right]\left[\dfrac{\sum y^2}{n} - \bar{y}^2\right]}}$$

$$= \frac{\frac{141}{8} - (4.5 \times 4.5)}{\sqrt{\left(\frac{204}{8} - 4.5^2\right)\left(\frac{204}{8} - 4.5^2\right)}}$$

$$= \frac{17.625 - 20.25}{5.25}$$

$$= -0.5$$

The method used in Example 1 is *not* usually used to calculate rank correlation. The measure used is **Spearman's rank correlation coefficient** (r_s).

The formula for r_s is

$$r_s = 1 - \frac{6\Sigma d^2}{n(n^2 - 1)}$$

where d is the difference between the rankings of each item and n is the number of paired observations.

Example 2

Find Spearman's rank correlation coefficient for the data in Example 1.

Solution

x	y	$d = x - y$	d^2
1	4	−3	9
7	3	4	16
2	6	−4	16
3	7	−4	16
5	1	4	16
4	8	−4	16
6	5	1	1
8	2	6	36
			$\Sigma d^2 = 126$

Putting the values in the formula with $n = 8$

$$r_s = 1 - \frac{6\Sigma d^2}{n(n^2 - 1)}$$

$$= 1 - \frac{6 \times 126}{8(64 - 1)}$$

$$= 1 - 1.5$$

$$= -0.5$$

Remember:
d is the difference between rankings.

as calculated earlier, but by a much quicker method.

Since Spearman's rank correlation coefficient is derived from the product moment correlation coefficient, we compare our value of 0.5 with +1 for perfect positive correlation, −1 for perfect negative correlation, and 0 for no correlation.

The result of −0.5 suggests some negative correlation between the two judges' scores.

Dealing with tied ranks

Sometimes more than one item is given the same rank. In this case new ranks are allocated to the items that have tied ranks as in the following example. (If there are more than a few ties Pearson's formula will give a more accurate answer.)

Example 3

Suppose that in the dance competition Judge 1 gave both dances E and F a rank of 4 and Judge 2 gave dances A, B and H a rank of 2, as shown in this table.

Dance	A	B	C	D	E	F	G	H
Judge 1	1	7	2	3	4	4	6	8
Judge 2	2	2	6	7	1	8	5	2

Allocate new ranks to the items with tied ranks.

Solution

If E and F had been slightly different Judge 1 would have ranked them 4 and 5, so we award each of the the mean of those ranks, that is $\frac{1}{2}(4 + 5) = 4.5$.

If A, B and H had been slightly different Judge 2 would have ranked them 2, 3 and 4, so we award each of them the mean of those ranks, that is $\frac{1}{3}(2 + 3 + 4) = 3$.

The rankings are now:

Dance	A	B	C	D	E	F	G	H
Judge 1	1	7	2	3	4.5	4.5	6	8
Judge 2	3	3	6	7	1	8	5	3

When asked to calculate Spearman's rank correlation coefficient of data given as numerical values, it is important to rank the data first.

Example 4

The marks of 12 pupils in geography and history essays are as follows:

Geography	15	16	19	17	17	15	18	16	18	18	14	10
History	10	12	12	13	11	9	11	13	11	12	8	7

Calculate Spearman's rank correlation coefficient.

Solution

First rank the data.

The lowest geography mark is 10. This mark is ranked 1.
The next mark is 14, which is ranked 2.
The next two marks are both 15 so they are ranked
$\frac{1}{2}(3+4) = 3.5$.
The next two marks are both 16 so they are ranked
$\frac{1}{2}(5+6) = 5.5$.
The next two marks are both 17 so they are ranked
$\frac{1}{2}(7+8) = 7.5$.
The top three marks are all 18 so they are ranked
$\frac{1}{3}(9+10+11) = 10$.

The lowest history mark is 7 which is ranked 1.
The next mark is 8 which is ranked 2.
The next mark is 9 which is ranked 3.
The next mark is 10 which is ranked 4.
The next three marks are all 11, so they are ranked
$\frac{1}{3}(5+6+7) = 6$.
The next three marks are all 12, so they are ranked
$\frac{1}{3}(8+9+10) = 9$.
The top two marks are both 13, so they are ranked
$\frac{1}{2}(11+12) = 11.5$.

Put the rankings in a table:

Geography, x	Rank, x	History, y	Rank, y	$\lvert d \rvert = \lvert x - y \rvert$	d^2
15	3.5	10	4	0.5	0.25
16	5.5	12	9	3.5	12.25
19	12	12	9	3	9
17	7.5	13	11.5	4	16
17	7.5	11	6	1.5	2.25
15	3.5	9	3	0.5	0.25
18	10	11	6	4	16
16	5.5	13	11.5	6	36
18	10	11	6	4	16
18	10	12	9	1	1
14	2	8	2	0	0
10	1	7	1	0	0
					$\Sigma d^2 = 109$

$n = 12$

Calculate Spearman's rank correlation coefficient.

$$r_s = 1 - \frac{6 \Sigma d^2}{n(n^2 - 1)}$$

$$= 1 - \frac{6 \times 109}{12(144 - 1)}$$

$$= 1 - 0.3811\ldots$$

$$= 0.619 \text{ (3 d.p.)}$$

This result suggests some positive correlation between the geography and history results.

When used with data which you first rank, Spearman's rank correlation formula is not used to find linear correlation but a more general correlation.

11.4 Spearman's Rank Correlation Coefficient
Exercise

Technique

1 Calculate Spearman's rank correlation coefficient for each of the following data sets:

a

x-rank	1	2	3	4	5	6	7
y-rank	5	4	2	6	1	7	3

b

x-rank	1	2	3	4	5	6	7	8	9	10
y-rank	10	8	9	6	7	3	4	2	5	1

2 The rankings for x and y are shown in the table below.

x	1	2	3	4	5	6
y	3	1	2	4	6	5

a Calculate Σd^2.
b Calculate Spearman's rank correlation coefficient.
c Comment on your value of Spearman's rank correlation coefficient.

3 At a local cookery competition, marks were awarded for cakes by two independent judges:

Cake	A	B	C	D	E	F	G
Judge 1	6.8	7.8	8.4	9.9	5.0	5.5	8.1
Judge 2	5.9	8.1	7.8	9.1	4.9	5.8	8.8

a Construct a table of rank for the two judges.
b Calculate the Spearman's rank correlation coefficient.
c Comment on your answer to **b**.

4 The following table shows the percentages given to 10 pupils for two tests in German and French. Calculate Spearman's rank correlation coefficient and comment on its value.

German	68	74	81	85	59	74	64	81	89	79
French	54	69	69	74	51	61	54	72	75	59

5 The following table shows the annual income per head in US$ and the life expectancy at birth in years for a sample of eight countries.

Country	A	B	C	D	E	F	G	H
Annual income per head (US$)	160	210	230	360	480	560	740	1290
Life expectancy at birth (years)	42	46	51	47	48	48	56	65

a Calculate Spearman's rank correlation coefficient.

b What does your answer to **a** suggest about the relationship between annual income per head and the life expectancy at birth?

11.5 Least Squares Regression Model

In Section 11.1, we looked at drawing lines of best fit; this was done by drawing a line through $(\bar{x}, \bar{y})$ with roughly the same number of points above and below the line. This line is called a **regression line**. We are now going to consider the equation of the regression line in order that we can use it to predict values of y for given values of x.

Consider the following example, which shows the correlation between the time a student spent on a homework task against the score for that piece of work:

In 1869, Francis Galton published *Hereditary Genius* which led to the formation of the Regression Law.

The regression line is a straight line and is of the form $y = a + bx$.

Looking at the diagram it is clear that not all the points lie on the straight line. In order that we can make the best possible prediction from this line, the distances $e_1, e_2, \ldots, e_n$ shown on the diagram need to be as small as possible. These values are the differences between the actual value of y and the predicted value of y using the line and are known as the **residuals**.

So, for example

$$e_1 = (a + bx_1) - y_1$$
$$e_1 = \text{predicted value of } y - \text{actual value of } y$$

Note the similarity with $y = mx + c$, remembering that m is the gradient and c the intercept.

Any point *on* the line $y = a + bx$ has coordinates $(x, a + bx)$.

The total of all the residuals needs to be as small as possible to ensure the best regression line. However, since some of the residuals are negative and some are positive the result of summing them would equal zero since they would all cancel each other out.

So, in fact we consider the sum of the *squares* of the residuals since these will all be positive and we make this as small as possible, in other words we *minimise* the following sum:

$$S = e_1^2 + e_2^2 + \cdots + e_n^2$$

This process is called finding the **least squares regression line** and involves minimising the sum of the squares of the residuals.

The resulting equation of the regression line that ensures S is as small as possible is given by:

$$y - \bar{y} = \frac{s_{xy}}{s_x^2}(x - \bar{x})$$

or

$$y - \bar{y} = \frac{S_{xy}}{S_{xx}}(x - \bar{x})$$

where $S_{xy} = ns_{xy}$ $S_{xx} = ns_x^2$

Remember: s_{xy} is the covariance of x and y and s_x is the standard deviation of x.

Remember:
$S_{xy} = \Sigma(x - \bar{x})(y - \bar{y})$
and
$s_{xy} = \frac{1}{n}\Sigma(x - \bar{x})(y - \bar{y})$

Example 1

For the following data find the equation of the least squares regression line y on x.

x	1	2	5	7	8	9	10
y	7	9	13	15	14	17	20

Use your regression line to estimate y when $x = 3$.

Solution

x	y	x^2	y^2	xy
1	7	1	49	7
2	9	4	81	18
5	13	25	169	65
7	15	49	225	105
8	14	64	196	112
9	17	81	289	153
10	20	100	400	200
$\Sigma x = 42$	$\Sigma y = 95$	$\Sigma x^2 = 324$	$\Sigma y^2 = 1409$	$\Sigma xy = 660$

$n = 7$

$\bar{x} = 6$ and $s_x^2 = 10.286$

$\bar{y} = 13.571$

$s_{xy} = 12.860$ (3 d.p.)

$s_x^2 = 10.286$ (3 d.p.)

The equation of the least squares regression line is

$$y - \bar{y} = \frac{s_{xy}}{s_x^2}(x - \bar{x})$$

So,

$$y - 13.571 = \frac{12.860}{10.286}(x - 6)$$

$$y - 13.571 = 1.250(x - 6)$$

$$y = 6.071 + 1.250x$$

When $x = 3$,

$$y = 6.071 + (1.250 \times 3)$$

$$= 9.821$$

$$s_{xy} = \frac{\Sigma xy}{n} - \bar{x}\bar{y}$$

$$= \frac{660}{7} - (6 \times 13.571)$$

$$= 12.860$$

$$s_x^2 = \frac{\Sigma x^2}{n} - \bar{x}^2$$

$$= \frac{324}{7} - 6^2$$

$$= 10.285\,714$$

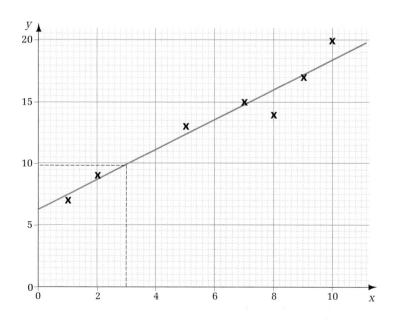

Note:
regression line crosses y-axis at 6.071 and has gradient 1.25.

Using regression lines

When using regression lines it is important to realise that it is only possible to predict, with a degree of confidence, values of y for values of x within the given range of the data; this is known as **interpolation**. Outside the range of the data extreme care must be exercised since attempting to predict such values of y for which no data has been collected may lead to incorrect conclusions. This process of predicting values outside the range collected is known as **extrapolation** and should, in general, be avoided.

Once a regression line has been calculated in the form $y = a + bx$, it is important to remember that both the coefficients a and b have meaning.

● a is the intercept on the y-axis, in other words the value of y when $x = 0$.

● b is the gradient of the line, that is the increase in y for every unit of x, sometimes known as the rate of change of y with respect to x.

Both these values have a meaning within a given context as can be seen in the following example.

Example 2

The following table shows the results of an experiment where eight similar plots of land were given different amounts of water, in centimetres, and the resulting yield of wheat in tonnes per acre was recorded for each plot.

Amount of water (x)	35	50	65	75	90	115	120	130
Yield of wheat (y)	4.2	5.68	5.90	6.10	5.85	7.10	7.54	7.6

a Find the equation of the regression line of y on x in the form $y = a + bx$.

b Interpret the coefficients of your regression line.

c What would you expect the yield to be for a plot where 70 cm of water was added and for a plot where 190 cm of water was added?

d Comment on the reliability of the results gained in **c**.

Solution

a

x	y	x^2	y^2	xy
35	4.2	1 225	17.64	147
50	5.68	2 500	32.26	284
65	5.90	4 225	34.81	383.5
75	6.10	5 625	37.21	457.5
90	5.85	8 100	34.22	526.5
115	7.10	13 225	50.41	816.5
120	7.54	14 400	56.85	904.8
130	7.6	16 900	57.76	988
$\Sigma x = 680$	$\Sigma y = 49.97$	$\Sigma x^2 = 66\,200$	$\Sigma y^2 = 321.17$	$\Sigma xy = 4507.8$

$n = 8$

$\bar{x} = 85$ and $\bar{y} = 6.246$

$s_x = 32.404$ and $s_x^2 = 1050$

$s_{xy} = \frac{4507.8}{8} - (85 \times 6.246)$

$= 32.565$

The equation of the least squares regression line is

$$y - \bar{y} = \frac{s_{xy}}{s_x^2}(x - \bar{x})$$

So

$y - 6.246 = \frac{32.565}{1050}(x - 85)$

$y - 6.246 = 0.031(x - 85)$

$y = 3.610 + 0.031x$

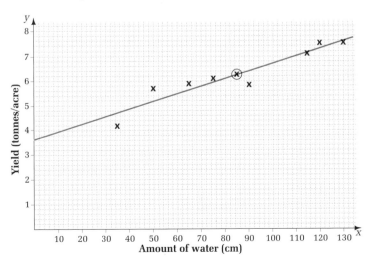

b   Interpretation of coefficients:

The gradient is 0.031 which can be interpreted that for every unit on the x-axis, that is for every centimetre of water added the yield of wheat increases by 0.031 tonnes per acre.

The y-intercept is 3.610 and can be interpreted that without any extra water added, 3.610 tonnes of wheat per acre will be produced.

This value has been obtained by extrapolation and must be treated with caution.

c   For 70 cm of water, using the regression line equation:

$$y = (0.031 \times 70) + 3.610$$
$$= 5.78 \text{ tonnes}$$

For 190 cm of water, using the regression line equation:

$$y = (0.031 \times 190) + 3.610$$
$$= 9.5 \text{ tonnes}$$

d   In **c**, interpolating for $x = 70$ cm would result in a good estimate for the amount of wheat produced. However, for $x = 190$ cm we are extrapolating outside the given data range and therefore cannot be confident that 9.5 tonnes is a good estimate for 190 cm of water added.

Many calculators can calculate the values of a and b in the equation of the regression line directly. Check *your* calculator to find out if it can do this.

11.5 Least Squares Regression Model

Exercise

Contextual

1 Calculate the equation of the least squares regression line in the form $y = a + bx$ for the following data:

x	1	2	3	4	5	6	7	8	9
y	5	4.7	5.8	6.2	4.6	4	3.5	5	4

2 Find the line of regression of y on x for the temperature and yield data on p. 293, Exercise 11.1, question **6**.

3 Calculate

a the covariance

b the equation of the least squares regression line for the following data:

x	2	4	5.6	3.8	2.7	5.6	5.9	8.2
y	4.8	7.6	6.2	7.4	6.2	9.6	11.3	14.3

4 Obtain the regression equation for y on x in the form $y = a + bx$ where $n = 8$ if:

$$\Sigma x = 38.45 \qquad \Sigma x^2 = 211.513 \qquad \Sigma y = 21.1$$

$$\Sigma y^2 = 63.19 \qquad \Sigma xy = 111.775$$

Use your regression line to estimate the value of y when $x = 3$.

5 Calculate the equation of the least squares regression line in the form $y = a + bx$ for the following data. Use your regression line to estimate the width of a leaf with length 138 mm.

Length (mm)	104	120	145	149	86	125	152	146	120	128
Width (mm)	34	38	42	54	33	37	51	41	30	42

6 The following table gives the results from research of a particular firm's profit relative to the size of an order made.

Size of order (units)	20 000	2000	5000	10 000	4000	3000	9000	20 000	18 000	500
Profit (£)	14 800	1200	2600	7700	2600	1500	5400	11 400	11 800	400

a Calculate the equation of the regression line of y on x, in the form $y = a + bx$.

b Find the expected profit from an order of 8000 units.

c State, giving a reason, whether or not you would use the line to find the expected profit from an order of 100 units.

Consolidation

Exercise A

1 What are the two main factors to consider when drawing a scatter diagram?

2 For the following data, calculate:

a the covariance

b Pearson's product moment correlation coefficient.

x	6.8	5.1	3.9	4.2	5.8	7.6
y	2.1	3.2	5.2	4.9	3.8	1.4

3 In a local craft competition the following marks were awarded to entrants in the junior section:

Entry	A	B	C	D	E	F	G
Judge 1	8.9	9.6	9.1	5.9	7.8	7.3	5.9
Judge 2	7.5	8.7	8.9	6.1	6.8	7.1	6.8

a Construct a table of ranks for the two judges.

b Calculate the Spearman's rank correlation coefficient.

4 The following data show the annual income per head, x, (in US$), and the infant mortality, y, (per thousand live births), for a sample of 11 countries.

Country	A	B	C	D	E	F	G	H	I	J	K
x	130	5950	560	2010	1870	170	390	580	820	6620	3800
y	150	43	121	53	41	169	143	59	75	20	39

Draw a scattergram of the data. Describe any relationships between infant mortality and income per head suggested by the scattergram. *(AEB)*

5 **a** State two conditions under which it might be more appropriate to use the Spearman rank correlation coefficient rather than the product moment correlation coefficient.

b At the end of a season a league of eight hockey clubs produced the following table showing the position of each club in the league and the average attendance (in hundreds) at home matches.

Club	A	B	C	D	E	F	G	H
Position	1	2	3	4	5	6	7	8
Average attendance	27	29	9	16	24	15	12	22

Calculate the Spearman rank correlation coefficient between position in the league and average home attendance. *(ULEAC)*

6 In a ladies' fashion competition, two judges gave marks to seven
contestants as follows.

Contestant	A	B	C	D	E	F	G
Judge X	64	65	67	78	79	80	96
Judge Y	70	63	61	81	80	78	98

(Use $\Sigma x = 529$, $\Sigma x^2 = 40\,751$, $\Sigma y = 531$, $\Sigma y^2 = 41\,239$, $\Sigma xy = 40\,948$)

a   Calculate the product moment correlation coefficient.
b   Calculate Spearman's rank correlation coefficient.

(*UCLES*)

7 An agricultural researcher collected the following data showing the annual
yield of wheat (in bushels per acre) and the annual rainfall (in inches).

Rainfall (x)	9.7	19.0	8.2	11.1	6.9	13.6	13.0	15.0
Yield of wheat (y)	28.0	35.1	23.8	25.6	20.1	30.2	28.5	33.7

a   Plot the data on a scatter diagram.
b   Evaluate the product moment correlation coefficient between x and y.
     (Use $\Sigma x^2 = 1272.11$, $\Sigma y^2 = 6501.80$, $\Sigma xy = 2843.23$)
c   Give an interpretation of your coefficient.
d   Find the equation of the regression line of y on x in the form $y = p + qx$.
e   Give an interpretation of your value for q.
f   State, giving a reason, whether or not you would use your regression
     equation to predict the yield in a year in which there was 30 inches of
     rain.

(*ULEAC*)

8 A farmer is investigating the relationship between the density at which a
crop is planted and the quality. By using more intensive methods he can
increase the yield, but he suspects that the percentage of high quality
produce may fall. The farmer collects the following data.

Seed per acre (x) in suitable units	120	130	140	150	160	170
Percentage of high quality produce (y)	31.3	28.9	25.4	21.3	21.0	10.7

$n = 6$, $\Sigma x = 870$, $\Sigma y = 138.6$, $\Sigma xy = 19\,443$, $\Sigma x^2 = 127\,900$, $\Sigma y^2 = 3469.24$

a   Draw a sketch to illustrate the data. Hence discuss how suitable a
     straight line model would be for the relationship between y and x.
b   Calculate the equation of the regression line of y on x.
c   Obtain from your regression line the predicted values of y at $x = 145$
     and $x = 180$. Comment, with reason, on the likely accuracy of these
     predictions.

(*MEI*)

9 In the chemical industry the yield of a batch process and the temperature at which the process was carried out are recorded. The following table gives the results for eight batches.

Temperature °C (x)	175	185	195	205	215	225	235	245
Yield tonnes (y)	142.4	146.2	159.2	164.1	172.1	186.2	194.3	206.2

$\Sigma x = 1680$, $\Sigma x^2 = 357\,000$, $\Sigma y = 1370.7$, $\Sigma xy = 291\,727.5$

a Plot the data on a scatter diagram.
b Calculate the equation of the regression line of yield on temperature and plot it on your scatter diagram.
c Estimate the yield for a temperature of 200°C.
d The residual is defined as the actual yield minus the yield predicted by the regression equation. Calculate the residual for each point.
e The yields at 175°C, 195°C, 225°C and 245°C were measured by Sharon while the yields at the other temperatures were measured by Ali. Comment on the residuals and make an approximate estimate of the yield at 200°C as measured by Sharon.

(*AEB*)

10 In an experiment on memory, five groups of people (chosen randomly) were given varying lengths of time to memorise the same list of 40 words. Later, they were asked to recall as many words as possible from the list. The table shows the average number of words recalled, y, and the time given, t seconds. The data are also shown in a scatter diagram.

t	20	40	60	80	100
y	12.1	18.5	22.8	24.6	24.0

$\Sigma t = 300$, $\Sigma t^2 = 22\,000$, $\Sigma y = 102$, $\Sigma y^2 = 2189.66$, $\Sigma ty = 6718$

a Calculate the equation of the regression line for y on t.

b Use your regression line to calculate y when $t = 20$. Comment on the result.

c Use your regression line to calculate y when $t = 160$. Comment on the usefulness or otherwise of this result.

d Discuss briefly whether the regression line provides a good model or whether there is a better way of modelling the relationship between y and t.

(*MEI*)

Exercise B

1 For the following data plot a scatter diagram to illustrate the data and if appropriate draw a line of best fit.

Rainfall (inches)	10.1	18.6	8.1	11.3	6.9	14.1	14	13.8
Yield of maize (tonnes per acre)	27.1	36.2	21.6	25.2	16.9	36.1	27.2	25.6

2 For the following data, calculate:

a the covariance

b Pearson's product moment correlation coefficient.

x	7	9	8	6	4	5
y	3	5	5	4	5	2

3 What is the difference between interpolation and extrapolation when using a regression line to estimate values of y for given values of x?

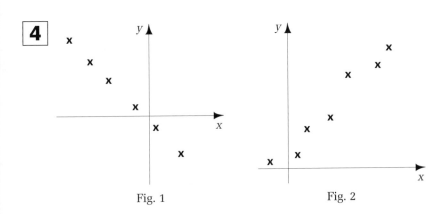

Fig. 1   Fig. 2

a For the scatter diagram shown in Fig. 1, state the value of the product moment correlation coefficient.

b For the scatter diagram shown in Fig. 2, state the value of Spearman's rank correlation coefficient.

(*UCLES*)

5 Two people, X and Y, were asked to give marks out of 20 for seven brands of fish finger. The results are recorded in the table.

Brand	A	B	C	D	E	F	G
X's mark	8	10	18	2	1	4	15
Y's mark	5	14	12	9	4	1	19

Construct a table of ranks and calculate Spearman's rank correlation coefficient.

(UCLES)

6 A random sample of students who are shortly to sit an examination are asked to keep a record of how long they spend revising, in order to investigate whether more revision time is associated with a higher mark. The data are given below, with x hours being the revision time (correct to the nearest half hour) and y being the percentage mark scored in the examination.

x	0	3	4.5	3.5	7	5.5	5	6.5	6	10.5	2
y	36	52	52	57	60	61	63	63	64	70	89

$n = 11$, $\Sigma x = 53.5$, $\Sigma y = 667$, $\Sigma x^2 = 338.25$, $\Sigma y^2 = 42\,129$, $\Sigma xy = 3366.5$

Obtain the value of the product moment correlation coefficient for the data.

(MEI)

7 a In addition to its full-time staff, a supermarket employs part-time sales staff on Saturdays. The manager experimented to see if there is a relationship between the takings and the number of part-time staff employed. She collected the following data on nine successive Saturdays.

Number of part-time staff employed, x	10	13	16	19	22	25	28	31	34
Takings, £100s, y	313	320	319	326	333	342	321	361	355

$\Sigma x = 198$, $\Sigma x^2 = 4896$, $\Sigma y = 2990$, $\Sigma xy = 66\,713$

i Plot a scatter diagram of these data.

ii Calculate the equation of the regression line of takings on the number of part-time staff employed. Draw the line on your scatter diagram.

iii If the regression equation is denoted by $y = a + bx$, give interpretations to each of a and b.

iv On one of the Saturdays, major roadworks blocked a nearby main road. Which Saturday do you think this was? Give a reason for your choice.

v The manager had increased the number of part-time staff each week. This was desirable from an organisational point of view but undesirable from a statistical point of view. Comment.

b The following table shows the percentage of part-time staff employed by the nine largest supermarkets in the area. It also shows their ranking in terms of weekly takings; the supermarket with the highest weekly takings was given rank 1.

Part-time staff (%)	45	56	38	29	54	33	36	33	22
Weekly takings (rank)	7	4	5	9	2	8	1	3	6

Calculate the value of Spearman's rank correlation coefficient for this set of data.

(AEB)

8 The following table shows the amount of water, in centimetres, applied to seven similar plots on an experimental farm. It also shows the yield of hay in tonnes per acre.

Amount of water (x)	30	45	60	75	90	105	120
Yield of hay (y)	4.85	5.20	5.76	6.60	7.35	7.95	7.77

(Use $\Sigma x^2 = 45\,675$; $\Sigma y^2 = 304.8980$; $\Sigma xy = 3648.75$)

a Find the equation of the regression line of y on x in the form $y = a + bx$.

b Interpret the coefficients of your regression line.

c What would you expect the yield to be for $x = 28$ and for $x = 150$? Comment on the reliability of each of your expected yields.

(ULEAC)

9 An A-level chemistry student was investigating whether there was a linear relationship between a metal's melting point and its boiling point. From a set of tables the results for four metals were obtained as follows:

Atomic number	20	21	22	23
Melting point (°C)	848	1541	1677	1917
Boiling point (°C)	1487	2831	3277	3377

Taking the variables x and y to be melting point and boiling point respectively, the following summary statistics were calculated:

$\Sigma x = 5983$, $\Sigma y = 10\,972$, $\Sigma x^2 = 9\,581\,003$, $\Sigma y^2 = 32\,368\,588$, $\Sigma xy = 17\,592\,785$.

a Calculate the product moment correlation coefficient between melting point and boiling point.

b State, with a reason, whether the results suggest that there is a linear relationship between a metal's melting point and boiling point.

(OCSEB)

10 A company monitored the number of days (x) of business trips taken by executives of the company and the corresponding claims (£y) they submitted to cover the total expenditure of these trips. A random sample of ten trips gave the following results.

x (days)	10	3	8	17	5	9	14	16	21	13
y (£)	116	39	85	159	61	94	143	178	225	134

a Plot these data on a scatter diagram. Give a reason to support the calculation of a regression line through these points.

b Find an equation of the regression line of y on x, in the form $y = a + bx$. (Use $\Sigma x^2 = 1630$ and $\Sigma xy = 17\,128$)

c Interpret the slope b and the intercept a of your line.

d Find the expected expenditure of a trip lasting eleven days.

e State, giving a reason, whether or not you would use the line to find the expected expenditure of a trip lasting two months.

(*ULEAC*)

Applications and Activities

1 Investigate the relationship between the common first names of adults over 50 years old and of children.

2 Round your waist is twice round your neck. Investigate.

Summary

- A scatter diagram shows whether there is any correlation between two variables.

- If as one variable increases so does the other, there is positive correlation.

- If as one variable increases the other decreases, there is negative correlation.

- A line of best fit is a line drawn on a scatter diagram, going through the mean $(\bar{x}, \bar{y})$ so that roughly the same number of points are above and below the line.

- The covariance between two variables, x and y, is

- Pearson's product moment correlation coefficient is r, where

$$r = \frac{s_{xy}}{s_x s_y} = \frac{\frac{\Sigma xy}{n} - \bar{x}\bar{y}}{\sqrt{\left(\frac{\Sigma x^2}{n} - \bar{x}^2\right)\left(\frac{\Sigma y^2}{n} - \bar{y}^2\right)}}$$

- Spearman's rank correlation coefficient is r_s, where

$$r_s = 1 - \frac{6\Sigma d^2}{n(n^2 - 1)}$$

(d is the difference between the rankings of each item.)

- A residual is the difference between the actual value of y and the predicted value of y.

$$e_i = (a + bx_i) - y_i$$

- The equation of the least squares regression line, y on x, is

$$y - \bar{y} = \frac{s_{xy}}{s_x^2}(x - \bar{x})$$

12 Estimation I: Point Estimators

What you need to know

- How to calculate the mean, variance and standard deviation.

- The properties of the normal distribution.

Review

Calculate the mean and variance of the following:

1   37   39   41   41   44   47   50

2   157   188   216   241   255   264

3   2.4   2.8   5.9   3.1   7.8   1.9   6.3   3.7

4   0.02   0.09   0.05   0.05   0.1   0.05   0.08   0.06   0.06   0.05

5   −1   −3   −6   −5   3   2   5   −1   6   6   6

6

x	0	1	2	3	4
f	12	36	49	29	14

7

x	−3	−2	−1	0	1	2	3	4
f	7	9	19	32	29	18	13	4

8

x	0–5	5–10	10–15	15–20	20–25	25–30
f	6	15	28	22	18	11

12.1 Point Estimator for Population Mean

We take a sample from a population in order to gain some information about the properties of that population, such as the mean and the variance. As the size of the sample increases so does the accuracy of the results, but a balance must be maintained between the size of the sample and the cost of sampling in terms of time, effort and money.

The mean and standard deviation of a sample are called **sample statistics** or simply **statistics**. If we calculate a single value (rather than an interval in which the value lies) for a statistic it is called a **point estimation** of that statistic.

Remember that different symbols are used to indicate the mean and standard deviation of a population and those of a sample.

		Symbol
Population	Standard deviation	σ
	Mean	μ
Sample	Standard deviation	s
	Mean	$\bar{x}$

If an *estimate* of the population mean and standard deviation is taken from a sample, then the following symbols are used:

Estimator	Standard deviation	$\hat{\sigma}$ (sigma hat)
	Mean	$\hat{\mu}$ (mu hat)

Example

Every week six numbers are selected as the winning line in the National Lottery. The choice of numbers is from 1 to 49 and every ball has an equal chance of being selected. One selection of six numbers was 5, 10, 17, 25, 40 and 43. Calculate the point estimator of the mean.

Solution

The mean value of the six numbers is:

$$\frac{140}{6} = 23.3$$

So the point estimator of the mean,

$$\bar{x} = 23.3$$

12.1 Point Estimator for Population Mean
Exercise

Technique

1 Calculate the mean and standard deviation of the numbers 1–49 inclusive.

2 Calculate the mean of the following winning National Lottery lines.

3, 4, 5, 16, 22, 25	24, 33, 42, 43, 44, 47
14, 27, 39, 40, 41, 43	13, 16, 17, 29, 40, 48
7, 24, 37, 39, 40, 43	3, 19, 24, 25, 26, 33
5, 8, 21, 38, 34, 49	2, 9, 13, 18, 27, 48
6, 10, 14, 25, 27, 38	8, 12, 17, 23, 34, 43
1, 14, 16, 25, 32, 37	2, 8, 16, 21, 29, 37
12, 19, 22, 23, 25, 44	1, 3, 28, 31, 41, 46
5, 12, 20, 29, 39, 42	7, 12, 20, 24, 28, 43
12, 19, 28, 31, 34, 43	6, 20, 29, 31, 35, 40
8, 10, 16, 17, 24, 40	5, 10, 17, 25, 40, 43

3 Comment on the spread of the mean values in question ②.

4 Group the results from question ② into a frequency table using the groups $10 \le x < 15$, $15 \le x < 20$, ..., $35 \le x < 40$. Comment on any pattern.

12.2 Central Limit Theorem

Using the example of the National Lottery it would be interesting to examine further the distribution of the mean value of the six numbers taken at random between the values of 1 and 49 inclusive. By obtaining further winning lines, or sets of six random numbers between 1 and 49 inclusive, calculate the mean value of a further fifty sets of numbers. Combine the mean values into a grouped frequency table and from this draw a frequency chart of the results. Comment on any pattern that develops.

The **Central Limit Theorem** states:

> For a sample size n drawn from a distribution with mean, μ, and variance, σ^2, the distribution of the sample mean is approximately normal with the same mean, μ, but with a variance of σ^2/n, for a sufficiently large n.

In the case of the National Lottery lines the parent population is rectangular, that is in a large sample each number would occur the same number of times, but the distribution of the mean values of the samples of size six should have been observed to become approximately normally distributed.

The parent population is the population from which the sample is drawn.

If the parent population is normal, then the sampling distribution (of the means), that is the distribution formed by the values of the means of the samples, will be normal, whatever the size of the sample. If the parent population is not normal, as with the Lottery numbers, the sampling distribution will still be approximately normal, and will tend to a closer fit to the normal distribution as the number of samples increases.

The Central Limit Theorem is extremely important in the study of statistics so it is important to examine all its implications.

The distribution of the sample mean is approximately

$$N\left(\mu, \frac{\sigma^2}{n}\right) \quad \text{for sufficiently large } n.$$

- Firstly, the mean of the sampling distribution is the *same* as the mean of the parent population. This may seem obvious but it is fundamental to sampling techniques.

- Secondly, the standard deviation of the sampling distribution is *different* from the standard deviation of the parent population.

In the example of the lottery lines the mean values of the lines were more closely grouped together than the original figures. So the standard deviation of the sampling distribution, $\dfrac{\sigma^2}{n}$, is often referred to as the standard error of the sample mean, or **standard error** for short.

Proofs

1. The mean of the sample distribution is the same as the mean of the population.

   If $X_1, X_2, X_3, X_4, \ldots, X_n$ is a sample of n independent observations from a distribution with mean, μ, and variance, σ^2, then:

   $$\bar{X} = \frac{1}{n}(X_1 + X_2 + X_3 + X_4 + \cdots + X_n)$$

   $$\therefore \quad E(\bar{X}) = E\left[\frac{1}{n}(X_1 + X_2 + X_3 + X_4 + \cdots + X_n)\right]$$

   $$= \frac{1}{n}E[(X_1 + X_2 + X_3 + X_4 + \cdots + X_n)]$$

   $$= \frac{1}{n}[E(X_1) + E(X_2) + E(X_3) + E(X_4) + \cdots + E(X_n)]$$

   $$= \frac{1}{n}[(\mu) + (\mu) + (\mu) + (\mu) + \cdots + (\mu)]$$

   $$= \frac{1}{n}(n \times \mu)$$

   $$= \mu$$

   The mean of $\bar{X}$ is μ, the same as the mean of the parent population.

2. The variance of the sample distribution is $\dfrac{\sigma^2}{n}$.

   $$\text{Var}(\bar{X}) = \text{Var}\left[\frac{1}{n}(X_1 + X_2 + X_3 + X_4 + \cdots + X_n)\right]$$

   $$= \frac{1}{n^2}\text{Var}(X_1 + X_2 + X_3 + X_4 + \cdots + X_n)$$

   $$= \frac{1}{n^2}[\text{Var}(X_1) + \text{Var}(X_2) + \text{Var}(X_3) + \text{Var}(X_4) + \cdots + \text{Var}(X_n)]$$

   $$= \frac{1}{n^2}(\sigma^2 + \sigma^2 + \sigma^2 + \sigma^2 + \cdots + \sigma^2)$$

   $$= \frac{1}{n^2}(n \times \sigma^2)$$

   $$= \frac{\sigma^2}{n}$$

   The variance of $\bar{X}$ is $\dfrac{\sigma^2}{n}$.

Example

In trials a researcher recorded the number of ears of wheat on 10 stalks as:

$$18 \quad 25 \quad 20 \quad 22 \quad 27 \quad 21 \quad 19 \quad 15 \quad 26 \quad 20$$

The wheat is from a population with a known variance of 2.25. Calculate the mean and standard error of the sample.

Solution

$$\text{mean} = \frac{\Sigma x}{n} = \frac{213}{10} = 21.3$$

$$\text{standard error} = \frac{\sigma}{\sqrt{n}} = \frac{\sqrt{2.25}}{\sqrt{10}} = 0.474 \ (3 \text{ s.f.})$$

12.2 Central Limit Theorem
Exercise

Technique

The following samples were taken from a normal population with the given variance. Work out the mean and standard error of the sample.

1 $\quad$ 48, 53, 58, 61, 64; $\quad \sigma^2 = 12$

2 $\quad$ 103, 109, 111, 111, 113, 115; $\quad \sigma^2 = 12$

3 $\quad$ 268, 268, 269, 270, 274, 274, 275, 275, 275, 276; $\quad \sigma^2 = 12$

4 $\quad$ 19.6, 24.8, 24.9, 32.1, 35.8, 42.5; $\quad \sigma^2 = 30$

5 $\quad$ 457.2, 489.1, 491.0, 495.6, 499.8, 501.9, 502.0, 505.6; $\quad \sigma^2 = 50$

6 $\quad \sigma^2 = 15$

x	20	21	22	23	24	25	26	27	28
f	5	11	17	21	19	12	10	7	4

7 $\quad \sigma^2 = 60$

x	100	120	130	140	150
f	23	47	68	49	35

8 $\quad \sigma^2 = 12$

x	104	106	108	110
f	42	69	104	35

9 $\quad \sigma^2 = 10$

x	−2	−1	0	1
f	13	15	18	9

10 $\quad \sigma^2 = 5$

x	99.5	100	100.5	101
f	5	17	9	4

Contextual

1 Students measured the heights of eight samples of Year 12 students who were chosen at random from a population with a variance of 81 cm². The mean of each sample was

144, 183, 192, 156, 179, 165, 151, 186

Find the mean and standard error of the sample.

2 Biologists investigating the growth of worms in a particular location measured their lengths to the nearest centimetre. The variance of the population was known to be 16 cm². The mean lengths of their samples were:

18, 12, 21, 19, 23, 17, 24, 16, 19, 15,
18, 22, 15, 17, 22, 20, 16, 19, 18, 18

Calculate the mean and standard error of the sample.

3 The IQs of 20 students were measured as:

130, 121, 113, 110, 135, 124, 141, 122, 114, 138
122, 127, 151, 119, 125, 134, 119, 111, 142, 137

The population is known to be normally distributed with a variance of 225. Calculate the mean of the sample and the standard error.

4 The following table shows the number of strokes taken by golfers at one particular hole.

Strokes	2	3	4	5	6	7	8
Golfers	2	11	38	33	25	9	2

If the distribution has a variance of 6.25, find the mean value and the standard error.

5 The number of children in families in a certain area were recorded as:

Number of children	0	1	2	3	4	5
Families	13	25	36	19	8	4

If the population has a variance of 10, find the mean and standard error of the sample.

12.3 Biased and Unbiased Estimators

An estimator for a population parameter, such as the mean or variance, is said to be **unbiased** if the mean, or expected value, of its sampling distribution equals the parameter it is estimating.

A **biased** estimator is one where the mean of its sampling distribution is not equal to the population parameter it is supposed to measure.

Population mean

From the Central Limit Theorem the mean of the sampling distribution, $\bar{X}$, is equal to the mean of the population, μ, which makes $\bar{X}$ an unbiased estimator of μ.

$$\hat{\mu} = \bar{X}$$

Population variance

If a sample of size n is taken from a population with an unknown variance σ^2, then the sample variance is denoted by S^2.

The mean of the sampling distribution of S^2 is $\dfrac{n-1}{n}\sigma^2$.

From this we can show that an unbiased estimator of the population variance from a sample is $\dfrac{nS^2}{n-1}$.

$$\hat{\sigma}^2 = \frac{nS^2}{n-1} \qquad \text{where } S^2 \text{ is the sample variance.}$$

To show $\hat{\mu} = \bar{X}$

For a sample $X_1, X_2, X_3, X_4, \ldots, X_n$

$$E(\bar{X}) = \frac{1}{n}\left[E(X_1) + E(X_2) + E(X_3) + E(X_4) + \cdots + E(X_n)\right]$$

$$= \frac{1}{n}\left[n \times E(X)\right]$$

$$E(\bar{X}) = E(X) = \mu$$

Therefore

$$\bar{X} = \hat{\mu}.$$

To show that $\dfrac{ns^2}{n-1}$ is an unbiased estimator of σ^2

$$s^2 = \sum\left(\frac{X}{n} - \bar{X}\right)^2 = \sum \frac{X^2}{n} - \bar{X}^2$$

So
$$ns^2 = \Sigma X^2 - n\bar{X}^2$$

$$E(ns^2) = E(\Sigma X^2) - E(n\bar{X}^2)$$

$$= E(X_1)^2 + E(X_2)^2 + \cdots + E(X_n)^2 - nE(\bar{X}^2)$$

$$E(X_1) = E(X_2) = E(X_3)\cdots = E(X_n) = \mu$$

and
$$\mathrm{Var}(X_1) = \mathrm{Var}(X_2) = \mathrm{Var}(X_3)\cdots = \mathrm{Var}(X_n) = \sigma^2$$

Now
$$\mathrm{Var}(X) = E(X^2) - [E(\bar{X})]^2$$

$$\sigma^2 = E(X^2) - \mu^2$$

$$\sigma^2 + \mu^2 = E(X^2)$$

Substituting $E(\bar{X}) = \mu$, and $\mathrm{Var}(X) = \dfrac{\sigma^2}{n}$ in $\mathrm{Var}(X) = E(X^2) - [E(\bar{X})]^2$

$$\frac{\sigma^2}{n} = E(X^2) - \mu^2$$

$$\frac{\sigma^2}{n} + \mu^2 = E(X^2)$$

From
$$E(ns^2) = E(\Sigma X^2) - E(n\bar{X}^2)$$

$$= n(\mu^2 + \sigma^2) - n\left(\mu^2 + \frac{\sigma^2}{n}\right)$$

$$= n\mu^2 + n\sigma^2 - n\mu^2 - \sigma^2$$

$$= n\sigma^2 - \sigma^2$$

$$= (n-1)\sigma^2$$

$$E\left[\frac{ns^2}{n-1}\right] = \sigma^2$$

Therefore $\dfrac{nS^2}{n-1}$ is an **unbiased** estimator of σ^2, the population **variance**.

If an unbiased estimator for the mean and variance of a population is to be calculated from a sample distribution $N(\bar{x}, s^2)$, then
$$\hat{\mu} = \bar{x}$$

and
$$s^2 = \frac{(n-1)}{n}\sigma^2$$

or
$$\hat{\sigma}^2 = \frac{nS^2}{n-1}$$

Unbiased estimators are used because, on average, they are not biased in one direction or the other.

Although $\hat{\sigma}^2$ is an unbiased estimator of σ and $\hat{\sigma}$ is used as an estimator of σ, it should be noted that $\hat{\sigma}$ is in fact a biased estimator of σ.

Population proportion

If p is the unknown proportion of success in a population an estimate for p can be found by taking a sample of size n, and calculating the proportion of success in that sample, denoted by P_s.

$$\hat{p} = P_s$$

To show $\hat{p} = P_s$

A population has probability of success p, and a random sample of size n is taken from this population. If X is the random variable 'number of successes in the sample' $X \sim B(n, p)$.

When n is large $X \sim N(np, npq)$, where $q = 1 - p$.

If P_s is the random variable 'proportion of successes in the sample' then $P_s = \dfrac{X}{n}$.

$$E(P_s) = E\left(\frac{X}{n}\right) = \frac{E(X)}{n} = \frac{np}{n} = p$$

Therefore P_s is an unbiased estimator for the population proportion.

Example 1

The lengths of a sample of 10 fish were measured to the nearest centimetre as follows:

23.7   28.9   32.1   24.5   29.2   30.5   24.1   22.6   27.4   35.5

Calculate an unbiased estimator of the population mean and an estimator of the population standard deviation.

Solution

sample mean, $\bar{x} = 27.85$

sample variance, $s^2 = 15.6805$

$$\therefore \quad \hat{\mu} = 27.85$$

$$\hat{\sigma}^2 = \frac{ns^2}{n-1}$$

$$= \frac{10}{9} \times 15.68$$

$$\hat{\sigma}^2 = 17.423$$

$$\hat{\sigma} = 4.174$$

Example 2

A sample of 40 students is chosen from a sixth-form college. Fifteen of these students wear glasses. Calculate an unbiased estimate of the proportion of students in the college who wear glasses.

Solution

Proportion of students in the sample who wear glasses is p_s.

$$p_s = \tfrac{15}{40} = 0.375$$

$$\therefore \quad \hat{p} = 0.375$$

12.3 Biased and Unbiased Estimators

Exercise

Technique

Calculate unbiased estimators for the mean and variance of the normal population from which the following samples were taken.

1   5   7   9   11

2   2   2   6   7   7   9

3   31   33   34   37   43   45   47   50

4   6.4   3.5   6.1   4.8   5.5   8.3   5.4   5.0   3.9   7.5

5

x	23	24	25	26	27	28	29
f	6	9	13	5	3	3	1

6

x	0	1	2	3	4	5
f	2	5	8	6	3	1

7

x	0–	3–	6–	10–	15–25
f	3	7	8	7	5

8

x	14–16	17–19	20–22	23–25
f	42	69	104	35

9

x	−3	−1	1	3
f	13	15	18	9

10

x	99	100	101	102
f	5	17	9	4

Contextual

1   A sample of students' marks in a test were:

    1   2   2   4   4   4   7   7   8   9

Find an unbiased estimator for the mean and an estimator for the standard deviation of all the students' marks.

2 The number of minutes that buses arrive late at a bus stop were recorded. The times were:

> 3   13   5   8   12   5   6   4   8   7   10   8

Find an unbiased estimator for the mean and an estimator for the standard deviation of the number of minutes late of all the buses.

3 The life expectancies of a sample of rats were recorded in days as

> 814   729   798   894   564   619   750   765
> 684   741   615   752   513   545   648

Calculate an unbiased estimator for the mean and an estimator for the standard deviation of the life expectancy of the rat population.

4 In a sample of netball goalshooters their percentage accuracy was found to be:

> 82   73   58   87   64   75   90   84

Find an unbiased estimate of the mean and variance of the accuracy level for all netball goalshooters.

5 As part of a survey, 16 Year 13 students were asked how many subjects they had studied as part of their courses. The results were:

Subjects	1	2	3	4	5
Frequency	2	3	5	5	1

Find unbiased estimates of the mean and variance of the number of subjects that Year 13 students study.

6 Twelve teenagers were asked to indicate the allowance they received each week from their parents. The results were (£):

> 8   12   5   9   4   10
> 6   10   8   8   6   10

Find an unbiased estimate of the mean and an estimator for the standard deviation of the allowance that all teenagers receive.

12.4 Pooled Estimates of the Mean and Variance of the Population from Two Samples

If two independent samples are taken from a population then the results can be pooled to find unbiased estimators for the mean and standard deviation.

A population has an unknown mean, μ, and variance, σ^2. Two samples of size n_1 and n_2 are taken and found to have means $\bar{X}_1$ and $\bar{X}_2$ with variances S_1^2 and S_2^2 respectively. This then gives an unbiased estimator for the mean of the population as:

$$\hat{\mu} = \frac{n_1 \bar{X}_1 + n_2 \bar{X}_2}{n_1 + n_2}$$

$\hat{\mu}$ is unbiased and uses all the sample values.

Proof

$$E\left[\frac{(n_1\bar{X}_1 + n_2\bar{X}_2)}{n_1 + n_2}\right] = \frac{1}{n_1 + n_2} E(n_1\bar{x}_1 + n_2\bar{x}_2)$$

$$= \frac{1}{n_1 + n_2}(n_1\mu + n_2\mu)$$

$$= \frac{1}{n_1 + n_2}\mu(n_1 + n_2)$$

Cancel by $(n_1 + n_2)$

$$\therefore \quad E\left[\frac{(n_1\bar{X}_1 + n_2\bar{X}_2)}{n_1 + n_2}\right] = \mu$$

An unbiased estimator of the variance of the population is then

$$\hat{\sigma}^2 = \frac{n_1 S_1^2 + n_2 S_2^2}{n_1 + n_2 - 2}$$

$\hat{\sigma}^2$ is unbiased and give almost as good an estimate of σ^2 as poolir the samples, but it can be calculated directly from S_1^2 and S_2^2.

Proof

$$E(n_1 s_1^2 + n_2 s_2^2) = E(n_1 s_1^2) + E(n_2 s_2^2)$$

As

$$E\left[\frac{ns^2}{n-1}\right] = \sigma^2$$

$$E(ns^2) = (n-1)\sigma^2$$

So

$$E(n_1 s_1^2 + n_2 s_2^2) = (n_1 - 1)\sigma^2 + (n_2 - 1)\sigma^2$$

$$= (n_1 - 1 + n_2 - 1)\sigma^2$$

$$= (n_1 + n_2 - 2)\sigma^2$$

$$\frac{E(n_1 s_1^2 + n_2 s_2^2)}{(n_1 + n_2 - 2)} = \sigma^2$$

Example

In random samples from a population, the following results were obtained.

Sample 1   11.2, 11.8, 11.6, 11.8, 11.8, 11.2, 11.2, 11.3, 11.7, 11.4

Sample 2   11.3, 11.4, 11.4, 11.5, 11.6, 11.3, 11.4, 11.3

Find the distribution of the normal population from which these samples are taken.

Solution

Sample 1 $\bar{x}_1 = 11.5$ $s_1^2 = 0.064$

Sample 2 $\bar{x}_2 = 11.4$ $s_2^2 = 0.01$

$$\hat{\mu} = \frac{(10 \times 11.5 + 8 \times 11.4)}{10 + 8}$$

$$= 11.46$$

$$\hat{\sigma}^2 = \frac{(10 \times 0.064 + 8 \times 0.01)}{10 + 8 - 2}$$

$$= 0.045$$

So the population is distributed approximately $N(11.46, 0.045)$.

12.4 Pooled Estimates of the Mean and Variance of the Population from Two Samples

Exercise

Technique

Find unbiased estimators of the mean and variance of the population from which the following samples were taken.

1 Sample 1   8.9, 9.0, 8.6, 8.3, 8.5
Sample 2   8.4, 8.6, 8.3, 8.9, 8.6, 9.1, 8.4

2 Sample 1   3.1, 3.7, 4.1, 4.5, 3.8, 3.9, 3.6
Sample 2   3.6, 3.9, 3.4, 3.3, 3.8, 3.8

3 Sample 1   52, 51, 56, 59, 56, 51, 64, 60
Sample 2   54, 56, 51, 48, 55, 59, 63, 61, 49, 52

4 Sample 1   0.49, 0.63, 0.31, 0.55
Sample 2   0.32, 0.59, 0.58, 0.47, 0.49, 0.52

5 Sample 1

x	0	1	2	3	4	5
f	1	3	6	5	3	2

Sample 2

x	0	1	2	3	4
f	2	2	5	4	2

6 Sample 1

x	0	1	2	3	4	5	6	7
f	2	8	15	23	19	9	3	2

Sample 2

x	0.5	1	1.5	2	2.5	3	3.5	4	4.5
f	3	5	7	12	15	19	10	8	5

7 Sample 1

x	15–	17–	19–	21–23
f	2	6	7	3

Sample 2

x	16–	18–	20–	22–24
f	5	4	2	1

8 Sample 1

x	0–5	5–10	10–15	15–20	20–25
f	4	8	13	15	6

Sample 2

x	13–17	17–21	21–25	25–29
f	10	16	22	4

Contextual

1 A sample of scores was taken randomly for boys and girls from the same population and the results were:

      Boys   94, 71, 59, 65, 74, 53, 88, 61, 72
      Girls   79, 83, 47, 62

From these results find the mean and variance of the boys and girls. Hence find unbiased estimators for the mean and variance of the whole population.

2 Samples of bags of sugar from a machine were weighed in two batches. The results were, in kilograms:

      Batch 1   2.07, 1.95, 2.03, 2.01, 1.97
      Batch 2   2.1, 2.07, 2.01, 2.02, 1.96, 1.97, 2.05

The weight of the bags is known to normally distributed. Find estimators of the mean and variance of each batch. Use these values to find unbiased estimates of the mean and variance of all the bags of sugar. If the mean weight is claimed to be 2 kg is there any evidence to suggest this may not be true?

Trout were released into two pools. During the first day's fishing the weight of each fish caught was recorded, in kilograms:

Pool A   0.55, 0.77, 0.87, 1.17, 1.54, 1.35
Pool B   0.86, 0.59, 1.48, 1.21

Find unbiased estimators of the mean and variance of all the trout released.

  Samples were taken from each of two consignments of gold coins to test for the purity of the gold. The percentage of non-gold elements was analysed and the results were:

Batch 1	9.4	8.3	9.7	11.4	10.6	8.3	9.2	10.1
	11.7	8.5	9.2	10.5	9.1	8.7	10.9	9.3
Batch 2	12.4	11.7	9.6	10.4	11.3	11.9	10.4	9.3
	8.5	8.1						

Using the means and variances of each sample, calculate an unbiased estimator of the mean and variance of the population.

  Two colours of ribbons are produced and sold in 1 metre lengths. The actual lengths of the ribbons in a batch of each of the colours were measured and the differences from 1 metre, to the nearest millimetre, recorded. The results were:

White	21	19	5	12	7	−3	−9	12
	18	−15	−22	7	−17	−24	−1	5
	−4	−1	18	−10				

Red	−16	8	11	16	−5	−9	−20	−9
	12	−11	27	−6	−7	−29	13	4

From the two samples find an unbiased estimator of the mean and variance of all the ribbon lengths, if it is known that the length is normally distributed.

12.5 Pooled Estimator for Population Proportions from Two Samples

Again when two independent samples are taken from a single population, the *proportion of each sample with a specific characteristic* can be pooled to obtain an estimate of the proportion of the population with the same characteristic.

For example, in a binomial distribution where the probability of success, p, is unknown and two samples of size n_1 and n_2 are taken, with proportions of success, P_{s_1} and P_{s_2}, then an unbiased estimator, $\hat{p}$, for the probability of success in the parent population is:

$$\hat{p} = \frac{n_1 P_{s_1} + n_2 P_{s_2}}{n_1 + n_2}$$

This is a very similar formula to that of the pooled estimator for the mean using two samples.

Proof

The estimator is unbiased because:

$$\frac{E(n_1 p_{s_1} + n_2 p_{s_2})}{n_1 + n_2} = \frac{1}{n_1 + n_2} [E(n_1 p_{s_1}) + E(n_2 p_{s_2})]$$

$$= \frac{1}{n_1 + n_2} [n_1 E(p_{s_1}) + n_2 E(p_{s_2})]$$

$$= \frac{1}{n_1 + n_2} (n_1 p + n_2 p)$$

$$= \frac{1}{n_1 + n_2} (n_1 + n_2) p$$

$$= p$$

$E(p_{s_1}) = E(p_{s_2}) = p$

Example

When canvassing, 75 out of 120 voters declared they would vote for the Labour Party. In a follow up survey 84 out of 150 voters declared that they would vote for the Labour Party. Calculate an unbiased estimator for the proportion of the population that would vote for the Labour Party, using the results from both samples.

Solution

$$\hat{p} = \frac{n_1\, p_{s_1} + n_2\, p_{s_2}}{n_1 + n_2}$$

$$p_{s_1} = \frac{75}{120}$$

$$= 0.625$$

$$p_{s_2} = \frac{84}{150}$$

$$= 0.56$$

$$\hat{p} = \frac{(0.625 \times 120) + (0.56 \times 150)}{120 + 150}$$

$$= 0.589$$

So 0.589 of the population would vote Labour.

This can also be calculated by combining both samples as follows:

$$\hat{p} = \frac{75 + 84}{120 + 150}$$

$$= \frac{159}{270}$$

$$= 0.589$$

There were 159 Labour voters out of a total sample of 270.

12.5 Pooled Estimator for Population Proportions from Two Samples

Exercise

Technique

From the data given by two samples, find an unbiased estimate of the population proportion.

	n_1	p_1	n_2	p_2
1	100	0.45	80	0.42
2	25	0.84	50	0.86
3	200	0.57	150	0.54
4	40	0.61	60	0.56
5	64	0.19	48	0.08

From the following samples calculate the proportion of success for each sample and a pooled unbiased estimation of the population proportion.

	Sample 1		Sample	
	Sample size	Successes	Sample size	Successes
6	120	90	150	80
7	30	18	50	24
8	75	12	84	18
9	2000	855	2500	1162
10	340	286	290	267

Contextual

1 A sample of Year 12 students indicated that out of 85 students, 30 did not eat red meat. In Year 13 out of 60 students, 26 did not eat red meat. From these results calculate an unbiased estimate for the proportion of all sixth form students who do not eat red meat.

2 In a random sample, 500 people were asked about the building of a new ring road. Of the sample 27% were opposed to the suggestion. In a follow up survey of 350 people, 23% said they were opposed to building the road. Calculate an unbiased estimate of the proportion of the population who were opposed to building the road.

3 A random sample of 400 people resulted in 240 positive responses for a reduction in the amount of sport shown on television. In a further sample of 550 people, a proportion of 0.45 were found to want a reduction in the amount of sport shown. From these results find an unbiased estimate of the proportion of the population who would like a reduction in the amount of sport shown on television.

4 The proportion of 320 people who felt that VAT was too high was found to be 0.79. A further survey of 480 people found 360 of them felt that VAT was too high. From these results find an unbiased estimate of the proportion of people who felt that VAT was too high.

5 Out of 2500 eighteen-year-olds, 1800 indicated that the age at which you are allowed to vote should be lowered to 16. In a further sample of 3000 eighteen-year-olds, a proportion of 0.7 indicated support for lowering the voting age. From these results find an unbiased estimate of the proportion of all eighteen-year-olds who are in favour of lowering the age at which people can vote.

Consolidation

Exercise A

1 Five observations of a variable X gave the following values:

  6.2   5.8   9.1   8.7   7.0

  a State one condition that allows for the calculation of the population variance.
  b Calculate an unbiased estimator of :
   i the mean
   ii the variance
  of the population.

2 The random variable X is normally distributed with mean 20 and standard deviation 6. Write down:

  a the mean
  b the standard deviation

  of a random sample of size 12 taken from this distribution.

  (ULEAC)

3 The following seven observations were made on a random variable X that is normally distributed:

  14.3   15.1   14.9   14.8   14.4   14.9   14.5

  Find unbiased estimators of the population mean and standard deviation.

  (WJEC)

4 A sample, of size 20, is selected from a population and the value of a particular variable is recorded for each member of the sample. The mean and variance for the sample are calculated and are found to be 59.4 and 196.74 respectively. After further investigation of the sample it is realised that one of the values was mistakenly recorded as 96 instead of 69.

  a Calculate the actual mean and variance of the 20 correct values.
  b Using the correct statistics you have calculated in **a**, estimate the corresponding parameters for the population.

  (NICCEA)

5 A food processor produces large batches of jars of beetroot. In each batch the weight is known to be normally distributed. Two samples of sizes 13 and 12 were taken and the number of jars with weights of over 500 g were found to be six and four respectively.

  a Calculated an unbiased estimate of the population proportion with weights greater than 500 g.

b The weights of the jars in the samples were:

Sample 1   514   485   501   486   502   496   509
               491   497   501   506   486   498
Sample 2   490   484   494   501   506   490
               487   507   496   505   498   499

By finding the mean and variance of each sample, calculate a pooled estimate for the population mean and variance.

6 Stud anchors are used in the construction industry. Samples are tested by embedding them in concrete and applying a steadily increasing load until the anchor fails. A sample of six tests gave the following maximum loads in kilonewtons:

27.0   30.5   28.0   23.0   27.5   26.5

Assuming a normal distribution for maximum loads, find unbiased estimates of:

a   the mean   **b**   the variance of the population.

(AEB)

7 The potencies of two different samples of aspirin were as follows:

Sample A   58.7   58.4   59.3   60.4   59.8   59.4   57.7   60.3   61.0
            58.2   58.1   58.8   59.4   60.1   58.9
Sample B   65.8   56.4   60.3   61.0   59.2   58.7   59.3   61.8   64.1
            61.9   62.8   60.7   55.2   59.9   63.6   60.4   59.9   61.5
            59.3   65.2   57.6   64.9   57.7   61.4   61.8   66.3   65.3

a   Calculate the mean and variance of both samples.
b   Using the answers from **a** calculate unbiased estimates of the population mean and variance.

8 A student is studying heights of five-year-old children. She has measured the height, h metres, of 36 children and found $\Sigma h = 37.8$ and $\Sigma h^2 = 39.8$. She wishes to estimate the mean, μ, and the variance, σ^2, of the height of a five-year-old child.

a   Find an unbiased estimate of μ.
b   Find an unbiased estimator of σ^2.
c   Explain briefly what is meant by saying that your estimate in **a** is unbiased.

(ULEAC)

9 A manufacturer of convenience foods has introduced a new type of cheesecake and wishes to test how successful it might be. Two expert panels of assessors rated the dessert on 10 different attributes such as tastiness, eye-appeal and quality of packaging, using a five-point scale for each attribute: a score of 1 corresponds to 'very poor' and a score of 5 to 'excellent'. The 10 attribute scores were added to produce a total score. The results are shown below.

Panel A	29	38	41	36	21	48	33	34	28	37	45	42
Panel B	28	24	54	42	24	39	22	27	23	37	35	30

a   Find the proportion of Panel A and Panel B who scored more than 40.
b   Using the answers from **a** find the proportion of the total population who would have scored more than 40.
c   Calculate the mean and variance of the scores of each panel.
d   From the answers to **c** calculate unbiased estimates of the population mean and variance.

10 The following data are the third and fourth round scores of a random sample of five competitors in an open golf tournament.

3rd round	76	75	72	75	79
4th round	70	73	71	68	76

a   Find the mean and variance of the scores of each round assuming the scores are normally distributed.
b   Using the results of **a** find unbiased estimators of the mean and variance of all scores for a round.

Exercise B

1 Nine observations of a variable X, distributed normally, gave the following values:

   16.5   22.9   18.7   21.3   17.0   20.5   19.7   22.4   16.8

Calculate an unbiased estimator of:

a   the mean
b   the variance

of the population.

2 The random variable X is normally distributed with mean 100 and standard deviation 15. Write down:

a   the mean
b   the standard deviation

of a random sample of size 20 taken from this distribution.

3 The following eleven measurements were taken of the kicking accuracy of rugby players (%).

65   72   90   84   76   79   85   60   73   88   70

Find unbiased estimators of the population mean and standard deviation.

4 A sample, of size 15, is selected from a population and the value of a particular variable is recorded for each member of the sample. The mean and variance for the sample are calculated and are found to be 16.4 and 18.5 respectively. After further investigation of the sample it is realised that one of the values was mistakenly recorded as 12 instead of 21.

a   Calculate the actual mean and variance of the 15 correct values.
b   Using the correct statistics you have calculated in **a**, estimate the corresponding parameters for the population.

5 A food processor produces large batches of packets of cereals. In each batch the weight is known to be normally distributed. Two samples of sizes 20 and 18 were taken and the proportion of packets with weights of over 500 g were found to be 0.25 and 0.33 respectively.

a   Calculated an unbiased estimate of the population proportion with weights greater than 500 g.
b   The weight of the packets in the samples were:

Sample 1   495   504   510   499   508   489   497   497   488   494
           489   498   493   509   489   502   499   495   487   494
Sample 2   505   498   509   497   491   510   509   496   499   498
           495   508   496   493   498   489   496   508

By finding the mean and variance of each sample, calculated a pooled estimate for the population mean and variance.

6 The covering of the soles of shoes were tested to destruction in a continuous test, to find their useful life span. A sample of size five was taken and the results, in hours, were recorded.

82.4   93.5   78.7   86.3   89.2

Assuming a normal distribution for the life span, find unbiased estimates of:

a   the mean   b   the variance

of the population.

7 The effectiveness at killing germs of two samples of bleach was recorded as a percentage. The results can be assumed to be normally distributed.

Sample A	92.4	87.3	92.5	96.7	97.1	91.3
	93.6	94.8	90.2	92.3	89.4	
Sample B	85.6	88.3	98.7	99.1	86.9	91.4
	97.2	89.0	97.5	92.6	91.4	

a Calculate the mean and variance of both samples.
b Using the answers from **a** calculate unbiased estimates of the population mean and variance.

8 A student is studying heights of five-year-old children. He has measured the height, h metres, of 24 children and found $\Sigma h = 28.4$ and $\Sigma h^2 = 38.1$. He wishes to estimate the mean, μ, and the variance, σ^2, of the height of a five-year-old child.

a Find an unbiased estimator of μ.
b Find an unbiased estimator of σ^2.

9 A car manufacturer wishes to assess how successful the launch of their new model will be. Two expert panels of assessors rated the car on a variety of aspects such as shape, comfort, road holding ability, and so on. The results were as follows.

Panel A	45	42	58	60	52	55	64	57
Panel B	61	58	41	65	55	49	55	43

a Find the proportion of each of Panel A and Panel B who scored more than 55.
b Using the answers from **a** find the proportion of the total population who would have scored more than 55.
c Calculate the mean and variance of the scores of each panel.
d From the answers to **c** calculate unbiased estimates of the population mean and variance.

10 The following data are the first and second round scores of a random sample of six competitors in an open golf tournament.

1st round	68	72	70	77	69	71
2nd round	74	69	78	70	67	73

a Find the mean and variance of the scores of each round assuming the scores are normally distributed.
b Using the results of **a** find unbiased estimators of the mean and variance of all scores for a round.

Applications and Activities

1 A **hand** used to measure the height of horses is $4\frac{1}{2}$ inches. By finding a point estimator of the width of peoples' hands, is this an accurate measurement?

2 The old measurement of a yard was from the tip of your nose to the tip of your middle finger with your arm outstretched. Is there any evidence to suggest that this is accurate?

Summary

- A statistic calculated from a random sample to give information about an unknown parameter of the parent population is called an estimator.

- If the statistic is a single value it is a point estimator.

- The Central Limit Theorem states that:

  for samples from a distribution which has a mean, μ, and variance, σ^2, the means of the samples will be normally distributed with a mean of μ and a variance of $\dfrac{\sigma^2}{n}$.

- The standard error of a sample mean is $\dfrac{\sigma}{\sqrt{n}}$.

- An estimator of an unknown parameter is unbiased if its expected value is the same as the parameter.

- The mean, $\bar{X}$, of a random sample is an unbiased estimator of μ, the mean of a population.

- An unbiased estimator for the population variance is

$$\hat{\sigma}^2 = \frac{nS^2}{n-1}$$

- A pooled estimator for the mean of a population from two samples is:

$$\hat{\mu} = \frac{n_1\bar{X}_1 + n_2\bar{X}_2}{n_1 + n_2}$$

- A pooled estimator for the variance of a population from two samples is:

$$\hat{\sigma}^2 = \frac{n_1 S_1^2 + n_2 S_2^2}{n_1 + n_2 - 2}$$

- A pooled estimator for the proportion of the population from two samples is:

$$\hat{p} = \frac{n_1 P_{s_1} + n_2 P_{s_2}}{n_1 + n_2}$$

13 Estimation II: Interval Estimation

What you need to know

● The properties of the normal distribution.

● How to approximate a binomial distribution by a normal distribution.

Review

Calculate the mean and variance of the normal distribution that approximates to each of the following binomial distributions.

	Sample size	Probability of success
1	200	0.4
2	4000	0.55
3	70	0.35
4	150	0.375
5	375	0.515

	Sample size	Number of successes
6	100	55
7	3000	1440
8	850	462
9	1250	348
10	80	63

13.1 Interval Estimation of Population Mean – Variance Known

When calculating a point estimate for the mean of a distribution, how confident can we be that the figure is totally accurate? However large a sample there will always be doubt as to the accuracy of a point estimator used for the mean value, which is why an interval estimate is often used. With an interval estimate the mean is given as being within a range of values, such as 10.5 ± 0.5, the mean being between 10 and 11 The width of the range is related to the standard deviation of the population.

The interval estimate of the population mean is often referred to as the **confidence interval** for the mean.

From Example 1 in Chapter 12, the point estimator of the mean of the six numbers in the winning line of the National Lottery was 23.3. This involves an error as the true mean is 25. As has already been said, this highlights the problem of a point estimator, as 23.3 cannot be stated as the mean value of the population with total confidence.

The true mean
$$= \frac{1 + 2 + \ldots + 48 + 49}{49}$$
$$= 25$$

The Central Limit Theorem states that the sampling distribution of the means is approximately normal, therefore we would expect the distribution of the lottery means to be approximately:

$$N\left(25, \frac{14.29^2}{6}\right), \text{ as } \mu = 25 , \sigma = 14.29 \text{ and } n = 6$$

Standard deviation of the numbers 1 to 49 inclusive is 14.29. Variance of a sample is S^2.

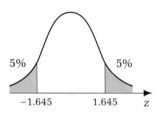

The diagram shows that when calculating the means of the six numbers it would be expected that 90% of the results would lie in the unshaded area. Using normal distribution tables at the 0.95 level gives a value of 1.645. To be 90% confident of quoting the population mean value, the range

$$\bar{x} \pm 1.645 \frac{\sigma}{\sqrt{n}} \text{ would need to be quoted.}$$

Check that the standard normal tables give 1.64 for 0.95: look up 0.95 in the body of the tables then check row and column position.

Proof

$$\bar{X} \sim N\left(\mu, \frac{\sigma^2}{n}\right) \quad \text{(approximately)}$$

Standardising

$$Z \sim N(0, 1)$$

$$Z = \frac{\bar{X} - \mu}{\sigma/\sqrt{n}}$$

For 90% confidence

$$P\left(-1.645 \leq \frac{\bar{X} - \mu}{\sigma/\sqrt{n}} \leq 1.645\right) = 0.9$$

$$P\left(-1.645\,\frac{\sigma}{\sqrt{n}} \leq \bar{X} - \mu \leq 1.645\,\frac{\sigma}{\sqrt{n}}\right) = 0.9$$

$$P\left(-\bar{X} - 1.645\,\frac{\sigma}{\sqrt{n}} \leq -\mu \leq -\bar{X} + 1.645\,\frac{\sigma}{\sqrt{n}}\right) = 0.9$$

$$P\left(\bar{X} + 1.645\,\frac{\sigma}{\sqrt{n}} \geq \mu \geq \bar{X} - 1.645\,\frac{\sigma}{\sqrt{n}}\right) = 0.9$$

It is important to understand what this actually means: 90% of the time, this interval will include the population mean.

Therefore the 90% confidence interval is $\bar{X} \pm 1.645\,\dfrac{\sigma}{\sqrt{n}}$.

Similarly for 95% confidence limits the interval is $\bar{X} \pm 1.96\,\dfrac{\sigma}{\sqrt{n}}$

and for 99% confidence limits the interval is $\bar{X} + 2.576\,\dfrac{\sigma}{\sqrt{n}}$.

Remember 1.96 and 2.576 come from the standard normal tables.

Example

One line from the National Lottery was 18, 19, 21, 30, 34, 46. It is known that the parent population has a standard deviation of 14.3. Calculate the:

a   90%   **b**   95%

confidence intervals for the mean of the population.

Solution

$$\bar{x} = \frac{18 + 19 + 21 + 30 + 34 + 46}{6} = \frac{168}{6} = 28$$

a   90% confidence limits are:

$$28 - 1.645 \times \frac{14.3}{\sqrt{6}} \leq \mu \leq 28 + 1.645 \times \frac{14.3}{\sqrt{6}}$$

$$18.40 \leq \mu \leq 37.60$$

So a 90% confidence interval for the mean is between 18.40 and 37.60.

b   95% confidence limits are:

$$28 - 1.96 \times \frac{14.3}{\sqrt{6}} \leq \mu \leq 28 + 1.96 \times \frac{14.3}{\sqrt{6}}$$

$$16.56 \leq \mu \leq 39.44$$

So a 95% confidence interval for the mean is between 16.56 and 39.44.

95% confidence limits are usually quoted to ensure accuracy. At this level of confidence the values have to be extreme to be outside the range quoted.

13.1 Interval Estimation of Population Mean – Variance Known

Exercise

Technique

Find:

a   90%   **b**   95%

confidence intervals for the population mean from the following samples, with the given standard deviation for the population. All the samples are from normal distributions.

1   12, 14, 15, 15, 17 $\sigma = 5$

2   48, 51, 55, 56, 63, 64, 65, 70 $\sigma = 20$

3   2, 3, 3, 4, 6, 7, 7, 9 $\sigma = 8$

4   21, 27, 28, 28, 28, 31, 32, 33, 35, 40 $\sigma = 16$

5   1.2, 1.2, 1.3, 1.3, 1.5, 1.5, 1.5, 1.6, 1.8 $\sigma = 0.5$

6   0.4, 0.5, 0.3, 0.1, 0.2, 0.1, 0.4, 0.5, 0.4, 0.6, 0.4, 0.6 $\sigma = 1$

7   0.01, 0.04, 0.03, 0.09, 0.03, 0.08, 0.04, 0.02, 0.07 $\sigma = 0.1$

8   12 005, 12 029, 12 031, 12 043, 12 047, 12 077, 12 083, 12 096, 12 099 $\sigma = 100$

9   −1, −4, −3, −8, 2, 1, 0, 0, −1, −3, 3, 3, 4, 1, −1, −2, 3, 3, 1, 0 $\sigma = 12$

10   988, 991, 985, 988, 990, 993, 982, 991, 993, 997, 993, 989, 986, 991, 990 $\sigma = 16$

11

x	0	1	2	3	4
f	3	5	4	3	1

$\sigma = 3$

12

x	−2	−1	0	1	2	3	4
f	3	7	9	13	11	4	3

$\sigma = 15$

Contextual

1 The heights of 10 students, measured to the nearest centimetre, are recorded below.

148 154 161 158 150 162 151 167 166 155

If the standard deviation of the population is known to be 9, calculate a 95% confidence interval for the population mean.

2 The IQs of 15 twenty-year-olds were found to be:

95 131 120 98 105 111 86 128
125 101 92 96 118 132 106

The test was known to have a variance of 144. Calculate a 90% confidence interval for the mean of the population.

3 The number of words in the sentences of a daily newspaper were recorded as follows:

Words	5	6	7	8	9	10	11	12	13	14	15
Sentences	2	8	15	28	37	21	16	10	7	4	2

If the variance of the sample is an accurate estimator of the variance of the population, calculate a 95% confidence interval for the mean length of sentence for the paper.

4 The scores of 10 golfers in a local competition were recorded as follows:

72 76 81 75 73 85 79 73 74 82

If the standard deviation of the scores is known to be 4, find a 99% confidence interval for the mean score of all the golfers in the competition.

5 The variance of the weight of a species of crab is known to be $6.25\,g^2$. A random sample of 12 crabs were weighed, in grams, and their weights recorded as follows:

20.1 23.3 30.4 17.3 25.1 28.4
26.3 28.4 26.7 22.9 23.8 15.4

Find 95% confidence limits for the mean weight of all the crabs of this species.

6 The number of pounds of weight lost by 25 slimmers in a four-week period was recorded as follows:

3 5 4 3 4 3 6 8 3 4
4 6 7 6 5 9 8 8 6 3
6 7 6 5 5

If the variance of the population is 81 pounds, find a 95% confidence interval for the mean weight lost by the population of slimmers.

13.2 Confidence Interval for the Population Mean – Variance Unknown, Large Sample

It is always better to take as large a sample of the population as time, money and effort will allow. The size of the sample is important. Firstly, how big does the sample have to be before the Central Limit Theorem means that the formulas in this section can be used? The answer is that a sample of size 30 is ample for most purposes. Secondly, how big does the sample have to be to get an acceptable estimate, that is a small enough confidence interval? This depends entirely on what is being estimated and why. For example, an opinion poll of 30 people might well be too small.

If n is large, and $\bar{x}$ and s^2 are the mean and variance of a random sample of size n, taken from a normal population, then an estimate of the mean of the population is $\bar{x}$ and an estimate of the population variance is s^2. A 90% confidence interval for μ is:

$$\mu = \bar{x} \pm \frac{1.645s}{\sqrt{n}}$$

This is only true for large values of n.

Compare with section 13.1, p. 352.

Example

A random sample of 200 Year 7 students was taken and their ages were recorded. The results were $\Sigma x = 2440$ and $\Sigma x^2 = 34\,000$. Find 90% confidence limits for the population mean.

Solution

$$\bar{x} = \frac{2440}{200} = 12.2$$

$$s^2 = \frac{34\,000}{200} - 12.2^2$$

$$s^2 = 21.16$$

90% confidence interval is

$$\mu = \bar{x} \pm 1.645 \times \frac{s}{\sqrt{n}}$$

$$= 12.2 - 1.645 \times \frac{\sqrt{21.16}}{\sqrt{200}} \le \mu \le 12.2 + 1.645 \times \frac{\sqrt{21.16}}{\sqrt{200}}$$

So
$$11.66 \le \mu \le 12.74$$

13.2 Confidence Interval for the Population Mean – Variance Unknown, Large Sample

Exercise

Technique

Calculate confidence intervals for the population mean from the following samples. For questions $\boxed{1}$ to $\boxed{3}$ use a 95% confidence interval and for questions $\boxed{4}$ to $\boxed{6}$ use a 90% confidence interval.

	Mean	Variance	Size
1	60	10	150
2	140	25	350
3	1.8	1	40
4	0.4	0.9	64
5	3440	225	90
6	9.76	4.5	115

Calculate confidence intervals for the population mean from the following samples. For questions $\boxed{7}$ to $\boxed{9}$ use a 95% confidence interval and for questions $\boxed{10}$ to $\boxed{11}$ use a 90% confidence interval.

	n	Σx	Σx^2
7	100	1 500	24 000
8	320	70 400	16 000 000
9	50	125	350
10	120	888	8 000
11	35	29 750	26 000 000

Contextual

1 The following are the number of goals scored in football matches in Divisions 1 and 2 in one week. Calculate 95% confidence intervals for the mean number of goals scored in each division and compare the results.

Division 1

Goals	0	1	2	3	4	5
Matches	4	15	13	9	8	6

Division 2

Goals	0	1	2	3	4	5	6
Matches	3	12	21	18	7	6	3

2 An office monitored the number of telephone calls received during 10-minute intervals between 9a.m. and 10a.m. daily. The results were:

Number of calls	0	1	2	3	4	5	6	7
Frequency	0	8	16	14	11	15	9	7

Calculate a 90% confidence interval for the mean number of all calls received within a ten-minute period.

3 The lengths of a variety of hen's eggs were measured and recorded in the following table:

Length (mm)	59.2	59.4	59.6	59.8	60.0	60.2	60.4	60.6	60.8
Frequency	5	19	62	98	123	84	75	31	3

Find a 95% confidence interval for the mean length of this variety of hen's eggs.

4 In an outbreak of a skin rash caused by a virus, sufferers were categorised by the approximate percentage of skin area affected. The results were:

% of skin area affected	0–5	5–10	10–15	15–20	20–25	25–30
Frequency	16	23	19	12	7	3

Find a 95% confidence interval for the mean percentage of skin area on the sufferers of this rash that was affected.

5 A meat packing firm wished to test the efficiency of their new vacuum sealing process. To do this they monitored how many days it took for the packed meat to spoil. Their results were:

Number of days	4	5	6	7	8	9	10
Frequency	2	8	9	13	16	11	1

Find a 90% confidence interval for the mean number of days it takes the meat to spoil.

13.3 Confidence Interval for the Population Mean – Variance Unknown, Small Sample

Unfortunately it is often difficult to take a large sample due to the nature of the study, such as testing to destruction to measure the life span of an item. Sometimes the cost in time, money and effort makes it difficult to obtain a suitably sized sample. In cases of this nature it is inappropriate to use values obtained from standard normal distribution tables as they are inaccurate.

This problem was studied by W S Gosset, who wrote under the pen-name 'Student'. Instead of using the standard normal variate:

$$Z = \frac{\bar{X} - \mu}{\sigma/\sqrt{n}}$$

Gosset used the variate t, where:

$$t = \frac{\bar{x} - \mu}{s\sqrt{n}}$$

$\bar{x}$ is the mean and s is the standard deviation of a sample, size n, taken from a normal population with mean μ.

and the sample is from a normal distribution.

The sampling distribution of t, called the Student t distribution, is similar in shape to a standard normal distribution, ($\mu = 0$, $\sigma = 1$). It is symmetrical about $t = 0$, but it becomes increasingly more spread out as the sample size n decreases. The shape of the t distribution depends on n, but when you use tables of the t distribution you select the values of t according to the number of degrees of freedom (ν) rather than the sample size, n. ν is related to n but the relationship depends on the particular problem and you will usually be told what value of ν to use.

Less information is contained in small samples and a greater variation in results is likely.

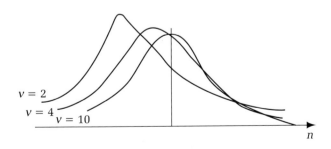

As $v \to \infty$, the t-distribution $\to$ standard normal distribution

Properties of the *t* distribution

Some properties of the t distribution are:

- the distribution is continuous

- the distribution is defined by one single parameter, ν, the number of degrees of freedom

- the distribution is symmetrical about its mean

- the mean of the distribution is always zero, the same as for standardised normal scores.

Using the symbols $X \sim t(\nu)$ means that the variable, X, has a t-distribution with ν degrees of freedom.

The method for small samples is similar to that for large samples. As the sample is small the variance of the sample is a biased estimator of the population variance so an unbiased estimator must be calculated first.

As σ^2 is unknown

$$\hat{\sigma}^2 = \frac{ns^2}{n-1}$$

where s^2 is the sample variance.

Substituting for $\hat{\sigma}$ in $\dfrac{\bar{X} - \mu}{\sigma/\sqrt{n}}$ gives

$$t = \frac{\bar{X} - \mu}{s/\sqrt{n-1}}$$

So $t = \dfrac{\bar{X} - \mu}{s/\sqrt{n-1}}$ with $n-1$ degrees of freedom.

The confidence interval for the mean value from a small sample where the parent population is normally distributed is then:

$$\bar{x} - \frac{ts}{\sqrt{n-1}} \leq \mu \leq \bar{x} + \frac{ts}{\sqrt{n-1}}$$

The value of t varies according to the confidence level and is read from a table of the t distribution.

The t-distribution was one of the techniques developed by William S Gosset to analyse statistical data. Gosset, who worked for the Guinness breweries in Dublin, published his work using the pseudonym 'Student', which has resulted in the t-distribution often being referred to as Student's t-scores.

Unbiased estimator

$$\hat{\sigma}^2 = \frac{ns^2}{n-1}.$$

Example

The lengths of a species of eel were known to be normally distributed. The lengths of a sample of eight eels were measured to the nearest millimetre and were found to be:

836   745   921   883   705   829   901   853

Find a 95% confidence interval for the mean length of the eel population.

Solution

$\bar{x} = 834.125$ and $s^2 = 4926.4$, so $s = 70.19$

$$\mu = 834.125 \pm t \times \frac{70.19}{\sqrt{8-1}}$$

Value for *t*

The number of *degrees of freedom* are found by $n - 1$, which in this case is $8 - 1 = 7$. Using the t distribution tables, find the value where the column $P = 0.975$ intersects with the row for seven degrees of freedom. This gives $t = 2.365$.

$$\mu = 834.125 \pm 2.365 \times \frac{70.19}{\sqrt{8-1}}$$

$$771.38 \leq \mu \leq 896.87$$

A 95% confidence interval for the mean length of the eel population is $771.38 \, \text{mm} \leq \mu \leq 896.87 \, \text{mm}$.

13.3 Confidence Interval for the Population Mean – Variance Unknown, Small Sample

Exercise

Contextual

1 The lengths of 12 bolts were measured in centimetres and found to be:

5.4   5.2   5.6   6.3   4.9   5.3
6.1   5.9   5.4   4.8   5.1   5.7

The lengths of the bolts are normally distributed. Calculate a 95% confidence interval for the mean length of the bolts.

2 The blades in 11 razors are changed after being used the following number of times:

8   12   7   11   11   8   9   13   9   8   12

Assuming a normal distribution, calculate a 90% confidence interval for the mean number of uses.

3 Science students attempted to estimate the mean error that occurred when measurements of length were taken. They measured a piece of wire of known length and recorded the difference between the actual and measured lengths to the nearest millimetre. The results were:

0.2   0.3   −0.2   −0.1   0.1   −0.3   −0.2   0.1
0.1   −0.3   −0.2   0.2   −0.3   −0.2   −0.3

Assuming the errors to be normally distributed, find a 90% confidence interval for the mean length of the errors.

4 The pulse rates of a group of science students were measured as follows:

75   91   68   72   94   86   84   82
74   80   89   69   75   85   84   72

If the pulse rates can be assumed to be normally distributed, calculate a 95% confidence interval for the mean pulse rate.

5 The marks gained by police constables when taking their sergeant's exam were:

82   73   81   85   79   87   95

If the results are normally distributed, find a 95% confidence interval for the mean score.

6 The journey times, in minutes, taken by trains between two stations were recorded as follows:

48   52   46   43   50
52   49   46   51   52

Assuming that the times are normally distributed, find a 95% confidence interval for the mean journey time.

7 The difference between the expected scores and the actual scores in a test were calculated as follows:

−8   7   −6   −4   9   5   5   −6   −8   11   7
−5   6   11   −14   8   8   13   5   6   12   −4

Assuming the differences are normally distributed, calculate a 90% confidence interval for the mean differences in the population scores.

8 The height reached by the water in eight successive high tides was recorded, in metres, as:

4.8   5.3   3.9   4.3   4.7   5.5   4.8   5.0

Assuming the heights of the tides to be normally distributed, find a 95% confidence interval for the mean height of all tides.

13.4 Size of Sample

Often before carrying out a test or survey it is useful to be able to calculate the size of sample needed to give the mean of the population within a certain accuracy. Suppose the mean height of a population was to be quoted to the nearest centimetre, with 95% confidence. What size of sample is required?

The factors that affect the limit of the mean are:

- the standard deviation of the population
- the confidence level
- the size of sample.

In this case the height has to be quoted to the nearest centimetre, which is ± 0.5 cm.

For a confidence level of 95% the standardised score, from the standardised normal distribution tables, is $Z = 1.96$

$$P(\bar{x} - 0.5 \leq \mu \leq \bar{x} + 0.5) = 0.95$$

$$P\left(\bar{x} - 1.96 \frac{\sigma}{\sqrt{n}} \leq \mu \leq \bar{x} + 1.96 \frac{\sigma}{\sqrt{n}}\right) = 0.95$$

By examining the two equations then

$$1.96 \frac{\sigma}{\sqrt{n}} = 0.5$$

$$1.96 \frac{\sigma}{0.5} = \sqrt{n}$$

$$\left(1.96 \frac{\sigma}{0.5}\right)^2 = n$$

Example

The mean height of a population, with a standard deviation of 5 cm, was to be quoted to the nearest centimetre, with 95% confidence. What size of sample is required?

Limit is $x \pm 0.5$ cm.

Solution

$$\frac{(1.96 \times 5)}{\sqrt{n}} = 0.5$$

$$\frac{(1.96 \times 5)}{0.5} = \sqrt{n}$$

$$19.6 = \sqrt{n}$$

$$384.16 = n$$

A sample size of 385 is required to be within ± 0.5 cm as the sample size must be an integer.

From this example it can be seen that to achieve a small limit the size of sample is quite large. A balance must be kept between the size of the limit and the size of the sample.

13.4 Size of Sample
Exercise

Technique

Find the size of sample required at the:

a 90%   **b** 95%

confidence limits for the following distributions and intervals.

1 $\sigma = 15\,\text{cm}$, interval $\pm 8\,\text{cm}$

2 $\sigma = 5\,\text{cm}$, interval $\pm 1\,\text{cm}$

3 $\sigma = 25\,\text{cm}$, interval $\pm 20\,\text{cm}$

4 $\sigma = 12\,\text{cm}$, interval $\pm 0.5\,\text{cm}$

5 $\sigma = 50\,\text{cm}$, interval $\pm 10\,\text{cm}$

6 $\sigma = 0.5\,\text{m}$, interval $\pm 0.1\,\text{m}$

7 $\sigma = 22.5\,\text{km}$, interval $\pm 8\,\text{km}$

8 $\sigma = 1000\,\text{mm}$, interval $\pm 50\,\text{mm}$

9 $\sigma = 0.1\,\text{mm}$, interval $\pm 0.001\,\text{mm}$

10 $\sigma = 3.4\,\text{m}$, interval $\pm 0.25\,\text{m}$

11 $\sigma = 13.54\,\text{mm}$, interval $\pm 0.5\,\text{mm}$

12 $\sigma = 14.5\,\text{mm}$, interval $\pm 3\,\text{mm}$

13.5 Confidence Limits for Population Proportions

In a sample, size n, of a population it was found that a certain proportion, p_s, were female. From this information the researchers wish to estimate the proportion of females in the population with 95% confidence. The distribution of females in the population is binomial and for a large sample it is approximately normally distributed with a mean np, and variance npq.

Remember $q = 1 - p$.

$$B \sim N(np, npq)$$

For 95% confidence limits for a large sample,

$$\bar{x} - 1.96\sigma \leq \mu \leq \bar{x} + 1.96\sigma$$

$$np_s - 1.96\sqrt{np_s q_s} \leq np \leq np_s + 1.96\sqrt{np_s q_s}$$

Replacing $\bar{x}$ with np_s and σ with $\sqrt{np_s q_s}$

Dividing by n throughout,

$$\boldsymbol{p_s - 1.96\sqrt{\frac{p_s q_s}{n}} \leq p \leq p_s + 1.96\sqrt{\frac{p_s q_s}{n}}}$$

This gives the 95% confidence limits for the proportion, p, within the population.

Example

In a sample of 500 children, 220 were girls. Find an interval estimate for the proportion of females in the population at the 95% confidence level.

Solution

$$p = \frac{\text{number of girls}}{\text{sample size}} = \frac{220}{500} = 0.44$$

$$q = 1 - 0.44 = 0.56$$

At 95% confidence level

$$0.44 - 1.96\sqrt{\frac{0.44 \times 0.56}{500}} \leq p \leq 0.44 + 1.96\sqrt{\frac{0.44 \times 0.56}{500}}$$

$$0.396 \leq p \leq 0.484$$

So the 95% confidence level for the proportion of females in the population is between 39.6% and 48.4%.

13.5 Confidence Limits for Population Proportions

Exercise

Contextual

1 During filming it was found that out of 500 extras only 120 were suitable for parts in a major film. Find the 95% confidence interval for the proportion of all film extras who may have been suitable for parts in the film.

2 In a sample of 200 students, 40 were found to have auburn hair. Find the 99% confidence interval for the proportion of students with auburn hair.

3 During a school reunion, out of a year of 180 students, only 72 were able to attend. Calculate a 95% confidence interval for the proportion of all past students who would have been able to attend.

4 During a phone-in programme on the local radio, 316 out of 815 callers were against the building of a proposed bypass. From this sample find a 95% confidence interval for the proportion of the population opposed to the scheme that was claimed by the programme presenter.

5 Of 610 blonde-haired people 464 were found to have blue eyes. Find a 99% confidence limit for the proportion of all blonde-haired people with blue eyes.

6 In a sample of 2350 shoppers 1687 regularly used out-of-town supermarkets to buy their food. Using this information, find a 95% confidence interval for the proportion of all shoppers who use out-of-town supermarkets to buy their food.

7 Out of 80 householders questioned, 34 said that they never read the free newspapers that came through their letterbox. Find a 90% confidence interval for the proportion of all householders who read the free newspapers.

8 In a survey of 1600 people, 586 raised no objections to light industry units being sited on the edge of residential areas. Find a 95% confidence interval for the proportion of the population who might agree to such siting of light industry units.

Consolidation

Exercise A

1 The tensile strength of vulcanised rubber is known to be normally distributed with a standard deviation of $0.106 \, \text{kg cm}^{-2}$. A random sample of 20 specimens has a mean tensile strength of $31.420 \, \text{kg cm}^{-2}$. Find 99% confidence limits for the population mean.

(ULEAC)

2 In a survey carried out among first year students at a large university, 242 students out of a sample of 400 students expressed satisfaction with the facilities provided by the students' union. Calculate approximate 95% confidence limits for the proportion of first year students satisfied with the facilities provided by the students' union.

(WJEC)

3 Solid fuel is packed in sacks which are then weighed on scales. It is known that if the full sack weighs μ kg the weight recorded by the scales will be normally distributed with mean μ kg and standard deviation 0.36 kg. A particular full sack was weighed four times and the weights recorded were 34.7, 34.4, 35.1 and 34.6 kg respectively.

a Calculate a 95% confidence interval for the weight of this full sack.
b State the width of the interval calculated in **a**.
c How many times would this full sack have to be weighed so that a 95% interval for the weight would be of width 0.3 kg?

(AEB)

4 Out of a random sample of 500 apples from a supermarket, 43 had sticky labels which did not come off easily and the other 457 had sticky labels which did come off easily. Calculate a symmetrical 90% confidence interval for the proportion of sticky labels which do not come off easily. Give your answer correct to three decimal places.

(UCLES)

5 The following seven observations were made on a random variable, X, that is normally distributed with unknown mean, μ, and standard deviation 0.3:

14.3   15.1   14.9   14.8   14.4   14.9   14.5

Calculate 99% confidence limits for μ.

(WJEC)

6 Batteries supplied to a large institution for use in electric clocks had a mean working life of 960 days with a standard deviation of 135 days. A sample from a new supplier had working lives of 1020, 998, 894, 921, 843, 1280, 782, 694, 1350 days respectively. Assume that the data may be regarded as a random sample from a normal distribution.

    a From the working lives of batteries from the new supplier, calculate an unbiased estimate of the variance. Use this to calculate a 95% confidence interval for:

        i the mean   **ii** the standard deviation.

    b The institution would like batteries with a large mean and little variability. Compare the two sources of supply.   (*AEB*)

7 **a** Explain what is meant by the *sampling distribution* of an estimator. If a random sample of n observations is drawn from a normal distribution with mean μ and variance σ^2, specify completely the sampling distribution of $\bar{X}$, the mean of such a sample. Explain what is meant by an unbiased estimator of μ. Explain what is meant by:

        i a point estimator of μ **ii** an interval estimate of μ.

    b A forensic scientist wished to obtain a reliable estimate of the true refractive index, μ, of a particular piece of glass. She decided to obtain 50 independent measurements, x, of the refractive index, which produced the summarised results: $\Sigma x = 76.25$ and $\Sigma x^2 = 116.287\,13$. The scientist knew that, using the available apparatus, measurements of the refractive index of the glass would be distributed with mean μ and variance σ^2. Obtain unbiased estimates of μ and σ^2.

    Calculate the estimated standard error of $\bar{X}$ based on the above data.

    In fact the scientist used her estimate of σ^2 to estimate the number, n, of measurements that she would need to make if she were to produce an estimate of μ with a standard error of approximately 0.001. Calculate her estimate of n.   (*NEAB*)

8 A youth club has a large number of members. In order to find the distribution of weekly allowances of the members, a random sample of 10 are questioned.

    a Describe a method of producing the random sample.

Such a random sample produced the following weekly allowances:

    £5.20   £4.40   £3.00   £2.00   £3.30   £7.50   £5.00   £6.50   £4.80   £5.70

    b Estimate the population mean and variance.

    c Find a 95% confidence interval for the population mean.

    d Explain how the width of the confidence interval may be reduced.

    Assuming the same variance as in **b**, what must the sample size be, to reduce the width to £2?   (*MEI*)

9 The mass of a certain brand of chocolate bar has a normal distribution with mean μ grams and standard deviation 0.85 g. The masses, in grams, of five randomly chosen bars are:

124.31   125.14   124.23   125.41   125.76

Calculate a symmetrical 90% confidence interval for μ giving the end points correct to two decimal places.

(*UCLES*)

10 **a** A box contains five cards numbered 1, 2, 3, 4, 5 respectively. A random sample of three cards is selected without replacement. Write down, in a table, the 10 different possible samples of three numbers selected. Calculate the mean $\bar{x}$ and the median M for each sample.

  i Verify that both $\bar{x}$ and M are unbiased estimators of the mean μ of the five numbers in the box.
  ii Calculate the variance of both $\bar{x}$ and M. State, with a reason, which of $\bar{x}$ and M you regard as the better estimator of μ.

b Another box contains n cards numbered $1, 2, 3, \ldots, n$ respectively. Three cards are selected at random without replacement and $\bar{x}$ denotes the mean of the three numbers on them. Assuming that $\bar{x}$ is an unbiased estimator of the mean of the n numbers in the box, show that $2\bar{x} - 1$ is an unbiased estimator of n.

In a particular case, the numbers on the three cards were found to be 1, 2, 6. Use the above result to estimate n and comment on your result.

(*WJEC*)

Exercise B

1 When a darts player aims at the centre of the darts board the distance from the centre to the point where the darts lands is R. The mean value of R will vary for players of different ability. The famous darts player Willy Jackson aims 50 darts at the centre of the board. The distances from the centre are summarised as $\Sigma R = 35.5$ and $\Sigma R^2 = 33.2$.

a Construct a 90% confidence interval for the mean value of R. What assumption(s) have you made about the set of 50 throws?
b Estimate the number of throws required if the 90% confidence interval for the mean of R for Willy Jackson is to be of width 0.1.

(*MEI*)

2 Out of 248 cars parked in a car park, 72 were fitted with an anti-theft device on the steering wheel. Assuming that the cars form a random sample of parked cars, calculate an approximate 95% confidence interval for the population of parked cars fitted with an anti-theft device on the steering wheel.

(*UCLES*)

3 When the alcohol level (in mg/100 ml) of a specimen of blood is measured, the reading obtained is a normally distributed random variable with mean μ and variance σ^2. The value of σ depends upon the precision of the measuring instrument being used.

a It is known that $\sigma = 2$ for a particular instrument. Using this instrument, six measurements of the alcohol level of a specimen were as follows:

    70.3 72.9 69.6 70.8 67.2 72.5

Calculate the 95% confidence limits for the value of μ for this specimen.

b Another instrument for which σ is unknown is used to make six measurements of alcohol level of a second specimen. It is found that, for these measurements, $\Sigma x = 489$ and $\Sigma x^2 = 39\,868$.

  i Calculate an unbiased estimate of σ^2.

  ii Find 95% confidence limits for the alcohol level of this specimen.

(WJEC)

4 Explain briefly, the Central Limit Theorem. Mary wishes to investigate the heights of 14-year-old boys. She writes to a number of schools and asks them to measure the heights of boys who are within seven days of their fourteenth birthday. The heights of 36 boys were found and a mean height of 164 cm and standard deviation of 9 cm were calculated. Assuming the sample to be unbiased, calculate the 99% confidence interval for the mean height of all boys within seven days of their fourteenth birthdays.

5 Employees of a firm carrying out motorway maintenance are issued with brightly coloured waterproof jackets. These come in five different sizes, numbered 1 to 5. The last 40 jackets issued were of the following sizes:

    2 3 3 1 3 3 2 4 3 2
    5 4 1 2 3 3 2 4 5 3
    2 4 4 1 5 3 3 2 3 3
    1 3 4 3 3 2 5 1 4 4

a Find the proportion in the sample requiring size 3.

b Assuming the 40 employees can be regarded as a random sample of all employees, calculate an approximate 95% confidence interval for the proportion, p, of all employees requiring size 3.

c Your estimate of p is $\hat{p}$. How large a sample would be needed to obtain an approximate 95% confidence interval of the form $\hat{p} \pm 0.1$?

(AEB)

6 The times taken by five-year-old children to complete a certain task are normally distributed with a standard deviation of 8 seconds. A random sample of 25 five-year-old children were given this task and their mean time was 44.2 seconds. Find 95% confidence limits for the mean time taken by five-year-old children from the school. *(ULEAC)*

7 The athletics coach of the Road Runners club monitored the number of miles, x, to the nearest mile, run in training by a random sample of 75 of the club members during a particular week. The results are summarised as $\Sigma x = 1876$ and $\Sigma x^2 = 50\,186$. Find approximate 90% confidence limits for the mean number of miles run that week by club members. *(ULEAC)*

8 A car mechanic measures the voltages of six batteries of the same type. The results (in volts) are:

    12.24   12.02   12.12   12.15   12.23   12.08

a Calculate unbiased estimates of the mean and variance of the voltage of the batteries of this type.

b Making appropriate assumptions, which should be stated, calculate 95% confidence limits for the mean voltage of batteries of this type.

    (WJEC)

9 A population of antelope has a mean mass denoted by μ kg. The standard deviation is denoted by σ kg. A random sample of size 57 is taken.

a State three facts concerning the distribution of the sample mean mass.

b The actual masses in the sample are summarised by $\Sigma x = 5273$ and $\Sigma x^2 = 493\,373$, where x kg is the mass of the antelope. Find unbiased estimates of μ and σ^2.

c Find a 95% confidence interval for the population mean mass, giving the end points of the interval correct to one decimal place. *(UCLES)*

10 An angling club owns a pond. The number of fish caught by an experienced angler fishing alone for three hours in this pond is a random variable X. The probability distribution of X is shown below:

X	0	1	2	3	4	5	6
$P(X)$	0.38	0.24	0.14	0.10	0.09	0.04	0.01

a Calculate the mean and standard deviation of X.

b The club holds a competition for 50 experienced anglers who fish together for three hours and catch a total of 38 fish. The random variable Y represents the number of fish caught by one experienced angler fishing in the pond at the same time as 49 other experienced anglers.

    i Give an estimate of the mean value of Y.

    ii The number of fish caught by each of the anglers in the competition may be regarded as a random sample of Y. Given that Y does have the same standard deviation as X, calculate a 90% confidence interval for the mean of Y. *(AEB)*

Applications and Activities

By examining the contents of packets of crisps, boxes of sweets, etc. is the manufacturer's claim stated on the package supported by an interval estimate based on your sample?

Summary

For variance known and either a large sample or from a normal distribution

- The 90% confidence interval for the population mean is

$$\bar{x} \pm 1.645 \frac{\sigma}{\sqrt{n}}$$

- The 95% confidence interval for the population mean is

$$\bar{x} \pm 1.96 \frac{\sigma}{\sqrt{n}}$$

- The 99% confidence interval for the population mean is .

$$\bar{x} \pm 2.576 \frac{\sigma}{\sqrt{n}}$$

Those for unknown variance but large samples have s in place of σ.

- Confidence intervals for the population mean (small sample from a normal population) are found using the Student t distribution, with v degress of freedom

$$\bar{x} \pm \frac{ts}{\sqrt{n-1}}$$

- The 90% confidence interval for the population proportion (large sample) is

$$p_s \pm 1.645 \sqrt{\frac{p_s q_s}{n}} \quad \text{where } p_s \text{ is the sample proportion and } q_s = 1 - p_s$$

- The 95% confidence interval for the population proportion (large sample) is

$$p_s \pm 1.96 \sqrt{\frac{p_s q_s}{n}}$$

- The 99% confidence interval for the population proportion (large sample) is

$$p_s \pm 2.576 \sqrt{\frac{p_s q_s}{n}}$$

14 Significance Tests I: Single Values

What you need to know

- How to calculate unbiased estimates for the mean and variance.

- How to find Z scores from normal distribution tables.

- How to find t scores from the tables.

Review

1 For the following samples find unbiased estimates for the population mean and variance:

   a   16, 24, 19, 19, 17, 23, 22, 15

   b   1.9, 1.2, 1.4, 1.4, 1.7, 1.5, 1.3, 1.8, 1.6, 1.6, 1.5, 1.4

   c   195, 204, 203, 198, 198

   d   1.03, 1.04, 1.02, 0.99, 1.00, 1.01, 1.03, 1.03, 0.98, 0.97, 1.02, 1.01, 1.00, 1.01, 0.97

   e   2.3, 2.2, 2.2, 2.2, 2.35, 2.21, 2.4, 2.5, 2.47, 2.35, 2.18

2 Find the Z scores for the following probabilities for the standard normal distribution.

   a   0.85   **b**   0.90   **c**   0.925

   d   0.95   **e**   0.99

3 Find the values from the Student t tables for the following degrees of freedom and the given confidence interval.

   a $v = 4$, at 90%   **b** $v = 8$, at 95%   **c** $v = 12$, at 98%

   d $v = 5$, at 80%   **e** $v = 9$, at 90%

14.1 Defining Terms

Michelle was certain she was telepathic, so she constructed a simple experiment to confirm this. She took a coin and tossed it, covering it with her hand as it landed. She then looked to see whether it was a head or a tail and thought hard about the result, trying to make a friend guess on which side the coin had landed. She was careful to ensure her friend had not seen the coin land. The friend guessed whether the coin had landed heads or tails and Michelle recorded whether her friend was right or wrong. The experiment was repeated 10 times with her friend managing to guess seven outcomes correctly.

Michelle thought that seven correct guesses might be a significant result, so she decided to test the hypothesis that the probability of her success was greater than that expected from pure guess work.

A **hypothesis** is an idea, theory or argument that is put forward for study, either from personal experience or from collected data.

The **null hypothesis**, H_0, is a statistical hypothesis put forward for testing. In Michelle's case the null hypothesis is that the probability of her friend guessing correctly is 0.5 or $\frac{1}{2}$.

The **alternative hypothesis**, H_1, is the hypothesis that is accepted if the null hypothesis is rejected. In Michelle's case the alternative hypothesis is that the probability of her friend guessing correctly is greater than 0.5.

The **significance level** will determine whether there is any difference in the data collected by experiment or survey and that found by calculation or from expectation.

The 5% level is normally used in significance tests, but more stringent tests can be applied at the 1% or 0.5% level.

For H_0 to be rejected and H_1 to be accepted, the results of any test used in comparing the data must give either a value *lower* than the *significance level*, or a value *greater* than a *critical value* normally found in tables linked to the type of test used.

Example 1

On the basis of Michelle's results do you think she is telepathic?

Solution

Michelle's results give:

H_0: $p = 0.5$ the probability of a correct guess is $\frac{1}{2}$.

This means Michelle is not telepathic and we can test whether the results rule out that possibility.

$H_1: \ p > 0.5$ the probability of a correct guess is greater than $\frac{1}{2}$.

This may indicate that Michelle is telepathic as the chance of her being correct is greater than $\frac{1}{2}$.

significance level: 5%

If the null hypothesis is true the results of the guessing can be modelled by the binomial distribution $B\left(10, \frac{1}{2}\right)$, where $P(X = x) =^{10} C_r (0.5)^{10-x}(0.5)^x$.

Correct guesses	Probability	Cumulative probability
0	0.000 976 5	0.000 976 5
1	0.009 766	0.010 741 5
2	0.043 95	0.054 681 5
3	0.117 188	0.171 868 5
4	0.205 078	0.376 946 5
5	0.246 09	0.623 036 5
6	0.205 078	0.828 114 5
7	0.117 188	0.945 301 5
8	0.043 95	0.989 241 5
9	0.009 766	0.999 006 5
10	0.000 976 5	1

The probability of guessing seven or more results correctly must be less than 5% for the result to be significant. The reason for considering seven or more correct, when Michelle got exactly seven correct is because all the people who guessed eight, nine or ten correctly *have* guessed seven correctly. The probability of guessing seven correctly must include the probability of guessing eight, nine or ten correctly. The chance of getting a score of 7 or above with a probability of 0.5 is:

$$1 - P(X < 7) = 1 - 0.828\ 114\ 5$$

$$P(X \geq 7) = 0.171\ 885\ 5, \text{ or } 17.19\%$$

Since 17.19% > 5% there is no reason to reject H_0. Therefore there is no evidence to suggest that the probability of success does not equal 0.5.

For a result of eight correct guesses out of 10 then:

$$P(X \geq 8) = 1 - P(X < 8)$$

$$= 1 - 0.945\ 301\ 5$$

$$= 0.546\ 985$$

$$= 5.47\%$$

Remember the binomial distribution is used to model situations where there are only two possible outcomes, success or failure. It has two parameters: n, the number of trials and p, the probability of success.

Remember:
$P(X \geq r) = 1 - (X < r)$

This means that the probability of guessing eight or more results correctly is still greater than the significance level of 5%. It is not until nine correct guesses are achieved that the probability is less than 5%. So to indicate that telepathy might exist a score of 9 or more correct guesses is required.

This is called the **critical value** of the test, which is the value at which the *null hypothesis* can be rejected and the *alternative hypothesis* accepted.

Example 2

Michelle carried out a further test where she placed four different coloured discs in a bag, selected one, ensuring her friend could not see it, concentrated on the colour and then asked her friend to guess the colour. She repeated the process 20 times and her friend managed to guess correctly nine times. Michelle felt this result indicated that she was telepathic. Would you agree?

Solution

H_0: $p = 0.25$ the probability of a correct guess is $\frac{1}{4}$.

H_1: $p > 0.25$ the probability of a correct guess is more than $\frac{1}{4}$.

significance level: 5%

The results of the experiment can be modelled by the binomial distribution, $B\left(20, \frac{1}{4}\right)$, where $P(X = x) = ^{20}C_r(0.25)^r(0.75)^{20-r}$.

The chance of getting a score of 9 or above is $1 - P(X \leq 8)$.

Using cumulative binomial probability tables look up the table for $n = 20$. Find where row 8 intersects with column 0.250, which should give a value of 0.9591.

$P(X \geq 9) = 1 - 0.9591$

$= 0.0409$, or 4.09%

As 4.09% < 5%, H_0 can be rejected and H_1 accepted.

There is evidence to suggest that $p > 0.25$.

Care must be taken when only one experiment is carried out. The evidence obtained in this case indicates the need for further research.

Example 3

Michelle repeats the experiment in example 2, but this time she uses five different coloured discs. She carries out the experiment 20 times and her friend guesses correctly only once.

Is there sufficient evidence to suggest her success rate is falling?

Solution

H_0: $p = 0.2$ Michelle's success rate is 20%.

H_1: $p < 0.2$ Michelle's success rate is less than 20%.

significance level: 5%

The results can be modelled by the binomial distribution $B(20,\ 0.2)$ where

$$P(X = x) =^{20} C_r(0.2)^r(0.8)^{20-r}$$

Using cumulative binomial probability tables, the probability of one success, or no successes, is

$$P(X \leq 1) = 0.0692 = 6.92\%$$

As 6.92% > 5% we do not reject H_0.

There is some evidence to suggest that Michelle's success rate has not fallen.

14.1 Defining Terms
Exercise

Technique

Using a cumulative binomial probability table, or otherwise, find the critical values at the 5% level of the following distributions:

1 $B(10, 0.25)$

2 $B(15, 0.7)$

3 $B(20, 0.1)$

4 $B(12, 0.5)$

5 $B(9, \frac{1}{3})$

6 $B(40, 0.5)$

7 $B(5, 0.15)$

8 $B(25, 0.4)$

9 $B(8, 0.07)$

10 $B(30, 0.15)$

11 By using tables, or otherwise, find the critical value at the:

    a   2.5% level

    b   1% level

for the distributions in questions 1 to 10.

Contextual

*In all the answers state clearly the **null** and **alternative hypotheses**.*

In all cases test at the 5% level.

1 An automatic bottle filling machine is expected to overfill 10% of the bottles. Of 20 bottles inspected, five were found to be overfilled. Is there evidence to suggest the machine needs to be reset, as it is overfilling too many bottles?

2 A bus company claim that 80% of their buses arrive no more than five minutes late. An inspector monitors 15 buses on a particular route and finds that six are more than five minutes late. Does this evidence disprove the company's statement?

3 It is claimed that $\frac{1}{3}$ of the population is overweight. In a small village a sample of 30 adults revealed that only three of them were overweight. Does this suggest that the village is healthier than the rest of the population?

4 A gardener expects 75% of a particular plant to be yellow. Out of 18 plants only 12 were completely yellow. Is there evidence to suggest the plant has produced fewer yellow plants than claimed?

5 In a board game a dice lands with 3 upwards seven times out of 15 throws. Is this evidence to suggest a biased dice, landing on 3 most often?

6 Rana normally passes 70% of her tests with a score of 60% or better. She has only gained more than 60% in seven of her last 16 tests. Does this indicate a drop in Rana's standard at the 1% level?

14.2 One- and Two-tailed Tests

In the examples covered so far, the results were tested for a significant difference at only one end of the distribution, that is the probability was greater or less than expected. These are **one-tailed tests**.

The graphs indicate the regions used to reject H_0.

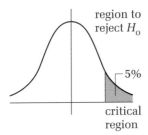

This shows the region where the probability of the events happening is significantly greater than expected.

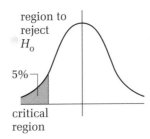

This shows the region where the probability of the events happening is significantly less than expected.

A **two-tailed** test considers significant differences at both ends of the distribution.

For a significance level of 5% the critical regions would consist of the combination of the two regions of 2.5% at each end of the distribution.

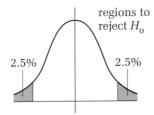

A two-tailed test is used when a significant difference is tested that does not specify that the result is greater or less than expected.

Example

Michelle's friends have the opportunity to pick a red or black card placed on the table. Twelve friends picked the red card and four picked the black card. Test at the 5% level whether they are more likely to choose one card than the other.

Solution

In this example the probability of picking 12 or more red cards must be combined with the probability of selecting four or fewer black cards.

$$H_0: \; p = 0.5 \quad \text{the probability of selecting a colour is } \tfrac{1}{2}.$$

$$H_1: \; p \neq 0.5 \quad \text{the probability of selecting a colour is greater or less than } \tfrac{1}{2}.$$

significance level: 5% two-tailed test.

$$P(X \geq 12) = 1 - P(X \leq 11)$$

$$= 1 - 0.9616$$

$$= 0.0384$$

$$P(X \leq 4) = 0.0384$$

$$\text{Total probability} = 0.0384 + 0.0384$$

$$= 0.0768$$

$$= 7.68\%$$

As the distribution is symmetrical the total probability could be calculated by $2 \times P(X \geq 12)$.

As 7.68% > 5%, H_0 is not rejected and we conclude at the 5% level that the black and red cards could be equally likely to be chosen.

Remember: steps in testing

● Decide the appropriate test

● State the null hypothesis, H_0 and the alternative hypothesis, H_1.

● From these determine whether a one or two-tailed test is required.

● Decide on the significance level, which fixes the critical values of the test statistic.

● Carry out the calculations to find the value of the test statistic.

● Draw a conclusion.

14.2 One- and Two-tailed Tests

Exercise

Contextual

1 The probability of a girl or boy being born is approximately 0.5. In one family with eight children, there are seven children of one sex. Is there sufficient evidence to suggest that they are more likely to have a child of one sex rather than the other?

2 A coin lands on heads 14 times out of 18 tosses. Is there evidence to suggest the coin is biased? Test at the 5% level.

3 In a multiple choice test, there are five possible answers. Of the 20 questions, eight of them had the middle choice as the correct answer. Does this show bias in the setting of the questions? Test at the 5% level.

4 The probability of Malcolm hitting a target is 0.7. He has 17 shots at the target and hits it eight times. Does the evidence suggest, at the 5% level, his accuracy has decreased?

5 In question **4**, what would be the critical values, at the 10% level, to indicate a change in Malcolm's accuracy?

6 Michelle asks her friends to guess the numbers she has written down on a piece of paper. The friends know that the numbers are from 1 to 5 inclusive. Out of 20 guesses her friends managed to obtain the correct number eight times. Is there any evidence to support the theory that the probability of success was greater than $\frac{1}{5}$?

7 In a raffle 30 tickets were sold. Of the 10 prizes, eight of them were won by holders of red tickets. Is there evidence to suggest the chance of winning with a red ticket was higher than 0.6?

8 On a golf course the chance of a player landing on the fairway with her first shot is usually 40%. During one round she gets on the fairway with her first shot six out of nine times. Is there any evidence to suggest that she is improving?

14.3 Tests using Normal Distributions or Student *t* Tests for Single Values

In the next five sections various tests are used to compare samples with population parameters using the properties of the normal distribution. These tests are used for:

- a single item – to see if the single item is from a normal distribution $N(\mu, \sigma^2)$

- a sample mean – to see if a sample mean is from a normal distribution with a particular mean, assuming:
  - σ^2 known
  - σ^2 unknown and large sample
  - σ^2 unknown and small sample

- a sample proportion to see if a sample with a certain characteristic comes from a given population.

A single item (Z test)

This test is used to determine whether a single item could come from a parent population with a given mean and variance. It tests whether the item is within reasonable limits when compared to the mean value and variance of the population. The test indicates whether or not the item *could* come from, not that it *must* or *could not* come from, the parent population. Care must always be taken when dealing with a single item.

If X is normally distributed with mean μ and variance σ^2, then the statistic $Z = (X - \mu)/\sigma$ is also normally distributed with a mean of 0 and variance of 1, $N(0, 1)$.

Z is the **standard normal variable** and is used in tests of significance.

Example 1

Test at the 5% level whether a sample value of 52 could come from a normal population with mean, $\mu = 40$, and variance, $\sigma^2 = 25$.

Solution

$$H_0: \quad \mu = 40 \quad \text{the mean of the distribution is 40.}$$

$$H_1: \quad \mu \neq 40 \quad \text{the mean is not 40.}$$

significance level: 5% two-tailed test, reject H_0 if $|Z| > 1.96$.

$|Z|$ is the modulus or absolute value of Z

$$Z = \frac{52 - 40}{\sqrt{25}} = \frac{12}{5} = 2.4$$

As $|Z| > 1.96$, H_0 is rejected.

At the 5% level there is significant evidence to indicate that the value does not come from a population with a mean of 40. We have not proved for certain that the value does not come from this population. But, as only 5% of the values from the population are as extreme as this, the chances are that this value hasn't come from the population.

Example 2

The length of a species of lizard is known to be normally distributed with mean, $\bar{x} = 28$ cm and variance $s^2 = 10$ cm. A lizard of length 24 cm was found. Test at the 10% level whether this lizard could be from the same species.

Solution

H_0: $\mu = 28$ the lizard is from a population with
mean length 28 cm.

H_1: $\mu \neq 28$ the lizard is not from the population.

significance level: 10%   two-tailed test, reject H_0 if $|Z| > 1.645$.

$$Z = \frac{24 - 28}{\sqrt{10}} = \frac{-4}{3.16} = -1.266, \text{ so } |Z| = 1.265$$

As $|Z| < 1.645$ then H_0 is not rejected.

There is some evidence to suggest that the lizard could be of the same species.

Example 3

Test at the 5% level whether the value 340 could be from a normal population with a mean of 320 and variance of 80, or whether the mean is greater than 320.

Solution

H_0: $\mu = 320$

H_1: $\mu \geq 320$

significance level: 5%   one-tailed test, reject H_0 if $Z > 1.645$.

$$Z = \frac{340 - 320}{\sqrt{80}} = \frac{20}{8.94} = 2.236$$

As $Z > 1.645$, reject H_0 and accept H_1.

There is significant evidence to suggest the value is from a population with a larger mean than 320.

14.3 Tests using Normal Distributions or Student t Tests for Single Values

Exercise

Technique

Test at the 5% level whether the sample value could have come from the normal population defined by the null hypothesis.

	Sample value	Null hypothesis	Alternative hypothesis	Population variance
1	18	H_0: $\mu = 12$	H_1: $\mu \neq 12$	16
2	42	H_0: $\mu = 34$	H_1: $\mu > 34$	16
3	140	H_0: $\mu = 125$	H_1: $\mu \neq 125$	200
4	85	H_0: $\mu = 100$	H_1: $\mu < 100$	150
5	88	H_0: $\mu = 120$	H_1: $\mu \neq 120$	225
6	200	H_0: $\mu = 225$	H_1: $\mu \neq 225$	400
7	56	H_0: $\mu = 52$	H_1: $\mu \neq 52$	25
8	118	H_0: $\mu = 105$	H_1: $\mu > 105$	40
9	80	H_0: $\mu = 72$	H_1: $\mu \neq 72$	30
10	66	H_0: $\mu = 60$	H_1: $\mu > 60$	9
11	35	H_0: $\mu = 42$	H_1: $\mu \neq 42$	9
12	0.6	H_0: $\mu = 0.5$	H_1: $\mu \neq 0.5$	0.04

Contextual

1 A machine filling bottles of liquid is set to have a mean of 440 ml with a variance of 20 ml^2. A sample measured contained 432 ml. Does this suggest that the machine is not working properly?

2 The pulse rate of adults has a mean of 72 beats per minute with a variance of 36 (beats per minute)^2. Is there evidence to suggest that a pulse rate of 85 beats per minute comes from a population with a faster pulse rate?

3 The time for a roulette wheel to spin is normally distributed with a mean of 0.75 seconds and a variance of 0.69 s^2. After the wheel had been overhauled the time taken for a complete revolution was 0.395 seconds. Is there evidence to indicate that the mean time has now been reduced?

4 The time that a species of rose produces flowers has been found to be normally distributed with a mean of 54 days and a standard deviation of six days. One plant was given additional fertiliser, which resulted in it flowering for 70 days. Is there evidence at the 10% level to indicate that the fertiliser has been beneficial?

5 A box of matches contains 52 matches. The manufacturer set up the packing machine to distribute the contents normally with a mean of 60 matches and a variance of 10 matches^2. Is there evidence at the 5% level to indicate that the mean is lower?

6 The time for a bus to complete a particular journey is normally distributed with a mean time of 48 minutes, and a variance of 30 minutes^2. A new one-way system is introduced on part of the route which, it is hoped, will reduce the mean time for the journey. The first journey along the new route took 40 minutes. Is there any evidence to suggest, at the 10% level, that the mean time has been reduced?

7 A basketball team has an accuracy rate which is normally distributed with a mean of 68.4% and a standard deviation of 5.8%. After a series of intensive training sessions the team's accuracy in the first match was 75.4%. Does this new figure suggest that the accuracy of the team has improved?

8 Lindsay is determined to improve her A-level grade. Her coursework marks are normally distributed, with a mean of 62.4% and a standard deviation of 7.2%. Her next coursework mark is 71%. Is there evidence at the 10% level to indicate an improvement in her scores?

Critical values for z scores

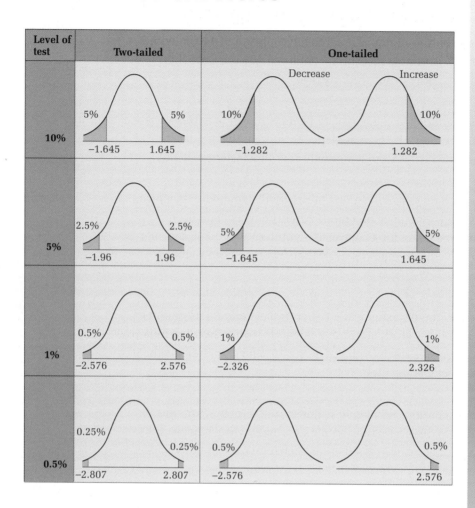

14.4 Testing a Mean – Population Variance Known

This test is used to determine whether the mean value of a sample is equal to the mean value of the parent population. The difference between the two values is compared to the known standard deviation of the parent population.

The parent population is assumed to be normal unless the sample is large, say over 30, when we do not have to assume the parent population is normal since the Central Limit Theorem tells us the sample mean has a normal distribution, approximately.

Using the null hypothesis that the population mean is μ then $X \sim N(\mu, \sigma^2)$.

- The sampling distribution of the means, $\bar{X}$, is normally distributed

$$N\left(\mu, \frac{\sigma^2}{n}\right).$$ ◀ **Central Limit Theorem**

Therefore standardising to $N(0, 1)$, we use

$$Z = \frac{\bar{X} - \mu}{\sigma/\sqrt{n}}$$

The null hypothesis, H_0, is that the true population mean is μ.

Example

The weight of chocolate bars is normally distributed with a mean of 50 g and a variance of 25. A sample of 40 bars was taken and found to have a mean weight of 51.5 g. Is there evidence at the 5% level to suggest that the mean value has increased?

Solution

$$H_0: \ \mu = 50$$

$$H_1: \ \mu > 50$$

significance level: 5%   one-tailed test, reject H_0 if $Z > 1.645$.

$$Z = \frac{\bar{X} - \mu}{\sigma/\sqrt{n}}$$

$$= \frac{51.5 - 50}{5/\sqrt{40}}$$

$$= 1.897$$

As $Z > 1.645$, reject H_0.

Accept H_1; there is significant evidence to indicate that the mean weight is greater than 50 g.

14.4 Testing a Mean – Population Variance Known

Exercise

Technique

Test at the 5% level whether the sample mean indicates that the sample could come from the given normal population with the mean given by H_0.

	$\bar{x}$	n	H_0	H_1	s^2
1	40	100	$\mu = 38$	$\mu \neq 38$	36
2	997	40	$\mu = 1000$	$\mu < 1000$	200
3	14.8	500	$\mu = 15$	$\mu \neq 15$	4
4	34.5	6400	$\mu = 35$	$\mu \neq 35$	100
5	504	300	$\mu = 500$	$\mu > 500$	225
6	3.4	50	$\mu = 3$	$\mu > 3$	3
7	0.65	85	$\mu = 0.6$	$\mu \neq 0.6$	0.5
8	32 425	125	$\mu = 32\,400$	$\mu > 32\,400$	2000
9	0.941	92	$\mu = 1$	$\mu < 1$	0.09
10	1.17	56	$\mu = 1$	$\mu > 1$	0.15
11	1487	44	$\mu = 1500$	$\mu \neq 1500$	2500
12	17.9	72	$\mu = 20$	$\mu \neq 20$	360

Contextual

1 The scores obtained in a specific test are known to be normally distributed with a mean score of 80 and variance of 49. A random sample of 40 students took the test, achieving a mean score of 82.5. At the 10% level is there evidence to indicate that these 40 students have performed significantly better?

2 A normal population has an unknown mean and a variance of 16. A sample of eight was taken with the results being:

22 21 26 24 29 22 26 24

At the 1% level, test whether the population mean could have been 26.

3 A javelin thrower finds the distance she throws is normally distributed with a mean of 65 m. She introduces a new training system, then measures five consecutive throws. The distances are 72 m, 62 m, 65 m, 63 m and 69 m. If the variance of her original throws is 12 m², is there any evidence at the 5% level that her new training has improved her throwing?

4 A production line is set to produce items with a volume of 600 ml. Assume that the volume is normally distributed with a variance of 16 ml². Is there any evidence at the 1% level that the mean is higher than 600 ml, if a sample of 15 items has a mean of 603 ml?

5 As part of a survey to assess how accurately witnesses can describe people, a group of 120 people was asked to estimate the age of a person shown to them. The estimated age was then taken from the real age and the difference calculated to the nearest five years. The results were:

Difference (years)	−15	−10	−5	0	5	10	15	20
Frequency	8	11	14	22	28	23	8	6

It was found that the standard deviation of the population was 15 years. Could this sample have been one from a population where the mean difference was zero years?

6 The weights and measures inspector was concerned that a shopkeeper's scales were faulty and measured 10 weights of 1 kg. In machines of the type tested the weights recorded were known to be normally distributed with standard deviation of 0.1 kg. The machine recorded the 10 weights as:

0.96 kg 0.99 kg 1.01 kg 1.00 kg 0.98 kg
0.94 kg 0.98 kg 0.92 kg 0.97 kg 0.98 kg

Could the sample of weights shown by the weighing machine have come from a population where the mean weight is 1 kg?

7 The age of a population is known to be normally distribution with a variance of 225. In a survey of the ages of shoppers to a newly opened shopping centre, designed to attract younger people, the results were:

Age	$0 \leq x < 10$	$10 \leq x < 20$	$20 \leq x < 30$	$30 \leq x < 40$	$40 \leq x < 50$
Frequency	5	18	39	28	10

Calculate the mean age of the sample and test at the 5% level whether the mean age of the shoppers at the new centre could be 25 years.

14.5 Testing a Mean – Population Variance Unknown, Large Sample

In most cases where sampling occurs the variance of the parent population is unknown, therefore an unbiased estimator of the variance has to be worked out. The test then proceeds in the same way as when the population variance is known.

Again, the sampling distribution of the means is $\bar{X} \sim N\left(\mu, \dfrac{\sigma^2}{n}\right)$ approximately.

Because σ^2 is unknown an estimator, $\hat{\sigma}^2 = \dfrac{ns^2}{n-1}$ is used, where s^2 is the sample variance and $\hat{\sigma}^2$ gives an unbiased estimator.

As n is large, $\dfrac{n}{n-1}$ is approximately 1.

So $\hat{\sigma}^2 = s^2$

The statistic $Z = \dfrac{\bar{X} - \mu}{s/\sqrt{n}}$ is used, which is distributed approximately as $N(0, 1)$.

The null hypothesis, H_0, is that the population mean is μ.

Remember that $n \geq 30$ is considered large.

Example

A supplier claims that the mean life expectancy of their light bulbs is 120 hours. A consumer organisation tested 200 bulbs and found the mean to be 117.5 hours, with a variance of $169\,\text{h}^2$. Is there evidence at the 1% level that the mean is lower than 120 hours?

Solution

$$H_0: \ \mu = 120 \text{ hours}$$

$$H_1: \ \mu < 120 \text{ hours}$$

significance level: 1%   one-tailed test, reject H_0 if $Z > 2.326$.

$$Z = \frac{\bar{X} - \mu}{s/\sqrt{n}} = \frac{117.5 - 120}{13/\sqrt{200}} = -2.720$$

As $Z > 2.326$, reject H_0 and accept H_1.

There is evidence to indicate that the mean life span is less than 120 hours.

14.5 Testing a Mean – Population Variance Unknown, Large Sample

Exercise

Contextual

1 In a sample of 60 students their heights were normally distributed with a mean of 165 cm and a variance of 289 cm^2. Is there evidence at the 1% level to indicate that the population mean could be 167 cm?

2 A sample of 40 trout had a mean mass of 2.42 kg with a variance of 0.005 kg^2. The population mean mass is thought to be 2.4 kg. Is there any evidence to support this assumption?

3 A school has a mean score of 78.3% in a national test, with a variance of 60. With 180 students taking the test, is there evidence that the school performed better than the national mean of 76.8%, at the 5% level?

4 A machine has been set up to produce metal rods of a mean length of 1 m. A sample of 50 rods produce a normal distribution with a mean of 1.05 m and variance of 0.025 m^2. Is there evidence to suggest the machine is producing rods with a greater mean length?

5 A large sample of 200 one-kilogram bags of sugar from a packing machine were weighed to test whether the machine was set up correctly. The sample weights were normally distributed with a mean of 0.981 kg and a variance of 0.05 kg^2. The machine was originally set to produce bags with a mean weight of 1.01 kg. Does the evidence suggest, at the 5% level, that the machine needs to be reset?

6 A company produces batteries with a mean lifetime of 2100 hours. After a new method of production is introduced 120 batteries are tested and found to have a mean life of 2130 hours and standard deviation of 115 hours. Is there any evidence at the 5% level that the new method of production has increased the mean lifetime of the batteries?

7

The manufacturer of tyres for a mountain bike claim the tyres can withstand the rigours of the roughest terrain. They tested this claim by measuring the amount of pressure required to puncture the tyre. They found, from a sample of 60 tyres, that the mean pressure required to puncture the tyres was 142.3 N. The manufacturer found that the pressure was normally distributed with a variance of 125 N^2, but had thought that the mean was 145 N. Test at the 5% level whether the mean pressure required to puncture the tyres in the sample could have come from a population with a mean of 145 N.

8 In an assessment of the ability of Year 10 students to compete in an inter-school radio quiz, a variety of general knowledge questions was set to the 136 students in the year. The national results were known to be normally distributed with a standard deviation of 9. The school's Year 10 students had a mean score of 72.32 while the national mean score was 70. Test at the 5% level whether the school's result was higher than that from a population with a mean score of 70.

14.6 Testing a Mean – Population Variance Unknown, Small Sample

The last section dealt with testing the mean of a large sample against the mean of a parent population, where the sample was large. Unfortunately, due to time, cost or other factors, many samples are unable to be considered as large. Again an unbiased estimator of the variance must be calculated and then student t values are used to compare the difference in the sample and population means with this estimation of the variance.

As in the previous examples, σ^2 is unknown, therefore an unbiased estimator is used.

$\hat{\sigma}^2 = \dfrac{ns^2}{n-1}$ is used where s^2 is the sample variance

$$Z = \frac{\bar{x} - \mu}{\hat{\sigma}/\sqrt{n}}$$

Replacing $\hat{\sigma}^2$ gives $Z = \dfrac{\bar{x} - \mu}{s/\sqrt{(n-1)}}$ and as the sample is small the test statistic is

Remember a small sample has less than 30 items.

$$t = \frac{\bar{x} - \mu}{s/\sqrt{(n-1)}}$$

where t has $(n-1)$ degrees of freedom.

The null hypothesis, H_0, is that the population mean is μ.

Example

Ten students prepared for an examination by attempting a 'mock' then reviewing the answers. The differences between their mock mark and final mark were recorded as follows:

22	−3	14	5	−4	11	9	4	−1	12

Test, at the 5% level, whether there is evidence that revision has improved the students' scores.

Solution

If no change took place μ would be zero, so,

H_0: $\mu = 0$ indicates no improvement

H_1: $\mu > 0$ indicates an improvement.

As the mean and the variance of the population are unknown the sample mean and variance have to be calculated.

significance level: 5%   one tailed test.

Using Student t-tables for $(n-1)$ degrees of freedom gives a critical value of $t_9 = 1.833$.

$$\Sigma x = 69 \text{ and } \Sigma x^2 = 1093$$

$$\bar{x} = \frac{69}{10} = 6.9$$

$$s^2 = \frac{1093}{10} - 6.9^2$$

$$= 61.69$$

$$s = 7.854$$

$$t = \frac{\bar{x} - \mu}{s/\sqrt{n-1}}$$

$$= \frac{6.9 - 0}{7.854/\sqrt{9}}$$

$$= 2.64$$

As $t > 1.833$, H_0 is rejected and H_1 is accepted.

There is significant evidence to indicate that revision improved the results.

14.6 Testing a Mean – Population Variance Unknown, Small Sample

Exercise

Technique

Test the following hypothesis at the level indicated.

	n	Σx	Σx^2	Hypothesis		Significance level
1	5	57	754	H_0: $\mu = 10$	H_1: $\mu \neq 10$	5%
2	8	26	142	H_0: $\mu = 0$	H_1: $\mu > 0$	2.5%
3	10	168	2870	H_0: $\mu = 18$	H_1: $\mu < 18$	10%
4	6	1.2	0.3	H_0: $\mu = 0$	H_1: $\mu > 0$	1%
5	8	50	548	H_0: $\mu = 5$	H_1: $\mu > 5$	2.5%
6	9	3.8	2	H_0: $\mu = 0.4$	H_1: $\mu > 0.4$	5%
7	3	0.48	0.08	H_0: $\mu = 0.15$	H_1: $\mu > 0.15$	5%
8	7	14 559	30 290 000	H_0: $\mu = 2050$	H_1: $\mu > 2050$	5%
9	20	2	0.3	H_0: $\mu = 0$	H_1: $\mu < 0$	5%
10	11	4.56	2	H_0: $\mu = 0.42$	H_1: $\mu < 0.42$	5%

Contextual

1 A manufacturer claims that his garden candles last four hours, on average. Six candles were sampled with the following time spans,

2.6   3.2   3.7   2.5   3.9   3.8

Carry out a test, at the 5% level, of the manufacturer's claim.

2 A new diet is claimed to increase the speed of weight loss. Ten volunteers followed the diet and recorded their weight loss in one week. The results were (in pounds):

2.7   2.3   1.1   2.4   2.7   3.1   2.0   2.5   2.2   2.3

A study with a large number of volunteers on a calorie-controlled diet showed a mean weight loss of 2.2 lb. Test, at the 1% level, whether the new diet increases the speed of weight loss.

3 The masses, in grams, of six components produced by a machine were measured as follows:

117   86   126   172   126   116

The components are supposed to weigh 150 g. Test, at the 5% level, whether the machine is operating properly.

4 The times that eight trains arrived at a station were recorded with respect to the timetable. The number of minutes early were classed as positive and the times late as negative. The results were:

1   −2   −5   −4   2   −3   −1   −7

The company claims that the trains arrive on time. Test this claim at the 1% level.

5 A school wishes to monitor the length of telephone calls made by students using the pay-phone during the school day. A sample of 15 student phone calls measured to the nearest minute were:

3   4   8   1   6   4   1   7   5   2   3   2   8   9   1

The school claims that the students spend an average of $2\frac{1}{2}$ min on a phone call. Test at the 2.5% significance level whether the evidence supports the school's claim or whether the average time is greater than $2\frac{1}{2}$ min.

6 The following are the results of a trial group of 10 adults who took part in a Swimathon for a national children's charity. The number of lengths of a 50 metre swimming pool that each individual completed was recorded. The results were:

16   19   23   24   25   26   26   32   34   37

The organisers thought that the mean distance for all the swimmers would be 23 lengths. Test at the 10% level whether the sample could have come from a population with a mean of 23 lengths.

7 The lengths of eight caterpillars were recorded in centimetres.

3.4   3.7   4.1   3.9   3.8   4.0   3.4   3.6

The lengths of a population of caterpillars were known to be normally distributed a with a mean value of 3.7 cm. Test whether there is any evidence to suggest that this sample comes from the same population.

14.7 Testing a Sample Proportion (Z Test)

A sample can be taken to estimate the proportion of a parent population with a special characteristic, such as left-handedness, blue eyes, etc. This test compares the sample proportion against the proportion within the parent population to determine whether the sample could have come from that population. The test is carried out in a similar way to the methods used in the previous tests.

The sampling distributions of proportions gives

$$p_s \sim N\left(p, \frac{pq}{n}\right) \text{ approximately}$$

where p_s is the proportion of success in the sample,
p is the proportion of success in the population,
$q = 1 - p$ and n is large.

The test statistic is

$$Z = \frac{p_s - p}{\sqrt{pq/n}}$$

which is distributed $N(0, 1)$ with H_0 that the proportion of success in the population is p.

Example

A brewery claimed that 25% of young women preferred the taste of white ciders to traditional drinks. In a survey of 400 eighteen- to twenty-one-year-old women, 88 said they preferred white cider. Does the evidence support the brewery's claim?

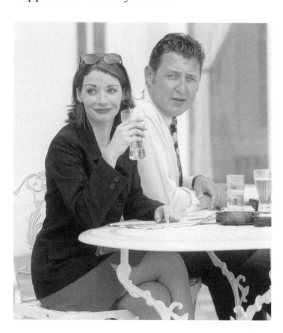

Solution

$$H_0: \quad p = 0.25 \quad \text{25\% prefer white cider}$$

$$H_1: \quad p < 0.25 \quad \text{less than 25\% prefer white cider}$$

significance level: 5% one-tailed test, large n, critical value 1.645.

$p_s = \frac{88}{400} = 0.22$

$q = 1 - 0.22 = 0.78$

$n = 400$

$$Z = \frac{p_s - p}{\sqrt{pq/n}}$$

$$= \frac{0.22 - 0.25}{\sqrt{(0.25 \times 0.75)/400}}$$

$$= -1.386$$

As $Z < 1.645$, H_0 is not rejected.

Note: If the significance level had been 10%, with a critical value of 1.282, then H_0 would be rejected.

14.7 Testing a Sample Proportion (Z Test)

Exercise

Technique

Test the following hypotheses using the appropriate significance test.

	Sample size	Number of successes	H_0	H_1	Level
1	80	24	$p = 0.4$	$p \neq 0.4$	5%
2	150	85	$p = 0.5$	$p > 0.5$	5%
3	120	100	$p = 0.75$	$p > 0.75$	1%
4	65	18	$p = 0.4$	$p > 1.4$	5%
5	320	210	$p = 0.6$	$p \neq 0.6$	5%
6	35	24	$p = 0.6$	$p > 0.6$	10%
7	82	60	$p = 0.75$	$p \neq 0.75$	5%
8	3000	1984	$p = 0.7$	$p < 0.7$	5%
9	560	172	$p = 0.35$	$p < 0.35$	5%
10	4500	638	$p = 0.15$	$p \neq 0.15$	5%
11	850	266	$p = 0.35$	$p < 0.35$	5%
12	40	23	$p = 0.5$	$p > 0.5$	5%

Contextual

1 In a test of indigestion tablets 164 out of a sample of 200 people found that the tablets were effective. The research team claimed that the tablet was 90% effective. Does the evidence support this claim?

2 In a general election the leading party gained 48% of the votes cast. After the publication of their first budget a sample of 400 voters was taken from which 158 indicated they supported the government. Is there evidence to suggest that there is a decrease in support for the government?

3 A machine normally produces defective items at a rate of one in 25. A sample of 250 items showed that 17 were defective. Is there evidence, at the 1% level, to suggest that the number of defective items is increasing?

4 In limited overs cricket, a statistician estimated that the probability of the team batting last winning is 0.7. In one season, out of 460 matches, the team batting last won 294 of them. Test whether the estimate of the statistician is supported by the evidence.

5 A school claims that its A-level results are above national averages resulting in more of its students going to university. Of the 75 students who completed A-level courses 62 carried on to university while, nationally, 78% of students carried on to university. Is the school's claim supported by the figures?

6 A publisher claims that by introducing students to a new series of teaching texts the students will be more motivated and will complete more work. The material was tested with 1438 students, with the result that 84.6% of all work was completed. Prior to the test an estimate of all work completed by students was given as 77.3%. Is there any evidence to suggest the new material encourages students to complete more of the work set? Test at the 5% level.

7 The percentage of defective components being produced by a factory was 6.23%. In an attempt to improve the performance a complete overhaul of the machines and working methods took place. This proved to be costly in terms of time and money. After the overhaul, a sample of 350 items was examined and of those 16 were found to be defective. Does the evidence suggest that there has been an improvement in performance in the factory?

Consolidation

Exercise A

1 A machine in a fruit canning factory puts quantities of sliced peaches into tins. The machine is set so that the mean mass of the contents is 120.4 g. The machine breaks down and after repair six tins are selected and their contents weighed. The weights of the contents were, in grams:

> 122.1 119.9 121.3 119.4 121.7 120.9

Stating any necessary assumptions and using a 10% significance level, test the hypothesis that the population mean is now greater than 120.4 g.

(UCLES)

2 At a large school there was an investigation of the distances from school to the students' homes. The distance from school, X km, measured to the nearest kilometre, was recorded for each of a random sample of 60 students. The results were summarised as $\Sigma x = 464$ and $\Sigma x^2 = 5769$.

a Calculate unbiased estimates of the mean and variance of the population from which the sample was drawn.

b It is claimed that students from the school live on an average less than 10 km away from the school. Stating any assumptions you make, use your results from **a** to test this claim. State clearly your hypotheses and use a 5% level of significance.

(ULEAC)

3 A leaflet from the Department of Health recently claimed that 70% of businesses operate a No Smoking policy on their premises. A member of the public who believed the true figure to be lower than 70% rang a random sample of 20 businesses to ask whether or not they operated a No Smoking policy. She then carried out a hypothesis test.

a Write down the null and alternative hypotheses under test. Explain why the alternative hypothesis has the form it does.

b Of the 20 businesses, k say that they do operate a No Smoking policy. Use tables to write down the critical region for a 10% test. (That is, write down the value of k for which the null hypothesis would be rejected at the 10% level of significance.)

c A second person decided to carry out a similar test, also at the 10% level, but sampled only four businesses. Write down the critical region in this case.

(MEI)

4 You are given a random sample of n observations from a normal distribution and you are required to test the null hypothesis that the distribution has a mean μ_0. Explain how you would decide whether to use a normal distribution or a t test when carrying out your test.

A hospital research team is studying the effects on the unborn child of its mother smoking throughout pregnancy. As part of its investigation the team chose a random sample of 12 pregnant woman who smoked throughout pregnancy. Each baby born to a woman in the sample had its birthweight, x kg, measured, producing the following values:

$$2.68 \quad 3.74 \quad 2.82 \quad 3.02 \quad 3.37 \quad 3.97$$
$$3.36 \quad 2.90 \quad 3.09 \quad 2.63 \quad 2.27 \quad 3.71$$

In recent years the birthweights of all babies born in the hospital have been normally distributed with mean 3.45 kg. Carry out an appropriate test to decide, at the 5% significance level, whether the mean weight of babies born to mothers who smoke throughout pregnancy is lower than 3.45 kg. You may assume that the babies, born in the hospital to mothers who smoke throughout pregnancy, have birthweights that are normally distributed with standard deviation 0.55 kg.

The length at birth, y cm, was measured for each of the 12 babies, producing the following data.

$$46.8 \quad 51.8 \quad 47.9 \quad 48.2 \quad 49.2 \quad 53.4$$
$$49.2 \quad 45.2 \quad 47.3 \quad 48.6 \quad 44.7 \quad 50.3$$

$(\Sigma y = 582.6$ and $\Sigma y^2 = 28\,354.44)$

Use these data to obtain a symmetrical 99% confidence interval for the mean length of babies born in the hospital to mothers who smoke throughout pregnancy.

(*NEAB*)

5 A machine is set to produce discs with mean diameter 14 mm. A random sample of six discs from a day's production yielded the following diameters, in millimetres.

$$13.1 \quad 15.0 \quad 14.4 \quad 13.4 \quad 16.1 \quad 17.4$$

Given that the diameters are normally distributed and using a 10% significance level, test whether the mean diameter is 14.0 mm:

a assuming that the population standard deviation of the perimeters is 1.3 mm

b without assuming that the population standard deviation is 1.3 mm.

(*UCLES*)

6 A pharmaceutical company claimed that a course of its vitamin tablets would improve examination performance. To publicise its claim the company offered to provide the tablets free to candidates taking a particular GCSE examination. This offer was taken up by some of the candidates. The average mark in the examination for all candidates who *did not* take the vitamin tablets was 42.0.

A random sample of 120 candidates from those who had taken the course of vitamin tablets gave a mean mark of 43.8 and a standard deviation of 12.8.

a Test, at the 5% significance level, whether the candidates who took the vitamin tablets had a mean mark greater than 42.0. State clearly your null and alternative hypothesis.

b Why was it not necessary to know that the examination marks were normally distributed before carrying out the test? (*AEB*)

7 Mr Robinson treated the ground in which eight of his strawberry plants were grown with a chemical soil conditioner. The yield in grams of each plant was as follows:

116   117   127   123   121   120   117   126

Experience had shown Mr Robinson that without the soil conditioner the mean yield was 116 g.

a State a null hypothesis if Mr Robinson wished to test whether the soil conditioner improves the yield.

b Carry out a suitable test and, and using the 1% level, draw a conclusion about the use of soil conditioner.

c State the necessary assumption made about the distribution of the yield of strawberry plants. (*NICCEA*)

8 When a scientist measures the concentration of a solution, the reading obtained can be modelled by a normally distributed random variable with mean m units, equal to the true concentration, and standard deviation 1.6 units. He is given a solution to analyse, which a colleague believes has a concentration of more than 25 units. He makes four independent measurements of the concentration of the solution, obtaining the following results:

25.1   27.8   26.9   25.8

a State appropriate null and alternative hypotheses for a test to determine whether there is sufficient evidence to support the colleague's belief.

b Calculate the sample mean.

c Carry out an appropriate test to determine whether the sample mean is significantly higher than 25 units. (*WJEC*)

9 The staff in a college have always assumed that 75% of students apply for university. A random sample of 100 students showed that 66 students intended applying to university. Stating clearly your null and alternative hypotheses, test whether or not the proportion of students applying for university has decreased. Use a 5% level of significance.

(ULEAC)

10 The lengths, in centimetres, of 21 adult trout of a particular variety were found to be as follows

    16.0 14.6 11.7 13.1 15.9 15.7 13.0
    11.5 13.4 14.1 15.8 14.8 12.5 12.7
    13.9 14.2 12.4 12.5 13.4 13.5 14.3

a Obtain a 95% two-sided confidence interval for the mean length of adult trout of this variety.

b A fish of length 15.5 cm has been caught. By using an appropriate test, do you think this fish is likely to be of the same variety as the other 21?

(OCSEB)

Exercise B

1 A production line is designed to produce 13 amp fuses. In practice the fuses will blow at a level of current which is normally distributed. A sample of 12 fuses is selected from the production line and tested to find the level of current at which they blow. The values of the current at which they blew are:

    13.102 12.971 13.053 13.056 13.173 12.548
    13.060 13.193 13.187 13.300 13.168 13.132

Carry out a suitable test to decide whether the production line is producing fuses which will blow at 13 amps.

(NICCEA)

2 A machine is known to dispense liquid into cartons such that the volume dispensed is normally distributed with a standard deviation of 3.4 ml. It is claimed by the manufacturer of the machine that the mean volume dispensed is 100 ml. In a series of trials on the machine the following values were recorded:

    104.4 101.7 103.6   99.2 102.2
    107.6   96.2 105.8 104.7   98.6

Use the results to test, at the 5% level, the manufacturer's claim.

(ULEAC)

3 A random sample of 10 independent observations of a normally distributed random variable X is taken from a population, and a test statistic, $t = 3.1$, is calculated. It is thought that the population mean is 110.0. Write down a suitable null hypothesis and a suitable alternative hypothesis for a two-tail significance test for μ. Use a t test to test your null hypothesis against your alternative hypothesis at the 1% significance level. *(UCLES)*

4 It is known that the cholesterol levels within the males of a population has mean 5.52 and standard deviation 1.25. A study of the cholesterol levels of upper and middle class males in the age range 45–64 was undertaken. In total 58 men were tested and their mean cholesterol level was found to be 6.2. Is the mean of this group significantly higher at the 1% level from the population mean? *(NICCEA)*

5 A certain brand of mineral water comes in bottles. The amount of water in a bottle, in millilitres, follows a normal distribution of mean m and standard deviation 2. The manufacturer claims that m is 125. In order to maintain standards the manufacturer takes a sample of 15 bottles and calculates the mean amount of water per bottle to be 124.2 ml. Test, at the 5% level, whether or not there is evidence that the value of m is lower than the manufacturer's claim. *(ULEAC)*

6 A newspaper article claims that in newly married couples the husband is equally likely to be younger or older than the wife. In the past it was far more likely that the husband was older than the wife. A vicar wishes to investigate whether such a change as this has taken place and he therefore decides to test the claim in the newspaper article.

  a Letting p denote the probability that the husband is older than the wife, write down the null and alternative hypotheses which the vicar should use.

  b In the next month the vicar marries 19 couples and finds that in 14 of these marriages the husband is older than the wife. The vicar carries out the hypothesis test at the 5% level of significance. What conclusion should he reach and why? *(MEI)*

7 A random sample was taken from a normal population with mean μ and known variance. The null hypothesis, $\mu = 80$, was tested against the alternative hypothesis, $\mu \neq 80$, at the 5% significance level. The calculated value of the standardised normal test statistic Z was -1.80. Carry out the significance test for μ based on this result, stating your conclusion clearly. *(UCLES)*

8 The values below are the scores obtained in a statistics test by a random sample of 12 students taught using an active learning approach.

36   26   30   34   42   24   30   45   32   19   35   38

It is known that the mean score for students taught by more traditional methods is 30. Test, at the 5% level of significance, the claim that students taught using the active learning approach achieve a higher mean score than those taught by more traditional methods.

(AEB)

9 The common toad appears in most parts of Britain. The sexes differ considerably in size, the females being much longer.

a A sample of 121 male common toads was taken and the sample mean length was found to be 6.2 cm. Given that the population of lengths of male toads has a variance $1.6\,cm^2$, test, at the 5% significance level, the hypothesis that the population mean length, μ, is equal to 6.0 cm against the alternative that
   i $\mu \neq 6.0\,cm$
   ii $\mu > 6.0\,cm$.
b Determine a symmetrical 95% confidence interval for μ on the basis of the sample in **a**.

(NEAB)

10 A manufacturer claims that the lifetime of its batteries is normally distributed with mean 21.5 hours. A laboratory tests eight batteries and finds the lifetimes, in hours, of these batteries to be as follows:

19.7   18.4   22.2   20.8   16.9   25.3   23.2   21.1

Stating clearly your hypotheses, examine whether or not these lifetimes indicate that the batteries have a shorter lifetime than that claimed by the company. Use a 5% level of significance.

(MEI)

Applications and Activities

The average number of children in a family has been recognised as being 2.4. Collect suitable data to examine whether this average is still correct (remember that some families have no children).

Summary

To test the significance of data the following steps must be carried out:

- Decide the appropriate test.

- State the null hypothesis, H_0, and the alternative hypothesis, H_1.

- From these determine whether a one- or two-tailed test is required.

- Decide on the significance level, and find the critical value(s) of the test statistic.

- Carry out the calculations to find the value of the test statistics.

- Draw a conclusion.

- To test whether a single item comes from a normal distribution use

$$Z = \frac{X - \mu}{\sigma}$$

- To test a mean with known population variance use

$$Z = \frac{\bar{x} - \mu}{\sigma/\sqrt{n}}$$

- To test a mean with unknown population variance (large sample) use

$$Z = \frac{\bar{x} - \mu}{s/\sqrt{n}}$$

- To test a mean with unknown population variance (small sample) use

$$t = \frac{\bar{x} - \mu}{s/\sqrt{n-1}} \text{ with } (n-1) \text{ degrees of freedom}$$

- To test a sample proportion use

$$Z = \frac{p_s - p}{\sqrt{pq/n}}$$

15 Significance Tests II: Two Values

What you need to know

- How to calculate unbiased estimates of the mean and variance of a population from two independent samples taken from that population.

- How to calculate population proportions from two samples.

- The properties of the normal distribution.

Review

Assume, in each question, that you have two samples from a single population. Calculate the sample mean and variance for each of the two samples, and use them to calculate unbiased estimates of the mean and variance of the population.

	Sample 1			Sample 2		
	n	Σx	Σx^2	n	Σx	Σx^2
1	5	60	900	8	88	1100
2	12	720	45 000	10	620	45 000
3	9	1.8	0.5	9	2	0.55
4	20	25	35	25	30	40
5	18	75.6	380	10	45	240

Two samples are taken independently from a population. Use these results to calculate an estimate for the proportion of the population with the specified attributes.

	Sample 1		Sample 2	
	n	p_s	n	p_s
6	15	0.3	12	0.32
7	240	0.63	270	0.59
8	164	0.47	124	0.48
9	48	0.95	85	0.92
10	30	0.5	60	0.52

Tests for two values

In the previous chapter one value was tested to see if it came from a specific population. This idea is now developed for two values to see whether they could be from the same distributions. There are a variety of different tests but the methods are similar and are based on the properties of the normal distribution (Z scores) or Student t tests.

The tests that will be considered are used to compare:

- Differences between two means   paired samples

unpaired samples

- Sample proportions   difference between two sample proportions

- Non-parametric   sign test – single values

                 – paired samples

       Wilcoxon test – single values

                   – paired samples

15.1 Testing the Difference between Means – Paired Sample

Usually tests of this nature are carried out on small samples where t scores are used, but Z scores can be used for larger samples. **Paired samples** are where one item of data from a sample has a corresponding item of data in another sample.

A sample $X_1, X_2, X_3, \ldots, X_n$ is taken from a normal population and a sample $Y_1, Y_2, Y_3, \ldots, Y_n$ is also taken from a normal population. Suppose we wish to test whether the two samples come from the same normal populations, or from normal populations having the same mean and variance. To do this the values X_1 and Y_1, X_2 and $Y_2, \ldots, X_n$ and Y_n are paired and the difference between each pair is found by calculating $X_1 - Y_1, X_2 - Y_2, \ldots, X_n - Y_n$. It is only possible to pair the results if such an operation is reasonable.

This gives a set of differences which we will call $D_1, D_2, D_3, \ldots, D_n$, which are also normally distributed.

The differences will have a mean $\bar{D}$ and a variance σ_D^2.

If we consider the parent population of all possible differences the mean would be μ_D.

The difference between $\bar{D}$ and μ_D is then tested to see whether it is significant. If the variance, σ_D^2, of the differences is known then the test statistic is:

$$Z = \frac{\bar{D} - \mu_D}{\sigma_D / \sqrt{n}}$$

Central Limit Theorem.

The null hypothesis, H_0, states that there is no difference between the two populations, so the mean of the differences, μ_D, must be 0. So the test statistic becomes:

$$Z = \frac{\bar{D}}{\sigma_D / \sqrt{n}}$$

which is distributed normally $N(0, 1)$.

However, the variance of the population of differences is usually unknown, so an estimate has to be calculated. When the samples are small, say fewer than 30 differences, t scores replace Z-scores and $\dfrac{s_D}{\sqrt{n}}$ is replaced by $\dfrac{s}{\sqrt{n-1}}$.

The test statistic is then $t = \dfrac{\bar{D}}{s/\sqrt{(n-1)}}$ for small samples.

$\bar{D}$ is the mean of the paired sample differences, s is the standard deviation of the paired sample differences, and n is the size of sample.

Example

As part of a training programme the number of press-ups a group of adults could complete at the start of the course was measured. After six weeks training the number of press-ups was counted again. Test the effectiveness of the training at the 5% level.

Before training	32	45	21	42	19	28	35	20
After training	37	53	23	42	25	28	37	17

Solution

These are paired data as the before and after numbers in each column refer to the same person.

$$H_0: \quad \mu_D = 0$$
$$H_1: \quad \mu_D > 0$$

significance level: 5% – one-tailed test.

Using $t = \dfrac{\bar{D}}{s/\sqrt{(n-1)}}$ with $(8-1)$ degrees of freedom

d	5	8	2	0	6	0	2	−3	20
d^2	25	64	4	0	36	0	4	9	142

$\bar{d} = \frac{20}{8} = 2.5$

$s^2 = \frac{142}{8} - 2.5^2 = 11.5$

$s = 3.391$

$t_7 = \dfrac{2.5}{3.391/\sqrt{7}} = 1.951$

Critical value for t_7 is 1.895.

As $t > 1.895$, H_0 is rejected and H_1 accepted. There is significant evidence to indicate that there is an improvement in fitness.

15.1 Testing the Difference between Means – Paired Sample

Exercise

Technique

Test the following paired samples at the level of significance given.

1 $\Sigma d = 30$, $\Sigma d^2 = 280$, $n = 5$, $H_1 > 0$ at 5%

2 $\Sigma d = 54$, $\Sigma d^2 = 820$, $n = 10$, $H_1 \neq 0$ at 2%

3 $\Sigma d = 16$, $\Sigma d^2 = 68$, $n = 13$, $H_1 \neq 0$ at 5%

4 $\Sigma d = 2.3$, $\Sigma d^2 = 3$, $n = 8$, $H_1 > 0$ at 2%

5 $\Sigma d = 1.6885$, $\Sigma d^2 = 114.05$, $n = 25$, $H_1 \neq 0$ at 5%

6 $\Sigma d = 21$, $\Sigma d^2 = 148$, $n = 19$, $H_1 \neq 0$ at 5%

7

x	9	7	13	11
y	12	11	15	14

$H_1: \mu_D \neq 0$ at 5%

8

x	10	15	20	23	27	30
y	17	20	17	26	34	30

$H_1: \mu_D > 0$ at 2.5%

9

x	9	7	8	6	8	8	6	8	6	5
y	6	5	7	7	4	6	4	3	6	8

$H_1: \mu_D < 0$ at 2.5%

10

x	0.3	0.7	0.3	0.6	0.4
y	0.2	0.9	0.8	1.1	0.5

$H_1: \mu_D \neq 0$ at 2.5%

Contextual

1 A school conducted two IQ tests for 200 students. The mean score of the first test was 115 while the mean score of the second test was 119. The variance of the differences between the tests was found to be 400. Test whether the second test is an improvement on the first test at the 1% level.

2 Six strands of wire were tested for their breaking points and then were retested after having a special coating applied. On the evidence of the results, does the coating strengthen the wire?

Before	7.2	5.4	7.1	8.1	7.0	7.9
After	9.4	8.1	6.6	9.9	8.7	8.3

3 In a sample comparing 10 pairs of measurements, $\bar{d} = 3.7$, and using a student t test was just significant at the 1% level. Find the standard deviation of the differences, s, if the test was:

a two-tailed **b** one-tailed.

4 An airline was concerned at the number of empty seats on their trans-Atlantic routes. They recorded the numbers of empty seats on 12 routes, then introduced price reductions. The numbers of empty seats on the same 12 routes were than recorded. From the evidence is there any indication, at the 0.5% level, that there is a reduction in the numbers of empty seats?

Before	24	22	31	24	15	29	8	18	17	21	11	21
After	18	18	25	23	12	21	10	16	16	12	13	19

5 In a school, boys and girls of the same age, weight and height were paired together and timed in running 200 m. The results were, to the nearest second:

Boys	25	39	34	34	43	26	30	40	37	37
Girls	28	36	38	33	41	30	34	41	36	30

Is there any evidence to suggest a difference in the achievements of the boys and girls?

6 A particular golf competition tests the ability of players to play different types of shots more accurately than their opponents. In the pitching competition, the players have to try to get the ball as near as possible to the hole and the distance from the hole is measured. The results of one competition were:

Team A	4.2	1.9	0.7	3.2	1.9	0.2	2.8	0.8	1.1	3.8
Team B	2.2	0.5	1.9	0.1	2.5	1.3	1.4	3.7	1.9	4.7

Is there a significant difference in the performance of the two teams?

15.2 Unpaired Tests

Known variance (Z test)

This test is similar to the previous test but the items of data are not matched as pairs. As there is no pairing the methods used in the previous test have to be adapted.

We have independent samples of sizes n_1 and n_2 from the same normal population or from populations with equal variances. The variance of the normal populations is σ^2. The random samples of size n_1 and n_2 have means of $\bar{x}_1$ and $\bar{x}_2$ respectively.

The two distributions are: $N(\mu_1, \sigma^2)$ and $N(\mu_2, \sigma^2)$ therefore $\bar{x}_1 \sim N\left(\mu_1, \dfrac{\sigma^2}{n_1}\right)$ and $\bar{x}_2 \sim N\left(\mu_2, \dfrac{\sigma^2}{n_2}\right)$. From the combination of normal distributions

$$\bar{x}_1 - \bar{x}_2 \sim N\left(\mu_1 - \mu_2, \ \frac{\sigma^2}{n_1} + \frac{\sigma^2}{n_2}\right)$$

with H_0: $\mu_1 = \mu_2$ or H_0: $\mu_1 - \mu_2 = 0$.

As $\mu_1 - \mu_2 = 0$, $\bar{x}_1 - \bar{x}_2 \sim N\left(0, \ \dfrac{\sigma^2}{n_1} + \dfrac{\sigma^2}{n_2}\right)$

Therefore the test statistic is

$$Z = \frac{\bar{x}_1 - \bar{x}_2}{\sigma\sqrt{\dfrac{1}{n_1} + \dfrac{1}{n_2}}}$$

which is normally distributed $N(0, 1)$.

Note: If n_1 and n_2 are large, or the populations are normal, and σ_1 and σ_2 known and are not equal, then

$$Z = \frac{\bar{x}_1 - \bar{x}_2}{\sqrt{\dfrac{\sigma_1^2}{n_1} + \dfrac{\sigma_2^2}{n_2}}}$$

Unknown variance

If the variance is unknown the test is often carried out using small samples which changes the statistic from a Z score to a Student t score.

An unbiased estimate of the common population variance is

$$\hat{\sigma}^2 = \frac{n_1 s_1^2 + n_2 s_2^2}{n_1 + n_2 - 2}$$

For small samples the test statistic becomes

$$t = \frac{\bar{x}_1 - \bar{x}_2}{\hat{\sigma}\sqrt{\dfrac{1}{n_1} + \dfrac{1}{n_2}}}$$

distributed as t with $(n_1 + n_2 - 2)$ degrees of freedom

$$H_0: \ \mu_1 = \mu_2 \text{ which is the same as } H_0: \ \mu_1 - \mu_2 = 0$$

This is the most often applied test for comparing two sample means. For large samples the test statistic is

$$Z = \frac{\bar{x}_1 - \bar{x}_2}{\sqrt{\dfrac{s_1^2}{n_1} + \dfrac{s_2^2}{n_2}}}$$

Example 1

A random sample of size 40 was taken from a normally distributed population with $\sigma^2 = 100$. A further sample of size 60 was then taken. The sample means were found to be 75.4 and 81.3 respectively. Test at the 5% level whether there is any significant difference between the two means.

Solution

$$H_0: \ \bar{x}_1 - \bar{x}_2 = 0$$

$$H_1: \ \bar{x}_1 - \bar{x}_2 \neq 0$$

significance level: 5% – two-tailed test, large n, critical value 1.96

$$Z = \frac{\bar{x}_1 - \bar{x}_2}{\sigma\sqrt{\dfrac{1}{n_1} + \dfrac{1}{n_2}}}$$

$$Z = \frac{75.4 - 81.3}{10\sqrt{\frac{1}{40} + \frac{1}{60}}}$$

$$Z = -2.89$$

As $|Z| > 1.96$ reject H_0, accept H_1. There is a significant difference between the mean values of the samples.

Example 2

The heights of eight boys in Year 9 were, to the nearest centimetre:

141   158   148   152   165   174   161   154

The heights of fifteen girls in Year 9 were such that $\Sigma x = 2295$ and $\Sigma x^2 = 355\,015$. Test at the 5% level whether the Year 9 boys are taller than the girls.

Solution

$$\bar{x}_1 = \frac{1253}{8} = 156.625$$

$$s^2 = \frac{196\,991}{8} - 156.625^2$$

$$s = 9.617$$

$$\bar{x}_2 = \frac{2295}{15} = 153$$

$$s^2 = \frac{355\,015}{15} - 153^2$$

$$s = 16.083$$

$$H_0:\ \bar{x}_1 - \bar{x}_2 = 0$$

$$H_1:\ \bar{x}_1 > \bar{x}_2$$

significance level: 5%   one-tailed test,

degrees of freedom $v = 8 + 15 - 2 = 21$

critical value 1.721

An unbiased estimator of the variance is:

$$\hat{\sigma}^2 = \frac{n_1 s_1^2 + n_2 s_2^2}{n_1 + n_2 - 2}$$

$$\hat{\sigma}^2 = \frac{8 \times 9.617^2 + 15 \times 16.083^2}{8 + 15 - 2}$$

$$= 219.992$$

$$\hat{\sigma} = 14.832$$

$$t_{21} = \frac{156.625 - 153}{14.832\sqrt{\left(\frac{1}{8} + \frac{1}{15}\right)}}$$

$$t_{21} = 0.558$$

As $t < 1.721$, do not reject H_0.

There is no significant difference in the mean heights.

15.2 Unpaired Tests
Exercise

Technique

For the following sets of data decide whether there is a significant difference between the mean values by performing the appropriate test.

	n_1	n_2	σ^2	Σx_1	Σx_2	H_0	H_1	Level
1	30	120	25.4	180	540	$\bar{X}_1 = \bar{X}_2$	$\bar{X}_1 > \bar{X}_2$	10%
2	50	35	33.32	12 650	8995	$\bar{X}_1 = \bar{X}_2$	$\bar{X}_1 \neq \bar{X}_2$	5%
3	42	33	58.5	8568	6963	$\bar{X}_1 = \bar{X}_2$	$\bar{X}_1 \neq \bar{X}_2$	1%
4	87	45	85.4	8978.4	5211	$\bar{X}_1 = \bar{X}_2$	$\bar{X}_1 < \bar{X}_2$	2.5%
5	110	92	100	3531	2750.8	$\bar{X}_1 = \bar{X}_2$	$\bar{X}_1 \neq \bar{X}_2$	5%
6	74	39	2.53	33.3	22.62	$\bar{X}_1 = \bar{X}_2$	$\bar{X}_1 \neq \bar{X}_2$	5%

	n_1	n_2	Σx_1	Σx_1^2	Σx_2	Σx_2^2	H_0	H_1	Level
7	6	4	37.2	246	20.4	115	$\bar{X}_1 = \bar{X}_2$	$\bar{X}_1 < \bar{X}_2$	10%
8	5	8	126.5	3500	182.4	4200	$\bar{X}_1 = \bar{X}_2$	$\bar{X}_1 \neq \bar{X}_2$	5%
9	15	16	4.5	1.5	9.6	6	$\bar{X}_1 = \bar{X}_2$	$\bar{X}_1 > \bar{X}_2$	1%
10	9	9	1.5	0.35	1.9	0.5	$\bar{X}_1 = \bar{X}_2$	$\bar{X}_1 \neq \bar{X}_2$	5%

Contextual

1 A company has two factories employing 52 and 75 workers respectively. The mean number of days absence per month is calculated at 3.02 days with an estimated variance of 2.84 for the first factory. The second factory has a mean of 2.76 days absence with an estimated variance of 2.44. Is there evidence to suggest the mean absences of the two factories are different?

2 The mean wages of the workers in the first factory in question ☐1 are £120 with a variance of 400. The second factory has a mean wage of £110 with a variance of 300. Is the mean wage of factory 1 significantly different from that of factory 2?

3 Two machines fill bags of flour, and samples of size 10 are taken from each machine. Machine A had a mean weight of 0.998 kg. with a variance of $4\,g^2$. Machine B had a mean weight of 1.006 kg. with a variance of $9\,g^2$. At the 5% level, test whether there is a significance between the mean weights of the bags filled by each machine.

4 Further samples were taken from each machine described in question ☐3. From machine A eight bags were weighed which produced a mean weight of 996.5 g with a variance of $6\,g^2$ while from machine B six bags were weighed with a mean of 1003 g and a variance of $8g^2$. Test at the 5% level whether the mean weight of the bags filled by each machine separately has fallen.

5 A group of students measured the diameter, in centimetres, of a number of mints from two different packs. The results were:

Pack A	1.073	1.071	1.073	1.074	1.073	
Pack B	1.076	1.071	1.077	1.076	1.073	1.074
	1.074	1.075	1.072	1.077	1.074	

Is there a significant difference between the mean diameters of the mints in each pack, with pack B being larger than pack A?

6 A record company wishes to test the accuracy of the running times given in the CD notes. They take a sample from discs produced by two of their factories, and measure the differences between the printed time and the actual running time, in seconds. The results are:

Sample 1	5	2	4	3	−2	−7	−4	−9	−6	0	3
Sample 2	7	3	2	6	4	4	5	−1	−3		

Is there any evidence to suggest that the mean differences in time are significant?

15.3 Testing the Difference between Proportions (Z Test)

If samples of sizes n_1 and n_2 are taken and the proportions with a certain characteristic, such as blonde hair, left-handed and so on, are found to be p_1 and p_2 respectively, then we might wish to find whether the samples are drawn from the same population, or from populations with the equal proportions of that characteristic.

The populations are both approximately normally distributed, so if p_1 and p_2 are drawn from the same population then $p_1 - p_2$ will have a mean of zero, and will be normally distributed.

If the proportion of the population with the required characteristic is $\hat{p}$ then the test statistic is:

$$Z = \frac{p_1 - p_2}{\sqrt{\hat{p}(1 - \hat{p})\left(\dfrac{1}{n_1} + \dfrac{1}{n_2}\right)}}$$

where the pooled estimator of the population proportion is
$\hat{p} = \dfrac{n_1 p_1 + n_2 p_2}{n_1 + n_2}$.

The null hypothesis is $H_0: P_1 = P_2$, that is the samples are from the same population or populations with equal proportions.

If the proportion in the population is known then the statistic is given by

$$Z = \frac{p_1 - p_2}{\sqrt{\hat{p}\hat{q}\left(\dfrac{1}{n_1} + \dfrac{1}{n_2}\right)}}$$

where $\hat{p}$ is the proportion of the population, with the required characteristic.

Example

A school claims that students are given equal access to all courses. There are 250 girls in the school of which 75 study science subjects, while 77 of the 220 boys study science subjects. Test at the 5% level whether there is a significantly greater proportion of boys in science than girls.

Solution

$$H_0: \ p_b = p_g$$

$$H_1: \ p_b > p_g$$

significance level: 5% one-tailed test, large n, critical value = 1.645

$$p_b = \tfrac{77}{220} = 0.35$$

$$p_g = \tfrac{75}{250} = 0.3$$

$$\hat{p} = \frac{n_b \, p_b + n_g \, p_g}{n_b + n_g}$$

$$\hat{p} = \frac{220 \times 0.35 + 250 \times 0.3}{220 + 250} = 0.323$$

$$\hat{q} = 0.677$$

$$Z = \frac{p_b - p_g}{\sqrt{\hat{p}\hat{q}\left(\dfrac{1}{n_b} + \dfrac{1}{n_g}\right)}}$$

$$= \frac{0.35 - 0.3}{\sqrt{\left(0.323 \times 0.677\left(\frac{1}{250} + \frac{1}{220}\right)\right)}}$$

$$= 1.157$$

As $Z < 1.645$, do not reject H_0. There is insufficient evidence to indicate a significant difference in the proportion of boys and girls studying science subjects.

15.3 Testing the Difference between Proportions (Z Test)
Exercise

Contextual

1 A company produced two flavours of cat food. In a sample of 100 cats, 60 preferred the fish flavour. while in a further sample of 120 cats, 60 also preferred that flavour. The company claimed that 60% of cats preferred fish flavoured food. Does the evidence suggest a difference between the two samples? ($\hat{p}$ known)

2 In a random sample of 600 students aged 18, it was found the 90 out of the 240 boys had full driving licences. Of the girls 150 had full driving licences. Is there a significant difference between the proportions of boys and girls who are licence holders?

3 The owner of a number of fishing-lakes was concerned as to the proportion of pike in the lakes. In a balanced system the ideal proportion was estimated to be 0.04. Two samples of fish were taken, the first of 82 fish had six pike in it, while the second of 63 fish had seven pike in it. Test at the 5% level whether there is a significant difference in the proportions of pike.

4 In a survey of youth unemployment samples were taken in two neighbouring towns. In town A a sample of 1736 under-21-year-olds showed an unemployment rate of 9.1%. In town B a sample of 1432 under-21-year-olds showed an unemployment rate of 15.36%. Is there evidence to suggest the rate of unemployment is lower in town A than town B?

5 A sample of 92 similar worms showed that the proportion that were over 15 cm in length was 0.326. A further sample taken later showed the proportion of worms, from a sample of 75, over 15 cm in length was 0.4. Is there evidence to suggest the two samples are from the same population?

6 In a darts match the winner managed to hit the treble 20, 108 times out of 128 attempts. In his next match he hit the treble 20, 137 times out of 154 attempts. By testing at the 5% level the difference between the proportion of successes in the first match and that in the second match, is there any evidence to support the claim that the player played better in the second match than the first?

7 In training to be a supermarket checkout assistant, Thomas was expected to recognise different fruit and vegetables that the supermarket sold. After training, follow-up tests were arranged to ensure that the level of proficiency that Thomas had achieved was maintained. Thomas managed to recognise 76 out of 84 products at the end of his training. After a month he was able to recognise 64 out of 75 products. Do the tests indicate a significant difference in Thomas's ability to recognise the different products? The company require checkout personnel to be proficient at recognising different products, and expect staff to have a proficiency rating of 90%. Does Thomas's second test differ significantly from the required 90%? Test at the 5% level.

15.4 Non-Parametric Tests – The Sign Test

The methods we have considered so far involve some assumptions about the distributions of the populations that have been sampled, for example assuming that the data is normally distributed, and are known as parametric methods. Sometimes it is necessary to analyse data from population distributions about which it is not possible to make such assumptions. The methods used to analyse these data are known as non-parametric. Such tests are often concerned with rank orders rather than the numerical value of the variables or observations.

The Sign Test – Single sample

Sometimes the mean is an inappropriate measure to use as an estimate of a population parameter due to the presence of outliers in the data. In such a case the difference of items from the median can be used.

From the definition of the median the probability of being above or below it is equal, that is $\frac{1}{2}$. Due to this property, when carrying out the sign test if an item is above the population median it is given a plus sign and if it is below the population median it is given a minus sign. Any item that is equal to the population median is given zero and not counted in the test, the sample size being reduced by 1.

Method 1 – Binomial

The plus and minus signs are assumed to have an equal probability of occurring so that the number of pluses (or minuses) are binomially distributed $B(n, 0.5)$ where n is the number of values excluding zeroes.

Example 1

The breaking strains of a sample of 10 strands of wire were, in kilograms:

   8.4   7.4   7.5   8.6   8.6   8.2   8.8   8.5   8.5   7.9

Is there evidence to indicate that the population median strength has increased from its previous value of 8.2 kg?

Solution

H_0: the population median $= 8.2$
H_1: the population median > 8.2 one-tailed test

We allocate a plus sign to those values above 8.2, a minus sign to those values below 8.2, and zero to those values that equal 8.2.

This gives:

$$+ \quad - \quad - \quad + \quad + \quad 0 \quad + \quad + \quad + \quad -$$

Altogether there are six pluses, three minuses and one zero. As the zero is not taken into account only nine results are counted.

If X is the random variable 'number of + signs', we are testing to see how likely six or more pluses are under the distribution $X \sim B(9, \ 0.5)$.

As we are using a one-tailed test at the 5% level, we will reject H_0 if $P(X \geq 6)$ is less than 0.05.

$$P(X \geq 6) = P(X = 6) + P(X = 7) + P(X = 8) + P(X = 9)$$
$$P(X \geq 6) = 0.1641 + 0.0703 + 0.0176 + 0.0020 = 0.2540$$

As $0.2540 > 0.05$ we do not reject H_0.

There is insufficient evidence to suggest the median has increased from its previous value of 8.2 kg.

Method 2 – Z scores

For larger samples the test statistic of non-parametric tests are approximately normally distributed.

The test statistic can be found from

$$Z = \frac{x - \mu}{\sigma} \quad \text{where} \quad \mu = \frac{n}{2} \quad \text{and} \quad \sigma = \frac{\sqrt{n}}{2}$$

Remembering that the normal distribution is continuous whereas the binomial distribution is discrete, a continuity correction must be used.

This gives $\quad Z = \dfrac{U \pm \dfrac{1}{2} - \dfrac{n}{2}}{\dfrac{\sqrt{n}}{2}} \quad$ which is distributed $N(0, 1^2)$ with

H_0: the population median is equal to some given value m.

U is the number of positive values, and n is the number of items having a value not equal to m.

The continuity correction is added or subtracted so that Z is moved away from the nearest critical region.

Example 2

Repeat Example 1 but this time use the Z scores.

Solution

$U = 6$ (six plus signs) $n = 9$ (nine results counted, as zero is ignored)

H_0: the population median $= 8.2$
H_1: the population median > 8.2

one-tailed test at 5% level.

As the critical region is to the right-hand side of the distribution, the continuity correction of $\frac{1}{2}$ is subtracted

$$Z = \frac{6 - \dfrac{1}{2} - \dfrac{9}{2}}{\dfrac{\sqrt{9}}{2}} = \frac{6 - 0.5 - 4.5}{\dfrac{3}{2}} = \frac{1}{1.5} = 0.6667$$

As $Z < 1.645$ (critical value at 5%) we do not reject H_0.

There is insufficient evidence to suggest the median is more than 8.2.

The Sign Test – Paired Samples

To compare two sets of paired items U is found by subtracting one item from its pair and recording the sign of the result. The test statistic remains the same.

Example 3

The time taken by 15 students to complete a task before and after practice was recorded to the nearest second. Test whether there is any evidence of improvement, using the sign test.

Before	47	49	51	53	36	55	41	40	38	36	35	42	38	41	40
After	41	44	50	54	36	49	42	35	36	38	34	42	36	39	42

Solution

M_1 is the median time taken before practice and M_2 is the median time taken after practice.

Test
H_0: the population median of the differences is zero.
H_1: $M_1 > M_2$

one-tailed test, at 5% level.

Find the difference between the before and after times and record the signs:

$$+ \quad + \quad + \quad - \quad 0 \quad + \quad - \quad + \quad + \quad - \quad + \quad 0 \quad + \quad + \quad -$$

$U = 9, n = 13$ (two zeros discarded)

$$Z = \dfrac{9 - \dfrac{1}{2} - \dfrac{13}{2}}{\dfrac{\sqrt{13}}{2}} \qquad \text{(continuity correction subtracted)}$$

$$Z = \dfrac{9 - 0.5 - 6.5}{1.803}$$

$$Z = 1.109$$

As $Z < 1.645$, do not reject H_0.

There is no significant evidence to show an improvement in the median time at the 5% level.

15.4 Non-Parametric Tests – The Sign Test

Exercise

Contextual

1 The incomes of 15 households in the Midlands were, to the nearest pound:

212 392 184 300 288 348 260 200
224 284 332 228 312 284 216

The median weekly income for the population in the UK was £250. Test, using a sign test, whether there is evidence to suggest the median income of the households in the Midlands is greater than £250.

2 The times recorded for a random sample of runners completing a half marathon were measured to the nearest minute. The results were:

59 75 63 70 61 74 91 62 68 63
71 61 68 73 84 67 90 70 62 65

Usually half of all runners complete the course in 70 minutes or less. Using a sign test, test whether the runners in this race were faster than expected.

3 The blood pressures of a sample of eight teachers from one school were taken and the lower values recorded. The results were:

72 93 88 105 97 91 75 83

The median blood pressure of all teachers is 75. Does the evidence from this sample suggest that the blood pressure of teachers in this school is higher than in other schools?

4 The number of eggs produced weekly by a sample of 12 free range hens was:

7 6 4 5 5 3 6 6 5 4 5 4

The median numbers of eggs usually produced by all free range hens is four per week. Is there any evidence to suggest that this sample of hens produces more eggs than the population of free range hens?

5 Two methods of manufacture are used to produce electronic resistances. Samples from each method were compared and the results were:

	Resistance (ohms)									
Method A	7.4	9.3	10.2	9.4	9.3	11.1	7.4	8.5	10.5	8.3
Method B	8.1	10.1	9.7	10.1	9.3	11.3	8.6	7.9	8.8	8.7

Test whether there is a difference between the two methods using the sign test.

6 Using the sign test, is there significant evidence to indicate a difference between the scores achieved by students in two tests?

Test 1	17	12	15	11	9	12	11	18	8	14	16	7	15	18	9	12	18	9
Test 2	15	11	9	12	9	15	10	19	12	15	16	9	13	13	10	13	19	9

7 Using the sign test at the 5% level, test whether there is significant difference between the weights of two samples of trout bred using different feeds.

	Weight in kilograms							
Group A	0.75	0.43	0.48	0.63	0.52	0.84	0.41	0.66
Group B	0.51	0.56	0.62	0.63	0.59	0.71	0.44	0.72

15.5 Non-Parametric Tests – Wilcoxon Signed Rank Test

The hypothesis tested by the Wilcoxon signed rank test is the same as that tested by the sign test. The Wilcoxon test, however, takes into account the magnitude of the differences as well as the signs.

Single values

The differences between each data item and the median are calculated. These differences are ranked, without regard to sign. Next, the rank of the positive differences, are added to give P, and the ranks of the negative differences are added to give Q. The test statistic T is the smaller of P and Q. Finally we must compare the value of T with the critical values given in the table, depending on the nature of the test and the level of significance at which we are testing.

Example 1

The ages in years, of a group of students entering university were as follows:

23   21   18   21   19   26   24   18   18   24   19   19

The median age was thought to be 20 years of age. Does this data provide sufficient evidence that the median is not 20?

Solution

H_0: the population median age $= 20$
H_1: the population median age $\neq 20$

two-tailed test at 5% significance level.

From tables the critical value of T is 13, when $n = 12$

Age – median	+3	+1	−2	+1	−1	+6	+4	−2	−2	+4	−1	−1
Ranking without regard to sign	−1	−1	−1	+1	+1	−2	−2	−2	+3	+4	+4	+6
Ranks	3	3	3	3	3	7	7	7	9	$10\frac{1}{2}$	$10\frac{1}{2}$	12

P (the sum of the ranks of the positive differences)
$$= 3 + 3 + 9 + 10\tfrac{1}{2} + 10\tfrac{1}{2} + 12$$
$$= 48$$
Q (the sum of the ranks of the negative differences)
$$= 3 + 3 + 3 + 7 + 7 + 7$$
$$= 30$$
T (the smaller of P and Q) $= Q = 30$

At $T > 13$ (the critical value) we do not reject H_0, and conclude that there is some evidence to suggest that the median is 20 years of age.

Paired Samples
Example 2

A group of 8-year-old children were timed to see how long they took to complete a puzzle. They were then shown a method for completing the puzzle, and timed to see how long they took to solve a similar puzzle. Is there any evidence to suggest the second test was completed more quickly? The times, recorded to the nearest second, were:

Before	12	15	29	19	14	24	18	12	16	17
After	15	13	22	20	15	18	14	14	12	12

Solution

H_0: the medians of the population differences is zero,
that is, median of before-score = median of after-scores
H_1: the median of the after-scores < median of the before-scores

one-tailed test at the 5% significance level.

From tables the critical value of T when $n = 10$ is 10.

Before	12	15	29	19	14	24	18	12	16	17
After	15	13	22	20	15	18	14	14	12	12
After – Before	−3	−2	−7	+1	+1	−6	−4	+2	−4	−5
Ranking without regard to sign	+1	+1	−2	+2	−3	−4	−4	−5	−6	−7
Rank	$1\frac{1}{2}$	$1\frac{1}{2}$	$3\frac{1}{2}$	$3\frac{1}{2}$	5	$6\frac{1}{2}$	$6\frac{1}{2}$	8	9	10

$P = 1\frac{1}{2} + 1\frac{1}{2} + 3\frac{1}{2} = 6\frac{1}{2}$

$Q = 3\frac{1}{2} + 5 + 6\frac{1}{2} + 6\frac{1}{2} + 8 + 9 + 10 = 48\frac{1}{2}$

$T = 6\frac{1}{2}$

As $T < 10$ we reject H_0, and conclude there is some evidence to suggest the median of the times after coaching is less than the median of the times before coaching.

15.5 Non-Parametric Tests – Wilcoxon Signed Rank Test

Exercise

Contextual

1 The incomes of 15 households in the Midlands were, to the nearest pound:

212 392 184 300 288 348 260 200
224 284 332 228 312 284 216

The median weekly income for the population in the UK was £250. Test, using the Wilcoxon signed rank test, whether there is evidence to suggest the median income of households in the Midlands is greater than £250.

2 The times recorded for a random sample of runners completing a half marathon were measured to the nearest minute. The results were:

59 75 63 70 61 74 91 62 68 63
71 61 68 73 84 67 90 70 62 65

Usually half of all runners complete the course in 72 minutes or less. Using the Wilcoxon signed rank test, test whether the runners in this race were faster than expected.

3 The blood pressures of a sample of 10 teachers from one school were taken and the lower values recorded. The results were:

72 93 88 105 97 91 80 78 74 83

The median blood pressure of all teachers is 75. Does the evidence from this sample suggest that the blood pressures of teachers in this school are higher than in other schools?

4 Two methods of manufacture are used to produce electronic resistances. Samples from each method are compared and the results are:

	Resistance (ohms)									
Method A	7.4	9.3	10.2	9.4	9.3	11.1	7.4	8.5	10.5	8.3
Method B	8.1	10.1	9.7	10.1	9.3	11.3	8.6	7.9	8.8	8.7

Test whether there is a significant difference between the two samples using the Wilcoxon signed rank test.

5 Using the Wilcoxon signed rank test, is there significant evidence to indicate a difference between the scores achieved by students in two tests?

Test 1	17	12	15	11	9	12	11	18	8	14	16	7
Test 2	15	11	9	12	8	15	10	19	12	15	15	9

6 Using the Wilcoxon signed rank test, test whether there is a significant difference between the weights of two samples of trout bred using different feeds.

	Weight in kilograms							
Group A	0.75	0.43	0.48	0.63	0.52	0.84	0.41	0.66
Group B	0.51	0.56	0.62	0.61	0.59	0.71	0.44	0.72

Consolidation

Exercise A

1 The manager of a large hotel has to decide which of two brands of light bulb, Brand A or Brand B, he should use in the hotel. The prices of the two brands are the same and he therefore decides to compare their lifetimes by monitoring samples of the two brands.

    a For each light bulb in a random sample of 100 Brand A bulbs, the manager measured its lifetime, x thousand hours, and found that $\Sigma x = 231.6$ and $\Sigma x^2 = 566.38$. Calculate unbiased estimates for:

        i the mean μ_A

        ii the variance s_A^2

        of the lifetimes of the Brand A bulbs.

    b Unbiased estimators of 2.408 and 0.3212 for the mean, μ_B, and the variance, s_B^2, respectively, of the lifetimes (in thousand hours) of Brand B bulbs were calculated from a random sample of 150 such bulbs. Stating suitable null and alternative hypotheses, and using a significance level of 10%, determine whether or not these results indicate a difference between the mean lifetimes of Brand A and Brand B bulbs.

(WJEC)

2 A liquid product is sold in containers. The containers are filled by a machine. The volumes of liquid (in millilitres) in a random sample of six containers were found to be:

    497.8   501.4   500.2   500.8   498.3   500.0

After overhaul of the machine, the volumes (in millilitres) in a random sample of 11 containers were found to be:

    501.1   499.6   500.3   500.9   498.7   502.1

    500.4   499.7   501.0   500.1   499.3

It is desired to examine whether the mean volume of liquid delivered to a container by the machine is the same after overhaul as it was before.

    a State the assumptions that are necessary for the use of the customary t test.

    b State the null and alternative hypotheses that are to be tested.

    c Carry out the t test, using a 5% level of significance.

(MEI)

3 A petrol company claims cars will achieve a higher mileage per litre if they use their Super unleaded petrol as opposed to the Ordinary unleaded petrol. Twelve cars of the same model were tested with 25 litres of each type of petrol and the miles travelled are shown in the following table.

	Miles completed	
Car	Ordinary	Super
1	165	168
2	164	164
3	172	176
4	160	163
5	178	175
6	159	166
7	162	162
8	169	167
9	173	178
10	166	174
11	164	168
12	170	172

Perform: **a** a sign test and **b** the Wilcoxon signed rank test at the 5% level, to investigate the hypothesis that the Super unleaded petrol gives a higher mileage than the Ordinary unleaded petrol. (*NEAB*)

4 A firm producing mugs has a quality control scheme in which a random sample of ten mugs from each batch is inspected. For 50 such samples, the number of defective mugs were as follows:

Number of defective mugs	0	1	2	3	4	5	6+
Number of samples	5	13	15	12	4	1	0

a Find the mean and standard deviation of the number of defective mugs per sample.

b Show that a reasonable estimate for p, the probability that a mug is defective, is 0.2. Use this figure to calculate the probability that a randomly chosen sample will contain exactly two defective mugs. Comment on the agreement between this value and observed data.

The management is not satisfied with 20% of mugs being defective and introduces a new process to reduce the proportion of defective mugs.

c A random sample of 20 mugs, produced by the new process, contains just one which is defective. Test at the 5% level, whether it is reasonable to suppose that the proportion of defective mugs has been reduced, stating your null and alternative hypotheses clearly.

d What would the conclusion have been if the management had chosen to conduct the test at the 10% level? (*MEI*)

5 A university department is deciding which of the two research proposals to support. It asked 11 members of staff to read the proposals and to award each of them a mark out of 100. The marks awarded were as follows:

Member of staff	1	2	3	4	5	6	7	8	9	10	11
Proposal 1	89	37	70	21	29	36	1	46	74	47	26
Proposal 2	95	49	69	86	30	99	19	52	30	45	80

a   Use: **i** a sign test **ii** the Wilcoxon signed rank test
at the 5% level to test whether Proposal 2 is better supported than Proposal 1.
b   In view of the erratic nature of the marks awarded it was decided to ask a further 10 members to award the proposals marks out of 100, but these staff were trained in the features to look for and the method of awarding marks. The new staff awarded the following marks:

Member of staff	1	2	3	4	5	6	7	8	9	10
Proposal 1	53	46	60	53	66	59	52	67	63	46
Proposal 2	75	67	69	51	76	59	65	68	72	59

Use a paired t test at the 5% significance level to test whether there is a difference in the mean marks awarded to the two proposals by the 10 members of staff who have received training.

(AEB)

6 One of the questions addressed as part of an investigation into the problems of adolescence was: 'Do boys worry more than girls?'. Following personal interviews, a score, based on the 'Worries Scale', was assigned to each adolescent in independent random samples of 16 boys and 12 girls. A summary of these results is tabled below. (High scores indicate a high level of worry.)

	Sample mean $\bar{x}$	Unbiased estimate of population variance σ^2
Boys	68.2	77.37
Girls	61.3	60.28

Scores based on the 'Worries Scale' may be assumed to be normally distributed. Test whether there is no significant evidence of a difference between the mean scores for adolescent boys and adolescent girls.

(NEAB)

7 The proportion of car drivers taking lead-free petrol at a particular filling station has been found to be 42%. Following an increase in the tax on other types of fuel, a random sample of 120 cars was observed at the filling station. The number of drivers taking lead-free petrol was found to be 58. Test, at the 5% level, whether there has been an increase in the proportion of drivers taking lead-free petrol at the filling station.

(*UCLES*)

8 The times, in minutes, taken by a group of seven trainee typists to perform a simple exercise were recorded both before and after a short course designed to improve their speed. The results are given in the following table.

Typist	A	B	C	D	E	F	G
Before	5.2	4.7	6.5	5.8	6.3	4.9	7.2
After	5.1	4.8	6.2	5.9	5.9	4.8	6.1

Test at the 10% significance level whether or not times taken by typists to complete the exercise tend to decrease after the course.

(*ULEAC*)

9 An inspector is examining the lengths of time to complete various routine tasks by employees who have been trained in two different ways. He wants to examine whether the two methods lead, overall, to the same times. Ten different tasks have been prepared. Each task is undertaken by a randomly selected employee who has been trained by method A and by a randomly selected employee who has been trained by method B. The times to completion, in minutes, are shown in the table.

Task	A	B	C	D	E	F	G	H	I	J
Time by method A employee	33.4	41.0	26.8	37.2	47.4	27.5	34.0	28.4	35.0	20.7
Time by method B employee	27.1	42.0	23.0	33.9	38.1	27.7	32.7	23.2	35.0	22.7

What underlying distributional assumption is necessary for the paired samples *t* test to be appropriate? Carry out the test at the 5% level of significance for the above data. Provide a two-sided 90% confidence interval for the true mean difference between times.

(*MEI*)

10 **a** A car mechanic measures the voltage of six batteries of the same type. The results (in volts) are given below.

12.24   12.02   12.12   12.15   12.23   12.08

  i Calculate unbiased estimates of the mean and variance of the voltage of batteries of this type.

  ii Making appropriate assumptions, which should be stated, test at the 5% level whether the mean voltage is greater than 12 volts.

b The birthweights (x kg) of each baby in random samples of babies born in two different countries were measured and the following results calculated:

Country A
Sample size = 100, $\Sigma x = 340.2$, $\Sigma x^2 = 1238.42$
Country B
Sample size = 120, $\Sigma x = 335.7$, $\Sigma x^2 = 1015.75$

Test at the 5% significance level whether the birthweight of children born in Country A is significantly greater than that of children born in Country B.

(WJEC)

Exercise B

1 The volume of paint, in litres, in a randomly chosen 2-litre can is denoted by the random variable V. Ten random observations of V are taken, with the following results:

1.99   2.12   2.03   2.07   1.99   1.95   2.01   2.00   2.08   1.94

Assuming that V has a normal distribution, use a single sample t test, at the 1% significance level, to test the claim that the mean volume of the paint in 2-litre cans is not 2 litres.

After installation of a new machine for filling the cans, there were worries that, on average, the new machine was dispensing less paint than the old machine. The volumes of paint dispensed by the new machine in a random sample of 20 cans were measured, and the results summarised by:

$$\Sigma w = 38.1 \text{ and } \Sigma (w - \bar{w})^2 = 0.0604$$

where w is the volume of paint, in litres, in a can. Use a two sample t test to test whether there is evidence, at the 10% significance level, that the new machine is dispensing less paint than the old machine.

(UCLES)

2 Following a claim by a company that its washing powder 'Washo' fades colours less than a leading brand of another company, a statistical experiment was set up to test the claim. Eight different pieces of cloth (A to H) were each cut in half. One set of halves was washed 20 times in Washo and the other set of halves was washed 20 times in the other brand, under the same conditions. A standard method of measuring strength of colour was used in which the stronger the colour the larger the measured value. After the washings the strength of colour was measured and the results shown in the table.

		A	B	C	D	E	F	G	H
Measured strength of colour	**Washo**	93	87	94	93	89	90	85	88
	Other	92	86	95	89	88	86	85	89

You may assume that the measured strength of colour in faded material follows a normal distribution.

a State the null hypothesis for a suitable statistical test to analyse the claim made for Washo.

b Carry out this test and briefly discuss your result. *(NICCEA)*

3 In an investigation to compare the effectiveness of open-learning to teaching on an adult computer desk-top publishing course, a random sample of 60 students was split into two groups of size 30. One group followed an open-learning package (Method A) for a period of three weeks. The other group was teacher led (Method B) for the same three week period. At the end of the three week period each student was timed to produce independently the same one page report. The summary of their times was as follows:

Method A: $\Sigma x = 222$ minutes, $\Sigma x^2 = 1730$

Method B: $\Sigma y = 195$ minutes, $\Sigma y^2 = 1360$

For each method calculate unbiased estimates of the mean and of the variance of the times taken.

The times taken to produce the reports by either method may be assumed to be normally distributed. Investigate, at the 2% level of significance, the claim that the teacher led method gives, on average, faster times than the open-learning method in producing the reports.

4 The proportion of patients who suffer an allergic reaction to a certain drug used to treat a particular medical condition is assumed to be 0.045.

a Each of a random sample of 90 patients with the condition is given the drug and X is the number who suffer an allergic reaction. Assuming independence explain why X can be modelled approximately by the Poisson distribution and calculate $P(X = 4)$.

b When 400 patients were treated, 25 suffered an allergic reaction. Using a normal approximation, test at the 5% significance level whether the quoted figure of 0.045 is an underestimation.   (*UCLES*)

5 Horticultural tests were carried out on a particular species of tomato plant grown in one of two different composts. A sample of 150 of the plants was grown in compost A, and for each plant the weight, x kg, of tomatoes produced was measured, giving the results: $\Sigma x = 487.5$ and $\Sigma x^2 = 1676.75$.

A second sample of 200 plants was grown in compost B, and for each plant the weight, y kg, of tomatoes produced was measured, giving the results: $\Sigma y = 572.0$ and $\Sigma y^2 = 1702.86$.

For each type of compost calculate, correct to three significant figures, unbiased estimates of the population mean and population variance of the weight of tomatoes produced.

The manufacturer of compost A claims that the mean weight of tomatoes grown in compost A will be 0.5 kg per plant more than those grown in compost B. State suitable null and alternative hypotheses and test, at the 5% level of significance, whether the above results support this claim.

(*NEAB*)

6 The effect of hypnosis on speech was investigated by hypnotising 10 randomly chosen individuals and counting the number of words each spoke over a period of 30 minutes. The numbers of words spoken by the same individuals during a period of 30 minutes when not hypnotised were also counted. The results are given in the table:

Not hypnotised	255	1250	126	480	371	308	688	345	264	306
Hypnotised	67	67	89	129	491	304	49	281	131	107

Use: **a** a sign test at the 1% level
b the Wilcoxon signed rank test at the 5% level
to test the hypothesis that people are less inclined to talk when hypnotised.

The mean number of words spoken in a period of 30 minutes by people not under hypnosis is μ_1. The corresponding mean for people under hypnosis is μ_2. Assuming normality, test, at the 5% significance level, the null hypothesis $\mu_1 - \mu_2 = 400$ against the alternative hypothesis $\mu_1 - \mu_2 < 400$.

(*UCLES*)

7 In a comparison of the times to develop two types, A and B, of time-zero film (film that begins to develop as soon as the picture is taken) the following developing times, in seconds, were recorded.

Film	Developing times (seconds)						
Type A	8.2	5.0	6.8	6.7	5.8	7.3	6.4	7.8
Type B	5.1	4.3	3.4	3.7	6.1	4.7		

By using an appropriate two sample test, investigate the claim that the mean developing time of type A film exceeds that of type B film.   (*AEB*)

8 Cloud Trek Airlines are doing some market research. Passengers in the concourse at Aldergrove were asked which is their favourite airline. One-twentieth of them said Cloud Trek. The management then paid for a marketing promotion, then the market research was repeated. This time, out of 100 passengers asked, eight said Cloud Trek. Carry out a test, using a 5% significance level, to see if there has been a significant improvement.

(*NICCEA*)

9 The times taken by five-year-old children to complete a certain task are normally distributed with a standard deviation of 8.0 s. A random sample of 25 five-year-old children from school A were given this task and their mean time was 44.2 s.

a Find 95% confidence limits for the mean time taken by five-year-old children from school A to complete the task.

b The mean time for a random sample of 20 five-year-old children from school B was 40.9 s. The head teacher of school B concluded that the overall mean of school B must be less than that of school A. Given the two samples were independent, test the headteacher's conclusion using a 5% significance level. State you hypotheses and conclusion clearly.

(*ULEAC*)

10 A central business district of a town is served by two railway stations, A and B. Part of a study is to examine whether the mean daily number of passengers arriving at station A during the morning peak period is the same as the corresponding average at station B. Counts were taken at station A for a random sample of eight working days and at station B for a separate random sample of 12 working days, with the following results for the numbers arriving during the morning peak period:

Station A	1486	1529	1512	1540	1506	1464	1495	1502				
Station B	1475	1497	1460	1478	1520	1473	1449	1480	1503	1462	1474	1486

a State formally the null and alternative hypotheses to be tested.
b State an underlying assumption concerning distribution.
c Carry out the test, using a 5% level of significance.

(*MEI*)

Applications and Activities

Ask a number of people to estimate:

a   the length of a piece of string
b   ten seconds.

Then compare the mean results from different groups, for example:

male/female
oldest students/youngest students
teachers/students

Summary

- To test the difference between population means using paired samples use

$$Z = \frac{\bar{D}}{\sigma_D/\sqrt{n}} \quad \text{and} \quad t = \frac{\bar{D}}{s/\sqrt{n-1}}$$

for large samples.   for small samples.

- To test the difference between population means using unpaired samples use

$$Z = \frac{\bar{x}_1 - \bar{x}_2}{\sqrt{\dfrac{\sigma_1^2}{n_1} + \dfrac{\sigma_2^2}{n_2}}}$$

for large samples, and

$$t = \frac{\bar{x}_1 - \bar{x}_2}{\hat{\sigma}\sqrt{\dfrac{1}{n_1} + \dfrac{1}{n_2}}}$$

for small samples.

- To test the difference between proportions use

$$Z = \frac{p_1 - p_2}{\sqrt{\hat{p}(1-\hat{p})\left(\dfrac{1}{n_1} + \dfrac{1}{n_2}\right)}}$$

- The sign test for the difference between paired and unpaired sample is

$$Z = \frac{U - \dfrac{n}{2} \pm \dfrac{1}{2}}{\sqrt{\dfrac{n}{4}}}$$

- The Wilcoxon signed rank test compares the smaller of the sum of the positive differences and the sum of the negative differences with the critical value given in the table.

16 Chi-squared Test and Analysis of Errors

What you need to know

- How to calculate the probabilities of a binomial distribution.

- How to calculate the probabilities of a Poisson distribution.

Review

1 Calculate the probabilities from binomial distributions with the following values:

a $n = 7, p = 0.7, P(x = 5)$

b $n = 10, p = 0.4, P(x = 3)$

c $n = 12, p = 0.55, P(x \leq 2)$

d $n = 5, p = 0.63, P(x > 3)$

e $n = 16, p = 0.21, P(x < 4)$

2 Calculate the probabilities for the following Poisson distributions:

a $\lambda = 3, P(x = 4)$

b $\lambda = 1, P(x = 2)$

c $\lambda = 3.5, P(x < 1)$

d $\lambda = 4.8, P(x > 2)$

e $\lambda = 2.1, P(x \leq 1)$

16.1 Chi-squared Test

The chi-squared test is widely used in geography, biology and the social sciences to test whether observed data are different from expected data found from calculation. The test is used to measure the differences between the observed and expected frequencies and to see if those differences are significant.

There can be two reasons for the use of the chi-squared test:

- to see whether the observed frequencies fit a particular pattern and are therefore predictable

- the differences between the observed and expected frequencies are significant and further study is required to explain why those differences might have occurred.

χ is the Greek letter chi, pronounced 'khi'.

Simple test of observed frequency against expected frequency

The shape of the chi-squared curve varies as the number of **degrees of freedom** (v) increases. As the number of degrees of freedom increases then the curve slowly approximates to the normal distribution.

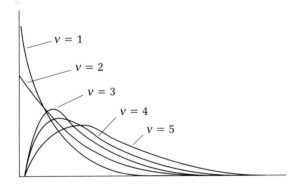

The **degrees of freedom** relate to the number of independent choices that are possible when calculating the expected frequencies.

degrees of freedom, ν

= the number of groups − the number of constraints

Example 1

A dice is thrown 120 times. What are the expected frequencies of the individual scores, and how many degrees of freedom are there?

Solution

Each score is equally likely so the expected frequencies are all $\frac{120}{6} = 20$.

The frequencies for 1, 2, 3, 4 and 5 are said to be independent but the frequency for 6 must make the total number of throws add up to 120. This gives five degrees of freedom.

Calculating the degrees of freedom (ν)

ν = number of classes − number of constraints

$\nu = 6 - 1$ (the total must be 120)

$\nu = 5$

To use the chi-squared distribution to test the data, the differences between the observed and the expected frequencies are calculated. If the differences are small then the two distributions are similar.

The greater the differences in the frequencies the greater the difference in the distributions.

H_0: the observed frequencies are a random sample from the hypothesised distribution.

H_1: the observed frequencies are not from the distribution.

The test statistic is: $\chi^2 = \sum \frac{(O - E)^2}{E}$

where O is the observed frequency

and E is the expected frequency

There is one important condition when using chi-squared tests. The expected frequencies of each group must be five or greater. Any group that has a frequency less than five must be combined with another group or groups.

Example 2

A dice is thrown 120 times and the scores recorded. The results are:

Score	1	2	3	4	5	6
Frequency	21	28	15	23	10	23

Is there evidence at the 5% level to indicate bias in the dice?

Solution

H_0: The dice is not biased $\left(p = \frac{1}{6} \text{ for each score}\right)$

H_1: The dice is biased $\left(p \neq \frac{1}{6}\right)$

$\nu = 6 - 1 = 5$

With $p = 0.95$ and $v = 5$, the critical value from chi-squared tables is 11.070.

Score	O	E	$(O - E)$	$(O - E)^2$	$(O - E)^2/E$
1	21	20	1	1	0.05
2	28	20	8	64	3.20
3	15	20	−5	25	1.25
4	23	20	3	9	0.45
5	10	20	−10	100	5.00
6	23	20	3	9	0.45
				$\sum (O - E)^2/E =$	10.40

$$\chi^2 = 10.40$$

Critical value of $\chi^2 < 11.07$, so do not reject H_0. There is no significant evidence to indicate bias in the dice.

16.1 Chi-squared Test
Exercise

Contextual

1 An ordinary dice was thrown 600 times. From the results, is there any evidence to indicate that the dice was biased?

Score	1	2	3	4	5	6
Frequency	82	109	121	54	97	137

2 The number of students absent each day of the week was recorded. The results were:

Mon	Tues	Wed	Thur	Fri
82	63	41	39	75

Does this indicate, at the 5% level, that the distribution of absence is not affected by the day of the week?

3 In a test of soil types 100 seeds were sown in strips in 10 different fields. The number of seeds that germinated in each strip were recorded as follows:

Strip	1	2	3	4	5	6	7	8	9	10
Number of seeds	65	82	43	48	75	91	55	68	47	89

Is there evidence to indicate that the type of soil affects the number of seeds that germinate?

4 A machine is set to produce sweets in the following ratio: three red, five green, six yellow and two orange. Twelve packets of sweets were opened and the colours counted as:

red	green	yellow	orange
32	88	98	22

Is there any indication that the machine is not dispensing the colours in the correct ratio?

5 The numbers of male students taking A-level subjects were as follows:

Maths	Physics	English	Geography	History	Social Studies	Art	Biology	Chemistry
22	14	28	12	7	8	11	8	15

Is there evidence to indicate bias in the choice of A-level subjects by male students? Test at the 5% level using the χ^2 distribution.

6 The totals scored by throwing two dice 720 times were as follows:

Total	2	3	4	5	6	7	8	9	10	11	12
Frequency	17	29	62	74	112	117	109	78	51	43	28

Compare the results with the expected frequencies and test at the 5% level whether there is any indication of a biased die.

7 The grades obtained by students at GCSE were compared to the estimated grades given prior to the examination. An analysis of whether the actual grades were significantly different was carried out. Using the actual grades as the observed data and the estimated grades as the expected data, carry out a suitable test to decide whether there is a significant difference between the two.

Grades	A	B	C	D	E	F	G
Estimated	15	25	56	74	45	34	11
Actual	11	19	48	98	56	17	11

16.2 Chi-squared Test for Binomial Distribution

This is a test to see whether the observed frequencies follow a known distribution. The most common distributions tested are the binomial, Poisson and normal.

If it is suspected that a sample is binomially distributed then by using the chi-squared test the observed frequencies can be compared to the expected frequencies calculated from binomial theory.

Example

At a fruit packing warehouse samples of five apples are selected at various times during the day. The number of rotten apples in each sample is given in the table.

Number of rotten apples	0	1	2	3	4	5
Frequency	18	27	16	9	6	4

a   Find the frequencies of the number of rotten apples, per sample, obtained from a binomial distribution with the same mean and total.
b   Test whether the results actually obtained follow a binomial distribution.

Solution

a $\bar{x} = \dfrac{\sum fx}{\sum f} = \dfrac{130}{80}$

$\bar{x} = 1.625$

Let X be the random variable 'the number of rotten apples in a sample of five apples'

$X \sim B(n, p)$ where $n = 5$

For a binomial distribution,

$$\bar{x} = n \times p$$
$$1.625 = 5 \times p$$
$$p = 0.325$$

so $X \sim B(5, 0.325)$

The expected frequencies can be found by using the binomial distribution function, with $p = 0.325$ and $q = 0.675$.

$$P(X = 0) = {}^5C_0(0.675)^5 = 0.140$$

expected frequency $= 80 \times 0.140 = 11.21$

$$P(X = 1) = {}^5C_1(0.325)(0.675)^4 = 0.337$$

expected frequency $= 80 \times 0.337 = 26.99$

$$P(X = 2) = {}^5C_2(0.325)^2(0.675)^3 = 0.325$$

expected frequency $= 80 \times 0.325 = 25.99$

$$P(X = 3) = {}^5C_3(0.325)^3(0.675)^2 = 0.156$$

expected frequency $= 80 \times 0.156 = 12.51$

$$P(X = 4) = {}^5C_4(0.325)^4(0.675)^1 = 0.0377$$

expected frequency $= 80 \times 0.0377 = 3.01$

$$P(X = 5) = {}^5C_5(0.325)^5 = 0.00363$$

expected frequency $= 80 \times 0.00363 = 0.29$

Retain all decimal places in probabilities when calculating the expected frequencies. Round expected frequencies to two decimal places.

Number of rotten apples	0	1	2	3	4	5
Observed frequency (O)	18	27	16	9	6	4
Expected frequency (E)	11.21	26.99	25.99	12.51	3.01	0.29

Notice that two of the groups have expected frequencies of less than five so the last three groups have to be combined.

Number of rotten apples	0	1	2	3 and over
Observed frequency (O)	18	27	16	19
Expected frequency (E)	11.21	26.99	25.99	15.81

Score	O	E	(O − E)	(O − E)²	(O − E)²/E
0	18	11.21	6.79	46.10	4.11
1	27	26.99	0.01	0.0001	0.00
2	16	25.99	−9.99	99.8001	3.84
3 or more	19	15.81	3.19	10.1761	0.64
				$\sum (O - E)^2/E =$	8.59

b H_0:   The distribution is binomial with $p = 0.325$.

   H_1:   The distribution is not binomial.

   number of degrees of freedom $v = 4 - 2 = 2$

   (Total must equal 80, and value of p was estimated from the sample, thus two constraints)

   From tables critical values of χ^2 are:

   $\chi^2(2)$ at 5% $= 5.991$

   $\chi^2(2)$ at 1 % $= 9.210$

   $\chi^2 = 8.59$

   As $\chi^2 > 5.991$ then H_0 is rejected at the 5% level.

   but as $\chi^2 < 9.210$ then H_0 is accepted at the 1% level.

At the 5% level the distribution does not fit a binomial distribution with $p = 0.325$. At the 1% level a binomial distribution with $p = 0.325$ could be a suitable model.

Note: If p is known, such as with coins, dice and so on, then that value is used to calculate the expected frequencies.

16.2 Chi-squared Test for Binomial Distribution

Exercise

Contextual

1 Three dice were thrown and the number of ones were counted. The experiment was repeated 648 times with the results:

Number of ones	0	1	2	3
Frequency	360	239	36	13

Using a 5% level of significance, test whether the observed frequencies fit those expected from a binomial distribution.

2 A distribution is thought to come from a binomial population with a probability of success of 0.4 The results of testing the population were:

x	0	1	2	3	4	5	6
Frequency	12	41	87	85	41	10	4

Test at the 5% level whether the claim for the population is true.

3 In a poker competition a player's probability of success is 0.25. When playing with friends he usually plays eight hands and over a period of time records the number of hands he wins.

Number of hands	0	1	2	3	4	5	6	7	8
Frequency	4	13	12	12	6	3	2	0	0

Does the evidence suggest that the poker player usually wins 0.25 of the hands he plays with his friends?

4 A weed killer is tested by applying it to batches of eight weeds and counting the number of weeds that survive. The results were:

Weeds	0	1	2	3	4	5	6	7	8
Frequency	8	12	19	27	23	18	9	4	1

By calculating the mean of the sample and hence an estimate for p, find the probability of a weed surviving the weed killer. From this, test whether the distribution fits a binomial distribution.

5 In a warehouse, samples of six components are selected at various times throughout the day. The number of defective components in each sample is recorded in the table.

Number of defective components	0	1	2	3	4	5	6
Frequency	35	52	18	12	8	3	2

By calculating the mean number of faulty components per sample, test whether these results follow a binomial distribution.

6 In a china factory samples of five items are checked and the number of undamaged items is recorded. Is there evidence at the 5% level that these results are binomially distributed?

Number of undamaged items	0	1	2	3	4	5
Frequency	6	36	84	198	186	90

16.3 Chi-squared Test for Poisson Distribution

The second test of distributions is to see whether the observed frequencies correspond to the frequencies from a Poisson distribution. The properties of the Poisson distribution are used as an initial check before proceeding with the chi-squared test. The Poisson distribution fits events occurring randomly over a set interval. For observed data the mean and variance should be approximately equal; a simple test to be carried out before proceeding with the χ^2 test. With a small sample in particular, the mean and variance can differ quite a lot even though a Poisson distribution is appropriate.

Example

The numbers of cars passing a point on a busy road over equal intervals of time were noted as:

Number of cars	0	1	2	3	4	5	6	7 or more
Frequency	7	24	26	28	13	12	10	0

Estimate the mean and variance of this distribution. Test the data for goodness of fit to a Poisson distribution.

Solution

$$\bar{x} = \frac{\sum fx}{\sum f} = \frac{332}{120} = 2.767$$

$$s^2 = \frac{\sum fx^2}{\sum f} - \bar{x}^2 = \frac{1248}{120} - 2.767^2 = 2.746$$

Mean and variance are approximately equal so the distribution could be Poisson, with $\lambda = 2.767$.

Expected frequencies of Poisson distribution are found by:

$$P(X = x) = \frac{e^{-\lambda}\lambda^x}{x!} \times 120$$

where $\quad \lambda =$ the mean (and variance)

$\quad\quad x =$ the size of the variable

$\quad\quad e =$ the exponential value

$\quad\quad 120 =$ the total frequency

Number of cars	0	1	2	3	4	5	6	7 or more
Observed frequency (O)	7	24	26	28	13	12	10	0
Expected frequency (E)	7.54	20.87	28.87	26.63	18.42	10.19	4.70	2.78

As the expected frequencies of the groups of 6 and 7 or more are less than five they are combined into a group of 6 or more.

Cars	O	E	$(O-E)$	$(O-E)^2$	$(O-E)^2/E$
0	7	7.54	−0.54	0.29	0.039
1	24	20.87	3.13	9.80	0.469
2	26	28.87	−2.87	8.24	0.285
3	28	26.63	1.37	1.88	0.070
4	13	18.42	−5.42	29.38	1.595
5	12	10.19	1.81	3.28	0.322
6 or more	10	7.48	2.52	6.35	0.849
				$\sum (O-E)^2/E =$	3.629

H_0: The distribution is Poisson.

H_1: The distribution is not Poisson.

number of degrees of freedom $= v = 7 - 2 = 5$

(Total must be 120, and mean was estimated from the data)

$\chi^2(5)$ at 5% level is 11.070.

$\chi^2 = 3.629$

As $\chi^2 < 11.070$, do not reject H_0. The observed frequencies could come from a Poisson distribution.

16.3 Chi-squared Test for Poisson Distribution

Exercise

Contextual

1 It is observed that the frequency of a certain distribution is:

x	0	1	2	3	4	5	6	7
Frequency	24	60	52	32	22	5	3	2

Estimate the mean and variance of x and explain why the Poisson distribution with mean 2 might be a good fit. Test the data for goodness of fit to the Poisson distribution.

2 In an experiment to measure traffic, the number of vehicles passing a point every 20 s was recorded. The results were:

Vehicles passing in 20 s	0	1	2	3	4	5
Frequency	33	57	42	21	9	3

Test whether the frequencies fit the Poisson distribution.

3 The distribution for the number of goals scored by teams in football matches was:

Goals	0	1	2	3	4	5
Teams scoring	5	13	18	12	9	3

Use the χ^2 test to compare the observed frequencies with those expected from the Poisson distribution. Comment on the agreement of the figures.

4 A switchboard monitored the number of calls made every hour. The results were

Number of calls	0	1	2	3	4	5	6	7
Frequency	18	29	41	33	24	15	9	1

Compare this with the frequency expected from a Poisson distribution and test the goodness of fit.

5 The table gives the distribution of the number of hits by flying bombs in 450 equal sized areas.

Number of hits	0	1	2	3	4	5
Frequency	180	173	69	20	6	2

a Find the expected frequencies of hits given by a Poisson distribution having the same mean and total as the observed distribution.

b Test at the 10% level of significance to the adequacy of the Poisson distribution as a model for these data.

16.4 Chi-squared Test for Normal Distribution

When testing that a distribution is normal the procedures are similar to those applied for binomial and Poisson distributions. Data have to be grouped to test for a normal distribution as a normal distribution is continuous. Usually from the data the mean and variance of the population are unknown and estimates have to be calculated. This restricts the degrees of freedom as the variances, means and totals of the observed and expected data have to be the same, so there are three constraints.

If the mean and variance of the population is known then there is only one constraint, namely the total.

Example

In a survey, the weights of 14-year-olds were recorded in a group frequency table. The results were:

Weight (kg) x	Frequency f
$24.5 < x \leq 29.5$	19
$29.5 < x \leq 34.5$	47
$34.5 < x \leq 39.5$	92
$39.5 < x \leq 44.5$	145
$44.5 < x \leq 49.5$	108
$49.5 < x \leq 54.5$	38
$54.5 < x \leq 59.5$	11

Calculate the mean and variance for this distribution. Test whether the sample fits a normal distribution with the same mean and variance.

Solution

Calculating the mean and variance

$$\bar{x} = \frac{19\,190}{460} = 41.72$$

$$s^2 = \frac{820\,770}{460} - 41.72^2 = 43.94$$

$$\text{unbiased estimator} = \frac{ns^2}{n-1} = \frac{460}{459} \times 43.94$$

so

$$\hat{\sigma}^2 = 44.04$$

and

$$\hat{\sigma} = 6.64$$

Retain all the decimal places in $\bar{x}$ when calculating s^2. Round to two decimal places in the answer.

In order to work out the expected frequencies for the normal distribution we must first find the true class boundaries and standardise these values, using μ as 41.72 and σ as 6.64.

1st interval
The upper class boundary for the first interval is 29.5.

Standardising gives

$$Z \leq \frac{29.5 - 41.72}{6.64}$$

$$Z \leq -1.840$$

We can now calculate

$$P(X \leq 29.5) = \Phi(-1.840)$$

$$= 0.032\,88$$

The expected frequency is found by multiplying the probability by the total frequency, that is:

$$0.032\,88 \times 460 = 15.12$$

2nd interval
The upper class boundary for the second interval is 34.5.

Standardising gives

$$Z \leq \frac{34.5 - 41.72}{6.64}$$

$$Z \leq -1.087$$

This time we need to calculate

$$P(29.5 < X \leq 34.5) = \Phi(-1.087) - \Phi(-1.840)$$

$$= 0.138\,52 - 0.032\,85$$

$$= 0.105\,64$$

The expected frequency for this interval is $0.105\,64 \times 460 = 48.59$.

Continuing in the same way we obtain the following results:

Interval	Standardised upper boundary	$P(a < x \leq b)$	Expected frequency
≤ 29.5	-1.840	0.03288	$0.03288 \times 460 = 15.12$
$29.5 < x \leq 34.5$	-1.087	$0.13852 - 0.03288 = 0.10564$	$0.10564 \times 460 = 48.59$
$34.5 < x \leq 39.5$	-0.334	$0.36919 - 0.13852 = 0.23067$	$0.23067 \times 460 = 106.11$
$39.5 < x \leq 44.5$	0.419	$0.66239 - 0.36919 = 0.2932$	$0.2932 \times 460 = 134.87$
$44.5 < x \leq 49.5$	1.172	$0.8794 - 0.66239 = 0.21701$	$0.21701 \times 460 = 99.82$
$49.5 < x \leq 54.5$	1.925	$0.97289 - 0.8794 = 0.09349$	$0.09349 \times 460 = 43.01$
$54.5 < x \leq 59.5$	2.678	$0.9963 - 0.97289 = 0.02341$	$0.02341 \times 460 = 10.77$

Testing at 95% level for normality.

H_0:   The data fit the normal distribution.

H_1:   The data do not fit the normal distribution.

O	E	$(O-E)$	$(O-E)^2$	$(O-E)^2/E$
19	15.12	3.88	15.0544	0.9957
47	48.59	-1.59	2.5281	0.0520
92	106.11	-14.11	199.0921	1.8763
145	134.87	10.13	102.6169	0.7609
108	99.82	8.18	66.9124	0.6703
38	43.01	-5.01	25.1001	0.5836
11	10.77	0.23	0.0529	0.0049
			$\sum (O-E)^2/E =$	4.9437

That is,

$\chi^2 = 4.9437$

$v = 7 - 3 = 4$ (total must equal 460, mean and variance calculated from data)

$\chi^2(4)$ at $5\% = 9.488$

As $\chi^2 < 9.488$, do not reject H_0. The data could fit a normal distribution.

16.4 Chi-squared Test for Normal Distribution

Exercise

Contextual

1 Test whether the following data fit a normal distribution with the same mean and variance.

x	0–15	15–20	20–25	25–30	30–35	35–40
Frequency	2	9	18	29	12	10

2 Test whether the following data fit a normal distribution with the same mean and variance.

x	0–5	6–11	12–17	18–23	24–29	30–35	36–41	42–47
Frequency	6	15	28	36	41	26	18	5

3 The heights of students in Year 9 were measured and the results were:

Height	150–154	155–159	160–164	165–169	170–174	175–179
Frequency	11	22	43	35	19	40

The distribution is thought to be approximately normal. Test at the 5% level whether this is true.

4 In studying the growth rate of Nile crocodiles their lengths were measured at the end of one year. The results were:

Length (cm)	<60	60–80	80–100	100–120	120–140	140–160	160–180	180–200	200–
Frequency	4	17	19	42	46	43	35	13	11

It is suspected that the population has a distribution which is approximately normal with a mean of 13 and a variance of 1156. The expected frequencies for this population would be

    5   12   27   45   52   45   27   12   5

Test at the 5% level whether the data supports what is suspected.

5 The ability of adults to estimate the size of an angle was part of the research into the use of mathematics. People were shown an angle and asked to estimate its size, the results were:

Angle (degrees)	56–60	61–65	66–70	71–75	76–80	81–85
Frequency	11	23	58	51	32	18

Test whether the distribution fits a normal distribution with the same mean and variance.

16.5 Contingency Tables

Sometimes it is necessary to classify results according to two factors rather than one. To do this a table is drawn up with one factor forming the rows in the table and the other factor forming the columns. If hair colour and eye colour are being considered then the eye colours can be listed to form the rows and the hair colour listed to form the columns. This is called a **contingency table**.

	Hair colour			
Eye colour	Brown	Black	Blonde	Auburn
Blue				
Brown				
Hazel				
Green				

The unshaded cell represents those people who have brown eyes and blonde hair. It is then possible to test whether the factors, hair and eye colour, are independent or are connected.

Example

In a survey of 350 farms the type of soil was compared with the type of farming. The results were:

	Type of farming			
Type of soil	Arable	Dairy	Mixed	Total
Chalk	11	41	30	82
Clay	25	39	32	96
Sand	24	36	15	75
Loam	42	17	38	97
Total	102	133	115	350

Test at the 5% level whether there is a significant link between the type of farming and the type of soil.

H_0: The type of farming is independent of soil type.

H_1: The type of farming is related to soil type.

Solution

Degrees of freedom

For a contingency table with h rows and k columns there are $(h-1)(k-1)$ degrees of freedom.

So,

$$v = (4-1) \times (3-1)$$

$$= 3 \times 2 = 6$$

To calculate the expected values for each cell in the table:

$$E = \frac{(\text{row total}) \times (\text{column total})}{\text{grand total}}$$

So for arable farms on chalk soil

$$E = \frac{102 \times 82}{350} = 23.90$$

For dairy farms on clay soil

$$E = \frac{133 \times 96}{350} = 36.48$$

Expected frequencies

Type of soil	Type of farming			
	Arable	Dairy	Mixed	Total
Chalk	23.90	31.16	26.94	82
Clay	27.98	36.48	31.54	96
Sand	21.86	28.50	24.64	75
Loam	28.27	36.86	31.87	97
Total	102.01	133.00	114.99	350

Note: Some rounding errors have occurred in the totals.

$(O-E)^2/E$ has to be calculated for each value in the table.

The $(O - E)^2/E$ values are:

Type of soil	Type of farming		
	Arable	Dairy	Mixed
Chalk	6.96	3.11	0.35
Clay	0.32	0.17	0.01
Sand	0.21	1.97	3.77
Loam	6.67	10.70	1.18

$$\sum \frac{(O - E)^2}{E} = 35.42$$

$\chi^2(6)$ at 5% is 12.592

As $\chi^2 > 12.952$, reject H_0. There is sufficient evidence to indicate that the type of farming is related to the type of soil.

16.5 Contingency Tables
Exercise

Technique

Test the following contingency tables at the 5% level to investigate whether X and Y are independent.

1

	X_1	X_2	X_3	X_4
Y_1	26	34	63	47
Y_2	19	11	32	23

2

	X_1	X_2
Y_1	5	37
Y_2	24	41
Y_3	16	22

3

	X_1	X_2	X_3
Y_1	6	15	10
Y_2	9	18	18
Y_3	7	19	14

4

	X_1	X_2	X_3
Y_1	84	75	25
Y_2	116	83	92

5

	X_1	X_2	X_3
Y_1	16	37	59
Y_2	7	43	81
Y_3	19	85	97
Y_4	4	29	103

Contextual

1 A survey was carried out to examine the connection, if any, between hair colour and eye colour. The results were:

Eye colour	Hair colour			
	Brown	Black	Blonde	Auburn
Blue	16	18	32	6
Brown	17	38	14	16
Hazel	18	29	5	12

Test at the 5% level whether hair and eye colour are independent.

2 The yields of tomatoes grown in four different soils using five different types of fertiliser were:

Fertiliser	Soil type			
	1	2	3	4
A	31	35	37	30
B	37	28	29	34
C	26	31	31	31
D	34	31	38	27
E	31	31	27	34

Is there evidence to indicate that the tomato yield is dependent on the soil type and fertiliser used?

3 Students in a school were given one of three tests on one day last week. The number of passes were recorded as:

Test	Day				
	Mon	Tues	Wed	Thur	Fri
A	66	41	35	34	39
B	57	47	34	27	64
C	50	35	27	22	41

Is the number of passes dependent on the test and the day on which it was taken?

4 The hair and eye colour of 200 people were recorded and the results are shown in the table:

Eye colour	Hair colour			
	Brown	Black	Fair	Ginger
Blue	18	12	26	11
Brown	22	20	11	8
Green	14	5	13	6
Grey	12	6	8	8

Is there any evidence to suggest that hair colour is dependent on a person's eye colour?

5 A group of farmers monitored the milk yields of six different breeds of cattle. The cattle were classed as having low, medium or high milk yields. The results were:

Breed	Yield		
	High	Medium	Low
1	16	19	15
2	26	14	10
3	20	42	28
4	8	50	24
5	38	42	94
6	12	6	26

Is there any evidence to indicate that the milk yield is independent of the breed of cattle, at the 5% level?

16.6 2 × 2 Contingency Tables

The number of degrees of freedom in a 2 × 2 table is:

$$(2 - 1) \times (2 - 1) = 1 \times 1 = 1$$

The approximation to the continuous χ^2 distribution can be improved by applying **Yates' continuity correction**, which involves subtracting $\frac{1}{2}$ from $|O - E|$.

The calculation becomes:

$$\chi^2 = \sum \frac{(|O - E| - 0.5)^2}{E}$$

Example

In a sample of 500 people the relationship between hair and eye colour was considered. The results were:

Hair colour	Eye colour		Total
	Blue	Brown	
Brown	95	138	234
Blonde	154	112	266
Total	250	250	500

Test at the 5% level whether there is an association between hair and eye colour.

Solution

H_0: Hair colour and eye colour are independent.

H_1: Hair and eye colour are dependent.

Estimated frequencies

Hair colour	Eye colour		Total
	Blue	Brown	
Brown	117	117	234
Blonde	133	133	266
Totals	250	250	500

Table of values for $\chi^2 = \sum \dfrac{(|O - E| - 0.5)^2}{E}$

Hair colour	Eye colour	
	Blue	Brown
Brown	3.95	3.59
Blonde	3.16	3.16

$$\chi^2 = \sum \frac{(|O - E| - 0.5)^2}{E} = 13.86$$

$\chi^2(1)$ at 5% is 3.841.

As $\chi^2 > 3.841$, reject H_0. There is significant evidence to indicate that there is an association between hair and eye colour.

16.6 2 × 2 Contingency Tables

Exercise

Technique

Test whether X and Y are independent:

1

	X_1	X_2
Y_1	59	21
Y_2	68	32

2

	X_1	X_2
Y_1	16	24
Y_2	35	56

3

	X_1	X_2
Y_1	81	95
Y_2	116	64

4

	X_1	X_2
Y_1	12	88
Y_2	26	61

5

	X_1	X_2
Y_1	25	18
Y_2	4	40

Contextual

1 In a test on the resistance of plants to disease two groups of 120 and 80 plants were used. The first group was treated in an attempt to increase resistance. Both groups where then examined for traces of infection. The results were:

	Group 1	Group 2
Disease free	78	47
Infected	42	33

Test whether the distribution is the same for both groups.

2 The pass rates of two driving examiners were tested for independence. The results of their driving tests were:

	Examiner A	Examiner B
Fail	24	11
Pass	78	59

Do the examiners have the same pass rate?

3 Two treatments for dandruff were tested on sufferers with the following results:

	Treatment 1	Treatment 2
Cured	22	63
Not cured	8	27

Is there any evidence to suggest that one treatment is more effective than the other?

4 The association of two plants to each other was examined by measuring the numbers of each plant in two locations. The results were:

	Location 1	Location 2
Plant A	137	208
Plant B	282	355

Is there evidence to support the hypothesis that the plants grow independently?

5 In an examination 83 out of 108 boys passed and 104 out of 142 girls passed. By constructing a 2×2 contingency table, test whether boys and girls show a difference in their ability.

16.7 Pearson's Product Moment Correlation Coefficient

In Chapter 11 we found that the value of the product moment correlation coefficient, r, ranges from -1 to $+1$. If the value is near 0 then it is apparent there is no correlation between the sets of data. If the value is near to -1 or $+1$ then it can confidently be assumed that the sets of data are either negatively or positively correlated.

It is assumed that the population correlation coefficient is ρ. The number of items used in the sample is important.

The number of degrees of freedom for r is $n - 2$. A table of critical values is then needed with a separate row for each individual degree of freedom. The value of r is then compared to the critical value taken from the table.

Example 1

In Exercise 3.6, question 2, the following information about the number of gold medals won in the Summer and Winter Olympics was given.

Country	Summer	Winter
USA	789	53
USSR/Unified	442	88
Germany	186	45
UK	177	7
France	161	16
Sweden	133	39
GDR	154	39
Italy	153	25
Finland	98	36
Japan	90	3
Poland	48	1
Canada	45	19
Netherlands	45	14
Switzerland	42	27
Belgium	35	1
S Korea	31	6

Does the correlation coefficient between the number of gold medals won in the Summer Olympics and the number won in the Winter Olympics show a significant difference in the numbers of medals won?

Solution

The correlation coefficient between the number of gold medals won in the Summer Olympics and those won in the Winter Olympics is

Summer (x)	Winter (y)	x^2	y^2	xy
789	53	622 521	2809	41 817
442	88	195 364	7744	38 896
186	45	34 596	2025	8 370
177	7	31 329	49	1 239
161	16	25 921	256	2 576
133	39	17 689	1521	5 187
154	39	23 716	1521	6 006
153	25	23 409	625	3 825
98	36	9 604	1296	3 528
90	3	8 100	9	270
48	1	2 304	1	48
45	19	2 025	361	855
45	14	2 025	196	630
42	27	1 764	729	1 134
35	1	1 225	1	35
31	6	961	36	186
$\sum x = 2629$	$\sum y = 419$	$\sum x^2 = 1\,002\,553$	$\sum y^2 = 19\,179$	$\sum xy = 114\,602$

$$\bar{x} = \frac{\sum x}{n} = \frac{2629}{16} = 164.3125$$

$$\bar{y} = \frac{\sum y}{n} = \frac{419}{16} = 26.1875$$

$$s_{xy} = \frac{\sum xy}{n} - \bar{x}\bar{y} = \frac{114\,602}{16} - 164.3125 \times 26.1875 = 2859.6914$$

$$s_x^2 = \frac{\sum x^2}{n} - \bar{x}^2 = \frac{1\,002\,553}{16} - 164.3125^2 = 35\,660.9648$$

$$s_y^2 = \frac{\sum y^2}{n} - \bar{y}^2 = \frac{19\,179}{16} - 26.1875^2 = 512.9023$$

so

$$r = \frac{s_{xy}}{s_x s_y} = \frac{2859.6914}{\sqrt{35\,660.9648} \times \sqrt{512.9023}} = 0.6687$$

From the table of critical values of the product-moment correlation coefficient, for a two-tailed test, the critical values are:

| 10% level | 0.4259 | 5% level | 0.4973 |
| 2% level | 0.5742 | 1% level | 0.6226 |

It can be seen that the value of r is significant at all levels.

There is positive correlation between the number of medals won in the Summer and Winter Olympics.

Example 2

In Exercise 3.6, question 3, the following data was given.

Year	Cinema audiences (000s)	TV licences (000s)
1950	9501	304
1955	8783	558
1960	7896	942
1965	7638	1264
1970	5401	1309
1975	4004	1637
1980	4861	1708
1985	4753	1686
1990	4409	1724
1995	4662	1950

Is the value of the correlation coefficient between the annual size of cinema audiences and the number of TV licences significant?

Solution

The correlation coefficient between the annual size of cinema audiences and the number of TV licences is:

Cinema (x)	TV (y)	x^2	y^2	xy
9501	304	90 269 001	92 416	2 888 304
8783	558	77 141 089	311 364	4 900 914
7896	942	62 346 816	887 364	7 438 032
7638	1264	58 339 044	1 597 696	9 654 432
5401	1309	29 170 801	1 713 481	7 069 909
4004	1637	16 032 016	2 679 769	6 554 548
4861	1708	23 629 321	2 917 264	8 302 588
4753	1686	22 591 009	2 842 596	8 013 558
4409	1724	19 439 281	2 972 176	7 601 116
4662	1950	21 734 244	3 802 500	9 090 900
$\sum x = 61\,908$	$\sum y = 13\,082$	$\sum x^2 = 420\,692\,622$	$\sum y^2 = 19\,816\,626$	$\sum xy = 71\,514\,301$

$$\bar{x} = \frac{\sum x}{n} = \frac{61\,908}{10} = 6190.8$$

$$\bar{y} = \frac{\sum y}{n} = \frac{13\,082}{10} = 1308.2$$

$$s_{xy} = \frac{\sum xy}{n} - \bar{x}\bar{y} = \frac{71\,514\,301}{10} - 6190.8 \times 1308.2 = -947\,374.46$$

$$s_x^2 = \frac{\sum x^2}{n} - \bar{x}^2 = \frac{420\,692\,622}{10} - 6190.8^2 = 3\,743\,257.56$$

$$s_y^2 = \frac{\sum y^2}{n} - \bar{y}^2 = \frac{19\,816\,626}{10} - 1308.2^2 = 270\,275.36$$

so

$$r = \frac{s_{xy}}{s_x s_y} = \frac{-947\,374.46}{\sqrt{3\,743\,257.56} \times \sqrt{270\,275.36}} = -0.9419$$

From the table of critical values of the product-moment correlation coefficient, for a two-tailed test, the critical values are:

10% level	0.5494	5% level	0.6319
2% level	0.7155	1% level	0.7646

From these values we see that r is significant at all levels. This value for r ($r = -0.9419$) suggests that there is a correlation between the two variables, that is as the number of TV licences increases the annual size of cinema audiences decreases.

16.7 Pearson's Product Moment Correlation Coefficient

Exercise

Technique

In Exercise 11.3, Technique, Pearson's product moment correlation coefficient was calculated. From the calculations, test at the 5% level, whether the values for r are significant.

The questions from Exercise 11.3, Technique are reproduced below for reference.

1   **a** $\sum x = 71.3, \sum y = 56, \sum xy = 573.4,$
$\sum x^2 = 703.53, \sum y^2 = 476,$
$n = 8$

     b $\sum x = 372, \sum y = 278, \sum xy = 14\,242,$
$\sum x^2 = 21\,258, \sum y^2 = 12\,467,$
$n = 7$

2

x	2	2.6	3.1	3.6	4.1	4.8	5.2	5.6
y	3.6	3.9	4.2	3.8	4.7	5.2	6	6.4

3

x	6	8	10	12	14	16	18	20	22
y	4.1	8.6	3.2	10.4	12	8.7	9.4	13.1	16

4

Goals conceded	16	20	23	25	40	46
Position in league	1	3	2	4	5	6

5

English	68	43	94	89	75	71	84	90	47	52
Maths	94	86	73	41	60	92	60	71	50	63

16.8 Spearman's Rank Correlation Coefficient

Spearman's rank correlation coefficient, r_s, is not distributed in the same way as Pearson's product moment correlation coefficient, so a different set of tables are required to test the significance of the coefficient. The value of r_s is tested against the critical value taken from these tables.

$$r_s = 1 - \frac{6\Sigma d^2}{n(n^2 - 1)}$$

Example 1

In Exercise 3.6, question [2], the following information about the number of gold medals won in the Summer and Winter Olympics was given.

Country	Summer (S)	Winter (W)
USA	789	53
USSR/Unified	442	88
Germany	186	45
UK	177	7
France	161	16
Sweden	133	39
GDR	154	39
Italy	153	25
Finland	98	36
Japan	90	3
Poland	48	1
Canada	45	19
Netherlands	45	14
Switzerland	42	27
Belgium	35	1
S Korea	31	6

Is Spearman's rank coefficient of correlation between the number of gold medals won in the Summer Olympics and those won in the Winter Olympics significant?

Solution

	Rank S	Rank W	d	d^2
USA	1	2	−1	1
USSR/Unified	2	1	1	1
Germany	3	3	0	0
UK	4	12	−8	64
France	5	10	−5	25
Sweden	8	4.5	3.5	12.25
GDR	6	4.5	1.5	2.25
Italy	7	8	−1	1
Finland	9	6	3	9
Japan	10	14	−4	16
Poland	11	15.5	−4.5	20.25
Canada	12.5	9	3.5	12.25
Netherlands	12.5	11	1.5	2.25
Switzerland	14	7	7	49
Belgium	15	15.5	−0.5	0.25
S. Korea	16	13	3	9
				$\sum d^2 = 224.5$

$d = \text{rank } S - \text{rank } W$

$\sum d^2 = 224.5$ and $n = 16$

$$r_s = 1 - \frac{6 \sum d^2}{n(n^2 - 1)}$$

$$= 1 - \frac{6(224.5)}{16(255)}$$

$$= 0.6699$$

From the table of critical values for Spearman's rank coefficient of correlation, for a two-tailed test, the number of gold medals for each games is different, the critical values are:

10%	0.4265	5%	0.5029
2%	0.5824	1%	0.6324

From this it can be seen that the value for r_s is significant at all levels. What is also apparent is that the critical values for Spearman's rank coefficient of correlation are higher than those at the same level for the product-moment correlation coefficient. So the value of Spearman's rank coefficient of correlation in this case being higher than Pearson's product-moment correlation coefficient does not make it more significant.

Example 2

In Exercise 3.6, question 3, the following data were given.

Year	Cinema audiences (000s)	TV licences (000s)
1950	9501	304
1955	8783	558
1960	7896	942
1965	7638	1264
1970	5401	1309
1975	4004	1637
1980	4861	1708
1985	4753	1686
1990	4409	1724
1995	4662	1950

Is the value of Spearman's rank coefficient of correlation between the annual size of cinema audiences and the number of TV licences significant?

Solution

	Rank C	Rank T	d	d^2
1950	1	10	-9	81
1955	2	9	-7	49
1960	3	8	-5	25
1965	4	7	-3	9
1970	5	6	-1	1
1975	10	5	5	25
1980	6	3	3	9
1985	7	4	3	9
1990	9	2	7	49
1995	8	1	7	49
				$\sum d^2 = 306$

$d = \text{rank } S - \text{rank } T$

$$r_s = 1 - \frac{6 \sum d^2}{n(n^2 - 1)}$$

$$= 1 - \frac{6(306)}{10(99)}$$

$$= -0.8545$$

From the table of critical values for Spearman's rank coefficient of correlation, for a two-tailed test, the size of cinema audiences and the number of TV licences are different, the critical values are:

10%	0.5636	5%	0.6485
2%	0.7333	1%	0.7818

From this it can be seen that the value of r_s is significant at all levels.

16.8 Spearman's Rank Correlation Coefficient

Exercise

Technique

In Exercise 11.4, Technique, Spearman's coefficient of rank correlation was calculated. From those results test, at the 5% level, whether the values of r_s are significant.

The questions from Exercise 11.4, Technique, are reproduced below for reference.

1 **a**

x	1	2	3	4	5	6	7
y	5	4	2	6	1	7	3

b

x	1	2	3	4	5	6	7	8	9	10
y	10	8	9	6	7	3	4	2	5	1

2

x	1	2	3	4	5	6
y	3	1	2	4	6	5

3

Cake	A	B	C	D	E	F	G
Judge 1	6.8	7.8	8.4	9.9	5.0	5.5	8.1
Judge 2	5.9	8.1	7.8	9.1	4.9	5.8	8.8

4

German	68	74	81	85	59	74	64	81	89	79
French	54	69	69	74	51	61	54	72	75	59

5

Country	A	B	C	D	E	F	G	H
Annual income per head (US$)	160	210	230	360	480	560	740	1290
Life expectancy at birth (years)	42	46	51	47	48	48	56	65

16.9 Analysis of Errors

In analysing data it is always possible to make errors. Attempting to make assumptions about a population from a single item or a sample does in itself carry a risk of mistakes occurring.

However, there are two definite errors it is important to understand:

- a **Type I error** is made when H_0 is rejected when it is in fact true, that is H_0 should have been accepted;

- a **Type II error** is made when H_0 is accepted when it is false, that is H_0 should have been rejected and H_1 accepted.

This is usually written as:

$$P(\text{Type I error}) = P(\text{rejecting } H_0 | H_0 \text{ is true})$$

and

$$P(\text{Type II error}) = P(\text{accepting } H_0 | H_1 \text{ is true})$$

The probability of a Type I error is the same as the significance level used in hypothesis testing.

Example 1

A gambler claims he can toss an unbiased coin and get it to land on heads seven tries out of eight on average. What is the probability of tossing six or more heads in eight throws if his claim is true, and what is the probability if he can only toss four heads on average?

His claim is tested and his claim is accepted if he tosses six or more heads out of eight. Find the probability that the test will accept the gambler's claim when he can only average four out of eight heads, or reject the claim when in fact he can average seven out of eight heads.

Solution
If claim is true

$$P(\text{head}) = \tfrac{7}{8}$$

$$X \sim B(n, p), \text{ where } n = 8 \text{ and } p = \tfrac{7}{8}$$

$$X \sim B\left(8, \tfrac{7}{8}\right)$$

$$P(X \geq 6) = P(X = 6) + P(X = 7) + P(X = 8)$$

$$= 28 \times \left(\tfrac{1}{8}\right)^2 \times \left(\tfrac{7}{8}\right)^6 + 8 \times \left(\tfrac{1}{8}\right) \times \left(\tfrac{7}{8}\right)^7 + \left(\tfrac{7}{8}\right)^8$$

$$P(X \geq 6) = 0.933$$

If claim is false

$$P(\text{head}) = \tfrac{1}{2}$$

$$X \sim B(n, p), \text{ where } n = 8 \text{ and } p = \tfrac{1}{2}$$

$$P(X \geq 6) = P(X = 6) + P(X = 7) + P(X = 8)$$

$$= 28 \times \left(\tfrac{1}{2}\right)^8 + 8 \times \left(\tfrac{1}{2}\right)^8 + \left(\tfrac{1}{2}\right)^8$$

$$= (28 + 8 + 1) \times \left(\tfrac{1}{2}\right)^8$$

$$P(X \geq 6) = 0.145$$

H_0: The gambler's claim is true, that is $p = \tfrac{7}{8}$.

H_1: The gambler's claim is false, that is $p = \tfrac{1}{2}$.

Type II error is

$$P(\text{accepting } H_0 | H_1 \text{ is true}) = P\left(X \geq 6 \,|\, p = \tfrac{1}{2}\right)$$

$$= 0.145$$

The probability of a type II error, accepting the gamblers claim when he can only average four out of eight heads, is 0.145.

Type I error is

$$P(\text{rejecting } H_0 | H_0 \text{ is true}) = P\left(X < 6 \,|\, p = \tfrac{7}{8}\right)$$

$$= 1 - 0.933$$

$$= 0.067$$

The probability of a Type I error, rejecting the gambler's claim when he can average seven out of eight heads, is 0.067.

Example 2

In a normal population with variance 100 and an unknown mean, a sample of size 400 is taken. The researchers wish to test whether the mean is 100 so they set up the null hypothesis:

H_0: $\mu = 100$

and the alternative hypothesis

H_1: $\mu > 100$

The criterion used to decide the outcome is accept H_0 if $x \leq 101$ and reject H_0 if $\bar{x} > 101$. Find the probability of a Type I error.

If the alternative hypothesis is

$$H_1: \quad \mu = 102.5$$

what is the probability of a Type II error?

Solution

H_0 true

$$\bar{x} \sim N\left(\mu, \frac{\sigma^2}{n}\right), \text{ where } \mu = 100$$

Therefore $\sigma = \sqrt{100} = 10$

H_0 is rejected if $\bar{x} > 101$, that is

$$P(Z > 2) = 1 - 0.977\,25$$

$$= 0.022\,75$$

The probability H_0 is rejected when H_0 is true (Type I error) is $0.022\,75$.

H_1 true

$$\bar{x} \sim N\left(102.5, \tfrac{100}{400}\right)$$

$$P(\text{Type II error}) = P(\text{accept } H_0 | H_1 \text{ is true})$$

$$= P(\bar{x} \leq 101 \,|\, \mu = 102.5)$$

$$= P\left[\frac{\bar{x} - 102.5}{\frac{10}{20}} \leq \frac{101 - 102.5}{\frac{10}{20}}\right]$$

$$= P(Z \leq -3)$$

$$= 1 - 0.998\,65$$

$$= 0.0001\,35$$

$$P(\text{Type II error}) = 0.001\,35$$

16.9 Analysis of Errors
Exercise

Contextual

1 A suggested test for deciding if a coin is fair is to toss it four times and call it biased if four heads or tails are obtained. A second test is to toss the coin seven times and call it biased if six or seven heads or tails are obtained. How likely is it for each test to conclude wrongly that a fair coin is biased?

Which of these two tests is better for correctly judging as biased a coin whose probability of coming down heads is 2/3?

2 A fair coin is tossed 180 times. By using a normal approximation, calculate the probability of there being:

a more than 100 heads
b more than 105 heads.

A significance test is constructed to test the hypotheses:

H_0: $p = 0.5$ – the probability of a head is 0.5.

H_1: $p = 0.58$ – the probability of a head is 0.58.

Construct a significance test using 180 tosses such that the probability of accepting H_1 when H_0 is true is as close to 0.05 as possible. For the test calculate the probability of accepting H_0 when H_1 is true.

3 A bag contains a number of different coloured discs. It contains either 60 yellow and 20 red discs or 40 yellow and 40 red discs.

The null hypothesis, H_0: the bag contains 60 yellow and 20 red discs.

The alternative hypothesis, H_1: the bag contains 40 yellow and 40 red discs.

Five discs are drawn and H_0 is accepted if four or more discs are yellow, otherwise it is rejected. Find the size of Type I and Type II errors in this test.

4 The breaking strain of a wire was expected to be 200 newtons. If this value falls below 190 then the wire must be rejected. The distribution of the breaking strain is normal with a standard deviation of 20. Samples are taken to test the hypothesis.

H_0: $= 200\,\text{N}$ $\qquad$ H_1: $m = 190\,\text{N}$

How many samples will be needed if $P(\text{Type I error}) = 0.05$ and $P(\text{Type II error}) = 0.1$?

Consolidation

Exercise A

1 A random sample of 930 companies quoted on the Stock Exchange revealed the information summarised in the table below, which shows the distribution of these companies, classified according to two attributes. In this table, D indicates that the company has diversified its product range during the previous financial year, and P indicates that there has been a significant rise in profits in the same year.

	D	Not D
P	148	106
Not P	299	377

The null hypothesis that the attributes D and P are independent is to be tested against the alternative hypothesis that they are dependent. Show that the null hypothesis can be rejected at all reasonable significance levels.

(UCLES)

2 An ophthalmologist does a small-scale study into colour blindness. The particular interest is to find out whether there is any connection between gender and colour blindness. Of 400 adult males tested, 20 were found to be colour blind and of 600 adult females tested, 20 were found to be colour blind. Perform a χ^2 test on a contingency table to see whether there is a connection. State clearly your null hypothesis, significance level and conclusion.

(NICCEA)

3 The table gives the numbers of new men and women psychiatric patients seen by a consultant in a six-month period classified by type of psychiatric illness.

	Men	Women
Depression	13	10
Anxiety state	3	18
Other	6	8

Perform an appropriate test to examine whether there is an association between sex of patient and type of illness. State carefully the null and alternative hypotheses and any assumptions needed for your test.

(OCSEB)

4 A factory has a large number of lights in it. Records are kept of the number of light bulbs which need to be replaced each day. The figures for a random sample of 100 days are as follows:

Number of bulbs, x	0	1	2	3	4	5	6	7+
Number of days, f	14	10	15	34	11	12	4	0

a Explain why the Poisson distribution might be thought to be a suitable model for the number of light bulbs which need to be replaced each day.

b Find the mean and variance of the given data. Hence give an additional reason for supposing that the Poisson model might be appropriate.

c Using the mean as calculated in **b**, calculate the expected frequencies corresponding to the given frequencies in the table. Comment further on the suitability of the Poisson test.

d By using a χ^2 test, determine whether the data fits a Poisson distribution.

(MEI)

5 It is claimed that when homing pigeons are disorientated harmlessly they will exhibit no particular preference for any direction of flight after take-off. To test this, 128 pigeons, from lofts in a particular region, were disorientated harmlessly and then all released from a position 100 miles south of the region. The direction of flight of each pigeon was recorded with the following results.

Flight direction	0°–90°	90°–180°	180°–270°	270°–360°
Number of pigeons	30	35	36	27

Use the χ^2 goodness of fit to determine whether or not these data can be used to discredit the claim.

(NEAB)

6 Six hens are observed over a period of 20 days and the number of eggs laid each day is summarised in the following table.

Number of eggs	3	4	5	6
Number of days	2	2	10	6

Show that the mean number of eggs per day is five.

It may be assumed that a hen never lays more than one egg in any day. State one other assumption that needs to be made in order to consider a binomial model, with $n = 6$, for the total number of eggs laid per day.

Calculate the expected frequencies using the binomial model for the above data and carry out a χ^2 goodness of fit test, using a 10% significance level.

(UCLES)

7 A random variable has a normal distribution with mean μ and standard deviation 8. The null hypothesis $\mu = 12$ is to be tested against the alternative $\mu > 12$ using a random sample of size 16. The null hypothesis will be rejected if the sample mean is greater than 14.7. Calculate the probability of making a Type I error.

(UCLES)

8 A weaving mill produces pieces of cloth. The lengths of a random sample of 150 pieces were measured. The mean length was 71.867 m and the standard deviation was 2.787 m.

a Assume that the lengths are normally distributed and that 2.787 m is an accurate estimate of the population standard deviation. Calculate a 90% confidence interval for the mean length.

b A statistician decides to check the assumption that the data are normally distributed. She obtains the original data and fits a normal distribution with the following results.

Length (m)	Observed frequency	Expected frequency
<65	0	1.04
65–67	2	5.02
67–69	24	16.73
69–71	39	33.89
71–73	29	41.99
73–75	29	31.74
75–77	27	14.67
>77	0	4.92

Use the χ^2 distribution at the 5% significance level to test whether the normal distribution provides an adequate model for the data.

(AEB)

9 A survey of the number of hours spent watching television each week was carried out. The sample, randomly selected from a large population, contained 240 males and 200 females. The results are summarised in the table.

	Male	Female
Under 10 hours	40.0%	32.5%
10–25	47.5%	51.5%
Over 25 hours	12.5%	16.0%

Use an approximate χ^2 statistic at the 5% level of significance to assess whether or not there is any association between gender and time spent watching television.

(*ULEAC*)

10 During a long motorway journey a statistician counted the number of red cars that drove past him in a series of two-minute intervals. The results were as follows:

Number of red cars	0	1	2	3	4	5	6	7
Observed frequency	12	15	17	12	11	8	4	1

a Show that the average number of red cars in each two-minute interval is 2.5.

b The statistician claims that the data could be described by a Poisson distribution. Using the table of the Poisson cumulative distribution function and giving answers to one decimal place, he obtained the following:

Number of red cars	0	1	2	3	4	5	6	7
Observed frequency	12	15	17	12	11	8	4	1
Expected frequency			20.5	17.1	10.7	5.3	2.2	1.1

Obtain the missing two expected frequencies.

c Test the statistician's claim at the 5% level stating your conclusion clearly.

(*ULEAC*)

Exercise B

1 A cubical dice is to be tested for bias by analysing the results of 120 throws.

a State suitable null and alternative hypotheses for testing whether even and odd scores are equally likely. Given that 53 out of the 120 throws resulted in the dice showing an even score, carry out this test, using a 10% significance level, and state your conclusions clearly.

b The number of times that each score is obtained is shown in the following table:

Score	1	2	3	4	5	6
Frequency	26	17	20	13	21	23

Write down the expected frequency for each score, assuming that each score is equally likely to occur. Carry out a goodness of fit analysis to test the hypothesis that each score is equally likely to occur, using a 10% significance level. Show full details of your method and state any conclusions clearly.

2 A dentist notices that most people have cavities on the right-hand side of their mouths. He conjectures that this is because they are right-handed and as a result they clean the left-hand side of their mouths more thoroughly.

To test his hypothesis he selects at random 30 right-handed and 20 left-handed patients and classifies them further on whether they have more cavities on the left or right side of their mouths.

	Side of the mouths with most fillings	
	Left	Right
Left-handed	12	8
Right-handed	7	23

Carry out a χ^2 test to find out whether there is sufficient evidence to support the dentist's claim. Use a 5% level of significance. (*NICCEA*)

3 An incurable illness, which is not life threatening, is usually treated with drugs to alleviate painful symptoms. A number of suffers agreed to be allocated into two groups. The members of one group would undergo a new treatment which involves major surgery and the members of the other group would continue with the standard drug treatment. Twelve months later a study of these sufferers produced information on their symptoms which is summarised in the following 2×4 contingency table:

	No change or worse	Slight improvement	Marked improvement	Information unobtainable
New treatment	12	32	46	44
Old treatment	36	39	12	33

a Test at the 5% significance level whether the outcome is independent of the treatment.

b Comment on the effectiveness of the new treatment in light of your answer to **a**.

c   Further analysis of the reasons for information being unobtainable from suffers showed that of the 44 who underwent the new treatment, 19 had died, 10 had refused to co-operate and the rest were untraceable. Of the 33 who underwent the standard treatment, three had died, 12 had refused to co-operate and the rest were untraceable.

Form a 2 × 3 contingency table but do not carry out any further calculations.

Given that for the contingency table you have formed $\sum |(O - E)^2/E| = 10.74$, test at the 5% significance level whether the reason for information being unobtainable is independent of the treatment.

(AEB)

4   The following table is the result of analysing a random sample of the invoices submitted by branches of a large chain of book shops.

	Novel	Textbook	General
Hardback	24	10	22
Paperback	66	110	18

Using an approximate χ^2 statistic, assess at the 5% level of significance, whether or not there is any association between the type of book sold and its cover. State clearly your null hypothesis.

(ULEAC)

5   In a survey 200 motorists, chosen at random, were asked how many attempts they took at the driving test until they passed. The results are summarised by the following frequency distribution:

Number of attempts	1	2	3	4	5	6	7	8+
Number of motorists	71	47	35	20	15	9	3	0

a   Calculate the sample mean x.

A statistician suggests that the number of attempts required to pass the driving test can be modelled by the random variable X defined as follows:

$P(X = r) = p(1 - p)^{r-1}$ for $r = 1, 2, 3, \ldots$

where p represents the probability of a motorist passing a particular test. You are given that, for this model, $E(X) = 1/p$, so that p can be estimated by $1/x$.

b   Calculate the expected frequencies according to the statistician's model.

c   Carry out an appropriate test, at the 5% level, to determine whether the model is a good one or not. State your hypotheses and conclusions carefully.

(MEI)

6 As part of a paired-sample signed test, the differences in the paired data were given the signs below. The (+) or (−) below each pair indicates whether the difference was positive or negative.

Pair	1	2	3	4	5	6	7	8	9	10
Sign	−	−	+	−	+	+	+	+	+	+

Test whether there is a difference in the population medians, using a two-tailed test at the 5% significance level.

(UCLES)

7 A dice is suspected of bias towards showing more sixes than would be expected of an ordinary dice. In order to test this, it is decided to throw the dice 12 times. The null hypothesis $p = \frac{1}{6}$, where p is the probability of the dice showing a six, will be rejected in favour of the alternative hypothesis $p > \frac{1}{6}$ if the number of sixes obtained is four or more. Calculate to three decimal places the probability of making:

a a Type I error   **b** a Type II error if, in fact, $p = \frac{1}{2}$.

Another way of testing the hypothesis is to throw the dice 120 times and reject the null hypothesis if the number of sixes obtained is m or more. Find the value of m for which the probability of making a Type I error is 0.01.

(UCLES)

8 A survey is to be carried out among hotel guests to discover what features they regard as important when choosing a hotel. In a pilot study guests were asked by the staff to rate a number of features as important or not important. The results for four features are shown below (the number rating each feature is not the same, as not all guests were asked to rate the same features).

	Adequate lighting for reading in bed	Comfortable beds	Courteous staff	Squash courts
Important	28	34	26	4
Not important	12	17	10	29

a Use the χ^2 distribution, at the 5% significance level, to test whether the proportion of guests rating a feature important is independent of the feature.

b Under what circumstances would it be necessary to pool the results from more than one feature in order to carry out a valid test?

c In the final survey 30 features were rated as unimportant, important or very important. The analysis of the resulting contingency table led to a value of 82.4 for $\sum |(O - E)^2 / E|$, with no features being pooled. Test, at the 5% significance level, whether the rating was independent of the feature.

(AEB)

9 The height, in centimetres, gained by a conifer in its first year after planting is denoted by the random variable X. The value of X is measured for a random sample of 86 conifers and the results obtained are summarised in the table.

X	<35	35–45	45–55	55–65	>65
Observed frequency	10	18	28	18	12

a Assuming that the random variable is modelled by a $N(50, 15^2)$ distribution, calculate the expected frequencies for each of the five classes.

b Carry out a χ^2 goodness of fit analysis to test, at the 5% significance level, the hypothesis that X can be modelled as in **a**.

(*UCLES*)

10 A survey in a college was commissioned to investigate whether or not there was any association between gender and passing a driving test. A group of 50 male and 50 female students were asked whether they passed or failed their driving test at the first attempt. All the students asked had taken the test. The results were as follows.

	Pass	Fail
Male	23	27
Female	32	18

Stating your hypotheses clearly test, at the 10% level, whether or not there is any evidence of an association between gender and passing a driving test at the first attempt.

(*ULEAC*)

Applications and Activities

1 From information gathered in geography, biology or social sciences, construct a contingency table and test whether the variables are independent.

Examples:
Geography – soil type against type of farming
Biology – hair colour against eye colour
Social Sciences – alcohol consumption against age.

2 Examine the relationship between GCSE grades and the sex of candidates.

Summary

- Observed data can be compared with expected outcomes using a chi-squared test:

$$\chi^2 = \sum \frac{(O-E)^2}{E}$$

- This test can be applied to data thought to follow a binomial distribution, a Poisson distribution or a normal distribution.

- For a 2×2 contingency table Yates' continuity connection must be used. This gives

$$\chi^2 = \sum \frac{(|O-E| - 0.5)^2}{E}$$

- A Type I error is made when H_0 is rejected when it is in fact true, that is H_0 should have been accepted.

- A Type II error is made when H_0 is accepted when it is false, that is H_0 should have been rejected and H_1 accepted.

Answers

All answers will be given to three significant figures or one decimal place unless stated otherwise.

2 Collection of Data

Review (p. 6)

1 a

Mark	Tally	Frequency
0	III	3
1	II	2
2	II	2
3	II	2
4	III	3
5	III	3
6	HII I	6
7	III	3
8	IIII	4
9	I	1
10	I	1
		30

b

Number of chairs	Tally	Frequency
1	I	1
2	HII	5
3	III	3
4	II	2
5	III	3
6	I	1
7	III	3
8	II	2
		20

2.1 Technique (p. 9)

1 a qualitative (blonde, brown, ginger)
b qualitative (male or female)
c quantitative, discrete
d quantitative, continuous
e qualitative (red, blue, green)
f qualitative (A, B, C)
g quantitative, discrete

2 a continuous   **d** continuous
b discrete   **e** discrete
c continuous   **f** discrete

2.2 Technique (p. 15)

4 Take 24 boys and 24 girls at random from the 20 classes. Take 6 boys and 6 girls at random from years 12 and 13.

5 a quota   **b** quota
c stratified   **d** stratified
or quota

2.2 Contextual (p. 15)

1 a Allocate a number to each student in the college starting 000 and finishing 599,

then generate 20 random numbers and the corresponding students constitute the sample.
b Take five at random from Year 7, three at random from each of Years 8, 9 and 10, two at random from each of Years 11, 12 and 13.
c Choose any five from Year 7, any three from each of the Years 8, 9 and 10, any two from each of Years 11, 12 and 13.

2 Take 45 at random from the first group, 90 at random from the second group and 15 at random from the third group.

2.3 Technique (p. 18)

2 a direct observation
b personal/postal/telephone survey
c personal survey

5 a Ambiguous, does it mean immediate or extended family?
b Offensive style of question and also very ambiguous, exactly what is meant by middle-aged?
c An emotionally worded style of question which is basically asking the respondent to agree.
d Too open, allows for too many responses that will be difficult to analyse.

Consolidation A (p. 19)

1 a qualitative   **b** quantitative
c quantitative   **d** qualitative

2 a discrete   **b** continuous
c discrete   **d** continuous

7 c Take a sample of 20 at random from the male students taking mathematics, 40 at random from the rest of the male students. Take 16 at random from female students taking mathematics and 24 at random from the rest of the female students.

Consolidation B (p. 21)

2 a qualitative   **b** quantitative
c quantitative   **d** quantitative

3 Data Analysis I

Review (p. 25)

1
a 64%	**d** 96%	**g** 28.2%
b 60%	**e** 120%	**h** 54.5%
c 135%	**f** 69.8%	**i** 48.1%
		j 146.2%

2
a 60% increase	**f** 15.1% decrease
b 25% decrease	**g** 20.2% increase
c 12.5% decrease	**h** 15.8% decrease
d 7.14% increase	**i** 20.6% decrease
e 71.05% increase	**j** 82.4% decrease

3
a 2304	**d** 36.69	**g** 5.0625
b 529	**e** 84.29	**h** 36
c 16	**f** 45.5625	**i** 4
		j 1.83

3.1 Contextual (p. 27)

1
a 10.6%
b 5.0%
c 1961 to 1971, 5.9% (0.59% per year)
d Scotland's population rises and falls throughout this period of time, with the general trend being downwards.
e 2031, 84.3%

2
a 45 to 59 year olds
b 1992
c 1992, 0.8%
d 16 to 24 year olds, 6.5%
e Relevant comments such as there being a decrease in the overall total from 1991 to 1994 then a small increase.

3.2 Contextual (p. 31)

1
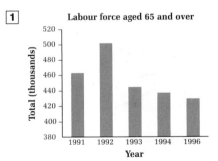
Labour force aged 65 and over

2
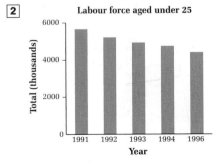
Labour force aged under 25

3
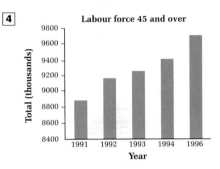
Labour force under 45

4

Labour force 45 and over

5 Relevant comments such as the number of under 25s has fallen at a similar rate each year.

6 The number of under 45s has fallen while the number of over 45s has risen.

3.3 Technique (p. 33)

1 and **2** a

1 and **2** b

1 and **2** c

1 and **2 d**

47° 89°
49°
51° 65°
59°

1 and **2 e**

22° 29°
76° 45°
69° 57°
62°

1 and **2 f**

65°
116°
78°
102°

1 and **2 g**

79°
180°
101°

1 and **2 h**

28°
129° 55°
65°
83°

1 and **2 i**

33°
103° 42°
42°
80° 59°

1 and **2 j**

23°
114° 50°
67°
105°

3.3 Contextual (p. 33)

1

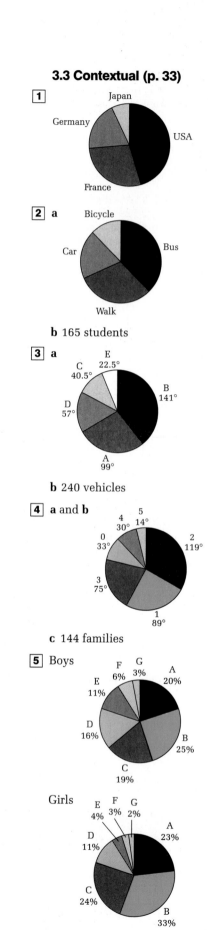

Japan
Germany
USA
France

2 a

Bicycle
Car
Bus
Walk

b 165 students

3 a

E 22.5°
C 40.5°
B 141°
D 57°
A 99°

b 240 vehicles

4 a and **b**

5 14°
4 30°
0 33°
2 119°
3 75°
1 89°

c 144 families

5 Boys

F 6° G 3%
E 11%
A 20%
D 16%
B 25%
C 19%

Girls

E 4% F 3% G 2%
D 11%
A 23%
C 24%
B 33%

Girls have achieved a larger proportion of grades A, B and C, particularly grade B. Boys have achieved a greater proportion of grade E.

3.4 Contextual (p. 36)

1

All items tend to show a sharp increase in cost in relation to their 1990 cost, but food less than others.

2

Most items show a slow increase or in some cases a decrease in relative cost.

3 Essential items seem to have generally increased while non-essential items have shown less of an increase or a reduction in relative costs.

3.5 Contextual (p. 41)

1 **a** 26 students **b** 8, 50, 42 (50 − 8)
c 29 (3 times) **d** 29

2

```
4 | 0 0
3 | 5 5 5 6 6 6 6 7 7 8 9 9
3 | 0 0 1 1 1 2 2 2 2 2 3 3 3 4 4
2 | 5 5 5 5 6 6 6 7 7 8 8 8 9 9 9 9 9 9
2 | 1 1 2 2 2 3 3 4 4 4
```
Key: 2|1 means 21 cm

a 57 eels **b** 19 cm **c** 29 cm **d** 30 cm

3

```
6 | 2
5 | 5 6 6
5 |
4 | 5 6 6 6 6 6 7
4 | 0 0 0 1 1 1 1 2 2 2 2 2 3 3
3 | 6 6 6 6 7 7 8 0 0
3 | 0 0 0 0 0 0 1 1 1 2 2 2 3 4 4 4 4 4 4 4
2 |
2 | 4 4 4 4 4
```
Key: 2|4 means 24 min

a 38 min **b** 37 min

4

Key: 5|0 means 5.0 cm

a 4.8 cm **b** 7.6 cm

3.6 Contextual (p. 44)

1 Some positive correlation

2 Some positive correlation

3 Negative correlation

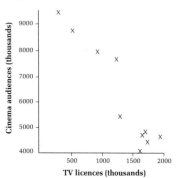

3.7 Contextual (p. 51)

1 Number of seeds germinating in 100 trays

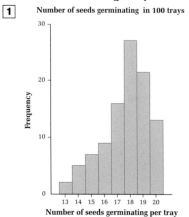

2 Distances travelled by commuters

3 Number of days between incidents of pollution on inland waterway

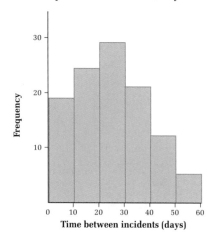

4 Group width 59.5–69.5, 69.5–79.5, 79.5–89.5, 89.5–99.5, 99.5–109.5, 109.5–119.5, 119.5–129.5, 129.5–139.5

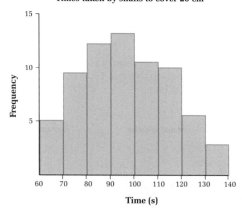

Times taken by snails to cover 20 cm

5

Group	0–2	2–4	4–8	8–12	12–18	18–24
Frequency density	6	12.5	4.5	4	1	0.5

Time intervals between trains

The scatter diagram appears to show negative correlation.

Although the crime rate is increasing over the period of time given, the unemployment rate fluctuates.

3 Death 25°, partnership split 32°, children leaving 47°, household move 216°, other 40°

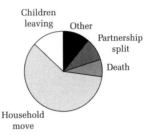

6 Group	Frequency density
332.5–	3
337.5–	17
339.5–	24.5
341.5–	12
342.5–	4.5
347.5–352.5	2

4 Height (cm)	Frequency	Width	Frequency density
110–	13	10	1.3
120–	18	10	1.8
130–	34	5	6.8
135–	27	5	5.4
140–	17	10	1.7
150–160	11	10	1.1

Volumes of 150 cans of lemonade

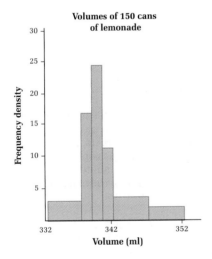

Consolidation A (p. 53)

1 a Bicycle 144°, bus 96°, car 43.2°, walk 76.8°

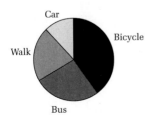

b 108 students

Heights of Year 7 girls

5 **a** 24

b C

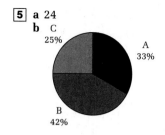

C

10–19	20–29	30–39	40–49	50–59	60–69
2	2	5	8	4	3

Test marks

6

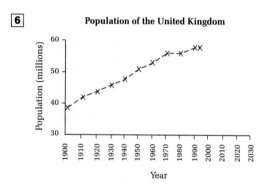

a 60 million, 62 million approximately
b 1900–1910, the steepest part of the graph

7

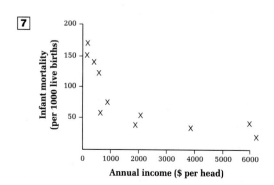

There is a negative correlation between infant mortality and income per head.

8 **a**

9	7				
9	0				
8	5	7	9		
8	3				
7	6				
7	2	3	3	3	3
6	5	7			
6	0	1	3	4	4
5	6	7	8		
5					
4	9				
4					
3	6	7			

Key: 3|6 means 36

b In most countries 55 to 75% of the population live in urban areas. The range is 61% from a minimum of 36% to a maximum of 97%. Only three countries have less than 50% of the population living in urban areas.

c Community   Others

9	7			9				
9	0			9				
8	5	7	9	8				
8	3			8				
7	6			7				
7	3			7	2	3	3	3
6	5	7		6				
6	3			6	0	1	4	4
5	6	8		5	7			
5				5				
4				4	9			
4				4				
3	6			3	7			

Key: 3|6 means 36

The indication from the diagrams is that the Community countries are more urbanised than the others, though the range of values for the community is larger. Half the Community countries are more urbanised than the maximum value of the other countries.

9 **a** 41 026, 42 188, 43 201, 43 611
There is a gradual rise in the number of people able to vote.
b 1979, 61.5%; 1983, 50.9%; 1987, 55%; 1992, 58.8%

c

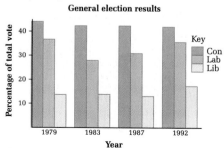

General election results

d The Labour share of the vote seems to fluctuate the most. The Conservative and

Liberal share of the vote remains fairly steady.

General Election Results 1992

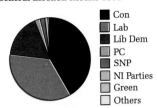

- ■ Con
- ■ Lab
- ■ Lib Dem
- ■ PC
- ■ SNP
- ■ NI Parties
- ■ Green
- □ Others

10 **a**

Age	Frequency
0	5
1	8
2	8
3	9
4	11
5	6
6	8
7	9
8	6
9	7
10	2
11	4
12	2
13	2
14	3
15	2
16	2
17	1
18	2
19	0
20	0
21	0
22	2
23	1

b

Ages of 100 cars

c

Age	Frequency
0–1	13
2–3	17
4–5	17
6–7	17
8–9	13
10–12	8
13–15	7
16–20	5
21–25	3

d

Ages of 100 cars

e Grouping the figures gives a distribution that is more evenly spread, but highlights the drop in numbers as the age increases.

Consolidation B (p. 56)

1 **a** Train 101°, bus 86°, car 126°, walk 47°

b 150

2

There is a positive correlation between unemployment rate and the number of crimes.

3 **a** 18°, 58°, 68°, 176°, 40°

b

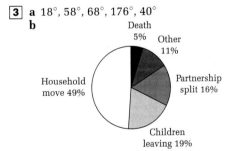

4

Height (cm)	Frequency	Width	Frequency density
115–	17	5	3.4
120–	28	5	5.6
125–	25	10	2.5
135–	19	10	1.9
145–	8	15	0.53
160–175	3	15	0.2

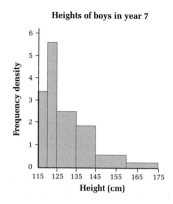

Heights of boys in year 7

5 a 35
b

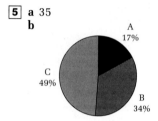

A 17%
B 34%
C 49%

c

Mark	Frequency
10–14	4
15–19	5
20–24	10
25–29	7
30–34	6
35–39	3
	35

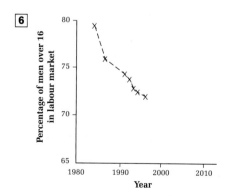

6

a 71%, 67%
b 1984–1986 the steepest part of the graph

7

There appears to be a positive link between the hours worked and the mortality rate from circulatory disease.

8 a Men

```
6 |
6 | 3
6 | 4  5
6 |
6 | 8  9
7 | 0  0  0  0
7 | 2  3  3  3
7 | 4  4  4  4  4  4  5  5  5  5
7 | 6  6
7 |
8 |
8 |
8 |
```
Key: 6|3 means 63

b Women

```
6 |
6 |
6 |
6 |
6 |
6 |
7 |
7 |
7 | 5  5  5
7 | 6  6  6  6  6
7 | 8  9  9  9  9
8 | 0  0  0  1  1  1  1  1  1  1
8 | 2  2
8 |
```
Key: 7|5 means 75

c From the diagrams the life expectancy of women is longer than men. Generally it seems that women live five years longer than men.

9 **a** 1168.3, 3171.5, 1522.6, 935.6 (thousands)
   b 30.3%, 19.3%, 36.1%, 28.7%

By-election results

c The Labour percentage of voters has fluctuated throughout the period while the Conservative percentage has remained constant and the Liberal percentage has steadily increased.

d
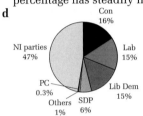

The indications are, from the table of results, that there were more by-elections in NI constituencies.

10 **a**

Tens	Units									
	0	1	2	3	4	5	6	7	8	9
1	0	3	2	3	1	0	0	3	2	3
2	3	5	0	1	2	5	0	3	3	3
3	2	0	1	3	3	3	3	7	2	3
4	1	3	3	4	3	1	0	1	3	4
5	2	0	1	2	0	1	2			

Frequency table: Numbers in the table represent the frequency of the number formed by the intersection of the row and the column.

b

Fuel consumption

c

Group	Frequency
10–14	9
15–19	8
20–24	11
25–29	14
30–34	9
35–39	18
40–44	14
45–49	9
50–55	5
56–59	3

d
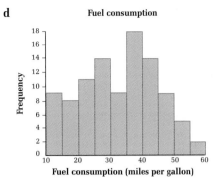
Fuel consumption

e The grouped data tend to indicate that there are two different sets of results centering around 20–29 and 35–44. In the original figures there seemed to be a wide spread of results.

4 Data Analysis II

Review (p. 62)

1 **a** 25, 165, 140, 140
   b 46, 182, 136, 136
   c 114, 1636, 1522, 152
   d 3.9, 1.63, −2.27
   e 27.56, 112.22, 84.66, 84.66
   f −2, 124, 126, 126
   g 12, 25.625, 13.625, 13.625
   h 52, 396.5, 344.5, 344.5.

In each case, the last two answers are the same. Therefore $\Sigma(x^2 - x)$, and $\Sigma x^2 - \Sigma x$ are equal.

2 **a**
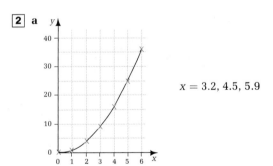
$x = 3.2, 4.5, 5.9$

b
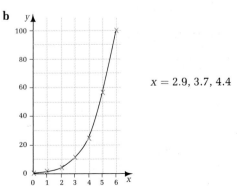
$x = 2.9, 3.7, 4.4$

c

$x = 2.6, 4.3, 6.3$

d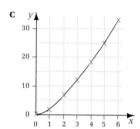

$x = 2.2, 3.2, 4.3$

4.1 Technique (p. 64)

1. 15.2, 15, 15
2. 33.8, 36, 35.5
3. −0.1, −1, −1
4. 4.95, 5, 5
5. 38.7, 47, 38
6. 0.6875, −2, 0
7. 29.9, 26 and 34, 27
8. 3.53, none, 4.25
9. 6.98, 7.4, 7.3
10. 0.687, 0.7, 0.7

4.1 Contextual (p. 64)

1. **a** 29, 29
   b 27.77
   c 29, as it represents the most frequently occurring score and the middle score

2. **a** 7.8 cm and 9.3 cm
   b 7.6 cm
   c 7.46 cm

3. **a** 34 min
   b 37 min
   c 37.78 min
   d It is difficult to give an accurate average for the times because of the wide range of values and because there is a group of values at each end of the range, but 37 minutes would be the best measure of an average to use.

4.2 Contextual (p. 67)

1. **a** 17.62 plants
   b 18 plants
   c 18 plants

   The mode, as it reflects what the most trays have.

2. **a** 17.97 km   **b** 15 km   **c** 15 km

3. **a** 70.65 kg   **b** 71 kg   **c** 70 kg

4. **a** 4.77 min   **b** 0 min   **c** 0 min

5.

Scores	Section 1	Section 2	Section 3
5.8	1	1	0
5.7	1	0	0
5.6	3	1	4
5.5	2	2	2
5.4	2	2	1
5.3	1	1	0
5.2	0	3	1
5.1	0	0	2
Averages			
Mean	5.54	5.41	5.42
Median	5.55	5.4	5.5
Mode	5.6	5.2	5.6

4.3 Contextual (p. 73)

1. **a** 30 to 40   **b** 36.5   **c** 35.54

2. **a** 10 to 12   **b** 11.58

3. **a** 340 to 341   **b** 340.8   **c** 340.6

4. **a** 80 to 100   **b** 83.8   **c** 85

5. 71.7%

4.4 Technique (p. 76)

1.

cf	6	25	46	70	86	90
Max	5	10	15	20	25	31

2.

cf	2	9	28	61	88	112	134	150
Max	15	20	25	30	40	50	60	80

3.

cf	Max
18	24.5
46	29.5
78	34.5
100	39.5
117	44.5
130	49.5
139	54.5
145	59.5
150	64.5

4.

cf	Max
4	5
15	10
47	15
93	20
137	25
166	30
183	35
194	40
200	45

5

cf	Max (£1000s)
5.5	4
12.6	6
21.9	8
37.8	10
49.0	12
63.6	15
82.5	20
91.9	25
96.0	30
98.8	50
100.0	100

6 a

b

c

d

e

7 **a** 14   **b** 35   **c** 34
   d 20.5   **e** £12 000

4.4 Contextual (p. 77)

1 **a** mean = 23.94 min

b

Group	Max	cf
10–14	14.5	8
15–19	19.5	30
20–24	24.5	64
25–29	29.5	94
30–35	35.5	120

c median = 23.9 min

2 **a** mean = 15.8 years

b

Group	Max	cf
13–15	15	48
15–16	16	132
16–17	17	222
17–20	20	240

Age (years)

c 16 years

3 **a** mean = 64.62 kg

b

Group	Max	cf
50–55	55	32
55–60	60	72
60–65	65	134
65–70	70	185
70–75	75	221
75–80	80	250

Weight (kg)

c median = 64.5 kg

4 median = 85

Score

5 median = 46.5 min

Time (min)

4.5 Technique (p. 81)

1 $Q_1 = 9.5$, $Q_3 = 20$, IQR = 10.5, 0–6 years, 24–30 years

2 $Q_1 = 26$, $Q_3 = 51$, IQR = 25, 0–21 cm, 58–80 cm

3 $Q_1 = 28.5$, $Q_3 = 43$, IQR = 14.5, 20–24 m, 49–65 m

4 $Q_1 = 15.5$, $Q_3 = 27$, IQR = 11.5, 0–11 s, 31–45 s

5 $Q_1 = 8300$, $Q_3 = 18\,000$, IQR = 9700, £0–£8000, £21 000–£100 000

4.6 Technique (p. 84)

1

2

3

4

5

4.6 Contextual (p. 85)

1

2

3

4

5

4.7 Technique (p. 89)

1
a 6, 3.46	**f** 0.42, 0.194
b 16.75, 9.44	**g** 0.13, 0.018
c 10.83, 6.18	**h** 2.70, 1.186
d 51.3, 5.75	**i** -1.19, 2.098
e 3.87, 0.367	**j** -0.656, 2.318

2
a 3.45, 1.55	**d** 0.31, 0.206
b 18.63, 3.29	**e** 1.143, 0.581
c 4.06, 0.99	

4.8 Technique (p. 92)

1 13.5, 6.63

2 32.78, 12.61

3 3.91, 1.74

4 3.922, 5.897

5 20.30, 16.20

4.8 Contextual (p. 92)

1 15.35, 1.52

2 a
Group	Max	cf
50–74	74.5	57
75–99	99.5	323
100–149	149.5	531
150–199	199.5	724
200–299	299.5	819
300–399	399.5	900
400–599	599.5	955
600–999	999.5	1000

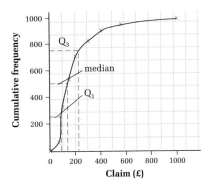

b £201.71, £170.11
c The standard deviation is relatively high compared to the mean.

3 35.3, 18.9

4 3.10, 6.23

5 47.38, 19.00

The mean value of the sample is within a reasonable range for the required mean of 50, that is $50 \pm 5\%$. However the standard deviation is double the value that is required, indicating that the spread of marks is too great.

Consolidation A (p. 94)

1 total weight of boys
$= 7 \times 58.1\,\text{kg} = 406.7\,\text{kg}$

total weight of girls
$= 13 \times 62.7\,\text{kg} = 815.1\,\text{kg}$

total weight $= 1221.8\,\text{kg}$

mean weight $= 1221.8 \div 20 = 61.09\,\text{kg}$

2 a median $= \frac{1}{2}(\pounds274 + \pounds329) = \pounds301.50$
$Q_1 = \pounds188$, $Q_3 = \pounds435$
b

c mean = £4816 ÷ 14 = £344

$$s^2 = \frac{\sum x^2}{n} - \bar{x}^2$$

$$= \frac{2\,069\,822}{14} - 344^2 = 29\,508.429$$

$$s = \sqrt{29\,508.429} = £171.78 \text{ (2 d.p.)}$$

3

Group	Width	Frequency	Frequency density
160–169	10	16	1.6
170–174	5	12	2.4
175–179	5	20	4
180–189	10	30	3
190–204	15	12	0.8

Competitors' times

modal group is 175–179

4 **a**

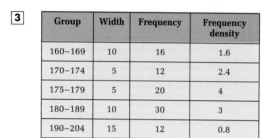

Contents of 220 match boxes

b mode = 65 matches, median = 65 matches, mean = 14 430 ÷ 220
= 65.59 matches
c mode, as most boxes contain 65 matches

5

Group	Max	Frequency	cf
80–84	84.5	12	12
85–89	89.5	38	50
90–94	94.5	45	95
95–99	99.5	32	127
100–104	104.5	23	150

a median = 92 min
b Q_3 = 97 min, Q_1 = 88 min,
IQR = 97 − 88 = 9 min
c 20%

new median is 94 min

6 **a**

Group	Width	Frequency	Height
0–4	0.5	260	$\frac{260}{50} = 5.2$
5–14	1	543	$\frac{543}{100} = 5.4$
15–44	3	1727	$\frac{1727}{300} = 5.8$
45–64	2	756	$\frac{756}{200} = 3.8$
65–79	1.5	577	$\frac{577}{150} = 3.8$
80 and over	2	135	$\frac{135}{200} = 0.7$

b

Ages in an area of the UK

c

Midpoint	Frequency
2.5	260
10	543
30	1727
55	756
72.5	577
90	135

mean = 153 452.5 ÷ 3998 = 38.38 years

d $\sigma^2 = \dfrac{\sum fx^2}{n} - \mu^2 = \dfrac{8\,023\,481.25}{3998} - 1473.2$

$= 533.67$ so $\sigma = 23.1$ years

7 a

```
9 │ 0   3   5   8
8 │ 1   5   6
7 │ 1   2   4   5   6   8
6 │ 2   5
5 │ 0   3   3   3   4   8   8   8
4 │ 0   0   4   4   5   6   7
3 │ 3   4   6   6   7   7   8   9
2 │ 1   3   6   7   7   8   9   9
1 │ 5   7   8   9
```

Key: 1│5 means 15 minutes

b median = 45.5 min, Q_1 = 33 min,
Q_3 = 71 min

c

Group	Midpoint	Frequency	Group total
10–19	14.5	4	58
20–29	24.5	8	196
30–39	34.5	8	276
40–49	44.5	7	311.5
50–59	54.5	8	436
60–69	64.5	2	129
70–79	74.5	6	447
80–89	84.5	3	253.5
90–99	94.5	4	378
	Totals	50	2485

d

mean = 2485 ÷ 50 = 49.7 min

e $s^2 = \dfrac{\Sigma fx^2}{n} - \bar{x}^2 = \dfrac{151\,552.5}{50} - 49.7^2 = 560.96$

$s = 23.68$ min

8 a mean = $(1 + 2 + 3 + 4 + 5) \div 5 = 3$

X	$X - \bar{x}$	$(X - \bar{x})^2$
1	−2	4
2	−1	1
3	0	0
4	1	1
5	2	4

$\sigma^2 = 10 \div 5 = 2$, so $\sigma = 1.41$

b Similarly, mean = 7.5, $\sigma = 1.12$

c

			X		
	+	1	2	3	4	5
	6	7	8	9	10	11
Y	7	8	9	10	11	12
	8	9	10	11	12	13
	9	10	11	12	13	14

Number	Frequency	fz
7	1	7
8	2	16
9	3	27
10	4	40
11	4	44
12	3	36
13	2	26
14	1	14
		Total = 210

d mean = 210 ÷ 20 = 10.5

$$S_z^2 = \frac{\Sigma fz^2}{n} - \bar{z}^2 = \frac{2270}{20} - 10.5^2 = 3.25$$

$S_z = 1.80$

e value is 10.5 ± 1.8 which is 8.7 to 12.3, frequency is 14, giving 70%

f $M_z = M_x + M_y$, $S_z^2 = S_x^2 + S_y^2$

9 a 14, 13, 8, 3

b median = 13 min, Q_1 = 6 min,
Q_3 = 21.5 min

c 8.5 min

d

e

f Data is positively skewed, that is there is a greater number of lower values than higher values.

10 a i 160.7, 4.16

ii 152.38–169.02, 175

b i Less

ii Less

c $a = 20$, $m_2 = 159.947$

Consolidation B (p. 97)

1 total height of boys
= 13 × 1.69 m = 21.97 m

total height of girls
= 12 × 1.62 m = 19.44 m

total height = 41.41 m

mean height = 41.41 ÷ 25 = 1.6564 m

2 a median = $\frac{1}{2}$(£357 + £396) = £376.50
Q_1 = £244, Q_3 = £559

b

c mean = £7226 ÷ 18 = £401.44

$$s^2 = \frac{\Sigma fx^2}{n} - \bar{x}^2 = \frac{3\,601\,222}{18} - 401.44^2$$

$$= 38\,913.82$$

$$s = £197.26$$

3

Group	Width	Frequency	Frequency density
200–219	20	36	1.8
220–229	10	65	6.5
230–249	20	158	7.9
250–269	20	84	4.2
270–300	30	45	1.5

Times in a marathon race

modal group is 230–249

4 **a**

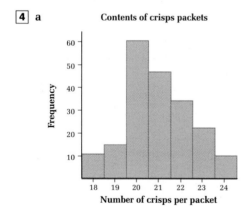

Contents of crisps packets

b mode = 20 crisps, median = 21 crisps,
mean = 4184 ÷ 200 = 20.92 crisps
c mode as most packets contain 20 crisps,
or median as that suggests more crisps per
packet

5

Group	Max	Frequency	cf
5–7	7.5	4	4
8–10	10.5	13	17
11–13	13.5	37	54
14–16	16.5	28	82
17–19	19.5	18	100

Times on obstacle course

a median = 13.2 minutes
b Q_3 = 15.8 min, Q_1 = 11.1 min,
IQR = 4.7 min
c 32%

new median is 14.1 min

6 **a**

Group	Width	Frequency	Height
0–9	2	531	$\frac{531}{200} = 2.7$
10–14	1	657	$\frac{657}{100} = 6.6$
15–29	3	1452	$\frac{1452}{300} = 4.8$
30–49	4	1899	$\frac{1899}{400} = 4.7$
50–69	4	740	$\frac{740}{400} = 1.9$
70 and over	6	463	$\frac{463}{600} = 0.8$

b

Ages in a UK region

c

Midpoint	Frequency
5	531
12.5	657
22.5	1452
40	1899
60	740
85	463

mean = 203 252.5 ÷ 5742 = 35.40 years
d $s^2 = \frac{\Sigma fx^2}{n} - \bar{x}^2 = \frac{9\,898\,581}{5742} - 35.40^2$

$$= 470.73$$

$$s = 21.70$$

7 **a**

```
9 | 0  1  1  8
8 | 2  2  3  3  4  5  5  6  8  9
7 | 2  3  4  6  6  7
6 | 1  3  3  4  4  4  6  7  7  8
5 | 0  2  3  4  5  6  8  8  8  9  9  9
4 | 0  0  1  1  2  2  2  3  5
3 | 0  2  4  4  6  6  7
2 | 2  3  4  4  5  8
1 | 1  3  4  5  6  6
```

Key : 1|5 means 15 cm

b median = 58 cm, Q_1 = 36 cm, Q_3 = 74 cm

c

```
        Q₁            Q₃
 ┌──────┬────────┬───────┐
─┤      │        ┊       ├─
 └──────┴────────┴───────┘
 min         median      max
 ├──┬──┬──┬──┬──┬──┬──┬──┬──┬──┤
 0  10 20 30 40 50 60 70 80 90 100
        Length (cm)
```

d

Group	Midpoint	Frequency	Group total
10–19	14.5	6	87
20–29	24.5	6	147
30–39	34.5	7	241.5
40–49	44.5	9	400.5
50–59	54.5	12	654
60–69	64.5	10	645
70–79	74.5	6	447
80–89	84.5	10	845
90–99	94.5	4	378
	Totals	70	3845

mean = 3845 ÷ 70 = 54.93 cm

e $s^2 = \dfrac{\Sigma fx^2}{n} - \bar{x}^2 = \dfrac{248\,687.5}{70} - 54.93^2$

$= 535.37$

$s = 23.14$ cm

8 **a** mean = $(2 + 4 + 6 + 8) \div 4 = 5$

X	$X - \bar{x}$	$(X - \bar{x})^2$
2	−3	9
4	−1	1
6	1	1
8	3	9
		Total = 20

$\sigma^2 = 20 \div 4 = 5$

$\sigma = 2.24$

b similarly, mean = 5, $\sigma = 2.83$

c

		X			
+	1	3	5	7	9
2	3	5	7	9	11
4	5	7	9	11	13
6	7	9	11	13	15
8	9	11	13	15	17

(Y down the left side)

Number	Frequency	fx
3	1	3
5	2	10
7	3	21
9	4	36
11	4	44
13	3	39
15	2	30
17	1	17
		Total = 200

d mean = 200 ÷ 20 = 10

$s^2 = \dfrac{\Sigma x^2}{n} - \bar{x}^2 = \dfrac{2260}{20} - 10^2 = 13$

$s = 3.61$

e value is 10 ± 3.61, which is 6.39 to 13.61, frequency is 14, giving 70%

f $M_z = M_x + M_y$, $S_z^2 = S_x^2 + S_y^2$

9 **a** 11, 9, 8, 1

b median = 14 min, Q_1 = 6 min, Q_3 = 23 min

c 20 min

d

```
     Q₁        Q₃
 ┌───┬─────┬─────────┐
─┤   │     ┊         ├─────────────
 └───┴─────┴─────────┘
 min median          max
 ├────┬────┬────┬────┬────┬────┤
 0    10   20   30   40   50   60
                     Time (min)
```

e

the data is very slightly positively skewed (caption: min median max, Q₁ Q₃)

f the data is very slightly positively skewed

10 **a** **i** 68.2, 6.45

ii 55.3–81.1

iii 51

b **i** greater

ii less

c **i** $a = 20$

ii $m_2 = 69.11$

5 Probability

Review (p. 102)

1 three – each team can win, draw or lose

2 **a** if today is Monday then 1, otherwise 0

b will depend on the current weather

3 $\frac{2}{3}$

4 **a** $\frac{2}{6} = \frac{1}{3}$ **b** 0 **c** $\frac{4}{6} = \frac{2}{3}$

5.1 Contextual (p. 106)

1 **a** $\frac{1}{3}$ **b** $\frac{1}{5}$ **c** $\frac{11}{30}$

2 **a** $\frac{4}{5}$ **b** $\frac{2}{25}$ **c** $\frac{2}{5}$

3 **a** $\frac{1}{15}$ **b** $\frac{19}{30}$

4 **a** $\frac{3}{28}$ **b** $\frac{19}{28}$ **c** $\frac{9}{28}$

5 **a** $\frac{2}{5}$ **b** $\frac{29}{30}$

6 **a** $\frac{3}{20}$ **b** $\frac{13}{30}$ **c** $\frac{23}{30}$

5.2 Contextual (p. 110)

1 **a** $\frac{4}{13}$ **b** $\frac{1}{2}$ **c** $\frac{7}{13}$

2 **a** $\frac{2}{5}$ **b** $\frac{3}{5}$ **c** $\frac{1}{2}$

3 **a** $\frac{5}{8}$ **b** $\frac{3}{8}$

4 **a** mutually exclusive and exhaustive
b not mutually exclusive nor exhaustive
c not mutually exclusive nor exhaustive

5 **a** $\frac{1}{2}$ **b** $\frac{1}{3}$ **c** $\frac{2}{3}$ **d** $\frac{2}{3}$

6 **a** 0.6 **b** 0.4 **c** 0.9

7 K and L are mutually exclusive as
$P(\text{K} \cup \text{L}) = P(\text{K}) + P(\text{L})$

5.3 Contextual (p. 113)

1 **a** $\frac{1}{6}$ **b** $\frac{1}{6}$ **c** $\frac{1}{12}$

2 **a** 0.12 **b** 0.58

3 **a** 0.2, 0.06
b B and C are not independent as
$P(\text{B} \cap \text{C}) \neq P(\text{B}) \times P(\text{C})$

4 $\frac{6}{25}$ **b** $\frac{12}{125}$

5 **a** $\frac{1}{16}$ **b** $\frac{1}{4}$

6 **a** $\frac{4}{15}$ **b** $\frac{1}{10}$

5.4 Contextual (p. 116)

1 **a** 0.4 **b** 0.5

2 $\frac{3}{4}$

3 **a** $\frac{3}{10}$ **b** $\frac{1}{2}$

4 **a** $\frac{1}{17}$ **b** $\frac{4}{51}$

5 **a** $\frac{8}{15}$ **b** $\frac{4}{15}$ **c** $\frac{8}{15}$

6 $\frac{4}{5}$

R and S are not mutually exclusive as
$P(\text{R} \cap \text{S}) \neq 0$

7 **a** $\frac{5}{12}$ **b** $\frac{5}{33}$ **c** $\frac{7}{11}$

8 **a** 0.2 **b** 0.25

9 **a** $\frac{7}{10}$ **b** $\frac{3}{5}$ **c** $\frac{1}{3}$

5.5 Contextual (p. 120)

1 **a** $\frac{9}{64}$ **b** $\frac{15}{32}$

2 $\frac{5}{14}$

3 **a** $\frac{1}{75}$ **b** $\frac{58}{75}$

4 **a**

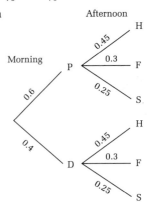

b **i** 0.1
ii 0.33

5 0.002 25

6 0.48, 0.288

Consolidation A (p. 121)

1 **a** $\frac{1}{17}$ **b** $\frac{25}{102}$ **c** $\frac{26}{51}$

2 **a** 0.02 **b** 0.45

3 **a** $\frac{1}{100}$ **b** $\frac{2}{5}$

4 **a** **i** Mutually exclusive because score
cannot be 1 or 2, *and* 3 or 4. Not
exhaustive because score could be
5 or 6.
ii C could be the event {score is greater
than 1}
b **i** 0.08
ii 0.75

5 **a** $\frac{7}{60}$ **b** $\frac{1}{2}$ **c** $\frac{13}{60}$

6 **a** $\frac{1}{4}$ **b** $\frac{2}{9}$

7 **a** 0.1 **b** 0.8 **c** 0.2
d 0.3 **e** $P(\text{B} \cap \text{C}) = 0$

8 **a** 0.55 **b** 0.18

9 **a** $\frac{1}{4}$ **b** $\frac{1}{4}$ **c** $\frac{9}{28}$

10 $\frac{1}{3}$

Consolidation B (p. 122)

1 **a** $\frac{9}{256}$ **b** $\frac{9}{16}$ **c** $\frac{5}{32}$

2 0.296

3 **a** $\frac{5}{8}$ **b** $\frac{5}{8}$ **c** $\frac{1}{4}$

4 **a** 0.09 **b** 0.24

5 **a** $\frac{7}{15}$
b A and C are not independent as
$P(\text{A}) \times P(\text{B}) \neq P(\text{A} \cap \text{B})$

6 a $\frac{4}{25}$ b $\frac{1}{5}$ c $\frac{18}{25}$

7 a $\frac{9}{20}$ b $\frac{21}{38}$ c $\frac{17}{38}$

8 $\frac{1}{12}, \frac{1}{9}$

9 a 0.004   b 0.604   c 0.006 62 (3 s.f.)

10 a 0.1   b 0.452

6 Permutations and Combinations

Review (p. 126)

1 $\frac{2}{3}$

2 $\frac{18}{29}$

3 $\frac{245}{696}$

6.1 Technique (p. 132)

1 a 11 880   b 720 720   c 41 186 376

2 a $\frac{8!}{5!}$ b $\frac{18!}{14!}$ c $\frac{12!}{10!}$

3 a 12   b 336   c 1 235 520

4 a 168   b 840   c 10 080

6.1 Contextual (p. 132)

1 40 320

2 a 24   b 360   c 50 400

3 720, 480

4 726 485 760

5 2520, 720

6 15, 2

7 336

8 747

9 5040

10 60

6.2 Contextual (p. 136)

1 28

2 a 210   b 185

3 2002

4 70, 5

5 675

6 a 120   b 112

7 56, 20

8 a 1287   b 525   c 420   d 756

9 15

10 a 462   b 210   c 200   d 281

Consolidation A (p. 138)

1 5040, 720

2 a i 16   ii 90
b 112

3 40 320, 4320

4 a 10   b 150   c 16   d 12

5 39 916 800, 7776

6 364

7 a 70   b 65

8 a 60 480   b 5040

9 a 360   b 180   c 120

10 a 210   b 60   c 105   d 100

Consolidation B (p. 139)

1 362 880, 17 280

2 84

3 a 495   b 225   c 15

4 a 12!   b 495

5 a 312   b 19 440

6 2520

7 a 30 240   b i 840
ii 2520
iii 240

8 a 300   b 786   c 396

9 a 1440   b 14 400

10 $\frac{11!}{2!\,2!\,2!} = 4\,989\,600$

7 Discrete Probability Distributions

Review (p. 142)

1 a 16.56   b 5.38   c 0.74

2 a 2.55   b 18.50   c 0.19

7.1 Contextual (p. 147)

1 a i

x	2	3	4	5	6	7	8	9	10	11	12
$P(X=x)$	$\frac{1}{36}$	$\frac{2}{36}$	$\frac{3}{36}$	$\frac{4}{36}$	$\frac{5}{36}$	$\frac{6}{36}$	$\frac{5}{36}$	$\frac{4}{36}$	$\frac{3}{36}$	$\frac{2}{36}$	$\frac{1}{36}$

ii $\frac{5}{6}$ iii $X = 7$

b

x	2	3	4	5	6	7	8	9	10	11	12
Expected frequency	1.9	3.9	5.8	7.8	9.7	11.7	9.7	7.8	5.8	3.9	1.9

2 a

x	0	1	2
$P(X=x)$	$\frac{4}{15}$	$\frac{8}{15}$	$\frac{1}{5}$

3 a

y	0	1	2	3
$P(Y=y)$	$\frac{1}{8}$	$\frac{3}{8}$	$\frac{3}{8}$	$\frac{1}{8}$

b $\frac{1}{2}$

4 a

x	10	20	50
$P(X = x)$	$\frac{1}{6}$	$\frac{3}{6}$	$\frac{2}{6}$

b

y	30p	40p	60p	70p	£1
$P(Y = y)$	$\frac{1}{5}$	$\frac{1}{5}$	$\frac{2}{15}$	$\frac{2}{5}$	$\frac{1}{15}$

5 a

x	0	1	2	3	4
$P(X = x)$	0.055	0.25	0.39	0.25	0.055

b 0.305

6 a $\frac{1}{15}$ **b** $\frac{2}{5}$

7 a $\frac{1}{7}$ **b** $\frac{6}{7}$

8 $\frac{3}{16}$

9

x		1	2	3	4
Expected frequency		96	24	48	72

10

c	1	2	3	4	6
$P(C = c)$	$\frac{3}{20}$	$\frac{1}{2}$	$\frac{3}{20}$	$\frac{3}{20}$	$\frac{1}{20}$

7.2 Technique (p. 154)

1 a $\frac{7}{6}$ **b** $\frac{5}{8}$

2 a 5 **b** 9

3 a 3 **b** 10 **c** 13

7.2 Contextual (p. 154)

1 7

2 a 28.3 **b** 56.7

3 2

7.3 Technique (p. 159)

1 a 2.34 **b** $\frac{23}{16}$

2 a 6.4 **b** 19.64

4 a 5 **b** 2.5 **c** 22.5 **d** 22.5

5 a

w	0	1	2	3
$P(W = w)$	$\frac{1}{8}$	$\frac{3}{8}$	$\frac{3}{8}$	$\frac{1}{8}$

b 1.5 **c** 0.75 **d** 3

6 a $\frac{1}{6}$ **b** 4.17 **c** 0.806

7.4 Technique (p. 164)

1 a 3.5 **b** 14 **c** 13 **d** 86

2 a −1 **b** cannot be found
c 1 **d** 9

3 a 1.3, 2.05 **b** 0.61, 1.75

4 a 0.6, 2.7 **b** 0.24, 0.21
c 3.5 **d** 7.89

5 a

r	1	2	3	4	5	6
$P(R = r)$	$\frac{1}{6}$	$\frac{1}{6}$	$\frac{1}{6}$	$\frac{1}{6}$	$\frac{1}{6}$	$\frac{1}{6}$

The above table for R_1 and R_2.

b

s	2	3	4	5	6	7	8	9	10	11	12
$P(S = s)$	$\frac{1}{36}$	$\frac{2}{36}$	$\frac{3}{36}$	$\frac{4}{36}$	$\frac{5}{36}$	$\frac{6}{36}$	$\frac{5}{36}$	$\frac{4}{36}$	$\frac{3}{36}$	$\frac{2}{36}$	$\frac{1}{36}$

c 7 **d** $5\frac{5}{6}$

Consolidation A (p. 165)

1 a

x	0	1	2	3
$P(X = x)$	$\frac{4}{91}$	$\frac{27}{91}$	$\frac{216}{455}$	$\frac{12}{65}$

b $1\frac{4}{5}$ **c** $\frac{108}{175}$

2 a

y	1	2	3	4	6	8	9	12	16
$P(Y = y)$	$\frac{1}{16}$	$\frac{2}{16}$	$\frac{2}{16}$	$\frac{3}{16}$	$\frac{2}{16}$	$\frac{2}{16}$	$\frac{1}{16}$	$\frac{2}{16}$	$\frac{1}{16}$

b $\frac{5}{16}$ **c** 4

d

y	1	2	3	4	6	8	9	12	16
Expected frequency	6.25	12.5	12.5	18.75	12.5	12.5	6.25	12.5	6.25

3 a $5\frac{1}{3}$ **b** 1.768

4 a 0.15 **b** 12 **c** 46.8, 14.31

5 b $\frac{11}{6}$, $4\frac{5}{36}$

6 a 4.38, 5.01 **b** 0.6

7 a $\frac{1}{4}$ **b** 3.5 **c** 1.917 **d** £1.05

8 b $\frac{49}{99}$

9 b

q	1	2	3	4	6
$P(Q = q)$	$\frac{1}{12}$	$\frac{1}{3}$	$\frac{1}{12}$	$\frac{1}{3}$	$\frac{1}{6}$

d $2\frac{7}{18}$

10 a $\frac{1}{13}$, $\frac{1}{13}$ **b** 2.769, 0.331

c

y	50	25	15	0
$P(Y = y)$	$\frac{1}{13}$	$\frac{1}{13}$	$\frac{1}{13}$	$\frac{10}{13}$
	$P(X = 1)$	$P(X = 2)$	P(3rd guess correct)	P(3rd guess incorrect)

$6\frac{12}{13}$

d £6.15

Consolidation B (p. 167)

1

z	0	1	2	3	4	5
$P(Z = z)$	$\frac{1}{6}$	$\frac{5}{18}$	$\frac{2}{9}$	$\frac{1}{6}$	$\frac{1}{9}$	$\frac{1}{18}$

1.94, 1.43

2 a 12.8 **b** 36

3 a 4.7 **b** 13 **c** 6.7 **d** 52

4 a $\frac{1}{16}$ **b** $3\frac{7}{16}$

5 a

z	2	3	4	5	6	7	8	9	10	11	12
$P(Z = z)$	$\frac{1}{36}$	$\frac{2}{36}$	$\frac{3}{36}$	$\frac{4}{36}$	$\frac{5}{36}$	$\frac{6}{36}$	$\frac{5}{36}$	$\frac{4}{36}$	$\frac{3}{36}$	$\frac{2}{36}$	$\frac{1}{36}$

b 7 **c** $5\frac{5}{6}$

6 2.449, 2.574

7 b i $Y = 4X - 8$
ii £8.80

8 **b** $6\frac{2}{3}$ **c** $6\frac{2}{9}$

9 $\frac{5}{9}$

10 **a** 24
   b $P(X = 3) = 0$ since impossible to get just one wrong matching
   c $\frac{1}{4}, \frac{1}{3}$

x	0	1	2	3	4
$P(X = x)$	$\frac{3}{8}$	$\frac{1}{3}$	$\frac{1}{4}$	0	$\frac{1}{24}$

   d 1, 1
   e 0.316

8 Binomial, Geometric and Poisson Distributions

Review (p. 171)

1 **a** 15   **b** 10   **c** 495
   d 8   **e** 10   **f** 1

2 1.75, 1.3875

3 $2\frac{1}{2}$, 1

8.1 Technique (p. 174)

1 $x^5 + 5x^4y + 10x^3y^2 + 10x^2y^3 + 5xy^4 + y^5$

2 $a^7 + 7a^6b + 21a^5b^2 + 35a^4b^3 + 35a^3b^4 + 21a^2b^5 + 7ab^6 + b^7$

3 **a** $924p^6q^6$ **b** $495p^8q^4$ **c** $66p^{10}q^2$

4 70

5 **a** 4   **b** 3060

6 **a** 15   **b** 1   **c** 20

7 $\frac{28}{729}x^2y^5$

8 $\frac{3}{8}a^2b^2$

9 $\frac{448}{6561}t^5$

10 $^nC_r\,p^r q^{n-r}$

8.2 Technique (p. 179)

1 Sample size 12, probability of success 0.72, 0.00503

2 **a** 0.1591   **b** 0.000 03

3 **a** 0.0112   **b** 0.7361
   c 0.999 999 9

4 **a** 0.0710   **b** 0.0617
   c 0.000 004

5 **a** 0.000 002   **b** 0.003 34

6 **a** $X \sim B(10, \frac{1}{2})$ **b** 0.2051

8.3 Technique (p. 183)

1 **a** 0.9997   **b** 0.2048   **c** 0.0579

2 **a** 0.1673   **b** 0.0425   **c** 0.0017

3 **a** 0.9803   **b** 0.2816   **c** 0.4709

8.3 Contextual (p. 183)

1 **a** 0.1157   **b** 0.1319

2 **a** 0.8906   **b** 0.8906

3 **a** 0.1596   **b** 0.266

4 0.1746

5 **a** 0.3111   **b** 0.8586

6 0.01280

7 **a** 0.0024   **b** 0.9795

8.4 Contextual (p. 189)

1 1.5, 1.125

2 7.2, 2.88

3 20, 3.16

4 7, 2.13

5 **a** 20   **b** 2.19

6 $n = 8, p = 0.1, 0.000\,41$

7 **a** 0.218   **b** 0.804

8 0.851, 13

8.5 Contextual (p. 192)

1 **a** 0.78
   b 0.39
   c 0.3721, 0.4758, 0.1521
   d 37.2, 47.6, 15
   e no

2 **a** 1.2   **b** 0.3

   c

Theoretical probability	Expected frequency
0.2401	14.4
0.4116	24.7
0.2646	15.9
0.0756	4.5
0.0081	0.5

   d fits quite well

3 mean $= 1.22, p = 0.41$

x	0	1	2	3
$P(X = x)$	37.0	77.1	53.6	12.4

8.6 Contextual (p. 196)

1 0.1029, 0.028 25

2 5, 0.488

3 0.065 536, 0.059 326

4 **a** 0.166 252   **b** 35

5 $3.\dot{3}, 7.\dot{7}$

6 **a** $0.0\dot{6}$ **b** 15   **c** 21   **d** Lost £3.20

8.7 Contextual (p. 201)

1 binomial
  a 0.0779   **b** 0.2525   **c** 0.0841
  Poisson
  a 0.0842   **b** 0.2510   **c** 0.0842

2 **a i** 0.2454
    ii 0.2427
    iii 0.8340
  b i 0.2466
    ii 0.2417
    iii 0.8335

3 **a** 0.0006   **b** 0.1373   **c** 0.0203

4 **a** 0.0025   **b** 0.0028

5 **a** 0.4724   **b** 0.0405

6 0.0034

8.8 Technique (p. 206)

1 **a** 0.0498   **b** 0.5768
  c 0.9962   **d** 0.7674

2 **a** 0.0001   **b** 0.0153
  c 0.9994   **d** 0.0803

3 **a** 0.8095   **b** 0.0041
  c 0.9890   **d** 0.2017

4 0.1689

5 **a** 4   **b** 3   **c** 9   **d** 5

8.8 Contextual (p. 206)

1 **a** 0.0009   **b** 0.0912
  c 0.9927   **d** 0.1730

2 **a** 0.0183   **b** 0.9576

3 **a** 0.224   **b** 0.0023

4 **a** 0.8753   **b** 9 computers

5 **a** 0.5665   **b** 0.0916

6 **a** 0.0424   **b** 0.1042

7 **a** 0.7149   **b** 12

8.9 Technique (p. 211)

1 mean $= 0.627$, variance $= 0.9247$;
  not suitable

2 mean $= 1.22$, variance $= 1.15$;
  Poisson model is suitable

3 $a = 17, b = 2$

8.9 Contextual (p. 211)

1 **a** 0.7
  b 0.4966, 0.3476, 0.1217, 0.0284, 0.005,
    0.0007, 0.0001
  c 44.7, 31.3, 10.9, 2.6, 0.45, 0.06, 0.007
  d quite a close fit

2 $\lambda = 0.51$

x	0	1	2	3	4	5
$P(X = x)$	0.6004	0.3063	0.0781	0.0133	0.0017	0.0002
Expected frequency	58.84	30.02	7.66	1.30	0.17	0.02

3 **a** 0.9, 1.0
  b 0.4066, 0.3659, 0.1647, 0.0494, 0.0111,
    0.002, 0.0003
  c 16.26, 14.64, 6.59, 1.98, 0.44, 0.08, 0.012
  d good fit

8.10 Contextual (p. 215)

1 **a** Po(6)   **b** 0.5543

2 **a** 0.997   **b** 0.0183   **c** 0.0993

3 **a** 0.1403   **b** 0.1912   **c** 0.1317

Consolidation A (p. 216)

1 **a** 0.0229   **b** 0.7384

2 **a** 4.5, 2.121   **b** 0.2971   **c** 5

3 **a** 0.3519   **b** 0.8961   **c** 0.1905

4 **a** 0.002 46   **b** 0.000 016 8
  c 0.001 64   **d** 0.001 64

5 **a** 0.2138   **b** 0.1378   **c** 0.0457

6 **a** the probability of it raining is the same for
    each day
  b 0.4, 0.6
  c 0.0280

7 **a** 0.7481   **b** 0.0254   **c** 2.1 belts
  d 0.3504   **e** 5 belts

8 **a** 0.1523   **b** 0.5669   **c** 0.2851

9 **a** 0.8692   **b** 0.0728

10 **a** $X \sim B(40\,000, \frac{1}{200\,000})$ n large, p small
  b i 0.819
    ii 0.164
    iii 0.018
  c 250 000
  d i 0.235
    ii 0.247

Consolidation B (p. 218)

1 **a** 0.0197   **b** 2.5

2 **a** 0.4164   **b** 0

3 **a** The geometric distribution would be most
    appropriate, as X is a discrete random
    variable and there are only two outcomes,
    success and failure, and the trials end
    when the first success is achieved.
  b i 0.1914   **ii** 0.5138   **c** 170 trials

4 0.1329

5 **a i** 0.311
    ii 0.959
    3.6, 1.2
  b i $^{5}C_4 p^4(1 - p)$
    ii $^{5}C_2 p^2(1 - p)^3$
    $p = \frac{2}{3}$

6 **a i** 0.9989
    ii 0.001
  b $(6 \times 0.7) + (14 \times 0.2) = 7$
  c 0.5503

7 **a** 0.8793   **b** 0.7731

8 **a i** 0.2226   **ii** 0.6201   **iii** 0.6163
  b 0.1380

9 **a** $X \sim \text{Po}(2.5)$
  b i 0.0821   **ii** 0.1088
  c distribution of sheep in each square is not independent; sheep will not occur singly

10 **a ii** 2.68, 1.52   **b** 6

9 Continuous Probability Distributions

Review (p. 223)

1 **a** discrete   **b** continuous   **c** discrete

2 **a** $x^4 + c$ **b** $\frac{2}{5}x^5 + \frac{3}{4}x^4 + c$
  c $\frac{1}{3}x^3 - 2x^2 + 5x + c$

9.1 Technique (p. 231)

1 **a**

  b 0.844   **c** 0.8

2 **a** 0.5625   **b** 0.4375   **c** 0.150

3 **a** $\frac{1}{9}$
  b

  c 0.451   **d** 0.124

4 **a** $\frac{1}{18}$
  b

  c 0.8125   **d** 0.0445

5 **a**

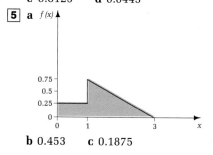

  b 0.453   **c** 0.1875

9.2 Technique (p. 237)

1 $$F(x) = \begin{cases} 0 & x < 0 \\ \frac{1}{8}(6x - x^2) & 0 \le x < 2 \\ 1 & x \ge 2 \end{cases}$$

  $m = 0.764$

2 $$F(x) = \begin{cases} 0 & x < 1 \\ \frac{1}{26}(x^3 - 1) & 1 \le x < 3 \\ 1 & x \ge 3 \end{cases}$$

  $m = 2.41$

3 $$F(x) = \begin{cases} 0 & x < 0 \\ \frac{1}{27}x^3 & 0 \le x < 3 \\ 1 & x \ge 3 \end{cases}$$

  $m = 2.38$

4 $f(x) = \frac{1}{20}(x + 3), \quad 0 \le x \le 4$

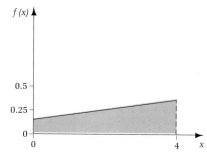

5 $k = \frac{3}{7}$

9.3 Technique (p. 241)

1 $E(X) = 0.833, \text{Var}(X) = 0.306$

2 $E(X) = 2.31, \text{Var}(X) = 0.259$

3 $E(X) = 2.25, \text{Var}(X) = 0.338$

4 $E(X) = 4.125, \text{Var}(X) = 0.434$

5 $E(X) = 1.375, \text{Var}(X) = 0.443$

6 **a** $c = \frac{1}{64}$ **b** $E(X) = 2.13$
  c $\text{Var}(X) = 0.782$

7 $k = \frac{4}{5}$

  $E(X) = 1.36, \text{Var}(X) = 0.150$

9.4 Technique (p. 245)

1 **a** 1.6   **b** 3.2   **c** 7.4
  d 0.107   **e** 0.96

2 **a** 0   **b** 2   **c** −3   **d** 0.238   **e** 0.952

3   **a** 0.8   **b** 1.6   **c** 2.4
   d 0.427   **e** 0.507

4   **a** 0.694

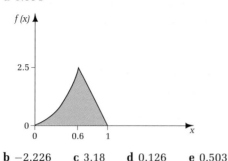

   b −2.226   **c** 3.18   **d** 0.126   **e** 0.503

9.5 Technique (p. 250)

1   **a** $f(x) = 0.5$, for $0 \leq x \leq 2$
   b $1, \frac{1}{3}$ **c** 0.375

2 $f(y) = 0.833$, for $1.2 \leq y \leq 2.4$
   a 1.8   **b** 0.12   **c** 0.25

3   **a** $f(m) = 0.263$, for $-1.3 \leq x \leq 2.5$
   b 0.6   **c** 4.8   **d** 0.263

4 $W \sim R(-2.5, 2.5)$
   mean $= 0$
   variance $= 2.083$

5   **a** $f(l) = 0.417$ for $2.4 \leq l \leq 4.8$
   b $3.6, 0.48$ **c** 0.25   **d** 0.875

Consolidation A (p. 251)

1   **a** $\frac{1}{4}$ **b** 1.07 or $\frac{16}{15}$

2   **a** $\frac{8}{3}, \frac{8}{9}$ **b** $\frac{1}{3}, \frac{1}{18}$ **c** $7\frac{1}{3}$ **d** $\frac{65}{18}$

3   **a** $F(t) = \frac{1}{2}k(t^2 - 4t + 4)$, $k = \frac{1}{2}$
   c $E(T) = \frac{10}{3}$, $Var(T) = \frac{2}{9}$

4   **a** 43 minutes

5   **a**
$$F(t) = \begin{cases} 0 & 5 < t \\ 0.004(15t^2 - t^3 - 250) & 5 \leq t < 10 \\ 1 & t \geq 10 \end{cases}$$

   b 0.496

6   **a**

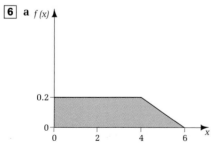

   c
$$F(x) = \begin{cases} 0 & x < 0 \\ 0.2x & 0 < x \leq 4 \\ -0.05(x^2 - 12x + 32) & 4 < x < 6 \\ 1 & x \geq 6 \end{cases}$$

   d 0.0125

7   **a** $1, \frac{1}{6}$ **b** 2, 2   **c** 7   **d** $8\frac{2}{3}$

8   3.2, 2.56

9   **a** $\frac{5}{16}$ **c** $f(t) = \frac{3}{2}t^2 - \frac{3}{4}t^3$, for $0 \leq t \leq 2$
   d $f(t)$

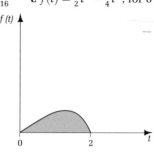

10   0.35

Consolidation B (p. 253)

1 $2, \frac{1}{2}$

2   **a** $k = \frac{1}{2}, \frac{4}{3}, \frac{2}{9}$
   b $\frac{8}{5}, \frac{8}{75}$
   c $\frac{16}{15}$ **d** $2\frac{32}{75}$

3   0.25
$$f(x) = \frac{1}{2\sqrt{x}}, \text{ for } 0 \leq x \leq 1$$
   b 0.0889 or $\frac{4}{45}$

4   **b** 1.8 years   **c** 1.10 (3 s.f.)   **d** 0.028

5   **b** $\frac{4}{49}$ **d** $2\frac{13}{18}$

6   **b** $\frac{8}{15}$ **c** $\frac{11}{225}$

7   **a** 6.27, 1.129
   b 0.75, 0.0375
   c 26.57   **d** 1.166

8   **c** $\alpha^2/18$

9   **a** 0.0140
   b 1200 litres, 400 litres

10   **b** 3   **d** 0.802

10 The Normal Distribution

Review (p. 257)

1   Poisson

2   binomial

3   binomial

4   binomial

5   Poisson

10.1 Technique (p. 266)

Answers are generally accepted to 3 s.f.

1   0.109 35

2   0.821 21

3   0.085 34

4 0.020 68

5 0.468 56

6 0.280 79

7 0.464 40

8 0.342 48

9 0.853 78

10 0.312 06

11 0

12 2.30

13 1.03

14 2.84

15 1.96

10.2 Technique (p. 270)

1 a 0.773 37   b 0.598 71   c 0.382 09
   d 0.337 24   e 0.127 02   f 0.199 71

2 a 0.738 91   b 0.374 48   c 0.673 64
   d 0.468 12   e 0.196 45   f 0.637 56

3 a 0.691 46   b 0.933 19   c 0.598 71
   d 0.644 31   e 0.233 54   f 0.224 25

4 a 20.24   b 17.74
   c 18.08   d 16.3

5 a 207.2   b 227.12
   c 230.96   d 205.28

10.2 Contextual (p. 270)

1 a 0.945 20   b 0.788 14   c 0.9545

2 0.066 81
   15.9% (1 d.p.)

3 53.2% (1 d.p.)

4 a 0.401 29   b 0.308 54   c 0.464 83

5 a 0.401 29   b 0.158 66   c 0.464 83

6 8.47 (2 d.p.)

7 24

8 54.28 cm

10.3 Technique (p. 277)

Answers obtained by interpolation from 4 d.p. for z.

1 a 0.274 25   b 0.100 27
   c 0.315 61   d 0.515 95

2 a 0.327 37   b 0.186
   c 0.464 38   d 0.429 01

3 a 0.609 26   b 0.710 45
   c 0.444 84   d 0.455 84

10.3 Contextual (p. 277)

1 $\mu = 363$, $\sigma^2 = 58$
   a 0.346 83   b 0.179 03

2 $\mu = 36$, $\sigma^2 = 34$, 0.753 64

3 0.099 30

4 $\mu = 7390$, $\sigma = \sqrt{240\,400}$, 0.491 86

5 a 0.274 25   b 0.579 26

6 $\mu = 136$, $\sigma^2 = 116$, 0.288 73

10.4 Technique (p. 283)

1 a $P(X < 10.5)$
   b $P(X > 37.5)$
   c $P(20.5 < X < 30.5)$

2 a $P(Y > 34.5)$
   b $P(Y < 41.5)$
   c $P(29.5 < Y < 37.5)$
   d $P(39.5 < Y < 40.5)$

3 a 0.144 41   b 0.999 69   c 0.198 03

4 a 0.078 59   b 0.089 22   c 0.687 06
   d 0.345 44   e 0.025 93

10.4 Contextual (p. 283)

1 a 0.077 37   b 0.214 59   c 0.744 42

2 a 0.138 04   b 0.018 79   c 0.445 61

3 a 0.093 44   b 0.093 44

10.5 Technique (p. 285)

1 a 0.254 18   b 0.388 40   c 0.056 63

2 a 0.176 27   b 0.176 27   c 0.527 75

3 a 0.247 56   b 0.040 80

4 0.135 67

5 0.087 63

Consolidation A (p. 286)

1 0.991 40

2 a 0.057   b 0.974

3 a 0.919 24   b 0.904 (3 d.p.)

4 0.133 63

5 a 0.308 54   b 0.440 05   c 163.8 (1 d.p.)

6 a 15.9%   b 80.1%   c 60.2 g

7 0.233 43

8 0.528 54

9 a 0.3828   b 0.90

10 a i 0.105 65
     ii 0.888 14
   b 972.088 g   c 0.053 66

Consolidation B (p. 288)

1 0.378 05

2 a 0.908 78
   b drug dose not appear to be effective for approx 10% of patients

3 **a** 0.884 93   **c** 0.304 22

4 **a** 0.629   **b** 0.839   **c** 0.686 19

5 **a** 0.1151 (4 d.p.),   **c** 0.123 76

6 **a i** 0.791
    ii 0.860
    iii 0.069
  b 10.26

7 **a** 0.657 (3 d.p.)   **b** 0.214

8 **a** 0.035 93   **b** 0.733 34
approx 28 vehicles

9 **a** $N(360, 2.16)$ **b** 0.001 40

10 **a** 275 g   **b** 1.3 g

11 Correlation and Regression

Review (p. 292)

1 **a** 34   **b** 4.778   **c** 0.316

2 **a** 6.00   **b** 4.714   **c** 0.042

11.1 Contextual (p. 296)

1 **a** wheat dependent, rainfall independent
  b French/German results are
    interchangeable
  c lung damage dependent, number of years
    smoking independent

2 positive correlation, example height and
weight

3 some positive correlation

4 some positive correlation, generally the
history marks are lower than the geography
marks

5 **a** 18.2, 56.1

6 **b** 133

11.2 Technique (p. 301)

1 **a** −1.96   **b** 4.18

2 **a** 22, positive
  b −90.8, negative
  c 0.894, slight positive

11.3 Technique (p. 305)

1 **a** 0.983   **b** −0.365

2 **a** 1.104   **b** 0.939

3 0.805

4 **a** 17.167   **b** 0.924

5 **a**

b −50.8   **c** −0.171
d no evidence of correlation

11.4 Technique (p. 311)

1 **a** -0.036 **b** -0.891

2 **a** 8   **b** 0.771
   c indicates strong positive correlation

3 **a**

Cake	A	B	C	D	E	F	G
Judge 1	3	4	6	7	1	2	5
Judge 2	3	5	4	7	1	2	6

   b 0.893
   c strong positive correlation

4 0.939, very strong positive correlation between German and French test results

5 **a** 0.851
   b strong positive correlation between annual income per head and life expectancy at birth

11.5 Contextual (p. 319)

1 $y = 5.581 - 0.165x$

2 $y = -24.361 + 0.928x$

3 **a** 4.85   **b** $y = 1.852 + 1.391x$

4 $y = 0.773 + 0.388x$, 1.937

5 $y = 4.353 + 0.281x$, 43.1 mm

6 **a** $y = -177.060 + 0.669x$
   b £5174.94
   c would not use the line since 100 units is outside the given range of data.

Consolidation A (p. 320)

1 Scale and choice of axes

2 **a** -1.756 **b** -0.96

3 **a**

Entry	A	B	C	D	E	F	G
Judge 1	5	7	6	1.5	4	3	1.5
Judge 2	5	6	7	1	2.5	4	2.5

   b 0.884

4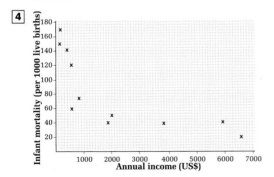

Negative correlation between infant mortality and income per head. As annual income per head increases, infant mortality decreases, although not a linear correlation.

5 **a** when no actual numerical data values are given, only the order, and when measuring non-linear correlation.
   b -0.429

6 **a** 0.952   **b** 0.714

7 **a**

   b 0.943
   c strong positive correlation
   d $y = 13.709 + 1.195x$
   e for every inch of rain yield of wheat increases by 1.195 bushels per acre
   f would not use the line to predict yield for 30 inches of rain since outside given data range

8 **a** linearity is good for x at the low end of the range, but is suspect at the high end of the range

   b $y = 77.289 - 0.374x$
   c $y(145) = 23.06$ likely to be accurate because in mid range
      $y(180) = 9.97$ suspect because out of range.

9 **a**

   b $y = -22.688 + 0.924x$
   c 162.112
   d 3.388, -2.052, 1.708, -2.632, -3.872, 0.988, -0.152, 2.508
   e Sharon had positive residuals throughout, whereas Ali always had negative residuals. 160 tonnes at 200°C

10 **a** $y = 11.43 + 0.150t$
b 14.43; a little larger than the actual observed value but a good estimate
c 35.43; since we are extrapolating value not very useful since trying to predict outside given range.
d it would seem from scatter diagram that a curvi-linear model might be better.

Consolidation B (p. 323)

1

2 **a** 0.667 **b** 0.338

3 interpolation – predicting y within given range of x
extrapolation – predicting y outside given range of x

4 **a** −1 **b** 1

5

X	4	5	7	2	1	3	6
Y	3	6	5	4	2	1	7

0.714

6 0.338

7 **a i**
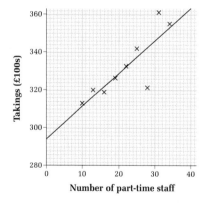

ii $y = 294.211 + 1.728x$
iii a – if no extra part time staff are working still get takings of £29 421
b – for every extra person an extra £173 is taken
iv seventh Saturday with takings of £32 100 does not follow trend as well
b 0.4375

8 **a** $y = 3.667 + 0.038x$
b a – 3.667 is the yield of hay when no water is added

b – 0.038 tonnes of hay are produced for every extra centimetre of water added
c $y(28) = 4.731$; reliable
$y(150) = 9.367$; not reliable since extrapolating way outside range

9 **a** 0.986
b suggests strong linear correlation

10 **a**
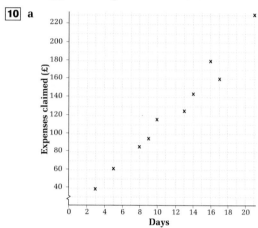

b $y = 8.640 + 9.893x$
c slope b; for every extra day £9.89 worth of claims are submitted
intercept a; for no days claim of £8.64 is submitted
d £117.46
e no, since extrapolating

12 Estimation I: Point Estimators

Review (p. 328)

1 42.71, 17.92

2 220.17, 1435.14

3 4.238, 4.025

4 0.061, 0.000 489

5 1.091, 18.628

6 1.98, 1.20

7 0.473, 2.83

8 15.7, 47.76

12.1 Technique (p. 330)

1 25, 14.142 136

2

12.5	38.83	34	27.17	31.67
21.67	25.83	19.5	20	22.83
20.83	18.83	24.17	25	24.5
22.33	27.83	26.83	19.17	23.3

3 max, 38.83; min, 12.5
range, 26.33; actual mean is 25
means of winning lines are
$12.5 \leq x \leq 38.83$, which is 25.66 ± 13.16

so the means of the winning lines are grouped around the actual mean of 25

4

Group	f
$10 \leq x < 15$	1
$15 \leq x < 20$	3
$20 \leq x < 25$	8
$25 \leq x < 30$	5
$30 \leq x < 35$	2
$35 \leq x < 40$	1

The means are most frequent in the middle two groups reducing in number either end of the distribution. Similar to normal distribution.

12.2 Technique (p. 333)

1 56.8, 1.549

2 110.3, 1.414

3 272.4, 1.095

4 29.95, 2.236

5 492.775, 2.5

6 23.63, 0.376

7 130.14, 0.5199

8 107.06, 0.219

9 -0.58, 0.426

10 100.17, 0.378

12.2 Contextual (p. 334)

1 169.5, 3.182

2 18.45, 0.894

3 126.75, 3.354

4 4.86, 0.23

5 1.96, 0.31

12.3 Technique (p. 338)

1 $\bar{x} = 8$, $s^2 = 5$, $\mu = 8$, $\sigma^2 = 6.67$

2 $\bar{x} = 5.5$, $s^2 = 6.917$, $\mu = 5.5$, $\sigma^2 = 8.30$

3 $\bar{x} = 40$, $s^2 = 44.75$, $\mu = 40$, $\sigma^2 = 51.14$

4 $\bar{x} = 5.64$, $s^2 = 2.0124$, $\mu = 5.64$, $\sigma^2 = 2.236$

5 $\bar{x} = 25.075$, $s^2 = 2.319$, $\mu = 25.075$, $\sigma^2 = 2.379$

6 $\bar{x} = 2.24$, $s^2 = 1.5424$, $\mu = 2.24$, $\sigma^2 = 1.607$

7 $\bar{x} = 9.58$, $s^2 = 33.301$, $\mu = 9.58$, $\sigma^2 = 34.45$

8 $\bar{x} = 19.58$, $s^2 = 7.787$, $\mu = 19.58$, $\sigma^2 = 7.818$

9 $\bar{x} = -0.16$, $s^2 = 4.173$, $\mu = -0.16$, $\sigma^2 = 4.250$

10 $\bar{x} = 100.34$, $s^2 = 0.739$, $\mu = 100.34$, $\sigma^2 = 0.761$

It should be noticed that as the sample size becomes larger then the variance of the sample and that of the population become approximately equal.

12.3 Contextual (p. 338)

1 $\bar{x} = 4.8$, $s = 2.638$, $\sigma = 2.78$

2 $\bar{x} = 7.417$, $s = 2.957$, $\sigma = 3.088$

3 $\bar{x} = 695.4$, $s = 105.23$, $\sigma = 108.93$

4 $\bar{x} = 76.625$, $s^2 = 111.484$, $\sigma^2 = 127.41$

5 $\bar{x} = 3$, $s^2 = 1.25$, $\sigma^2 = 1.33$

6 $\bar{x} = 8$, $s = 2.273$, $\sigma = 2.374$

12.4 Technique (p. 342)

1 8.633, 0.08

2 3.731, 0.13

3 55.389, 23.90

4 0.495, 0.013

5 2.4, 1.713

6 2.939, 1.587

7 19.067, 3.599

8 17.33, 22.44

12.4 Contextual (p. 343)

1 Boys 70.78, 159.062
Girls 67.75, 205.688
Overall 69.848, 204.94

2 2.017 kg, 0.002 489 1

The mean weight is slightly above 2 kg with a very small variance.
The mean weight seems to be at least 2 kg.

3 1.039 kg, 0.145 kg

4 9.942%, 1.54%

5 -0.083, 206.27

12.5 Technique (p. 347)

1 0.437

2 0.853

3 0.557

4 0.58

5 0.143

6 0.75, 0.53, 0.630

7 0.6, 0.48, 0.525

8 0.16, 0.214, 0.189

9 0.428, 0.465, 0.448

10 0.841, 0.921, 0.878

12.5 Contextual (p. 347)

1. 0.386

2. 0.254 (25.4%)

3. 0.513

4. 0.766

5. 0.709

Consolidation A (p. 349)

1. **a** parent population is normally distributed
   b i $\mu = 7.36$
   ii $s^2 = 1.75$, $\sigma^2 = 2.183$

2. **a** $\bar{x} = 20$
   b $s = 5.745$

3. $\mu = 14.7$, $s^2 = 0.077$, $\sigma = 0.3$

4. **a** $\bar{x} = 58.05$, $s^2 = 132.548$
   b $\mu = 58.05$, $\sigma^2 = 139.524$

5. **a** $p = 0.4$
   b Sample 1 $\bar{x} = 497.846$, $s^2 = 75.822$
   Sample 2 $\bar{x} = 496.417$, $s^2 = 53.243$
   $\mu = 497.16$, $\sigma^2 = 70.635$

6. **a** $\mu = 27.08$
   b $s^2 = 4.951$, $\sigma^2 = 5.942$

7. **a** Sample 1 $\bar{x} = 59.23$, $s^2 = 0.849$
   Sample 2 $\bar{x} = 61.19$, $s^2 = 8.095$
   b $\mu = 60.49$, $\sigma^2 = 5.783$

8. **a** $\bar{x} = 1.05\,\text{m}$
   b $s^2 = 0.00306$, $\sigma^2 = 0.00314$
   c An estimator is unbiased if the mean of
   its sampling distribution equals the
   parameter it is estimating.

9. **a** Panel A $= 0.33$
   Panel B $= 0.17$
   b $p = 0.25$
   c Panel A $\bar{x} = 36$, $s^2 = 53.5$
   Panel B $\bar{x} = 32.08$, $s^2 = 85.08$
   d $\mu = 34.04$, $\sigma^2 = 75.589$

10. **a** 3rd round $\bar{x} = 75.4$, $s^2 = 5.04$
    4th round $\bar{x} = 71.6$, $s^2 = 7.44$
    b $\mu = 73.5$, $\sigma^2 = 7.8$

Consolidation B (p. 351)

1. **a** $\mu = 19.53$
   b $s^2 = 5.269$, $\sigma^2 = 5.9275$

2. **a** $\bar{x} = 100$
   b $s = 14.62$

3. $\mu = 76.55\%$, $s^2 = 84.43\%$, $\sigma = 9.637\%$

4. **a** $\bar{x} = 17$, $s^2 = 18.26$
   b $\mu = 17$, $\sigma^2 = 19.564$

5. **a** $p = 0.2879$
   b Sample 1 $\bar{x} = 496.8$, $s^2 = 46.56$
   Sample 2 $\bar{x} = 499.72$, $s^2 = 42.201$
   $\mu = 498.183$, $\sigma^2 = 46.967$

6. **a** $\mu = 86.02$
   b $s^2 = 26.566$, $\sigma^2 = 33.207$

7. **a** Sample 1 $\bar{x} = 92.509$, $s^2 = 8.066$
   Sample 2 $\bar{x} = 92.518$, $s^2 = 21.852$
   b $\mu = 92.514$, $\sigma^2 = 16.455$

8. **a** $\mu = 1.18$
   b $s^2 = 0.187$, $\sigma^2 = 0.195$

9. **a** Panel A $= 0.5$
   Panel B $= 0.375$
   b $p = 0.4375$
   c Panel A $\bar{x} = 54.125$, $s^2 = 48.859$
   Panel B $\bar{x} = 53.375$, $s^2 = 62.484$
   d $\mu = 53.75$, $\sigma^2 = 63.625$

10. **a** 1st round $\bar{x} = 71.167$, $s^2 = 8.472$
    2nd round $\bar{x} = 71.833$, $s^2 = 13.139$
    b $\mu = 71.5$, $\sigma^2 = 12.967$

13 Estimation II: Interval Estimation

Review (p. 355)

1. 80, 48

2. 2200, 990

3. 24.5, 15.925

4. 56.25, 35.156

5. 193.125, 93.67

6. 55 24.75

7. 1440, 748.8

8. 462, 210.89

9. 348, 251.12

10. 63, 13.39

13.1 Technique (p. 358)

1. **a** 14.6 ± 3.68 **b** 14.6 ± 4.38

2. **a** 59 ± 11.63 **b** 59 ± 13.86

3. **a** 5.125 ± 4.65 **b** 5.125 ± 5.54

4. **a** 30.3 ± 8.32 **b** 30.3 ± 9.92

5. **a** 1.43 ± 0.27 **b** 1.43 ± 0.33

6. **a** 0.375 ± 0.47 **b** 0.375 ± 0.57

7. **a** 0.046 ± 0.055 **b** 0.046 ± 0.065

8. **a** $12\,057 \pm 54.83$ **b** $12\,056 \pm 65.33$

9. **a** -0.1 ± 4.41 **b** -0.1 ± 5.26

10. **a** 989.8 ± 6.80 **b** 989.8 ± 8.10

11. **a** 1.625 ± 1.23 **b** 1.625 ± 1.47

12. **a** 0.92 ± 3.49 **b** 0.92 ± 4.16

13.1 Contextual (p. 359)

1 $\bar{x} = 157.2, 151.62 \leq \mu \leq 162.78$

2 $\bar{x} = 109.6, 104.52 \leq \mu \leq 114.68$

3 $\bar{x} = 9.35, 9.02 \leq \mu \leq 9.68$

4 $\bar{x} = 77, 73.74 \leq \mu \leq 80.26$

5 $\bar{x} = 24.01, 22.60 \leq \mu \leq 25.42$

6 $\bar{x} = 5.36, 1.83 \leq \mu \leq 8.89$

13.2 Technique (p. 361)

1 60 ± 0.506

2 140 ± 0.524

3 1.8 ± 0.310

4 0.4 ± 0.195

5 3440 ± 2.601

6 9.76 ± 0.325

7 $14.24 \leq \mu \leq 15.76$

8 $215.62 \leq \mu \leq 224.38$

9 $2.26 \leq \mu \leq 2.74$

10 $6.882 \leq \mu \leq 7.918$

11 $810.33 \leq \mu \leq 889.67$

13.2 Contextual (p. 362)

1 Division 1 $\quad 1.975 \leq \mu \leq 2.752$
Division 2 $\quad 2.293 \leq \mu \leq 2.965$
The spread of the confidence interval of the mean in Division 1 is much wider than that of Division 2, but the point estimator is higher in Division 2.

2 $3.468 \leq \mu \leq 4.132$

3 $59.988 \leq \mu \leq 60.044$

4 $9.755 \leq \mu \leq 12.745$

5 $6.859 \leq \mu \leq 7.475$

13.3 Contextual (p. 366)

1 $5.181 \leq \mu \leq 5.769$

2 $8.703 \leq \mu \leq 10.933$

3 $-0.171 \leq \mu \leq 0.0246$

4 $75.707 \leq \mu \leq 84.293$

5 $76.77 \leq \mu \leq 89.516$

6 $46.677 \leq \mu \leq 51.123$

7 $-0.261 \leq \mu \leq 5.533$

8 $4.355 \leq \mu \leq 5.217$

13.4 Technique (p. 369)

1 **a** $n \geq 9.51, n \geq 10$
   b $n \geq 13.5, n \geq 14$

2 **a** $n \geq 67.2, n \geq 68$
   b $n \geq 96.04, n \geq 97$

3 **a** $n \geq 4.2, n \geq 5$
   b $n \geq 6.0025, n \geq 7$

4 **a** $n \geq 1549.2, n \geq 1550$
   b $n \geq 2212.76, n \geq 2213$

5 **a** $n \geq 67.62, n \geq 68$
   b $n \geq 96.04, n \geq 97$

6 **a** $n \geq 67.65, n \geq 68$
   b $n \geq 96.04, n \geq 97$

7 **a** $n \geq 21.405, n \geq 22$
   b $n \geq 30.39, n \geq 31$

8 **a** $n \geq 1082.41, n \geq 1083$
   b $n \geq 1536.6, n \geq 1537$

9 **a** $n \geq 27\,060.25, n \geq 27\,061$
   b $n \geq 38\,416, n \geq 38\,416$

10 **a** $n \geq 500.51, n \geq 501$
   b $n \geq 710.5, n \geq 711$

11 **a** $n \geq 1984.40, n \geq 1985$
   b $n \geq 2817.1, n \geq 2818$

12 **a** $n \geq 63.22, n \geq 64$
   b $n \geq 89.7, n \geq 90$

13.5 Contextual (p. 371)

1 $p = 0.24, q = 0.76; 0.203 \leq p \leq 0.277$

2 $p = 0.2, q = 0.8; 0.127 \leq p \leq 0.273$

3 $p = 0.4, q = 0.6; 0.328 \leq p \leq 0.472$

4 $p = 0.388, q = 0.612; 0.354 \leq p \leq 0.421$

5 $p = 0.761, q = 0.239; 0.717 \leq p \leq 0.805$

6 $p = 0.718, q = 0.282; 0.700 \leq p \leq 0.736$

7 $p = 0.425, q = 0.575; 0.334 \leq p \leq 0.516$

8 $p = 0.366, q = 0.634; 0.342 \leq p \leq 0.390$

Consolidation A (p. 372)

1 $31.36 \leq \hat{\mu} \leq 31.46$

2 $p = 0.605, q = 0.395; 0.557 \leq p \leq 0.653$

3 **a** $34.35 \leq p \leq 35.05$
   b 0.7056
   c $n = 22.128; n \geq 23$

4 $p = 0.086, q = 0.914; 0.065 \leq p \leq 0.107$

5 $\bar{x} = 14.7; 14.41 \leq \mu \leq 14.99$

6 **a** $\bar{x} = 975.8$ days; $s^2 = 42\,145.5$;
   $\hat{\sigma}^2 = 47\,413.7$
   i $833.5 \leq \mu \leq 1118$
   ii $47\,271.4 \leq \sigma^2 \leq 47\,555.96$
   $217.4 \leq \sigma \leq 218.1$
   b For first batteries, mean is 960 days with standard deviation 135 days. For second batteries mean is $835 \leq \hat{\mu} \leq 1178$ with a mid value of 975.75 days. So the second supplier may have batteries of a higher mean value but has greater variability.

7 **a** The sampling distribution is the distribution of the mean values of the sample statistic.

The distribution is $N\left(\mu, \dfrac{\sigma^2}{n}\right)$

An estimator for a population parameter is unbiased if the mean of its sampling distribution equals the parameter it is estimating.

  i A point estimator is when a single value is used to estimate μ.

  ii An interval estimate is when a range of values is given in which μ must lie.

b $\bar{x} = 1.525$, $\sigma = 0.011$; standard error $= 0.001\,53$; $n = 118$, $\hat{\mu} = 1.525$, $\hat{\sigma}^2 = 0.000\,12$

8 **a** Choosing 10 names from all the names in a draw. Choosing randomly from membership numbers using a random number generator. Any other suitable method.

b $\bar{x} = £4.74 = \mu$, $s^2 = 2.4644$
$\sigma^2 = 2.74$, $\sigma = £1.65$

c $4.74 \pm 1.96 \times \dfrac{1.65}{\sqrt{10}}$

d By taking a larger sample $n = 10.46$, $n \geq 11$

9 $\bar{x} = 124.97$; $124.34 \leq \mu \leq 125.60$

10 **a**

Cards	Mean (x)	Median M
123	2	2
124	2.$\dot{3}$	2
125	2.$\dot{6}$	2
134	2.$\dot{6}$	3
135	3	3
145	3.$\dot{3}$	4
234	3	3
235	3.$\dot{3}$	3
245	3.$\dot{6}$	4
345	4	4

  i mean of $\bar{x} = 30/10 = 3$
mean of $M = 30/10 = 3$
therefore $\bar{x}$ and M are unbiased estimators of μ, as $\mu = 3$

  i variance of $\bar{x} = 0.3$, variance of $M = 0.6$
$\bar{x}$ is a better estimator of μ as the variance of $\bar{x}$ is smaller than the variance of M

b $\mu = \dfrac{1 + 2 + 3 + \cdots n}{n} = \frac{1}{2}n(n+1)/n$

$= \frac{1}{2}(n+1)$

As $\bar{x}$ is an unbiased estimator of μ then
$\bar{x} = \frac{1}{2}(n+1)$
Substituting in $2\bar{x} - 1$
$2\left(\frac{1}{2}(n+1)\right) - 1 = n + 1 - 1 = n$
$2\bar{x} - 1$ is an unbiased estimator of n, the number of cards

$\bar{x}(1, 2, 6)$ is $9/3 = 3$
$n = 2 \times 3 - 1 = 5$
The cards are supposed to show $1, 2, 3, \ldots, n$ respectively. If you have only five cards, then how can the number 6 be selected?

Consolidation B (p. 374)

1 **a** $\bar{x} = 0.71$; $\sigma = 0.4$; $0.617 \leq R \leq 0.803$
The distribution of R is normal. The variance of the sample is an unbiased estimator of the variance of R.
b $n \geq 174$

2 $p = 0.29$; $q = 0.71$; $0.234 \leq p \leq 0.346$

3 **a** $\bar{x} = 70.55$; $68.95 \leq \mu \leq 72.15$
b $\bar{x} = 81.5$; $s = 1.55$; $\sigma^2 = 2.90$; $80.14 \leq \mu \leq 83.86$

4 For a sample size, n, from a distribution with mean μ and a finite variance σ^2 the distribution of the sample means is approximately normal with mean μ and variance σ^2/n.
$160.14 \leq \mu \leq 167.86$

5 **a**

Size	1	2	3	4	5
Frequency	5	8	15	8	4

b $0.225 \leq p \leq 0.525$
c $n \geq 91$

6 $41.064 \leq \mu \leq 47.336$

7 $23.761 \leq \mu \leq 26.27$

8 **a** $\sigma^2 = 0.00732$, $\bar{x} = 12.14$
Sample comes from a normal distribution with mean μ and variance σ^2
b $12.07 \leq \mu \leq 12.21$

9 $\hat{\mu} = 92.51$, $\hat{\sigma}^2 = 99.54$, $89.92 \leq \mu \leq 95.10$

10 **a** $\bar{x} = 1.44$, $s = 1.56$
b $\bar{y} = 0.76$
c $0.398 \leq \bar{y} \leq 1.122$

14 Significance Tests I: Single Values

Review (p. 378)

1 **a** 19.375, 11.125 **d** 1.007, $0.001\,21$
b 1.525, 0.042 **e** 2.305, 0.0136
c 199.6, 14.3

2 **a** 1.036 **b** 1.282 **c** 1.441
d 1.645 **e** 2.326

3 **a** 2.132 **b** 2.306 **c** 2.681
d 1.476 **e** 1.833

14.1 Technique (p. 383)

1 5

2 14

3 4

$\boxed{4}$ 10

$\boxed{5}$ 6

$\boxed{6}$ 26

$\boxed{7}$ 2

$\boxed{8}$ 14

$\boxed{9}$ 2

$\boxed{10}$ 8

$\boxed{11}$

	a 2.5%	b 1%
1	5	6
2	15	15
3	5	6
4	9	10
5	6	6
6	26	27
7	3	4
8	15	16
9	2	3
10	9	9

14.1 Contextual (p. 383)

$\boxed{1}$ H_0: $p = 0.1$; H_1: $p > 0.1$; reject H_0 (4.32%)

$\boxed{2}$ H_0: $p = 0.2$; H_1: $p > 0.2$; do not reject H_0 (9.82%)

$\boxed{3}$ H_0: $p = 1/3$; H_1: $p < 1/3$; reject H_0 (0.33%)

$\boxed{4}$ H_0: $p = 0.75$; H_1: $p < 0.75$; do not reject H_0 (28.25%)

$\boxed{5}$ H_0: $p = 1/6$; H_1: $p > 1/6$; reject H_0 (2.05%)

$\boxed{6}$ H_0: $p = 0.7$; H_1: $p < 0.7$; do not reject H_0 (2.57%), rejected at 5% level

14. 2 Contextual (p. 387)

$\boxed{1}$ H_0: $p = 0.5$; H_1: $p \neq 0.5$; two-tailed test; do not reject H_0 (7.04%)

$\boxed{2}$ H_0: $p = 0.5$; H_1: $p \neq 0.5$; two-tailed test; reject H_0 (3.09%)

$\boxed{3}$ H_0: $p = 0.2$; H_1: $p > 0.2$; one-tailed test; reject H_0 (3.21%)

$\boxed{4}$ H_0: $p = 0.7$; H_1: $p < 0.7$; one-tailed test; reject H_0 (4.03%)

$\boxed{5}$ Critical regions $h \leq 8$ and $h > 15$ two-tailed test.

$\boxed{6}$ H_0: $p = 0.2$; H_1: $p > 0.2$; one-tailed test; reject H_0 (1%)

$\boxed{7}$ H_0: $p = 0.6$; H_1: $p > 0.6$; one-tailed test; do not reject H_0 (5.47%)

$\boxed{8}$ H_0: $p = 0.4$; H_1: $p > 0.4$; one-tailed test; reject H_0 (2.5%)

14.3 Technique (p. 390)

$\boxed{1}$ $Z = 1.5$; do not reject H_0

$\boxed{2}$ $Z = 2$; reject H_0

$\boxed{3}$ $Z = 1.06$; do not reject H_0

$\boxed{4}$ $Z = -1.224$; do not reject H_0

$\boxed{5}$ $Z = -2.133$; reject H_0

$\boxed{6}$ $Z = 1.25$; do not reject H_0

$\boxed{7}$ $Z = 0.8$; do not reject H_0

$\boxed{8}$ $Z = 2.055$; reject H_0

$\boxed{9}$ $Z = 1.46$; do not reject H_0

$\boxed{10}$ $Z = 2$; reject H_0

$\boxed{11}$ $Z = 2.333$; reject H_0

$\boxed{12}$ $Z = 0.5$; do not reject H_0

14.3 Contextual (p. 391)

$\boxed{1}$ $Z = -1.789$; H_0: $\mu = 440$; H_1: $\mu \neq 440$; do not reject H_0 at 5% level

$\boxed{2}$ $Z = 2.167$; H_0: $\mu = 72$; H_1: $\mu > 72$; reject H_0 at 5% level

$\boxed{3}$ $Z = -0.427$; H_0: $\mu = 0.75$; H_1: $\mu < 0.75$; do not reject H_0

$\boxed{4}$ $Z = 2.667$; H_0: $\mu = 54$; H_1: $\mu > 54$; reject H_0

$\boxed{5}$ $Z = -2.530$; H_0: $\mu = 60$; H_1: $\mu < 60$; reject H_0

$\boxed{6}$ $Z = -1.460$; H_0: $\mu = 48$; H_1: $\mu < 48$; do not reject H_0

$\boxed{7}$ $Z = 1.207$; H_0: $\mu = 68.4$; H_1: $\mu > 68.4$; do not reject H_0

$\boxed{8}$ $Z = 1.194$; H_0: $\mu = 62.4$; H_1: $\mu > 62.4$; do not reject H_0

14.4 Technique (p. 394)

$\boxed{1}$ $Z = 3.33$; reject H_0

$\boxed{2}$ $Z = -1.342$; do not reject H_0

$\boxed{3}$ $Z = -2.236$; reject H_0

$\boxed{4}$ $Z = -4$; reject H_0

$\boxed{5}$ $Z = 4.619$; reject H_0

$\boxed{6}$ $Z = 1.633$; do not reject H_0

$\boxed{7}$ $Z = 0.652$; do not reject H_0

$\boxed{8}$ $Z = 6.25$; reject H_0

$\boxed{9}$ $Z = -1.886$; reject H_0

$\boxed{10}$ $Z = 3.285$; reject H_0

$\boxed{11}$ $Z = -1.725$; do not reject H_0

$\boxed{12}$ $Z = -0.939$; do not reject H_0

14.4 Contextual (p. 394)

1 $Z = 2.259$; H_0: $\mu = 80$; H_1: $\mu > 80$;
reject H_0

2 $Z = -1.237$; H_0: $\mu = 26$; H_1: $\mu \neq 26$;
do not reject H_0

3 $Z = 0.775$; H_0: $\mu = 65$; H_1: $\mu > 65$;
do not reject H_0

4 $Z = 2.905$; H_0: $\mu = 600$; H_1: $\mu > 600$;
reject H_0

5 $Z = 1.887$; H_0: $\mu = 0$; H_1: $\mu \neq 0$;
do not reject H_0

6 $Z = -0.854$; H_0: $\mu = 1$; H_1: $\mu \neq 1$;
do not reject H_0

7 $Z = 1.333$; H_0: $\mu = 25$; H_1: $\mu \neq 25$;
do not reject H_0

14.5 Contextual (p. 397)

1 $Z = -0.911$; H_0: $\mu = 167$ cm;
H_1: $\mu \neq 167$ cm; do not reject H_0

2 $Z = 1.789$; H_0: $\mu = 2.4$ kg; H_1: $\mu \neq 2.4$ kg;
at 5% do not reject H_0

3 $Z = 2.598$; H_0: $\mu = 76.8\%$; H_1: $\mu > 76.8\%$;
reject H_0

4 $Z = 2.236$; H_0: $\mu = 1$ m; H_1: $\mu > 1$ m;
at 5% reject H_0

5 $Z = -1.834$; H_0: $\mu = 1.01$; H_1: $\mu > 1.01$;
at 5% reject H_0

6 $Z = -2.302$; H_0: $\mu = 97\%$; H_1: $\mu \neq 97\%$;
do not reject H_0

7 $Z = -1.871$; H_0: $\mu = 145$; H_1: $\mu \neq 145$;
do not reject H_0

8 $Z = 3.006$; H_0: $\mu = 70$; H_1: $\mu > 70$; reject H_0

14.6 Technique (p. 401)

1 $t_4 = 0.613$; do not reject H_0

2 $t_7 = 3.207$; reject H_0

3 $t_9 = -1.650$; reject H_0

4 $t_5 = 4.472$; reject H_0

5 $t_7 = 0.610$; do not reject H_0

6 $t_8 = 0.300$; do not reject H_0

7 $t_2 = 0.433$; do not reject H_0

8 $t_6 = 2.00$; reject H_0

9 $t_{19} = 6.16$; reject H_0

10 $t_{10} = -1.173$; do not reject H_0

14.6 Contextual (p. 401)

1 $t_5 = -2.8415$; reject H_0: $\mu = 4$

2 $t_9 = 0.774$; do not reject H_0: $\mu = 2.2$

3 $t_5 = -2.304$; do not reject H_0: $\mu = 150$

4 $t_7 = -2.224$; do not reject H_0: $\mu = 0$

5 $t_{14} = 2.476$; reject H_0: $\mu = 2.5$

6 $t_9 = 1.55$; do not reject H_0: $\mu = 23$

7 $t_7 = 0.406$; do not reject H_0: $\mu = 3.7$

14.7 Technique (p. 405)

1 $Z = -1.826$; do not reject H_0

2 $Z = 1.633$; do not reject H_0

3 $Z = 2.108$; do not reject H_0

4 $Z = -2.025$; reject H_0

5 $Z = 2.054$; reject H_0

6 $Z = 1.035$; do not reject H_0

7 $Z = -0.383$; do not reject H_0

8 $Z = -4.622$; reject H_0

9 $Z = -2.126$; reject H_0

10 $Z = -1.545$; do not reject H_0

11 $Z = -2.265$; reject H_0

12 $Z = 0.949$; do not reject H_0

14.7 Contextual (p. 406)

1 $Z = -3.771$; reject H_0; accept H_1; $p < 0.9$

2 $Z = -3.403$; reject H_0; accept H_1; $p < 0.48$

3 $Z = 2.259$; do not reject H_0; $p = 0.04$

4 $Z = -2.849$; reject H_0; $p < 0.7$

5 $Z = 0.976$; do not reject H_0; $p = 0.78$

6 $Z = 6.608$; reject H_0; $p > 77.3\%$

7 $Z = 1.284$; do not reject H_0; $p = 6.32\%$

Consolidation A (p. 407)

1 The weights are normally distributed.
$\bar{x} = 120.88$; $s^2 = 0.915$; $s = 0.956$
H_0: $\bar{x} = \mu$; H_1: $\bar{x} > \mu$; critical value $= 1.476$;
$t_5 = 1.24$; do not reject H_0

2 **a** $\bar{x} = 7.733$; $s^2 = 36.35$; $\sigma^2 = 36.962$
b H_0: $\bar{x} = 10$; H_1: $\bar{x} \neq 10$;
critical value $= 1.96$; $Z = -2.888$;
reject H_0

3 **a** H_0: $p = 0.7$; H_1: $p < 0.7$;
testing lower values
b from tables $k = 11$
c $k = 4$

4 **a** normal distributions are used for large
samples while t-tests are used for small
samples, if the variance is unknown.
$\bar{x} = 3.13$; $s^2 = 0.240$; $s = 0.490$
H_0: $\bar{x} = \mu$; H_1: $\bar{x} > \mu$; critical
value $= 1.796$; $t_{11} = -2.015$; reject H_0
$\bar{y} = 48.55$; $s^2 = 5.768$; $s^2 = 6.29$;
$\bar{y} = 48.55 \pm 1.865$

5 **a** $\bar{x} = 14.9$; $s = 1.3$
H_0: $\bar{x} = 14$; H_1: $\bar{x} \neq 14$;
$Z = 1.696$, reject H_0

b $\bar{x} = 14.9$; $s = 1.497$; $t_5 = 1.345$; do not reject H_0

6. **a** $\mu = 42$; $\bar{x} = 43.8$; $n = 120$
H_0: $\bar{x} = 42$; H_1: $\bar{x} > 42$;
critical value $= 1.645$; $Z = 1.540$;
do not reject H_0
b because it is a large sample

7. **a** $\bar{x} = 120.875$; $s = 3.919$
H_0: $\bar{x} = 116$; H_1: $\bar{x} > 116$
b critical value $= 2.998$; $t_7 = 3.291$; reject H_0
c the yield is normally distributed

8. **a** H_0: $\bar{x} = 25$; H_1: $\bar{x} > 25$
b $105.6/4 = 26.4$
c $t_3 = 1.516$; do not reject H_0

9. $p_s = 0.66$; H_0: $p = 0.75$; H_1: $p < 0.75$;
critical value 1.645; $Z = -2.078$; reject H_0

10. **a** $\bar{x} = 13.76$; $s = 1.356$; $\bar{x} = 13.76 \pm 0.580$
b H_0: $\bar{x} = 13.76$; H_1: $\bar{x} \neq 13.76$;
critical value $= 2.086$; $t_{20} = 5.733$; reject H_0
There is no evidence to suggest the fish is of this species.

Consolidation B (p. 410)

1. $\bar{x} = 13.079$; $s = 0.179\,997$
H_0: $\bar{x} = 13$; H_1: $\bar{x} > 13$;
critical value $= 2.201$; $t_{11} = 1.448$;
do not reject H_0

2. $\bar{x} = 102.34$; $s = 3.36$
H_0: $\bar{x} = 100$; H_1: $\bar{x} > 100$;
critical value $= 2.262$; $t_9 = 2.118$; reject H_0

3. H_0: $\mu = 110$; H_1: $\mu \neq 110$;
critical value $= 3.25$; $t_9 = 3.1$;
do not reject H_0

4. H_0: $\bar{x} = 5.52$; H_1: $\bar{x} > 5.52$;
critical value $= 2.33$; $Z = 4.143$; reject H_0

5. H_0: $\mu = 125$; H_1: $\mu < 125$;
critical value $= -1.549$; $t_{14} = -1.497$;
do not reject H_0

6. **a** H_0: $p = 0.5$; H_1: $p > 0.5$; $p = 0.737$
b $Z = 2.065$; reject H_0

7. critical value $= 1.96$; $Z = -1.80$;
do not reject H_0

8. $\bar{x} = 32.583$; $s = 7.112$
H_0: $\bar{x} = 30$; H_1: $\bar{x} < 30$;
critical value $= 1.796$; $t_{11} = 1.2048$;
do not reject H_0

9. **a i** H_0: $\mu = 6.0$; H_1: $\mu \neq 6.0$;
critical value $= 1.96$; $Z = 1.739$;
do not reject H_0
ii H_0: $\mu = 6.0$; H_1: $\mu \neq 6.0$;
critical value $= 1.64$; $Z = 1.739$;
reject H_0
b 6 ± 0.225

10. $\bar{x} = 20.95$; $\hat{\sigma} = 2.674$
H_0: $\bar{x} = 21.5$; H_1: $\bar{x} < 21.5$;
critical value $= 1.895$; $t_7 = -0.582$;
do not reject H_0

15 Significance Tests II: Two Values

Review (p. 414)

1. 11.38, 28.36
2. 60.91, 418
3. 0.21, 0.0153
4. 1.22, 0.180
5. 4.31, 3.845
6. 0.309
7. 0.609
8. 0.474
9. 0.931
10. 0.513

15.1 Technique (p. 418)

1. $t_4 = 2.683$, reject H_0
2. $t_9 = 2.229$, do not reject H_0
3. $t_{12} = 2.212$, do not reject H_0
4. $t_7 = 1.407$, do not reject H_0
5. $t_{24} = 0.155$, do not reject H_0
6. $t_{18} = 1.830$, do not reject H_0
7. $t_3 = 7.348$, reject H_0
8. $t_5 = 1.929$, do not reject H_0
9. $t_9 = 2.002$, do not reject H_0
10. $t_4 = 2.058$, do not reject H_0

15.1 Contextual (p. 419)

1. $Z = 2.828$, reject H_0; second test is better
2. $t_5 = 2.826$, reject H_0 at 5% level; the wire is strengthened
3. **a** 3.415   **b** 3.935
4. $t_{11} = 3.079$, do not reject H_0
5. $t_9 = 0.172$, do not reject H_0
6. $t_9 = 0.0688$, do not reject H_0; there is no evidence to indicate any difference

15.2 Technique (p. 423)

1. $Z = 1.458$, reject H_0
2. $Z = 3.144$, reject H_0
3. $Z = 3.934$, reject H_0
4. $Z = 7.425$, reject H_0
5. $Z = 1.557$, do not reject H_0
6. $Z = 0.413$, do not reject H_0
7. $t_8 = 0.9395$, do not reject H_0
8. $t_{11} = 0.788$, do not reject H_0

9 $t_{29} = 7.198$, reject H_0

10 $t_{10} = 0.846$, do not reject H_0

15.2 Contextual (p. 423)

1 $Z = 0.886$; no significant evidence to indicate difference

2 $Z = 2.977$, reject H_0; there is sufficient evidence to indicate the mean wage of the workers in the first factory is higher

3 $t_{18} = 6.656$, reject H_0; there is significant evidence to indicate the mean weights of the bags are different

4 Machine A, $t_{16} = 1.348$; indicates no change
Machine B, $t_{14} = 1.850$, decrease

5 $t_{14} = 1.175$, reject H_0 at 10%, do not reject H_0 at 5%

6 $t_{18} = 2.104$, reject H_0; there is evidence to indicate a significant difference between the means

15.3 Contextual (p. 427)

1 $|Z| = 1.508$, do not reject H_0

2 $|Z| = 1.021$, do not reject H_0, $p_b = p_9$

3 $|Z| = 1.156$, do not reject H_0, $p_1 = p_2$

4 $|Z| = 5.41$, reject H_0, accept H_1: $p_A < p_B$

5 $|Z| = 0.991$, do not reject H_0, $p_1 = p_2$

6 $|Z| = 1.136$, do not reject H_0, $p_A = p_B$

7 $|Z| = 0.998$, do not reject H_0, $p_A = p_B$
$|Z| = 0.979$, do not reject H_0

15.4 Contextual (p. 433)

1 $U = 9, Z = 0.516$, do not reject H_0: median is £250

2 $U = 7, Z = -0.707$, at 5% level do not reject H_0

3 $U = 6, Z = -1.152$, do not reject H_0

4 $U = 8, Z = 2.000$, reject H_0, the hens do lay more eggs

5 $U = 6, Z = 0.667$, do not reject H_0

6 $U = 9, Z = 0.516$, do not reject H_0

7 $U = 5, Z = 0.756$, do not reject H_0

15.5 Contextual (p. 437)

1 $T = 39$, do not reject H_0

2 $T = 67\frac{1}{2}$, do not reject H_0

3 $T = 3\frac{1}{2}$, reject H_0

4 $T = 20$, do not reject H_0

5 $T = 36\frac{1}{2}$, dop not reject H_0

6 $T = 14\frac{1}{2}$, do not reject H_0

Consolidation A (p. 439)

1 **a** $\bar{x} = 2.316, s^2 = 0.300, \sigma^2 = 0.303$
b H_0: $\mu_A = \mu_B$, H_1: $\mu_A \neq \mu_B$, critical value = 1.645, $Z = -1.2776$, do not reject H_0

2 **a** the volumes are normally distributed
b $\mu_1 = 499.75, s = 1.2907, \mu_2 = 500.2909$, $s = 0.9140$, H_0: $\mu_1 = \mu_2$, H_1: $\mu_1 \neq \mu_2$
c critical value = 2.13, $t_{15} = 0.942$, do not reject H_0

3 **a** $n = 10, U = 8$, H_0: $s = 0$, H_1: $s > 0$, critical value = 1.645, $Z = 1.581$, do not reject H_0
b $T = 5\frac{1}{2}$, reject H_0

4 **a** $\bar{x} = 100 \div 50 = 2, s = 1.183$
b $p = 0.2$, $P(X = 2) = 0.3020$; the observed frequency is almost exactly equal to the expected frequency.
c H_0: $p = 0.2$, H_1: $p \leq 0.2$, critical value = 1.645, $Z = 1.291$, reject H_0
d reject H_0

5 **a** H_0: $p_1 = p_2$, H_1: $p_1 < p_2$,
  i critical value = 1.645, $Z = 1.809$, reject H_0
  ii $T = 12\frac{1}{2}$, reject H_0

b

d	22	21	9	-2	10	0	13	1	9	13

$\bar{d} = 9.6, s = 7.8$, critical value = 1.833, $t_9 = 3.69$, reject H_0

6 H_0: $\mu_b = \mu_g$, H_1: $\mu_b \neq \mu_g$, $t_{26} = 2.157$, reject H_0

7 $p_s = 0.483$
H_0: $p_s = 0.42$, H_1: $p_s > 0.42$, critical value = 1.65, $Z = 1.4057$, accept H_0

8

d	0.1	-0.1	0.3	-0.1	0.4	0.1	1.1

$d = -0.257, s = 0.3849$, critical value = 1.440, $t_6 = 1.636$, reject H_0

9 the differences in the times are distributed normally H_0: $d = 0$, H_1: $d \neq 0$, critical value = 2.262

d	6.3	-1	3.8	3.3	9.3	-0.2	1.3	5.2	0	-2

$\bar{d} = 2.6, s = 3.430, t_9 = 2.274$, reject H_0

10 **a i** $\bar{x} = 12.14, \hat{\sigma} = 0.0856$
  ii the voltage is normally distributed
  H_0: $\bar{x} = 12$, H_1: $\bar{x} > 12$, critical value = 2.015, $t_5 = 3.657$, reject H_0

b

Country A	$\bar{x}_A = 3.402$	$s^2 = 0.8106$
Country B	$\bar{x}_B = 2.7975$	$s^2 = 0.6386$

H_0: $\bar{x}_A = \bar{x}_B$, H_1: $\bar{x}_A > \bar{x}_B$, critical value = 1.645, $Z = 5.192$, reject H_0

Consolidation B (p. 443)

1 $\bar{x} = 2.018, \hat{\sigma} = 0.0575$
H_0: $\bar{x} = 2$, H_1: $\bar{x} > 2$, critical value = 2.821, $t_9 = 0.9899$, do not reject H_0
$\bar{x} = 1.905, s^2 = 0.003\,02$
H_0: $\bar{x}_1 = \bar{x}_2$, H_1: $\bar{x}_1 \neq \bar{x}_2$, critical value = 1.313, $t_{28} = 0.9717$, do not reject H_0

2 **a** H_0: $\bar{d} = 0$, H_1: $\bar{d} > 0$
b

d	1	1	-1	4	1	4	0	-1

$\bar{d} = 1.125, s = 1.833, t_7 = 1.624$, at 10% reject H_0, else accept H_0

3 Method A: $\bar{x} = 7.4$, $s^2 = 2.907$, $\hat{\sigma}^2 = 3.007$
Method B: $\bar{x} = 6.5$, $s^2 = 3.083$, $\hat{\sigma}^2 = 3.190$
$H_0: \bar{x}_A = \bar{x}_B$, $H_1: \bar{x}_A \geq \bar{x}_B$, critical
value $= 2.054$, $Z = 1.98$, do not reject H_0

4 Poisson is a good approximation to the
binomial for small p and large n.
$\lambda = 4.05$, $P(X = 4) = 0.195$, $p = 0.0625$
$H_0: p = 0.045$, $H_1: p > 0.045$, critical
value $= 1.65$, $Z = 1.688$, reject H_0

5 $\bar{x}_1 = 3.25$, $s^2 = 0.616$, $\sigma_1^2 = 0.6200$,
$\bar{x}_2 = 2.86$, $s^2 = 0.335$, $\sigma_2^2 = 0.3364$
$H_0: \bar{x}_1 - 0.5 = \bar{x}_2$, $H_1: \bar{x}_1 - 0.5 > \bar{x}_2$,
critical value $= 1.645$, $Z = -1.44$, do not
reject H_0; claim not supported

6 **a** $U = 9$, critical value $= 2.33$, $Z = 2.214$,
reject H_0
b $T = 4$, reject H_0

7 A: $\bar{X}_1 = 6.75$, $s_1 = 0.9747$
B: $\bar{X}_2 = 4.55$, $s_2 = 0.8977$
$H_0: \bar{x}_A = \bar{x}_B$, $H_1: \bar{x}_A > \bar{x}_B$, $t_{12} = 4.002$,
reject H_0

8 $H_0: p = 0.05$
$H_1: p > 0.05$, critical value $= 1.645$,
$Z = 1.376$, do not reject H_0

9 **a** $\bar{X} = 44.2 \pm 3.136$
b $H_0: \bar{x}_A = \bar{x}_B$, $H_1: \bar{x}_A > \bar{x}_B$, critical
value $= 1.645$, $Z = 1.375$, do not reject H_0

10 **a** $H_0: \bar{x}_A = \bar{x}_B$, $H_1: \bar{x}_A \neq \bar{x}_B$
b normally distributed

c

	$\bar{x}$	$\hat{\sigma}$	s
Sample A	1504.25	23.897	22.354
Sample B	1479.75	19.66	18.824

critical value $= 2.101$, $t_{18} = 2.507$,
reject H_0

16 Chi-squared Test

Review (p. 448)

1 **a** 0.318   **b** 0.215   **c** 0.007 88
d 0.391   **e** 0.558

2 **a** 0.168   **b** 0.184   **c** 0.030
d 0.857   **e** 0.380

16.1 Contextual (p. 452)

1 $\chi^2 = 43.4$, reject H_0, at 5% level accept
H_1: the dice is biased

2 $\chi^2 = 25.33$, reject H_0, at 5% level accept
H_1: absences are related to the day of the
week

3 $\chi^2 = 42.69$, reject H_0, at 5% level accept
H_1: germination is related to soil type

4 $\chi^2 = 8.85$, reject H_0 at 5% level, accept
H_1: the machine needs resetting

5 $\chi^2 = 28.43$, reject H_0, at 5% level accept H_1:
choice is gender biased

6 $\chi^2 = 11.14$, do not reject H_0 at 5% level

7 $\chi^2 = 22.62$, reject H_0, at 5% level accept
H_1: there is a significant difference between
actual and estimated grades

16.2 Contextual (p. 457)

1 $\chi^2 = 1.492$, accept H_0 [classes 2 and 3
combined]

2 $\chi^2 = 3.949$, accept H_0 [classes 5 and 6
combined]

3 $\chi^2 = 5.918$, accept H_0 [classes 4, 5, 6, 7 and
8 combined]

4 mean $= 3.33$, $p = 0.416$, $\chi^2 = 16.98$,
reject H_0

5 $\chi^2 = 14.87$, reject H_0, results do not fit a
binomial distribution

6 $\chi^2 = 12.257$, reject H_0, data does not fit a
binomial distribution

16.3 Contextual (p. 459)

1 mean $= 2.025$, variance $= 2.094$, $\lambda = 2$,
$\chi^2 = 2.43$, do not reject H_0

2 mean $= 1.545$, variance $= 1.45$, $\lambda = 1.5$,
$\chi^2 = 0.592$, do not reject H_0

3 mean $= 2.27$, variance $= 1.73$, $\lambda = 2.3$,
$\chi^2 = 1.88$, do not reject H_0

4 mean $= 2.6$, variance $= 2.78$, $\lambda = 2.6$,
$\chi^2 = 11.93$, reject H_0

5 **a** E: 182.96, 164.66, 74.10, 22.23, 5.00, 1.05
b mean $= 0.9$, variance $= 0.91$, $\lambda = 0.9$,
$\chi^2 = 1.67$, do not reject H_0

16.4 Contextual (p. 465)

1 mean $= 26.75$, variance $= 42.56$, $\chi^2 = 3.13$,
do not reject H_0

2 mean $= 23.62$, variance $= 99.658$,
$\chi^2 = 1.815$, do not reject H_0 at 5% level

3 mean $= 166.38$, variance $= 59.77$,
$\chi^2 = 12.73$, do not reject H_0

4 $\chi^2 = 15.29$, do not reject H_0

5 mean $= 71.21$, variance $= 42.53$,
$\chi^2 = 12.73$, do not reject H_0

16.5 Technique (p. 469)

1 $\chi^2 = 3.21$, $v = 3$, do not reject H_0
2 $\chi^2 = 10.41$, $v = 2$, reject H_0, accept H_1
3 $\chi^2 = 0.82$, $v = 4$, do not reject H_0
4 $\chi^2 = 20.85$, $v = 2$, reject H_0, accept H_1
5 $\chi^2 = 33.74$, $v = 6$, reject H_0 accept H_1

16.5 Contextual (p. 469)

1 $\chi^2 = 31.88$, $v = 6$, reject H_0, accept H_1
2 $\chi^2 = 5.93$, $v = 12$, do not reject H_0
3 $\chi^2 = 7.65$, $v = 8$, do not reject H_0
4 $\chi^2 = 0.99$, $v = 6$, do not reject H_0
5 $\chi^2 = 78.98$, $v = 10$, reject H_0, accept H_1

16.6 Technique (p. 474)

1. $\chi^2 = 0.46$, $v = 1$, do not reject H_0
2. $\chi^2 = 0.00$, $v = 1$, do not reject H_0
3. $\chi^2 = 11.48$, $v = 1$, reject H_0, accept H_1
4. $\chi^2 = 8.12$, $v = 1$, reject H_0, accept H_1
5. $\chi^2 = 21.4$, $v = 1$, reject H_0, accept H_1

16.6 Contextual (p. 474)

1. $\chi^2 = 0.56$, $v = 1$, do not reject H_0
2. $\chi^2 = 1.12$, $v = 1$, do not reject H_0
3. $\chi^2 = 0.013$, $v = 1$, do not reject H_0
4. $\chi^2 = 1.72$, $v = 1$, do not reject H_0
5. $\chi^2 = 0.25$, $v = 1$, reject H_0, accept H_1

16.7 Technique (p. 480)

1. **a** $r = 0.983$, $n = 8$, critical value at 5% 0.7067, at 1% 0.834; therefore the two variables show a high degree of correlation
   b $r = -0.365$, $n = 7$, critical value at 5% 0.7545, at 20% 0.5509; therefore the two variables show no significant correlation.
2. $r = 0.939$, $n = 8$; as question 1, the two variables show a high degree of correlation
3. $r = 0.805$, $n = 9$, critical value at 5% 0.6664, at 1% 0.7977; therefore the two variables show a high degree of correlation
4. $r = 0.924$, $n = 6$, critical value at 5% 0.8114, at 1% 0.9172; therefore the two variables show a high degree of correlation
5. $r = -0.171$, $n = 10$, critical value at 5% 0.6319, at 20% 0.4428; therefore the two variables show no significant correlation

16.8 Technique (p. 484)

1. **a** $r_s = -0.036$, $n = 7$, critical value at 5% 0.7857, at 20% 0.5714; therefore there is no significant correlation between the two variables.
   b $r_s = -0.891$, $n = 10$, critical value at 5% 0.6485, at 1% 0.7818; therefore the two variable show a high degree of correlation
2. $r_s = 0.771$, $n = 6$, critical value at 5% 0.8286, at 10% 0.7714, at 20% 0.6571; the coefficient is not significant at a level that can be quoted with confidence
3. $r_s = 0.893$, $n = 7$, critical value at 5% 0.7857, at 1% 0.8929; there is a strong positive correlation between the rankings of the judges
4. $r_s = 0.939$, $n = 10$; as in question 1 there is a very strong positive correlation between German and French test results

5. $r_s = 0.851$, $n = 8$, critical value at 5% 0.7381, at 2% 0.8095, at 1% 0.8571; there is a strong positive correlation between annual income per head and life expectancy at birth

16.9 Contextual (p. 488)

1. H_0: $p = 0.5$, P(Type I error) in both cases $= 0.125$
   H_1: $p = \frac{2}{3}$ (heads), first test $P(H_0) = 0.79$, second test $P(H_0) = 0.73$; second test is better
2. **a** 0.0588
   b 0.010, P(Type I error) $= 0.05$
   If heads > 100 reject,
   P(Type II error) $= 0.278$
3. P(Type I error) $= 0.367$,
   P(Type II error) $= 0.188$
4. $n = 11$, $n = 7$

Consolidation A (p. 489)

1. Expected frequencies

	D	Not D
P	122.1	131.9
Not P	324.9	351.1

$\chi^2 = 14.02$, $v = 1$, reject H_0, accept H_1, dependent

2. Observed

	CB	Not CB
Male	20	380
Female	20	580

Expected

	CB	Not CB
Male	16	384
Female	24	576

$\chi^2 = 1.329$, $v = 1$, accept H_0, independent

3. Expected frequencies

	Men	Women
Depression	8.7	14.3
Anxiety state	8.0	13.0
Other	5.3	8.7

$\chi^2 = 8.6$, $v = 2$, reject H_0, accept H_1, independent

4. **a** randomly occurring variable within a set time limit
   b $\bar{x} = 2.7$, $s^2 = 2.67$; as mean and variance approximately equal then a condition for Poisson

c $\lambda = 2.7$, expected frequencies: 6.72, 18.15, 24.50, 22.05, 14.88, 8.04, 5.67
$\chi^2 = 25.16$, $v = 5$, reject H_0, accept H_1, not Poisson

5 expected frequencies = 32
$\chi^2 = 1.6875$, $v = 3$, accept H_0; flight random

6 $\bar{x} = \frac{100}{20} = 5$, $p = \frac{5}{6}$, expected values:
1.2451, 4.0188, 8.0376, 6.698
$\chi^2 = 0.856$, $v = 1$, accept H_0, binomial

7 $P(\text{Type I error}) = 0.0885$

8 $\bar{x} = 71.867 \pm 0.374$
$\chi^2 = 13.7$, $v = 3$, reject H_0, accept H_1; not normal

9 $\chi^2 = 2.9774$, $v = 2$
Some evidence to suggest there is some association between gender and time spent watching TV.

10 a $\bar{x} = \frac{200}{80} = 2.5$ **b** 6.6 and 16.4
c $\chi^2 = 8.92$, $v = 4$, accept H_0

Consolidation B (p. 492)

1 $H_0: p = \frac{1}{2}$, $H_1: p \neq \frac{1}{2}$, $p = 0.44$, $Z = -1.31$, accept H_0, not biased
$\chi^2 = 5.2$, $v = 5$, accept H_0, not biased

2 H_0: cavities equally likely to occur on left and right sides
Testing at 5% level, $\chi^2 = 5.3799$, reject H_0, there is some evidence to suggest cavities do not occur equally on each side.

3 a $\chi^2 = 33.5$, $v = 3$, reject H_0, accept H_1, dependent

b new treatment is an improvement

c

	Died	Refused	Untraceable
New treatment	19	10	15
Old treatment	3	12	18

$\chi^2 = 10.74$, $v = 2$, reject H_0, accept H_1, dependent

4 $\chi^2 = 39.06$, $v = 2$, reject H_0, accept H_1, dependent

5 a $\bar{x} = \frac{500}{200} = 2.5$
b $p = 0.4$, expected frequencies: 80, 48, 28.8, 17.28, 10.368, 6.208, 9.3312
$\chi^2 = 5.27$, $v = 4$, accept H_0, model fits

6 $Z = 10.4$, accept H_0, machines equal

7 $P(\text{Type I error}) = 0.125$,
$P(\text{Type II error}) = 0.073$, $m = 30$

8 a $\chi^2 = 35.31$, $v = 3$, reject H_0, accept H_1, dependent
b when the expected frequency is less than 5
c $\chi^2 = 82.4$, $v = 29$, reject H_0, accept H_1, dependent

9 a expected frequencies: 13.6, 18.2, 22.2, 18.2, 13.6
b $\chi^2 = 2.54$, $v = 4$, accept H_0, normal fits

10 H_0: passing is independent of gender
H_1: passing is dependent on gender
$\chi^2 = 2.586$, $v = 1$, at 10% accept H_0; independent

Formulas

This is a list of formulas you should **remember**. Each formula has been referenced to the chapter in which it **first appears** in the text.

TOPIC	FORMULA	CHAPTER
Mean of raw data	$$\bar{x} = \frac{\Sigma x}{n}$$	4
Mean of frequency distribution	$$\bar{x} = \frac{\Sigma fx}{\Sigma f}$$	4
Variance of raw data	$$s^2 = \frac{\Sigma(x - \bar{x})^2}{n}$$ or $\quad$ $$s^2 = \frac{\Sigma x^2}{n} - \bar{x}^2$$	4
Variance of frequency distribution	$$s^2 = \frac{\Sigma f(x - \bar{x})^2}{\Sigma f}$$ or $\quad$ $$s^2 = \frac{\Sigma fx^2}{\Sigma f} - \bar{x}^2$$	4
Complementary probability	$$P(A') = 1 - P(A)$$	5
Addition rule	$$P(A \cup B) = P(A) + P(B) - P(A \cap B)$$	5
Product rule for independent events	$$P(A \cap B) = P(A) \times P(B)$$	5
Conditional probability	$$P(A|B) = \frac{P(A \cap B)}{P(B)}$$ or $\quad$ $$P(A \cap B) = P(B) \times P(A|B)$$	5
Permutations	$${}^nP_r = \frac{n!}{(n - r)!}$$	6
Combinations	$${}^nC_r = \frac{n!}{(n - r)!r!}$$	6
Mean/ expected value of discrete distribution	$$\mu = E(X) = \Sigma xP(X = x)$$ $$E(aX + b) = aE(X) + b$$ $$E(X \pm Y) = E(X) \pm E(Y)$$	7

TOPIC	FORMULA	CHAPTER
Variance of discrete distribution	$\sigma^2 = \text{Var}(X) = E[(X - \mu)^2]$ or $\quad \text{Var}(X) = E(X^2) - \mu^2$ $\text{Var}(aX + b) = a^2 \text{Var}(X)$ $\text{Var}(X \pm Y) = \text{Var}(X) + \text{Var}(Y)$	7
Binomial distribution $X \sim B(n, p)$	$E(X) = np$ $\text{Var}(X) = npq$ where $q = 1 - p$ $P(X = r) = {}^nC_r \, r^p (1 - r)^q$	8
Poisson distribution $X \sim Po(\lambda)$	$E(X) = \lambda$ $\text{Var}(X) = \lambda$ $P(X = r) = \dfrac{e^{-\lambda} \lambda^r}{r!}$	8
Geometric distribution $X \sim G(p)$	$E(X) = \dfrac{1}{p}$ $\text{Var}(X) = \dfrac{q}{p^2}$ where $q = 1 - p$ $P(X = r) = q^{r-1} p$ $P(X \le r) = 1 - q^n$	8
Mean/expected of continuous distribution	$\mu = E(X) = \displaystyle\int_{-X}^{X} x f(x) \, dx$	9
Variance for continuous distribution	$\sigma^2 = \text{Var}(X) = \displaystyle\int_{-\infty}^{\infty} x^2 f(x) \, dx$	9
Cumulative distribution function	$F(x) = \displaystyle\int_{-\infty}^{\infty} f(x) \, dx$	9
Median of continuous distribution	$F(m) = 0.5$	9
Standardising a normal distribution	$Z = \dfrac{X - \mu}{\sigma} \sim N(0, 1^2)$	10
Normal approximation to binomial distribution	$X \sim N(np, npq)$	10
Normal approximation to Poisson distribution	$X \sim N(\lambda, \lambda)$	10

TOPIC	FORMULA	CHAPTER
Covariance	$$s_{xy} = \frac{\Sigma xy}{n} - \bar{x}\bar{y}$$	11
Pearson's product moment correlation coefficient	$$r = \frac{s_{xy}}{s_x s_y} = \frac{\frac{\Sigma xy}{n} - \bar{x}\bar{y}}{\sqrt{\left(\frac{\Sigma x^2}{n} - \bar{x}^2\right)\left(\frac{\Sigma y^2}{n} - \bar{y}^2\right)}}$$	11
Spearman's rank correlation coefficient	$$r_s = 1 - \frac{6\Sigma d^2}{n(n^2 - 1)}$$	11
Least squares regression line	$$y - \bar{y} = \frac{s_{xy}}{s_{xx}}(x - \bar{x})$$	11
Standard error	$$\frac{\sigma}{\sqrt{n}}$$	12
Unbiased estimator for population variance	$$\hat{\sigma}^2 = \frac{ns^2}{n - 1}$$	12
Unbiased estimator for mean of a population from two samples	$$\hat{\mu} = \frac{n_1\bar{x}_1 + n_2\bar{x}_2}{n_1 + n_2}$$	12
Unbiased estimator for variance of a population from two samples	$$\hat{\sigma}^2 = \frac{n_1 s^2 + n_2 s_2^2}{n_1 + n_2 - 2}$$	12
Unbiased estimator for proportion of a population from two samples	$$\hat{p} = \frac{n_1 p_1 + n_2 p_2}{n_1 + n_2}$$	12

TOPIC	FORMULA		CHAPTER
Confidence intervals for population mean – large sample	90%	$\bar{x} \pm 1.645\dfrac{\sigma}{\sqrt{n}}$	13
	95%	$\bar{x} \pm 1.96\dfrac{\sigma}{\sqrt{n}}$	
	99%	$\bar{x} \pm 2.576\dfrac{\sigma}{\sqrt{n}}$	
Confidence intervals for population mean – small sample	where and	$\bar{x} \pm \dfrac{ts}{\sqrt{(n-1)}}$ $X \sim t(v)$ $t = \dfrac{\bar{x} - \mu}{s/\sqrt{(n-1)}}$	13
Confidence limits for population proportion	90%	$p \pm 1.645\sqrt{\dfrac{p_s q_s}{n}}$	13
	95%	$p \pm 1.96\sqrt{\dfrac{p_s q_s}{n}}$	
	99%	$p \pm 2.576\sqrt{\dfrac{p_s q_s}{n}}$	
Testing difference between means of paired samples	Large samples Small samples	$Z = \dfrac{\bar{D}}{\sigma_D/\sqrt{n}}$ $t = \dfrac{\bar{D}}{s/\sqrt{(n-1)}}$	15
Unpaired samples	Large sample sizes	$Z = \dfrac{\bar{x}_1 - \bar{x}_2}{\sqrt{\dfrac{\sigma_1^2}{n_1} + \dfrac{\sigma_2^2}{n_2}}}$	15
Unpaired samples	Small sample sizes	$t = \dfrac{\bar{x}_1 - \bar{x}_2}{\sigma\sqrt{\dfrac{1}{n_1} + \dfrac{1}{n_2}}}$	15
Testing difference between proportions		$Z = \dfrac{p_1 - p_2}{\sqrt{\hat{p}(1-\hat{p})\left(\dfrac{1}{n_1} + \dfrac{1}{n_2}\right)}}$	15

TOPIC	FORMULA	CHAPTER
Sign test	$$Z = \dfrac{U - \dfrac{n}{2} \pm \dfrac{1}{2}}{\sqrt{\dfrac{n}{4}}}$$	15
Chi-squared (χ^2) Test	$$\chi^2 = \sum \dfrac{(O - E)^2}{E}$$	16
Yates continuity correction	$$\chi^2 = \sum \dfrac{(|O - E| - 0.5)^2}{E}$$	16

Statistics Tables

Binomial Cumulative Distribution Function

The tabulated value is $P(X \leq x)$, where X has a binomial distribution with index n and parameter p.

$p =$	0.05	0.10	0.15	0.20	0.25	0.30	0.35	0.40	0.45	0.50
$n = 5, x = 0$	0.7738	0.5905	0.4437	0.3277	0.2373	0.1681	0.1160	0.0778	0.0503	0.0312
1	0.9774	0.9185	0.8352	0.7373	0.6328	0.5282	0.4284	0.3370	0.2562	0.1875
2	0.9988	0.9914	0.9734	0.9421	0.8965	0.8369	0.7648	0.6826	0.5931	0.5000
3	1.0000	0.9995	0.9978	0.9933	0.9844	0.9692	0.9460	0.9130	0.8688	0.8125
4	1.0000	1.0000	0.9999	0.9997	0.9990	0.9976	0.9947	0.9898	0.9815	0.9688
$n = 10, x = 0$	0.5987	0.3487	0.1969	0.1074	0.0563	0.0282	0.0135	0.0060	0.0025	0.0010
1	0.9139	0.7361	0.5443	0.3758	0.2440	0.1493	0.0860	0.0464	0.0233	0.0107
2	0.9885	0.9298	0.8202	0.6778	0.5256	0.3828	0.2616	0.1673	0.0996	0.0547
3	0.9990	0.9872	0.9500	0.8791	0.7759	0.6496	0.5138	0.3823	0.2660	0.1719
4	0.9999	0.9984	0.9901	0.9672	0.9219	0.8497	0.7515	0.6331	0.5044	0.3770
5	1.0000	0.9999	0.9986	0.9936	0.9803	0.9527	0.9051	0.8338	0.7384	0.6230
6	1.0000	1.0000	0.9999	0.9991	0.9965	0.9894	0.9740	0.9452	0.8980	0.8281
7	1.0000	1.0000	1.0000	0.9999	0.9996	0.9984	0.9952	0.9877	0.9726	0.9453
8	1.0000	1.0000	1.0000	1.0000	1.0000	0.9999	0.9995	0.9983	0.9955	0.9893
9	1.0000	1.0000	1.0000	1.0000	1.0000	1.0000	1.0000	0.9999	0.9997	0.9990
$n = 20, x = 0$	0.3585	0.1216	0.0388	0.0115	0.0032	0.0008	0.0002	0.0000	0.0000	0.0000
1	0.7358	0.3917	0.1756	0.0692	0.0243	0.0076	0.0021	0.0005	0.0001	0.0000
2	0.9245	0.6769	0.4049	0.2061	0.0913	0.0355	0.0121	0.0036	0.0009	0.0002
3	0.9841	0.8670	0.6477	0.4114	0.2252	0.1071	0.0444	0.0160	0.0049	0.0013
4	0.9974	0.9568	0.8298	0.6296	0.4148	0.2375	0.1182	0.0510	0.0189	0.0059
5	0.9997	0.9887	0.9327	0.8042	0.6172	0.4164	0.2454	0.1256	0.0553	0.0207
6	1.0000	0.9976	0.9781	0.9133	0.7858	0.6080	0.4166	0.2500	0.1299	0.0577
7	1.0000	0.9996	0.9941	0.9679	0.8982	0.7723	0.6010	0.4159	0.2520	0.1316
8	1.0000	0.9999	0.9987	0.9900	0.9591	0.8867	0.7624	0.5956	0.4143	0.2517
9	1.0000	1.0000	0.9998	0.9974	0.9861	0.9520	0.8782	0.7553	0.5914	0.4119
10	1.0000	1.0000	1.0000	0.9994	0.9961	0.9829	0.9468	0.8725	0.7507	0.5881
11	1.0000	1.0000	1.0000	0.9999	0.9991	0.9949	0.9804	0.9435	0.8692	0.7483
12	1.0000	1.0000	1.0000	1.0000	0.9998	0.9987	0.9940	0.9790	0.9420	0.8684
13	1.0000	1.0000	1.0000	1.0000	1.0000	0.9997	0.9985	0.9935	0.9786	0.9423
14	1.0000	1.0000	1.0000	1.0000	1.0000	1.0000	0.9997	0.9984	0.9936	0.9793
15	1.0000	1.0000	1.0000	1.0000	1.0000	1.0000	1.0000	0.9997	0.9985	0.9941
16	1.0000	1.0000	1.0000	1.0000	1.0000	1.0000	1.0000	1.0000	0.9997	0.9987
17	1.0000	1.0000	1.0000	1.0000	1.0000	1.0000	1.0000	1.0000	1.0000	0.9998
18	1.0000	1.0000	1.0000	1.0000	1.0000	1.0000	1.0000	1.0000	1.0000	1.0000

Poisson Cumulative Distribution Function

The tabulated value is $P(X \leq r)$, where X has a Poisson distribution with parameter λ.

$\lambda =$	0.5	1.0	1.5	20	2.5	3.0	3.5	4.0	4.5	5.0
$r = 0$	0.6065	0.3679	0.2231	0.1353	0.0821	0.0498	0.0302	0.0183	0.0111	0.0067
1	0.9098	0.7358	0.5578	0.4060	0.2873	0.1991	0.1359	0.0916	0.0611	0.0404
2	0.9856	0.9197	0.8088	0.6767	0.5438	0.4232	0.3208	0.2381	0.1736	0.1247
3	0.9982	0.9810	0.9344	0.8571	0.7576	0.6472	0.5366	0.4335	0.3423	0.2650
4	0.9998	0.9963	0.9814	0.9473	0.8912	0.8153	0.7254	0.6288	0.5321	0.4405
5	1.0000	0.9994	0.9955	0.9834	0.9580	0.9161	0.8576	0.7851	0.7029	0.6160
6	1.0000	0.9999	0.9991	0.9955	0.9858	0.9665	0.9347	0.8893	0.8311	0.7622
7	1.0000	1.0000	0.9998	0.9989	0.9958	0.9881	0.9733	0.9489	0.9134	0.8666
8	1.0000	1.0000	1.0000	0.9998	0.9989	0.9962	0.9901	0.9786	0.9597	0.9319
9	1.0000	1.0000	1.0000	1.0000	0.9997	0.9989	0.9967	0.9919	0.9829	0.9682
10	1.0000	1.0000	1.0000	1.0000	0.9999	0.9997	0.9990	0.9972	0.9933	0.9863
11	1.0000	1.0000	1.0000	1.0000	1.0000	0.9999	0.9997	0.9991	0.9976	0.9945
12	1.0000	1.0000	1.0000	1.0000	1.0000	1.0000	0.9999	0.9997	0.9992	0.9980
13	1.0000	1.0000	1.0000	1.0000	1.0000	1.0000	1.0000	0.9999	0.9997	0.9993
14	1.0000	1.0000	1.0000	1.0000	1.0000	1.0000	1.0000	1.0000	0.9999	0.9998
15	1.0000	1.0000	1.0000	1.0000	1.0000	1.0000	1.0000	1.0000	1.0000	0.9999
16	1.0000	1.0000	1.0000	1.0000	1.0000	1.0000	1.0000	1.0000	1.0000	1.0000
17	1.0000	1.0000	1.0000	1.0000	1.0000	1.0000	1.0000	1.0000	1.0000	1.0000
18	1.0000	1.0000	1.0000	1.0000	1.0000	1.0000	1.0000	1.0000	1.0000	1.0000
19	1.0000	1.0000	1.0000	1.0000	1.0000	1.0000	1.0000	1.0000	1.0000	1.0000

$\lambda =$	5.5	6.0	6.5	7.0	7.5	8.0	8.5	9.0	9.5	10.0
$r = 0$	0.0041	0.0025	0.0015	0.0009	0.0006	0.0003	0.0002	0.0001	0.0001	0.0000
1	0.0266	0.0174	0.0113	0.0073	0.0047	0.0030	0.0019	0.0012	0.0008	0.0005
2	0.0884	0.0620	0.0430	0.0296	0.0203	0.0138	0.0093	0.0062	0.0042	0.0028
3	0.2017	0.1512	0.1118	0.0818	0.0591	0.0424	0.0301	0.0212	0.0149	0.0103
4	0.3575	0.2851	0.2237	0.1730	0.1321	0.0996	0.0744	0.0550	0.0403	0.0293
5	0.5289	0.4457	0.3690	0.3007	0.2414	0.1912	0.1496	0.1157	0.0885	0.0671
6	0.6860	0.6063	0.5265	0.4497	0.3782	0.3134	0.2562	0.2068	0.1649	0.1301
7	0.8095	0.7440	0.6728	0.5987	0.5246	0.4530	0.3856	0.3239	0.2687	0.2202
8	0.8944	0.8472	0.7916	0.7291	0.6620	0.5925	0.5231	0.4557	0.3918	0.3328
9	0.9462	0.9161	0.8774	0.8305	0.7764	0.7166	0.6530	0.5874	0.5218	0.4579
10	0.9747	0.9574	0.9332	0.9015	0.8622	0.8159	0.7634	0.7060	0.6453	0.5830
11	0.9890	0.9799	0.9661	0.9467	0.9208	0.8881	0.8487	0.8030	0.7520	0.6968
12	0.9955	0.9912	0.9840	0.9730	0.9573	0.9362	0.9091	0.8758	0.8364	0.7916
13	0.9983	0.9964	0.9929	0.9872	0.9784	0.9658	0.9486	0.9261	0.8981	0.8645
14	0.9994	0.9986	0.9970	0.9943	0.9897	0.9827	0.9726	0.9585	0.9400	0.9165
15	0.9998	0.9995	0.9988	0.9976	0.9954	0.9918	0.9862	0.9780	0.9665	0.9513
16	0.9999	0.9998	0.9996	0.9990	0.9980	0.9963	0.9934	0.9889	0.9823	0.9730
17	1.0000	0.9999	0.9998	0.9996	0.9992	0.9984	0.9970	0.9947	0.9911	0.9857
18	1.0000	1.0000	0.9999	0.9999	0.9997	0.9993	0.9987	0.9976	0.9957	0.9928
19	1.0000	1.0000	1.0000	1.0000	0.9999	0.9997	0.9995	0.9989	0.9980	0.9965
20	1.0000	1.0000	1.0000	1.0000	1.0000	0.9999	0.9998	0.9996	0.9991	0.9984
21	1.0000	1.0000	1.0000	1.0000	1.0000	1.0000	0.9999	0.9998	0.9996	0.9993
22	1.0000	1.0000	1.0000	1.0000	1.0000	1.0000	1.0000	0.9999	0.9999	0.9997

Normal Distribution Function

The tabulated value is $\Phi(z) = P(Z \leq z)$, where Z is the standardised normal random variable, $N(0, 1)$.

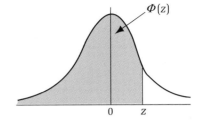

z	.00	.01	.02	.03	.04	.05	.06	.07	.08	.09
0.0	.50000	.50399	.50798	.51197	.51595	.51994	.52392	.52790	.53188	.53586
0.1	.53983	.54380	.54776	.55172	.55567	.55962	.56356	.56749	.57142	.57535
0.2	.57926	.58317	.58706	.59095	.59483	.59871	.60257	.60642	.61026	.61409
0.3	.61791	.62172	.62552	.62930	.63307	.63683	.64058	.64431	.64803	.65173
0.4	.65542	.65910	.66276	.66640	.67003	.67364	.67724	.68082	.68439	.68793
0.5	.69146	.69497	.69847	.70194	.70540	.70884	.71226	.71566	.71904	.72240
0.6	.72575	.72907	.73237	.73565	.73891	.74215	.74537	.74857	.75175	.75490
0.7	.75804	.76115	.76424	.76730	.77035	.77337	.77637	.77935	.78230	.78524
0.8	.78814	.79103	.79389	.79673	.79955	.80234	.80511	.80785	.81057	.81327
0.9	.81494	.81859	.82121	.82381	.82639	.82894	.83147	.83398	.83646	.83891
1.0	.84134	.84375	.84614	.84849	.85083	.85314	.85543	.85769	.85993	.86214
1.1	.86433	.86650	.86864	.87076	.87286	.87493	.87698	.87900	.88100	.88298
1.2	.88493	.88686	.88877	.89065	.89251	.89435	.89617	.89796	.89973	.90147
1.3	.90320	.90490	.90658	.90824	.90988	.91149	.91309	.91466	.91621	.91774
1.4	.91924	.92073	.92220	.92364	.92507	.92647	.92785	.92922	.93056	.93189
1.5	.93319	.93448	.93574	.93699	.93822	.93943	.94062	.94179	.94295	.94408
1.6	.94520	.94630	.94738	.94845	.94950	.95053	.95154	.95254	.95352	.95449
1.7	.95543	.95637	.95728	.95818	.95907	.95994	.96080	.96164	.96246	.96327
1.8	.96407	.96485	.96562	.96638	.96712	.96784	.96856	.96926	.96995	.97062
1.9	.97128	.97193	.97257	.97320	.97381	.97441	.97500	.97558	.97615	.97670
2.0	.97725	.97778	.97831	.97882	.97932	.97982	.98030	.98077	.98124	.98169
2.1	.98214	.98257	.98300	.98341	.98382	.98422	.98461	.98500	.98537	.98574
2.2	.98610	.98645	.98679	.98713	.98745	.98778	.98809	.98840	.98870	.98899
2.3	.98928	.98956	.98983	.99010	.99036	.99061	.99086	.99111	.99134	.99158
2.4	.99180	.99202	.99224	.99245	.99266	.99286	.99305	.99324	.99343	.99361
2.5	.99379	.99396	.99413	.99430	.99446	.99461	.99477	.99492	.99506	.99520
2.6	.99534	.99547	.99560	.99573	.99585	.99598	.99609	.99621	.99632	.99643
2.7	.99653	.99664	.99674	.99683	.99693	.99702	.99711	.99720	.99728	.99736
2.8	.99744	.99752	.99760	.99767	.99774	.99781	.99788	.99795	.99801	.99807
2.9	.99813	.99819	.99825	.99831	.99836	.99841	.99846	.99851	.99856	.99861
3.0	.99865	.99869	.99874	.99878	.99882	.99886	.99889	.99893	.99896	.99900
3.1	.99903	.99906	.99910	.99913	.99916	.99918	.99921	.99924	.99926	.99929
3.2	.99931	.99934	.99936	.99938	.99940	.99942	.99944	.99946	.99948	.99950
3.3	.99952	.99953	.99955	.99957	.99958	.99960	.99961	.99962	.99964	.99965
3.4	.99966	.99968	.99969	.99970	.99971	.99972	.99973	.99974	.99975	.99976
3.5	.99977	.99978	.99978	.99979	.99980	.99981	.99981	.99982	.99983	.99983
3.6	.99984	.99985	.99985	.99986	.99986	.99987	.99987	.99988	.99988	.99989
3.7	.99989	.99990	.99990	.99990	.99991	.99991	.99992	.99992	.99992	.99992
3.8	.99993	.99993	.99993	.99994	.99994	.99994	.99994	.99995	.99995	.99995
3.9	.99995	.99995	.99996	.99996	.99996	.99996	.99996	.99996	.99997	.99997

Percentage Points of the Normal Distribution

The table gives the values of z satisfying
$P(Z \leq z) = p$ where Z is the standardised
normal random variable $N(0, 1)$.

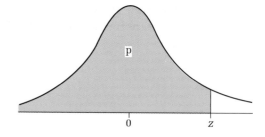

p	.00	.01	.02	.03	.04	.05	.06	.07	.08	.09
0.50	0.000	0.025	0.050	0.075	0.100	0.126	0.151	0.176	0.202	0.228
0.60	0.253	0.279	0.305	0.332	0.358	0.385	0.412	0.440	0.468	0.496
0.70	0.524	0.553	0.583	0.613	0.643	0.674	0.706	0.739	0.772	0.806
0.80	0.842	0.878	0.915	0.954	0.994	1.036	1.080	1.126	1.175	1.227
0.90	1.282	1.341	1.405	1.476	1.555					

p	.000	.001	.002	.003	.004	.005	.006	.007	.008	.009
0.95	1.645	1.655	1.665	1.675	1.685	1.695	1.706	1.717	1.728	1.739
0.96	1.751	1.762	1.774	1.787	1.799	1.812	1.825	1.838	1.852	1.866
0.97	1.881	1.896	1.911	1.927	1.943	1.960	1.977	1.995	2.014	2.034
0.98	2.054	2.075	2.097	2.120	2.144	2.170	2.197	2.226	2.257	2.290
0.99	2.326	2.366	2.409	2.457	2.512	2.576	2.652	2.748	2.878	3.090

Percentage Points of the Student t Distribution

The table gives the values of x satisfying
$P(X \le x) = p$ where X is a random variable
having the Student t distribution with v
degrees of freedom.

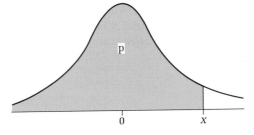

p / v	0.9	0.95	0.975	0.99	0.995
1	3.078	6.314	12.706	31.821	63.657
2	1.886	2.920	4.303	6.965	9.925
3	1.638	2.353	3.182	4.541	5.841
4	1.533	2.132	2.776	3.747	4.604
5	1.476	2.015	2.571	3.365	4.032
6	1.440	1.943	2.447	3.143	3.707
7	1.415	1.895	2.365	2.998	3.499
8	1.397	1.860	2.306	2.896	3.355
9	1.383	1.833	2.262	2.821	3.250
10	1.372	1.812	2.228	2.764	3.169
11	1.363	1.796	2.201	2.718	3.106
12	1.356	1.782	2.179	2.681	3.055
13	1.350	1.771	2.160	2.650	3.012
14	1.345	1.761	2.145	2.624	2.977
15	1.341	1.753	2.131	2.602	2.947
16	1.337	1.746	2.120	2.583	2.921
17	1.333	1.740	2.110	2.567	2.898
18	1.330	1.734	2.101	2.552	2.878
19	1.328	1.729	2.093	2.539	2.861
20	1.325	1.725	2.086	2.528	2.845
21	1.323	1.721	2.080	2.518	2.831
22	1.321	1.717	2.074	2.508	2.819

p / v	0.9	0.95	0.975	0.99	0.995
23	1.319	1.714	2.069	2.500	2.807
24	1.318	1.711	2.064	2.492	2.797
25	1.316	1.708	2.060	2.485	2.787
26	1.315	1.706	2.056	2.479	2.779
27	1.314	1.703	2.052	2.473	2.771
28	1.313	1.701	2.048	2.467	2.763
29	1.311	1.699	2.045	2.462	2.756
30	1.310	1.697	2.042	2.457	2.750
31	1.309	1.696	2.040	2.453	2.744
32	1.309	1.694	2.037	2.449	2.738
33	1.308	1.692	2.035	2.445	2.733
34	1.307	1.691	2.032	2.441	2.728
35	1.306	1.690	2.030	2.438	2.724
36	1.306	1.688	2.028	2.434	2.719
37	1.305	1.687	2.026	2.431	2.715
38	1.304	1.686	2.024	2.429	2.712
39	1.304	1.685	2.023	2.426	2.708
40	1.303	1.684	2.021	2.423	2.704
45	1.301	1.679	2.014	2.412	2.690
50	1.299	1.676	2.009	2.403	2.678
55	1.297	1.673	2.004	2.396	2.668
60	1.296	1.671	2.000	2.390	2.660

Percentage Points of the χ^2 Distribution

The table gives the values of x satisfying
$P(X \le x) = p$ where X is a random variable
having the χ^2 distribution with v degrees of
freedom.

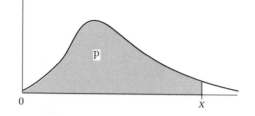

p / v	0.005	0.01	0.025	0.05	0.1	0.9	0.95	0.975	0.99	0.995
1	0.00004	0.0002	0.001	0.004	0.016	2.706	3.841	5.024	6.635	7.879
2	0.010	0.020	0.051	0.103	0.211	4.605	5.991	7.378	9.210	10.597
3	0.072	0.115	0.216	0.352	0.584	6.251	7.815	9.348	11.345	12.838
4	0.207	0.297	0.484	0.711	1.064	7.779	9.488	11.143	13.277	14.860
5	0.412	0.554	0.831	1.145	1.610	9.236	11.070	12.833	15.086	16.750
6	0.676	0.872	1.237	1.635	2.204	10.645	12.592	14.449	16.812	18.548
7	0.989	1.239	1.690	2.167	2.833	12.017	14.067	16.013	18.475	20.278
8	1.344	1.646	2.180	2.733	3.490	13.362	15.507	17.535	20.090	21.955
9	1.735	2.088	2.700	3.325	4.168	14.684	16.919	19.023	21.666	23.589
10	2.156	2.558	3.247	3.940	4.865	15.987	18.307	20.483	23.209	25.188
11	2.603	3.053	3.816	4.575	5.578	17.275	19.675	21.920	24.725	26.757
12	3.074	3.571	4.404	5.226	6.304	18.549	21.026	23.337	26.217	28.300
13	3.565	4.107	5.009	5.892	7.042	19.812	22.362	24.736	27.688	29.819
14	4.075	4.660	5.629	6.571	7.790	21.064	23.685	26.119	29.141	31.319
15	4.601	5.229	6.262	7.261	8.547	22.307	24.996	27.488	30.578	32.801
16	5.142	5.812	6.908	7.962	9.312	23.542	26.296	28.845	32.000	34.267
17	5.697	6.408	7.564	8.672	10.085	24.769	27.587	30.191	33.409	35.718
18	6.265	7.015	8.231	9.390	10.865	25.989	28.869	31.526	34.805	37.156
19	6.844	7.633	8.907	10.117	11.651	27.204	30.144	32.852	36.191	38.582
20	7.434	8.260	9.591	10.851	12.443	28.412	31.410	34.170	37.566	39.997
21	8.034	8.897	10.283	11.591	13.240	29.615	32.671	35.479	38.932	41.401
22	8.643	9.542	10.982	12.338	14.041	30.813	33.924	36.781	40.289	42.796
23	9.260	10.196	11.689	13.091	14.848	32.007	35.172	38.076	41.638	44.181
24	9.886	10.856	12.401	13.848	15.659	33.196	36.415	39.364	42.980	45.559
25	10.520	11.524	13.120	14.611	16.473	34.382	37.652	40.646	44.314	46.928
26	11.160	12.198	13.844	15.379	17.292	35.563	38.885	41.923	45.642	48.290
27	11.808	12.879	14.573	16.151	18.114	36.741	40.113	43.195	46.963	49.645
28	12.461	13.565	15.308	16.928	18.939	37.916	41.337	44.461	48.278	50.993
29	13.121	14.256	16.047	17.708	19.768	39.087	42.557	45.722	49.588	52.336
30	13.787	14.953	16.791	18.493	20.599	40.256	43.773	46.979	50.892	53.672
31	14.458	15.655	17.539	19.281	21.434	41.422	44.985	48.232	52.191	55.003
32	15.134	16.362	18.291	20.072	22.271	42.585	46.194	49.480	53.486	56.328
33	15.815	17.074	19.047	20.867	23.110	43.745	47.400	50.725	54.776	57.648
34	16.501	17.789	19.806	21.664	23.952	44.903	48.602	51.966	56.061	58.964
35	17.192	18.509	20.569	22.465	24.797	46.059	49.802	53.203	57.342	60.275
36	17.887	19.233	21.336	23.269	25.643	47.212	50.998	54.437	58.619	61.581
37	18.586	19.960	22.106	24.075	26.492	48.363	52.192	55.668	59.892	62.883
38	19.289	20.691	22.878	24.884	27.343	49.513	53.384	56.896	61.162	64.181
39	19.996	21.426	23.654	25.695	28.196	50.660	54.572	58.120	62.428	65.476
40	20.707	22.164	24.433	26.509	29.051	51.805	55.758	59.342	63.691	66.766
45	24.311	25.901	28.366	30.612	33.350	57.505	61.656	65.410	69.957	73.166
50	27.991	29.707	32.357	34.764	37.689	63.167	67.505	71.420	76.154	79.490
55	31.735	33.570	36.398	38.958	42.060	68.796	73.311	77.380	82.292	85.749
60	35.534	37.485	40.482	43.188	46.459	74.397	79.082	83.298	88.379	91.952

Critical Values of the Spearman Rank Correlation Coefficient

The tables gives the critical values, for different significance levels, of the Spearman rank correlation coefficient r_s for various sample sizes n.

One tail Two tail	10% 20%	5% 10%	2.5% 5%	1% 2%	0.5% 1%
4	1.0000	1.0000	1.0000	1.0000	1.0000
5	0.7000	0.9000	0.9000	1.0000	1.0000
6	0.6571	0.7714	0.8286	0.9429	0.9429
7	0.5714	0.6786	0.7857	0.8571	0.8929
8	0.5476	0.6429	0.7381	0.8095	0.8571
9	0.4833	0.6000	0.6833	0.7667	0.8167
10	0.4424	0.5636	0.6485	0.7333	0.7818
11	0.4182	0.5273	0.6091	0.7000	0.7545
12	0.3986	0.5035	0.5874	0.6713	0.7273
13	0.3791	0.4780	0.5604	0.6484	0.6978
14	0.3670	0.4593	0.5385	0.6220	0.6747
15	0.3500	0.4429	0.5179	0.6000	0.6536
16	0.3382	0.4265	0.5029	0.5824	0.6324
17	0.3271	0.4124	0.4821	0.5577	0.6055
18	0.3170	0.4000	0.4683	0.5425	0.5897
19	0.3077	0.3887	0.4555	0.5285	0.5751
20	0.2992	0.3783	0.4438	0.5155	0.5614
21	0.2914	0.3687	0.4329	0.5034	0.5487
22	0.2841	0.3598	0.4227	0.4921	0.5368
23	0.2774	0.3515	0.4132	0.4815	0.5256
24	0.2711	0.3438	0.4044	0.4716	0.5151
25	0.2653	0.3365	0.3961	0.4622	0.5052
26	0.2598	0.3297	0.3882	0.4534	0.4958
27	0.2546	0.3233	0.3809	0.4451	0.4869
28	0.2497	0.3172	0.3739	0.4372	0.4785
29	0.2451	0.3115	0.3673	0.4297	0.4705
30	0.2407	0.3061	0.3610	0.4226	0.4629
31	0.2366	0.3009	0.3550	0.4158	0.4556
32	0.2327	0.2960	0.3494	0.4093	0.4487
33	0.2289	0.2913	0.3440	0.4032	0.4421
34	0.2254	0.2869	0.3388	0.3972	0.4357
35	0.2220	0.2826	0.3338	0.3916	0.4296
36	0.2187	0.2785	0.3291	0.3862	0.4238
37	0.2156	0.2746	0.3246	0.3810	0.4182
38	0.2126	0.2709	0.3202	0.3760	0.4128
39	0.2097	0.2673	0.3160	0.3712	0.4076
40	0.2070	0.2638	0.3120	0.3665	0.4026
41	0.2043	0.2605	0.3081	0.3621	0.3978
42	0.2018	0.2573	0.3044	0.3578	0.3932
43	0.1993	0.2542	0.3008	0.3536	0.3887
44	0.1970	0.2512	0.2973	0.3496	0.3843
45	0.1947	0.2483	0.2940	0.3457	0.3801
46	0.1925	0.2455	0.2907	0.3420	0.3761
47	0.1903	0.2429	0.2876	0.3384	0.3721
48	0.1883	0.2403	0.2845	0.3348	0.3683
49	0.1863	0.2377	0.2816	0.3314	0.3646
50	0.1843	0.2353	0.2787	0.3281	0.3610
60	0.1678	0.2144	0.2542	0.2997	0.3301

Critical Values of the Product Moment Correlation Coefficient

The table gives the critical values, for different significance levels, of the sample product-moment correlation coefficient r based on n independent pairs of observations.

| One tail | 10% | 5% | 2.5% | 1% | 0.5% |
Two tail	20%	10%	5%	2%	1%
4	0.8000	0.9000	0.9500	0.9800	0.9900
5	0.6870	0.8054	0.8783	0.9343	0.9587
6	0.6084	0.7293	0.8114	0.8822	0.9172
7	0.5509	0.6694	0.7545	0.8329	0.8745
8	0.5067	0.6215	0.7067	0.7887	0.8343
9	0.4716	0.5822	0.6664	0.7498	0.7977
10	0.4428	0.5494	0.6319	0.7155	0.7646
11	0.4187	0.5214	0.6021	0.6851	0.7348
12	0.3981	0.4973	0.5760	0.6581	0.7079
13	0.3802	0.4762	0.5529	0.6339	0.6835
14	0.3646	0.4575	0.5324	0.6120	0.6614
15	0.3507	0.4409	0.5140	0.5923	0.6411
16	0.3383	0.4259	0.4973	0.5742	0.6226
17	0.3271	0.4124	0.4821	0.5577	0.6055
18	0.3170	0.4000	0.4683	0.5425	0.5897
19	0.3077	0.3887	0.4555	0.5285	0.5751
20	0.2992	0.3783	0.4438	0.5155	0.5614
21	0.2914	0.3687	0.4329	0.5034	0.5487
22	0.2841	0.3598	0.4227	0.4921	0.5368
23	0.2774	0.3515	0.4132	0.4815	0.5256
24	0.2711	0.3438	0.4044	0.4716	0.5151
25	0.2653	0.3365	0.3961	0.4622	0.5052
26	0.2598	0.3297	0.3882	0.4534	0.4958
27	0.2546	0.3233	0.3809	0.4451	0.4869
28	0.2497	0.3172	0.3739	0.4372	0.4785
29	0.2451	0.3115	0.3673	0.4297	0.4705
30	0.2407	0.3061	0.3610	0.4226	0.4629
31	0.2366	0.3009	0.3550	0.4158	0.4556
32	0.2327	0.2960	0.3494	0.4093	0.4487
33	0.2289	0.2913	0.3440	0.4032	0.4421
34	0.2254	0.2869	0.3388	0.3972	0.4357
35	0.2220	0.2826	0.3338	0.3916	0.4296
36	0.2187	0.2785	0.3291	0.3862	0.4238
37	0.2156	0.2746	0.3246	0.3810	0.4182
38	0.2126	0.2709	0.3202	0.3760	0.4128
39	0.2097	0.2673	0.3160	0.3712	0.4076
40	0.2070	0.2638	0.3120	0.3665	0.4026
41	0.2043	0.2605	0.3081	0.3621	0.3978
42	0.2018	0.2573	0.3044	0.3578	0.3932
43	0.1993	0.2542	0.3008	0.3536	0.3887
44	0.1970	0.2512	0.2973	0.3496	0.3843
45	0.1947	0.2483	0.2940	0.3457	0.3801
46	0.1925	0.2455	0.2907	0.3420	0.3761
47	0.1903	0.2429	0.2876	0.3384	0.3721
48	0.1883	0.2403	0.2845	0.3348	0.3683
49	0.1863	0.2377	0.2816	0.3314	0.3646
50	0.1843	0.2353	0.2787	0.3281	0.3610
60	0.1678	0.2144	0.2542	0.2997	0.3301

Wilcoxon Rank Sum Test

The table below gives the largest value for the signed rank statistic T leading to statistical significance at the level shown, on a one-tailed test.

Sample Size	Significance level			
	0.05	0.025	0.01	0.005
5	0			
6	2	0		
7	3	2	0	
8	5	3	1	0
9	8	5	3	1
10	10	8	5	3
11	13	10	7	5
12	17	13	9	7
13	21	17	12	9
14	25	21	15	12
15	30	25	19	15
16	35	29	23	19
17	41	34	27	23
18	47	40	32	27
19	53	46	37	32
20	60	52	43	37

Index

Salesman ... out of ...
and of the man w ... ... McCarthy's wi... ...
by defying the Ho... ...merican Activities Committee and by
exposing its corru... ...on in *The Crucible*.

Born in 1915, a year after the outbreak of the First World War,
aged 14 at the time of the Wall Street Crash, a teenager during
the Depression, a student under the New Deal, Miller's story,
told with astonishing vividness and skill, is already the story of
America in the twentieth century. In becoming a writer of plays
that probed at the very essence of what it is to be an American,
he also became the conscience of his country. As a brilliant
intellectual with Broadway at his feet and Marilyn Monroe at his
side, he seemed to reconcile impossible opposites and turn the
American dream into reality. And with the collapse of that
dream, Miller has become a citizen of the world, travelling
widely – frequently in the company of photographer Inge
Morath, his wife for the past 25 years – and working tirelessly for
the physical and intellectual freedom of writers everywhere.

Complete with 32 pages of photos, most never before published,
Timebends already bids fair to become a classic of autobiographical writing. Arthur Miller seems to have had rather
more than his share of what the twentieth century has to offer –
both good and bad. But as his book, and many of his plays, seek
to demonstrate, he sees it as our universal task to cease denying
personal responsibility for our own history.

Arthur Miller was born in Manhattan, New York City in 1915.
After graduating from the University of Michigan, he began
work with the Federal Theatre Project. His many award-
winning stage plays include *The Man Who Had All The Luck* (1944);
All My Sons (1947); *Death of a Salesman* (1949); *An Enemy of the People*
(1950), adapted from Ibsen; *The Crucible* (1953); *A Memory of Two
Mondays* and *A View from the Bridge* (presented as a double-bill in
1955); *After the Fall* (1964); *Incident at Vichy* (1964); *The Price* (1968);
The Creation of the World, and Other Business (1972); *The American
Clock* (1980); *The Archbishop's Ceiling* (1977); the double-bill *Danger:
Memory!* (1987); and *Broken Glass* (1994). His prose writing includes
Focus, a novel (1945); *The Misfits*, first published in 1957 as a short
story and made into a film and published as a novel in 1961; a
collection of short stories, *I Don't Need You Any More* (1967); and
three works of non-fiction, *In Russia* (1969); *Chinese Encounters*
(1979); and *'Salesman' in Beijing* (1984), an account of directing his
best-known play in China.

Arthur Miller

TIMEBENDS

A LIFE

Methuen

Published by Methuen 1999

5 7 9 10 8 6 4

First published in hardback in the United Kingdom in 1987 by Methuen London
First published in paperback in 1988 by Methuen London and then reissued
in 1990 in a Minerva edition published by Mandarin Paperbacks

This paperback published in 1999 by Methuen Publishing Limited
215 Vauxhall Bridge Road, London SW1V 1EJ

Methuen Publishing Limited Reg. No. 3543167

A CIP catalogue record for this book is available from the British Library

ISBN 0 413 77340 X

Printed and bound in Great Britain by
Cox & Wyman Ltd, Reading, Berkshire

For Inge

ONE

The view from the floor is of a pair of pointy black calf-height shoes, one of them twitching restlessly, and just above them the plum-colored skirt rising from the ankles to the blouse, and higher still the young round face and her ever-changing tones of voice as she gossips into the wall telephone with one of her two sisters, something she would go on doing the rest of her life until one by one they peeled off the wire and vanished into the sky. Now she looks down at me looking up at her from the foyer floor, bends over and tries to move me clear of her foot. But I must lie on her shoe, and from far up above through skirt and darkness I hear her laughing pleasantly at my persistence.

Then, later, a slightly more elevated view, from about two and a half feet above the floor: she sits at a sixth-story window that overlooks Central Park, her profile emblazoned against the afternoon sun, hair still long but gathered in a bun, her full arms pressing against the gauzy cotton of her shirtwaist sleeves above a shorter skirt now and velvet pumps. Both hands rest on an open book in her lap as she listens intently to a young man with a pipe, thick glasses, and a short beard, a student from Columbia to whom she pays two dollars an afternoon each week simply to come and talk with her about novels. She knows hardly anyone in or out of the family who has ever read a book, but she herself can begin a novel in the afternoon, pick it up again after dinner, finish it by midnight, and remember it in detail for the rest of her life. She also remembers the names of the entire British royal family and their German cousins. But her secret envy, made evident by her con-

3

tempt, is for Madame Lupescu, the Jewish paramour of King Carol of Rumania, and also, she believes, his brains.

Still later, there is the view from about five feet above the floor: from here she is in high heels with rhinestone buckles, a black beaded knee-length dress, and a silver-and-black cloche hat over her bobbed hair. Her lips are red with lipstick. She is high-busted and round-armed, already in the habit, whenever she dresses up to leave the house, of drawing her upper lip down in order to slim her pudgy nose. There are diamonds on her fingers, and she trails a silver fox across the floor as she promises to bring home the sheet music of the show they are off to see, Kern or Gershwin or Herbert, which she will play the next morning on the Knabe baby grand, and sing in the happy, slightly hooting soprano so proper and romantic and fashionable. She is holding her head high to flatten the double chin but also out of the insecure pride of moving along-side him, a head taller than she, blue eyes and skin so white it is nearly translucent, reddish blond curly hair enhancing his inno-cent alderman's look, a fellow whom policemen are inclined to salute, headwaiters to find tables for, cab drivers to stop in the rain for, a man who will not eat in restaurants with thick water glasses, a man who has built one of the two or three largest coat manufac-turing businesses in the country at the time and who cannot read or write any language.

A still later view: in the little Brooklyn house where she shuffles about in carpet slippers, sighing, cursing with a sneer on her lips, weeping suddenly and then catching herself, in the winters feed-ing the furnace with as scant a shovelful of coal as will keep it burning, making meal money at high-stakes professional bridge games all over Midwood and Flatbush, which are sometimes raided by the police, whom she talks into letting her go home to prepare supper. She had arrived at the bottom of the Depression, when to get arrested for trying to make a buck was not the total eclipse of respectability it so recently would have been. My mother moved with the times.

This desire to move on, to metamorphose—or perhaps it is a talent for being contemporary—was given me as life's inevitable and rightful condition. To keep becoming, always to stay involved in transition. It was all she and my father had ever known. She was born on Broome Street on the Lower East Side of Manhattan, her father, Louis Barnett, a clothing contractor, one of the struggling mass down there climbing over each other to grab the brass ring as it went by. Like Samuel, my father's father, Louis came from the

Polish hamlet of Radomizl, and they were probably distantly related, I have always thought, because they so resembled one another: both were very fair-skinned, stolid types—though Grand-father Samuel with his severely curved spine was a tiny man whose wife and sons, very exceptionally at the time, were over six feet tall. They had all been transforming themselves since they were children in Europe, even before their emigration in the 1880s seemed possible, living as they did in a cultural twilight zone between the Austrian-German language and influence, the Polish peasantry, and their Jewish identity. The height of culture for them was anything German.

Louis Barnett wore a vandyke beard, had his remaining hair clipped closely, bathed twice daily in summer, got his ties pressed along with his shirts, kept his hats in their original boxes, and folded his handkerchiefs and socks before dropping them into the laundry basket. And he slept on three pillows, a great wide one with a narrower one on top and a tiny cushion on top of that. He slept with his white satin yarmulke on his head, and it too was pressed, with a crease straight up the front and over its crown, and he lay down at night flat on his back with his hands folded over his ample stomach and never moved until he awoke in the morning with the bedclothes as flat and frozen as they had been when he parted them the night before. I know all this because during the Depression he no longer had a home of his own, and he and I shared the same small room in the tiny house in Brooklyn. His soul left his body when Louis Barnett slept, had no use for it until it returned in the morning for breakfast. Not a word did I ever hear from him that might have some attachment to a thought, not a sound that was not immediately useful or a mere greeting or a goodbye. When, in 1940, my mother told him that I was marrying a gentile girl, he said nothing, but as she waited for a response across the twelve-foot width of the Brooklyn living room, he reached over to a heavy alarm clock that someone had left on a nearby table and threw it at her, just missing his daughter's head. He had owned a prosperous business in the twenties, though, and then too was known for a tendency to direct action. Union organizers in his work force he would invite to the top of a stairway and, while talking to them reasonably, would suddenly knock their heads together and throw the stunned men down the stairs. He thought Franklin Roosevelt should not be allowed to run against Herbert Hoover for the presidency because Roosevelt had never run a business. He had invented that idea, soon to be common among Republicans, all by himself. Five years later, however, he thought Roosevelt should be crowned king and all elections canceled during his lifetime. Louis considered elections insulting to those in power, such was the strong German streak in him. In time he came to dislike my gentile wife, Mary, somewhat less, but only because her continued presence within the family represented a kind of orderliness; it was against disorder that he had thrown the clock.

But all that was after the collapse, the Great Crash of 1929 that would once again transform their transformed lives. In the twenties in the apartment at the edge of Harlem, six stories above the glorious park, from whose windows we could see far downtown, even down to the harbor, it seemed, we had no thought of politics. My father, Isidore, thought it odd that people like Morris Hillquit, the Socialist leader, were called "freethinkers." This amused and perplexed him. "He thinks free!" Free of charge, that is. On Sundays the *New York Times* was spread over the Oriental carpet in the living room, the warm sepia rotogravure section especially friendly, with its reassuring photographs of the handsome Arrow Collar man and especially his seated, ears-up German shepherd at his side; Commander Byrd with his valorous white uniform and his polar expeditions, which I dreamed of joining as soon as they would let me into the Boy Scouts (for he took a few lucky Scouts along); and President Hindenburg of Germany on a gigantic black stallion leading a parade, the bags under his eyes like the King of England's bags and even the Prince of Wales's, just exactly like my father's and both grandfathers'. My mother was the only reader of the news sections, which she at least skimmed before turning to the interesting stuff about the theatres, of which there were sixty or seventy on Broadway, and the society pages, whose great families and their lineages, the Rockefellers, Morgans, Biddles, she knew as though she were in some way connected to them. At Easter time President and Mrs. Calvin Coolidge posed on the White House lawn with their aristocratic collie dogs in lordly attendance and the American flag right up there at the top of the pole over their fabled home. He the pallid, expressionless ex–Massachusetts governor and she his proper lady posing in elegant dignity exactly as my mother would have done under the circumstances. On less formal occasions Coolidge was photographed fishing in a stream, dressed in black business suit, gray fedora, and high starched collar and tie, the very icon of solid dignity that would shortly disintegrate in the Crash. There would also be our little mayor, James J. Walker, with his handsome Irish grin and nattily tailored jackets, shown entering a nightclub for some relaxation after a hard day of looting the city, and before him Mayor Hylan, who had bought—or was it sold?—all the sidewalks of Staten Island, thefts that everyone seemed to find hilarious, stealing being the politicians' natural game. In fact, there was a feeling of security in the repetitiousness of their thefts, a kind of warming dishonesty. But at the same time, mysteriously, a president or for that matter the governor was above the mire, ranking in the mind alongside bishops and the Pope as no laughing matter. On a summer's day in the early twenties in Far Rockaway—we rented a wonderful bungalow there for many summers, ours the first one on the street with a view of that deserted white beach and the pure ocean—I saw in a store window a black-draped photograph of President Warren Gamaliel Harding, that handsome white-haired actorish man, and I went past solemnly, for he was the president and had died. It would be many years before I learned that he had presided over a corruption of the federal government unknown since at least the time of President Grant.

The rotogravure seemed to take special pleasure in frequent photographs of the British in Africa and India, in Malaya and among Chinese-looking people and Pygmy tribes, and for weeks and weeks with the Egyptians, whose gold-laden tomb of King Tut they had just opened. The map of the world in school was covered with reassuring British pink to indicate the Empire, whole subcontinents and hundreds of islands in every kind of climate. In the rotogravure Englishmen stood posing in their pith helmets and beautiful straight noses under palm trees or in furs among the Eskimos, in harsh dark forests and on burning deserts. It was not, in fact, until these early years of the twenties that the United States became a creditor nation rather than one of the many in debt to the British banks, as we had been since the Revolution. But of course I did not think of banks, lying there under the Knabe and turning those warm pages, but of adventure among the natives, of being the first to peer, flashlight in hand, through the fresh hole in the wall of King Tut's burial chamber—how frightening that was to imagine. What if he awoke! One of the first newspaper articles I ever read was about the mysterious deaths, one after another, of the explorers who had broken into his tomb—felled by a curse, the papers thought, wafted toward them from the dark air of the violated sanctuary. Frightening as the curse was, it also had a certain attraction for my mother, and consequently for me, since it confirmed in some remote but implicit way her belief in spirits. The air was far from empty, and to the end of her days she would be trying to penetrate the future. In the twenties it was the Ouija board craze. Three or four people would sit with this magical board touching their knees, one of them holding out his hands to make it levitate. A lot would depend on weather, wet air being a better spirit conductor, and especially upon the tranquility of the participants' concentration. If she never succeeded in getting the thing to rise off her knees, it proved only that she was not doing it right, not that it was a fraud. She knew perfectly well that the whole business was imaginary, but it was her nature to be blind and sighted at one and the same time, to leap off the cliff and stand there watching herself fly downward through the air, and I was learning that credulousness and detachment even when I was still spending much of my time on the floor. In effect, of course, she was being an artist, but it was a process that could wreak havoc upon the search for authenticity any child's mind must crave.

Much later I would see that there was a certain direction to the tide we were all so unknowingly riding in those years of sublime confidence. My father, deep in his Sunday nap on the living room couch, toward whose kindly face I looked up from the floor as to a bison, an albino buffalo that blinked softly at my loudest outcries and moved in measured pace when everyone else was rushing around hysterically, had arrived in New York all alone from the middle of Poland before his seventh birthday. Nowadays he had a National and a chauffeur waiting for him at the curb to take him downtown to the Seventh Avenue garment district every morning. Such a transformation had nothing strange, nothing even noteworthy about it then, nor would it for many years to come, life being accepted as an endless unfolding, a kind of scroll whose message was surprise and mostly good news.

Logically, I suppose, Isidore's lone-boy trip across Europe and the ocean should have evoked all kinds of negative feelings in us, like outrage at the parents who had left him behind, or resentment toward the three brothers and three sisters who had been taken along on the big exodus to the New World. But it was just part of the saga, unquestioned like everything else in our fable. The official explanation was that Grandpa couldn't afford to buy Papa's ticket and figured on sending the money as soon as he had made some in America, a matter of a few months at the most. Meanwhile, the little left-behind boy was stashed with an uncle who would soon die. The child was then passed from family to family, allowed to sleep with the aged grandmothers and the feebleminded, who soiled their beds and howled half the night and didn't mind who they slept with. Poor Izzie, after many months of this, must have felt effectively orphaned, something I have only lately come to surmise, after over sixty years of knowing the story. Indeed, his orphanhood may well have contributed to the special warmth my second wife, Marilyn Monroe, never ceased to feel toward him; she was able to walk into a crowded room and spot anyone there who had lost parents as a child or had spent time in orphanages, and I acquired this instinct of hers, but not as unerringly. There is a "Do you like me?" in an orphan's eyes, an appeal out of bottomless loneliness that no parented person can really know.

My father's ticket arrived at last, and he was put on a train for the port of Hamburg with a tag around his neck asking that he be delivered, if the stranger would be so kind, to a certain ship sailing for New York on a certain date. Europe was apparently still civilized enough for such an arrangement, and after three weeks in steerage—the bottom deck where the light of day never shone, an area near the chains that operated the steering gear, where twice a day a barrel of salt herring was opened for the scores of emigrant families, from which, naturally, a child traveling alone got no more than the leavings—he arrived in New York with his teeth loose and a scab on his head the size, they used to say, of a silver dollar. His parents were too busy to pick him up at Castle Garden and sent his next-eldest brother, Abe, going on ten, to find him, get him through Immigration, and bring him home to Stanton Street and the tenement where, in two rooms, the eight of them lived and worked sewing the great long many-buttoned cloaks that were the fashion then. Abe, a scamp, walked my father uptown pointing out building after building that their father, he said, already owned. Izzie was put into school for several months and then removed to take his place at one of the sewing machines in the apartment, never to see the inside of a school again. By the time he was twelve he himself was employing two other boys to sew sleeves on coats alongside him in some basement workshop, and at sixteen he was sent off as salesman by his father, Samuel, with two big steamer trunks filled with a line of coats for the Midwest stores. But, as he explained on my back porch more than half a century later, "I got to the train station, but I come back home—I was still too lonesome for my mother. So I started out again the next year, and then I could do it." He told me this in his seventies and still, even then, felt somehow embarrassed by his dependency on his mother, a woman to whom, until he married at the age of thirty-two, he handed over his sizable weekly pay in return for an allowance. His three brothers had done the same. A formidable woman, she would decline, at a particularly desperate moment during the Depression, to loan him money—but that was still far away from my time on the floor, and far behind us when we were having our quiet conversation on my porch.

My brother, Kermit, lived only on the periphery of my life until I was five and faced the exciting prospect of going to school too. Until then he was merely a nuisance who kept getting in my way whenever I wanted to write on something or cut something out of a magazine or drive a nail through the phonograph cabinet. Now that I would be joining him in school he became my ideal, which required that I love him. As the eldest son he had all the responsibility, and I had all the fun, but he was handsome and I was funny-looking, with ears that stuck out and forced me to endure my mother's brother Moe's inevitable salutation when he came to visit, "Pull in your ears, we're coming to a tunnel." As for my father's side of the family, they invariably greeted me by staring at me with supercilious smiles—they were all very large white blue-eyed bison, and extremely satisfied with themselves as they grazed—and saying, "Where did *he* come from?" I alone being dark, with brown eyes and dark hair. Of course my mother had the same coloring, a mistake of nature in their view, she being the sole dark woman to have married into that immense family. They were an unusually inbred clan and married only people who resembled them. In fact, one of my most beautiful cousins married her flesh-and-blood uncle against the rabbi's warnings, and though they lived in love for years, holding hands and endlessly admiring one another, I think the guilt finally got to her, for she withered strangely in her early forties with something no one could then diagnose, and died looking like a bent hag, her hair gone, her eyes nearly blinded by some inner calamity, having no known disease. My dark mother seemed somehow alien to them, perhaps even an embarrassment, especially since she was the brightest one in the family; they all owned identical Knabe baby grands, but she was the only one who could play, at which they affected amusement. Each time I called to announce the birth of a child of mine, my father's first anxious question was "Is it dark?" The racist implications angered me, but by then, from the clan's reaction to me and to my mother, I had long known the meaning of rejection, the kind that hits you when you've walked into a room and haven't even said anything.

It may be that even if half consciously, we choose our personalities to maintain a certain saving balance in the family's little universe. Kermit, three years my senior, I early on paired with our father as a force for order and goodness. With his blue eyes and fair skin he so resembled the old man, while my dark mother and I were linked not only in appearance but in our unspoken conspiracy against the restraints and prohibitions of reality. If I came up from the street and announced that I had just seen a policeman on roller skates, she would stand amazed and ask for more details, my father would frown slightly as he tried to keep from laughing, and Kermit would roll his eyes ceilingward, scandalized by such horseshit.

And of what importance, I have so often asked myself, is any of this absurdity, not only in my life but in anyone else's? It is simply that the view from the floor, filled though it is with misunderstandings, is also the purest, the matrix whose content is so difficult to change later on. The impact of things seen and heard from the carpet is red-hot and returns with a far greater shock of truth when recalled because those visions are our very own, our private misunderstandings of reality shared by no one else, and are thus the soil of poetry, which is our freedom to alter mere facts. From misunderstandings, more than from anything dutifully learned out of respect for culture, the threads unwind that spin the uniqueness of each artist's vision, promising implicitly to remake the world all new. Unknowingly, almost from the beginning, I have sought to reconstruct my life, becoming my brother from time to time, my father, my mother, putting on theirs and others' forms and faces in order to test the view from angles other than my own. And incidentally, it sometimes took years before I could painfully strip myself of such disguises and find myself again. In a word, at the very time we are most vulnerable to impressions, we are least able to avoid outrageously misjudging what they mean. At a minimum, therefore, life will never lose its mystery.

The mystery, for example, of what made me decide that my position was second base. Somehow I came to make this choice, just as one day I would "decide" I was a playwright. Second base was "me," while Kermit was a pitcher and a track man. These identities had a fate behind them, were inexorable, came down from on high. I have to wonder what other elements of my being I chose, took off the rack, for no good reason. Why did Kermit nearly always fall just a step or two before the finish line in the Central Park races we were constantly running? The crowd of boys from the row of apartment houses facing the park on 110th Street was cheering him on, his powerful legs were pumping along at a good steady pace, and just as he spread out his arms, down he went and lost. What choice of his lay behind this? Was it unrelated to his volunteering for the army in World War II and as an infantry captain finding himself carrying a man on his back for hours in zero weather until they could reach an aid station, while his own toes were freezing and becoming gangrenous? Whence come these fateful images that might lose a man his feet, or his life—or be your salvation if he happens to be near when you need saving?

Kermit was always a good man to have around at such times. But his pathological honesty could sink my mother on occasion, like the time his teacher assigned the class an original picture to draw and he chose a house, which he managed decently enough, but the chimney's perspective he could not get right. He erased and re-drew the chimney time after time, but it was never right, never seemed to be attached to the roof. At ten o'clock the night before the assignment was due, my mother (talented enough to catch a person's likeness with startling accuracy) took courage in hand and, sweetly smiling, suggested that she be allowed to draw the chim-ney. His yells of horrified protest woke me up, and I hurried down the corridor into the dining room, where he sat clutching his draw-ing to his breast while my mother, half hysterically now, pleaded to be allowed to add one single perspective line that would make the chimney look like a chimney and not a box kite that had gotten stuck on the roof. My father, of course, was deep in sleep, what with the stock market continuing its apparently endless climb and the coat business better than ever. His father's firm, S. Miller and Sons, had recently been dissolved, and a veritable wave of brothers and their outriding relatives had descended on Isidore and his Miltex Coat and Suit Company, which he had broken away to establish after the Great War. Family loyalty had forced him to make jobs for all of them, something my mother would blame for his firm's collapse a few years hence. But it pleased him to have been trans-formed from left-behind Izzie to the chief source of livelihood for the entire clan, he whom they had always scoffed at and who bore the scar, his illiteracy, of their barely concealed contempt through-out his life. But for now, he happily slept.

I joined my mother in pleading with Kermit to let her finish his drawing. "But she can't! It's supposed to be mine!" Corrupt con-spirators, my mother and I tried to argue that he had certainly drawn everything but the chimney and chosen the colors and painted them in himself, but he would have none of this sophistry. The solution, as is so often the case, was exhaustion; so many tremendous decisions in life are made because it is five o'clock. He would go to sleep, we all would, and think about it again before breakfast. Kermit agreed, hardly able to hold his head up after spending days drawing his house, changing the coloring, the location of doors and windows. As he went down the corridor to our bedroom, the drawing remained behind on the dining room table and I sensed what was going to happen. Did he as well? And when, at breakfast, he rolled up his picture, which now had a very nicely drawn chimney on it, did he not notice? Did one have to be evil, like me, to notice?

About forty-five years later that very dining room table was on the stage for the first Broadway production of my play *The Price*. In 1968 I had no idea that our old dining table still existed, and could hardly recall what it had looked like. But the set designer, my old friend Boris Aronson, liked to take off from reality and kept after me to describe each piece of furniture that would be piled up, one piece on top of another, in the room of the deceased father when his two sons returned to divide up the family's possessions after many years of not seeing each other. The characters were not based on Kermit and me, we were far different from these two, but the magnetic underlying situation was deep in my bones.

It was my sister, Joan—not yet born in this narrative—who, on hearing that the set required furniture of the twenties, reminded me that our old dining table had been given to my father's baby sister Blanche, then in her seventies; my mother had no room for it in the small apartment she and my father occupied in the last years of their lives. I hurried out to Brooklyn and Aunt Blanche's apartment. The youngest in my father's family, Blanche was sweet and pretty and soft, and now she was old but still good-heartedly ready for laughter. As it turned out, she had recently been talking to secondhand dealers about selling the table and eight chairs because she and her husband, Sam, my father's Depression-era partner in one of his ill-fated attempts to get another coat business going, were about to move into a smaller apartment themselves.

I looked at the table, still solid and sound and somehow amusing with its heavy harp trestle legs deeply carved and a scalloped border running around its top. My mother had gotten up and danced on it on more than one New Year's Eve (also her wedding anniversary), although I had never been allowed to witness these riotous displays, which only took place in the small, evil hours, long after my bedtime. But I was not sure its style would fit into Boris's design, so I phoned him then and there and described it to him.

Boris generally didn't take kindly to outside suggestions; in fact, he found it hard to hear anything at all without instinctively taking exception to it. Years before his great success as designer of *Cabaret, A Little Night Music,* and other hit musicals, as well as *The Crucible, A View from the Bridge,* and *A Memory of Two Mondays,* we were sitting beside the swimming pool of a mutual friend who had invited us up to his swank Westchester estate to escape the terrible heat of the city. Stretching out in the cool shade, I lamented the fate of the poor folk who had to stay in the city in such weather. Boris was instantly spurred to invent his demurrer.

"I don't know, I like New York in the heat; even better I like it than in good weather."

"How can you like New York in the heat?" I asked.

"Because it's so relaxing. I mean, when I'm walking down a street on a hot July day in New York, I know that whoever I'm going to meet is also a failure."

Boris's Russian-Yiddish accent and his plastic attitude toward language were among my sources for Gregory Solomon, the eighty-nine-year-old used furniture dealer in the play. Though the true model for the character was a quite different man, it was still rather strange to be standing in sight of the dining table asking Boris what he thought of our buying it for the set of *The Price,* which was of course a play about selling old furniture to a dealer whose distinctive mangled English was exactly like Boris's. I was standing, as it were, between slices of mirrors going off into infinity reflecting my image, and within my image that of Boris, my play, my parents, their table . . .

"Vat style is it?" Boris asked.

I had no idea what to call it and turned to Blanche, who was standing there thrilled by the idea that the table might end up on a Broadway stage. "What style is this, do you know?"

"Well, one of the dealers who looked at it said it was Spanish Provincial."

"You're kidding."

She laughed at the idiocy of the description and assured me it was what the dealer had actually said.

"Boris? One of the dealers who looked at it says it's Spanish Provincial."

"That's it! Take it!" he instantly and delightedly replied.

And so it was that table that David Burns, a comic genius, struck

with the flat of his little hand as he tipped back his dusty black
fedora, brushed cigarette ashes off the lapels of his drooping black
overcoat, and explained, "Listen! You can't move it. A man sits
down to such a table he knows not only he's married, he's got to
stay married—there is no more possibilities. . . . You're laughing,
I'm telling you the factual situation. What is the key word today?
Disposable. The more you can throw it away the more it's beautiful. The car, the furniture, the wife, the children—everything has
to be disposable. Because you see the main thing today is—shopping. . . ."

Once the table was on the stage, I was strangely unable to feel
sentimental about it. Nevertheless, it had once been a center of life,
where my brother sat and did his lessons and I learned to read
while Mother sketched us in a silence warmer than blanket or fire.
The only sounds were the scrape of her pencil on paper and the
hissing of the radiators. And if very occasionally a sharp shot
echoed from some Harlem rooftop farther uptown, no one so much
as looked up.

There was of course no television, and our superheterodyne
radio pulled in KDKA, Pittsburgh, as well as WJZ, New York, but
no one would think of simply turning it on and letting it foul the
air with a background of shapeless music. One either listened or it
was shut off, probably because the sound was so tinny, a mere
facsimile of music. As often as not, though, it was out of order as
a result of Kermit's attempts to fix it. Once Kermit laid hands on
a clock or a machine of any kind it died, as though of fright, its
leftover parts hidden under vases and inside the piano, where
suddenly he would rediscover them, after months had passed, and
attack the ailing machine again, finishing it off forever if it had
survived his first ministrations. I soon knew that I could fix things
better than he, with his tendency to storm a mechanical problem
in the hope that by sheer righteous determination it would yield
to him. But what I envied him, as I did my mother, was the ability
to memorize. Like her, he could read a text a couple of times and
embed it in his brain at will while I would go wandering off after
irrelevant associations.

On my first day in school the teacher, a Miss Summer, showed
us a cardboard clockface to teach us to tell time, mysteriously
manipulating the hands to cue us into calling out the hours and
minutes. All I was really interested in was how she got the clock
hands to move. I managed to creep around until I could see her
turning a handle behind the face, and at the end of the lesson she

allowed me to turn it myself. But I finally had to get my mother
to teach me how to tell time. Equally distracting were Miss Summer's admirable horn-rimmed eyeglasses; no one I knew wore
glasses, and I now took to walking around squinting as though I
were going blind, until my mother, to avoid a breakdown, talked
the oculist into fitting me with an unneeded pair of glasses, which
I wore about a week and lost in the park grass. Nothing was more
enjoyable than mimicry. I was about the height of my father's back
pocket, from which his handkerchief always hung out, and for
years I pulled the corner of my handkerchief out exactly the same
distance. I had noticed early on—from my vantage close to the
floor—that men, though not women, often leaned to one side to
fart; experimenting, I never managed the output, only the position,
but it was yet another enticement to grow up, one of the great
things in store once the helplessness of childhood was ended.

The new excitements of the Jazz Age, perceived from a few feet
off the floor, came to me chiefly through women, my mother and
her friends. When she bobbed her long hair it shocked Kermit and
made him weep in his room and scold her for days, particularly for
not forewarning him. As innocent as I was at five or six, I was still
aware of an exciting secret life among the women, and I found
myself one warm evening taking one of my father's straw hats and
going down the elevator to sit on a box in front of our apartment
building, hoping somehow to attract female notice. But this kind
of sexuality is a colored cloud rather than a physical state, and I
lived on that cloud much of the time. It was, perhaps, part of my
inability to forgo, to wait until a wish could be fulfilled; I had to
have what I wanted at once. To see an interesting thing was to
need to possess it, and my life consisted of explosions of desires that
could not wait to be satisfied, in contrast to my brother's self-
control and responsibility. I would soon be haunted by what I
suppose were guilt images, naive but real. Our apartment windows
on the top floor of the building took the unobstructed force of
wind-driven rains, and the flickering lights from neighboring
apartments flashed the shape of a furious large monkey against the
outside of the glass, his teeth bared and his dripping arms out-
spread as he tried to get into my bedroom. (An organ grinder's
monkey I had patted on a street in Rockaway the previous summer
had suddenly bitten my finger and held it tenaciously between his
teeth until its master slapped it loose.) I was gradually turning into
a habitual sleepwalker, haunting the apartment corridor, staring,
fast asleep, into my parents' bedroom. Once I awoke leaning far

out the window looking six stories down into the depths of the
interior courtyard. As I came awake, the terror of the height whis-
tled up through my veins, a fear I have never lost.

When I first heard—probably not until I left home for college—
Jews referred to as "the people of the Book," I mistook it to mean
books in general rather than the Bible, and the description, compli-
mentary as it was, was news to me. Brought up among Jews until
the age of twenty, I could recall none but my mother who ever
read anything. My friends' apartments on 110th Street had no books
on the shelves, only knickknacks—porcelain ladies in eighteenth-
century hoop dresses, figurines of horses, the Little Dutch Boy in
wooden shoes getting ready to put his finger in the dyke, a bucket
hanging over a well, perhaps a bust of Lincoln. Even my mother
rarely bought a book, borrowing instead from the public library
down the street near Fifth Avenue or, after our move to Brooklyn,
for two cents a day from the Womrath Lending Library in the
drugstore.

Nevertheless, one learned very early that books had to be respected; they were all putative Bibles and to some small degree
had a share in holiness. When I laid an open book face down, my
brother would reprimand me; like a person, a book had a spine that
could be broken. *The Book of Knowledge* came early into the
house, and one page in it for the first time introduced me to the
concept of a writer: a full-page illustration of Charles Dickens in
profile, with oval vignettes of Mr. Pickwick and David Copperfield
and the rest surrounding his head. My mother was already reading
to us from *Oliver Twist*, and the notion amazed me that real people
able to talk and walk and feel could come out of a person's head,
for the fictional and life were merged in one wonderful mirage. I
would not have questioned that *somewhere* Oliver did actually
live.

Thirty years later, in the early fifties, I would visit the homes of
longshoremen in the Red Hook area of Brooklyn while preparing
a never-to-be-made film on waterfront racketeering, and the
nearly total absence of books in those homes was not only disabling
but almost spectrally strange.

Loyal as she wished to be to my father, speaking of him almost
always with praise and respect—except when she helplessly lashed
out at some clumsiness of his—my mother, I couldn't help knowing, also subverted him. She was a woman haunted by a world she
could not reach out to, by books she would not get to read, concerts
she would not get to attend, and above all, interesting people she'd

never get to meet. In effect, she had been traded into an arranged marriage within months of graduating *cum laude* from high school. But even such human barter could have its charms: she would laugh warmly as she told how "Grandpa and Grandpa Miller went into our living room and compared their account books. They were in there for hours, and finally they came out and"—how she laughed!—"said I was getting married!" The two clothing manufacturers were making sure that they had comparable assets, just as two landed barons might have done centuries earlier. Then, suddenly, her look would blacken as she clenched her jaws in anger. "Like a cow!" she would mutter, with my father often sitting there listening along with my brother and me, even nodding his head to confirm the story, so accepting was he of the unchanging tradition. Even so, my heart went out to him in his humiliation, however imperturbably he seemed to bear it; somehow it had become my job to distract them from their conflict, already a kind of artful acting.

But there were compensations for her. She could put her sons into the National and drive downtown with them behind the chauffeur to visit the Miltex Coat and Suit Company, where Papa, in shirtsleeves and vest, vastly tall and competent, manifestly in charge, showed us off to the rows of workers sitting at their machines, the clerks and the salespeople, many of whom were his overpaid relatives.

In the mid-twenties all was hope and security in this mammoth place, so dimly lit, with its immense rolls of cloth stacked on racks to the ceiling, and wonderful lumbering iron carts rolling past, which I loved to ride on, and a cavernous freight elevator, and in the front office men with sleeve garters and green visors over their eyes. The gazes of the help upon us were filled with respect and a kind of congratulation for being who we were, the sons of the boss and our clever and pretty mother. Here was the concord, the happiness I seem always to have been trying to press my parents toward—my father in his full power and she content with a mixture of glories, her admiration making him proud and strong, his strength keeping her safe. And besides, there was a world here—his workers and staff—to witness this ennoblement along with my brother's and my role in what became in my mind an orderly and primordial pageant. Such pleasures—not merely the oppressions—of hierarchy would one day be useful to understand. And the worms of paradox, too: even as she received all this goodwill with happy grace and near royal appreciation, I knew how she despised

the meanspirited, money-mad "cloakies," Jews who cared for nothing but business. If my father escaped such definition by virtue of
a certain loftiness she saw in him, he also came pretty close, dangerously so, I thought, since he was so ignorant of what she regarded as culture. It would take decades until I understood that his
taste, if more naive, was finer than hers, more personal and authentic; his illiteracy was merciful, keeping him from worrying about
what was in or out, stylish or old-fashioned, so that he could react
simply and in a wholly human rather than media-washed way to
what he saw or heard. A song, a show, a play, had to satisfy his
sensuously utilitarian aesthetic no differently than his hats did. Art
had to touch him. But of course "culture," as with most American
families, was the wife's affair, the men providing the wherewithal
and the naps, and it never dawned on him that his opinion on
anything artistic was even worth mentioning, as acute as some of
his untutored perceptions were. His illiteracy set me in a conflict
with learning for many years, since I so wished to be like him, and
long before I knew anything about psychoanalysis I had to tell
myself consciously that after all I was not him and was perfectly
capable of memorizing some necessary text or passing an examination. To become a reader meant to surpass him, and to claim the
status of writer was a bloody triumph; it was also a dangerously
close identification with my mother and her secret resentment, if
not contempt, for his stubborn incapacity with words.

There was never a lack of reasons to wonder on fate's capricious-
ness, and one of these was made clear to me in the 1920s when my
mother remarked for the fiftieth time how stupid they had been
in turning Bill Fox down for a loan back in 1915. It seems I had
narrowly missed an entirely different life as the son of a Hollywood
mogul, a fate not worse than death, perhaps, but close. Fox, a
former wool "sponger," was having trouble raising capital to set up
a movie studio in California and was scouring the garment industry
for funds. To hear my father tell it, the reason for his difficulty was
not hard to find—spongers were not noted for their honesty, the
very nature of their trade practically inviting sharp practices.
Woolen cloth had to be preshrunk before it was cut into garments.
The manufacturer would therefore send his bolts of cloth to a
sponger, who unrolled them over vats of steam. But who was to
know how much a seventy-yard roll had really shrunk? Two yards,
ten, fifteen? The sponger might report the truth, or then again he

might snip off a few yards and return a short roll to the manufacturer as a bad case of shrinkage. Belief in a sponger's word required a whole lot of faith, and here was one of them asking my father to invest fifty thousand dollars to make movies, and in far-off California, no less. By the time he got to my father, Fox had all but exhausted his garment business contacts and was offering a sizable piece of the company for this last chunk of cash he needed.

My father loved shows, and to actually meet a live actor would have overwhelmed him. He was tempted. But finally his good sense triumphed—he simply could not trust Fox and turned him down. It would have been inconceivable to him that afternoon, as he told Fox the bad news, that in not so many years he would be finding it hard to scratch up the price of a ticket to a Twentieth Century Fox movie. Had he taken the risk, I would have been raised in Los Angeles, never learned what I did in Central Park and the streets of Harlem and Brooklyn, been spared the coming Depression, and arrived no doubt at a different personality. On a trip to Poland many years later, I had a similar realization: had my grandfathers not decided before the turn of the century that there was no future for them in that country, I would not have survived to the age of thirty. Hardly a Jew was left in that part of Poland once the Nazi war machine had swept across its flat and dreary landscape.

But in 1918 and after, the atmosphere in our house denied that even war was the spiritual defeat it is and should appear to be. Of course I am speaking of my own sense of things as they trickled down to my homeland, the floor. I was three when the Great War ended, and if I was unconscious of my mother's worrying about her two brothers—Hymie in the navy, who never got to sea, and the other, Moe, who was gassed in France—I can still feel the aura of cheer and self-congratulation that the Armistice brought into the house. I am sure I heard my mother phoning all her sisters and friends, none of whom was likely to have read the newspapers, to announce the end of the war. She hated the Kaiser in a personal way, more or less the way she hated Mikush, the superintendent of our building, a Pole of depressing hauteur. We had to beg to get him to open a painted-in window, we knew he was breaking into the apartment when we were away in the summer, but without him no life was possible since he was the only human who could handle a tool or break open a trunk whose key had been lost, move the piano, and turn off the gas when one of the stove spigots got jammed in the open position. Unlike the Kaiser, Mikush had never been defeated, so my mother could hate the Kaiser with the added satisfaction of imagining Mikush in his position, having to chop his firewood in Doorn, Holland, exiled there for the rest of his life. The Kaiser's photo in the *Times* weekly rotogravure section was the signal that another year had passed—for some reason, on the anniversary of the Armistice he was inevitably shown chopping wood in Doorn, a stolid-looking fellow with a pointy mustache, knickerbockers, high shoes, a short jacket, and the dead-eyed stare of a Doberman.

From the floor, the defeat of Imperial Germany meant Uncle Moe coming to visit with a black suitcase full of German marks in hundred-thousand denominations—totally valueless now, but my mother wanted to hold on to them just in case. He also brought a German helmet wrapped in brown paper and twine with its spearpoint sticking out on top. Merely to touch and smell it brought images, such as I had seen in the press, of fields of dead men and frightening explosions. And to think that a living man who was now dead had worn this! The effect on me, quite naturally, was to make me dream of becoming a soldier and, with luck, going to war. I imagined the smell of earth and sweat in the inner leather headband of the helmet. Its rough exterior, rusting now, must surely have been covered by a fall of dirt from an Allied shell exploding. ("Allies"—what rolling waves of warmth and confidence in that word! How deep into our brains the suds washed, right down to floor level. Soon there would be *The Boy Allies,* kids' books ranging us in our short pants against the brutal Boche.) But the helmet was too large and slid down over my face, so I walked around holding it over my head with both hands until it dawned on me that I was being proud to be a German, a horrible idea. The last I saw of the helmet was when I opened a closet years later and it fell off a shelf and struck my shoulder, like the head of a dead man who had come back to reprimand me. It was also, somehow, Moe's head, for he had died by then of tuberculosis contracted in France, exacerbated by the gassing he had endured. But I had always known from my mother's tone of voice whenever she spoke of him that he was doomed to a short life. From France he had sent her Victorian stiff-upper-lip letters, "penned" rather than written, containing "lore" rather than stories; things of "great import" were "noted," and he had "witnessed scenes not meet to speak of." Writing in more or less the language one spoke was a sign of poor education and vulgarity. Uplift was the inevitable purpose of writing at all, and propriety the aim of any written style.

This was a concept handed down by the public schools. Even at P.S. 24 on 11th Street, we were at school in order to become ladies and gentlemen; we were not to read Whitman or Dreiser or Sinclair Lewis but Keats and Shelley and Wordsworth—writers who wrote English English. What was wanted was sanctified elegance and finish—why else would you be going to school? We were taught the discipline of the Palmer Method of handwriting, which required shaping each letter according to a pattern of prescribed height and width. As in old China, moral virtue clung to clear and good handwriting, a connection that opened new vistas of guilt, evil, and even civil disorder: one of the sure signs of a criminal disposition was crabbed and illegible writing. Good conduct, called deportment, was part of the curriculum, graded like arithmetic. Mornings began with an inspection of hands and fingernails and the shine of shoes, each pupil turning to face the aisle nearest him (two shared a seat in P.S. 24) as the teacher, most often an Irish spinster wearing a long dark dress and black shoes, with hair knotted in back in a bun, and smelling, if you were lucky, of cherry soap, and if unlucky, of laundry, turned each pair of palms down and slammed a steel-edged ruler across the knuckles of a dirty hand. With two in a seat there was a temptation to whisper, but that could get your head cracked against your neighbor's—the teacher would creep up silently from the rear, and then you'd see what we called stars for a moment or two.

Summoned to the blackboard, you would automatically gather up all your belongings—pen, pen wiper, blotter, notebook, galoshes, sweater—depositing them on the floor as you wrote and carting them back to your seat again. Nothing out of sight was safe, and this accounted for my confusion at my first Chaplin pictures, which so often showed him filching an apple from a fruit stand or a wallet from a pocket. I joined nervously in the laughter, for it was a doubtfully comic situation to me. When I was thirteen we moved to Brooklyn, and in James Madison High School, where my mother had talked them into admitting me a full term before I graduated from grammar school "so he can be with his cousins," my first sight of kids leaving their stuff behind on their desks when they went to the blackboard was a powerful shock. Our P.S. 24 track team had all their street clothes stolen from lockers while they proudly ran in their shorts in a meet in Central Park. Foolishly roller-skating in the park alone one day at the age of seven or eight, I was ambushed by some Italian kids and would long remember the fist coming up fast to my nose as they held me down; then they ran off with my skates. When I got home, my mother sighed and shook her head. The black and Puerto Rican kids, most of them first-generation migrants from rural places, were never feared as thieves. They were still shy and overawed by the city and the police, who swung the club first and asked questions later. Roller-skating in the park was prohibited, and if spotted by a strolling cop, you could expect to get knocked down from behind by his flying club, a technique some of them really had fun with.

But a cop could also be a hero; between waves of cars, the young one directing traffic on the corner of 110th and Lenox would retrieve and, lefthanded, throw back batted balls that got past us into the street. Occasionally somebody hit a hard high fly out his way, and Lefty would race after it, causing awesome squeals of brakes and the delightful swerving of cars on broad 110th. He could be crude, but the New York cop was also your friend in need whom you were instructed to ask for a nickel in case you lost your fare on some voyage. Their gallant troops of twenty or more horses passing by left knobs we had to move aside in the afternoons to make paths for our marbles, the much valued immies, which we knuckled along the curbs, coming upstairs later with frosty cheeks and the invigorating smell of manure on our hands. Horses still pulled the milkman's wagon and the iceman's, and once in a while we would stand mystified watching their lengthening erections as they waited for their masters in front of the apartment house, their eyelashes softly opening and closing like underwater coral fans.

Most of the time anguish was absorbed into the games that came around with each changing season, but something happened now and then that could burn your insides. Because Kermit had a library card, I too had to have one. When I was enrolled in school and entitled to join the library near Fifth Avenue on 110th, I finally walked into the place one hot spring afternoon. It was so dark and cool in there, like no other place I had ever been, and the pink-cheeked lady leaning over her polished mahogany counter spoke in such a funereal whisper that something supernatural seemed to be present, something sacred that must not be disturbed by ordinary tones of voice, and so I stood on tiptoe as close to her ear as possible and whispered back the answers to her questions. My name, my address, my age, school, my mother's name—Augusta. At this something began knotting up inside my belly; no one had ever called her anything but Gus or Gussie, so I was already telling a kind of untruth, donning a disguise. Now the lady asked my father's name. I had not expected any of this, thinking I was simply going into this place to happily claim my rightful card, the same as my brother had done. It was going to be my turn not to be a baby anymore. Looking up into her blue eyes, I could not bring to voice my father's so Jewish name, Isidore. I was paralyzed, could only shake my head. "What does your mother call him?" I was trapped. The smile went from her face, as though she suspected me of something. My cheeks were burning. "Izzie" being impossible, I finally managed "Iz." She looked puzzled. "Is?" she asked. I nodded. "Is what?" I rushed out into the street, and I am sure that within minutes I was back with the gang playing ring-a-levio or banging a ball against a building in a game of stoopball.

I was six the year I entered school, and I could not, myself, ever have heard an anti-Semitic remark. Indeed, had I thought about it at all, I would have imagined that the whole world was Jewish except maybe for Lefty the cop and Mikush. Through those short years on the floor studying peoples' shoes, the lint under the couch, the brass casters under the piano legs, my skin had been absorbing some two thousand years of European history, of which, unbeknown to me, I had become part, a character in an epic I did not know existed, an undissolved lump floating on the surface of the mythic American melting pot. To use the latter-day jargon, I had already been programmed to choose something other than pride in my origins, and this despite my father's seemingly confident authority and his easy way with police and yelling cab drivers and even Mr. Mikush, who could put the fear of God into a brown bear. From my father some undefinable authority emanated, perhaps because his great height, fair skin, blue eyes, square head, and reddish hair cast him as an important Irish detective. Holding his hand, I often saw him simply pause at an alleyway and with his blank look disperse a crap game. He assumed without thought that he would be well served in restaurants, where he need hardly lift a finger to attract a waiter, and he never hesitated, but without fuss, to send back a dish that wasn't right. Knowing his past, I could never understand where this baronial attitude came from. He even had a way of listening that without any show of skepticism would cause the speaker to stop exaggerating. His open, relaxed stare, blue-eyed and innocent, brought blushes to the faces of people unsure of themselves. It would have astonished him to be credited as some kind of moral force—if indeed he could have understood such an idea. Life was just too hard to allow most people most of the time to act unselfishly, least of all himself. Nevertheless, his minority anxiety had moved into me, I am sure, though among his very few words of advice only one sentence explicitly conveyed it. We were passing an automobile accident on 110th Street, my hand in his and my brother on his other side. When we both pressed forward to see what had happened, he drew us back and steered us gently on, saying, "Stay away from crowds." That was all. It may have been enough.

Yet I doubt that such fright as I showed the librarian had come from him, at least not mainly. Throughout his life he declined instinctively to sentimentalize Jews, unlike my mother, who tended to expect a higher sensitivity and even morality from them, thus being endlessly and angrily disappointed. He sometimes was impatient with these idealizing waves that would repeatedly rise and break over her, and even laughed and shook his head at her naiveté. But there was no discernible apprehension disturbing his air of quiet confidence. My mother's father, Louis Barnett, once instructed me never to walk under a large lighted cross overhanging the sidewalk outside a Lenox Avenue church; if by accident I did, I must spit when I realized what I had done, in order to cleanse myself. There was a certain mild fear of that particular cross after this, but mainly that it might break loose and fall down on me. Nothing of the theology or history behind such admonitions was ever mentioned, leaving them in the realm of superstition or in a kind of immanent symbolism of menace.

There was, in fact, a certain disinclination to explain rationally anything at all that might impinge on the sacred, even in the Hebrew teacher who came to the house a few days a week to tutor Kermit and me in preparation for our bar mitzvahs, still years off. This bearded ancient taught purely by rote, pronouncing the Hebrew words and leading us to repeat after him. In the book, the English translations of the passages from Genesis faced the Hebrew, but there were no English translations of the English: what did *firmament* mean? The worst of it was that when I spoke a passage correctly, the old man would kiss me, which was like being embraced by a rosebush. Once he leaned over and, laughing, gave my cheek a painful pinch and called me *tsadik*, wise man, a compliment whose cause I understood neither then nor later. I would have to pump up all my self-control to appear to welcome his furry arrival. The lessons were boring and meaningless, but my rebellion may simply have been caused by an undisciplined spirit: I hated piano lessons, too, or any set of rules that interfered with fantasies of magically quick accomplishment. When the violin suddenly became "my" instrument, as mysteriously and irrevocably as second base had become my position, my mother found a teacher who, poor man, loaned me a small violin to begin on. I found that a rubber ball would take a lively bounce off the back of it as well as causing all the strings to hum, and I went downstairs to use it as a tennis racket until the neck broke in my hand. My mother carefully laid the pieces in the case and returned the instrument, and I went back to walking in my sleep, which was far more interesting than studying. So the root of that choking fear that suddenly gripped me as I looked into the face of the kindly librarian is so deeply buried that I can only imagine I had been denying, quietly and persistently, what I surely must have been hearing from my position on the floor—stories, remarks, fear-laden vocal tones that had been moving me by inches into a beleaguered zone surrounded by strangers with violent hearts.

Mikush was doubtless one of those, the sole mythic enemy who had a face and a name, as far as I knew. But fears of Mikush sprang far less from mythic antagonisms than from the cat-and-mouse game all the boys in the building played with him on the roof. A favorite sport, of which my brother was a master, was to stand up on a parapet and leap across a shaftway to the other side over a drop of six stories. Terrified as I already was of such a drop from my sleepwalking experiences, I could not bear to watch Kermit standing tall on the parapet. Mikush was endlessly popping up out of the hatchway to chase us, not that he cared if one of us went into the abyss, but our heels made holes in the tar roofing material. "No touch-a roof!" he would roar as we dodged him and clattered down the iron stairway into the building. As we flew down into the lower stories, his Polish war yells echoed along the ceramic-tiled floors of the hallways.

Because he was a Pole, the Jews in the building had to believe he hated them just as his countrymen for the most part had in Radomizl, where pogroms and tales of pogroms were woven into the very sky overhead, and where only the Austrian emperor Franz Josef and his army kept the Poles, egged on by their insatiable priests, from murdering every last Jew in the land. But I nevertheless had an ambiguous relation of sorts with Mikush; I brought my badly bent almost-new bike to him after an experiment of no-hands riding banged the front fork into a lamppost in the park. He straightened it with his bare hands, a memorable feat of strength that I imagined no one else in the whole world was capable of. I must have had some faith in his goodwill toward me, Pole or no Pole; my fear of him was less than total. Such a relationship made it understandable, a decade or so later, that German Jews—even those who could afford to—did not immediately leave when Hitler came to power. Had we lived in Germany, Mikush would likely have been the Nazi representative in the building, but it would have been hard to imagine even Mikush, anti-Semitic as he undoubtedly was, going from apartment to apartment with a list of names and ordering us out into trucks bound for a concentration camp and death. After all, he had straightened the fork of my bike.

Perhaps I was so unprepared, so surprised by my own terror in the library, because of what was to be a lifelong inability to believe that all reality was of the visible kind. We all are taught how to receive our experiences, and my mother, my prime teacher, saw secret signs of other worlds wherever she looked; she was talked to by people far away without benefit of telephone, and even by the dead. As with others so inclined, this gave her, I suppose, an enhanced sense of her importance in the scheme of things and helped make life more interesting. Whatever the cause, I had clearly put out of mind a certain childish recognition of infinite human brutality until suddenly the librarian seemed to challenge me to identify myself as a candidate for victimization, and I fled. I had been taught to recognize danger—even where it did not exist—but not how to defend against it. The dilemma would last a long time. The same quandary, and the effort to locate in the human species a counterforce to the randomness of victimization, underlie the political aspect of my play *Incident at Vichy*. But as history has taught, that force can only be moral. Unfortunately.

For me, my mother's mysticism set death lurking everywhere. It has prejudiced me against teaching children religion; too often God is death and it is death that is being worshiped and "loved." If I learned early on how to disregard her dark and pessimistic surges, the fact was that they too often turned out to be prophetic. Her brother Moe, who had been a mule driver carrying ammunition up to the front in France, returned from a funeral with her one rainy afternoon, and as he sat on the pinkish satin Louis Something straight chair in the living room, she screamed and her hands flew up to her hair: he must immediately go out the apartment door and wipe a smear of gray cemetery mud off one of his heels lest it bring death to this house. They were beautiful brown calf shoes with a white bead around the seam between soles and uppers. He quickly left the living room, limping to keep the heel off the carpet.

In appearance, I would grow up to resemble Moe, a tall, thin man of great gentleness whose spirit the Great War seemed to have broken. It was as though in more than the physical sense he could never quite catch his breath. Even then I noted that joy never seemed to collect around him, even for his wedding there was no great party, no welcoming of his tiny wife, Celia, who was barely five feet tall. He was constantly bending to her as they walked, with one gentle hand against her back as though she were a child. Trying to get with the spirit of the twenties, he made it down to Florida to speculate in real estate, but his nerve soon waterlogged, his investment melting into the sea during a great land boom in which immense fortunes were made and innocents like himself fleeced. All Moe returned with was a nice tan that encouraged my mother to believe that his health was permanently restored, but he was soon back in the Veterans Hospital at Saranac Lake, where he died. The cemetery mud on his shoe could not help but cross my mind, and with it the lurking suspicion of some validity in the superstition. That only my mother knew the rules and regulations tended to leave me with all of the attendant apprehensions and none of the satisfactions of prediction—"I knew, *I knew!*" she wailed when we heard the news of his death.

It was the same when, out of a deep sleep in an Atlantic City hotel where we were spending the High Holidays, she suddenly sat up and said, "My mother died"—which she had, it turned out, and at approximately that hour of the night. Of course, her secret powers were not all negative and would as often send her into prescient highs of optimism, especially about me. I need only draw a straight line to hear myself praised as a coming da Vinci; my failures she simply swept aside as the fault of my teachers or a momentary fogging of my mind. This worked pretty well until Miss Fisher, the principal of P.S. 170, summoned her to a conference about my unruliness.

Miss Fisher had been the principal when my mother was a pupil in the same school. Holding me by the hand in the office, my mother seemed to blush in girlish shame as her onetime goddess said, "I do not understand, Augusta, how a fine student like you can have brought him up so badly." Miss Fisher wore a lace net collar with little ivory stays that pushed into the flesh under her jaw hinges and kept her from bending her neck. It was hard to look up at her without grimacing with pain. She was white-haired and wore ankle-length skirts and white long-sleeved blouses with starched pleated fronts. Tears formed in my mother's eyes. "Kermit is such a well-behaved boy," the great lady went on, "and so quick in his studies . . ." I began crying too, already feeling the sting of my mother's hand on the side of my head and imagining the stars I was about to see, but worst of all was her face wracked with disappointment. What was the matter with me? Why was I like this? Dear God, please let me be good like my mother and father and brother! At times like this all life seemed like rowing forever through a sea of remorse.

Between my terror in the library and Miss Fisher's condemnation, I seemed to have joined some underworld of disapproved people. My father and brother lived well beyond the sparkling blue line of demarcation—they were wholly good—but placing my mother was not so simple. We had hardly gotten out onto 111th Street when she violently shook me, holding my wrist, gave me a clout on top of the head with her pocketbook, and then bent over me and screamed into my face, "What are you doing to me!" A double condemnation, since even at that moment I knew she wasn't condemning for her own sake—she adored everything I did—but as an agent for Miss Fisher and implicitly my father and Kermit and the whole United States of America. Thus it was even more painful for her to have to be cursing me when deep within her she thought I hadn't done anything very wrong. And so we were closer than ever as we reentered the apartment and I pretended deep remorse and she pretended black despair, and in a little while we both had some hot chocolate. Only then did a conspiratorial practicality enter her voice as she said, "Listen"—I looked up from my cup—"I want you to behave." I said, "I'm going to," and I meant it. And I did, for a while.

Of course there are models, avowed and surreptitious, that we mythologize and make into gods, and in enfolding their attributes into ourselves we muddy whatever character they may have really possessed. My mother's youngest brother, Hymie, was an extremely good-looking young man of no great intelligence or imagination, yet she so loved beauty in women and handsomeness in men that Hymie excited her more than any other relative. In the style of the times he knotted his tie very tight and small, and his collars were so tight that his skin overlapped them, and his hats were tilted over one eye, and when he laughed, his straight white teeth against his swarthy complexion flashed like lights. He had started a small factory to make artificial flowers and brought bouquets of them when he visited. Touching them made me feel itchy, but they were marvelous imitations.

One afternoon he appeared with a thin blonde woman wearing a black fur collar on a white coat, his beloved, he said, his Stella, whom my mother instantly, as I could see, disapproved of. She disapproved of all the wives of all her brothers. Myron's Minnie was fat and short and stupid and wore artificial fruits on her hats and was dumb enough to sleep with her own son just because he was sick with tuberculosis and needed comfort. My mother had never heard of Freud, but she knew there was something funny about this, something disgusting, in fact, and would go around imitating Minnie's whiny way of speaking, frowning intensely and narrowing her nasal passages to sound like a cat. Harry's wife was also far from what he might have had—they had all undervalued themselves in the spouses they picked. Betty had been a dancer in burlesque, and if her beautiful and buxom body was an understandable attraction for mild Harry, he might at least have found somebody more respectable. In fact, mild as he was, Harry had been crazed by this woman, enough to creep into his father's office one night to steal money from the safe.

My mother's dislikes, of course, were merely expressions of her sense of entrapment in her own marriage, and during the second half of her life—after the Depression had laid low every last hope of ever really changing her condition—all these women were transformed into her dearest and closest allies and friends. Minnie might go on sleeping with her son into his twenties, when he married, but her valiant support of her husband after he'd lost his money showed her to be a wonderful person, as the phrase went, and if Betty had danced practically or altogether naked in sleazy halls, her valor during the Depression and after the birth of her first child—a helpless mongoloid whose condition she interpreted as God's admonition, causing her to take up religion—showed that she too was a woman of seriousness and real quality.

Stella had been brought up in an orphanage, which my mother seemed to feel was somehow her own fault. She got Hymie alone one day and demanded that he not sink his whole life with this clearly unworthy mate, who, aside from her obviously bleached hair, was bony-looking and had big feet and hands, horse teeth, an enormous mouth, and a honking baritone laugh. Stella, she naturally assumed, must be pregnant, and when Hymie swore that she was not, the whole liaison became incomprehensible. How could so handsome a man marry an uncomely orphan, and one, moreover, who must be leading a pretty low life—why else would she be so vulgarly dying her hair? Unlike brother Moe, an introverted man who seemed to search for me in my eyes and made me feel extant, Hymie paid me little attention, being too busy admiring himself in windowpanes or in the glass of the pictures on the walls. His narcissistic self-involvement was not different from that of his father, Louis Barnett, who in the worst months of the Depression, when every cent in his pocket came from my father, who himself had next to nothing, would still stroll down to the barber's every single week to get his little vandyke and mustache properly trimmed and powdered and his bald head sprinkled with perfume. Even the Italian barber thought his vanity a bit much.

Louis was hot stuff, and so was Hymie, but what Hymie had that nobody else did was the ability to shoot bird shot through his front teeth clear across a room while he went right on smiling. This talent must have been honed in the navy, where he had been surrounded with hunter types, of which there would not have been any in Harlem. Hymie's shooting gallery showed up at family celebrations. Both the Barnett and the Miller families were large, and just as a quarter-century later hardly a month would pass without a funeral, so now in the youth-time of this clan there were clumps of weddings and bar mitzvahs to attend. Women wore out evening gowns in those years. Hymie would enter the big ballrooms where these functions were held, his blonde and bony wife cheerfully yelling out her hoarse greetings and whispering things to the men that made them roar with laughter while the women looked at one another with the semi-grins of the left-out, and as he turned in all directions he would gracefully smile. Magically, an epidemic of what seemed to be fleas would erupt around him, with people brushing hands down backs of necks or across foreheads until pretty soon everybody in the ballroom was scratching as they danced or stood around drinking. My mother would rush up to Hymie and pound him on the chest yelling, "Stop it!" but he would plead innocence and kiss her and carry her off to dance, which she loved, and then, as they waltzed, he would smile at the other dancers, who would begin brushing fleas off their faces, driving her into a hysteria of protesting laughter. Hymie could pouch a whole palmful of bird shot in his cheeks, and his aim was perfect. He never hit an eye but did manage to penetrate ears at will, and of course once pinked, people had a tendency to start scratching other places as well. He tried teaching me his art, but I could never master it, so we settled for my learning to blow a fierce whistle with two fingers in my mouth, one of the greatest gifts anyone ever handed me, surely one of the most useful.

Hymie resembled George Raft, the actor-gangster, and I remembered him one afternoon some thirty years later when Raft walked onto the set of *Some Like It Hot* flanked by a few bravos, debonair with the inner tips of his eyebrows cranked up high, his protectors turning left and right with warning looks at any who might menace his life, dignity, or shoeshine. A purely social visit to pass a few words with Billy Wilder, the director of the film, and to eye Marilyn Monroe for a minute or two before turning around and leaving, as completely in charge of the entire world as he had been on his entrance. It was a kind of challenging saunter, as though his arrival had instantly created a situation of top- and underdoggery—much the style Sinatra and Mailer would later affect on entering a crowded room. Hymie had had no bravos to accompany him; he might have, one day, except that at the age of twenty-seven he walked into the drugstore around the corner on Lenox and 111th to order an Alka Seltzer, and when the pharmacist turned around to serve it, he found him lying dead on the floor.

My mother wore a black veil for his funeral and would not allow my brother or me to attend, it being too intimate a proximity with death, especially one so untimely and unjust. Twenty-four hours after the news, she still could not take a full breath without breaking into sobs. Her second young brother dead before reaching thirty. "That goddamned druggist," she said, fixing the veil over her face as she looked in the mirror of her dressing table, "if he'd served him quicker he'd have saved his life . . ." Later she would concede, reluctantly, that it had probably been a heart attack and not the druggist's fault at all. Still, she could never after be at ease with the man, never again stayed in the store to chat, and she would send me alone to get a dose of sarsaparilla and castor oil, something he was delighted to watch me agonize over and finally drink. (She once also sent me down alone—I was seven at the time—to the dentist, a Dr. Herbert on the ground floor, at two o'clock in the morning when I got a sudden toothache. I rang his bell and he opened his door in his pajamas and looking down saw me in mine and almost without a word shuffled in his slippers into his office, where he turned on the light, motioned me to sit in the chair, took out a pair of forceps, asked, "Which one?" and following my finger, pulled it out. So rapidly did it all happen, with none of the preparatory reassurances and time-consuming, apprehension-feeding preliminaries, that I hardly had time to yell before I was out his door and ringing the elevator button to go back upstairs, where I found everybody fast asleep.)

Stella became a manicurist after Hymie's death, and as a year passed and another with no sign that she wanted to marry again, my mother came to love her deeply, quite as though her noble loyalty were demonstrated. In fact, Stella dealt with countless men in the barbershop and never married and said to me once many years later as I bent forward to get my neck hair cut, "Kid, there was one Hymie and that was it." As they used to say, a tough broad. She never lost her loud, cynical, wide-mouthed laugh—as though what she was finding funny was the whole world. I lost track of her for decades, until one pessimistic late afternoon in 1961, walking down Broadway at Twenty-fourth Street, I saw a barbershop and was seized with the hopeful idea of a haircut. Looking in the window to check the place out, I was shocked to see what could only be Stella's back, slightly arched at a certain familiar angle of defiance as she conversed with a customer smoking his cigar while his few hairs were being trimmed. I walked in. She did not turn. Now I saw that she had her manicuring tray in one hand. Her hoarse voice, that exciting and embarrassing yappy sound. She had to be nearly seventy by now. My stomach went cold at the thought of her recognizing me. I had only recently separated from Marilyn and could not bear questioning on the subject, which I was sure would fascinate her, but neither could I walk away from one more meeting with Stella. The barber indicated the chair next to where she was standing. I sat in it and quietly said, "Stella?"

Forty years had passed since Hymie's collapse, and now my mother and all the other Barnetts—the only family she had ever had—were dead. And I became aware as she began turning toward me that in my resemblance to the Barnetts I was the last of the line she'd be likely to see. Her face as she turned showed an ironic readiness to banter with another customer, but when she saw who it was, there was a softening around her hard mouth, an instant's loving vulnerability that she quickly banished behind a tough grin. "Arthur," she said, in a level, comradely voice. My clothes as usual were unpressed, and once again I was overdue for a haircut, so unlike the far worthier Hymie, a man of style and class, who would never be seen in public looking as stale as this. I found myself sharing her doubtless rekindled amazement at life's injustice that the wrong man had been allowed to survive. All the fascinated timidity I had felt in her exotic presence so many years ago returned, and I was at her mercy.

Which she instantly sensed, asking, "What're you doin' around here?" "Here" was a second-rate office area that successful people

fled at five o'clock. Naturally I could not be living in such a neighborhood, which at the time also consisted of seedy apartment
houses and a few hotels ranging from ruined to rank.

"I live near here," I said. Instantly the winds of my social descent
went whistling past my ears as I plummeted into oblivion. "In the
Chelsea Hotel."

Her expressions moved through shock, disbelief, amusement,
and finally a kind of pity. But at least I was not beneath her very
interested notice; I was glad to see the shifting focus of her questioning mind—is he down, broke, hiding out, maybe off his nut?
Her steady and absolutely unsentimental gaze humbled me. "I
been readin' about it," she said, referring to the recent breakup of
my marriage. I nodded, acknowledging that we were both sitting
in the same bath of life. "It's too bad," she commiserated.

She seemed to assume that I must be in a state of unrequited
longing. "It is and it isn't," I said, looking into her gray eyes. "It
couldn't go any further than it did."

Surprise lit up her face, and a certain disapproval, I thought, that
I was not going to lean on the piano and ask Sam to play it again—a
reaction I would find repeated through the years. Her tone
changed, cooled, as she asked after my children, whom she had
never seen, and my brother and sister. She had been in touch with
Joan, whose career as a stage and film actress she said she was
avidly following. When the barber came over and began working
on me, she wandered back to her little table in a corner of the shop,
where she fell into conversation with a middle-aged man who with
infinite care was getting his jacket buttoned around his belly while
inspecting his newly shaven face in the mirror. I could hear her
glassy laughter with him, her professional interest in his case, and
I wondered then why her approval seemed to mean so much to
me. She was a crass woman whose idea of heaven would undoubtedly have been to get the nod from a George Raft or even an Al
Capone or Bugsy Siegel, to be publicly honored by one of their
sincere looks and a "How ya doin', toots?"

Her stout customer was now leaving, and she began packing up
her equipment. I noticed that a sign had been hung in the door
pane, so I was the last customer. There would be time for a chat
now. But she was implicitly refusing. Could I have reminded her
too powerfully of Hymie and the life she damn near had? I could
see her in the mirrors that faced each other along both walls,
slipping out of her white coat, putting some finishing brush strokes
to her thinning hair, for the ten thousandth time inspecting herself
like a girl of eighteen with the whole world in front of her. She

seemed like some legendary bird whose slain mate remains an image in her eye forever. How strange that this woman, with whom I could not have spent more than a few hours in my entire life, should be so important to me. How terrible it seemed then that she should have been so transfixed by a man for a lifetime, a man she had known for hardly more than a year, yet as she leaned into the mirror pressing her rouged lips together it seemed she was preparing to meet him tonight in her empty apartment—the flashed image of Hymie so quickly gone was still, I thought, upholding her morale and strength. And the image came of her standing in the light of a 110th Street window in a fur-collared white cloth coat while Hymie, with his magical dexterity, floated an accordion of connected picture postcards back and forth in front of my seated mother, showing the Florida resorts of their honeymoon tour. I had not wanted Hymie to notice my mother's coolness to Stella, and so I managed to get the cards out of his hands and to ooh and aah about each beach and swimming pool they were going to visit, and for the first time succeeded in making him notice me. In the barber chair I could still recall the thrill of his attention, which I suppose was his gratitude. Hymie liked, admired me!—the brother my mother loved by far the best, the one whose death she would never forgive God. In that instant he and I shared the same unearthly light of her love.

"'Bye, dear," Stella said, pausing behind me on her way out. In the mirror I saw that she was wearing a nicely cut British raincoat and a mannish felt hat and a dark purple foulard. Terrific morale. When I insisted on turning to reach for her hand, she stepped around the barber and stood for a moment beside me, relenting, it seemed. And all at once I saw that I had brought all her losses into the shop with me, including my recently dead mother, whom she had come to adore and who in so many ways was like her. They shared a lust for foul jokes, filthy punch lines, sex scandals, *relationships,* the whispered world of frank women and their scents.

I took her hand, but all I could manage was a grin. I was thankful when she leaned down and kissed my cheek.

"I'll come by again," I said, with the foreboding that I would not because nothing was left of any life between us, or that if I did she would not be here. She nodded and seemed to know this too, and walked to the door and into the dark street at the end of another day. The barber, finishing up, slipped off my semi-shroud and shook the hair off it onto the floor, saying nothing. He had caught her coolness, the disturbance I had brought to her.

Twenty-third Street was already deserted though the sun had

hardly set. The wholesale toy stores with their cheap Hong Kong windups and fake silverware, the secondhand office supply places and used electric motor stores, were all shut for the night. Embedded in the concrete in front of a parking lot a few yards off Seventh Avenue were the large brass letters P R O, the word breaking off at a seam in the sidewalk. So many years since my father had reminisced about Proctor's Opera House, which had stood here in his youth, the most exciting theatre in New York for vaudeville and the big shows. The parking lot now was empty for the night. The city kept plucking out its memory as it fled hysterically toward the future. I stood waiting for the light to change and saw quite simply that my style as a playwright had been influenced by Stella no less than by my mother, that somewhere down deep where the sources are was a rule never if possible to let an uncultivated, vulgarly candid, worldly, loving bleached-blonde woman walk out of one of my plays disappointed. . . . How odd these underground connections always are; I begin with a library lady unintentionally frightening me and end with a widow, with cemeteries and death, a veritable delta fanning out into the sea, and somehow it is all propelled, far, far back, by the anti-Semitic quandary.

But the more overtly Jewish memories, in fact, are suffused far less with fear and flight than with power and reassurance: sitting in the lap of my long-bearded great-grandfather Barnett in the 114th Street synagogue, his basso voice resounding in my ears as he prayed, swaying back and forth and moving me with him like a horse on a merry-go-round, and occasionally putting his big hand on my head to press me aside as with a great expulsion of breath he spat out the open door beside his special seat a stream of tobacco juice that I would watch dripping off the fire escape. Naturally I could not read at four or five years of age, let alone Hebrew, but he would keep turning my face toward the prayer book and pointing at the letters, which themselves were magical, as I would later learn, and apart from their meanings were lines of an art first inscribed by men who had seen the light of God, letters that led to the center of the earth and outward to the high heavens. Though I knew nothing of all that, it was frightening at times and totally, movingly male—the women having been consigned to the balcony with the privilege of looking on and admiring, captive and saved, until they got home, where of course they ran everything.

From where I sat, on my great-grandfather's lap, it was all a kind of waking dream; the standing up and then the sitting down and the rising and falling of voices passionately flinging an incomprehensible language into the air while with an occasional glance I watched my mother up in the balcony with her eyes on me and Kermit, on my great-grandfather and grandfather and father all in a row. She sometimes wept, I think, with the pride of it up there. Even my inability ever to find out what was happening seemed inevitable and right, every question of mine being greeted with a holy and violent "Shhhhh!" lest God turn an impatient eye my way. So I shut up and invented my own religion composed of close-up views of beard roots, eyebrows, nostrils, backs of hands, fingernails, and longer shots of the Torah scrolls being sometimes touched or lifted out of their Ark, where they lived together and talked when the doors were shut, or tenderly removed from the Ark and carried around the whole congregation for everyone to kiss, for they were the Law, the heart of hearts, that which the earth kept trying to hurl away into space so that it could fly apart and die of its sins, but could never let go of. Without fear, of course, there can be no religion, but if one small life in the 114th Street synagogue means anything, the transaction called believing comes down to the confrontation with overwhelming power and then the relief of knowing that one has been spared its worst. But I learned this, as I did most things, apparently, in a somewhat odd fashion.

Great-grandfather, I later came to believe, liked me and enjoyed having me by his side in *shul,* as totally out of everything as I was. He would pray with his big hand resting on my shoulder, his powerful smells so bracing and unique, a mixture of musty linen, tobacco, slivovitz, and humanity—and there was a good dose of humanity by Friday night when he had not bathed since the previous Saturday. People seemed to depend more on smells in order to recognize or identify one another in those days. Certainly to a small boy every individual had a different scent, and my great-grandfather was an orchestra of scents—when he lifted his arm around me, flapped his prayer shawl over his powerful broad shoulders, combed fingers through his beard, or leaned over to one side to get his handkerchief out of his back pocket, each gesture smelled different.

I had entered into what seemed a dark and beautiful tapestry whose patterns both flowed and remained unchanged in their relationships to each other. At the center, of course, there was me under the high dark ceiling, beside Great-grandfather and his deep voice unspinning the Hebrew language from the book, my brother

beside me already understanding everything, handsome, clean,
and unspeakable in his rectitude, more and more resembling my
father. As he would throughout his life when in a synagogue, my
father, however, was searching the prayer book for "the place." He
could piece out enough Hebrew to feel good about it, but whenever our glances crossed he'd give me a poker-faced blue-eyed
wink, as though to say, "Hang in there, it'll be over soon." As for
Louis Barnett, my grandfather, I could even then get little from
him but a boring solemnity, as humorless and ungenerous as his
own father's spirit was free and flowing and smiling. The human
race is forever taking one step forward and one step back.

The climax of my thus far fascinated but unilluminated religious
life came one late afternoon when Great-grandfather, with whom
I seem to have been alone that day, instructed me to cover my eyes
and not look, and then did an inconceivable thing. He took off his
shoes, showing his naked white socks. Standing up, he raised his
prayer shawl over his head, gave me final warning not to look,
waited for me to place my fingers over my eyes, and then, evidently, walked off and left me alone in the short pew facing the side
of the altar and quite close to it, his honored elder's seat.

I obediently waited there in my darkness, hearing deep male
voices gathering in greater and greater number near the altar a
few yards ahead of me. Above the altar, which bore the weighty
candelabra and the tasseled cloths of red velvet and gold braid, was
the Holy Ark, a small shoulder-high closet with two carved doors
behind which rested the great scrolls of the Torah as in a miniature
toy house. Naturally, what fascinated were the small doors, about
three feet tall, just big enough for me to pass through, which I'd
have loved to do. I had always enjoyed watching them being
opened and shut, and the tender way the scrolls, which were just
about my size too, were carefully laid against the shoulder of the
man who'd been given the honor of carrying them, a ritual that had
always made me hold my breath, since I knew that I would have
dropped them and been banished straight into darkness, no question about it.

Now, my fingers pressing with all the power of religious obedience against my closed lids, I heard, of all things, the voices of men
beginning to sing! Not in unison like a chorus, but a dozen or more
individually, softly, all kinds of different melodies, and then I heard
muffled thumps, and then more, deeper thumps and the voices
rising louder, some of them seeming to be calling out above an
undertone of baritone worrisomeness, and then a sudden tenor

flight taking air like a pigeon and the thumping getting faster. My rising fear separated two fingers over one eye, and I peeked through the fuzz of eyelashes and saw the most astonishing thing—about fifteen old men, bent over and covered completely by their prayer shawls, all of them in white socks, *dancing!* I gasped in fright. One of them must be Great-grandfather, and I was seeing the forbidden. But exactly what was the forbidden part? That they had their shoes off? Or maybe that they were so undignified! Or maybe that in some hidden and mysterious way they were being happy even though they were old. For I had never heard a music like this, so wild and crazy, and each man dancing without any relation to another but only toward the outer darkness that enveloped the spaces beyond family and men, the spaces you might say listened to prayers.

Now the heads began to uncover and I quickly hid my eyes, a faker who would have to sit there and wait for Great-grandfather to return and permit me to see again. Especially wounding, this particular fraudulence, when I had undoubtedly sensed even so early—as the vividness of memory about him attests—that he loved me much, and that in some osmotic way it was he I would strive to imitate as a writer though he died before I even started to go to school.

The man's reputation for telling stories was very big, and while I understood no Yiddish I would sit beside my mother after dinner, with a dozen or more family listening to him there at the end of the table going on and on through his great beard, pausing only to spit or drag on a cigarette, no doubt enjoying the center of the stage he had so securely won, and when I asked my mother to interpret something he had said, she would wave down at me and yell, "Shhh," so I was left to concentrate on the pure spell he wrought and the music of his expressive voice. I can only recall a fragment of one story that my mother did take the time to translate for me as the old man spoke. A man in the old country was taking a shortcut home one night through a cemetery when out from behind a gravestone stepped a . . . "Wait, wait!" she said, breaking off to hear what my great-grandfather had to say next, her eyes as wide as a child's, her lips open. One minute passed as the old man spoke, two minutes. Unable to wait anymore, I pulled her sleeve for the translation. "Shhh!!" she shot down at me. It was hopeless, and I could only stare down the length of the table at that spellbinder and those grownups he held so helpless in the palm of his hand.

Through the decades I have watched these dancing men cross my memory, each time resolving to find out what their ceremony was all about and forgetting to follow through, until recently, in writing this, I finally had to decide whether it was real at all or a dream. A rabbi friend, hearing the scene described, laughingly apologized, explaining that he was a Reform rabbi and that this sounded like a real old-time Orthodox service. But what time of the year was it? he asked. I searched for clues in the clothes I was wearing but could not recall. Then I remembered the open door to the fire escape through which the tobacco juice had streamed, which meant that it had to have been either spring or fall, because in summer we'd have been away in Far Rockaway. My friend now decided it had been fall and the occasion Simchat Torah, one of the three great festivals—the last day of Succoth, "The Rejoicing in the Law," that is, in the Lord's gift of the Torah to the people. On Succoth the congregation dances with joy, and indeed it is the only occasion when all the Torah scrolls are removed from the Ark and carried around the synagogue to be kissed. The only baffling part was the instruction to keep my eyes covered, something the rabbi had never heard of before. As integral as this has always been to my memory of the scene, my friend's mystification made me wonder if the old man had been pulling my leg or if watching was really forbidden; either way, something so frightened me—and it certainly was frightening and thrilling and wonderful all at once—that I only dared recall it as though I had glimpsed it for an instant. Further inquiry has indicated, however, that the ritual was most likely the Priestly Benediction, when the Kohanim, or priestly caste, invoke the Lord's blessing on the congregation, which indeed is forbidden to watch so close an approach being made to the center of all life. In any case, he must have been the only old, old man who loved me so and whom therefore I cannot think of, sixty-five years later, without warmth flowing into me.

His death, while not quite exemplary, has always thrown a certain poetic light on his nature. In his late eighties, believing he was close to his end, he one morning summoned his little wife to his bedside and told her to bring the young rabbi. And indeed he looked to her as he had never looked in their seventy years together. As soon as she could, she brought the rabbi, apparently a new one to the 114th Street synagogue, who sat with the old man and accompanied him in prayers until he fell asleep, whereupon the rabbi left. Hours passed while my distraught great-grandmother summoned her children to the Harlem apartment two stories up in a brownstone. The old man slept and slept. The doctor who was brought in examined him without waking him and could only confirm what everybody knew, that like everybody else, but sooner than most, he was on his way to Abraham's bosom. The doctor left, and so did the children, who all had their lives to attend to. As the sun was setting, the old man awoke. His wife asked him how he felt, and he lay there trying to understand, apparently, why his head seemed lower than it had before. He slowly turned on his side, massive fellow that he still was, felt under his pillow and felt again, sat up and lifted the pillow and the bedclothes, and finally faced his uncomprehending wife, asking, "Who took them?"

Following custom in those roughriding years, Great-grandfather kept much of his assets in the form of diamonds, which took less space than cash and were easier to hide. He was apparently in that large minority who did not consider any financial institution a hundred percent honest or safe, along with W. C. Fields, another turn-of-the-century man who made no bones about his cold-eyed view in many a quip and script motif, as well as in his near paranoid distribution of his own money in an enormous number of banks across the country, against the inevitable day when some of them would abscond or plead a fake bankruptcy. In point of fact, just at the time Great-grandpa was reaching under his pillow for his life's savings, colorful or absurd as it may seem, Richard Whitney, head of the New York Stock Exchange and widely esteemed leader of the financial community, was quietly stealing enough to earn him a sentence in Sing Sing—he would not lack for colleagues there— once the Great Crash had confirmed the suspicions of my great-grandfather and Fields and exploded the illusions of the trusting majority.

Ill as he was, Great-grandpa definitely remembered stashing his whole little fortune under his pillow and now demanded to know who had been to visit him. His trembling wife reeled off the list, plus, of course, the new rabbi. Commanding her, despite her protests, to help him dress, he took his oak walking stick and, refusing her touch on his elbow, plodded up Madison Avenue from 112th to 114th and into the synagogue, where he found the rabbi seated at a table writing. He said to the rabbi that he would like to have his jewelry back. The rabbi looked up and with a blank expression repeated, "Your jewelry?" With which the old man raised his stick and brought it down on the rabbi's neck before the poor man could dodge out of the way. Bedlam. But new life had sprung into the old man's sinews as he pursued the rabbi around the room with people trying to grab his flailing rod of righteousness. At last the rabbi

faced him, both of them gasping for breath, and with hands raised
he backed to the coat draped over his chair, reached into a pocket,
and produced a knotted linen cloth. The old man unknotted it with
his bent fingers and after a glancing count stuffed it into his own
coat and walked out. He got home but barely made it back upstairs
through the narrow brown-painted hallway and into his bed. The
news had flown, and my mother and her father and a whole troop
of heirs quickly assembled and watched as from his pillow he distributed his life among them, then sighed and closed his eyes,
never to wake again.

Thirty years later, on a cold spring day in 1952, I was the only
visitor in the Historical Society "Witch Museum," the exhaustive
collection of papers on witchcraft in Salem, Massachusetts, at the
time an institution known to few outside scholarly ranks but far
more widely frequented when my play *The Crucible* had registered in the public mind. My eye had been caught by some framed
etchings and woodcuts made in 1692 during the lethal court proceedings of Salem's tragedy. The pictures showed the goings-on in
Salem so the people in Boston and other remote locations might
have some firsthand idea of how fantastically people were behaving under the prickings and seducing tricks of witches. Portrayed
were the afflicted innocent girls pointing in terror at some farmer's
wife who was secretly persecuting them and yet stood in proud
contempt of their Christian accusations. Nearby, in front of an
enormous window indicating a church or courthouse, loomed a
judge and some fifteen subordinate officials and Christian ministers
dressed in floor-length robes, with long prophetic beards, looking
wildly outraged at the incredible Devil-driven adamancy of the
accused. The shafted light on the scene sharply contrasted with the
sinister shadowed areas.

I was researching *The Crucible* then, and in this handful of pictures I suddenly felt a familiar inner connection with witchcraft
and the Puritan cult, its illusions, its stupidities, and its sublimity
too, something more mysteriously personal than even a devotion
to civil liberty and justice, reaching back much further into my life.
I had all but committed myself to writing the play, but only at this
moment did I realize that I felt strangely at home with these New
Englanders, moved in the darkest part of my mind by some instinct
that they were putative ur-Hebrews, with the same fierce idealism,
devotion to God, tendency to legalistic reductiveness, the same
longings for the pure and intellectually elegant argument. And
God was driving them as crazy as He did the Jews trying to main-

tain their uniquely stainless vessel of faith in Him. And now, in these pictures, they also had the beards and, oddly, a building and lighting suggestive of the somber synagogue on 114th Street, where light—and I had done a lot of looking up there—seemed to vanish into dim paradisaical indefinition before the eye reached the man-made ceiling, so that all the humans moved as though suspended in a luminescence not quite of this world, lacking a hardness of outline—an impression derived, I suppose, from my having first seen that incantatory dancing through the fuzziness of my own eyelashes. More than once in the future, on crossing paths with some Ancient of Days, some very old man with a child's spirit, I would sense an unnameable weight upon our relationship, the weight of repetition of an archaic reappearance. Perhaps one of these is Gregory Solomon in *The Price,* another, the silent Old Jew in *Incident at Vichy.*

Large families inevitably mean a constantly renewed supply of deaths that at some point set up a resonance, a certain rhythm of trips to cemeteries, of ingatherings in living rooms to finish off the coffee and cake and to say one more goodbye to a rarely encountered aunt or uncle from the Bronx or Cleveland who thereupon promptly walks out of one's life forever. Few occasions are as joyous to small children as funerals, almost better than the big wedding blowouts that take place at night when it's hard to stay awake. A small boy will never be harshly criticized at a funeral; he is more treasured as death comes close and all his wickedness vanishes before the inescapable fact that, thank God, he is healthy.

In truth, a small boy can make use of deaths to discipline his more uncontrollable outbreaks if he wishes to. Among the infractions that led Miss Fisher to summon my mother to school were the fits of giggling that came over me at the most inappropriate times, as when half a dozen of the black boys in our class, missing from their seats one beautiful spring day, attracted our mass attention by waving to us from a rooftop across 112th Street. At the same time, Miss Daniels, a teacher of sixty or more, was reading from *Julius Caesar,* of which not one word or syllable was comprehensible to any of her pupils. Just as she was being quite carried away, she sensed a rush of suppressed energy flowing through the children. Looking up and seeing the miscreants across the street, she indignantly instructed us all not so much as to glance at them but to give our entire attention to her and to Shakespeare. Like everyone else, I tried, perhaps even a little harder than the others be-cause my mother and Kermit were so depending on me to behave. Besides, by now I had a new baby sister, a whole new responsibility, another psychic mouth to feed.

Probably because the six escaped inmates were our worst incit-ers, the class was able to obey Miss Daniels and even to take her side, more or less, against these guys who were snubbing her good efforts to educate them. I fixed her in my gaze, resolved not for an instant to look out the window, and I was doing wonderfully when the vicious rippling began in my belly and I knew I was in for one of my worst fits, the kind where your mouth begins reaching back to swallow your ears. Desperately clenching my jaws and gripping the desk, I was suddenly visited by thoughts of Uncle Hymie, who was dead. Who had died. Who was actually under the ground covered with dirt and being rained on. Handsome Uncle Hymie, and my mother, my poor mother having to weep so hard for him. My stomach flattened out, the fit passed me by, and from that time on I could control my giggling by forcing myself to think of my handsome dead uncle. There were occasions when I was driven not only to think of Hymie but to hold him in my arms as he was dying, and a few times I even got into his coffin with him and patted his cheek. He was always a reliable resource.

And so the years as they passed were marked off by rhythmical repetitions—the funerals, the weddings and bar mitzvahs, the cy-cles of games that, for some reason no one understood, could be played only in their proper seasons. Shooting checkers into chalked-off squares on the sidewalk was strictly for spring, and immies rolling along the curb only happened in fall. There were always one or two boys who, unlike my brother or me, saved their last year's checkers and immies and sold them to the other kids when the season rolled around. Joe Rubin was one of these hateful bankers and naturally became an important lawyer on Wall Street, and another was my best friend, Sid Franks, whose father actually was a banker; he became a New York cop. Sid was already capable of building crystal radio sets that could bring in broadcasts, and on rainy afternoons, rather than running up and down the hallways of the building like a crazy person, he would be trying to unravel math texts he had found in the library. He was the first person I met who talked concretely about the future as a kind of stairway, each step to be mounted in its turn—certain scientific courses to be followed by others, certain schools to be applied to, fields of science to consider as one's specialty.

Sid's father, president of a downtown bank, emerged each morning from the apartment house and strode confidently to a line of
chauffeur-driven cars waiting at the curb for him and the other big
men, whose daily departure was also rhythmical. Mr. Franks
smoked a pipe with half a cigar sticking up out of it and wore a fur
coat. He had a Locomobile, the most beautiful of all the cars, an
open beige tourer with gorgeous wire wheels and two beige can-
vas-covered spare tires mounted in its front fender wells. It was so
aristocratic a car that it did not deign to put its name on the hubs
or radiator. Automobiles then, the more pretentious of them, were
close to being handmade objects; their owners wanted them to
look different from those of the neighbors. We could hang out our
sixth-floor window, Sid and I, and call out the names of every car
passing on 110th, recognizing them from above, so distinctive were
they; at the time there was a far longer list of makes than there
would be after 1929. To see a chauffeur-driven Minerva going by,
or a Hispano-Suiza or even one of the greater Packards or Pierce-
Arrows, the Marmon, Franklin, Stearns-Knight, some of them with
the chauffeur's compartment exposed roofless to the sky, was to
feel the electric shock of real power. These were rolling sculptures,
steel totems polished like lenses to throw back the light of the stars,
and there was no question that the social power they represented
could ever weaken or pass from the earth, for they spoke their own
rumbling, deep-throated reassurance that within their glinting
panes of glass sat the very rich who were so rich their chauffeurs
were rich. The wealthy had not yet been frightened, as they would
be after the Crash, into feeling guilty.

Some cars had not only a chauffeur but also a footman to sit
beside him in matching uniform, both looking stalwartly straight
ahead. Their uniforms were often wonderful candy shades of lav-
ender, chocolate, white, blue, as well as black. I loved talking to the
chauffeurs as they awaited their bosses, and I hoped to be allowed
to sit behind a steering wheel for a moment or two, or to get a
glimpse of an engine. I was forever trying to find out how a car
worked, but nobody would tell me, and I think this kind of trifling
with me built a frustration that later made school so difficult,
though for the opposite reason: it took forever for teachers to
explain what I could have understood in a few minutes, and I
would lose track and wander mentally and then have to rush to
catch up. Sitting once as a very small boy in the front seat between
my father and Uncle Abe, who was driving his Packard—the same
Abe who as a boy had been sent to greet my father fresh off the

boat—I heard my father ask him how the car was running. "Oh, she runs beautifully," Abe replied, and looking through the windshield down the blue surface of the long hood to the silver-encased thermometer sticking up from the nickel radiator, I envisioned a running woman attached to the car underneath, making it go. "Is there a lady in there?" I asked Uncle Abe, and he and my father burst out laughing, but of course they didn't understand how an engine worked either. Since obviously there was no woman in there and yet the car ran, I was left with its she-ness to account for its motive power, a living persona of its own. This ignorance around me of how anything worked made Sid Franks, with his analytical, scientific attitude, more and more useful to me, even necessary.

In the mid-twenties, whites were not necessarily vacating houses into which black and Puerto Rican families moved. It was by no means taken for granted that all of Harlem was to be a black ghetto—in fact it was inconceivable when some of the best restaurants in the city were doing great business on Seventh and Lenox and along 125th Street too. The Cotton Club, after all, was deep in black Harlem but largely patronized by whites. There was at least one Shubert Theatre on Lenox at around 115th, as well as other legitimate theatres scattered through Harlem playing what in effect were road company productions of the hits down on Broadway. My mother loved to drop in on matinees at the Shubert, and that was where I saw my first stage play, at about the age of eight, she and I alone, my brother probably too busy either studying or going to a dentist downtown where, among his other drudgeries, he was having braces put on his teeth. This was still a novel procedure and an extremely expensive way of discoloring one's teeth for life. My teeth were no less prognathous, but I was not the eldest son and to my great relief even then was not regarded as worth the money. If this put me down, it also freed me from Kermit's weighty responsibilities, which I had much respect for but no desire to share. Everything would climax at his bar mitzvah when the poor boy had to deliver the same speech in three languages, English, Hebrew, and German (still the classy language of culture), in order, I suppose, to declare my mother's contempt for the stupidity and arrogance of the Miller clan, who still imagined, even after so many of them were in my father's employ, that he was somehow their inferior. Kermit's speeches, while making them uncomfortably de-

fensive as they congratulated him, did not prevent them from
turning to me and asking each other, as they always had, "Where
did *he* come from?" This was a valuable early lesson in how not to
belong, and one of the reasons why I resolved, about three times
a month, to run away from home.

I was caught between Joan, who had clearly taken my place as
chief baby, and my brother, whose stature I could not begin to
match. Joan had also introduced a new element of competition
between Kermit and me, for it quickly developed that two boys
could not hold the same baby at the same time, and there were
constant outbreaks of fighting between us, as there would be for
years to come. Running away from home, a form of suicide designed to punish everybody, was an idea I had picked up from
Oliver Twist, the only one of whose habits I could not hope to share
was his holding up his empty bowl asking for "more," a heartbreaking plea immortalized in the Cruikshank drawing; for me the problem was getting rid of the food they kept forcing on me. One of
the greatest explosions occurred over my refusal one morning to
eat the lumpy oatmeal served by our Polish-speaking maid, Sadie,
who always gave us breakfast while my mother slept. She finally
pushed my face into the hot cereal. The volume of sound from
Sadie, who screamed in Polish, as well as my own screams, my
brother's and finally my mother's—she had joined us in her negligee and rapped me on the head a couple of times while wiping
my face—this concatenation of tonalities rearranged molecular
structures in my brain that finally clicked into a plan to leave
forever, to create vacant space where until now I had been in the
house, to deprive them all of my unwanted presence.

There must have been sources other than the Dickens novel for
the idea of running away; the notion was always in the air, along
with the conviction that one was really an orphan. Since I resembled no one except, in a remote way, my mother, this made thrilling sense and explained why nothing I did came out right: I was
laboring hopelessly under a prenatal prejudice that nobody would
acknowledge, at least not to my face. I simply did not belong to this
family. In pulp novels and movies and comic strips, boys left home
with a notched stick from which hung a napkin containing all their
earthly goods plus, probably, a sandwich. Such runaways disappeared for many years, finally returning under new names, rich,
handsome, powerful, and magnanimously prepared to forgive
their properly chastised parents. In the Horatio Alger stories—by
no means a joke as yet—the solitary boy was generally, and cer-

tainly in my mind too, a capitalist-to-be. The truculent desire for freedom of Huckleberry Finn seemed not a fantastic and literary creation but a realistic version of my own state of mind.

Instead of a raft I had only my bike, and for the Mississippi either Central Park to the south or Lenox Avenue and Harlem to the north. I chose Harlem. I left no note to embarrass me in case I changed my mind and decided to return home; besides, leaving with no explanation would hurt them all the more. Of course I had to finish school that day and didn't get home until a little past three, but there was still enough daylight left to put plenty of distance between myself and this hated house before dark. Sadie, whose kinky red hair stood up like springs, was boiling some linen in the kitchen, which made it impossible to secretly make myself a sandwich, so I casually asked her to make me one, which she was happy to do as there was nothing she enjoyed more than to see me eating. Folding the sandwich in a linen napkin, I made my way out, and in short order I was on the road. I had no notched stick, there being none on 110th Street, and to go into the park to cut one off a bush risked getting myself clubbed by a cop, so I hung the sandwich on the handlebars.

Runaway boys in stories were soon picked up and adopted by millionaires whose carriages had almost run them down, but the farther north into Harlem I got the less likely it was, I realized, that I would be running into rich people. I had never ventured beyond 116th Street before, except with my family, to eat in one of the restaurants on 125th or to attend a track meet along with my brother in one of the grammar schools uptown. Beyond a small apprehension as to what I would do once darkness fell, I felt no fear as I rolled along the side streets off Lenox Avenue winding my way uptown, even though I knew that between the black people and us there was supposed to be some foggy hostility. But I had had no conflicts with black kids in school. They seemed softer and quicker to react and readier to laugh than some other kids, especially the Puerto Ricans, who were tense and constantly chattering in their incomprehensible language. Still, one of my best friends was a boy named Carillo, whom I envied because he would be leaving school at twelve or thirteen to learn the glazier's trade. I would have loved to cut glass even while I felt superior as one of those heading for the "Academic" courses that led to college. The system was unabashedly class-conscious, which seemed perfectly natural and practical. Our myths were already in possession of our minds, our roles and even our costumes laid out into the far future. My one

caution as I coasted through Harlem was not to stray east of Madison Avenue, where the Italians lived. Unlike any other group, they
were ferocious for some incomprehensible reason, always carrying
a challenge. It would be possible to be knocked off my bike in East
Harlem but not very likely west of Madison.

The farther uptown I went, the more black faces there were on
the streets and stoops; there was a kind of crowdedness that one
never felt downtown. I could not yet know that in this superdensity
lay the secret of Harlem's degeneration into a slum. A few years
hence, even my father would be angered that fine apartment
houses all around ours were being "broken" by landlords renting
single apartments to two and three black families. When we moved
to Brooklyn in 1928, our landlord was happily planning to lease our
six-room apartment to two families, thus increasing his take, regardless of the inevitable deterioration of the building.

If menace was not with me as I pedaled past 130th Street heading
uptown, and if the few black people who paid me any attention
seemed warm and affable, it in no way meant that I felt they and
I were alike. Since I had had fights with white boys but never once
with blacks and had never been robbed or threatened by them, I
felt safer among them than in a white neighborhood where I was
the stranger. But black people were mysterious nonetheless. For
one thing, I found it hard to understand their speech and as a born
mimic had often found myself exaggerating it comically. In the
movies, of course, they were always stupid, lumbering creatures
rolling their eyes in terror of ghosts but certainly never dangerous.
This last was the perverse contribution of Hollywood to my image
of the Negro—he totally lacked menace, a figure apart or beneath
the white people. A rich friend of my father's had a Negro servant
wear his new shoes to break them in, and I thought that as funny
as he did.

On one of the streets above 130th I stopped to see why a small
crowd of people had gathered, and saw a black man lying on the
sidewalk with his head twisted toward a stream of dirty water
flowing along the curb, his tongue stretching out to it. Someone
said the word *gas*, and I thought he must have inhaled some from
his stove inside his house and been made so terribly thirsty by the
fumes. His red tongue was only an inch from the water, but nobody
was helping him to get closer. They stood there quietly staring
down at him, watching him struggle for a drink. I rode away under
the overarching boughs of the trees, past the clean stoops and
washed windows of the black people's houses, which looked no

different here than they did downtown, except that there were more people in them.

Remembering my sandwich, I stood straddling the bike and eating as dusk began to fall. I had forgotten my anger. At that hour the streets were filled with older black women shopping for dinner. So many of them were heavy and seemed to have painful feet. There were a lot of kids running around with no shoes on, not, I thought, because of poverty but because in the South where they came from they were used to running barefoot. Or so they had told me. Calmed by Harlem, I had a leisurely ride home, and by the time I got my bike parked in our foyer I was looking forward to meeting my mother again and finding out what was for dinner. The runaway linen napkin I slipped back into a drawer.

Nearly fifty years later, in the seventies, I left the campus of City College, where I had given a lecture, and found myself strolling alone on Convent Avenue on a lovely spring afternoon at about half past four. I had come close to this hill on my runaway bike ride. After my lecture, student actors had treated me to several scenes from my plays, and I had been surprised and moved by a remarkable performance of a scene from *A View from the Bridge* played by a Korean Eddie, a Jewish Beatrice, a black Marco, and a Chinese as his brother Rodolpho. The raw force of their acting was still with me as I walked away from the imitation Tudor campus where for about two weeks in 1932 I had tried to begin my night school education but had had to quit because I could not stay awake after eight hours on a job in an auto parts warehouse. My memories of City College were of falling asleep at a chemistry lecture, and once even while standing up in the jammed main library with an open reference book in my hands. Every seat in that immense library was filled, every space at the deep sills of the leaded windows where one could rest a book and write one's notes. I was among the late arrivals who could not even get to a windowsill. It was nearly midnight, and I had been up since six, had traveled an hour and twenty minutes by trolley and subway from Brooklyn to my job on Sixty-third and Tenth Avenue—where Lincoln Center would one day stand—and was now in Harlem trying to memorize facts about the Versailles Treaty. That was the night I returned the reference book to the librarian and walked out into the darkness knowing that I could not make it.

Now I was walking out of City College again, but this time enjoying the memory of the scenes I had watched and admiring that elevated area whose apartments provide some of the most striking

views of the city. I came to a corner and stood looking around for
a sign of a taxi. There was remarkably little traffic, merely a car or
two, and not many people on the broad streets either. My eye
moved upward toward the clear, cloudless sky, and I noticed that
in several apartment windows people, all of them black, were
observing me. A group of four or five young black men in their
early twenties came toward me, talking intensely among themselves. Seeing me, they went instantly silent, looks of near shock
passing over their faces as they parted ranks to walk past me. I
turned and saw them glancing back at me. What was up? Why was
I such a curiosity? Now two middle-aged black women approached
from the direction of the college. They were nicely dressed, neatly
turned out, and smiled as they neared me.

"Looking for a subway?"

"I thought I'd catch a cab."

"A cab? Up here? No, no, you can't find cabs up here."

They worked at administrative jobs at the college, had attended
my lecture, and had watched the scenes the students played for
me. Beforehand they had looked up my 1932 academic record and
laughingly reported that I had made all D's for the two weeks I had
been, at least bodily, present. We chatted for a while, but I noticed
a tenseness in their smiles—they were not eager to relax with me
on the corner, and after only a brief exchange one of them offered
to escort me to the subway a few blocks away. Stout black women
had always been good to me. I thanked them, embarrassed at the
idea of their protecting me even as I guessed that they were
tougher than I was, as middle-class and overweight as they appeared to be.

"I think I'll stick it out for a few minutes. But thanks anyway,"
I said.

They walked off, their anxiety undisguised now. Alone again on
the corner I glanced up at the windows where the black faces were
still watching me, waiting no doubt for the chicken to be plucked.
I knew, of course, that I was caught in the remote past when as a
boy I had sweated up these grades on my bike in order to coast
down. It may also have been that I still associated the facades of
many of the apartment houses, the emblems on cornices and window frames, with a certain upper-middle-class stylishness (some
are similar to the buildings in the Sixteenth Arrondissement in
Paris, that elegant if boring neighborhood). In any case, I could not
penetrate my unwillingness to face facts and flee, nor can I now.
It was as though I was home on that Harlem street. If I have a

psychic root it is sunk in those sidewalks, and those facades still emanate a warm and enfolding energy toward me. How could I run from them like a stranger, an invader? Nevertheless, as I realized that I had been standing there for more than fifteen minutes and that the sun was going down, I thought of returning to the college to try to call a cab. And I belatedly realized that the two women had not only been offering to lead me to the subway but to accompany me downtown, where they said they also were headed, implying that it was even unsafe for me to enter the subway alone.

Now I saw what appeared to be a taxi three blocks away, moving slowly in my direction; it had a broad white stripe around its middle and was painted brown, not a taxi color in New York, but there was a broken sign on the roof that I assumed had at one time read "Taxi." As it came closer I saw the cracked side window, the wires holding the fenders on, and the absence of a radiator grill, and I saw that the driver was a black man. The car slowed to a stop in front of me. The passenger in the back seat paid the driver, then opened the door and stepped out, one of the most beautiful women I had ever seen in my life. As she straightened up, her grocery bag clutched to her side, I exchanged a glance with her. A model, I thought. Her chocolate skin and straight teeth, the wit in her eyes, her mink hat and beige cloth coat—her soaring femininity caught me by the throat. I was enslaved then and there.

With a slightly arched eyebrow and a grin of mock amazement she asked, "You getting in *there*?"

I laughed. "If he'll let me."

"Huh! I have now seen everything." And she walked off in the spikiest heels I had seen since the fifties, on a thrilling pair of legs.

I leaned in to the driver, a small bearded man in his thirties who was folding up his money and barely glancing at me, so unwilling was he even to begin a conversation.

"Can you take me downtown?"

"How am I going to go downtown?"

"Why not?"

Now he looked at me, his money stashed. "Where downtown you goin'?"

"Well"—I thought quickly—"you can go as far as Ninety-sixth Street, can't you?" This was a gypsy cab, unlicensed and technically illegal, I knew.

"I can, but I probably be stuck down there. I won't get nobody coming back up."

The hard border between the two civilizations is Ninety-sixth

Street; I had known this for years, of course, and had simply put it out of mind. Something in me still refused to admit how definite the frontier was.

"How about you take me down," I said, "and I'll pay you double so you won't lose getting back up here?"

He turned and stared through the windshield for a moment and then agreed. I got in. The seat was situated on the floor some distance from the backrest, and I wrestled it into its more or less correct position, but it was still uncomfortably low. Rubber foam was sticking out of the upholstery as though chickens had been plucking at it. One door had no handles at all. We drove slowly downtown. I was happy.

"Quite a car," I said.

"This? This is not a car, this is history." The remark seemed more educated than I had expected. "What are you doing up here?" he asked suddenly, an edge of suspicion in his tone.

There was on his skin a kind of powder-gray dust. And I saw now that he seemed terribly tired. His fingers were as long as pencils, his nails were long flat yellow ovals and very clean. He wore two cable-knit sweaters and drove with both hands clutching the wheel as though he expected the front end to twist off the road any minute.

"I gave a talk at the college," I explained.

He drove on in silence for a block. Then he asked, "Talk about what?"

"About the theatre. I write plays for the theatre."

He drove another block in silence. "Ever give a talk at Columbia?"

"Actually, yes, a few years ago. Why?"

He said nothing for another block or so, then decided to speak. "I was a teaching fellow in sociology."

Then I was right not to have fled!

"The government cut the program I was involved with, so I'm doing this."

"You making out?"

"It slows the decay a little."

"What program were you on?"

"A study of Ethiopians in New York—I'm Ethiopian."

"Born there?"

"Yes. I'm only staying on here because I've got rank in the army and they'd have their hands on me the minute I stepped off the plane."

"But how long can you go on driving the cab?"

"That's it—I don't know. I don't really make enough. But I'm not going back to that senseless war."

"What's it all about? I haven't kept up."

"Officers like wars, that's all. They get to be important and rich." His voice was soft, like a light breeze.

When we got to Ninety-sixth he offered to take me all the way to Twenty-third, to the Chelsea Hotel, and then we had a beer at the bar next door. I asked him if I had been foolhardy to stand on that corner all alone. He had grayish eyes and a narrow face, an ascetic air. He looked down at his drink and then up at me with a shrug and a silent shake of the head, as baffled as I was, as reluctant to give up a deeply held faith, and at the same time as incapable of belief, as morally paralyzed. The ultimate human mystery may not be anything more than the claims on us of clan and race, which may yet turn out to have the power, because they defy the rational mind, to kill the world.

One lovely evening not long afterward, my wife Inge and I came out of a theatre and decided to walk home to the Chelsea instead of taking a cab from the West Forties theatre district. Below Forty-second Street life thins out around midnight, but south of Thirty-fourth there is nothing at all at that hour, hardly a car on Seventh Avenue, the fur district deserted, and not a single pedestrian. Apart from the occasional newspaper delivery truck or cruising cab there is no movement, and you could pitch a tent without being disturbed on that broad thoroughfare, which in daylight is jammed with commercial traffic. We were strolling southward, chatting about the play we'd just seen, when I noticed three or four men standing on the corner of Twenty-seventh Street. Half a block distant I heard a burst of laughter that had, I thought, the loosened clang of drink. I drew Inge closer, and we passed the group. They were black and young, in their twenties, but a quick glance was vaguely reassuring—their hair was rather neatly clipped. On the other hand, they had gone silent as we passed. We continued walking, and I could not help looking down the avenue for possible help in case we needed any. There was nothing, a dark empty boulevard. And yet it was not fear I felt but a curious suspension of soul, a kind of dying of life inside me. I supposed that to really fear them at this moment I would have to feel some hatred, but hatred, along with all other feeling, was absent. Now I heard running behind us. Several pairs of feet were slapping down hard on the pavement at high speed. I moved Inge toward the curb, thinking that our only safety might be to draw them into the middle of the street rather than be thrust into a doorway.

A deep baritone voice shouted, "Mr. Miller! Mr. Miller!"

I turned around, incredulous, as four tall black youths bore down on us calling my name. How wonderful to be famous! Breathless, they came to a halt before us.

"You *are* Mr. Miller, aren't you?"

"I sure am!"

"I knew it!" one of them shouted triumphantly to the others and, turning to me, said, "I recognized you."

"Well, frankly, you guys had me scared there for a minute."

We all laughed, and the one who had recognized me shook my hand and said, "Man, I have always enjoyed your music!"

What to say? "You fellas in school?" I asked.

"We go to NYU."

"Well, you've got the wrong Miller. I think you mean Glenn, the bandleader who died a long time ago. I'm a writer."

Embarrassment, apologies, but they had studied my plays and sweetly pretended to be as enthusiastic as if I had played trombone. We shook hands all over again to validate my revised recognition and parted happily waving to one another.

The shock of release from tension lifted us in a momentary surge of self-satisfaction, as though not luck but my talent had drawn a charmed protective circle around us—a response I recognized to be ridiculous. But if it was not fear I had felt with those running feet bearing down on us, it should have been, I told myself. Was I incapable of real despair? Or was it possible that things in this city were not as bad as advertised?

I knew that my memories of Harlem were deceptively warm. Even in my dreams black people surfaced most often as sufferers and injured, though sometimes obscurely threatening. Like the figure in one dream I had in the sixties, a man at a café table bent over a glass of wine, the brim of his straw hat concealing his face from above—for I was hovering in midair looking down at him— and as I floated closer I saw that a hole had been cut in the side of his hat through which the eyes of a black man were staring at me with an expression neither menacing nor friendly, just frighteningly open to interpretation. He had eyes in the side of his head, saw in all directions, the silent symbol of the force of judgment or the measurer of my high-flying presumptions, or both.

An ambiguous place, Harlem was packed nevertheless with the living and much hope. As darkness fell in the warm evenings, Sid Franks and I would release captured fireflies from jars and watch them swoop down the six stories from our front windows and cross 110th Street to vanish in the park. We would sit impatiently waiting at those windows in the dead of winter, eyes on the flagpole above the boathouse until the red ball flag went up announcing the hardening of the ice, which sent us yelling our way down the elevator and across to the edge of the lake to sit struggling with clamp-on skates that never stayed on very long. It was the Harlem of Joe Aug's bike store on East 111th, a sensual place in my mind after my fourteen-year-old cousin Richard began hanging around there with a condom drooping out of his breast pocket, the first such apparatus I had seen, the size of it intimidating and promising at the same time. Richard was the one who slept with his mother because he had an incipient case of tuberculosis—the mystery of the connection was never to be solved in my mind—and as if these pied signals of the forbidden were not enough, he had also appointed himself Joe's helper and clerk, fascinated as he was by the bicycle, a machine that by the age of seven I also found deep pleasure in riding or just thinking about. It would be thirty years or so before a dream gave me the reason: I saw a bicycle turned upside down, and under the sprocket bearing-housing there were three holes, and under them a word lighting up one letter at a time like a theatre marquee—"M-U-R-D-E-R." That was a hard period with women for me, and the triangular frame of the machine was the female.

But one of my missions to Joe's store, the most vivid one, had a far more tragic connection with womankind. My mother's adored mother had had a leg amputated as a result of her diabetes, and something was needed to keep the sheet raised off her wound. I thought the rear fender of my bike might work and, encouraged by my mother, went to Joe to have it removed. Joe was a friend of our family, and his sister Sylvia, still in high school, had been hired by my mother as our all-around helper, museum guide, and spirit of encouragement. She was our baby-sitter, pinner of my mother's hems, exclaimer of praise for my singing, fetcher to my schoolroom of books I had forgotten, and awestruck audience for any elaborate tale I came home with.

As Joe, a kindly thin little man forever with a cigarette, squinted one eye and unbolted the fender, Cousin Richard held the bike firm, and despite the solemnity of the occasion I found it indecently hard to keep my eyes off the condom hanging from his pocket. Richard, who would become a solid businessman one day, was not yet respectable; through a most pleasant and relaxed cat's grin he ceaselessly dropped obscenities that had Joe laughing and me embarrassed. He was cool decades before Cool. As I rode off, my fender under my arm, Richard called after me from the doorway of the store, "Ride careful! Watch out for your *pipik!*"—a particularly sacrilegious farewell when I was bound for the house of my dying grandmother with an object that might well prolong her life. When I arrived at her apartment and softly knocked and the brown mahogany door slowly opened to reveal my mother looking down at me, I knew she had forgotten our plan about the fender. I entered the living room, the eyes of half a dozen anxious faces looking uncomprehendingly down at me and my invention, which I managed to stash next to the doorway before backing out of the apartment like an irreverent disturbance. When Grandmother Barnett died, a few days later, it did cross my mind to ask for my fender back, but it was beyond me to raise the issue. I suspected that it had never even been used, a hard lesson but maybe a necessary preparation for the future's rejection of so much of my creation.

My first movie was a haunting experience that deepened my misunderstanding of the real. One night, for some reason, the roof of our apartment house was turned into a makeshift theatre, with a few long benches and camp chairs facing a large suspended sheet. I was not yet in school, small enough to look straight ahead at my father's pocket, from which he took coins to pay our admission. It was a balmy evening, the first time I had been on the roof at night. (Had they gotten Mikush's permission to walk on his cherished black tar?) A light suddenly blasted the sheet, and large people moved about on it, laughed, chased one another, threw pails of water, and then, drenched, turned to face us and slipped on the sidewalk and fell, and a woman seemed to be weeping but then laughed when a friendly man walked into her room.

Now the light went out—the whole thing had lasted only ten minutes or so—and I asked my father where those people were. Of course he had no idea. So I gripped his fingers and made him follow me around the benches as the small audience was getting up, and we approached the sheet. Why was it so silent back there? I did not let my father's hand go as I peered behind the sheet, still expecting some wonderful vision full of light and strange scenery and a room where the action I had just witnessed had taken place. But there were only the pipes sticking up from the roof, and overhead the

usual stars in the night sky. "Where are the people?" I asked my
father again. He shook his head in bewilderment and softly
laughed. I felt anger, not at his inability to explain, but at his failure
to take the problem I was trying to solve seriously. Had it been my
mother, she would doubtless have cooked up an explanation that
at least showed some respect for the dilemma.

Three years later in the Shubert Theatre on Lenox Avenue there
was a different kind of shock when I saw a curtain go up for the
first time. Here were living people talking to one another inside a
large ship whose deck actually heaved up and down with the swells
of the sea. By this time I had been going to the movies every
Saturday afternoon—Chaplin's little comedies, Fatty Arbuckle,
Pearl White's serials that always ended in frustration, with her
head an inch from a buzz saw or the train roaring down the tracks
toward her trussed body or her canoe poised on the edge of a
waterfall. I had seen the great cowboys: William S. Hart, looking
just like his horse with his long expressionless face and flat cheeks,
and later William Boyd and Tom Mix, always cheerful and ready
to help everybody—except Indians, of course. Yet once you knew
how they worked, movies, unlike the stage, left the mind's grasp
of reality intact since the happenings were not in the theatre
where you sat. But to see the deck of the ship in the Shubert
Theatre moving up and down, and people appearing at the top of
a ladder or disappearing through a door—where did they come
from and where did they go? Obviously into and out of the real
world of 115th Street, of Harlem, and this was alarming.

And so I learned that there were two kinds of reality, but that
of the stage was far more real. As the play's melodramatic story
developed, I began to feel anxious, for there was a cannibal on
board who had a bomb and intended to blow everybody up. All
over the stage people were searching for him, a little black man in
a grass skirt, with two bones knotted into his hair, who would show
up, furtive and silent, as soon as the white people went off. They
looked for him behind posts and boxes and on top of beams, even
after the audience had seen him jump into a barrel and pull the lid
over him. People were yelling, "He's in the barrel," but the passengers were deaf. What anguish! The bomb would go off any minute,
and I kept clawing at my mother's arm, at the same time glancing
at the theatre's walls to make sure that the whole thing was not
really real. The cannibal was finally caught, and we happily walked
out onto sunny Lenox Avenue, saved again.

It was not only blacks but also Orientals who were depicted on the stage as sinister. The Hearst press went periodically frantic about an oncoming "Yellow Peril," with the Tong Wars in Chinatown as proof that Chinese were bloodthirsty, sneaky, and—as I would learn in one special vaudeville show put on to combat drug addiction—lustful for white women. Many were the front pages with the immense black headlines "TONG WAR!!"—accompanied by drawings of Chinese cutting each other's heads off and holding them up victoriously by their pigtails. It made me wonder why anybody went to Chinatown at all. I would ask my parents what tongs were, and they preferred not to talk about them, doubtless having no real notion that they were in fact fraternal organizations. Actually, as in the larger American society, there were feuding racketeers in Chinatown, which would have been reassuring had I known of their existence.

At the vaudeville show on Saturdays, always the most anticipated day of the week, the opening acts—the mildly amazing Chinese acrobat families with their spinning plates and flying children, fairly boring after you had seen them twenty times—were always followed by the equivalent of a visit to the dentist: the classical soprano and the grand piano accompanying her. At the first sight of that piano being pushed onto the stage every kid in the house groaned and began beating his friends and crawling around under the seats. "The Last Rose of Summer" would be followed by one endless "rendition" after another from sopranos who all seemed to share the same high bust and the habit of folding their hands in genteel poise over their ample stomachs. Later I would see them as a punishment demanded by our Puritan conscience and approved by the audience as penance for its otherwise enjoyable two hours.

These included jokers and singers like Eddie Cantor and George Burns and Al Jolson and George Jessel, the black tap dancers Buck and Bubbles and Bill "Bojangles" Robinson, and the headline acts like Clayton, Jackson and Durante, whom my father all but revered. He was a connoisseur, having seen these performers so often during his days on the road that he could tell me how their routines had changed. He loved to whistle, and good numbers could keep him happy for weeks whistling the tunes around the house. His highest accolade for a performer was "He puts it over, I tell ya," and his worst condemnation was "dry." His judgment was accurate within its limits, and those limits were not narrow. He would hardly have been expected to sit through an hour of Shakespeare, but one day, after my plays had begun to be produced, he recalled a Yiddish theatre production he had come upon years before in the Midwest. He could not recall the play's title, but the great Jacob Adler was its star.

"He played some kind of king. You know, it was the olden days. And he had these three or four daughters, I think it was three, maybe four. And he's going to give each one some of his money, and the one that really loves him the most he thinks don't love him. So he ends up half out of his mind looking for his buttons, and he's got nothin' and he's left standing there in the rain, it was some story. But that Adler, there was an actor, he put it over, I tell ya. I seen that show, must've been over forty times, because he was touring for years in it. What I would do I would go past the theatre and ask them when the last scene goes on, because that was the best scene, when he's out there in the rain. He would belt out a roar that you couldn't bear to look at him."

He took performances personally sometimes, and if he adored Jacob Adler, he could almost literally not bear to watch Monty Woolley, a sophisticated bearded comedian who had a big hit in *The Man Who Came to Dinner*. The movies were low-cost balm and surcease for large audiences during the Depression and into the forties, and he and my mother would always find the quarter or fifty cents for tickets to the local movie house. When Woolley appeared, my father could not sit still and to my mother's amused annoyance would keep changing seats, moving back and forth across the theatre hoping to get a less irritating view of the actor from a different spot. Not only had he failed to understand how movies worked on the rooftop, but ever after too. Long before our marriage, I first met Marilyn Monroe on the set of a film in which she had a bit part—a movie starring Monty Woolley, my father's nemesis.

One afternoon at the Regent Theatre on 116th and Seventh—the acrobats having come and gone, and the soprano mercifully finished torturing us—a man in a business suit, the house manager, appeared before the lowered curtain in an unprecedented interruption of the flow of acts. We were now to "witness" a powerful play, he announced, brief but daring, as a warning to all our young people and even some adults about the evils of narcotics. Promising a thrilling and educational drama, he walked off, and the curtain rose on a Chinatown "crib" where foolish uptown white people surreptitiously came to indulge in opium smoking in order to enter "the land of dreams." Along the back wall were double-decker bunks that, except for their untidy bedding, resembled

those in a summer camp dormitory. A couple of Chinese wearing
long pigtails and wide sleeves and black pumps packed pipes with
opium and fed them to customers who entered, lay down, and
smoked with hardly a word to these evil clerks.

A beautiful young woman in a pure white evening gown entered
with two fair young fellows wearing white tuxedos and straw boat-
ers. They were all having a night on the town. First one fellow, the
cocky one, took a pipe and lit up, then sat on the edge of a bunk
and gaily fell back into it, giggling as though he had entered dream-
land with one puff. The Chinese quickly wore down the mild resistance of the second, more judicious fellow, and even I understood
that with both of her friends out for the count she would be totally
unprotected against these slimy Chinks, which was exactly what
happened. She in turn was handed a pipe, but she seemed a bit
worried. I had all I could do not to rush up to the stage and knock
the filthy thing out of her hand. How horrible it was to harm a girl
so beautiful! But nothing could stop her from also taking a puff, and
her eyelids instantly started drooping. Another puff and she was
staggering to the bed. Two Chinese instantly pushed her onto it
and conferred excitedly in their strange language. The house manager reappeared at the edge of the stage and announced, "They
are discussing her introduction into white slavery and are planning
to ship her to a house of ill repute in *Singapore*!" I was so desperate
I wondered why the manager didn't stop it, but it was not to be.
He turned and walked off the stage.

Now one of the Chinese started to climb into the bunk with her.
The audience whispered in horror. Gangrenous green light covered the whole scene. Why oh why had she gone to Chinatown?
She could have stayed on Park Avenue in her warm, safe home!
The Chinese had one leg over the edge of her bunk. Ah, she was
still apparently awake, if doped up, and resisted him, but so weakly,
poor thing. His confederate reached in to hold her arms. A struggle. Gasps from the poor girl. And not a sign of life from her two
idiot companions. Oh, how I hated them. Then, suddenly, offstage
excitement, shouts and bustle, and on came an elderly but ener-
getic gentleman and two policemen. Her father! A rich, clean,
white, and hearteningly indignant man who, aided by the men in
blue, pummeled the Chinks and collared them both, driving them
off the stage. Shaking the two companions awake, the father up-
braided both and warned them never, never, ever to touch opium
again. With his ashamed and deeply grateful daughter supported
by his strong arm, he exited, causing the green light to turn to

reassuring rose. Thank God. I, certainly, had learned my lesson. It would be many a year before I discovered that it was the English who had forced the Chinese government to lift its ban on shipments of opium from India, causing the Opium Wars, the failed Chinese resistance to the white man's poison. But no such perplexing news disturbed our feelings of white uplift as we, my mother and I, walked confidently down Lenox toward 110th Street and home.

Then as now the miracle of New York City was the separation of one group from the experiences of others. The city is like a jungle cut through by a tangle of separate paths used by different species, each toward its own nests and breeding grounds. Except for our teachers and Mikush our family knew almost no gentiles, and our prosperity helped seal us inside our magical apartness. It was my mother in her imagination and reading, and my father in his travels, who brought news of that other world where Jews were not the center of interest. His refusal to attribute naturally superior virtues to all Jews and anti-Semitism to all gentiles may have set up in me, if not a faith in, then an expectation of universal emotions and ideas. When it came to ethnic traits he was believer and skeptic at the same instant; the conflicting claims of family and vagrant sexuality, idealism and advantage, were as prevalent among Jews as among the gentile men he met on the road, whom his fair, blue-eyed appearance allowed him to get close enough to observe.

In the twenties, when he flourished, the Ku Klux Klan was riding high, swelling its membership immensely from year to year, and the Jews were their prime targets where there were few Negroes to threaten. The time was still far off when racism and bigotry would seem anything but natural and even praiseworthy ideas equated with patriotism and pride of ancestry. If ever any Jews should have melted into the proverbial pot, it was our family in the twenties; indeed I would soon be dreaming of entering West Point, and in my most private reveries I was no sallow Talmud reader but Frank Merriwell or Tom Swift, heroic models of athletic verve and military courage. As it turned out, we were building a fortress of denial that would take two massive onslaughts to crack—the Depression and Hitler's war. Nor was it only a question of Jews denying the world's reality, as events would show, but also a failure in practice of the most sacred claims of our democracy itself to a more perfect decency and sensitivity toward injustice. By the early 1940s the world knew that the Jews en masse were being hunted down by the Germans, and by 1942 that they were being incinerated, but such was the grip of anti-Semitic bigotry on the American State Department and the British Foreign Office that even the official immigration quotas—which, small as they were, might have saved at least some thousands of Jews—were never filled, and the rail lines into the killing camps were never bombed even after other equally distant installations were. And the American Jewish community did not dare to demand that rescue efforts be put in motion, such was the fear of exacerbating the American people's hostility not only to Jews but to foreigners in general. If it was that bad in 1942 at a time when Democracy was avowedly embattled against Nazism, whose most prominent sin was its racism, what must the unacknowledged truth have been in the late twenties, with the Klan parades so well attended all over the country? Yet there I was dreaming of pitching the winning game for Yale or joining Tom Swift against the Germans in our own World War I boys' submarine. But as I said, escape and denial are hardly the monopoly of the Jews; one of the strongest urges in the writer's heart, and perhaps most especially the American's, is to reveal what has been hidden and denied, to rend the veil.

I suppose my sallies into Harlem began a pattern of retreating into myself when the competition had overwhelmed me. As I coasted through Harlem on my bike, everything between 110th and 145th seemed under my control, for when I turned a corner into a new block the one behind me was wiped out of mind and I kept riding into the future forever, practicing a defiant loneliness—that cousin of revolt—blindly groping for the beginning of the lifelong voyage toward myself. Years later would come a dream of a long procession of praying people, my relations, imploring the heavens as they slowly progressed, and when I saw with amazement that the leader was me as a teenager, I fled—my departure noticed by none of them. Even early on I noted with my blood, so to speak, that when Moses climbed up the mountain to receive the Law from God, he went alone, without his brother, his wives, or a committee, and when I stretched out on the carpet with *The Book of Knowledge* and the etching of Dickens circled by the vignettes of his Oliver Twist, Mr. Pickwick, Little Dorrit, and a dozen others, the main marvel was their having come *out of his head, with no need of anyone's help*. The time would come, long years later, when I rebelled against such lonely grandeur and the cult of the autonomous hero-author, but not yet—I still had all I could do to create him.

Had I been asked before the age of thirteen whether I was happy—but of course no one would as yet have conceived of asking such a question of a child; if he had escaped diphtheria, scarlet fever, polio, pneumonia, tuberculosis, blood poisoning, deep ear infections, and all the other lethal diseases, he was lucky and hence happy—but had I been asked, I would have been astonished that my opinion mattered. Life might be frustrating, but it was exciting, and people in general seemed not to be bored. It was partly that progress was always in the air but also that to do anything at all still required so much effort. All day Saturday the kitchen was dense with steam from the enormous tin tubs boiling the laundry on the stove as Sadie or my grandmother or my mother or all of them by turns pushed a long round wooden staff into the water to keep the clothes stirred. Then the heavy linen sheets had to be carried to the lines on the roof to dry and carried down to the apartment again for pressing with irons that had been heated on the stove. On Fridays my mother would make the noodles, which I enjoyed drap-ing over the backs of the wooden kitchen chairs to dry. Then she was chopping three or four kinds of fish to make gefilte fish. Before vacuum cleaners, the carpet had to be periodically rolled up, car-ried to the roof, and beaten mercilessly. Women were always lean-ing out of windows to wash them or crouching under the piano to polish its legs. For refrigeration the iceman had to bring cakes of ice up on his shoulder from his horse-drawn wagon in the street, and he was always showing up too late, when the butter was melt-ing, or too early, when there wasn't enough room in the ice com-partment for so large a cake, and Sadie always had to follow him, muttering Polish curses, down the foyer to mop up after he had dripped all over the floor. Icemen had leather vests and a wet piece of sackcloth slung over the right shoulder, and once they had slid the ice into the box, they invariably slipped the sacking off and stood there waiting, dripping, for their money.

People did not merely buy a chicken but went to the butcher's, looked over the live beasts in their slatted cages, and pointed to an unfortunate, and as the butcher reached into the feathered hys-teria and gathered a pair of legs in one hand and with a twist of the knife slit an artery and hung the bird for plucking, a small boy was profoundly entertained. It was even better when he could help point out a swimming pike or carp or flounder in the water tank and make sure it was the one the net caught. And the thump of the club on its head, the scaling of the sides, the scissor snipping off fins and tail, the silvery knife slicing up the belly and the entrails plopping out—it was all so deftly done that it secured the world. There was even something satisfying in being sent at the last minute before the store closed for some fresh horseradish and seeing the vegetable man toss two or three second-class roots back in the bin before picking out the one he seemed to love most, which he then ground up, sometimes permitting the boy to turn the crank. These transactions took up time, and involved life and death and transformation—like this long white root turning into a mushy pulp that flung out a gorgeous, eye-tearing smell. Pickles had to be selected from the barrel they floated in, and choosing the right ones involved the spirit of decision, just as at the fruit stand—since no one expected an absolutely unblemished apple or pear or cherry—a lot of feeling and calculating went on as to exactly how spoiled the innards would turn out to be.

Except for light switches nothing worked by pushing a button. The phonograph had to be wound, a lot of the cars had to be cranked, coffee was ground by cranking, too, and the hand still had uses beyond separating pieces of paper money and pointing. Transforming things by hand always bordered on the miraculous. I would spend months in school decorating a cigar box with the American eagle copied from the masthead of the Hearst paper. In the veneer of our phonograph I had carved with the point of a nail a picture of Nipper, the Victor Company's fox terrier trademark, and at the age of six, by attaching a set of baby carriage wheels to a wooden soapbox, I built a wagon I could ride, if not steer. A few years later in the basement of our little Brooklyn house I was laying out the plans for a glider when my father, who barely understood how to open a window—although he could expertly operate a sewing machine, a skill he had learned as a child—came downstairs and innocently asked how I was going to get my plane out of the basement. It was hard to accept, being grounded by a man who hadn't a clue about the principles of flight.

TWO

"I still feel—kind of temporary about myself," Willy Loman says to his brother Ben. I smiled as I wrote the line in the spring of 1948, when it had not yet occurred to me that it summed up my own condition then and throughout my life. The here and now was always melting before the head of a dream coming toward me or its tail going away. I would be twenty before I learned how to be fifteen, thirty before I knew what it meant to be twenty, and now at seventy-two I have to stop myself from thinking like a man of fifty who has plenty of time ahead.

It was in my twenties that I felt old, that was when time was an abrasive wheel grinding me down. But it was not so much death I feared as insignificance. In 1940 I had hardly been married more than a week when I was off alone on a freighter touching the Gulf ports, and if my solo honeymoon seemed somewhat odd even to me, it also had a certain logic of the inevitable. Mary Grace Slattery and I stood on the fantail of the SS *Copa Copa,* a Waterman Line freighter about to cast off from a Hoboken pier; my parents, who had also come to see me off, stood nearby at the rail staring at the New York skyline. Mary and I had been living partners during the two years since our graduation from the University of Michigan, although I still kept my room in a decrepit rooming house on Seventy-fourth Street and Madison Avenue and she her shared apartment on Brooklyn Heights. I had outlined a play about a group of Germans in the South Pacific who under the pretext of exploring for minerals were secretly arranging to set up Nazi bases. I thought I needed to know something about ships and the sea, but it was also my divided desire for settled order and a lust for experience that sent me off. Far too much of what I knew I had merely read about, and I was in a rush to meet life and my nature.

Before the war Brooklyn Heights was like a quiet, leafy village, and from Mary's windows on Pierpont Street one could watch the ships moving in all their stately mystery out into the world. I wanted to go, at least for a little while, and alone. In any event, her secretarial job in a publishing house would not allow her to accompany me. The longer we stood on that hot, sunny dèck the stranger it seemed that I should be leaving now, even if only for a couple of weeks. But Mary trusted me more than I trusted myself; she had a stubborn integrity and once she had committed herself would countenance no qualms. She strengthened me with her clear-eyed support, and I loved her more in the leaving than if I had hung around merely dreaming of the sea. This early parting, like our marriage—and perhaps most marriages in our time—was a refusal to surrender the infinitude of options that we at least imagined we had. I would not yet have believed that our characters leave us far fewer choices than we like to concede.

There was a deep shadow then over intermarriage between Jews and gentiles, and still deeper if the gentile was Catholic. Mary had stopped considering herself a Catholic as a high school student in Ohio, just as I was struggling to identify myself with mankind rather than one small tribal fraction of it. Both of us thought we were leaving behind parochial narrowness of mind, prejudices, racism, and the irrational, which were having their ultimate triumph, it seemed to us, in the fascist and Nazi movements that were everywhere growing in strength.

There was no doubt in our minds that it somehow mattered in the world what we—or anyone—thought, and that our actions were perfectly accurate reflections of our inner lives. We enjoyed a certain unity within ourselves by virtue of a higher consciousness bestowed by our expectation of a socialist evolution of the planet. It was to be the last moment for such an inner order: when by siding with the inevitable victory of the new and just system, you bought a kind of righteousness ticket. Among its other benefits, it allowed you to suppress any contradiction that tended to cast doubt on socialism, and as important, upon your own motives or virtue.

In truth our god of Reason concealed an unacknowledged machinery as hieratic and otherworldly as any religion. For we shared with religions, which of course we despised as superstition, the belief that the power to choose was entirely within us, and I even harbored the millenarian suspicion that with our generation history might have come to its end. On some exhilarating days the blind dominating power of habit and of culture itself seemed to be blowing away like a fog before the sunrise of our triumphant consciousness. Judaism for me and Catholicism for Mary were dead history, cultural mystifications that had been devised mainly to empower their priesthoods by setting people against one another. Socialism was reason, and now it was in fascism that the rank pools of instinct collected, with Hitler and Mussolini and later Francisco Franco reaching down to the dark atavisms within man to rule by unreason and war. It was the Soviet Union that upheld reason's light by doing what was best for the majority and by repeatedly calling for a pact of collective security that would join the West and Russia together against fascism. If the one-party Soviet system seemed doubtfully democratic, there was plenty of denial available to turn the gaze away (no less than there would be decades later for Castro's Cuba and, on the right, for the dictatorships in Chile and Argentina and Turkey). It was really quite simple: we had to hope, and we found hope where we could, in illusions, too, providing they showed promise. Reality was intolerable, with its permanent armies of the unemployed, the stagnating and defeated spirit of America, the fearful racism everywhere, the waste of everything precious, especially the potential of the young. And if Roosevelt was doubtless on the side of the angels, even he was merely improvising to fend off the day of complete collapse. All that could save us was harsh reason and socialism, production not for profit but for use.

The deck paint was getting tacky under the rising heat of the sun, and the bitter smell of hot steel repelled us. We kissed one last time, and my guilt at leaving was lessened by our having gone through a kind of testing the week before at our strange wedding in Ohio. And I had just sold my first radio play to Columbia Workshop, the prestigious CBS experimental series under Norman Corwin. It was a political satire called *The Pussycat and the Expert Plumber Who Was a Man* and would be broadcast while I was at sea. In this, too, there was a strange sense of power at being able to leave my voice, in effect, speaking in my absence. Still, there was the element of unacknowledged escape that I knew I would be carrying in my valise.

As sensibly progressive as we appeared to each other and to our friends, the wedding had dramatized how conflicted both of us were inside. With our marriage decided upon, Mary soon asked, for the sake of her foolishly pious mother, that we marry in Ohio with a priest conducting the ceremony, though not inside the church. We would be not so much under the wing of the Church as only under one of its feathers. With a mother like mine I could easily understand Mary's wish to appease hers, and I agreed, all ritual and ceremony having already been consigned to our mutual mental museum.

Like my mother, Mrs. Slattery was a woman wasting away under customs she was forced to obey. Intelligent and sympathetic, she could see, for example, past the Church's support of Franco in Spain to the sufferings that the fascist rebellion had caused, and past her husband's fierce denunciation of Roosevelt's welfare agencies to the suffering they alleviated, but she found it necessary or advisable to adopt the profession of illness. Still only in her late forties, she had already perfected a wistful, rather elderly manner of referring to herself in the emotional past tense, as one whose remaining days were being counted on the fingers of God, her future a slippery chute, only slightly inclined, on which her body was sliding toward the grave, whose momentary darkness would receive her in a state of gratitude at the completion of her earthly trials. She was prodigiously repressed, had a shriek for a laugh—its utterance would bring a covering hand to her mouth while her other hand tugged at the hem of her skirt, drawing it over her knees. But she had intelligence: she was able to identify with people who were not Catholic. Stupidity, the want of empathic power, was reserved for Mr. Slattery, a retired boiler inspector for the city of Cleveland. Now living on a meager pension, he could identify only with the rapacious, the wealthy, and anyone in a uniform. He had fiddled around at the edges of a German-American anti-Semitic organization in Cleveland whose meetings he liked to attend, and I therefore must have been his bitterest pill, though he never let on lest Mary be lost to them altogether. While she had made it clear that she was bringing her bridegroom home for the wedding as a gesture of family reconciliation rather than out of any revival of her Catholic faith, Mary only gradually revealed what to her was doubtless of little importance but rather chilled me to learn. We would have to be given a special dispensation from Rome, no less, to carry out even the minimal ceremony that had been planned.

We arrived at the Cleveland railroad station during the hottest week of that scorching summer. Mrs. Julia Slattery was already close to tears as she leaned stiffly forward from the waist in her flowered cotton dress to touch lips to her daughter's cheek. Flushing with anger when the rear door of his Dodge remained stuck, Mr. Matthew Slattery turned to me to say, "It's the unions, you know—they forbid their members to do a good job." I now began to sense an atmosphere of civilized duplicity that was already edging toward farce if not outright hysteria. As we rode from Cleveland toward suburban Lakewood, I heard for the first time bridges, corporate headquarters, and public installations referred to with the possessive—"And here is our Standard Oil Building, and there is our Cuyahoga County Highway Department, and there is our Lake Erie. The last time we drove to New York we drove over your George Washington Bridge . . ."—leaving me with a feeling of foreignness that was entirely new. But here was the prewar Middle West in all its pristine innocence, that real America to which every political piety was addressed. Here were the Adamic people in the land of the unalienated, these were the folk who had to be appeased lest they rise from dim sleep and most indignantly evacuate the halls of Congress.

In the rooms of their ample house on the leafy street was no bright picture but only, in the living room, a brown statuette of Christ crucified hanging from the wall. Something parched touched everything, and even the fruit in the bowl on the dining room table seemed to have been counted. We had, it now appeared, to wait out the week until Friday and the wedding, and though there were plenty of beds in the house, I was not, in propriety, to sleep there under the same roof as my intended but in a rooming house some sterilizing blocks away. The farce of this separation when Mary and I had more or less lived together for two years, as her parents must certainly have been aware, was sustained in all seriousness. Infinite was everyone's capacity, including mine, to dissimulate. Nevertheless, here was the source of Mary's self-discipline, which I—or part of me—had such respect for.

As distant as all this was from the effulgent heat and color of Jewish life, the real surprise to me was a certain deeper similarity. At breakfast Mrs. Slattery, reading in the *Plain Dealer* that a man had been arrested for falsifying his company's books, said, "I hope he isn't Catholic," just as my mother would have, only substituting "Jewish" as her worry. For the first time, Catholics, despite their Christianity, their cathedrals, and their political clout, appeared as a minority to me, and a defensive one at that. And I saw Mary and myself more deeply related than I had until now imagined. It was only dawning on me what courage she must have had to break from this, and all alone, with no allies in some surrounding of dissent! From this vantage America seemed an unbroken tapestry of conforming obedience, of clenched teeth, of exhausted sleep from days and years of submission.

The "relationship" gathered in the evening on the front porch, aunts and uncles and cousins, to look me over, their first heathen. (The scheduled ceremony came under the official heading "For Moslems, Heathen, and Jews" who were marrying a Catholic.) Some stayed an hour or so, others just shook hands, nodded a welcome, and left. All in all there must have been more than twenty visitors, and the strain was telling on everyone. The women fanned themselves in the rockers and Mr. Slattery spat tobacco juice onto the lawn while his wife nearly groaned in despair and glanced over at me as I pretended not to have seen. Relief from it all came with the arrival of Mary's cousins, young men and women her own age who were simply glad to see her and talked with me as though we were all citizens of the same nation.

And now the young parish priest who would be marrying us arrived for his formal visit. He happened to appear at an interesting moment: Uncle Theodore Metz, recently retired as chief of police, a small, jocular, muscled man, was telling how he had put one over on his son, Barney, a new police lieutenant and Mary's favorite cousin. Through high school, she had been his frequent shipmate aboard the many small boats he loved to sail on nearby Lake Erie. Theodore had ordered Barney, as a neophyte cop, to don civilian clothes and investigate a report of systematic ripoffs of customers at the local whorehouse. Utterance of the word itself sent all eyes flitting my way to see whether I could bear up under the sound and roused a fluctuating burble of giggles and a nervous exhaling of pent-up air from the lungs of the ladies. Then all went silent as Theodore Metz unraveled his plot; he had sent a detail of cops to the whorehouse while Barney was inside, ordering them to rush the building suddenly, burst into the rooms, and collar everyone in sight—including his son, whose protests could not convince the cops that he was in the place on business. The uproar from the crowded porch clamored up and down the quiet block as Barney's indignant explanations were repeated by his laughing father. "I had the fellas put him in the paddy wagon with the girls!" Oh, it was all delicious, but anxious glances were still coming my way to see if my opinion of the family had collapsed.

It was when the laughter was billowing up that the priest appeared. I was surprised by his youthfulness; he seemed younger than my twenty-five. But more surprising was the suddenness of the awed silence at their first sight of him, so pale and adolescently thin, coming up the stoop from the narrow path to the street. He said his good evenings, shook my hand and, immediately turning away, held Mary's hand a bit longer and sat down. A propriety approaching real anxiety seemed to grip them as they leaned forward to catch every one of his softly spoken remarks, and his least attempt at humor brought immensely relieved laughter. "I have had a very long day" was greeted by a long sympathetic "Aaahh," and "It's been so hot I've been tempted to take a swim in the lake" created a thrilled flutter of amazed laughter, a vastly appreciative compliment to his simple humanity. After ten minutes or so he said his good nights and left, allowing the former chief of police to finish his whorehouse story.

Later that evening, after the relatives had gone, Mary and I escaped for a walk through the neighborhood. She seemed grim and daunted by the lengths to which her parents were carrying their inane notions of decorum and their subservience to what they thought the Church required of them. I now saw them, however, as victimized people with whom we could end up as friends. She apologized for putting me through all this, but her mother would probably collapse with guilt if some touch of the Church's sanction, however slight, was not set upon her daughter's marriage. In the unremitting heat of the night a kind of desiccation of the spirit oppressed both of us at the prospect of this pretense we had to continue to play out.

A new surprise each day. Now it appeared that we were to take instruction from the young priest in the Church's rules of family life. Growing grimmer by the minute, Mary led me to the priest's office next morning, where we sat listening to him asserting the ban on birth control and the Church's insistence that our children be baptized and raised as Catholics, none of which we had any intention of carrying out. Youthful as he was, after a few minutes he got the message of our silence, hurried through a few more rote sentences of admonition, and asked if we had any questions. I did, in fact—a genuine one. Several years earlier, Brooks Atkinson, the *New York Times* drama critic, had reported a front-porch conversation with a Kentucky farmer. Atkinson asked the farmer, a devout churchgoer, if he had any idea what the Holy Ghost was. The farmer thought a moment and replied, "I figure it's sort of an oblong blur." For some reason the Atkinson story had set me off on a brief, fruitless search for a clear definition of this mysterious entity. Now that I had this expert before me, I eagerly asked what was meant by the Holy Ghost.

He pursed his lips and glanced out the leaded windows, whose watery light emphasized the gauntness of his cheekbones and his tight skin. Turning, his blue eyes flickered away from mine in clear resentment. "I think we'd better conclude now and maybe take that up on some other occasion. But I have a duty to tell you"—and now he turned to Mary, seated beside me—"that our experience shows these marriages never last."

Both of us were so stunned we could not answer or even move. The priest stood up and took Mary's hand and said goodbye, then nodded a distant farewell to me and left us to walk out of the office into the open air alone. Outside, Mary laughed as though a cord had at last been cut by something real, an authentic expression that had brought life back. She seemed to straighten up, shedding a furtiveness that was so uncharacteristic of her. "Aren't they something?" she said, grinning. She knew where she was again. Once more the line had been drawn for her, the old line that she had crossed at fifteen and would not cross again. The priest's challenge had clarified her loyalties and her present duty, which was simply to do a kindness to her mother's sensibilities. And so all that remained now was to go on avoiding conflict for two more days until Friday and the wedding.

Or so we thought. After an agonizingly empty day of driving us aimlessly about in the killing heat, Mr. Slattery announced, as napkins were being folded following the sliced ham dinner, that there was apparently some foul-up with the dispensation. It was even possible, although not yet sure, that the wedding would have to be postponed over the weekend, from Friday to Monday. The prospect of three additional enforced days in what by now threatened to become a corrupting dishonesty snapped something in my head, and I heard myself telling Mr. Slattery across the table that I couldn't possibly stay past Friday since I had important business in New York first thing Monday morning, a happy invention that seemed to raise my standing at the table. Mrs. Slattery's eyes remained demurely lowered to her hands, which were smoothing a napkin. I was surprised and confused by Slattery's nodding encouragingly as I spoke.

The reason for his agreement soon appeared—he would lose his two-hundred-dollar deposit on the reception he had arranged in the local hotel, and two hundred dollars was not easily come by in those days for a retired city employee. This thin bald man, who had been as nervously formal with me as if I were a large bird that had flown into his house, now rather mechanically strove for intimacy, stretching his lips away from his dentures and touching my elbow with his fingers as he asked me, in an almost conspiratorial hush, to have patience. But wasn't there anyone he could appeal to? I asked. Yes, he was thinking of trying to call on the monsignor—but this was clearly something he had just that minute dredged up out of his shame.

Next morning at breakfast we were all quickened by the prospect of action, and the mood lasted through the ride downtown and up to the top of a tall office building in the Cleveland business district where we sat for an hour in a dark oak waiting room. His name called, Slattery nearly leaped up and soundlessly hurried through a door. Twenty minutes later, after his interview, he apologetically explained that he was still not sure we would have the dispensation by Friday as the papal delegate in Washington, who alone could issue it, was on a golfing vacation and could not be reached. Only halfheartedly now, he swiped at making this excuse seem reasonable, and riding back to Lakewood, I realized in the silence between him and his daughter that he was experiencing a deep humiliation before me, a stranger. Getting out of the car in front of his house, I could not bear to meet his flushed, evasive gaze.

Alone with Mary, I felt that she too was humiliated but as powerless as her father. Her submission was intolerable. I went to the phone book and found the number and called the monsignor's office. Slattery, standing only a few feet away unabashedly eavesdropping, looked on wide-eyed as I asked to speak to the monsignor himself.

The unperturbed voice on the other end replied that the monsignor was occupied. I felt an uproar rising in me, an anger fed in part by the long hot train ride from New York, the tasteless unseasoned food in this house, the idiocy of sleeping in a hot furnished room, the appalling mood of unrelieved blame that emanated from my crucified kinsman hanging on the wall, the repression of every human instinct in these people, my insecurity about my unknown future as a writer, the fall of France to the Nazis just weeks before, and guilt about marrying without my family present—for they had made no mention of wanting to come, and the expense of it all was beyond my means anyway. Anger created a new reality here, the reality of Mary, whom I felt myself falling in love with in a way I had not when she had seemed so strong and resolute a girl rather than the foundering and vulnerable young woman she was now. I was happy.

"I am calling," I said as quietly as I was able, "to inform you that we will be married tomorrow whether there is a dispensation or not."

"Just a moment," said the voice, quite as routinely as a moment before, when it had announced the monsignor unapproachable.

During the wait it was probably inevitable that I thought of the constitutional prohibition against the establishment of religion. Suddenly, the obvious fact that one could, if one desired, marry outside the Church, that its writ was limited to those who professed belief in it, was a miracle and a blessing.

Another voice, announcing itself as the monsignor's: "What seems to be the problem?"

I explained that Slattery had this deposit and that we had come from New York and all the rest.

"But the papal delegate has gone for the weekend and can't be reached," the monsignor explained with a certain blind reasonableness.

"Well then, we'll have to be married by a justice of the peace."

"*She* can't do that."

"But can't a telegram be sent to Washington? This is very important to the family."

"My dear sir, the Catholic Church has been doing business this way for nearly two thousand years, and you are not going to change that before tomorrow."

"I am not trying to change it."

"You will have to make up your mind to wait through the weekend."

"We are marrying tomorrow, sir. If you want it done with a dispensation, it will have to be here before then."

There was silence. "I'll inquire again, but I am sure there is nothing to be done."

"Well then, thank you very much."

In his excitement, Slattery unloosed a veritable flood of spit into his cuspidor, and a new energy seemed to charge Mrs. Slattery, who forgot her weakness and marched into the kitchen to make some cheerful iced tea. They wanted to know exactly what the monsignor had said, and I had to reenact the conversation several times. Suddenly the phone rang. Hardly an hour had passed. Slattery picked it up, and his small blue eyes widened. As he covered the mouthpiece he loudly whispered the caller's identity: the young local priest. Back into the phone, all he could say was "Thank you, Father. Yes. Thank you. Yes. Thank you. Yes. Thank you." The dispensation would be arriving in time for the wedding tomorrow. Oddly, my having to win Mary like this had blasted away whatever doubts I had that we belonged together.

But Mrs. Slattery's fears were not so easily downed. As the pale priest next morning read off his special service, her tensioned fingers managed to break her rosary and the beads bounced all over the polished floor, causing everyone to look around for them while the reluctantly uttered words rolled on. She looked guiltily at me, paralyzed by this prophetic symbol of destruction that her hands, all by themselves, had unloosed upon the ceremony.

But all was changed again by lunchtime. After the morning reception ended, with its scant few whiskey bottles and canapés spread as far as they could go on a table, we were off inland to Berea and the old family farm where Mrs. Slattery was born and raised. The square Victorian house stood under elms and old maples whose limbs stretched over a broad yard surrounded by flat fields of hay and sugar beets and corn. Braces of small children raced in and out among some fifty people, including a dozen of Mary's adult young cousins, some of them broad thigh-slapping laughers and others with introverted and sad faces, and immensely fat farmers and small-town folk, all of them feeding on slices of roasts and turkeys and chocolate cakes six inches thick.

Overlooking the crowd, seated on the deep porch rocking rapidly back and forth, Mrs. Slattery's eighty-year-old mother, Nan, looked with darting eyes from face to face, her expressions changing as she recognized some rarely encountered member of the clan. She wore a flowered blue cotton print dress that was obviously brand-new and still stiff, and an old-fashioned, high-crowned tucked bonnet of the same material with a visor ten inches deep. Thin as a whip, she gripped the chair arms with her gnarled hands as she excitedly rode it back and forth. When we arrived Mary had kissed her feelingly and she had looked into Mary's eyes and said, "You were always smart." Now, when I happened to be alone on the lawn for a moment some yards from the porch, I heard her shriek, "Arthur!" I turned and saw her beckoning me surreptitiously, and I came up onto the porch and sat beside her as she began to tell me her life. At a table not far off in the crowd, Mary's mother kept glancing over at us with a nervous smile, but Mr. Slattery seemed an altogether different man, waving to me from time to time with the secret smile of a co-conspirator. In his eyes,

I was now a go-getter, a type he looked up to from the shafts he had been strapped to all his life.

When I said the farm looked beautiful to me, Nan told me it had been rented out for years now; all the girls had married and gone off—there had been six daughters and no sons, a calamity for a farm couple—and her husband had not lived a long life.

"We come out here on a wagon from New York State, don't y'know, and we arrived over there by the lake and I liked it fine right there, but he wanted a heavier soil so we come back in here, and the clay was what killed him. The spot I wanted to settle turned into the middle of Cleveland." She chuckled, stared out at the mob, and suddenly yelled toward a passing man at the top of her lungs, "Bertie!"

Mary's mother was instantly on her feet coming over in embarrassment to tell her not to scream like that. The old lady listened studiously to this instruction, and Mary's mother returned to her table and sat again, but her eyes were open in the back of her head.

The old lady continued. "My husband liked that heavy soil they had in Alsace, that's in the old country where he come from, but the clay is what killed him . . ." She seemed to see something to one side of the porch and got to her feet, and I followed her over to the railing where a chicken house stood fenced around with wire. Now I could hear some restive clucking from within. She went to a glider couch standing against the house wall and, bending far over, drew a hatchet out from underneath and went back to observe the chicken house. I asked her what was happening, and she said, "They's rats been gettin' in there."

"What do you do with the hatchet?"

"Why, I throw it," she said, as though I must be stupid.

Mary's mother was suddenly behind us, blushing and taking the hatchet from the old lady. "Now, Mother, you don't have to today . . ."—and led her back to her rocker, where I sat beside her again. Quite mortified, Mrs. Slattery climbed back down the stoop and returned to her table, wearily wiping her hair away from her face, stretched in a slow agony between her husband's spitting and her mother's throwing hatchets at rats.

"Who're you voting for?" Nan suddenly asked me. I told her it would be Roosevelt.

"Yes. Well, he's the best around, I guess. But I always voted Farmer-Labor, and always for Bob La Follette when I could, although he never got close for president. But I was a member of the party, and he was always my man."

"Are you a socialist?"

"Oh, sure. But them"—she waved toward the party of people—"they're all conservative and Republicans now." Suddenly she half stood up and started to scream someone's name but stopped herself and sat, impatiently waiting for the person to turn her way. Then she waved properly and said, "Hi!" in a softened voice and returned to rocking rapidly as though she were on horseback with her eyes roving across an interesting horizon.

Without warning she turned to me and said, "I like you bein' so tall, my husband was a tall man."

"I like you too, Grandma."

She patted my knee and went back to looking over the crowd. Mary came up and sat down on her other side, and they held hands. After a moment the old lady turned to me and said, "She was always the smart one, don't y'know." An immense feeling of safety crept over me as we sat there in the middle of America.

But the serenity of that scene begins to tremble as I look at it more closely after nearly half a century. I was far less secure than I have accustomed myself to believe, and the reasons were in great part political. Ohio was deep in isolationism in 1940, and I knew that most of the people on the lawn were persuaded that after a mere twenty years of peace America had no business entering another European war. I felt the same, but my reasoning, unlike theirs, was radical; I saw the conflict between Germany and the Anglo-French as a new version of the old imperialist conflict of the previous world war, another last gasp of an expiring, self-destroying capitalist system. The people on the lawn, even if temporarily denied its bounty, believed in capitalism. Some of them had also bought the idea that by standing against America's involvement in the war they were foiling the international Jewish banker conspiracy to get us into it.

This message had gradually evolved into the main theme of a radio preacher with the largest audience in the world, Father Charles E. Coughlin, who by 1940 was confiding to his ten million Depression-battered listeners that the president was a liar controlled by both the Jewish bankers and, astonishingly enough, the Jewish Communists, the same tribe that twenty years earlier had engineered the Russian Revolution and was sworn to repeat it in "Washingtonsky," as he called it. I could just see Mr. Slattery with his ear to his Philco, shaking his head with a deeply pleasured grin at the padre's wicked wit. He was being educated, as were an unknown number of others on that lawn, to understand that Hitlerism was the German nation's innocently defensive response to the threat of Communism, that Hitler was only against "bad Jews," especially those born outside Germany, just as he was against "bad gentiles," the ones who had radical ideas. That Coughlin was broadcasting word-for-word translations of Nazi propaganda minister Joseph Goebbels's editorials in *World Service,* the German government's official propaganda sheet, was not known to the people on the lawn, and for some of them would not have been shocking news. That I shared with them an opposition to entering the war while disagreeing with everything else they believed in was a gnawing unhappiness for me and a rather new experience with ambiguity. Every generation looks back longingly to an earlier age when things were simpler and clearer, a time before degeneration began, but the year 1940—the end of my bachelor-youth and of the Depression—does still seem to me to have marked the end of a simple democratic idealism handed us by the overwhelmingly obvious evil of Hitlerism. At least it was obvious to us in New York. The further into the country one moved, however, the more human Hitler seemed to look, simply another warlike German leader who was out to avenge his country's defeat of 1918, a not entirely dishonorable ideal, come to think of it, and in any case not our business to interfere with.

In short, my conscience was muddled, as tends to happen when one knows one's agreement with a friend or ally is not at all as unconflicted as it purports to be. I still believed in the goodness of a Soviet Union that in the official Catholic view of my new in-laws and their friends was the chief creation of the Antichrist. But I refused to despair, because I thought that it was simply their longing for peace that had allowed them to be misled by demagogues into what seemed a sympathy for fascism.

The end of all this inner turmoil was that it reinforced the weld between my personal ambition as a playwright and my hopes for the salvation of the Republic. More, it deepened the presumption that should I ever win an audience it would have to be made up of all the people, not merely the educated or sophisticated, since it was this mass that contained the oceanic power to smash everything, including myself, or to create much good. By whatever means, I had somehow arrived at the psychological role of mediator between the Jews and America, and among Americans themselves as well. No doubt as a defense against the immensity of the domestic and European fascistic threat, which in my depths I interpreted as the threat of my own extinction, I had the wish, if not yet the conviction, that art could express the universality of human beings, their common emotions and ideas. And I already had certain clues here in Ohio that at bottom we were all pretty much the same.

Slattery was actually going around spreading the news of my refusal to accept the delay in the granting of the dispensation. It seemed now that as a New Yorker and a "writer," and possibly even as a Jew, there was something almost glamorous about me, dead broke as I was and altogether uncertain of my future. Sitting beside the old lady on the porch, I now began to enjoy acceptance of myself not only as a person but as a symbol of suspect strangeness beneficently transformed. Now people began recommending Mary to me, recalling what a great reader she had always been, practically the only kid who had loved school, as though her marrying an intellectual had been fated. The relaxed bursts of laughter of honest folk along the banquet tables on the grass, the high nasal women's voices, the overeating of the roasts and turkeys and cakes and all the creamy goodness of that countryside, spoke to me of the oneness of mankind. My father had been right in his refusal to deny gentiles a capacity for justice and warmth toward the stranger.

And at the same time, of course, running parallel with this euphoric hopefulness was my certainty that if I should suddenly stand up and announce that it was all a mistake and that I was leaving alone for New York, Mary's mother would thank me rapturously, followed by the whole clan.

As usual, it was dialogue that combed out my muddle. People now had momentarily ceased to come up to us on the porch, and turning to me with the vaguely apprehensive look in her eyes that old people sometimes show when addressing the opaque young, Nan asked, "What're you making of this pact?"

The Nazi-Soviet Pact had stunned the world; Hitler's archenemy had been Bolshevism, whose threat to Germany had justified all his barbarities and had won him support from many conservatives in the West. Partisans of the Soviet Union who had not quit the ranks in disgust were defending the pact by recalling that for years the Russians had been pleading with France and England for a treaty against the Nazis and had gotten nowhere; now they had simply turned the tables and from their point of view neutralized Germany in order to give themselves time to prepare for the inevitable German attack later on. In other words, the myth still held that these were not only different but absolutely opposite systems.

Before I could answer, the old woman said, "Looks like the

Russians just got fed up with those French." *French* sounded slightly distasteful, she being of German Alsatian background. "I wouldn't blame them at all."

Coming from so authentic a native of the heartland rather than from a New York radical, this was a relief to me. The truth was that with the pact there had come, as some such moment does to every generation, an end to innocence, the sunny air of youth clouding over with an ambiguous weather. Throughout the Depression years, whatever the frustrations and political twists and turns, one's pure words had had no need to be colored by unacknowledged reservations: one had simply and directly reached out to the rational and landed on the left. The alternative was to justify insanities like the destruction of crops to keep prices up when people in the cities were starving for food. But nothing was that clear anymore.

"Well, I hope we can stay out of this one," she went on, "but you just wait and see—those British are going to work around us till we're bailing them out of trouble with our boys again . . ."

For a moment her simple common sense promised to settle my uncertainty about this single most crucial issue of the hour. In effect, she was saying that no conflict of values stood between the Nazis and their Western opponents: it was merely the everlasting old power fight, this time over the redivision of empire as a result of a resurgent Germany having recovered from her defeat twenty years ago in the First War.

The issue itself is of course long gone, but the human process that underlay my rationalizations (and probably those of most Americans at the time) is still very much with us, now applied to other issues. For seven years I had literally been having nightmares about the Nazis, if only because they seemed in the profoundest sense to be unopposed, truly the wave of the future, as Anne Morrow Lindbergh had called them, a wave of total darkness as I envisioned it, a government of perverts, hoodlums, and the raving mad. How could I possibly have tolerated the idea that a Nazi victory would be no worse than that of the British and French, corrupt and decadent as they were, and craven as they had been during the decade in knuckling under to Hitler's demands? This paradox was very much part of the radical mind-set of the thirties.

Part of the national confusion as to how to view the oncoming war grew out of an uncustomary American cynicism resulting from the Crash. The stock market, far more than a mechanism of investment or even legalized gambling, had carried for a great many middle-class people the prestige of capitalism itself. The market was the visible symbol of the rising line of "values" of property, even the proof of some sort of classless society in the making, since investing had spread so widely through the country. When the market collapsed practically overnight, with none of the great leaders or institutions capable of stopping it or even understanding what was happening, a panic deep in the spirit made questionable any and all belief in everything official. In an act of contempt, someone thrust a midget onto the lap of the great and formerly sequestered investment banker J. Pierpont Morgan while cameras flashed. Other financiers landed in prison or jumped out of windows. The uncontrollable slide of the market also took with it what had remained of the noble mythology justifying the First World War, which now became but another proof of the power of the moneybags to brutally squander innocent lives in order to make the rich richer. In this light the revolution in Russia, which had pulled the czarist army out of the war and its mindless slaughter, made terrific sense; from a distance it seemed a sublime instance of man's intelligence.

Now, in 1940, they were going at it again, and again it was the Russians who were opting out of yet another war. And if it seemed a cynical turnabout to have allied themselves with the very fascists they had inveighed against, there was also more than a semblance of consistency in the pact, if that was what you wished to see. Russia in 1940 had no colonies, had annexed no neighbors (the division of Poland with Germany and the occupation of the Baltic republics were explained away as defensive acts), and could therefore claim a clean anti-imperialist record; and it had no unemployment, unlike every major European country. Could her alliance with Germany not demonstrate either that she was determined to stay out of a rotten war even at the cost of having to embrace the loathsome Nazis or that she was buying time in order to prepare to fight them?

The difficulty of understanding human illusion is the difficulty of discovering its premises, the logic of the illogical. Once the Western democracies, led by men like Chamberlain of England and Daladier of France, had simply handed Hitler the Czechs, who with one of Europe's strongest and best-prepared armies could quite possibly have stopped the Germans, once it was perfectly evident in the refusal of the Allies to sell arms to the Spanish Republicans that they were accomplices of Italian and German fascism in the destruction of the first democracy in Spain's history, it was not a difficult step to believe that the secret dream of the governments of France and Britain was a German victory in Russia, and afterwards a long future without any Communists at all in a world comfortably divided into spheres, none of them socialist, all of them held in place by German Nazis, English aristocrats, French millionaires, and their mercenary armies. That the Russians should now have drawn the teeth of this burgeoning new dragon by shaking its claws, leaving its tail to slash at Paris and London instead of Moscow and Leningrad, was certainly comprehensible.

What was omitted from this scansion was power, in place of which we injected moral considerations. It was our desire for a moral world, the deep wish to assert the existence of goodness, that generated, as it continues to do, political fantasy. Given the depth of our alienation from the failing capitalism of the time, it would have been intolerable to see the clear parallels between the social institutions of the fascist and Nazi regimes and those of the Soviet Union. Captive trade unions, mass youth organizations, secret police, informers in the workplace and the home, masses of political prisoners, and at the center of it all idolatry of the state and its leader—all of these had originated in the Soviet system. Fascism and Nazism were imitations of Soviet forms, with manic nationalism and racism replacing international proletarian solidarity as their central "spiritual" content. The generic enmity between the two systems turned out to be no deeper than the enmity of England for France at certain times in history, or of Germany for England. The moral conflict, which we preferred to take to heart, concealed the nationalism and geopolitics that were the driving engines of the time.

The fear of drift, more exactly a drift into some kind of fascism, lay hidden somewhere in the origins of *The Man Who Had All the Luck*, an early play of mine—seemingly a genre piece about mid-America that has no connection with any of these political questions. It was, so to speak, handed me by a woman who climbed up on the porch and seated herself beside Mary, Nan, and me. She was Mrs. Slattery's younger sister Helen, whose husband had hanged himself not long before. Like every writer, I am asked where my work originates, and if I knew I would go there more often to find more. But there simply are circumstances in which plays collect and form, like bacteria in a laboratory dish, later to kill or cure.

Helen was eager to meet the stranger Mary was bringing into the clan and seemed to long for news of the world outside. Slender, with a small pale face and brown button eyes, she had a certain absentminded integrity in her unselfconscious way of crossing her legs and leaning on her thigh, in her unawareness of the hairpins dangling from her bun and the crookedness of her blouse neckline. She emitted the power of the distracted, the air of a Middle American searcher.

Mary had told me about Helen's awakening one morning to see through her bedroom window the open barn door and her young husband hanging from a rafter. "I was sorry to hear about your husband," I said. "I hear he was a fine man."

With no hesitation she moved right into the subject, as though by telling it again and again her story might turn out to be less real.

"We were together in the same classes since kindergarten, don't y'know, and right through high school, although Peter had to quit and get some work and I went on and graduated. Everybody'd always liked him, so he never wanted for a job, I mean people just liked having him around, he was so cheerful, don't y'know . . ."

Like a litany, her story seemed to have been often told, reminding me of the prisoners' wives at Michigan's Jackson State Penitentiary, the largest in the country, where as a student I had spent many weekends visiting a friend who had gotten the job of psychologist there after a single psychology course in Ann Arbor. Those women, too, seemed to have spent years repeating the same stories of injustice to anyone who would listen.

"Then he changed. Overnight, just all of a sudden started this getting up out of bed and putting on his clothes and going out."

"Where'd he go?"

"A lot of the times to the filling station . . ."

Peter had owned a very lucrative gas station, only one of the properties he had developed while still in his twenties, and he liked to make surprise inspections to balance the cash against the gallons pumped. That no discrepancies ever turned up did not lessen his panicky conviction that his employees were pilfering. "You couldn't contradict him, he'd get mad if you did," Helen said.

Naive as they were, his friends realized he was ill and finally managed to get him to doctors in a Cleveland hospital. For a time he seemed better, but just when Helen and he were planning a vacation to Canada, he killed himself.

The story swept through me with a certain familiarity that I could not understand. I was almost nakedly ignorant of formal psychology, and it never occurred to me to write Peter off as a case, a paranoid psychotic; instead I sensed the mysterious motion of spirit in his illogical behavior, and like Helen, who still could not recover her confidence in the reality of the daylight world, I was preoccupied by the unanswerable. Why would so successful a young man be drawn to his own death? Especially in this pristine countryside far from the crush and competitive pressures of the city? What logic required his death, a logic we ordinarily never notice ruling our lives?

First as a novel, which I never found a publisher for, then as a play, *The Man Who Had All the Luck* hounded me for the next three years, until its 1944 production, my first on Broadway, which lasted four sad performances and disappeared. But it was through the evolving versions of this story that I began to find myself as a playwright, and perhaps even as a person.

To begin with, Helen moved me through an odd resemblance to my cousin Jean, Aunt Esther's daughter, who lived across the street from us on East Third Street in Brooklyn. Both were mild-spoken young women with intrepid and smiling natures that sudden death had struck down. Jean's husband, Moe Fishler, a strikingly handsome man with straight and sparkling white teeth, a fascinating black mole on his flawless white cheek, glistening black hair, and a small, perfectly proportioned body, had also been a great success by his early thirties. He radiated an unmistakable aura of competence and good fortune. During the Depression, when everybody else was financially gasping, he had steadily risen to become a prosperous textile executive. But something had apparently come between him and his wife, and they barely spoke to one another anymore.

They were an extremely fastidious family, and now they seemed to be kept together by all the polishing they did. Moe would even polish his red Buick's engine until it shone like the body paint. Jean came from a family of three daughters whose recreation was to cover their heads with bandannas and clean their tiny house under the leadership of their mother, my aunt Esther, a woman who could not sit down in a chair without first giving it a swipe with the side of her palm and was forever dusting her décolletage with the tips of her fingers lest a snowflake of dandruff had drifted down on its expanse.

On a hot summer afternoon Moe decided to drive alone to Brighton Beach, some two miles away, for a swim. By sundown he had not returned. As the sky turned a darker blue, with the last yellow rays of the sun still flashing on the windows of their house, Jean stood alone on their high brick porch looking toward the corner, worried but too timid to call the police. Now a lone car, one she'd never seen before, rounded the corner, and she watched, motionless as a deer that has seen a hunter, as it slowed to a halt in front of her stoop. Out of the driver's side a tiny hunchbacked man in a bathing suit slid himself off the seat onto the pavement. Like a large broken doll, he limped around the car to the bottom of the five steps. Looking up at Jean, he seemed apologetic in his tone and movements, his hands turned up toward her. "I have him in the car," he said, without introduction or explanation, apparently sure from her widened eyes, as much as from Moe's identification in the wallet he held in his hand, that she must be the new widow he was looking for.

She came down the steps into the final dream of her life and looked into the car window and saw her beautiful Moe dead. The hunchback was a physician who had been lying on the beach when he saw Moe collapse and had tried to save him. Now Moe's mother came out through the screen door and the screaming began, the helpless and furious wailing. All the neighbors came out onto the sidewalk—old people, kids, women carrying babies, young couples, and the one gentile on the street, little gray-haired Mr. Clark, who lived next door and worked in a bank and normally carried a small pistol. (This evening he was in his old wash trousers and undershirt, having just lubricated his Model A Ford. It could be seen shining in his garage, the floor of which he had dug out so that he could stand in the pit and grease the car himself. When he died a few years later, Moe's sister Mae and her husband bought this car from Mrs. Clark. In a half-dozen years of ownership the Clarks had put less than three hundred miles on the Ford. It had been less an auto than an icon. The childless couple had nowhere they wanted to go; they merely needed something to care for and worry about and protect from the elements.)

Moe was lifted out of the car with Mr. Clark's awed help, but the hunchbacked doctor was fended off by Jean, who in her hysteria kept him from touching him. Moe's mother, furious, was screaming incoherently at him; why had he come, this misshapen midget in a bathing suit bringing them a dead, still-beautiful son? "Who are you!" she kept yelling at him, as though Moe might revive if she could deny that this deformed creature had any connection with him. And they never let the little doctor enter the house, as though he were cursed, and I saw him waddle back to his car on his crooked skinny legs in his droopy bathing suit, weeping openly as he drove away.

Oddly, Jean and her mother-in-law, near collapse and needing support, each took on a kind of stunned naysaying tic at the grave-side, a ceaseless back-and-forth motion of denial. And Helen, on the Ohio porch, had the same attitude of denial, if without the tic. It would take months for Jean to lose it, and longer for the old lady, who would continue to stand at the porch railing at sundown, her head motioning no-no-no as she looked toward the cemetery, some blocks away.

From Moe's sudden and incredible death, and from the suicide of Helen's husband, emerged *The Man Who Had All the Luck,* which wrestled with the unanswerable—the question of the justice of fate, how it was that one man failed and another, no more or less capable, achieved some glory in life. Perhaps I was refracting my own feelings of a mysterious power gathering within me, contrasting it with its absence in others. But already in 1939, before the war began and fresh out of college, I had written a large tragedy about Montezuma's destruction at the hands of Cortez, with a related inner theme. As the successful David Beeves, the hero of *The Man Who Had All the Luck,* was destroyed by an illusion of his power-lessness, Montezuma convinced himself that the strange white creatures who had come out of the ocean were fated to be his masters and at the same time to apotheosize him to godhood now that he had, as he believed, led his Aztecs to the conquest of all the known world and had nothing left to do with his life. Very differently put, the same question is raised in both plays—the dreamlike irreality of success and power. Both plays, it should be said, were at the same time referring to the paralysis of will in the democracies as Hitler moved week by week to the domination of all Europe.

The Man Who Had All the Luck, through its endless versions, was to move me inch by inch toward my first open awareness of father-son and brother-brother conflict. David Beeves was initially an orphan who had made his way up the ladder rather miraculously in his small town. His friend Amos was a young local baseball pitcher whose father, Pat, had fanatically trained him practically from childhood; even in the long winters he had his boy pitching against a target in their basement. In short, Amos's life was to be totally fenced off from insane chance. But after a game to which, at long last, Pat has inveigled a Detroit Tigers scout, Amos is turned down for the big leagues. The scout believes he is psychologically paralyzed whenever men are on base behind him—down in the basement he had nothing to worry about but the target in front of his eyes. The very thing that was supposed to guard him against failure is what brings him down. The effect on David is powerful, dangerously isolating him as a shining success among his peers in the town.

One day, quite suddenly, I saw that Amos and David were brothers and Pat their father. There was a different anguish in the story now, an indescribable new certainty that I could speak from deep within myself, had seen something no one else had ever seen.

I had written four or five full-length plays by 1940, had won two successive Avery Hopwood Awards at Michigan, and had attracted the interest of a few producers and some actors in New York. My first play, *No Villain,* using members of my family as models, was the story of a strike in a garment factory that set a son against his proprietor father. Another was about a prison psychiatrist's doomed struggle to keep the sane from moving over into madness. In that story, there had also been a conflict between brothers, but I had not thought of it as such.

As I said, I had spent many weekends visiting Jackson State Penitentiary, where my former classmate Sid Moscowitz, who had graduated a year before me, had gotten himself appointed on the basis of one elementary psych course as the lone psychologist of the country's largest prison, with the responsibility of keeping some eight thousand inmates from going crazy. In those Depression years it did not take much insight to notice that most crimes were preeminently economic, people stealing in order to eat. I met several prisoners who had murdered sheriffs for attempting to confiscate their livestock for a foreclosing bank, and dozens of small businessmen with seven-year sentences for kiting not very large checks.

But it was the incomprehensible cases—those with only the remotest connection to economic causation—that kept me coming back to Jackson. These were men like one I'll call Droge, an Indianapolis Speedway champion driver who had no real need to turn criminal and yet for a dozen years had secretly been running a ring of car thieves. I met Droge in the machine shop at Jackson, where he was teaching auto repair to the inmates. In his midforties, he was a handsome, trim, and intelligent thief, wittily morose, usually with his embittered self as his irony's target. In talking to him, as to other inmates, I had the advantage of access to his records and could check on his truthfulness. His story was true.

An especially valuable foreign or American car would be spotted by Droge's gang and driven a short distance to a waiting truck with a lowered ramp. Then, as the truck sped along the highway to some other city, mechanics inside would change engine numbers, provide new plates, spray the car a different color, and unload it at a cooperating dealer's premises by evening. They could work a car a day and often a second one through the night for delivery in the morning. Droge had several groups operating across the Midwest; one gang member was an unemployed printer in Lorraine, Kansas, who could turn out perfect registration certificates with false numbers. Over a decade Droge had become a rich thief even as his car racing fame grew.

His downfall came as a result of absolute chance. After lifting a Rolls-Royce in Flint, Michigan, he garaged it behind a rooming house where he had arranged beforehand to stay the night, figuring to depart before dawn when the alarm for the missing car had begun to cool and he could quickly run it up onto his waiting van. Unfortunately, he had managed to pick probably the only rooming house in Flint owned by a cop, who on returning home saw the beautiful Rolls in his garage. Worse yet, Droge had had an instinctive flash and had quietly come downstairs; he was in the car starting to back it out of the driveway when he saw the cop with drawn revolver in his mirror and gunned the engine in the hope of running him down. He got a fifteen-year sentence, cars being sacred in Michigan, but the worst of it was that he knew who to blame for his concrete environment.

One day I found him in the vast open yard of the prison, an area several blocks square, where men strolled about, tossed baseballs, or just sat facing the spring sun. Droge was looking up at the top of the surrounding wall, a straight concrete slab about five stories high, over the top of which four prisoners had made their incredible escape a week earlier. Now workmen were moving about against the sky up there, installing a system of electric eyes so that anyone crossing the beam of light would set off an alarm. The recent escapees had worked in the prison's electrical department and had managed over a period of weeks to collect twelve-foot lengths of one-inch electrical conduit pipe, threaded at both ends, which they buried in the yard length by length each day, plus a long rope that they had cut off the curtain of the prison theatre auditorium. Early one morning they had uncovered the pipes, screwed them together after bending one end, and raised the resulting pole, hooking it onto the top of the wall. Then they had shinnied up and let themselves down on the other side with the rope. Within a week they were all shot dead in St. Louis.

Watching the workmen on top of the wall, his eyes narrowed in thought, Droge shook his head and sighed.

"What's the matter?" I asked.

"Waste of time. All a guy'd need would be a three-cell flash-light—if he was stupid enough to try getting out of here, I mean."

"A flashlight?"

"Sure. Shine it into the receiving cell, walk past it, then shut off your light. You never interrupt the beam and you're home free, till they catch you and blow out your brains."

"God!" I exclaimed. "Maybe you ought to tell them."

"What's the difference? It gives them a little work. Anyway, they'll find out sooner or later."

Droge was definitely not mad, but men in different stages of delusionary dreams were wandering everywhere in the prison, a place I came to regard as more an asylum for the insane than a place to punish criminals. In fact, the sanest of all were the con men, the forgers, safecrackers, and high-level car thieves like Droge who had simply matched skills and wits against the system and had momentarily lost in a game that was purely technical, with no more hard feelings than a pole vaulter has against the force of gravity.

The Great Disobedience, the play I eventually wrote about the prison, was the first I had ever researched; I wanted to get out of myself and use the world as my subject. And here was the sys-tem's malign pressure on human brains waiting to be exposed. After winning the two Hopwood Awards, I did not win a prize in my senior year, this play having been thought "turgid" by the judges, as indeed my feelings about Jackson were. It was reputed to be the most progressive prison in the nation, but I could never sleep easily after returning to Ann Arbor until I had managed to put out of mind that city of caged men, the musky zoo smell of those hot, humid cellblocks with tier on tier of humans, over eight thousand of them, and the echoing of their hollow bass rumbling that never ceased, the wild, insane laughter and threat-ening uproars that periodically arose. No guard dared walk within arm's length of the cells for fear of being strangled by hands darting out between the bars. The worst of it was that had I been given charge of that prison I knew I would have been helpless to change it, short of opening the gates and letting ev-eryone go. Yet one couldn't do that either. I thought that at least a quarter of them were totally mad.

My play's failure did nothing to weaken my conviction that art ought to be of use in changing society. This was, of course, a com-mon idea in the thirties, in part because it was so simple to under-stand. Stalin had called art a "weapon" of revolution and writers "engineers of the soul," and indeed something like that concept goes far back in human history. The medieval and Renaissance works that glorified Christianity through the formulas of biblical imagery, as well as Shakespeare's repeated affirmations of monarchy's divine rights, were different aspects of this same demand upon art to confirm the sublime validity of a regime. And closer to our own time, the two greatest writers I knew of, Tolstoy and Dostoyevsky, were neither of them "free" in the British or American sense of detachment from all social and religious responsibilities; for both, in their different ways, the confirmation of Christ's message, not entertainment or escape, was the ultimate end of art. Chekhov's adored plays were usually approached then as specimens of a generically gloomy Russian personality, but just as the Greek tragedies—which I was coming to love in the way a man at the bottom of a pit loves a ladder—sought to transform the vendetta and the blood feud into the institutions of law and justice, so Chekhov was voicing a social need to break out of the Russian tradition of indolence into a brisk new age of purposeful work and scientific analysis of problems. In short, these were not mere authorial "angles" to sell arbitrarily fashionable causes but natural eruptions of mankind's will to evolve.

In the thirties Ann Arbor was regarded as a radical enclave in the heart of the Middle West, registering the largest number of student signers of the so-called Oxford Pledge, a promise never to bear arms in war, which had originated at the British university. Of course it was really the bygone world war we were swearing not to participate in: by the time the next one came along, the same committed pacifists, with few exceptions, would present themselves for battle against Germany and Japan.

Change is of the essence, but some things change more ironically than others. The head of the campus peace movement was a senior named G. Mennen Williams, an heir to the shaving cream fortune, nicknamed "Soapy" then and thereafter. His wry, acerbic letters to the editor put antimovement conservatives in their place at least once a week. Soapy could often be found, in 1935 and 1936, haranguing the doubtful from the library steps.

At the worst of the McCarthy time, in 1953, less than twenty years later, the editor of *Holiday* magazine, Ted Patrick, asked me to go back to Ann Arbor to report the changes since the thirties. In many ways the campus was unrecognizable. A member of the

Student Council told me that as a resident of a cooperative rooming house she was running into more and more people who thought she must be a Communist for not living in a privately owned house or an official university dormitory; Erich Walter, my old English professor who had become dean, told me that the FBI was asking teachers and students to inform on each other and suggested that I confirm this by talking to the current "orientation professor"; members of the Socialist Club, an anti-Communist group, said that people no longer came to the club's weekly meetings by car because a state policeman was outside taking down license numbers. But the climax of my little investigation came during a visit to my beloved offices of the *Daily*.

In the thirties the building was home to every disputatious radical splinter group, along with the liberals and conservatives shouting back at them, since all political groups inevitably wanted to dominate *Daily* editorial policy on the issues of the day. Competition for reporters' jobs was fierce. But now the building seemed deserted at two in the afternoon, and I soon learned that the paper, incredibly, was forced to advertise for applicants to the staff. To refresh my memory of the old days, I asked for some *Dailies* of the thirties from the morgue, sat down at the large round oak table at the end of the editorial room on the second floor, and began riffling through the musty pages. Soon a burly middle-aged man appeared and seated himself at the table to peruse some recent issues of the paper and take notes. A student reporter materialized at my elbow, whispering to me to come with him if I wanted to know what was happening in the place.

In a distant corner of the deserted editorial room, the student introduced himself with evident pride as the author of a recent four-part series, "Communism on Campus," which had exposed a couple of student radicals who, he said—not without some pity— might face expulsion soon. The result of his exposé, he was happy to inform me, was a job offer from a Los Angeles paper. He was a tiny, dwarfed young man with stretched, parchmentlike skin, wearing a fedora tipped to one side like a character in *The Front Page*. Now he got down to business, indicated the middle-aged man, who was still turning pages at the round table, and whispered, "He's state police. He comes in once a week and goes through the letters columns and the news and picks up the names of anybody who says stuff that sounds leftist."

"And what happens then?"

"Well, it all goes into the master file in the governor's office. The governor in Michigan is the direct commander of the state police, you know."

The governor now, of course, was G. Mennen "Soapy" Williams. I could not help smiling as I returned to the table and sat at my old papers with the thick-necked cop across the table scanning the columns for dangerous names. I began looking through the papers with the vague hope of finding one of Soapy's letters to the editor. Fate had me by the elbow: the very editorial page open before me had a letter apparently in response to a complaint the previous day by someone signing himself "Conservative" who had expressed "dismay" at learning that "only radicals attend these so-called Peace meetings."

"Dear Conservative," went the reply of the peace movement chairman, "if you Conservatives would bother coming to our meetings it goes without saying they would not only be attended by radicals." Signed, G. Mennen Williams. I picked up the yellowed paper, walked around to the state police officer, laid it beside the fresh one he was reading, and pointed at the ancient letter. He glanced up at me questioningly, then read the nearly twenty-year-old type, looked up at me again, and said, "Who're you?"

I gave him my name, which meant nothing to him, and explained my *Holiday* assignment. "McCarthyism" meant nothing to him either, and he went back to dutifully scanning the papers for dangerous names.

In the McCarthy years, a kind of unacknowledged underground mentality had permeated all kinds of places. A week or two after my *Holiday* piece on Michigan came out, Ted Patrick asked me to write still another about anything I wished. Since I did little magazine writing, I thanked him but almost automatically declined. A few days later came another request, and then another, until I finally did manage to write a short memoir of life in Brooklyn in the thirties, which he duly published. Years later, after Patrick's death, I learned the reason for his strange persistence. The advertising department of the Pontiac division of General Motors had warned Patrick that Pontiac would cancel all its advertising in *Holiday* if they ever published another piece by Arthur Miller. As it turned out, my second piece did not dry up the Pontiac account, but the air in those days bristled with such threats, and I regretted being unable to congratulate Patrick for his defense, particularly courageous at the time, of editorial integrity. More often the threats had their intended effect, as was illustrated by one of the documents I used for my Michigan piece: a mimeographed in-house release from the president of the National Association of Manufacturers advising members to cease their attacks on the university faculty for its alleged radicalism—a time-honored NAM custom—because the radicals had by now been "cleaned out" with the help of organizations like theirs.

Nevertheless, with all the radical turmoil on the campus in the thirties, it was a myth that the student body, let alone the faculty, was predominantly leftist. Most students by far, and almost all the faculty, were mainly interested in their careers, just as they always are. I might editorialize in the *Daily* against the university's refusal to allow John Strachey to speak on his famous book *The Coming Struggle for Power,* but I had no illusions that I was in anything other than the tiny minority that was even aware of his book or point of view.

If Michigan was not in fact a leftist institution, it did earn its reputation for democratic attitudes, witness its willingness to accept me, if only after I had written a couple of imploring letters promising to mend my academic ways. In the twenties the faculty had been open to socialists, birth control advocates, and other oddballs who had found themselves unwanted in more traditional schools, and it was one of the few universities in the thirties where Marxism as such was openly discussed in classrooms, with the teacher usually opposed to its tenets but at least willing to debate them.

The symbolic Marxist for me at the time was a brilliant student named Joe Feldman; I still consider him one of the most intelligent people I have ever known. I first met Joe around midnight one freezing February evening when he came loping into the *Daily* editorial room in his sneakers, which, like his bushy brown head of hair, were covered with snow. He was wearing a good tweed jacket over a pajama top and had a fistful of paper in his hand. Tall and loose-jointed, he stepped onto a desk top to greet all the editors and reporters, who looked up from their typewriters and sat back to await his performance, Joe being a phenomenal speaker on almost any subject. Though he rarely attended a class, he never got less than perfect grades because he could devour texts at incredible speed, preparing in a day or two for any exam. "Compared to the witlessness of this university's educational system, Ed Wynn is Molière and Jack Benny is Falstaff . . ." He had a charming snigger and whole bushels of facts.

I no longer recall what brought him to us that night, but it was usually some editorial he objected to and insisted on being given space to rebut. In reality, he was trying to humiliate the managing editor, with whom he was competing for the beautiful Leah Bloom, who usually trailed him, exhausted, into the building along with Mrs. McCall, his landlady, maternally carrying his overcoat and standing below him as he harangued the staff, pleading with him to put it on before he caught his death as Leah pressed his galoshes or a muffler on him. As often as not it was the *Daily*'s attempts at objectivity that drove him wild, especially in regard to Spain. Sniggering down at the little managing editor, who sneered up at him between heavy sarcastic sighs directed at Leah, Joe shouted, "What is this about Nazi planes 'allegedly' flying for Franco? Are you trying to become the *New York Times*, for Christ's sake? Do we not have photographs showing the wreckage of shot-down fighter planes with Nazi German identification on the engines?" But the editor thought that anybody could take a picture of anything, and how did he know the picture hadn't been snapped in Hamburg? "You mean they crash planes on purpose in Hamburg? *Erwachen Sie!* Rouse yourself from this protofascistic funk you're in, stop playing with yourself, and turn this into a newspaper. So what if you don't get tapped by the *Times*? Aren't you too young to be so corrupt?" And so forth, until the editor was unable to hold back any longer and they were fighting down in the icy street, with the landlady and Leah trying to keep Joe from getting a chill.

Leah ended up marrying neither of them, and I lost track of Joe after my graduation in 1938, until one day in 1940 I ran into him on a midtown New York street, shaved and neatly dressed and with his hair combed. By this time Spain had succumbed to Franco and two of our classmates had died there fighting for the Loyalists. I was about to go out to Ohio to get married, and Joe had decided to become a stage designer, having simply walked in on Cleon Throckmorton, one of the most respected designers of the time, and convinced him to take him on as his chief assistant even though Joe's interest in set design was only a few weeks old. During this brief time he had read everything on the subject available in English and was probably beginning to instruct Throckmorton and correct his mistakes.

I congratulated him on his swift rise, but he stared at the passing traffic on Fifth Avenue and said he was on the verge of quitting. I was surprised. "I'm joining the Air Corps." The Air Corps! How could he join the Air Corps for an imperialist war? "I think we're going to get into it," he said, all the merry gloss gone from his eyes. "I think we'll have to." And would he be fighting the Soviets—still

Germany's allies at the time—in that case? He nearly ceased breathing, and a peculiar deathlike density packed his eyes. "I don't think they're going to stay with the Germans, but if they do—yes, we'll have to fight them too." We shook hands without smiling, aware that he was, in a way, betting his life on a vision of reality.

He died over Burma. One early evening in the sixties I found myself on Ninety-sixth and Madison on my way to a friend's house for dinner, and suddenly noticing the Feldman Pharmacy sign over the corner store, I recalled that his father had been a pharmacist in the area. It was now thirty years since Joe had stepped onto the desk in the *Daily* office, and more than twenty since he had been shot down. His father would probably be retired or dead by now. At the counter a small white-haired woman looked at me through the banks of lipsticks and combs. I said I had been a friend of Joe's, and was she by any chance his mother? Her tired, bored face quickly flushed with energy, and she instantly reached down into a drawer and pulled out an envelope with an eight-by-ten photograph that I expected would show Joe's merry face, his satiric eyes, and the pain. But it showed a large gravestone, perhaps six feet high, in a clearing surrounded by jungle flora, engraved with some dozen names including Joe's. She reached over and pointed at it. "This is in Burma," she said. We talked for a few minutes. He had been their only child. She thanked me for stopping in and was curious to know why I had done it. I said I wasn't sure but that I could never forget him. Her eyes began to fill with tears, and she turned away.

They were dying in Vietnam then. Not long before, I had returned to Ann Arbor to speak at the first teach-in: the whole university had closed down for three days to discuss the war and how to protest it. I had no prepared speech; with experts like Jean Lacouture among the participants, my presence represented purely symbolic support for the protest. Standing on the stage of Hill Auditorium, a vast place donated in the twenties by a lumber baron, I remembered the afternoon in 1935 when I had sat in the same hall listening to the Japanese evangelist Toyohiko Kagawa, a merchant of the sublime, as I saw it then, and had witnessed some fifty Chinese students standing up and walking out because he had referred to Manchuria, which the Japanese army was then occupying, as Manchukuo, its Japanese name. On the steps of that auditorium I had one day been accosted by a Chinese student with a little pail of tickets he was trying to sell to raise money to bring over a famous Chinese who would, he said, tell what the Japanese were doing to his country. I had asked, "Why do you need a famous person? Why don't you tell the story yourself?" His hooded eyes barely widened with surprise at my suggestion. "Who, me? I just a little shit."

Now, in the sixties, I thought I noticed something like a festive air among the students protesting the war, an atmosphere of delighted mutual discovery and a breaking down of personal defenses that I thought slightly unreal, I knew not why. And so when the applause for me died away—there was too much of it, I felt—I found myself saying; "I remember some other protests in this building, and I have to tell you that it's wonderful how these things bring people together, but you mustn't forget that the FBI is among you and someday you may have to account for being here."

It was the wrong moment to be saying such a thing, here at the budding of a noble movement to end an unjust war, a moment when this generation had just begun to reach out and find its partners in protest. Silence greeted my remark, a confused silence. And so I went on and said that despite the presence of spies and the possibility that people might one day be called on to renounce and condemn the passions they were feeling today, it was the essential risk of living at all to feel what they were feeling now. And more: that even if this movement should end, not in some climactic thunderclap of victory but in pale distraction and remorse for wasted time, it should not be the occasion for disillusion, because we must go on groping from one illusion of virtue to another; the fact was that man could not act at all without moral impulse, however mistaken its identification with any particular movement might eventually turn out to be.

Standing there at fifty, so close to young and determined men like Carl Oglesby and Bob Moses, Jean Lacouture and Tom Hayden, I soon realized, however, that they had passed beyond the reach of such warnings, for this was not the generation of the thirties, not at all. These young people were talking up an organization, totally American and in a certain sense not even political, that would throw down its bodies in the path of tanks. This was not the symbolic ideological rhetoric of another time when Hitlerism, however threatening, was very far away and few people really believed the United States would enter a new European war. The students packing Hill Auditorium knew they were personally up for grabs and that they might be killed if America did not change course. They were not saving somebody else, and that was the difference between them and their fathers in the thirties, when with all the poverty and dislocation of life it still took a leap of the imagination for a student to be radicalized. The ticket to radicalization in the sixties was the draft card in the wallet.

Like the American campaign for the Oxford Pledge against bearing arms, the phenomenon of the anti-Vietnam War teach-in was initiated at Michigan. For three days and nights classes were suspended and lecturers talked about Southeast Asia, about the history of Vietnam, the language and poetry and religion, and a sad exhilaration spread over everyone, or almost everyone, for I could not believe that students and intellectuals could halt a war. Listening to the speakers, I could not help placing my own father in the audience; as in the theatre, even he should be able to understand and be moved.

One evening after midnight, as I was walking with some students, a young soldier in uniform who had been enrolled here until his service in Vietnam came up to me and walked along under the trees with our group. "You people are wrong, you know. The war can be won. It really can be."

Since this was what I had been privately saying to Oglesby and Jean Lacouture—that they were underestimating America's stomach for this war—I was curious to know what this young veteran thought. "All you have to do is put one million men in there." The other students laughed—a million men! The veteran grinned with cool irony. "A million men could do it, and I wouldn't kid myself that they won't try. I don't think the administration knows it now, but they will sooner or later. But short of a million, it's no go."

It was so like the thirties: the alienated had the prophecy but not the power. In '36 and '37 we had been certain that if Franco could only be defeated a new world war might be averted, since a democratic Spain on Hitler's flank would act as a brake upon him, while a fascist ally would surely bring on a general European war. But the British and French had sold themselves on the democracy-is-Communism-in-embryo idea, and Roosevelt had kept hands off, and Franco ended up in Madrid declaring his solidarity with the Axis powers, and it was merely a matter of time before the big bang sounded. In a hundred ways Spain was the matrix for the next half-century's Western dilemma. The central unadmitted falsehood then was that the lesser breeds like the Spaniards, and later on the Iranians and the peoples of the Middle East and Latin America, were perfectly satisfied with right-wing dictatorships, while democracy was the proper mode only for the old Western European states and the United States. Thus, any local threat to the right had to be an opening wedge of the Communists, for an authentic democrat rising out of a poor country was simply not conceivable and his claim to being a democrat was a mere disguise and a fraud.

Of course it was impossible to predict in 1965 that before the Joint Chiefs, the Congress, the president, and the majority of the American people could be awakened to the facts presented so lucidly in that teach-in, some fifty-eight thousand Americans would have to die and our society be brought to its knees, an alienation unimaginable in its depth and scope having overwhelmed a generation of youth because of the war. Nevertheless, even in those three days and nights one understood that this was not going to be a repeat of the thirties. I walked past 411 North State Street, the house where, thirty years before, I had written my first play, and past a little pizza joint in the center of town where, a dozen years ago on my visit for *Holiday* in the McCarthy time, I had sat talking with students who were afraid of speaking up without plenty of cautionary thinking beforehand lest they be branded radicals. The atmosphere of the teach-in was a new and quickened world, with professors addressing full classrooms in the middle of the night, openly explaining that the United States had thwarted a national Vietnamese election that would undoubtedly have made Ho Chi Minh the president of the country, and that Americans were now being called on to frustrate the Vietnamese people's will.

The organizers of the anti–Vietnam War movement, which was born in those days and nights in Ann Arbor, would one day believe they had failed because the war, regardless of everything, continued for ten more years. Still, I saw the teach-in as the exploding moment of alienation, the time of the opening of the eyes to the corruption of the soul in high places. In this it was much like the Crash of 1929. Lying in bed in the Michigan Union, where I had spent my first night at college thirty years before, I wondered how many times a country could be disowned by a vital and intelligent sector of its youth before something broke, something deep inside its structure that could never be repaired again. The systole and diastole, the radicalization and the return of cautionary thinking, the bursts of idealism followed by equally quick swerves back to skepticism and the acceptance of things as they are—how many times before memory catches up with the latest swelling of the ideal and squashes it with cynicism before it can mature? In a word, how long is freedom? Is this the way America grows, or is this the way she slowly dies? Are these the spasms of birth or of death?

The Man Who Had All the Luck, my first professionally produced play, hardly seemed a Depression story, but it was, with its obsessive terror of failure and its guilt for success. By 1941, when I began writing it, despite every outward sign of failure my secret fate was full of promise. The two Hopwood Awards were still my encouragement, along with the far more important imprimatur of the Bureau of New Plays Prize, twelve hundred and fifty dollars given by the prestigious Theatre Guild in New York after a nationwide collegiate competition. One of the other winners was a fellow from St. Louis with the improbable name Tennessee Williams, whom I envisioned in buckskins, carrying a rifle.

When *The Man Who Had All The Luck* reached Broadway in 1944, it managed to baffle all but two of the critics (New York had seven daily newspapers then, each with its theatre reviewer). It must be said, nevertheless, that whatever its shortcomings, in a different theatrical time this play might well have stuck to the wall instead of oozing down. But Broadway in the forties was in what might be called a "classical" phase, such as occurs in every art, when there were absolutely definite rules of playwriting whose nonobservance brought failure. There was supposed to be nothing so impersonal as playwriting; after all, with each individual character having his autonomous viewpoint toward the common theme, the author could only be a sort of conductor who kept order rather than a sneaky deviser of some meaning at which the play would finally arrive. This spurious objectivism was taken so seriously that as late as the sixties, even so perceptive a critic as Walter Kerr could declare that plays that developed social or moral concepts rather than seeking simply to entertain would ultimately drive the audience out of the theatres. *The Man Who Had All the Luck* was manifestly nonobjective in this sense, and therefore "unnatural." Moreover, neither I nor its director, a dear fellow named Joe Fields, really understood its antirealistic thrust.

Joe's father had been part of a famous vaudeville team of the twenties, Weber and Fields. The brother of lyricist Dorothy Fields, he had written many successful musical comedies and seemed the last man in the world to be attracted to what in Broadway terms was an arcane work. But while his *Doughgirls,* a big, brassy farce, was raking in a fortune, Fields himself was spending much time in art galleries or reading his favorite French writers, especially Charles Péguy, one of whose books was always in his jacket pocket. He believed in my play and enlisted the backing of Herbert H. Harris, founder of Charbert, the perfume company that supplied the money for the production.

Trying to explain their uneasiness, one after another of the critics latched onto what they considered the absdurdity of a baseball pitcher as great at throwing a ball as Amos Beeves being turned down by a big league scout merely because of his ineptitude at pitching with men on base. Surely he could have been taught this skill! On the other hand, the critic Burton Rascoe, a former sports reporter, wrote a long piece in the *World-Telegram* assuring his colleagues that he had known many athletes who had been destroyed by a single defect, and going on to predict great things for me. Even so, it was slightly embarrassing to win my first professional encouragement on the grounds that I did indeed know something about baseball.

A more important if mystifying boost came from a source I would have thought unlikely. John Anderson, the critic for the *Journal-American*, a reactionary and sensational Hearst paper, invited me for a drink at the New York Athletic Club to talk about my play. I had never laid eyes on a critic before. He was in his early forties, handsome and well tailored and very earnest. There was an unclarity in the play, he felt, "but I sensed some strange shadow world behind the characters, a fascinating gathering of darkness that made me wonder if you have thought of writing tragedy. A doom hangs over this play, something that promises tragedy."

I said that I didn't think I would write another play. "This is now my fifth or sixth, and I seem to have gotten nowhere."

Anderson looked down at the floor. As I remember him he had wavy brown hair and a searching, deeply serious look. "You've written a tragedy, you know, but in a folk comedy style. You ought to try to understand what you've done."

This was the first of perhaps three or four conversations I have ever had with critics, and though I did not return to playwriting until three years had passed—during which I published my only novel, *Focus*—I nevertheless held his words dear. Only three months after our talk, Anderson was suddenly dead of meningitis.

One other question of Anderson's nagged at me, and still does. "Are you religious?" he had asked. Blind not only to myself but to what my work was trying to tell me, I thought the surprising question absurd. If anything, *The Man Who Had All the Luck*

seemed an antireligious play about a young man who had re-
nounced his own power to the heavens and could only be saved by
recognizing himself in his work. But drama, if allowed to follow its
premises, may betray even its author's prejudices or blindness; the
truth was that the play's action did seem to demand David's tragic
death, but that was intolerable to my rationalist viewpoint. In the
early forties such an ending would have seemed to me obscuran-
tist. A play's action, much like an individual's acts, is more revealing than its speeches, and this play embodied a desperate quest on
David's part for an authentication of his identity, a longing for a
break in the cosmic silence that alone would bestow a faith in life
itself. To put it another way, David has succeeded in piling up
treasures that rust, from which his spirit has already fled; it was a
paradox that would weave through every play that followed.

Standing at the back of the house during the single performance
I could bear to watch, I could blame nobody. All I knew was that
the whole thing was a well-meant botch, like music played on the
wrong instruments in a false scale. I would never write another
play, that was sure. After the final performance and the goodbyes
to the actors, it almost seemed a relief to get on the subway to
Brooklyn Heights and read about the tremendous pounding of
Nazi-held Europe by Allied air power. Something somewhere was
real.

I suppose it is inevitable that the thought of religion should call up
memories winding back to the first mention of Marxism I ever
heard. On a clear fall day in 1932 I for some reason found myself
rather hesitantly venturing into the Avenue M temple, looking, if
the truth be known, for God. A few years before, I had made a
terrific hit with my bar mitzvah speech, which had drawn highest
praise from my father—"Ya sure put it over!"—and possibly because I was in the throes of a sexual explosion with no permissible
outlet, my mind had made a connection between the synagogue
and that sparkling day when I had successfully asserted myself,
even if only with a speech. In any case, what I found inside the
building, scene of my triumph, was three old men in an office
smoking Turkish cigarettes, kibitzers who looked at me in mystification through watery eyes as I tried to explain that I would like
to ask somebody a few questions about religion, a subject obviously
far from their minds when they were no doubt swamped by building deficits and a falling off of attendance and other vital matters.

Since I was probably the only adolescent ever to ask such a question, especially in the middle of the week, they were dumbfounded. Recovering, they glanced at one another as though for inspiration until one of them came up with the suggestion that I return on Saturday and join the sabbath service. But I knew all about that rote exercise, which was really for people already certain about themselves, I thought. What I needed was something that would reach into my chaos and calm it and make me like everybody else.

So I wandered the two blocks to our house, my inner thirst as unslaked as it was undefined. The house meant much to me. Some rainy afternoons with nothing to do I enjoyed vacuuming the carpets, gluing a loose chair rung, or in spring planting tulips in the backyard—and digging up tin cans and old boots, for it was all filled-in land under a layer of cosmetic topsoil. At such times I had to work close to the ten-foot fence surrounding the kennel of Roy, the wolf kept by the Lindheimers next door. Roy would snarl and fling himself against the fence, his eyes red and his jaws lathering. He really *was* a wolf. Mr. Eagan, Lindheimer's father-in-law, who, in top hat and boots, drove a hansom cab stationed in front of the Plaza Hotel, would take Roy for his walks holding him by a heavy chain in one hand, a riding crop in the other. At Roy's slightest attempt to deviate left or right, the crop would hit him square across the eyes.

I was digging among my tulips one day when I noticed the quiet. Roy was not behind the fence. Straightening up to rest my back, I caught out of the corner of my eye the sight of Roy standing in our yard behind me, unchained, unaccompanied, empty space all around him, and he was looking up at me. I froze. We looked at each other a long, long time. I knew that if I so much as moved a finger to change my grip on the shovel he'd be at my throat. I doubt if I even blinked. After several months he turned, perfectly relaxed but looking rather baffled, and walked around their garage and back into his kennel area. Step by careful step, I managed to get into our house and phoned next door, and powerful Mrs. Lindheimer, a high school swimming teacher, came out and locked Roy's gate. A broad-shouldered woman, Mrs. Lindheimer always seemed unhappy. Mr. Lindheimer was a wholesale butcher, and they both seemed full of meat. They had recently bought a new Packard, a beautiful car and expensive, but it turned out to be hardly three or four inches narrower than the driveway. She had already gotten it stuck trying to back it out and had become nearly hysterical, caught inside with no possibility of opening the door for rescue or escape. She finally inched it into the street, but not without cracking our stucco and gouging a streak along one shiny fender. She seemed to blame us for having our house so close to theirs, and I could never pass her on the street without feeling I ought to apologize for something. But I lacked the retaliatory spirit and never dreamed of her drowning.

Our furnace also meant a lot to me. It was mysterious. We were never sure of precisely how to bank it to keep it from going out overnight, so I deeply loved the fire when blue flames played evenly over the whole bed of black coal rather than licking at one corner and leaving whole areas of it dead and ashy, a condition you knew was going to spread and spread until the fire went out and you were left with all that perfectly good coal, which had to be rescued from the ashes piece by piece.

I loved to see the coal truck backing up to the house and the driver setting the chute through the cellar window and then tilting the truck body so that the coal slid into the bin with a satisfying and even warming and tasty whoosh. With a full bin we could keep warm for a long time.

It was thrilling to go down to the cellar at about four in the morning and, opening the furnace door, find that it had not gone dead in there, that this time I had mastered the mystery of banking the fire for the night. Then, walking the block and a half to my job at the bakery with my woolen skating socks pulled up over my mackinaw sleeves, I would feel that the family was secure and safe.

The baker was a friendly but worried overweight man who breathed hard. From a list scrawled with a stubby pencil whose point he was always having to sharpen because he leaned on it too hard, he inscribed addresses on each brown paper bag he had packed with rolls, bagels, and rye breads in various combinations to suit each customer. I curled the bags shut and carefully stowed them in the immense wire basket hanging over the front wheel from the heavy delivery bike's handlebars. In spring or fall it was glorious riding down the silent empty streets past the sleeping houses; you could almost hear the people breathing in their beds. Despite my newly explosive sexuality, I did not yet imagine them making love. I simply did not think of it. Stopping, I would carefully lean the bike against a lamppost, with a flashlight find the right bag for that house, and gently lay it on the back porch near the kitchen door. When it rained I would find some sheltered place for the bags; a few of my customers set out lidded wooden boxes.

On winter mornings the temperature was sometimes around zero at that early hour, and cats would follow me in troops, desperate for the heat of my body, rubbing urgently against my trouser legs and howling imperatively up at me, sending chills up my back with their accusations.

There were mornings when Ocean Parkway, six lanes wide, was entirely covered with ice as unblemished as a frozen country pond, and occasionally there would be a taxi playing on the otherwise deserted road, jamming on the brakes to make the car spin happily over the glaze. At about half past four one such morning, I saw two cabs waltzing around like this trying to come as close to each other as they could without crashing. Sometimes it was nearly impossible to keep my balance on the ice, and I would have to walk the bike for the entire route. One time it toppled over and all the bags spilled out of the basket and opened, shooting naked bagels skidding like hockey pucks over immense distances into the darkness, rolls and rye breads fanning out over the sidewalk and into the road. I had to find them with my flashlight and then try somehow to match the bags' swellings with the right number of bagels, rolls, and breads. By the time I got back to the bakery the phone was already ringing, with people demanding to know what they were supposed to do with four rolls and two bagels when they always got three of each. The outrage in their voices leaped out of the receiver and I feared for my job, but the baker forgave me.

As it had been in childhood, my bike was my solace, my feminine, my steed of escape carrying me forever toward some corner around which would suddenly appear the magic of myself at last, mere ectoplasm no more. One day I found myself straddling the bike and watching a big round-robin handball game against the wall of Mr. Dozick's drugstore. Four boys were playing doubles, and a dozen others were standing around cheering or offering screams of advice or quietly conspiring to lay somebody's sister or trying to figure out how to steal penny candy from Mr. Rubin's store or, failing that, how to go on a militarily disciplined Boy Scout camping trip up to Newburgh. I sat on the bike's saddle, absorbed in the game and all the conversations at the same time, while beneath this level of murmuring excitement ran the ever present anxiety about my and my family's future.

By the fall of 1932 it was no longer possible in our house to disguise our fears. Producing even the fifty-dollar-a-month mortgage payment was becoming a strain, and my brother had had to drop out of NYU to assist my father in another of his soon-to-fail coat businesses. There was an aching absence in the house of any ruling idea or leadership, my father by now having fallen into the habit of endlessly napping in his time at home or occasionally looking at me and asking, "What do you think you're going to do?" With my life, that is. What I would dearly have loved to do was to sing on the radio and become a star like Crosby and make millions. In fact, by the time I graduated from high school, I already had an agent of sorts, a squat, cigar-smoking neighborhood character named Harry Rosenthal, who peddled songs to publishers and sometimes got singers jobs in clubs.

I had a high, steady tenor voice, "slightly Irish" in Rosenthal's judgment and not bad for ballads, especially Irving Berlin's stuff. But these were songs I thought made me sound like Eddie Cantor, who sang part-time, in my opinion. In the months to come Rosenthal would take me into Manhattan on the subway, to the Brill Building on Broadway near Fiftieth Street, the heart of Tin Pan Alley, to get me auditioned for singing jobs. On each floor there were tiny cubicles with upright pianos where a songwriter could play his new song for a publisher, and the sounds intermixed through the skimpy partitions so that in any one cubicle you heard everything going on everywhere on the floor. In the midst of this pandemonium I tried to sing some tender ballad by my favorite, Lorenz Hart, before a harried, droopy-eyed man to whom I was not even introduced, so lowly was my position in this world. I could hardly hear my own voice, and I was scared and sang badly and in the middle of the number wondered what I was doing there. No, this did not feel like me, but Rosenthal nevertheless managed to arrange a fifteen-minute radio show of my own on a Brooklyn station—without pay, of course. A blind pianist was provided, an aging man whose strangling emphysema was probably being broadcast along with my singing, and whose arthritic fingers could strike chords but few individual notes, so cemented were his joints. Covered with cigar ashes, his half-dozen hairs wetted down for the occasion and combed laterally across the top of his head, he seemed moved by my singing, and after our second program—which turned out to be our last—he advised me to bill myself as "The Young Al Jolson," which I thought might be reaching a bit, though not outrageously so.

But I was already at the end of my singing career. At sixteen, for the first time in my life, I found my brain translating the song lyrics into reality, and they embarrassed me when I realized with some amazement that almost every one of them implied the attempt of a man to make love to a woman. Here I had been innocently throwing my heart into these sung poems without the remotest idea of their having any meaning at all—they were simply sweet sounds to carry my voice and might as well have been in another language—when I was really singing to a girl, no less, and saying, "If I had a motion picture of you-oo . . ." It was simply intolerable and closed my throat forever, at least as an aspiring professional, and by the time I could make use of the ideas behind those lyrics I had all but lost my voice.

Like most abrupt turnings in the path of life, my introduction to Marx that day outside Dozick's drugstore came out of an absurdly unexpected moment, and it has frozen in my memory to the stillness of a painting. The brick wall of the store was being pounded by the ball, the bane of that mild, unoffending man's existence, for not only was his large store window occasionally hit, but he also had to give out free glasses of ice water from his fountain. Dozick was tiny, with thick eyeglasses and a piping voice, and was too kind to refuse thirsty boys. Finally, in desperation, he had his soda fountain removed altogether, and when that failed he put up a big six-by-ten-foot metal sign advertising bottled Moxie, the popular soft drink. The sign stuck out of the wall several inches and if struck would deflect the ball, ruining a shot, but we quickly learned to play around it quite expertly as though it weren't there at all. Of course when a ball did hit it, the sign resonated, bringing Dozick out of his door on the run to plead with us to stop, simply stop hitting the sign for God's sake, and we always apologized and tried to play more accurately. On top of all that he had to sew up our wounds, complaining right through some fairly intricate emergency operation that he shouldn't be doing it. "I am not qualified!" he would cry out when some bloodied boy staggered in from the street, as my brother once did after chasing a ball and putting his head through the side window of a passing Ford, nearly severing his left ear. Almost twenty years later Dozick would write me a note of appreciation for *Death of a Salesman,* doubting that I would remember his name, as though it were not engraved an inch deep in my brain, especially after watching him sew up Kermit's ear as he lay flat on Dozick's desk in the back of the store. (Right next door was another tiny Jewish man, Mr. Fuchs, who ran a minuscule tailor shop. For a dollar he would let out your trouser bottoms and insert a gore that made the cuffs as wide as your shoes; a lot of sewing went on in that block.)

On this particular day there were no accidents, and sunlight shone over the street as I straddled my bike watching the game while an older boy, whose name has long since left me, stood beside me explaining that although it might not be evident to the naked eye, there were really two classes of people in society, the workers and the employers. And that all over the world, including Brooklyn, of course, a revolution that would transform every country was inexorably building up steam. Things would then be produced for use rather than for someone's personal profit, so there would be much more for everyone to share, and justice would reign everywhere. No image remains of his face, only the certainty that he was already in college. Why had he picked me for this revelation? What clue had I given him that I was fertile ground for his amazing ideas? For I understood him instantly, and I remember giving up my turn to get into the game and saying to him, "Everything is upside down!"—meaning that in my family workers had always been a nuisance; necessary though they might be, they were always getting in the way of businessmen trying to make and sell things. Life's structure was so fixed that it was not only Grandpa Barnett, a Republican, who was full of indignation at this Roosevelt even, presuming to contest President Hoover's right to another term—I felt the same way. The truth, I suppose, was that we were really royalists to whom authority had an aura that was not quite of this world.

It would be a long time before I understood anything of the spin my soul had been given by this anonymous college student. For me, as for millions of young people then and since, the concept of a classless society had a disarming sweetness that called forth the generosity of youth. The *true* condition of man, it seemed, was the complete opposite of the competitive system I had assumed was normal, with all its mutual hatreds and conniving. Life could be a comradely embrace, people helping one another rather than looking for ways to trip each other up. This day's overturning of all I knew of the world revolutionized not only my ideas but also my most important relationship at the time, the one with my father. For deep down in the comradely world of the Marxist promise is parricide. For those who are psychically ready for that age-old adventure, the sublimation of violence that Marxism offers is nearly euphoric in its effects; while extolling the rational, it blows away the restraints on the Oedipal furies, clothing their violence with a humane ideal. Its impact brings to mind Jesus' direction to his disciples to turn away even from their parents in order to follow him, for it really is impossible to serve two masters, and in his words too there is a shadow of hidden parricide.

I had never raised my voice against my father, nor did he against me, then or ever. As I knew perfectly well, it was not he who angered me, only his failure to cope with his fortune's collapse. Thus I had two fathers, the real one and the metaphoric, and the latter I resented because he did not know how to win out over the general collapse. Along with a desire to help, I was filling with pity for him as first the chauffeur was let go and then the seven-passenger National went and the summer bungalow was discarded—as the waiting began for the past to return and the unreality of the present wound itself around us all like some dusty vine that had taken root in the living room carpet and could not be kept down for more than a day before it grew again. Never complaining or even talking about his business problems, my father simply went more deeply silent, and his naps grew longer, and his mouth seemed to dry up. I could not avoid awareness of my mother's anger at this waning of his powers; when a system fails, people will seek out each other's weaknesses to account for their troubles, just as ancient kings slew the messenger who brought evil news. It was my father who was our link to the outside world, and his news was bad every night. I must have adopted my mother's early attitudes toward his failure, her impatience at the beginning of the calamity and her alarm as it got worse, and finally a certain sneering contempt for him that filtered through her voice.

At the same time she was valiantly pitching in to save us all, cutting down on every expenditure and intelligently budgeting the household, which up to then had always been run by sheer chance. And finally, when her mother died and there was nothing left to keep us in Harlem, the move to Brooklyn, initially to an ample half of a two-family house with a broad closed-in porch and airy rooms, and then another step down, to the little six-room house on East Third Street that cost five thousand dollars and was bought with an enormous mortgage besides. There could hardly have been a cheaper way to live, but by 1932 she was having to charm the man in the bank on Kings Highway to extend one month's mortgage payment into the next. By the early thirties the last of her disposable pieces of jewelry had been pawned or sold, all but a diamond brooch of her mother's and a few wedding presents she refused to part with, as though to shed them would have extinguished her last hopes, which, like the seeds for next year's crop, must not be eaten.

Had I been able to side with her wholeheartedly in her disappointment with my father, my course would have been straightforward and probably fairly painless. But I couldn't help blushing for him when she made him her target, since I admired his warm and gentle nature as much as I despaired of his illiterate mind. And her way was never straight and simple; she could veer suddenly and see with a blast of clarity and remorse that what had happened to him had happened to a man of a certain honor and uncomplaining strength. For love of me and all of us she divided us against ourselves, unknowingly, innocently, because she believed—as I was beginning to believe myself—that with sufficient intelligence a person could outwit the situation. Why couldn't he do that? Because his mother's selfishness had forced him to work before he was twelve so that he could lay his weekly pay on her dinner plate every Saturday night. She hated his mother—who continued to live two miles away in a great old Flatbush house, apparently knowing nothing of hard times—and through his mother womankind, which she saw as born to suck out the marrow of men, although there were exceptions depending on how she felt that particular day. There was no contradiction, in this or anything else, that fazed her; she could be moved to tears by her husband's endurance and dignified refusal to complain, and within an hour make a remark about his blockheadedness. One minute we must all pray for President Hoover, an honest Quaker who, after all, was as much a victim of the collapse as anyone else, and the next he was a son of a bitch who had no heart—imagine his still repeating again and again that prosperity was just around the corner, didn't he realize people were going absolutely *crazy* and that it was happening *now*? Real desperation was seeping in under the doors—by the end of 1932 there was the unspoken fear that we might even lose this chicken coop of a house. And then what?

It has often been said that what kept the United States from revolution in the depths of the Great Depression was the readiness of Americans to blame themselves rather than the system for their downfall. A fine dusting of guilt fell upon the shoulders of the failed fathers, and for some unknown number of them there would never be a recovery of dignity and self-assurance, only an endless death-in-life down to the end. Already in the early thirties, within a year or two of the collapse, the papers were reporting that in New York City alone there were nearly a hundred thousand people who had been psychologically traumatized to the point where they would probably never be able to work again. Nor was it only a question of insufficient food; it was hope that had gone out of them, the life illusion and the capacity to believe again. America, as Archibald MacLeish would write, was promises, and for some the Crash was in the deepest sense a broken promise.

If Marxism was, on the metaphorical plane, a rationale for parricide, I think that to me it was at the same time a way of forgiving my father, for it showed him as a kind of digit in a nearly cosmic catastrophe that was beyond his powers to avoid. But the poor man had to be radicalized, had to concede that it was not his fault that he had failed, instead of answering my lectures with measly and ungainly facts that simply angered me more at his stupidity.

"But," he would say, "if there's not going to be a profit . . ."

"Profit is evil, profit is wrong!" I would plead with him in my sixteen-year-old tenor.

"Yeah, but where's the money to do business? Who's going to pay for new machines when the old ones wear out, for instance? Or maybe you didn't have such a good year last year, you gotta have money to keep going till things pick up . . ."

The next time I would hear these counterpunching arguments was in China half a century later when they were trying to pick themselves up off the floor after the profit-hating decades of Mao Zedong.

But of course the Depression was as much an occasion as a cause of such father-son collisions. It would strike me years later how many male writers had fathers who had actually failed or whom the sons had perceived as failures. Fitzgerald, Faulkner, Hemingway (his father was a suicide), Thomas Wolfe, Steinbeck, Poe, Whitman, Melville and Hawthorne, Chekhov and Dostoyevsky and Strindberg—the list is too long to consign the phenomenon to idiosyncratic accident. As different as these writers are, they share an ambition to create a new cosmology, not merely to describe the visible world around them. If they could, they would devise a new order of perception that would make the world all new, as seen through their eyes. If the Americans on such a list differ from most of the Europeans, it is in the absence of a grand vision of revolution, whether social or religious or political. Among the Americans, only Steinbeck, who matured in the thirties and experienced social struggle in the West, contains a political aspect and a sometimes revolutionary one. Indeed, no writer anywhere else seems to arrive on the scene in quite the American style—as though the tongue had been cut out of the past, leaving him alone to begin from the beginning, from the Creation and the first naming of things seen for the first time. He is forever Cortez standing on the fabled peak, always Columbus on his heaving deck hearing across oceanic distances the first rumblings of an unseen surf upon an undiscovered shore. Writers in other places may casually drop the names of their youthful models, their Strindbergs and Tzaras, their Tolstoys or Waughs, taking for granted that there is honor as well as custom in continuing a tradition. But American writers spring as though from the ground itself or drop out of the air all new and self-conceived and self-made, quite like the businessmen they despise. It is as though they were fatherless men abandoned by a past that they in turn reject, the better to write not the Great American Novel or Play, but verily the First.

At the time it was beyond me to rationalize my feelings, but I knew that the Depression was only incidentally a matter of money. Rather, it was a moral catastrophe, a violent revelation of the hypocrisies behind the facade of American society. And that is why facts, for those who turned left—now as then—could mean so little. Nothing is as visionary and as blinding as moral indignation. Adolescence is a kind of aching that only time can cure, a molten state without settled form, but when at the same time the order of society has also melted and the old authority has shown its incompetence and hollowness, the way to maturity is radicalism. All that is is falsehood and waste, and the ground is cleared for the symmetrical new structure, the benign release of reason's shackled powers, which is what Marxism claimed to offer and still claims now. If it stood as the enemy of religion, it nevertheless engaged some of the very same sinews of faith within me, and it provided the same privileges of joining the elect that enthrall religious communities. The sleepers awaken, and their song is the voice of the future, and when it is required of them they will bring not peace but the sword. Two decades after that fateful handball game, when I was at the Salem Historical Society studying the record of the witch trials of 1692, I could fairly hear the voices of those hanging judges, whom it was only possible really to understand if one had known oneself the thrill of having been absolutely right. In fact, I would probably not have been in Salem at all had I not found Marx in the midst of that handball game.

Once having experienced salvation, I would have become completely intolerable at home if anyone had had the decency to listen to me for very long, but my father had trouble staying awake, and my brother, agreeing in principle, was too busy mobilizing himself to save our father, whom he had romanticized into a fallen giant. Kermit was intent on rebuilding the family fortunes, or at least as much of them as could be rebuilt before capitalism collapsed altogether, a by no means remote possibility when everyone knew that not radicals but the bankers' association had asked Roosevelt to nationalize the banks, the system having spun completely out of their control. It was certainly an odd one as revolutionary situations go in the twentieth century, but we were far from being alone in the way our minds moved along several planes of credulity at once. As it became clearer and clearer that this was not to be another recession like the one at the beginning of the twenties, and that Roosevelt's stirring rallying cries, while they called forth brandnew government agencies to absorb the worst of the emergency needs of the unemployed, were not visibly lifting production, the prospect of deep social change became less and less the subject of intellectual conversation and more the common property of almost everyone. Things simply could not go on this way. There is a limit to the time a ship can lie dead in the water before people start screaming and doing peculiar things to bring on the wind.

"Mr. Glick," as he was usually called—not "Glick" or "Harry"—was the hardware store man who had the distinction of still being unmarried in his thirties. In Brooklyn, in this part of it anyway, everybody was married. But red-haired Mr. Glick, able-bodied except for his myopia, seemed content to live alone over his store on Avenue M frying his own fish and, when business was slack, sitting out front in a camp chair taking the sun and nodding to passersby with a wink and a barely perceptible ironic smile. His hardware business, probably because it involved repairing things, managed to survive on a block of failed, empty stores. I had already formed a deep connection to hardware and loved to hang around Mr. Glick, as did several other boys, especially Sammy the Mongoloid, who was probably Mr. Glick's closest friend. Sammy, also in his thirties then, knew every family in every house in those blocks of little houses, but not by name, only by phone number.

"D'ja hear about Dewey nine–six. five five seven?"

"No, what?"

"She's getting engaged to Navarre eight–three two eight zero."

Then Glick, putting on a dread look of scandal, would ask, "What happened to Esplanade seven–four five seven nine?"

"Oh, she hasn't gone out with him since I don't know when."

"I heard different," Glick would say, "I heard that Dewey nine–six five five seven's going with Navarre eight–three two eight *one*."

"*One!* Three two eight one is a girl!"

"A girl! Since when?"

"Since always!"

Sammy began to look like he was about to cry, but Glick was remorseless and took these dialogues to the edge of their possibilities before backing away. Teasing made his day. Until I caught on I would always answer when I passed his store near Fifth Street and he asked, "Raining on Third Street?"

"No, it's just like here."

"Well, that's nice."

But women were like the ripest fruit to be savored as he slowly consumed their credulousness. The few stores on Avenue M formed a village with boundaries invisible to the stranger's eye but hard and fast nonetheless. The main occupation of that village was worrying, at least it was what occupied most people most of the time. There was a lot of shuffling along the sidewalk in bedroom slippers by people who hadn't the morale left to put on shoes when they went out for a paper or a can of sardines, and in the warm months housewives would go out in negligees and flapping housecoats, the sight of which set Glick off on flights of inventiveness that my friends and I reinforced by keeping straight faces.

A woman would come into the store carrying an electric broiler, which she would plunk down on the counter, announcing, "It don't broil."

"What don't broil?"

"This. It don't broil, Mr. Glick," she would say, drawing together her negligee.

"You cold? I could send up some heat, I own the building."

"Cold? It's July!"

"You're so beautiful I nearly forgot. Now, what's the problem with this broiler, what do you mean it don't broil?"

"It don't get hot."

Now looking deeply and attentively into her eyes: "And you don't know what to do if it don't get hot?"

"Listen, I'm talking about the broiler."

"Absolutely, darling. Now, what did I tell you to do first thing if it don't heat up?"

"I did it, I plugged it in."

"You plugged it in?" He leans closer to her chest.

"It got a little warm, but that's all."

"Tell me, what were you wearing at the time?"

"What I was wearing! My clothes!"

"Good, because these broilers are very sensitive."

"Well, I'm not going to cook with no clothes on."

"You'd be surprised what goes on in the neighborhood. I've had women—I'm not going to mention names—you wouldn't believe it, but they come in here and tell me they're broiling without a stitch on."

"Who're you talking about?"

"Now she wants to know who I'm talking about! Blondes! Brunettes! Black-haired! *Broiling naked in this neighborhood!*"

"You crazy? I would never broil naked!"

"Well, that's good. Now tell me, what do you put in?"

"What do you mean, what I put in? Chops, a hamburger . . ."

"Did you say hamburger?"

"Yes, hamburger. Why?"

With immense sadness, shaking his head, he now turns the broiler upside down and points to the Underwriters Laboratory number. "You see here the number ends in a nine? You know what that means?"

"No, what does it mean?"

"Any Underwriters number ending in nine means no hamburger allowed. *But*"—before she can protest—"for you I am not going to count it, and I'm giving you a brand-new broiler right this minute!"

". . . because I know I didn't do anything wrong."

"Darling, a woman looking like you *can't* do anything wrong." Now, producing a new broiler, he becomes grave. "But this is an improved model. With this one you can broil naked."

"Are you crazy? I never heard of such a thing!"

He cuts her off, his grin turning familiar and relaxed. "I'm only kidding you, darling, because you make me so unhappy."

With a half-smile, dizzy by now, she asks, "*I* make you unhappy?"

"Because you're married."

Now she catches on and gives him a soft slap on the cheek and shuffles off in her slippers, the new broiler under her arm.

One spring a few years later, returning from college, I passed the hardware store and saw Mr. Glick seated out front with a baby carriage beside him and a short, stubby woman, also red-haired, standing in the doorway. And then, many years after that, I returned again, this time with a CBC film crew directed by Harry

Rasky, who was making a documentary about me. Mr. Glick's store was gone; the whole building had vanished, replaced by an apartment house that was already showing signs of age.

Merchants like Mr. Glick were spending a lot of time sitting out in front of their stores waiting for customers, but they were the lucky ones; wherever one walked For Rent signs were pasted across empty store windows, and there was hardly an apartment house without a permanent Vacancy sign on it. People were doubling up, married children returning to their parents with their own children. There were touch football games in the side streets between teams whose members were twenty or older, fellows with no jobs or even hopes for one anymore, playing the days away like kids and buying their Camels or Luckies one cigarette at a time, a penny apiece, from Rubin the candy store man on Avenue M. The normal rites of adolescent passage tended to be skipped over; when I graduated from Abraham Lincoln High School in 1932, mine was by no means the only family that failed to show up for the ceremony, nor did I expect them to attend. I knew that with my education at an end I was but another new young man on the long line waiting for work. Anyway, with a master's degree, as the saying went, you might get hired to sell ties at Macy's.

If there was a national pastime I suppose it was hanging out, simply standing there on the street corner or on the beach waiting for something to appear around the bend. Evenings, before I had begun to feel embarrassed about any self-display, I'd be out there in front of Dozick's drugstore with half a dozen others singing the latest hits, sometimes in competition with anyone else who thought he sang better (for a couple of pennies you could buy pirated mimeoed lyrics of the newest songs). After I had turned fifteen these competitions seemed childish, but I continued as one of the star comics of the gang, improvising inanities, doing imitations of the Three Stooges, who even then were on the verge of our contempt as idiotic shadows of the Marx Brothers. We always had a sandlot football team going, and one of our halfbacks, a giant with a heavy lower lip named Izzy Lenowitz, whom nobody dared tackle for fear of his bowling ball knees, would clap me on my thin back and implore me, "Oh, come on, Artie, enjoy us." And with sufficient encouragement I would ad-lib a monologue that with a little luck might stay airborne for five minutes or more. Without plan or awareness of what I was doing, I had begun the process of separating myself: I was moving out of the audience to face them alone.

My mother and brother excepted, as I've said, I cannot remem-

ber a person in the neighborhood who willingly read a book, there
being no practical reason for doing so. The boys on those blocks had
other things on their minds; mainly how to get girls, those innocent
victims of male lust—in my day specifically Mary Costigliano, already nearly thirty, with enormous breasts and just possibly feebleminded, who was reported to fall stunned and helpless before
anybody who brought her a box of Whitman's candy. True or not,
this caused sniggers when she walked by, and occasionally she
would stop in the street to scream at some insulting boy. I once
walked into a basement to find our whole football team masturbating each other, which seemed to contradict a certain idealism that
I thought the team stood for, not to mention that I was far too shy
to join in. Besides, I preferred my own private visions of women.

My mother having gotten me enrolled in high school a year
before I had finished grammar school, I suffered under the curious
idea that I was too young for everything, by about a year, and it
was probably in order somehow to become mature that I managed,
despite my thin, gangling body, to make the second squad of the
Abraham Lincoln High football team as an end. I could run fast and
snatch a ball with my long arms, but at a hundred and twenty
pounds it was no joke being tackled by boys fifty pounds heavier.
I dreaded the kick in the face when I tackled and had to steel
myself to dive for a runner's ankles, most of the time thankfully
missing, but in one important scrimmage with our A-team I closed
my eyes and flew at our number one halfback, a mean little bastard
whom everyone considered to have a real football future. By some
mischance I landed on his feet and brought him down with a bang
that amazed him and even more me. As we were getting up he
ground his cleats into my neck, but the longed-for opportunity to
tackle him again never came up. Instead, catching a pass a few
minutes later, I was tackled from the side and brought down with
a ripped ligament that for many years thereafter clicked my knee
into the bent position and prevented my leg from straightening
without intense, tearing pain. Some eight years later, this injury
would keep me out of the army.

I seem always to have known that I was a carpenter and a mechanic. At fourteen or fifteen I bought lumber with my savings
from my bread delivery job—a painful twelve dollars accumulated
from work that earned four dollars a week—and built a back porch
for the little house on Third Street. For advice I first approached

one of my two pioneer uncles who had moved their families to Brooklyn in the early twenties when the Midwood area was so empty they could watch their kids walking all the dozen blocks to the school across the scrubby flatlands. Manny Newman and Lee Balsam were both salesmen, and unlike us, they owned hammers with which they repaired things around their attached houses on their days off. But only Lee would lend me a hammer, since he did not take manual work seriously. Manny not only had a policy of never lending tools but would blatantly deny that he even owned a shovel, for example, when he knew I could plainly see it hanging on the wall behind him in the garage where in warm weather he liked to play cards with the neighbors in his underwear.

Lee Balsam, all kindness, had a soft voice and a bad heart that caused him to move meditatively and with deliberation. He improvised a porch design with me that worked pretty well except that, as I discovered only after it was finished, there was no connection between the porch and the house. Still, it lasted for two decades, only gradually creeping inch by inch away from the kitchen. It was my first experience with the fevers of construction, and I could not fall asleep for anticipation of tomorrow; and it was exactly the same one cold April in 1948 when I built a ten-by-twelve studio near my first house in Connecticut where I intended to write a play about a salesman. The idea of creating a new shadow on the earth has never lost its fascination. Since the implicit ambition of the middle class is to avoid manual labor, I have a hard time tracing the origins of my love for it as well as my respect for craftsmen.

In the twenties, when the Millers came out from Manhattan in their limousine to visit, the Newman-Balsam connected houses were flanked by only four other pairs, a line of little wooden homes with flat roofs and three-step stoops, surrounded by open flatland where tall elms still grew, and wild roses and ferns, and the grass was crisscrossed with footpaths that people used instead of the unpaved streets without sidewalks. With no stores closer than a couple of miles, they bought potatoes by the hundred-pound sack and canned the tomatoes they grew, and their basements smelled hauntingly of earth, unlike Manhattan basements with their taint of cat and rat and urine. Before moving to Brooklyn, both families had lived for years in cold upper New York State small towns and spoke with hard rural *r*'s and a twang, in the women's voices especially. They were different from New Yorkers in their small-town rhythms of thought, their willingness to spend time sitting around just talking, and an untroubled self-acceptance as ordinary Americans, their Jewishness having somehow lost any power to separate them. Next door to them lived gentile families with whom they socialized intimately, and unlike the Manhattan Jews I knew, they never called in plumbers or roofers but did the work themselves.

It was Lee and Esther's three daughters who, until they married and left, seemed to spend their lives with bandannas around their heads cleaning the little house and polishing the Nash and even scrubbing the stoop with soapy water. The Newmans did all these things too, but there was a shadowy darkness in their house, a scent of sex and dream, of lies and invention, and above all of contradiction and surprise.

Manny Newman was cute and ugly, a Pan risen out of the earth, a bantam with a lisp, sunken brown eyes, a lumpy, pendulous nose, dark brown skin, and gnarled arms. When I walked into the house, he would look at me—usually standing there in his one-piece BVD's, carrying a hammer or a screwdriver or perhaps a shoebox filled with his collection of pornographic postcards—as though he had never seen me before or, if he had, would just as soon not see me again. He was a competitor, at all times, in all things, and at every moment. My brother and I he saw running neck and neck with his two sons in some race that never stopped in his mind. He had made two daughters and two sons: the eldest, Isabel, a real beauty despite her resemblance to him, and the youngest, Margie, a tender girl bedeviled by a pustular acne that kept her at home, sad but still bravely witty. But in that house even she dared not lose hope, and I would later think of it as a perfection of America for that reason—because something good was always coming up, and not just good but fantastic, transforming, triumphant. It was a house without irony, trembling with resolutions and shouts of victories that had not yet taken place but surely would tomorrow. Both boys could be Eagle Scouts and win all the badges and make their beds and clean up after themselves and speak often and gravely of the family's honor and then, with Bernie Crystal and Louis Fleishman, go into Rubin's candy store and distract him long enough to make off with his three-foot-high globular glass display vase filled with penny candy. Or spend weeks preparing a camping trip to Bear Mountain with the portentous gravity of explorers planning an expedition to the South Pole, and once up there, having followed every honorable rule of scouting, find an old whore in a local tavern and spend the night taking turns with her in the pup tent and in the morning cut her reward by half, figuring that as brothers they should only be charged one fee. Everybody envied them, especially Buddy, the eldest, who played baseball and basketball and football and got mentioned in the Brooklyn *Eagle* two or three times and took two hours to get himself dressed for a date, oiling his black hair and talcing his face and punching himself in the stomach and snarling into the mirror to peruse his teeth. Like his father, he was dark, but taller, and had Grandpa Barnett's heavy shoulders, as did Annie, his mother, a most moving woman who bore the cross of reality for them all. People pitied her having to insinuate carefully to Manny that perhaps orange was not the right color to paint the house even though he had got a bargain on several gallons of orange paint in a fire sale on Fulton Street, all the while keeping up her calm, enthusiastic smile lest he feel he was not being appreciated. With the girls she could be more candid, naturally, as she worked year after year to guide them like leaky ships safely into the marital port, Margie with her depressing skin problem, and Isabel being tempted to give away too early what might more profitably be held back, at least for a while.

I actually spent no more than a couple of hours in Manny's presence in my life, but he was so absurd, so completely isolated from the ordinary laws of gravity, so elaborate in his fantastic inventions, and despite his ugliness so lyrically in love with fame and fortune and their inevitable descent on his family, that he possessed my imagination until I knew more or less precisely how he would react to any sign or word or idea. His unpredictable manipulations of fact freed my mind to lope and skip among fantasies of my own, but always underneath was the river of his sadness. He and Annie were clucked over as hopeless people, but they were the most interesting to talk about, among other reasons because they were still in love. In fact, they had eloped against Grandpa Barnett's wishes, and as big and broad-chested as she was, and as overweight now, with her gale of a laugh, her pink pockmarked face often reddening with the hypertension that would kill her at sixty, and he with his burnt Indian look, his head always half in some other world, they were still, even now, obviously bound to each other sexually. The great thing on New Year's Eve was for eight or ten couples to sit at a riotous dinner down in that narrow Newman basement next to the coal furnace and wait for Manny to bring out his shoebox of postcards, but only after we boys were sent upstairs—as if we hadn't examined each and every picture fifty times during the year, as Manny well knew. Like every social occasion, these parties finally turned into card games, and when Manny got bored he would curl up in Annie's expansive lap and pretend to suckle, an embarrassment to her but not enough to make her stop him. That house seemed dank with sexuality, especially compared to ours or the Balsams' or any other I knew of; ours were light and airy, while the Newmans' was secretly obsessed, as though they were obscenely involved with one another—a fantasy of mine, of course.

As fanatic as I was about sports, my ability was not to be compared to his sons', and since I was gangling and unhandsome into the bargain I lacked their promise, so that when I stopped by I always had to expect some kind of insinuation of my entire life's probable failure, even before I was sixteen. But this did not diminish the lure and mystery with which my mind unaccountably surrounded the Newmans. I could never approach their little house without the expectation that something extraordinary was about to happen in there, some sexual lewdness, perhaps, or an amazing revelation of some other kind.

No sensible person could take Manny seriously—he loved to clown—but it was hard to remain unmoved by him, I suppose because an inch below his mad imaginings people sensed the common suffering that in his case never healed over with the customs of indifference. If it was typical of him to look up at me from his casino hand, with his shovel hanging in open view just behind his head in the garage, and say, "I don't have a shovel," it was normal, too, and Lee and my father and whoever else was playing with him would never think of openly mentioning the obvious contradiction. Everyone knew that his solution for any hard problem was always the same—change the facts. And everyone took a certain delight in him, as though that was really what they would love to do themselves if only they dared. Beneath the general scoffing at him there was something like intense curiosity if not respect and envy for his crazy courage in turning away from the ordinary rules of sane intercourse. For me, I think, he also seemed to contain multitudes, subtleties of meaning and implication absent in everyone else; in his straightforward denial of owning a shovel, for example, he was actually implying the theme of his life, the competitiveness that drugged his mind. In effect he was saying, "Why don't your father buy his own shovel? If he's important enough to look down on me"—as he was sure conservative types always did—"then he's got no call asking me to lend him a tool. Is he too high-class to own a shovel? Is he such a success that he can go around not even thinking of a shovel except when he desperately needs one, or his son does, and then he thinks you can just drop over and pick up mine? I've got money tied up in this shovel. So for the Millers I have no shovel." But it went even further; in his mind's eye the shovel hanging behind his head had really ceased to exist at that moment.

Of course I learned from my father and Uncle Lee and the other men in the family to despair of Manny, but I could never keep my eyes off him either, nor could they. A gin game was only a gin game without Manny, half a dozen or more mildly bored people sitting around a table and talking in spurts about operations or pregnancies or the endless rain or lack of rain or who was likely to get elected or, above all, a fortune somebody had made or lost and how much Bing Crosby or Rudy Vallee made in a single week. But from Manny there was bound to come an assertion sometime in the first ten minutes, the announcement of a theme for the evening, like "Friend of mine in Providence tells me this Rudy Vallee guy broke all the records up there, they took in thirty million dollars in two nights."

"Thirty *million*?"

"Thirty million not counting matinees."

And they were off, figuring the probable number of seats in the theatre and dividing that into thirty million . . . But mercy softened them before anyone would declare the outright absurdity of the take, and anyway Manny had changed the subject with some joke, along with a certain self-confessing psychic wink that charmed his listeners into wondering whether he was really serious after all, and he managed to finish a card game with everyone's emotions having been stirred to outrage, laughter, and finally comradeship with this imp of a man who continuously slipped in and out of every category. Through it all, the fair skin of his wife, Annie, alternately flushed and paled as she dreaded and was relieved of the fear that he was making too much of a fool of himself, something she would have to pay for later, when with no audience to confirm his existence his agonizing uncertainty of identification flooded him with despair. If such black moods hung on, she would sit beside him all the way through New England in his little car, which in winter was barely kept above freezing by its primitive heater, and she would persistently talk him into sunnier thoughts. In those days, before the parkways and superhighways, he had to drive through every town, stop at every traffic light, and he carried a short-handled shovel in the trunk to dig his way out of drifts, since there were no snow tires as yet and many towns only plowed their roads once in a storm.

It was the unpredictability of his life that wove romance around it. He was not in some dull salaried job where you could never hope to make a killing. Hope was his food and drink, and the need to project hopeful culminations for a selling trip helped, I suppose, to make life unreal. Fifty years later, in my Chinese production of *Death of a Salesman,* Ying Ruocheng, the actor playing Willy, was trying to imagine an equivalent to this romance of hope in some Chinese occupation, selling having always been a disreputable pursuit for Chinese, and certainly not something to be romanticized. He finally seized on the outriders who in the old times had accompanied caravans across China, protecting them from bandits. These hired guns had all kinds of adventures and formed a kind of bragging brotherhood, meeting in faraway places from time to time to trade tales of victories and defeats. With the coming of the railroads the need for their services vanished, and they ended up in local fairs firing at targets, swallowing swords, and drinking to forget (rather like our Buffalo Bill).

Much more than a single model would ultimately go into Willy Loman. Indeed, since I saw so little of Manny he was already, in my youth, as much myth as fact. But there are images of such defined power and density that without offering concrete information to the writer they are nevertheless the sources of his art.

Actually, a friend of his, another salesman whom he had brought home at the end of one of his trips, was more vivid to me than even Manny. One evening he was sitting in the Newman kitchen when I suddenly came on him, no doubt on one of my expeditions to see what was going on in that feverish household. I remembered him well from one of his previous visits, but I was certain he would not recall a kid like me. I started to pass him to go into the living room when he said, "Hello, Arthur, how are things?"

I stopped and turned back to him. He had two vivid distinctions for me: although middle-aged, he was unmarried, and he had a wooden leg, which at the moment was propped across the seat of a chair. Unlike Manny, he was a listener, a quiet and unsmiling man with quizzical brown eyes, sparse hair, and a reflective air. Imagining his stump, I felt some of his pain and wondered if it was what gave him his somewhat tired and thoughtful look. I also knew that he was unable to drive and had to move by train, wrestling bags and dealing with porters, valiantly pressing his way across the country like a wounded soldier. Like any traveling man, he had to my mind a kind of intrepid valor that withstood the inevitable putdowns, the scoreless attempts to sell. In a sense, these men lived like artists, like actors whose product is first of all themselves, forever imagining triumphs in a world that either ignores them or denies their presence altogether. But just often enough to keep the game going one of them makes it and swings to the moon on a thread of dreams unwinding out of himself.

"I'm fine," I said, flattered. And not knowing what to do next, I stood there waiting as his tired eyes searched my face. Actually, I was feeling tense from trying to keep my eye from lingering on his fascinating artificial limb, its shoe stiffly pointing to the ceiling from the seat of the chair it was resting on.

"You've changed, haven't you?" he said. "You've gotten serious."

With one sentence he had handed me the dignity of a history of my own. Until that moment, like everything else around me, I had simply been inevitable, as enveloped by time and as helpless as a leaf on a river's surface. "Changed" meant I was not as I had been before. Somehow this was hopeful, but why I could not imagine. For days and weeks afterward I replayed this moment in my mind, trying to understand how I had "changed." I studied my face in the bathroom mirror, looking for some sign of my "seriousness" and trying to recall what I had looked like before I gained this little distinction. If I ever knew that salesman's name I forgot it long ago, but not his few interested words that helped crack the shell of suffocating subjectivity surrounding my existence.

Manny had managed to make his boys into a pair of strong, self-assured young men, musketeers bound to one another's honor and proud of their family. Neither was patient enough or perhaps capable enough to sit alone and study, and they both missed going to college. Buddy joined the Seabees during the war and welded landing mats for aircraft on Pacific islands, married an older woman who had her own children, and died at forty of cancer, an entrepreneur at last, serving aircraft workers sandwiches from a small fleet of vans he had managed to buy or lease. Abby fought with the infantry at Anzio, one of the worst-conceived landings of the war, his outfit pinned down on the beach by German artillery fire from surrounding heights. He said he had lost his mind, finally, and had climbed out of his foxhole and walked around on the exploding battlefield as though nothing were happening, and was never even grazed. Like everything else he ever recounted, this story had some holes in it—certain dates he dropped seemed to place him elsewhere than at Anzio—but the possibility was very great that as a Newman he had indeed turned his back on reality and gone for a stroll on a battlefield.

The last I saw of Abby was a number of years before he died, in his early forties, like his mother, of hypertension. He had invited me to his bachelor apartment in Manhattan after I phoned him. I had not seen him since before the war. Wearing blue silk pajamas and slippers, he ushered me into his small living room overlooking lower Lexington Avenue. It was a late Saturday afternoon. *All My Sons* was running on Broadway, *Focus* had been published a year or two earlier, and I had a wife and two children. What he had came out of his bedroom on two pairs of spike heels, two startlingly beautiful young women who dashed over to him where he sat and kissed him on each cheek, pausing only long enough to nod to me as he introduced me with a display of pashalike satisfaction. Buttoning up blouses and straightening stockings, they hurried out of the apartment. They were late, they said, for work. "I love it with two," he chuckled as the door slammed shut.

He very much resembled our long-dead uncle Hymie the shotspitter, with the same aquiline nose, the brown eyes witty with lust, the thick wavy dark hair, and the straight white teeth. He had always looked oiled. Had he arranged this demonstration of his sexual powers to stoke my envy? He certainly succeeded. We had made our date three days earlier, and he would have had time to attend to the staging. His face as he sat there smiling at me seemed to declare his superior potency. I realized that absurd as it might seem on the level of reality, on a deeper path we had been jostling one another for a very long time to see who would lead. And that was why I thought he had timed the girls' presence. He must have deeply resented my success, as he doubtless saw it, with a prizewinning play. In short, he couldn't write but he could certainly fuck. Of course his face showed nothing but his sweetly imagined superiority, which, however, I knew to be fragile. As always, his lifelong narcissism made me uneasy with him; to remain friends with such people one has to be false to oneself, since they must always be praised. The only mystery is why one bothers. But of course one doesn't in the end.

I had a purpose here that I had not told him about. Before very long we were talking about the war and his outbreak of temporary irrationality at Anzio. "They took me out of the line as soon as we broke through, and I made lieutenant in the military police. We were trying to track down missing freight cars full of tires that kept disappearing below Rome around Foggia, and I finally traced a whole new track these guys had laid out—the cars were driven off into a forest and unloaded and then put back on the main track." He laughed his gutty laugh. "There was plenty of dough to be made, but naturally I didn't." By which I was to understand that he had come out of the war with money in his pocket, and simultaneously that he was far too honorable to accept bribes. In the delightful Newman physics two things could occupy the same space with ease. What the reality was only God knew, but in any case his basic message was clear: he was a success.

And now, with a sudden turn toward philosophical unhappiness: "I don't think I could ever stay with one woman. How can you do it?"

"Who says you have to?"

"I don't know . . ." He glanced disconsolately out the window. "I might want a kid sometime." He turned to me, joyfully unhappy. "Can you figure it out?"

"Not really. Once in a while everybody wants both."

"I don't know if I could ride it out, though. I mean if I began to get bored . . . What do you do if she bores you?"

"Wait till it passes."

He sighed. "That's what I figured."

But he did marry and have a child before he ended.

"What did your pop want?" I asked him. This was what I had come for.

I was obsessed these days by vague but exciting images of what can only be called a trajectory, an arched flow of storytelling with neither transitional dialogue nor a single fixed locale, a mode that would open a man's head for a play to take place inside it, evolving through concurrent rather than consecutive actions. By this time I had known three suicides, two of them salesmen. I knew only that Manny had died with none of the ordinary reasons given. I had also totally forgotten that ten years earlier I had begun a play in college about a salesman and his family but had abandoned it. I would only discover the notebook in which I had written it some nine years hence—long after the first production of *Death of a Salesman*—when my marriage broke up and I had to move my papers out of my Brooklyn house.

"I mean if you had to say the one thing he wanted most, the one thing that occurred to him most often, what would it be?"

My cousin Abby, big, dark, filled with the roiling paradoxes of love for me and competitive resentment, of contempt for his late failed father and at the same time a pitying love and even amused admiration for the man's outrageousness—my cousin sitting there had also entered my dreams not long before, and possibly it was the dream that had caused me to ring him up after so many years.

A vast purple plain blends on the horizon into an orange sunset sky. My bare white foot is lowering into a shallow hole at the bottom of which is a little pool of crystal clear water beneath whose surface are stretched five silvery strings, thick as harp strings. My foot descends and touches them, and the air fills with a bloom of music that even ripples the water. Now in the near distance appears a white concrete wall on the purple plain, and as I approach I see two goatlike fawns walking on their hind legs. They are playing handball against the wall. They are my cousins, Abby and Buddy. The smack of the hard black ball against their forehooves is tremendous, thrilling.

"He wanted a business for us. So we could all work together," my cousin said. "A business for the boys."

This conventional, mundane wish was a shot of electricity that switched all the random iron filings in my mind in one direction. A hopelessly distracted Manny was transformed into a man with purpose: he had been trying to make a gift that would crown all those striving years; all those lies he told, all his imaginings and crazy exaggerations, even the almost military discipline he had laid on his boys, were in this instant given form and point. To be sure, a business expressed his own egotism, but love, too. That homely, ridiculous little man had after all never ceased to struggle for a certain victory, the only kind open to him in this society—selling to achieve his lost self as a man with his name and his sons' names on a business of his own. I suddenly understood him with my very blood.

It was an accidental meeting almost a year earlier that had set me up for the particular question I asked and for the resonances of the answer my cousin gave. On a late winter afternoon I had walked into the lobby of the old Colonial Theatre in Boston, where *All My Sons* had just opened, its Broadway premiere a few weeks away, and I was surprised to see Manny among the last of the matinee audience to leave. He had a nice gray overcoat on his arm and his pearl gray hat on his head, and his little shoes were brightly shined, and he had been weeping. It was almost a decade since I had last laid eyes on him. Despite my name on the marquee he clearly had not expected to see me here.

"Manny! How are you? It's great seeing you here!"

I could see his grim hotel room behind him, the long trip up from

New York in his little car, the hopeless hope of the day's business. Without so much as acknowledging my greeting, he said, "Buddy is doing very well." Then I saw a passing look of embarrassment on his face, as though, perhaps, he had not always wished me well.

We chatted for a moment, and he went out of the vast lobby and into the street. I thought I knew what he was thinking: that he had lost the contest in his mind between his sons and me. An enormous welling sorrow formed in my belly as I watched him merge into the crowd outside. Years later it would seem a spectral contest for a phantom victory and a phantom defeat, but there in the lobby I felt some of my boyhood need of his recognition, my resentment at his disparagements, my envy of his and his sons' freed sexuality, and my contempt for it too. Collected in his ludicrous presence was all of life. And at the same time in some isolated roving molecule of my mind I knew I had imagined all of this and that in reality he was not much more than a bragging and often vulgar little drummer.

But it was the absence of the slightest transition to "Buddy is doing very well" that stuck in my mind; it was a signal to me of the new form that until now I had only tentatively imagined could exist. I had not the slightest idea of writing about a salesman then, totally absorbed as I was in my present production. But how wonderful, I thought, to do a play without any transitions at all, dialogue that would simply leap from bone to bone of a skeleton that would not for an instant cease being added to, an organism as strictly economic as a leaf, as trim as an ant.

And more important than even that, a play that would do to an audience what Manny had done to me in our surprising meeting—cut through time like a knife through a layer cake or a road through a mountain revealing its geologic layers, and instead of one incident in one time-frame succeeding another, display past and present concurrently, with neither one ever coming to a stop.

The past, I saw, is a formality, merely a dimmer present, for everything we are is at every moment alive in us. How fantastic a play would be that did not still the mind's simultaneity, did not allow a man to "forget" and turned him to see present through past and past through present, a form that in itself, quite apart from its content and meaning, would be inescapable as a psychological process and as a collecting point for all that his life in society had poured into him. This little man walking into the street had all my youth inside him, it seemed. And I suppose because I was more conscious than he, I had in some sense already created him.

* * *

But the business at the moment was *All My Sons.*

The play had already run in New Haven and had shown its impact, but Elia Kazan continued rehearsing sections of it every day even now, driving it to ever more intensified climaxes, working it like a piece of music that had to be sustained here and hushed there. To keep the cast from routinizing their characters' conflicts, he would stimulate arguments among them by seeming to favor one over the other, seeding little fungi of jealousy that made them compete all over again for his affection. A small, compact man who walked on the balls of his feet, he had the devil's energy and knew how to pay attention to what the writer or his actors were trying to tell him; he could make each actor think he was his closest friend. I think his method, if it can be given so self-conscious a name, was to let the actors talk themselves into a performance. Far more by insinuation than by command, he allowed the actors to excite themselves with their own discoveries, which they would carry back to him like children offering some found object to a parent. And he respected rather than scoffed at actors' childishness, knowing that it was not a grown-up occupation and that the sources of their best inventions were in their earliest years. Instinctively, when he had something important to tell an actor, he would huddle with him privately rather than instruct before the others, sensing that anything that really penetrates is always to some degree an embarrassment. Unlike Harold Clurman, who adored talking and led his actors by sending them a message of his own amiable helplessness, calling to them, in effect, for rescue, Kazan grinned a lot and said as little as possible. A mystery grew up around what he might be thinking, and this threw the actor back upon himself.

Kazan came from close-knit people of intense feelings, people of clannish propriety and competitiveness who knew that no feeling is alien to man. His most reassuring side, for me, was a natural tendency to seek out the organic and hew to its demands. I believed by this time in a kind of biological playwriting—nature abhors the superfluous, and whatever does not actively contribute to the life of an organism is sloughed off. This same predilection may be why Kazan was not suited to Shakespeare and would have his difficulties with Tennessee Williams, who sometimes showed a weakness for verbal adornment for its own sake. In a play, as in personal relations, Kazan knew that the making and the breaking was done by the needs of people and not by their avowals and disavowals. In the same spirit he listened to music, classical and jazz, seeking to experience what was naked in it and expressive of the composer's secret outcry. He had cast Ed Begley to play the father, Keller, in *All My Sons* not only because Begley was a good actor (although not as yet of great distinction) but because he was a reformed alcoholic and still carried the alcoholic's guilt. Keller is of course a guilty man, although not an alcoholic; thus traits could be matched while their causes were completely unrelated. As Kate Keller he cast a long-unemployed leading lady, Beth Merrill, not only because he thought she could act but because she had a certain pathetic pretension as the last of David Belasco's stars, whom that outlandish genius had forbidden to show herself on the street, putting a chauffeured car at her disposal lest she lose her mystery for the public. Indeed, I had come to the theatre the afternoon I met Manny because we were having a bit of a crisis with her: she had been deeply insulted by what she considered a lack of attention and was talking of quitting. But when I looked in on her in her dressing room after the matinee, she was feeling splendid, and I noticed an immense mass of flowers nearby, which I soon learned Kazan had sent her, in true Belasco style. Kazan had also put on a tie and jacket to present this offering, sensing her longing for some sign of class, however spurious, in the surrounding environment, for we all dressed like steamfitters. On the first day of rehearsal she had glanced at her fellow actors, who looked like street people, and with a grimace of pain had asked Kazan, "Is this the *cast*?"

Kazan was already a well-known but far from famous director at this time, still a year away from the mystique that would come with his production of *A Streetcar Named Desire,* and I was almost totally new to the critics and newspaper theatrical columns, so despite very good Boston reviews, the enormous Colonial was never really filled. The Boston audience was still in a condition of what might be called stubborn spiritual stateliness, and it was hard for me to read their largely silent reactions. One tall and dignified man I saw standing in the lobby crowd at the intermission after the second-act curtain was quite visibly shaken by that climax, his eyes red with weeping. To his companion, who had asked what he thought of the play, he muttered through thin, barely moving lips, "I like it."

Something in the play seemed to have departed from tradition. It is possible that Mordecai Gorelik's set, a disarmingly sunny suburban house, as well as the designedly ordinary and sometimes jokey atmosphere of the first ten minutes, made the deepening threat of the remainder more frightening than people were culturally prepared for; this kind of placid American backyard was not ordinarily associated, at least in 1947, with murder and suicide. Ward Morehouse, the *New York Sun* drama critic, came up to see the play in New Haven and invited Kazan and me to have a drink with him so that he could ask us straight out, "What's it about?" Coming as it did a few months after the famous producer Herman Shumlin had said, "I don't understand your play," Morehouse's question mystified me, and I could only grope for an explanation of a story that, to me and Kazan at any rate, was absolutely clear. On top of this, in the coming weeks I would be asked by Jim Proctor, our press agent, to write a piece for the *Times* "to explain the play" and what I was after in writing it. Apart from the embarrassment of presuming to tell critics what to think, I was at a loss as to what needed elucidation.

After the play opened, one recurring criticism was that it was overly plotted, to the point of implausible coincidence. At a crucial moment, Annie produces a letter written to her during the war by her fiancé, the Kellers' son Larry, presumed dead; in the letter Larry declares his intention to commit suicide in his despair at his father's much publicized crime of selling defective plane parts to the army. With one stroke this proves that Larry is indeed dead, freeing Annie to marry Chris, his brother, and at the same time that Joe Keller not only caused the deaths of anonymous soldiers but, in a manner he never imagined, that of his own son. If the appearance of this letter, logical though it might be, was too convenient for our tastes, I wondered what contemporary criticism would make of a play in which an infant, set out on a mountainside to die because it is predicted that he will murder his father, is rescued by a shepherd and then, some two decades later, gets into an argument with a total stranger whom he kills—and who just happens to be not only his father but the king whose place he proceeds to take, exactly as prophesied. If the myth behind *Oedipus* allows us to stretch our commonsense judgment of its plausibility, the letter's appearance in *All My Sons* seems to me to spring out of Ann's character and situation and hence is far less difficult to accept than a naked stroke of fate. But I have wondered if the real issue is the return of the repressed, which both incidents symbolize. Whenever the hand of the distant past reaches out of its grave, it is always somehow absurd as well as amazing, and we tend to resist belief in it, for it seems rather magically to reveal some unreadable hidden order behind the amoral chaos of events as we rationally perceive them. But that emergence, of course, is the point of *All My Sons*—that there are times when things do indeed cohere.

In later years I began to think that perhaps some people had been disconcerted not by the story but by the play's implication that there could be something of a tragic nature to these recognizable suburban types, who, by extension, were capable of putting a whole world to a moral test, challenging the audience itself. This thought first crossed my mind in 1977 when I visited Jerusalem with my wife, Inge Morath, and saw a production of tremendous power. *All My Sons* had broken the record by then for length of run by a straight play in Israel, and the audience sat watching it with an intensifying terror that was quite palpable. On our right sat the president of Israel, Ephraim Katzir, on the left the prime minister, Yitzhak Rabin, who had arrived late because, as would be announced the next morning, he had just lost his post to Menachem Begin. At the end of the play the applause seemed not to dispel an almost religious quality in the audience's attention, and I asked Rabin why he thought this was so. "Because this is a problem in Israel—boys are out there day and night dying in planes and on the ground, and back here people are making a lot of money. So it might as well be an Israeli play." I would have added that the authority of the play was enhanced by the performance of Hanna Marron, a very great actress whose leg had been blown off in a terrorist bombing of an El Al flight in Zurich in 1972, the year of the Munich Olympics massacre. Perhaps it was only my imagination, but her disfigurement as the result of war, which of course everyone knew about though her limp barely showed, seemed to add authenticity to Kate Keller's spiritual suffering in another war at a different time.

· The play in this production was centered on Kate, the mother, which was an emphasis our original production had bypassed in favor of the father-son conflict. In London a few years later the same shift was made by Michael Blakemore directing Rosemary Harris in the role and Colin Blakely as the father, and it made me wonder whether it was a certain ambiguity in Kate Keller that had confused both Shumlin and the critic Morehouse. For while trying to put it out of her mind, she knows from the outset that her husband indeed shipped faulty plane engine elements to the army. Her guilty knowledge, so obdurately and menacingly suppressed, can be interpreted as her wish to deny her son's death but also, and perhaps even primarily, to take vengeance on her culpable husband by driving him psychically to his knees and ultimately to suicide.

Parenthetically, Morehouse's visit to see the play a month before reviewing it on its Broadway opening, while unusual if not unique, indicated a relationship to the theatre on the part of some critics in those days that has largely gone by the board; there was, I think, less of an arm's-length attitude toward writers and actors and directors, leading in some instances to friendships such as George Jean Nathan's with Eugene O'Neill. I am not sure why there has been such a hardening of the pretense that the critic is somehow virginally distanced from the vulgar enterprise of theatre, that his responsibility ends with the delivery of his impressions of the play. This might be the case if it were absolutely certain that praise and blame were always deserved, always correct, but with their demonstrable prejudices for or against artists, themes, and styles, the critics are at least as fallible and as vulnerable to misjudgment as the works they criticize. Why, then, this antiseptic removal from the problems of the theatre's devolution? After all, even judges at law often address themselves to the mundane housekeeping problems of the courts over which they preside, as they ought to in a democratic society, acknowledging that they themselves may indeed contribute to injustice and may even be part of the problem of achieving justice. To a very important degree the theatre we have is the theatre the critics have permitted us to have, since they filter out what they consider we ought not see, enforcing laws that have never been written, laws, among others, of taste and even ideological content.

It is not a universal condition. In England, for example, critics routinely air their prejudices: a reviewer will tell his readers that he personally detests plays with heavy political content or that he is tired of absurdist styles or that he would like to see a return to more romantic approaches to sex and love—or the contrary. English critics put their cards on the table; they by no means pretend to the authority of sublime universalism, to the purity of no preferences a priori, and are consequently liberated from a posture of perfect objectivity that is not and never has been a real human response to art. It may be that such acknowledgment of membership in the human race is itself a result of a social situation very different from ours. There are still a number of British papers competing for readers' attention, and their critics are thus obliged, if only implicitly, to defend their own validity. But in a New York theatre community on its knees before a single great newspaper, a certain ex cathedra tone, what might be called an automatic response mechanism, soon takes over the style of whatever critic happens to be on duty in any particular season, and we who work in the silly business are stuck with whatever his slant may be. It is a very old habit among us to move in droves, something Tocqueville noticed a hundred and fifty years ago; the American wants to be one of the crowd, and when condemnation is leveled against a play by the only newspaper whose authority he accepts, the critic's influence, along with outrageous ticket prices and the phenomenal expense of parking, becomes lethal. For all intents and purposes the contemporary American repertoire comes out of New York and represents the taste of whoever is writing the *New York Times* review, only slightly mitigated by other reviews. The *Times* did not invent the situation, but there it is, a dictatorship as effective as any cultural control mechanism in the world. Indeed, when the Soviets close down a show, it is a committee that makes the decision, rather than one man—at least since Stalin died.

Monopoly in anything is not only an evil but an insidious one, and there was actually a moment, in 1967, soon after the *Herald Tribune* vanished, when Clifton Daniel, then the *Times* managing editor, convoked a meeting of some hundred authors, newspeople, producers, and actors in a midtown restaurant to discuss what might be done to mitigate the paper's awesome new power and its unhealthy, undemocratic potentialities. The *Times*, Daniel declared, did not create this monopoly and did not wish to hold the power it had been handed by history. After some wayward discussion, I suggested that since the nub of the issue was the danger of injustice in a single critic carrying all the immense prestige of the *Times*, perhaps the solution was to send two or three critics to write independent notices, maybe even on occasion asking an informed theatregoer to write his impressions of a show in a paragraph or two. As a playwright I naturally saw the risk of ending up with not one but three bad notices in the *Times*, but I was willing to take the chance in the interest of a more consensual criticism. Another benefit, I thought, was that differing reviews would make very interesting reading and would broaden the public's awareness of how fictional, rather than a matter of plain fact, all criticism really is, which is to say, how subjective. It was not, I said, that critics knew more than others but that they could write better about the little they did know, and this fact might emerge from such an exercise in comparative criticism by two or three informed minds focused on the same subject.

Daniel thought for a moment and said that my idea was impossible, and when I asked him his reasons, he replied, "But who would be speaking for the *New York Times*?" There may have been one or two in the room who laughed, but not more, for we are so completely sold on the inevitability if not the rightness of the monopoly of power in everything that we are beyond the point where we even notice it anymore. I could only ask Daniel why we had assembled if not to find a way to dilute the dominance of the *Times.* Was his objection not simply a reaffirmation that the *Times* did indeed want to keep the power it had been handed by history? But the meeting simply wandered back down into the street.

All this in face of the fact that the *Times,* far more often than not, has been very kind to me and to my work. It was Brooks Atkinson's campaign for *All My Sons* that was responsible for its long run and my recognition as a playwright. And if I cannot prove it, I still believe that one of his motives in supporting the play and me was his concern that the New York theatre be made hospitable to work that was not socially trivial. Had he not respected the play, he would not have championed it, of course, but I think he used it as a lever to open the door to other voices that he hoped would come. In short, he was not oblivious to a responsibility for the whole theatre enterprise.

In any case, the audience confirmed his judgment, and by spring the production was a fixture on Broadway and received the Drama Critics Circle Award and a few others. After some weeks, realizing as I sat down to dinner with Mary in our Brooklyn Heights house that the Coronet Theatre was about to fill up yet again that evening with paying customers and that my words had a power beyond my mere self, I felt a certain threat along with the inevitable exhilaration. As a success I was occasionally greeted by people on the street with a glazed expression that was pleasant but made me feel unnervingly artificial. My identification with life's failures was being menaced by my fame, and this led me, a few weeks after the opening of *All My Sons,* to apply at the New York State Employment Service for any job available. I was sent out to a factory in Long Island City to stand all day assembling beer box dividers for the minimum wage. The grinding boredom and the unnaturalness of my pretense to anonymity soon drove me out of that place, but the question remained as to how to live without breaking contact with what theatre folk called the civilians, the ones in the audience who made the pants and filled the teeth. It was not merely a question of continuing to draw material from life but also a moral one. I had not yet read of Tolstoy at the height of his renown spending days in a Moscow shop making shoes, but I shared his impulse.

I was not the first to experience the guilt of success (which, incidentally, was reinforced by leftist egalitarian convictions), and though I suspected the truth, I was unable to do much about it: such guilt is a protective device to conceal one's happiness at surpassing others, especially those one loves, like a brother, father, or friend. It is a kind of payment to them in the form of a pseudo remorse. But this is not altogether a phantom exercise, for the psyche knows that those who have been surpassed may harbor thoughts of retaliation that can be dangerous in reality. So one speaks through such guilt—"Don't bother resenting me, I've failed too." In due time my laments receded as my play began to be produced all over Europe and *Focus* was published in England, France, Germany, and Italy, but I counted myself lucky that *All My Sons* had created a decent number of enemies as well as a great many friends, and thus kept reality in equilibrium.

We were living then in a converted brownstone on Pierpont Street whose normal quiet was blasted one afternoon by a yelling argument in the hallway outside. Thinking violence was about to break out, I opened the door to find a small young man in army uniform sitting on the stairs with a young and beautiful woman whom I recognized as our upstairs neighbor. They went silent on seeing me, so I figured everything was under control and went back into our apartment. Later the young soldier, by now out of uniform, approached me on the street and introduced himself as a writer. His name, he said, was Mailer. He had just seen my play. "I could write a play like that," he said. It was so obtusely flat an assertion that I began to laugh, but he was completely serious and indeed would make intermittent attempts to write plays in the many years that lay ahead. Since I was at a time when I was hammering out my place in the world, I made few friends then, and Mailer struck me as someone who seemed to want to make converts rather than friends, so our impulses, essentially similar, could hardly mesh. (I am at the age when it is best to be charitable.) In any event, although we lived for years in the same neighborhood, our paths rarely crossed.

THREE

With *All My Sons* more and more firmly established, the question was, as always, what to do next. Though I had resolved never to change my level of living, it soon seemed illogical for Mary and our two young children, Jane and Robert, to be stuffed into a small apartment, so I bought an old but handsome house with two duplex apartments on Grace Court close to the river. We moved into the upper one, the other continuing to be held by longtime tenants, the Davenports. Henry Davenport was president of the Brooklyn Savings Bank. Each evening he and his wife unfailingly dressed for dinner, she in an evening gown, and he, ruddy-faced and slender, in black tie and velvet dinner jacket and pumps, looking exactly like the Harvard overseer that in fact he was. The street was lined with waiting limousines when they had one of their infrequent dinner parties, and he adored phoning upstairs to the Drama Critics Circle Award winner to report that his window would not open or his faucet leaked. I could not wait to sell the house and buy another, but that would take another play and, with luck, more money.

It occurred to me three or four times a day that if I did no work I would still be earning a lot of money and by the end of the week would be richer than at the beginning. My mind worked at this anomaly, trying to get used to it. If I simply went outside and walked around the block the cash would still come in. Even if I took a nap or read some stupid magazine for half an hour or went to the movies. The word *royalty* took on a more exact meaning. I had been scratching on the glass from the outside for thirty-one years, until now I was scratching on it from the inside, trying to keep contact with the ordinary life from which my work had grown. For the slow dread was descending on me that I might have nothing more to say as a writer.

As always the world and I were full of problems, but *All My Sons* had exhausted my lifelong interest in the Greco-Ibsen form, in the particular manner in which I had come to think of it. Now more and more the simultaneity of ideas and feelings within me and the freedom with which they contradicted one another began to fascinate me. I even dabbled with the notion of studying music in the hope of composing, for the only art in which simultaneity was really possible was music. Words could not make chords; they had to be uttered in a line, one after the other.

I began to walk endlessly, often across the Brooklyn Bridge into lower Manhattan. Success seemed to have deepened a sense of my own contradictions, and my new feelings of power made me wish to acknowledge them. The beauty in the tension of opposites I saw everywhere—the pull of gravity actually strengthening the bridge's steel arches by compression. (This was before the reconstruction lay crude reinforcing girders laterally over the roadways, destroying the birdlike air of winged flight to the bridge's outline.) I was growing rich and attempting to think poor, to persist in a sternly leveling view of myself, even as my spirit was opening to its own sensuality. But to frankly acknowledge one's inner paradoxes is already a sensual action and a defeat for monolithic puritanism. I knew that with *All My Sons* I had won a new freedom to create, and I would stand on the high point of the bridge's arch facing the wind from the ocean, trying to embrace a world larger than I had been able to conceive of until this time. If I had no subject, I had an indescribable feeling of a new form; it would be both infinitely compressed and expansive and leisurely, the story both strange and homely. It would be something never seen on any stage before. The very thinking of it filled me with sexual desire, with love for my wife and, incredibly, for all women at the same time. I began to think that true art must be an overflowing of love. But of course love can be faked through techniques and stylistic persuasiveness, and I would have none of that. I longed for a way to deliver onto the stage all the raw complexity I felt swirling within me. The problem with *All My Sons* was not that it was too realistic but that it left too little space and time for the wordless darkness that underlies all verbal truth. But again, this was something that perhaps only music could suggest.

I had made no bones about being a rather impatient moralist, not even in interviews, where I was naive enough to confess that to me an amoral art was a contradiction and that an artist was obliged to point a way out if he thought he knew what it was. I had unknowingly picked up where my beloved Russians had left off, but without Tolstoy's and Dostoyevsky's privilege of a god whose unearthly resolutions, as in *Crime and Punishment,* one did not have to believe in reasonably but only sense to validate. I was striving toward a sensation of religious superreality that did not, however, depart the conditions of earth, a vision of avoidance of evil that would thrill even atheists and lead them "upward," and perhaps even shame priest and rabbi into realizing how their "spiritualizing" of raw life had made a trifle of religions. The more exactingly true a character or dilemma was, the more spiritualized it became.

My walks, it gradually seemed to me, were in themselves indicative of some personality failure. I loved the city, was feverishly curious about all the lives lived in it, but moved through it alone, unconnected. My shyness tortured me. Life was always elsewhere. And yet, paradoxically, out of my aloneness I was communicating my feelings to thousands of strangers every week in the theatre. Still, I was fending off too much, condemning too much. Naive as I was, I knew that there was almost no space for me between sexuality and art. I even sensed, without being able to explain the reasons, that while fiercely protective of what I wrote, I was also vaguely ashamed of it, as though it were a sexual secret. On these walks flashes of accusatory truth would sometimes fly at me, showing up my fraudulent pretensions to monogamous contentment when my lust was truer and bewilderingly taunting. At moments it seemed that my relation with Mary and all women was thin and cautious out of some fear that surpassed sex itself. With no more Freud than rumor brought me, I could afford to admit into consciousness what a bit more sophistication might have caused me to suppress: I knew that somewhere behind my sexual anxieties lay incestuous stains that spread toward sister and mother. Playfully my mind would set up chessboard arrangements, the pieces being father, mother, brother, sister, each with different powers and rights-of-way, imperious in one direction while vulnerable and paralyzed in another. Regardless of how the game played out, it had to end the same way, in a confrontation with the father after I had picked off sister and mother and pushed brother beyond reach of effective action. The father could move in all directions, and his decree of punishment, of course, was always death.

Six or seven years on, trying to repair a marriage that mutual intolerance was slowly destroying, I would learn in analysis far less than what it simply confirmed. Somehow, relations between family members that are usually too fearsome to be made conscious had been matters of ordinary observation to me since childhood, and if it was "sinful" to acknowledge their existence, they were always clear to my secret vision. But they had only incidental identifications with my actual parents and siblings; I had, it seemed, always moved on two planes at the same time, the actual reality and a metaphoric one in which, for example, my father appeared as a deanimated and forbidding avenger who I knew was and was-not my actual father. My mother was and was-not the woman who was tempting me sensually to capture her from my father, and was both culpable of disloyalty to him and, as herself, perfectly innocent. Until I began to write plays my frustration with this doubleness of reality was terrible, but once I could impersonate all conflicts on a third plane, the plane of art, I was able to enjoy my power—even if a twinge of shame continued to accompany the plays into the world.

But a sense of power without a theme is one hand clapping, and I walked endlessly trying to find my way into the city and into myself. One day it registered on my mind that for weeks now I had been passing graffiti on walls and sidewalks saying, "Dove Pete Panto?" without ever bothering to try to figure out that it meant "Where is Pete Panto?" It was down near the piers that this mysterious question covered every surface, and it was not hard to guess that it was still more evidence of the other world that existed at the foot of peaceful, old-fashioned Brooklyn Heights, the sinister waterfront world of gangster-ridden unions, assassinations, beatings, bodies thrown into the lovely bay at night. Now the sentence began showing up in subway stations and chalked on Court Street office buildings. Finally the liberal press took up the cry, with *PM*, the progressive daily that lasted for a few years after its birth during World War II, explaining that Pete Panto was a young longshoreman who had attempted to lead a rank-and-file revolt against the leadership of President Joseph Ryan and his colleagues, many of them allegedly Mafiosi, who ran the International Longshoremen's Association. Panto, one evening during dinner, had been lured from his home by a phone call from an unknown caller and was never seen again. The movement he had led vanished from the scene.

I took to wandering the bars on the waterfront to pick up what-

ever I could about Panto. It was a time when the heroic had all but
disappeared from the theatre along with any interest in the tragic
tradition itself. The idea of a young man defying evil and ending
in a cement block at the bottom of the river drew me on.

It took only a couple of days on the piers to discover that men
were afraid to so much as talk about Panto. Most of them were of
Italian descent, many of them born in the old country and completely dependent on the favor of their leaders for jobs. As I realized after a trip to southern Italy and Sicily the next year, the hiring
system on the Brooklyn and Manhattan waterfronts had been imported from the Sicilian countryside. A foreman representing the
landowners would appear in the town square on his horse; a crowd
of job-seeking peasants would humbly form up around his spurs,
and he would deign to point from favored face to favored face with
his riding crop and trot away with the wordless self-assurance of a
god once he had lifted from hunger by these barely perceptible
gestures the number of laborers he required for that day. In troubled times one more element was added—the armed *carabinieri*.
During my time in Calabria and Sicily I once saw half a dozen
soldiers with slung rifles standing by to silently instruct the peasants that this time-honored way of casually employing human beings was never to be changed.

But Italy was yet to come; now in Red Hook, Brooklyn, at four-
thirty on winter mornings, I stood around with longshoremen huddling in doorways in rain and snow on Columbia Street facing the
piers, waiting for the hiring boss, on whose arrival they surged
forward and formed up in a semicircle to attract his pointing finger
and the numbered brass checks that guaranteed a job for the day.
After distributing the checks to his favorites, who had quietly paid
him off, the boss often found a couple left over and in his generosity
tossed them into the air over the little crowd. In a frantic scramble,
the men would tear at each other's hands, sometimes getting into
bad fights. Their cattlelike acceptance of this humiliating procedure struck me as an outrage, even more sinister than the procedure itself. It was as though they had lost the mere awareness of
hope. Carlo Levi, the Italian-Jewish writer and painter who for
years was banished by Mussolini to a godforsaken place called
Eboli, had written a memoir of his exile, *Christ Stopped at Eboli*,
that resonated in my head on those dark mornings on Columbia
Street. America, I thought, stopped at Columbia Street.

On the Brooklyn Bridge the waves of traffic moved serenely
above the heads of men who were enduring what without exagger-

ation were medieval conditions. The idea of a longshoreman standing up to the arrogance of such power chilled me with awe, especially when the comfortably placid looks on the passing policemen's faces showed that anyone who had thoughts of change
would have little to hope for from the men of power in the city.
Pete Panto had become heroic for me. But after a couple of weeks
I saw that I could never penetrate the permanent reign of quiet
terror on the waterfront hardly three blocks from my peaceful
apartment. I had all but put the waterfront out of mind as a hopeless project when, a few months later, a man I had never heard of
phoned and asked to see me to talk about the subject.

Vincent James Longhi and his friend Mitch Berenson arrived
that very afternoon. Berenson, I would shortly learn, was attempting to carry on Pete Panto's work of organizing opposition to the
Ryan domination of the longshoremen's union. His base was the
young American Labor Party in the Red Hook area, a dangerously
inhospitable one for men of his views since they were fair game for
the Mafia, which, in the antileft fever of the later forties, would
hardly be reprimanded for making them disappear. The evolution
of these two men remained for me for decades to come a kind of
measure of radicals in our time.

Berenson, in his late twenties then, was a round, bullish worker
with a pockmarked face, totally bald, with a high arching nose and
a forehead as broad as Beethoven's, an overweight but powerful-
looking man whose poverty showed in his rotted shoe soles, his
frayed shirt cuffs, a stained, permanently knotted tie, and the five-
cent stogie jammed between his teeth. Cheap food had distended
his belly over his belt, and he walked like a barrel on wide-apart
legs. It was impossible then to guess what a turmoil of conflicts was
rushing through him when he seemed so tough and certain of his
ideas. At moments I thought I noticed fleeting signs of some poetic
fragmentation going on in his head.

Vinny Longhi, a new member of the bar with political ambitions,
was of another sort. Over six feet tall and darkly handsome, he was
a smooth talker who, at least in speaking to me, was clearly trying
to jostle Italianate street accents out of his delivery in favor of
something more cultivated. His awe for my novel, *Focus,* and *All
My Sons* was somewhat embarrassingly overdone, but he was unconscious of his glamour-struck effusiveness. Unabashedly romantic, he reminded me of cousins of mine as well as guys in high
school who lived for the single purpose of bringing girls down to
bed level. His helpless sensuality moistened his gaze like a syrup.

He wore a lawyerlike blue suit that day, the sleeves snug around his strong, thick wrists. He would not feel pain too acutely.

They had "worked with Pete," they said, to organize a rank-and-file anti-Ryan movement in the locals, and they outlined some of the fascinatingly corrupt rackets on the docks, the kickbacks forced from men who had to pay off gangsters for the privilege of being allowed to work, the specially designated neighborhood stores and barbershops where a worker rented a job for a day with a ten-dollar payment for a two-dollar bottle of wine or a seventy-five-cent haircut. It was like an isolated village ruled by a feudal lord, within sight of the traffic on the Brooklyn Bridge and the vaulting skyscrapers of lower Manhattan. The main reform being touted by Berenson and Longhi was the establishment of a hiring hall where the men would register and get their jobs first come, first served, no favorites. Of course this would mean the end of a racket and was a dangerous idea to propagate, so they were trying to launch a campaign to raise money for a new longshoremen's movement to clean up the waterfront. I was their first prospect, being unquestionably a millionaire, what with a hit on Broadway, and undoubtedly pals with others of my ilk who might be patsies for this kind of pitch. In reality my only contacts in the theatre and film were with a few ordinary actors and would-be playwrights, but if I couldn't raise money I would love to find some way of writing about this sealed-off area of the city, which aside from everything else had always seemed so photogenic. They were eager to show me around, and I had my entry at last into what had become for me a dangerous and mysterious world at the water's edge that drama and literature had never touched.

Now, looking back, I see how volcanic this decision was for me. Out of it would come a movie script (never to be produced); a play, *A View from the Bridge;* and a trip to Hollywood, where I would meet an unknown young actress, Marilyn Monroe, and at the same time come into direct collision with the subterranean machine that enforced political blacklisting and the ideological disciplining of film writers, actors, and directors.

At the moment, of course, I was simply following instinct toward what I sensed was a tragic tale. But probably there was also something more; by 1947 I believe I felt the beginnings of a cultural shift that was completely new in my experience. It may be that I was trying to fend off a certain rising ambiguity, both in my own life and in the city and the world, where nothing like a hero was any longer really conceivable. And so it was challenging to be in the company of what I took to be unambiguous men striking out heroically against unjust power. But of course in that also I was in for some surprises.

It did not take me long to learn that the waterfront was the Wild West, a desert beyond the law. An electrical generator big enough to light a city in Africa, where it was bound, standing two stories high on a flatcar and worth millions, simply vanished one night from a Brooklyn pier. The exploitation of labor was probably a minor matter compared to the Mob's skimming of commerce moving through the world's greatest port, a form of taxation, in effect. And in this part of Brooklyn the name that stood atop it all like the name of a duke of the realm was Tony Anastasia, Tough Tony to the man on the Red Hook street.

But nothing was ever quite what it seemed in this Brooklyn Byzance. Tough Tony, it turned out, was fearsome mainly because his brother Albert had headed Murder, Inc., and was credited with having assassinated over a hundred men. Nine or ten years later, Albert would make the mistake of coming over from Jersey, where he was exiled by the New York authorities, and stretching out on a barber chair on Seventh Avenue and Fifty-third Street, where he was hamburgered by two killers while his eyes were covered with a hot towel. But at this point Albert was still very much alive, and kid brother Tony could bask in his bloody glory as head of the ILA local that covered this part of the Brooklyn waterfront. Thus, Berenson and Longhi understood that it would only be a matter of time before Tony was heard from, since it was his workers they were trying to organize into a rump faction that would contest his power and through him that of Joe Ryan, who ran the entire union from Manhattan.

Like dictators before him and after, Tough Tony saw himself as protector of the decent, hardworking longshoreman, not at all as an oppressor. Indeed, he would make ferocious speeches to his local demanding more for the workers and less for the shipping companies. The men knew how to keep straight faces, and he could hardly be grinned at openly when he carried a thirty-eight-caliber Smith and Wesson revolver in a holster hitched up high enough to show the butt at the fold of his left lapel. But Tony was a complicated enough man to make Berenson wonder if he might one day be the means by which a revolt of the members could be mounted against the Ryan leadership. It was an idea that would come very close to getting him killed, and perhaps Vincent Longhi along with him.

Berenson was for me an unorthodox kind of radical for having sprung from the working class rather than being an intellectual. His father, a carpenter, had emigrated from Russia with a sister after the violent reaction following the failed 1905 revolution. Berenson himself had been a full-time organizer for the Ladies Garment Workers by the time he was fifteen. In fact, he had been used to carry out some of the more athletic organizing tactics, not uncommon at the time, like shinnying up drainpipes or jimmying a window to let union inspectors into a boss's office for a peek at the company books or some crucial piece of information. Long before they got respectable, the unions had been handing the boy Berenson and his gymnastic expertise around to break many a stalemate in an organizing drive.

But as he was arrested more and more often, his thoughts grew longer, partially under the influence of his aunt Riva, one of those unlettered women of wisdom that great revolutionary experiences always seem to create. She broadened his education, turning him to novels and poetry out of the rich Russian store of words, and of course to Marx. At around the same time he pursued a beautiful painter whom, despite his unhandsome appearance, he won by the strength of his conviction that she belonged with him, just as he belonged with the militant labor movement that would transform America—an imprecise vision that was still coiled in history's womb. It would be two or three years before he understood it himself, but he was at a turning point in his life as he moved in to take the place of a man who had been thrown into the bay. If I saw no sign ever of fear in his face, it was probably that at this point he still saw himself as an invulnerable and disembodied undulation of the wave of history. With his rolling gait and cheap cigar and his manic explosions of crude laughter, he went around the piers looking for an opening in a bout with an octopus.

For Vinny Longhi it was less easy to stand apart and objectify, because unlike Berenson, he could not help identifying himself—and maybe even hating himself for doing so—with the stylish *gravitas* of some of the waterfront power figures, who mimed or rather parodied the code-driven gallantry of feudal Italy. Like most radical materialists and Marxists, these two were romantics in analytical clothing; they thought they could see around their more naive bourgeois opponents, whose vision was narrowed by selfish interests, while they had no personal interests, only historical ones, and were thus freer to maneuver than those in the game for the purpose of gain. Thus their power—provided men would follow them—would be a kind of spiritual self-satisfaction at having assisted history to give birth. Morally they were puritanical, barring a few lapses Longhi could not help, because after all he was so handsome.

Periodically over the next six months I would join up with one or both of them as they sought to penetrate the fiefdoms of the waterfront. Longhi was a powerful, rather operatic speaker on the piers, attracting larger and larger crowds of longshoremen in the predawn mists as they stood around on Columbia Street waiting to be picked for a day's work. Chopping the air like Lenin in October, he expanded on his main theme, the degradation of honest sons of Italy by an unjust union machine. The problem, of course, was that the men knew this better than he did, but it was nice to hear somebody saying it anyway. It did not take long to realize that only a power equal to what held them down could gain their trust, and I could see no hope that any such thing would be allowed to come to life here.

But in the meantime I was moving in and out of longshoremen's houses and making some friends and tuning my ear to their fruity, mangled Sicilian-English bravura, with its secretive, marvelously modulated hints and untrammeled emotions. In the course of time Longhi mentioned a story he'd recently heard of a longshoreman who had ratted to the Immigration Bureau on two brothers, his own relatives, who were living illegally in his very home, in order to break an engagement between one of them and his niece. The squealer was disgraced, and no one knew where he had gone off to, and some whispered that he had been murdered by one of the brothers. But the story went past me; I was still searching for a handle on Pete Panto.

I fiddled with a screenplay, dropped it and picked it up again, wandered back into Red Hook searching for what I did not realize I already had—*A View from the Bridge*.

Melodrama stirred me once—Tony Anastasia appeared suddenly one afternoon in the loft where Berenson had his headquarters and threatened then and there to kill him and Longhi. There was even the requisite operatic crowd gathering in the street below to observe the festivities. Tony was outraged because, comically enough, he had been hired by a large corporation to sail two tugboats up the Hudson River with a couple of hundred strikebreakers who were to enter its plant from the water side, the land entrances being heavily picketed by the United Electrical Workers. He had pleaded beforehand with Berenson and Longhi, who had been feeling him out for an alliance against the Ryan leadership, to call their friends in the union and persuade them not to fight his strike-breakers. To this incredible request the two had replied with a lecture on working-class solidarity that left the gangster's mind boggled.

His attempted naval invasion of the plant was thwarted by union motorboats—there was actually a little gunfire between the two armadas until the tugboat captains decided they'd had enough and brought the men back to Brooklyn—and Tony soon found Red Hook sniggering at his humiliation, and of course he was now being referred to behind his back as "the Admiral." It was all too much, and he marched over to Berenson's loft in full sight of the neighborhood to demand satisfaction for his betrayal by the radicals. He was very confused.

Forced into confrontation, sweating Longhi and Berenson turned on the eloquence—which Tony was a sucker for and Longhi especially a master of—castigating him for dishonoring the memory of his late and beloved father, who, as Tony adored to memorialize at the drop of a hat with real tears in his eyes, had hit the docks every morning for a hundred and fifty years and raised his hordes of children from the sweat off his back as a longshoreman, and whose son, Tony, was now betraying workers by breaking strikes when he had all the makings of a truly great workers' leader and, if he chose, could be an honor to the persecuted Italian people, to say nothing of the whole human race. They ended up in a state of abeyance if not as friends, and the climax was their offering to get him two tickets for *All My Sons*. Indeed, I met him in front of the theatre a few days later, and when he looked up at the marquee and saw my name, then looked at me and said very little, he reminded me of my uncle Manny in Boston. He got into his car beside his driver and drove off without seeing the play. I figured he simply wanted to be sure Longhi and Berenson weren't kidding him about me, insulting him all over again.

The uncomfortable truth was that I was finding the waterfront as absurd as it was tragic, and it was out of one of its absurdities that I ended up traveling to Italy and France with Longhi—a trip whose echoes would inform much of my life to come.

By the time I met them, Berenson and Longhi were veterans of many frustrated, nearly fruitless organizing attempts. In 1946, realizing that they lacked the political clout to guarantee protection for any workers who dared confront the union-Mafia combination, they had come up with the idea of running Longhi for Congress. But the Democratic Party in the district was owned by Congressman John Rooney, who in turn was in Joseph Ryan's pocket. This bred a fantasy in Berenson's maverick imagination that the Republicans, perhaps out of amused desperation, since they had never in history won an election in the district, might be sold on running Longhi in this Italian working-class area.

Putting one of his bowed legs in front of the other, Berenson took Longhi over to Court Street to see Johnny Crews, the Republican leader, a witty Scot who quickly saw that an Italian candidate, even if he was radical, might be the answer to a Republican prayer in this predominantly Italian district. The deal to back Longhi was quickly made.

The absurdity of one day glancing right and left for whoever was about to throw them into the river and the next owning the Republican nomination for Congress sent the two of them into incredulous laughter, but such situations are never so totally without meaning; time would show that Berenson might have gone into Crews's office an opportunistic buccaneer but he was something different when he came out. His and Longhi's relation to themselves and the country had begun a subtle change that would lead to unimaginable consequences. Hopeless though his chances for election were, Vinny had now stepped out of the dark and frozen world of the feudal waterfront into daylight America, where, quite literally, the most amazing things could still happen.

For Johnny Crews a Vincent Longhi candidacy might be a merely symbolic and even wry piece of theatre by which to throw Rooney off balance for a few weeks, but Vinny actually intended to win and be photographed with the president on the White House steps and send the photo by special delivery to his lavishly adoring mother. Running as a Republican, with the endorsement of the American Labor Party, he stumped the Twelfth Congressional District tirelessly, making a powerful appeal for reform. It was a hot, bitter campaign, with Rooney denouncing the Republicans for backing a left-wing upstart, and when the votes were counted, Vinny pulled in 31,000 to Rooney's 36,000—an amazingly close result considering that a few thousand votes could easily have been stolen from him.

Encouraged by his first foray into mainstream politics, Longhi decided to take Rooney on again in the '48 elections. This time the Republicans were playing it safe with a party regular, and Longhi was running on the ALP line. Now he really begged me to raise some money, and for the first and only time in my life I approached another person for a political contribution. I had been seeing Tennessee Williams on and off over the past year and had mentioned my interest in the waterfront. It now turned out that Frankie Merlo, with whom he lived in a Manhattan apartment, was the son of a Mafia chieftain in New Jersey. Frankie knew the waterfront story better than I, having sat as a young boy at his father's feet during meetings when such matters were discussed and dealt with by the old man. He insisted that Tennessee write a check for five hundred dollars, a good piece of money then. Tennessee, I thought, regarded my interest as remote from him as a writer and yet quite parallel to his lifelong sense of living among the unjust and the cruel. He sat listening to my descriptions of waterfront indignities holding his gnarled white English pug on his lap—as much to keep it from pissing on his bed again as to pet it—and with Merlo explicating for him as his adept social specialist, he seemed moved, although it was particular persons and words that touched him more than any general condition of men.

Despite Vinny's speaking ability, it was soon obvious that only some fantastic coup could dislodge Rooney, something so grandiose as to be unanswerable. And he soon hit upon it—he must make a trip to Calabria and Sicily, look up as many relatives of longshore families as he possibly could, and return with their best wishes, which he would personally deliver to several hundred households. Apart from its characteristic but efficient sentimentality, the plan had·another even more useful feature—hundreds of Italian longshoremen had two families, two wives and two sets of children. In most cases they had not deceived either the American second wife or the original in Italy, whom they continued to support and even to visit periodically in order to beget another child. But in their financial straits these trips home were often very far apart, five or six or more years. They would be in profound debt to someone bringing firsthand news of the original wife and kids—a debt most natural to repay with a vote.

With Vinny's decision to go my own took shape. America was where you got rich, but Europe was where the thinking was going on, or so you tended to imagine. America was becoming suspiciously unreal. An imaginative builder named Levitt was building wonderful, not unreasonably priced houses in a town named for himself, with two bathrooms and even attic two-by-sixes of finished lumber that made the previous generation's homes seem primitive. I was running into old atheist friends and cousins who, bizarrely, were now contributing to something they called "temple";

before the war I would not have imagined that anyone of my generation would ever go to *shul* again. From Europe, however, one heard of new men like Sartre and Camus who had come out of the Resistance and the European night with a new, politically usable democratic vision that was not bound to Moscow, apparently. I was thirsting for a new sense of the future now that fascism was dead, and with it, ironically enough, the form it had given my life in resistance to it. The yin and the yang of existence had gone slack. Italy in 1947–48 was the focus of speculation as to Europe's future, what with her immense Communist Party, the largest outside the Soviet Union, and Vinny would be useful with his ability to speak Italian.

Jane was just beginning school and Bob was even younger, and with travel abroad not yet the easy option of ordinary people, it seemed inevitable that I should make the trip of three or so weeks alone. The very leaving behind of the familiar is implicitly erotic and renewing, an opening of the soul to the unknown, a kind of expectancy that calls for aloneness, and besides, with so little confidence that I could write another commercially successful play, I needed to conserve money. In short, I fled to the future as I had once done on my bike into Harlem when life was tangling up my feet and I wanted nothing I knew around me.

The SS *America*, the least expensive way to cross the Atlantic, was two-thirds empty and rode high and vicious on rough February seas. I was desperate enough to spend my time as lone swimmer in the pool, pretending it was merely the real ocean, where one never got seasick, until it got so rough that the pool had to be closed down before I was bashed to death against the tile walls. I spent most of the last twenty-four hours at the bar standing with Albert Sharpe, who had just quit as the star of *Finian's Rainbow*, having earned all the money he would need for the rest of his life in his Irish country cottage. I let him shower my head with one gorgeous Irish story on top of another until dawn broke into the lounge portholes and we went out on deck to greet the land fog.

The first shock of Europe was a series of very simple absurdities. The great concrete piers of Cherbourg were brokenly tilted into the water; passengers were taken in by lighter to a temporary dock. Here was civil ruin rather than the wreckage of armies, and it was somehow ungraspable. I had never before thought of myself as in any way an innocent, but I did now. (The next time I had this same feeling was many years later, walking through the streets of a Harlem whose familiar apartment houses were burned out, standing in ruin.) Next, the gigantic nineteenth-century railroad station, whose stories-high, cathedrallike vaulted roof of glass panes, stretching several blocks, was totally smashed, an eyeless structure all that remained. It was all a monstrous vandalism, a rage and a spite so awesome as to strike fear into the heart for the species.

A young American in our train compartment, after fifteen minutes of inaction, suddenly called out, "When is this shootin' match supposed to start!" We all laughed, the Europeans and Vinny and I, embarrassed at his insensitivity to the deprivation all around. Absurd, too, the obsequiousness in the trainmen toward us, the *Übermenschen*, the lords of the earth, Americans. I enjoyed the feeling, unearned though it might be, even as I saw us through their resentful and envious eyes.

The sun never seemed to rise over Paris, the winter sky like a lid of iron graying the skin of one's hands and making faces wan. A doomed and listless silence, few cars on the streets, occasional trucks running on wood-burning engines, old women on ancient bicycles. Who that I passed had collaborated with the Nazis and who had hid in a cellar accompanied by his heartbeat? And what would I have done? I ordered an orange, toast, and two fried eggs for breakfast in Les Ministères across the street from the hotel, and the woman in charge and the cook and two waiters came out to watch me eat this massive amount of food, and to watch me pay for it out of a roll of cheap francs. The concierge at the Pont-Royal on the rue du Bac wore tails, but the sleeves were unraveling, and his chin always showed little nicks from having shaved with cold water. A hungry-looking, garishly got-up young woman in black lace stockings with a fallen hem on her skirt was allowed to sit in the lobby all night for the convenience of the guests, and she watched my approach with a philosopher's superior curiosity. The round brass bars across the revolving door were missing, like a lot of the plumbing and metal fittings, stolen by the Germans in the last desperate months. The concierge had to rush across Paris and back once a day to feed his rabbits. Rabbits were saving a lot of people.

In the streets no man seemed to have a matching jacket and trousers, and many who looked like professionals wore mufflers to hide bare shirtless chests. Bicycles and bicycles—which I would recall in Beijing thirty-five years later—and people hanging from crowded buses that stank like the ones in Cairo. Later on in China, Egypt, Venezuela, so much would remind me of this time in the

City of Light; the genius of Europe had been to bomb itself into what was not yet named the Third World. There were still fresh bouquets of flowers lying on sidewalks beneath plaques set in buildings to memorialize some Resistant shot there by the Nazis, who after all were also Europeans; had there been, in effect, two civil wars, in 1914 and 1939? I wrote to Mary, lonely for her, that the country seemed a wounded animal that would never rise to its feet again—France was finished. Sartre was said to hang out in the Montana Bar, but I never found him. The papers were relying on America to rearrange a new civilization, it seemed to me—as though we had the slightest idea of what to do with this failed continent. It was disappointing; I would have to go back to thinking myself into a future that certainly did not promise to exist here.

There was a *réunion* of writers in a palais near the rue de Rivoli to which I was invited by Vercors, founder of Éditions de Minuit, the French publisher of *Focus*. Catholic, Communist, Gaullist— artists and the unaffiliated were going to attempt to rebuild their wartime resistance unity, joining once more in reading their poems and making speeches into the government radio microphone that was set up in the grand eighteenth-century entrance hall of the palais, overseen by Frenchified busts of blind Eros and rounded curly-haired lovers like Pyramus and Thisbe. It was very cold standing on the marble floor, even with a couple of hundred men and women there and a glass of red wine. What joy these intellectuals drew from this gesture was not evident; their wartime spiritual unity and political toleration had been cracked by the new and rapidly deepening Cold War.

Vercors, a novelist and essayist and one of the most universally respected heroes of the Resistance, had befriended me and led me through some of the alleyways where he had evaded Germans to deliver Resistance literature and newspapers on his bicycle. If he had been discovered by those other Europeans, they would have shot him dead in the street. It was strange to think that on these lovely Parisian boulevards Frenchmen had been hunted down, shot like vermin. Again I had to wonder how I would have behaved under those circumstances, for the moral, the literary, and the political were one and the same then. As the meeting wore on in the echoing chamber of marble, the readings seeming interminable, without expression, dour, Vercors explained in whispers that this would probably be the last attempt to maintain some semblance of French culture, which would soon be completely fractured by political polemic. He pointed out Louis Aragon and Elsa

Triolet, Camus and Sartre, Mauriac and other Catholic writers. I saw people finish their readings and quietly leave.

With Soviet prestige still tremendous, Russian armies having, by common consent, saved Europe from a thousand years of Nazism, it was not easy to credit tales of Stalinist terror. People like Vercors, a slim and athletically handsome man, tolerant and just, simply went silent before reports of such events, which eviscerated the last fifteen antifascist years of all meaning. That Manichean world, with its simple and unflickering flame, the light against a surrounding darkness, was dying away just then. Truth was hung on the wall like a picture of an old country scene that was neither discarded nor looked at. The heroism of the Soviets and the allied left still went deep; during the war, in labor with Jane, our first child, Mary had wept, half-conscious and in pain, crying out, "Oh, those poor Yugoslavs!"—who at the moment were suffering the Nazi invasion of their snowy mountains.

In a freezing theatre Louis Jouvet, in *Ondine* by Jean Giraudoux, had to play the whole evening in an armchair due to illness, wrapped in muffler and sweater. People were working their toes inside their shoes and blowing on their hands, and everyone sat in his coat. It was another moving page in the sad tale of the death of a country—the heat would never be turned on again in a French theatre, there was doom everywhere, and there really was such a thing as a defeated people. But Jouvet connected with the audience in a personal way I had never experienced before, speaking *to* each of them individually in their beloved tongue. I was bored by the streams of talk and the inaction onstage, but I could understand that it was the language that was saving their souls, hearing it together and being healed by it, the one unity left to them and thus their one hope. I was moved by the tenderness of the people toward him, I who came from a theatre of combat with audiences. They were communing with Jouvet, who I thought stepped out of the role now and then to admire the author's turning of a phrase, something the audience applauded with delight. One element stuck with me, although at the time it was simply one more French strangeness—Jouvet's emotions seemed real, concrete and continuous, but he was surrounded by the unreal, a fantasy. So that words were in themselves the event, they and his emotions. I had gone so far as to cut out some lines in *All My Sons* that were too flashy, too *written,* rather than a phenomenon of what I thought of then as nature.

No day passed without the Marshall Plan somehow featured in

a headline. But the French and British governments were furious that the Germans were also to receive American aid money and have their industries rebuilt before they had restored every single brick they had smashed in England and France. The Germans clearly were to be our new friends, and the savior-Russians the enemy, an ignoble thing, it seemed to me. The new tangle was beginning to coil around itself—in twenty years I would meet Theodor Adorno in Frankfurt and be told that at this very time the German schoolbooks that contained the story of Hitler were being withdrawn under American pressure and replaced with new ones that simply left a void in the Nazi years, that hiatus for which a new German radical generation would revile the United States.

It seemed to me in later years that this wrenching shift, this ripping off of Good and Evil labels from one nation and pasting them onto another, had done something to wither the very notion of a world even theoretically moral. If last month's friend could so quickly become this month's enemy, what depth of reality could good and evil have? The nihilism—even worse, the yawning amusement—toward the very concept of a moral imperative, which would become a hallmark of international culture, was born in these eight or ten years of realignment after Hitler's death. For myself I wanted to stand with those who would not give way, not because I was sure I was good but because of a sense that there could be no aesthetic form without a moral world, only notes without a staff—an unprovable but deeply felt conviction.

My introduction to Italy was a prosciutto and pepper sandwich on Italian white bread, the best thing I had ever tasted in my life, bought from a stand in the Milan railroad station. Already I was more at ease with the Italians and Italy, where, compared to France, nothing was serious.

Ezio Tedei, an anarchist short story writer who had spent fourteen years in a Mussolini prison, owned neither shirt nor socks nor underwear, went about Rome in the February cold in only trousers, shoes, and an ancient tweed overcoat, and slept outdoors on an open balcony loaned to him by the half-dozen poor families, with a total of some twenty children, who had simply taken over a palazzo that had belonged to a high Fascist official. After I had insisted on his accepting a shirt, shorts, razor blades, and socks, he appeared some days later in his customary nudeness, explaining that he had given my gifts to some people who needed them. He would sit writing at a desk on this balcony amid the comings and goings of countless families, oblivious to conversations and shouts a yard away from his ears. The elegant desk, liberated from some sequestered drawing room, had dozens of drawers and compartments where people kept bread and groceries and he his manuscripts and his treasured Parker pen.

I noticed on one of our walks through Rome that here and there a heavy chain held the shutters of a window shut—the legal requirement, Ezio explained, for all bordellos. I wanted to visit one immediately, and he had a favorite to which we now proceeded. Just inside the entrance doorway to what must once have been a grand palace stood a column topped by a pair of copulating bronze lovers, the woman's hair streaming out as though in a high wind. A deep crimson carpet led up a marble stair to what had been a grand ballroom with floor-to-ceiling baroque mirrors. Vast bushels of crystals hung from the deeply carved ceiling, lighted, albeit dimly, by dusty bulbs. Along one wall sat some twenty-five men of all ages, some of them reading newspapers, some playing chess, some asleep, some staring across the room at a line of a dozen women who stood leaning against the mirrored wall, women dressed in Moorish vests with veiled trousers, in pure white confirmation dresses, in ordinary housewifely costumes, in panties with and without bras; with long hair, short hair, piled-up hair; barefoot, in high heels, sandals, street shoes, or shoes sparkling with sprinkles of diamondlike glass. Our century of theatre and actors. Tedei and I sat with the men and waited. The chess games continued, the newspapers kept being folded and unfolded, and the women waited vacantly, as though on line at a bus stop. Apparent indifference united us all. Now a man stood up, with no more evident motivation than a single gull rising out of the flock to take the air, and walked across the parquet to a woman who disappeared with him through a doorway as though she were going to fit him for shoes. It was as stimulating as an auction of old costumes. I remembered Chekhov's writing of his disgust with himself for having visited such a house, and my own sensation of vacancy and remoteness when, at sixteen, I was taken by my brother and his friends to an apartment on the Upper West Side for my first time. But I felt no disgust here. Tedei grinned like a proud host at one of his native city's more interesting attractions; sex, it was obvious, at least just now after twenty-five years of fascism and a terrible war, was interesting, to be sure, but far less important than eating, having a roof over one's head and clothes to keep the body warm. These women may have been a necessity, and they received the respect that necessities deserve, but that was all. The great neorealistic movies of postwar Italy that were coming out, *Open City*, *Bicycle Thief*, and the like, reflected this same integration of sexuality into life, a life that was grounded in necessity, the coherencies of food-gathering and the sustaining of family and friendships and human solidarity. In 1948 Italy did not yet know the problems of surplus, let alone glut, and the accompanying fantasies of unbounded, limitless self. Here in this grimy ballroom was a certain sharing of humility before the nature of mankind, a chastening acceptance.

But the glimpse of the West's future that I had imagined I would find in Europe was as confusing there as it was in Brooklyn. The Italian Communist Party might be the largest in Europe, but it was quietly advising people to vote for the Christian Democrats in the upcoming election lest America cut off its food shipments and the country starve, the Russians having nothing to send in the event of a Red electoral victory. I was still under the sway of an apocalyptic idea of history and constantly had to remind myself that the crowds in the streets and the people we met, far from being the innocent victims of Mussolini's stupidity and arrogant posturing, had for the most part supported fascism or not resisted it. Surprisingly few were, like Ezio Tedei, dangerous enough to have been put away, and he seemed even now a supremely innocent if not naive man awaiting a revolution whose signs I could find nowhere.

There was a so-called Ring around Rome where thousands of homeless families were living in lightless caves dug into precipices and hillsides. We climbed up and sat with them, skin-and-bones people living in their own filth, lugging pails of water up from hydrants far down below in the streets. From some of the caves they had a view of brand-new apartment houses going up across a highway as the rain of February swept across their faces. This was the Rome of *Bicycle Thief*. Of course it could not have dawned on me that in forty years New York would admit to even more homeless than Rome had after the devastation of war. Nor would I have easily believed then in the erosion of outrage, including my own most of the time, to the point where I am used to this catastrophe as a merely sad consequence of life in imperial New York, the world's most exciting city.

South of Foggia the red flag flew over one city hall after another, and Longhi and I would sit with peasants who drew out from under their beds maps of the latifundia, the estates that would be divided up among them once the Communists had won the oncoming national election. They had their names written on parcels on these maps and were already sure where each one's boundaries were going to be and with their dark fingers were glad to trace them for me. Moving up and down the country that winter, almost three years after the end of the war, I realized one day that we had not seen a single fat Italian. Where were the ample mamas and the belly-heaving papas? It was all over in Italy, finished. People everywhere were asking if we thought Italy could be admitted as the forty-ninth state in the American Union, and they weren't kidding either.

Still, it was not sad in the way France seemed to be; Italian energy was like a weed that took root anywhere, no matter what. In a small town in the southeast, every afternoon about four, Vinny's maiden aunt Emilia, a schoolteacher in her fifties, would rush out into the square, where loudspeakers erupted with speeches phoned in from the Christian Democratic Party headquarters in Foggia, the provincial capital, while a few yards away another loudspeaker bawled out a fiery speech by the Communists, wired from Rome. The cacophony was spectacular. A passionately sincere string of a woman, Emilia would try to herd strollers to collect around the Demo-Christian loudspeaker and turn their backs on the Communist one. By five-thirty the loudspeakers cut out so that the evening promenade could begin; the party lines melted as people did as they had done for a thousand years, walked around and around the piazza, the marriageable young stopping to chat and look one another over like penguins. Emilia was fascinated to learn that I was a Jew, having taken for granted that they no longer existed—not because of what was not yet called the Holocaust but out of some unexamined belief that they had all been converted after the resurrection of Christ or had somehow vanished into the pages of the Bible. "But," she smiled reassuringly, "you believe in Christ, too, of course." I thought, when I informed her otherwise, that a flicker of terror passed over her devout eyes as she stared at me, but we were soon friendly again, it being part of her faith that not everything in life was supposed to be comprehensible. I, on the other hand, still imagined that nothing was beyond the reach of the mind.

One afternoon a church procession appeared on the street and stopped what little traffic there was, and as we waited while the golden crucifix and the saint's statue were carried past by chanting choirboys, I wondered if indeed the old ways were as dead as people thought. A middle-aged man in front of us stood with bowed head, his hat over his heart, and after the procession passed, Longhi delicately asked him what sacred occasion was being celebrated. "Who the hell knows?" he replied, stuck his hat back on, and hurried impatiently across the street. That, to me, was Italy then, a touching performance wrapped around a cynical joke. The French took collapse far more to heart, as though they had been cheated unfairly of some victory or had bad consciences for having collaborated. The Italians seemed to understand that as usual they had kidded themselves with Mussolini's grandiosity. And anyway the main idea was to live, not die for something.

On the lovely Adriatic breakwater in Mola di Bari, just above the heel of the boot, was a different sort of procession at around five in the afternoon. Longhi had a number of addresses from Red Hook longshoremen's families to look up here, and he went from house to house, a one-man Red Cross, bringing news of Brooklyn, making notes on the ages of the children and how the women were faring. The husbands' second families back in Brooklyn were of course never mentioned, but their existence was understood. These women's dramas were being ground out grain by grain between the molars of economic necessity, and if some of the "first wives" were now grim and aging, others were still in their thirties, and their doe's eyes revealed how fearful they were of ultimate abandonment. But Vinny loved few things more than to reassure women, and they adored looking up at him, so unusually tall for an Italian and so full of good, healthy food.

At around five we saw a promenade at the seafront consisting of an unusual number of single men walking together, some arm in arm, a common custom, but not dressed like other Italians; they wore dark New York overcoats and gray New York hats with brims turned up all around, and buttoned white shirts without ties, and pointy, thin-soled, brilliantly shined city shoes. In one of the cafés facing the sea we accosted four who were having their coffee. At first they spoke Italian, but Vinny's witty grin brought acknowledging smiles and they happily lapsed into Brooklynese. Clearly they were on the lam, "the boys" waiting out some threat of prosecution in New York, Chicago, Philadelphia, or LA, condemned to watch the profitless sun going up and down in this beautiful but boring exile until the fix was in and they could hit the States again.

Italy was giving me courage for the play forming in my head, *A View from the Bridge,* but I was not yet sure I dared write as intimately about Italians as it would demand. All I was sure I understood was that the difference between America and Europe was that Europe was full of relatives and in America the pull of the blood connection was gone. In Rome, Vinny felt compelled to visit a cousin, a captain who worked at the top staff level of the War Department of Italy. Formal, foot-clomping guards in white spats and white gloves crisscrossed balletically in front of the entrance of what amounted to their Pentagon, rifles in firm grips held before them. At the tiny information wicket Vinny asked to see Captain Franco Longhi, but the attendant behind the thin bars was sorry, there could be no visitors here without previous notification.

"Captain Longhi is my cousin."

The face of the man behind the window went still. "Your *cousin*?"

"I'm from America. Brooklyn."

"Brooklyn!"

Instantly he was on the phone, and I thought I saw his eyes growing moist. In a moment we were in an elevator and, emerging from it, were greeted by three or four colonels, a couple of generals, and weepy women secretaries looking on with hands clasped under their chins as Captain Longhi embraced Vinny—Italians instantly divide up into audiences and actors—and all work halted here in the heart of the Italian military as we sat around on desks for at least half an hour listening to the cousins exchanging news of various relatives, some of whom had died in this or that Italian battle or of old age and disease. A general finally ordered the captain to take us to lunch, and over our salad he asked Vinny if he had an in with the Parker Pen Company in America; the one thing you could surely sell in Italy in 1948 was a genuine Parker pen. There were unfortunately a lot of fakes made in Naples, but people were on to them now . . .

"This is the way the world ends" kept revolving in my head as we walked on the Neapolitan promenades, which, with their baroque lampposts, were either tilted toward the bay or had been bombed to rubble even as the facing hotels kept enough lights on to invite nonexistent guests. The young whores roved in chattering packs and reached down between our legs and laughed, calling us fags for not taking them on. In daylight, women balancing laundry baskets on their heads walked through the street crowds near the foreigners' hotels and with magical hands snatched the hats off passing strangers, quickly popping them into their baskets and leaving the victims to turn around and around looking for a hat that had vanished in air. Once I was sitting in a carriage alone, waiting for Vinny to change some money in a nearby bank, when a young guy came over and began pulling our valises literally from under my feet, quite as though he had some instruction from us to take them. I complained in English, and he looked up with a certain civilized recognition but went right on trying to pull the bags out of the carriage until I kicked his hands with the heel of my shoe, at which he looked up at me again and shrugged and went his way, no hard feelings. Another performance.

And the wicked Neapolitan stories then. Of the parish priest who came upon a long line of neighborhood people in front of a house and followed it up the stairs into a second-floor apartment. Entering, he found one of his elderly parishioners charging people a few cents each to go into the bedroom to get a look at his unmarried young daughter in bed with her new baby, which was black. There were many black American troops in Naples then, and a black baby born to a white woman was both scandalous and somehow unbelievable, like a miracle. The priest, of course, exploded in outrage. "It's bad enough your daughter is not married, but you are brazen enough to profit from her misfortune before the whole neighborhood!" The girl's father took the priest aside and whispered, "Don't worry, Padre, it's not really her baby."

It was finished in Italy, all over, but just outside Rome was an improvised backyard restaurant with four or five wobbly tables and a sign overhead reading, "Come In. Eat! Nobody Ever Died Here!" For a moment in history we were in a place where people most enjoyed the distinction of being alive and not dead, an aristocracy of survivors.

A different kind of survivor, though, at the windy Mola di Bari littoral. The town mayor confided that the *"ebrei,"* Jews out of the German death camps, had been given shelter in the line of grand seafront palazzos that had been built by prominent Fascisti who had fled or were now in prison. Vinny found the way, which was difficult because the British were pressuring the Italian government not to allow concentration camp Jews into the country or, once in, to prevent them from taking ship to Palestine, and no one wanted to mention their presence to strangers. All Mola di Bari and Bari conspired to keep the secret. Finally at evening we found them, hundreds of people camped in perhaps twenty large houses facing the Adriatic, many nearly piled one on top of the other in corridors. When we walked in I felt an icy hostility such as I had never known, a sense of my nonexistence, of my being transparent. The women turned away from us to look after children, men and boys passed us by like draughts of air. But I knew that to make a wrong move that could be interpreted as aggression would mean being torn to pieces. I approached two young men, unshaven but clean, who watched me with looks of undisguised threat. I tried English, Vinny did some Italian, and finally I attempted some pidgin Yiddish-German, simply to wish them well and to identify

myself as a Jew. They were not interested in my problem and could
see no help in me for their own, which was simply to get aboard
a ship to Palestine and leave the graveyard of Europe forever.
Their mistrust was like acid in my face; I was talking to burnt wood,
charred iron, bone with eyes. In coming years I would wonder why
it never occurred to me to throw in my lot with them when they
were the product of precisely the catastrophe I had in various ways
given my writing life to try to prevent. To this day, thinking of
them there on their dark porches silently scanning the sea for their
ship, unwanted by any of the civilized powers, their very presence
here illegal and menaced by British diplomatic intervention, I feel
myself disembodied, detached, ashamed of my stupidity, my failure to recognize myself in them.

It reminds me of a similar hole in my heart regarding my response to the first report of Hiroshima. How could I have felt such
wonder? Such relief, too, that the war was over at last? How could
I have dared study the first descriptions of the workings of the
bomb and feel some pride in man's intellect?

Whence this detachment? One day it would seem the very soul
of the matter: a failure to imagine will make us die.

In his passionately intimate Italian, Vinny asked the hotel clerk
where we could find a place to eat lunch. Foreigners were still so
rare at the Hotel des Palmes that the man was embarrassed to
inform us that no restaurant existed as yet in Palermo, except one
on the other side of town that served only dinner. Indeed, as we
could see, even our hotel was only half standing after the misfortune with that American bomb. By this time Europe to me was a
middle-aged concierge in tails with a wing collar and a stained gray
silk tie and broken fingernails. The lobby, surrounded by elaborate
archways with heavy buttresses suitable for masking trysts and
quiet business conversations of doubtful legality, ended abruptly at
a vast brown shroud of canvas beyond which lay the ruins of the
fallen half of the building.

Now the bell captain, a younger and more up-to-date man, intervened; he thought the one restaurant on the other side of town
might serve lunch, but it was hard to spot, there being no sign on
the window as yet. Holding both palms vertical, he instructed us
how to traverse the broken city. Except for our morning coffee we
had not eaten since yesterday when we boarded the little boat
to cross the Strait of Messina along with a lot of Sicilian workers

who had had the sense to bring their own food. We set out briskly.

From the outside the hotel's windows were immaculately clean, a reassuring sign of the will to live, but a mountain of rubble leaned against the side wall, on which elegant wallpaper still clung, and carved plaster vines arched over bricked-up doorways. Puffs of cement dust blew up under every step we took, and eyebrows were white with lime. On every street men were climbing up and down ladders carrying hods, backbreaking loads of wet cement; occasionally a waiter in apron climbed a ladder carrying a tray of coffee and bread for some boss above. A donkey loaded with iron rods was trying to bite the arm of a boy attempting to make it move over rubble, a tiny Fiat truck with gears whining seemed about to capsize with a load twenty feet high. Stately black-clad women with faint mustaches commanded whole streets with their husky baritone complaints and spanked girls as old as sixteen for various infractions, forever sending them home. The men spoke only to other men. Two stories up, a woman in a window hefted her infant son, showing the city one of its naked little gods. But unlike Naples, Palermo had no whores in the streets. Along the broken harbor, whose piers lay overturned in the water, squadrons of brown rats worked over a fallen palm tree, as undisturbed by our passing as if licensed by the city. On the sunlit water under the perfect blue sky a lone freighter was unloading onto lighters the bags of American wheat that alone kept the city alive. With the national elections only weeks away, the American ambassador had come and made a speech and, it was said, had taken a handful of grain and poured it over the head of a small laughing boy and announced, quite needlessly, that if the Communists were elected this grain would naturally cease to arrive—merely one more sign that it was all over here, Italy was finished, a mendicant and a whore. Now and then a horse-drawn carriage went clopping by, a *carrozza* out of the nineties back in service as the country slid down into its past. But the workers still hurried up and down the ladders rebuilding and plastering walls in the sun with the immemorial Italian affection for wet cement.

The restaurant was the only completely reconstructed building on the shattered little square, and indeed it had no sign in its window. Coming in from the glare outside, we thought that the eight or ten white-clothed tables were all empty. The proprietor, the first fat Italian we had so far seen, looked surprised as he came out to greet us from behind a blue cotton curtain at the back and somewhat nervously asked what we wished, as though we might be his first postwar patrons. Not until we had taken our seats did

I happen to glance about and see this amazing row of silent people seated behind a banquet of a dozen tables that had been pushed together along one wall. The mere glance left me bewildered by their totally mismatched social levels. A bleached platinum night-club blonde with deep rosy cleavage beside a traditional dark Sicilian mama wearing a black shawl over her head; a ruddy young boy of fourteen beside a peasantlike worker in denim shirt; a rather wan man with eyeglasses, possibly a newspaperman or an intellectual, between a thick laborer and a pallid businessman with a heavy mustache; two men who had to be gangsters in double-breasted suits and trimmed mustaches; another hooker with pearls in her hair beside a mild-looking family doctor type . . .

And all in absolute silence, unabashedly observing us in the otherwise vacant room. Everything was suddenly reversed; we were the actors, the Sicilians the audience. The menu was also a surprise, with the first lamb and mutton we had been offered in Italy; even in Naples and Rome there had been only fowl and fish. The proprietor rubbed his hands together in the usual welcoming gesture, but his charged eyes were still more preoccupied than warm. He left us and went—I was about to write "upstage"—and disappeared behind the blue curtain at the back.

Longhi was turning beet red as he studied his menu, and seemed to be forcing his eyes to stay on it. Between expressionless lips, he said, "Don't look now, but you know who's behind you?"

"Mussolini."

"Stop fucking around, this is serious."

"King Victor Emmanuel. Balzac. Louis B. Mayer."

"Lucky Luciano."

Like most newspaper readers, I was aware that Luciano had been exiled to Italy after Special Prosecutor Thomas E. Dewey had nailed him as a Mafia chief, brutal killer, and head of prostitution, gambling, and other assorted rackets. Winning Luciano's conviction, at first thought impossible, had made Dewey a national figure; now he was favored to become, for the second time, the Republican nominee for president and to beat Truman in the coming election. Luciano was the prince of thieves, the worst, a veritable horned monster.

"Don't order that stuff."

I heard Brooklyn and looked up to see the unforgettable face, which I recognized from photos, telling the proprietor, "Bring them my lunch," whereupon he drew up a chair and sat at our table and the proprietor happily fled as though released from anxiety now that he had the permission he required.

"Cholly! God! . . ." Vinny thrust his hand at Luciano—whose proper name was Charles—as though the honor of it all was nearly beyond his powers to bear. Vinny's face, however, was perspiring.

"Where yiz from?"

"The States, Cholly."

"Whe'bouts?"

"Brooklyn, Cholly. My name is Vincent Longhi, this is my friend Miller."

I got only a passing nod as I was obviously not Italian. It was Longhi who interested him since, for one thing, Brooklyn had been his home base. It managed to occur to me that Vinny must no doubt have been the first Italian from Brooklyn of whose arrival in Sicily he had not been forewarned.

"Whe'bouts in Brooklyn?"

"Well, I'm spending a lot of time in Red Hook now, Cholly," Vinny said, and laughed familiarly. "Home, huh?"

"Right, that's right. What do you do?"

"I'm a lawyer."

Luciano gave a very short nod and turned to me. "You a lawyer too?"

"No, I'm a writer."

"Wha' paper?"

"No, he writes plays, Cholly . . . you know, the theatre."

Luciano nodded doubtfully. "What're you got in there?" He pointed to the leather box in which lay my eight-millimeter Kodak movie camera.

"That's my camera," I said.

"I see it?"

As though up from the floor I felt body heat and, turning, saw beside me a six-footer standing over my camera box. He had a big pistol sticking out of his jacket, probably a thirty-eight. He was looking down at the box, which I now opened, taking out the camera. This he promptly removed from my hand and, making a half-turn so that it faced away from his master, opened it, then closed it and handed it back to me and said, "Thanks."

My eye following his turning body, I saw that the entire line of diners along the wall had simply disappeared, were gone, vanished, and without a sound, not the scuff of a sole on the floor or the scrape of a chair. We were all alone.

Luciano's spring had ever so slightly slacked off, and he gave us an ordinary civilized depressed smile. "So what're yiz doin' here?"

"Just sort of touring around," I said.

He nearly laughed at my joke. "Touring in *Palermo*?"

As our lunch was served by the now reassured proprietor, Longhi explained his plan to locate the families and his ambition to be a congressman. Like Anastasia, Luciano took very seriously this manifest of the achieving spirit in a young Italian and gave it a deep look and many commendatory nods. I had a chance now to realize that I had never seen a face so sharply divided down the center. The right side was hooded, the mouth downturned and the cheek drawn flat. This was the side he killed with. The left, however, had an eye not at all cold but rather interested and intelligent and inquisitive, his social eye, fit for a family dentist. And he wore rimless middle-aged glasses. Lincoln was the only other man with so divided a face, at least that I could think of.

"Who do you know?" Luciano asked Vinny, who took a breath and ran off a list of Mafiosi none of whom, I was convinced, he had ever actually met but whose names were golden in the community as the great successes. Again like Anastasia, Luciano was aggrieved by injustices done him in the name of law, for he was even forbidden to set foot on the Italian mainland, let alone to visit his beloved Naples, where he claimed an aunt of his mother's lay dying, calling desperately for one last look at him. He insisted on paying our bill, dropping a lump of money on the table without counting it ("Shit, it's all funny money anyways"), and when I got up and said we were going to continue our little exploratory walk, he first offered and then insisted on driving us back to the hotel, where we had no desire to go for a few more hours.

I now invented: "I'm thinking of writing about Sicily, and I want to take a look around."

"No, no, no, come on, we got the car, we drive you," he persisted, and it was clear that we were not as yet to be let out of his sight. At this point the street door was unlocked by the bowing proprietor; I had not noticed it being locked in the first place.

"Beautiful car," I said, admiring his sporty big green Lancia as we got in, the bodyguard behind the wheel with me beside him, and Vinny next to Luciano in the backseat.

"Gimme a Chevy anytime," he said. He certainly was homesick. And in such captivity we were driven back to the hotel, an irritating comedy to me but from Vinny's anxious levity not to him.

Following Vinny's lead, I went to the desk, where we asked for our key just as Luciano was handed his. "You're in the next room!" he said and looked into my eyes. I could only confirm that, yes, our key numbers indicated we had adjoining rooms. With no desire to go upstairs I nevertheless found myself getting into the elevator ahead of Luciano rather than behind him, as I had offered to do, he being my senior, and there was no talk at all as we waited to reach our floor, he with his back pressed against the elevator wall. At our doors we nodded farewell to him, unable to think of anything to say.

Vinny fell on his back on the bed holding his head. "Jesus Christ! And we got the next room, too!" His genuine worry surprised me. "But, man! We could be the FBI or some Mob guys who came to put a hole in his head! . . ."

If there was danger, it was making me sleepy, along with the uncustomarily elaborate lunch, and I lay down and napped. Vinny went on talking for a while but finally gave up and fell asleep too. I believed in a great many things in those days, among them the mystical protections of an American passport.

A knock woke us. Vinny was on his feet listening. Another knock. He glanced at me and swallowed. I started to laugh, and it began to infect him, and he bent over to smother his paroxysms. The third knock straightened him up. Somebody most definitely intended to see us and knew we were in here, and that could only be Luciano or a representative. Vinny opened the door.

A tall, marvelously handsome young man stood there in a blue navy watch cap and neat plaid mackinaw and peasant's brogans. "Signor Longhi," he said, smiling, his whole being emanating command and ease of soul, a young man for whom the world was made. "I understand," he said as he sat with us and removed his knitted cap with the casual confidence of one who owned everything south of Rome, "that you wish to tour Sicily."

"That's right," Vinny said, "but we are told there is no gasoline to be had." Luciano was the only one who knew of our wish to tour the island.

"There is *some* gasoline," the young man said.

"But we have no car, and it is difficult to rent . . ."

"There are *some* cars. When do you wish to start?"

"Well, how's tomorrow morning, is that possible?"

"Yes, it is possible."

"We have some money but not too much. How much will it cost, do you know?"

"Oh, no, no, you are my guests. Unless you have some American cigarettes?"

We certainly did, and opened our bags to give him a few packs. When he saw our four cartons he took three of them, which he tucked under his arm. This offering of ours warmed his pride, and with some prompting from Vinny he began to tell his story. His teeth were a row of square pearls, and his hands could knock a horse down, yet he seemed lithe and flat-bellied, a hero proud of his apparently fabulous rise in life.

He was now twenty-four, but as a mere teenager when the Germans had occupied the country he had managed to control the entire vegetable supply of Palermo "with the cooperation of the peasants," in short, by dominating the roads into the city with his peasant gunmen. By the last year of the occupation he so totally controlled the gasoline dumps on the island that the Germans—he laughed with sly joy at this—had decided to give up trying to fight his men, whom they called bandits, and simply paid him a tax for every tank truck that moved into the city limits. This was entirely satisfactory.

His story finished, he rose, shook our hands, thanked us for the cigarettes, and left.

"He never gave us his name," I said.

Resuming our walking tour of the half-ruined city, toward evening we headed in the direction of the single "nightclub-restaurant" and, rounding a corner, nearly ran into a man hardly five feet tall wearing a black cape and a beret and sporting a ferocious mustache and walking stick.

"Louie!"

"Vinny!"

Lifting him up off the ground, Vinny kissed the little fellow, who had been a New Yorker for more than a decade after Mussolini exiled him in the thirties. Now he was back with a vengeance, having been elected to the Senate of the Sicilian Parliament.

His welcome at the restaurant was princely, and we were given a ringside table. Vinny could hardly wait to tell the senator about our adventure. He had spent half a decade in one of Mussolini's jails as a political prisoner and listened with what I took to be diminishing amusement to Vinny's excited reenactment of the terrors of actually meeting Lucky Luciano and later the mysterious young man.

A small party of guests was now being seated at another ringside table some twenty feet away. A vaguely familiar round-busted woman with pearls in her hair, and—was it possible?—Luciano and his strongarm guy. The great killer saw Vinny and just barely nodded as he sat down. I turned as calmly as I could to interrupt. "He's here," I muttered.

Vinny took one glance and then lowered his head. "Jesus! He's going to think we're following him!"

"Following who?" the senator asked.

"Luciano. That's him over there!"

The little senator looked across at Luciano's table, reached into his breast pocket, drew out a pearl-handled snub-nosed revolver as smoothly as if it were a fountain pen, and laid it on the white tablecloth next to his wineglass. Grinning contemptuously under his luxuriant mustache, in a voice loud enough to hail a taxi, he called out, "Luciano? Luciano is my *prick*!"

I have always lacked a flight reflex; in its place I have a denial reaction that refrigerates me and slows down all my movements. I looked down at my plate, memorizing its border pattern, while through the corner of my eye I saw that Luciano, his bravo, and the pearl-haired woman were also not reacting and that the waiters were continuing to move about and the maître d' smoothly guiding another party to a table.

Not yet returning his pistol to his pocket, the senator explained that the Mafia had recently killed a number of Socialist organizers and Communists and that he would be perfectly happy, as he thought Luciano was aware, to fight it out with him right here and now. Longhi and I, needless to say, were not as happy as he was at the prospect, but some wonderful spaghetti and a broiled fish with spicy sauce cheered us, and presumably Luciano and his party as well. We all finished our meals as though nothing had happened.

"We are in Luciano's power," I said as we lay down to sleep. "What's going to happen in the morning? Do we accept the car?"

"Maybe he called it off now," Vinny surmised, half hopefully. Worried but full of good food and fine red wine, we slept soundly despite what I now concluded was the waste of three cartons of cigarettes.

Next morning as promised, a little Fiat with driver was waiting at the front door of the hotel. The driver, a middle-aged depressive in a rumpled business suit, with no hat and a green tie that seemed to have been nibbled by mice, understood immediately that we wished to travel the whole island, and off we went.

A mountainous if often water-hungry Eden, Sicily was possessed by secretive people. As we went through villages and hamlet streets, they glanced at us from fields and houses as though we were to be executed shortly and were best left alone. But Vinny went on happily searching out his families, made his little speeches, collected the names of the living and the dead. It was all perfectly cynical and finally quite moving. The truth was that he was fulfilling a desperate need in these people to communicate over an ocean not only of water but of indifference to their awful loneliness. The women, many of them young and strong and initially greeting us suspiciously like frightening visions out of the sky in this place where few strangers meant them well, were soon won over and sat in prayerful adoration of Vinny's cheering reports of husbands and brothers and sons far off in Brooklyn, and of course he loved his noble role.

The way we got our fuel troubled me. We would pull up to an isolated grocery store out in the country with a lone dust-covered gas pump beside the road, and our driver would cut his engine and in the silence simply wait. No sign of life for a few moments, but presently a man would appear and wordlessly walk to the hose, stick it into the tank, crank out the gas, replace the cap, and walk back into his store without a lira being paid or a syllable exchanged. It was beginning to look like the swamp called Something for Nothing, from which there is no return. Meanwhile the driver, despite Vinny's being able to understand him, would utter not a word mile after mile, hour after hour. But suddenly in Siracusa, a town still in partial ruin as a result of the war, he stopped the car, shut off the engine, got out and opened the door, and with a gesture behind him said, *"Teatro."*

I got out, and there indeed was the steel-fenced ruin of the tremendous ancient Greek theatre. Why had he stopped here?— unless Luciano or the young bandit had instructed him to, for me, a writer of plays. I made my way down the stone tiers of that vast, vine-grown, sun-blasted amphitheatre chiseled out of the mountain, and at last stood on the rock stage that ended with a sheer drop to the blue sea just behind it and the arch of sky overhead. I felt something close to shame at how suffocatingly private our theatre had become, how impoverished by a psychology that was no longer involved with the universalities of fate. Was it possible that fourteen thousand people had sat facing the spot on which I stood? Hard to grasp how the tragedies could have been written for such massive crowds when in our time the mass audience all but demanded vulgarization. If the plays were not actually part of religious observances, it is hard to imagine what it was that fenced them off from the ordinary vulgarity of most human diversions. Still, religion alone does not entirely explain the foreverness of the architecture, the sculpture, and the plays themselves—the inexhaustible tension of their unadorned straight line from intention to the exploding flare of consequences realized at last. Amazing that the past's domination of the present should have inspired in me a reassurance of order in this colony of Greece, a city that had never known more than a few periods of peace, a land never tranquil, fought over since the end of the Stone Age by nearly every tribe in Europe, from North Africa to Denmark. Yet amid such chaos such symmetry—how was it possible? What had kept them from despair, why are those plays so filled with sun? Surely they knew no less than we the betrayal of human hopes, the deaths of children? In Ezra Pound's translation of *Ajax*, the hero's final, agonized cry, "IT ALL COHERES!," victoriously declares life justified, and even his betrayal and death. Was coherency the triumph, the system's manifestation and therefore God's okay, while our flux of choices merely soothes the entrepreneurial loneliness of the untribed, self-warring soul? Surely one sound was never in this place—applause; they must have left in amazement, renewed as brothers and sisters of the moon and sun.

Almost ten years later I found myself sitting on a plane next to the young director Peter Brook, who was showing me newspaper clippings on a subject he wanted to make into a movie: the hunting down of Salvatore Giuliano, the fearsome Sicilian bandit, by a virtual Italian army. He had finally been gunned down in the courtyard of a country house. Giuliano by this time was a legend all over Europe. The journalists could not quite decide whether he had stolen from the rich to give to the poor or, a mere bum, from everybody without discrimination. Was he a Mafia stooge? Not quite, apparently. A hero, then? Certainly not, he was far too bloodthirsty. But women, it was said, so adored him that he must have had real charm. I turned a page to a large close-up of the dead face. In the grainy blowup I was sure I saw our friend in the mackinaw.

Longhi lost the election, this time by a landslide—only one among many signs that the political climate was changing. I was off on another tack by now: the salesman was crowding the piers out of my head.

But Italian images would always hang behind my eyes like painted scenes. In a town whose name I have forgotten, somewhere in central Sicily on a beautiful sunny day in winter, I saw a dozen men standing around a well in the middle of a dusty piazza. They were in their twenties and early thirties, strong-bodied, with hard, hoe-curved hands and the burnt skin of peasants, masons, woodcutters. We had paused at a rotting country café for a glass of juice and learned that it was customary for men to come to the well around noon, just in case one of the surrounding latifundia might need an extra worker in the middle of the day, and for lack of anything else to do they just hung around until it got dark, when they went home. Always hungry, they were offering themselves, but all they were eating was time. Suddenly this image locked into place, connecting itself to the story Vinny had told me months before about the Red Hook longshoreman who had betrayed some illegal immigrant relatives and had disappeared. This glimpse in Sicily of desperate, workless men standing in their hunger around that well made monstrous the idea of their betrayal after they had succeeded in escaping this slow dying in the sun. And somehow their story attached itself in my mind to the theatre on which I had climbed around in Siracusa. But I was not ready to write such a play, not yet.

Back in New York it was a hard cold winter. One afternoon, after attending to some business in midtown, I was about to head for the subway and a bit of warmth when my eye caught *The Testament of Dr. Mabuse* on one of the Forty-second Street marquees. I decided to look in on it again. It was one of the films that over the years since I had first seen it had become part of my own dream tissue and had the same intimacy as something I had invented myself.

·The dingy theatre at three o'clock in the afternoon was almost empty, and seeing a movie during working hours still felt vaguely sinful. Even worse, I had been making preliminary sketches of scenes and ideas for a salesman play and should have been home at my desk. I was still at the stage of trying to convince myself that I could find a structural arch for the story of the Lomans, as I called the family. The name had appeared suddenly under my hand one evening as I was making my vagrant notes, still unconvinced that I would take up this project for my next work. "Loman" had the sound of reality, of someone who had actually lived, even if I had never known anyone by that name.

Now, watching Fritz Lang's old film, I was drawn into the astounding tale, gradually recalling it from the past. From time to time, Paris is experiencing fires, derailments, explosions, but the chief of the Sûreté is baffled because he can find no motive for these catastrophes, which he has come to believe are not accidental but the work of criminals. But to what end and for whose profit he cannot imagine. He visits a great psychiatrist, Dr. Mabuse, who heads a famous clinic outside Paris. After hearing the chief out, the doctor explains that indeed these are probably not accidents but that the perpetrators will be very difficult to find. They may be lawyers, clerks, housewives, mechanics, people of all classes who have one thing in common—a disgust with civilization and the wish simply to destroy it. Being psychological and moral, the profit is impossible to track.

The chief, played by Otto Wernicke, a massive actor the size of Lee J. Cobb (whom, incidentally, I had not yet met or heard much about), proceeds to send out men to keep watch on the crowds that collect at fires and other calamities. In time one young detective notices a man watching a particularly awful fire in an orphanage and recalls having observed him at a previous fire. He begins to track this fellow through the city and is led into a great printing plant closed for the night. The tension under Lang's direction is almost unbearably visceral as the detective moves around the massive printing machines in the darkness, keeping his eye on the suspect, who now opens a steel door and vanishes through it. The detective follows, opens the door, goes down a flight of steel stairs, and finds himself in a basement auditorium that is about a quarter filled with men and women representing every class of people in Paris, from pretentious business types to common laborers, students, and shopkeepers. They seem unrelated and sit quite apart from one another, all watching a curtain drawn across a stage. From behind it now is heard a voice that in quiet, rather business-like tones instructs the audience on the next objective, a Paris hospital that is to be dynamited and set afire. The detective rushes the stage, parts the curtain—and discovers a phonograph playing a record. The chase is on.

He slips into a tiny office, quietly shuts the door, switches on the light, and sits down at a phone to call his boss, the chief played by Wernicke. The camera moves into a close-up on the young detective's desperate face as he clamps the receiver to his ear and whispers, "Hello? Hello! Lohmann? Lohmann!" The light snaps out and the screen goes black before he can give his location. The next shot finds him in an asylum in a white gown, seated on a bed with his hand up to his ear gripping a nonexistent phone receiver, a look of total terror in his face, repeating, "Lohmann? Lohmann? Lohmann?"

My spine iced as I realized where I had gotten the name that had lodged so deep in me. It was more than five years since I had last seen the film, and if I had been asked I never could have dredged up the name of the chief of the Sûreté in it. In later years I found it discouraging to observe the confidence with which some commentators on *Death of a Salesman* smirked at the heavy-handed symbolism of "Low-man." What the name really meant to me was a terror-stricken man calling into the void for help that will never come.

Memory inevitably romanticizes, pressing reality to recede like pain. When the escaping Hebrews saw the waters rushing in to cover the God-dried seabed, drowning the pursuing Egyptian army, they sat down on the shore to catch their breaths and promptly forgot all their previous years of miserable argufying and internecine spitefulness.

Now, with only the serene blue sea before them, they were soon telling their children how wonderful life used to be, even under the Egyptians, when at least they were never allowed to forget they were all Jews and therefore had to help one another and be human. Not like now, when everybody's out for himself, etc. . . . The brain heals the past like an injury, things were always better than they are now.

Already in the sixties I was surprised by the common tendency to think of the late forties and early fifties as some sort of renaissance in the New York theatre. If that was so, I was unaware of it. I thought the theatre a temple being rotted out with commercialized junk, where mostly by accident an occasional good piece of work appeared, usually under some disguise of popular cultural coloration such as a movie star in a leading role.

That said, it now needs correction; it was also a time when the audience was basically the same for musicals and light entertainment as for the ambitious stuff and had not yet been atomized, as it would be by the mid-fifties, into young and old, hip and square, or even political left and middle and right. So the playwright's challenge was to please not a small sensitized supporting clique but an audience representing, more or less, all of America. With ticket prices within reason, this meant that an author was writing for his peers, and if such was really not the case statistically, it was sufficiently so to support an illusion that had a basis in reality. After all, it was not thought particularly daring to present T. S. Eliot's *The Cocktail Party* on Broadway, or Laurence Olivier in a Greek tragedy, or Giraudoux's *The Madwoman of Chaillot,* or any number of other ambitious works. To be sure, such shows had much shorter lives than the trash, but that was to be expected, for most people would much rather laugh than cry, rather watch an actor being hit on the head by a pig bladder than by some painful truth.

The net of it all was that serious writers could reasonably assume they were addressing the whole American mix, and so their plays, whether successfully or not, stretched toward a wholeness of experience that would not require specialists or a coterie to be understood. As alienated a spirit as he was, O'Neill tried for the big audience, and Clifford Odets no less so, along with every other writer longing to prophesy to America, from Whitman and Melville to Dreiser and Hemingway and on.

For Europe's playwrights the situation was profoundly different, with society already split beyond healing between the working class and its allies, who were committed to a socialist destiny, and the bourgeois mentality that sought an art of reassurance and the pleasures of forgetting what was happening in the streets. (The first American plays I saw left me wondering where the characters came from. The people I knew were fanatics about surviving, but onstage everyone seemed to have mysteriously guaranteed incomes, and though every play had to have something about "love," there was nothing about sex, which was all there was in Brooklyn, at least that I ever noticed.) An American avant-garde, therefore, if only because the domination of society by the middle class was profoundly unchallenged, could not simply steal from Brecht or even Shaw and expect its voice to reach beyond the small alienated minority that had arrived in their seats already converted to its aims. That was not the way to change the world.

For a play to do that it had to reach precisely those who accepted everything as it was; great drama is great questions or it is nothing but technique. I could not imagine a theatre worth my time that did not want to change the world, any more than a creative scientist could wish to prove the validity of everything that is already known. I knew only one other writer with the same approach, even if he surrounded his work with a far different aura. This was Tennessee Williams.

If only because he came up at a time when homosexuality was absolutely unacknowledgeable in a public figure, Williams had to belong to a minority culture and understood in his bones what a brutal menace the majority could be if aroused against him. I lived with much the same sense of alienation, albeit for other reasons. Certainly I never regarded him as the sealed-off aesthete he was thought to be. There is a radical politics of the soul as well as of the ballot box and the picket line. If he was not an activist, it was not for lack of a desire for justice, nor did he consider a theatre profoundly involved in society and politics, the venerable tradition reaching back to the Greeks, somehow unaesthetic or beyond his interest.

The real theatre—as opposed to the sequestered academic one—is always straining at the inbuilt inertia of a society that always wants to deny change and the pain it necessarily involves. But it is in this effort that the musculature of important work is developed. In a different age, perhaps even only fifteen years later, in the sixties, Williams might have had a more comfortably alienated audience to deal with, one that would have relieved the pressure upon him to extend himself beyond a supportive cult environment, and I think this might well have narrowed the breadth of his work and its intensity. In short, there was no renaissance in the American forties, but there was a certain balance within the audience—a balance, one might call it, between the alienated and the conformists—that gave sufficient support to the naked cry of the heart and, simultaneously, enough resistance to force it into a rhetoric that at one stroke could be broadly understandable and yet faithful to the pain that had pressed the author to speak.

When Kazan invited me up to New Haven to see the new Williams play, *A Streetcar Named Desire*—it seemed to me a rather too garishly attention-getting title—I was already feeling a certain amount of envious curiosity since I was still unable to commit myself to the salesman play, around which I kept suspiciously circling and sniffing. But at the same time I hoped that *Streetcar* would be good; it was not that I was high-minded but simply that I shared the common assumption of the time that the greater the number of exciting plays there were on Broadway the better for each of us. At least in our minds there was still something approximating a theatre culture to which we more or less pridefully belonged, and the higher its achievement the greater the glory we all shared. The playwright then was king of the hill, not the star actor or director, and certainly not the producer or theatre owner, as would later be the case. (At a recently televised Tony Awards ceremony, recognizing achievement in the theatre, not a single playwright was presented to the public, while two lawyers who operated a chain of theatres were showered with the gratitude of all. It reminded me of Caligula making his horse a senator.)

Streetcar—especially when it was still so fresh and the actors almost as amazed as the audience at the vitality of this theatrical experience—opened one specific door for me. Not the story or characters or the direction, but the words and their liberation, the joy of the writer in writing them, the radiant eloquence of its composition, moved me more than all its pathos. It formed a bridge to Europe for me, to Jouvet's performance in *Ondine,* to the whole tradition of unashamed word-joy that, with the exception of Odets, we had either turned our backs on or, as with Maxwell Anderson, only used archaically, as though eloquence could only be justified by cloaking it in sentimental romanticism.

Returning to New York, I felt speeded up, in motion now. With *Streetcar,* Tennessee had printed a license to speak at full throat, and it helped strengthen me as I turned to Willy Loman, a salesman always full of words, and better yet, a man who could never cease trying, like Adam, to name himself and the world's wonders. I had known all along that this play could not be encompassed by conventional realism, and for one integral reason: in Willy the past was as alive as what was happening at the moment, sometimes even crashing in to completely overwhelm his mind. I wanted precisely the same fluidity in the form, and now it was clear to me that this must be primarily verbal. The language would of course have to be recognizably his to begin with, but it seemed possible now to infiltrate it with a kind of superconsciousness. The play, after all, involved the attempts of his sons and his wife and Willy himself to understand what was killing him. And to understand meant to lift the experience into emergency speech of an unashamedly open kind rather than to proceed by the crabbed dramatic hints and pretexts of the "natural." If the structure had to mirror the psychology as directly as could be done, it was still a psychology hammered into its strange shape by society, the business life Willy had lived and believed in. The play could reflect what I had always sensed as the unbroken tissue that was man and society, a single unit rather than two.

By April of 1948 I felt I could find such a form, but it would have to be done, I thought, in a single sitting, in a night or a day, I did not know why. I stopped making my notes in our Grace Court house in Brooklyn Heights and drove up alone one morning to the country house we had bought the previous year. We had spent one summer there in that old farmhouse, which had been modernized by its former owner, a greeting card manufacturer named Philip Jaffe, who as a sideline published a thin magazine for China specialists called *Amerasia.* Mary worked as one of his secretaries and so had the first news that he wanted to sell the place. In a year or two he would be on trial for publishing without authorization State Department reports from John Stewart Service, among a number of other China experts who recognized a Mao victory as inevitable and warned of the futility of America continuing to back her favorite, Chiang Kai-shek. *Amerasia* had been a vanity publication, in part born of Jaffe's desire for a place in history, but it nevertheless braved the mounting fury of the China lobby against any opinion questioning the virtues of the Chiang forces. At his trial, the government produced texts of conversations that Jaffe claimed could only have been picked up by long-range microphone as he and his friends walked the isolated backcountry roads near this house. Service was one of many who were purged from the State Department, leaving it blinded to Chinese reality but ideologically pure.

But all that was far from my mind this day; what I was looking for on my land was a spot for a little shack I wanted to build, where I could block out the world and bring into focus what was still stuck in the corners of my eyes. I found a knoll in the nearby woods and returned to the city, where instead of working on the play I drew plans for the framing, of which I really had very vague knowledge and no experience. A pair of carpenters could have put up this ten-by-twelve-foot cabin in two days at most, but for reasons I still do not understand it had to be my own hands that gave it form, on this ground, with a floor that I had made, upon which to sit to begin the risky expedition into myself. In reality, all I had was the first two lines and a death—"Willy!" and "It's all right. I came back." Further than that I dared not, would not, venture until I could sit in the completed studio, four walls, two windows, a floor, a roof, and a door.

"It's all right. I came back" rolled over and over in my head as I tried to figure out how to join the roof rafters in air unaided, until I finally put them together on the ground and swung them into position all nailed together. When I closed in the roof it was a miracle, as though I had mastered the rain and cooled the sun. And all the while afraid I would never be able to penetrate past those two first lines. I started writing one morning—the tiny studio was still unpainted and smelled of raw wood and sawdust, and the bags of nails were still stashed in a corner with my tools. The sun of April had found my windows to pour through, and the apple buds were moving on the wild trees, showing their first pale blue petals. I wrote all day until dark, and then I had dinner and went back and wrote until some hour in the darkness between midnight and four.

I had skippéd a few areas that I knew would give me no trouble in the writing and gone for the parts that had to be muscled into position. By the next morning I had done the first half, the first act of two. When I lay down to sleep I realized I had been weeping—my eyes still burned and my throat was sore from talking it all out and shouting and laughing. I would be stiff when I woke, aching as if I had played four hours of football or tennis and now had to face the start of another game. It would take some six more weeks to complete Act II.

My laughter during the writing came mostly at Willy's contradicting himself so arrantly, and out of the laughter the title came one afternoon. *Death Comes for the Archbishop,* the *Death and the Maiden* Quartet—always austere and elevated was death in titles. Now it would be claimed by a joker, a bleeding mass of contradictions, a clown, and there was something funny about that, something like a thumb in the eye, too. Yes, and in some far corner of my mind possibly something political; there was the smell in the air of a new American Empire in the making, if only because, as I had witnessed, Europe was dying or dead, and I wanted to set before the new captains and the so smugly confident kings the corpse of a believer. On the play's opening night a woman who shall not be named was outraged, calling it "a time bomb under American capitalism"; I hoped it was, or at least under the bullshit of capitalism, this pseudo life that thought to touch the clouds by standing on top of a refrigerator, waving a paid-up mortgage at the moon, victorious at last.

But some thirty-five years later, the Chinese reaction to my Beijing production of *Salesman* would confirm what had become more and more obvious over the decades in the play's hundreds of productions throughout the world: Willy was representative everywhere, in every kind of system, of ourselves in this time. The Chinese might disapprove of his lies and his self-deluding exaggerations as well as his immorality with women, but they certainly saw themselves in him. And it was not simply as a type but because of what he wanted. Which was to excel, to win out over anonymity and meaninglessness, to love and be loved, and above all, perhaps, to *count.* When he roared out, "I am not a dime a dozen! *I am Willy Loman, and you are Biff Loman!*" it came as a nearly revolutionary declaration after what was now thirty-four years of leveling. (The play was the same age as the Chinese revolution.) I did not know in 1948 in Connecticut that I was sending a message of resurgent individualism to the China of 1983—especially when the revolution had signified, it seemed at the time, the long-awaited rule of reason and the historic ending of chaotic egocentricity and selfish aggrandizement. Ah, yes. I had not reckoned on a young Chinese student saying to a CBS interviewer in the theatre lobby, "We are moved by it because we also want to be number one, and to be rich and successful." What else is this but human unpredictability, which goes on escaping the nets of unfreedom?

I did not move far from the phone for two days after sending the script to Kazan. By the end of the second silent day I would have accepted his calling to tell me that it was a scrambled egg, an impenetrable, unstageable piece of wreckage. And his tone when he finally did call was alarmingly somber.

"I've read your play." He sounded at a loss as to how to give me the bad news. "My God, it's so sad."

"It's supposed to be."

"I just put it down. I don't know what to say. My father . . ." He broke off, the first of a great many men—and women—who would tell me that Willy was their father. I still thought he was letting me down easy. "It's a great play, Artie. I want to do it in the fall or winter. I'll start thinking about casting." He was talking as though someone we both knew had just died, and it filled me with happiness. Such is art.

For the first time in months, as I hung up the phone, I could see my family clearly again. As was her way, Mary accepted the great news with a quiet pride, as though something more expressive would spoil me, but I too thought I should remain an ordinary citizen, even an anonymous one (although I did have a look at the new Studebaker convertible, the Raymond Lowey design that was the most beautiful American car of the time, and bought one as soon as the play opened). But Mary's mother, who was staying the week with us, was astonished. "*Another* play?" she said, as though the success of *All My Sons* had been enough for one lifetime. She had unknowingly triggered that play when she gossiped about a young girl somewhere in central Ohio who had turned her father in to the FBI for having manufactured faulty aircraft parts during the war.

But who should produce *Salesman*? Kazan and I walked down Broadway from the park where we had been strolling and talking about the kind of style the production would need. Kazan's partnership with Harold Clurman had recently broken up, and I had no idea about a producer. He mentioned Cheryl Crawford, whom I hardly knew, and then Kermit Bloomgarden, an accountant turned producer, whom I had last seen poring over Herman Shumlin's account books a couple of years before when Shumlin turned down *All My Sons.* I had never seen Bloomgarden smile, but he had worked for the Group Theatre and Kazan knew him, and as much because we happened to have come to a halt a few yards from his office building as for any other reason, he said, "Well, let's go up and say hello." When we stood across the desk from him and Kazan said he had a play of mine for him to read, Bloomgarden squeezed up his morose version of a smile, or at least a suggestion of one he planned to have next week.

This whimsical transforming of another person's life reminds me of a similar walk with Kazan uptown from a garage on Twenty-sixth Street where he had left his old Pontiac to be repaired. He began wondering aloud whom he should ask to head a new acting school to be called the Actors Studio, which he and Clurman and Robert Lewis and Cheryl Crawford were organizing. None of these founders was prepared to run the place, Kazan, Clurman, and Lewis being too busy with their flourishing directing careers, and Crawford with her work as a producer. "Lee Strasberg is probably the best guy for it. He'd certainly be able to put in the time." In due course Strasberg became not only the head of the Actors Studio but also its heart and soul, and for the general public its organizer. So his work there was made possible by his having been unemployable at the right moment. But that, come to think of it, is as good a way as any to be catapulted into world fame.

Willy had to be small, I thought, but we soon realized that Roman Bohnen and Ernest Truex and a few other very good actors seemed to lack the size of the character even if they fit the body. The script had been sent to Lee Cobb, an actor I remembered mainly as a mountainous hulk covered with a towel in a Turkish bath in an Irwin Shaw play, with the hilarious *oy vey* delivery of a forever persecuted businessman. Having flown himself across the country in his own two-engine airplane, he sat facing me in Bloomgarden's office and announced, "This is my part. Nobody else can play this part. I know this man." And he did indeed seem to be the man when a bit later in a coffee shop downstairs he looked up at the young waitress and smiled winsomely as though he had to win her loving embrace before she could be seduced into bringing him his turkey sandwich and coffee—ahead of all the other men's orders, and only after bestowing on his unique slice of pickle her longing kiss.

Ground zero: Augusta and Isidore Miller before World War I.

Beautiful Mama, handsome Kermit, and me (*left*).

Kermit, the chief baby, and me.

Navy days.

In Harlem, before the Crash.

The Russian stage version of my years in the auto parts warehouse; character based on me is second from left. 1960s production of *A Memory of Two Mondays*, Moscow.

The Dolls' house, 411 North State, Ann
Arbor, forty years later.

Recording talc miners' wives' speech patterns while they wait for their men to surface, North
Carolina, 1940.

On Brooklyn Heights.

The original *All My Sons* cast, 1947: Arthur Kennedy, Karl Malden, Beth Merrill, Ed Begley, Lois Wheeler.

The powerful Israeli production of *All My Sons*, 1976, with Yossi Yadin, Lea Schwartz, and Hanna Marron, who had lost a leg in a terrorist attack.

The *Salesman* studio.

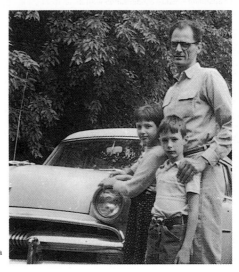

With Jane, Bob, and a
new Ford.

Mildred Dunnock, Lee J. Cobb, Arthur Kennedy, Cameron Mitchell. The original Mielziner set caught *Salesman*'s reality-condensation with its six-foot bedroom, tiny kitchen table, and lone appliance, the hated refrigerator.

With Elia Kazan, rehearsing *Salesman*.

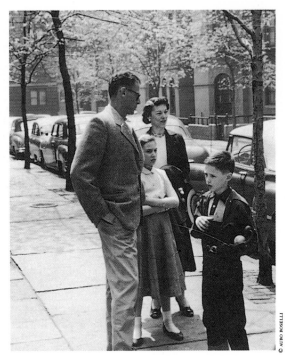

The Miller family, Willow Street, 1953.

Kay Brown, agent, indisputably in charge of everything for nearly forty years, beginning with *All My Sons*.

The best of times.

John Huston peering down the *Misfits* tunnel.

Montgomery Clift making it real before
mounting a very bad bronco.

Some Misfits trying to seize a Nevada afternoon: Marilyn, Eli Wallach, Gable. Symbolically or not, the wall could be unbolted and the house dismantled in a matter of minutes.

Kevin McCarthy and Paula Strasberg during an early pause.

Inge Morath by Henri Cartier-Bresson at the time we met.

Preparing to plant six thousand pines and firs on a barren Connecticut hillside.

The Calders' kitchen in winter: Louisa, sculptor Bill Talbot, and Sandy.

My shop: cherry dining table under construction.

Rebecca in swimming oufit, with gold chain and great hat.

After the Fall, early rehearsal: Kazan with Jason Robards; in background, Faye Dunaway, Jon Voight, Michael Strong, Barbara Loden, and other members of the young Lincoln Center Repertory Company, soon to be destroyed by the combined arrogance of bankers impatient for a big hit, a newly influential and resentful sixties avant-garde, and a press ignorant of public theatre's necessities.

Midnight script talk with Robert Whitehead and Kazan, Chelsea Hotel, 1963.

Jason Robards as Quentin and Barbara Loden as Maggie: on some nights they discovered a reality between them that was almost too painful to watch.

Franco Zeffirelli's production, with Monica Vitti and Giorgio Albertazzi, Naples, Rome, Genoa, 1964.

Luchino Visconti during his Paris production of *After the Fall*, 1965.

Bibi Andersson and Max von Sydow, Stockholm, 1964.

Harold Clurman's production of *Incident at Vichy* at Lincoln Center, 1964: Ira Lewis, Joseph Wiseman, Will Lee, David Stewart, David Wayne, Michael Strong, and Stanley Beck. Hal Holbrook as the German officer is off camera. I thought the storm against *Fall* clouded the reception of this remarkable ensemble performance coming so soon afterwards.

Clurman explaining; he thought that nothing would endure without some form of love in its creation. In heaven he would spend eternity explaining to God—with enormous enthusiasm—why He is quite right.

But while I trusted his and Kazan's experience, I lacked any conviction of my own about him until one evening in our Grace Court living room Lee looked down at my son, Bob, on the floor and I heard him laugh at something funny the child had said. The sorrow in his laughter flew out at me, touched me; it was deeply depressed and at the same time joyous, all flowing through a baritone voice that was gorgeously reedy. So large and handsome a man pretending to be thoroughly at ease in a world where he obviously did not fit could be moving.

"You know—or do you?—," Lee said to me one day in Bloomgarden's office a week or so before rehearsals were to begin, "that this play is a watershed. The American theatre will never be the same." I could only gulp and nod in silence at his portentousness—which I feared might augur a stately performance—and hope that he would make Willy come alive anyway.

But as rehearsals proceeded in the small, periodically abandoned theatre on the ratty roof of the New Amsterdam on Forty-second Street, where Ziegfeld in the twenties had staged some intimate revues, Lee seemed to move about in a buffalo's stupefied trance, muttering his lines, plodding with deathly slowness from position to position, and behaving like a man who had been punched in the head. "He's just learning it," Kazan shakily reassured me after three or four days. I waited as a week went by, and then ten days, and all that was emerging from Lee Cobb's throat was a bumpy hum. The other actors were nearing performance levels, but when they had to get a response from Lee all their rhythms slowed to near collapse. Kazan was no longer so sure and kept huddling with Lee, trying to pump him up. Nor did Lee offer any explanation, and I wondered whether he thought to actually play the part like a man with a foot in the grave. Between us, Kazan and I began referring to him as "the Walrus."

On about the twelfth day, in the afternoon, with Eddie Kook, our lighting supplier, and Jimmy Proctor, our pressman, and Kazan and myself in the seats, Lee stood up as usual from the bedroom chair and turned to Mildred Dunnock and bawled, "No, there's more people now.... There's more people!" and, gesturing toward the empty upstage where the window was supposed to be, caused a block of apartment houses to spring up in my brain, and the air became sour with the smell of kitchens where once there had been only the odors of earth, and he began to move frighteningly, with such ominous reality that my chest felt pressed down by an immense weight. After the scene had gone on for a few minutes, I glanced around to see if the others had my reaction. Jim Proctor had his head bent into his hands and was weeping, Eddie Kook was looking shocked, almost appalled, and tears were pouring over his cheeks, and Kazan behind me was grinning like a fiend, gripping his temples with both hands, and we knew we had it—there was an unmistakable wave of life moving across the air of the empty theatre, a wave of Willy's pain and protest. I began to weep myself at some point that was not particularly sad, but it was as much, I think, out of pride in our art, in Lee's magical capacity to imagine, to collect within himself every mote of life since Genesis and to let it pour forth. He stood up there like a giant moving the Rocky Mountains into position.

At the end of the act, Del Hughes, our sweet but hardheaded, absolutely devoted, competent stage manager, came out from a wing and looked out at us. His stunned eyes started us all laughing. I ran up and kissed Lee, who pretended to be surprised. "But what did you expect, Arthur?" he said, his eyes full of his playful vanity. My God, I thought—he really *is* Willy! On the subway going home to Brooklyn I felt once again the aching pain in my muscles that the performance had tensed up so tightly, just as in the writing time. And when I thought of it later, it seemed as though Lee's sniffing around the role for so long recapitulated what I had done in the months before daring to begin to write.

The whole production was, I think, unusual for the openness with which every artist involved sought out his truths. It was all a daily, almost moment-to-moment testing of ideas. There was much about the play that had never been done before, and this gave an uncustomary excitement to our discussions about what would or would not be understood by an audience. The setting I had envisioned was three bare platforms and only the minimum necessary furniture for a kitchen and two bedrooms, with the Boston hotel room as well as Howard's office to be played in open space. Jo Mielziner took those platforms and designed an environment around them that was romantic and dreamlike yet at the same time lower-middle-class. His set, in a word, was an emblem of Willy's intense longing for the promises of the past, with which indeed the present state of his mind is always conflicting, and it was thus both a lyrical design and a dramatic one. The only notable mistake in his early concept was to put the gas hot-water heater in the middle of the kitchen, a symbol of menace that I thought obvious and Kazan finally eliminated as a hazard to his staging. But by balancing on the edges of the ordinary bounds of verisimilitude, Jo was stretching reality in parallel with the script, just as Kazan did by syncopating the speech rhythms of the actors. He made Mildred Dunnock deliver her long first-act speeches to the boys at double her normal speed, then he doubled that, and finally she—until recently a speech teacher—was standing there drumming out words as fast as her very capable tongue could manage. Gradually he slacked her off, but the drill straightened her spine, and her Linda filled up with outrage and protest rather than self-pity and mere perplexity. Similarly, to express the play's inner life, the speech rate in some scenes or sections was unnaturally speeded or slowed.

My one scary hour came with the climactic restaurant fight between Willy and the boys, when it all threatened to come apart. I had written a scene in which Biff resolves to tell Willy that the former boss from whom Biff had planned to borrow money to start a business has refused to so much as see him and does not even remember his working for the firm years ago. But on meeting his brother and father in the restaurant, he realizes that Willy's psychological stress will not permit the whole catastrophic truth to be told, and he begins to trim the bad news. From moment to moment the scene as originally written had so many shadings of veracity that Arthur Kennedy, a very intelligent citizen indeed, had trouble shifting from a truth to a half-truth to a fragment of truth and back to the whole truth, all of it expressed in quickly delivered, very short lines. The three actors, with Kazan standing beside them, must have repeated the scene through a whole working day, and it still wobbled. "I don't see how we can make it happen," Kazan said as we left the theatre that evening. "Maybe you ought to try simplifying it for them." I went home and worked through the night and brought in a new scene, which played much better and became the scene as finally performed.

The other changes were very small and a pleasure to make because they involved adding lines rather than cutting or rewriting. In Act I, Willy is alone in the kitchen muttering to himself, and as his memories overtake him the lighting brightens, the exterior of the house becomes covered with leaf shadows as of old, and in a moment the boys are calling to him in their youthful voices, entering the stage as they were in their teens. There was not sufficient time, however, for them to descend from their beds in the dark on the specially designed elevators and finish stripping out of their pajamas into sweaters and trousers and sneakers, so I had to add time to Willy's monologue. But that was easy since he loved talking to himself about his boys and his vision of them.

The moving in and out of the present had to be not simply

indicative but a tactile transformation that the audience could feel as well as comprehend, and indeed come to dread as returning memory threatens to bring Willy closer to his end. Lighting was thus decisively important, and Mielziner, who also lit the show, with Eddie Kook by his side, once worked an entire afternoon lighting a chair.

Willy, in his boss's office, has exploded once too often, and Howard has gone out, leaving him alone. He turns to the office chair, which in the old days was occupied by Frank, Howard's father, who had promised Willy shares in the firm as a reward for all his good work, and as he does so the chair must become alive, quite as though his old boss were in it as he addresses him: "Frank, Frank, don't you remember what you told me? . . ." Rather than being lit, the chair subtly seemed to begin emanating light. But this was not merely an exercise in theatrical magic; it confirmed that we had moved inside Willy's system of loss, that we were seeing the world as he saw it even as we kept a critical distance and saw it for ourselves.

To set the chair off and make the light change work, all surrounding lights had to dim imperceptibly. That was when Eddie Kook, who had become so addicted to the work on this play that his office at his Century Lighting Company had all but ceased operations, turned to me and said, "You've been asking why we need so many lights. [We were using more than most musicals.] The reason is right there in front of you—it takes more lights to make it dark." With fewer lights each one would have to be dimmed more noticeably than if there were many, each only fractionally reduced in intensity to create the change without apparent source or contrivance.

Salesman had its first public performance at the Locust Street Theatre in Philadelphia. Across the street the Philadelphia Orchestra was playing Beethoven's Seventh Symphony that afternoon, and Kazan thought Cobb ought to hear some of it, wanting, I suppose, to prime the great hulk on whom all our hopes depended. The three of us were in a conspiracy to make absolutely every moment of every scene cohere to what preceded and followed it; we were now aware that Willy's part was among the longest in dramatic literature, and Lee was showing signs of wearying. We sat on either side of him in a box, inviting him, as it were, to drink of the heroism of that music, to fling himself into his role tonight without holding back. We thought of ourselves, still, as a kind of continuation of a long and undying past.

As sometimes happened later on during the run, there was no applause at the final curtain of the first performance. Strange things began to go on in the audience. With the curtain down, some people stood to put their coats on and then sat again, some, especially men, were bent forward covering their faces, and others were openly weeping. People crossed the theatre to stand quietly talking with one another. It seemed forever before someone remembered to applaud, and then there was no end to it. I was standing at the back and saw a distinguished-looking elderly man being led up the aisle; he was talking excitedly into the ear of what seemed to be his male secretary or assistant. This, I learned, was Bernard Gimbel, head of the department store chain, who that night gave an order that no one in his stores was to be fired for being overage.

Now began the parade of the visiting New York theatre people to see for themselves, and I remember best Kurt Weill and his wife, Lotte Lenya, who had come with Maxwell Anderson's wife, Mab. We had coffee in a little shop, and Weill kept shaking his head and staring at me, and Mab said, "It's the best play ever written," which I dare repeat because it would be said often in the next months and would begin to change my life.

Of the opening night in New York two things stick to memory. At the back of the lovely Morosco, since destroyed by the greed of real estate men and the city's indifference, Kazan and I were sitting on the stairs leading up to the balcony as Lee was saying, "And by the way he died the death of a salesman . . ." Everything had gone beautifully, but I was near exhaustion since I acted all the parts internally as I watched, and suddenly I heard, ". . . in the smoker of the New York, New Hahven and Hayven." Surely the audience would burst out laughing—but nobody did. And the end created the same spell as it had in Philadelphia, and backstage was the same high euphoria that I had now come to expect. A mob of well-wishers packed the corridors to the dressing rooms. For the first time at a play of mine the movie stars had come out, but my face was still unknown and I could stand in a corner watching them unobserved—Lucille Ball and Desi Arnaz, Fredric and Florence March, and faces and names I have long forgotten, putting me on notice that I was now deep in show business, a paradoxically uncomfortable feeling indeed, for it was too material and real to have much to do with something that was air and whispers.

Finally, edging my way onto the stage, where I hoped to find a place to sit and rest, I saw as in a glorious dream of reward and high success three waiters in rich crimson Louis Sherry jackets arranging plates and silver on an extraordinarily long banquet table stretching almost the entire stage width. On its white linen table-cloth were great silver tureens and platters of beef, fowl, and sea-food along with ice-filled buckets of champagne. Whose idea could this have been? What a glorious climax to the triumphant evening! Anticipating the heady shock of cold champagne, I reached for a gleaming glass, when one of the waiters approached me and with polite firmness informed me that the dinner had been ordered by Mr. Dowling for a private party. Robert Dowling, whose City Investing Company owned the Morosco along with other Broadway theatres, was a jovial fellow turning sixty who had swum around Manhattan Island, a feat he seemed to memorialize by standing straight with his chest expanded. I liked his childishness and his enthusiasms. I said that Mr. Dowling would surely not begrudge the play's author a well-earned glass of wine in advance of the celebration, but the waiter, obviously on orders, was adamant. I was dumbfounded, it must be somebody's joke, but a bit later, as Mary and I were leaving with the cast and their friends, we all stopped for a moment at the back of the theatre to watch with half-hysterical incredulity as this rather decorous celebratory dinner proceeded literally inside Willy Loman's dun-colored Brooklyn house, the ladies in elaborate evening gowns, the men in dinner jackets, the waiters moving back and forth with the food under a polite hum of conversation suitable for the Pierre Hotel dining room, and the diners of course totally oblivious to the crowd of us looking on laughing and cracking jokes. It reminded me of scenes from Soviet movies of the last insensible days of the czarist court. Dowling, an otherwise generous fellow, was simply exercising the charming insensitivity of the proprietor, something Broadway would begin to see more and more of, but never perhaps on so grandly elegant and absurd a scale.

Secretly, of course, I was outraged, but sufficient praise was on the way to put offense to sleep. An hour or so later, at the opening-night party, Jim Proctor grabbed my arm and pulled me to a phone. On the other end was the whispered voice of Sam Zolotow, that generation's theatrical inside dopester and a reporter for the *Times,* who was actually reading our review directly off Brooks Atkinson's typewriter as the critic wrote it—I could hear the clacking of the typewriter on the phone. In his Noo Yawk voice he excitedly whispered word after word as Atkinson composed it under his nose—"Arthur Miller has written a superb drama. From every point of view, it is rich and memorable . . ."—and as one encomium was laid upon another Sam's voice grew more and more amazed and warm and he seemed to reach out and give me his embrace. The conspiracy that had begun with me and spread to Kazan, the cast, Mielziner, and all the others now extended to Zolotow and Atkinson and the *Times*, until for a moment a community seemed to have formed of people who cared very much that their common sense of life in their time had found expression.

Driving homeward down lower Broadway at three in the morning, Mary and I were both silent. The radio had just finished an extraordinary program, readings of the play's overwhelmingly glowing reviews in the morning papers. My name repeated again and again seemed to drift away from me and land on someone else, perhaps my ghost. It was all a letdown now that the arrow had been fired and the bow, so long held taut, was slackening again. I had striven all my life to win this night, and it was here, and I was this celebrated man who had amazingly little to do with me, or I with him.

In truth, I would have sworn I had not changed, only the public perception of me had, but this is merely fame's first illusion. The fact, as it took much more time to appreciate, is that such an order of recognition imprints its touch of arrogance, quite as though one has control of a new power, a power to make real everything one is capable of imagining. And it can open a voraciousness for life and an impatience with old friends who persist in remaining ineffectual. An artist blindly follows his nose with hands outstretched, and only after he has struck the rock and brought forth the form hidden within it does he theorize and explain what is forever inexplicable, but I had a rationalist tradition behind me and felt I had to account to it for my rise.

I came to wish I had had the sense to say that I had learned what I could from books and study but that I did not know how to do what I had apparently done and that the whole thing might as well have been a form of prayer for all I understood about it. Simply, there is a sense for the dramatic form or there is not, there is stageworthy dialogue and literary dialogue and no one quite knows why one is not the other, why a dramatic line *lands* in an audience and a literary one sails over its head. Instead, there were weighty interviews and even pronouncements, and worst of all, a newly won rank to defend against the inevitable snipers. The crab who manages to climb up out of the bucket causes a lot of the other crabs to try to pull him back down where he belongs. That's what crabs do.

The fear once more was in me that I would not write again. And as Mary and I drove home, I sensed in our silence some discomfort in my wife and friend over these struggling years. It never occurred to me that she might have felt anxious at being swamped by this rush of my fame, in need of reassurance. I had always thought her clearer and more resolved than I. Some happiness was not with us that I wanted now, I had no idea what it might be, only knew the absence of it, its lack—so soon. In fact, the aphrodisiac of celebrity, still nameless, came and sat between us in the car.

And so inevitably there was a desire to flee from it all, to be blessedly unknown again, and a fear that I had stumbled into a dangerous artillery range. It was all an unnaturalness; fame is the other side of loneliness, of impossible-to-resolve contradictions—to be anonymous and at the same time not lose one's renown, in brief, to be two people who might occasionally visit together and perhaps make a necessary joint public appearance but who would normally live separate lives, the public fellow wasting his time gadding about while the writer stayed at his desk, as morose and anxious as ever, and at work. I did not want the power I wanted. It wasn't "real." What was?

Outlandish as it seemed, the Dowling party in the Lomans' living room came to symbolize one part of the dilemma; the pain and love and protest in my play could be transformed into mere champagne. My dreams of many years had simply become too damned real, and the reality was less than the dream and lacked all dedication.

From time to time in the following months I would stand at the back of the theatre watching sections of the performance, trying to understand what there was about it all that bothered me. It was marvelously effective—although I could drive a truck through some of Lee's stretched-out pauses, which were tainting his performance with more than a hint of self-indulgence. With Kazan off to a new project, Lee had taken to re-directing Arthur Kennedy and Cameron Mitchell and to enjoying rather than suffering the anguish of the character. But these problems only reinforced my belief that with my complicity the production concept itself had somehow softened the edges of my far more aseptic original intention. I knew nothing of Brecht then or of any other theory of theatrical distancing; I simply felt that there was too *much* identification with Willy, too much weeping, and that the play's ironies were being dimmed out by all this empathy. After all, I reminded myself, I had written it for three unadorned black platforms, with a single flute in the air and without softening transitions—a slashing structure, I had thought. But at the same time I could not deny my own tenderness toward these characters.

I put myself to work on *The Hook,* the screenplay about Panto's doomed attempt to overthrow the feudal gangsterism of the New York waterfront. After reading the script, Kazan agreed to direct it but felt we must first go to Hollywood together and try to get the backing of a major studio. Kazan was then under contract to Twentieth Century Fox, but they would have nothing to do with this grimy story and its downbeat ending. So we decided to approach, among others, Harry Cohn, president of Columbia Pictures and himself a tough graduate of the Five Points district of the lower Manhattan waterfront who would be likely to know what the script was about.

Departing on the Super Chief on a morning in the spring of 1950, Kazan and I were back in the conspiracy again, two minority men plotting to hit the American screen with some harsh truths. If we were already out of date and the country was now about to spend its idealism on the battle with Communism in Korea, the news had struck us only abstractly. I had been out of touch with Longhi and Berenson for some months now and would not learn for half a year to come that they had been barred from the waterfront under a new Coast Guard security system that required individual passes for anyone wishing to enter a pier.

Riding west on the Super Chief, we studied the script on our laps. The movie, Kazan thought, should take off from the tradition of *Open City* and the other neorealist Italian films. But was it really possible that the studios would put up money for a film that would so violently cut against their notions of entertainment? There had indeed been social problem films made in Hollywood, rather generalized and packed with abundant goodwill, but this was not a problem picture; it was closer to fact since the union involved had to be the ILA and none other, the port had to be New York, the deaf and blind cops had to be New York cops. The odds against us were almost hopeless, but if we could manage somehow to make this picture, we would be bringing ourselves some glory and even in a small way helping the future to arrive. In 1950 the future was even less definable than before, but one belonged to it anyway, as even slack, unfilled sails belong to the wind.

FOUR

My feel for the reality of longshoremen's lives had been enriched by the Italian trip, which gave me their earlier European background. But I had also spent almost two years during the war in the Brooklyn Navy Yard, where probably a near majority of the workers were Italian. Working thirteen out of fourteen nights, from four in the afternoon to four in the mórning, I had made connections with their family-centered concerns. But they could also be elaborately treacherous to one another, and the Yard was full of Sicilian dramas, guys caught in the arms of somebody's wife and escaping over rooftops, or maneuvering a friend out of the way the better to get to his girlfriend. Ipana Mike was my boss, so called because he had no front upper teeth. He wore his cap sideways, ate six spinach sandwiches on Bond bread at midnight (by which time the bread was green and wet), and was constantly on the phone with his girlfriends, one of whom was a packer on the night shift at Macy's; I often had to go outside the Yard to call her and help arrange their trysts. From her hot arms he would hurry home to his wife, who was keeping his bed warm, and sometimes by noon he was sniffing up a third woman on her lunch hour from the Abraham and Straus department store. Mike was a busy man, apart from helping to win World War II.

He deeply resented his wife, whom he had been tricked into marrying in the late thirties by his immigrant grandfather, who had arrived from Calabria with a trunk full of money, a fortune, it was believed, paid him for property he sold not long before emigrating. Promised the dowry if he married a good respectable woman despite his crazy-making adoration of an Irish bimbo, a "baloney" violently disapproved of by the old man, Mike discovered on his wedding night that the immense bundles of lire in the trunk came to about three hundred and five American dollars, and so he refused to "have relations." His grandfather took to sitting out in their living room at night waiting for the wife to emerge and report that she had been penetrated. For Mike the alternative was to get beaten up by his grandfather, a "gi'nt" with iron fists and a lead-pipe sense of propriety. Mike was not bad with his fists either, but nobody could attack a grandfather.

Like hundreds of others in the Yard, Mike had made an art of avoiding work on board warships by finding inaccessible corners to sleep in, but this was as much a sign of his realistic appraisal of the navy's need for his services as a fuck-you attitude, which of course was mixed into it. For the Yard was vastly overmanned, planning was often chaotic, and one man more or less in this beehive could not mean too much. One genius who had rigged himself a bed high in the dark upper reaches of a heavy cruiser's engine room awoke one morning to leave for home only to find himself at sea beyond sight of land. He did not return to his Red Hook crap game for six weeks.

Still, Mike had his morals, and when he really believed he was not being suckered he could turn into a phenomenally resourceful worker, especially when we were trucked out of the Yard at night to repair navy ships lying in the Hudson River waiting to sail out among the German submarines known to be lurking beyond Sandy Hook. With raw winter winds biting into our faces, we many times straightened steel and welded cracked struts on depth-charge platforms with never a complaint from him. We were drawn together then, since we relied on each other's help in avoiding falls into the icy waters, but this did not mean I was ever to be an honorary Sicilian. Besides, Mike was probably put off by my evasiveness about my pre-Yard work experience, a gap I left because I knew that neither he nor the others in our shipfitters' gang would believe that I had given up what would have seemed lucrative work writing radio scripts in order to freeze aboard a ship in the river.

With Sammy Casalino, another of my age and rank, shipfitter third, I had gradually become too friendly to continue avoiding my past, especially when it was noised about that I must have spent some years in prison. I was a writer, I finally told Sammy. He was a high school graduate and in his own view a man sensitive to culture and art, a rebel of a kind who had married a Jewish girl. "I hate race prejudism," he would say, disapproving not only the widespread anti-Jewish talk in the Yard but the occasional beatings of British seamen by Italian-American workers who would ambush them on Adams Street in the middle of the night because Britain had "betrayed" Italy by declaring war on her. That they were at the same time repairing and building ships to destroy Italy just showed how tough it was to earn a living in this particular world, but the fact was that while rooting for Mussolini they were also deeply attached to Roosevelt and the America with which Il Duce was at war. It was all a mere anarchy loosed upon the world and would now and then break into its underlying absurdity, as when the yardmaster put up a notice asking workers to avoid wasting cadmium, which had to be imported over the water at great risk and cost. Cadmium nuts and welding flux were used on underwater hull areas because cadmium did not rust. The very next night men were hunched over everywhere filing rings for their women out of the nuts, which could be brought to a high silvery sheen, and making bracelets out of the rods of flux.

Sammy's and my disgust drew us closer together, and that midnight over our lunch sandwiches he told me a troubling dream. "I come into my cousin's bedroom—Rita—and there she is layin' on a bed lookin' up at me, and you know what? I fell down right on top of her. *Right on top of her!* I woke up I was sweatin' like a pig! Now what the hell is that supposed to mean?" I delicately suggested that it could mean he liked his cousin. "Oh, yeah, I always liked her a lot." And maybe down deep in his mind he might dream of making love to her? "To *her?* Chrissake, I told you she's my *cousin!*" And that ended that.

As I had anticipated, telling Sammy that I was a writer was simply an additional proof to him that I probably had a prison term to hide, and now instead of avoiding my past I was drawn into trying to impress him with the truth. It happened that a script of mine about Amelia Earhart, the flyer who had disappeared in the South Pacific some years back under mysterious circumstances, was to be broadcast on the Du Pont Cavalcade of America radio series on a Monday night, our off-night, starring the movie actress Madeleine Carroll. As we were walking out of the Yard that Monday at a little past four in the morning, moving past the marine guards at the gate, I said, "A play I wrote will be on tonight, Sammy. You'll hear my name mentioned."

The look he gave me was half suspicion of my sanity and half fear that in some unfathomable way I was setting him up. "Yeah?" he said.

"Yeah," I said, "it's on NBC at eight. My name comes at the end."

When I reported for work on Tuesday and as usual ran into Sammy on board the damaged British cruiser we were assigned to, I waited in vain for him to mention the program, and after some hours of suspense I finally asked if he had remembered to listen. Oh, sure, he'd listened. And had he heard my name? Yeah, he'd heard it. Well?

"But it was all true," he complained.

"What do you mean?"

"The story. Except the end, nobody knows how she came down or where, so I figured you wrote that part."

"No, I wrote the whole thing, Sammy. It's based on known facts, but those are actors in a studio in Manhattan, and somebody has to write down what they say. I mean, Madeleine Carroll isn't Amelia Earhart."

"I know that, for Chrissake."

He stared cloudily into space—"writing" meant inventing. And I think he realized as he stood there that he had believed Madeleine Carroll really was Amelia Earhart speaking and at the same time that this was impossible since Earhart was dead. Adding to the confusion was my having said that I had voluntarily come down to the Navy Yard to contribute to the war effort when he knew I could have made far more money in radio, which was glamorous besides. All these truths left him feeling deceived, and from now on he became rather formal with me. That is, until he could no longer hold back news of another of his dreams of Cousin Rita, whom he now saw taking the garbage pail out to the curb in front of her house, and bending over to set it down, "she let her bathrobe fall open." Another time she was climbing a ladder that he was steadying in place below, and she started to sway, "so I had to look up and . . . Jesus!" Clomping into the Yard every afternoon at a quarter to four in his regulation steel-toed work shoes, bundled up to his neck in his dun mackinaw, his earlaps down, opening his tin lunchbox to the marine inspectors as he entered the gate, Sammy looked just like the sixty thousand indistinguishable others, each with his identical tin lunchbox and his unique and mystifying dreams.

Whenever a drydock was finally flooded and a ship instead of sinking floated safely into the harbor and sailed out into the bay, I was not the only one who stared at it thinking it miraculous that out of our chaos and incompetence, our bumbling and goofing off and our thefts and our dedicated moments in the wind, we had managed to repair it. More than one man would turn to another and say, "How the hell'd it happen?" as the ship vanished into the morning mists and the war.

* * *

Rejected for military service, I had tried to justify my existence by throwing myself into writing patriotic war plays for radio, mostly sponsored by Du Pont and U.S. Steel. We were all one big happy family fighting the common enemy, but the more expert I became the more desiccated I felt writing the stuff, which was more like a form of yelling than writing. Still, it was an easy dollar and allowed me to continue working at plays and stories and took less time than teaching or some other job. An enormous, rotund blond man named Homer Fickett produced and directed Cavalcade from the Madison Avenue offices of Batten, Barton, Durstine and Osborn, probably the largest ad agency of the time and a voice box of corporate America in helping to refashion the necessary profit motive into themes of high-minded service. It was Bruce Barton who had announced that Jesus Christ was the world's greatest salesman, implying, one supposed, that admen were disguised missionaries and BBD&O a seminary brought up to date. The secretaries washed in Pears Soap, and Homer's fair cheeks blushed as he made me bury my copy of the *Nation* or *New Masses* or even *Partisan Review* in my coat pocket before some closely shaved executive found me out.

Homer needed me; I had become his utility man, whom he could phone in an emergency for a half-hour script to be conceived and finished in a day. Two or three times a year he would find himself rehearsing a script too substandard to broadcast on Cavalcade, radio's class act, but these alarming revelations often came to him only two or three days before the broadcast date. There would then be a desperate phone call, and on my agreeing to pitch in he would messenger a book about some incident in American history, and I would read it by Wednesday evening, cook up a half-hour script on Thursday, and get it to him on Madison Avenue by Friday morning. He would cast and rehearse it and be ready for broadcast on Tuesday evening, with a thirty-piece orchestra doing the bridges live. For this I received five hundred dollars, a good solid piece of money at a time when my used Nash-Lafayette had cost me two fifty and my Grace Court house came to twenty-eight thousand. (The last of its prices that I know of, in the sixties, was three-quarters of a million.)

But occasionally a worthwhile theme came along, like the story of Benito Juárez, the nineteenth-century Mexican leader—which, unaccountably, BBD&O thought would be a grand idea to do since Du Pont did a lot of business and owned plants south of the border.

There was no rush with this one, and I decided to amuse myself by writing the script in verse, more gracefully to condense the innumerable events of Juárez's affecting life.

Juárez was a coeval of Lincoln, whom he worshiped, a peasant revolutionary unusual for his democratic convictions. For once I wrote with some excitement, the form being rather novel with its organic need of imagery that would help to telescope an epic career into twenty-eight minutes. Finishing the script one afternoon, I decided to amble up to Manhattan and show it to Homer before having it typed.

NBC Studio 8-A was the big one from which the important shows were broadcast. Opening the soundproof doors, I walked into an enormous area the size of a basketball court and heard a tremendous but vaguely familiar baritone-basso voice. At first I assumed it was that of an actor performing a scene of raging fury, but moving closer, I saw that the cast of six or eight actors wore expressions of very real anxiety, some with eyes lowered to avoid looking at the giant orator, who, I now realized, was Orson Welles.

He was not acting but roaring in the direction of the sound booth, from whose depths on the PA system feeble rejoinders were brokenly emerging whenever he momentarily paused for breath. The voice from the booth was Homer Fickett's trying to soothe the star. "Now, come on, Orson, it really isn't all that bad . . ."

Welles's fists moved from the vicinity of his knees toward the ceiling. "It is a TRAVESTY, I tell you, a LIE, a purposeful and contemptible distortion of KNOWN FACTS in order to justify the unforgivable!"

"But, Orson . . . ," poor Homer's voice meekly tried to interrupt. The outrage continued. Everett Sloane, Joe Cotten, Mercedes McCambridge—practically the whole Mercury Theatre Company was apparently here, stopped in its tracks.

Welles's real adversary, it appeared, the cause of his outrage, was another man in the booth, a Professor Monaghan, a Yale historian who normally vetted the American history scripts for accuracy and who, according to Welles, had either been drunk or was so corrupt that the distortions he was protesting had been allowed to stand. Welles could roar with such authority because an ancestor, Gideon Welles, was the navy secretary involved in the very incident that had been dramatized as a great American success in Latin America when in reality it had been a catastrophe and a disgrace.

Fury spent, Welles now stood silent as Homer emerged from the booth to plead with him to go on with rehearsal. Again Welles absolutely refused. Homer went white; it was only a day or two before the broadcast, and this could end in court. Welles still refused.

Homer's eye fell on me, and I gestured him to a corner of the vast studio. I had the Juárez script folded up in my jacket pocket and whispered that I thought Welles would be a great Juárez, especially since he loved doing accents. Homer, presently a beached sea lion, glanced at the unbound script I handed him, walked over to Welles, and offered him the clump, muttering an introduction to me. Welles looked very skeptically at the messy, pencil-marked dialogue but noticed that the play opened with a half-page-long narration in verse, the sight of which seemed to surprise him. Now the actors watched in silence as he read to himself; his lips began to move as he tried the fit of the words, and without glancing at me he walked to a microphone and read the page, ringing out the syllables like a rebuke to the professor, who had remained behind in the sound booth. Enormously relieved, the actors gathered around the one microphone. Passing sheets to one another and craning over each other's shoulders to read, they played out the story. I went into the booth with Homer and listened amazed at Welles's genius with the microphone; he seemed to climb into it, his word-carving voice winding into one's brain. No actor had such intimacy and sheer presence in a loudspeaker. He was then a lithe young guy, like me in his twenties, but he already had his loose and wicked belly laugh and the noble air of a lord. At the end of the reading I came out of the booth and he pulled me to him in a loving embrace, and I went home on the IRT in triumph.

I had hardly come through the door to report my incredible afternoon to Mary, who was as delighted as I was, when Homer was on the phone saying there might be a couple of problems with Du Pont on the script and that I had to meet the next morning with a small committee from the company.

There were three or four of them up there high above Madison Avenue, and they had come up specially from Delaware to talk with me since there was so little time before the broadcast. They were led by Russ Applegate, a gray-haired man of good but firm temper, in charge of the company's public relations. One objection was to the words "where parrots flew," there being no parrots in the particular jungle through which Juárez had fled his persecutors. I immediately agreed to find some other image for the line, but the executive whose point had been so well taken felt so victorious that he continued to discuss the jungle, in which he had been a tourist, for the better part of an hour. I marveled at the spectacle of these grown men sent all the way from Delaware to remove a phrase. But now came the good part.

In one scene, taken from the book sent me by BBD&O, Juárez's troops crossed the Rio Grande at night to pick up a great pile of rifles left on the U.S. side by order of Lincoln, who was supporting Juárez against Emperor Maximilian, the Hapsburg princeling whom the French had made puppet ruler of the country. This scene had to go.

"But I got it from the book you sent me, and it's a good scene. Besides, it shows how friendly the U.S. was to the Mexican revolution and justifies Juárez's faith in Lincoln."

In fact, BBD&O had seized on the Juárez story to celebrate Pan American Day, which coincided with the day of our broadcast. Applegate was adamant. The scene could not stand. I persisted. It would be difficult to supplant it with another so late in the day, when we were broadcasting in about twenty-four hours, and anyway I hadn't an alternative idea in my head. I kept asking what was wrong with the scene.

Applegate hesitated and then said that they did not want Du Pont accused once again of gunrunning in Latin America.

But it was Lincoln who had ordered arms to be left there, not Du Pont.

"They were Remington arms, and Remington is linked to Du Pont," Applegate said, "corporately."

More than forty years later it is impossible to remember whether I pulled the scene or not, but I tend to think that they finally let it stand—trembling, no doubt, at the possible consequences. Like many power people here and in other countries, they often made the strangest and most unlikely decisions. Another time they assigned me to write the story of the Merritt brothers, providing me with two books documenting what seemed to me the most brutally rapacious corporate tale I had ever heard. Briefly, the Merritt brothers were miners up in Minnesota before the turn of the century who had been led by an Indian—as though, they said, by Providence itself—to outcroppings of pure iron ore on the earth's surface, which they promptly laid claim to. This turned out to be nothing less than the largest opencut iron deposit on the face of the earth, the legendary Mesabi Range. The news spread quickly to New York and the first John D. Rockefeller, who immediately dispatched his personal Baptist minister to convince the brothers to sell him the rights. For John D. was a religious man, and his agents had informed him that the Merritt boys were steeped in God. But the Merritts did not want to sell, planning instead to exploit the mine themselves and give the proceeds to the Indians and the poor, an idea whose nobility stirred Rockefeller down to his depths. In short order, of course, having constructed enough of the mine to begin operations, the simple brothers ran out of money, and Rockefeller's minister promptly reappeared, this time with an offer to finance their efforts to help the poor. Little by little, Rockefeller held out more and more of the tempting bait, gathering up their IOU's to the point where the Merritt brothers awoke one day to learn, as they testified to a U.S. Senate investigating committee a couple of years later, that "Rockefeller was the owner of Mesabi and they did not have the nickel for carfare on the trolley across Duluth." Ownership of this limitless supply of ore made possible the starting up of the U.S. Steel Corporation across the lake and was the real reason for the burst of industrial production in the Midwest cities of Michigan and Ohio. It was a fabulous tale, and incredibly, it was not only to be sponsored by Du Pont, but on the night of the broadcast the top executives and other personnel of the corporation all over the country were going to hold dinners and listen en masse.

I called Homer to ask if he had read the research. Yes, he knew the story. "And they're going to broadcast this?" I asked.

"Write it and let's see."

I wrote the story straight, hewing very faithfully to the sources. The script was quickly approved, rehearsed, and broadcast, and the local Du Pont klatches loved it. The Du Pont family, many of whom suffered from deafness and had to have special hearing apparatus connected to their radios, were also very enthusiastic, it was said.

Later I asked Homer to explain it to me. "They don't see it the way we do," he said. "To them the story shows Rockefeller's foresight and acumen and ability to organize one of the largest mining operations—in fact, it was the largest—efficiently and for the good of humanity. To them it shows what enterprise and imagination can accomplish."

"But," I said, "his minister really conned them, saying that John D. was going to devote the wealth to the poor and all that. He gulled those guys. The Senate investigating committee was outraged."

"True," replied Homer, "but that's not the way they see it. The

Merritt boys were just unable to manage this kind of wealth, and it was in the country's interest, and humanity's interest, that the one who could manage it should."

"In other words, God's in his heaven."

"He sure as hell is."

That we see what we wish to see was dramatized again a few years later when *The Man Who Had All the Luck* opened its pre-Broadway run in Wilmington, Delaware, the home of the Du Pont corporation. The actor playing David Beeves was Karl Swenson, who had for years been a leading actor on Cavalcade shows, so we were invited by Russ Applegate to have a drink with him in the Du Pont Hotel before one of the performances. He showed up with his wife and two of his subexecutives and their wives, pleased that we alumni of the Du Pont show were now to be on Broadway. Inevitably, the talk turned to politics, since Roosevelt was running for his fourth term in an exceptionally bitter campaign against Thomas Dewey. Applegate, the eyes and ears of Du Pont in its relations with the public, now turned to Swenson, who as a rich actor was bound to be a Republican, and with an anticipatory smile of satisfaction asked, "Well, Karl, how do you see the election?"

Swenson, actually a secret Democrat, looked uncomfortable as he pretended to think for a moment. In those days employees of banks and big businesses hid their Roosevelt buttons until they got out into the street. Besides, Du Pont was the money behind the Liberty League, a far-right pressure group. Applegate's question, therefore, was carrying a certain load, especially given his supremely confident smile. Swenson decided to dive off the board.

"Well," he drawled, swiping back a platinum lock and flashing his handsome grin, "I guess I'd have to say my impression is that most people are going for Roosevelt."

"Roosevelt!" Applegate nearly shouted, a bitterness narrowing his eyes. "Why, that's impossible—nobody *we* know is voting for him!" And he glanced about at his two subordinates for a confirmation that they did not begrudge him. Of course Roosevelt did win handily.

I had no doubt that Applegate was being blinded by self-interest and his ideological commitment, and to a nearly comical degree. His hatred of Roosevelt and the New Deal was almost religious in its intensity, yet no hint of it ever appeared in his company's advertising or publicity or in the normal course of his daily business life. With an opposing ideological slant I behaved much as he did, however, and this doubleness, this obedience to a civil code of behavior, created a certain unreality. I suppose that it was a civility imposed by the war itself, for with victory and Roosevelt's passing, with the United States the most powerful nation on earth and the only solvent one, the restraining hand was struck away and a new age of unbridled and even joyous accusation opened, the age of the political investigating committees of Congress, of McCarthyism, of openly antileft legislation like the McCarran-Walter Act, which set up a political means test for any foreigner wishing to so much as visit the country. I would have cause to recall this little scene in coming years when the people "we know" were having their revenge for the two decades of political and cultural isolation imposed on them by liberal and left assumptions about the real and the true. Russ Applegate's comic narrowness, in fact, would one day remind me of my own.

My first attempt at a play, rather inevitably, had been about an industrial conflict and a father and his two sons, the most autobiographical dramatic work I would ever write. I was gunning for a Hopwood Award, which at Michigan was the student equivalent of the Nobel. But I had two jobs and a full academic schedule, and between dishwashing three times a day and feeding three floors of mice in a genetics laboratory in the woods at the edge of town, I would fall into bed each night exhausted. I had used up almost all of the money with which I had come to Michigan the year before as a freshman—one had to show a bankbook with a minimum balance of five hundred dollars to assure the school that one would not become an indigent ward of the state. The mousehouse job was my cash source, fifteen dollars a month paid out by Roosevelt's National Youth Administration, which subsidized student jobs administered by the universities. Every afternoon at four I would walk the two miles out to the lab, where another student, Carl Bates, and I would break open crates of rotting vegetables garnered from Ann Arbor grocery stores and distribute them in the hundreds of wire cages stacked on shelves from floor to ceiling. Wired to each cage was a steel identification tag, and when the thousands of mice heard us entering the silent, tree-surrounded building, they would rush around, and the jangling of the tags on the cages would send chills up my spine. Two biologists, a young man and woman in white coats, worked on the ground floor in a small room and never seemed to speak. They were carrying out long-range genetic research that required absolute separation of the mice families, each of which was branded by differently shaped holes punched in their ears, a code that placed every individual in the total scheme. A violent electric bell had to be rung immediately if a stray mouse was discovered running loose, lest it get into the wrong cage and screw away a whole year's work. Naturally, it was I who volunteered to design a trap that would capture mice without injury, but after half a semester of tinkering I had to give up. There was every imaginable size mouse in the place, some so tiny a hair would hardly bend if they stepped on it, so that a gate that would shut behind a very light fellow would be so sensitive that it would chop the tail off a heavier guy or come down on his neck.

There were other distractions as well, like the occasional copulations of the two silent researchers on the desk in their little office, excitingly echoing what the mice were doing, as the delicate tinkling of the cage tags constantly made evident. I was also detailed about once a week to carry a cageful of mice that had outlived their usefulness out to a shack behind the laboratory, small, low-ceilinged, windowless, and black dark, where two owls sat on a shelf snapping their beaks together as I entered carrying their prey. The birds would hum and hoot threateningly, fluffing out their wings and stamping about on their shelf, impatient for me to release the mice—not an easy job when they clung to the wire mesh and had to be shaken violently until they dropped out onto the hay-strewn ground and occasionally scampered up my leg for safety. As I danced out through the splintery old door, fearful of stepping on a hysterical mouse underfoot or letting an owl escape, I had to remind myself that this too had research significance—every week some graduate student would come riffling around in the hay on the floor and proceed to count the surviving mice in order to determine which color mouse was better protected. Duly noted was the fact that the white, orange, and yellow mice, indeed all the lighter-colored ones, were gobbled up, while the plain gray and dark brown were more likely to survive. This conclusion seemed fairly predictable to me, but I was still in awe of scientific types making notes on clipboards and thought there must be something here that I did not understand. There wasn't.

A concrete cube set off by itself in the dense woods, the mousehouse was as often as not empty of humans when I hurried in to work in the late afternoons, and it was a strange feeling to think of these thousands of rodents, each with his little conniving brain, sitting in his cage trying to figure a way of getting out. Besides, there was Carl Bates giving me the creeps by making a meal for himself out of the mouse salad, cutting away the rotten parts of grapefruit, carrots, and lettuce. Carl had to save pennies in order to send home a couple of dollars a week for his family, aside from supporting himself. He had a bad case of acne but was always cheerful in a stunned sort of way, which may have come from having been raised on a northern Michigan potato farm where, I supposed, the days were long and silent. Contrasting with the volatility of New York and the Jews I had known, Carl's depth of undemonstrated emotion broadened my education. His older brother had converted to Christian Science and insisted on praying over his crushed right thumb, which had gotten caught under a toppled auto engine in the Engineering School. Once I accompanied Carl when he went to sit with him, quietly trying to persuade him to go to the hospital as the thumb seemed to be dying on the hand, but he silently read on and on in Mary Baker Eddy until, in a week or so, it began to heal. As materialists, Carl and I remained unconvinced. In 1935, America was as far beyond the reach of prayer as a collapsed bridge.

I decided to remain in Ann Arbor rather than go home for the spring vacation and to use the week to write my play. Why it had to be a play rather than a story or novel I have never been sure, but it was like the difference, for an artist, between a sculpture and a drawing—it seemed more tangible. One could walk around a play, it excited an architectural pleasure that mere prose did not. But it may mainly have been my love of mimicry, of imitating voices and sounds: like most playwrights, I am part actor.

I had actually seen only a few plays, and those so many years before in Harlem, plus a recent college production of *Henry VIII* in which I played a bishop who thankfully had no lines but merely nodded gravely on cue. I was living at 411 North State Street in a house owned by a family named Doll. One of the sons, Jim, lived in a room across the corridor where he made the costumes for the theatre on his sewing machine, from his own designs. On a budget of pennies he generated a flood of Renaissance clothes of incredible richness, even Henry's famous S-hook necklace, which he made of common drapery hooks bought from the five-and-ten and painted gold. When spring vacation drew near I asked Jim how long an act was, and he said half an hour or so. I began to write and in about a day and a night had finished what felt to me like Act I. I set my alarm clock for half an hour and read the act aloud to myself, and exactly as the curtain fell the bell, to my amazement, went off. The very notion of a fixed form like this was of course normal for that era. It was only later on that I became aware of Strindberg, the mystical rather than social reformist side of Ibsen, and the German expressionists. In a few of the avant-garde theatre magazines, almost all politically on the left, I had begun to read one-act protest plays about miners, stevedores, and the like, but nothing came near the work of Clifford Odets, the only poet, I thought, not only in the social protest theatre but in all of the New York theatre. And the only theatre there was was in New York, the academic theatres being devoted almost exclusively to restaging the latest Broadway hits, usually the comedies at that. The more ambitious would occasionally stage one of the Greek classics or a Shakespeare play, in productions that put everyone to sleep.

From the beginning, the idea of writing a play was entwined with my very conception of myself. Playwriting was an act of self-discovery from the start and would always be; it was a kind of license to say the unspeakable, and I would never write anything good that did not somehow make me blush. From the beginning, writing meant freedom, a spreading of wings, and once I got the first inkling that others were reached by what I wrote, an assumption arose that some kind of public business was happening inside me, that what perplexed or moved me must move others. It was a sort of blessing I invented for myself. Of course the time would come, as it had to, when the blessing seemed to have been withdrawn from me, but that was far down the road.

Working day and night with a few hours of exhausted sleep sprinkled through the week, I finished the play in five days and gave it to Jim to read. I was close to despair that he might make nothing of it, but I had never known such exhilaration—it was as though I had levitated and left the world below. Like my father in times of unresolvable stress, having handed over the manuscript, I fell sound asleep. I was awakened by laughter. It was coming from Jim's room. My stomach went hard with terror and hope.

Jim Doll was about six feet eight inches tall, as were his mother and father and brother, a family of giants bending over to pass through the doorways of their tiny nineteenth-century Midwest house. I was drawn to Jim, who was the first practical theatre man I had ever met. When he talked about them, the published plays I was reading lost some of their monumental inevitability and he led me to see their flaws and stumbles. He was also the first homosexual I had known, and his suffering—at that time and in the Middle West besides—created a kind of kinship of misfits. He had a vast acquaintance with the European playwrights and pointed me toward their works, especially Chekhov, whom he worshiped.

Finally his door opened, and he came across the corridor into my room and handed me the manuscript. Aesthetic pleasure makes people vulnerable, and Jim's long, bony face was like a child's now, despite a smile made crooked by his forcing down the left side of his upper lip to cover missing incisors, a not uncommon condition in those hard times. "It's a play, all right. It really is!" He laughed with a naiveté I had not seen in him before. "What's surprising is how the action flows and draws everything into it instead of chasing after its meanings. I think it's the best student play I've ever read." Something like love shone in his face, something, incredibly enough, like gratitude.

Outside, Ann Arbor was empty, still in the spell of spring vacation. I wanted to walk in the night, but it was impossible to keep from trotting. My thighs were as hard and strong as iron bars. I ran uphill to the deserted center of town, across the Law Quadrangle and down North University, my head in the stars. I had made Jim laugh and look at me as he never had before. The magical force of making marks on a piece of paper and reaching into another human being, making him see what I had seen and feel my feelings—I had made a new shadow on the earth.

And if I should win a Hopwood, imagine! Two hundred and fifty dollars for one week's work! I was still accustomed to thinking like a laborer: it had taken me two years to save up the five hundred dollars to come to Michigan, two years on the subway morning and night, living through the summer heat and the freezing cold in that auto parts warehouse.

The Chadick-Delamater warehouse, on Sixty-third Street and Tenth Avenue, where the Metropolitan Opera House now stands, was my entry into the big world beyond home and school. It was the largest wholesale auto parts warehouse east of the Mississippi, an old firm that sold to retail parts stores and garages all over the Eastern seaboard. Stashed away in its five floors of bins and shelves were parts for all the latest models, as well as some, their records long vanished, that fit cars and trucks built by forgotten manufacturers long before the First War.

Joe Shapse, a schoolmate at Lincoln High, was the son of a parts retailer whose shop, just at the end of the Fifty-ninth Street Bridge in Long Island City, repaired the gas company's trucks, among

others, and was a good customer of Chadick-Delamater. I had
driven Sam Shapse's delivery truck for a few months after graduation, making many pickups of parts from Chadick, and had come
to understand something about the business, although I managed
to get myself lost in Long Island City several times a day and was
not in general Sam's greatest find as a truck driver. The summer
of 1932 was probably the lowest point of the Depression, and Sam's
business had almost come to a complete halt. It was all very simple,
nobody had any money. What would be the last Republican administration for twenty years was at its gasping end, without ideas,
and for us at the bottom, without even the rhetoric of hope. My
memories of that year especially, as I moved the truck through the
streets, back and forth across the bridges, up into the Bronx and out
to Brooklyn, were of a city under a spell, being slowly covered with
dust, block after block sprouting new For Rent signs on the dirty
windows of long-established and now abandoned stores. That was
the year of the breadlines, too, of able-bodied men standing six and
eight abreast along some warehouse wall waiting to be handed a
bowl of soup or a piece of bread by one or another improvised city
agency, the Salvation Army, or a church.

People then had a way of looking movingly at one another on the
streets, there always seemed to be a kind of question in their
eyes—"Are you making it? What are you doing that I could do? Are
you in? How can I get in? When does this end?" Only in that sense
were people more unguarded with each other, especially in working-class neighborhoods like Long Island City, for there was ferocity, too. We were all on a ship that had run aground and were
walking around on the deck staring out at a horizon that every
morning was exactly the same. And that was when Sam had to let
me go. He was a small man with an easygoing temperament, a
Hoover supporter and lifelong Republican who had given up trying to justify his president. Like a lot of other people in 1932, he
simply stopped talking about politics—it was all too baffling, an
epidemic of rolling catastrophes that no one could stop.

So I was back hanging around the house again, despairingly
scanning the few help-wanted ads in the *Times* each morning. In
those days it was routine for an ad to specify "White" or "Gentile"
or sometimes "Chr." And the eye soon trained itself to zip down
a column and to stop only at the ads with no such warning—for that
is what it was to me, a warning to stay away. It was a time when
to be a Jew was to be a little bit black too; the two groups still
understood one another. There were even ads specifying "Protes-

tant" and, very rarely, "Cath. firm," as though the city consisted of clans terrified of each other's impurities. My disdain for such clannishness probably helped move me later to marry a gentile girl.

One morning I was excited to see an ad with no warning symbols calling for a stock clerk at fifteen dollars a week in an auto parts warehouse in Manhattan. The phone number and address seemed familiar. It was Chadick-Delamater. I instantly called Sam Shapse to ask permission to use him as a reference, and he of course agreed. "But I want you to be sure to let me know what they tell you when you apply." I had no idea what lay behind his instruction.

I recognized Wesley Moulter, the manager, from my frequent pickups there in the past. I sat beside his desk all scrubbed and wearing my one tie, feet flat on the floor to conceal the hole in my shoe sole, and told him about my experience working for Shapse. Moulter at thirty was in charge of the whole place, at a salary of thirty-six dollars a week. As a sign of his executive status he wore a striped tie, had his collar buttoned, and rolled his sleeves neatly up two turns to mid-forearm; the ordinary help rolled their sleeves up above the elbow. A serious fellow but not cheerless, he had dense, tightly curled reddish hair and a square flat face and a thick neck. His desk was set beside a window overlooking the street, a few feet from where the bookkeepers, three women and one man, bent to their tasks. The walls of this white-collar area were bare cement block, and my eye as I talked with Moulter detected some daylight in the mortar joints. He gave me five minutes, nodded once or twice, took my phone number, and said he would let me know.

I did nothing all next day but hang around near the phone in our dining room, which, like anything one stares at long enough, began to become animate, the living spirit of a mockingly obdurate silence. My desire for the job spread over me like an itch that I was trying to forget. The fifteen-dollar salary was not only three more than the going rate for a "boy" but proof of how high-class a firm Chadick was. And indeed from my vantage point as a truck driver it had always had a certain panache, handling the best brands— Bear ignitions, Timken roller bearings, Detroit axles, Brown and Lipe transmissions, Packard-Lackard ignition wires, Prestone antifreeze, Gates gaskets and radiator hoses, Perfect Circle piston rings and wrist pins—these were heavy names that bespoke grave and established firms solid as rock. On entering Chadick, one walked on a concrete floor unlike the splintery floors in other auto warehouses. The place was always swept and had a banklike decorum, as in the offices of Brooklyn Union Gas, where we would go to pay our monthly bills. Obviously they were offering fifteen dollars instead of twelve because they expected more from whomever they hired, and I, standing at the starting line, was crouched and ready to go in this, the beginning of my eighteenth year, but the phone did not ring.

As I sobered up, the inevitable reason for that silence was plain, but it did not particularly dishearten me, I think; such exclusion was not yet given the name of discrimination and was merely the natural order of things. It simply meant that I would have to probe for another way into the American world.

That evening Sam Shapse phoned to ask if I had been hired, and when I told him I hadn't, he said, "You are going to have that job. You know more about the business than any boy they're likely to find. It's because you're Jewish. But most of their customers are Jews, and I am going to call them first thing in the morning. You get ready to go down there, you hear?"

Moulter called in the middle of the next morning and gave me the good news, and I was on the trolley rocketing down Gravesend Avenue to the subway stop at Church and then up to Times Square and a change to the local train to Sixty-sixth Street, then a short trot over to Sixty-third and up the steel stairs into that quiet, cool establishment. Except for Moulter and one other, they were all Irish, all of them to a man and woman, and as I began to move among them I practically had to stand still to be sniffed, for there had never been one of my kind in this pen before.

The three women bookkeepers were the first to relent; one of them, Dora, found me working behind a pile of axles. A spinster (as thin and with the same nearly transparent wrists as the Baroness Blixen, with whom, a quarter-century on, I would spend an afternoon), Dora whispered through her buck teeth and what I got to know as the perpetual cold in her nose that I would like it here, that it was an awfully nice place to work. I was grateful to her for that, but I realized that my job of locating parts in five stories of bins to fill the orders impaled on a spike on the desk of the sixty-five-year-old packing boss, Gus—he had the same mustache as Kaiser Wilhelm and fierce white eyebrows and a belly that looked as solid as a medicine ball—the job would only be easy once I knew where the stock was. Such welcome as I had been given soon wore thin as the other workers grew tired of being asked where I should look for various items. So at quarter past five, when everyone had left, I started at the end of one aisle of storage bins, climbed the rolling ladder, and peered into each one to see what lay inside. Soon I heard heel taps on the concrete floor and, looking down, saw Wesley Moulter making his way around the foot of my ladder toward the bathroom, a linen towel over his wrist. I nodded a greeting to him, about to explain my no doubt praiseworthy purpose in staying late, but before I could speak he grinned up at me with a cool, untroubled gaze and said, "Figuring on owning the place?" and continued on down the aisle to the toilet.

The coldness in my belly did not warm up until I was halfway back to Brooklyn. Maybe I shouldn't try to buck the dislike I now realized must be the general feeling for me there. Dora's little visit, it occurred to me, had been meant to show me that she was not like the others, but what a frail ally! I said nothing to the family at dinner; there was no point spoiling their relief at my landing a job. Kermit, always romantic about business, thought I had taken a fabulous step forward in being employed by such a fine company. Of course we all knew that without Sam Shapse's intervention I would not have been hired, but the psychological principle of reality denial was already doing its work. I desperately wanted the Chadick job and feared that a season of idleness would weaken me, as it was doing to so many guys in the neighborhood who had no money to continue in school, and the objective need created the necessary attitude—I denied that Wesley Moulter, my boss, hated my presence, and when I came in to work next morning I cheerfully nodded to anyone who looked like a candidate for a friendly hello, and went around the place energetically filling orders. In the quiet periods, when there were no orders to fill and men stood around the packing table in the back of the loft, I quickly learned how to stand on the sidelines, looking and listening and uncharacteristically keeping my young mouth shut rather than seeming to ask for their friendship or even toleration.

But in a few weeks I was trading inanities just like the rest of them. They had caught on that I was really no smarter than they were, dumber in some ways, in fact; for the fear of the Jew is first of all the fear of his intelligence, which is mysterious and devilish and can embarrass and ensnare the unwary. It is the fear, too, of people who appear not to live by one's own rules, a mirror image of the Jew's estimate of the gentile. I would learn at Chadick's how to hold the hand of a man whose wife had almost lost her newborn baby's life in their unheated Weehawken flat the night before; he was so distressed—hours afterward, when he had time to realize what had nearly happened—that he suddenly began to shake, his face looking split as if by a stroke. This was Huey, a large blond lisping stock clerk of twenty-eight who even normally was in a suppressed state of desperation from trying to feed his four children on eighteen dollars a week.

As time went by and season followed season outside the filthy windows of the packing room, which overlooked both the ailanthus trees growing up out of the backyards and a newly installed five-story bordello—we could wave to the naked young whores taking their sunbaths sitting cross-legged like Hindus on their beds in the morning—the sheer endurance and self-discipline of Chadick workers came to move me, although I knew enough not to have illusions about our being "the same." On the hour-and-a-half trip in from Brooklyn every morning I was reading novels or the *Times*, a paper they would sometimes peruse with a certain suspicious daintiness, turning a page with their fingertips as though it were satin. And when Dora, in whom I had confided, let it out that I was saving to go to college, the moral they drew was that Jews did not drink up their pay, so that once again we were set apart. Besides, by intending to go to college I was not only trying to escape their common fate but implicitly stating that I was better than they. Still, their questions about my strange people were mostly about our family practices, for what impressed and baffled them a little was that an able-bodied guy like me was not being required to contribute to the family's upkeep but was instead allowed to save for his education. Most weeks, in fact, I banked thirteen out of my fifteen dollars' pay, figuring I could just make the required five-hundred mark by July or August of 1934, in time for the September semester at Michigan.

Only once did the mask of acceptance—if indeed it ought to be called that—slip. Fetching parts as usual out of a bin in the middle of a corridor, and failing to hear Huey's footsteps coming up behind me, I stepped back to clear the ladder's path and sent its wheel rolling over his toe. He was a heavy, flat-footed, slope-shouldered man and usually wore shoes with razor slits to ease the joints of his big toes. The pain shot his fist straight at my nose as he yelled, "You fucking . . ." I could hear "Jew" almost but not quite as I ducked and his fist jammed into a bin. It took a couple of minutes to free it, and his knuckles were bleeding from the shallow scratches of the sheet metal. Walking away with his handkerchief wrapped around his hand, he looked very peeved, but nothing more was ever said about it.

By the time I left Chadick-Delamater in August of 1934, I had broken in Peter Damone, the first Italian to work there, a dour and proper young Sicilian who never smiled and was rapidly cordoned off from *all* intimate confidences, as I had been from some; and Dennis MacMahon, fresh off the boat, a young giant with a lovely brogue who pasted sheets of wrapping paper over the windows so that he would not have to be looking at whores all of his God-given days here. Dennis was soon struggling against becoming a drunk, as most of them had had to do at some time in their working lives, understandably, I thought, given that they knew there was absolutely no future for them here and at the same time that they had to be thankful for working at all in those days. The repression of anger, though, was not always successful.

With a figurative line of eager unemployed waiting to take our jobs should we ever complain about conditions, we learned to absorb blows to the ego without flinching. If one of us, for example, happened to pick up an order for brake lining, we had to cut it to size ourselves on an abrasive wheel without a guard, with no mask or goggles, even though the brake material was compressed asbestos as hard and brittle as brick. A cloud of stinking asbestos dust filled the work area and even drifted out to the front office from time to time, and once in a while the abrasive wheel would shatter and glass-sharp slivers would fly all over the packing room. It never occurred to me or anyone else that the risk involved might be abnormal. A piece of broken wheel hit me in the chest once, but since it was winter and never warmer than the high fifties or low sixties in the place, I had kept my windbreaker and sweater on and hardly felt the blow and simply proceeded to attach a new wheel and went right on cutting brake lining. The papers reported new unions being organized in various industries, but when I mentioned this to Huey and the other workers they looked at me with a certain apprehension at the prospect of conflict with the big boss (whom I would name "Mr. Eagle" in a play about this place written twenty years later, and whose real name I have long forgotten). Anyway, we knew we were unskilled and easily replaceable. The fact is we were quite like other workers then, even some skilled ones, in our lack of pride in what we were doing for a living. Had an organizer appeared we would have thought ourselves beneath consideration as union members.

Mr. Eagle was said to own several other firms, which was why he only appeared here one or two days a week. According to Dora he had gone to Princeton and was a yachtsman, which one could ascertain by glancing through the only clean windows in the place, in the partition surrounding his little office up front; on the wall was a large etching of a sailboat at sea, a taunt to the eye in the heat of summer, for we of course not only had no air conditioning but also no fans, and the temperature on the three-foot-long thermometer with "Prestone" printed on it in blue and red hanging near the front counter often went over ninety degrees. It never occurred to anyone to ask Moulter to ask Eagle for a fan. Instead, a steady line of people kept moving in and out of the single toilet next to the packing table overlooking the whores, to lave their faces using the one tepid water tap over the grimy brown sink in there, the same that Mr. Eagle used himself. Nor did it seem an indignity when, on occasion, Mrs. Eagle, a rather sweetly polite young woman who always seemed airily dressed for a party in the middle of the day, would leave their two large and insane springer spaniels tied to the big cast-iron floor scale while she went off for a few hours of shopping. Since under the scale lived a venerable colony of gray mice with dozens of members, the tied dogs never ceased attacking the steel base and howling as though in the hunt over the countryside that was imprinted on their brains. Naturally the male of the pair occasionally pissed on the scale, leaving the question of who among us was supposed to clean this up, and our one sign of revolt was the unspoken decision to let it dry slowly all by itself. We had the pleasure of watching Mrs. Eagle having to negotiate the puddle when she returned to untie her animals and to thank us all for bearing with them, unaccustomed as they were to city life.

In·A Memory of Two Mondays, my one-act play written as the fifties got under way, I tried to paint the picture, but it was only abroad that the play made a mark for itself—in Latin America, Italy, Czechoslovakia, and the less affluent countries of Europe, which still had such workers and conditions of work or could remember them. In New York in 1955 the stock market was on the rise and the dollar was the only legitimate money in the world and a play about workers was the last thing anybody wanted to think about. By the time I wrote the play I had had five plays produced on Broadway and had been embraced and, as I knew in my gut, rejected by what I still imagined was the peculiar aberration of American society known as the Eisenhower time. A play like this, I felt, with its implied assertion of human solidarity, was one way of insisting that something besides money-getting had to be real, if only as a memory of a long-gone era. But nostalgia, I suppose, is reserved for memories of pleasure, not pain or mere reality.

In any case, on the day I left Chadick-Delamater at the end of the summer of 1934, Dora alone seemed to register the fact, just as only she had noted, two years earlier, that I had arrived. Even Dennis, my closest friend there, barely glanced up as I said good-bye to him while he wrapped up an axle. Jim Smith, the octogenarian onetime Indian fighter, went padding by with his cigar stub centered in his pursed mouth, his head tilted up as he read an order in his hand through his bifocals, and Johnny Drone, with the same blackheads around his nose that he had had two years earlier, wearing one of his three dark blue ties stiffened with soil, gave me a slight nod, shifted from one foot to the other as though standing on a hot boiler, and said, "You ought to look into accountancy." There were now two new Irish parts clerks whom I had never gotten to know at all since they did hardly any work and disappeared for hours into the freight elevator to shoot craps with suckers they had found in the street. In order to aggravate the naive and pure Dennis, who, however, had long since lost the Irish country bloom of his cheeks, these two one late afternoon sat themselves down on his packing table and gave a loud and circumstantial account of how, on the previous weekend, they had taken a girl home from a dance in Paterson and each in turn had raped her while the other drove the borrowed truck. Dennis's outrage had led to the first and only knockdown fight in my time there. It brought Wesley Moulter running down from the front office hollering at Roach, one of the two clerks, who was pounding on Dennis's belly, while I pulled on Dennis, and Dora and a couple of other women screamed and threatened to call the cops, before the ordinary torpor of the place was restored.

One day in the mid-forties, some ten years after I had walked out of there to go to Michigan, I found myself a few blocks away, and for the first time in many years feeling a tug of curiosity about my relationship with these people, I decided to pay a sentimental visit. I walked over from Broadway, climbed the stairs, opened the steel door, and was surprised to see a wholly new atmosphere. The counter was now faced in dark plywood, and a paneled wall, declaring a new gentility, blocked off the public from the aisles of bins as well as from the office area that must still have existed somewhere behind it. A couple of mechanics were waiting to be served at the counter, and presently an overweight blond man came through the door from the rear to wait on them. It was Huey, but swollen with middle age, disguised by a decade of time. He wore a respectable shirt and tie now and had his shirt sleeves neatly rolled to mid-forearm in executive style, and without being able to see his feet I was sure he was no longer wearing shoes with slits in them. The mechanics left with boxes of parts, and I came to the counter and nodded to him. He waited for me to give my order, and I said, "How are you, Huey?"

Nonrecognition flattened his gaze, and a surprising suspicion, too. I was embarrassed to have to tell him my name. He was busy, obviously. "What'd you want?" he asked, still expecting me to order. I explained that I had worked here for two years. Like the Depression itself, my time at Chadick was a dream now; he not only did not remember me but seemed irritated at being forced to wonder what I was up to. His honed lack of interest in even trying to recall depressed me, and the conversation began to stumble, and after only a couple of minutes I left, closing the steel door behind me for the last time. There was the same anonymous scent of steel as on my first arrival and my departure, a scent that reminded me of the Navy Yard and factories, and one that I would always find stimulating, promising a kind of comradeship of makers and builders, but depressing in the end as each man is left exactly where he began—alone.

Walking away that afternoon, I wondered what I had expected from a return to Chadick-Delamater. To show off to them that I had made it and was a writer now, with a failed Broadway play and a novel, *Focus,* that a surprising number of people had bought? Yes, but it was more than boasting; I had really wanted somehow to stop time, I think, perhaps to steal back from it what it had stolen from us, but Huey's failure—or refusal—to remember had thrown me right back on myself again. It was terribly strange that the whole crew should have stayed so fixed in my mind while I had vanished from theirs. How could Huey have wiped out so completely the memory of my gripping his hand to steady him during his sudden fit of fear after his baby had nearly died in his freezing flat, or even that he had thrown a punch at me? Is this, I wondered, why writing exists—as a proof against oblivion? And not just for the writer himself but also for all the others who swim in the depths where the sun of the culture never penetrates?

I bought a paper and walked down Broadway reading it. The bleeding of Russia was of staggering proportions, but the war was slowly turning against Germany. There was talk of losing half a million Americans in the onslaught against Japan that would be coming up one day soon. I had been turned down for military service twice now. My brother was somewhere in Europe. Yet the city seemed weirdly unaffected. What meaning had all this blood-letting? If my brother died, would it make a difference? As a non-combatant I had time for such questions. And I thought that in secret people did worry about the meaning of things but were too unsure to admit it, going along instead with the official pretensions to an overwhelming national purpose that would someday justify everything. I wished I could speak for those people, say what they lacked the art to say.

In the eight years since winning my first Hopwood Award in 1936, I had written four or five full-length plays; the novel version of *The Man Who Had All the Luck; Situation Normal,* a book of reportage about army training drawn from my research for my screenplay *The Story of GI Joe;* and some two dozen radio plays on which I had been making my living. I was walking through the city in wartime feeling the inevitable unease of the survivor. I had even tried to serve by applying for a job with the Office of War Information, the propaganda and intelligence agency, but with my school-book French and no connections I apparently had nothing to offer and was turned down. I seemed to be part of nothing, no class, no influential group; it was like high school perpetually, with everybody else rushing to one or another club or conference with a teacher, and me still trying to figure out what was happening. I was only sure that writing was not a matter of invention; I could not be the Dickens of *The Book of Knowledge,* his head surrounded with portraits of characters that had miraculously sprung from it. The city I knew was incoherent, yet its throttled speech seemed to implore some significance for the sacrifices that drenched the papers every day. And psychologically situated as I was—a young, fit man barred from a war others were dying in, equipped with a lifelong anguish of self-blame that sometimes verged on a pathological sense of responsibility—it was probably inevitable that the selfishness, cheating, and economic rapacity on the home front should have cut into me with its contrast to the soldiers' sacrifices and the holiness of the Allied cause. I was a stretched string waiting to be plucked, waiting, as it turned out, for *All My Sons,* which, as I have said, was set off by the last person in the world I could imagine being inspired by—Mary's mother, Mrs. Slattery.

No work of any interest has a single source, any more than a person psychologically exists in only one place at any one time. Nevertheless, as Tolstoy thought, in an artist's work we want to read his soul, and for that, the artist must commit himself and stand still for his self-portrait. I was trying to make of spirit a fact, to make a circumstance of what I took to be a common longing for meaning.

I wanted to write a play that would stand on the stage like a boulder that had fallen from the sky, undeniable, a fact. I had come a particular road to the point of making such a demand not only of myself but of the drama.

On the day my name was called out before the assembled contestants and their guests as a Hopwood winner, in the spring of 1936, I felt pleasure, of course, but also something close to embarrassment, praying that everybody would soon forget my poor play in favor of my next one, which would surely be better.

I immediately called my mother, who screamed and left the phone and rushed outside to arouse relatives and neighbors to the new day dawning while my new wealth trickled away into the phone company's vault. On Third Street I was now famous and no longer in danger of watching my life shrivel up in touch football games on the streets all day, and there is no fame more gratifying. In particular the prize let me relish a certain vengeance upon a woman, my aunt Betty, widow of my mother's brother Harry, self-appointed seer, card reader, and mystic, whom my mother had had do my cards on the eve of my departure for Michigan two years before. Betty had been a very buxom and good-looking woman, at one time a burlesque dancer. When she had realized, twenty years ago, that her baby son was mongoloid, she turned to religion and expectantly watched for spooks out of the corners of her eyes as she wiped poor Carl's chin, by turns flying at him in a rage, mocking his fluffy speech to his face, and dressing him up in expensive suits and ties to proudly walk with him, teaching him how to take her arm and act like a real gentleman.

On the last night before my trip west, Betty had sat me down at the dining room table and dealt the cards. My mother kept a certain distance from us lest her own vibrations of anxiety confuse those emanating from me. My father was in the living room playfully baiting Carl. "So you like Mae West, Carl?" "Oh, yeah, I love him." "What do you love about him?" "He beautiful." My sister, Joan, now entering her teens, was probably upstairs trying on Mother's clothes with her best friend, Rita, whom I suspected, rightly as it turned out, of pilfering our loose change, and who was graduating into Mother's costume jewelry, heading no doubt for the few valuable diamond trinkets that were still left. Kermit, I suppose, was either off on a date or in the bedroom writing me one of his heartfelt hortatory notes, his style a continuation of poor

Uncle Moe's Victorian World War I letters from the front. In short, I was leaving them all behind, the Joseph packing up to cross the desert to bamboozle Pharaoh one day. I knew that this last evening at home was a cresting of my life's small wave.

An expectant silence as Betty carefully snapped down the last card in the row and proceeded to match arcane correspondences in the series of cards, which she now placed one on top of the other. Pause. More shifting of cards in a thickening silence. Obsessively neat Aunt Esther walked in to say goodbye and wish me luck but before she could speak was *shhh*ēd by my mother and stood awed, brushing specks of dandruff off her nearly nonexistent bosom as she watched Betty's operation.

Now Betty shook her head mournfully from side to side. "He's not going to do very well there. He's going to flunk out in a few months." Electric horror flashed into my mother's eyes. Betty now looked directly at me, reaching over with a commiserating touch of her hand. "Save your money. Stay home. There's no use going there."

Naive though I was at the time, it occurred to me as I looked into her round, sensual face that there might be less a question of spectral visitation here than jealousy. But I quickly shook off the accusatory thought—after all, she was family and must wish me well. The truth was that she had touched the naked nerve of superstition in me, depressing me by saying exactly what I feared myself. Valiantly recovering, my mother immediately whipped out coffee and one of her deep yeast cakes and turned the occasion into a party, to which news of the cake's appearance drew a houseful of well-wishers before the night was out. Next morning Kermit and my father were at the bus to see me off as though the nether parts of Asia were my destination, and at the very last moment Kermit suddenly took off his hat—he always looked handsome in hats, and I ridiculous—and stuck it on my head as a parting gift. It was a hat I would only lose four years later on my last hitchhike home, in a wheat field near Oneonta, New York, on a day filled with sunshine and spring gusts, when a sudden wind lifted it off my head and away into the distance like a child's balloon as I hurried to a car that had stopped for me on a very lonesome road.

By the spring of '36 and the Hopwood Award I no longer feared academic failure, but I wanted Betty to acknowledge this distinction, in order, I suppose, that I might also believe it, since she had done no more than express my own doubts that evening. Only fitfully was my victory a promise of things to come; hardly had I cashed the Hopwood check when I started the habit, which I have never lost, of worrying whether I had anything left to write. I had exhausted all I knew about the family in this first play, and I knew very little about anything else. More, its central drive had been an attack on a father by his eldest son for his antisocial attitude in fighting a strike in his plant. But having laid my fictional father low, I had the satisfaction of winning the approbation of my real one, no longer needing to pretend to him that I was studying journalism—a real profession with a boss and salary. As for Kermit, toward whom I felt some guilt for having left him to prop up the family while I, the inferior student, went off to college, the prize might help him to feel his sacrifice had not been wasted, even as he must have privately wondered why he was not a recipient too. But he was in service to the idealized father just as I was enlisted in that ideal's destruction.

The prize had all sorts of benefits. It earned me the pained pleasure of listening to Professor Erich Walter give an unprecedented reading of my play to his essay class as an example, he said, of the condensation of language. This absentminded, lovable man—whose tie as often as not came out from under the side of his shirt collar, and who habitually forgot that he was slipping out of his overcoat on entering the classroom and simply walked away from it to his desk, from where, half an hour later, he would notice it lying on the floor and stare down at it through thick rimless glasses, wondering how it had climbed off the hook—Erich Walter insisted on reading my New York dialogue in his Midwestern twang, which tore my ears, especially when he pronounced "Oh, yeah" as "Oh, yay." But his horrible rendition was so loving that when a line got a laugh from the class he would look up with apple cheeks shining to beam proudly down the long table at me. A while earlier in the term he had surprised me by inviting me to walk with him after class. So awed was I by professors that this individual notice raised my sophomore self-regard by several yards even before he spoke. What he wished to tell me was that my essays indicated a bent for criticism and that I might become a critic if I studied, let's say, for ten years. Ten years! I would be thirty before I could begin being a critic! I could only nod gravely as though I would consider it, but I was secretly thinking I would break through as a playwright in a year, or at most two—certainly not nine, as it turned out. Walter sent me to Kenneth Rowe, who taught playwriting and welcomed me to his class. Rowe soon became for me a combination of critical judge and confidant. Aside from his friendship, which meant much to me, his chief contribution to my development was his interest in the dynamics of play construction, something not normally the subject of college courses. His scholarship and support were greatly important, and when he became a consultant to the Theatre Guild, reading new plays for them, this professional recognition added weight to his encouragement.

It was the same Erich Walter who in the early fifties took me into his office in the new administration mini-skyscraper to help me with my *Holiday* article. Dean of the university now, he wore a smartly tailored business suit and a sedate tie that no longer came out from under the side of his collar but obediently from the front, and he had a couple of secretaries in the outer office, but he still lisped and had pink cheeks and listened intently, always ready to be delighted. He was hoping, he said, that McCarthyism would be part of my article, for its paranoid spirit was paralyzing communication between students and faculty and, combined with the current corporate competition for college graduates, was inculcating a smooth and featureless psyche in the young. The students' highest goal, he felt, was now to fit into corporate America rather than to develop some skill in separating truth from falsehood. "They become experts at grade-getting, but there's less hanging round the lamppost now, no more just chewing the fat," or speculating about the wrongs of the world and ideal solutions, something no employer was interested in and might even suspect. It was Walter who sent me over to the orientation professor, who in all innocence, with no idea of the sinister implications, revealed as a matter of course that the FBI was actually enlisting students to report any radical remarks by their professors and at the same time asking professors to inform on students who expressed dangerous thoughts. The shadow of the faceless informer had not quite darkened the entire university of the fifties, but the dean was beginning to seriously dread the future.

With the 1936 Hopwood Award, my psychic sun on the rise, I had no difficulty pitting myself in imagination against the reigning writers of the Broadway theatre—Clifford Odets, first of all, and Maxwell Anderson, S. N. Behrman, Sidney Howard, Sidney Kingsley, and Philip Barry, and a dozen others whose names have disappeared with their seasons. However, there were no Americans who seemed to be working a vein related to what I had come to sense was mine, except for Odets and for a few weeks Anderson, who I thought was attempting to break out of the dusty Broadway naturalistic habit. But there was something artificially antiqued in his work that soon wore thin for me.

As for Eugene O'Neill, his work seemed archaic in the mid-thirties with its mawkish twenties slang and, along with a deadly repetitiveness that sometimes lulled me to sleep as I tried to read his plays, a suspicion of self-willed grandeur. One approaches writers from one's own historical moment, and from where I stood O'Neill seemed the playwright of the mystical rich, of high society and the Theatre Guild and escapist "culture." It would take many years before an entirely opposite side of him emerged, when his disgust appeared more absolute and beyond earthly solace than any strain in Odets, who alone had seemed pure, revolutionary, and the bearer of the light. This, of course, by virtue of his commitments to socialism and the Soviet idealization that was so widespread in the West, as much as for his plays' lyricism of hopeful despair. O'Neill had begun his decade of silence just as Odets's rocketlike career was taking off, and this seemed to prove the withering up of his fossilized individualism, his dirgelike longing for private salvation redolent of the alcoholic twenties, in contrast to Odets's comradely outcry against the intolerable present. As always, we were trapped into estimating writers by what they apparently stood for rather than by what they were actually doing, by the critical propaganda surrounding them rather than by their literary deeds.

It would await the end of the forties, a quite different decade, for me to realize that I had been had; despite the extremely weak original production of *The Iceman Cometh* in 1946, the same season *All My Sons* opened, I was nevertheless struck by O'Neill's radical hostility to bourgeois civilization, far greater than anything Odets had expressed. Odets's characters were alienated because—when you came down to it—they couldn't get into the system, O'Neill's because they so desperately needed to get out of it, to junk it with all its boastful self-congratulation, its pious pretension to spiritual values when in fact it produced emptied and visionless men choking with unnameable despair. If content had been the gauge of radicalism rather than certain automatic journalistic tags like "Catholic," "Jewish," "tragic," and "class-conscious," it would have been O'Neill who was branded the anticapitalist writer first and foremost. Odets, after all, would have reformed capitalism with a dose of socialism; O'Neill saw no hope in it whatsoever, but unlike

Odets he was not part of any political movement, at least not since his socialist youth. It was O'Neill who wrote about working-class men, about whores and the social discards and even the black man in a white world, but since there was no longer a connection with Marxism in the man himself, his plays were never seen as the critiques of capitalism that objectively they were.

The real Odets was also not quite as advertised at the time. He might wave a red flag and for a while be happy to take to the air as a "stormbird of the working class," but this was gesturing toward a hoped-for certainty that he did not really possess, as it turned out. He was an American romantic, as much a Broadway guy as a proletarian leader, probably more so. To call him contradictory is merely to say he was very much alive and a sufferer. Harold Clurman, his director and closest friend, visiting him in Hollywood, once read him a sentence he had written about him—"For Odets Hollywood is Sin"—and laughed as he quoted himself. "What are you laughing about? It is," Odets rebuked him, like a man who had lost his moral bearings.

One could easily blame him for squandering himself in screenplays, most of them never produced, but to what theatre was he supposed to remain faithful? The Broadway commercial theatre is an organism that rejects its hearts; Odets felt mocked and discarded in his last years, quite like Williams and O'Neill. I came to taste their species of bitterness myself, but not as devastatingly, perhaps because my illusion of having been truly accepted in the first place was always thin—I was not raised to be surprised when a marriage between commerce and art collapsed. The story of American playwrights is awfully repetitious—the celebratory embraces soon followed by rejection or contempt, and this without exception for any playwright who takes risks and does not comfortably repeat himself.

In the mid-thirties, with what Clurman would call his "poster play," *Waiting for Lefty,* followed by *Awake and Sing!,* Odets had sprung forth, a new phenomenon, a leftist challenge to the system, but even more, the poet suddenly leaping onto the stage and disposing of middle-class gentility, screaming and yelling and cursing like somebody off the Manhattan streets. For the very first time in America, language itself had marked a playwright as unique, for the context of his advent was a nonpolitical and nonlyric theatre, with the hits of the hour plays like *Dinner at Eight, Stage Door, The Children's Hour, The Petrified Forest,* and *The Philadelphia Story. Our Town* was the nearest to a reaching for lyricism, but its language in comparison to Odets's was timorous. And because he was so rough a diamond, Odets's image was instantly loaded with a moral and social responsibility that he would wrestle with through a lifetime. It was not his radicalism, actual and alleged, but his art that was the real cross he bore in a popular culture demanding instant and painless entertainment. The apolitical F. Scott Fitzgerald would founder within much the same conflict, in Odets's case symbolized by Joe Bonaparte of *Golden Boy,* who, according to Clurman, is Odets himself, a man torn between the quick buck and notoriety of boxing-Hollywood-Broadway and his violin, an art expressive of his private soul.

Returning to New York on vacations, I had my brain branded by the beauty of the Group Theatre's productions. With my untamed tendency to idealize whatever challenged the system—including the conventions of the Broadway theatre—I was inspired by the sheer physical spectacle of those shows, their sets and lighting by Boris Aronson and Mordecai Gorelik, and the special kind of hush that surrounded the actors, who seemed both natural and surreal at the same time. To this day I can replay in memory certain big scenes acted by Luther and Stella Adler (children of Jacob, my father's hero), Elia Kazan, Bobby Lewis, Sanford Meisner, and the others, and I can place each actor exactly where he was on the stage fifty years ago. This is less a feat of memory than a tribute to the capacity of these actors to concentrate, to *be* on the stage. When I recall them, time is stopped. They seem never to have been tempted to make an insignificant gesture. The closest to these productions that I ever saw was the Abbey Theatre's *Juno and the Paycock* with Sara Allgood and Barry Fitzgerald, who humbled the heart as though before the unalterable truth. There is also color in my recollection; Gorelik and Aronson used color interpretively, like painters, for its subjective effects and not merely its realistic accuracy. I would later learn of the feuds within the Group, the nervous breakdowns and the selfishness and arrogant ambitiousness of various members, but from my fifty-five-cent balcony seat it was all a dream of utter integrity of aims and artistic means, as indeed it often really was. It was not the first time that the art was nobler than the artist.

Lillian Hellman's work didn't seem to me and other younger writers I knew to belong with these impassioned, challenging plays. Despite her dissection of its moral pretensions, the middle class in her plays seemed as unshakable as it was unworthy, enough so to make it a surprise to learn that personally she was on the left.

There was also a certain elegance in her dialogue that set her apart from the theatre of protest, which was so brash and exciting then. No doubt unjustly, she seemed to some of us preeminently Broadway rather than an outsider, with plots that never faltered and a certain deliberateness that we were probably too young and careless as writers to appreciate. Not slow revelation but the renewing blaze of righteous anger was what we were looking for. Moreover, the heart of decadence was Hollywood, and she seemed too welcome there to be trusted with one's hopes. Which may simply be another way of saying that as rebels we did not know how to idealize successful people, but it did seem unlikely that a genuine light-bearer could be spending so much of her life working for Sam Goldwyn and the other merchants.

My purity was still breathtakingly unmarred through the thirties, so much so that at a certain point in 1939, only months out of college and conniving to get myself a twenty-three-dollar-a-week job on the Federal Theatre Project, which was already coming to its end, I had no qualms about turning down a two-hundred-and-fifty-dollar-a-week offer by a Colonel Joy, representing Twentieth Century Fox, to come to work for them—along with dozens of other young writers who, as the saying went, were being shipped to California in cattle cars at the time. There was a going-away party for a few of them one afternoon, all left-wingers, some of them contributors to *New Masses* magazine's literary page. Two in particular had written unproduced plays that I thought showed talent, and when I asked them why they were leaving the theatre, one of them replied, "Do you realize the number of people who see a movie? We want to reach the people." But with *what* were they being reached? Everyone knew how closely controlled films were. Since there was obviously no contradiction between this man's social convictions and his newfound eagerness to hire himself out, I asked, "But would any of you be talking like this if Fox were paying thirty-five dollars a week?" It was still beyond my understanding, this rush to unfreedom. The very idea of someone editing a play of mine or so much as changing a word was enough to make my skin crawl, and to actually submit pages to a producer who became the owner of what one wrote the moment one wrote it—this was unconscionable. Indeed, the very process itself of exchanging art for money was repulsive. Even as far along as the late forties I was shocked and incredulous to hear an actor referring to his accountant–business adviser. An artist having an *accountant*! And a *business* adviser!

Naturally, I was not above dreaming of success and the power that went with it, a power expressed in wealth and fame, its inevitable accompaniments in the theatre, but success was only legitimate if won without sacrificing independence, a word one particularly connected to the theatre. Odets, one heard, had moved into One Fifth Avenue, one of the most elegant apartment houses in New York, and owned *hundreds of records*. I could never roam the streets of the Village without glancing up at that elegant apartment house overlooking Washington Square and thinking of him with shelf upon shelf of classical music at his fingertips, and probably beautiful actresses stretched out on one of his numerous couches, and him with his shock of wavy hair staring moodily down at the city that waited upon the clacking of his typewriter for scenes that would mesmerize and save. An Odets play was awaited like news hot off the press, as though through him we would know what to think of ourselves and our prospects. But in those years of the "high" thirties when the prestige of the Communists was cresting, there were rumors that even Wall Street analysts were consulting with Communist Party intellectuals for clues as to the system's next crisis. In Marxism was magic, and Odets had the wand, and of course it was an impossible act of levitation to sustain for very long.

For four or five years there was no writer who so concentrated in himself the symbolic uniqueness of his era. O'Neill came out of Jeremiah, Odets out of Isaiah; prophetic spirits both, they were playwrights of political consequence, not merely theatrical talents.

Of course my impressions were filtered by the vast distance from the top of One Fifth Avenue to the street, and the even vaster one from New York to Ann Arbor, where, in addition to schoolwork and jobs, I was writing a full-length play a semester. Confronting dramatic problems myself now, I read differently than I had before, in every period of Western drama, pretending that the works of Chekhov or Euripides or Ernst Toller were brand-new or not yet finished, still open to revision and improvement, trying out choices different from those their authors had made. I imagined them no longer marble masterworks but improvisations that their authors had simply given up trying to perfect. Regarding them as provisional, I could not find as common an identity among various Greek plays as Aristotle described, *Ajax*, for example, being of an entirely different nature than *Oedipus at Colonus*, and so it all devolved into the practical and familiar business of storytelling and the sustaining of tension by hewing to inner theme or paradox. My mind was taken over by the basic Greek structural concept of a past stretching so far back that its origins were lost in myth, surfacing in the present and donating a dilemma to the persons on the stage, who were astounded and awestruck by the wonderful train of seeming accidents that unveiled their connections to that past. (To possess the past is to achieve importance!) But the discovery of connection was also the revealing of their characters; it was each person's uniqueness that paradoxically revealed his union with the fate of all.

And of course the purpose of the whole event was to prove the power of the invisible world, expressed in the long arm of vengeance upon violators of the moral law; and what was the moral law but man's sacred ongoing social survival? And that retribution was beautiful because it proved that something out there cared. The Erinyes, howling furies of the gods' police force, were put in the world to sustain the symmetry of Nature's endless self-correcting urge, her aversion to man-destroying waste.

I could find no such air of process in Odets, only individual explosive scenes with no strong momentum driving the whole, excepting always *Rocket to the Moon,* his one real success as a writer, and one with a central symbol that emits an integral power, not merely a rhetorical one, and does it naturally. I find it interesting that like O'Neill, he was working within and against an orthodoxy, but O'Neill had wrestled loose of his Catholicism, while Odets's Marxism still—in the thirties—pressed him into deforming gestures.

·I encountered Odets the first time in 1940, when I glanced up from a rack of secondhand books in Dauber and Pine's shop on Fifth Avenue and Twelfth Street and recognized him from his photographs, though he looked more wraithlike than I expected. He was just leaving with two thick tomes lovingly clasped to his chest, and since I had only come in to browse, my income from the radio plays being nearly nil at the moment, I followed him outside, something I had never done before. His hair grew thin and soft, like feathery ferns, and his gaunt face had a rather startled look. I was so supremely naive as to mention that I was a playwright too, news that to my surprise seemed to slam a door between us then and there. I had no way of knowing how boringly often this approach must have been made to him, but I did manage to ask what he was writing now, and hefting the books he was carrying, he said, "I'm doing a play about Woodrow Wilson."

Eighteen years later he met Marilyn Monroe in a Hollywood studio and made a date to meet us both for dinner, but first our paths would cross again in 1949, at the Cultural and Scientific Conference for World Peace, in the Waldorf-Astoria Hotel, where we both found ourselves on the arts panel at what would turn out to be a hairpin curve in the road of history.

It was dangerous to participate in that fateful attempt to rescue the wartime alliance with the Soviet Union in the face of the mounting pressures of the Cold War, and one knew it at the time. For me, however, the conference was an effort to continue a good tradition that was presently menaced. To be sure, the four years of our military alliance against the Axis powers were only a reprieve from a long-term hostility that had begun in 1917 with the Revolution itself and merely resumed when Hitler's armies were destroyed. But there was simply no question that without Soviet resistance Nazism would have conquered all of Europe as well as Britain, with the possibility of the United States being forced into a hands-off isolationism at best, or at worst an initially awkward but finally comfortable deal with fascism—or so I thought. Thus, the sharp postwar turn against the Soviets and in favor of a Germany unpurged of Nazis not only seemed ignoble but threatened another war that might indeed destroy Russia but bring down our own democracy as well. The air was growing hot with belligerence. I thought one must either speak out against it or forfeit something of honor and the right to complain in the future.

Paradoxically, however, I might not have agreed to chair one of the panels had *Salesman* not continued to be such a universally acclaimed success. I simply felt better with one foot outside the standard show business world, and once invited, I could not refuse.

There was no denying the probability of retribution against the conference participants as its opening day drew near. If some were obviously only concerned liberals like Harvard astronomer Harlow Shapley, composer Aaron Copland, and painter Philip Evergood, or literary stars like Lillian Hellman, Norman Mailer, Mark Van Doren, Louis Untermeyer, Norman Cousins, and a score of others, the radical Odets would be speaking, as well as some real live Soviets, including the composer Dmitri Shostakovich and the writer A. A. Fadeyev.

The House Committee on Un-American Activities by this time had become a permanent kind of thought police in Hollywood but made forays into New York for a crack or two at a few prominent stage actors, and with all the famous names at the conference the Committee would doubtless be most interested. In addition, on the eve of the conference *Life* magazine published two facing pages of passport-sized photos of the several dozen Americans listed as supporters or participants, a veritable gallery of rogues. And indeed, as the months passed, "Supporter of Waldorf Conference" or "Participant" would become an important key to the subject's disloyalty. On top of this, it was big news in the press that every entrance of the Waldorf-Astoria would be blocked by a line of nuns praying for the souls of the participants, who had been deranged by Satanic seduction. And on the morning of the conference I actually had to step between two gentle sisters kneeling on the sidewalk as I made for the Waldorf door. Even then it was a bewildering thing to contemplate, this world of symbolic gestures and utterances.

The audience for the panel I was chairing—my duty turned out to be simply to announce the name of the next speaker and to recognize people who wished to speak from the floor—was surprisingly sparse, testimony to the fear in the air. Not more than twenty or thirty people showed up, of whom some eight or ten were angrily hostile to the whole occasion. Mary McCarthy was there, along with the composer Nicholas Nabokov, who in later years would become a good friend, and a number of others from the intellectual anti-Communist and Trotskyite camps. Never having attended such a meeting, I did not know exactly what to expect. A couple of speakers read statements pleading for the world not to allow the American-Soviet wartime alliance to disintegrate. Dmitri Shostakovich, small, frail, and myopic, stood as stiffly erect as a doll and without once raising his eyes from a bound treatise in his hand read a *pro forma* statement affirming the peaceful intentions of the Soviets. When he finished he sat down, his gaze directed over the heads of the audience, an unapproachable automaton. The man accompanying him made no attempt to even introduce him to the rest of us on the panel. I can no longer recall what the anti-Soviet contingent actually said, only that I recognized three or four of them who stood up and, mainly addressing Shostakovich, raised the issues of Soviet persecution of artists and the Russian occupation of Eastern Europe. The great composer, who unbeknown to me was at that very moment in a deadly duel with Stalin, kept his silence, and no real debate occurred at the conference, which ended in futility except for its setting a new and higher level of hostility in the Cold War. That a meeting of writers and artists could generate such widespread public suspicion and anger was something brand-new in the postwar world.

Even now something dark and frightening shadows the memory

of that meeting nearly forty years ago, where people sat as in a Saul Steinberg drawing, each of them with a balloon overhead containing absolutely indecipherable scribbles. There we were, a roomful of talented people and a few real geniuses, and in retrospect neither side was wholly right, neither the apologists for the Soviets nor the outraged Red-haters; to put it simply, politics is choices, and not infrequently there really aren't any to make; the chessboard allows no space for a move.

Odets now took his turn. By this time he had spent practically the whole decade in Hollywood, although he still spoke of writing more plays and indeed would in a few years write his last, *The Flowering Peach*. Until this very moment I had not gotten more than a cool nod from Odets, because of his competitive resentment toward me, I assumed. *The Crucible*, still four years in the future, would be the only Broadway play to take on the anti-Communist hysteria; Odets denigrated it to Kazan as "just a story about a bad marriage." There was a slightly more generous acknowledgment by Lillian Hellman, who, after a twenty-minute all but silent walk with me following a performance of the play in its pre-Broadway week in Wilmington, Delaware, let drop, "It's a good play." If we on the left were engaged in a conspiracy, as was almost daily reported, it certainly did not overflow into mutual generosity and support among the participants. It is no great credit to me to say that I felt no such hostility toward either of them, probably because I was sure that if there was a competition among us I had won it. But I was never more conscious of resentment from my fellow writers than from those on the left, no doubt the consequence of my own arrogance as much as theirs.

The audience was quieting down to hear Odets. I had absolutely no idea what he would say, no idea what his present orientation toward the Soviet Union actually was, any more than I knew my own beyond a belief in resisting the burgeoning new anti-Soviet crusade.

He seemed distracted as he rose to his feet, tieless, with his shirt collar open and his sports jacket hanging unbuttoned. I recalled how, years before, I had assumed him to be a determined militant, but he seemed so thin-skinned and childishly sensitive. The roles we play! Striving to achieve an authoritative stance, he now began an amazingly theatrical speech that I have never forgotten, and one that makes me despair of history as more than a circumstantial fiction.

The point is that we were now in 1949, some fifteen years past

Odets's springtide of theatrical rebellion against the failed America of the Depression. Yet not only was he still generally identified with that period, but despite his ten years of Hollywood luxury, he himself evidently felt as he faced this audience that he should sound as though it were still 1935; helpless before his own past, he felt bound to reidentify himself as "Odets."

And what of myself? If I was unsure of my own posture, why was I risking attack by chairing this session, something that I indeed sensed would do more to interfere with my freedom in the coming years than anything I had done until then?

I had tried two years before to define once and for all my philosophical position vis-à-vis Marxism. *All My Sons* had received some very good but also some lukewarm notices, and its fate was doubtful; at this point the *Daily Worker* had nothing but praise for it, noting that its truthfulness would doom it to commercial failure. But once Brooks Atkinson turned it into a popular success with a couple of articles in the *Times*, the *Worker* re-reviewed it and found it a specious apology for capitalism—after all, Chris Keller, the son of the boss who has shipped faulty parts to the army, causing fighter planes to crash, accepts to inherit the business rather than turning into a revolutionary himself. Among other things it now occurred to me that for the left the best proof of artistic purity was failure.

To clarify my own thoughts on the subject, I wrote an essay arguing that if Marxism was indeed a science of society, a Marxist writer could not warp social probability and his own honest observations to prove an a priori point of political propaganda. In short, Chris Keller would not become a revolutionary in real life, and in any case that was not what the play was about. The preconceived conclusion, after all, is detestable to science. I then read my essay to a large meeting of writers in the midtown theatre area and found that it caused massive confusion. For what I seemed to be saying was that art, at least good art, stands in contradiction to propaganda in the sense that a writer cannot make truth but only discover it. Thus, a writer has first to respect what exists or else abandon the idea of unearthing the hidden operating principles of his age. Marxism is in principle neither better nor worse than Catholicism, Buddhism, or any creed as an aid to artistic truth-telling. All one could say was that a philosophy could help an artist if it challenged him to the sublime and turned him from trivializing his talent.

In fact, I pointed out to this audience of writers of various shades of leftist opinion, most of whom no doubt admired *All My Sons*, that the play would not have been written at all had I chosen to abide by the Party line at the time, for during the war the Communists pounced on anything that would disturb national unity; strikes were out of the question, and the whole social process was to be set in amber for the duration. Like everybody else, of course, I knew that this was nonsense and that profiteering on a vast scale, for one thing, was rampant and that the high moral aims of the antifascist alliance, if they were to be given any reality at all, had to be contrasted to what was actually going on in society. The truth was that as I worked on *All My Sons* for better than two years, I expected that if it was ever produced the war would more than likely still be going on. The play would then explode, most especially in the face of the business community with its self-advertised but profitable patriotism—and of the Communists!

As it was, within a few weeks of the play's opening, a letter to the *Times* from an engineer flatly stated that the plot was technically incredible, since all airplane engine elements were routinely X-rayed to detect just such defects as Joe Keller manages to slip past army inspectors. The letter went on to accuse the play of being Communist propaganda, pure and simple. And in August 1947, hardly seven months after *All My Sons* opened, its presentation to U.S. troops in Germany was canceled after blistering protests by the Catholic War Veterans, whose commander, a Max Sorensen, admitting he had never seen the play as he was "too busy to go to the theatre," nevertheless condemned it as a "Party line propaganda vehicle" and demanded the identity of "who in the War Department was responsible for this outrageous arrangement." (Joe McCarthy was still some five years in the future, but his entrance music was wafting through the air.) Sorensen was quickly joined by the socialist *New Leader*, whose fiery anti-Stalinism led it into amnesia about the simplest American realities of the time such as the play presented.

But I was spared having to reply to such accusations when a Senate committee exposed the Wright Aeronautical Corporation of Ohio, which had exchanged the "Condemned" tags on defective engines for "Passed" and in cahoots with bribed army inspectors had shipped many hundreds of these failed machines to the armed forces. As Brooks Atkinson pointed out in one of several defending articles, the Wright Corporation had "succeeded in getting the Government to accept defective motor materials by falsification of tests, forging reports and failing to destroy defective materials." Atkinson could smell the future; my attackers, he wrote, were "working in the direction of censorship and restriction. They would feel happier if all art were innocuous and never touched on a real idea."A number of officials went to jail in the Wright case, while in my play poor guilt-ridden Joe Keller blew his brains out. Even worse for the Wright Corporation, it would hardly have collapsed had it withdrawn its defective engines, while Keller's small company would have been knocked out of business for manufacturing defective parts, let alone for shipping them.

If my little essay touched a nerve, it started no debate on the left, but the exercise did clear up some questions in my mind anyway.

Meantime, as chairman of the arts panel at this "pro-Soviet" conference, I was being pegged by the anti-Communist left as quite simply a Stalinist. But it is the memory of Shostakovich that still haunts my mind when I think of that day—what a masquerade it all was! As the recent target of a campaign by Stalin attacking "formalism," "cosmopolitanism," and other crimes against the official line, he had abjectly promised to reform; were his rote statement here and his silence additional payments of dues to avoid worse punishment? It would be thirty years before the full details emerged of the physical threats and spiritual torture he had had to endure under the very regime he purported to represent at the Waldorf. God knows what he was thinking in that room, what splits ran across his spirit, what urge to cry out and what self-control to suppress his outcry lest he lend comfort to America and her new belligerence toward his country, the very one that was making his life a hell.

In any case, whatever my misgivings about doctrinaire Marxism, it was beyond me at the time to join the anti-Soviet crusade, especially when it seemed to entail disowning and falsifying the American radical past, at least as I had known and felt it. The sum of it all was that with no answer at hand I grew more stubbornly determined to resist the wind; so here I was waiting for Odets to begin, surer than ever that my part in this storm was to hang in there and wait it out.

The stillness in the room as Odets made ready to speak spread even to the anti-Communist contingent, which sat clustered in a group separated by empty chairs from the others. Now, in a voice very close to being inaudible, Odets asked, "Why is there this threat of war?"

Silence deepened and he lengthened the pause. Slight apprehension danced across my mind that he might overtheatricalize. But so far the audience was unquestionably held.

"Why," he went on in his near whisper, "are we so desperately reaching out, artist to artist, philosopher to philosopher, why have our politicians failed to insist that there cannot and must not be war between our countries? What is the cause? Why is this threat of war?"

The question hung in silence, and the audience pressed forward, straining to hear his voice. Now, slowly, his hand rose above his head and his fist closed, and at the raging top of his voice he yelled, "MONEEY!"

Astonishment. A few grins breaking out. But on the whole his inner urgency was having an effect.

There was another pause, and again a series of questions demanding the source of our danger, and once more the scream: "MONEEEY!"

Four or five repetitions had the audience tittering, and even worse was Odets's apparent unawareness that he was stepping over the edge into the ridiculous. I sat there thinking unjust thoughts: what had he been doing in Hollywood but wasting his talent making money? Had this *cri de coeur* come from a man who had stuck with the stage and his art rather than hiring himself out under the delusion that Hollywood would ever allow him an honest word, he would have swept the audience. Why were there so few Americans so far beyond corruption that their voices were undeniable by any honest person? The question transcended Odets, obviously. Was it simply that we consumed everything including our truth-tellers at such a rate that none of them ever seemed to mature? Still, this outlandish gesture of defiance had taken some courage, what with most of the powerful columnists in Hollywood sniffing up the left for blood.

In 1958, preparing to shoot *Some Like It Hot,* Marilyn met Odets and gave him a script of *The Misfits;* he suggested they have dinner to talk about it and—more important—about a project of his own in which she could star. I was then splitting my time between Connecticut and California, trying to get on with a play between attempts to be of what help I could to her. On the afternoon of their date Odets called our bungalow at the Beverly Hills Hotel to confirm the time and place, and I had to tell him that she did not feel up to dinner that evening. It was her day off, and she was at the moment attempting to fall asleep, having slept poorly the night before. The agonies she suffered in the making of every film of hers during our nearly five years together were even now moving toward a climax. She liked Odets and felt bad about standing him up, so she asked me to see him alone. Naturally he was disappointed, but I looked forward to a quiet talk with this man who had meant so many contradictory things to me and the theatre of our time.

Outside the hotel I got into his dusty old Lincoln. He seemed to have aged little in the decade since the Waldorf Conference; there was still something movingly boyish about his manner, despite a touch of disingenuousness at having wound up with only me for dinner. Nine years his junior, I found myself feeling older or at least not as desperately uncertain, and indeed he turned to me in the car and asked, "Where do you like to eat?"

Since it was he who had been living here for the last two decades, I said that any place he liked would be all right with me, but he persisted—"I don't know the town that well." This feigned unfamiliarity, so childishly transparent rather than crafty and expert, made him vulnerable to the point of fragility, and I wondered if he was even trying to make it a bit more believable to himself that he had not squandered himself over so many years in this industry he claimed to despise. Earlier, while waiting for him to arrive, I had resolved to tell him how much his work meant to me as a student in the thirties, but it was impossible to praise his past now that I found him so painfully defensive.

After more hesitation he managed to think of a restaurant but even then made a couple of mistaken approaches to it, peering up at the names of the main avenues as though he had never seen them before. Our dinner died before it could be born since, as I had suspected, he had little interest in *The Misfits;* only when Marilyn came into the conversation could he let his natural warmth flow, his defensiveness forgotten, as he asked his fan's questions with wide-eyed wonder. "She *reads,* doesn't she?" he asked, as though she were a prize gazelle or a genius chimp. I said she did, and let it go at that. With the possible exception of Colette's *Chéri* and a few short stories, however, I had not known her to read anything all the way through. There was no need to: she thought she could get the *idea* of a book—and often did—in a few pages, and most of those she opened she found unnecessary or untrue to her experience. With no cultural pretensions to maintain, she felt no need to bother with anything that did not sweep her away. She could not suspend her disbelief toward fiction, wanting only the literal truth, as though from a document. A story by Bernard Malamud upset her because it seemed to regard rape as something less than a catastrophically tragic and contemptible event. "That author doesn't know what a rape is, and he shouldn't pretend he does." I suggested that he might be understating in order to lead the reader to feel it more deeply, but her outrage could not accept literary irony about a humiliation she had experienced. And in many another situation, her sense of humor would collapse whenever painful images were evoked. Beneath all her insouciance and wit, death was her companion everywhere and at all times, and it may be that its unacknowledged presence was what lent her poignancy, dancing at the edge of oblivion as she was.

She was a born Freudian in this: there were no accidents of speech, no innocent slips; every word or gesture signaled an inner intention, whether conscious or not, and the most innocuous-seeming remark could conceal some sinister threat. I had always erred in the other direction, canceling out hostilities around me for the sake of getting on with life, a habit that had already created some serious misunderstandings between us. This golden girl, who was like champagne on the screen and whose very ability to read at all was a surprise even to so sensitive a man as Odets, was of another sort, but for Odets as for many shrewder observers before and after him, it was the happiness she emanated that was her whole nature. As we sat having our dessert and coffee in the rather ordinary, New York–like Italian restaurant, Odets seemed to me to share something of Marilyn's special kind of perceptive naiveté; like her, he was a self-destroying babe in the woods absentmindedly combing back his hair with a loaded pistol.

By this time, in 1958, it was some six years since Odets had "cooperated" with the House Un-American Activities Committee, and two years since I had refused to and been sentenced to jail for contempt. But his performance in Washington had always seemed more a pathetic coda to me than a climax. The overwhelmingly significant truth, I thought, as I still do, was the artist-hating brutality of the Committee and its envy of its victims' power to attract public attention and to make big money at it besides. To his generation Odets was more than an individual: he typified what it meant to survive as an artist in America, especially in the so-called big time. There was something so utterly American in what had betrayed him—he had wanted everything. His longtime friend, set designer Boris Aronson, mused once, "Odets has one trouble; he has to be the greatest everything. The biggest lover, the best family man; best friend to Billy Rose and then go downtown to sit with the Communist big shots; the biggest experimental artist in the theatre and at the same time the highest-paid movie writer. Who can be everything without exploding? The only thing he never liked was to hurt other people. And that's unusual for such a fellow."

Similarly, testifying before the Committee, he would roundly castigate them at one moment and without at all changing his indignant tone proceed to corroborate for them the names of people he had known in the Party. His tentative grip on the real was with him even on his deathbed. His body wasted by cancer, he suddenly raised a fist, tried to sit up, and gasped to a friend at his bedside, "Odets is coming back! Odets is only beginning!" America was promises, and Odets bought them all, with everything he had.

Harold Clurman, who was more clear-eyed but occasionally climbed up to sit with Odets on his cloud, kept exhorting him to leave Hollywood and "return," as though to some religion in whose bosom he would revive his spirit. Of course there was nothing to return to, no theatre or theatre culture, only show business and some theatrical real estate, and even that doomed to vanish soon as garish new hotels tumbled one grand old house after another into piles of bricks. In American theatre the moral is always so boringly the same: the quickest route to failure is success, and if you can't get there yourself, there are plenty around who'll be happy to give you a lift.

A play, even the angry and critical kind, is always on one level a love-letter to the world, from which a loving acknowledgment is eagerly awaited. The trick, of course, is how to face the turndown and go back and write another letter—and to the same lover, no less. This is an enterprise for a very young man, obviously, and a man with both feet solidly planted in his garden of Narcissus. Within two years after leaving Michigan I had written six plays, one of them a tragedy in grand style about Montezuma and Cortez, all of them rejected by the only producers there were in those days, the ones on Broadway. My Montezuma play, sent to the Group, did not even merit a reply.

Nearing thirty, having added two or three more unproduced plays to the pile, I began *All My Sons* as my final shot at playwriting. I knew playwrights nearing forty who were still awaiting their debut, but life was too interesting to waste it hanging around producers' doors. I laid myself a wager: I would hold back this play until I was as sure as I could be that every page was integral to the whole and would work; then, if my judgment of it proved wrong,

I would leave the theatre behind and write in other forms. When, in 1947, after two years of work, I sent *All My Sons* to my agent, Leland Hayward, I was an American playwright, which is to say, a Darwinian who had learned to expect no mercy (although he might still secretly hope for a little).

It was a pridefully tough profession in the forties. *Time* magazine referred to playwrights who wrote hits as "crack," implying something like target shooting, brisk and very technical, with big money prizes for hitting the bull's-eye, no sissy literary nonsense in cranking a play together, but a job for cigar-chewing mechanics serving—according to the going myth of the time—the whole American people.

It was an audience impatient with long speeches, ignorant of any literary allusions whatever, as merciless to losers as the prizefight crowd and as craven to winners, an audience that heard the word *culture* and reached for its hat. Of course there were people of great sensibility among them, but a play had to be fundamental enough to grab anybody, regardless. One healthy consequence of this audience's makeup, both actual and fancied, was a shift toward full-blown plays with characters and story that asserted as little as possible verbally and dramatized as much as possible by action. This tended to keep speeches short and the stage active rather than reflective. Different as we were as writers, Tennessee Williams and I both thrived on these stringent demands. The time was far, far off when a character could be permitted to sit in one place indulging in pages of monologue while surrounding actors stood absolutely still and mute awaiting the end of his aria. (When O'Neill so indulged, his storytelling never stopped, and if it did he failed.) Even further off was the time when a certain span of sheer boredom was thought to be a signal that a culturally rare event was taking place on a stage. The revolutionary newness of *The Glass Menagerie,* for example, was in its poetic lift, but an underlying hard dramatic structure was what earned the play its right to sing poetically. Poetry in the theatre is not, or at least ought not be, a cause but a consequence, and that structure of storytelling and character made this very private play available to anyone capable of feeling at all.

The time would come when storytelling seemed old-fashioned; the Bomb had blown away credibility in all such continuities. The world would end with neither bang nor whimper but two people on a slag heap each trying unsuccessfully to make out what the other was implying. If it was hard to disagree, I could still not walk for long in New York streets without running into people whom I hadn't seen in decades and who had left their tracks mixed into mine or my father's or brother's; the city still seemed to be built of time, time in the process of decay and transformation, just as it had always been.

When I pass Forty-seventh and Sixth Avenue now, it is as grimy as it was in 1938. But in those days there was an old tobacconist's shop with dusty pipes, untouched for years, behind an unwashed window on the ground floor of a four-story walk-up. From the second-floor landing as I climbed the dark stairs Mr. Franks was already leaning waving down to me with his kindly and distracted greeting. I had just graduated from the university, and my mission here was theoretically going to get me into the WPA Theatre Project.

"Well, say!" he chuckled, offering his hand and leading the way into the small apartment. "Sidney isn't here yet, but he shouldn't be more than a couple of minutes. Just went downtown to pick up his uniform." He had always called him Sidney when the rest of us were Bernie or Danny or Artie or Sam, and he was still a formal man with his starched collars and silk ties. With his outdated gentility and the eager appetite for company of a man alone all day, he gestured me to sit on the worn, once elegant wing-back chair that I remembered from childhood when Sid and I played in their apartment on 110th Street, the park, magical and mysterious, spreading out below us as we leaned out the sixth-floor windows at dusk to free our captured fireflies.

Mr. Franks, so long as he was not talking, looked healthy with his round, untroubled face and his gently polite smile, the neatly arranged dark blue tie flowing out of his stiff collar, and his gold cufflinks glittering even in the gray light that came through the grimy back windows. The place was a furniture dump filled with eleven rooms' worth of stuff from their old apartment, including the carpets, rolled up and standing like pillars against a high pile of chests and trunks that touched the ceiling.

I asked if the inspector had come.

"No, nobody. Maybe today."

"You don't mind me waiting?"

"Oh, no, glad to have you. Like some tea?" It was the only cooking he knew how to do seven years after moving in here, in 1931.

I had forgotten, even since yesterday when we had sat waiting here like this, how doll-like he had become in those years. He sat there, implicitly subservient, content to wait for me to move the conversation another step forward or to sit in silence. I had also forgotten how frequently he repeated, "Well, say," and what variations he had invented for it.

"They're predicting a very hot summer."

"Well-say." (That's to be expected.)

"Although no water shortage."

"Well, say!" (Mild surprise.)

"Business seems to be picking up."

"Well . . . say." (Chuckling disbelief.)

In later years he would seem the perfection of the Crash experience. Until 1930, he was a wealthy banker surrounded by an active, intelligent family. Then, in a few short months, his bank's assets evaporated, his wife died, and his daughter committed suicide. That he sat here smiling like this was something I found myself wishing to flee from, like a dark prophecy, all the worse because he was so placidly cheerful with me.

I had been coming here every day from my home in Brooklyn in order to demonstrate to the Welfare Department inspector that I lived in this place. To join the WPA Theatre Project it was necessary to get on the welfare rolls first, in effect to be homeless and all but penniless. And to get the bureaucratic process started I had brought my father to the Welfare Department's requisitioned old warehouse near the Hudson River, where we put on a fine scene of parental indignation against filial rebellion. The welfare worker looked on as we demonstrated why I would never be allowed to sleep in my family home, and simply sighed and judged the performance adequate, without necessarily believing anything more than our economic desperation. The final step was to be an unannounced visit by an inspector to see whether I actually lived at this address with people who were unrelated. My alleged cot, on which I had never slept, stood under a window here, and my winter overcoat hung on a hanger hooked over a gas fixture on the wall. A nice touch was the pair of sneakers placed under the cot, for by this time I was down to one pair of leather shoes.

With Mr. Franks incapable of initiating the least conversational effort, we soon fell silent. After 1930 there was simply nothing more for him to say. On the shelf of a breakfront behind his head was propped Sidney's bachelor of science diploma from Columbia, and beside it his *cum laude* certificate. He was presently on a subway coming up from a shop near the Centre Street police headquarters with his first cop's uniform. I noticed that Mr. Franks was no longer smoking and recalled him with his cut-off cigar stuck into his pipe as he crossed the 110th Street sidewalk in front of our building early in the mornings to be ushered into his beige Locomobile touring limousine by Alfred, his chauffeur, for the ride down to Wall Street.

Steps on the stairs coming up two at a time. Sidney burst in before Mr. Franks could get out of his chair. He had a long cardboard box under his arm. "Hi!" We were laughing as he undid the twine and took out the blue jacket. Sid was tall, with coal black hair and eyes, long lashes, and full curved lips. It was a face alive with a forward-moving curiosity, a quick-to-pun, put-down intelligence. He pinned the badge on his jacket and stood there for our inspection, looking at himself in the mahogany-framed floor-length tilting mirror. Then he turned to me, and we fell around the room laughing. The jacket collar stood away from his neck, the sleeves were slightly too long. I made him put on the cap, and there was space between his temples and the inner rim.

"What the hell are you going to do if something happens?"

"I've got a whistle, for Christ's sake, I'll call a cop."

There was a knock on the door. We shut down instantly. They never had visitors. It had to be the inspector. Sid went and opened the door. The man came in already asking for me, obviously accustomed to entering without being invited, but Sid's uniform jacket dampened his surly assurance, though he seemed confused by the light tan trousers. Drenched in disbelief, he asked to be shown where I slept, where my clothes were. We showed him everything, even my towel in the tiny box of a bathroom. He left abruptly, almost in my mid-sentence. When the door closed behind him, Mr. Franks turned to me. "Well, say!" (That came off all right, didn't it!)

Now Sid hung up his uniform, took his new revolver out of its carton, and loaded it with cartridges. Mr. Franks watched. "Well, say," he said gravely, registering that his son's life was seriously changing. The smile was leaving Sid's face as he loaded the gun. I saw now that he really was a policeman.

Since his graduation two years earlier, his life had gone through a typical devolution for these times. How to live had started out as an analytical problem of how to place himself so as to intercept the flow of money in the society. He thought in such objective abstractions. With production jobs nonexistent, advertising, words—what he called bullshit—were at a premium. Sid went to the Forty-second Street library to analyze the possibilities, took some free courses somewhere, and as an exercise analyzed the Fruit of the Loom underwear ads, attempting to come up with better ideas of his own for the product. This petered out, and he joined a team selling vacuum cleaners door to door. Analyzing that problem now, he rapidly climbed to top grosser for the company and was given his own team and the entire southwest quarter of the Bronx. His success, he believed, was the result of his objectifying what moved women to buy vacuum cleaners, which by and large they needed, he said, like a hole in the head.

He had discovered, working door to door, that people, women especially, would much rather placate a stranger than move into conflict with him. The trick, therefore, was to ask questions whose answers were bound to be positive. "Is this Nine ten Fairview Avenue?" "Yes." "Are you Mrs. Brown?" "Yes." "Do you have carpets or rugs?" "I do, yes"—and so on.

"By the time I got to my cleaner I had them nodding so fast they couldn't stop. The second stage is guilt. You unlimber the machine, always a new one in a new carton, which you cut open; cutting open the new carton creates an obligation, and the effort involved in unpacking puts them in your debt. By the time you're massaging the rug, the hook is in—you've done work for them, they owe you something, they've taken up your precious time . . ."

After a year or so disgust overwhelmed him even though—or perhaps because—the higher echelons of the company were opening up to him. He was attending conferences in Albany, the regional headquarters, and was invited to lunch with a vice-president. This seemed to threaten him further, and he now analyzed his position and was unable to deny to himself that he was telling lies all day six days a week, inventing a need where for the most part none really existed. He gave up smoking cigarettes not because of the health hazard, of which at the time there was little mention, but out of resentment at his responding to cigarette advertising. He went over to cigars, but an unlabeled and unadvertised brand sold by the tobacconist downstairs. By the time he passed the police exams, he had come to certain fixed conclusions, all objectively arrived at. We had sat in the Automat on the corner over two blueberry muffins and two cups of coffee as he explained.

"I am not an unusually talented person. I know I could be a good engineer, but they're a dime a dozen now and probably will be unless there's another war. By that time, if I go on the cops, I could save enough to go back to school and get an engineering degree.

There are two things I can't stand—insecurity and bullshit. An engineer is real, but I can't make that now. There's security on the cops, and from what I can tell so far the amount of bullshit involved is minimal."

Perhaps that was what had made us laugh so hard when he put on his uniform for the first time; it was so blatantly a masquerade and a mere costume, an absurdity and a childishness. And that was why we stopped laughing when he came to load his revolver—there was something in both of us that sensed this was really him.

We continued seeing each other two or three times a year during the early forties. Initially he still seemed to see it as a temporary job, but once he married, that kind of talk thinned out, and with the war on he figured he might as well be in this uniform as the other, although he had been shot at a few times in Harlem and could almost as easily have ended up dead there as in the army.

After a while it dawned on me that I was the one who always initiated our meetings. It was uncomfortable to admit, but our lives were diverging as I became better and better known as a writer. But there was also a kind of obsessive bitterness in him toward corruption in the LaGuardia administration, which was conventionally regarded as liberal and honest. With less and less humor he talked about Roosevelt's cynicism and in the president's fourth and final campaign revealed that he had given up voting altogether. Finally I could no longer imagine his idea of a future, either for himself or the country.

We had a beer one evening at an Irish bar on Third Avenue not far from his precinct station. Silences between us had grown longer. Something unrelentingly negative in him was pushing me away. And yet I occasionally glimpsed him as I had known him in our childhood, that bright-eyed little boy, the rare one with the foresight to save his marbles from one summer to the next. Now he said, "When I go into a dark alley after some bastard I am not thinking about his shitty upbringing and his deprived childhood." At the same time he had not a single friend on the force. "I bring my body in in the morning and take it home with me at night." The other cops were incurably reactionary, anti-Semitic, and ignorant. But the idea of resuming his education was gone. "I'm going to the end; I want the pension and that's it. I may try to become an engineer after that or maybe just sit home and cut up paper dolls, I don't know."

Still, something of his old joyfulness returned whenever he met my parents, with whom he could sit and talk about his own children or about the pre-Crash years. He seemed like an orphan on these visits. My mother, who drew all conversations toward intimate things, had him confessing that in his total refusal to compromise with the duplicities of business he had betrayed himself into another position that was just as false and inauthentic. They would sit together on our porch on a Sunday afternoon facing the backyard, over which my pear and apple trees—as whips, I had paid thirty-five cents apiece for them on Cortland Street in 1930—now spread their branches, his heels resting on the railing as he stretched out his legs with his open poplin jacket revealing the holster on his hip. Every few months he would come out like this to hear my mother talk about his mother, whom he found impossible to recall no matter how he tried. It was an illogical hole in his life. "Oh, she was elegant and so smart. But the minute it rained she would go with your rubbers to school and meet you coming out. Her Sidney!—my God, you were all she thought about . . ." At this his face would soften and almost glow as through my mother's voice he felt his own mother near him. He adored my mother for these recitations that gave him back some sweetness in his life, even though she kept at him remorselessly to change his career.

"But if you have no special talent . . . ," he tried to explain all over again.

"For God's sake, Sidney, a boom is starting, you're a young man. With that head you could make a wonderful career in something!" And I saw the temptation stir in his black eyes, and it hit me that he may have gone on strike against life out of spite, because his mother had deserted him by her death.

These visits would end with him staring out at the backyard chewing his cheap cigar, and I think I saw what he was seeing—not the current boom but the collapse that was bound to follow later; the Depression had left a knife cut across his brain. My mother would draw his head down as he was about to leave and kiss him on his eyelids, as soothingly as if he were a child being put to sleep.

We ceased seeing each other altogether sometime in the midforties. He always managed to be busy on the evenings I suggested we meet, until I gave up. Then, sometime in 1955, I was walking up Lexington Avenue when I thought I spotted him with a group of eight or ten men I took to be police, in light zipper jackets and sleeveless shirts. It was a perfect spring evening at around dusk, when the light is purple, the same kind of light we would wait for to release our fireflies.

For three or four weeks now the *World-Telegram* and the Hearst *Journal-American,* along with Walter Winchell and Ed Sullivan in his *Daily News* column, had been running patriotic attacks on my left-wing background. I had spent half the summer in the rough streets of Bay Ridge gathering material on warring youth gangs— what was then called juvenile delinquency—for a film that was to have been made with city cooperation. As I learned only later, a Mrs. Dolores Scotti had been sent from Washington by the House Un-American Activities Committee to secretly warn the city officials who were dealing with me and the project that the Committee was trying to "place" me as a member of the Communist Party, and though they had not yet succeeded, it would be best to break off any relations with me. Alerted, the Committee's press mouthpieces wailed in chorus until the city withdrew its cooperation, effectively destroying the project. It was the blacklisting time when the careers of many of my actor friends were being destroyed and any effective resistance to this bloodless American fascism was hard to detect.

The troop of cops was heading for the Sixty-seventh Street precinct off Lexington, having an animated discussion as they momentarily slowed to a halt on the corner. I approached from behind them. It was years since I had seen Sid, and all I felt was the joy of finding him again. From ten yards away I called out his name.

I was sure he recognized my voice, but he only half turned to me as I approached with my hand extended. With a strained grin he lightly returned my grasp and immediately let go. The other men had moved off by this time and were glancing at us from up the block. "I've got to report in," Sid said, turning away to join them as they rounded the corner toward the precinct.

I now recalled that my photo had been in the *Daily News* twice in the past few weeks, and just a few days before, the *World-Telegram* had actually published an editorial to the effect that I should be "allowed" to write the delinquency movie—after all, it was billed as a liberal newspaper—but that my name should simply not·appear on it. There had been no reaction from any side to this perfectly Soviet strategy of dealing with recalcitrant writers.

Over the next thirty years I could never pass that police precinct without wondering whether Sid was afraid of contamination or had been genuinely converted, a premature neoconservative. I remember how I continued up to the corner in time to see him mount the steps, the doorway flanked by two green globes that cast a sheen of iridescence over the cluster of young cops climbing the stoop. Sid was still busy talking to one of them. It looked to me like he had made friends at last.

His hostility still heated my face, and at the same moment I recalled him shaking out his jar of fireflies over 110th Street. Walking away down Lexington, I wondered if we were more conscious than in earlier times of such concatenations of experience, rather than its gradual unfolding, and whether it was this awareness that had exploded forms in the arts. In my own work I felt a need to hurry from climax to climax as in film montage, or even in Joycean prose with its strings of firecracker words, or in Picasso's figures seen from several angles superimposed, closing up the intervals of time. Life itself was a continuous multiple exposure. Did it seem like this because everything kept changing so quickly now and truth was far more a fluid than a fact? And was this why, at least in America, one lived in such anticipation and unease?

The Arab calls the Crusaders "accursed"—as did the Jews of medieval Europe, who were so frequently massacred by them on their way to redeem Jerusalem, the City of God—while the Christian image of the Crusader is all nobility, the epitome of the ideal man. Which view is properly history?

One's time is one's experience in it, and part of mine was Smedley D. Butler, a retired marine major general who came to Ann Arbor to deliver a lecture one day in 1935.

I went up to his hotel room to interview him for the *Daily*. He was a chesty little man who had had to stretch himself by an inch to make the marine height requirement and had climbed from private to one of the highest ranks in the corps by combining street toughness and intelligence. For several years he had led marine expeditions into Nicaragua, Haiti, Cuba, the Dominican Republic, and Honduras to put down rebellions against American-favored regimes, never questioning that like any policeman, he was preserving the peace for the good of the majority. But the time came when he was ordered to land a force on Mexico and was greeted on his arrival in port by a gentleman who represented the National City Bank in that country. The city, the general recalled, was quiet and peaceful as he drove through it seated beside the bank executive, who now led him into his inner office, where several other important men were waiting. Spread out on a table was a map of the country with areas marked off where oil was known to exist underground. The inhabitants, however, had refused to obey the government's orders to move off the land to make way for drilling equipment, and this, explained the banker, was contrary to law since the land had all been confiscated by the government under its constitution. Moreover, organized bands were continuing to hold off government troops, and it was these armed guerrillas whom the marines were to suppress.

The general, foreseeing marine casualties, said that he would have to consult with the American embassy before he could agree, in effect, to start a war. But the American embassy was already represented in the room by a high official who said that the ambassador had the same view as the man from National City and would certainly give him the go-ahead.

Butler's lecture that evening was basically a repeat of what he had written: "I helped make Mexico and especially Tampico safe for American oil interests. . . . I helped make Haiti and Cuba a decent place for the National City Bank to collect revenues in. . . . I helped purify Nicaragua for the international banking house of Brown Brothers in 1909–1912. I brought light to the Dominican Republic for American sugar interests in 1916. I helped make Honduras 'right' for American fruit companies in 1903." But this naked use of his troops by the bank, jeopardizing American lives for private profit, finally turned him around totally.

He developed the idea of a constitutional amendment to prohibit any U.S. navy ship from sailing beyond the twelve-mile limit. It was a concise and absolute formula for a nonimperial and militarily isolated America. He sat facing me smoking his cigar, unsmiling, jut-jawed, straight in his chair. I knew even then that his dream was not possible, but I shared it with him. What he confirmed that afternoon was that the men of money were disposing of our lives.

Hill Auditorium was barely half filled for his speech. My *Daily* story ran with a picture of him and summarized the details of his pitch. I do not recall ever hearing of Major General Smedley Butler again, but I have often thought of him—especially in recent years, when I read of our ships once more lying off some Latin American coast and hear the piety and benevolence of our policies being declared yet again. And if the resistance to those policies has deepened in the intervening half-century, so have the complications of the reality involved. Now, unlike in 1935, Communism and the Soviet challenge have become the only issue, but the substance seems hardly to have changed—the poverty and misrule in Central America, the rebellion against it, and an American resolve that nothing fundamental ever change except to our liking.

Though Butler had no politics and was clearly no radical, the purity of his outrage that soldiers were being sacrificed for somebody's profit confirmed all the more that the world must evolve

beyond the dictates of privately held capital. As he was telling that
simple story to his student audience in Hill Auditorium in 1935, the
New York audiences at Odets's *Waiting for Lefty* were jumping
to their feet with raised fists and throwing back the actors' cries of
"Strike! Strike!" as though a strike of taxi drivers held some symbolic key to all freedom. Such were the times. And so, when fourteen years later Odets rose at the Waldorf Conference to proclaim
"MONEEEY!" the source of Soviet-U.S. tensions, it may have been
simplistic as political analysis, but to me it was a reminder that our
consciences were not anywhere near as good as they had once
been. How could they be, when by 1949 no one knew of a country
that had freely voted a Communist regime into power and everyone knew that only recently the Communist Party of Czechoslovakia, which indeed had a large following, had nevertheless
conducted a coup to overthrow the legitimate government of that
democratic country.

The point is that for a time in the thirties a future still seemed
to beckon upward, but with the war's end, the existence of the
Bomb, and the deepening hatred between East and West, there
seemed nothing left to look forward to but the next beat of one's
heart. To believe in a political philosophy was like agreeing to have
all one's teeth pulled out or a limb amputated or an eye removed,
and for no tremendously sufficient reason. But there still had to be
something better than this uncertainty. And so one tried to deny
what one knew or suspected to be the facts, and instead of facts one
spoke of refusing to lose hope.

Such was the psychological terrain surrounding a dinner to
which Lillian Hellman had invited me about a year earlier, in order
to meet two young Yugoslav United Nations delegates. She thought
it would be a rare opportunity to get some inside dope about the
recent expulsion of Yugoslavia from the Comintern, an event that
had broken like a thunderclap upon the whole world. This was the
first crack in the still-new postwar front of Communist border
states created by the Russians, and it was such an astonishment that
many still thought it a ruse of some kind, just as a few years later
people would refuse to believe that the Chinese Communists had
really broken with the Russians. The assumption on both pro- and
anti-Soviet sides had been that all Communists were joined by a
kind of blood bond to Stalin, a Lucifer in absolute control of his
warlocks, who would go up in smoke should an anti-Russian
thought so much as cross their servile minds. Instead, gut nationalism, a force all but read out of existence by both Marxist and
capitalist rationalism, was now taking the stage.

I was surprised at the two delegates' youth—they could hardly have been thirty. With their square, unsmiling Slavic faces and their eagerness not to displease Lillian, they sat at her elegant table as though at some school exam, speaking carefully, never ragging Stalin or the Russians but mournfully regretting the necessity of Tito's declaration of independence from Russian tutelage. Their news was that the Soviets had been bleeding Yugoslavia white by literally absconding with machinery and anything else that could be carted off, and by forcing economic deals that were in every case to Yugoslavia's disadvantage and favorable to Russia. The theory, which Tito had finally branded a mere excuse and a fraud, was that in order to ensure the survival of socialism anywhere, it had first to be secured in Russia, the great protector.

But tonight the ulterior point they wished Lillian to understand was that Yugoslavia had not become anti-Soviet. It was simply a desperate case of national survival, and they hoped the day would come when they could once again stand with the Soviets side by side, but as equals, not as a sort of colony.

Asking very few questions, Lillian listened with uncustomary silence and seemed almost inanimate in her cloud of cigarette smoke. Emotionally, she must have been as impressed with these men as I was; they were not middle-class intellectuals disappointed by practical socialist discipline but former guerrillas who had fought the Nazis in the mountains. As they spoke, a flame bent and sputtered and threatened to be extinguished. They were reporting the breakup of what had been advertised as a comity of states that for a thousand years had been warring upon one another but had finally joined on a socialist basis in mutual aid and peaceful development. Such had been the dream rising out of the worst war in the history of Europe, and here were these two young veterans describing Russian behavior no different from that of the British imperium in exploited Malaya or India. And besides being Yugoslavs first and Communists second, they were implying that nationalism—that bogey of the left and traditional home of the right—was not only appropriate in a Red but also the last defense of small peoples against rapacious great powers, of which the Soviet Union was plainly one. In short, the old Adam was back, and running the world quite as it had been run before the war, nothing learned, nothing really changed. The futility of it all was crushing. And unacceptable. That a socialist state could so exploit a sister socialist state, especially the heroically anti-Nazi Yugoslavs, was an unconscionably outrageous proposition.

Any profound commitment tends to lift itself toward the sublime, and Russia's unimaginable sacrifices in the war still seemed to outbalance charges of ruthlessness toward dissidents and rumors of anti-Semitism. It turned out that even Orwell, with all his animus toward the Soviets, had no idea of the gulag—neither its vast extent nor the hellishness of its atrocities—and that he too had been giving Stalin some degree of credit.

Nevertheless it was impossible to dismiss these two young men, who, having finished their story, were looking to Lillian for her reaction. In their ill-fitting suits too tight for their squat, muscled frames, with their wrinkled shirt collars and ruddy faces, they seemed like dressed-up peasants supplicating a great lady in this richly furnished East Side living room. And I too looked to Lillian, wondering at the same time why her reaction should seem so tremendously important to them. I had been to France and Italy a year earlier and for the first time had witnessed the Europeans' rather amazing reverential respect for writers in the political arena, but for purely political men like these to be placing so much store in what Lillian Hellman thought of their policy still seemed very odd.

We were now seated facing her on her couch as she toyed with her glass, her lioness head tilted up in stubborn deliberation. For me, some ten years her junior, she had a certain mystique born of her unique flash as a southern American noblewoman who at the same time espoused pro-Soviet positions. She ran a kind of salon through which what could be called the significant world passed—everybody from leftist lawyers and labor leaders and Marxist theoreticians like Leo Huberman to her companion Dashiell Hammett to great surgeons, famous psychiatrists, statesmen, UN diplomats, wealthy businessmen, writers of all sorts, Hollywood producers and screenwriters, and of course the Broadway professionals, her peers. I was never quite at my ease there, I suppose partly because it was still difficult for me to relax with people of distinction, for there was inevitably a kind of ranking in the air that tended to disturb concentration upon whatever the subject was at the moment; one felt the depressing obligation to shine with a clever remark or some rare story, preferably of life beyond or beneath this rarefied social level. Confronted with high style, I tended to clam up and look rugged in defense against the sheer competitive self-awareness of it all.

But tonight it was a whole other story as the cold air of the Yugoslav mountains blew through the uncustomarily empty living room, with its tall velour drapes and carved moldings, the silver mementoes on the gleaming rosewood side tables, the photo of a younger Lillian on the piano staring loftily into space, her long hair brushing her shoulders. On the couch sipping her drink as the delegates' story came to its end was a Lillian subdued as I had not seen her before; she always had a sharp rejoinder, a cackling laugh, a brutally frank appraisal in her endless war against humbugs. People, she seemed to feel, almost always knew more than they let on, and life was less a mystery than a matter of willful self-deception in order to evade responsibility. Her task in life, then, was to confront people with what they already knew but hadn't the courage to come out with. And she was impatient of the unconscious as an excuse, just as she was of all innocence, the very scent of which made her pounce. Which is not to say that she could not see the ridiculous in herself, but it was most often from a particular quadrant; she saw herself sometimes as a rather poetical and unknowledgeable young girl who had been forced to assume an outsized authority she really did not feel she possessed. Forced, that is, by other people, mostly weak men who lacked courage and willpower, but also some empty-headed, coquettish women whose cowardice compelled her to grab the tiller and defiantly steer the ship away from the rocks of untruth. In these more fragile, feminine moods she seemed to call out for a leader, a master, like a wayward filly that gallops up to a trainer's hand and stops, only to fly off when it is touched. But she would quickly return from such affectation of girlish naiveté and even laugh at her attempt to escape from herself, the self that in the end could not resist claiming some exemplary role of leadership, if not domination.

As the Yugoslavs waited, she turned to me with a questioning look in which I thought I saw for the first time her helplessness to reply. But for me it was her opinion that mattered, not mine—what did I know about the Balkans or high policy except what I read in the papers? It was she who was on the inside.

I have only one memory of the delegates' exit; they both had exactly the same gray felt hats, probably bought in New York together, which they were both unthinkingly crushing in their hands as they bowed endlessly at the door, their eyes full of uncertainty. Back in the living room after they had left, Lillian insisted we have one more drink. We did not speak as she poured. Then she sat down again on the couch and with a load of portentous doubt clogging her voice asked, "You believe them?"

I could hear the wagons drawing up in a circle around the camp, and the clanking of rationalizations being piled up on the barricades. I did believe the delegates, absolutely, but I also felt the deep pull of loyalty to the past and the antifascist, pro-Soviet sentiments of years gone by. We were not truth-seekers but defenders of a beleaguered, crumbling orthodoxy, within which, however, a certain holy truth still lay cradled in whatever sublime confusion. In later years I blamed myself for a misplaced loyalty far more than I did Lillian, because I was aware that I was split in half by what I strongly suspected or already knew, while she seemed obdurate and wholly convinced; so if she was more mistaken than I, she was probably more honest, for she had always found it easier to deny any embarrassingly contradictory point of truth that might disturb her loyalty to her beliefs. What she feared more than untruth was fear itself; the main thing was always to defy. Her loyalty to the Soviet idea was on some level much the same to her as loyalty to a friend. Integrity meant staying with the ship, even if it was veering in an unscheduled direction that would bring disaster to all the passengers. Indeed, her loyalty was her most touching side, as in her enduring friendships with Dashiell Hammett and Dorothy Parker in their horrible declining years.

Replying to her question, I said that they had sounded truthful. She said something to the effect that it might all blow over—unless, of course, it turned out that Tito was an American agent. But she was merely repeating a speculation one heard all over the place in those days.

In Moscow two decades later, when I visited Russia with my wife, Inge, I sat face to face with Ilya Ehrenburg and other Soviet writer-survivors who at the very time of Lillian's dinner were living in terror of jail or worse and were being spiritually crucified by the Stalin regime—"We slept with one ear cocked for the sound of the elevator coming up at three in the morning, holding our breaths until it went past our floor," he told Inge. To think back at such a moment to evenings like this one with Lillian was a trip into the surreal; from that vantage we seemed history's fools, fleas in the mane of a galloping horse whose route we thought to influence by what we decided to believe or not believe.

As I put on my coat to leave Lillian's house I did not dare tell her or acknowledge fully to myself how depressed by doubt and uncertainty I was. But when we shook hands to say goodbye I saw that she had apparently recovered and was once again looking strong, straight, and prideful, as though something had already been solved for her. I think I knew then, consciously for the first time, that I had some fear of ever really crossing her. She lacked the guilt that was my lifelong companion, looked outward with her blame far more than into herself. But if we could never be comfortable friends it was probably due more to our competing in the theatre. I believed she deeply resented my success. There may also have been an archaic uneasiness on my part with people of high style and panache, a legacy of my father's shy embarrassment with the extroverted Newmans and their like. And finally, like many men, I had an abiding fear of women who were quick to turn anything unexpected into a moral issue. "Shocking!" came so easily to Lillian's lips that even she could be made to laugh at her repetitious outrage at the spread of aberrant behavior as the fifties twisted the simplicities of the past two decades into indescribably alien new shapes.

All in all, to put it charitably, there was enough self-delusion, if not dishonesty, in those years of the great historical crunch for everyone on every side to take his portion.

No one of my generation can be understood without reference to his relation to Marxism as "the God that failed," but I have come to think the phrase is wrong. It was an idol and no God. An idol tells people exactly what to believe, God presents them with choices they have to make for themselves. The difference is far from insignificant; before the idol men remain dependent children, before God they are burdened and at the same time liberated to participate in the decisions of endless creation. The dilemma has many surfaces and is no closer to being disposed of now than it was in the early thirties, nor will it be while Western society continues to leave so many of its people spiritually alienated, so empty of the joys of life and culture that they long for a superior will to direct their lives.

I was reminded all over again of idol and God in Turkey, where I went in 1985 with Harold Pinter on a mission for International PEN and the Helsinki Watch Committee. It was a long time since the thirties, but I had a few conversations with Turkish writers that threw me back five decades, to Brooklyn and Ann Arbor and New York. They were conversations that could have happened in many other places, from Beijing to Havana to New York, from Moscow to Phnom Penh to Prague, at that moment in history.

Some of these writers had been severely tortured in ghastly Turkish prisons for being members of a peace organization opposed to Turkey's dependency on both the United States and the

Soviet Union. They were more or less conventionally leftist, as most of the educated are in the Third World, and scornful of American pretensions to democratic principles when all they knew of us was our support of right-wing dictatorships everywhere, including the Turkish military government that had put them behind bars.

Some twenty of them had arranged a dinner for us in a restaurant one evening, and over food and a lot of drink a certain hostility began to appear, hard to understand when we had come here to draw world attention to their situation. One man stood up with raised glass and a mocking look and announced, "To the day when we are rich enough to go to America and investigate civil rights conditions!" Talking with him later, I found it hard to judge if he was an agent of the reactionary government trying to ridicule our mission or simply a Communist attacking me as an American, the archenemy.

Another writer, sitting beside me holding his vodka-loaded head in his hands, said, "If they rearrest me I will escape the country. I could not face torture like that again." He wore a plaid sports jacket and slacks and a rep tie, and his hair was cut short in fifties college style. "Are you a Marxist?" he suddenly asked.

"What is a Marxist?" I replied.

He looked at me incredulously. "What is a Marxist! A Marxist is a Marxist!" But there was more pain than anger in him.

"You mean a Chinese Marxist is the same as a Soviet Marxist with the two largest mobilized armies in the world facing each other on the border?—something like two million men up there, and each side has a picture of Karl Marx nailed to a stick. And what about a Chinese Marxist fighting Vietnamese Marxists on *their* border? Or Vietnamese and Cambodian Marxists in a battle to the death? Or a Cambodian Pol Pot Marxist against a Cambodian pro-Vietnam Marxist? I won't mention the Israeli Marxist and the Syrian."

I could see I had hurt his feelings; he had never wanted to think of it this way, and he was filling up with despair, bearing as he did the marks of torture on his body for the sake of a monolithic faith whose existence I was disposing of so airily. He got angry. "No, no, there is only one Marxism!" he nearly shouted over the mandolin playing nearby and the lilting voice of a folk singer.

I pressed no further but thought of the "one Christianity" clubbing itself to death in Ireland, or the "one Islam" in Lebanon. And of the seventeenth century, when in the name of Christ they nearly destroyed all Europe in the Thirty Years War. Or the "one

Judaism" in Israel, with the murderous hatreds between Orthodox and secular Jews.

"Maybe we are living through the retribalization of the world," I said. "One after another the remnants of ancient cultures are waking up from their long sleep, and maybe Marxism is the rationale that gives a modern sound to this upsurge of atavistic tribalism . . ."

A new voice interrupted; this was Aziz Nesin, author of some ninety books of humor and poetry, a Marxist since his youth and now a Socialist. He had been imprisoned many times and had once, a few years before, served six months for insulting the Shah of Iran in one of his pieces. Every Turk knew his name and his story: how he had left military school and ended up struggling against the American-backed military dictatorships of his former schoolmates. At fifty he was a short, reputedly rich man of imposing dignity.

"Stalin tried to grab an eastern province and the Bosporus right after the last war," he said, "and right now Russia is still pressuring us for parts of our side of the border, a tremendous area."

I was somewhat confused now; it was slightly odd that a man of the left, speaking to an American, should be slamming the Soviets. I said that Marxism had apparently not managed to curb Russian expansionism, at least in this part of the world, and he mournfully agreed, if with a troubled uncertainty in his eyes.

The first man, the one in the sports jacket who had been tortured, nodded mournfully too and without seeming to change the subject said, "Yes, American imperialism has missile bases all along the border, dozens!" As he elaborated on the size of the U.S. military presence in Turkey, the Soviet demand for the cession of a Turkish province quickly sank out of sight.

"Then as Marxists," I said, trying to trace their thinking process, "how do you locate yourselves between the two giants here? Both menace Turkish independence, right?"

They now stared at me with a peculiar blankness. Not exactly a denial nor yet an affirmation that they were truly between the hammer and the equally blameworthy anvil, it seemed more like a metaphysical suspension, a meeting point between the logic of an argument and the inadmissibility of its approaching conclusions. I had run into a phenomenon—the mystery of alienation—that had plagued the postwar years in so many places.

People of principle, confronting evidence that their beliefs are mistaken, dig themselves further into their convictions to stand off the threat of despair. To lose hope is to become corrupt. Here were two Marxists a few hours' drive from a Soviet border that they thought the Russians wished to bend southward into Turkish territory, but almost the entire weight of their resentment was against the United States. Never mind Soviet reality; Russia was the enemy of their enemy, and that was enough—enough, that is, to keep them from submission to the evils around them.

I knew their despair, for that is all it was or can be if alienation is the prize of moral thought and fact is set aside as mere detail.

The resurgent American right of the early fifties, the assault led by Senator McCarthy on the etiquette of liberal society, was, among other things, a hunt for the alienated, and with remarkable speed conformity became the new style of the hour.

As the fifties dawned I already knew radio scriptwriters who could no longer find producers to hire them. Initially one assumed that if they were not Party members they must be very close to it, and so society as a whole remained, one supposed, intact. But now, as America tested the first hydrogen bomb, condemned by many as immoral, and the expectation grew that the Russians would soon have one of their own, and Mao Zedong chased out Chiang Kaishek, a heaving dough began to displace the solid liberal earth underfoot, and one did not know from day to day when it would all fall in like a soufflé. On Brooklyn Heights one day it all seemed to have done just that.

Louis Untermeyer, then in his sixties, was a poet and anthologist, a distinguished-looking old New York type with a large aristocratic nose and a passion for conversation, especially about writers and writing. Forty years before, he had left the family jewelry business to become a poet. He had married four times—twice to the same woman, the poet Jean Starr—had taught and written and published, and with the swift rise of television had suddenly become nationally known as one of the original regulars on *What's My Line?*, a popular early show in which he, along with columnist Dorothy Kilgallen, publisher Bennett Cerf, and Arlene Francis, would try to guess the occupation of a studio guest by asking the fewest possible questions in the brief time allowed. All this with wisecracking and banter, at which Louis was a lovable master, what with his instant recall of every joke and pun he had ever heard.

Louis loved poetry and young women, not necessarily in that order; on his eighty-fifth birthday he would say, "I'm still chasing them. The only difference is that now I can't remember why." He had old friendships with many of the great American poets—among them William Carlos Williams, Robert Frost, Edna St. Vincent Millay, and Marianne Moore—and was a fellow who could easily spend an afternoon just talking and witticizing with kindred souls. One evening I saw unusual deference paid him by the kingly and much older Robert Frost, who sat still for a lengthy lecture from Louis on etymology. That afternoon my young springer spaniel, Red—an unteachable animal I later gave away to my Ford dealer, fleeing his showroom before he could change his mind—had rushed through our Willow Street doorway down the stoop and smashed into the side of a passing car, stunning his brain still further and sending him hysterically running, with me behind him, way up to Borough Hall. In the evening, Frost listened to the story of my chase and then, staring out like one of the heads on Mount Rushmore, drawled, "Sounds like a comical dog."

Louis very much enjoyed life, most especially now that he was such a success and making real money on the television. His present and final wife, Bryna—named by populist parents after William Jennings Bryan—was the editor of *Mademoiselle* and had her own arch wit to match his, although nobody had Louis's energy; he could pun in whole streams that she could only dam up by screaming from the middle of the room with hands clapped over her ears. In the ensuing silence he would go to the piano and play some extremely loud Beethoven. Urbane and cultivated, and now with an amazing check coming in every week, they lived in a snug and cluttered Brooklyn Heights apartment.

As the obverse side of his confidence in the world, Louis seemed not to know what guilt was. The only self-recrimination I ever heard from him was once, in his nineties, when he suddenly said, "I wrote too much," and presumably too often superficially. I suppose his innocence was what left him so unprepared when one day he arrived as usual at the television studio an hour before the program began and was told by the producer that he was no longer on the show. It appeared that as a result of his having been listed in *Life* magazine as a sponsor of the Waldorf Conference, an organized letter campaign protesting his appearance on *What's My Line?* had scared the advertisers into getting rid of him.

The producer had actually been one of Louis's students in a literature course in years past and was unhappy at having to fire him, especially when it had been his idea to hire him in the first place. But as Louis quoted him years later, after he had recovered from the experience, the producer said, "The problem is that we know you've never had any left connections, so you have nothing to confess to, but they're not going to believe that. So it's going to seem that you're refusing to be a good American."

Louis went back to his apartment. Normally we ran into each other in the street once or twice a week or kept in touch every month or so, but now I no longer saw him in the neighborhood or heard from him, and when I did call, Bryna always answered and talked obscurely about him not wanting phone conversations anymore, preferring to wait until we could all get together again. But that didn't happen. As a very infrequent television watcher I was still unaware of his absence from the program and figured he would call me when he felt like it.

Louis didn't leave his apartment for almost a year and a half. An overwhelming and paralyzing fear had risen in him. More than a political fear, it was really that he had witnessed the tenuousness of human connection and it had left him in terror. He had always loved a lot and been loved, especially on this TV program where his quips were vastly appreciated, and suddenly he had been thrown into the street, abolished. This was one of the feeds that went into the central theme of *After the Fall,* a play I would write more than ten years later.

A man like Louis Untermeyer broke down not, I think, for purely personal reasons but for historical ones too—the reassurances of the familiar past had suddenly been pulled out from under him. The question is whether there ever were such reassurances.

In the thirties, one of Ann Arbor's small-town charms for me was its reassuring contrast with dog-eat-dog New York, where a man could lie dying on Fifth Avenue in the middle of an afternoon and it would take a long time before anybody stopped to see what was the matter with him. A short ten or twenty years later people were looking back at the thirties nostalgically, as a time of caring and mutuality.

Whence came the notion that solidarity had once existed and that its passing was sinister? It often seems that the impoverished thirties are the subliminal fixed point from which all that came afterward is measured, even by the young who only know those years from parents and reading. It was not that people were more altruistic but that a point arrived—perhaps around 1936—when for the first time unpolitical people began thinking of common action as a way out of their impossible conditions. Out of dire necessity came the surge of mass trade unionism and the federal government's first systematic relief programs, the resurgent farm cooperative movement, the TVA and other public projects that put people to work and brought electricity to vast new areas, repaired and built new bridges and aqueducts, carried out vast reforestation projects, funded student loans and research into the country's folk history—its songs and tales collected and published for the first time—and this burst of imaginative action created the sense of a government that for all its blunders and waste was on the side of the people. Hemingway would write, "A man alone ain't got no bloody fucking chance"—amazing recognition from a professional loner that a new kind of hero had walked on the scene, a man whose self-respect demanded solidarity with his fellow men. For a while in school every other guy seemed to be studying to be a social worker.

By 1936, in my junior year, I had had more than a taste of life at the bottom, and there was no room for sentimentality there. Pushing hand trucks in the New York garment center—one of my summer jobs—you had to fight to hold your place in the post office line against chiselers breaking in to beat the closing time for mailing packages; my nine-hour days driving Sam Shapse's truck through city traffic had been a ceaseless struggle for parking spots and entries onto bridges, lined with spikes of anxiety that the truck would be rifled while I left it to deliver or pick up parts. The bathos of the popular songs and plays and movies of the day seemed weirdly misplaced even at the time. A scene in Steinbeck's *The Grapes of Wrath* in which a storekeeper lets a hungry family keep a ten-cent loaf of bread without paying for it might be inspiring, but it was an amazing departure from any reality I had experienced.

So that by the time I went up from Ann Arbor to Flint, Michigan, on New Year's Day 1937, to report for the *Daily* on the outbreak of sit-down strikes in the General Motors Fisher Body Plant Number 1, I identified with the workers in no abstract way; in fact, my work experience may account for my amazement at their new solidarity. It was nearly incredible to me that hundreds of ordinary factory workers, a large number of them recruited in the southern states, where hostility to unions was endemic, had one day simply stopped the machines, locked the factory doors from within, and refused to leave until their union was recognized as their bargaining agent.

I arrived at midday after getting a ride up from Ann Arbor with a young test-driver for Ford, whose job was to put mileage on a new model coupe to be introduced in two years, and to report to the factory in Dearborn by telephone when something in the car went wrong. Ford, of course, was the most violently anti-union shop of them all, and this southern boy, happy for some company as we drove north to Flint, talked about the tear gas that everybody knew Henry Ford had pumped into the factory's sprinkler system in case his workers decided to pull a sit-down. "Man, they pull a strike in Ford's and I'm headin' back down home, 'cause somebody goin' to get killed in *that* place," he said, laughing. The spirit of fascism had alarming vitality in the world then, and the scene in Flint seemed to stand in direct opposition to it.

The Fisher Plant stretched out along a broad avenue facing the General Motors administration building, where the office help and executives worked. The two buildings were connected by an enclosed overpass bridging the dividing avenue. Afraid of involvement in anything connected with unions, the Ford driver took one look down that street and drove off, leaving me standing there. And indeed, practically at my feet three National Guardsmen, two of them on their haunches and one sprawled on his belly on the sidewalk, were tending a machine gun on a tripod pointing up toward a two-story projection of the plant building. I learned later that they had fired at three workers taking the air on the roof, wounding one of them. Other soldiers moved around silently, rifles unslung, and a couple of army trucks filled with young troopers blocked both ends of the street. Two overturned police cars lay at odd angles, upended, I was informed, by a powerful stream of water from firehoses manned by workers who had connected them to hot-water outlets to keep police and soldiers at bay. To prevent invasion through the covered overpass, they had welded it shut with several Chevrolet bodies set vertically on end. This was the third day of the strike. There was a silence broken only by a muffled saxophone from inside the plant, where an improvised jazz group would periodically blow up a few numbers and then evaporate. At the moment the saxophonist seemed to be doing a practice solo. Jammed in a window on the second floor, many heads looked down as several wives appeared with boxes of food that the workers hoisted up on lines, chatting all the while and occasionally laughing at some remark; then the women waved and walked away. Inside, I was told, the men were sitting and sleeping on car seats but taking great care to cover them with paper; odd as it seemed, the rights of property were still quite sacred to them.

I found the union office in a side street and went up a flight of steps to a tiny room over an empty store, from which, so I had heard, a couple of brothers were running the strike. A young man wearing a baseball cap was staring out the window. He glanced at me and introduced himself as Walter Reuther (his brother Victor, who had made a trip to the Soviet Union, was rumored to be a Socialist). I asked Walter how things were. He was a pale and reflective man with red hair and a simple, direct quality of respectful attention to me, a mere student reporter from the university. I had expected a tough guy with no interest in what I was trying to do.

"Well, let's see," he said, leaning back in his chair. "I think we've got over three hundred members right now . . ."

Three *hundred*! An amazing number, I thought. There were many reports in the press that the whole thing was a fluke and would soon collapse, for it was a practically unheard-of attempt to organize unskilled workers rather than machinists, toolmakers, and carpenters, whose elite unions had been started at the turn of the century.

"But we're signing up more and more all the time."

"Then you think you can win recognition? How long will they stay in there before they get sick of it?"

"I think they'll stay in."

"Can I ask you why?"

He let a grin pass over his lips. "They've kind of got to like it in there." We both laughed. "They've been through a lot together, you know. They've got their pride going now, and there's a lot of good feeling in there."

Talking to Walter Reuther, I realized that he did not think of himself as controlling this incredible event but at best guiding and shaping an emotion that had boiled up from below. I had heard that some of the hard organizing was being done by the Communists, but no one seemed to know where I could find them, so I never found out.

I had to return to school before victory day, February 11, 1937, when the company caved in and recognized the United Auto Workers. It made me feel safer on the earth, and as it did to others trying to write or make art in that time, it seemed to me a new beauty was being born. It would not have crossed my mind that a new power to coerce was also being created here, certainly not one that would often turn a cynical gangster face to the world and, incidentally, suppress a movie I had written—but that was a decade and a half later. It must be said, however, that the UAW itself remained remarkably democratic.

The twisting of meaning proceeds. It was the spirit of the thirties that Odets—unfashionably, by 1949—was trying to shout up out of its grave at the Waldorf Conference. When I recall the nuns with their scrubbed, frightened faces glancing up at me as I picked my way between them, and almost four decades later when I read about Catholic clergy in the Third World ministering to the poor and often leading revolution rather than serving as outriders of the rich, the world seems to be evolving. Now, too, a council of American Catholic bishops condemns the ruthless strain in a federal policy content to let illiteracy, racism, and hunger erode immense sectors of society, and I think of the hopelessness of trying to so much as discuss such matters with that line of kneeling sisters at the Waldorf entrance. They and I see the same world at last, but I have changed as much as they.

Finishing *All My Sons* after two years, I sent it to Herman Shumlin, who had produced and directed Lillian Hellman's plays. After three or four days I was told that he "didn't understand it." Herman was as prestigious a producer as Broadway had, a rather severe man of terrifying principle, but gentle and extremely soft-spoken—until, so I was told, he lost his temper. Apparently he had lost it with Lillian, as she had lost hers with him, and they had parted company. Notwithstanding his great need for a new social playwright, my play was evidently beyond him. I could not imagine what it was that baffled him, and it was a crisis for me to be judged a failure after two years of the most careful work, especially since I had vowed to abandon playwriting if *All My Sons* failed.

Mary and I and our first child, Jane, were spending summers in a rented bungalow near Port Jefferson, Long Island, where I had finished the play on the porcelain-topped kitchen table. I had given a copy to my old friend and summer neighbor Ralph Bell, who had been in my Michigan class and was a stage and radio actor now. His wife, Pert Kelton, older than Ralph, had been born into show business, had been in the Ziegfeld Follies, and was an opera singer as well as a Broadway comedienne. She became the first TV wife of Jackie Gleason on his *Honeymooners* show, the original Mrs. Kramden. She read my play and said it was a big one, "like an opera," and that compliment, along with the wide-eyed look of wonder in her face, strengthened me against Shumlin's rejection. Pert, to whom Charlie Chaplin had presented his famous bowler and cane back in the twenties as tokens of his admiration for her imitation of him in the Follies, had a raw backstage wit and a caustic laugh. She was studying Christian Science, trying to cure herself of epileptic seizures. In that summer of 1946 we couldn't have guessed that four or five years later, as the nationally known female star of the country's biggest hit TV program, she would be notified by telegram—in a Chicago hospital bed where she was recovering from a minor illness—that she had been fired from the show. As a long series of inquiries finally revealed, the cause was that Ralph had once participated in a May Day parade, many years before. Ralph, I knew, had had absolutely no leftist connections whatever but had simply thrown himself in with a gang of actors protesting whatever it was that year, and Pert had never even voted in her life.

It was a situation not dissimilar to Untermeyer's, and the brutal coldness with which she had been thrown down, as it were, to hit the concrete frightened her so deeply that she always thereafter seemed to have a reserve of furtiveness, even though she continued rather successfully in the theatre and in films long after the blacklisting madness had died away. In 1946 I do not think we could have believed that such a blacklist was possible, that the current of one's life and career could simply be switched off and the wires left dead.

As I mentioned, I had also sent the play to glamorous Leland Hayward, my agent at least in name. There was no response at all. After a week or so I went to his offices, only to be told that he hadn't read it, was in California, and could not be reached. To his anxious secretary I announced that I wanted all my old scripts back then and there and that I was leaving the agency. I mention this at all because it tells me that I had somewhere found a certain confidence that I could no longer be stopped. It may merely have been the pride of desperation, but I actually gathered up the scripts of my earlier plays and off I went. Not, however, before the secretary convinced me to leave the new play for a Miss Brown to read.

Kay Brown would be my agent for very nearly forty years. She phoned me next day in Port Jefferson to tell me that the play was terrific and that she would be honored to handle it and had some ideas about where to send it now that Shumlin had turned it down. Mary and Jane and I were moving back to New York that very day. I pushed the pedal down on the old Nash-Lafayette two-door, which was crammed with Jane's crib and toys and our stuff, and blew a tire as we came off the Southern State Parkway. Like a sign of good things to come, there was a tire store twenty yards away where I bought a new one for twelve dollars, an expense I really could not afford.

I had heard of Elia Kazan and of course of Harold Clurman, who had been one of the heads of the Group Theatre and its most literate figure. The Group had vanished five years before, and they had recently started up a partnership to produce plays commercially. Kay thought they might be interested, as well as the Theatre Guild. In a day or two both organizations wanted to option *All My Sons.*

The Guild's head, Theresa Helburn, had a claim on my loyalties because it was she who had been the chief officer of the Bureau of New Plays when it had selected me for a national award back in 1937. And the Guild had been O'Neill's initial producer, although in recent years its reputation was rather more glamorously "theatrical" than I felt comfortable with.

Kazan and Clurman, in contrast, had been among the creators of that thirties mixture of Stanislavsky and social protest which was the real glamour to me. The choice of their new organization did not take me long to make, but I was not prepared to be asked which of them I wanted as director. Clurman, it was my impression, had been the Group's chief thinker; he had directed all of Odets in the thirties and was already a legendary figure to outsiders like me. Kazan, however, was said to be the more aggressive and vital director although he was younger than Clurman, his mentor, and had fewer credits. By this time I knew many actors, and the picture they were giving out was of a Clurman who might be inspired but could often fumble, and a Kazan who was wily and could punch directly to the point with actors.

Naturally, to meet both of them in their offices with the purpose of choosing between them was heady stuff. If such a thing as a directorial expert existed, here were two of the greatest. I suppose I loved them both after the first five awkward minutes. They were heaping compliments on the play and were grateful I had chosen them over the Guild, already a triumph for their new company. The energy in the air was fierce. Kazan grinned under his enormous nose, his head tilted down like a fighter's, and Clurman leaned back rubbing his hands together as though about to sit down to a roast turkey. The place was simply happy. And it was eager. This was a time when it was still imagined that with the possible exception of a doctor saving a life, writing a worthy play was the most important thing a human being could do.

It was just about ten years since I had asked Jim Doll across the hall how long an act normally lasted. In those Depression times Harold Clurman had come forward as a priest of a new kind of theatre that would cry down injustice and heal the sick nation's spirit. Kazan had played in *Waiting for Lefty,* and I had seen him in *Golden Boy* as Fuseli, the gangster who appears in the doorway of the gym and, watching Luther Adler punch a bag, leans menacingly far forward without raising his heels and says, "I want a piece of that boy." Ah, what glamour, what hard and clear strokes of theatrical characterization! And here were both of them fairly lusting after my play. I had arrived.

I had led a nearly isolated life, still turning out the occasional radio play to pay the bills and working every day on *All My Sons* until it seemed as tight as a drum. It was exhilarating, as it usually is the first time around, merely to come to the production office on East Fifty-seventh Street every morning to watch Clurman and Kazan interviewing actors. Of course none seemed to resemble "real" people like the ones I had modeled the characters on, the young women being too beautiful and the young men too handsome; even when they looked ordinary they had the performer's charge of energy that normal people lacked. I feared artificiality taking over. And I suppose I learned more about the theatre in that five or six weeks of casting than I ever would again.

Kazan's capacity to objectify actors' personalities was really an exercise in clinical psychology. At one and the same instant he could seem intimately and lovingly involved with an actor while standing back to gauge the impression he might make in the role. Those we ended up with he had known or observed onstage before, so there was no real question of acting ability. Clurman, smelling like a barbershop, took charge of interviewing the ladies, a daily toil that filled him with a zest and happiness that all but foamed. He seemed never to notice a woman's flaws, only her good points—she might have two pairs of ears, but then again she had terrific legs or fantastic eyes or an engaging laugh. Walter Fried, their cigar-smoking business manager, himself not immune to the parade of females passing his desk, added his lisping anticipation of a hit to the prayers of Clurman, who, as soon as the office was empty, would have his young secretary, another of his adoring worshipers, on her knees buffing his shoes while he rubbed his hands gleefully together, laughed unscrupulously, and commanded God, "I want a hit, a hit!"

This diktat had its own historic significance in 1947, for it was flung at the memory of the always impoverished Group Theatre years, which with this commercial production were officially declared over and done with. Now each part would go to the most fitting and attractive actor rather than being cast out of the Group itself, which had sometimes been more necessary than desirable. Clurman was also acknowledging a new realism about theatre; this play would ask for no allowances from a clique audience willing to overlook some dull stretches for the sake of artistic or social points. Despite his apparent—at least to me—disappointment at not having been chosen to direct it, Clurman, in one of his uncontrollable seizures of enthusiasm, would suddenly bang the flat of his hand down on a desk and stand up and yell, "Goddamit, this play is *built*!"

Kazan, who had been Clurman's stage manager in the Group and still saw him as the father-master, was no less hot about the possibilities of success but was far more calculating, remorselessly grasping an objectifying view at whatever cost. What counted was what came over to the audience, no excuses and no mercy to be expected. Clurman's mind implicitly appealed to some high court of culture at whose feet he lay his offerings of artistry; if he failed in the real theatre, he could find solace in a transcendent judgment of his work's higher, if mundanely unappreciated, value. Kazan looked to the sky only for weather, not supportive judgments, and it was more training than directing that his actors got from him. He pointed an actor and then walked along beside him with an arm over his shoulder in a gentle embrace of steel. "Casting is ninety-five percent of it," he would say, for the audience knows only what it sees and hears, not what author or director have tried to set before it. He drove the actors relentlessly in *All My Sons*, as I had driven myself in the writing. At one rehearsal he pressed Karl Malden—as the outraged lawyer son of the unjustly imprisoned partner of Joe Keller—closer and closer to such an actual explosion of emotions that he burst onto the stage and stood facing the actress playing his sister, Lois Wheeler, unable to speak at all, swaying dizzily and nearly collapsing. Kazan was thereupon satisfied that he had hit Malden's outer limits of indignation.

Likewise with Arthur Kennedy, whose sweet idealism in the first act must turn to murderous anger at the climax of the second, a scene Kazan knew would make or break the play. He had staged it so that Ed Begley, the guilty father, was sitting remorsefully with head in hands just as Kennedy brought his fist down on his back. After much rehearsal Begley's back was very painful and he had to strap a rubber pad on under his jacket to protect himself, such was the closeness to reality of the emotions in that production.

Approaching the height of his powers, Kazan was eating fire in those days, working with great certainty and discretion. He had asked for one important excision, of a long speech by the doctor-neighbor lamenting the closing down of his youthful idealism—advice I resisted until I began to hear it, as Kazan had, as an authorial exercise rather than an authentic outgrowth of the play's essential structure. He relied, although by no means as totally as was rumored, on his wife Molly's analytic capacities in this. In my experience, she was very good at tracing the lines of force of a play's story and character structures but sometimes tended to crop excrescences dangerously close to a play's nerve. Kazan was far more the poet but was sometimes uncertain whether to unleash a play's fancifulness or scramble back for safety to its main plot lines. In a sense, nevertheless, and not only in the theatre, Molly was his conscience, a figure he had both to rely on and to slyly evade on occasion.

Life in a Kazan production had that hushed air of conspiracy I've described before, a conspiracy not only against the existing theatre but society, capitalism—in fact, everybody who was not part of the production. People kept coming up to whisper in his ear, and they were whispering in each other's ears too, with sideways glances. It was all new to me and immensely challenging, even if I could hardly guess what it was all about. What I did feel was a love for this man in his insatiable rooting out of the least weakness. You knew you were on the first team and that the idea was to win, and no margin of safety was too great. The audience was an enemy that had to be overwhelmed and dominated like a woman, and only then loved. The path to victory was opened up by clarity about the play's mission, its reason for existing, as well as about the actor's motives and the shape of his personality and talent. But Kazan's was no mere technical virtuosity; from the Group and its Russian and European antecedents, he had learned that a theatrical production is, or should be, a slice through the thickness of the culture from which it emerges, and that it is speaking not only to its audience but to other plays, to painting and dance, to music and to all forms of human expression by which at any moment we read our time. And so he would send one actor to listen to a particular piece of jazz, another to read a certain novel, another to see a psychiatrist, and another he would simply kiss. And more, though he never mentioned political people or ideas, it was assumed that he identified himself with the idealism of the left and that his emotional and intellectual loyalties lay with the workers and the simple and the poor. Like Odets, he wore the fading colors of the thirties into the forties and fifties, the resonances of the culture of antifascism that had once united artists everywhere in the world.

Even in 1947, however, one understood that Kazan stood alone in this implicitly principled ambience. His old friend and co-director Clurman, who had pretty much the same outlook on life and the theatre, never offered either his personal comradeship beyond the theatre's walls or any kind of political example. Harold tacitly let you know that he was on the train for as long as he could bear it but that his interests might prompt him to get off a stop or two before yours. Oddly, while Kazan on the whole was warm but quiet onstage, Harold could rant and shriek and literally howl to the flies, but his enthusiasms would never make him forget a dinner date. At the same time, without mentioning it to anyone, he would visit a sick or unstable actor and hold his hand for a couple of hours. But work for him was work, and he was careful not to promise any more of himself than he could deliver—perhaps a little less. Clurman's selfishness, in short, he wore on his sleeve along with his loving heart.

I learned from Kazan's production the beauty that lay in the expressive integration of means. When the set was first brought in, I was puzzled by a low hump in the middle of the grassy backyard, around which the actors were forced to make their way lest they trip. The women were especially inconvenienced because their heels caught on it, and I asked Kazan why it was there. Suppressing a persecuted grin, he quietly confided, "It's a grave."

"A grave! This is their backyard!"

"But the set signifies a graveyard. I'm not sure, maybe Max is right. Why don't you ask him to explain it, and tell me what he says." ·

Mordecai Gorelik, known as Max, was another Group veteran, a choleric genius who designed sets that might seem to be a dentist's office or a gym or whatever but were organized, at least in his mind, around a metaphoric statement condensing the central image of the play at hand. I went to Max with the worry that the actors were going to fall over his bump and destroy my play. He was a beardless Abraham, a ramrod-straight fanatic with the self-certainty of a terrorist and the smile—when he demolished an opponent in argument it just managed to flicker over his mouth—of a blood-covered avenging angel.

"Tripping? I didn't see anybody tripping."

"Well, they have slightly, and it makes them uncertain."

"Talk to the director if they're uncertain, uncertainty is his job."

"But what is the point of it, Max—a rise like that in the middle of the stage?"

"You have written a graveyard play," he said as categorically as if he were reading each word in lights behind my eyes, "and not some factual report. The play is taking place in a cemetery where their son is buried, and he is also their buried conscience reaching up to them out of the earth. Even if it inconveniences them it will keep reminding them what the hell all this acting is really *about.* The bump stays!" In fact, I gradually had to admit that in some indefinable way the mound did seem to unify the performances around a single subliminal preoccupation that had a certain power. And if one of them tripped on it occasionally, perhaps it did serve to remind them that the play was indeed about a bad conscience. But whether it worked or was meaningless, Max terrorized Kazan and me and everyone else into believing that it did, the alternative being to confront him, a suicidal act.

Kazan, Clurman, Gorelik, Arthur Kennedy, Karl Malden—these were all men connected to the now deceased Group, whose influence on theatre, however distorted and convoluted, continued for decades to come and extended far beyond the United States. Inevitably, I took their idealism more seriously than they did, but I was not an actor and could afford to be saddened by opportunism; they had to make a living, and when the money wagon came, many of them jumped on before it passed them by. In rehearsals they were like a football team, helping one another, advising, and criticizing, for the Group's idea had emphasized the coherence of the whole over the stardom of any individual, something they regarded as a symptom of artistic cynicism.

The play's first performance, in New Haven, in addition to gripping the audience, reawakened the dimmed idealism of the war years, and the prospect of so serious a work actually becoming a popular success pushed the cast into a feverish search for the least detail that might not contribute to the whole effect. By the time it opened in Boston and then New York, the production was like a bullet on a straight, clean trajectory that rammed the audience back into its seats.

It can take a long time to accept that celebrity is merely a different form of loneliness. Especially in that era when playwriting was considered as much a craft as an art, a play that was serious and could still win a Broadway audience was an achievement to envy, the more so when every such attempt normally failed. No longer purely the observer but the observed, I denied at first that anything could change in my life, and that was when, a month or two after *All My Sons* opened on Broadway, I took that job at the Long Island City factory, as though to insure my continuity with the past. I spent the better part of a week working around a circular counter alongside six or eight men and women standing as silent as prisoners doing time, assembling the dividers in wooden beer boxes. My play was bringing in some two thousand dollars a week, and my wage here was the minimum, forty cents an hour. After a few days the irreality of my flight from and toward myself simply spent my energy and I quit. I can only surmise that without at the time rationalizing my feeling, I was attempting to be part of a community instead of formally accepting my isolation, which was what fame seemed to hold. But there really was no community; those workers had never been inside a theatre in their lives, and probably never would be. If on some sublime level I thought I was speaking for them, it was purely my illusion, which they would hardly have understood.

But I was also reacting to my having excelled, and the contradictions of the old fraternal competition flamed up, for they could neither be openly acknowledged nor set aside. I wanted and did not want to excel over my brother, or more precisely, the little boy in me did not want to, even as I knew perfectly well what pride Kermit took in my success. But the first church is in the skull, and there the gods face in two directions. In any case, having laid a week's ill-paid and mind-numbing work at the foot of the idol, I went home and returned to my life of writing. I had paid some other dues as well with *All My Sons,* which in fact was my only tightly made play among seven or eight of a far looser and more vagrantly poetic form; now I hoped to open up the side of my vision that was, so I imagined, a path into my own chaos.

The box factory was not the first time that I had tried to turn my back on the isolate life of the writer. My wartime year in the Navy Yard, completely voluntary as it had been, was in part an expression of the same wish for community, since arguably my radio work for various government agencies aided the war effort more than anything I contributed to repairing ships. I left the Yard early in 1943 when Herman Shumlin recommended me to Lester Cowan, a Hollywood producer looking for a young writer to make a screenplay of *Here Is Your War,* a collection of columns by America's best-loved war reporter, Ernie Pyle of the United Press. I was still almost two years away from the production of *The Man Who Had All the Luck,* and totally unknown, but Shumlin's prestige as a producer-director convinced Cowan to offer me seven hundred and fifty dollars a week to invent a movie based on Pyle's book. Far, far down the road this project would finally emerge as *The Story of GI Joe,* but only after some four or five other writers had hauled and pushed and recarved my original screenplay about an infantry company moving through the war.

With my prejudice against screenwriting as an art—it was produced by the will, not the soul—I found it difficult to feel more than a cool technical involvement, but I would learn more than I bargained for in the next months as I went from Fort Benning to Camp Campbell to half a dozen other training camps trying to understand soldiers and a war that only a handful of cadremen, returned from combat to train others, had as yet experienced. In the European theatre of operations our only serious engagement had been in North Africa, the Battle of Kasserine Pass, where the Germans had mauled us badly.

In contrast to the quite different wars that were to come in Korea and Vietnam, I recall no sign that the tankmen, glider troops, paratroopers, and foot soldiers in the stateside camps ever questioned our ultimate victory, which was merely a matter of time. And for many the army was a distinct step upward from the Depression life, which a majority were fairly sure would return when the fighting was over. I kept searching for some ideological conception animating them, but the war was "about" little more than what a game of football is "about"—something that had to be won for pride's sake. Nevertheless, I wrote a work of reportage, *Situation Normal,* my first published book, in which I tried to see a higher purpose operating among these men. In truth, the minority who did grope for some meaning in the war beyond America's responding to the Japanese attack ended up figuring that somebody else must know what it was, but even so, this was a world away from the nihilism of Vietnam or even the Korean War. Though unable to define it in words, they shared a conviction that somehow decency was at stake in this grandest slaughter in history, literally a war on every continent of the planet and in the air overhead and under the seas.

My screenplay reflected my instinctual democratic suspicion of stardom; I tried to make every man in the company the center of the war, equal in importance. After working for five or six weeks at home alone, piling up not less than a hundred and fifty pages of manuscript, I was summoned to Hollywood by Cowan. But first I had to accompany him to Washington to meet the chiefs of the Army Ground Forces and explain our film, which would require much army cooperation and equipment, not to mention a few submarines and a small naval battle squadron. Why the latter I had no idea, having written no naval scenes whatsoever, but Cowan moved in mysterious ways. He was a small former basketball coach from Ohio with a flattened nose and a grin like a canteloupe slice.

In Washington, my naiveté impregnable as ever, I spent three nights and days being introduced to generals and colonels who were apparently convinced that they were personally to be made world-famous by this movie. That there was no character of their rank in the script was a fact I knew enough not to mention. With war raging everywhere, Cowan could pick up a phone and cause coveys of the highest army officers to assemble in order to hear me unwind about this movie, whose main virtue, he endlessly repeated, was that it would put the "ordinary GI in the front row of the war and show that he is what it's all *about*," to which startling new conception there could only be patriotic agreement. I was gritting my teeth, trying not to quit with every dawning day.

But Washington had its pathos, too. Joe Liss, a friend and radio writer then working for the Library of Congress Folklore Division, took me to dinner with his wife and a young woman friend of theirs whose husband had been reported missing on the Murmansk run a few months earlier; his destroyer had been either damaged or sunk escorting merchant ships going to Russia with Lend-Lease supplies. As I looked into her distracted face, the war suddenly became real to me. She was keeping up almost daily inquiries at some naval office as though there was still hope for her young husband. I danced with her. She told me she was sleeping with young sailors now. I found this admission astonishing, and very moving, since it persuaded me that through them she was reaching into the sea where her beloved lay dead. I wanted to sleep with her myself, stimulated almost as much by the poetry of the idea as by her body, for she was not really my notion of a beauty. But the brush of death had made her sensually attached to life, to sex, had given her a taste for the catastrophic. My own vulnerability, which normally I kept carefully shielded, responded to hers, and I knew that I was no longer as safely high-minded as I had tried to imagine.

So absorbed with myself was I that on the long train ride to Hollywood I blithely told Mary of my attraction to this woman, saying that had I not been married I would have liked to sleep with her. It seemed not at all an explosive announcement and in another culture might have been passed off as one more male inanity or simply a report on human nature, but it was received with such a power of disgust and revulsion—as though I had longed to use a toothbrush found in a railroad washroom—that her confidence in me, as well as my mindless reliance on her, was badly damaged. If her reaction was silly and overblown, she had nevertheless sensed a truth; I had announced the existence of the part of my nature nearly absent from our marriage. Like most such announcements, it had scorched my face, and our arrival in Hollywood was strained and sad.

Still, my congenital optimism soon swept even this cloud away, believer that I was in the permanence of marriage—here I was, past twenty-five, and none of my friends had been divorced. The American trivialization of marriage had not yet become a fact of life, and it weighed on me that I had shaken my own, especially so stupidly and unnecessarily.

Meanwhile, I worked, or tried to, in an office in the General Service Studios, a rambling one-story building whose windows looked out on a wide lawn and beyond it to the immense sound stages where two or three films were then being shot. Copies of my script were being shown to various directors, one of whom had participated in the perilous British commando raid on Dieppe; he arrived each day, conferred with Lester privately, and finally, after some weeks, took me aside and asked if I was being paid, since he was not. He was the earliest of several whose minds would be sucked for ideas before they were allowed to simply wander away, drained. At the same time Lester was having the army send along one hapless foot soldier after another to sit and tell me his battle experiences, none of which I could possibly fit into the script. I became ashamed to look at these boys, so excited by the hope of being in the movie, sitting out in the waiting room all day until they too drifted off.

· At last, one evening, appeared Laurence Stallings himself, among the most famous of screenwriters, co-author of *What Price Glory?* with Maxwell Anderson, and author of other war films including my boyhood favorite, *The Big Parade*. Stallings had lost a leg in World War I and walked with a severe limp that enhanced his martial authority for me. As the chauffeur solemnly drove us through the Hollywood dusk, I felt myself privileged to have won my way into this life and this work, through which I could put my talent to use for the antifascist war.

Stallings spoke in a soft, rather kindly voice. "Your script is surprisingly good, considering you've never been in battle. The device of not featuring any one man above the others could be moving and would gradually impose the idea of a company, maybe of an army. It's a very unusual approach. I've never seen it done before."

Swimming in my happiness, I explained that I had wanted to symbolize, through a nearly equal emphasis on the whole group, the democratic ideals of the war. I went even further and pointed out the then incredible turnabout on the eastern front, where the Russians were beginning to look like they might well roll back the Germans, until now widely believed to be the inevitable winners due to their technological superiority and warmaking ability. "It's the Russians' belief in their ideology that's helped make the difference," I said.

"That's not exactly the way it is," Stallings replied, giving me a faint elder man's grin. "They're using their Guards Divisions. A Guards Division man is not thinking about socialism, he's in there with his mustache and his special uniform and is not going to retreat, ever, because he is a Guards trooper. This is one thing you've got to watch in your script—don't try to make it mean too much. Battle is never about beliefs or ideas, it's about your buddy and you and not coming off a shitass or a coward. War is the whole world turned into a drunken barroom. And there's one other thing."

I realized now that Lester had put him up to talking to me. We were not having an idle conversation. My future on this project was the subject, and my work of months suddenly hung in the balance.

Stallings said, "They are never going to make your script the way it is." I was shocked. Why would they not make it when Lester seemed so enthusiastic? "He should be enthusiastic, it's very well done. But all war movies, Arthur, are the same movie. There is a big guy and a little guy; they are different sizes so you can recognize them quickly in the smoky battle scenes. There is a girl whom one of them gets, but it's the other guy she loves, and she finally gets *him*. In the end they have to leave her behind because she's a foreigner, and it breaks your heart. One of them can get shot, preferably in the arm, or a wound that requires a head bandage."

The car halted before my rented house. Stallings touched my knee. "You could fix it. Try."

I watched the car drive into the darkening blue night. Standing there in the rising sexual damp of Hollywood, I was embarrassed at having wasted so much hope and effort, for there was no wish in me to remake *The Big Parade,* which was essentially what he had been describing. If nothing else, I had a commitment to Ernie Pyle not to glamorize him or the men he loved in precisely the kind of film Stallings had outlined.

The film rights to *Here Is Your War* had been sought by all the big companies, but Cowan, an independent, had won Pyle's agreement—provisional, as I soon learned—because he alone had pledged to feature not Pyle but the soldiers. Pyle had a singular position in the public mind; far more than any other correspondent, he was trustingly read each day by soldiers' families desperate for news, because he always gave the names and addresses of the men he ran into overseas. In fact, he not only shared their dangers but saw more combat than almost any soldier, moving from unit to unit to remain in battle when troops were withdrawn for recuperation.

Pyle did not seek out colorful characters or men of great patriotic consciousness. The killing was a human catastrophe for all sides. Before the war he had toured the Midwest with his wife beside him in his little Ford, talking to Main Street people, gathering the most common stories and ordinary emotions to share with his readers. The atmosphere of his daily column was benign, warmly humorous, small-town. The war was simply Main Street with sudden death added.

I had no idea until I arrived in Albuquerque, New Mexico, to visit him that Pyle had declined to sign a contract with Cowan until he could see a script of the film. But at that point, a few months before my fateful talk with Stallings, there was nothing more to show him than some sequences and detailed notes of scenes I had not yet written. Sitting with him in his Albuquerque living room, I realized only gradually that I had been sent to convince America's best-loved reporter of Cowan's integrity and the film's high intentions. As the picture's reigning innocent, I had first beguiled the army brass, and now it was Pyle's turn—a much harder job when the very word "Hollywood" meant fraud to him.

The C-47 on which I had flown in from Hollywood landed with a load of vomit, not only from me but from about two dozen navy fighter pilots on leave from the Pacific. An electrical storm over the Rockies had sent the plane screwing through the air, dropping and rising several hundred feet in a matter of seconds, wings flapping visibly and at one point scraping treetop level along a mountain slope. The sole undisturbed passenger was a woman in her late sixties who sat in the single-seat righthand row with her legs crossed, reading a paper while nearly upside down and eating Hershey bars with almonds. So severe had our punishment been that the pilots were sent onward by train. Once on the ground, I, like them, kept turning my ankles as I made my way to the interior of the simple airport building, where I sat and waited to be picked up by a taxi Pyle had sent. On my hotel bed I lay on my back only to find my legs rising straight in the air. I sat myself up and then lowered down on my back again, but up they swung out of control. Finally I lay on my side and let them rest extended at right angles to my body. A week later, when I was in the airport waiting for a plane back to New York, Ernie introduced me to the woman who tended the souvenir counter, and she recognized me. "I really thought you were having an attack last week and was just about to call an ambulance when the taxi man came. I couldn't believe you could get up and walk out. You looked dead."

As is so often the case with American heroes, Pyle was a tortured man, uncertain of himself and ridden with guilt. Slight of build, with sandy hair thinning to baldness, gentle and self-effacing, he seemed the last man in the world to bring himself willingly into battle. He lived with his wife, who was at the moment in the hospital being treated for—he insisted on uttering it—alcoholism. Their home was a small tract house, one among twenty or thirty recently put up at the outer edge of the town. The place seemed somehow airless and unhappy, but when one stepped off his stoop and faced the mesa, the endless scope of New Mexico spread out in all its marvelous painterly colors, always changing, always new. On our after-dinner walks the main street was empty by sundown, an occasional passing car only emphasizing the amazing silence of this small city. One evening we saw a lone Indian man standing on a corner with a bundle under his arm, staring straight ahead toward the setting sun. I thought he was waiting for the traffic light to change, but when it did he remained motionless. Many years later I wrote him into *The Misfits,* but John Huston, impatient with this symbol of the American displaced person, swept the camera past him without really registering him. I guess the man's symbolism was too personal to mean much to others.

It was on these blue-lit evening walks that I came to realize that Cowan was using me to get Ernie to sign the contract, so I informed him that I had no control over the final script and that he shouldn't base his decision on a favorable impression of me. But such was his desire to immortalize the American GI that he convinced himself my presence guaranteed the script would not be cheapened. I was so flattered that I convinced myself likewise, and we embraced this happy illusion together.

One evening I told him the story of my play *The Man Who Had All the Luck,* which had been optioned for production the next year. Facing the fire in his sparsely furnished living room, I acted it all out for him, revising as I went along, and discovered a look of amazement and baffled awe forming on his face. When I was done he asked, "Where'd you get that story?" I had invented it, I said, based on my wife's relative. "That's the story of my life," he said.

As he described himself, he had been too modest and shy to imagine becoming the star reporter he was now. Indeed, it was his inwardness that had moved him to invent the greatly successful idea of touring the small towns with his wife, thus avoiding major stories and the journalist's usual need to impose upon people. He had managed to create the public image of a romantic pair of comrades savoring the everlasting truths of the unsung American majority. Luck had been his lifelong companion, he thought, and he had never understood why his professional life had been so successful. In the back of his mind disaster waited for the moment when it was least expected.

We were drinking and warming to our unexpectedly interesting lives when, staring into the fire, he began a long story about an experience in Italy. Not many months before, he had come upon "a pile of dead Italians and some German troops. They were just stacked up and must have been killed at about the same moment, because *rigor mortis* had set in and they nearly all had enormous erections. Some of their cocks were popping through the buttons. Must have been nearly two hundred of them facing up to the sky." I recalled reading the column, but he had of course not mentioned the erections. And then, hardly glancing at me, "I had this accident as a boy . . ." He broke off before adding the unnecessary.

It was my turn to confess now, and I surprised myself by talking about the woman in Washington whose husband had been lost at sea, but he was ahead of me and cut me off. "Don't, don't do anything like that ever. The marriage is everything. That sex stuff is no good, it won't get you a thing. . . . You think you have to do it, but you don't. Your wife sounds like a wonderful woman . . ." What amazed me suddenly was the depth and innocence of his caring, and what I imagined was a certain envy for my good physical luck.

But the main news he gave me on that and the other nights was his refusal to hate the enemy soldiers, men trapped as ours were in this killing. Through that respectful and suffering vision of his, of a human disaster transcending politics, I saw his tragic nature for the first time. It bound me never to betray his hopes for a valid film, one that could certainly not be about a big guy and a little guy and a girl.

Back in Brooklyn a few days later, I got a call from Lester announcing that Ernie had signed the contract and the film was now "definite"—quite as though he had ever informed me it wasn't—and that United Press was having a celebration to which I was invited by Lee Miller himself, the head of the organization of which Ernie, of course, was the star. I got on the subway trying to forget Stallings's realism of some weeks before and looking forward to seeing Pyle again.

It was after ten o'clock in the evening when the drinking in the UP office paused long enough for ten or twelve of us to escape to 21 for some dinner. There, in the dining room already half empty, seated alone at a table chewing on crumbs from a broken piece of bread, was another American hero, John Steinbeck. He turned out to be an old friend of Miller's, who had sent him to Russia and elsewhere as a correspondent. Nothing would do but that we join him.

I had never seen Steinbeck before, and it struck me that like Ernie Pyle, he could easily blush, but unlike Pyle, he seemed to want to expand himself physically, to present a strong and able and heartily Western image, his basic sensitivity and sentiment covered by an aggressively cynical wit that could move over the edge into cruelty. He had written—in *The Red Pony, Of Mice and Men,* the story "The Daughter," and of course *The Grapes of Wrath*— scenes that were engraved on America like the Indian's profile on the nickel, and I felt a faint disappointment to find him idling in this decadent place. I sat, as was natural, at the foot of the table and had no conversation with him. Pyle was neither eating nor drinking, and I imagined that he had for some reason lost the desire to celebrate. When the check came Steinbeck grabbed it, and only when Lee Miller protested that UP would pay did he relent enough to toss a coin for it. He lost the toss and paid whatever hundreds of dollars it all came to. It seemed an excessive gesture and left the others feeling some awkwardness as he did the business with the waiter.

On the sidewalk Pyle took me aside and said, "I hope you stick with this. Don't let them ruin it, will you?" I promised to do all I could, and he said that he probably wouldn't be seeing me again till the picture was finished because he had decided to return overseas—this despite Lee Miller's pleading that he had risked himself enough and could stay at home and do anything he liked for UP for the rest of his life. But his unhappiness here was sunk in his eyes, the more so now at the end of a night of false gaiety. We shook hands. In 1945, during the invasion of a tiny island off Japan called Ie Shima, he died in a foxhole, a bullet through his head. He had had enough of having all the luck. Maybe he could not bear surviving his dead or his time.

I walked with Steinbeck up Sixth Avenue toward his apartment. Something almost frenetic betrayed his anxiety and discontent with himself. His drinking wife had recently fallen off a balcony of their apartment, and he bore the special conflict of the cele-brated—the desire to confide and the distrust of all confidants. He seemed an ungainly small-town fellow out of his element, grabbing the check like a provincial—a New York writer would not have thought to pay for ten people he had not invited for dinner, it smacked more of inner uncertainty than confident noblesse. It was cold but he wore no overcoat and enjoyed breasting the sharp wind as we walked toward the park. He seemed a shackled giant of a man fit for sun, water, and earth and not sidewalks and smart people. His face was no longer blotched with embarrassment, and he had ceased to guffaw sardonically at some bitter truth about people—in the restaurant he had been all laughing irony—but he was still jumpy and unhappy and restless. I did not know then that he had just broken up with his wife. That the author of prose so definite and painterly could be so personally unsure was beyond my experience.

I said good night to Steinbeck and walked on to the subway station. Waiting in the nearly empty train for the doors to close, I saw an old Orthodox Jew enter, clutching the inevitable bundle wrapped in brown paper and twine. A long white beard and broad-brimmed black felt hat, the traditional sidelocks and all the anxious energy of the survivor. Such men had always seemed like atavisms, fossils of a long-dead past. My father had run into Orthodox Jews in the garment industry and showed some irritation with their way of life; they were either collecting alms or were too sharp as busi-nessmen, a charge I found hard to listen to.

The man seemed in a sweat of anxiety as he glanced up and down at the few passengers. Finally he chose me to sit next to. The redness of his cheeks reminded me of Steinbeck's flush in the restaurant. An evening full of anxious men. Suddenly he leaned toward me and, putting his lips close to my ear, asked, "Are you Jewish?"

"Yes."

"You're Jewish?" he repeated, wanting some added assurance, balanced on the knife edge of trust.

"I said yes."

His eyes widened with apprehension as he took the plunge: "Does this stop at Canal Street?"

I wanted to laugh but nodded and assured him that it did, and he seemed to relax in contentment, which relieved me as well. I could feel the heat of his body through my sleeve. That people like him were being hunted down like beasts was once again incredible. I determined to conquer whatever problems there were in the screenplay and to make sure it strengthened support for our men fighting the enemy, but to do so by giving each character his own viewpoint and space in the film.

Back in Hollywood in a few weeks, I was discouraged to find yet another putative director wandering about in the Cowan offices, also unpaid. One afternoon I was staring in futility out the studio window when, as in a dream, about twenty perfectly shaped chorus girls carrying identical metal lunch boxes appeared on the green lawn, sat down under a two-story-high white Grecian arch supported by Doric columns, remnant of some set or other, and proceeded to eat. Their faces were painted half white and half green to match similarly divided tights and two-color stockings and shoes. One of them rose now and then on long, gorgeous legs and moved like some humanoid gazelle to chat with another. They were beyond earshot, and the silence loaned the scene an added air of hallucination. A tractor appeared pulling a wheeled circus wagon with an enormous brown bear behind the bars. It halted amidst the girls, who laughed and waved happily to the bear, who looked down at them as though he too were in a dream.

A bulky old Minerva open touring car driven by a uniformed chauffeur now moved into view and came to a glistening halt just below the cage. It was the kind of glorious limousine Sid Franks and I had loved to watch lining up along the curb on 110th Street. A white-uniformed nurse stood up from the backseat and helped an old gentleman to his feet. He was then handed to the ground by two men who had hurried out of one of the sound stages in the background to meet the car. The passenger, I now made out, was W. C. Fields.

A portable stair was set in place beside the cage, and the great comedian, wearing a straw hat despite the wintry chill, made it up the three or four steps to a platform level with the floor of the cage, where a photographer stood focusing a Graflex. Fields was handed an apple, which he held up between the bars to tempt the bear to its feet. The bear blinked uninterestedly at the apple. Fields tossed it to him, and the bear gulped it down but did not rise. Fields took another apple and held it high between the bars, still with no results. Suddenly, without apparent reason, the bear stood and gripped the bars with his gigantic paws, stretching his muzzle toward the apple, which Fields held just beyond his reach. The flashes went off: a picture of Fields and the bear a few inches apart, Fields's expression astonishingly bearlike as he traded looks with the animal.

As the bear held his position stretching for the apple, Fields carefully drew from his breast pocket a water pistol and with an expression of infinitely vicious joy squirted it directly into the bear's astounded face. The animal reared back and nearly fell over. Fields hurried with amazing agility down the stair and into his car and was instantly driven away, the nurse covering his lap with a blanket.

It was not easy to turn my mind back to the World War II epic lying on my desk. Anyway, I had come to the end of my invention and was simply moving elements of the story from one place to another, with Cowan cryptically hinting that the script "still had a way to go." But where and to what end? The contrast between the holiness of the sacrifices in the war and the absurdity of Hollywood began eating into me now that I had exhausted my imagination. The girls had left the lawn, the bear and his cage were gone, and only the flat, empty Grecian arch remained.

I was surprised now by the sound of a motorcycle engine right under my window. A rider dressed in black leather, black helmet, emblazoned gauntlets, and black leather puttees was swinging off the black machine. A truly Hollywood-type messenger, I thought. Again I tried to concentrate on the script, but there was a knock on my door. Opening it, I found the motorcycle rider with his helmet under his arm, removing his gauntlets. To my surprise he wore eyeglasses and was middle-aged. I imagined he carried a special message to me from Cowan, who was at the moment back in Washington, doubtless arranging for the use of a hundred thousand tanks and a million men.

"You're Miller, right?"

"That's right." I expected him to hand me an envelope.

"My name is LeMay. I'm your collaborator."

"My collaborator?"

"Didn't Lester tell you? He's put me on the script with you."

"No, he never mentioned it. Come in, sit down."

I had in that instant decided, without conflict or even effort, to quit the project, but I wanted to find out how this procedure worked.

We sat at the lone desk. Alan LeMay, whose name I gradually recalled in connection with action films, seemed a contented technician happy to tackle yet another problem job. He now took out of his pocket a brand-new deck of file cards, which he laid on the desk. "I think the best way would be to put the name of each character on a card . . ."

"Excuse me," I said, "but have you read my script?"

"No, not yet, but I will. But I think we can save time if you give me the names of each of the characters and we make up a card for him."

"And what do we do with the cards?"

"What we do, we combine them to reduce the number of characters. In other words, under each name we put his main story actions and see if we can take several actions and give them to one guy instead of three or four."

"I see. So we can end up with . . . like a big guy and a little guy?"

"Not necessarily only two. We might end up with three or even four, but there'd be one major guy and a sidekick, sort of. On that order. But have you had lunch?"

"Not yet. How about a ride on your motorcycle?"

"Great. I know a place about a mile away."

On the way out of the office I felt, for the first time in Hollywood, thoroughly at home with myself. I paused at the desk of Cowan's secretary to ask her to send him a wire in Washington thanking him for the opportunity to write this film but saying that I had never agreed to a collaborator and was returning to New York tomorrow, my services at an end.

LeMay was a terrific maneuverer through traffic, and the ride on the back of the British Triumph was glorious. We leaned way over on turns and came to such a stylishly sudden halt in front of the restaurant that I nearly slid up his leather back and over his head.

LeMay probably did some good work on the picture and was naturally replaced by another writer and yet another, but *The Story of GI Joe* was finally made and turned out to be surprisingly good. Of course it had lost almost all relation to the original scheme and had become the plain story of a caring infantry captain, played by Robert Mitchum, who in the end is killed. It was a moving tale but totally without any formal invention or interest for me. Ernie was played by Burgess Meredith, then a youthfully lyrical actor with a sweet American intelligence. I sensed, however, that a dimension of Pyle was missing, not from the performance but from the conception of the script. I only realized what it was decades later, during the Vietnam War, when I recalled Pyle's insight that all war was civil war between brothers and that this fratricide overshadowed all compensatory glory and threatened any claim to meaning itself. The film, understandably, was about a fight between enemies, for it was very nearly impossible at the time to equate the Germans with those who fought them. Yet with his ordinary Main Street language, Pyle had glimpsed the war on the awful plane of tragedy—a word he would have shied from as far too intellectual—and if Cowan brought off a respectable achievement that honored Pyle and Americans, it was a far shallower portrait than they deserved.

My name, of course, never appeared on the film, but half a dozen years later—after *All My Sons* and *Death of a Salesman*—I was surprised one afternoon by a call from Cowan, complete with his transparently rote little laugh, asking if I wouldn't like to have my name added to the re-release. I said that I didn't think it was my script anymore.

"But a lot of your stuff is in there, Arthur. In fact, most of the best of it is yours."

"Really? I don't recall recognizing anything, but maybe so." Then, half as a joke, but only half, I said, "Tell you what, Lester. You pay me twenty thousand and you can put my name on it."

He laughed and I laughed, and for me that was the end of *The Story of GI Joe*.

FIVE

FIVE

Albuquerque again, but Pyle was now some five years dead and nearly a decade had passed since we strolled together down an empty moonlit main street trading uncertainties. Now the Super Chief rested on the sunlit siding, taking on water. I walked back to the last car and stood staring down the empty track stretching away across beige New Mexico. This silence would always excite me, the wide sky as clear and blue as Creation. For a man of thirty-five, I seemed to have done nothing but work; I had had, as Thornton Wilder put it in *The Matchmaker,* a lot of adventures but no experience. When, I wondered, does one cease to work and start to live?

.I was conscious of time fleeing and my waste of it, unable as I was to embrace the greatness of the American story that I knew was all around me on this haunting continent. I was proud of *All My Sons* and *Salesman,* but they were already the past. The vision returned of that lone Indian man Ernie and I had noticed looking off toward the sunset on an Albuquerque street corner. Absurdly enough, I felt lonesome for the sight of him and imagined that if I could find that corner, even after all these years had passed, he would still be standing there lost in the motionless staring that was so full of his sadness. He had become in my imagination a natural feature of this landscape.

I felt the excitement of approaching Hollywood tomorrow, this time with some successful plays behind me and a challenging movie script that I was glad to have written even if it should never reach production. It too was an attempt to hack out a road that would penetrate to the American center, the point of creation beyond which there was nothing.

Sitting on a beer box someone had left near the tracks, I tried to imagine myself a local man who had come to watch the trains passing. The lure of another identity and of losing oneself in America. There was something mistaken in my life. Maybe I had simply married too young.

Kazan was studying the waterfront script in our compartment. It was a persuasive story I had created, yes, but one I had not really lived and therefore did not quite trust.

A gray cat appeared from under the train and looked at me. For him, perhaps, I belonged here. Thin as a fan, he arched pleasurably against the train's sun-warmed wheel. If I let the train leave me behind, I thought, I would know no one in New Mexico. A feeling of freedom and infinite choices touched me.

I had known, in fact, only one native of New Mexico, and I thought about him now, the only man I had ever met who wore octagonal glasses and parted his hair in the middle. He had a snub nose and a rather stolid Dutch look. In 1950 it would have been very difficult to explain to Americans why Ralph Neaphus had had to die—and may even have chosen to—at twenty-three, in the spring of 1937.

Raised on a New Mexico ranch, Ralph had never been east of the Mississippi before coming to the University of Michigan. With his rather schoolteacherly look, he was one of those soft-spoken Westerners who come slowly to a decision and thereafter cannot be budged. He had hardly ever talked politics with me as we washed dishes side by side month after month in the Co-op cafeteria kitchen. Anyway, there was little to dispute about Spain—for us the issue was beyond doubt, the fascists had to be stopped. It never occurred to me to ask him if he was a Communist; it hardly mattered then. And by no means were all the volunteers Party members.

As I·drove east with him across Ohio—in my little 1927 Model T coupe we were much too big for, which I had recently bought from a graduate student for twenty-two dollars—I carried my own indecision within me like a kind of sinfulness. One moment I was ready to break loose and go off with him to join the Abraham Lincoln Brigade in Spain, the next I was too appalled at the idea of not living to write a great play. Worst of all was the blinding prospect of informing my mother that I was off to war. It never occurred to me that if I went I might survive. I already thought of Ralph as dead, sitting there next to him as the car's iron engine ticked faithfully on, he as silent as New Mexico itself. Night came on, and it began to rain. We were on Route 17 east of Buffalo, climbing into the mountains. The single windshield wiper had to be operated manually, and a bump would send the wheel spinning if only one hand was gripping it while the other was swinging the wiper. The rain came heavier and heavier until I could see nothing at all, so I pulled cautiously to the side and felt earth under the wheels. Figuring we were in a field somewhere, I stopped and switched off the engine and cut the lights. The cloth roof sounded like shrapnel was falling on it in waves.

Sitting there shoulder to shoulder steaming in the dark, I had my first chance to ask about the procedure. He had an address in downtown New York where he would report. The Party would give him the papers he needed. He did not know if they had uniforms in the brigade, but he doubted it and expected to wear his own clothes into battle, an odd image to me. "I'm pretty good with a rifle" was his first and only statement that approached self-description. But I did not think it unusual for someone of the left to suppress personal feelings, which after all were of no real significance—only duty was. There was something of the psychology of priests in this. I tried to pump him; had he informed his parents he was going?

"Yes," he said, and that was all.

"How do they feel about it?"

In the black darkness I could only sense him turning his head to me with what I took for surprise. "I don't know," he said, as though the question had never occurred to him. He had become the bridegroom of war.

In the half-century to come, the shadow upon all the wars of liberation would always be Spain, and the long, faith-lifted gaze of Ralph Neaphus would hover above China and Vietnam, the Maquis and the Algerian FLN, and all the scores of wars of untrained, passionate men against regular armies.

The rain was not letting up, and I had been driving all day. Both of us couldn't possibly sleep inside the car, so I took my yellow slicker out of the trunk and let Ralph have the seat. I stretched out on the sodden ground, put my arm under my cheek, and quickly fell asleep, the rain pouring on my head.

Sunlight woke me. Opening my eyes, I saw a pair of woman's shoes, thick ankles, and legs a few inches away. Above me an angry middle-aged face glared down. Behind it was her house. We were on her waterlogged lawn, and the tracks of the car were deeply gouged into it. I tried to explain, but she was too furious, so I got in and we quickly drove off.

In a few miles the forward band of the planetary transmission began slipping, and I opened the gearbox and tightened it. Now the engine roared, but midway up the hills we were almost standing still. So I turned the car around and went up in reverse. Drivers overtaking us, seeing us apparently heading down the mountain on the wrong side of the road, jammed on their brakes to avoid colliding, then started up tentatively behind us and passed, often cursing out their windows at us, though one or two urged us playfully on. Then the battery died and the brakes wouldn't hold, so as we descended into towns I had to use the reverse pedal to slow down while both of us banged on the outside of the doors and yelled to warn people away. I had about three dollars, and Ralph had agreed to split the gas with his four, so repairs were out of the question. We had to get to New York and the Spanish war so that Ralph could die there, and we would have to do it in this car in this condition. I was already mourning him, and he began to look beautiful, which he really was not, with his slightly turned-up nose and peering eyes and rather forbiddingly straight neck, a naive neck, too, somehow.

Finally, heading across the George Washington Bridge, the front wheels suddenly broke into a violent shimmy, like a circus fun car. I could hardly hold on to the wheel at all. The sun was shimmering on the Hudson on this gorgeous June day. As we approached the New York end of the bridge, a cop appeared, wearily raising his hand, and I jammed down the reverse pedal to be sure to come to a stop before running him over. The car whined when you did that, but it did stop, although breathing hard. In that leisurely way they have, the policeman walked up to my window looking the car over. He was kind of naive too.

"You don't want to bring that thing into the city, you're liable to kill somebody. There's a lot of people in this city, you know, a lot of cars and things." The Michigan plates had obviously convinced him that we were from a town with maybe two streets.

"Well, I just want to get to Brooklyn, and then I won't drive it anymore . . ."

He could not think of anything to do or say and just stood there nodding, but I thought to demonstrate my innocence by asking how to get onto Riverside Drive. With the Michigan plates and two valises tied with clothesline to the running board on Ralph's side, we apparently deserved some commiseration, and pointing up at a lamppost, the cop said, "See that sign?"

"Yep," I said, as hicky as I dared.

"That says One hundred sixty-nine Street, got it? Well, you turn right and you keep an eye on each corner which is gonna say One hundred sixty-eight, One hundred sixty-seven, One hundred sixty-six, One hundred sixty-five . . ."

"I got it. Those are streets, you mean."

"Tha-a-t's right, those are streets. When you get to where it says Hundred sixty-fourth, turn right and that'll put you onto the drive. But go very slow, will ya? Don't rush. Brooklyn'll take you about an hour. Take your time, and good luck."

"Thanks very much."

"Try not to kill anybody."

Ralph wanted to see Forty-second Street, so we turned and crossed town, and on the corner of Broadway he revolved in a circle taking it all in for his first and last time. This was before the blessings of cocaine and heroin, but the garish lights of the theatre marquees were on in the sunshine, and the hoarse, self-advertising atmosphere was as fraudulently cheerful as ever. There were the same drifting midday crowds on Broadway, the young down from the Bronx or up from Brooklyn to hit the Paramount and the Palace, munching the nickel hotdogs with a hunger for the hopeful glamour of these movie palaces so unlike the barren drabness of their neighborhood theatres.

Up six-lane Ocean Parkway the Model T, like a horse nearing its barn, lost its shimmy and behaved, and we could relax on the nearly empty road. The horses on the bridle path confused Ralph, who could hardly believe that people would pay money to ride, let alone to head nowhere. I told him that I had done it myself pretty often, at two dollars an hour. He leaned forward to observe the miles of neat one-family houses, like a man in a foreign country. At home, my mother welcomed us and made up a bed for him on the couch but stiffened when she heard what his mission was, fearing its contagion. Her eyes threatened whenever I mentioned his imminent transatlantic voyage to Spain. Ralph himself kept silent about it, the Lincoln Brigade being an illegal recruitment organization. On his third and last night with us, his silence spread to everyone despite our awkward attempts to enliven the conversation. I began to hate my mother for her unprincipled selfishness in restraining me and reminded myself that I was past twenty-one, old enough to decide for myself; but I fell back on Ralph's having already graduated while I still had a year to go before my degree—as though one had to have a degree before dying in a war. Actually, most of the time I was not afraid to die; no one at twenty-one or -two would ever really die, certainly not in perfect health. Except maybe Ralph. Anyway, I could not find the trigger in myself that would propel me, as Ralph had clearly done. Eating in silence on this last evening, none of us any longer attempted to keep up the polite chatter, for Ralph seemed to be enveloping himself in a kind of membrane, the isolation of the committed. Maybe he was steeling himself against deviating from his path, but I felt that even in these few days together he had gradually hardened against the trivialities of ordinary life.

Next morning I walked him the three blocks to the elevated Culver Line that I had ridden for two years to my warehouse job, its cars still the drafty old wooden kind with iron coal stoves around which in winter the handful of passengers would sit with gloved fingers outstretched. I wanted to break through Ralph's distance from me as we walked, for it was like a form of distrust between us now; after all, he was doing an illegal thing. The word *fate* was not in my vocabulary then, but by this morning I knew that I was not to go to Spain, my drift was in another direction. At the turnstile Ralph glanced back and gave me a dry, silent wave and was gone into the rickety train, his heavy valise packed with all he owned in the world banging against his leg. So wrapped in his mission was he that I wondered for that instant if he would mind dying. I bounded down the long steel stairway to the sidewalk and strolled toward home, past the two empty lots where we used to play football, glad for the spring sun and the clear blue sky and the clean snuggling silence of Brooklyn at midday, glad for the sense of some spreading power in me, and turning into Third Street from Avenue M, I broke into a run at top speed, arriving at our stoop with heart pounding. I walked into the house and saw my mother at the stove in the back kitchen. She glanced up at me placidly, having won. For which I resented her, and even more deeply my own complicity with her. I could not stay in the room with her. I opened the back door and walked out on the gray porch, the porch I had built seven years before, which continued—only I was secretly aware of it—to part from the house by fractions of an inch each year.

When I returned to school for my senior year, the news that Ralph Neaphus had been captured was all over campus. Then he was safe! I was immensely happy, as though some blame had been lifted from me. And then, two or three weeks later, came the report that Franco's Moorish troops had shot their prisoners and that he had been among them. This was one of the debts I would carry in my heart, an invisible force that pressed me more than a decade later to cross the line of nuns around the Waldorf, one of the many secret debts borne by all of us whose souls had been enlisted in that consensus or coalition or, rather, condition of anti-fascism. Or perhaps not even a condition but an atmosphere of alienation from what seemed the worldwide drift into what Odön von Horváth called the "age of the fish," where grinning, killing, and feeding were the only signs of human life.

Hollywood for me will always evoke a contradictory mixture of certain scents. A sexual damp, I have called it, the moisture in the clean creases of a woman's flesh, combined with a challenging sea-salt smell; the exciting air surrounding a voyage on water and the dead ozone inside a sound stage; raw gasoline and lipstick perfume; swimming pool chlorine and the scentless smell of rhododendron and oleander, nature's attempts at plastic flora, plants that really belong in mountains, not in the rescued desert of Los Angeles where their artificiality adds its evergreen shine to the oppressive perfection.

We were met at the station by a man from Twentieth Century Fox who handed the keys of the small black Lincoln to Kazan and with barely a nod left us to drive off with it.

In my mid-thirties, I still looked out at the world half as an adolescent. Hollywood in 1950 had not lost the tags of mystic glamour, success, and escape that it had once had for kids in a Brooklyn high school. At the same time, as we drove through Los Angeles toward Beverly Hills, my feelings were satisfactorily different from what they had been when I arrived, an unknown, to work on Cowan's movie almost eight years before; now the place was all about power for me, about using the power I had presumably earned with my plays. In the unwavering sunshine I found myself turning grave precisely as the boy within smelled sexuality and the adventure of making a film. The studios then were still in full command, and the notion of the writer's control over his script—or, for that matter, the director's over his film—was simply beyond discussion. I took for granted that we were heading into a struggle in the coming days, but the prize was worth it: a truthful film about a dark cellar under the American Dream. Everything was contradictory, inside me and without. And with Kazan, too, my relation was complex.

Not unlike other writers who had worked with him, I felt a partnership without ever forgetting that it was an illusion, for in making a play or film people come together primarily as elements of a creating organism and not out of love or mutual regard. I had never known Kazan to chat, to call for no specific reason, in those times when, in his mid-forties, he was building his career. But if he was honed down to an instrumentality of his work, that was part of his attraction for writers, who are forever trying to ward off aimlessness in their attempt to penetrate to some systematic core that generates the bewildering sparks and fires of chaotic life.

We drove into Beverly Hills, perfection to right and left, the nests of the famous and the rich impressing my ambitious heart and leaving an uneasiness in the mind. The place was so depressingly completed—maybe that was it, the sheer end-of-the-road materiality. The Tudor castle divided by a hedge from the New England farmhouse divided by a driveway from the French provincial. To each his individual dream, connected only by the silent little Japanese gardener and his son padding from lawn to immaculate lawn picking up the browned fallen palm frond, the crisp, dead, adventurous leaf, while nothing whatsoever moved, stirred, cried out, each house suspended in its spell of total achievement and guaranteed against ever becoming a ruin, all too perfect to die. And here was I carrying into this deep dream of peace a script about an old waterfront where the sun shone through dust and the acrid smell of steel, a slum where nothing looked completed or else was broken and falling apart. So young in comparison, Beverly Hills seemed frozen in timeless self-approval. Of course they were going crazy inside the houses, but I knew nothing of that yet.

I planned to stay a week. We settled into the house of Charles Feldman, formerly an agent and now one of the leading producers (*A Streetcar Named Desire,* his latest film, had been directed by Kazan), a handsome, suave man close to fifty and eager to make himself useful to Kazan. I was still revising the screenplay, which was far too long but in sufficiently good shape, Kazan believed, for its feasibility as a film to be determined. He had sent a copy to Harry Cohn, the Columbia chief. I could continue working on it for a couple of days while Cohn made up his mind.

But it was impossible to concentrate. As I sat at a glass table beside Feldman's swimming pool, the waterfront kept vanishing into the sun sparkling on the eggs Benedict, the very effort to conjure it up whispering of fraud. A Filipino houseman provided coffee and whatever else I could imagine eating. I finally gave up and lay staring at the birdless foliage wondering if this was what being "in" meant. It was a question I would never be able to answer; it may be that Hollywood is merely a living Escher drawing with no inside at all, only an outside, since everyone I met regarded himself as an outsider perpetually passing through, like politicians in Washington.

Meantime, there was a "party" each evening. Although his

young wife's photos remained all over the house, Feldman was divorced or separated, and there were usually eight or ten for dinner. The folkways excited and puzzled me; even when they arrived together, couples turned out to be only recently met, some as recently as an hour earlier, and women—many of them, if not all, ambitious for stardom—arrived and left alone in their own cars. It took a while to realize that some were mine to select from. I would later write in a poem, "Lines from California," that to succeed in Hollywood a woman had to have a car. The company would sit around after dinner in the lavishly plain living room or wander out to the pool for more intimate conversation or to dance to succulent big band records. At one point I danced with an elegantly tall young woman, an heiress, I was told, who had come to Hollywood to be a star. But it was hard to know whether her unshakable silence meant contempt or awe or some stupendous inertia brought upon her by the oppression of great wealth. Jack Warner came one evening, looking amazingly like the comedian Victor Moore playing Wintergreen, the sappy presidential candidate in *Of Thee I Sing,* as he sat broadly grinning in a high-backed chair for over an hour telling one joke after another, a ritual of Hollywood parties, evidently. Yet Warner Brothers, slightly more socially conscious than the other studios, had made some good topical and biographical movies. I wondered for a fleeting moment if I was merely a snob trying to suppress a perverse attraction to his cultural type, for he reminded me of my father, who might have inspired similar deference if he had decided to lend Bill Fox some money.

Warner was clearly interested in talking seriously only with Kazan, whom he would have liked to employ whatever his leftist reputation. Soon, as a friendly witness before the Un-American Committee, Warner would gravely reassure the members that he had always made it a policy "to turn my back whenever I see one of those Reds coming." (Which, a quarter-century further on, would aid me in understanding some of the ferocity of ostracism in the Chinese Cultural Revolution.)

The all but announced themes of these evenings seemed to be sex and employment. On reflection many years later, I was reminded of the court of Louis XIV, with its similar shuttlings and weavings of people trying to intercept the trajectories of power. At Versailles, however, women often held and administered power, while in Hollywood they never had more than the pleasure of momentary contact with it, and the memories of service to it for their old age. But the part of me that was still a boy was nevertheless dazzled by men and women I had seen on the screen and directors whose names I had long known, and as we awaited Harry Cohn's decision on the script, I began to look forward to these dinners and their famous guests. Since my normal environment was four walls surrounding a typewriter on a desk, all this excitement was unreal but fascinating, and the conversation was by no means always vapid; the political drift of the country, for example, had a direct bearing on the movies one could expect to make, so there was more than an academic interest in what was really going on underneath the headlines. As nowhere else, there was a hunger here for the inside dope. And I had never before seen sex treated so casually as a reward of success; the immemorial right of the powerful to bed women of choice, a right claimed by men around the world, from Darryl Zanuck to Mao Zedong, was the practice here to the point of boredom, but a provocation nevertheless.

On one of these evenings a young woman to whom Kazan had introduced me some days before created a quickened center for the company's interest, attended by its barely suppressed sneer. Her agent and protector, Johnny Hyde, had recently died, but not before managing to get her a few small roles that had led to John Huston's using her in *The Asphalt Jungle* as Louis Calhern's mistress. In a part practically without lines, she had nevertheless made a definite impact. I had had to think a moment to recall her in the film. She had seemed more a prop than an actress, a nearly mute satirical comment on Calhern's spurious propriety and official power, the quintessential dumb blonde on the arm of the worldly and corrupt representative of society. In this roomful of actresses and wives of substantial men, all striving to dress and behave with an emphatically ladylike reserve, Marilyn Monroe seemed almost ludicrously provocative, a strange bird in the aviary, if only because her dress was so blatantly tight, declaring rather than insinuating that she had brought her body along and that it was the best one in the room. And she seemed younger and more girlish than when I had first seen her. The female resentment that surrounded her at Feldman's approached the consistency of acrid smoke. An exception was the actress Evelyn Keyes, a Huston ex-wife, who managed to draw Marilyn out, sitting with her on a settee, and who softly said to me later as she watched her dancing with someone, "They'll eat her alive." The eye sought in vain to find the least fault in the architecture of her form as she moved with her partner, her perfection seeming to invite the inevitable wound that would make her more like others. And so it was a perfection that aroused a wish to defend it, though I suspected at the same time how tough she must be to have survived here for so long and with such relative success. But apparently she was now alone in the world.

A few days earlier I had gone to the Twentieth Century Fox studio with Kazan, who was under contract there and had many friends working on the sound stages. One of them, his former film editor, was now directing *As Young As You Feel*, a comedy with my father's bête noire Monty Woolley and, in a bit part, Marilyn. Moviemaking was still an exotic and fantastic affair for me, and full of mysteries. We had just arrived on a nightclub set when Marilyn, in a black openwork lace dress, was directed to walk across the floor, attracting the worn gaze of the bearded Woolley. She was being shot from the rear to set off the swiveling of her hips, a motion fluid enough to seem comic. It was, in fact, her natural walk: her footprints on a beach would be in a straight line, the heel descending exactly before the last toeprint, throwing her pelvis into motion.

When the shot was finished she came over to Kazan, who had met her with Hyde on another visit some time before. From where I stood, yards away, I saw her in profile against a white light, with her hair coiled atop her head; she was weeping under a veil of black lace that she lifted now and then to dab her eyes. When we shook hands the shock of her body's motion sped through me, a sensation at odds with her sadness amid all this glamour and technology and the busy confusion of a new shot being set up. She had been weeping, she would explain later, while telling Kazan that Hyde had died calling her name in a hospital room she had been forbidden by his family to enter. She had heard him from the corridor, and had left, as always, alone.

Her slight role in the movie finished, she tagged along with us the next day to Harry Cohn's office at Columbia Pictures. It was a vast space, his office, but something makeshift about its cheap lumberyard stained paneling declared his stubborn grip on reality, a reminder that he had come up out of the waterfront slums of lower Manhattan. A tough dreamer who prided himself on having no important stockholders, Cohn was the last of my father's breed, along with Jack Warner and one or two dying others. He could hardly keep his eyes from Marilyn; trying to recall where he had seen her, he marched around in front of her hitching up his pants like a Manhattan cab driver getting ready to fight. His face has receded from memory, but not his flowing brutality and candor as he peered at her, growling, "I t'ink I know whose goils you were," while she sat there in her special agonized mixture of amusement and shame. In a shaft of sunlight poking through the edge of the brown Venetian blind, her face seemed puffed and not especially beautiful, but she could hardly move a finger without striking the heart with the beauty of its curving line.

"This picture won't make a dime," Cohn aggressively announced once he had settled himself behind his desk. But he kept hearing messages through the air, it seemed, and would interrupt himself to punch a button and yell into an intercom to his secretary beyond the closed door. He knew every yard of the studio complex and what was happening everywhere and sent commands and questions down the barrackslike halls as we went on talking about our picture. "But I come from back there, though," he said, jabbing a hairy finger down at the script, "and I know the whole story. But it won't make a dime, but I'll go in with yiz, pervided yiz don't take any money unless it makes money. And I'll back it because"—he turned and pointed straight at Kazan—"I want you to make a picture for me after this."

Then, suddenly, he turned to Marilyn and said, "I remember you!" It was, apparently, an unpleasant memory; in fact, he had wanted her aboard his boat a time ago, and she had refused to go unless his wife came along—a grievous insult that for a moment passed a reddened blush of anger over his forehead.

His memory seemed to move him again to his buttons. Bending over the desk, he punched and yelled, "Get me fear!" For a moment he stood in calculation, growing angrier, and now he pushed the button and roared with all his force, "I want fear! Now!"

There were running footsteps outside the door, which opened to admit a small sixtyish man in collar and tie and cufflinks: Joe Fier, Cohn's majordomo. He was heaving for breath and perspiring, having no doubt run some distance.

"Yes, Mr. Cohn," he was able to gasp, cheeks red and bald head blanched white.

With such open contempt that it was hard to watch, Cohn gave him some perfunctory command and then turned his back on him and quite calmly picked up our conversation where we had left off, his eyes again gazing at Marilyn, who sat apart, not saying a word, her eyes lowered. Fier departed soundlessly, having played out his role as victim of Cohn's power, a demonstration to us of our coming subjection.

"Is it a deal? No money till we're in profits, okay? I mean if yiz are so fucking idealistic, right?" His gleeful grin cut, but his challenge seemed to me acceptable enough: he would gamble his money and studio; I would throw in my script, and Kazan his work.

With the terms set, Cohn announced that the script had to be vetted by his labor relations man since the story dealt with a union. This seemed rather strange, but in a world so new to me I had no precedents and did not object. Whereupon Cohn yelled down at his desk for said executive, who promptly showed up, an Ivy League gentleman unusual at first glance for his collar and tie and blazer reminiscent of the formality of the East. He negotiated union contracts for Columbia. With a trim, imperturbable Yankee face, he seemed a man of some depth who did not spend emotions lavishly but grinned only slightly or allowed a twinkle to slip into his eye. Cohn had given him the script the day before, and now, to Cohn's request for his opinion, he replied that he thought the script terrific and in his experience an accurate depiction of the New York waterfront situation. For the first time Cohn looked impressed, glancing over at me with some small deference now that I had been complimented by a tough-minded civilian rather than some show business ignoramus.

A relaxed air seemed to surround Cohn now, doubtless because he imagined he had pulled off a coup in getting Kazan and me on spec, with the added prospect of winning points for producing an unprecedentedly realistic movie about a major social issue that no other studio would touch. Looking pleased with himself, he pulled a book out of his drawer and handed it to me, asking me to consider doing a screenplay based on it. I had no intention of hiring out but agreed to read it. I was still trying to believe that we had accomplished what we had come for and were going to expose the long-shoremen's condition in the bargain; I was high on the thought of what was about to happen to something that had begun as graffiti chalked on the walls of Brooklyn Heights. I looked over at Marilyn, who was staring at me, smiling secretively lest she draw Cohn's attention to herself again. Kazan was talking about shooting dates and the unusually long schedule he hoped to be allowed for the film. I desperately wanted her and decided I must leave tonight, if possible, or I would lose myself here.

"I just have to check it with the FBI." I heard Cohn's gruff voice and for a moment wondered what he meant to check with the FBI. It turned out to be the script.

I thought for a moment that he was kidding. "What's there to check?" I asked, astonished.

Cohn shrugged. "They've got a good man here, I'd like him to look at it. Being it's about the waterfront."

Driving away in that everlasting sunshine, I wondered what precisely we were in for. If he meant that Kazan and I were being checked for background, they hardly needed to look at the script. This was threatening to become the briefest triumph I had ever experienced, but I still hoped for the best, if only because Cohn now seemed positively attached to the story, possibly as a result of his own youthful waterfront experience and his labor relations man's objective enthusiasm for it. I remembered reading about gangsterism in the Hollywood unions and wondered if *The Hook*, as the screenplay was called, might be a roundabout blow he thought to strike.

In any case, we did not yet have Cohn's commitment, and I thought I had better stay on a day or two more until the FBI had given its judgment. And so we went the rounds, the three of us, visiting Kazan's friends—waking the Robert Ardreys in the middle of the night, having a drink with Alfred Newman, the *Streetcar* musical director, laughing hilariously at our own silly remarks, released not only by Marilyn's beauty but, I thought, by her orphanhood, which heightened her charged presence; she had literally nowhere to go and no one to go to.

The three of us wandered through a bookstore, Marilyn wanting to find *Salesman*. When I turned to hand her a copy I had found on the drama shelf, I saw out of the corner of my eye a man, Chinese or Japanese, staring at her from the next aisle while masturbating in his pants. I quickly moved her away from the man, whom she had not seen. She was wearing an ordinary blouse and skirt, not at all provocative, but even here, with her attention on other things than herself, the air around her was charged. She had said she liked poetry, and we found some Frost and Whitman and E. E. Cummings. It was odd to watch her reading Cummings to herself, moving her lips—what would she make of poetry that was so simple and yet so sophisticated? I could not place her in any world I knew; like a cork bobbing on the ocean, she could have begun her voyage on the other side of the world or a hundred yards down the beach. There was apprehension in her eyes when she began to read, the look of a student afraid to be caught out, but suddenly she laughed in a thoroughly unaffected way at the small surprising turn in the poem about the lame balloon man—"and it's spring!" The naive wonder in her face that she could so easily respond to a stylized work sent a filament of connection out between us. "And it's spring!" she kept repeating on our way out to the car, laughing again as though she had been handed an unexpected gift. How pleased with her fresh reaction Cummings would have been, I thought, and resolved all over again to leave California as soon as possible.

There was still silence from Cohn. I gave up altogether trying to concentrate on the script, which kept cracking up and blowing away in the relentlessly beautiful days beside the pool. Instead I swam endlessly back and forth trailing blood from barbs of lust but confused by some sublime, trackless spirit in this incomprehensible young woman with whom—hardly touching—I had exchanged something secret, and something like hope, it seemed, for each of us. Rummaging for some skeptical explanation, I wondered if maybe no one had ever given her a book before and told myself for the last time that I must go.

At the airport, Kazan and Marilyn and I waited for my plane to board. It was early evening. I went to the ticket counter to recheck the flight, which should have been called by now. Marilyn came with me, and as I waited for the clerk to show up, she strolled away a few yards, looking around, and then came back; there were a dozen people in the lounge, and almost all were watching her. She was in a beige skirt and a white satin blouse, and her hair hung down to her shoulders, parted on the right side, and the sight of her was something like pain, and I knew that I must flee or walk into a doom beyond all knowing. With all her radiance she was surrounded by a darkness that perplexed me. I could not yet imagine that in my very shyness she saw some safety, release from the detached and centerless and invaded life she had been given; instead, I hated my lifelong timidity, but there was no changing it now. When we parted I kissed her cheek and she sucked in a surprised breath. I started to laugh at her overacting until the solemnity of feeling in her eyes shocked me into remorse, and I hurried backwards toward the plane. It was not duty alone that called me; I had to escape her childish voracity, something like my own unruly appetite for self-gratification, which had both created what art I had managed to make and disgusted me with its stain of irresponsibility. A retreat to the safety of morals, to be sure, but not necessarily to truthfulness. Flying homeward, her scent still on my hands, I knew my innocence was technical merely, and the fact blackened my heart, but along with it came the certainty that I could, after all, lose myself in sensuality. This novel secret entered me like a radiating force, and I welcomed it as a sort of proof that I would write again, but not the dutiful drudgery of a movie script, which is a form of knowing rather than being and feeling; I sensed a new play in me, and a play was my very self alive.

Back in Brooklyn, I veered between congratulating myself on having escaped destruction and wondering why I had left. A day and another day with no word from Kazan, and I began to feel relief. Cohn must finally have turned the script down, which meant that I needn't return to Hollywood again; maybe writing was too sexual to be truly done for hire. Mary, meantime, was doubtless reading my uneasiness, and I was as helpless to forgive myself as she was. At last the phone rang. It was Kazan speaking in his softest tone, I thought, almost as though others were in an office with him, which was probably not true at all; I may simply have caught a kind of public apprehension in him.

Cohn wanted some changes; if I agreed, the film would be do-able, he said. The main one was that the bad guys in the story, the union crooks and their gangster protectors, should be Communists. I started to laugh even as my heart froze. Kazan said he was merely transmitting what Cohn had told him, in the belief that I should have it uninflected by his own comments. Roy Brewer, the head of all the Hollywood unions, had been brought into the matter—by the FBI, presumably; he had read the script and said flatly that it was all a lie, that he was a personal friend of Joe Ryan, head of the International Longshoremen's Association, and that none of the practices I described took place on the piers. Finally, he informed Cohn that if the film was made he would pull all the projectionists across the country out on strike so that it could never be shown. The FBI, moreover, regarded it as a very dangerous story that might cause big trouble on the nation's waterfronts at a time when the Korean War was demanding an uninterrupted flow of men and matériel. In effect, unless Tony Anastasia was turned into a Com-munist, the movie would be an anti-American act close to treason.

Nearly speechless, I said that I knew for a fact that there were next to no Communists on the Brooklyn waterfront, so to depict the rank and file in revolt against Communists rather than rack-eteers was simply idiotic, and I would be ashamed to go near the waterfront again. His voice even and hopeless, Kazan repeated that idiotic or not, it was what Cohn-Brewer-FBI insisted on. In an hour or two I wired Harry Cohn that I was withdrawing my script as I was unable to meet his demands. Next morning a boy delivered a telegram to my Brooklyn Heights door: "ITS INTERESTING HOW THE MINUTE WE TRY TO MAKE THE SCRIPT PRO-AMERICAN YOU PULL OUT. HARRY COHN."

Once again I was roaming Brooklyn Heights, crossing the liberat-ing bridge on foot or bike, finding my way down to the Battery to watch people boarding the ferry to the Statue of Liberty. By now years of grimy rain had washed away the "Dove Pete Panto" graffiti, and I knew I would never rescue this man whom I had never seen from his fate as anonymous fish food at the bottom of the bay. That the trade union idea, into which my generation had poured so much idealistic hope, was in this case just another racket was a commonplace, but that it should be so systematically protected from one coast to another, and under the name of patriotism to boot, was something to gag on. It was not even a question of my personal credibility; the corruption on the waterfront had by now been documented in a Republican newspaper, the *New York Sun*, by an investigative reporter named Malcolm Johnson, who had laid out the whole skein of racketeering controls for all to see and had been awarded a Pulitzer Prize on the same day I received mine for *Salesman*. In fact, Joe Ryan himself would shortly be sent to Sing Sing for his crimes as head of the ILA. So there was no longer a duty to cry out the facts. That had been done. But the blind tides of traffic continued to roll mindlessly over the bridge, above the scenes my screenplay had portrayed and the conditions Johnson had meticulously exposed. The country clutched corruption to its breast while it sent its sons to cleanse the earth eight thousand miles away in Korea.

A perpetual night of confusion was descending, I thought. Years later I came to see this as a narrow view when I learned from new and younger friends—William Styron and James Jones in particular—that the early fifties was their budding time and America to them seemed destined to guide, if not to lead, the world. For them, as writers living in Rome or London or Paris, the heirs of a victorious war, it was an America that might on bad days win the booby prize but withal was still liberty's home.

It did not look quite like that from the bridge where I did my walking. I thought of writing an article about my Hollywood misadventure to demonstrate the state of freedom in America, but it seemed an absolutely pointless exercise in self-pity when in the face of Johnson's exposés a Brewer could still call my script an untruth and make tough Harry Cohn fold up and run with him, cloaking his retreat in the American flag. If I did speak out, I thought, I must do so where it would count and not be brushed aside like yesterday's paper. I did not expect anybody to be outraged because a playwright had had his film script suppressed; on the contrary, I might even have to face new attacks for having conceived a story that might obstruct the smooth delivery of arms to Korea. Such were the times. I was all alone, as so many felt who could not quite make it aboard the American Century, that train one sensed was bound for nowhere, its tracks ending in the desert where the vast pauperized majority of mankind lived.

Behind my despairing sense of being treed there were more than general impressions. A year or so earlier I had been invited by Jack Goodman, a senior editor at Simon and Schuster, to join a weekly discussion on what writers might do to combat the rising hysteria in the country, the spreading fear of uttering any opinion that could be remotely interpreted as left or even liberal, let alone pro-Soviet. We were heading straight into the time when an American senator could just about call Defense Secretary George C. Marshall, former general of the army and secretary of state, a Communist in league with Stalin, and without arousing a convulsion of disgust for doing so.

Each Tuesday evening in his comfortably worn ground-floor Greenwich Village living room, Jack managed to collect a couple of dozen stars of the magazine and fiction worlds. Edgar Snow, then an editor of the *Saturday Evening Post,* Jack Belden, novelist and reporter on China, John Hersey, novelist and *New Yorker* reporter, Richard Lauterbach of *Life,* Ira Wolfert, novelist and *Reader's Digest* reporter, and Joe Barnes, foreign editor of the *Herald Tribune,* were some of the regulars, and photographer Robert Capa was among the faces that came and went each week. Soon there were lawyers and businessmen, people disturbed by the know-nothingism of the hour, twenty or thirty of us sitting around drinking and smoking and trying to conceive a countertide in the media to the overwhelming propaganda of the right. Essays were suggested, themes kicked around, and some of us contacted other writers outside New York asking for their ideas. The novelist Louis Bromfield, then scientifically farming in Ohio, wrote back angrily damning us all as conspiring Communists. Such were the times.

After many months, many proposals, many actual attempts to publish one or another reply to the prevailing paranoia, not a single line from any of us had seen print anywhere. The shock, if not dramatic, was noticeable: whatever our reputations, we were little more than easily disposable hired hands. Everywhere teachers were being fired for their associations or ideas, real or alleged, as were scientists, diplomats, postmen, actors, directors, writers—as though the "real" America was rising up against all that was not simple to understand, all that was or seemed foreign, all that implied something slightly less reassuring than that America stood innocent and pure in a vile and sinister world beyond the borders. And from this there was no appeal. One lived in an occupied country where anyone at all might be a spy for the enemy. Indeed, within a year, Goodman would be hauled before HUAC, not accused of Communism but called to explain why these gatherings had been held and how as a non-Red he could have sponsored such an anti-American campaign involving so many first-class authors and editors. In short, within our little hard-drinking band there had been an informer, for the Committee knew the name of every participant.

Ten, twenty, thirty years later it became clear that a good part of what drove this domestic campaign was a conscious decision, first by a sector of the Republican Party, out of power for nearly two decades, to equate the basic New Deal ideas with disloyalty, and then by acquiescent Democrats to see the light. But at the time, to most people, it all had the feel of a natural phenomenon, an unstoppable earthquake rolling through the political landscape. Despite the Democrats' only spotty resistance to him, McCarthy would soon be calling the whole Roosevelt-Truman era "twenty years of treason." And indeed, by the eighties under Reagan, the structural supports of the New Deal had largely been repudiated even if they could not be totally dismantled without the country collapsing.

My wife, Inge, as yet unknown to me, arrived in 1951 as a photo-journalist on brief assignment in Hollywood, to find herself harshly interrogated by an immigration inspector, under suspicion of Communist connections because she had a novel in her suitcase published by the Left Book Club of London. Having spent the war in Nazi Germany, part of the time as a forced laborer under the bombs at Berlin's Tempelhof airport, she could finally take no more and, polite as she was, had to inquire how the inspector imagined a Communist would have survived the war in Nazi Germany, and why she was never asked if she perhaps had some Nazi sympathies. But of course we were too busy admitting Nazi war criminals under patently false identities, men and a few women who in later decades would at last be extradited and tried for war crimes in Europe. Such were the times.

I had grown used to living with a rage that had no form. Apart from I. F. Stone, whose four-page self-published weekly newsletter persistently examined the issues without obeying the rule that every question had to be couched in anti-Communist declarations, there was no other journalist I can now recall who stood up to the high wind without trembling. With the tiniest Communist Party in the world, the United States was behaving as though on the verge of bloody revolution. In my lawyers' office on some business prob-

lem that had no connection with politics, I happened to say that the
Broadway theatre was becoming "corrupt," with its galloping commercialism, and one of the attorneys glanced up from a document
and reprimanded flatly, "That's a Communist position." For an
instant the breath went out of me, not from fear, but in astonishment at how this blanket of suspicion was really smothering any
discussion at all. Was I now to take care never to use that word in
reference to Broadway's commercialization, which I sensed was
going to end where it has, in the present sterility?

But along with rage marched guilt, the guilt of the naysayer
whose very skepticism implies his betrayal of the credulous mass.
The threat of public obloquy caused a defensiveness in me that
I came to hate. As if this were not enough unreality, I had still
another level of existence, as celebrated playwright treated to every
kind of glorification, including Father of the Year—an honor too
ironical when I was so at odds with myself, with Mary, and with the
undeniable inner pressure to break out of what had come to seem
an emptied, self-denying carapace. I wanted to stop turning away
from the power my work had won for me, and to engorge experience forbidden in a life of disciplined ambition, at the same time
dreading the consequences—less to myself, perhaps, than to those
I loved. What Freud had named the return of the repressed I was
unwittingly inviting up from the depths. Cautiously at first, or so
I fatuously thought, I let the mystery and blessing of womankind
break like waves over my head once or twice, enough to shatter
for me the last belief that social arrangements, including marriage,
had something to do with inevitability. Fluidity and chance soon
poured in to swamp all law, that of the psyche as well as the courts.
We were all mythmaking creatures, it seemed, who created not
only art but lives no less fictional, no less willed into existence, if
only we knew it.

I saw the civilities of public life deftly stripped from the body
politic like the wings of insects or birds by maniac children, and
great and noble citizens branded traitors, without a sign of real
disgust from any quarter. The unwritten codes of toleration were
apparently to be observed no longer. I might resolve not to relinquish my public self, the only part of America I could hope to
control, but the chaos within remained; a youth was rising from a
long sleep to claim the feminine blessing that was the spring of his
creativity, the infinite benediction of woman, a felicity in the deepest heart of man, as unmaterial, unrepayable, and needful as the
sky. It was as though great success, like an immense hot fire that
sucks all the oxygen out of the air, had used up all the love that my

life had collected around me, and if I blamed myself or my wife or the confusions of a seductive mother from one moment to the next, it would later, much later, all come toward me from the past as simply the price I was called upon to pay for what I had been given.

If under the pressures to go to the right I moved even further left for a time, it is explicable, if it is at all, as a willful act of self-abandonment and defiance of my new-won standing in the world. Respectable conformity was the killer of the dream; I was sick of being afraid, of life and of myself and of what on many days seemed the inexorable march of the cheerful totalitarian patriots.

I attended a few meetings of Communist writers in living rooms, but I felt as unreal there as I had as a loner. Decent enough middle-class people, they were probably searching out much the same species of self-realization that would later be sought in one or another of the cults or self-improvement klatches. But in this time, self-cleansing came through sacrificing the present to the perfect socialist future in order to banish emptiness, contradictions, ambiguities, and arrive at a solid and straightforward moral position. A certain smugness and mutual congratulation on the left was hard to reconcile with all the uncertainties bedeviling me, distant as I felt from self-knowledge then. In any case, it was one of my paradoxes that I could call for community and human solidarity while finding it all but impossible to sit at any kind of meeting or really to accept the leveling implied. And when I was finally unable to return, I had to wonder what had happened to the possibility of a philosophical, transpolitical ideal of the kind attributed to an Ibsen or a Chekhov. What seemed to have displaced the nobility of the ideal was a tactical or strategic maneuvering, vis-à-vis oneself as well as the nation and the world. Later I came to think of the dilemma in terms of the absence of transcendence, but I was not yet at a point where politics was an evasion in a particular sense; it still seemed like the ultimate reality to which one ought to be attached. If I turned away from it here, it was as much from a sense of bewilderment and dissatisfaction with myself as from disillusionment with others.

By this time, the early fifties, the woods were filling up with ex-radicals disillusioned not only with the Soviets but with liberalism and even the promise of science itself as an enhancement of the spirit. Jews were embracing Catholicism, socialists were joining the Communist witch-hunt with no regard for its civil liberties implications, and lifelong pacifists were banging the Cold War drums. It all seemed another version of escape from the moral tangle we all knew life had become. Some distaste clung to the spectacle of the born-again anti-Soviet ex-radical, in part because the time was so opportune for such conversions. Besides, I was taunted by my own tenuous hold on steadfast faithfulness in general, and my fears aroused the self-accusation of egoism that I had carried with me since early years. In any case, castigating the Soviets, fashionable as it had become, was not the issue, it seemed to me; the question was what one was *for*. How had these conversions transformed these people, lifted them from the dead flat plane on which most lived? If the left was telling its beads, repeating its ritual prayers to the always receding future of a classless and just society, the new orthodoxy of the right was demanding a confirmation of American society that I could hardly give, with such examples before me as the forbidden screenplay in the drawer, revealing not only the mass oppression of thousands of people under the bridge but now the repressive power of a right-wing union reaching across the country into the studios of Columbia Pictures.

I should have exulted in my aloneness and taken heart from Ibsen's signature line in *An Enemy of the People*—"He is strongest who is most alone." But the Jew in me shied from private salvation as something close to sin. One's truth must add its push to the evolution of public justice and mercy, must transform the spirit of the city whose brainless roar went on and on at both ends of the bridge.

In the early fifties the so-called theatre of the absurd was still in the offing, and I would resist most of its efforts as spurious, but each generation of writers has an investment in its accomplishments that it is obliged to defend. Had I really obeyed the logic of my daily observations, however, I would have been an absurdist myself, for most of the time I was shaking my head at what was going on and laughing the dry laugh of incredulous amazement.

I had sold *Salesman* to Stanley Kramer, who made the film for Columbia. My sole participation was to complain that the screenplay had managed to chop off almost every climax of the play as though with a lawnmower, leaving a flatness that was baffling in view of the play's demonstrated capacity for stirring its audiences in the theatre. Stanley Roberts, the author of the screenplay, flew east to sit with me and bring me to reason, and I recall one response of his that may illuminate the problem.

In the first act, after Linda pleads with her sons to have compassion for their father, Biff relents and agrees to stay on in New York and look for a job, saying that he will simply keep out of Willy's way. But Linda rejects this as inadequate; he must give his father psychological support. To Biff this means relinquishing his opposition to Willy's ideas about how he should live his own life, and he explodes, "I hate this city and I'll stay here! Now what do you want?" To which Linda replies, "He's dying, Biff," and proceeds to describe Willy's preparations for suicide.

This small but important step toward the approaching climax was simply skipped over, and I was mystified. "But," Roberts explained, "how can he shout at his mother like that?"

This was only part of the trouble with the film and with Hollywood films in general, but it may have been related to the main and deeper difficulty: Fredric March was directed to play Willy as a psycho, all but completely out of control, with next to no grip on reality. March had been our first choice for the stage role but had turned it down—although he persuaded himself in later years that he had not been offered it formally. He could certainly have been a wonder in the film, but as a psychotic, he was predictable in the extreme; more than that, the misconception melted the tension between a man and his society, drawing the teeth of the play's social contemporaneity, obliterating its very context. If he was nuts, he could hardly stand as a comment on anything. It was as though Lear had never had real political power but had merely imagined he was king.

But such were the times that even this weakened version was thought too radical. I was first asked by Columbia's publicity department to issue an anti-Communist statement to appease the American Legion, which warned that my failure to take an ad in *Variety* castigating the Reds, a ritual of the period, would bring on a picketing campaign against the film nationwide. I declined the request. The next thing I knew, I was invited by Columbia to the screening of a twenty-five-minute short they had just completed, which they proposed to run as a preface to the *Death of a Salesman* film wherever it played.

This small masterpiece had been shot on the campus of the Business School of New York's City College and consisted mainly of interviews with professors who blithely explained that Willy Loman was entirely atypical, a throwback to the past when salesmen did indeed have some hard problems. But nowadays selling was a fine profession with limitless spiritual compensations as well as financial ones. In fact, they all sounded like Willy Loman with a diploma, fat with their success, to which had been added, of course, Columbia Pictures' no doubt generous pourboire for participating in this admirable essay of elucidation. When the lights came on in the screening room on Seventh Avenue, the two or three executives watching the film with me waited for my reaction in what I interpreted as a vaguely defensive if not chagrined silence.

Sitting there with these well-paid men, I was caught in a barrage of contradictory sensations, but over everything hung an inexpressible horror at the charade it all represented. The unseen presence in the room was the patriots' threat to kill the film commercially with a yahoo campaign against me. Fear was the only genuine emotion here, but this of course could not be acknowledged. Instead, I was pressed to admit that the short was "not really bad" and that "it would help sell the picture." But no one, probably right up to Harry Cohn, their employer, really believed I was a menace to the country, and certainly the film wasn't.

"Why the hell did you make the picture if you're so ashamed of it?" I asked. "Why should anybody not get up and walk out of the theatre if *Death of a Salesman* is so outmoded and pointless?"

I wasn't sure, but I thought my tirade was a relief to them, and I muttered something about suing the company for destroying the value of my property with this defamatory short. I began to think as I became aware of a certain defeated lassitude in their arguments that privately they might even be admiring my stand. But that would only make it worse, and not only for them and for me but somehow for the country in which we were carrying on this massive pretense. If I shared some of their terror, I also had what they did not, a pride in my play that was not possible to betray and that finally was my anchor, for at bottom I was being asked to concur that *Death of a Salesman* was morally meaningless, a tale told by an idiot signifying nothing. And to that it was easy to say no. We all parted in polite good spirits, and if the short was ever shown I never heard about it. They had done their duty and could now report back that I was threatening a lawsuit, which was probably enough to get Columbia off the hook with the Legion—doubtless the whole point of the entire exercise, which must have cost the company a couple of hundred thousand dollars.

Thus, while I still held some cards in this game of Let's Kill Miller, I had no illusions about the fact that powerful people had me in their sights and were only awaiting a clear shot. But I have a strong forgetter and managed to turn to my work despite what often felt like a glacial pressure to knuckle under. There were even times when the whole atmosphere turned truly comical. A man whose name I vaguely recalled from the distant past called me one morning, saying he had been an officer in the Lincoln Brigade, had known Ralph Neaphus in Spain, and had something important he wished to discuss with me. I supposed he must be in some political trouble and had the unfortunate idea that I was respectable enough to help him out of it, a big mistake that was still being made in those days. But when he sat on my living room couch with his black briefcase on his lap and announced with an uncertain look of cheerful affability that he wanted to sell me stock in some Texas oil wells, I knew that times were changing. He explained that he had taken up this line of work after being blacklisted from a union job but that gradually he had come to enjoy it and was starting to make some real money at it. Then came the kind of line that history itself sometimes writes to set the theme of a period. "I mean," he said, with genuine earnestness now, "let's not forget that when the workers take over the country they're going to need oil. And even more than now because socialism will expand production!" Calvinism is immortal and is reborn in the strangest places; the important thing always is to be sure one is doing others some good.

These were the days when a frightened and despairing Louis Untermeyer shut the door of his Remsen Street apartment and did not come out again for a year. And I would not realize until thirty years later, when I learned it from Harrison Salisbury of the *New York Times,* how wonderfully mirrorlike the reflection of paranoia was on the other side of the world. The Stalin censorship at this very time had been screwed down so tight that it had become impossible to report more than official handouts, and the Western press departed Moscow in total frustration, leaving the city to a handful of agency reporters. Salisbury, then the *Times* Moscow correspondent, was determined to stay on and penetrate the frozen Soviet terror. To report any real news at all, he had to resort to a kind of impromptu code in his dispatches. In America, damages might be limited by constitutional safeguards, but the main question of political discussion in both countries was reduced to loyalty; in the eighties, Salisbury learned—thanks to the Freedom of Information Act—that he himself had been under heavy FBI suspicion as a Red agent, in part because he had insisted on remaining in Moscow after so many of the other reporters had left. Such were the times.

But how to say all this, how to find the form for outcry? Little in current novels and nothing in the theatre so much as hinted at the burgeoning calamity, and the movies were dancing the country

into happy time. Beneath the bridge, though, there was no attempt
to disguise that a new era had come to pass, or at least that a certain
continuity with the past was being disassembled and smashed.

Barred from the waterfront for lack of a Coast Guard pass under
the new Korean War regulations, Mitch Berenson had to find a job
in private industry. For the first time in his adult life, all of which
he had spent as an organizer, he found himself confronting a
strange dog-eat-dog society for which he was as ill equipped as a
seminarian who had quit the priesthood. He had literally no conventional social history, no conventional employment background,
no social security card, and no training. He had surfaced into a
raging competitive torrent where he quickly had to learn to swim
or sink.

Certain he had wasted his life (he could not know that in a few
years Tony Anastasia, doubtless as a consequence of his and
Longhi's influence, would build the first medical facility on the
waterfront for longshoremen, the Anastasia Clinic), his mood was
oddly ebullient nonetheless. For if he lacked all experience in a
competitive society, he now discovered with growing surprise that
his life as an organizer had certain tangencies to that of an entrepreneur. Both had to decide where to go in the mornings, whom
to call or see, and in general what to do with time. Routine was as
alien to him as to any capitalist, spontaneous risk-taking everything; the awful truth dawned that selling a revolution was not
totally unrelated to selling anything else.

As an organizer Mitch had earned twenty dollars a week, if he
got paid at all, and this meagerness in his pockets had bred a
certain aristocratic superiority toward money, which he had never
imagined accumulating and which therefore had no emotional
value for him; when he was desperate enough he could always hit
one of his friends all over the city, men beside whom he had fought
union organizational battles over the years.

But he had to have a job now, and it occurred to him that the
only boss he had ever known at all well was Krauss, a sweater
manufacturer on the Lower East Side, who, however, hated him
for having led a long strike against his plant nine years before.
Every morning for more than fourteen months he had marched his
chanting workers around and around in front of the miserable
factory, forcing Bernie Krauss to fight his way through to his office.
And every morning Krauss had paused long enough to shake his
fists at Berenson and scream, "You goddamned Bolshevik, may you
rot in hell with cats up your ass!" Berenson would spread out his
arms, giggling, and reply, "Bernie! Settle!"

So he was anxious as he approached the factory, but as he opened the street door the smell of charred wool and burnt wood distracted him. There, amidst puddle and stench, sat Bernie Krauss, a man of fifty now and aging fast, overweight and bald and looking as blank as death. But when he saw Mitch Berenson standing before him, the old resentment began to flow into his eyes.

"Wait, take it easy, Krauss. I just came to ask you for a job."

"A job! *Me* you're asking for a job?" Krauss would have risen in fury, but he had just had a fire and the insurance company was refusing to pay for more than a fraction of his stock, claiming that the rest was not sufficiently damaged, so his spirits were low.

By the end of the afternoon Krauss had hired Berenson as a salesman and in no time at all was offering him a partnership. Berenson first turned the fire hose on the undamaged sweaters, reporting to a grateful fire department that he had quenched a new smoldering blaze, and thereby getting the insurance company to pay up. Next, he sold a bill of goods to Gimbels in Philadelphia, which, as was the frequent practice, they promptly canceled, causing the naively outraged Berenson to return to Philadelphia and make a speech of such powerfully eloquent indignation that the stunned executives rescinded the cancellation—an unheard-of triumph in the sweater business—and offered him a job at Gimbels.

Within five years Berenson was a millionaire several times over, having designed housing for the elderly that was immensely popular. Still chewing the cheapest cigars he could find and driving a wreck of a car, he all but ran the small suburban village he had moved to. "What I found out," he said to me once, "is that the thing really is a democracy. The people really make the basic decisions in the end. It takes too long and they get fooled too often, but it does work finally, and it's beautiful."

Almost inevitably he turned to mysticism once he had proven his power but had lost the heartwarming Marxist prophecy of doom and the redemptive promise that accompanied it; he had won the world and lost a religion, had become a normally happy, uneasy man.

At the end of his final lecture to our sophomore psychology class, the venerable Professor Walter Bowers Pillsbury looked out over the faces of the undergraduates and created an uncustomary pause. As the distinguished author of our textbook he had great authority in his field, but for me his fascination came from his having been institutionalized for some years himself. A tall, white-haired, tragically dignified presence out of an earlier America, he wore dark ties and stiff collars, and his gaze went deep. In the silence we all realized he was saying his farewell not only to us but to his career, for he was nearing retirement age. He said, "I do not presume to give you advice about your mental health, but there is one truth I hope you will always try to keep before you: never think about any one thing for too long."

In 1935, when I was trying to concentrate my mind on my new craft and the country seemed scatterbrained in the face of its awful problems, this seemed silly advice. But now, in the early fifties, some fifteen years later, the old man's voice kept returning to me as I realized that there was something obsessional in my thoughts about my marriage and my work; great swellings of love and hope for my future with Mary were followed by a cycle of despairing resentment that I was being endlessly judged, hopelessly condemned. In an attempt to break out, I had begun analysis with Rudolph Loewenstein, a Freudian of great skill, but it was ultimately impossible for me to risk my creativity, which he was wise enough not to pretend to understand, by vacating my own autonomy, however destructive it might continue to be. And so I have never pretended to a valid estimate of analysis even though it gave me a good man's friendship, above all, and a way of assessing human behavior perhaps more dispassionately than before. But I could not escape the fear of being bled white by a gratifying yet sterile objectivity that might be good for critics but not so good for writers whose fuel is the chaos of their instinctual life.

I have always resisted a final judgment on psychoanalytic claims for two reasons in particular. I had entered analysis in order to save a marriage, a distorting premise that raised the suspicion of self-examination for the sake of marital concord. But I was also being nagged by a suspicion born of that particular historic moment. While the country seemed to be happily exulting in Joe McCarthy's homegrown American paranoia toward all that was unfamiliar, including the mind itself, I was rooting about in my cobwebs, clearly a self-indulgence, even if only, as I hoped, a temporary one. Nor could I dispel my commonality with the flocks of liberal and left people excitedly discovering analysis just as a sharp and threatening turn in history was flinging us into space. My difficulties were surely personal, but I could not help suspecting that psychoanalysis was a form of alienation that was being used as a substitute not only for Marxism but for social activism of any kind. My conscience, in short, was at odds with my improvement.

New York, that riverbed through which so many subterranean cultures are always flowing, was swollen with rivulets of dispossessed liberals and leftists in chaotic flight from the bombarded old castle of self-denial, with its infinite confidence in social progress and its authentication-through-political-correctness of their positions at the leading edge of history. As always, the American self, a puritanical item, needed a scheme of morals to administer, and once Marx's was declared beyond the pale, Freud's offered a similar smugness of the saved. Only this time the challenge handed the lost ones like me was not to join a picket line or a Spanish brigade but to confess to having been a selfish bastard who had never known how to love. Whether psychoanalysis could have meant some glorious liberating conjunction of sensuality and responsibility I would never find out, if only because I was being forced back into defending the narrowing space where I could simply exist as a writer; I had to save myself in society before I could reorder my brains, for society was not being passive with me.

Again, it was not just the things I read in the papers that informed my feelings of anxiety and threat. *Cock-a-doodle Dandy*, a new play by Sean O'Casey, was announced for New York production, and the American Legion promptly threatened to picket the theatre. This alone would have been enough to make any producer think twice about the play's commercial possibilities, but in addition the chief backer, Mrs. Peggy Cullman, had not long before converted to Catholicism, and after reading the script, she decided it was anti-Catholic and withdrew her money. No doubt it was anticlerical, although not anti-Catholic, but the Legion was probably more interested in O'Casey's custom of wearing a hammer-and-sickle button in the lapel of his rumpled jacket, proclaiming that Communism had captured his Irish heart. He sounded like no other Communist I had ever heard of, and I rather suspected he was putting on the conservatives, especially the British, who of course remained irritatingly oblivious, while the Irish in Ireland, whence he had exiled himself, affected to forget his existence as they had that of Joyce before him, preoccupied as they were with emigrating from the country. In any case, given the gorgeousness of some of his plays and his wonderful autobiography, I was outraged that this genius should be hounded by Legion thuggery. When the producer of the play appealed for help from the Dramatists Guild—the Legion's threats having dried up his money sources, menacing the production altogether—I cooked up a motion and presented it to my fellow

Guild officers one afternoon. In attendance were Moss Hart, our natty chairman, whose beautiful pipes I envied, although they were too dainty and small for my taste; Oscar Hammerstein II, whose avuncular presence belied his sharp libertarian views; and Robert Sherwood, playwright, Roosevelt speechwriter, and activist for civil liberties, some of whose early work outspokenly raised the question of the individual being flattened by the steamroller of modern civilization. Also present, among a few others who escape memory, was Arthur Schwartz, producer and composer of numerous hit musicals like *The Little Show, The Band Wagon, Flying Colors,* and *A Tree Grows in Brooklyn,* and a man of quick humor and a caring charm.

I proposed we announce immediately that in the event the Legion picketed O'Casey's play, we would call upon playwrights to form a counter–picket line in support of freedom of the theatre. An embarrassed shock went around the table, but Hammerstein looked seriously interested, and if no one was ready just yet to rush out and carry a sign up and down Shubert Alley, it did seem to me that our discussion was moving toward some statement in O'Casey's defense. At this juncture Arthur Schwartz, visibly upset to the point of unwanted vehemence, warned that if one penny of Guild money was spent to defend a Communist, he would lead whatever members would follow him out of the Guild to form a new playwrights' organization. The sudden prospect of such a split brought all discussion to a dead halt, and the subject died then and there. I now had no reason to doubt that should the Legion decide to picket my next play to death, I could look for no meaningful defense from my fellow playwrights, for these were the most powerful names in the theatre and they were either scared or bewildered about how to act. Such were the times. Indeed, it was not at all difficult to imagine an ideological committee of Legionnaires especially empowered to move their lips through all new plays and decide which should or should not be permitted on the New York stage. I had already had a taste of the Legion's power, for they had not only threatened the movie version of *Salesman* but had managed in two or three towns to close down the road company production with Thomas Mitchell as Willy, Darren McGavin as Happy, Kevin McCarthy as Biff, and June Walker as Linda—what the Boston critics had called the best Irish play ever. In one Illinois town the picketing was thorough enough to have left but a lone customer in the theatre. Mitchell insisted on playing the show just for him, but I never found out what he thought of it.

I was possibly more scared than others because I was scared of being scared. But it was also that given my nature and time, I aspired to a rather exalted image of the dramatist as a species of truth-revealing leader whose brandished light would blind the monster Chaos in his approach. Dramaturgy was the physics of the arts, the one that failed when it lied and succeeded when it cut to the first principles of human life. With so joyously painful a burden, it was not easy to think of slipping away and taking to the hills.

When Bobby Lewis came to me with the idea of a new adaptation of Ibsen's *An Enemy of the People,* with Fredric March and his wife, Florence Eldridge, as the Stockmanns, it bucked me up that these veteran theatre people, whom I had never connected with radical politics, had awakened to the danger. I soon learned that the Marches were suing a man for libeling them as Communists; the charge had cost them film roles, and they saw themselves in the shoes of the Stockmanns, who were also crucified by a mob in the throes. Bobby Lewis, a veteran of the Group Theatre, whose tenderly imaginative staging of Saroyan's *My Heart's in the Highlands* I had vastly admired years before, had a witty detachment that had kept him out of partisan politics, and I tended to trust him as a showman despite my feeling that the project would do little more than move the lot of us closer to the bull's-eye of the Red-hunters' target.

The play, now that I read it again, seemed musty despite its thematic relevance to the current situation. But the producer, a wealthy young businessman named Lars Nordenson, the son of a Swedish senator, saw a swelling prefascist tide running in the United States and pressed me to work on the script. He would provide his own word-by-word rendering of Ibsen's original Norwegian, which he claimed was not at all wooden, like the translations, but slangy and tough, with scatological outbursts. After all, it had been written in fury and, for Ibsen, in an unusually short time. With Nordenson's first tentative pages of translation, in pidgin English with no attempt even to form sentences, I began the work and was soon convinced that I might capture Ibsen's spirit in the kind of fight I was sure he would have enjoyed.

As always, I would find out what I really believed through my attempts to dramatize my sense of life. The more familiar I became with the play, the less comfortable I felt with one or two of its implications. Though Dr. Stockmann fights admirably for absolute license to tell society the truth, he goes on to imply the existence of an unspecified elite that can prescribe what people are to believe. For a democrat this was rather a large pill, until I recalled myself telling the meeting of Marxists years earlier that an artist had the duty to claim new territory, and that if I had obeyed either the Party line or the shibboleths of the national press during the war, I could not have written *All My Sons*—which, now that the war was over, was being praised for its courage, its insights, and its truth. Ibsen-Stockmann was simply making the artist's immemorial claim as point man into the unknown.

Still, it is indefensible in a democratic society, albeit the normal practice, to ascribe superior prescience to a self-elected group, and the tangle only gets worse when Ibsen draws a parallel with biological selection, even introducing an element of breeding into the matter. Indeed, the great man himself had found it necessary to back away from the play's implied social Darwinism by going before a trade union meeting in Norway and assuring the resentful members that he was only calling for recognition of a spiritual avant-garde with no power over other people but merely the right to advance new ideas and discoveries without a majority vote. In the play, however, this demurrer remained somewhat less forthright, it seemed to me.

And so I cut across the problem to its application to our moment in America—the need, if not the holy right, to resist the pressure to conform. It was a full-blown production with solid sets and a Freddie March in the flood of his considerable art, and bristling with his private anger besides. Eldridge did her damndest to rub some color into the rather gray role of Stockmann's worried, faithful wife. If Lewis erred, it was in encouraging a certain self-indulgent picturesqueness and a choreographed quality, especially in the stirring crowd scenes where March stood over the townspeople with arms spread out like Christ on the cross, something dangerously off-putting in what was a teaching play to start with. But these were quibbles of my own. The production was strong and forthright, and in dozens of other productions in coming years the same script would electrify audiences, though on Broadway it never caught fire.

The play had always been a message work, Ibsen's furious reply to the vilification in press and society of his play *Ghosts*, a scandal in its time. George S. Kaufman had warned long ago that a playwright with a message had better send it by Western Union, given Broadway's historic allergy to uplift masked as entertainment, but my own feeling was that the play could have established itself with its natural public, the sizable number of people who resisted the threatening atmosphere of the time. Instead, the press reacted defensively, as if its virginity had been fingered. Some of the critics, clever as could be, claimed to have detected my anti-U.S. propaganda hand in the line spoken by the Stockmanns' one consistent supporter, the Captain, a rugged fellow who at the end of the play commiserates with them in their mob-wrecked living room, where they sit dejectedly wondering what to do next: "Well, maybe you ought to go to America," life being freer across the water. According to these critics, such Miller-injected irony was a typically heavy-handed misuse of the sainted Ibsen's play for the purpose of sneering at American pretensions to civic freedom. I was tempted to point out that I had simply taken the line from Ibsen's original Norwegian text, but I refrained, hopelessly aware that nothing would burn off the fog of suspicion that I had used Ibsen as a front for the Reds. That the critics sprang to the defense of Ibsen's purity without bothering to read him was one more testimony to the power of the obsessive fear that we had hoped our production of the play might penetrate.

The failure in 1950 of *An Enemy of the People* opened wide the door to my time of confusion, and as always, it was through my work that I tried to find clarity. I began sketching what I called *An Italian Tragedy*, which after several months I laid aside. Initially, I had the bones of the story from Vinny Longhi, but in its first murky draft in 1950 it was more a probe into the mysterious world of incestuous feelings and their denial, leading to a murder-suicide. I could not really understand why I was writing it, but growing more and more anxious for light, I threw open any and every window; it was a painful time of rebirth, perhaps even a second adolescence when I seemed to be turning into a stranger to myself and everyone else in a world I had unaccountably made. But the trail of the play vanished before I could complete it, and I felt defeated again. It was some five years before it resurfaced as *A View from the Bridge* in its original one-act form. And it was more than a decade before I finally glimpsed something of myself in this play, when I saw Robert Duvall, a young actor I had never heard of until then, in Ulu Grosbard's powerful off-Broadway revival. As I watched Duvall, the most unimaginable of incarnations came through to me from his Eddie Carbone—I suddenly saw my father's adoration of my sister, and through his emotion, my own. When I wrote the play, I was moving through psychological country strange to me, ugly and forbidding. Yet something in me kept to the challenge to push on until a part of the truth of my nature unfolded itself in a scene, a word, a thought dropping onto my paper.

Another of these unfinished probes of 1950 was the story of a group of research physicians employed by a wealthy pharmaceuticals maker who inspires them to important discoveries while suborning them to his business interests, subtly taking over their very wills as he strokes their ambitions. Alternately mocking his crude commercialism and sucking up to him, they typify what I then saw as the captive artist-creator.

Into their midst comes the mistress of Dr. Tibbets, Lorraine, a character modeled rather distantly on Marilyn, whom I still barely knew. With her open sexuality, childlike and sublimely free of ties and expectations in a life she half senses is doomed, she moves instinctively to break the hold of respectability on the men until each in his different way meets the tragedy in which she has unwittingly entangled him—one retreats to a loveless and destructive marriage in fear of losing his social standing; another abandons his family for her, only to be abandoned in turn when her interests change. Like a blind, godlike force, with all its creative cruelty, her sexuality comes to seem the only truthful connection with some ultimate nature, everything that is life-giving and authentic. She flashes a ghastly illumination upon the social routinization to which they are all tied and which is killing their souls—but she has no security of her own and no faith, and her liberating promise is finally illusory.

Behind the whole story stands an idealistic image of the humane role they had originally believed their science to play, a redemptive power they no longer have the strength and faith to grasp. They have matured into the ego-time when there is no ideal that cannot be seen through, no belief that can fill its adherents with creative hope in a culture that has prized man's sexuality from his social ideals and made one the contradiction of the other.

The play remained unfinished because I could not accept the nihilistic spiritual catastrophe it persisted in foretelling. That is, I believed it as a writer but could not confess to it as a man. I could not know, of course, that in the coming years I would live out much of its prophecy myself. Putting it aside, I adapted Ibsen's play, which of course is a clear statement of resistance to conformity but also an affirmation of hope and human integrity, and a play, incidentally, with no sensual eruptions. It was in some part a reflection of my own split, which I could not stop from widening, between the willed determination to keep my family together and fulfill my role as father and the corrosive suspicion that family, society, all "roles," were just that—conventions that would pour me in concrete, forbidding my nature and vision their evolutionary changes. What I had repressed was indeed returning, and the self-accusations of insincerity that hounded me were deserved. For I knew in my depths that I wanted to disarm myself before the sources of my art, which were not in wife alone nor in family alone but, again, in the sensuousness of a female blessing, something, it seemed, not quite of this world. In some diminished sense it was sexual hunger, but one that had much to do with truthfulness to myself and my nature and even, by extension, to the people who came to my plays. I deeply wanted to be one, not divided, to speak with the same voice in private and publicly. I did not see why marriage and family necessarily imposed strategies of subtle self-censorship, not so subtle subterfuge, and implicit betrayal. But I lacked the courage to declare in so many words that I was no longer speciously whole, as I had been, and that the future for me was no longer known. I retreated into silence, uncertain of what I might say and what was prohibited, for I had already passed beyond the conventions, beyond a commonsensical awareness of what one's partner could or should be called upon to bear. My life was havoc, seizures of expansive love and despairing hate, of sudden hope and quick reversals of defeat.

By now, even after only those few hours with Marilyn, she had taken on an immanence in my imagination, the vitality of a force one does not understand but that seems on the verge of lighting up a vast surrounding plain of darkness. I was struggling to keep my marriage and family together and at the same time to understand why I felt as though I had lost a sort of sanction that I had seemed to possess since earliest childhood. Whom or what was I writing for? I needed the benediction of something or someone, but all about me was mere mortality. I came to see that I had always assumed I was writing in the service of some worthy cause in which I no longer believed. I had learned how to be alone for very long periods, but someone, I had always supposed, was secretly watching over me unseen. It was of course the mother, the first audience—actually the concept of her in a most primordial sense that perhaps only the boy-child, half lover and half rebel against her dominion, really knows in his mythifying blood. My own mother was mortally flawed by her very normal expectations for a successful son, far too grossly material to leave intact the gossamer of her ancient authority; her love was too real, too mixed with the needs of her own impure, transactional self. I could not live, not happily, without the myths of childhood, which at bottom feed our everlasting becoming and our faith in self and world. The muse has always been a sanctifying woman, God help her. And she was gone.

Finally sick of pretending to be a landlord, especially Henry Davenport's landlord, I managed to sell our Grace Court house and buy a mid-nineteenth-century single-family house on nearby Willow Street, one block from the river. (I learned later that the anonymous purchaser of our house, acting through an agent for fear that no one would sell to him directly, was W. E. B. Du Bois, the great black historian.) Trying to send up all the signals of a confident marriage, I spent a week installing a new subfloor in the entrar·ce hall, laid a cork floor on that, built all sorts of conveniences in the kitchen, did fifty things a man does who believes in a future with his family, but the ease of mutual trust had flown from us like a bird, and the new cage was as empty as the old where no bird sang.

Occasionally I got a note from Marilyn that warmed my heart. In strangely meandering slanted handwriting that often curled down margins and up again on the other side of the paper, using two or three different pens with a pencil thrown in, she talked about hoping we could meet again when she came east on business, and offered to come without any excuse if I gave her some encouragement. I wrote back a muddy, formal note saying that I wasn't the man who could make her life happen as I knew she imagined it might, and that I wished her well. Still, there were parched evenings when I was on the verge of turning my steering wheel west and jamming the pedal to the floor. But I wasn't the man who was able to do that either.

At the same time that I was wrestling with this inner turmoil, rumors of weird games going on under HUAC pressure were rocking the theatrical community. There was still nothing like a blacklist in the theatre, no doubt because there was no single group of powerful producers to be bulldozed, as the controlling companies in Hollywood had been, into policing their artists. In the theatre, financing came from dozens of small investors, and most producers were simply temporary occupants of tents that were struck and vanished with the end of each show. Furthermore, few theatre actors were known across America where the votes were, and the Committee was manifestly uninterested in "investigating" if the results would land on the back page with the crossword puzzle. But there were a few HUAC forays into New York, and one heard now of prospective witnesses making deals to name each other before the Committee, thus to ease their consciences about informing. Inevitably, some individuals refused to play and were named without their agreement, but their resistance only justified their newly reborn former comrades in nailing them as hardcore Communists.

For me the spectacle was depressing, and not only for the obvious reasons. Certainly I felt distaste for those who groveled before this tawdry tribune of moralistic vote-snatchers, but I had as much pity as anger toward them. It bothered me much more that with each passing week it became harder to simply and clearly say why the whole procedure was vile. Almost to a man, for example, the accused in 1950 and 1951 had not had a political connection since the late thirties or early forties, when in their perfectly legitimate idealism they had embraced the Russian Revolution as an advance for humanity. Yet the Committee had succeeded in creating the impression that they were pursuing an ongoing conspiracy. For another thing, they were accused of having violated no law of any kind, since the Communist Party was legal, as were its fronts, which most often espoused liberal positions that did not so much as hint at socialist aims.

Swirling about the hearings was a moral confusion that no one seemed able to penetrate and clarify, even by bending history now and then; for example, there were militant actors who defied the Committee by taking the Fifth Amendment, imagining themselves heirs of Georgi Dimitrov, the hero who in a Nazi courtroom, in the face of torture and the threat of summary execution, threw the charge of setting fire to the Reichstag back at the Nazis and accused them of having torched it themselves, as they doubtless had. (Amazingly, he survived and became, after the war, the premier of Communist Bulgaria.) This act of defiance was a thrilling legend in the thirties and had stamped itself upon the radical movement as the ideal way to confront the fascists. The problem was that in New York the Committee members had all been elected democratically and were not plotting to take over the republic by violent terror. At least some of them, moreover, were genuinely alarmed by the recent Red victory in China, the Russian demonstration of the atomic bomb, and the expansion of Soviet territory into Eastern Europe. The mixture, in other words, of authentic naiveté, soundly observed dangers, and unprincipled rabble-rousing was impossible to disentangle, especially when the public exposure of a bunch of actors who had not been politically connected for years would never push one Red Chinaman out of the Forbidden City or a single Russian out of Warsaw or Budapest.

Perhaps more disturbing to me than all the rest was the atmosphere being created, a pall of suspicion reaching out not only to radio and television and movie studios but into Holy Trinity Church in Brooklyn Heights, whose minister, Reverend William Howard Melish, was hounded out of his pulpit, and his family out of their home, by an anti-Communist campaign among a divided vestry. While his aged father, John Howard Melish—in former years the handsome, popular minister of this immense and beautiful Episcopal church, the clergyman who for decades had sworn New York's mayors into office—lay bedridden on the top floor, the son and his family were put out in the street. As head of a section of Russian War Relief, he had become a rather naive believer in the goodness of Soviet aims, if not of the system. That he had never ceased being a devout Christian no one seemed to question, and over the many long months of his self-defense, ending in a civil court case upholding his bishop's right to fire him, I could only conclude that the country was intending to become a philosophical monolith where no real differences about anything important would be tolerated. In terms of my work, however, I had already adapted *An Enemy of the People*—which the Melish case almost amazingly duplicated, down to a certain muddleheaded stubbornness in the main characters—and that play had not worked.

I would not have put it in such terms in those days, but what I sought was a metaphor, an image that would spring out of the heart, all-inclusive, full of light, a sonorous instrument whose reverberations would penetrate to the center of this miasma. For if the current degeneration of discourse continued, as I had every reason to believe it would, we could no longer be a democracy, a system that requires a certain basic trust in order to exist.

I had known about the Salem witchcraft phenomenon since my American history class at Michigan, but it had remained in mind as one of those inexplicable mystifications of the long-dead past when people commonly believed that the spirit could leave the body, palpably and visibly. My mother might believe it still, if only in one corner of her mind, and I suspected that there were a lot of other people who, like me, were secretly open to suggestion. As though it had been ordained, a copy of Marion Starkey's book *The Devil in Massachusetts* fell into my hands, and the bizarre story came back as I had recalled it, but this time in remarkably well-organized detail.

At first I rejected the idea of a play on the subject. My own rationality was too strong, I thought, to really allow me to capture this wildly irrational outbreak. A drama cannot merely describe an emotion, it has to become that emotion. But gradually, over weeks, a living connection between myself and Salem, and between Salem and Washington, was made in my mind—for whatever else they might be, I saw that the hearings in Washington were profoundly and even avowedly ritualistic. After all, in almost every case the Committee knew in advance what they wanted the witness to give them: the names of his comrades in the Party. The FBI had long since infiltrated the Party, and informers had long ago identified the participants in various meetings. The main point of the hearings, precisely as in seventeenth-century Salem, was that the accused make public confession, damn his confederates as well as his Devil master, and guarantee his sterling new allegiance by breaking disgusting old vows—whereupon he was let loose to rejoin the society of extremely decent people. In other words, the same spiritual nugget lay folded within both procedures—an act of contrition done not in solemn privacy but out in the public air. The Salem prosecution was actually on more solid legal ground since the defendant, if guilty of familiarity with the Unclean One, had broken a law against the practice of witchcraft, a civil as well as a religious offense; whereas the offender against HUAC could not be accused of any such violation but only of a spiritual crime, subservience to a political enemy's desires and ideology. He was summoned before the Committee to be called a bad name, but one that could destroy his career.

In effect, it came down to a governmental decree of *moral* guilt that could easily be made to disappear by ritual speech: intoning names of fellow sinners and recanting former beliefs. This last was probably the saddest and truest part of the charade, for by the early 1950s there were few, and even fewer in the arts, who had not left behind their illusions about the Soviets.

It was this immaterial element, the surreal spiritual transaction, that now fascinated me, for the rituals of guilt and confession followed all the forms of a religious inquisition, except, of course, that the offended parties were not God and his ministers but a congressional committee. (Some of its individual members were indeed distinctly unspiritual, like J. Parnell Thomas, whose anti-Communist indignation was matched only by a larcenous cupidity for which he would soon do time in a federal prison, not far from the cell of Ring Lardner, Jr., who had been jailed for contempt of

Congress—namely, for refusing to answer Thomas's questions.) We were moving into the realm of anthropology and dream, where political terms could not penetrate. Politics is too conscious a business to illuminate the dark cellar of the public mind, where secret fears, unspeakable and vile, rule over cobwebbed territories of betrayal and violent anger. McCarthy's rise was only beginning, and no one guessed that it would grow beyond the power of the president himself, until the army, whose revered chiefs he tried to destroy, finally brought him down.

My decision to attempt a play on the Salem witchcraft trials was tentative, restrained by technical questions first of all, and then by a suspicion that I would not only be writing myself into the wilderness politically but personally as well. For even in the first weeks of thinking about the Salem story, the central image, the one that persistently recurred as an exuberant source of energy, was that of a guilt-ridden man, John Proctor, who, having slept with his teenage servant girl, watches with horror as she becomes the leader of the witch-hunting pack and points her accusing finger at the wife he has himself betrayed. The story's lines of force were still tangled, but instinct warned that as always with me, they would not leave me untouched once fully revealed. And so, in deciding to make an exploratory trip up to Salem, Massachusetts, where the original court records of the witch trials were still available, I was moving inward as well as north, and not without a certain anxiety in both directions. The day before I was to leave, Kazan phoned and asked to see me.

Since he was not a man to idly chat, at least not with me, and since this was his second or third such call in the past few weeks, I began to suspect that something terrible had come to him and that it must be the Committee. I drove into a dun and rainy Connecticut morning in early April 1952 cursing the time. For I all but knew that my friend would tell me he had decided to cooperate with the Committee. Though he had passed through the Party for a brief period fifteen years before, as he had once mentioned to me, I knew that he had no particular political life anymore, at least not in the five years of our acquaintance. I found my anger rising, not against him, whom I loved like a brother, but against the Committee, which by now I regarded as a band of political operators with as much moral conviction as Tony Anastasia, and as a matter of fact, probably somewhat less.

The sun briefly appeared, and we left his house to walk in the woods under dripping branches, amid the odor of decay and regeneration that a long rain drives up from the earth in a cold country forest. He was trying, I thought, to appear relieved in his mind, to present the issue as settled, even happily so. The story, simple and by now routine, took but a moment to tell. He had been subpoenaed and had refused to cooperate but had changed his mind and returned to testify fully in executive session, confirming some dozen names of people he had known in his months in the Party so long ago. He felt better now, clearer about everything. Actually, he wanted my advice, almost as though he had not yet done what he had done. Confirmation was what he needed; after all, he had no sympathies with the Communists, so why should he appear to by withholding his testimony?

But as much as the issue itself mattered, it was our unreality that I could not grasp. I was never sure what I meant to him, but he had entered into my dreams like a brother, and there we had exchanged a smile of understanding that blocked others out. Listening to him now, I grew frightened. There was a certain gloomy logic in what he was saying: unless he came clean he could never hope, at the height of his creative powers, to make another film in America, and he would probably not be given a passport to work abroad either. If the theatre remained open to him, it was not his primary interest anymore; he wanted to deepen his film life, that was where his heart lay, and he had been told in so many words by his old boss and friend Spyros Skouras, president of Twentieth Century Fox, that the company would not employ him unless he satisfied the Committee. It would be easy, I thought as he spoke, for those with less talent to sneer at this, but I believed he was a genius of the theatre, where actors and scripts were concerned a seer who worked along an entirely different trajectory than other directors. To be barred from his métier, kicked into the street, would be for him like a nightmarish overturning of the earth itself. He had always said he came from survivors and that the job was to survive. He spoke as factually as he could, and it was a quiet calamity opening before me in the woods, because I felt my sympathy going toward him and at the same time I was afraid of him. Had I been of his generation, he would have had to sacrifice me as well. And finally that was all I could think of. I could not get past it.

That all relationships had become relationships of advantage or disadvantage. That this was what it all came to anyway and there was nothing new here. That one stayed as long as it was useful to stay, believed as long as it was not too inconvenient, and that we were fish in a tank cruising with upslanted gaze for the descending crumbs that kept us alive. I could only say that I thought this would pass and that it had to pass because it would devour the glue that kept the country together if left to its own unobstructed course. I said that it was not the Reds who were dispensing our fears now, but the other side, and it could not go on indefinitely, it would someday wear down the national nerve. And then there might be regrets about this time. But I was growing cooler with the thought that as unbelievable as it seemed, I could still be up for sacrifice if Kazan knew I had attended meetings of Party writers years ago and had made a speech at one of them. I felt a silence rising around me, an impeding and invisible wash of dulled vibrations between us, like an endless moaning musical note through which we could not hear or speak anymore. It was sadness, purely mournful, deadening. And it had been done to us. It was not his duty to be stronger than he was, the government had no right to require anyone to be stronger than it had been given him to be, the government was not in that line of work in America. I was experiencing a bitterness with the country that I had never even imagined before, a hatred of its stupidity and its throwing away of its freedom. Who or what was now safer because this man in his human weakness had been forced to humiliate himself? What truth had been enhanced by all this anguish?

As I got into my car to leave, Molly Kazan came out of the house into the drizzle that had begun again; she could tell, I suppose, that it had not gone well. It was impossible to keep looking into her distraught eyes. History prints certain lines directly on the mind that stay there into the grave. She was a rather moralistic woman who had, as I've said, an analytical talent for spotting where a play's theme had managed to slip out of sight or the author's exuberance had led him away from the central conflict. She had repeatedly pressed me, long before the *Salesman* rehearsals began, to eliminate Uncle Ben and all the scenes in the past as unnecessary in the strictest sense. It was, I thought, an amazing example of the "nothing-but" psychoanalytical reductionist method of peeling away experience only as far as its quickly recognizable conventional paradoxes, in the misconceived belief that color, tone, and even longing in themselves do not change fate.

I was half inside the car when Molly came out and asked, unforgettably, if I realized that the United Electrical Workers union was entirely in the hands of Communists. Standing in the drizzle there, a woman fighting for her husband's career, she seemed to have been lashed to this frantic question, which in a calmer time would have made her laugh at its absurd remoteness from the dilemma before us. I muttered that I had heard about the UEW many years ago. Then she pointed out toward the road and told me that I no longer understood the country, that everybody who lived on that road approved of the Committee and what had been done. I didn't know what to say anymore across the crevasse widening between us. In the awkward predeparture moment, after I had said that I could not agree with their decision, she asked if I was staying at my house, half an hour away, and I said that I was on my way to Salem. She instantly understood what my destination meant, and her eyes widened in sudden apprehension and possibly anger. "You're not going to equate witches with this!" I told her I wasn't at all sure I could write the play but I was going to look into the stuff they had up there. We all waved rather grimly as I pulled away.

Once on the road nosing the car north, I thought she was probably right about the people in the comfortable homes I was passing, and felt myself drifting beyond the pale. The strangeness was sharper because as usual I was carrying several contradictions at the same time, my brother-love as painfully alive in me as it had ever been, alongside the undeniable fact that Kazan might have sacrificed me had it been necessary. In a sense I went naked to Salem, still unable to accept the most common experience of humanity, the shifts of interests that turned loving husbands and wives into stony enemies, loving parents into indifferent supervisors or even exploiters of their children, and so forth. As I already knew from my reading, that was the real story of ancient Salem Village, what they called then the breaking of charity with one another. The gray rain on my windshield was falling into my soul.

Salem then was a town dribbling away, half-forsaken. It was originally the salt lick of the mother colony of Plymouth to the south and had been bypassed by the modernization of industry a generation before. Lapped by the steely bay, it was dripping this afternoon in the cold black drizzle like some abandoned dog. I liked it, liked its morose and secret air. I went to the courthouse, asked the clerk for the town records for 1692, and had to wait a few minutes while he got out similar tomes for last year and three or four years earlier, handing them to a pair of real estate agents searching deeds for a property deal. The room was silent, and I found good gray light near a tall window that looked out over the water, or so I remember it now, the same hard silver water that the condemned must have beheld from the gallows on Witch Hill, of whose location no one is any longer sure.

In fact, there was little new I could learn from the court record, but I wanted to study the actual words of the interrogations, a gnarled way of speaking, to my ear—and some ten years later the subject of a correspondence with Laurence Olivier, who was seeking an accent for the actors in his magnificent London production of *The Crucible*. After much research he decided on a Northumberland dialect, which indeed is spoken through clenched jaws. And I heard it so in the courthouse, where it seemed from the orthography to be a burred and rather Scottish speech. After a few hours of mouthing the words—often spelled phonetically in the improvised shorthand of the court clerks or the ministers who kept the record as the trials proceeded—I felt a bit encouraged that I might be able to handle it, and in more time I came to love its feel, like hard burnished wood. Without planning to, I even elaborated a few of the grammatical forms myself, the double negatives especially, which occurred in the trial record much less frequently than they would in the play.

"When I passed his house my wagon was set [stuck] in the plain road," a complainant testified, "and there he stood behind his window a-staring out at me, and when he turned away again the wheel was free." A wagon bewitched by a stare. And so many other descriptions were painterly, action stopped as though by a camera—a man unable to rise from his bed, caught with uplifted head by a woman who floated in through his window to lay her body on his, just like that. Reading the testimony here beside the bay was an experience different from reading about the trials in New York. Here, it could have happened. The courthouse closed at five, and there was nothing to do in the town but walk the streets. In the early darkness I came on a candy store where a crowd of teenagers was hanging out, and excited laughter went up as two girls appeared around the corner snuggled one behind the other, hopping in time with a broomstick between their legs. How, I wondered, had they known I was here? Salem in those days was in fact not eager to talk about the witchcraft, not too proud of it, and only after *The Crucible* did the town begin exploiting it with a tourist attraction, the Witch Trail, a set of street signs indicating where so-and-so had been arrested or interrogated or condemned to hang. At the time of my evening walk, no Massachusetts legislature had passed so much as a memoir of regret at the execution of innocent people, rejecting the very suggestion as a slur on the honor of the state even two and a half centuries later. The same misplaced pride that had for so long prevented the original Salem court from admitting the truth before its eyes was still alive here. And that was good for the play too, it was in the mood.

Like every criminal trial record, this one was filled with enticing but incomplete suggestions of relationships, so to speak, offstage. Next day in the dead silence of the little Historical Society building, two ancient lady guardians regarded me with steady gazes of submerged surprise; normally there were very few visitors. Here I found Charles W. Upham's quiet nineteenth-century masterpiece *Salem Witchcraft*, and in it, on my second afternoon, the hard evidence of what had become my play's center: the breakdown of the Proctor marriage and Abigail Williams's determination to get Elizabeth murdered so that she could have John, whom I deduced she had slept with while she was their house servant, before Elizabeth fired her.

". . . During the examination of Elizabeth Procter, Abigail Williams and Ann Putnam both made offer to strike at said Procter; but, when Abigail's hand came near, it opened,—whereas it was made up into a fist before,—and came down exceeding lightly as it drew near to said Procter, and at length, with open and extended fingers, touched Procter's hood very lightly. Immediately, Abigail cried out her fingers, her fingers, her fingers burned. . . ."

The irony of this beautifully exact description is that its author was Reverend Parris, who was trying to show how real the girls' affliction was, and hence how dangerous people like Elizabeth Proctor could be. And irony, of course, is what is usually dispensed with, usually paralyzed, when fear enters the mind. Irony, indeed, is the supreme gift of peace. For it seemed obvious that Parris was describing a girl who had turned to look into her former mistress's face and experienced the joyous terror of the killer about to strike, and not only at the individual victim, the wife of a lover who was now trying to deny her, but at the whole society that was watching and applauding her valiant courage in ridding it of its pestilential sins. It was this ricocheting of the "cleansing" idea that drew me on day after day, this projection of one's own vileness onto others in order to wipe it out with their blood. As more than one private letter put it at the time, "Now no one is safe."

To make not a story but a drama of this parade of individual tragedies—this was the intimidating task before me, and I wondered if it would indeed be possible without diminishing what I had come to see as a veritable Bible of events. The colors of my determination kept changing with the hour, for the theme of the play, the key to the compression of events, kept its distance as I groped toward a visceral connection with all this—since I knew that to simply will a play into existence was to insure a didactic failure. By now I was far beyond the teaching impulse; I knew that my own life was speaking here in many disguises, not merely my time.

One day, after several hours of reading at the Historical Society, where it now seemed no one but I had ever entered to disturb the two gray guardians' expressionless tranquility, I got up to leave, and that was when I noticed hanging on a wall several framed etchings of the witchcraft trials, apparently made at the time by an artist who must have witnessed them. In one of them, a shaft of sepulchral light shoots down from a window high up in a vaulted room, falling upon the head of a judge whose face is blanched white, his long white beard hanging to his waist, arms raised in defensive horror as beneath him the covey of afflicted girls screams and claws at invisible tormentors. Dark and almost indistinguishable figures huddle on the periphery of the picture, but a few men can be made out, bearded like the judge, and shrinking back in pious outrage. Suddenly it became my memory of the dancing men in the synagogue on 114th Street as I had glimpsed them between my shielding fingers, the same chaos of bodily motion—in this picture, adults fleeing the sight of a supernatural event; in my memory, a happier but no less eerie circumstance—both scenes frighteningly attached to the long reins of God. I knew instantly what the connection was: the moral intensity of the Jews and the clan's defensiveness against pollution from outside the ranks. Yes, I understood Salem in that flash, it was suddenly my own inheritance. I might not yet be able to work a play's shape out of this roiling mass of stuff, but it belonged to me now, and I felt I could begin circling around the space where a structure of my own could conceivably rise.

I left Salem in the late afternoon, and the six o'clock news came on the radio with the black night like a cloak thrown over the windshield. The rain had not ceased. The announcer read a bulletin about Elia Kazan's testimony before the House Un-American Activities Committee and mentioned the people he had named, none of whom I knew. I had almost forgotten him by now, so deep had I been in the past. The announcer's voice seemed a violent, vulgar intrusion into a private anguish; I remember thinking that the issue was being made to sound altogether political when it was really becoming something else, something I could not name.

I was heading down toward New York, back into the world. A numbness held me. The bulletin was repeated again on the half-hour. I wished they would stop. I felt something like embarrassment, not only for him, but somehow for all of us who had shared the—comradeship, I suppose the word is, born of our particular kind of alienation. The political element was only a part of it, maybe even a small part. We had all cheered the same heroes, the same mythic resisters, maybe that was it, from way back in the Spanish war to the German antifascists and the Italians, brave men and women who were the best of our identity, those who had been the sacrifices of our time.

What we had now seemed a withering parody of what was being advertised as high drama. When the Committee knew all the names beforehand, there was hardly a conspiracy being unveiled but rather a symbolic display that would neither string anybody up on a gallows nor cause him to be cut down. No material thing had been moved one way or another by a single inch, only the air we all breathed had grown somewhat thinner and the destruction of meaning seemed total when the sundering of friendships was so often with people whom the witness had not ceased to love.

Approaching New York, I felt as always the nearness of the circumstantial, the bedrock real. As I headed downtown toward the Brooklyn Bridge on glistening wet roads, I found myself keeping to the slow side of the speedometer as though to protect what truth there was in me from skidding into oblivion. That I was committed to this play was no longer a question for me; I had made the decision without thinking about it somewhere between Salem and this city.

Molly's instant reaction against the Salem analogy would be, as I already sensed, the strongest objection to such a play. "There are Communists," it would be repeatedly said, "but there never were any witches." I did not wish to evade this point, there was no need to; my obligation was still solely to myself and to the material. But I did not want it to sidetrack me either, not before I clearly knew the theme. All I had so far was a mass of stories, evidence of an imploded community that distrust and paranoia had killed—literally so, for it was a hundred years before people bought some of the farms owned by those who had been hanged, such was the reality of the curse upon them.

It was thus not true that "there never were any witches." I had no doubt that Tituba, Reverend Parris's black Barbados slave, had been practicing witchcraft with the girls, but more important, the best minds of the time, here and in Europe, inside and outside the

churches, would have been indignant to be told there were no
witches when the Bible on three different occasions warns against
dealing with them. Addison, Dr. Johnson, King James, and the
entire British church hierarchy shared the view of Blackstone, the
voice of English jurisprudence himself, who declared, "To deny
the possibility, nay the actual existence, of witchcraft and sorcery,
is at once flatly to contradict the revealed Word of God, in various
passages both of the Old and New Testament; and the thing itself
is a truth to which every nation in the world hath in its turn borne
testimony, either by examples seemingly well attested, or by
prohibitory laws, which at least suppose the possibility of commerce with evil spirits." John Wesley summed it up: "The giving
up witchcraft is, in effect, giving up the Bible." As always, these
affirmations had a cause: an alarming rise in what was called "infi-
delity," which is to say, skepticism, deism, even atheism—and
witchcraft was the ultimate sneer at God. The witch-hunt was a
way of saying, "You must gather to us in the church since we alone
stand between you and the Devil's overwhelming the world." Beneath high moral dudgeon, then as now, lay our old friend power,
and the lust for it. When several hundred thousand people had
been executed in Europe for witchcraft, it was hardly wisdom to
say that the cause was merely imaginary.

But a theme is not an idea; it is an action, an unstoppable process,
like a fetus growing or, yes, a cancer; it is a destroyer as it changes
and creates or kills, a paradox that nothing can keep from unwinding through all of its contradictions down to its resolution, which
in its right time illuminates the whole from the beginning. After
weeks of attacking from every side, writing scene after experimental scene, I came on the layers of internal parallelisms in the Salem
experience that suggested a path toward a climax, and I found
myself asking what, if it had been present in Salem, would have
made it impossible to set these people against one another like this.

Almost every testimony I had read revealed the sexual theme,
either open or barely concealed; the Devil himself, for one thing,
was almost always a black man in a white community, and of course
the initial inflammatory instance that convinced so many that the
town was under Luciferian siege was the forced confession of the
black slave Tituba. But apart from that, men rarely accused another man of having bewitched them, and almost all the bewitched
women were tempted by a warlock, a male witch. Night was the
usual time to be subverted from dutiful Christian behavior, and
dozens were in their beds when through window or door, as real

as life, a spectral visitor floated in and lay upon them or provoked them to some filthy act like kissing or bade them sign the "Devil's book," a membership roll of the underground party of the damned. The relief that came to those who testified was orgasmic; they were actually encouraged in open court to talk about their sharing a bed with someone they weren't married to, a live human being now manacled before them courtesy of God's lieutenants.

Here was guilt, the guilt of illicit sexuality. (And indeed, blessed as they were by their godly crusade, august New England judges soon took to playing shovelboard with their holy adolescent witnesses and sharing an ale with them in the local tavern—devilish business certainly, but permissible now that they were battling for God in this open war with Hell.) Had there been no tinder of guilt to set aflame, had the cult and culture of repression not ruled so tightly, no outbreak would have been possible. John Proctor, then, in being driven to confess not to a metaphoric guilt but to actual sex with an identified teenage partner, might save the community in the only way possible—by raising to consciousness what had been suppressed and in holy disguise was out to murder them all.

The political question, therefore, of whether witches and Communists could be equated was no longer to the point. What was manifestly parallel was the guilt, two centuries apart, of holding illicit, suppressed feelings of alienation and hostility toward standard, daylight society as defined by its most orthodox proponents.

Without guilt the 1950s Red-hunt could never have generated such power. Once it was conceded that absolutely any idea remotely similar to a Marxist position was not only politically but morally illicit, the liberal, with his customary adaptations of Marxist theory and attitudes, was effectively paralyzed. The former Communist was guilty because he had in fact believed the Soviets were developing the system of the future, without human exploitation and irrational waste. Even his naiveté in seeing Russia not as an earthly empire but rather as a kind of spiritual condition was now a source of guilt and shame.

The House Un-American Activities Committee had been in existence since 1938, but the tinder of guilt was not so available when the New Deal and Roosevelt were openly espousing a policy of vast social engineering often reminiscent of socialist methods. But as in Salem, a point arrived, in the late forties, when the rules of social intercourse quite suddenly changed, or were changed, and attitudes that had merely been anticapitalist-antiestablishment were now made unholy, morally repulsive, and if not actually treasonous then implicitly so. America had always been a religious country.

I suppose I had been searching a long time for a tragic hero, and now I had him; the Salem story was not going to be abandoned. The longer I worked the more certain I felt that as improbable as it might seem, there were moments when an individual conscience was all that could keep a world from falling.

By midsummer I had found the moment when Proctor, able at last to set aside his guilty feelings of unworthiness to "mount the gibbet like a saint," as I had him say, defies the court by tearing up his confession and brings on his own execution. This clinched the play. One of the incidental consequences for me was a changed view of the Greek tragedies; they must have had their therapeutic effect by raising to conscious awareness the clan's capacity for brutal and unredeemed violence so that it could be sublimated and contained by new institutions, like the law Athena brings to tame the primordial, chainlike vendetta.

"Every playwright has to have Jed Harris once," George Kaufman had said, "like the measles." After two productions with Kazan and our sharing of ideas about plays and life, finding a new director was a hard thing to face. Jim Proctor, who had done the publicity for *All My Sons* and *Salesman,* was old enough to recall, as I was not, the string of triumphs Harris had directed in the late twenties and early thirties, when, as sometimes happened on a Broadway that still had dozens of straight plays running at the same time, a star director would rise and spin off show after show for years and even decades and dominate an era with his personality. Harris had produced *Coquette* with the ingenue Helen Hayes, *Broadway*, *The Royal Family*, and *The Front Page*, and had directed *Uncle Vanya*, *The Inspector General*, *A Doll's House*, *Our Town*, and Sartre's *Red Gloves*, among others, but by the fifties his legend had all but faded. A couple of years earlier, however, he had taken over and revised a failing production of *Washington Square*, retitled it *The Heiress*, and turned it into a success. He had fathered a son with Ruth Gordon and had fought with practically everybody who was anybody in the Broadway theatre, something I was not privy to when Jimmy brought us together for the first time on a gleaming sixty-foot motor yacht in the Westport, Connecticut, harbor.

Jimmy Proctor had a flattened nose, a thick neck, a bald head, and the pigeon-toed lope of a myopic wrestler, which he had been at Cornell in the mid-twenties. He also had a lisp and, like so many newspapermen of his era, was incurably sentimental, especially about people with talent, whether for tightrope walking or playwriting. His father had showed up periodically during his boyhood on home leave from one or another South American revolution, or sometimes from an expedition into some gold-rumored jungle. Early on, therefore, Jimmy had developed a tendency to romanticize people with unusual or exotic personas—of whom Jed Harris, as it turned out, was one of the foremost examples in the twentieth century. "A lot of people will badmouth Jed," warned Jimmy in one of his rare understatements, "but he's a kind of genius, and I don't believe a man can ever lose that."

As I later learned, Harris had temporary use of the yacht, a venerable and immaculately kept vessel, pending his decision to buy it (although surely not with money, of which he had none). There was also a totally silent and lovely young woman on board, doubtless on a similar trial basis. I quickly surmised that what was good about Jed was what was bad, a visceral, physical power and an appetite that brooked no denial. When it was Sunday and he said it was Tuesday and you corrected him, he would grin mischievously with his heavy lower jaw jutting forward and say, "I never argue with talent." I had suspicions from the outset that he was just too classy for me and would be trouble, but he was also refreshingly knowledgeable about plays and actors, as well as a self-confessed connoisseur of poetry and literature in general. He was one of those men who, without saying it in so many words, could get up from dinner and leave you with the feeling that he had rather intimately known Winston Churchill, Mahatma Gandhi, and maybe Gertrude Stein. Jed had style, which is always suspicious, especially when it is not only a form of entertainment but also a weapon.

But like all stylish fellows he had his blind, naive side, as when I drove him up to Boston in my Ford and he yelled for me to stop just as I was passing through a tollbooth after paying the attendant. I braked and asked him what the problem was. Gesturing back to the tolltaker, Jed said, "You didn't tip him." As an introduction to a new director this boded ill for a shared sense of reality, but even better news was on its way. I was taking him to Boston to see Arthur Kennedy in a new show there. Kennedy had been in two plays of mine, and I thought of him as a possible John Proctor. But Jed had detested the idea from the moment I first mentioned it.

"Where's he come from?" he asked.

"Worcester, Mass."

"I thought so. He's got those feet."

"What feet?"

"Those *feet*! Didn't you ever see his feet, for Chrissake, and you had him in two shows?"

"I don't understand what you're talking about."

Seeing Kennedy onstage that evening, Jed nudged me and pointed. "There! You see? He's a fucking potato farmer, see how he puts his feet down? He's in mud, clump, clump, clump!"

On the way down to New York I insisted that Kennedy was capable of great lyricism, and we ended up hiring him, but Jed's ludicrous objection to his feet was a signal of his misconception of the play, which with my usual optimism I preferred to overlook. Kennedy was too common, he felt, ignoring the fact that John Proctor is not an actor but a Salem peasant. Indeed, Harris saw the production as a "Dutch painting," a classical play that had to be nobly performed—an invitation to slumber, I thought. But he was correct about the rest of the casting, which was decidedly on the majestic side, with the eighty-year-old Walter Hampden a magnificent presence as Danforth, knife-mouthed Philip Coolidge as Hathorne, E. G. Marshall as Reverend Hale, Beatrice Straight playing Elizabeth, and an aged vaudevillian named Joseph Sweeney with a knowing and bitter wit as the octogenarian farmer Giles Corey, who is pressed to death with stones for refusing to testify.

After ten days of rehearsal with this powerful company something leaden and dead lay on the stage, and I remembered an old saw to the effect that there had never been a hit in Puritan costumes. (Which may have been a takeoff on Max Gordon's declaration after the flop of a Napoleon play he had produced: "I will never do another play where a guy writes with a feather!") There was little spontaneity in the performances, and I knew that the players were simply scared of Harris, who would sometimes break into a scene to ridicule an actor nastily for moving beyond a certain fixed point on the stage. He would even mouth their lines to emphasize a vowel, or turn them bodily so that whole passages were performed without their looking at one another, this to underline some classical depersonalized restraint he insisted on imposing. The whole thing was becoming an absurd exercise not in passion but in discipline. It would not work, and one morning Jed did not appear for rehearsal at all.

I got him on the phone in his borrowed Central Park South apartment and thought he was not exaggerating when he whispered, after a long half-minute's silence, "Arthur, I am dying."

"What does the doctor say?" I asked a few minutes later, after rushing to his bedside.

Jed shook his head hopelessly. "Doesn't know," he answered. I might have known that any illness of Jed's would be beyond the ordinary reach of medical science. "I want you to take rehearsal," he whispered, his teeth chattering as he reached a hairy arm from under the cover and took my hand. "You're a good boy," he said solemnly, as though this was to be our final moment together on earth.

Assuring him that we would all be eager to see him again once he had recovered—a lie for which I instantly found it perfectly possible to forgive myself—I returned to the theatre, where after half an hour of rehearsing, I turned and saw Jed sitting behind me in his overcoat, collar up, teeth still chattering, a hostage to his art. Within the hour he was back on the stage telling Kennedy exactly where to place his cloddish feet and how many degrees to turn as he spoke a line.

Of the large troupe only E. G. Marshall ever stared Jed down, unafraid. Arriving for an evening rehearsal, he carried a quarter-full bottle of whiskey that he insisted on keeping in his hand as he played Reverend Hale in the scene where he presses Proctor to recite the Ten Commandments to prove his piety. E. G. stood there as Kennedy reeled off his catechism, and when Jed climbed on the stage and asked him to move forward a few inches, he first tipped the bottle straight up, drained it, turned at his leisure, and joyously flung it across the entire orchestra up into the darkness of the balcony, where it crashed. Then, turning to Jed and smacking his lips, he asked, "Now, what is it you'd like me to do?" Jed, so far as I know, never gave him another direction.

Jed was a charming man living at the raveled edge of his self-control, and I suppose that was the source of his authority. We tend to obey the crazy. Nevertheless, he could be wonderfully funny. I arrived in his apartment one day to find him on the couch reading an enormously thick book. I said that one rarely saw new books that size. "Oh, yes," Jed said, "and although long, it is not interesting." But his shifts of mood were severe. A few minutes later we were standing at his elevator waiting for it to open, chatting and relaxed. Without warning he began kicking and pounding on the sheet-metal door with all his force until it boomed, yelling, "Come up here!" over and over again. After a minute or so the operator, a fragile old man in his seventies, appeared at the open door with frightened eyes, trying to explain the delay, but Jed could not keep himself from grabbing the man by his lapels and roaring, "I've been ringing!" as he banged him violently against the wall of the elevator before I could pull him away. By the time we reached the street he was himself again, talking about buying a used Chrysler, one with a divider between chauffeur and passengers. It was obvious by now that he hadn't the money to maintain a chauffeur-driven car, but on our way to the theatre he insisted on showing it off to me in the showroom on Broadway, getting in and out of it a couple of times, closing and opening the doors, and giving the dealer the impression of an imminent sale.

By the time we were ready to leave for the first public performance in Wilmington, Delaware, Jed, I thought, knew that he hadn't found the play's key, and so for several days he made one incredible demand after another—the firing of some of the actors, for example—until the producer, Kermit Bloomgarden, thought the time had come to separate. This proposal clearly pleased Jed, who, however, insisted on being given a large percentage of the show in return for pulling out—an impossibility.

An enthusiastic tumult greeted the first performance in Wilmington, home of the Du Pont empire, which I had regarded as a provincial company town since my last visit with *The Man Who Had All the Luck*, nine years before. At that time the audience there had seemed like a summer theatre crowd, unengaged and remote, but now these people were on their feet at the end calling for the author. I was standing at the back of the house beside Lillian Hellman and Bloomgarden, still unhappy with the stifled spirit of the production, with no real confidence in its New York fate, when Jed appeared on the stage, flanked by an obviously startled Kennedy and an openmouthed E. G. Marshall, and took an author's bow: The curtain came down on a genuine demonstration of affection for me, even if I looked a decade or two older up there than I had in this morning's local paper. Lillian, who had taken a fancy to Jed, was doubled over with her choking laughter, and Bloomgarden, having learned the word from her, kept repeating, "Shocking! Shocking!" Immediately Jed appeared, holding out the palm of his hand and showing me some torn threads on his jacket. "The actors pulled me onto the stage. Look, they tore off my button!" he explained. Something seemed to have penetrated at last, telling him his attempted impersonation was not too classy. I grinned at him and patted him on the shoulder, with which he turned to Lillian and Kermit to repeat his button-and-jacket act as proof that he was still one of nature's noblemen. Kennedy and Marshall, of course, hadn't pulled him onto the stage at all.

I have never been surprised by the New York reception of a play, and opening night in the Martin Beck, some four years after *Salesman*, was no exception. I knew we had cooled off a very hot play, which therefore was not going to move anyone very deeply. It was not a performance from within but a kind of conscious rendering. Jed indeed had intimated more than once that he detested the emotionalism of Kazan's productions and was going to do *The Crucible* with his customary style. What I had not quite bargained for, however, was the hostility in the New York audience as the theme of the play was revealed; an invisible sheet of ice formed over their heads, thick enough to skate on. In the lobby at the end, people with whom I had some fairly close professional acquaintanceships passed me by as though I were invisible.

The reviews were not as bad as I had expected, although the *Times* calling the play cold reminded me of Jed's claim to have taken Brooks Atkinson to lunch during the rehearsals of Thornton Wilder's *Our Town*, hoping to prime him for what was then the revolutionary idea of a setless play. "I invited him into rehearsals so he could learn about the theatre, and I told him, I said, 'Brooks, you don't know anything about the theatre, why don't we start giving you lessons with this play?' And he kind of chuckled and said he would love it but the *Times* critic just couldn't do anything like that." And in fact, in his review of *The Crucible*, Atkinson could not separate the play from the cold production at all.

Business inevitably began falling off in a month or so, and Kennedy and Beatrice Straight would shortly leave for films. The rest of the cast insisted on playing even with little or no pay, especially after one performance when the audience, upon John Proctor's execution, stood up and remained silent for a couple of minutes, with heads bowed. The Rosenbergs were at that moment being electrocuted in Sing Sing. Some of the cast had no idea what was happening as they faced rows of bowed and silent people, and were informed in whispers by their fellows. The play then became an act of resistance for them, and I redirected it with Maureen Stapleton as Elizabeth Proctor and E. G. Marshall taking Kennedy's place. I had the sets removed to save stagehand costs and played it all in black, with white lights that were never moved from beginning to end. I thought it all the stronger for this simplicity. We managed to extend the run some weeks, but finally a sufficient audience was simply not there. After the last curtain I came out on the stage and sat facing the actors and thanked them, and they thanked me, and then we just sat looking at one another.

Somebody sobbed, and then somebody else, and suddenly the impacted frustration of the last months, plus the labor of over a year in writing the play and revising it, all burst upwards into my head, and I had to walk into the darkness backstage and weep for a minute or two before returning to say goodbye.

In less than two years, as always in America, a lot would change. McCarthyism was on the wane, although people were still being hurt by it, and a new *Crucible*, produced by Paul Libin, opened in one of the first off-Broadway productions in New York's history, at a theatre in the Martinique Hotel. It was a young production, with many of the actors neophytes who had none of the original cast's finish, but it was performed this time as it was written, desperate and hot, and it ran for nearly two years. Some of the critics inevitably concluded that I had revised the script, but of course not a word had changed, though the time had, and it was possible now to feel some regret for what we had done to ourselves in the early Red-hunting years. The metaphor of the immortal underlying forces that can always rise again was now an admissible thing for the press to consider.

In time, *The Crucible* became by far my most frequently produced play, both abroad and at home. Its meaning is somewhat different in different places and moments. I can almost tell what the political situation in a country is when the play is suddenly a hit there—it is either a warning of tyranny on the way or a reminder of tyranny just past. As recently as the winter of 1986 the Royal Shakespeare Company, after touring *The Crucible* through British cathedrals and open town squares, played it in English for a week in two Polish cities. Some important government figures were in the audience, by their presence urging on its message of resistance to a tyranny they were forced to serve. In Shanghai in 1980, it served as a metaphor for life under Mao and the Cultural Revolution, decades when accusation and enforced guilt ruled China and all but destroyed the last signs of intelligent life. The writer Nien Cheng, who spent six and a half years in solitary confinement and whose daughter was murdered by the Red Guards, told me that after her release she saw the Shanghai production and could not believe that a non-Chinese had written the play. "Some of the interrogations," she said, "were precisely the same ones used on us in the Cultural Revolution." It was chilling to realize what had never occurred to me until she mentioned it—that the tyranny of teenagers was almost identical in both instances.

In the late fifties a touching film version was made by the French director Raymond Rouleau, with Simone Signoret and Yves Montand, who had reportedly had a big impact in the stage production (I was prevented from seeing it under a State Department travel ban). Jean-Paul Sartre's screenplay, however, seemed to me to toss an arbitrary Marxist mesh over the story that led to a few absurdities. Sartre laid the witchcraft outbreak to a struggle between rich and poor peasants, but in reality victims like Rebecca Nurse were of the class of relatively large landowners, and the Proctors and their like were by no means poor. It amused me to see crucifixes on the farmhouse walls, as they would be in French Catholic homes but never, of course, in a Puritan one. Nonetheless, Simone Signoret was immensely moving, and the film had a noble grandeur, Salem and the Proctors sharing a wonderfully French sort of sensuality whose repression trembled with imminent disaster.

In 1965 I had the curious satisfaction, sitting behind a young British couple at Olivier's production, of catching a remark the woman made to her escort after the second-act curtain: "I believe this had something to do with that American senator—what was his name?" The play had now become art, cut from its roots, a spectacle of human passions purely. Overhearing, I felt as though I had returned from the dead, and it felt good.

But at the time, *The Crucible* was still another defeat—about which, however, I was far from regretful. I had spoken my piece into the teeth of the gale. People now assumed I had some claim on leadership, and though that was the last thing in my mind, it was hard to avoid an occasional speech, as when the Newspaper Guild asked me to address them on John Foster Dulles's recent declaration that his State Department had a perfect right to refuse newsmen passports for a trip to China: "If the Government has the right to forbid businessmen from helping Chinese Communism by doing business with them, the obligation of writers is no different." He apparently imagined his ban on information about it would cause the world's most populous nation to drop out of history. Paraphrasing Hitler on war, I called this "total diplomacy," and the *Times* ran a respectable report of my remarks. But one would have had to be a fool to think the American people did not agree with Dulles. Huey Long's "fascism arriving as antifascism" kept coming to mind as we kept losing track of first principles; for the people's right to know was definitely not the same as its right to buy and sell. I had no doubt such speeches of mine were simply going into J. Edgar

Hoover's dossier on me. I spoke to a quasi-radical group, the National Council of Arts, Sciences, and Professions, saying that in view of the almost total absence of movies, plays, or books about blacklisting and the onslaught against civil liberties in America, one had to wonder if self-censorship was not the real problem before us. But then as now, speeches always left me emptied, with only feelings of futility. The work was all that mattered in the end, and good work would last long after speeches were forgotten.

Still, it was not easy to go back to the desk again, especially when I felt that though *The Crucible* had failed as a commercial production it had succeeded as a play. I could not help thinking in 1953–54 that time was running out, not only on me but on the traditional American culture. I was growing more and more frighteningly isolated, in life as in the theatre.

It was around this time that Montgomery Clift called, asking if I would come and watch rehearsals of a production he and Kevin McCarthy were doing of *The Seagull* at the Phoenix Theatre. With no director, I thought this well-meant effort had no concise center, and even with Sam Jaffe playing Dr. Dorn it never lifted off. I talked to the actors a couple of afternoons, searching out some consistent metaphoric line they might follow, but nothing took except one remark that Monty repeated for years to come, even into the shooting of *The Misfits* some seven years on. As Treplev, he was not quite sure why he commits suicide, and I suggested that he think of Treplev aiming the revolver through his own head at Arkadina, his mother. This idea absolutely delighted him and made him wish his suicide occurred onstage instead of off.

But all this was a diversion; I had no drive to be a director, if only because it was difficult to be in the company of others for such long periods with my own narcissism having to make way for theirs. Besides, the written word travels gratifyingly farther than anything else and can be invested with surprising new meanings, some that illuminate the writer to himself. I had an unexpected example one evening as I was leaving the theatre lobby after a rehearsal with Monty and Kevin.

A downpour that wouldn't stop was flooding Second Avenue. Just inside the otherwise empty lobby, a wet umbrella at his side, stood a strikingly odd young man in rubbers, white shirt and black tie, black overcoat, and black suit, with black eyes and a curly helmet of black hair. A feverish, fanatical look in his eye as he approached, spittle in the corners of his mouth.

He reminded me that he had phoned some weeks before, asking

for a few minutes to explain a problem, and then I recalled him, a Columbia sophomore from Argentina who wanted to discuss *The Crucible*. I let him sit beside me in my car, figuring to get rid of him more quickly there than in a living room, for he was terribly strange and made me uneasy.

The downpour continued mercilessly, waves of water pushed by the wind across the empty avenue. He sat formally with his umbrella between his knees, and I noticed he was wearing a ring with a large diamond. After some chitchat about art—he was a painter, he said—I pressed him to his question, which was whether I believed that one person can "influence" what another person does. Assuming he was talking literature or painting, I said that I had been influenced by various writers, but he meant something different.

"I mean that one person can . . ." He hesitated.

"Control?"

"Yes, that's it, control."

"Somebody controlling you?"

"Yes, always."

"Do you know who it is?"

"My aunt."

This lady, he said, had practically raised him in the family's great house, bathing him, teaching him, dressing and undressing him, until in his early teens he experienced an insidious shift of focus and realized that what she had secretly decided to do was to murder him. "I knew when she was approaching the house from even five blocks away, her influence was so strong on me."

But now in New York he surely had nothing to fear? On the contrary, at a party only last week he had started across the room to greet a girl student he liked when he was suddenly pushed against a piano, breaking two of his front teeth and disfiguring his upper lip. He showed me two tooth shards nestling in a blood-spotted handkerchief.

"But who pushed you?"

"My aunt. She does not wish me to be a friend to girls."

"All the way from Argentina?"

"The distance is not important, she can be anywhere."

"You've been to see doctors, I suppose."

"Yes, they don't know anything."

"Why did you pick me to tell this to?"

"Because of *The Crucible*."

I was flabbergasted. "But what in *The Crucible* would lead you to think . . ."

"The girls. They are tormented by these witches."

"Oh, yes. I see. But you understand that I don't believe they were telling the truth."

"But of course they were."

A chill went up my back. I denied it, trying as best I could to straighten the poor boy out.

"But I saw this play in Buenos Aires, and I knew that you would understand me because you know that this happens."

It was the end of the following summer before he finally walked out of my life, hospitalized, his delusions beyond the reach of psychiatry. Yet he had detected a reality in the play that I had not vouched for in writing it but that he made me realize was certainly there.

Still at loose ends, I accepted, despite misgivings, an invitation from the Arden, Delaware, summer theatre to direct a production of *All My Sons* with Kevin McCarthy and Larry Gates as Chris and Joe Keller, and my sister, Joan Copeland, as Ann. (Joan had become a gifted actress; she appeared in many Broadway productions, including *Detective Story* and *The Diary of Anne Frank*.) I was feeling disoriented and weak then, the demise of *The Crucible* having bitten deeper than I had let myself believe, and so it was unsettling to find actors investing me with authority. It had never dawned on me before how exposed and vulnerable the actor feels onstage, and how easy it really is to make him a dependent and oneself a person of importance.

But the whole process was repellent, and less than ever did I want to be a director, the provider of reassurance that for the most part I did not possess myself. The very idea of authority was fraudulent. I seemed to have passed over the line where I could trust myself to another person. It was not a question of being angry at life but of recognizing its plainest terms. Ibsen's line, "He is strongest who is most alone," kept coming to mind.

A phone call from Martin Ritt, an actor I had heard of as one of the younger Group Theatre people but had never met, was an exciting invitation to come out of isolation. He was appearing in *The Flowering Peach*, Odets's latest—and, as it turned out, his last—play; it was probably going to close in a month or two, and Robert Whitehead, its producer, had agreed to let the cast have the theatre for Sunday evening performances of anything they wanted to play. Did I perhaps have a one-act they could do?

Under the illusion that I was writing for an impromptu group of actors rather than a Broadway opening, it took me hardly two weeks to finish *A Memory of Two Mondays,* a kind of elegy for my years in the auto parts warehouse. I suppose I chose the material out of a need to touch again a reality I could understand, unlike the booming, inane America of the present. In a trivial time that delighted in prosperous escapism, I had managed to seize on the one subject nobody would want to confront, the Depression and the struggle to survive.

Stout and cheerful, a gifted poker and horse player, Ritt was high on the new one-act but thought I needed a curtain raiser for it, something to round out a full evening. I loved this promising atmosphere of sheer play and enjoyed my own power to give actors roles without commercial worries to dampen the happiness of work. Besides, one-act plays were never done in the Broadway theatre, and rarely in the rest of the country, and this added to the attraction of the project. Even better, the people who came on Sunday nights would probably not be the proverbial businessmen but real lovers of the theatre. If I noticed any contradiction between democratic ideals and this comforting exclusion of all but aficionados, it was drowned in the pleasures of composition.

I walked around for a few days trying to think of something short and wonderful, and then, suddenly, my old *Italian Tragedy* seemed to fall into place as a one-act with a single rising line of intensity leading inevitably to an explosive climax. For this informal production, *A View from the Bridge,* which I had been worrying over for years as a projected full-length play for the Broadway theatre, now came to hand in ten days. Reading it, Marty burst into his deep belly laugh at the idea that I had begun it as a curtain raiser, since it was obviously now the main event.

But reality soon flowed back, rapid and destructive. *The Flowering Peach* had to fold sooner than expected, making its theatre unavailable to us. On the other hand, the two new one-acts, performed by a single group playing parts in both, suddenly became attractive to Broadway. Naturally, I was torn between the original pristine notion and Kermit Bloomgarden's enthusiasm for a major new production. Instinct warned against Broadway, where I did not think these plays belonged, but vanity won out. And there were also good reasons for a full-fledged Broadway attempt, especially the availability of quality actors, far less obtainable for an unpretentious production in some corner of town. In 1955 the off-Broadway theatre was still in its infancy.

Nevertheless, casting, as always, was the nemesis. *A View from the Bridge* had come out of the piers and my time in Calabria and Sicily, yet we ended up with mainly WASP actors—among them, only Jack Warden had the lingo and the feel. It was my own fault, for Marilyn Monroe had finally moved into my life, and the resulting mixture of despair for my marriage and astonishment with her left little room for concentration on casting. I had accepted the chestnut that good actors, regardless of type, can surmount anything. They can't. Van Heflin, the son of an Oklahoma dentist, was filled with doubts about his ability to portray an Italian longshoreman and asked me to take him around in Red Hook and introduce him to people. He studied their speech like a foreign language, which was unfortunately how it sounded on his tongue, and it was his preoccupation with accents and mannerisms that kept him from feeling the part in the end.

J. Carrol Naish, an actor who had been taking his repertoire of ethnic characterizations off the rack in Hollywood for decades, did so again here despite Ritt's desperate attempts to make him into a personage resembling someone in real life. Playing Gus, a barrel-shaped warehouse foreman in *Memory,* Naish had eight-pound weights built into his shoes to give him a grotesque anthropoid walk, but as the narrator-lawyer of *View* he had no physical gimmick to cling to and on opening night scrambled his lines like a juggler who keeps dropping his Indian clubs: referring in one speech to Frankie Yale, a famed gangster who had once walked the bloody streets of Red Hook, he instead said "Frankie Laine," naming the popular crooner while looking pleased with himself for remembering the rest of that particularly lengthy speech at all.

If *A View from the Bridge* more than thirty years later has a vigorous life on stages all over the world, it is no thanks to the original production, which made it appear at best an academic and irrelevant story of revenge. That I could blame no one but myself made matters even worse. Deeply involved with Marilyn, I was alternately soaring and anxious that I might be slipping into a new life not my own. My will seemed to have evaporated, and I could only accept Bloomgarden's longing for a Broadway hit when what I had written was something very different, something plain and elementary and frightening in its inexorability. Marty Ritt, who became a successful director of films like *Edge of the City, The Long Hot Summer,* and *Hud,* was on his first time out and went along, as he thought he must, rather than aggressively pursuing his own vision of what the production ought to be. In a word, the play on the stage had no tang; it lacked the indefinable webbing of human involvement that can magically unify many otherwise dismally ordinary separate parts.

Watching the production, I felt remote from it, as though I had dropped into the theatre as a visitor. Even *A Memory of Two Mondays,* avowedly a reminiscence, seemed to strain for effects rather than strolling through a panorama of time recalled. Less than two years later, Peter Brook did a new, revised, full-length production of *View* in London, and I remember best something he said just before we opened at the Comedy Theatre, after I had asked what he thought the British would make of it. "I'm not at all sure its inexorability won't put them off; the English tend to flee from Ibsen and the Greeks and anything else that shows some underlying logic to life so that if one thing happens it is almost certain to cause something else. If they took that to heart, I suppose they would flee this country, which everybody knows has no future. We are relying here on the arrival of happy accident, and in *View* it just doesn't work that way."

And indeed the play's main significance for me lay in its unpeeling of process itself, the implacability of a structure in life. For around me I felt a wasting vagrancy of mind and spirit, the tree of life turning into a wandering vine. The much celebrated "end of ideology," which some influential ex-Marxists were elaborating, seemed to me to dissolve the very notion of human destiny. At bottom, people were to be left to their loneliness, each to himself and for himself, and this compounded the sadness of life, although it might liberate some to strike out on their own and make more money. In America we were then at the very beginning of the Beat movement, which gave a name to the nameless and a form to the formlessness of our existence, and toward which I had no sympathy at all at the time. How to live and how to relax were not the same problem, not if you had children and the anxiety, which would never leave me, that something life-mocking and mean was stirring in the American spirit—something that had to be outmaneuvered and thwarted by the strategies of art. It took me a while to see that the Beats had an eye on the same monster and were foiling him with an entirely different bag of tricks.

The reception of *View* was actually a good deal better than I judged at the time and than lodged in my memory. But I have yet to meet the artist who has not on occasion believed that his critics have plotted against him. Perhaps it was also a negative memory because something in me was disowning the play even as its opening approached. I was turning against myself, struggling to put my life behind me, order and disorder at war in me, in a kind of parallel of the stress between the play's formal, cool classicism and the turmoil of incestuous desire and betrayal within it.

I no longer knew what I wanted—certainly not the end of my marriage, but the thought of putting Marilyn out of my life was unbearable. My world seemed to be colliding with itself, the past exploding under my feet. And on top of everything else I was once more under attack.

The first barrage had come in 1953. I had received a cable from the Belgo-American Association, a business group, inviting me to attend the premiere of *The Crucible* in Brussels, all expenses paid. It was the first production of the play on the Continent, and one that I hoped might at last prove its vitality. I wired my acceptance, only to discover that my passport had expired. Monty Clift accompanied me downtown to the Wall Street passport office, and then we went to a rehearsal of *The Seagull* across town on Second Avenue. I had asked for a rush processing since I would have to leave for Brussels by Friday in order to make the opening on Saturday evening and it was already Monday.

When I heard nothing for two days, John Wharton, my lawyer, contacted a colleague in Washington, Joseph L. Rauh, Jr., who by Thursday managed to elicit from Mrs. Ruth B. Shipley, the chief of the Passport Division of the State Department, that in her opinion my going abroad was "not in the national interest" and so she was not going to renew my passport. She sounded to me like the Duchess in *Alice in Wonderland,* with the same chance of appeal from her edicts—a matter in any case of weeks or months or even years. I had to cable the Belgian National Theatre that I could not get a passport in time and would not appear. Mrs. Shipley doubtless had my dossier, of which she doubtless distinctly disapproved, with its lump of left-wing entries, petitions I had signed and meetings I had attended, and of course my much publicized break with Kazan, which had received broad press coverage.

The Brussels newspapers had reported that I would be present at the premiere, and when the final curtain fell, a call went up for the author. It showed no sign of decreasing, and finally a man stood up in one of the first orchestra rows to acknowledge the reception. The audience cheered him heartily, naturally mistaking him for the playwright. It was the American ambassador, who was probably present in deference to the pro-American association that had sponsored the evening. Once the odd substitution was discovered, however, the papers took off against American policy, using my forced absence to embrace my play as their protest against McCarthyism. This Belgian strand would emerge again in the late seventies, twenty-five years later, when I found myself in our Belgian embassy at a reception in my honor. In 1953 the notion of being greeted with applause as I walked into an American embassy would have been madness to conceive.

As *View* was moving into rehearsal, I was hammered by a second attack. Even at the time the wild swings of my life alternately alarmed and amused me. I would be with Marilyn in her subleased apartment high up in the Waldorf Tower while below in the streets the *Daily News,* the *World-Telegram,* and the *Journal-American,* each running all the shots of her they could get as many times a week as they could get them, were indignantly calling on Mayor Wagner and the City Council to dissociate themselves from my subversive, un-American presence.

The issue this time was that film on juvenile delinquency, the one I had spent two months researching in the streets of Brooklyn and was now close to sitting down to write. Though Bloomgarden, Ritt, and I had completed the principal casting of *View* and *A Memory of Two Mondays* in the spring, we would not be going into production until fall, and so I had a long hiatus before me. A young producer unknown to me had proposed that I write a screenplay on the recent outbreak of gang warfare, the dynamics of which nobody seemed to understand. He had a contract with the city, which in exchange for police cooperation with the author and the film crews—in particular, access to precinct stations—would receive five percent of the film's profits, a very liberal cut indeed. Especially vital was the cooperation of Mobilization for Youth, a new city agency that was placing young street workers among the gangs in an attempt to lead them back to civilization. I had turned down many far more lucrative film offers in the past, but this challenge excited me, and I accepted a few thousand dollars as a fee, plus a percentage of the profits should there ever be any.

After months in the streets I had come up with a broad outline that was heartily approved by, among others, the Catholic Welfare Agency, whose longtime involvement with the poor youth of the city had given its leadership a grounding in the perplexities of the gang phenomenon. But the project was not to be: Mrs. Scotti, the HUAC investigator, had quietly shown up in New York to warn the

city administration that only embarrassment awaited any association with me because sooner or later I was going to be destroyed.
But she made the nearly fatal mistake of contacting the head of
Mobilization for Youth, whose name and background alone assured
her of his political sympathies. James McCarthy, although a
thoroughly Irish Notre Dame graduate, detested his namesake's
assaults on democracy and was a firsthand witness of my rather
hard-won views on delinquency, which he enthusiastically shared.

I was subjected to a political means test in a session with the
nominal board of Mobilization, which had never before met. It
consisted of the chiefs of every city department, including Sanita-
tion, none of whom had the slightest acquaintance with social
work. They were now called upon to question me and to vote on
whether I should be allowed to write this screenplay. Ever optimistic, if not quixotic, I had the sense as we assembled in a large City
Hall room that most of them were somewhat embarrassed by being
forced into the position of adjudicating a case in which they had
no claim to the slightest competence. But one woman, looking
distraught and undernourished and literally wearing tennis shoes,
shrieked that Arthur Miller had killed our boys in Korea and kept
fingering a four-inch-thick folder filled, she said, with the government's record of my treason—no doubt Mrs. Scotti's contribution
to world knowledge. In my turn, I said that I thought my qualifications to write such a film were demonstrated by my work and that
I was not going to discuss my political opinions in order to gain a
right with which I had been born. The board made its decision in
private, and I lost by one mere vote, a happy and even invigorating
surprise at that moment in history. Such were the times.

So there was a certain halo of imminent catastrophe, a super-
charged ozone of jeopardy around our hours in the Waldorf, but
not only because of my situation. Marilyn was absenting herself
from Hollywood in an all but acknowledged strike until her business partner, the photographer Milton Greene, could renegotiate
her Twentieth Century Fox contract so she could periodically
make independent pictures with her own new company, Marilyn
Monroe Productions. Her hopes were immense for this arrangement, which promised both decent roles and personal dignity.
Naturally, the then powerful movie columnists were taking shots
at Marilyn, the non-actor floozy, for the preposterous chutzpah of
making artistic demands on so great and noble a corporation as
Twentieth Century Fox.

She was also beginning to sit in on Lee Strasberg's classes at the

Actors Studio, not daring as yet to open her mouth, awed as she was by Strasberg's weighty authority and the entire atmosphere of New York actor talk, which, in contrast to Hollywood preoccupations, probed the slippery concerns of the actor's art rather than the shapes of noses or breasts. I knew little of Strasberg beyond a nod and a handshake and the pervasive tales of his terrible temper in the Group Theatre—he was said once to have thrown an actor off the stage. Actors I respected, including my sister, Joan, revered him, although Monty Clift, a most astute analyst of acting and its problems, thought him a charlatan. Marilyn's dealings with Strasberg were her own business, I felt, especially at this early stage of our relationship, and if she slipped into hushed reverence when uttering his name, I figured she needed that kind of faith after years in the cynical Hollywood jungle. Idealization might lead to disillusionment, but without ideals there is no life. It was not yet clear to me that I, too, was being idealized beyond all human weakness.

She was a whirling light to me then, all paradox and enticing mystery, street-tough one moment, then lifted by a lyrical and poetic sensitivity that few retain past early adolescence. Sometimes she seemed to see all men as boys, children with immediate needs that it was her place in nature to fulfill; meanwhile her adult self stood aside observing the game. Men were their need, imperious and somehow sacred. She might tell about being held down at a party by two of the guests in a rape attempt from which she said she had escaped, but the truth of the account was far less important than its strange remoteness from her personally. And ultimately something nearly godlike would emerge from this depersonalization. She was at this point incapable of condemning or even of judging people who had damaged her, and to be with her was to be accepted, like moving out into a kind of sanctifying light from a life where suspicion was common sense. She had no common sense, but what she did have was something holier, a long-reaching vision of which she herself was only fitfully aware: humans were all need, all wound. What she wanted most was not to judge but to win recognition from a sentimentally cruel profession, and from men blinded to her humanity by her perfect beauty. She was part queen, part waif, sometimes on her knees before her own body and sometimes despairing because of it—"Oh, there's lots of beautiful girls," she would say to some expression of awed amazement, as though her beauty betrayed her quest for a more enduring acceptance. For myself it was beyond rationalizing; I was in a swift current, there was no stopping or handhold, she was finally all that was true. What I did not know about her life was easy to guess, and I suppose I felt the pain of her memories even more because I did not have her compensating small pride at having survived such a life.

It was an ironical summer packed with powerful images that I would never forget. Many mornings I spent with Marty and Bloomgarden planning the new production and meeting actors for the remaining parts, or in Boris and Lisa Aronson's Central Park West apartment studying his endlessly revised set designs for the two plays, my soul only half there, but still exhilarated with life and at the same time ridden by guilt, a spinning whirl in my head, a drunkenness with the blasted, limitless beauty of existence. In the late afternoons I would be out in Brooklyn, in the Bay Ridge hotbox where I had attached myself to Vincent Riccio, who was teaching me how to maneuver in an area exploding with some of the worst violence in the city. The summer nights were the best for war, and the mindlessness of it all somehow reflected my own humbled pretensions to an ordered life.

The part of Bay Ridge where Riccio was based was a white slum made up of Irish, Italians, and some families of German and Norwegian background, and the houses did not look bad from the street. The vast black ghetto of Bedford-Stuyvesant was not far away, but race conflicts were not the problem. Occasionally, in fact, black boys would take long subway rides to join in a white rumble, just to see some action when things got too quiet back home. Of course, all-black gangs were warring with each other no less than the whites were, and for no better reasons. The strife was so bewildering partly because it seemed utterly profitless; a tall, good-looking black eighteen-year-old, a physician's son from the Bronx, who had traveled all the way to Bay Ridge to join a fight, simply shrugged when I asked him why and gave me an opaque look edged with contempt for my powerlessness to penetrate his mind. They drew a certain perverse sense of dignity from the very purposelessness of their wars, a gallant kicking over of society's tables of loss and gain. The spirit's logic was the mind's irrationality.

With Riccio my guide, it was not hard to map what from the outside seemed a sealed-off jungle. Fairly soon it was obvious that tribal organizations with boys instead of adults at their head were being substituted for weak or absent fathers. These youths had reverted to an age of chivalry whose misread pennants fluttered in their confused heads. But they were not without pathos. The gang had its president, treasurer, secretary of war—a government in miniature, but one based on respect, especially for their leaders, rather than on any material motive. In America they believed in nothing, in the gang they doubted nothing. Guys might suddenly decide to go over to Fulton Street to rob some passerby on the street, but they went as individuals, not as gang members, and did not look for gang support in these forays. As gang members they were a shadow military who saw themselves fighting for something like honor and the sublime spoils of victory. The problem, it soon seemed to me, was that in trying to suppress these gangs society had assumed that gain was the only real motive for human action, while the gang, albeit in a distorted and desperate way, considered itself useful to the community. The gang members longed for pride; money was something each would try to get on his own time. Like all idealisms, theirs made it difficult to figure out what they really wanted and what would satisfy that want.

A former slum kid himself, the youngest of twenty-one brothers and sisters brought up in respectable poverty, Riccio understood this. In his mid-twenties, he was a graduate of St. John's, a subway university, had no advanced degrees or prospect of earning any, and at least in his own mind was in a demeaning conflict with the more intellectually sophisticated leadership of Mobilization for Youth, which was administering this infiltration program. He had boxed as a lightweight in the navy—"where I won my dentures," as he put it—and his handy combination punches more than anything else had won him respect among the boys. His approach was theoretically simple: "They've got no fathers, so I'm the role model, so they keep testing me for the soft spot where I cave in to their threats or join in some gang bang. They'd like me to turn phony on them, and at the same time they secretly hope I don't; it's like you'd like to be good without you have to stop being bad." And so there was a keen tension between their incipient cynicism toward him and a touching hope for their own salvation through his example and help.

Riccio had a very fine line to walk between his roles as society's representative and the boys' trusted ally. The police had never really accepted Mobilization's demand that its street workers not be required to divulge knowledge of a crime, although there had been an agreement on that touchy point. In effect, the police wanted the street workers to act as informers, something that clearly would crush the boys' confidence in them. Some individual cops understood and respected this confidentiality, but most resented it; it gradually eroded, and for this among other reasons the program was eventually undermined.

A tide was turning in 1955, and one felt it even then: for one thing, it was the first time narcotics were noticed in the neighborhoods, though I thought this only symptomatic of a wider but impossible-to-define disorientation that far transcended the gangs. One evening at dinner with Jim McCarthy and Mobilization's chief theoretician, Richard Cloward of the Columbia University School of Social Work, the question arose as to how this generation of youth differed from our own of the thirties. We were sitting in a spaghetti joint on the Lower East Side next to a housing project where a particularly destructive outbreak was taking place. Fires were being set in hallways, elevators sabotaged, windows smashed, feces strewn on stairways. But relatively few attacks were directed at people. The police were overwhelmed and had asked McCarthy to come in and make suggestions, since he by now had had some publicity as Mayor Wagner's troubleshooter on youth problems.

Tall, overweight, and cheerful, now and then wearing a baseball cap when he approached the gangs, McCarthy was quick to laugh, but his rather innocent Irish eyes never lost their seriousness; during a conversation, he would keep nodding and saying, "Right, right." He thought there was some connection between the vandalism and events of the past few months in the project. A tenants' union had been organized, with committees that were put in charge of keeping order on each floor, the members visiting families whose kids were troublemakers and generally acting as adjudicators of disputes between one apartment and another. It had been working very well until the district's state assemblyman launched an investigation of the union as a Red front and within a short time managed to disband it, scaring off the membership. The political organization of the buildings, Jim theorized, had lifted the morale and sense of responsibility of the tenants, many of them menial workers and some periodically unemployed. Of course it was understood among us at the table that Mobilization, a city agency, could hardly come to the defense of the tenants' union, which indeed might be a left-led organization, even if in this instance it had done socially useful work. What, we wondered, could substitute for it? The Democratic and Republican parties were hardly about to organize tenants' committees in housing projects; it wasn't their style. In a word, this particular outbreak, and perhaps some others, could be traced to the frustration of self-expression.

The depoliticalization of the project led to the broader question of what social ideals would be moving people in the immediate future, for the fifties were baffling, a time, at least so far, without a dominant accent or form. The three of us had grown up during the Depression, when it had been all but impossible to think of one's individual fate apart from that of society. The rise of this obscure tenants' union seemed like a throwback to a perfectly normal and ordinary reaction, thirties-style, of a community of people caught in a common problem—namely, to deal with it by mutual action and responsibility. It might well be that Communists were behind this union, but if collective action itself was to be forbidden, then collective responsibility would obviously have no community support, and things would inevitably end with every man for himself and desperate phone calls to the overwhelmed or indifferent police.

We sensed that we were at the edge of a gulf that would have to be crossed. "If common action of this kind is out, how are people going to visualize their evolution?" I asked Cloward in particular, since he was more the theoretician than McCarthy or I.

"The question is going to be lifestyle," he replied.

I had never heard the expression before. "What's that mean?"

"There will be competing styles of life, symbolic and essentially meaningless differences in clothing, speech patterns, tastes in food, cars, and so forth. The class struggle is over for now, and maybe even the conception of rank-and-file organizing. People are less and less interested in common action, which even now is getting to seem strange and kind of pointless. Identification will be more and more in terms of style—the self-image will be politically neutralized that way. It's going to be style-conscious, not class-conscious."

It seemed an empty idea to me, but it returned to mind early one evening in July when I saw Billy, a boy I knew, slumped in a Bay Ridge doorway, unconscious. He was one of six children of a longshoreman, Tommy Flaherty, a small man who lived with his family above a bar and who loved to stand out on the sidewalk and challenge anyone who showed up to a footrace around the block. He never lost, even against young guys. His fast feet were his pride. More than once I saw Billy and his older brothers forcing their father upstairs against his will because his childishness was an embarrassment to them, and for the sake of their mother, a startlingly lovely and dignified woman now nursing her sixth infant. They were a handsome family, blue-eyed and flaxen-haired, the boys tall and straight, and Margaret, the mother, a proud woman still in her early forties. Billy was the apple of her eye, the one who had never stolen and never been arrested and seemed destined, with his delicate hands and fine features, for something like his uncle Raymond's career as a successful stockbroker on Wall Street, whose clean towers across the bay could be seen beyond the end of the street.

To me, as to his friends, Billy's behavior during the past weeks had begun to seem weird; he had become furtive, with an absent look, and no one could understand his sudden transformation. Then he began disappearing when the gang went to war, and it was finally realized that drugs—once they had learned he was on a drug—made a guy useless to them. Beer was something else, it unshackled you sometimes, but heroin encased a man within himself. Of course it wasn't a question of their disapproving of narcotics but a matter of the practical loss of a good fighter. Narcotics menaced even their subculture with its ultimate privatism, and they consciously understood the threat quite soon. My memory of this in the sixties made it seem untrue and absurd when the new revolutionaries began touting drugs as a challenge to society and a pathway toward liberation.

Billy died of an overdose, the result either of poor information or of despair, but hardly of protest, I thought; it was an end still so novel that it did indeed seem arbitrary. Its fundamental pointlessness, the unredeemed waste, connected with Cloward's speculation about "lifestyle," how accurately I could not yet fully understand. At Billy's wake, in the family's small apartment above the bar, his beautiful mother sat with her youngest infant on her lap, staring into space with a fixed dead smile and neither bitterness nor anger in her eyes, for she was beyond those feelings. The sons, all in their best clothes, sat sighing with boredom but protective of their mother, while their father, his performer's instinct fired up as he faced the little crowd of a dozen or so mourners, went around showing off a new tie he had bought for the occasion. He leaned over me, stroking it. "Like the tie, Art?" His ineptitude clouded his sons' faces with hopeless pain. In his open coffin Billy looked his old surprised self, with skin too fair to bury and a face hardly marked by his eighteen years. I would not have been able to believe then that he was only the first victim of a scourge.

After three or four weeks in the streets with the gangs, I became cautiously optimistic about being able to write a film script. For one thing, I loved their mangled English. One burly Italian boy, nicknamed Mungy, had a sweet nature and masturbated incessantly. He was happy to show his immense penis to anyone who asked, like a valuable gift that some stranger had unaccountably handed him on the subway. That spring, along with some thirty other boys, he had been bussed up to a YMCA camp near Peekskill—their first time out in the country. Here, where they were immeasurably safer than down in the neighborhood, they were frightened of being alone and insisted on sleeping several to a cot. Mungy alone seemed content, as though his penis were company enough, wandering off by himself to peer up at a bird in a tree or lose himself staring at the running brook. There he captured a large painted turtle and tied a string around its neck, waiting patiently for it to move and taking a few steps at a time beside it as if it were a dog on a leash. Looking up at me, he said, "I'm commutin' with nature."

The YMCA camp was normally closed so early in spring but had been especially opened for the gang's weekend at a time when no other children would be there, the management having been apprised of the boys' reputation. Gang boys in Harlem in the twenties had usually been pretty good athletes, and I expected the same now, but when these boys managed to hit a ball they were breathless by the time they got to first base and had to lie down. In the lake they floundered about, none daring to go out over his head, and they refused to play the outfield except in a mob of half a dozen at a time, afraid of derision should they miss a fly ball. They would protectively conceal whoever missed the catch, even here moving together like a gaggle of geese.

A busload of girls from some middle-class Manhattan school showed up unexpectedly, and the camp manager quickly summoned Riccio to tell him to get the gang on its bus and out as fast as possible. But Riccio guaranteed him peace and tranquility, which I thought was distinctly in danger when the girls suddenly appeared around the swimming pool, bursting out of their skintight swimsuits. Rape was one of the occasional sports the gang indulged in, and I glanced around for signs of trouble. The gang had magically disappeared, and the pool was entirely given over to this female visitation. Imagining a council of war going on, I went off looking for the boys. Only a few yards into the surrounding shrubbery, I found them crouching like a band of frightened aborigines on an uncharted island peering out through the foliage at incredible invading creatures. I had never seen them so serious, so awed, as when a girl made a high arching dive from the board, followed by others slanting into the water in racing form and speeding up and down the length of the pool. Here were two civilizations, divided between those who could breathe and those who could barely do so, between the fed and trained and the deprived and ashamed.

From life on the streets to Marilyn high in the Waldorf Tower was a cosmic leap, but not such a discontinuity as it would seem. Of course it was strange for me to see boys in the Bay Ridge candy store staring hungrily at some photo of her in today's *News* when I knew that I would be telling her about it in a few hours, but she was no stranger in spirit to what was happening down below. Movie stars' salaries were beginning to take off now, but hers was fixed by an old contract, and she had the resentment of a revolutionary. In her long fight with Fox for the freedom to make her own films, she positioned herself against the studio's exploitation of her popularity, which had been soaring over the past couple of years. What she thirsted for was not so different from what the gang boys so ineffectually plotted and fought to win, a sense of self-respect in a world that called them zeros. She could hardly find a sentence in any piece about her, even those written in praise, that was not condescending at best, and the majority seemed to have been written by slavering imbeciles who liked to pretend that her witty sexuality marked her as little better than a whore, and a dumb one at that.

Now that I knew her somewhat better, I began to see the world as she did, and the view was new and dangerous. We were still a decade and a half away from the end of the sixties, and America was still a virgin, still denying her illicit dreams, still living up to some standard image of the pure and the real. When a calendar of nude color photos of Marilyn was discovered, the studio went berserk, spinning off one plan after another to squelch it, even frantically pressuring her to deny that it was she who had posed for the pictures. Instead, she calmly confirmed that she had needed the money and that that amazing body was indeed hers, her most precious possession, in fact. Though the hurricane quickly receded and she was even admired for not running for cover, she knew down deep that hypocrisy was the order of the hour and that she had not ceased being its target.

Marilyn lived in the belief that she was precisely what had to be denied and covered up by the conventional world. She did not expect that to change. But when I began to know her she was just starting to attract the public's curiosity and sometimes its affection, and this made her tentatively imagine that she might somehow create a rooted, respectable life. She relied on the most ordinary layer of the audience, the working people, the guys in the bars, the housewives in the trailers bedeviled by unpaid bills, the high school kids mystified by explanations they could not understand, the ignorant and—as she saw them—tricked and manipulated masses. She wanted them to feel they'd gotten their money's worth when they saw a picture of hers.

"A character is defined," I once wrote in a notebook, "by the kinds of challenges he cannot walk away from. And by those he has walked away from that cause him remorse."

But what I had omitted out of inexperience was the overwhelming power of the past to overflow the dam of lifelong restraints so that choice itself floats off in the debris. In the Bay Ridge streets life had burst the last respect for rule in the gang boy's brutal revolt against such specious moral rationalizations as his school and parents had bothered to give him. At the same time I was groping day by day toward a similar romantic vision of a more authentic life, one that would welcome its own evolution rather than trying to deny it. I had become estranged from my own past, which now seemed a parade of impersonations. And I was helplessly aware of moving in parallel to a breakdown around me of old credos and restrictions, all somehow connected to the wild thrashings of the untamable rogue force of paranoia in the political life of the country. The rules had been revoked, the ropes around the ring cut, and the fight had spilled out into the crowd itself. Such was my sense of life then.

One night on an abandoned pier from which the Wall Street skyline could be seen, two gangs assembled for a new kind of battle that Riccio had invented. A war had been brewing between the gangs, insults had been exchanged, satisfaction refused, and Riccio had convinced the leaderships (replicating the knightly jousts of individual horsemen, a tradition he knew nothing about) that each side should elect a champion to represent it and stage a "fair fight." Weeks of negotiation followed, culminating in this night, when some fifty guys, ages twelve to eighteen, congregated on the splintered pier. There were to be no weapons, only fists and feet. Few could box well; they were street fighters who always handled weapons, chains or knives or sometimes a bag of steel bearings.

There was no moon, and it was hot even beside the river. A few freighters lay out in the roads, and from one of them a Puerto Rican radio commercial could be heard floating across the water. "This music I heard across the water," I thought, incorrectly recalling a lovely line so separate from this ugly time. Kenny Costello—a thin boy of sixteen with an uncontrolled temper, already an ex-jailbird, and a fair player of the guitar, an instrument he had taken up after stealing it from a Fulton Street pawnshop—came dancing from among his cohorts in the lights of a police cruiser that obligingly appeared just as he and his opponent, a much heavier, clumsy Italian boy whose name I never got, faced each other with Riccio between them as referee. Costello broke open a bees' nest of short sharp jabs that sent the larger guy falling backwards, and the fight was finished in a minute, no more. The relief was almost wide open on all sides that something had been settled, no one quite knew what. Riccio made a charming speech beginning with "Listen, fellas, I gotta say this—you make me proud," praising all of them for inventing a world-shattering new way of settling disputes. Calling the leaders together to shake their hands and congratulate them for their wisdom in safeguarding the honor of their troops, he shortcut any smoldering objections of the frustrated young brawlers by promising both gangs nothing less than a city-paid-for mass bus ride to Coney Island the following evening, with a free hotdog and a soda for each guy, and maybe more if there was money left over.

I caught a glimpse of the two cops in the cruiser as it turned and majestically moved away into the darkness. They were not amused by Riccio's display of an authority that had always been exclusively theirs. They had been accustomed to prowling the neighborhood and, on finding a clot of boys on a corner, getting out and batting them around for a few sporting minutes to "disperse an unruly crowd."

It was about then that strange men began appearing on those same corners, unmolested by the police, men who would take a curious boy into an alleyway and make him a present of some powder he might want to try. What was in those glassine bags would make this time of the gangs seem like high good health, the last period of dignity that many such neighborhoods would ever know.

They were boys nobody wanted, that much was as clear to them as to any observer. They were excess, and in the bars after they got out of jail they would pridefully unfold their newspaper clippings, accounts of their arrests and trials, which they carried around carefully folded in an envelope, like actors with their notices. Everything was publicity; if your name was in the paper you existed, and your photo on top of that was immortality—you had made it out of this throttling anonymity, this nothing.

Since I was married and Marilyn could hardly peek out of her hotel room door without being photographed, we spent much time alone together, drawn into far lengthier talks than if we had been able to move freely amid the usual distractions. The bond of shared silences, as mysterious as sexuality and as hard to break, also began to form. Looking out over the sparkling city at night, we were each, I think, finding the presence of the other difficult to tear away from dream. Our connection seemed about to vanish, it was obviously a wrong fit, as though we had come out of two climates that could not correspond. But beneath the clash of dissimilarities there seemed a dark carpet of wordless being on which we could walk at our ease together. In each stood an image that could not yet be turned and seen full face but only obscurely, from an angle that drew us on, at first with curiosity, and gradually with the hope of being transformed by our opposite, as light longs for dark and dark for light. Many years later in the temples of Angkor Wat in Cambodia, the relief sculptures of full-bodied crowned goddesses, with their stone stares and their faint but confident world-containing smiles, would bring back to me the silent tumult of those evenings, when the nowness of life seemed alive around us and there was no future and no past.

After one of those silences I said, "You're the saddest girl I've ever met."

She first thought this a defeat; men, she had said once, only wanted happy girls. But then a smile touched her lips as she discovered the compliment I had intended. "You're the only one who ever said that to me."

We were confirming new roles for each other as people do in love, renewing the world as we saw each thing freshly, like people reborn. From those windows the whole city below seemed recently constructed from someone's dream. In the streets I had come to feel a strange new tenderness toward others, reminding me of the births of my own children, when I had brought them home from the hospital driving the car with anxious care in traffic that suddenly seemed dangerously heedless.

My mind kept discarding her and then rushing to bring her

back—fleeing the brutalized woman I now knew was in her and returning again to the child.

They were often inseparably mixed. "I never intended to make all that much about being an orphan. It's just that Ben Hecht was hired to write this story about me, and he said, 'Okay, sit down and try to think up something interesting about yourself.' Well, I was boring, and I thought maybe I'd tell him about them putting me in the orphanage, and he said that was great and wrote it, and that became the main thing suddenly."

Of course she had not been an orphan, not really, not with a mother and maybe even a father somewhere, like lots of other kids who were never called orphans. But they had parked her in an orphanage when her mother was institutionalized and there was no other place she could stay. Gradually her orphanhood had taken hold as a fact that Hecht confirmed in his story. Actually, the real shock had come when on approaching the orphanage she realized what it was and dug in her heels and yelled, "But I'm not an orphan! I'm not an orphan!"—the terror of being denied by her own mother and given to strangers. As the years passed and I saw her continuing need for unstable older women, whose exploitation of her found some perverse pleasure center deep inside, it seemed one more inevitable stone in the wall of her monument. But that was not yet.

To me now she bore the news of the grungy, Byzantine demiworld of southern California, from whose sunny and rotting moonscape she had fled. During our rehearsals of A View from the Bridge—held like Salesman's in the dust-filled and collapsing New Amsterdam roof theatre on Forty-second Street—I passed a lifesize cutout of her in the lobby every day, the famous laughing shot from The Seven Year Itch, in a white dress with her skirt blowing up over a subway grate, whereupon I would sit for six hours as Van Heflin–Eddie Carbone struggled with a compulsion he could not nail and destroy. How to get up on the stage and describe to Van the sensation of being swept away, of inviting the will's oblivion and dreading it? For that was what the production lacked, and perhaps the play too at that stage of its writing. How could one walk toward the very thing one was fleeing from?

I could not understand how she had come to symbolize a kind of authenticity; perhaps it was simply that when the sight of her made men disloyal and women angry with envy, the ordinary compromises of living seemed to trumpet their fraudulence and her very body was a white beam of truth. She knew she could roll into a party like a grenade and wreck complacent couples with a smile, and she enjoyed this power, but it also brought back the old sinister news that nothing whatsoever could last. And this very power of hers would eat at her one day, but not yet, not now.

It was impossible to guess what she wanted for herself when she herself had no idea beyond the peaceful completion of each day. When she appeared the future vanished; she seemed without expectations, and this was like freedom. At the same time the mystery put its own burden on us, the burden of the unknown.

One evening as we sat staring down at the city, she said, apropos of nothing in particular, that when she was fourteen or fifteen her elderly "aunt" Ana, a Christian Scientist who was the one intelligent and kind woman she had known, took ill and died; loving her, Ana had been for a while an impromptu guardian, and Marilyn had come to rely on her. She had not been living with Ana for some time, but the shock of her death was terrible. "I went and lay down in her bed the day after she died . . . just lay there for a couple of hours on her pillow. Then I went to the cemetery and these men were digging a grave and they had a ladder into it, and I asked if I could get down there and they said sure, and I went down and lay on the ground and looked up at the sky from there. It's quite a view, and the ground is cold under your back. The men started to try to fool around, but I climbed out before they could catch me. But they were nice and kidded me. And then I went away."

Oddly enough, she seemed not to know fear as she went about rearranging her life; it was when she tried to assert herself and act that the terrors she was born to had to be downed. Strasberg had suggested she study the part of Anna in O'Neill's *Anna Christie,* and one evening she tried a few pages out on me. Here was the first inkling of her inner life; she could hardly read audibly at first, it was more like praying than acting. "I can't believe I'm doing this," she suddenly said, laughing. Her past would not leave her even for this private affirmation of her value, and that past was murderous. Something like guilt seemed to suppress her voice.

It was not merely her mother's malign influence—the woman had always been paranoid, an institutionalized schizophrenic who had tried to smother her in her crib as an infant; it was also the condemnation of religion that she had had to defend herself against. And the stain kept reappearing like a curse.

She was only five or six years old when the fundamentalist church to which her foster family belonged held a vast open-air service in which hundreds of children, all dressed alike, the girls in white dresses and the boys in blue trousers and white shirts, stood ranged against the sides of a tremendous natural amphitheatre somewhere in the mountains in the Los Angeles area. Each girl had a cape, red on one side and white on the other, and at the start they wore the red side out. On signal during a revivalist hymn they were all to turn their capes inside out, from sinful red to the pure white of the saved. Magically the mountainside turned white on the proper verse of the hymn, all except one red dot in the middle of the expanse. She would laugh with affection for the little girl, herself, caught there in the wrong. "I just clean forgot. It was all so interesting, everybody turning their capes inside out, and I was so glad that they all remembered to do it on cue that I just clean forgot to do mine!" And she bent over laughing, as though it had been yesterday rather than twenty-five years before. But she was beaten for her failure anyway, condemned by Jesus himself, she was told, and it was only one instance of God's irremediable dislike. "Jesus is supposed to be so forgiving, but they never mentioned that; he was basically out to smack you in the head if you did something wrong." Of course she could laugh about it, but something in the back of her eyes was not laughing even now.

Everything speeded up. In Boston the play seemed more moving than I had expected, but I still doubted we had found its voice. I reread the first act of *Hamlet* in my hotel room, and in the business of his seeming insanity I suddenly saw not madness but a silliness, the way one gets when a dilemma is at once obvious and absolutely insoluble; he must avenge his father, but at the same time he feels joy at the thought of taking his place. What can you do but laugh? He is sure everyone around him is lying even as he feels himself false too. He has no way of cleanly and loosely expressing affection without fear of betraying—what, he no longer even remembers. All he knows is that he is more truthful than anybody else, but once alone he knows his own duplicity. More and more estranged from my family, I nodded at his self-condemnation and resentment, his grinding hatred for his guilt, his repeated failure to step outside it.

Marty Ritt took me to the racetrack several afternoons and explained the dope sheets, which I couldn't begin to understand, and we won a few dollars. His mother had been a professional gambler. He could always come away at least a little ahead. I had never realized how light, almost toylike, racehorses are.

He was modest about directing, somewhat like Kazan in this,

totally the opposite of Jed and his bragging. Marty, I thought, saw the director as an essential force but basically an assistant to God rather than the Boss himself. The first job, he said, was to discover what the script was saying, not what it reminded you of. He had few cultural pretensions—too few, in fact, since he read considerably—and he did his work with his shoulders as much as his head; he feared making actors think too much at the expense of instinctively sniffing out the role and situation. Again, this was a lot like Kazan's approach. I thought it might have been their acting background that made them so earthy.

Thirty years later, Dustin Hoffman would say it—"You always win by the skin of your teeth"—but in that first production of *View* we were unable to make the ultimate demand on ourselves and tended to let "pretty good" stand. In 1965 Ulu Grosbard's off-Broadway production would magically catch this play's spirit, helped by a combination of good judgment in the casting and amazing luck. Two unknown young actors, Robert Duvall and Jon Voight, played Eddie and Rodolpho. I could not imagine how a type right off the Brooklyn piers like Duvall could give such a profound performance. Backstage afterwards, he introduced me to his parents, his father an admiral standing there in his stiff white uniform, and Duvall himself speaking perfectly cultivated English. There was also an adenoidal young assistant stage manager popping in and out whom Grosbard, incredibly, told me I should keep in mind to play Willy Loman in a few years. My estimate of Grosbard all but collapsed as, observing Dustin Hoffman's awkwardness and his big nose that never seemed to get unstuffed, I wondered how the poor fellow imagined himself a candidate for any kind of acting career. Grosbard, however, was looking not at Hoffman but at an actor, at a spirit, and this kind of naked skin-on-skin contact with essentials was what his production had in every role.

After the play had been running a while the actors noticed a man who kept showing up night after night in one of the front rows a few feet from the stage. He was always deeply moved and among the last of the audience to leave. One night an actor came down and talked to him. "I knew that family," he said, wiping his eyes. "They lived in the Bronx. The whole story is true, except the end was changed." How had it ended in real life? "The girl came in when Eddie was having his nap and stabbed him in the heart." Of course, I knew nothing of this Bronx family, but what an ending!

Marilyn came up to Boston for the day. No one recognized her in her heavy cable-knit sweater, a deep white knitted hat that came down over her forehead, a black-and-white-checked woolen skirt, and moccasins. At twenty-nine, she could have been a high school girl. Her sunglasses attracted a few glances on the street since the weather was so dark and overcast. We took a long walk, saw a new movie, *Marty,* in a neighborhood theatre, and ate in a diner where the waitress, mysteriously drawn to her, kept talking at her, instinctively smelling out something unique about her even in those unexceptional clothes.

A podiatrists' association, she said, wanted to take casts of her feet because they were so perfectly formed, and a dental school wanted one of her mouth and teeth, which were also flawless. Not without fear we sat looking at each other waiting for the future to come closer.

"I keep trying," I said, "to teach myself how to lose you, but I can't learn yet."

Her face filled with an unspoken anxiety. "Why must you lose me?" And she removed her glasses with a compassionate smile.

The waitress, a middle-aged woman with bleached hair, happened to pass our table just then and overheard Marilyn. Her mouth dropped open in recognition, and she turned fully to me with a mixture of amazement and resentment, perhaps even outrage, that I would be so stupid or cruel as to cause her idol the slightest unhappiness. In that second her proprietary sheltering of Marilyn, whom she knew only as an image, sprang forth. In a moment she was back with a piece of paper to be autographed.

As we walked back to the hotel, Marilyn sensed an amorphous weight on me. "What is it?"

"It's as though you belong to her." I left out the rest of it.

"It doesn't mean anything."

But on that empty sidewalk we were no longer alone.

SIX

Pyramid Lake, Nevada, was a piece of the moon in 1956, long before the marina, the hotdog stands, and the roar of outboards blasted away its uninhabited, enigmatic enchantment. It was a gray, salty lake miles long, surrounded by a Paiute Indian reservation, a forbidding but beautiful place occasionally favored by movie companies shooting scenes of weird monsters in outer space. I had come here to live out the six-week residency required for the otherwise easy Nevada divorce, the New York State law still requiring a finding of adultery. Saul Bellow, with whom I shared an editor, Pascal Covici of Viking Press, was in Nevada for the same reason, and Covici had asked his help in finding me a place to stay. Bellow had taken one of the two cottages facing the lake. I took the other. He was then working on his novel *Henderson the Rain King*. I was trying to make some personal contact with the terrain where I had landed after exploding my life.

Fittingly, this being Nevada, home of the rootless, the wanderers, and the misfits, the only phone between our cottages and Reno, some forty miles away, was in a lone booth standing beside the highway, a road traveled by perhaps three vehicles a day and none at night. Nearby were the empty cottages of an abandoned motel for people waiting out their divorces. Only its owners lived there now, a troubled couple, the man a fairly scrupulous horse breeder whose half-dozen thoroughbreds grazed untied along the lakeshore. He, his wife, or their hired man would drive over to summon one or the other of us to the phone booth for one of our rare calls from what had come to seem an increasingly remote United States.

Surrounding us was a range of low, iron-stained mountains per-petually changing their magenta colors through the unbroken si-lence of the days. Saul would sometimes spend half an hour up behind a hill a half-mile from the cottages emptying his lungs roaring at the stillness, an exercise in self-contact, I supposed, and the day's biggest event. He had already accumulated a library here large enough for a small college.

A mile across the lake an island—full of rattlers, we were told—could be seen as though it were a hundred yards away, so clear was the air. The Indians kept removing the federal warning signs from an area of quicksand at the shoreline, hoping to do in any Reno fishermen who might venture out too far in their hip boots, but visitors were rare and only a few were said to have been sucked under, their bodies sinking for miles into the gorge that the lake had filled, to rise periodically over months or years and sink again, borne by a clockwise current. Strange broad-mouthed fish lived in the lake, whiskery and forbidding, of an unevolved kind found only here, it was said, and in a lake in India. I had a vision of an Indian eagle flying the ocean and dropping one of its unique eggs here. Once a week we would drive to Reno in Saul's Chevrolet to buy groceries and get our laundry done. No car ever passed us during the forty-mile trip, and we overtook none. It was a fine place to think, if you dared, plenty of space in which to hope and privacy to despair. I had moved into the unknown, physically as well as spiritually, and the color of the unknown is darkness until it opens into the light.

But there were only glimmers so far. Divorce, I suppose, is to some degree an optimistic reaching for authenticity, a rebellion against waste. But we are mostly what we were, and the turtle stretching toward delicious buds on high does not lighten his cara-pace by his resolve. I had to wonder sometimes if I had managed to evade rather than to declare the reality of myself. Marilyn was shooting *Bus Stop,* directed by Joshua Logan, and in her scrawled notes to me she sounded harried too. The play had been a great hit, and the role seemed made for her. Despite her usual trepidation, she had looked forward to working with Logan, the respected director of a great many Broadway hits, among them *South Pacific* and *Mister Roberts.* That nothing I could say seemed to cheer her up was bewildering, although the promise of our coming new life, she said, made her look ahead with a kind of hope for herself that she had never felt before.

The motel owner woke me one night to tell me I was wanted on the phone. It was after eleven, well past Marilyn's bedtime while filming. The truck bumped along the sandy path to the phone booth, lit inside only by the greenish glow of the moon. Every star seemed to crowd the sky across the great Western vault. The air seeping in under the door of the booth was cold on my bare ankles.

Her voice, always light and breathy, was barely audible. "I can't do it, I can't work this way. Oh, Papa, I can't do it . . ." Jokingly at first, then as a habit, she had been calling me this, but there was no joking here; she was desperate and near weeping. She sounded strangely private, almost as though she were talking to herself, not even bothering with pronouns. "Says I did the scene with vulgarity. What is it, a registered nurse? Can't stand women, none of them can, they're afraid of women, the whole gang of them. Vulgar! Supposed to rip off my tail, this thing I have sticking out of my costume in the back, but angrily so it makes a mockery of me so I can *react,* instead of like just lifting it away I didn't even know he'd done it. So I said rip it off, be angry with me so I can make it real when I react, but they're afraid to act nasty because the audience might not approve, you see what I mean? I'm no trained actor, I can't pretend I'm doing something if I'm not. All I know is real! I can't do it if it's not real! And calls me vulgar because I said that! Hates me! Hates me!

"Supposed to run out into the rodeo and my shoe came off and I could see him start to call cut, but then he saw the crowd laughing and so happy so he let me run back and get my shoe and go on with the scene, but he was ready to cut if I hadn't of gone on! Because I knew the minute it happened it would be good, and it was, but he doesn't know!"

But all this was overlay, a swollen sea of grief heaved under it, and now she began to sound high and inspired. "I don't want this, I want to live quietly, I hate it, I don't want it anymore, I want to live quietly in the country and just be there when you need me. I can't fight for myself anymore . . ."

I asked if her partner, Milton Greene, couldn't help, and her voice went deeper into secrecy; he was there in the room with some other people. But he was afraid to stand up to Logan for her.

As such, her complaints about Logan—which smacked a bit of frantic actor talk—mattered less to me than a new terror I was hearing, an abandoned voice crying out to a deaf sky, and the dead miles between us choked me with frustration; whatever the truth about Logan, her sincerity was unquestionable, for she was dancing on the edge and the drop down was forever. This was the first time she had sounded so unguardedly terrified, and I felt the rush of her trust in me. She had concealed her dependency before, and I saw suddenly that I was all she had. I recalled her telling me months ago that she was putting off signing a contract that Greene and his lawyer had been pressing on her to set up her new company; it gave Greene fifty-one-percent control against her forty-nine. In return for his share he would bring in new recording and film projects that would not require her participation, but so far the new company's assets consisted only of her and her salary. She had not wanted to dwell on this, had tried to turn from the implicit betrayal, and even now as she reported her disappointment in Greene's failure to protect her from Logan, she seemed to shy from any open anger with him. For myself, I wished she could trust him; I had had only the minimum necessary interest even in my own business affairs, leaving most of the decisions to lawyers and accountants to keep myself free to work. I hardly knew Greene; it was faith itself I instinctively did not want to see her lose.

I kept trying to reassure her, but she seemed to be sinking where I could not reach, her voice growing fainter. I was losing her, she was slipping away out there, and with partner and friends so close by. "Oh, Papa, I can't make it, I can't make it!" Her suicide leaped up before me, an act I had never connected with her before. I tried to think of someone I knew in Hollywood who could go and see her, but there was no one, and suddenly I realized I was out of breath, a dizziness screwing into my head, my knees unlocking, and I felt myself sliding to the floor of the booth, the receiver slipping out of my hands. I came to in what was probably a few seconds, her voice still whispering out of the receiver over my head. After a moment I got up and talked her down to earth, and it was over; she would try not to let it get to her tomorrow, just do the job and get on with it. Lights were still revolving behind my eyes. We would marry and start a new and real life once this picture was done. "I don't want this anymore, Papa, I can't fight them alone, I want to live with you in the country and be a good wife, and if somebody wants me for a wonderful picture . . ." Yes and yes and yes and it was over, and the healing silence of the desert swept back and covered it all.

I left the highway behind me and walked toward the two cottages and the low moon. I had never fainted before. A weight had fallen and my lungs felt scored, as if I had been weeping for a long time. I felt healed, as though I had crossed over a division within me and onto a plane of peace where the parts of myself had joined. I loved her as though I had loved her all my life; her pain was mine.

My blood seemed to have spoken. The low lunar mountains outside my window, the overarching silence of this terrain of waste and immanence, the gloomy lake and its unchanging prehistoric fish swimming longingly toward India forever—I felt my happiness like a live glow in all this dead, unmoving space. I tried to recall a play about people who suffer but do not fail and saw suddenly the inexpressible happiness that tragedy reveals. Suddenly the hidden order, life's grin of continuity; as I had felt it tonight, as though her being had been maturing in me since my own birth. The anguish of this past year, the guilty parting with children and the wrenching up of roots, seemed now the necessary price for what might truly be waiting just ahead, a creative life with undivided soul. For the first time in months or maybe years, a fierce condensing power of mind moved in me, the signal to write, but only something as simple and as true as tonight. To be one thing, sexuality and mind, appetite and justice, one. All our theatre—my own of course included, but that of the masters too—seemed so paltry now beside the immensity of human possibilities. It had all been written by unhappy men—Ibsen, a paranoid with a lust for young women he could not dare acknowledge; Chekhov, fatally ill and all but abandoned by an unfaithful wife; Strindberg, in terror of castration. Where was the broad marble brow of the Greek vision, the sunlit wholeness of a healthy and generous confrontation with catastrophe? She, in her fogged, blundering search, was an unaware exemplar. She had accepted the role of outcast years ago, even flaunted it, first as a casualty of puritanical rejection but then with victorious disorder; from her refusal to wear bras to her laughing acknowledgment of the calendar photos, her bracing candor—so un-American especially now in the new empire preparing to lead the war-crippled West—was health, the strength of one who has abandoned the illusions of a properly ordered life for herself. With all her concealed pain, she was becoming enviable, the astonishing signal of liberation and its joys. Out of the muck, the flower. And soon, an amazing life . . .

Nevada was easy to define, hard to grasp. On the left of the highway to Reno a black tar-paper box about twenty feet square stood on stilts with a roughly made ladder descending from the middle of the floor and disappearing into a hole in the ground. A Cadillac, dusty but new, was parked nearby. The owner was a small man dressed in boots and jeans and a sweaty broad-brimmed hat, cheerful and friendly. When he needed a little cash he would descend the ladder from his living room and go down the hole into his silver mine. It was simple but hard to absorb, somehow. Especially when I learned that he kept a grand piano in his stilt house and played only chopsticks on it. None of this thought particularly noteworthy among Nevadans.

After a week or so out on the desert with two rodeo men whom I had met in Reno, hunters of wild mustangs in their off times, we came on an abandoned shack in the middle of nowhere, a shelter put up by some long-gone rancher and used now for a lie-down by anybody who happened by. The lone window had lost its panes, the door hung open on one hinge. Several hundred magazines lay strewn about. They were of two types, *Playboy* and its clones, and Western stories. In the corners the piles were a foot thick, indicating that hundreds of cowboys must have come by with their magazines over many years, to rest and read and dream. My two friends couldn't understand why I thought it strange that men who had lived on horseback for years looked to the movies for their models and could imagine no finer fate than to be picked up for a film role. The movie cowboy was the real one, they the imitations. The final triumph of art, at least this kind of art, was to make a man feel less reality in himself than in an image.

Four years later, one of these men showed up on location when we were shooting *The Misfits,* and after a good reminiscing talk, he watched from beside the camera as Clark Gable happened to be telling Marilyn some details of his character's past, which I had drawn from this cowboy's life. When the scene was finished he turned to me shaking his head, excited and pleased: "Sounds real as hell." But he clearly showed no sign of recognizing his own biography as the source, or even the possibility of such a metamorphosis. Nevada thus became a mirror to me, but one in which nothing was reflected but a vast sky.

Out on the desert, far from any vehicle track, there were sometimes signs of life underground: in the midst of sage and sand a pair of shorts hung on a stick to dry in the sun, or a T-shirt. My friends never ventured close, although they claimed to know some of these residents of holes in the ground. They were men wanted by the law, for murder more often than not. The state police knew they were out there, and nobody inquired why they were never picked up, but payoffs were inevitably suspected.

* * *

In Reno on our weekly shopping and laundry expeditions we saw the town differently than tourists do looking for fun; after a few weeks the tawdriness of the gambling enterprise grew depressing. Next to the supermarket checkout counter, women carrying babies would drop their change into waiting slot machines, but from the indifferent blankness of their faces they had no anticipation of winning. It was as joyless a routine gesture as discarding a Kleenex out a window, tired and blind and thoughtless. Just a lot of women in jeans and worn sneakers giving away money.

Toward dusk one night in a tiny town of some eight or ten houses on a single dogleg street, the two cowboys and I bought stringy steaks from a little grocery store at the edge of the desert. The grocer simply reached up to a side of beef hanging over his cash register and started cutting. We also bought a long spongy white bread and some salt, and went outside and built a fire of dried sagebrush and roasted the meat on sticks. The juices, spiked with sage, drenched the bread. Each of us must have eaten several pounds of beef, and it was one of the best meals I have ever had. The moon rose while we were digesting beside the fire, and the two men admired its appearance as though it were a woman, with those faint smiles that show a man is imagining something.

There was an occasional week when they did the rounds, servicing two or three women waiting in various beds in the area, but they almost always referred to them with respect. There was always a nice trickle of would-be divorcées flowing in from all the states, and the variety of their personalities fascinated my friends. Being divorced themselves, they sympathized with the difficulties of staying married. Under all that sky and amid those eternal mountains they understood weather and animals and each other, but the women were forever the mystery. The older of the two, Will Bingham, a rodeo roper in his early forties, had left a wife and a six-year-old daughter whom he occasionally stopped by to visit in a small town in the north of the state. He led a lone, self-sufficient life that he seemed to think inevitable if not ideal, but the guilt of having left his child was always with him. The sensitivity of some of these brawny Western men was somehow reassuring, something I did not recall reading about, except for hints of it in Frank Norris's forgotten masterpiece, *McTeague.*

* * *

I ran out of a few staples one day, and rather than make the long trip to Reno, I decided to try to locate the Indian store a few miles inside the reservation. I found it hidden in a valley several miles from the lake, a general store in front of a cluster of tilting cabins surrounded by rusting debris, the busted bikes, washing machines, and automobile shards of the other civilization. Beside the dirt road stood a lone gas pump. Inside the barren store a middle-aged Indian woman was just laying out a display of homemade moccasins in the food case next to the cheese, butter, and milk. I asked if I could buy some milk and bread and butter, and she was setting out my purchases with her dark peasant's hands when a heavy-bellied middle-aged Indian with a worn Stetson tilted back on his head came out of the back room and asked if I was being taken care of. As soon as I answered, his eyebrows went up. "What part of Brooklyn you from?" he asked with a happy grin. He had lived for twenty years on Atlantic Avenue, worked on the George Washington and other New York bridges as a high-altitude painter, saved his money, and come back to buy this store. But he felt strangely out of place now and was restless. "These people are very discouraged. They gave up trying to improve themselves," he confided disappointedly once we were outside and I was getting back into the car.

I asked him his name as we were saying goodbye.

"Moe."

"That's not an Indian name, is it?"

"No, but nobody can pronounce my Indian name, so everybody in Brooklyn start calling me Moe, so now this is Moe's Store. I'm going to put up a sign."

I saw through the rearview mirror as I slowly drove away that the woman had come out of the store and he was pointing down the dirt track at me, another man from Brooklyn. He looked animated but probably went back inside regretting having left the excitements of Atlantic Avenue. There was a kind of universal homelessness in Nevada that was somehow beautiful, maybe because it tended to impart an air of inquisitive longing to the people, rather than the smugness usually found in quiet places. I wished I could write about it.

Once a week I would fly into Los Angeles, a technical illegality since my period of residence in Nevada had to be unbroken, but the risk seemed negligible when the whole business was a fantasy of formality anyway, patently devised to draw divorce-hungry visitors to the state and fees to the lawyers.

Marilyn's tension concerning *Bus Stop* was relentless, but she seemed to be growing less hostile to Logan, slightly more willing to see the possibility of being good in the film. Selfishly, I could not imagine her being anything but fantastic on film and thought her worries exaggerated. Her coach, Lee Strasberg's wife, Paula, had the next room in the Chateau Marmont and was acting as Lee's proxy, with daily phone calls to him in New York on Marilyn's problems.

I tended to find Paula comical, if vaguely threatening around the edges, a Molièrian character who apparently believed that whether an actor had sat in on one or two of Lee's classes out of curiosity or had committed himself over a training period of years, he somehow belonged to the Strasbergs as a Cambridge man belongs forever to his college. "Our people are now all over the world," she told me one day, mentioning actors filming in various countries, some of whom I happened to know had spent the briefest of moments at the Studio. She once even referred to the famous film dress designer Jean Louis as "one of our best designers," suggesting the possibility that he had learned the needle trade from Lee.

On one of my visits she grabbed me by the arm and said I had to sit down right now and listen to a tape of Lee's lecture on Eleonora Duse, which he had recently given on the anniversary of the legendary Italian actress's birth or death. Paula stood by, hands clasped together in divalike formality, chin raised, and a far-off look in her eye as Lee's voice came through the tape machine.

"Now, most people think that we revere Duse because she was a great actress," he began suspensefully. "But that is not why we revere her." A lengthy pause. Why, I began to wonder, *do* we revere Duse? "It is not that at all," he continued. "There are many great actresses, living and dead, American and foreign. Many who created spectacular theatrical images and stage life over the generations. Some are English, some Swedish, some German, Italian, Dutch, Spanish, French, men and women of every country and in all generations." My mind began to wander as I waited for him to say why we revere Duse. But the parenthesis continued, expanded, ran over in all directions, and the question itself began to fade into the background until I was able recall Duse as the principal subject only with the most muscular effort. The lecture went on for at least twenty minutes.

Marilyn sat there pathetically attentive, her reverent gaze

mixed with some mystification. How could I tell her that I was definitely wondering if her inspiring mentor did not harbor some disconcerting Willy Lomanism, a tendency to spitball, to improvise facts. But the dependency on him was far too profound for any such direct contradiction of his authority; if this crutch was kicked out now, she might fall. And who was I to make such a judgment when quite good actors of high intelligence had great faith in him? I could only sit there listening to the bubble he was inflating on tape and trying to keep from kidding Paula for holding her near salute while we were not told why we revere Duse. And since I was also being idealized at the time, uncomfortable as the unreality of it occasionally was, I said nothing, at least not yet. Anyway, I still imagined, just as Marilyn did, that I would not be involving myself with her career—unnecessary, we thought, what with Greene managing her business affairs while Lee helped to deepen her confidence as an actor. By now her relationship with Greene had been straightened out, their percentages in Marilyn Monroe Productions having been reversed to fifty-one for her and forty-nine for him, thus restoring her to control. Meanwhile, he would be generating new projects for the company in order to establish its separateness from her work, a necessity for the Internal Revenue Service if she was to begin, as she hoped, saving some of her income by paying corporate rather than individual taxes. For she had more doubts than belief that her popularity would last into the long future.

In the new company's first production Laurence Olivier was to direct and act with her in Terence Rattigan's *The Prince and the Showgirl,* a very light comedy based on his play *The Sleeping Prince.* Shooting was to begin in England shortly after we married in June. Happily, Binkie Beaumont, the most successful producer in the thriving if then mostly trivialized British theatre, had decided to do a new production of *A View from the Bridge* under Peter Brook's direction, to be rehearsed at the very same time. I was planning on expanding the one-act play to full length. My vision had been of each of us doing our own work side by side, drawing strength from one another, and it seemed to be coming true.

A packed New York press conference with Olivier standing beside her announced their collaboration, the most unlikely combination in movie history according to most commentators, he representing high art and she little more than near pornographic photogenia from the rear. Suddenly her gown's shoulder strap broke, sending up excited gasps at the prospect of further revelations. But she blithely asked if anyone had a safety pin instead of demurely blushing and fleeing from the platform. *Time,* characteristically, had no doubt the whole thing had been prearranged. It was then that she was asked if it was true she wanted to do *The Brothers Karamazov,* and if so, which part, a brilliant provocation that brought down the house, quite as though she were planning to wear a beard and play one of the brothers. She replied that she wanted to play Grushenka, adding, "She's a girl," and stopped there rather than openly suggest that a fair number of the reporters who were the loudest to laugh had probably been too busy going to journalism school to read the book. One of the geniuses in the room asked if she could spell "Grushenka," and of course Marilyn got the message; even with Sir Laurence crossing the Atlantic to stand beside her at a press conference she could not be accorded the simple dignity of a performer announcing a new project. Of course sex and seriousness could not exist in the same woman, and this American illness was not about to end, or so it seemed. The fact was that it was she who had originated the idea of working with Olivier, but not at all because it would give her a new public persona; her present one was quite good enough. It was the very preposterousness of the pairing that struck her as amusing and even possibly enlightening, given the right script. And if it led to some additional decency toward her in the press, all the better.

As the end of my Nevada residence period approached, I began to be anxious about the publicity our marriage would break over our heads, and realized one morning how much I had underestimated it when a camera truck appeared on the lake road in front of my cottage and a crew got out with an interviewer prepared to fire off a dozen questions about our plans. It had not yet dawned on me that one can become public property in the most literal sense under such circumstances. My only excuse as I look back is that I had probably seen a half-dozen television programs in my life—I didn't even own a set, and in 1956 a lot of people could still say the same. It was a painful business, but for more than the obvious intrusion; I quickly realized that something in me was proud of identification with Marilyn—and aware, too, that our seeming so ill assorted was part of what made us such news.

But I was sure the media would tire of us and latch onto something new in a few weeks. Early on the forty-second day of my residency I packed the few things I had brought in a valise, put my typewriter in its case, said goodbye to Saul, and at ten o'clock entered the Reno office of a lawyer, Edwin Hills, whom John Wharton had selected in far-off New York to shepherd my divorce through the courthouse routine. On the drive to Reno in the motel owner's pickup, I stared out at the bony hills that I was sure I would never see again and found a kind of remorse in myself for the lost silence I had come to depend on each morning when I woke, and their changing colors at dusk and dawn. Noise awaited me—was it all a mistake? I wiped out the thought, condemning my own vice of self-sufficiency.

The lawyer's large waiting room was reassuringly plain, without the usual pretensions. Its windows overlooked the Mapes Hotel across the street, its walls of low-grade imitation mahogany plywood buzzed in resonating complicity with the window air-conditioner. The inverted bottle on the water cooler was still full at this early hour. One man, a client, I assumed, sat on a shiny black plastic-covered couch staring into space and smoking. I had hardly set down my valise and typewriter when lawyer Hills hurried out of his inner office, asked me to wait for just a few minutes, and before I could get a proper look at his face, returned to his office and shut the door.

Over that door hung a steer's head bearing horns as thick as a flue pipe and spanning at least ten feet, the tips pointing downward toward my face. A couple of dozen plaques, diplomas, and citations covered one sector of wall. Mr. Hills had been honored not only by the American Legion, the Veterans of Foreign Wars, and the Catholic War Veterans, but also by the National Rifle Association and an organization of pistol fanciers, the Grange, the Rotarians, the Knights of Columbus, the Order of Fire Fighters, and the Sons of the White Rose; he had a Cutting Horse Breeders Commendation as well as personal letters of gratitude for patriotic services from Nevada's Senator Pat McCarran (co-sponsor, with the present chairman of HUAC, of the McCarran-Walter Act to keep "subversives" out of the country), Senator Joseph McCarthy, and Representative Richard M. Nixon, who had all been impressed by Mr. Hills's fervid defense of American values at various times and locations. I had come to exactly the right place for a quiet morning of divorce. It gave me a certain perverse happiness that a couple of the organizations that had honored my new lawyer had picketed plays of mine from time to time. But a desiccated irony by now was bread and wine, the daily diet of the American hour.

Taking a chair a dozen feet away from the lone other client, I wondered if Hills's air of preoccupation was perhaps a way of showing his patriotic distaste at having to represent me. On the other hand, John Wharton must surely have chosen him because he was a reliable technician in this sort of action, and he was probably just overworked. After all, he was also making the other client wait, and this guy was not from my side of the political tracks but had the look of a rich cowboy.

In fact, now that I studied him, he had a remarkable resemblance to John Wayne, with that same densely aggressive pout. In a dove gray Western outfit, he looked to be at least six foot six, and his muscles were thick as a cobra under the fine, pressed cloth of shirt and trousers. His boots cost at least five hundred dollars the pair, I figured, and the gray Stetson resting on the cushion beside him seemed to look at me without approval. Surprisingly, when our eyes happened to meet, I imagined I saw an agreeable softening there, but I could not drop my guard, not in this castle of blind nationalism.

Hills hurried in again and gestured toward me with one finger raised. We converged at a window overlooking a Reno street as empty as a dream street, roasting in the ferocious ninety-degree sunshine. He was clearly in a state of tension as we came together, a man in his sixties with a few strands of hair across his rosy scalp from a part on the left, wearing thick rimless lenses, a blue pin-striped suit, and a slim, shiny tie of some silvery material that he might have worn on horseback in a patriotic parade. His eyes looked up at me with the opaque innocence of an angelfish passing a swimmer's face mask. Gripping my elbow tightly between thumb and forefinger, he asked so intimately that I could barely hear, "Has he found you?"

"Who?"

"He hasn't found you?" he asked with a surge of hope.

"Who do you mean?"

Light kept flashing across his dense lenses as he tightened his fingers on my elbow. "An investigator from the House Un-American Committee has been here looking for you with a subpoena." He waited, motionless, watching me with slightly open mouth, floating beside me in the silent sea.

Anticlimax relaxed me, the arrival of fate at last, the raised axe finally falling.

"Is there anything to it?" he asked with touching naiveté.

The dove gray cowboy had turned his head toward us. The question had changed from getting divorced to getting lynched. "I can't imagine why they'd be after me now," I said, but broke off before a tangle of history he would never understand; the Committee had been on the wane for some time, and if they had not bothered me in years past when I had been far more politically noticeable, it seemed senseless now when I had trouble keeping interested in politics at all. I suppose that historically we were in the narrow trough between the grandiose anti-Communist domestic crusade and the next ennobling cause, the war in Vietnam that awaited us some seven years on.

"He said he'd be back later this morning; he knows you were due here today."

"Well, I guess there's nothing I can do about it."

"Do you want to accept the subpoena?"

"What do you mean?" I realized with some small shock that Hills regarded this country as so much his own that he need not necessarily accept all directives from its hand.

"Well, there's a back door to this building. You can stay inside in my office, and I'll get the judge to come over here instead of you having to show up in the courthouse. 'Cause I think this fellow is probably going to be waiting for you over there."

This unexpected conspiracy moved a flood of gratitude through me, and in a flash I realized that the framed citations on his wall were in fact testimonials to his thoroughly American anarchism, for which, over the past few years, I had developed a lot of respect as our last stand against fascist decorum.

But for the moment I had no resolve, and seeing that I was floundering, he said he had to make a phone call in his office and would be right back.

I stood staring out the window at the empty street below. My brain had died. Exhaustion suddenly drained my legs and I sat down, realizing too late that I had chosen a chair directly facing the dove gray cowboy. His jaws stood out like angle irons. Now he looked me in the eye. "I'm Carl Royce. I know who you are." Surprised, I said I was glad to meet him, and he leaned powerfully across the space between us and shook my hand. His calloused palm was hard enough to slap a nail through a board. For the first time I noticed a large American flag on an eagle-topped staff in the corner of the room, its colors menacing. In the silence I waited for the emptiness in my head to fill.

"What are you going to do about it?" His tone was dead neutral. I had to be careful.

"I haven't had a chance to think," I stalled. What did he want? Who was he?

"I hope you're not going to tell those bastards anything." We were beyond pleasantries now; he had wrath in his sky blue eye.

I supposed he could see my surprise. Still cautious, I hedged, since a confidence misplaced could have consequences. "I've always opposed the Committee."

"Do you know Dashiell Hammett?"

"Of course. Sure." What in God's name could a radical like Hammett have to do with John Wayne?

"He was my sergeant in the Aleutians; we lived in the same tent a couple of years. He taught me everything I know." I felt numbed. A few years earlier, Hammett had spent time in jail for refusing to give investigators the names of contributors to the bail fund of the Civil Rights Congress.

I had never been close to Hammett, if only because he so rarely spoke—a reticence I sometimes thought was a strategy of putting everyone else on the defensive before his raised-eyebrow silence. But he was rare, a man with a code whom one was bound to respect, and of course he had written wonderfully. For all his repute as an action man, I often used to wonder if he was not in reality painfully bottled up. Everything that was new in the postwar climate he seemed to greet with a supercilious grin, as though the past were just around the corner and the present not a serious matter. Like Lillian Hellman, his longtime companion, he was a putative aristocrat whatever his leveling convictions, and while affecting to denigrate the immature politics and personal derelictions of Hemingway and Fitzgerald, he plainly felt closer to them than to the left-wing writers. The twenties were still his frame of reference, with their happy deference to talent and the interesting rich, and what got a rise out of him more quickly than anything else was the present indifference to quality in human relations.

I began to feel light-headed as Royce joined the conspiracy too. "I'm only here for the day to buy cattle. My place is in Texas. I could fly you out of here in about an hour and a half; my plane and pilot are waiting at the airport. I have a couple of thousand acres, and one of the houses is empty, right in the middle of it. They'd never find you there. You can just wait this out down there till they get tired of it. In fact, Dash stayed in that same house when they were after him, but then he got foolish and left, and that's when they got him. He would never have gone to jail if he'd stayed there. You can stay as long as you like, maybe use the place to write something for a couple of months. You could just forget about them."

"I'm wondering if it'll seem like I'm trying to escape a subpoena. They could blow that up into something even bigger."

But Royce dismissed this as a mere detail—with his thousands of acres it seemed ridiculous to be concerned with what anyone thought of him. "I wouldn't worry about that; the main thing is not to let them get you. All it is is a publicity stunt for them anyway."

Hills came out of his office to tell Royce that he could go over to another law office down the street now to sign the cattle deal. We all walked to the outer door together. "It's a Cessna Barron, red with white wings, just ask for Royce's Cessna. The pilot is Bill Sisley. I'll call over to tell him you're coming. Think about it, and I hope you do it. I'll be out there in about an hour, hour and a half. Wait in the plane if you like, they won't touch you in there."

"You can leave by the back door," Hills added. "I have a car and driver parked behind the building. I'll tell him now that you might be coming, and he can drive you to the airport. I've got the judge coming over in about twenty minutes, so there won't be any need to go to court."

"I don't know," I muttered. Royce grabbed my hand, gave me a wonderful stare of encouragement, turned, and went out.

"Let me know," Hills said, and returned to his office.

I stood at the window again trying to think clearly. My disappearance would cause a tremendous sensation now that it was known that Marilyn and I were to be married sometime soon, and the brunt of it all would fall on her. A new, lurid chapter of her life, but this time with overtones of disloyalty. And there would be no chance to explain to my children. But the image of a lone house on a couple of thousand acres made me yearn for its peace. Perhaps there I could begin to write again . . .

I had to move my legs, I was all tightened up. I went out to the elevator and rang. I could see an open filigree cage rising to the gate before me. A man was in it. The gate opened, and he glanced at me and proceeded toward Hills's door. The words were out of my mouth before I could think.

"Are you looking for me?"

He turned and came back to me: a comfortable man of the suburbs in his late forties, almost my height, a stranger to agony in a checked linen sports jacket of pinkish hue, slacks, and a good snug haircut. I thought there was a look in his eye of surprised disadvantage at being taken unawares. Maybe this was why I had made the move when I could have gone down the elevator and out into Texas. I did not want to be running, I guess, from myself or anyone else, and I resented being afraid.

He took the pink onionskin subpoena out of his breast pocket and, while asking me if I was Miller, touched it to my lapels, technically serving me. I looked at the paper, seeing nothing. Now he relaxed and asked if I would join him for a cup of coffee, two ordinary citizens again. Out of curiosity I agreed, and we went down into the coffee shop on the ground floor of the Mapes across the street.

His name, William Wheeler, rang a bell; I had read about this diabolically clever investigator, who had had much success in bringing film people to see the light. I wanted to know what it felt like to be worked over by a talent like that. And it may also have been a thirst for reality in this dreamlike affair that made me want something more than a mere piece of paper as executioner.

After a few falsely relaxed preliminaries about the weather and Nevada's gambling-dominated society, of which he was amusingly disapproving, he said, "I'd like to talk this over. There's really no need to make this overly public."

I nodded, said nothing.

"By the way," he interjected awkwardly, as though he had only this moment thought of it, a not too persuasive bit of acting, "I'm a very close friend of Lee Cobb's. Do you ever see him?"

"No, but he lives in California, doesn't he?"

"Yes, but I just wondered. He thinks the world of you."

This, apparently, was one of his deft ploys to smoke out my attitude toward Lee, who had informed to the Committee three years earlier, an act for which I might denounce him now or with darkened brow refuse to discuss his treachery. But Lee, of course, was incidental; the real question on the table was how I would behave before the Committee, as pussycat or rattler, and it pleased me not to let on just yet. In fact, I could not help thinking of Lee, my first Willy Loman, as more a pathetic victim than a villain, a big blundering actor who simply wanted to act, had never put in for heroism, and was one of the best proofs I knew of the Committee's pointless brutality toward artists. Lee Cobb, as political as my foot, was simply one more dust speck swept up in the thirties idealization of the Soviets, which the Depression's disillusionment had brought on all over the West.

"What do you think of him as an actor?"

"Well, he certainly was my favorite Willy."

My praise seemed to surprise him; apparently he had expected moral indignation against an informer. I decided to match blandnesses and revealed, "In fact, I offered him the part of Eddie Carbone in *A View from the Bridge.* He was my first choice."

Wheeler's face showed a real confusion whose unconcealment lowered my estimate of his professional cool. Could this really be the subtle genius, the Svengali, who had turned so many actors and directors to his gods?

"I never knew about that," he said rather skeptically.

"Why don't you ask his agent?"

"An actual offer?"

"Oh, yes."

"You talked to him yourself?"

"No, Bloomgarden talked to his agent. You see," I added, "there was no doubt in my mind that Lee would have made the best Eddie Carbone I could imagine, and since I don't believe in blacklisting artists for their political opinions, even when I absolutely disagree with them, I told Bloomgarden to make the offer. Marty Ritt had no objection either," I put in, since he must have known about Ritt's low opinion of his old friend's having broken before the Committee.

Wheeler was silent, seemed unsure where to put his foot down next. "You're different than I expected," he finally said.

"You should check this with Lee's agent."

"He'd have been good in that part."

"Oh, yes. He wanted to do it, too. But the agent told Bloomgarden that Lee was afraid to act in one of my plays because the Legion would make it hot for him again." As I didn't need to remind Wheeler, *View* was, among other things, about a man who informed on his own relatives to the immigration authorities. Cynically or not, I had thought that under the circumstances Lee would bring the pain of the harried longshoreman onto the stage rather than some studied impersonation.

"Maybe you'd like to talk to me again," Wheeler said. "I could see you in New York or LA, either one."

"What I have to say I'll say to my lawyers."

"I see." He seemed to want to press on but gave it up quickly. "Well, okay." In short, I would get the full treatment from the Committee.

We got up from the table, and I gave him an unsmiling goodbye. He wandered off into the lobby, where even at this early hour the slot machines were thumping away. Ridiculously, I could not help wondering as he was swallowed up by the lobby crowd whether this event had had any meaning for him or was simply a government-paid junket from LA to Reno for a little chat that would fill up quite a nice report before he got back to his golf game. But few are that jaded; we all believe in something, I suppose. Of course in our brief exchange of words there was no mention of my having broken a law. Purely a matter of my agreeing to a public rite of contrition was what it came to, an obligatory kowtow before the state, the century's only truly credible god, for having had in the past certain thoughts that I had indeed harbored, and for having met, as I had also done, with other like-minded writers in an attempt to advance the idea of socialism, or more especially human brotherhood, however muddled and profoundly unexamined the means. That all of this was now long gone with the wind was beside any conceivable point, there being no trace of an American left anymore and nothing in reality to be loyal or unfaithful to. Nothing, that is, except the most generous thoughts of one's youth, which, to be sure, had turned out to be badly mistaken in practical terms, but whose impulse had had some touch of nobility; it was youth's ample heart that was now up for betrayal or disavowal or mockery. From such Marxism as I had once espoused I had not wanted anything for myself, that was certain; it had been far less a political than a moral act of solidarity with all those who had failed in life, an abnegation of power in the guise of a materialistic thrust for it, a redemption from the self. Just as I had gone, a week after the success of *All My Sons,* and offered myself to the employment service for a menial job that I could bear for a week and no more, so I had from time to time thrown myself toward one or another Party front and stayed long enough to be bored and frustrated all over again by its rote emptiness. However, by this time, 1956, I had learned to trace the leveling impulse to less exalted arenas than morality and public reform, back to the ancient competitions with my brother and illiterate father, whose metaphoric retaliation for my victories I had dodged by declaring my equality with the least of the citizenry while in the real world working day and night to achieve what glory and superiority my art might win me.

In twenty-two years I would hear my own story—from the mouths of Chinese writers returning from exile after the Cultural Revolution. Of course their punishment had been immeasurably greater, but my own experience made their emotions uncomfortably easy to grasp.

* * *

The plane to New York was half empty, and I could stretch out across a couple of seats. There was time now for fear, not so much of what would become of me but of being unable to answer this summons to explain my life and justify it as an authentically American one when in fact I didn't understand my life. It was one of those moments when unfinished recollections return with their embarrassing unanswered questions. Maybe I had simply been a conformist and not a radical at all, fearful of the left's opprobrium for those who failed to fail and proved thereby that a robust pulse remained in the body of America. For example, I had realized long ago what lay behind the Communists' disapproval of *Salesman* and *All My Sons:* their success and critical acceptance had thrown doubt on the shibboleth that American theatre could not, and theoretically should not be able to, support socially truthful plays. A work that really told how it was could not succeed. The left had been living in the Last Days before the Coming, a pleasing mental environment for the passive moralist who need only know Truth to experience Salvation, a fix as old as Pauline theology and as seductive as justification by faith alone. But as an artist I knew that creation demanded a forward motion, an assault upon the world's slothful sleep of sensibility. My whole life had been a struggle between action and passivity, creation and detached observation. Flying toward New York, I made a note recalling a dream I had had some years before, of a theatre where I was watching one of my plays with an audience that I suddenly realized was motionless as death, and in one sweeping glance I saw the faces of family, friends, all the people I had ever met in my life, and I shouted, "My God, I have killed them all!" as though to create likenesses was to steal the spirit out of the bodies of those portrayed; yet I felt an illicit exhilaration, too, at having violated the Commandment, for I had made life, just like God.

I now recalled my six months on the WPA Theatre Project after graduating from Michigan; there had been some forty or fifty playwrights who, in 1939, were drawing $22.77 a week to turn out plays, most of which I read and found execrable, totally incompetent— and indeed, not one of these people was heard from again once the project closed down as the war drew closer. Shrouding my secret dissociation from their untalented ranks, I had posed as a fellow victim of Broadway commercialism's contempt for real art, all the while believing that those with some modicum of talent were simply too lazy to press it to its limits and preferred to go on blaming the system for the sloppy raggedness of their scenes. The truth was that I had always lived in the belief that a good man could still make it, capitalism or no capitalism.

But the subpoena in my pocket was too blunt an instrument to allow delicate nuances: in defense of honor I must confound the Committee, a stand that would inevitably force me not only to seem pro-Soviet when I had long since lost the last shred of faith in the Soviet system but also—more privately and painfully—to pose as one content with submergence in the community of the ineffectual and the artistically failed, the sentimental drones of the literary left from whose ranks I had forever been separating myself. There was no doubt in my mind, however, that I would never give the Committee the names of people, all of them writers, whom I had known to be Communists, and this had nothing to do with anything but myself; I might have every rational reason to conform to the fashion of the time except for a single overriding consideration: I simply could not believe that anything I knew or any individual I could name was in the remotest sense a danger to democracy in America. My real view of American Communists was of a sect that might as well be praying somewhere in the Himalayas for all the relevance they had to any motion in the American world. But I could not think they had particularly harmed me personally, and I had no need for either revenge or even some impassioned break when they were simply inconsequential, fellow loiterers on the platform waiting for the Redemption train to come through.

But how to make any of this comprehensible, especially to a booming and increasingly self-satisfied country, was beyond me. Indeed, I was sure that the failure of *A Memory of Two Mondays* and *A View from the Bridge* was in some part due to their images of privation and even desperation; as usual, America was denying its pain, and remembering was out. My inarticulateness would be repeated down the road when the people of the Vietnam War sixties found it impossible to pass on their cataclysmic visions to an indifferent new generation. MacLeish was right: America was promises—and it was not interested in recalling those that had failed.

On top of everything, the news about the coming marriage was out; clearly, Wheeler would hardly have come all the way to Nevada except to make sure that the imminent publicity would include the Committee, which badly needed it now in its threatening ebb time.

In certain situations one can get scared enough to grow calm. Since I was damned already, I felt worse for Marilyn than for myself. Besides, it was all unreal, something unserious about it kept panic away; Carl Royce in his beautiful dove gray cowboy outfit sat beside me now. He must be back on his Texas land by this time, but his simple manly skepticism, his blessed American anarchy of heart, was flying with me. From somewhere I had inherited a reliable tendency to slow down in the face of menace, maybe from our two thousand years of tenting on the lip of the abyss, and I lay back and let the earth's inertia take me. I was an American, after all, a citizen of the unexpected isle, the roller-coaster society. Who knew?—maybe something good was on its way. Or should I have confronted reality by fleeing to Texas?

To paraphrase Winston Churchill's characterization of the Germans, the press with Marilyn Monroe was either at her feet or at her throat. Papers like the New York *Daily News,* then in its far-right incarnation, were bound to resent my entry on the scene, but even apart from that ungrateful lapse, her breaking up what they had decided was the perfect American marriage, with Joe Di-Maggio, had simply been unforgivable. Thus, on her return from making *Bus Stop,* they thought it vital that not only her persona be destroyed but her beauty defaced, the more so now that her dream of acting with Olivier was about to come true. Instead of joining in limbo the innumerable overreaching starlets with pretensions to art, she would be leaving for England shortly after our wedding to shoot *The Prince and the Showgirl.* Something had to be done about this.

We were temporarily living in a Sutton Place apartment house at whose entrance a crowd of photographers had begun to appear as early as eight o'clock each morning. A tribute to her amazing popularity, I first thought. But even after the two of us finally held an impromptu press conference on the sidewalk in hopes of getting them to leave, the documentarians of the *News* and *Post* (then in its liberal phase) returned each day at the crack of dawn. Why? we wondered. The answer came one morning when Marilyn, spotting them from within the lobby, backtracked and went down into the basement in an attempt to escape through the service entrance. She had no makeup on and was dressed in a sloppy oversized sweater, with a bandanna wrapped over her hair and knotted under her chin as though she had a toothache, a getup she often used in order to make it across town to her analyst without attracting notice.

The working press came tearing down the alley, cornered her amid the trash cans, and got the shot they were fixing to get for days, the *News* giving it all of page one. And there she was, this so-called beauty, America's sweetheart, snarling, puffy-eyed, brandishing a hand at the reader like some crazy bag woman cursing out an innocent passerby, surrounded by garbage. The same newspapers, quite naturally, gave over practically entire editions to their editors' unbearable expressions of grief upon her death hardly six years later.

Once again Twentieth Century Fox mysteriously reached into my life; Spyros Skouras paid us a surprise visit the evening before I left for Washington, in a try at getting me to cooperate with the Committee. He had called from Hollywood to ask Marilyn if he could stop by as soon as he got to New York. I knew what this meant, of course, since the president of Twentieth Century Fox was not in the habit of making such flying visits, not to see Marilyn, at any rate, when the studio was still at odds with her. He would be trying to get me to avoid a possible jail term for contempt of Congress. Not that I mattered to him, but if the rumors that we were going to marry were true, the patriotic organizations might well decide to picket her films. Such were the times. If there was any surprise in his phoning, it was that he had not done so earlier. He was reputed to have worked over many an actor and director with his persuasive mixture of real conviction, paternalism, and the normal show business terrors of bad publicity.

When she returned to me from the phone, I must have looked disconcerted at her announcement that it was Skouras, for she quickly asked me not to refuse to see him. And this was curious.

By turns she resented him, hated him, and spoke of him warmly as a friend of last resort at the studio. Although she was furious at his denying her the ordinary perquisites of a great star, which she unquestionably was by this time—the best dressing room, her choice of cameraman and director, and the respect due her as by far the public's favorite performer—she could still be moved by his repeated reassurances, often accompanied by actual tears, that she was closer to him than even his own adored daughter. At the same time she was sure it was his obduracy that denied her recognition as the number one Fox draw.

The company insisted on binding her to her old contract, which paid her a hundred and fifty thousand dollars a picture, a fraction of her market value even at the time. This was a figure negotiated before her amazing cult had formed and the studio's profits from her pictures had commenced soaring. But despite everything, her resentment lost its steam when Skouras took her by the arm and said, "You are my daughter." I was encouraged when she felt warmly toward him; we were to be married soon, and I found myself welcoming any of her feelings that were at all positive and unworried. In any case, it would be up to me how to respond to Skouras, and about that I had no uncertainty, although his coming increased my uneasiness that my public condemnation might harm her career.

Spyros Skouras, I estimated then, might be an eel but was not really a bad fellow because his deviousness was obvious enough to be almost reassuring. One never had the slightest doubt where he stood—right next to Power. If he indulged himself in passionate self-promoting speeches about honor, compassion, and truth, it was much in the Mediterranean or more specifically the Achillean tradition of rhetorical excess accompanying all of life's grand shifts, such as weddings and births—especially of boy babies—as well as the more stunning betrayals that Power periodically necessitates. I had met Skouras a few times before, but only once when I could watch him in full rhetorical flight, and I never forgot it.

One afternoon about five years earlier, I had happened to meet Kazan a few yards from the Fox building on Forty-sixth Street, where he had an appointment with Skouras. He invited me to join him, and having nothing better to do, I agreed. Kazan was still in the early stage of his movie directing career and was excited about the work; his fellow Greek Skouras was his friend, boss, and godfather.

Skouras's office was about the size of a squash court, with the entire wall at one end covered by a map of the world as a backdrop for the coffin-length executive desk in front of it. On the map, Latin America was some ten feet long and the other continents proportionately immense, all marked with many large red stars where Fox offices were located. Alone on the desk top of beige marble a low baroque statuette supported a golden pen and pencil.

On a hassock at the foot of this desk sat George Jessel, then in his fifties, who greeted Kazan and me with both his hands wrapped passionately around each of ours in turn. At a wave of Skouras's hand we sat on beige sofas from whose deep, downy cushions it was nearly impossible to rise again.

For no reason I could imagine, Skouras, from a standing start behind his desk, launched—in a hoarse, shouting voice that seemed to address several thousand people in his mind—into a tirade against Franklin Roosevelt, who by then was already six years dead. Slapping the stone desk top with the palm of his hand for emphasis, occasionally throwing his head back defiantly or shaking his finger at Kazan, apparently in reprimand, he portrayed the late president as a man without honor, decency, or courage.

"He was terrible!" Jessel suddenly piped up from his hassock in front of the desk.

"He was not terrible, he was goddam sonabitch!"

"That bastard," Jessel concurred, shaking his head angrily with a glance over at Kazan and me as though something had to be done immediately about this vile person. "I could tell you things, Spyros, that you . . ."

"You don't know nothin'! *I* know!"

"I know you know, Spyros, but I was in Des Moines once when he . . ."

"Don't tell me Des Moines!" Skouras commanded in outrage. "This man sold out million pipple to Stalin! He was agent of Stalin! He was absolutely agent!" And he slammed his desk.

"He was worse than an agent!" Jessel yelled, thrilling himself visibly.

Now, with not the slightest warning or tonal change or shift of emphasis, Skouras declared, his head thrown back pridefully, "Without Franklin Roosevelt the United States would have been revolution in spring of 1935. He saved America!"

"Goddamned right!" Jessel shouted, likewise without so much as an eyeblink at this abrupt reversal. "Chrissake," he amplified in pity-filled tones, "people were starving, dying in the streets . . ."

Skouras now soared into praise of Roosevelt with encomia worthy of a graveside while tears of mourning bubbled up along the lower lids of Jessel's eyes, and shaking his head, he added his loving recollections of the dead president's fineness of character, his humor and generosity. It took me some weeks to realize that Skouras relished this performance as his way of informing Kazan, and perhaps me as well, that his power was so immense that he could blatantly contradict himself in front of us without losing one ounce of his domination. He was a bull walrus on the beach, just howling his joy of life to the sun.

When I opened our apartment door to let Skouras in, I saw that he was tired, a weary old man in a dinner jacket. He may also have had a drop too much. His handshake was limp, and he let his gaze slide across my face without his usual electric greeting, as though he did not expect much of the evening. A bald man with a deep chest and a bull neck, he stood tilted slightly to the rear of his center of gravity, back straight and chin tucked in like a boxer's. He could smile warmly while his eyes darted about for signs of the enemy. Marilyn immediately came into the foyer, and they embraced, almost tearfully on his part, probably because of all the favors he had had to deny her. "Won'erful, won'erful," he kept repeating with eyes closed, his nose in her hair.

She was moved, surprisingly so. But I did not know then how aged men often evoked in her so intense an awareness of her own power over them that it turned to pity within her and sometimes even love. Her nearness could make such men actually tremble, and in this was more security for her than in a vault full of money or a theatre echoing with applause. Holding her hand to his lips, Skouras took her to the couch and sat beside her, but she immediately sprang up and insisted on getting him a cognac, which he accepted despite his asthmatic protests and sipped. Beside him on the couch again with her knees drawn up, she faced him with her upper lip ever so slightly flicking like the lip of a bridled horse, a prideful tic of self-possession. He could not have helped being struck by her beauty in a beige satin blouse with high Byronic collar and a tight white skirt and sparkling white patent leather spike heels. It had been months since he had seen her, time enough to have forgotten the impact of the force wave that her beauty seemed to displace.

Sitting on one cheek like an awkward circus bear, he kept sliding off the couch cushion as with his rather adolescently charming hoarseness he touched on the illnesses and deaths of mutual Hollywood friends, problems with his Rye estate, and developments in his daughter's life. Marilyn was charmed and happy as emotion alone could make her happy, almost without regard for its hostile or benevolent significance, for only in emotion was there truth. Incredibly now he began pleading with her to renounce her own company and return to the studio, something that had been settled by contract almost a year before, but she understood the diversion—he had come with something difficult for him to say, and this roundabout way of getting down to business, absurd as it was, showed a certain respectful deference that moved her to listen and react as though he were talking about something real.

"Hones'-to-Gah-dahlin', I worry about you personally. I can't help what some of those people out there doin' to you these years,

I'm not Twentieth, I'm only the president. I speakin' to you from my heart, I promise you gonna be happy again with Twentieth. I'm absolutely serious, Mahlin dahlin', you make such a mistake, come back with us we are your own family, you fadder and mudder." On he went, like certain fish who spray an alkali before laying their eggs in acidic waters. Now he talked of his cathedral, which he had built in Los Angeles for the Greek Orthodox Church, the pride of his life. You could hate Spyros, but you had to like him, if only for the naiveté of his disregard for truth, which was at least not surgical and dry but had a certain ardor; he always meant what he said while he was saying it.

Out of the blue, he took Marilyn's hand, and with an envelopment of privacy between them he asked, "You in love, swithar'?"

She seemed to fill up, caught a breath, and nodded that she was. "You sure?"

Not without guilt she confronted him eye to eye, he who knew her story, and nodded again.

"Gah-bless-you-won'erful," he said, patting her hand with fatherly benediction; if it was really love and marriage, especially the latter, then God had entered the case and the fooling around was over. Skouras sat there nodding in active calculation as he studied his short black shoe on the carpet. Turning to me, he said, "Gah-bless-you-Artr-won'erful. I know you fine man, you goin' take good care this girl, she's like my own daughter, hones'-to-Gah."

Now that he had to believe we were not merely shacking up, the Company was inevitably and menacingly involved. With two pictures still owing them before she was totally free, her marrying at all was bad enough for her image of sexy availability, but to marry me in my situation was disaster.

He sighed. "Artr, I hopin' very much you not goin' to make some terrible mistake with the Committee."

I had every reason to think he would carry back to the Committee whatever I said, so I could only shrug and mutter something about doing what I thought was right.

He came wide awake now, watching for my reaction. "I know these congressmen very well, Artr, we are good friends. They are not bad men, they can be reasonable. I believe personally, Artr, that in your case they would take you privately in executive session, you understand? No necessity to be in the public at all. I can arrange this if you tell me."

In the code of the hour this meant that in exchange for "clearing" myself by naming names and engaging in the formulas of obeisance to the Committee, such as publicly thanking the members for helping me to find my way back to America, I would be questioned *in camera,* spared an open hearing.

"I'm against the Committee, Spyros. How can I come out and thank them for anything?"

Mixed into my response I heard "Socrates," and when I finished he said, "You must read this man's book."

"Socrates! Spyros, Socrates was condemned by the same kind of committee . . ."

"Yes, but he had the courage to say what he thinks, Artr."

For a moment this had me puzzled, until I realized that he meant I should use the hearing to declare my differences with the left and the liberals, an "attack" on my part that would take the sting out of my caving in to the Committee. It was more or less what Odets had been beguiled into doing, and something he never ceased regretting to the last day of his life.

"I don't need a congressional committee to give me a platform to attack the left, Spyros, I can do that on my own time." Privately I thanked my stars that I worked in the theatre, where there was no blacklist; as a film writer, I would now be kissing my career goodbye.

Getting up with his finger pointed to the ceiling, he tried to seem propelled by burning conviction, but repetition, I judged, had emptied his speech of real feeling. "Stalin," he began, "crucified the Grik pipple, Artr. I know what I'm talkin' about! The Grik Communist Party made civil war, torture, and shootin' pipple . . ." And he poured out a knowledgeable capsulized history of the postwar Greek political catastrophe between the right and the left, naturally with all the blame on the latter and all the good with the former. But even had I known or been able to acknowledge the truth of the left's brutalities at the time, it would not have changed what I saw as the issue in 1956, and that was the manifestly anti-democratic contempt for basic American rights on the part of the Committee, something impossible to support.

"It's out of the question, Spyros, I can't do it. I don't like those people."

How the rage hit me or what exactly triggered it I never could recall later, but in his persistence I felt myself cornered; it was as though he was trying to exercise control over my work, and it was intolerable. I got off only a sentence or two, but he quickly caught the idea and held up both his hands and went to his coat, which was lying over the back of a chair, and incredibly enough, I was sure I heard him mutter, "You are a Socrates." He embraced Marilyn again, but now with a real sadness, and I walked him out to the elevator. By the time it arrived he was his earlier sleepy self, and his last glance toward me as he disappeared behind the closing door was forgetful, as though I were a complete stranger he had met in the building corridor, for he was not a man to waste emotions.

Marilyn was sipping a scotch when I got back, in a mood of uncertainty; I felt he had moved her, not by his argument but by his feeling, for in some crazy way he did care about her. A few years later, Skouras would invite her to sit at the main table when Nikita Khrushchev visited the studio, presenting her to him as a great star. The Soviet chairman was very obviously smitten with her, and she in turn liked him for his plainness. Spyros then declaimed, for the thousandth time, the epic story of how he and his brothers had arrived in America with a few carpets on their backs as their only capital and now he was president of Twentieth Century Fox, such was the reality of opportunity in America. Khrushchev got up and countered that he was the son of a poor coal miner and was now the head man of the whole Soviet Union. Marilyn thought that a fantastic reply; like her, Khrushchev was odd man out.

My mother and Marilyn and I were sitting on a Penn Station bench waiting for the Washington train to be called. All I could think of was the waste my trip implied. It was all for absolutely nothing, except that it would cost tens of thousands of dollars in legal fees even after a great part of them were forgiven by my lawyers and friends at the Paul, Weiss, Wharton, Garrison office. Marilyn was gallantly trying not to seem unhappy, and since I was trying for her sake to maintain an even mood, neither of us could express anything we were really feeling, in particular about our failure to find an hour's peace since deciding to make a life together. Right now, I hated having brought her this trouble. My mother actually succeeded in pretending nothing ominous was happening and talked about Marilyn's clothes, which I thought made her seem insensitive in Marilyn's eyes. She had a complicated and fluctuating relation with older women, veering from sentimental idealization to black suspicions that they disapproved of her. She had been sentimentalizing my mother, but now there was a suggestion of an undertow in her feeling, a dark negative pull. Still, when I turned at the platform stairway and waved a final goodbye, they were arm in arm and seemed a pair. Waving back, Marilyn had to keep one hand holding the collar of her mink against her cheek lest she be recognized and draw one of the sudden crowds her appearance usually generated. The gesture told something about the unreality of the two disjointed worlds in which we were trying to live—here she was being serious about a serious matter, but if she was recognized she would have to start laughing, the happy carefree blonde.

We were having a drink before dinner in the Rauhs' Washington living room when Joe was called to the phone in the foyer by his wife, Olie. Returning, he began to laugh even more boyishly than usual.

A giant of a fellow who somehow looks even broader and taller because of his bow ties, Joe Rauh is a combative lawyer, formerly head of Americans for Democratic Action, a liberal pressure group whose adherents included men like Hubert Humphrey and Adlai Stevenson. Joe is anti-Communist for no other reason than his passionate love of democracy; he is uninterested in ideology or even philosophy except as they lead people to a respect or disdain for individual human rights. He is interested in American power abroad, but without the double standard of those who shut their eyes to the crimes of "our" dictators while hurling their thunderbolts at the ones who follow the Soviets' lead. He has an unswerving faith in the Bill of Rights as a guarantee of democratic life in America. In his public interest law firm he has made a fraction of what his ability would have earned him in business law.

Now he sat on one of the chintz-covered chairs and, solemnizing his expression, asked, "How would you like to *not* have to go into the hearing tomorrow?" And proceeded to report that he had just been talking to someone representing Representative Francis E. Walter of Pennsylvania, chairman of the Committee, who had proposed that the hearing could be canceled provided Marilyn agreed to be photographed shaking hands with him.

I burst out laughing. Why I was not even tempted I don't know. It certainly would have saved a lot of grief. We could only sit there shaking our heads at how fundamentally simple politics was—just as in show business, you kept your name in the paper no matter what.

My memories of the hearing itself are always scattered, like those that follow violence.

I remember the furled flag behind the tribunal where the members of the Committee sat looking down at me and Joe and co-counsel Lloyd Garrison, seated behind us, his patrician stare not unnoticed by Chairman Walter. Now the flag seemed reassuring rather than threatening, as it had in Nevada. In some places under other flags, I would have been facing a death sentence for exactly the same infractions I was being charged with today.

I remember the pile of papers on a table, from which the interrogator, Richard Arens, took one sheet and then another and another, reading off petitions I had signed so many, many years ago, almost in another country—protests, pleas to free some prisoner, appeals for friendship with Russia (which Joe insisted on seeing in order to read off some of the other names, among them Mrs. Roosevelt's)—and I remember wondering if he meant to go down the whole pile, asking with each one, "Did you sign this?" Yes, of course, I had signed everything, and after a dozen or so submissions I began answering yes before he had even identified the petition.

Some years later, I read that Arens had been fired from this job when it was reported that he was on retainer from a racist "foundation" as an adviser, pamphlet writer, and expert on the genetic inferiority of blacks. It didn't surprise me all that much; he was a short fellow with a shaved head and a square pug face, and he looked as though life had nastily disappointed him in every conceivable way. A bachelor, he was said to keep a beautiful flower garden in his Washington backyard.

I remember feeling, as I glanced at one after another of the protests he handed me for identification, how fatuous it had all been. I remember thinking that my influence on my own history had been nil. The simple truth was that I myself could barely recall a great many of the organizations or causes to which I had given my support. And perhaps the worst of it all was that while these were "facts" Arens was establishing about my life as a sympathizer, it would have been impossible under the circumstances to tell the larger truth even had I been given the freedom to do so. I had indeed at times believed with passionate moral certainty that in Marxism was the hope of mankind and of the survival of reason itself, only to come up against nagging demonstrations of human perversity, not least my own. How to explain that even if he had produced a Party card with my signature on it, I could only have said yes, I had probably felt that way then, had made up my mind that day or week that the only way to stand against fascism abroad and at home was to do what so many others of my generation also thought necessary. In the plays and novels about the heroism of the

Spanish Civil War and of the now long-forgotten German resistance to Hitlerism—in the whole left-wing liturgy—to be Red was
to embrace hope, the hope that lies in action. So it had seemed for
a time. But I have come to see an altogether different reality after
traveling in the Soviet Union, particularly, and in Eastern Europe
and China. Deep within Marxism, ironically enough, lies a despairing passivity before History, and indeed power is forbidden to the
individual and rightfully belongs only to the collective. Thus the
individual requires no rights, in the sense of protection from the
state, any more than a pious person needs rights against the powers
of his god. Passivity, before a revolution, derives from the belief in
the Last Days whose coming no man can slow or stop; and after the
revolution, from the New Law itself, which fundamentally absorbs
the individual into the collective.

History bends; the ease with which I could, in the sixties, understand the fear and frustration of the dissident in the Sovietized
world was the result, in some great part, of my experience before
the Un-American Activities Committee in the fifties.

I remember Chairman Walter's brown-and-white shoes with
perforated wing tips, and his blue blazer, a costume for a wedding
in Scranton, Pennsylvania, and his pleasant nod to me as he made
his entrance amid the stern faces of his Committee. He took no
pains to conceal his surprise and interest in the large number of
reporters present (including, of course, I. F. Stone, perhaps the
hardest-working and best reporter in Washington), and especially
in the unprecedented appearance of more than twenty foreign
journalists, all seated at a long table not far from me. This had not
happened before. It was not yet common for American plays to be
published and widely performed in Europe, as mine had been, and
I thanked my right hand for the work it had done over the years.
Of course I knew that they were thinking that what had almost
murdered European culture was sitting in this room under the
almost palpable power of the American flag, and I wanted to reassure them that it was not going to happen here, at least not today.

I remember only a couple of disappointing colloquies with the
Committee members. Arens produced a comment I had made
soon after the end of the war in answer to a questionnaire cir-
culated by *New Masses* magazine about the arrest of Ezra Pound,
asking various writers their opinions on what should be done with
him. I had said that he had clearly committed treason by broadcasting and writing for Mussolini in an attempt to demoralize American troops fighting in Germany and Italy, and that he should be

treated like anybody else who had committed the same crime.

Arens brought this up as a curious contradiction of my claim to believe in freedom of speech, a subject that also arose in an exchange with a Cincinnati congressman named Gordon Scherer. Once, on the subject of Pound, Scherer sternly asked whether "a Communist who is a poet should have the right to advocate the overthrow of this government by force and violence? In his literature, in poetry?"

I replied that "a man should have the right to write a poem about anything," wondering at his provincial foolishness in choosing poetry as an incendiary form; he was probably unaware that nobody read poets in America except other poets or students under compulsion and that he'd have made a much more forceful point by using film or the novel as an example.

When I confirmed that I did think a poet could legally write such a subversive poem, Mr. Scherer actually threw up his hands and turned to the other members as though to say, "What more do we have to ask?"

I was shocked when Arens, a far more sophisticated fellow, pressed me to explain how I could deny Pound his right to speak. It was terribly strange to equate a poet writing a subversive poem in peacetime America with a man broadcasting month after month to American troops in order to undermine their morale in time of war. But whatever the theoretical considerations, mine went far deeper.

I must have been one of the few Americans who had actually heard an Ezra Pound broadcast from Axis Italy, and I could still recall the cold that had flowed into my heart while I was listening to him. Back during the war I had bought a new radio, a handsome Scott offered me at cost—still a considerable sum—by Irving Aranoff, a friend who was then the furniture buyer at A&S, the big Brooklyn department store. It had a powerful shortwave band, and one evening in our Willow Street house I turned it on and heard a clearly Midwestern voice. I assumed I had picked up an American station until the voice started talking about the necessity of killing the Jewish people. This was so arrantly vile and at the same time so calmly spoken that I thought at first it was some lame bad-taste satire by a desperate comic. But gradually the man's jolliness of spirit, his sheer ebullience, convinced and appalled me. Left to herself, he blithely explained, Europe, composed as she was of closely interrelated peoples, would easily solve all her problems; it was purely the work of the Jews that this war had happened, for they were sworn to take vengeance on the gentiles while carrying out their plot to take over the entire world. The only solution, which he thanked God Hitler had had the intelligence to grasp, was to utterly destroy this hidden nation once and forever.

When Arens looked at me with his tight little pug face and asked if I didn't think it strange that in Pound's case I was so ready to abrogate my pristine principles of freedom of speech, I saw the face I had been fighting all my life and the blood came into my head. I regretted it and fought to down my anger, but he saw it happening and realized he had overstepped, since I was obviously one of those Jews who did not go into the gas without a complaint. Pound had been calling for racial murder and, judging from the broadcast I had heard, would have happily killed me as a Jew if he could have. The questioning petered out before Arens's hypocritical question could be exposed for what it was, but in a way I was glad for this little episode; it cleared the air. I had been against men like Pound who stood for wrong, and I was proud of it.

Still, leaving the room with Joe, I felt the flatness of anticlimax. If the Committee's basic interest in me was merely publicity rather than a serious defense of the republic, I nevertheless felt I had projected much more self-certainty than I really possessed, and at the same time a remoteness from the long-ago years of the thirties and forties when I had still connected the Soviets with socialism, and socialism with man's redemption. But such passions had no place in hearings conducted like some political tennis match whose narrow rules demanded that the ball bounce inside certain boxes; the Committee in order to win had to show I was dominated by the Party, and I had to show the opposite to prove that I had never skirted what now was treason.

Was it really enough to appear thoroughly selfish, their ultimate test of Americanism? Tolstoy as a Christian had once declared that he would rather be a Communist believer than a man of no beliefs. As Arens produced one after another of those petitions, protests, declarations—I seemed to have signed one a day— it crossed my mind how hopeful I must have been in those distant times! Had I signed nothing and cared less, I would not be here. But that was not the whole of it either. That pile of protests six inches thick, I realized, was as much a denial of reality as a commitment to the future. In truth, I had supported these various causes to express my fear of a looming victory of fascism and my alienation from the waste of potential in America while knowing nothing about life under any socialist regime. All I was sure of now, in 1956, was the desire to acknowledge myself in the present, and perhaps by ceasing to repress what was ambitious and sensual and, yes, selfish, to assume responsibility for my moment and my space in the world.

In coming years my mind would pick out themes of this symphony and leave me with one or two that I could whistle, but they turned out to be variations created by shocked memory. "Why do you write so tragically about America?" was what I had for years recalled as the chairman's final remark to me; but in looking up the record, I find that it was Congressman Doyle asking, "Why do you not direct some of the magnificent ability you have to fighting against ... Communist conspiracies? ... Why do you not direct your magnificent talents to that? ..."

But there was no mistaking what they wanted of me; it was reassurance and not the downbeat stuff I had been turning out. Nor did it dawn on anyone present that a congressman might not have the license to put such a question to a writer in America, and all their faces were placid as he asked it. And so for years to come his voice would echo far beyond himself or even his Soviet counterparts; it was the voice of state power everywhere, the voice of the club, the tribe, the spirit of unfreedom wherever organized society has existed. Walter and the Committee were simply a little less sophisticated, perhaps a little less intelligent than some other theologians of the idolatry of the state, and showed their hands when they need not have. Walter could not resist the temptation to cast his vote for optimism—at the end of the hearing he took a moment to thank me and to hope that in future I would write more happily about America.

And what came to mind in response was my luck: to have been born in a country whose founders had foreseen that Power was fundamentally an idiot who at all cost had to be restrained by a net of rules so basic and so clear that even he could be instructed in them before, in one of his rages, he tore down the house.

But before the end I had to be asked if a certain writer had been in the room when I arrived at a meeting of Communist writers a decade before, and as Arens probably anticipated by now, I of course had to ask not to be asked that question as I would not violate what on the spur of the moment I said was my sense of myself. I lacked the wit to inquire what investigative purpose the question could serve when he had already used the man's name in asking it, and when in addition it had been a perfectly legal meeting of a legal group. But of course it was all a game of power entirely; they had the power and were bound to make me concede that I did not by trying to force me to break an implicit understanding among human beings that you don't use their names to bring trouble on them, or cooperate in deforming the democratic doctrine of the sanctity of peaceful association. I was warned that I was in contempt of a congressional committee—since I had chosen not to claim the protections of the Fifth Amendment in the belief that I had done nothing against which I needed them. After repeating my request not to be asked that question, which had no conceivable legislative or investigative purpose, I was warned once more of my jeopardy in refusing to answer it, and that was that: having claimed no constitutional protections, I could now be sent to jail.

Marilyn had come to give moral support during the last days of the hearing, spending her time with Olie Rauh hidden from the press in their home. It had never been easy for me to share trouble—weakness—with a woman, just as my father had always kept bad news to himself, and even when my eyes were the height of the handkerchief drooping out of his back pocket, this stoicism had seemed like strength. Something like fear was filling her up at my closing myself off. I was protecting a wound, defensively turning inward, but she glimpsed herself an unwanted wife cooped up for days in a strange house. I tried to see a good challenge in her need, if a somewhat scary one. It was the first time I had had to apologize. Like a child, like me, she wanted to dissolve the boundaries of her mind and body in another person, in the world, and I had seemed to throw her back on herself.

But we'd soon be off to England, to a new kind of film for her with perhaps the most respected actor in the world, and a new chance for *View* with an extraordinary young director. I must get to work at once on the full-length version, a fascinating test of the play's structure. I had originally designed it as bare as a telegram, its story in the foreground, its appeal essentially to the mind's awe at its amazing concatenations. But I thought differently now, that it could move people too with pity for the protagonist and even identification with him, a man who does so many unworthy things. Perhaps, in the nearly two years since writing it, I had learned to suspend judgment somewhat and to cease holding myself apart from the ranks of driven men—and not as a matter of principle but for real.

* * *

Exhausted sleep in a strange bed after twelve hours over the Atlantic in a piston plane and a confrontation at the airport with what Laurence Olivier, near to giggling with excitement, described as the largest press conference in English history. There had to have been at least four hundred journalists from all over the British Isles as far away as the remotest mists of Scotland, as well as a contingent from the Continent including two dour Basques in berets, the whole mob surrounded by a cordon of police. At one point the camera flashes formed a solid wall of white light that seemed to last for almost half a minute, a veritable aureole, and the madness of it made even the photographers burst out laughing. Naturally not a word of what was asked or answered remains in memory, but it hardly mattered then or later, everyone so astonished that Marilyn was among them, a goddess risen from their cold sea. When she smiled they did, and frowned when she frowned, and if she so much as giggled they roared with delighted laughter, and listened in churchly silence when she took a moment and actually *spoke!* with her voice so soft and soothing that grown men went limp as lichens at the living sound of it.

It was a bracing new tone for her to experience, of respectful adoration undermined by no insinuation of the puritanical sneer; whatever sexual problems these journalists may have had, they were not trying to pretend that they would not gladly have rushed into the dungeon for life in return for her favors, or plucked a rose for her from the face of a vertical stone cliff overhanging the fires of Hell. There was little else in any newspaper next day, and on certain other days too during her months in England; the country could have been towed into the Indian Ocean without anyone noticing, if she simply went shopping or made even a remotely quotable remark that would justify yet another front-page photo of her. Queen and Parliament may have run the country, but she commanded its heart. When she visited Marks and Spencer a few weeks after arriving, the entire store was vacated of customers and closed for fear of an uncontrollable stampede of people trying to get a look at her. She shattered a thousand years of British imperturbability.

In rolling green Surrey a rambling and not too unreasonably damp country house was rented from Viscount Moore, the publisher of the *Financial Times*, in his forties and very tall and very thin and narrow-headed and very unable to take his eyes off her as he sat in the music room, having taken the morning off to introduce us to the house, pointing a finger and saying, "And there is that boring dining room. Which you reach through that boring corridor and through the boring salon," lengthening out the interview as long as it would stretch. There was a servant couple, Hungarian refugees who had not long before fled Budapest, and they waited breathlessly in one spot when called, like a pair of bewildered pigeons. I found a desk to work at in the music room, just behind the French doors opening onto the hundred feet of carpet that was called a lawn, which ended at a brick wall marking the boundary of Windsor Great Park, the vast estate surrounding the royal castle where the Queen occasionally stayed.

Staggering with weariness on our first English night, we slept like the stunned, and now I dreamed that I was hearing an angelic chorale, male voices singing in all the octaves and colorations, blending into a rounded hush of pure, unearthly sound. I seemed to float on it, immensely moved as one is when aware of dreaming superbly. But the gorgeous persistence slowly began to alarm me, and as my brain gradually surfaced and the sound did not cease to pour through the quiet air, I opened my eyes thinking I had gone mad, for even now that I was fully awake it surged through the room. Sitting up in darkness, terrified of lost sanity, I traced the swelling refrains to the vicinity of the heavily draped window, got out of bed, carefully parted the drapes, and over the railing of a small balcony saw spread out in ranks in the bright moonlight some hundred unsmiling boys and young men in blazers, standing at attention and singing reverentially up toward our window. I quickly woke Marilyn, and she, barely conscious, came and peeked out with me.

With no lights on behind us, we could not be seen from outside and stood listening with the cold night air numbing our flesh. The music and knightly lyrics sounded wet with schoolboy innocence.

"What do we do?" she asked.

Still cobwebbed in a half-real, half-dream state, my mind declined to operate at all; we might step out on the balcony and wave, but with no clothes on it could be awkward. Ought we get dressed? That seemed too much to ask. Besides, wasn't there something absurd in waving down from a balcony like some royal pair? Or was it ungenerous not to?

"Maybe you put on a robe and just wave down to them."

"Me?"

"Well, they're not singing to me, darling."

She sighed in her exhaustion, and I began to feel undefended now that reality was flowing in; a Scotland Yard plainclothes officer accompanying us from the airport had warned that there were all kinds of crazies in England and that she must not under any circumstances confront a crowd without security around her. A hundred maddened choirboys could be trouble.

"Maybe just stand pat," I said, instantly realizing that I had never used this expression in my life before, and inevitably thinking of Groucho Marx replying, "I can't stand Pat, never could." And so we stood there planless, she swaying in half-sleep, while a hundred devoted voices, rising to a pitch of divine glorification, continued to float up toward us through the cool damp of the English night.

Before we could decide anything, the final major chord trailed softly to a stop, and peeking out through the drapes, I saw the chorus in totally silent deference stepping carefully over hedge and fence, vanishing into the night like the Little People returning to the shade of their mushrooms, apparently satisfied that they had infiltrated Marilyn Monroe's dreams. But I had also feared something in them—as sweet and wholesome and worshipful as they were, they were also a crowd.

Once I dreamed of a gigantic chrome machine in a fairgrounds with a crowd around it waiting to be served hamburgers it was emitting at one end, and Marilyn was suddenly caught and drawn into the machine's gears, and I frantically ran around to the open end to rescue her and saw a hamburger emerging as the crowd scrambled for it, and one man pulled it free and ate, blood dripping from his lips. I was forever saving her from crowds, crowds she could handle as easily and joyfully as a minister moving among his congregation. Sometimes it was as though the crowd had given her birth; I never saw her unhappy in a crowd, even some that ripped pieces of her clothes off as souvenirs.

Olivier came to visit on our first morning, a courtesy call on a fine English day that seemed full of hope, with the sun pouring through the windows and a mildness in the air. He was clearly enchanted with Marilyn and eager to show her the Edwardian costumes designed for her by Edith Head, the best in the business then, and photos of the sets. But she was leaving everything to him and wanted most of all to rest thoroughly before shooting started in a week or so. She seemed preoccupied and more deeply tired than I had realized.

He asked what plays I was interested in seeing, offering to get tickets for us, and handed me the morning paper, which he had kept folded in his jacket pocket. There must have been sixty or seventy plays listed, an amazing profusion compared to the twenty or so normally open in New York, but running my eye down the page, I could not find any I'd ever heard of, or their authors either. Many of the titles sounded rather silly.

"What's good?" I asked.

"No, no, you pick, I don't want to influence you."

"But I don't know anything about any of them," I protested. He still declined to give advice. There was one title that purely as a title was striking. "How about this? *Look Back in Anger.*"

His reaction was quick and surprisingly negative, even angry. "No, no, you don't want to bother with that, find something else."

"Why? What's wrong with it?"

"Oh, it's just a travesty on England, a lot of bitter rattling on about conditions, although some people think it's fairly good satire." He seemed to have been offended by the play, his patriotism apparently wounded.

"It sounds interesting. Frankly, I haven't felt any connection with British theatre since Shaw and Wilde, and they were both Irishmen."

He gave up. "All right, I'll have a seat there for you tomorrow evening." Marilyn had decided to stay home and rest.

Next evening, after the hour's drive to London with the chauffeur assigned us by the studio, I stepped out of the hired Jaguar and to my surprise found Larry Olivier facing me. "I've decided to see it again!" he said, laughing. Entering the lobby, I saw for the first time how admirably adept the British were in their ability to notice a star like Olivier without intruding upon him by so much as a lingering stare. By this time, people in public places, Americans anyway, had become a very ambiguous promise-threat that left me bewildered as to how to behave toward them. Something in me groaned at their approach even if, against my will, I couldn't deny the animal fun of being noticed. The English seemed to accept Olivier with a certain prideful, looking-away warmth that did not imply that they owned him. It was a fine and gentle thing to experience for the first time, altogether different from the crowd aggressiveness back home and its humiliating assumptions.

I loved the play's roughness and self-indulgences, its flinging high in the air so many pomposities of Britishism, its unbridled irritation with life, and its verbal energy. Kenneth Haigh, Mary

Ure, Alan Bates, Helena Hughes, and John Welsh moved around on the set in an abandonment of self-preoccupation that suggested a very American kind of realism and turned London inside out for me, making it seem a familiar place. And the writing reminded me of Clifford Odets in his youth, when he was so lyrically bitter at Depression New York and the life of failure it seemed to have consigned him to. *Look Back in Anger* gave me my first look at an England of outsiders like myself who ironed their own shirts and knew about the great only from newspapers.

At the interval Olivier asked what I thought, and I said it was wonderful. At the end of the play he asked again, and I said there were a lot of hanging threads, but who cared? It had real life, a rare achievement.

George Devine, the modest, cheerful little fanatic who ran the Royal Court Theatre, hurried over to ask if we would mind coming upstairs to meet the author, who was eagerly awaiting us. In a moment we were all seated at two tiny tables next to a bar, I facing Devine, and Olivier, the institution, confronting the rebellious Osborne, who I assumed was his artistic and ideological adversary. Devine was beloved of the then disorganized and uncertain British modernizing movement in theatre, for which he was trying to create a home in the Royal Court. He had just done *The Crucible*, and I was listening with pleasure as he reported on its reception by his eager young audience when a few inches to my right I overheard, with some incredulity, Olivier asking the pallid Osborne—then a young guy with a shock of uncombed hair and a look on his face of having awakened twenty minutes earlier—"Do you suppose you could write something for me?" in his most smiling tones, which could have convinced you to buy a car with no wheels for twenty thousand dollars.

I was sure that Olivier represented for Osborne the bourgeois decadence of the British theatre, but his eyes were shining now, and he would indeed write something for Olivier soon—*The Entertainer*. As Olivier later said, that evening marked the end of a long and painfully sterile chapter of his career. It was then that he began to turn away from a trivial, voguish theatre slanted to please the upper middle class, and entered the mainstream of his country's theatrical evolution. Later, heading the new National Theatre, he strove to make it a reflection not of a comfortable society but of the alienation and fumbling search for a future that were beginning to find voice in Britain. Olivier had many reincarnations, and this was perhaps his most significant one; at the

point of vanishing as an artist, he drew himself up and miraculously fought for his maturity.

The Prince and the Showgirl, however, was still part of his past,
and Marilyn soon verged on the belief that he had cast her only
because he needed the money her presence would bring. I
wanted to believe that this was only half the truth; I was sure he
saw the legitimate dramatic contrast between their social and
cultural types, and if his motives were indeed partly cynical, that
did not cancel his valid artistic judgment in casting her. The
theatre is always part beast. But as she had done with so many
people, she had idealized Olivier, who as the great and serious
artist must be above mortal considerations of the kind so common among the Hollywood fleshmongers she thought she had escaped with this, her own company's first filmmaking partnership.
The Hollywood she knew was so vile that the legitimate theatre
had to be sublimely pure. Inevitably, the time soon came when in
order to keep reality from slipping away I occasionally had to
defend Olivier or else reinforce the naiveté of her illusions; the
result was that she began to question the absoluteness of my par-
tisanship on her side of the deepening struggle.

Paula Strasberg was with her on the set every day and in the
early weeks of shooting tried, I thought, to reassure Marilyn, who
increasingly perceived a menace in Olivier. Finally she came to
believe that he was trying to compete with her like another
woman, a coquette drawing the audience's sexual attention away
from herself. Nothing could dissuade her from this perilous vision
of her director and co-star. How much of it was true I could not
know, since everybody was on his best behavior during my visits
to the set at Shepperton. And I had to admit that I couldn't set aside
Olivier's greatness; in New York I had seen his *Oedipus Rex,* which
he had played on the same bill with Sheridan's *The Critic,* as inspiring a theatrical experience as I could conceive of. It was simply
impossible to agree that he could be the cheap scene-stealer she
was talking about.

I had to face the fact that she was right in one respect—I did feel
a cultural bond with him—but she was mistaken in imagining that
she was being condescended to from some high aesthetic altitude.
What gradually began to dawn on me through all this friction was
her expectation of abandonment all over again; it was the blood of
this terror that engorged what might have been a mere conflict of

opinions. We were trying to hear each other through the echoes between two arguments—one about Olivier, and the deeper subterranean struggle against what she saw as her fate. I did not understand at first. She could not bear contradiction in any detail on this question of Olivier's knowing betrayal of her expectations, but far worse than that, she was laboring with how I fit into the pattern of disappointment. I could hardly help my alarmed protests for my own sake and the truth as I saw it. She was felled by my stubbornness, everything was over; if she was so opposed she could not be loved. I was unable to grasp until much too late the imminence of humiliation in the very position of the actor vis-à-vis director, author, cameraman. Unlike them, he had no métier with which to armor himself; he stood naked and easily mocked, if not in reality, then in his own imagination, and Marilyn was by no means alone in viewing herself this way.

Still, on the afternoons when I showed up at the studio, her face lit up as it always had; so it was all a challenge, I thought, to both of us. We had to learn how to live very close to our real feelings without burning up. Too much truth can kill. But what more exhilarating way to risk one's life when to win out meant, as I visualized it, a nearly miraculous joining of body and mind and feeling. In a matter of days we were closer than ever and also more cautious. And there were times when quite suddenly she seemed to have healed toward Olivier, her suspicions downed. Perhaps my insistence had opened an eye. For periods she worked more easily and dared to take satisfaction from some moment here or there that she could not deny having done brilliantly. Seizing on anything positive, I probably overdid my praise, sending new uncertainty stealing across her gaze like a thief. Absolute truthfulness, pure as light—nothing less was the aim. But underneath yawned the old terror of abandonment, the deafness in the stranger's stare . . .

Meanwhile, I had to get on with my work and was sure things would straighten themselves out with a director as experienced as Olivier. As I had promised Peter Brook, I was revising *A View from the Bridge*, making it into a full-length play principally by opening up the viewpoint of Beatrice, Eddie Carbone's wife, toward his gathering tragedy. It was also necessary to spend days in London looking at actors for the secondary parts, and I had all I could handle.

But the situation worsened. Paula, no doubt without design, was forced into a double game, having to maintain her authority with

Marilyn by not contradicting her too openly or often, while keeping her hand in with Olivier. Thus she became a go-between, the interpreter to him of Marilyn's acting intentions, and to Marilyn of his direction. At best this would have been an almost impossible task even for a selfless person, but for one as vain and ambitious as Paula it quickly curdled into a nightmare, like a marriage of three people; at what point are two of them to be left alone, and will the one who is left out resent it? Bad faith was inevitable, and it began to spread its rot everywhere.

Discovering that he was only to be allowed to direct Marilyn through the humiliating intercessions of an acting coach, Olivier was soon prepared to murder Paula outright, and from time to time I would not have minded joining him, for Marilyn, a natural comedienne, seemed distracted by half-digested, spitballed imagery and pseudo-Stanislavskian parallelisms that left her unable to free her own native joyousness. She was being doused by a spurious intellection that was thoroughly useless to her as an acting tool, like a born jazz player being taught to rationalize what he instinctively knows how to do. Paula understood that what Marilyn needed to play this showgirl was what she already had when she arrived at Croydon airport; but between Marilyn's belief in a magical key, a flash of insight that would dispel all doubts, and Paula's inability to supply it, Paula had to keep talking, and the more she talked the more impervious the role became. At the same time, like most English actors, Olivier had little patience with acting systems—although he prepared himself for his roles not really very differently from Stanislavsky actors. But to him such preparation was simple common sense, the imitation of life, and something that did not bear all this portentous introspective palavering.

Applied to Marilyn, Paula's "method"—and Lee's—was beginning to seem sinister, a dangerously closed circle of reasoning; if you had not studied with Strasberg and were not one of his adepts, you were not in a position to criticize, and since neither Olivier nor I was in this category, we were barred from applying experience and common sense to a steadily degenerating situation whose arcane depths were by definition beyond us. If Paula could not help her, no one else must be allowed to. To add another complication, Marilyn's trust in Paula was by no means complete: she regarded her merely as Lee's stand-in who was indeed capable, however unintentionally, of misleading her. But Paula at least was hip to the Method and knew when to nod sagely as though she understood. In Paula's repeated refrain—"I'm only Lee's representative"—I also heard the coded warning that she was not to be held directly responsible for Marilyn's confusion. And neither was Lee, who after all was not even present. Who then was responsible? I gradually began injecting myself into this vacuum—a mistake when I had no power to change anything.

Only Lee could set Marilyn right; without him she had no certainty about anything she was doing. But her long daily transatlantic conversations with him seemed to help little. Inevitably I began feeling locked out, a helpless observer. Thus, candor became more and more difficult. She wanted a magical reassurance that was not of this world.

What was real? I was ready to believe that wittingly or not Olivier might be victimizing her, but she had had similar crises with Josh Logan, another accomplished director. One could dismiss it all as her way of energizing herself for work, but the pain she felt was real and debilitating. The worst of it was that any attempt to reduce the problem to reason implied that she was following a fantasy. And so the great wobbling wheel of emotions was setting itself into place, turning around the axial question of good faith. Truth-telling, all that could rescue us both, could also be dangerous when she needed every shred of reassurance to get through a working day.

Where to get a handhold when I could hardly deny my resentment at her clinging to Paula's fruitless instructions and turning against Olivier as some kind of competitor or enemy? Olivier too seemed to be growing more and more resentful. Only Paula showed no resentment, and why should she? She had become the ultimate authority by more and more openly lamenting Olivier's perfidy while privately assuring everyone but Marilyn that she did not believe it but was forced to pretend lest she lose Marilyn's trust and leave the poor girl with no allies at all, something none of us could bear to contemplate.

As for Olivier, with all his limitations in directing Marilyn—an arch tongue too quick with the cutting joke, an irritating mechanistic exactitude in positioning her and imposing his preconceived notions upon her—he could still have helped her far more than Paula with her puddings of acting philosophy and her stock of odds and ends of theatrical inside stories, always about the greatest names in the business coming in desperation to Lee or herself for help in acting a role under this or that totally incompetent director. Nevertheless, Marilyn's fate and the picture's were finally in Paula's hands, and this unacknowledged power made her an uncanny force for Olivier to deal with.

There was a genuine conflict, it seemed to me, between two

different styles not merely of acting but of life. The comedy of the script came from the timeworn dilemma of the powerful representative of society, the prince, reduced to helplessness in the hands of the innocent prole ignorant of all but sex and ending with all the power. Marilyn knew more than most about such circumstances. But her want of training, as she saw it, in high comedy, not to mention her unrelenting uncertainty, pressed her to try to delve too deeply into a character that was essentially a series of lines crafted to address a situation, an outside with no inside. Olivier, who had mastered most of the great roles, knew how little there was in this one, but to say outright that all she needed for it was herself would be demeaning. And for Paula this admission would mean that the Method had no application here. So the heart of the matter was that nobody could tell the truth, and Marilyn was finally in no position to hear it if it was told.

I did not know how to help her, not least because in the rushes she seemed so perfectly delectable, despite all her anxiety, even lending the film a depth of pathos it did not really have. Mistakenly, I thought that in the end it would all even out into a great success for her, although the movie itself could not be more than a trivial entertainment.

On top of everything else, Marilyn believed that Milton Greene was buying English antique furniture, shipping it home, and charging it to Marilyn Monroe Productions—this at a time when her salary was still the sole income of their company. It was yet another betrayal, and all the more infuriating to her because he was not facing Olivier down as she thought he should.

Somewhere in her mind, I thought, she knew that all this would pass, but it still fueled something frantic and frighteningly thematic in her life that she was less and less able to control; she had idealized Greene's ability to set up her financial life and now felt deceived; she had idealized Olivier as a grand artist without egoistic envy of her, a kind of actor-escort or father who would think only of safeguarding her; I too was crumbling because I could not smash her enemies with one magic stroke. And her frustration was agony: Greene she could not confront until they were back in the States because she needed his executive help while the picture was being made, and she could not show her full anger to Olivier when he still had to direct her. Toward me her disappointment could flow, since she probably knew that I would take it and come back, but she was testing my loyalty to her nevertheless.

As for Paula, Marilyn could tolerate her vacuousness and confusing advice primarily because Paula was her bridge to Lee, on whom she felt a nearly religious dependency, the more so, perhaps, as he was not present and his solutions—unavailable and therefore free from reality's tests—could remain ideal. But there was more to it than that. "Paula doesn't mean anything to me," Marilyn would say when I dared suggest that her instructions were contradictory and confusing, but without Paula she was lost. This subtly unstable woman was the latest of a number of such matronly advisers in her life; according to Marilyn her predecessor, Natasha Lytess, an earlier coach whom I had not met, had been forced to exit, with her wild and threatening delusions. A blatant fantast who could weave soothing, if improbable, triumphant tales about herself and her legendary husband, Paula in effect was the mad mother all over again, and irresistible even when Marilyn could see through her to her overweening ambition. She was a fantasy mother who would confirm anything that Marilyn wished to hear, including what her vulnerability and lack of acting sophistication disposed her to believe—in this case, that Olivier was in fact so competitive with her that he was not above making her look ludicrous in the picture, the better to set off his own performance. Why he should risk ruining a film that carried his hopes for financial revival nobody of course could say, but to mention the contradiction was to appear to be taking the enemy's side. The circle, as so often happens in such airless situations, was all but closed, and the real, murderously deranged mother proceeded with her work from ten thousand miles away.

It all peaked soon; one morning Paula announced that she must return for a week or so to America. At company expense, of course, much to Greene's chagrin and my own incredulity, since her fee was already outrageous. (On a future film, *Let's Make Love,* she actually cleared more than Marilyn.) But she was apparently sure enough of her hold on Marilyn to risk leaving her in Olivier's care, something that far from distressed him.

I never really discovered what the facts were, but when Paula wanted to return a week or two later, the British authorities refused to renew her work permit on some ground or other, thus denying her entry into the country. Marilyn instantly concluded that Milton and Olivier had conspired to keep her away for the remainder of the picture—a not unreasonable view since they both, for different reasons, hated her. Outraged, Marilyn now threatened to quit unless Paula was given a work permit, a matter of her personal self-esteem, and refused to hear either Greene's or

Olivier's pleas of innocence. She was ready to take a plane home. The permit was soon issued, Olivier claiming that he had gone to the top of the government for it. But Marilyn was unable to relax her suspicions of both men, and the event confirmed that she was among enemies. Our own relationship was also further wounded, for the truth now was that she was beyond my reassuring or anyone else's. She had no means of preventing the complete unraveling of her belief in a person once a single thread was broken, and if her childhood made this understandable, it did not make it easier for her or anyone around her to bear.

Still, there were what the British call "fine" days when the rain fell only lightly, when we would bicycle in the misty silence of Windsor Great Park and its enormous trees, or drive to Brighton and walk the deserted streets along the sea in what to us was a quaint, old-fashioned resort. She was struggling against seeming like a patient who had to be handled carefully, and we talked about positive, active things like buying a country house to replace the one I had sold. She wanted to be a wife and at peace once this film was over with. Filming was a kind of siege during which she needed eyes in the back of her head. Nor was she the first actor to believe that betrayal was all about her. But for me this suspicious-ness was tiring and fruitless, since I was inclined to throw my work like bread upon the waters, and if it sank so be it, I had done what I could. She could not imagine such yielding to fate, it seemed like inertia to her, and she struggled against it even in sleep, which still would not come without too many pills, barbiturates that were more lethal than I then realized. I had taken a few of them in the past but found myself numbed for half the day after. She had to fight for alertness through the day in that same way, I thought. But it would all end soon; we were in a holding action until the film was done and a real life could begin.

In the few relaxed hours when her thoughts could go outward toward society or politics or some novel she had dipped into, when she was for the moment not a competitor or even an actor, the toll of her stardom seemed terrible. It rained a little almost every day, but on a few Sundays we could sit out on the dense lawn, and in those uncustomarily purposeless moments she seemed like a crea-ture pursued, wounded now and sore inside. She would talk of going to school in New York and studying history and literature. "I'd love to learn how things got to be how they are." There were flashes then of some other woman inside her, a woman of cultiva-tion, resourceful in the conventional sense, educated to fend off the lesser challenges to existence. She seemed to have a mind of immense capacity that had been assaulted by life, bludgeoned by a culture that asked only enticement of her. She had acted that role, and now she was petitioning for permission to display another dimension, but in some difficult-to-grasp way she could not get a hearing, and this was hurtful when like any actor she was almost totally defined by what was said and written about her. If on the screen and to most observers she was, except for her wit, all enticement, to herself she was this and some deeper promise besides. And the secret of her wit's attractiveness was that she could see around it, around those who were laughing with her, or at her. Like almost all good comics, she was ruefully commenting on herself and her own pretensions to being more than a rather dumb sex kitten; like most comics, she despaired of her dignity, and her remarks and her wryness itself were self-generated oxygen that allowed her to breathe at all. Comics on the whole are deeper, are somehow closer to the crud of life and suffer more than the tragedians, who are at least accorded professional credit for seriousness as people.

But by this time, with the film in sight of completion, there was much more to deal with than her career. It was clear that she bore a guilt for her failure to be useful to me, and I felt no differently toward her for the same reason, that I had not been able to change very much for her, although at moments she claimed I had changed everything.

Our one relief was an old college friend of mine, Hedda Rosten, the wife of Norman, a poet and playwright who had also been at Michigan. She was acting as Marilyn's secretary, and although given at times to a certain poetic vagueness, she made up for everything by her unconditional love. To Hedda, her charge was—long before feminism's rise—the quintessential victim of the male and also of her own self-destroying perversities. Hedda had been a half-willing bride who loved her man even as she really preferred a solitary life of coffee and cigarettes and the silk of time passing across her palm as quietly as sunset and dawn. "Oh, my darling, is it all worth it?" And Marilyn would laugh sadly, lost, and they would enjoy sharing their womanly hopelessness. Alone with me, Hedda, who had been a psychiatric social worker at the Hartford Retreat, despaired of Marilyn's being able to heal her lifelong wounds while making films. "She is constantly having to test what she hasn't been able to put together yet." We had always had one of those understandings given to people with similar traits; a solitary streak ran through both our natures, silence was space, and we could be in each other's company without saying very much and still communicate.

"You are both very guilty," she said one afternoon as we had our tea together in the music room.

"I can't understand why."

"You both have the same conscience."

"What does that mean exactly?"

"You can't accept what you don't think you deserve; you take exception to each other when it was supposed to be perfect. So you're punishing yourselves." And she sighed then, as one of life's chief self-punishers, and shook her blonde head and laughed. She was a beautifully made woman who had held onto her innocence into her middle twenties, and I had railed against her general naiveté, which seemed to rebuke my attempts at reasoning her into a victory over failure. "Oh, God, Arthur, what unfits us all for life?" Hedda, born Hedwiga Rowinski, often sounded like a Chekhov character. She was good to have around, although one knew she could stand only so much trouble. In not too many years she would die of the smoke she was so deliciously inhaling and that she understood but refused to believe was going to kill her.

There were startling moments when suddenly it was impossible all over again to judge how real or unreal Marilyn's perceptions were. On the set one day, in a momentary lull in the talk and noise as a new shot was being set up, the voice of the venerable Dame Sybil Thorndike, a very great actress over many decades, was heard saying, "That little girl is the only one here who knows how to act before a camera." In a flash, all of Marilyn's suspicions seemed to turn true, her efforts to deepen a shallow role became praiseworthy and correct, and the trouble was simply that she was surrounded by mediocrity, petty jealousies, and maddening reassurances of "It's good enough." At such moments I visualized myself faced by an actor paraphrasing one of my speeches instead of speaking it accurately, and I recalled my own wild-headedness at this stupidity, my sense of being trod upon and disdained, my vision mocked by idiots. Once I made such an identification with her, I could sit and remorsefully hold her, certain once again that we could make it through to some area of peace. One could easily go mad shuffling about in this darkness, looking for something real. But the real comes like a bird lighting on a branch after a very long and wayward flight, not reasoned down out of the air.

Amazingly, Lee was still in his thirties.

1965, sixteen years later: Cobb cutting the *Salesman* record album, with Dustin Hoffman playing Bernard and obviously studying his future model.

1984, the future arrives: Hoffman as Willy, with John Malkovich, Kate Reid, and Stephen Lang.

Ying Ruocheng, *Salesman*'s translator and a brilliant Willy, with Uncle Ben (Zhong Jiyao, wearing Ying's genuine Texas hat), the boys (Mi Tiezeng and Li Shilong),and Linda (Zhu Lin, *left*) in my 1983 Beijing People's Art Theatre production, the first by a foreign director in post-Mao China.

Walter Hampden, Jed Harris, Kermit Bloomgarden. A moment of calm in the first *Crucible* production, Jed in a characteristically disarming attitude.

With designer Boris Aronson, unhappy that his modernist set has been shouted down by Jed in favor of a conventional one, and Bloomgarden, doubtless scheming unavailingly to outwit the director.

Mary Warren turning on Proctor, original production, 1953: (*counterclockwise from left*) Donald Marye, Madeleine Sherwood, Dorothy Jolliffe, Barbara Stanton, Jenny Egan as Mary, Joseph Sweeney (*back to camera*), E. G. Marshall, Philip Coolidge (*behind Marshall*), Arthur Kennedy, Walter Hampden, Fred Stewart, Don McHenry.

Crucible in Shanghai, directed by Huang Zuolin.

Original cast of *A View from the Bridge*, 1955: Van Heflin, Gloria Marlowe, Richard Davalos, Jack Warden, Eileen Heckart.

Raf Vallone in Sidney Lumet's *View*, a strong film shot in Brooklyn and Paris, 1961.

My father on a visit to the *View* location, apparently recalling something remote and important.

Anthony Quayle as the psychiatrist and Alec Guinness as Prince Von Berg, with the painter Lebeau (Dudley Sutton) and the Boy (Derek Carpenter): Peter Wood's London production, 1966.

Vichy in Moscow's Sobremenik Theatre, 1987, after twenty years' suppression; its first production, in 1968, was closed down on opening night. Rehearsal photo: Grigori Ostrin as the Old Jew, Valentin Nikuli as the Prince, Igor Kvasha as Dr. Leduc; Marlen Khutsiev directed.

The best sleigh ride ever, Russia, 1965. Inge, laughing, not yet aware that her shutter has frozen.

At Ilya and Lyuba Ehrenburg's table in their Moscow apartment, 1965. Surviving "the lottery" of life under Stalin, he returned from reporting the Spanish Civil War to find that almost all his fellow newsmen had disappeared after coming home, for they had "mixed with foreigners".

Signing Yuri Lyubimov's Taganka Theatre wall, a few years before he chose exile abroad.

In Cologne, Heinrich Böll's hometown, 1972, before his election as international president of PEN.

Rebecca Miller in her Brooklyn studio, 1987.

Inge and Henri Cartier-Bresson still arguing layouts: his apartment, Paris.

Addressing New York PEN Congress as president, 1966.

Pablo Neruda in Dauber and Pine's now vanished bookstore, looking for Shakespeare sonnets and Whitman editions.

A breather at the '66 PEN Congress: with Saul Bellow and John Steinbeck after Bellow's speech.

© GILBERT JONAS

Democratic Convention, 1968: with fellow Connecticut delegate Paul Newman as our hopes for a Vietnam peace plank in the party platform were dying.

© INGE MORATH/MAGNUM

Reverend William Sloane Coffin, Jr., Steve Minot, and I getting ready to address a New Haven rally against the slaughter in Vietnam.

The greatest used furniture dealer in human history, David Burns, hypnotizes Kate Reid, Arthur Kennedy, and Pat Hingle in *The Price*, 1967, Ulu Grosbard, director.

Directing *Up from Paradise*, my musical version of *The Creation of the World and Other Business*, with Seth Allen and Kimberly Farr.

Sister Joan as her "mother" in the 1980 *American Clock*, with John Randolph.

Peter Wood's *American Clock* in Britain's 1986 National Theatre production: Judith Coke, Barry James, and Adam Norton.

Vanessa Redgrave and Melanie Mayron in *Playing for Time*, my 1980 teleplay based on Fania Fenelon's memoir of the Auschwitz women's orchestra. A stage version followed.

Clara, Lincoln Center, 1987: Kenneth McMillan and James Tolkan; Gregory Mosher directed.

With Alan Ayckbourn, who directed *A View from the Bridge* at the National in 1987, and Michael Gambon, who played Eddie Carbone.

Roger Allam, Jane Lapotaire, and John Shrapnel in the RSC's *Archbishop's Ceiling*, 1986; Nick Hamm directed.

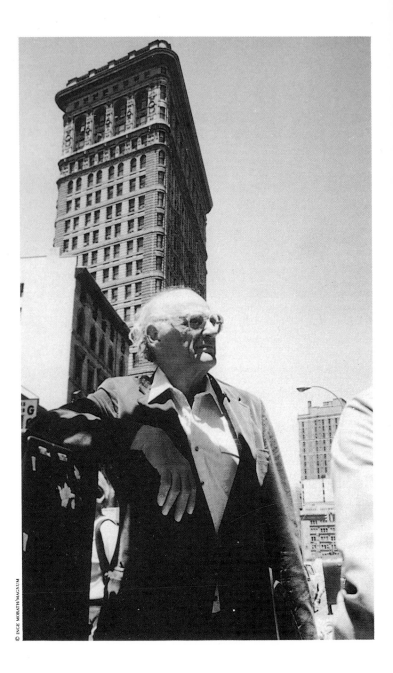

* * *

And through it all, to make matters even more encouraging, a contingent of reporters never left the entrance gate before the house, a steady column of them traipsing to and from a lovely pub on the country corner a few hundred yards up the road. As British technological inventiveness has receded before the originality of the Americans and then the Germans and Japanese, the creativity of her journalists has correspondingly increased; in their typewriters we were two characters in a novel of manners, with little domestic dialogues popping up at least twice a week in one or more of the papers, harmless chatty bits, fairly moronic, of course, but never vicious and all totally invented. I had saved her, it seemed, from a nasty fall off her bicycle, or the Hungarian maid had burned the toast and Marilyn had patiently taught her how to do it just right in a half-column of print, advising her how to change her hairdo in the bargain.

But one morning a paper reported a conversation we had actually had a few days earlier, and pretty much word for word. It was eerie reading it, an inconsequential and meaningless verbal exchange, to be sure, but one that had happened within the house. Were we tapped? Was someone outside, in the pub perhaps, tuning in to our conversations?

A tall security man in raincoat and mustache, brogans, and burr drove up from the studio soon after I had told Larry of our problem, and promptly summoned the Hungarian couple, who appeared before him in the salon. Without even taking off his raincoat or introducing himself to them, he fixed them in a stare of ice. My heart went cold at the first sounds of his growling voice strained between clenched teeth while he kept a grin on his face that emphasized the threatening glaze of pleasure in his eyes.

With no preliminaries whatsoever: "There is a plane on Thursday to Budapest. You have nothing but temporary permits to remain in this country, so you will be on it and will not be allowed another entry again in your lives." The couple stood wide-eyed, terrified, white with horror. Turning to the man, who had always been soft-spoken with us, if not timorous, he asked, "How much were you paid to betray Mr. and Mrs. Miller?" The ferocity in him was like a hot wind in the Hungarian's face.

"We did not know . . ."

"Don't lie to me, you little bastard!"

I started to interrupt, there having been no evidence, no right of rebuttal, nothing but this terror tactic, but the security man quickly got to his feet, gave me a warmly civilized smile, and said, "I don't think there will be any further problem with these people." And turning to the pair, "Will there?"

"No, sir," man and wife said in unison, and looked wonderfully relieved to have made this sudden if oblique confession.

"How much was it?"

"Five pounds, sir," the man said flatly, the cloth of his trousers shaking.

"And how much more have you told them?"

The woman tried to mitigate. "It was only . . ."

"Don't use that word with me! *Only* is not a word for you to use, at all!" She looked at the carpet with bulging eyes. "How much more will there be, then?"

"Nothing more," the man said, desperately now.

"Very good. You will go out to them at the gate and explain that if a single word more of what you have told them sees print, you are both on the plane to Budapest, have we got that straight?"

"Yes, sir. I will tell them now."

Nothing more was ever quoted again. The instantaneous transformations of the security man from such ferocity to the most sensitive British politeness stunned me. You need a long-lived empire to create such characters to police it.

Daily the bags of mail arrived, affording a view of English society that was probably unique. A movie star of Marilyn's magnitude is obviously no longer human, but what she is instead is hard to define without calling up the supernatural; she is a form of longing in the public's imagination, and in that sense godlike. The public holds her up before the sun to collect its rays to a burning point that will somehow stop time for them and make them feel her life on their flesh. Some of the letters addressed her as an institution, quite confidently asking for money for an operation, a mortgage payment, an education. But occasionally a container of feces would arrive, or a worn gardener's hat offered her as a keepsake now that the old rose fancier was dying. And always the bewildered queries about sex and marriage. Something like fifteen percent were quite insane; several offered to put her out of her misery, free of charge in some cases, for a fee in others. One man invited her to meet him "with the boys" in a coal mine, another to go fishing in a Scottish lake. Perhaps the most pathetic were from baffled women wanting to know how they could become wonderful "like you," as though she were a fairy who might touch them with the tip of her wand, all sparkly and nice, like Billie Burke in *The Wizard of Oz*. Though Marilyn rarely had the peace of mind to look at the bags of letters, Hedda handed her the ones she knew would move and encourage her, and invented replies that Marilyn insisted on signing herself.

But gradually Hedda was wearing down, as much because she found it too painful to witness her friend's seemingly endless anguish as because Marilyn was slowly becoming impatient with her; Hedda seemed to be withholding the total support she had formerly given and would blurt out, referring to some slight Marilyn was angry about, "But are you *sure* Larry meant that?" Hedda felt a trap closing; by declining to support everything Marilyn believed, she risked the charge of unfaithfulness, and yet she could not in principle reinforce her friend's unhealthy illusions. She returned home before the film was finished, but Marilyn would always remain her poetic girl, the golden feminine whose power over the male imagination Hedda joyfully celebrated as a kind of revenge on life's injustices to all women. "Oh, my dear," she would wistfully say as she looked at Marilyn in a new dress or momentarily caught in a pose of perfect, flaring beauty, "you have everything!"—leaving unsaid her question as to why she could not be happy. But Marilyn understood, and they would end in laughter, helplessly shaking their blonde heads as they fell into each other's arms.

I seemed unable to take a step without running into governments; now the lord chamberlain's office announced that *A View from the Bridge* could not play in a British theatre because Eddie Carbone accuses his wife's cousin Rodolpho of homosexuality and to prove it grabs him and kisses him on the lips. No doubt because it was so widespread, if not yet accepted as commonplace, homosexuality in 1956 could not be referred to directly on the stage.

Binkie Beaumont, head of H. M. Tennent, the venerable and still the most active theatrical producing firm in London, almost instantly conceived a solution that was not only elegant but characteristically profitable, at least for him. Under the law a private theatre club was permitted almost complete freedom. The Comedy Theatre, in all respects a normal commercial enterprise, he forthwith transformed into the Comedy Theatre Club, and the equivalent of about forty cents was added to the ticket price for a

club membership, which one had to buy to get in. Even Bob Whitehead, one of the play's American co-producers, never thought until
it was too late to demand a cut of this added price. And when he
did, Binkie produced one of his smiles—what I called "English
impish," of which he had a stock in hand—wearing down with it
not only Bob but also my agent in his demands for my percentage.
I liked Beaumont because he was uncomplicatedly ambitious for a
hit even if the show was literary or artistic. There was only one
audience for him, not several of varying sensibilities, and as in
Elizabethan times, the challenge was to conquer it. A tough negoti-
ator, he seemed to love the theatre and good plays and knew what
good acting was and wanted that too. There were long months
when he put another new play into rehearsal every Monday morning, and he had casts rehearsing all over the city. When I complimented him on his beautiful Rolls, in which we were all driven to
my play's opening, he had a one-word response, "Rented" (no
doubt to sidetrack any further discussion of percentages). He was
a producer who could simply say yes and proceed to put a play into
production without consulting anyone else, one of the last of a
breed that had not only money but also faith in its own judgment.
But of course the English were probably the best audience in the
world, and that helped a lot.

The *View* auditions were held in a theatre whose back faced the
vegetable stalls of Covent Garden. I would sit beside Peter Brook
listening in some pain as one actor after another who seemed to
have arrived fresh from Oxford recited the words of Brooklyn
waterfront Italo-Americans. One day in desperation I asked Peter
if we couldn't interview some of the Cockney hawkers in the hive
of working-class types behind the theatre, exactly the kind of men
the play needed. "Doesn't a grocer's son ever think of becoming
an actor?" I asked.

"These are all grocer's sons," Peter replied, indicating the group
of young gentlemen awaiting their turns at one side of the orchestra, "but they have trained themselves into this class language.
Almost all the plays are written in that language and are about
those kinds of people." It was a moment that returned to me in
China almost thirty years later when I insisted that the actors in my
Salesman production not attempt to disguise their Chinese identities with Western wigs and makeup. They were shocked at first by
this departure from the traditional conventions of a theatre that
had little connection with actual life; people in China went to the
theatre hoping to escape into poetry and music and interpretation,
not for any imitation of reality.

There being no way for them to learn a deep Sicilian-American accent, Anthony Quayle, Mary Ure, and the rest of the cast worked out among themselves an accent never heard on earth before, but as it turned out, it convinced British audiences that they were hearing Brooklynese. The actors also thought they were speaking it correctly, and I did nothing to disabuse them, for this newly minted language along with their mode of acting created a wholly fictional world, but one that was internally consistent and entirely persuasive even if its resemblance to the Brooklyn waterfront was remote or nonexistent. *View* came over under Brook's direction as a heroic play of great emotional force, the working-class characters larger than life, grand and rather strange. The play began on a Red Hook street against the exterior brick wall of a tenement, which soon split open to show a basement apartment and above it a maze of fire escapes winding back and forth across the face of the buildings in the background. On those fire escapes the neighbors appeared at the end like a chorus, and Eddie could call up to them, to his society and his conscience, for their support of his cause. Somehow, the splitting in half of the whole three-story tenement was awesome, and it opened the mind to the size of the mythic story.

And something else was novel about this production. On the day the set was first erected, a dozen or so wives and children of the stagehands, invited by Peter, sat watching while their husbands proudly described and demonstrated the mechanics of the scene changes; especially impressive was the rolling apart of the tenement. The families oohed and aahed. In New York I had never noticed the faintest interest of this kind on the part of the back-stage people, and the realization was saddening. With us it was all pure bucks.

It seemed an exotic play to the English at the time, especially when their own theatre was so middle-class and bloodlessly polite. The reception in the press was very favorable, and the acting community especially found it a sufficient challenge that within a few weeks a large meeting was held at the Royal Court Theatre to discuss what might be done about the condition of the British stage.

I had not expected to be the one to whom most of the audience's questions were addressed, for among those present on the stage were a number of top actors and directors, along with such local celebrities as Colin Wilson, an interesting rebel, rucksack and all, and Kenneth Tynan, the best critic of that period, if not of the whole postwar era. But in the fifties and into the sixties it was to America that England looked for vitality in the theatre, a small historical fact that American critics, especially of the learned academic variety, have almost succeeded in suppressing.

The same basic question was asked by one after the other of the audience—why is the English theatre so uninteresting? Fresh as I was from our frustrating casting sessions, I thought the answer might be not only that it drew practically all of its themes and material from a narrow section of the middle class, but that even these, at least to my alien mind, seemed to have been filtered through a mesh of propriety; it was good taste constantly looking over its shoulder. The reception of *Look Back in Anger* showed that something was stirring, but as original a work as it was, it had appeared in England some two decades after very similar attitudes of rebellion had broken onto the American stage through a not dissimilar cordon of middle-class proprieties. Actually, questioning American values and society had been the hallmark of our serious drama for even longer, starting in the twenties with O'Neill, although he was not usually regarded as a social critic. In a word, I wondered if British theatre was still comfortably oblivious to its own social mythology.

But when I thought about the problem later, it seemed to me more complicated; the class or caste system had to be involved. I recalled visiting the House of Commons one day in 1950, during the London production of *Salesman* with Paul Muni, and watching from the empty visitors' gallery as Winston Churchill and Anthony Eden, then in the opposition to Labour, sat on the front bench looking up with rather lordly condescension at the lone Communist in Commons, Willie Gallacher of Clyde, who was addressing the members with his thumbs hooked in the pockets of his unpressed trousers. Just as Gallacher was reaching the climax of his speech, I heard Churchill growl sotto voce but audibly enough, without moving his cigar-distorted mouth, "Take your hands out of your pockets, man!" And Gallacher instantaneously jerked out his thumbs—and no doubt hated himself for weeks after. That was class talking and being obeyed, and it was not something I had ever witnessed in America or thought possible, either the incredible command or the reaction to it.

The theatre meeting took place, I recall, on a Sunday evening, and Marilyn sat in the first row. It was the first time I felt she was being treated as a human, an actress more or less like any other in the profession, in the midst of people concentrating on a serious issue, with no one staring at her or burbling over her. I was not sure how she felt about this casual acceptance, but I thought while driving home that if we could only survive into some such normal atmosphere we might make a good life together. She was quiet in the car, allowing herself a fine silence. A great star's isolation from the calming inattention of ordinary people leaves a kind of unhealing wound. But at home in Roxbury after a time the people were unlikely to treat her very differently from anyone else.

Invited—or summoned—to attend a movie benefit at which the Queen and her entourage would be present, we had two unmarked London police cars fore and aft on our ride to the theatre, and a Scotland Yard plainclothesman sitting beside our driver. Marilyn had been sewn into a spectacular red velvet dress with a Gay Nineties look that barely allowed her to sit. Earlier, at Olivier's apartment, she had been warm and funny with him, and he was excited by her presence, even after all these months of conflict. About fifty open oysters were on a platter on the mantle, and I stood there eating away and hoping we would not have to leave for the theatre too soon.

In the lobby some twenty or so notables were presented to the Queen, Prince Philip, and Princess Margaret. Among them was a quite small and shy girl with long hair piled onto her head; she stood just behind me, and I caught her name, Brigitte Bardot. The Queen had arrived in a blasting glare from the diamonds in her tiara, political theatre in the theatre. But we were all performing, she with her extended hand and we with our grateful smiles, bows, and curtsies. The world as theatre is not metaphor but naturalistic description, in this case of a ritualized formality regulated at every step of the way by precedent and rehearsal.

Nearly thirty years later it would be a different story when I was waiting around at the Kennedy Center until it was time to emerge onto the balcony for the honors ceremony. In came the broadly grinning President and Mrs. Reagan, to shake hands all around with us honorees—Isaac Stern, Danny Kaye, Lena Horne, Gian Carlo Menotti—and our spouses. Reagan immediately began giving advice about how to survive shaking hundreds of hands in a short time, something he had just had to do. He had come from a conversation somewhere else and was simply continuing it with us, and he had me hold out my hand so that he could press his forefinger against the inside of my wrist while grasping it, which allowed him to press down and slip his hand free whenever he decided to. "It's hell when they hold on to you, especially some of

those old ladies," he laughed. "They can bring you to your knees."
An altogether different kind of theatre, that, but it was no less a
performance, a relaxed, offhand American type of acting as contrasted with the Queen's. She created far more awe—but awe is
her line of work, and rather a triumph considering how few operational battleships she has anymore.

Work on the film had its good weeks. I would sometimes bicycle
the ten or so miles to the Shepperton studios to look in at the end
of an afternoon, and find Marilyn laughing and kidding with the
other actors. Now it was Larry who seemed preoccupied and not
too happy. I had given up trying to keep score by this time, still
convinced that when the picture was in the can we were going to
start living. I even made a trip back to the States to be with my
children over their school vacation and returned certain we were
over the hump. But things had begun to change for the worse
again, and Larry decided to invite us to the theatre, doubtless to
break the renewed tension.

Going out with Marilyn in London was still a major logistical
operation. In this case, we were driven up to the stage door and
slipped directly into our seats in the darkness just as the curtain
commenced to rise, lest the performance be disturbed. Either I
had not been paying attention or, more likely, Larry had not
deigned to mention the name of the play or its director or actors,
and with no program or possibility of glancing at a marquee I was
totally ignorant of whom or what I was seeing as the curtain rose.
The setting was the veranda of an elegant house in what looked like
a Caribbean locale. I tried to make out what the actors were saying,
but between the extremely British speech and a plot that was all
words and very little action, I was soon barely able to keep my
brain alive. Why had Larry invited us to this?

Occasionally a surprisingly brilliant line would pop out, and suddenly I noticed that the leading woman was Vivien Leigh, his wife.
So that was it! Now I listened more closely, but to hardly greater
effect than before. It all seemed as lifeless and artificial as a glass
flower. At the interval I leaned past Marilyn and asked Larry,
"Who wrote this play?" The slightest grin tensioned his lips, and
he would not reply. "Every now and then there's a kind of Noel
Coward line, but not often. Who's the author?"

"It is *South Sea Bubble* by Noel Coward."

"Really!"

"Quite." He laughed.

"Great God, what'll I say next!"

"You already have!"

We bent over laughing. Then I asked, "And who directed it?" I was unable to keep a hint of disappointment out of my tone, the direction seeming rather wooden to me, with Vivien rushing to the right and to the left and back again.

Again Larry waited to answer, again with his grin wryly restrained.

"Really, who directed it?"

"I did."

I grabbed my stupid head and made to bang it on the back of the seat in front of me. But our friendship survived. This again was part of his dead past, a play without consequence except as an echo of a now vanished time.

It was terrible to see her anger returning, not only at Olivier, who she was absolutely convinced was condescending to her, but also at Milton Greene, with whom she could barely speak anymore, and finally at herself. I found myself being swept into her disappointment, if only because I was powerless to change anything for her and she could not simply walk away from the film. Anger, relentless and unending, at last refused to give way to any ameliorating word. In my trying to gentle her torment, she thought her cause was being trivialized. And indeed, to me no film was worth this kind of destruction, while to her a performance was almost literally worth a life. In a sense, I thought later, that was the difference between the performer's art and the writer's; the performer *is* his art, the writer can step away and leave it for the world to make of it what it will. I was still certain her performance in this picture was wonderfully witty and that she was overlooking this in her anxiety, but she could not rest or really sleep, and the barbiturates were drawing a distorting film over everything.

In such unremitting frustration, guilt emerged as the principle of life from which neither of us could escape. Each had failed with his magic to transform the other's life, and we were as we had been before, but worse; it was as though we had misled one another. She had no resources to rally against our failure, lived as always without reservation, holding nothing back, none of her hopes and none of her despair, and finally none of her suspicions of everyone around her with the exception of Hedda and Paula, neither of whom would contradict her, the one out of love, the other out of manipulative ambition.

By this time she had been in psychoanalysis for more than a year with a woman doctor in New York, and there would later be two more analysts, first Marianne Kris and then Ralph Greenson, both of them physicians of integrity and unquestionably devoted to her. But whatever its fine details, the branching tree of her catastrophe was rooted in her having been condemned from birth—*cursed* might be a better word—despite all she knew and all she hoped. Experience came toward her in either of two guises, one innocent and the other sinister; she adored children and old people, who, like her, were altogether vulnerable and could not wreak harm. But the rest of humankind was fundamentally dangerous and had to be confounded, disarmed by a giving sexuality that was transfigured into a state beyond even feeling itself, a purely donative femininity. But that too could not sustain forever, for she meant to live at the peak always; only in the permanent rush of a crescendo was there safety, or at least forgetfulness, and when the wave dispersed she would turn cruelly against herself, so worthless, the scum of the earth, and her vileness would not let her sleep, and then the pills began and the little suicides each night. But through it all she could rise to hope like a fish swimming up through black seas to fly at the sun before falling back again. And perhaps those rallies—if one knew the sadness in her—were her glory.

But England, I feared, had humbled both of us.

Another collision with government. I was in the music room one morning working on the original version of *The Misfits,* as a story, when as in a dream I saw a helmeted policeman walking his black bicycle toward the house along a path at the edge of the lawn. He stopped at the open French door and peered in, blinded by the sudden darkness of the interior. I got up and said hello.

"Are you Mr. Arthur Miller?"

"Yes." Dread stabbed my heart—something had gone wrong with my children or with Marilyn!

"I am to bring you to the Foreign Office, sir."

"You are to bring me to the Foreign Office."

"That is correct, sir."

"Where is the Foreign Office?"

"The Foreign Office is in London, sir."

"Why do you want to bring me there?"

"I have been ordered to do that, sir."

"Why? What's the reason?"

"I have no idea, sir."

The insanity of the moment caused me to wonder if I was to ride to London on his handlebars, which he still gripped. "But I've had no notice of this," I said.

"They would like you there today, sir. We have a car. Will you come now? It can be brought round in a few minutes."

There he stood holding his handlebars, a provincial policeman out of Agatha Christie, with his tall black helmet and innocent blue eyes—mindlessly carrying out his orders. I said I could use my own car and driver and agreed to leave shortly.

A man was waiting by the curb when we arrived an hour or so later at the Foreign Office, but his job was merely to lead me through a maze of corridors, past dozens of suppliants of various races and costumes, and finally into an office with one window at head level that opened into the grayish light of an airshaft. It was Dickens country. The officer greeting me had a Guards mustache, an eyepatch, and a bad limp and was held upright by a corset whose outlines I could make out beneath his expensive broadcloth shirt. A shot-down Spitfire pilot, no doubt, and now a cheerful man—to start with.

"And how is the filming going? Are you liking it in Surrey? Saw a photo of you both on bicycles, good cycling down there, don't you think? There's a fairly decent pub on your road, I recall. Are you writing? Good! Hope it's something we'll get to see over here. I enjoyed your *Salesman* play, at the Phoenix, wasn't it, Paul Muni? Extraordinary, yes." And when that ran out, a slightly smiling, rather effervescent pause, as though we were both looking forward to a roast pheasant on a platter, and then the direct look in the eye. He had red hair.

"Your passport will expire next month, Mr. Miller."

"Oh? I guess it does, I hadn't looked lately." So that was it: I had been allowed only a limited six-month passport because my trial in federal court for contempt of Congress was coming up in a few months. The long arm of the State Department and the Committee and all my admirers in the U.S. government was stroking my neck. "What about it?"

"We were wondering about your plans once the film is finished."

"My plans? We're going home."

"I see. That was really all."

"I understand. I couldn't figure out what the hurry was in my appearing here."

He chose not to register my soft rebuke. "You have children in America, I believe."

"Yes."

"And do you own property in this country?"

"No."

"And of course no relatives here."

"I can't wait to get home."

"I should think so. Well, thanks very much for coming." He rose. We shook hands.

"Frankly, it didn't sound like I had much choice." We now laughed. He decided to explain, a little.

"There have been people who have decided not to return under circumstances like yours, and we would rather avoid anything like that in your case . . ."

In other words, the mortifying of America should I decide I'd had enough badgering and wanted to live in England, as Chaplin had, and Joseph Losey, Larry Adler, and quite a long line of other artists during the past five or so Cold War years. A really hot flush of international embarrassment, come to think of it, if Marilyn were to set up house here too. The poor things in Washington must not have slept for nights before deciding to gather me into their arms again.

On the drive back to Surrey I warded off disillusionment with an England whose freedoms I had come deeply to admire. But they were so politically helpless now that their economic independence was washing away. A pity. One less reassurance in the world. And of course it was never far from my mind that withal I was being driven by a uniformed chauffeur to a lovely English country house. Surrealism was naturalism in 1956. In another, more logical time I would have been skulking along hedgerows to escape notice, a political pariah. No wonder it was so difficult to name the real, to touch it, and to feel one's bedrock authenticity. John Proctor and even Eddie Carbone had had God and a community announcing an orderly and a full-throated condemnation. Now? I had my twin in the car with me, an impersonator whose face I shaved every morning and whom I sent out to speak to reporters when that was required, or to the Foreign Office if need be, but who apparently had only the barest resemblance to me, else how could I have been imagined a candidate for flight from the United States, a country I loved as much as my twin was reputed to hate it.

That afternoon I returned to my desk and *The Misfits*, a story of three men who cannot locate a home on the earth for themselves and, for something to do, capture wild horses to be butchered for canned dog food; and a woman as homeless as they, but whose intact sense of life's sacredness suggests a meaning for existence.

It was a story about the indifference I had been feeling not only in Nevada but in the world now. We were being stunned by our powerlessness to control our lives, and Nevada was simply the perfection of our common loss.

Whatever Marilyn was she was not indifferent; her very pain bespoke life and the wrestling with the angel of death. She was a living rebuke to anyone who didn't care.

And there was a political refraction in all this; with the worst war in history only a decade past, the two main allies against Hitlerism were at each other's throats, or almost. Pointlessness was life's principle, and it spread its sadness.

England's kindness would be withdrawn if I should ever ask for shelter here. I thought of the security man and his brutal interrogation of the Hungarian couple.

Surrey resembles some of the Westchester suburbs above New York City—the quiet wealth, the clipped hedges, the comfort. I was really an outlaw, or would be in a few weeks when my passport ran out. Once I got home I would be tried in federal court and probably convicted—everybody cited for contempt was—and might go to jail. I wondered how I could be so unmoved by it all. It came at me like mere information.

One night at Pyramid Lake I had stretched out on the shore, unable to sleep. It was like lying down in a Douanier Rousseau painting, with a motionless moon hanging low over a vast black landlocked sea from whose edges rose the spectral mountains. Deep in the water swam the unchanging prehistoric fish. The island owned by rattlesnake colonies lay off there in the darkness. Nothing moved. I could be part of someone else's dream and might fall out of it into the void. My children must be wondering what had really become of me. Who could explain this world? What was the right question? The moon knew, that one unblinking eye. There was something Nevada-like about England now. Or had I detected some slight hint of regret in the crippled Spitfire pilot's manner as he settled in to question me? It would be nice to think so . . .

One of the minor satisfactions of having survived so long is to realize that the names of Hedda Hopper and Louella Parsons are all but unknown to anyone but relicts of the show business past. If Hollywood before its disintegration into smaller particles was an imperial confederation of half a dozen powerful production com-

panies whose tentacles wrapped around the globe, these two syn-
dicated gossip columnists were the guardian Furies, the police
matrons planted at the portals to keep out the sinful, the unpatri-
otic, and the rebels against propriety unworthy to breathe the
same pure air as such apostolic exemplars as Louis B. Mayer, Harry
Cohn, Jack Warner, Darryl Zanuck, Sam Goldwyn, and a handful
of others. Millions read their dispatches every day, received their
opinions from them, learned whom to hate and whom to applaud.
It would have been a joke except that a real campaign against an
individual, such as they had waged against Chaplin for his links
with liberals and leftists, could sink a film like *Monsieur Verdoux*
and help drive him from the country altogether.

The treasure these two ladies guarded was many-faceted, but its
name could be summed up in one word, *entertainment*. Without
theorizing about it they understood in their bones that in the
oncoming decades ours would become a nation whose primary
business was, in fact, to be entertained. With extremely few honorable exceptions, American movies had simply ignored the rise of
fascism, the depth and degree of suffering in the Depression, the
Spanish Civil War, and the breadth of civic corruption in the country, or if these topics were mentioned, it was with a thick syrup of
sentimental reassurance that leveled out the bumps and covered
the sores.

The ladies' ferocity toward Communism was matched only by
their duplication of some of its practices—as I was reminded in the
Soviet Union a decade later when I read the Party's directions to
Soviet writers to cease linking wisdom to criticism of the country
and either praise or shut up. The American movie was there to
praise American values, which coalesced in the idea of entertainment; indeed, I have wondered over the years whether the real,
if half-conscious, reason for HUAC's fixation on Hollywood leftists
was not that their politics imperiled the nation but that they were
a menace to entertainment. And in fact, for their part, some
screenwriters voluntarily brought stacks of their scripts into the
hearings as evidence that they had never introduced a political,
nonentertaining idea into any of them. They apparently took for
granted that the more vacuous the writing the more American it
was.

Terence Rattigan, for many years a highly skilled and successful
writer of high comedies, gave a party for Marilyn at his home in
London. At one end of a vast salon of some considerable formality,
with a small orchestra soothingly playing American musical hit

tunes while the cream of British theatrical society danced or stood chatting, Louella Parsons, a wide woman in black lace mantilla, looked on from a raised carved armchair that gave her the aspect of a priestess in her tabernacle. She received, never got to her feet. I was astounded, once I learned her identity, that her influence could have spread even to this island, but one after another the actors and directors and their companions made obeisance to her. And she was clearly excited; this was real British class, not Hollywood schlock.

Amazingly enough, a look of pleasure spread across her stout face as I was introduced. It was a face worn and tired from searching other faces for the secrets of dereliction whose exposure had been her daily travail for decades. She actually leaned toward me with outstretched hand and in a mid-American whine invited me to sit beside her. "How wonderful to meet you! Please! Sit down!" I took the much lower chair beside her and looked up as to a papal presence. "How marvelous that you two have come together. We all love Marilyn, it's so wonderful to know she's happy at last. And she does look really and truly happy." I could only nod, recalling that her columns had never been free of a sneering contempt for Marilyn's ambitions to escape the starlet's fate—thereby menacing entertainment.

I looked out at the dazzling company. It was like a dream of being caught in a locked theatre with a hundred actors doing scenes, dancing, calling to one another forever and ever. Yet there were some very gifted people present who doubtless genuinely welcomed Marilyn. I suddenly felt exhausted with trying to read anyone's sincerity; I simply wanted to get out of this theatre and go home.

SEVEN

A play title that occurred to me at the time, *Music for the Deaf,* might symbolize my feelings about our return to the States and what followed. Beethoven conducted the Ninth Symphony's premiere after he had gone totally deaf, and during the performance lost the tempo; so there he was waving his arms and hearing what he was hearing while the audience heard something quite different.

I could not hear the tempo of the time anymore; the theatre and the country seemed to confuse art with self-indulgence, as though the naive alone had truthfulness in it. On some days there was the flowery whiff of nihilism in the air, but who was I to level judgments? Laying judgment was getting harder even than it had been before. But on some days this seemed to me a good thing, for I was no longer able to romanticize the moralism of the thirties and forties.

We found a surprisingly inexpensive but spacious apartment right off the East River. Soon there was a routine, with Marilyn off to her analyst in the mornings and to the Strasberg's apartment in the afternoons for hours of private lessons with Lee. Occasionally we went out to Brooklyn to visit my parents, who would bring in the neighbors to shyly adore Marilyn. The street out front would be full of kids who cheered her when she came out of the little house. She took much pleasure in these ordinary folk and especially loved my aging father, who simply lit up at the sight of her. He had always been mad for light-skinned people and appreciated beautiful women, but it was his unquestioning fatherly indulgence that

4 4 5

was a kind of reassurance for her. He carried around a worn newspaper picture of himself with her, showing it to anybody who would stop and look. He had the vulnerability of age, which moved her to a flowing tenderness with him, and all the strain seemed to leave her when she sat comfortably on the couch at his side. In touch with her his fading feelings lost their pallor. She opened my eyes to his uninstructed sensitivity and good taste in theatre and his level-headed judgments of performers. Once again I saw how refreshingly unsentimental he was compared to my mother, how much harder to fool by fraudulent acting and dumb screenplays. The truth was that I had always been able to tell from his reaction to any story I told him whether it would register in its finished play form. Since he could barely read and write, he had developed an aural intelligence and listened avidly, like a peasant; with no pretensions to taste or learning, he could give back a native human reaction of great purity to what he heard. I found that if I could not make something clear to him, it was not really clear to me or had become too mental and lost its heart, and when I saw his blue eyes *seeing* what I was describing, I knew I had something real and alive to say.

It was strange to think that I would soon be facing a federal prosecutor and judge in Washington and might conceivably go to jail. In the meantime I was trying to straighten out the tangled lines of a new play. I had written only *A View from the Bridge* in the city, the rest in various country places, and I went scouting for a house we might buy, sometimes with my young son, Bob, beside me in the car.

I wrote an experimental scene about a young genius, Carlo, the physicist son of a great physicist, who reveres his father but objects to his advising the military about new weapons. He has developed a theory about a ray that could be directed from the atmosphere and stop all electrical activity in its path, which means it could stop the heartbeat. He dreads what he has discovered and decides to ask his father for advice. But when he begins describing his ray, he realizes that he cannot trust his father not to give the information to the military.

The scene was the perfection of stalemate. Retreating into silence, Carlo becomes his own hostage, deprived even of the ego gratification of the tremendous scientific victory he knows he has earned. The secret, inevitably, begins burning him up, and he is tempted to reveal the incredible power he has created to a colleague who he deeply suspects is in contact with the Russians; he wants the thing stolen from him, he wants it to materialize no matter what. But as with his father, he breaks off before he has unburdened himself to this man.

His self-estrangement moves him into a dappled world of light and shade; he feels omnipotent one moment and helpless the next, even wondering at times if some buried and unacknowledged rage in him has wrought merely an imagined weapon of total destruction that has no reality except as a projection of his own wish to destroy. But the objective truth is impossible to ascertain without disclosing his discovery and risking its release into a world he simply cannot trust with it. Keeping the secret rots him as it possesses him, spreading to his every waking moment and his dreams. He quite literally becomes his secret, until there is nothing left of him but a story that cannot be told.

One stormy afternoon I offered to drive over to the Strasbergs' to pick Marilyn up after her lesson, cabs being almost impossible to find in such heavy rain. When I entered the foyer of the immense Central Park West apartment, I was surprised by what sounded like Stravinsky played on a saxophone and jazz trumpets. Lee came out to greet me, and I immediately asked what this wonderful record was. His reply was an incomprehensibly secret grin as he said that it was a very special recording. "But what is it? Who's playing?" I asked. Once again there was no answer but his slightly private, superior grin and a repeat of his initial description of the record as something unique.

In the next room Marilyn was putting on her coat, a beige camel's hair that I loved, and the record was just coming to an end on the turntable near her. I started to reach for it, but Lee suddenly gestured to keep hands off and lifted it up with infinite care. Holding it vertically before him, he prevented me from reading the label, but I could see that it was gray, the Columbia color.

"It's Woody Herman," he said now.

"Really! I didn't know he played classical music."

Marilyn was watching him reverently. "Oh, yes, of course. He gave this to me."

"What's the title? I'd like to get it."

"No, no, you see this number?" He now held the record flat and indicated a long serial number of the kind stamped on all classical records. "This is a special number. It means that it can't be bought normally, the way you just go out and buy a record."

"But it's got a standard label. And I think all my records have numbers engraved into them."

"Oh, no," he persisted, but now with a tinge of embarrassment, I thought.

"How do you get it, then?"

"I told you. Woody gave it to me."

I looked into his eyes. Marilyn stood there with a certain pride in his being on such terms with the famous musician. I felt a wave of despair at this silly charade. Perhaps he was growing worried that he had taken things dangerously far, for he now broke the silence.

"Of course, if you really wanted to buy one, you could copy down this number and order it." And so it was a private sort of record and a sort of publicly available one, both at the same time. Willy Loman, I thought, rides again.

It was all so very strange. She seemed more and more to be surrounded by something like untruth, and neither I nor anyone else could expose it to her. She was spinning a web that hung from temporary rafters, and I feared it would simply have to be dismantled one day. I could only hope that she would be stronger soon. Lee was so crucial to her and therefore to me that I prayed I was wrong, that he was not the mountebank I thought him then. I saw that I did not understand actors. If he was able to instill faith in them, it was a great thing, and I kept reminding myself that I knew many bright and able actors who swore by him. On the other hand, there were actors of similar caliber who thought him a fraud. Kazan had said of Strasberg once that his great fault was to make his actors more and more rather than less and less dependent on him. But the actor's capital is his faith in himself, and if Lee could deepen hers it would be a blessing, whatever the means.

It was also strange how with each week she seemed to be gaining power all over the world while the swamp of doubt within her showed no sign of drying up. She seemed sometimes like one of those leaders Tolstoy describes in *War and Peace*—people who are given a power over others by some mysterious common consent, no one is sure exactly why, and who come to half believe and half mistrust it as an expression of their authentic nature. But deep within them is the usual vulnerable and mystified human being, in her case a mere child, an abused little girl. She never stopped probing the world and the people around her for the least sign of hostility, and everyone sensed her desperation for reassurance, witty and quick to laugh and winning as she was, and so they reassured her, and truth moved further and further away. But she would be strong enough for it one day, the day she could accept that she was beloved . . .

One day, she would be like the unhappily disturbed woman in Rilke's poem who walks to the window of her room and looks down into the courtyard and sees an immense tree that she has seen a hundred times before—*"Und plötzlich ist alles gut."* It would arrive, the balance, the healing, inflowing silence, possibly through me, possibly not, but suddenly she would know that everything was good.

There had been scores of such trials during the past five or six years of the great American Red-hunt, and none of them had taken more than an hour or two to complete. The routine was simple: the questions that the accused had declined to answer before the Committee of Congress were read; an "expert on Communism" testified that in his opinion the defendant was under "Communist discipline"; and a conviction and sentence for contempt were handed down by the judge. Some, like the Hollywood Ten—screenwriters and directors caught up ten years earlier in the virulence of the first hearings on the movie industry—had gone to jail for a year, but in more recent times a certain therapeutic boredom on the part of the public had tempered the proceedings, and the penalty was more likely to be a fine and suspended sentence, although not by any means in every case. Given the intense publicity about my case, I had reason to fear harsher rather than more lenient treatment, for the Committee would probably want to justify itself by punishing me.

Federal District Court Judge Charles McLaughlin sat behind the high tribunal looking like President Warren Gamaliel Harding, whose handsome face I had memorized so long ago in Far Rockaway when his black-draped photograph was displayed in all the store windows the week of his death. McLaughlin, with his silvery, neatly combed hair, glanced down at his fellow Democrat, my lawyer Joe Rauh, and at Prosecutor Hitz, and amiably contemplated aloud that give or take a few minutes the trial would doubtless be over by noon, about an hour and a half hence. Just as amiably Hitz assured him that the government's case would not require much time at all, and with equal cheerfulness Joe Rauh, giving his little baritone chuckle and touching his finger to his polka-dot bow tie, announced that *his* case would require a minimum of four and possibly five *days* to present.

The shock in Hitz's face I recall aurally rather than visually, as the kind of clicking sound made by a windup toy when it is lifted off the carpet and allowed to spin itself out. The judge was likewise absolutely astonished, having grasped, like Hitz, what Rauh's declaration meant—for the first time a lawyer intended to win a contempt case rather than hopelessly conceding it. As for me, I was too stupid to understand any of this until Joe explained it later; all I knew was that from then on a negative electricity began flowing toward me from the bench and the government table, whereas I had hardly been noticed before the incredible announcement was made. A defendant planning actually to win such a case was evidently an unconscionable affront to all decency and venerable tradition.

One reason for Rauh's imagining that he might if not win then make a record that would reverse the decision on appeal was the Watkins case. In that one he had established a precedent that forbade the Committee to ask questions of a witness unless the answers would serve a legislative purpose. A committee of Congress, in other words, could no longer simply reach out and pick people off the street, as HUAC had been delightedly doing for years, but had to show that their testimony was relevant to some piece of legislation the committee was actively contemplating for submission to Congress. In questioning me, the Committee had made a couple of passes at asking me about my passport in order, as was now amply demonstrated by the prosecution, to line themselves up with the requirement of Watkins. Indeed, my hearing had actually been labeled an inquiry into "the misuse of United States passports."

Naturally, there was not the slightest connection between my refusal to name a writer at a meeting I had attended years earlier and my passport, used or misused. But to my growing amazement—and, as the days passed, my sinking despair—Mr. Hitz opened each of his orations with one or another variation of "Now, when Mr. Miller went into Czechoslovakia, he knew he was forbidden by the stamp on his passport to enter that country . . ." Which indeed would have been a misuse of a passport, but since I had never been in or near Czechoslovakia in my life, it was hard to fathom how they expected to prove anything by this false assertion. Yet every time he took to his feet we had a repetition of it. And when, each time, Rauh rose on a point of order to wearily repeat that I had never been in that country, the judge simply turned back to Hitz and asked him to continue.

After each hard day in court—during which I drew many fine sketches of all the personnel in order to stay awake, while agonizing, like all amateurs, at the snail's pace of the proceedings—we normally returned to Joe's house, where we rushed to the bar and sat drinking as I, for one, had never drunk before. On about the third such evening, our first scotches under our belts, Rauh suddenly screwed his broad face up, pointed at me, and said, "Hey!"

"Yes, sir. Hey what?"

"Hitz keeps putting you in Czechoslovakia in 1947—isn't it '47?"

"Yes, '47."

"But Czechoslovakia was still a democratic country in '47. It was Eduard Beneš who was president then, wasn't it? They weren't Communist yet!"

"My God! I almost visited a free country and did something good! But I wasn't there anyway."

Next morning Rauh sat waiting for Hitz to start his daily prayer for vengeance on me for having gone to the forbidden land. And now it came. "When Mr. Miller went into Czechoslovakia knowing he was forbidden to do so by the terms of his passport . . ." Rauh was on his feet with his basketball shooting arm raised high in the air. "Your honor . . ."

Once recognized by the now wearying Warren Gamaliel Harding on high, Joe paused as before a double-thick lamb chop lying centered on his plate with a piece of parsley on either side and a baked potato with sour cream nudging it, and repeated that Mr. Miller was never in his life in Czechoslovakia, but that even if he had been, Czechoslovakia at the time was a democratic state whose President Beneš was our friend. This, he said, was a matter of history.

Well, now. A pause. Warren Harding looked down at Hitz, and Hitz looked up at Warren Harding, and Rauh sat down and straightened his bow tie with both hands and gave it an additional pat.

And now the judge spoke, saying, "I think it falls under the four corners of the indictment. Proceed, Mr. Hitz."

I leaned urgently toward Rauh and whispered, "What does that mean, 'four corners of the indictment'?" I had the image of a four-cornered tent under which I was suffocating.

Rauh bent to me now and beckoned my ear to his mouth. "Nothing," he said, and laughed. His enjoyment was so infectious that I found myself laughing too, about what, however, only God knew.

Time's fade-outs and fade-ins and cross-fades. More than a quarter-century after my hearing before the Un-American Activities Committee I was seated at a festive table with my wife, Inge Morath, and my guests, Joe Rauh and his wife, Olie, in a dining room in the Cannon office building, improvised for the occasion of the Kennedy Honors opening banquet because the State Depart-

ment dining room was then under reconstruction. A hundred or
more people, many of great distinction, were present, with Secretary of State George Shultz the official host. As we had entered
within a mob of celebrants, I'd had no chance to look at our sur-
roundings, but I noticed now that the walls and ceiling were newly
painted in decorator colors rather than the usual federal drab. Joe
Rauh suddenly turned fully around in his chair to study the room
and then leaned past Olie and told me that I was being honored
in the same room where my HUAC hearing had been held so many
years before.

Of course the layout was all different now, with a score of banquet tables covering the floor, but even after mentally reconstruct-
ing the old layout I could not connect to the place. Irony was all
I seemed able to feel, and it seemed so coldly metallic a thing when
I recalled the hot gases that had poured over me in this very room.
I looked around at the happy guests and the healthily smiling
secretary of state and the famous faces of my fellow honorees, and
again I felt on the outside looking in, and more, that it all lacked
reality. I had supposed that after the kind of merciless rejection I
had known it would never be easy to accept the smooth self-congratulation of such ceremonies. Still, I could enjoy this good-spir-
ited occasion—sort of. Maybe I had the illusion of having lost my
fear of power, having been close enough to it to know there was
nothing power had that I wanted. But a lot of my former faith in
the system's enduring beneficence had been burned out of me, too.
All that was the same on both occasions was the flag, which now
as then hung from a staff near a wall. It might even have been the
same one that had hung behind Congressman Walter's head so
long ago, and I recalled now how it had reassured me then, although I knew that to many in the world it signified cruel wealth
and arrogant blindness. But how to put all this together in a coherent sense of my life? Or maybe I ought to settle for it all having
been a dream, a dream of perpetual exile and perpetual returns.

The most interesting talk I recall having in that barren week of my
trial was with former senator Harry P. Cain, whom Rauh had
brought up from his semi-retirement in Florida to testify as my
"expert witness on Communism." He had read my plays and did
not believe I had been "under the discipline of the Communist
Party." Normally in such trials it was the government alone that
produced "expert testimony," usually from ex–Communist offi-

cials, to prove that the defendant showed all the necessary hoof-marks of the Communist Lucifer. This routine, incidentally, was an all but exact duplication of the use of clergy as experts on witch-craft in the Salem of 1692; one of them, Reverend Hale of Beverly, is a character in *The Crucible*. Hale in my play, like his original in history, defected from the prosecution's side on realizing that he had been had by the "afflicted girls" and, filled with remorse, tried unsuccessfully to save the people his earlier "expertise" had helped condemn to hang. Harry Cain's story, I now learned, was amazingly similar.

A much decorated marine who had fought in the Korean War, Cain was one of a very few Red-hunters to have turned against the whole business, in his case with a vengeance. He had ridden the anti-Communist tide out of his native state of Washington when, with no trace of any political background, he was picked up by the Republicans and run for the Senate. His sole campaign theme was the Communist menace, about which he had such powerful feelings that he would demand Chaplin's deportation for having asked "the self-admitted Communist Picasso" to help organize French protests against American repression.

Joe McCarthy came out to help him, and even then, in the full flood of his fervor, Cain noticed something disconcerting about Joe's paranoid vindictiveness. One night they were both on the platform in an American Legion hall when "some guy got up in the back and began heckling McCarthy. The boys threw him out in the street, but you couldn't help noticing how really mad McCarthy was at the guy—I mean he was mad *personally*, he was damn near shaken. It was weird.

"Anyway, some years passed, and we were playing poker with the wives one evening, and suddenly Joe looks at me and says, 'What'd you do about that guy?'

"I didn't know who he was talking about. 'That guy in the Legion hall that night who was bugging me.'

"It took me a minute to recall, it had been so long ago. I couldn't believe he'd even remember it, but it still really bothered him that somebody way, way back there in Tacoma hadn't gone along with him. And I said something like, 'I don't know, I guess they just tossed him out of the hall. Why?'

" '*Why!* For Chrissake, the son of a bitch was heckling me!'—and he was mad as hell all over again. I couldn't believe it, because Joe was not all that bad a guy, you know. He could be awfully sweet and good to a person if he wanted to be. He just got onto the

Communism thing and ran with it, and I think he was always scared it was going to collapse under him, so he kept looking for enemies.... Tell you the truth though, Arthur, the really vindictive ones were the wives. We'd be playing cards with some of these senatorial wives and their husbands, and more likely than not the wives'd be the ones who'd say, 'When are you going to get this one or that one? Why do you let him get away with saying this or that? Go get the son of a bitch!' They were the *real* haters."

In court Cain testified that he had read my plays and found that politically they were so contradictory that they could not have been written under Party control. It was pleasant testimony, but obviously the tracks were laid and the train was going to its appointed station no matter what.

Cain's transformation had grown out of his former job as head of the Subversive Activities Control Board, to which he was appointed by President Eisenhower after his defeat for a second term as senator. The board's mandate was to see that no Reds were hired by government or held government positions. In an ordinary day he received a bushel of letters of denunciation of one citizen by another for real or imagined subversive views, plus a small but steady number of complaints by accused people claiming innocence of Communist associations or sympathies, which went into the files with little ado.

A persistent man in Baltimore, however, caught Cain's bored attention with a semiliterate protesting letter about every third day claiming that he had been unjustly fired as a subversive from his job at the post office. A real Red, Cain imagined, had to know how to spell better than this, and he wrote agreeing to see the man to discuss the matter, figuring he would probably not dare to show up and face his interrogation.

But he did appear one morning and convinced Cain of his innocence. He had the same name as a man known to have contributed to some Party front. Cain got him his job back, but he now found himself staring at his massive files containing the hundreds of denials, partial denials, remorseful confessions, denunciations—the whole mixed detritus of thousands of Americans who had lived through the New Deal years and had been tainted with what was simplistically branded subversion. Beginning by attempting to sort out the obvious from the less obvious Reds, the far leftists from the more conservative leftists and the mere left liberals, he arrived in some worried weeks at the point where he no longer believed that the government should be in the ideological policing business at all. He got an appointment with Eisenhower, to whom he confided his deep misgivings that they were assembling a governmental structure of a totalitarian, mind-controlling bent. Eisenhower listened and Cain was promptly fired.

At the time of my trial he was doing regular political commentary on some Florida TV station. Sitting and talking with him in the Rauh living room, I saw a man with the special kind of tired, thin laugh that comes to those who have been spewed out by power and know they are not ever coming back.

When Judge McLaughlin looked down at me and asked if I had anything to say before sentencing, I thought I saw a look of embarrassment on his kindly Midwestern small-town face. I could think of nothing to add, and he sentenced me to pay a five-hundred-dollar fine and serve a month in jail, with the prison term suspended. The case was reversed by the court of appeals a few months later, with only the briefest technical comment. Spyros Skouras was quick to send a superlatively congratulatory telegram.

With the sentence delivered, McLaughlin quickly left, explaining to Rauh that he had a funeral to attend. And so Joe and I gathered up my doodles and his few documents and ambled out onto the broad steps of the courthouse into the bright Washington sunshine, where he suddenly grabbed my arm. "Wait! You can't leave this building, you're a convicted criminal! We've got to get you bailed out!"

With which we rushed down one empty marble corridor after another looking for a bail bondsman and a clerk to set me free. We were now in Kafka country, it being a few minutes after five, when no proper clerk would be found dead in a federal court. What to do? To depart might be to invite a whole new charge of flight from justice. Luckily, we happened on a wandering clerk on his way home who agreed to reopen his office and fix me up with the necessary stamps and documents.

In the early eighties, some twenty-five years later, I received a letter from a literature professor at a Midwestern university identifying himself as the nephew of Judge McLaughlin, now deceased, whom he rather feelingly described as having had an important and good influence on his development, as a man of warm human sympathies and a certain quality of intellect. Would I mind telling him how I felt about his uncle, who had confided to him that my trial had troubled him greatly and left him with some regrets about his part in it? Particularly, what had my impressions of him been during the actual trial?

I wrote the professor that I honestly felt no rancor toward the judge, regarding him now as simply one more deanimated cog in the gears. After all, no civil liberties organization had offered me its help then, any more than two years earlier when I had been barred from writing the screenplay on delinquency despite the *World-Telegram*'s suggestion that I be "allowed" to finish it but that my name not appear on the screen. To this benign outrage there was also no public reaction whatever, neither from the literary world and the civil libertarians nor from the reborn leftists and libertarian Trotskyites, who were now giving their all to fight Soviet totalitarianism and its contemptuous treatment of writers. It was simply that having once been pro-Soviet, I had failed later on to make the right exculpatory noises, the passionate anti-Soviet protestations, fearing as I still did a blind anti-Communism that could easily overflow into a primitive fascist spirit at home and fling us into war abroad; had failed, in short, to close my eyes to what was happening in my own country, something that would cost me over the years in certain influential literary quarters where such things mattered quite as much as literature—indeed, a lot more.

The hearing and trial seemed an artistically barren experience for me—I had already written *The Crucible* five years before, and the dynamics of the phenomenon were too repetitious to teach me much more. Yet in the long run it too served my education; a decade later, well before such concerns became the common property of Western intellectuals—if for some merely a chic exercise—I would accept the international presidency of PEN, an organization of poets, essayists, and novelists, and at the time a virtually expiring institution. Its London leadership, under David Carver, came to me in Paris while I was there on a long visit, in a last desperate hope that having a known working writer as president might help PEN to survive. No writer whose typewriter was still warm could want such a job, I thought, but after weeks of trying I finally found it impossible to turn down; my American experience had given me too clear an idea of what writers were going through in Eastern Europe and the benighted, ignorant, brutalized parts of the globe where there were few to hear and fewer to offer a helping hand once government had decided that they must be silenced. I thought by the mid-sixties that perhaps I could help hasten the time when a human principle unclouded by the Cold War, then temporarily in abeyance, might be seriously asserted. The Un-American Activities Committee had provided me with the desire to make its like impossible here anymore, and maybe on some far-off day, everywhere else in the world.

* * *

Our rented house in eastern Long Island faced broad green fields that made it hard to believe we were so near the ocean. Next door lived a painter and her husband who cherished their own privacy and thus defended ours. Now we could take easy breaths in a more normal rhythm of life. Marilyn had decided to learn how to cook and started with homemade noodles, hanging them over a chair-back and drying them with a hair dryer, and she gave me hair trims out in the sunshine, and we walked the empty Amagansett beach in peace, chatting with the occasional commercial fishermen who worked their nets from winches on their rusting trucks. These local men, Bonackers, so-called, greeted her with warmth and respect, even though she perplexed them by running along the shore to throw back the gasping "junk" fish they had no use for and had flung from their nets. There was a touching but slightly unnerving intensity in her then, an identification that was unhealthily close to her own death fear. One day, after throwing a couple of dozen fish one by one back into the water, she was losing her breath, and I finally had to distract her and draw her away to keep her from working the shoreline until she dropped.

The doctor, having administered a series of treatments over a period of weeks, had confirmed that she was pregnant, but could still not rule out the possibility of an ectopic pregnancy. I thought in talking to him that he really feared this danger at least as much as he hoped for a term pregnancy. But she was deaf to his caution-ary tone. A child of her own was a crown with a thousand dia-monds. I did all I could to throw myself into her anticipatory mood, at the same time trying to keep reality within sight should a crash be awaiting us. But the very idea of her as a mother ultimately swept me along with her, for already there were moments of a new kind of confidence, a quietness of spirit that I had never seen in her. For the first time she was being the hostess in her own home rather than defensively shying away from inconsequential visits by people whose good intentions she might normally not have trusted. She was beginning to feel a safe space around herself, or so it seemed. Becoming a father again in my forties would take some getting used to, but the almost visible process of learning about herself that the pregnancy had triggered was enough to convince me that if a child might intensify her anxieties, it would also give her, and hence myself, new hope for our future.

But her reprieve was short; the pregnancy was soon diagnosed as tubal and required an operation to end it, and as she lay recovering in her hospital bed, her vulnerability was almost impossible to bear: I would surely turn away from her, wounded as she was—a fear that was incredible to me. Returning to the apartment after a visit one night, I realized that this might be a chance to demonstrate what she meant to me, for her defenselessness moved me deeply. But I could think of nothing, and words of reassurance were clearly not enough.

The photographer Sam Shaw came to visit in the hospital one afternoon, and we took a walk along the East River afterward and sat on a bench talking about her. I knew Sam only slightly; he was an unaffected man who had never exploited his friendship with her, admiring her for her valor in taking life on so unarmed, with no allies and no reservations. I said that I thought there was a greatness of spirit in her, even a crazy kind of nobility that the right role might release, and if that happened she might step out of herself and see her own worth. Psychoanalysis was too much like talking *about* something rather than doing it, which was the only thing she had ever believed in anyway—her life had all been put up or shut up.

Sam began talking about my story *The Misfits*, which he had read in *Esquire* magazine. "It would make a great movie," he said, "and that's a woman's part she could kick into the stands."

The ambulance ride back to Amagansett took a seemingly endless three hours or more, and it was nearly impossible to speak. There could be no assurance that another pregnancy would succeed. Somehow, the past once again seemed to be reaching out its dead hand to drag her down. There were no words anymore that could change anything for her. She lay there sad beyond sadness, watching the traffic pass the cautiously driven ambulance. I felt an urgency about making something for her.

After a few days I began sketching out a screenplay, for the first time since our marriage working from breakfast to dinner. There was a studio detached from the house where I could be alone. My mother came out to visit, but a strange distrust soon arose between them, and she cut her stay short and returned to the city on the train, troubled and, I thought, frightened. Marilyn, it turned out, had sensed something like disapproval in her—maybe only disappointment, which came to the same thing—and was as upset with her as if she had been menaced. While I attempted to reassure her otherwise, I saw that she was not altogether wrong. My mother could be superstitiously put off by ill people; she wanted Marilyn whole and beautiful. This had gone past me, but Marilyn had dug at it until it dominated their time together. She had an uncanny instinct for threat and wanted it out in the open, having no reserves to withstand it. And of course with an older woman she had no means of sexually disarming it.

Still, a few days later she could laugh about it. Soon we could drive to isolated beaches and swim together. Strangely, she had never properly learned to swim; it was the only awkward thing she ever did, and her clumsy attempts ended in laughter. Emerging from the water, her powerful body threw back the sun like Botticelli's Venus, and sometimes she even had the same saltwater-washed, sea-emergent stare.

Life sent a helicopter to take her to be photographed at a promotional celebration in their New York headquarters; she was back in a few hours, descending past my studio window and stepping out onto the lawn. I came out and we both stood there waving to the rising pilot and an executive who had escorted her. She was wearing a full-skirted yellow cotton dress and high-heeled shoes and still carried a couple of roses someone had thrust into her hand. Her makeup seemed too artificially white in the sunlight, and when the copter was gone we looked at one another awkwardly; what a mixture of feelings! There could not have been another woman in the country they would have flown to New York and back like this for a couple of photographs; there was some madness to the desperation of their need for her. What frightening power she had! The event seemed like the intrusion of a gross iron hand into the vulnerable flesh of our existence and yet at the same time signified her triumph, a proof of the immense public importance she had won. She was distracted as we walked across the lawn back to the silent house, as though she needed time to be quiet and alone, to drive the vibrations of the helicopter out of her bones. I resolved to regard the publicity question purely as a work condition, which it was, but one had to face the inbuilt paranoid opening in the ups and downs of her standing with her public; she, the woman, could not send herself out to perform and make appearances while remaining at home to create a life. Having to look at herself with two pairs of eyes, her own and a hypothetical public's, was as inescapable as it was enervating in the end.

She would read parts of the screenplay and laugh delightedly at some of the cowboys' lines but seemed to withhold full commitment to playing Roslyn. My own interest in the project was by now as much technical as it was a matter of feeling: I was constructing a gift for her. In the end, however, it was she who would have to play the role, and this inevitably began to push the project into a different, coolly professional sphere. If my intention was as authentic as I wished to believe it was, she had the right to decide not to play the part—after all, I was not writing it to enslave her to something she had no excitement about doing. Nevertheless, her caution had to hurt a bit.

As I neared the end of the first draft, I thought of John Huston as the film's director. He had been the first to see some potential in Marilyn when he cast her in *The Asphalt Jungle,* and she had never forgotten his brusque kindnesses to her. Huston was one of her few good Hollywood memories, which encouraged me to think that a movie production could be as happy as some of my theatre productions had been, without the dark paranoid clouds that seemed to overhang the making of every movie of hers I knew about. I sent him a script at his home in Ireland as soon as it was typed. While we waited for his response, the implication began to grow that without Huston she might well not play the role, and I wondered when she spoke this way whether she was at all aware . . .

But I had joined my life with hers and still expected her to come to believe it one day—it was inevitable. The problem was that permanence with another person was a missing part of her, but it could be planted in her and would grow until we were partners in a common life. At the same time it was difficult to deny what her nerves signaled to her: that although with *The Misfits* I was preparing to dedicate a year or more of my life to her enhancement as a performer—I would never have dreamed of writing a movie otherwise—I was sometimes apprehensive and unspontaneous with her. This she might interpret as disapproval, but it was simply that I was off balance and could no longer confidently predict her moods. It was almost as though the fracture of her original idealization of me in England had left no recognizable image at all, and if what remained was to humbly accept reality, it meant junking the ideal, a difficult thing to do when, paradoxically, her energy rose out of her idealizations of people and projects. Still, hope was by no means fading; most marriages, after all, are conspiracies to deny the dark and confirm the light.

The source of it all lay in history—ancient roots had sprung these strange blossoms. I had joyously accepted the role she had long been fashioning for someone who would save her, and so far I had not made it happen; just as she had seemed the all-forgiving and sensuous beloved that a self-denying life had been preparing me for long before she arrived. In the void that had opened up between these dreams and reality worked the immemorial worms of guilt, the guilt each of us felt at having been naive and foolish, or even worse, having misled the other. But absolute commitment could still heal, I thought, and I was ready. That I had always looked down on screenwriting and had refused offer after offer to write pictures helped persuade me that something of importance was being sacrificed in this venture, and sacrifice is the essence of commitment. Thus *The Misfits* was loaded with a freight that needed a very strong vessel to bear; nothing else was possible, since I longed for her as much as for peace. She still blanked out the sun.

From Ireland, Huston quickly agreed to direct the picture. Casting would have to begin soon, but I wanted time to go over the screenplay carefully. He and I would meet in a few months to arrive at a shooting script.

Meanwhile, she still owed Twentieth Century Fox two pictures, at least one of which they insisted she complete before she could work independently, as she would on *The Misfits*. I welcomed the delay. Before too long, another non-Fox film would intervene, when Billy Wilder chose Marilyn for *Some Like It Hot*. But again I was in no rush, wanting the best possible cast around her, something that always took more time than anyone was willing to anticipate. While I waited, perhaps I could begin a new play.

I assumed that Huston would dictate most of the technical factors going into the film, so the producer should be someone who above all would be willing and able to gain Marilyn's complete confidence. I had known Frank Taylor since before the war when he had worked in the same publisher's office as Mary. Later, at Reynal and Hitchcock—a new firm he quickly provided with a prestigious list of authors—he had been my first editor, publishing *Situation Normal,* the book on army camps stemming from my research for the Ernie Pyle film, and my novel, *Focus.* I knew he had recently put in a couple of years as a producer for Fox, but his ideas had been too lofty to reach production—among them a script on Gauguin by James Agee and Fitzgerald's *Tender Is the Night.* A gaunt, sophisticated man of great height, he was an imaginative mixture of aggressive entrepreneur and aficionado of literature. Naturally he was delighted by my invitation, and when he came to meet Marilyn in our apartment, he quickly seemed to dispel her chronic uncertainty about a new person entering her life. I was sure I could rely on him, and she soon sensed that she could too.

A sly eagle named Lew Wasserman, the head man at MCA, seconded my desire for an ideal cast and proceeded to line up Clark Gable, Montgomery Clift, Eli Wallach, and Thelma Ritter.

Wasserman was the only man I ever knew who offered to shake hands with the side of his hand against his flat stomach and his palm straight up, but he understood what an agent should be doing, and that was what he effortlessly did.

The first problem was that for all his interest, Gable simply did not understand the script. Face to face with him in Hollywood a few months later, I thought there could be no other actor playing Gay Langland; he was born for it. But after several readings the script still evaded him.

"It's supposed to be a Western, but it's not, is it?" he asked in his high nasal voice. He had a craftsman's seriousness. His mystification gave that mythically confident face an attractive vulnerability.

I had never been too good at explaining my own work, especially not to actors looking for bread-and-butter answers while I was doing my skywriting extrapolations. I could not think of a reply that would not sound philosophical and therefore like box-office death. "It's sort of an Eastern Western," I said hesitantly. That got a laugh, and better yet, his quickened curiosity. "It's about our lives' meaninglessness and maybe how we got to where we are." I had never really rationalized the story to myself, but his fascinated eyes encouraged me. "Westerns and the West have always been built on a morally balanced world where evil has a recognizable tag—the black hats—and evil always loses out in the end. This is that same world, but it's been dragged out of the nineteenth century into today, when the good guy is also part of the problem. And if you want me to keep talking I'll get both of us so mixed up I won't know what I wrote."

He read the script again and next day agreed to be in it. Unknowingly I may have struck a chord that he himself had only lately begun to play. Many times married and a playboy for most of his life, Gable at nearly sixty had recently become a prospective father for the first time, and a fanatical one at that. He had also become more introspective, according to those who knew him.

Monty Clift was a different kind of problem. His surges of self-destructiveness had sent him driving his car into a pole one night, partly disfiguring his face. (I was of course charged by one of Monty's self-appointed entourage with exploiting that injury by casting him as Perce, whose face has been damaged in a rodeo accident, even if the original story as well as the screenplay long antedated Clift's smashup.) The insurance companies would no longer underwrite Monty in a film. But between my vouching for him and the insistence of Huston and Wasserman on his playing Perce, the insurance came through. As a matter of fact, I never even discussed with Monty the question of his reliability but merely offered him the part, which he enthusiastically accepted. He was so pleased to be working with me and Huston and Marilyn on this film that I couldn't believe he would betray his responsibility. And indeed he never missed an hour's work: he had his entire part memorized before shooting began and was always on time despite the long delays in finishing the picture.

A man sits down at a typewriter with some blank paper on which he types image-describing words, and at a certain point turns around and confronts some four or five hundred people, and trucks and food wagons, airplanes, horses, hotels, roads, cars, lights, all of which he has by some means, untraceable now in its complexity, evoked from nowhere and nothing. Oddly, he ends up with little power over these results of his imagination; they go their own way with not the slightest awareness that they owe their current incarnation to him.

On some days amid all this production I had to smile to myself, recalling that I had set out to create the feeling of a few isolated, lost, and lonely people on the vast mythic plain of existence. Now wherever you looked there was somebody eating a sandwich.

Right off, on our first day of shooting on a Reno street, I had trouble with the literalness of the camera, whose unacknowledged middle name is "merely." For me the streets of Reno might be a feeling, but the camera made them a thing; even commonplace scenes that I had known from my Nevada time nearly four years earlier took on a theatrical self-consciousness as soon as the camera turned on them. In part to avoid this, Huston decided on using black and white rather than color, but to me it was still there. The camera has its own kind of consciousness; in the lens the Garden of Eden itself would become ever so slightly too perfect.

Still naive about film, I kept comparing what we were shooting with my original image. To the eye the background context, even if not consciously noticed, is always in a tension with the focal center of what one sees. But the camera vastly emphasizes the foreground and in close-ups eliminates background completely; thus the it-ness of a person or object comes forward, and its super-detail cuts it off from the contextual life that the eye sees. The illusion of a context that is not really there must be created by editing and montage.

In her first shot Marilyn stood on a Reno bridge over the Truckee, a stream into which newly divorced women customarily tossed their wedding rings to celebrate freedom. Thelma Ritter, her inept, tough-sounding landlady, is trying to lift her low spirits. Watching Marilyn, I couldn't help feeling her disappointment not only in her character's marriage but in her own, and probably in herself. After the finish of the second take I went to her and told her it looked good; she glanced up at me ironically, as though I were lying. When she did that, she could make you feel you were. And to a degree it was true—I had sensed something withdrawn in her, not merely in the character she was playing. But I insisted it was only her insecurity showing; surely we still had a future, and the work on this film would somehow help to make it happen. It was far from accidental that by the end of the film Roslyn does find it possible to believe in a man and in her own survival.

Huston, heartily satisfied and bubbling with congratulations, overrode her wish to shoot the scene a third time, thereby unwittingly suggesting to her that he might be intending to settle for "good enough," and setting off an alarm bell in her mind. The miasma was threatening to swirl in again, but this time I felt as she did, that the scene lacked vitality. As simple and direct as it was, I wondered if she was not trying to give it too much meaning; already it was verging on the effortful. Huston probably sensed it would only get heavier the more times he shot it, and rather than register a backward step on the first day, he elected to push on. From her viewpoint, however, she had not been exhaustively *used*.

Huston seemed to be implicitly laying down his rules—let the actor do the acting while the director supplied overview and commented on the effect, but he was not going to tear her apart, remake her, transport her beyond her skin; was not going to be Lee or any other teacher. He was going to be Huston and she was going to be Marilyn, and beyond that there was no reality he was interested in entering. By the day's second shot, in which she meets Gable and Wallach in a bar, his approach seemed correct; she was fun, flirty, while keeping her inner preoccupation with fate in play underneath. She was professional, accurate, happy; I was ready to celebrate her accepting my gift of words that she would make live.

Never far from sight stood Paula, dressed for the heat of Reno in a black sack dress; black, she insisted, was cooler than the white the laws of physics would seem to have indicated. The crew promptly named her Black Bart, or simply Bart. Between takes she would retire with Marilyn to her trailer, where, when I entered, they would usually fall silent, just as they would before Huston. But I understood that an actor in creating his role recapitulates in a specific sense what an author has gone through to conceive it, reaching out in many directions to find its bounds and shape; it was not unreasonable now that in her absorption she could not see me, or anyone else either. All I knew for certain was that she was becoming something other than I had known before; on the screen at moments she seemed bright and alive, but in life she seemed opaque to everyone, as though she had all but disappeared into herself. But I was not a stranger to this same process in myself when at work.

I knew the rumors of Huston's sadism with actors, as well as writers, but by this time I was discounting anything I heard second- or thirdhand. Like most who are photographed and written about, I had encountered too many people who were sincerely persuaded that they were related to me, had been my classmates, had helped me write my plays, had been taken to bed by me, treated very well, very badly, ignored, pursued, and so on. A very large percentage of mankind seems to live in imaginary proximity to famous people with whom they carry on complex relationships, illusory conversations, scenes of conflict, and love affairs that even include heartbreaking partings and joyous reconciliations. The famous are balloons far up in the sky, to be envied for their quiet freedom or shot down as enemies. I had learned to take people in the business as they came and to ask nothing more than that they do their jobs faithfully. Huston, as far as I could see, was very nearly the perfect personality for this film and this cast. He quickly took to ignoring Paula's presence by offering absurdly elaborate congratulations —on her wearing a black dress in this terrible heat, for example— and by listening to everything she had to tell him with a seriousness so profound as to be ludicrous. It took her a while to catch on, and when she did it brought on one of the many crises awaiting us down the road. From the outset he insisted on treating Marilyn not as a patient but as a professional actress who did not need any condescending encouragement from him. This seemed to show signs of fortifying her and revived the illusion with which I had begun writing the film, that it would provide us our chance to live and work in partnership. The Huston I saw, whatever his reputed faults, relied on a certain ultimate resiliency or even courage in people, probably because he saw himself as a lifelong fighter against impossible odds. He would present Marilyn with the bracing challenge of fighting her problems through to a fine performance in a role for which she had every resource.

He had to have known that in her previous film, *Some Like It Hot,* under Billy Wilder's direction, she had given a marvelous comic performance that belied her agony during its production.

He was assuming that she had elected to proceed in torment through her life. He never begrudged people their temperament—the unconscious was not his business, nor could he afford to take it into directorial consideration. The job of an actor was acting, and how he managed to act was his own and no one else's affair, least of all the director's. It was a breath of fresh air, it seemed to me, calculated to put Marilyn on her mettle, and she responded as he hoped she would, at least for the first few days. But soon the signs of inner disquiet appeared again, except that there was no fault found with either Huston or her fellow actors.

I knew by this time that I had initially expected what she satirized as "the happy girl that all men loved" and had discovered someone diametrically opposite, a troubled woman whose desperation was deepening no matter where she turned for a way out. By the start of *The Misfits* it was no longer possible to deny to myself that if there was a key to Marilyn's despair I did not possess it.

During the shooting of *Let's Make Love* and *Some Like It Hot* I had all but given up any hope of writing; I had decided to devote myself to giving her the kind of emotional support that would convince her she was no longer alone in the world—the heart of the problem, I assumed. I went so far as to do some rewriting on *Let's Make Love* to try to save her from a complete catastrophe, work I despised on a script not worth the paper it was typed on. It was a bad miscalculation, bringing us no closer to each other. She seemed to take for granted what for me had been a sacrifice of great blocks of time, and if it was plain that her inner desperation was not going to let up, it was equally clear that literally nothing I knew to do could slow its destructive progress.

As *The Misfits* went into production, I clung to an expectation of change, not knowing quite why. Maybe it was that the role of Roslyn, her first serious one, had the womanly dignity that part of her longed for. And Roslyn's dilemma was hers, but in the story it was resolved. I hoped that by living through this role she too might arrive at some threshold of faith and confidence, even as I had to wonder if I could hold on to it myself after we had both been let down from expectations such as few people allow themselves in a marriage.

Yet despite everything, I felt we were still a challenge for one another, a challenge I believed we could meet. It might take a miracle, but I had not surrendered my sense of a total relation with at least one side of her being, nor had she with something in me. For each of us, in this limited sense, there was no substitute for the other, as is true for any idealized person or cause, however tarnished by time. Marilyn possessed a revolutionary idealism, regardless—or probably because—of her difficulties. We had come together at a time when America was in yet another of her reactionary phases and social consciousness was a dying memory, and that was an important element in her disillusionment with the country and herself and all she dealt with. The public knew little or nothing about what forces were manipulating their lives, and movies and plays and books were doing nothing to educate them. At moments, talking about this indifference, she seemed to have a Robespierre inside her awaiting an angry, righteous entrance. Wherever she turned she saw what she called "lallygagging," temporizing, the absence of strong and even miraculous liberating blows. She demanded a hero, and at such times nothing material mattered to her, including herself.

By now, 1960, we had patched up an old house we had bought half a mile up the road from my former place in Roxbury, Connecticut, and she had thrown herself into its remodeling with all her immense visionary energy. That we could not really afford all of her ideas I did my best not to dramatize, but it was inevitable that some of my concern showed, as well as that her sense of her own value would get tangled up with any estimate of how far we could objectively go. Money for her—as with the extremely wealthy and the very poor—was not something to be husbanded against a problematic future but to be spent as it came in, and rather grandly at that; to me it meant liberty, the freedom to write without hiring out to studio or producer.

We had begun a year or so earlier by merely fixing up the worst faults in the old house, with the idea of building a new one on a crest of woodland within sight of it. She had contacted Frank Lloyd Wright to come up with a plan. Her impulse was royal, in part a kind of gift to me of a unique home. Thus it had to seem like ingratitude to question whether we could ever begin to finance any Wright design, since much like her, he had little interest in costs. I could only give him his day and let her judge whether it was beyond our means or not.

Wright, then near ninety, promptly curled up in the back seat of the car when we picked him up in Manhattan one gray fall morning, sleeping soundly the two hours it took to get to Roxbury. He was tall and theatrically handsome and wore a wide-brimmed

Western hat and a vast broadly checked overcoat, and rather than merely speaking tended to deliver resonant declarations in a tone reminiscent of W. C. Fields's nasal drawl. On entering he looked around at the living room and said with amused disparagement, "Ah, yes, the old house. Don't put a nickel in it." We shared some smoked salmon and bread, but he declined pepper. "Never eat pepper, the stuff will kill you before your time. Avoid it."

Leaving Marilyn behind, I led him up the long, steep grade to the crest of the low mountain where the house would be sited, a walk of half a mile or more. He never asked to pause. At the top, turning toward the magnificent view with the wind at his back, he peed and said, "Yes. Yes, indeed." Then, quickly glancing about, he struck out down the hill at a fast pace over rocks and hummocks and broken ground. When we finally reached dead level and slowed down across a field of stubble, I thought the time had come to tell him something he had never bothered to ask, that we expected to live fairly simply and were not looking for some elaborate house with which to impress the world. I saw that this news had not the slightest interest for him.

His plan, actually a rather impressionistic watercolor, was not a complete surprise: a circular living room with a dropped center surrounded by ovoid columns of fieldstone some five feet thick, and a domed ceiling, the diameter no less than sixty feet, looking out toward the view over a swimming pool seventy feet long with fieldstone sides that jutted forth from the incline of the hill. The pool's supporting walls at the far end would have to be something like twenty feet high, and to hold water in addition to simply standing there, they would require, I judged, heavy construction on the order of the Maginot Line. When I asked what the house would cost, Wright said something about two hundred fifty thousand dollars, which, having done some building, I guessed might cover the cost of the swimming pool, if that. There were two lovely touches to his watercolor fantasy, a long 1920s-style limousine in the curved driveway with a uniformed chauffeur in the open driver's compartment, and a pennant flying stiffly from the top of the building, no doubt to signal that the owners were at home. His pleasure-dream of Marilyn allowed him to include in this monster of a structure only a single bedroom and small guestroom, but he did provide a large "conference room" complete with a long board-room-type table flanked by a dozen high-backed chairs, the highest at the head, where he imagined she would sit like the reigning queen of a small country, Denmark, say. On the whole it would have been useful as a hideaway for corporate executives to plot illegal stock deals and illicit mergers.

When I went to his office in the Plaza Hotel and saw his design, I said it was far too elaborate for what we had in mind, more news that had no visible effect on him. Indeed, he proceeded to show me immense watercolor sketches of an entire new city he had designed, if I recall, for either the Shah of Iran or the ruler of some oily sheikdom, with dozens of dreamy pink towers and minarets and interconnecting roadways strung across the sky from one building to another. I naturally looked for what would support these concrete ribbons and found nothing.

As scene followed scene in the shooting of *The Misfits,* my main worry continued to be that the context—the immense dead spaces of Nevada in which man seems lost—too often was blanked out by close-ups. Still, I saw a point in cinematographer Russell Metty's insistence that "they're not going to pay to get into this movie to see scenery." A tough old hand, he rarely used more than three lights for his shots and set them up in a matter of minutes. Contemptuous of "artistic" lighting that took expensive time, he relied on his adeptness to give the film the look of a reported event rather than a fiction, a good thing. I soon gave up trying to prime him with the thematics of the piece; between shots he was usually hovering near a phone awaiting news of an oil well he had put money into. A movie was a movie, but a gusher was real beauty. The technical people seemed isolated, each in the narrow circle of his own craft, in which he strove for perfection, nothing less. Disdaining all European theorizing, as pridefully pragmatic as a Ford or an Edison and as nonintellectual, such men had nevertheless created some of the most original films ever made.

They reminded me of a property man during the original stage production of *Salesman* more than ten years before, a cigar smoker named Hymie. One of his tasks was to see to it before each performance that the ashtray on the refrigerator had half-smoked Chesterfield cigarettes in it: playing Willy's son Biff, Arthur Kennedy had to light a cigarette at the end of Act I and put it out in this ashtray, which Hymie had decided should be full so as to add to the impression of Biff smoking heavily out of deep worry for his father. Hymie watched every show and had an opinion about how good or bad each performance was. Each night he would fill the ashtray with *new* cigarette butts to give it realism. This was his contribution to the tragedy. Actors might kid Hymie for his henlike fussing, but when they missed a cue or a line they avoided his gaze coming off the stage.

At some point, the rhythm of our workdays began to stumble as Marilyn was unable to appear until later and later each morning. I had no inkling of what to do or say anymore and sensed she was in a rage against me or herself or the kind of work she was doing. She seemed to be filling with distrust not only for my opinions of her acting but also for Huston's. It all gradually passed beyond anger or resentment, the way a natural calamity leaves one in a pause of powerless amazement. Still, she took an occasional drive out to country antique shops alone with Paula and bought one or two knickknacks for the house, a surprise since she seemed barely able to speak to me. We were like two people trying to occupy a single space, that of the provider who for innumerable reasons is unable to accept what the other offers; the frustration was thus mutual and was cutting a groove of its own.

Each day now brought strange events, but some surprises were hopeful, like Clift's turning out to be so staunchly reliable. Huston and I had feared that he might begin to drink and would have to be propped up, but instead, along with Wallach, he was a pillar of the production. On his first day of work, a week or so into the film, he did his scene in the phone booth alongside the highway, a solid page of talk, without an error or a hesitation, and on the first take. Huston and I congratulated each other on our persistent confidence in him despite the insurance company's misgivings. I chose to see it as proof that when he had something to do that he respected and knew he was not simply being exploited, Monty could pull himself together. It was as much the irrelevance and sheer stupidity of most of the work they had to do that was wilting the sanity of so many actors whose self-certainty was pretty tentative to begin with.

The heat on the salt lake sometimes touched above a merciless hundred and eight degrees. We worked as though on a glaringly lit moon. To pass the time I threw and punted a football with some of the crew. Paula would sit writing letters inside her air-conditioned Cadillac limousine. She and Marilyn would rehearse lines together in Marilyn's limousine on the trip up from Reno every morning, but Paula insisted as a matter of face on a personal limousine and chauffeur to follow behind. Glancing at her through the car window, I recalled *The Prince and the Showgirl;* her Byzantine obsession with rank and her pointlessly secretive ways seemed less comical now. She could hardly say what time it was without seeming to suggest it was secret information, and to engender awe in the innocent onlooker she wore several watches—a pendant hanging from her neck, a wristwatch, and another in her bag so she would know what time it was in London and Tokyo, Mexico City and Sydney, implying that she and Lee had important interests all over the world.

During some of the long waits I would talk with Gable, who liked to sit in the sun outside his trailer on the lake bed. He behaved as though Marilyn was a woman in physical pain, and despite his having to spend what might have been humiliating hours each day waiting for her to start working, no hint of affront ever showed on his face. Those who knew him were surprised by his uncharacteristic patience. Once or twice, however, his agent reminded us that his contract called for him to be paid twenty-five thousand dollars for each day over schedule, so he had begun well prepared for the worst. I couldn't help feeling somehow responsible for his enforced idleness, especially when I was the one who had convinced him to do the part, but he knew everyone was helpless, including Marilyn herself, and that it was not merely a case of a star trying to show who had the supreme power. Maybe he was softened, too, by Marilyn's having told him that he had been her girlhood idol; in fact, his framed photo stood on her equally worshipful mother's bureau, and in her very earliest years Marilyn thought he was her father. He and I would sometimes sit beside the trailer saying nothing for a long half-hour at a time in the Nevada silence, a kind of unacknowledged mourning. I could feel his commiseration, as, I was sure, he could feel my regret.

I would ask about the old movie years when he had worked for MGM. "We'd finish a picture most often on a Friday, and there'd be some parties over the weekend, and I'd come back to start a new picture on Monday—it was really like a stock company. My 'coach' over here"—he indicated his valet, a sixtyish man with a long doggy face who liked to sit in the trailer doorway listening to him and anticipating his need for a pack of cigarettes or a fresh filter for his holder or a cold drink, as he had been doing for decades now—"my coach would get me out of the tuxedo and under the shower, and while I was drying off he'd give me my first lines of dialogue, and on the way to the studio I'd be trying to wake up and listen to him reading to me. They'd have my costume ready, and I'd get into it and go out onto the set and say hi to the director and meet whoever was playing the girl in the picture and try to figure out where the locale was supposed to be—you know, Hawaii or Nome or Saint Louis or wherever. Then we'd have about twenty minutes to move into the shot and do it, that's all. By the end of the week you'd have a pretty good idea of what the character was, and then you'd have two more weeks till it was finished, and by the time you really understood anything it was over. But most of the pictures didn't have any character to speak of anyway, so you sort of just made up something as you went along, or maybe you didn't make up anything because there was nothing *to* make up. This one's altogether different, though."

He had brought his silver Mercedes gull-wing coupe from California and kept trying to improve his time driving up the mountain road from Reno every morning. Surely his face was as well known as any in world history, he was worth millions and could possess just about anything he wished, but he was not world-weary, not lacking in curiosity, and asked about my life and how I worked, and I thought I saw something like my father's animal simplicity in this interest. Perhaps he so *existed* onscreen because he was so fundamental. Great actor-personalities, I have come to think, are like trained bears in that they attract us with their discipline while their powerful claws threaten us; a great star implies he is his own person and can be mean and even dangerous, like a great leader.

I had written the rodeo scene to take place in a certain town, its name faded from memory now, far out in the desert. I had come across it one day with the two cowboy horse-hunters: a string of slatternly houses made of unpainted gray pine boards, and another string of bars, about eight or ten in all, facing an impromptu rodeo ring in front of a rough bleachers. Beyond the ring was a church atop whose steeple a wooden cross tilted over, ready to fall into the street, a reasonable symbol of what I was after in the film. The line of bars had one long dent in front where drunks had banged cars and trucks into them, men from the nearby wallboard plant who worked in clouds of white gypsum dust all day. Inside bullet holes showed in the ceilings and walls, with whole pockets dug out of some wooden bars by quick fire. It was the only town in Nevada where a man could legally carry sidearms, and a great many did, big forty-fives strapped to their thighs. During my Nevada time I had been there one Saturday night when the sheer fury of the customers was like a fever in the air, and I had to wonder if the grinding emptiness of their lives had driven them to want to kill or threaten to kill or be killed. It was never a question of robbery, just of two men starting a brainless argument that ended in shooting, a kind of mass sex, it seemed, with bloodshed as the climax of the rodeo itself.

As it turned out, we could not work in that town because there was insufficient water to supply cast and crew, and because of its distance from Reno and our hotels. We found another town, with better facilities and plenty of room for us: it had been deserted decades before by its entire population when some nearby mine gave out. Weathered signs were applied on the store windows or hung askew over the street. It was all very strange to think we were shooting where a real population had once lived, people who had doubtless had great hopes for a good life and now had vanished.

But another place where I had spent some time with my cowboy friends—a house owned by a Mrs. Styx—was used as Roslyn's temporary Nevada residence. It overlooked one of the rare green valleys in that desiccated area, with some trees and enough good grass for a few cattle. Anticipating a need for more space in which to move the camera around, production people had sawed through the corners of the house to make them removable at a moment's notice by turning a few bolts. In a morning a vegetable garden was set in place out front, as the story required, and shrubs planted. One quickly forgot these were all new. The oddness about it was that like demented gods, we had taken a reality and created a fake.

And I was finding it hard to remember that in reality Clark Gable was not the cowboy who had inspired the Gay Langland character. It was during this part of the shooting that the original cowboy suddenly showed up to look on for a few hours, and I could not help feeling disappointed by a certain thinness about him as compared to Gable's more satisfying roundness and density. Of course I was part of Gable's character, as I was not of the cowboy's.

There was also something disturbing in the fact that the walls of the very house in which I had sat a few years before with the real cowboy and a girlfriend he had brought along could now be unbolted and simply slipped out of position to reveal an open sky. Perhaps the secret alarm in this was its echo of the willfulness of our way of constructing our lives, and deconstructing them, too.

I kept trying to rewrite the last few minutes of the film, which had never been quite right. Aware of the hopefulness with which I had conceived the story and my uncertainty about my future now, I still could not concede that the ending had to be what I considered nihilistic, people simply walking away from one another. At the same time, contrary to my story, I could not deny that a certain indeterminacy of life was really all these characters had to rely on. In fact, taking uncertainty to heart left them feeling free. Life betrayed, and that was all there was to it, but I willed it to be otherwise in this film. Besides, it could also have been true that they had found one another and stuck.

One afternoon Marilyn, with no evident emotion, almost as though it were just another script, said, "What they really should do is break up at the end." I instantly disagreed, so quickly, in fact, that I knew I was afraid she was right. But the irony was too sharp: the work I had created to reassure her that a woman like herself could find a home in the world had apparently proved the opposite.

Briefly I wondered if this could be a call for help, but I could detect nothing in her eyes beyond a cool, professional look. I could no longer offer what I believed she could not accept. The terrible fact was that as she moved through the shooting she seemed at one moment all inwardness, not noticing anyone around her, and at the next wonderfully social with absolutely everyone she laid eyes on—as though the stream of her emotions had shattered into a spray of anger falling endlessly through her heart; it was impossible to sense at all what she was feeling and what her mood was until she spoke.

Huston at a certain point began to stir as the hours grew longer when she simply could not get ready to work. Her lifelong wrestling with the fact of time had thrown her to the mat finally, had nearly immobilized her now; she had always been one of those people for whom time is a sticky entanglement that they don't want to touch, perhaps in denial that a past exists.

Huston seemed to have resigned himself after the first month or so of shooting, but now he took Paula aside and asked what she proposed to do about her charge. He had begun staying up all night at the craps table, losing immense sums and winning them back and showing his mettle that way, occasionally falling asleep in his chair behind the camera and losing track of which scene he was shooting. Chaos was on us all. He was working on sheer muscle now, his control amazing.

I thought he had been simply blanking out Paula's existence for some weeks, refusing her intercession as demeaning and unprofessional. Her control over Marilyn was now so complete that Marilyn had moved from our apartment in the hotel into hers; Paula had finally won our long undeclared war. Still, this might clear the air, I thought, and free Marilyn to concentrate solely on the work as she now said she wanted to do. But I was under no illusions that any of us were really doing what we wanted to do; a force of pure destruction was thrashing around among us, beyond anyone's control. I was only going through the motions of caring about the rest of the picture. It now seemed a hateful thing that had cost me too much, and I could only hope it would not turn out too badly. The one real dread I had was that Paula would accede too easily to Marilyn's demands for more and more sleeping pills, but she promised she would not give in, and I tended to believe her because she was clearly in fear of a catastrophe herself.

One evening after dinner I walked to a small park near the hotel and sat on a bench watching eight young girls play tennis on adjoining courts. That people could still be doing something as simple as hitting a ball back and forth across a net seemed miraculous. The sheer good health of the girls drove tension out of me, just watching them take their untroubled deep breaths and wipe their wet pink upper lips and scream now and then. Longing to stretch out, I lay down on the grass propped up on one arm and soon fell fast asleep. I awoke in a silent city without traffic; the girls were gone, and it was a balmy three o'clock in the morning.

In the hotel's casino Huston was shooting craps at a table with a glass of scotch in his hand, his bush jacket as crisply pressed as if he had put it on ten minutes before. He was behind twenty-five thousand dollars. He grinned and I grinned back. It did not seem important to him, although I knew he would find it awkward paying out that much. I went up to bed. In the morning at about seven I came down for breakfast, and he was still shooting craps, still with a glass of scotch in his hand. He had won back the twenty-five grand and was now trying to win more. His bush jacket looked as neat as it had before. Just thinking about standing up all night exhausted me all over again.

Metty's worry that close-ups were showing Marilyn's exhaustion finally forced matters to a head. Paula, now in control and thus unavoidably open to blame, quickly announced that Lee was at last coming out from New York. Such was Huston's desperation that he very nearly welcomed this news. I certainly did, if only because Lee would now have to assume at least some direct responsibility for her unrelenting uncertainty as an actress in this role. Despite her utter reliance on his every word, he had managed to keep a safe distance through all her difficulties.

But there was another reason for welcoming his arrival: Marilyn had taken to paraphrasing speeches and omitting words and sentences. Huston, a writer himself, refused to accept her revisions, and to get the words right he had reshot sections as many as ten times. Looking on, I had assumed she was having memory lapses, but at one point she explained that the words in themselves were not important, only the emotion they expressed. In short, she was conveying Strasberg's teaching as she understood it, a crippling attitude that I had seen in other actors and that I believed contributed to her unresolved tension in acting. Regarding the words as a hurdle, she was seeking spontaneity and freshness of feeling despite them instead of through them. If this approach occasionally did free her, it most often compounded her uncertainty when the actor opposite her was working on a different principle, of fidelity to the text, as of course the director was as well. Huston saw it all as arrant self-indulgence. I had asked how she and Paula proposed to work on classic roles, as Strasberg often predicted she would one day, when everyone was familiar with the texts and would not easily tolerate their being paraphrased. But it was obvious she was simply repeating what she had been given by high authority, and the pathos of it was heartbreaking, though no longer penetrable by me or anyone else. The fact was that she had done her best work with scripts, like Billy Wilder and I. A. L. Diamond's for *Some Like It Hot,* from which she had not been allowed the slightest deviation because the comic dialogue had to be precise or would fail to work at all. That the same precision was necessary in a dramatic role, her first ever, seemed elementary, but with the encouragement of her mentors she was losing her way in an improvisational approach that might belong in an acting class but not in an actual performance.

In any event, Lee's imminent arrival was at least something new happening, and as a onetime director himself, he would surely see that his teaching, if correctly understood, was incapacitating, and if misunderstood, must now be corrected.

With the schedule lengthening out and nothing I could do to cure things, my function on the film grew thin and more and more formal, and most of the time I spent alone. I thought of leaving, but Huston now and then wanted to talk about something in the script or make a change. One day we shot two silent scenes at Pyramid Lake, one of Gable-Langland teaching Marilyn-Roslyn to ride horseback, the other of them swimming. The two cottages where Bellow and I had lived—could it have been almost four years ago?—had once looked down across the lonesome highway upon the rocky beach and the primordial lake, but not anymore; a marina and fast-food stand had been installed, and motorboats aimlessly dashed about blasting the unearthly silence that in the script was supposed to help restore Roslyn's hope for herself and her life. Everything seemed to symbolize; the motorboat drivers had to be asked to stop their engines while the scene was shot in this once enchanted place, observed by the chewing customers at the hot-dog stand that now stood a hundred yards away. I looked back along the highway for the phone booth where I had momentarily fainted once, but it was gone; there was probably a phone in the marina now. The booth's absence kept me staring into the distance trying to revive the empty highway and the mutual idealization that had swept through me here.

It was hard watching her walk out of the water to be embraced by Gable when I could see no joy in her. As valiantly as she tried to appear in love, I knew her too well not to notice her distraction. But to approach her was to see her stiffen incredibly. I could only look on, praying that my estimate was wrong, but the marks of a living performance are moments of surprise, and it was a painfully willed performance, it seemed to me, the wild notes too worked out and premeditated. I was almost completely out of her life by now, but from my distant view the film seemed purely a torture for her. As it was for me when I thought back to my walk along the East River with Sam Shaw, when I had first imagined it as a kind of gift.

The whole make-believe business seemed detestable now, a destroyer of people, especially of those actors unable to settle for an ounce less than the full measure of truthfulness. Whatever it was that Paula and presumably Lee had been teaching her, she seemed less than ever able to feel, as opposed to thinking *about* her feelings, and thoughts are very hard to act. To be fair, her work in the film looked far more authentic to me in later years than it did during that bad time. I now marvel at how she managed, under the circumstances, to do as well as she did.

But at the time I wondered if acting had merely become a socially acceptable excuse for narcissism, an unholy absorption in the self rather than a joyous celebratory observation of mankind, which is all that can ever ennoble it. In my too many hours spent alone, the whole country seemed to be devolving into a mania for the distraction it called entertainment, a day-and-night mimicry of art that menaced nothing, redeemed nothing, and meant nothing but forgetfulness.

One evening I switched on the TV in my hotel room and found Nixon and Kennedy about to begin one of their presidential election debates. For some reason the country seemed to be continuing despite *The Misfits*. I ordered dinner and a bottle of whiskey and sat down to watch. There they stood, two more actors, but looking as uncomfortable as high school argufiers, Nixon apparently wearing his brother's suit with the collar riding up his neck. How patently ambition-driven they were, these performers, each putting on a self-assured authority that he could not possibly have. Next to the TV the window showed blue night spreading over the everlasting mountains toward California, far easier to look at than the two on the screen. Weeks before, an arsonist's forest fire out there had blackened the skies of two states and cut off Reno's power, and our electricians had rigged a single cable six stories up to our room from a truck generator parked below in the street—the only lighted bulb in the city for Marilyn's comfort. That had been good of them. Movie crews love the impossible, it makes them feel real.

Alone with the screen now, I caught something stale and prearranged about this debate. I could not get myself out of the movies, out of the theatre, out of the fake of this unbelievably important TV casting session by which the American people were to pick the star of their unending feature movie, trying to sense which scenes each would play well and which not so well, since there was no substantive difference between the candidates beyond a few cult words addressed to their partisans. Nixon seemed the foxy self-pitier who could also be tough, though Kennedy could probably threaten other countries better with that square Irish jaw and that good suit. But much of their performance depended on the script, which was always being rewritten. I hoped for Kennedy, of course, but mainly, I suppose, because we had read some of the same books.

The phone in the morning. "Lee is here. He wants to see you right away."

At last. Now we could at least get straight the line Marilyn ought to follow to complete the film.

"Has he spoken to John yet?"

"Oh, no."

It was the "oh" that troubled me. Why "*oh*, no"? Was Lee already positioning himself against Huston when they would surely have to cooperate if things were to change?

In the elevator to the Strasbergs' apartment I rehearsed my complaints. Lee answered my ring. The absurdity of his costume blew all my plans out of my head; in this hundred-degree weather he was dressed in a stiff brand-new cowboy outfit—shiny boots, creased pants, ironed shirt with braided pockets and cuffs—but with the same whitish intellectual face and unexercised body.

"That's quite a getup," I said.

He grinned adventurously. "Yes, it's very comfortable."

"The boots too?" I doubted that pointy Western boots could be comfortable on first wearing.

"Oh, they're wonderful," he said, bending his knees.

Paula had not risen from the couch, where she lay on her side in a dragoned kimono with her head propped up on her hand, a smile of proud assurance on her face now that her champion had come to take up her burden, her hair let down intriguingly over her shoulder, an odalisque in the round.

Lee's expression turned to a frown. "We have to have a serious talk, Arthur."

"Yes, I've been hoping to do that for some time."

"Yes, the situation has become impossible."

"I know." He must already have worked out a new approach that would save the day, such was the impacted drive I sensed moving within him. For an instant I happily thought I had had him wrong and that he indeed possessed a secret that could restore a Marilyn whose soul was falling through space even as we spoke.

"Yes. If something isn't done immediately I will have to take Paula off the picture." He looked directly at me, as though demanding a statement.

Paula? Was this about Paula? I glanced over to her on the couch, where she was grinning contentedly as though she had at last ceased to be ignored.

"I don't get you, Lee."

"Huston has been refusing to talk to her. This is insulting! I won't permit her to go on unless it is agreed that he show her respect. I will not tolerate this kind of treatment of her. She is an artist! She has worked with the greatest stars! I simply will not allow her to be treated this way!"

Stunned, I floundered trying to grasp his meaning. Had Paula not told him that Marilyn was *in extremis,* that perhaps her very life was in danger, and certainly her ability to finish the film in question? How else could he stand here complaining about his wife's not getting respect from a director? Or was it possible that Paula was so insanely self-obsessed as not even to have noticed that Marilyn was in very bad trouble? And had Lee finally agreed to come out here simply to assert his authority on the pointless problem of his wife and thus distract from his being totally at sea as to how to help Marilyn?

It was too terrible to think that. Seeing him here in his crazy costume, like a jolly tourist on vacation, I suddenly wondered if maybe I was taking everything far too seriously, had reacted too personally to Marilyn's anger, which might simply be her normal frustration as an actress creating a role. Total confusion.

On he went . . . how Paula had been feeling abandoned and insulted, how she had put a life into coaching great performers, how he himself had not wanted to interfere but now had to "for Marilyn's good as well." It was impossible to address him, it was demeaning to speak seriously to him, infatuated as he was by his own importance and his wife's. Marilyn's suffering was a distant star that might occasionally be glimpsed as it dimmed out far, far away, but not more.

"I must get this settled before I can do anything else, Arthur."

"You can't expect me to settle it. It's between her and John."

"It's your picture, you must act."

"My script, not my picture. There's nothing I can do about it, Lee. John is not used to dealing with an actor through a third party, and I doubt he'll change. Are you going to be talking to Marilyn?"

"Then I will have to take Paula home with me."

"It will probably mean the end of the picture"—and of Marilyn, I needn't have added, if she failed to finish it—"but I guess you have to do what you have to do. But I hope you get to talk to Marilyn, she needs help now. Will you?"

"I'll talk to her, yes," he conceded. I understood the rules he was laying down—he would do what he could but was not going to take responsibility for her under any circumstances, most especially not when she was on the ropes. And he was the only person she trusted. Such was the perfection of her fate.

Shooting had ground to a complete halt. There was no point transporting scores of crew members across the mountains to the salt lake when there was so much uncertainty about getting any work done. The crisis was upon us. Whatever Lee said to her, it had apparently left her unchanged as far as her ability to work was concerned, and now he had gone back to New York. I went up to

Paula's apartment, afraid that in her opaque, absentminded way she might be failing to at least keep watch. It was still unclear whether Paula understood how sick Marilyn was. I was never sure that she was truly listening.

She let me into the living room with her finger against her lips, then walked into the bedroom, and I followed. Marilyn was sitting up in bed. A doctor was feeling the back of her hand, searching for a vein into which to inject Amytal. My stomach turned over. She saw me and began to scream at me to get out. I managed to ask the doctor if he knew how much barbiturate or other medicine she had already taken, and he looked at me helplessly, a young scared fellow wanting to give the shot and get out and not come back. Paula was standing beside the bed in her black shift, hair freshly brushed and pinned up, looking healthy and powdered and maternal, and vaguely guilty, I thought; yes, now she must know that she had made a bad bargain and was not in control anymore, and she wanted help and she wanted credit for her mothering love even as something in her could not care less because it was all hopelessly disconnected. I thought to move the doctor away from the bed to stall off the injection, but the screaming was too terrible, and her distress in my presence canceled out any help I could hope to give, so I left and stood in the living room and waited until the doctor came out. He was astonished that she could remain awake, having given her enough for a major operation, but she was still sitting up and talking. He believed he was the last doctor in the area to be called in, but he would not agree to any more shots of anything, fearing for her life now that he had seen what he had seen. I went back into the bedroom and she looked at me, ravaged but slowing down at last, merely repeating, "Get out," as in a dream.

Paula was warm to me now. "I'd like to get some dinner . . ." I felt a rush of warmth toward her, too, I suppose because I was so desperate for help and because in the corners of her eyes I saw fear, and if she was afraid she must be sane, and if she was sane and was still hanging in here she must have some feeling left for someone other than herself. I said thanks to her apropos of nothing in particular, and she touched me with her hand and left for dinner with one of the cast.

Marilyn lay down and shut her eyes. I watched for signs of labored breathing, but she seemed at peace. She was a flower of iron to survive this onslaught. I despaired at my presumption, the stupidity of thinking that I alone could keep her from harm, and I cast about for someone else whom she might permit to take responsibility. I was exhausted and without hope that I could reach her anymore; I had doubtless stayed too long, had nothing left but a stubborn holding on to responsibility when what she wanted was to ride the next wave thundering toward the shore, a mystic goddess out of the sea. Scoffing at magic, she still wanted her subjects to glow joyously at her touch, a sacred sort of artistry and power that was as much part of her as her eyes. I thought of her Los Angeles doctor, but he could hardly leave his practice to come here—and stopped myself again; why could she not take responsibility herself? Of course she could, and in fact it was her only hope . . . and yet she could not, not when she was still so dependent on sleeping drugs, chemicals I had been very slow to realize had removed her from me altogether . . . and the circle turned again, and I found myself believing that no one else would really stick with her. But I was worse than useless to her now, a bag of nails thrown in her face, a reminder of her failure to pull herself out of her old life even when she had at last truly loved someone.

It was the first quiet time we had had together in so long, and in the silence the idea of her trying to work in this condition was plainly monstrous—we were all crazy, what could possibly justify it? I must find some way to halt the picture. But I could see her indignant fury at what she would interpret as an accusation that she had caused the picture to be canceled, something that might break her career besides.

I found myself straining to imagine miracles. What if she were to wake and I were able to say, "God loves you, darling," and she were able to believe it! How I wished I still had my religion and she hers. It was suddenly quite simple—we had invented God to keep from dying of reality, yet love was the realest reality of all. I summoned a vision of her harsh, suffering eyes turning to their old thrilling softness, for this was the look of hers that to me would always be her very self, her unique sign; on the other side of love, everything else about her, about people, in fact, was appetite and frightening.

What, I wondered, if she no longer had to be this star, could we live an ordinary decompressed life down on the plain, far away from this rarefied peak where there was no air? For an instant the thought of it was like a crutch pulled from under me; she seemed to lose her whole identity. An ordinary person and hardly able to spell—what would she do with herself? But pressing into that vision, I began to imagine a wonderfully quieted Marilyn no longer backed into a terrifying corner, a young and natively intelligent woman piecing her way through each day to evening and then going unremarkably to bed. Was it possible? Surely she had been most dear to me when she was hardly known.

And then the shocking egotism of my thought stared me in the face—her stardom was her triumph, nothing less; it was her life's achievement. How would I feel if the condition of my marriage was tractability, the surrendering of my art? The simple fact, terrible and lethal, was that no space whatever existed between herself and this star. *She was "Marilyn Monroe," and that was what was killing her.* And it could not be otherwise for her; she lived on film and with that glory forsworn would in some real sense vanish. If she loved to fool in a flower garden and endlessly move furniture around the house and buy a lamp or a coffee pot, these were pleasing preparations for a life she could not live for long without a new flight to the moon in a new part and a new film. Since her teens she had been creating a relationship with the public, first imaginary and then real, and it could not be torn from her without tearing flesh.

I realized now, as I longed for a miracle, that I had come to believe no analysis could reach into her. Perhaps only a shock of recognition, a quick but convincing sight of her own death, could rouse her to a desperate attempt to trust again. Somewhere in her she seemed to know this, inviting these drugged temporary deaths whose threat would deliver her at last.

I had no saving mystery to offer her; nor could her hand be taken if she would not hold it out. I had lost my faith in a lasting cure coming from me, and I wondered if indeed it could come from any human agency at all.

One thing only was sure; she must finish the picture. To fail would confirm her worst terror of losing control of her life, of going under the pulverizing wave of the terrible past. She went on sleeping. I wished again that I knew how to pray and invoke for her the image of that which only knows love. But it was too late for that too.

A year or so earlier, in Hollywood during the shooting of *Let's Make Love,* a stupefying comedy that Fox had forced upon her, Walter Wanger had come to our bungalow to discuss my writing a screenplay for him based on *The Fall,* the novella by Albert Camus. I had reread it at his bidding, but I had no desire to write a film, and so we just chatted for a while about the book. I had heard of Wanger as the producer who had filmed *Blockade,* with Henry Fonda and Madeleine Carroll, during the Spanish Civil War; one of the few attempts by Hollywood to deal with that catastrophe for democracy, it had been picketed by the patriots despite its equivocal support of the Republican side. He seemed serious and well educated. But he was a movie producer above all, a man of the older Hollywood scene, who some years before had shot his wife's lover, as I vaguely recalled reading.

Apart from its philosophical conundrum, *The Fall* is about trouble with women, although this theme is overshadowed by the male narrator's concentration on ethics, particularly the dilemma of how one can ever judge another person once one has committed the iniquitous act of indifference to a stranger's call for help. The antihero, a self-described "judge-penitent," has on his conscience his failure to come to the aid of a girl he saw jump off a bridge into a river.

It was a beautifully carved story whose conclusion, however, had left me in doubt of its willingness to face something perhaps worse than mere indifference to a call for help. What if the man, at risk to himself, had attempted her rescue and then discovered that the key to her salvation lay not in him, whatever his caring, but in her? And perhaps even worse, that strands of his own vanity as well as his love were entwined in the act of trying to save her? Did disguised self-love nullify the ethical act? Could anyone, in all truth, really save another unless the other wished to be saved? Was not the real question how to evoke that wish? And if it refused evocation, when did one confess failure? And how was failure justified, or could it be? *The Fall,* I thought, ended too soon, before the worst of the pain began.

Finally, suicide might not simply express disappointment with oneself but hatred for someone else. The Chinese custom was for the suicide to hang himself in the doorway of the person who had offended him, clearly a form of retaliation against others as well as an act of self-destruction. In Christian custom it is forbidden to bury the suicide in sanctified ground; is this because he has died in hatred not only of himself but of God and God's gift of life?

Her sleep was not sleep but the pulsation of an exhausted creature wrestling some demon. What was its name? She seemed able to see only that she had been victimized and betrayed by others, as though she were a mere passenger in her life. But like everyone else, she was also the driver, and how could it be otherwise? I suspected that she knew this but could not bring herself to admit it to me. And that was why I was useless to her now, an irritant at best. The terrible irony was that I had reinforced the idea of her innocent victimization because I could not bear to accept her life as it was, because I had wanted to heal her of it rather than acknowledge it as hers. I had rejected the horrors she had lived, denied their power over her, but she saw herself rejected. Only some sublime act of grace could transcend this. And there was none. All that was left was for her to go on defending her innocence, in which, at the bottom of her heart, she did not believe. Innocence kills.

Huston took the bull by the horns, the unfinished film being now at the point of abandonment, and arranged to have Marilyn flown to a private hospital in Los Angeles where she could go off barbiturates under the care of her analyst. In some ten days she was back—her incredible resilience was almost heroic to me now—and looking wonderfully self-possessed if not yet bright-eyed. But perhaps that would come if she remained clean of the sleeping drugs. Days of concentrated work sped by now, and we could talk again. If she regarded me remotely, it was at least no longer with open rancor. Without discussion we both knew we had effectively parted, and I thought a pressure had been removed from her, and for that much I was glad.

The final shot was also the closing scene of the picture. Langland stops his truck so Roslyn can untie his dog, which was left behind while the mustangs were being rounded up. It was a studio process shot done in Los Angeles; a filmed track in the desert rolled away through the truck's back window, coming to a stop when Marilyn jumped out to go to the dog. Gable was supposed to watch her with a mounting look of love in his eyes, but I noticed only a very slight change in his expression from where I stood beside the camera, hardly ten feet away.

"Cut! Fine! Thanks, Clark; thanks, Marilyn." Huston was brisk and businesslike now, in effect refusing any sentimental backward look; hardly lingering, he said he had to be off to work with the film editor. I asked Gable if he thought he had shown sufficient expression in the final shot. He was surprised. "You have to watch the eyes. Movie acting is all up here"—he drew a rectangle around his eyes with his finger. "You can't overdo because it's being magnified hundreds of times on the theatre screen." He turned out to be right, as I was relieved to see in the rushes of the scene; he had simply intensified an affectionate look that was undetectable a few feet away in the studio.

Now, about to say goodbye, he told me that he had seen a rough cut the night before and that he thought *The Misfits* was the best picture he had made in his life. He was grinning like a boy and gripping my hand and warmly touching my shoulder, with an excitement in his eyes I had never seen before. A friend of his was standing by to drive him up north for a week of fishing and hunting. We looked at one another for a moment more with a sense of relief and perhaps of accomplishment, then he turned and got into a big Chrysler station wagon and was off. He was dead in four days of a sudden heart attack.

As his car pulled away, I glanced about for Marilyn and spotted a brown limo with Paula sitting inside looking straight ahead and, I thought, avoiding me. A healing indifference was moving into me very fast, a numbed cutting of losses. For all I knew, maybe Paula had been doing her damndest to prevent things from getting any worse than they were.

Marilyn came out of the building as I was opening the door of my car, moving so well and with such an alertness in her face and manner that I wondered again whether I had made too much of her difficulties. After all, she had suffered in much the same way in each of her last three or four pictures. Maybe I had let myself feel guilty about her necessary travail and anger, and in that way had failed her. "Men like happy girls." Anyway, we were leaving in separate cars, which struck me as very nearly funny.

Except that I believed she could not be done with her mother's curse. Now that she was serious about acting, she was asserting her value through her art, and that was forbidden, sinful. No less a conflict could have been the cause of such torture in this role through which she was, in a word, proclaiming herself a dignified woman.

I drove down Sunset Boulevard in my clunky rented green American Motors mess, which I liked because no heads ever turned to see who was in it. A restaurant slipped by, and I recalled that we had suddenly decided to go there for dinner around the time of *Let's Make Love,* rather than eat the boring food in the hotel apartment again. We went in disguise, she wearing dark sunglasses and a bandanna and I removing my glasses, and without a reservation we were refused a table. I thought somewhat indignantly of putting my glasses back on and having her take hers off. We laughed about it a moment later, but something about the incident was not amusing to her. Driving past the place now, I remembered my own feeling of affront as we backed out into the street, and the chastening realization that I had subtly come to depend on the power conferred by publicity to go to the head of any line. It was a relief now to be driving this wretched little anonymous car.

In a few blocks I stopped for a light, and the brown limo pulled up beside me. Both women were facing front, Paula talking animatedly, as always, and it crossed my mind that my old tendency to form team allegiances had distorted my vision again. I had always felt a twinge when one of my productions came to its inevitable end and the actors went their separate ways.

A long shoot like *The Misfits* is a daily marching around in a courtyard with high walls. Sometimes it was hard to remember whether it had been two years or three since I began the screenplay. Suddenly the big gate opens and there is a delightful, well-lighted world outside. I went up to San Francisco, where I knew no one—a good feeling, a new start. But disorienting. The sixties were beginning. In the hungry i, the first political cabaret I had seen since Café Society in the late thirties, Mort Sahl's mordant cool was out of a world I had never known, the young audience a well-washed happenstance gathering of detached individuals; I seemed to recall a sort of community of strangers in the old days, probably because we were unified against Hitler's approach while they were only waiting for Godot. But I now suspected all such generational positionings as myths invented to comfort us in our time, like the octopus blackening his surrounding water with his ink.

Eisenhower now, Kennedy coming up. Very strange. I moved about wonderfully uninvolved in anything at all, without even a home for the first time in decades. It was a good town to walk around in, safer than New York, I thought, but strange places always seem safer in America than the places you know.

I sensed I would be all right, but every few hours I wondered about Marilyn in the hands of strangers. I began to see that I had thought that everyone but me was a stranger to her—she had been with me so much longer than with anyone else in her life—and my egoistic presumption again embarrassed me. She had tried so hard to give but found it unreal to receive, as had I. Realizing slowly, day by day, that she had always known how to survive, I allowed myself the luxury of being cut off. I thought of going to the Connecticut house to live and maybe even farm, if I dared.

There were dark moments when suddenly I did not believe she really knew how to survive. But my uselessness to her confronted this fear and dissolved it twenty times a day. That was what I had to learn, how to believe she'd surface and stay there. Sentimental as it sounded, perhaps she really did belong to the world. I put it all out of mind—it could no longer be my business, you save yourself, no one does it for you or can. But it kept coming back. I wondered again if the analysis was peripheral. Did her doctor know the mortal danger she was in from sleeping pills? Maybe he was reassured by her showing up at his office looking like a milk-fed high school girl hours after peering over the edge into death's very jaws. Her unbelievable physical endurance, did he understand that? Even her stamina conspired against her.

I drove back down to Los Angeles, wondering at the instinct that had moved the first film people to select this artificially lush area for the industry, a desert that had to be watered before it would green up, a fake to start with, and I recalled Fox asking my father for an investment. It had never been anything but a money machine. What made people continually expect something more sublime from it?

There was a knock on the Hollywood hotel room door. A woman in her twenties stood in the hall, staidly dressed in a plaid skirt and blouse, a kind of pretty imitation college girl with a slack, overused mouth.

"Do you have some ink?" The nerved look straight in the eye; how touchingly inventive a way of telling me she recognized me and knew that I was now alone.

"Ink?"

"Yes. I want to write something."

"Well, no, but I can lend you a ballpoint."

"No, I only write with a real pen."

"Ah. You're a writer?"

Thin ice. Her cheeks pinked up. "Well, I'm starting to. I'm trying to learn." She smiled faintly.

"Good. I'll be glad to let you have a ballpoint."

"Thanks. I really wanted ink."

"Sorry."

"That's all right." She turned away, voice thinned out by the rejection.

I walked to the window and looked down eight stories to the swimming pool. A young woman was doing the crawl. She slipped out of the water and dried herself in a stripe of sunlight, bending over to pat her hair dry. She had heavy thighs, a broad bottom. Woman, that worshiped, tortured species. In youth I had always felt they were being endlessly lied to, why didn't they know?

I drove out to the beach, but there was a cold breeze and few

people were around. There was always something listless, almost
forlorn, about the lazy Pacific, unlike the sharp and cold and saltier
Atlantic that was so full of anger and ideas.

A girl walked out of the sea leading a Newfoundland on a leash.
"There's a million beautiful girls," she had said once when I marveled at her in a new navy blue skirt. She wanted everything, but
one thing contradicted another; physical admiration threatened to
devalue her person, yet she became anxious if her appearance was
ignored.

I took off my shoes and walked in the lobes of tepid water softly
washing up the slant of the beach. There was nowhere I had to be
tomorrow, yet something kept pushing me to hurry and make up
lost time. But lost to what? Who finds time that is lost? Time is
never lost, we give it away, dump it out, character is everything,
and I had not wanted to withhold myself anymore, that was all.
And hadn't, period. I had to try from now on to command an inner
motionlessness, to recover by spreading out my energy, opening to
all things, rather than keeping myself pointed at a target that was
not there anymore.

It was not really possible to understand oneself, let alone another
human being. Only irony was certain. The setting, cooling sun I
was looking at was rising somewhere else, all hot and new.

Did anyone ever feel he belonged in this place? It was odd to
recall that she had been born here. By even that much I could
never understand her—she thought this city was real rather than
an apparition recently summoned up out of nowhere.

With the sun going down on just such an evening "they said we
were going for a ride in the car but when we got out and I saw it
was the orphanage I grabbed the door and kept yelling, 'I'm not
an orphan, I'm not an orphan!' They had to tear my fingers open
to get me inside. And left me there." She had learned to laugh at
the poor incompetent people who had abandoned her.

I went back to my car and sat brushing sand off my feet. The
rapid night-cooling of California, like a refrigerator door opening
in a warm room. Her first night in the orphanage must have withered up the blessing of life, and it died in her there. For she did
have a mother, and a father too, although neither one at home; she
had roots and a recognizable being. So it would never matter again
what you really were, you could get dumped in the alley by what
some stranger said about you, you could get lost in his dead stare
upon you. So you'd better be sweet to him, or look sweet and sing
the orphan's anthem that charm was life.

But did her outcry mean she had known she had a real father and even that he was married to her mother, although they had broken up? Had it been her mother on one of her wild returns from the hospital who had spun out the idea of the unknown father, handsome and rich, who had refused to acknowledge her? Bedeviled by sin, smacked to the floor by religion's violence, had the poor woman come up with the story of illegitimacy and its curse, her own cue to murder, snatching the brand from her own heart and slaking it in her daughter's dreams? Where it would live on, yes.

Ben Hecht had been the first to seize the idea of her orphanhood and run with it, but she was never clear in telling about it whether she intended to be known as a real orphan or only as a child who had been left temporarily in an orphanage. Maybe it had always been much the same muddle for her as for her mother who the father was or was not, leaving only one thing clear, that illegitimacy was sin and sin made you worthless. Hecht must have sensed the attraction, for if you were worthless and so innocently babylike too, you were a defenseless sex object, or if you preferred, a free spirit with no one in the world to account to for your actions.

But it had left a quandary: to the end she would be crying out the contradiction that she had a real address and roots and a being and was in no way a defenseless orphan and did not deserve the concealed contempt such discarded people feel they inherit; and at the same time that she was as you desired her, a sexy, charming swinger with no home address. Who to be? It would not have been so painful a choice if one side of her had not been so serious about how to live usefully.

On the plane back to New York, *The Misfits* out of my life, I braced myself when a fat man in his sixties making his way down the aisle to the toilets stopped at the sight of me and pointed. "Say . . ."

"I know, but I'm not him. I look like him, but I'm not."

"Morris Green?"

"No." But I could not forbear. "Who's Morris Green?"

"Who's Morris Green!"—as though he were Bob Hope. "*Morris Green*, Poughkeepsie. Green's Hardware?"

"Oh! Well. No, I'm not him."

"I could have sworn. Excuse me," he said, continuing on his way and knocking my arm off the armrest. I had become part of the background, thankfully, fading fast into the national river of faces tumbling into the American gorge.

EIGHT

We met for the first time in Reno, where she had come with Henri Cartier-Bresson to photograph the goings-on. There can hardly have been many film productions more journalistically saturated than *The Misfits*, and they were the latest of a score of Magnum photographers who had been spelling one another over the months of shooting. Marilyn had liked her at once, appreciating her considerate kindness and the absence—remarkable in a photographer—of all aggression. She doted a little on the pictures Inge Morath had taken of her, sensing real affection in them.

I walked into the Mapes bar and found John Huston at a table laughing his head off with a photographer, a slender, noble-looking young woman with bobbed hair and a European accent, who seemed both shy and strong at the same time. I noticed the bob, her transparently blue eyes, and a conflicted sensitivity in her, but I was preoccupied by endings then, everything had gone out of control, and what words were spoken at the table I could never more than vaguely recall. That Inge and I have been married for twenty-five years as I write this sentence is not something I would have been able to believe that day. How to combine our quarter-century together, the best of my life, with my reasoned resolve never to marry again, surely not a third time! Past convictions, more often than not, are possible to recall but as difficult to relive as the future is unknown. I had been sure it would never come to me again, but it came and it stayed for days, and then weeks and months, the need to reach out and find the same person, to rely and be relied upon. Almost fifty years ago in Catholic Austria her parents had turned Protestant just before their wedding in order to be able to divorce legally should the need arise. A marriage should last as long as it lasted, she thought. So we got married in a state of spiritual modesty, with firm if minimal expectations of our predictabilities. It was all permanently temporary, and would stay that way, to our surprise, a reed to be admired rather than carelessly leaned on; marriage, after all, is a case of mutual forgiveness, and she knew she would need to dispense a lot of it.

But it was a mere glimpse of Inge Morath then; we would hardly speak more than a few words together until months later in New York, where we became friends. Although much younger than Cartier-Bresson, she had been a kind of editorial conscience to him for years in Paris and had joined him to cross the country in a rented car hoping to see the real America. They had searched in vain for something to eat from New York right into Reno. She an Austrian who had lived long in France, and he a Frenchman, they had made the fatal assumption that they would find marvelous provincial cooking along the way and had discovered the same hamburger tracking them everywhere. Luckily he had brought a little electric coil with which to heat water in a cup, and they practically lived on tea and a few lettuce leaves.

Huston would later explain what they had been so tickled about in the bar that day. She had photographed the making of *The Unforgiven*, a film he shot up in the Mexican backcountry just before *The Misfits*. She was working then for *Paris-Match* and *Life*. The picture starred Audie Murphy, the World War II infantryman turned movie actor, America's most decorated hero, who had killed endless ranks of Germans single-handed. One morning while John and a few friends were hunting ducks on the shore of the enormous high-country lake, Inge, who Huston insisted had to sit right behind him to photograph his kills dropping out of the air, grew bored with the noise and the pellets falling down on her and her new telephoto lens and went wandering off by herself. A couple of specks far out on the water and what looked like erratic thrashing drew her range finder to her eye, and she made out what she thought was someone struggling around a rocking boat. She called to the hunters, who refused to worry, knowing it was Audie out there with the company's plane pilot, a pair of machos who could survive anything. But she saw two helpless men. After a few more minutes she got out of her clothes and in panties and bra slipped into the cold lake and after swimming nearly half a mile found Murphy flailing desperately in the final stages of exhaustion, too weak to climb into the boat he had fallen out of; the pilot, also unable to swim, was hysterical and could not hold on to him from within the boat. She got Murphy to grasp her bra strap and towed him back to land. It took a long time, during which the onshore hunting never paused. Gasping for breath herself, she turned to the men and called them all bastards. In Reno these months later, Huston guffawed with happiness at seeing her again, showing the special respect for this handsome young woman that he reserved for people who had looked death in the eye. In gratitude Murphy had given her his dearest possession, a watch that had seen him through the entire war, a wonderful chronograph that she still wore. The other thing Murphy treasured was a revolver he always kept under his pillow and occasionally fired at the tent flap when he awoke out of one of his nightmares.

In New York, where she was temporarily staying between assignments, Cartier-Bresson and Gjon Mili, also a great but a very different photographer, were carrying on an amazing struggle of long standing for acknowledgment as her exclusive photographic godfather. The main issue at the moment was whether Inge should be using a tripod. Mili insisted she absolutely had to, Cartier-Bresson that she must not on any account, and all of this in French, up and down Sixth Avenue with the snow falling on us, and into Mili's vast studio on Twenty-third Street, and there were moments when it really looked like violence on the way. Meantime she, in the middle, was doing variations on "Oh, my God, stop it, stop it, stop it!"—but of course what she had to say was of small importance next to the towering authority over her that they were grappling for. They were pros but definitely not cool. Their fanaticism created a purity of feeling around them; egos and all, they were innocents because they cared so much. I wanted to be that way again myself. *"Moi, je déteste . . . moi, j'adore . . . moi, je . . ."*—they were endlessly shifting pieces of the world around to place themselves within its pattern, taking for granted that what they thought was of some decisive importance to the human condition. This refreshed me, so recently come from Hollywood, because none of it was for sale; it was simply their zealot's caring. Once, Cartier got so furious he began to take out his penknife. They loved one another, and she was glad to be their common sense, intolerable as they were. When she did a wonderful picture, each took it as an example of what he had been trying to tell her all along despite the other.

Gjon Mili was tall, with a drooping mustache under a long bulb of a Middle Eastern nose, and hair that was cut by Sammy, another unmarriageable Albanian who ran Mili's errands and from the looks of the haircut was easily distracted. Apart from photo supplies Gjon never bought anything and could nibble on the same cheese or stale bread all week. A mountain goat. *Life* gave him a one-room office in their building after his studio burned down, a major catastrophe, what with his thousands of photographs and gifts and old hats and letters from Picasso and everybody else who had mattered in the past fifty years. He loved folk dancing and went to lower Broadway every week and jumped around with a lot of other Albanians, most of them half his height. To him, everything was marvelous. He was a little like Saroyan, essentially an unattachable man with a great appetite for friendship and loneliness and no idea of the value of a dollar; although he pretended to be a shrewd trader he really didn't care about it. In his last years, two decades hence, he talked a lot about his mother, whose approval he still needed: in his late seventies he was still becoming a success in America so she, in her nineties, could boast way up there in those sequestered Albanian mountains.

Cartier-Bresson was from yet another planet, a Norman of high family who had read a lot, was always shaved, and dressed a bit on the English side in fine muted tweed jackets. He had been taken prisoner by the Germans during the war, finally escaping on the third attempt, and had hardly stopped traveling since. China, the Soviet Union, Africa, India—the world's elegant muteness had been caught by his Leica. Like Inge and Gjon, he lived painting, but unlike her, politics too.

These three simply could not or would not connect with the coming generation's inability to understand that photography was somehow, in some secret way, an extension of prophecy. They had no way of explaining that a photograph had to move the heart toward the sea of spirit and, however remotely, provoke bad, selfish, bigoted, narrow people to want to destroy it. The enemy was indifference always, and all the disguises of vulgarity in this, one of the most vulgar of the arts. I felt good near Inge's long view of everything, which still allowed her an involved uninvolvement with the latest thing.

What repeatedly surprised me was the austerity of her pride. "I am a snob," she once said, meaning that she would never stand in the middle of a crowd, only on the edge where she could see the whole. Balenciaga had made a broad gray hat and roomy gray coat and given them to her along with a rack of other clothes in return for her photographs and for the way she spoke Spanish like a Spaniard and disagreed with him when she felt like it. She had an earned suspicion of sentimentality about large-hearted humanity, raised as she had been in Nazi Germany with its fraudulent populism. For refusing to join the Nazi student organization, she was forced to assemble plane parts at Tempelhof airport in Berlin at a time when it was being bombed daily, working alongside Ukrainian women no one was likely to miss when they went up.

A year after we met, we were crossing the Rhine on a tiny ferry when she was suddenly approached by a bowing gentleman, well dressed in a fedora and tweed coat. I was at the rail watching the shoreline and, turning, saw him bend slightly forward with a fixed, wheedling smile. Back in the car driving off the ferry, Inge explained that he had been asking whether she could help him find a publisher for a book he was writing.

"He was the one who had me sent to Tempelhof."

"He tried to kill you."

"Yes, you could say that." She whitened.

We drove on up a mountain and stood before a castle overlooking the Rhine. Majestic. It had all been run by the Ku Klux Klan, on the same level of argument. But Heine had stood here once. Maybe the past really had been severed and the avant-garde was right. Even so, I had to search out a continuity. One had to explain all this so that people could understand it and not do it again, but the avant-garde was talking mainly to its converts, it seemed to me, and that simply could not be right. On the other hand, no conventional realism could illuminate this murder-by-civilization.

This quite ordinary-looking fellow politely wondering if she could help him find a publisher, both of them standing in the wind on the tiny ferry deck—it only held four cars and a few passengers, an idyllic little ferry under the brow of the chesty castle from whose crenellated tower a beer-bellied baron had long ago commanded cannonades upon ships below that failed to stop and pay his toll. It was a normal way of making a living in those days, they say. If you owned a castle, that was what you did, and you were a member of the nobility and had a crest and pride.

I would have been one of those on board the ship being shot at, not one of the shooters. The Jewish view of things is sometimes irritating.

We drove down the mountain. The Rhine can be frightening if you let yourself think about it. But so can everything. "Do not think about any one thing for too long," said old gray Professor Pillsbury in 1935, having not too long before been caught inside his own brain trying to get out and into the world. So we drove down the mountain and talked about something other than the man on the ferry. I was slowly getting to understand why she called herself a snob.

Johnny Langenegger, my driver and recording engineer, steered the new green 1940 Chevy van carefully along the barely perceptible trail through the pines, branches scraping at the top of the government vehicle. Suddenly we were at the edge of a vertical drop of granite that went ten stories down to a mile-wide floor. We could see little moving dots of men working the quarry. The air smelled of resin, like rotting oranges.

Johnny's head was close-cropped. He was trying to enlist in the marines for the big war that he was sure was coming soon, certainly by 1941 at the latest, and he didn't want to be in the army. We sat in the truck trying to figure what to do about getting down to the quarrymen, whom I would ask to talk into the microphone that was attached to the immense record-cutting machine in the back of the van. I was collecting dialect speech for B. A. Botkin of the folklore division of the Library of Congress, and we had been traveling around North Carolina for the past ten days talking to all kinds of people. It was wonderful how speech patterns could change so suddenly out in these backwoods places from one mile to the next, and they said the quarrymen spoke in a way all their own. In desperation I had gotten the job through my friend Joe Liss, who worked in the radio division of the library. Hardly two years out of college, with the WPA Theatre Project dissolved by Congress, I had not yet been able to connect in commercial radio on any regular basis, and my two Hopwood Awards were no longer resonating in my or anyone else's mind.

"Why don't we try going back to the paved road and see if it leads to an office or something. There must be a way to get down there," I said to Johnny. As he turned toward me, I saw his eyes go wide open and his mouth fall apart. I turned to my window and looked into the octagonal barrel of a shotgun. It was wavering. At the other end of it was a red-faced old man in denim shirt and overalls sitting in a truck—it was weird and dreamy that it had got there without our hearing it—and next to him a stringy woman was pulling at his right arm and saying something and looking angry and terrified at the same time.

The old red-faced man was speaking with lips drawn back over his enormous horsey false teeth. The woman kept pulling at him and calling his name, something like Martin or maybe Carter.

"You get out of here, you Jew bastards, or I'll blow your goddam heads off!" He released the safety, and my head pitched forward against the windshield as Johnny gunned the Chevy in reverse and went down the dirt track backwards doing at least twenty miles an hour.

The man had read the gold federal seal saying "United States Government" on the van's door, and that meant Roosevelt, who in some places down here was Rosenfeld, and we were all Jews out to get the races mixed, niggers in bed with white and so forth, because that was what the kikes were after, to destroy the Christian and so on. By this time he might also have heard that I had been in the town square interviewing black people who had nowhere to go after being fired from the shipyard they had recently finished building in the swampland mud.

The wavering barrel of that shotgun remained an afterimage in my brain, as if I had stared into a blindingly bright light. I saw it again, that black steel hole, as we drove down the mountain toward the Rhine. It was no good simply saying the past was canceled. But why did it seem to have no particular connection with the present and who I was now? Cancellation was the beginning of the sixties for me, the great disconcerting wipeout of all that had gone before.

Inge and I were walking down Madison to the Waldorf-Astoria. She would be off to some mountain in Argentina soon to photograph the making of a Yul Brynner film. She had photographed refugees with Brynner in North Africa for the United Nations a couple of years before.

We walked fast. Winter was blowing into New York, making the shops look cozy behind the store windows. A moment comes when you realize that you are friends and may separate or come together and part again quite happily, with no dependency. A good moment.

It was about six years since I had slipped into the Waldorf after days in the Bay Ridge streets with the wild boys, and about twelve since the Waldorf Conference. Now I was going inside to answer questions, along with the novelist James T. Farrell, before a convention of the American Psychological Association. Inge thought it should be interesting; her father had been a professor and scientist, and academies were serious business. But for me it was merely another attempt to look into the window of the time, a time that I could still not feel was mine. A time is yours when you and your friends are taking the same things for granted without thinking about it. I seemed unable to take anything for granted anymore, and I kept trying to figure out what others were taking for granted. The country had become foreign to me, and I did not understand why or how I had become this culturally hard-of-hearing fellow.

An audience of hundreds, surprisingly mostly women. This was not yet Vietnam, World War II was long gone. The Depression had not come back. There were still big fins on the cars. It was before Kennedy was shot, but Castro had beaten us at the Bay of Pigs, and men still had short haircuts. Milton Berle and Sid Caesar were on television. Sinatra was still a Democrat, like most of the showbiz folks. Even so the colors were beginning to run on the big cartoon; the liberal consensus was disintegrating, but the process still had no name.

Farrell and I sat side by side. Trying to concentrate on the speeches, I no longer knew why I had come here, but since he, a most honest and intense man, seemed absorbed in what was happening, I felt I should be too. I may have been hoping that someone would say something that would accidentally strike the beat of the time for me.

With the two formal speeches finished, somebody asked me about the place of morality in science. Everybody has a tag, and I was still the moralist, even now that I was not too regular what with one divorce behind me and a new one coming up.

All I could think to say was that morality could not be divorced from science—a reply that seemed to groan with the obvious if only we recalled the example of the Nazi doctors who, under the pretext of studying the physiology of drowning, had people bound hand and foot, thrown into pools, and then fished out for autopsies. Just because you had built a cathedral or synagogue, it did not mean you had a religion, and cutting people up did not mean you had a science. I kept my answer brief, hoping that we could now get on to something more interesting.

But there seemed to be some uneasiness in the audience at my answer. It left me bewildered. And when everyone was getting up to leave, a crowd, mostly women, surrounded me and asked why throwing those trussed people into the water was not science. Were they serious? Apparently. I could only answer that if it was science I preferred the Middle Ages. But mainly I was speechless. This was the first time I had faced Cool, the truthfulness without truth, the blankly interested posthumanist faces. I was surrounded by twenty or thirty women who were not at all satisfied that drowning people was not science and wanted further explanation. I may have been mistaken, but it crossed my mind that this could not have been so before the war, before it had been thoroughly done in the camps. Again I was at a loss. "Supposing some doctors said that they had to burn up a few million people to scientifically measure if human smoke had some special effect on the atmosphere, since it had never been done before, at least on that scale? Would that be science?"—but my words got lost in the chattering cross talk, and as we left, I wasn't so sure myself that there was any way of establishing what science was anymore. I thought the color had gone out of Inge's cheeks, as it had near the Rhine.

Science was reason's triumph, we had been so pridefully taught, the defeat of the Beast. But what happened when the Beast learned science? This had ceased to be an intellectual problem for me, had crossed over into my heart. I was living in a hotel, with no distractions—unusual for me—and with perhaps too much time alone, I had come to fear something I could not define or name.

Brooks Atkinson came up one afternoon with no special mission or interview in mind and sat talking for an hour or so. I felt I was a disappointment to him; as I read his mind, he may have expected that after my nearly five-year spell of Hollywood and notoriety, I would now be resolutely turning back to the theatre. It was nice of him to think it needed me—he was another of those who cared a lot—but my main feeling these days was something like embarrassment. Why, I wasn't sure, but it was certainly not a mood in which to start a new play.

The end of the past struck me wherever I looked. I knew hardly anyone of my generation anymore. In my mid-forties, I seemed to be the oldest one in the room. It was very strange that few remembered what I remembered.

I projected onto the city this same dislocation: people were in the wrong bodies with the wrong mates, saying things they did not really believe or understand. They were speeding around in motorboats, tossing things overboard to bob around in the wake—children, pots, pans, dogs and cats, houses and husbands and wives, all roiling around in the frothy water and then sinking out of sight and mind.

The theatre's serious work now was all about devastation, which is not the same as tragedy. I didn't accept it, even as I could hardly argue with it, given what had become of my own life.

Oddly enough, as the sixties began, the decade was being heralded as a time of acceptance of human nature, man shorn of illusions, but to me it seemed a time of denial. But of what? What had we done that we could not face?

I got to thinking again about Camus's *The Fall,* about the moralist unable to forget that he had not tried to stop the girl from jumping to her death in the river. I would put it differently. The question was not so much whether one had failed to be brave. It was something else. You can't oblige people to be brave, they either are or they aren't. What was there to say about this?

In Roxbury, spending more and more days of each week alone, I began to fear I was loving solitude and silence too much. My decaying barns, idle since the previous owner had departed, and my fallow fields, which for two centuries had supported families, cried out to be used again, just as my own spirit now seemed to have been left to the uses of chance for too long. Like my own interior terrain, the land longed for purpose and the forms that only loving work can bestow.

Inge, filled with purposefulness, was on assignment in France. I missed her sense of the hour's importance, the possibilities waiting in the unfolding day. I needed an ordered space around me if I was to work again, and when Inge was off on one of her jobs, I took on a tendency to walk into doors. But I must never form another commitment again, we were all too much like music, sounding illusions of hope from the mere pressures of air upon the ear, which last a moment before vanishing. The despair I felt was impossible to face or flee, and my only certainty was the hunger for long stretches of uninterrupted time to find my feet as a writer again. No partner ought to be asked to contribute to silence. In this year of knowing one another the simplest of ideas—that I needed help in order to live—became not only obvious but honorable and even a kind of strength. Maybe Ibsen had been wrong: he is not strongest who is most alone, he is just lonelier.

Down the road lived the Calders, Sandy and Louisa, whom I had known since moving into the area in the late forties. Their presence had always been a kind of reassurance for me, but they had begun to spend a lot of time in France. I had liked to come in the afternoons and drink wine with Louisa or go out and gossip with Sandy in his studio as he twisted wire and cut tin for a mobile. One day he sat drawing shapes for acoustical panels to be hung from the ceiling of the great concert hall in Caracas—Inge and I would see

them there twenty years hence—for he had graduated from the
Stevens Institute as an engineer, with the highest grades on record.
Like the painter Peter Blume and his wife, Eby, who lived over in
Sherman close to Malcolm Cowley, the Calders had come up here
in the Depression when small, bony farms still covered the landscape. All these people had known how to live happily on little
money—the Calders' place had cost thirty-five hundred dollars,
and the hundred-dollar down payment had been borrowed from
Bob Josephy, one of the finest book designers of the time. Even
then the farms were dying off, but the area still wore its pleasing
air of relaxed rural decay. I still had in my barn the gig in which
the farmer who sold me my place had driven to church.

Sandy transcended no matter what he did because his spirit
was a child's, as was his seriousness; he never theorized, either
about art or politics, and glancing at a canvas he didn't like, he
would simply say, "Poopy-doopy," without lingering on it long.
But he was shrewd about what was going on and went out of his
way to show me welcome in the bad time when I lost my passport and was being pushed around. He and Louisa were more
than a decade older than I, and I found a certain historical pleasure in their witness to the twenties and thirties, when she, a
great-niece of Henry James, and he, son of the sculptor of the
great arch in Washington Square, had experienced a New York so
different from the one I knew, a city not of striving immigrants
but of old families and quiet, powerful men. They continued to
live in the relaxed style of bohemian acceptance, judging no one,
curious about everything, but not far beneath the surface was a
stubborn and somehow noble sense of responsibility for the country, a sure instinct for decency that, in the wildly experimental
and super self-indulgent sixties, seemed in its quality of unpretentious simplicity all but lost to history. In another quarter of a century I would try to express my love for them both in *I Can't
Remember Anything*, a one-act play.

Sandy's slurred speech was as hard to understand as it was unmistakable, and coming through my bedroom window early one Sunday morning in the fifties, it shocked me out of sleep—could he be
out on the road speaking *French*? I went outside and found him in
his cutoffs and broken sandals walking slowly along with Oskar
Nitschke, a French architect who had recently lost his hearing;
Sandy had rigged up a piece of garden hose attached to a tin
funnel, into which he was making conversation while Nitschke
held the end of the hose to his ear and complained that Sandy was

yelling too loud. From Nitschke's neck hung a cardboard sign inscribed in Calder's inimitable hand, reading, "I AM DEAF." Each was carrying a bottle of red wine. They were in a very serious discussion the subject of which I have forgotten, but I remember joining in for a while, until they turned and walked the mile back to Calder's place. It was the end of one of their all-night parties. The two of them strolled down the middle of the road, on which no more than two or three cars a day passed in those days.

The Calders were hardly here anymore, and the men and women I had known who worked the land were almost all gone. Still, in the cold mornings there was the old softening whiff of a country spring in the air, a weather that had always triggered new works in me. But I was unready for even that much commitment, and in such a mood one invites new escapes: I must go to Paris, where Sidney Lumet was about to begin shooting a film of *A View from the Bridge* with Raf Vallone and Maureen Stapleton. Vallone had had a greatly acclaimed success with the play through two seasons there. Even better, I had accumulated enough royalties in London to buy a Land Rover and drive it down to Paris. That all this was a ruse to meet Inge I was perfectly aware, but sometimes even weak self-delusion is better than none. The truth was that I simply wished to praise the day and hope another one would follow, and Inge was a fine partner for that. Happy the man who need never assert more than he knows or less than he believes. I found in myself a novel respect for sheer fact, wanted to go with the facts and that was all. Perhaps I also longed to see Inge again because she so respected muddle, but being an artist herself, she could easily combine muddle with resolve. Besides, she seemed more and more beautiful, which is to say, undefinable. I knew, in short, that I was in trouble.

The Pont-Royal, where I had stayed after the war, was under renovation now, and its old golden patina of French bourgeois elegance shone once again through the grime of the war years. Gone was the concierge with frayed cuffs rushing across Paris once a day to feed his rabbits. Gone too, by the first of the sixties, the vistas of avenues and streets: parked cars blocked the view of all the lower stories and the grand entrances. Cars were now the foreground of Paris, architecture the background, and people were fragments worriedly maneuvering through the maze of bumpers and fenders and fumes. But the oysters and the color of the Paris sky were glorious still.

And Inge savored life as only one can who has nearly been killed. In this age survivors understand one another. It all seemed quite simple to her: there was little to expect from people, but what there was one had a right to demand and they an obligation to give.

At Tempelhof, a gate had been bombed open, and she had simply walked out, heading south toward Austria, more because she had to have a destination than from any belief that the family had survived and still lived in Salzburg. It was the story one heard a hundred times then: the exploding end of the Reich, the rides on trucks, the streams of people pressing in both directions, the unexpected decencies and the usual betrayals. Until at last she stood on a little bridge and, starting to climb the rail to let herself drop to her death in the water, was stopped by an older man, a soldier on crutches, who lectured her never to give up and made her follow him, and finally after days and nights on the road they arrived in Salzburg.

But her memory failed, she could no longer recall the house where she had lived, and now it seemed certain the parents could not possibly be living there still. The crippled soldier led her down one block after another, but nothing came to her until, at the edge of an affluent part of town, she had a warming sense of familiarity. But he scoffed at this—there were only prosperous people here to whom a scabby girl in rags could hardly belong—and they started to go on when suddenly she recognized a brass knocker and knew it was her house and rushed up to it and banged on the door, and there stood her mother, amazed. A miracle. They embraced, and she turned to thank the soldier and invite him in, but he was gone. She ran into the street, looked up and down, but there was nothing. As though she had dreamed of an angel. She was sure she hadn't. Why had he hurried away? Had he seen that he could not fit in with these elegant folk? Maybe he hated wealthy people or feared them.

It was not that she lacked all self-pity in the telling but that she seemed to take it absolutely for granted that you had to find the strength to save yourself; a bracing implication of self-reliance made for tragedy rather than mere pathos. She was neither optimist nor pessimist; sufficient unto the day was the evil thereof, and why go looking for more? She welcomed the good in people despite expecting the worst; indeed, a realistic philosophy had to allow for her soldier or it was false to life, and to mourn the world totally was to evade the terrifying contemplation of goodness. Such a war should not have tempered one such woman, but it had. It was hard to think of an American as cheerful as she.

And so, some four years after Walter Wanger had asked me to

write a film of *The Fall*—the story of a man who had failed to save a woman leaping from a bridge—a woman was telling me of a man who had held her back from just such a leap.

How strange, though, that he should have vanished in air!

One midday Marilyn showed up at the country house with her half sister, Berneice Miracle, and Ralph Roberts, an actor friend profoundly devoted to her, during the war an officer in Carlson's Rangers, now a masseur, a powerful, gentle half-Indian giant with wide cheekbones. He drove them up in a borrowed station wagon to get the big TV set from the second floor, a gift from RCA a couple of years before, as well as some other things of Marilyn's.

Marilyn wanted to show Berneice the house and all the changes she'd made in it. She took her upstairs and down and then out on the lawn to see the endless view. She described how she had dormers put in and raised the roof over one wing to make a room above the kitchen, and so on. Roberts was meantime carrying things to the station wagon. I gave them some tea and left them, thinking she wanted privacy with Berneice, a demure young woman from Florida. I gathered that they had met for the first time only recently, and Marilyn presented her to me with a certain pride in her relatedness. As far as I could recall, Marilyn had never mentioned her before, and if I had ever known she was Marilyn's mother's daughter by her first marriage, I had put it out of mind.

After half an hour I heard the tailgate slam shut and came down from my studio and said goodbye to Roberts and Berneice, who were just getting into the car. Standing alone in front of the garage, I faced Marilyn, and we grinned at each other and at the absurdity. I wondered what she remembered of our years and what she could not. And later I asked myself how much I had been unable to retain once denial had done its scrubbing job. She noticed the new tan Land Rover I had brought back from Europe a month before and assumed from it that I intended to live up here, which intrigued her. She wanted to know what *that* was sticking out of the back of the chassis, and I told her it was a power takeoff shaft to drive spraying equipment for fruit trees I intended to plant. She gave me a look of surprise in which I thought I saw some regret, considering all the hope we had put into this place; she had pressured me to buy more and more land, and I had resisted at first, saying it was unnecessary and would put us in debt, but it had turned out to be a clever investment as well as a beautiful one. Nevertheless, I had just had to sell some of my manuscripts to pay off our taxes. Yet here I was, apparently settled in, while she was in midair again, just as she had always been and as I could not be if I was to resume a working life. We had simply unveiled the austere perseverance of the past, and I knew now that one was never cleansed of it—not without the risk of suicide or murder in the attempt to escape it. What we are is what we were, give or take a few small crucial improvements if we're lucky, and Marilyn and I had pressed it all to the limit.

She seemed to delay leaving. Behind her the broad dogwood tree was losing the last of its dry little leaves, and the light on her was the gray color of its bark and of fall. She was wearing moccasins, which had always made her look fourteen, and a tan sweater, which she suddenly pulled up to reveal a dressing wrapped around her torso.

"See my bandage?" She grinned mischievously, as though it proved some point she wanted to make.

"What happened?"

"I had a pancreas operation. That's why I was in pain all the time."

I knew she did not mean to sound this rebuke—as though I, and probably Huston as well, had not taken her ill health seriously enough in our impatience with her endless delays on the picture; she was only trying to say that her behavior was not due to trivial malice or bad character or addiction. But it made me wonder if she realized even now how close to the end she had brought herself. For in her voice and in the demonstrative way she held up the sweater she seemed to see the disease as a visitation and not a consequence of immense dosages of barbiturates; she did not know she was still endangered by her very self and by her anger, however rightful it might be; she was still utterly the child and the prey. I felt the old admonitions branching out inside me but corrected myself and let them subside. And despite these tattered old signal flags fluttering at each other, I think we both felt vaguely silly waving goodbye as the car pulled out of the driveway, whose specific curve we had laid out together with the architect almost five years before. Alone, I stood there staring down at the tiny black stones imbedded in asphalt and recalled how unhappy she had been that we were not going to have the elegant crushing sound of loose stones under a car's wheels like they had in California; it snowed here, and the plows would have pushed them out into the road every winter. But of course you could always get more. And she was right, too—you could get more if you didn't mind the waste. I went back into the house still arguing with myself about it. Nothing really ends.

Too many honors are invented for the glorification of the donor for them to be accepted without a certain salt of skepticism, but this time it was easy to feel good about being in attendance. Among the crowd waiting in the Blue Room to go in to dinner were some of the best artists and writers in the country, as well as scientists, composers, and musicians. The White House dinner was in honor of André Malraux, currently De Gaulle's minister of culture, whose work I had admired since the thirties, but it was also manifestly a show of American intellectual pride. To my great surprise and pleasure I learned that I would be sitting with Jacqueline Kennedy and Malraux. Marine ushers in blue dress uniforms deftly shepherded the happy crowd into a long line, as if we were schoolchildren, and guided us toward the dining room, where we would go to our assigned tables. I found myself at the very end of the line, as had been my fate since grammar school due to my height, and as I slowly moved forward, I saw one lone man remaining outside. Of towering height, wearing a ruffled pale blue shirt, he was almost demonstrably disdaining the occasion, standing with one knee raised and a shoe pressed against the immaculate wainscoting, studiously cleaning his fingernails with a file like an idler in front of a country store. He looked friendless, if not peeved. I only gradually recognized his face. He was Lyndon B. Johnson, the vice-president of the United States, and clearly not in his element tonight. It was the only time I ever felt sorry for a vice-president.

Despite having been scorched by government power in the past, I was moved by Kennedy: at last a president who understood that a country needed not only its showbiz stars but its brains and its imaginative people. But my recent immersion in Hollywood may have cautioned me against Kennedy's high-speed, on-the-make inner spirit; his hard glazed eyes I found mechanized and a little frightening. He might have a quick mind, but I had to wonder about his compassion. Still, his excitement and happiness with the company he had attracted tonight swept everyone.

Malraux spoke in passionate bursts of French at a speed that defied comprehension by the president's wife much of the time and by me at any time. He was a star fencer flicking his foil before you had a chance to get set. He smoked almost violently and had a fascinating and disconcerting tic that made you wonder how he ever relaxed enough to sleep. The French ambassador, Hervé Alphand, deftly managed to loft an occasional translation toward me. Some two years later I was reminded of the subtlety of his performance and of Malraux's unrelenting intensity by another Frenchman, Cartier-Bresson. Sitting on the dock of my pond in Connecticut, Henri would read aloud for half an hour at a time to Rebecca, Inge's and my daughter, from his pocket edition of the memoirs of Saint-Simon, the superb chronicler of the machinations at the court of Louis XIV. It was his way of amusing himself and at the same time his admired Inge's daughter, even if she could understand nothing of what he was saying, let alone in French, since she was hardly more than a year old. Watching him down there by the placid water patiently turning the tiny pages while Rebecca cooed and kicked at the sky, I thought of our one American approximation of a royal court, and of Kennedy himself, who by this time had been murdered.

When it happened, we were in a large Connecticut hardware store. A radio was playing. "The President has been shot," came the voice through the shine and glitter of housewares. At first none of the two or three other customers seemed to hear. I felt an urge to laugh, maybe at the absurdity. The two clerks continued waiting on people. Nobody had been listening. For about a minute I couldn't locate the radio in all the clutter of mixers, irons, appliances. My mind kept saying, No, it's going to change, it's a mistake. Then I found the radio. Gradually the others were turning toward it. I knew what was in Inge's mind—that it was all happening again.

Like the headline about the bombing of Hiroshima, done and done. A tree struck by lightning, with split, still-living limbs swaying aimlessly against the sky, and the question "Why?" fluttering toward the blackened grass, and then the silence.

Driving back to the house with Inge, I thought of Roosevelt, who had also died unexpectedly, but the shock was of a different order. Roosevelt had so dominated my generation that we wondered who could take his place in the conduct of the war. Radio reporters describing the cortege passing down Pennsylvania Avenue suddenly broke into helpless sobbing, as though their own father had gone. The loss seemed far more intimate. Or was it simply that I had been younger then? Kennedy, on the other hand, was a contemporary of mine, and his death pushed a finger through the delicate web of the future. Even in the thirties, as bad as things got, there was always the future; certainly in all my work was an implicit reliance on some redemptive time to come, a feeling that the cosmos cared about man, if only to mock him. With Kennedy's assassination the cosmos had simply hung up the phone.

An image remaining to me from his inauguration ball, which I attended with Joe and Olie Rauh, was of Frank Sinatra and his pack in a special box overlooking the festivities. Lounging in magisterial isolation above the excited crowd, Sinatra seemed not so much to rise to the honor of presidential favor as to deign to lend his presence to the occasion. A singer for all seasons, he proceeded to do the same for Ronald Reagan, as high above politics as royalty while transitory presidents arrived and departed. Could this signify that the business of America was not business, as an innocent Calvin Coolidge had said, but show business, symbolic display, the triumph at last of metaphor over reality and the domination of the performer with his pure and pointless charm?

But maybe my lack of reverence was due to the fact that I could remember Sinatra in the late thirties, a skinny kid with a chicken neck, surrounded by screaming girls at the Paramount stage door after his first sensational breakthrough. We too were the same age.

It was hard to understand why, but a strange futility had crept into the very idea of writing a play. I am not sure whether it was the age we were entering or my own evolution, but wherever I looked there seemed to be nothing but theatre rather than authentic, invigorating experience. Practically everything—plays, department stores, restaurants, a line of shoes, a car, a hair salon—was being reviewed as though it had become a self-conscious form of art; and as in art, style was the thing, not content. One did not, after all, select a restaurant for nutrition but for taste and service, or a brand of shoes for durability or even comfort but for fashion. The tradition that a play of any significance had to address human destiny seemed ludicrously presumptuous, was going the way of values themselves. In the theatre, it was said, we were in the age of the director, with the playwright his assistant, in effect—but didn't this flow from the fascination not with what was being said but how? The very existence of the playwright was under challenge now; it was as though he represented the concept of predictability itself, with his preset speeches and plots that ended in some approximation of order. One avant-garde critic, to much applause, announced that it was much harder to write a good review than a good play. Only in spontaneity could truth be found, the mind being a congenital liar, and words but persuasive deceits. Gesture, preferably mute, was truth's last refuge, and even there it could only be a suggestion open to all kinds of interpretation, the more the better.

It was also taken for granted now that the audience was mortally bored, distracted, its attention splattered everywhere but on the stage it was facing. Nor was this purely an American phenomenon, as I would shortly learn, for they were also having trouble holding public interest in theatres across Europe. For one thing, nobody seemed to want to hear a story anymore; a story, I theorized, meant some continuity from past to present, and in our gut we knew there was no such continuity in a life where absolutely anything was perfectly possible for every kind of character. The only reliable recurring element in existence was the perverse, and the only sane reaction to it was bitter laughter, cousin to disgust.

In Peter Brook's Paris studio one afternoon in the mid-sixties, I watched his troupe of some two dozen actors perform for a class of deaf-mute schoolchildren. The troupe moved austerely through a series of dancelike formations, each actor carrying a baton to create patterns of contact and disconnection, design and confusion rearranging itself into new designs. It was pleasant to look at, communicating some aspect of longing, perhaps, but I could not be sure.

The schoolchildren now performed for the actors. Unable to speak or hear, they were condemned to the condition the actors aspired to, having nothing but gesture with which to communicate. They proceeded to present a mimed detective story of a child kidnapped from its parents, acting out the police investigation, the child's recovery, and the punishment of the criminals. There was suspense, a beginning and end, and a range of individual characterizations—the policeman identified himself by constantly saluting, the parents rushed about striking their chests and affecting attitudes of prayer for their child's safe return, the police dog sniffed everywhere for a scent of the criminals, and the kidnapped child rubbed her eyes as though permanently weeping. But what was striking was the children's anguished voiceless attempt to communicate with each other, the exaggerated gestures forced upon them by their inability to speak—gestures that seemed neither more nor less filled with feeling than the words they might have used had they not been mutes.

It seemed utterly wrong for those with all their senses to strive to eliminate some of them in the name of a closer contact with truthful expression. This experience typified for me the theoretical exhaustion of our artistic attitudes; here was a kind of admission that there was nothing worth saying anymore, and therefore nothing but mode or style to pursue and perfect. The deaf and dumb were desperate to convey an experience, to tell a story, hackneyed though it might be; those who could hear and speak were desperate to create a mood, a *feeling* pure and simple.

I suppose the theatre disgusted me because it seemed merely a sordid ego exercise, nothing more, and I hated egoism now, my own no less than others'. Truth-telling, I had once thought, was all that could save, but now it only seemed another disguise for the common brutality. Without mercy there was no truth, and without faith—in man, let alone God—mercy was merely one option among many others.

One laid one's work at the feet of a god unknown, without whose invisible presence there was no point in striving. "Ask not what your country can do for you; ask what you can do for your country," Kennedy had declared on that blustery inauguration day, with ancient Robert Frost trying to rescue the pages of his speech from the wind. The young president knew exactly what was wanted because he knew that it wasn't there. Why write?

Inge usually stayed at the old Chelsea Hotel in her numerous passages through New York, at the recommendation of her friend Mary McCarthy, to whose *Venice Observed* she had contributed photographs. For her it was the closest thing in America to a European hotel. The place was not yet as renowned for its famous artist residents as it would become in the mid-sixties, and I rented an apartment in part on the assurance of Mr. Bard, the owner, that nobody would know I was living there. With the same delightfully straight face, he claimed total innocence a few weeks later when the news began popping up in papers here and abroad, but it was hard to stay mad at Mr. Bard when he was so incapable of registering one's disapproval. A short, fair-haired Hungarian refugee with sublime self-confidence and a bad heart, he would vanish for days of fishing at Croton Reservoir between bouts of card playing with his fellow old-country survivors, the stakes often being hotels they owned, some as large as the New Yorker. But the Chelsea was his favorite of all his properties. "I like to be around artists, creative people," he would say. One needn't believe him to like him, if only because, like his hotel, he tolerated everything, except, quite naturally, a deficit.

I felt at home there almost at once, relaxing in the Chelsea charm, its unique air of uncontrollable decay. It was not part of America, had no vacuum cleaners, no rules, no taste, no shame. Bard's two partners, Krauss and Gross, did all the plumbing repairs, and that was why the hot water faucets were on the right, as in Hungary, and if some unwary bourgeois American happened to wander in, it served him right if he was scalded. On the ninth floor Virgil Thomson, at the time a reassuring sign of intelligent life, served drinks in his oak-paneled rooms that should have looked out on Fifth Avenue, potions that paralyzed Inge and me one forgettable evening; down the hall another composer, George Kleinsinger, aroused his girlfriends by scaring them with his collection of pythons, South American lizards, and tortoises, all dreaming away in their slimy floor-to-ceiling tanks; a defrocked minister nearly seven feet tall impatiently awaited cold, miserable weather to provide him with the new customers whose last rites would help pay his rent; Charles James, the once celebrated couturier, wandered the corridors in anguish at the old decay of the place being supplanted by the new decay of vulgar dope-dizzy artists, pseudo and legitimate, poisoning the atmosphere with their self-publicizing funk, not a lady or gentleman among them; and keeping order over the whole circus, the diminutive house detective sat in his room behind quadruple locks, surrounded by television sets, hi-fi equipment, typewriters, and fur coats he had stolen from guests, as was only discovered when the fire department had to smash down his door because the adjoining room caught fire after a drunk fell asleep with his cigarette burning.

The surreal had its citadel in the Chelsea long before its spirit was lifted by the Vietnam War into radical protest. To get to breakfast in the old Automat near the corner of Twenty-third and Seventh, I stepped carefully over the bloodied drunks sprawled on the sidewalk and had a Danish with Arthur Clarke, who lived half the year in Sri Lanka, which he thought the world's garden, and half in the Chelsea, its compost bin, whose nutrients, however, were far from wasted on the resident creative types. Clarke, surrounded by bag ladies nursing cups of coffee under broken noses and night workers with eyes glued to racing forms, excitedly confided that according to the most recent computations, vastly increasing carbon dioxide pollution threatened earth's end much sooner than was previously predicted. In the Automat ambience this news seemed perfectly inevitable.

The Chelsea, with all its irritants—the age-old dust in its drapes and carpets, the rusting pipes, the leaking refrigerator, the air-conditioner into which you had to keep pouring pitchers of water—was an impromptu, healing ruin that reminded me of William Saroyan's superbly American sentence spoken by an Arab in a saloon, a sentence totally forgotten by the sixties revolutionaries busy inventing a new nonsociety that would outlaw memory of all that had gone before: "No foundation all the way down the line." In his Armenian pursuit of amiable chaos, Saroyan had smelled the future way back in the forties and, posing as an uncultured minor comedian, had announced the authentic American optimistic absurd rather than aping the morbid European brand. Saroyan laced the absurd with the dark outsider-immigrant's unquenchable hope of finding his very own pillow on which to take his ease amid the rocks of the sunny American landscape.

I watched the new age, the sixties, stagger into the Chelsea with its young bloodshot eyes and made a few attempts to join the dance around the Maypole, but I could not help myself: to me it all felt self-regarding, self-indulgent, and not at all free. That included the Beats, who looked to be rehearsing a latter-day Lost Generation moan, for until Vietnam began to murder them, their complaints seemed to lack Necessity. The dope was a pure destroyer to me, not social protest, a mournful pleasure that would not lay one brick of the new church for whose absence they were making lamentation. It was their assault on sexual prudery that won respect, but otherwise they were part of the self-destruction that I was seeing everywhere, not least in myself and my life. America's unacknowledged religion was self-destruction, both politically and personally, and I spent my time in the Chelsea groping for a concise paradox that would hold a play in place on that theme.

It was not only Marilyn on my mind; in this very hotel in the early fifties, I had sat in one of these tall gray rooms trying to fathom Dylan Thomas as he methodically made his way out of this world, a young man who with a week's abstinence would have been as healthy as a pig. Much later, when I read his confessional about his father, it seemed to me that he had been throttling himself for having conquered fame with his art while the sweet father, a writer-teacher, remained an unknown, failed man. Thomas was making amends by murdering the gift he had stolen from a man he loved. I knew about that transaction, the struggle to hold off the guilt of power in the face of a father shorn of it. Patricide came with the territory as an urge; the question was how to live with it. Or how not to.

Later there was another who came to the Chelsea to die, the

Borstal boy himself, Brendan Behan, on his last legs then, asking me to come to the room where Katherine Dunham had put him up for a couple of nights to help him make it through the week. He sat there, his wet hair haphazardly plastered down, his face blotched, lisping through broken teeth, laughing and eating sausages and eggs while black dancers moved in and out of the room not knowing how to help him or whether even tenderly to try, and he said with his fixed uneasy chuckle, "I'm not really a playwright, you know—and you'd know that, of course—I'm a talker. I've a room upstairs where I'm talking a book to a secretary the publishers keep hounding me with. I've done a good bit of it in the hopes they'll empty another purse over me head. . . . But I did want to say hello to you, Art'r . . ." Hello and goodbye, that was clear; he was on his way out of it.

He would hold forth on the sidewalk outside, the vomit coming up and dripping on his tie as he joked and told his stories and sang a few ditties, rustling meanwhile through a *Post* to see if he was in Leonard Lyons again today, the columnists delighting in him now that he would soon be gallantly supplying them with the story of his rousing poet's death. There were so many ways you could help them kill you.

And the surest was to blame the system or somebody else; even if it was true, you dared not believe you had no part in it, or you would finally accept the victim's role and die too young. The part one played in one's own destruction was the mystery under the beauty of the American sky.

These men dreaded to hold the power they had won, and found the only way to be freed of it.

Charley Jackson, a bald-headed waif, would offer his tender smile of greeting whenever we passed in the lobby—a long time now since the power of *The Lost Weekend* had swept him up to a quick view from the amazing top of the wave. On the wagon now, he was clearly trying to walk the center line. Until it got so terribly narrow that he stepped off into a permanently liberating sleep in the Chelsea bed with the pill bottle beside him. He was nothing but kind, except to himself.

There were other casualties of the ceaseless Chelsea party that went on celebrating something no one could name. In the lobby once an angry young woman stood handing out mimeographed statements in which she described her intention to shoot a man, no one in particular, just one of the persecuting species that had ruined her life. People accepted the leaflets and then stood there chatting pleasantly with her. I heard one man disputing a point of syntax with her. I said to the management that this woman was going to kill somebody and maybe something ought to be done about her before she exploded, but she was a member of the party, it seemed, and it wouldn't do to be too square about it. She found Andy Warhol one day and she shot him, reportedly in the groin; the party slowed for a moment, but it soon picked up again.

Ever since Hiroshima I had been thinking about a play that would deal with the atom bomb. Now, fifteen years later, it was less a feeling of guilt than of wonder at my having approved the catastrophe that moved me to try to investigate firsthand how the scientists themselves felt about what they had created. The accounts of their struggles to convince President Truman to first drop a demonstration bomb at sea off Japan suggested that they had qualms at taking responsibility for so much death. Through Jim Proctor's friendship with a Cornell physicist, I gained an introduction to Hans Bethe, who had designed the lens without which the bomb could not have been detonated. I set out for Ithaca one misty fall day from the Roxbury house, with no inkling that in fact I was actually preparing to write quite a different play, *After the Fall,* but one with a related theme.

The murderous ironies in the story of the atomic bomb were familiar by this time. The German refugee scientists who were the main engine of the Manhattan Project had been afraid that Hitler's capable scientists, whom they had known in Germany as colleagues, might develop an atomic weapon with which to hold America hostage and change the course of history. But by the time they had the American bomb ready Germany had been beaten, and there turned out to have been no serious atomic project under way in the Third Reich. In that sense the bomb had been unnecessary.

Many of these scientists were Jews, antifascists, leftists, and a few were actual Marxists, and with the war's end they saw their weapon being brandished at the Soviet Union, their onetime spiritual home. In the supreme irony, J. Robert Oppenheimer was shadowed by U.S. security services as a radical while he was the very soul of the new power being forged for American dominance of the postwar world.

Some fifteen years after the successful explosion of Fat Man, Hans Bethe was a fit-looking fifty-five, a squarely constructed man, the Alpine type who loved taking long hikes in knickerbockers and sturdy shoes. The house was fit for a monk, with a small Oriental carpet in the middle of a large, dark living room almost bereft of furniture, and a glassed-in porch with a single table and chair standing in the gray light of an Ithaca afternoon.

Once a week an army plane still flew him to Washington for consultations. He had a somber curiosity to which some sadness clung, and I hesitated to wound him further with my main question. His world, I assumed, had become brutally ironical, due in no small part to his own inventions at Los Alamos; how did he deal with this? I knew there was no concise answer to such a question, but it was the surrounding emotion I was after, for it was the same question I was asking myself. I had created my own life dilemma, that much was clear; how to go on without a crippling bitterness?

He seemed a decent, feeling man, and I knew that he had strongly opposed dropping the bomb on living people but had failed to dissuade Truman. He had worked desperately on the Manhattan Project to preserve life against the Hitlerian death. Somewhere in the air must be an inexhaustible laughter now. As a physicist he had happened to stand on the burning point where the pure search for truth was touched by the hot iron of political and state power.

In Europe, he explained, as well as here in prewar times, a physicist was a lonely man. Who in his right mind would go in for this science, which had hardly any practical application and therefore held no prospects of financial or other advancement? The physicist was the priest of science, a pure inquirer likely to be recognized by a few others of his kind, no more. I asked him how he worked.

"Well, I come down in the morning and I take up a pencil and I try to think, to put things together in a new way. Sometimes something happens, most often not. This can go on for months, years sometimes. Then one might trip on a curb, and a connection is made in the brain. Or perhaps nothing comes at all. It is very lonely work, walking the edge. Or it was, before the bomb and all the developments."

He was describing a writer's work exactly—before the movies and mass entertainment, before truth had to be "useful." I realized after a few hours that it was all as mysterious to him as to me, that we were not to transcend the prison of irony into which we had rationalized ourselves in our time. One did what one did not intend. One did not intend what one had done. And yet one was responsible, if only because someone had to be.

Why was one responsible if one had no evil intention?

But if one had no evil intention, then where did the evil come from?

Could there have been, deeply concealed under monkish ideals, a nerve that tingled when Power passed by? Was this his mortality, his equality with the least of us, the stupidest, the most vile of us? Where was the heart of evil if not within us?

I went down to Princeton and found in Robert Oppenheimer a gaunt, obviously depressed man—indeed, he would be dead in not too many years and may have known it then. This, of course, was long after he had been barred from government work as a security risk despite having fathered the atomic bomb. We talked in his unadorned office, and I was reminded by it and his tweed jacket and pipe that he was an academic, though I had always connected him with power and war. Unlike Bethe's Spartan home, Oppenheimer's, as I recall it now, seemed to befit a renowned singer or artist who had surrounded himself with mementos, photos, statuettes, carpets and honors and gifts from around the world. It had once been a comfortable, unpremeditated house that spoke of the triumphant years when all was promise and the great had come from everywhere to pay him homage. But there was an aura of devastation now. His dying wife, Kitty Dallet, a fragile, petite woman in a tweed suit too large for her wasted frame, was still remarkably pretty, her face not at all aged. But her air of alert anxiety brought to mind the grueling governmental inquiries that had hammered her for her past radical connections. Even ill and scared, she looked like she'd had a lot of zip once. At a small gathering of university people she kept watching me with some fearfulness, I thought, and I sat beside her to reassure her that I was not searching out a new angle with which to torture them all over again in yet another magazine piece or television show. There was something pert about her, reminiscent of the aging Dorothy Parker and her forlorn wit. The air of the house was darkened by the shadows of better days.

It was emphatically not mere blame or guilt I was interested in but the scientist's connection, or the absence of it, with his own life. Looking back, I could not altogether find myself in my own romantic pursuit of something like total personal expression, my determination to find an absolute truth while blinding myself to facts. Had these idealizing scientists experienced a similar discontinuity? On an absurdly lesser scale the same human dilemma might reveal itself: I had changed the lives of others, my wives and children certainly, and maybe even people across the world in the audiences of my plays, and yet I could only dimly glimpse myself in my work, as the physicists might be denying themselves in theirs. It seemed impossible to evolve at all without a more complete, more living vision of one's responsibility for oneself, a surgically painful investigation. I did not see it as a moral question but almost as a biological one; as always I began with behavior, and there was something wraithlike and frustratingly disembodied in the way most people managed to live to one side of their lives, as though there were two of them, one that acted, the other condemned (or was it privileged?) to stand apart and observe, thirsting to partici- pate in his own existence, and afraid of it too.

I even wondered if this split underlay our common fascination with violence, the commercialization of sex by separating feeling from it, and the limitless desire for entertainment—the country's purpose sometimes seemed to be a massive, swarming search for new diversions. The past was no longer a guide in such matters, now that the impersonator of other humans, the movie star, was the most envied, most celebrated, and best-paid person in the country and his triumph, a fabricated escape from the self, was apparently the goal of life. More and more certainly now, the widely accepted virtue of the drugged life seemed an aspect of the same urge, the urge to fuse, however spuriously, the two sides of man into a single unity of action and consciousness, if not in social reality, then only inside the head, by substituting a chemical un- consciousness that would shut out the world and manufacture a transcendence without values.

This quest for the total self now seemed to define the search in *Hamlet,* in *Oedipus Rex,* in *Othello:* the drive to make life real by conquering denial, the secret thrust of tragedy.

Talking with these scientists, I entered a dark and unknown land ruled by the cruel tyrant Irony; having set free the most awesome forces of nature, they now found themselves imprisoned in narrow contradictions, chiefly that basic decisions were not theirs to make but were left to politicians whose minds and motives were too often petty and unwise. The great good science was doing in medi- cine had justified it as a lifesaving art, but it could extinguish all life. To which side of this equation did an inventing physicist connect himself?

In the end, Oppenheimer's protective caution made intimate discussion difficult; I supposed he had good reason to be suspicious of writers. Still, my questions seemed to interest him, even though he allowed himself mostly noncommittal replies, except to the central one—whether we all tended to deaden our connections, and hence our psyches, to those actions we found it difficult to justify. Plainly moved, his eyes filled with what I took for vulnerability, he looked directly into my eyes and said with quiet emphasis that this was not always true. In other words, he was indeed suffering, was not merely a man who had known power and was able to distract himself by recollecting his unique accomplishments. It was sufficient response for me at the moment.

I came away with the belief that to put the question was to answer it. Men had to deny, and the palpable gloom around these truth-seekers seemed to me now the gloom of denial; they had finally to believe that the great swath of history had simply swept them up much as an immense gravitational force sucks new stars into its gorgeous path. And yet the fact would not go away that all their marvelous craft had placed in the hands of ignorant, provincial men the destroying power of the gods.

Back in Roxbury I wrote page after page of a play in blank verse about an Oppenheimer-like character preparing to signal the fateful test explosion of Fat Man, the first experimental bomb. The scenes had a certain elegance but would not bleed—I was too remote from the character's daily life. But in the process of writing, it occurred to me that guilt of this kind might be a spurious, slyly invented pseudo-relationship with a person or event, something we fabricate to deny our real responsibilities. Guilt supplies pain without the need to act and the humiliation of contrition; by feeling guilt, in short, we weaken the need to change our lives.

It was clearer now why Camus's *The Fall* had left me unsatisfied; it seemed to say that after glimpsing the awful truth of one's own culpability, all one could do was to abjure judgment altogether. But was it enough to cease judging others? Indeed, was it really possible to live without discriminating between good and bad? In our eagerness to accept the fecund contradictions of life, were we no longer to feel moral disgust? And if we were to lay no more judgments, to what could we appeal from the hand of the murderer?

The bomb play was interesting when it should have been horrifying. I did not know how long I would live, and I longed to leave something absolutely truthful; this play might well illuminate the dilemma of science, but it failed to embarrass me with what it revealed, and I had never written a good thing that had not made me blush (nor did I think anyone else had either).

I began to search for a form that would unearth the dynamics of denial itself, which seemed to me the massive lie of our time—while

America, as I could not yet know, was preparing to fight a war in Vietnam and methodically deny it was a war and proceed to deny the men who fought the war the simple dignity of soldiers. I saw American culture, the most unfettered on earth, as the culture of denial; even as the drug, in expanding the mind, denied that it was destroying the mind, and the new freedom of sexuality denied that it was dissolving the compassionate self-restraint that made any human relationship conceivable over time. Costume and fashion allowed the stockholder's mind to deny the wearer of worker's jeans and secondhand clothes, whose free-flowing hair denied personal uninvolvement masquerading as liberated sensibility.

Inevitably the form of the new play was that of a confession, since the main character's quest for a connection to his own life was the issue, his conquest of denial the path into himself. It seemed neither more nor less autobiographical than anything else I had written for the stage. From the play I had abandoned a decade before, about a group of researchers suborned by a pharmaceuticals magnate, the figure of Lorraine emerged as the seeming truth-bearer of sensuality, contrasted with the constricted, mind-bound hero who looks to her for the revival of his life as she more and more comes to stand for the catlike authenticity of a force of nature.

Some weeks after the completion of *The Misfits* Marilyn had returned to New York, phoned me in the hotel where I was living before I moved to the Chelsea, and asked, "Aren't you coming home?"

It was a long moment before I could speak. She seemed genuinely surprised not to find me in our apartment, even though I had said I would be living elsewhere; had she forgotten her fury against me, or had it not meant to her what it did to me? Her voice now had its old softness and vulnerability, as though nothing at all destructive had happened in the past four years, years that seemed to blanch out as she spoke, like a color photo of violence that had been left too long in the sun. Suddenly the real past was as holy to me as life itself; this amnesia seemed like trying to die backwards. Now the unstated question posed in *The Fall* was not how to live with a bad conscience—that was merely guilt—but how to find out why one went to another's rescue only to help in his defeat by collaborating in obscuring reality from his eyes. *The Fall* is the book of an observer; I wanted to write about the participants in such a catastrophe, the humiliated defendants. As all of us are.

* * *

I was quickly piling up pages, too many for a normal play. I worked in the Chelsea and half the time in Roxbury, in the house that Marilyn, in her way, had longed to make her home, just up the road from my first house, where I had lived with Mary and the children for half a decade; but the past was no less mysterious for being so close by. In the curve of the road approaching that first house was a certain maple tree gradually dying of a wound inflicted by a car that smashed into it on the day Marilyn and I married. In an attempt to avoid the press, we had had the cere- mony at the Westchester home of Kay Brown, my agent and friend of many years. She and her husband, Jim, my parents and Joan and Kermit and their spouses, the Rostens, and a cheerful Rabbi Robert Goldberg could not dispel Marilyn's tension, which by now I had come to share, if only because the world, quite literally, was out searching for us. Returning home later in the afternoon, we came on a Chevrolet askew in the road a quarter of a mile from the house, its front end mangled around this tree. We stopped, and I got out and looked and saw a woman stretched out on the front seat, her neck obviously broken. At the house, which we reached in a moment, an ambulance was al- ready pulling up, and a mob of some fifty newspeople, camera- men, and onlookers was directing the driver to the accident. The unfortunate woman, Mara Scherbatof, a Russian of high birth, was head of the New York bureau of *Paris-Match* and had hitched a ride with an American photographer. Inquiring for my house from a neighbor, he had mistaken a passing car for mine, roared off in pursuit, failed to make this turn, and collided with the tree. It was so useless a death, and so pointless a mission in the first place, that a pall of disaster fell over both of us. The struck tree slowly rotted and after half a dozen years finally top- pled over, leaving a stump that my eye could not avoid looking for in the weeds whenever I drove past.

One learns to listen to what a developing play is trying to say. The theme of survivor guilt was emerging from the gargantuan manuscript. Months earlier, after our tour of the Rhineland, Inge and I had found ourselves in Linz, Hitler's Austrian birthplace, still famous for its anti-Semitism. Just outside the city, high on the crest of a low, forested mountain, stood the Mauthausen concentration camp, which Inge thought I might want to see. She had suffered under the Nazis, but she had also survived them, and her mind kept sifting through a past with which she wished to make peace.

As we drove by the small farms, it seemed strange that none of the people so much as glanced up to see who was passing on this rarely traveled road to a long-empty concentration camp. Naturally, I assumed they had been doing precisely what they were doing now when the trucks packed with people whined up this road during the years the camp was in operation. Nor could I blame them altogether, and that was the troublesome part. I inevitably wondered what I would have done in their place, powerless as they were to intervene—if indeed such a thought had ever entered their heads.

Built like a castle fortress, the camp was surrounded by a massive twenty-five-foot-high stone wall instead of the usual barbed wire fence on poles. This place was obviously to be a permanent killing ground for the Thousand-Year Reich. Beside the tall gates, locked shut, was a small wooden door. We knocked and waited in the country silence. The loveliness of the countryside falling so soothingly away in undulating waves of dense woodland mocked everything one knew. Where every prospect pleases and only man is vile.

Presently an inquisitive, roundly overweight Austrian appeared, smoking a long bent pipe just as in the cartoons, accompanied by his smiling overweight dachshund, perky and as full of curiosity as her master. The man, doubtless bored by his watchman's job, was happy to let us look inside. Not without deference to the thousands who had been murdered here, he was nonetheless lively as he showed us through barracks buildings and courtyards, pausing to explain about the stone slab, with its carved cradle to fit the head and the funnel at one end to let out the blood, on which cadavers were shorn of hair and their gold teeth knocked out. The living were also worked over here. Neither flooding with sympathy and remorse nor cooled by indifference, he was as interested in the horrors he described as he was respectful toward the victims, and clearly blameless in his manly heart. (And what else should he be? Was he not to live?) In an open alley between two barracks he pointed out a pyramidal stone obelisk recording that here a Russian general had been forced to stand in below-zero weather while water was poured over him until he froze to death in a column of ice.

Down below in a little roadside bar where we sat having coffee shortly afterwards, a burly fortyish workingman with fat hands sat at a table with a girl of eight or nine and with a caring sternness corrected her arithmetic in her school notebook. Probably he had lived here in the killing time only twenty years before, had known what those trucks constantly climbing up the hill each day were carrying. Through it all, Inge moved very straight, saying little, but pale and fighting her fear. Tears were constantly threatening the rims of her eyes. The builders of this place and the indifference we saw about us now—to say the least—had destroyed her youth and laid on her for the rest of her life a debt that she did not owe and could never pay and yet carried always, because of her humanity. It was a mystery. Though she saw that the world beyond the German lands left little more room for confidence in the human animal, she was apparently able to stand fast against pessimism. There were always, it seemed, a few individuals to whom one could appeal . . .

And if, as I thought, I would have done anything not to be one of the people inside the trucks grinding up that hill, was that why I felt something less than a purely mournful union with the dead?

Shortly after our trip to Linz, the *International Herald Tribune* reported in a four-line squib that a trial of former Auschwitz guards was going on in a Frankfurt courthouse especially built for these proceedings. I had never laid eyes on a Nazi, and I thought it worth a few hours' drive to do so.

In the new and impressively sedate tan marble courtroom, we sat down among a sparse dozen or so curious onlookers. After only a few minutes a reporter from one of the wire services came over to say that he hoped I'd be writing about the trial since he and his colleagues were having trouble getting their stuff into the European, American, and British press, there being a distinct absence of interest in the Nazi phenomenon now, more than fifteen years after the war. I had not come to the trial intending to write about it, but at the request of the *Tribune* I ended up doing a long piece, which was also published in the *New York Herald Tribune*.

Shards of that day remain. Facing the judge's high tribunal and the witness box, some twenty-three defendants, all men in their fifties and sixties by now, sat on a raised platform behind their lawyer, a tall, portly man named Laternser, who represented General Motors in Germany—too expensive a man, I would have thought, for these former guards, who were obviously neither educated nor well-to-do. Fritz Bauer, the chief prosecutor, explained this puzzle; he had learned that the accused guards had threatened to expose the murderous role of the head pharmacist at Auschwitz in the so-called medical experiments unless the pharmacist, a scion of a wealthy German family, provided them with a top attorney. Indeed, the pharmacist was seated right next to me, a nearsighted man of perhaps fifty, with a studious expression and a very good greenish tweed suit, who followed every word of the trial with understandably intense concentration. He was not yet indicted and was clearly hoping not to be.

One of the guards, responding to Laternser's questions, which were designed to portray him as a perfectly respectable family man of blameless habits, described his fatherly guidance of his four children into useful adulthood. Laternser, satisfied, began to turn away, but the guard continued, "Except for my youngest daughter. I don't speak to her." This seemed a real surprise to Laternser, who quickly tried to cut his client off. But the former Auschwitz guard, filled with naive indignation, insisted on showing the court what a faithful German he was, and went on to tell how he had broken off relations with his daughter once she decided to marry an Italian. The treacherous Italians, of course, had folded before the Allied advance, deserting the Reich, and anyway were dark, untrustworthy folk.

Another guard, famously sadistic in Auschwitz, had fled at war's end and was one of the few to go east rather than west. He produced witnesses from Polish hospitals who testified that as a nurse in Warsaw the past few years he was known as "Mother" because of his remarkable tenderness with patients. His specialty at Auschwitz was beating people tied to a bar in the "parrot's perch" position.

Privately Bauer confided what everyone knew—that local police authorities were dragging their feet in the matter of searching for subpoenaed witnesses to Nazi crimes, at the same time that West Germany was spending a lot of money pursuing these trials. Until the Nazis took power, Bauer had been the youngest Supreme Court justice in the state of Hesse. He was not immediately decommissioned by the Nazi judiciary, but because he could not in conscience administer "laws" that were little more than written prejudices, he fled to Sweden and spent the war there. Returning, he vowed to hunt down Nazis, but he was now a disillusioned man; it was not so much that the Nazi idea was holding on, he thought, but that people simply wished to avoid the past altogether, and certainly to deny its horrors. He was usually regarded as an enemy of

Germany, since he was its conscience—which is not, of course, an unheard-of state of affairs in other countries.

Inge and I had lunch with Laternser, a smoothly sophisticated man with a very quick mind, and unbending in his defense of the guards. "As Americans are the first to point out, there can't be a just trial when the prosecution's witnesses are all dead or so old they can hardly recall anything." That his clients had helped to kill these possible witnesses was certainly not his affair, only the evidence was.

I wrote a long piece about the trial that was played over two pages in the *International Herald Tribune* and only slightly cut in the New York edition. For a time, there was more coverage of such trials, but the fact remained as heavy as a gravestone—important though it might be to memorialize the Holocaust lest it fade away, its built-in human causation remained largely unexplored terrain for most people, who continued to nurture their fear of tribes and persuasions other than their own like something sacred. In any case, regardless of what one wrote or read, to so much as contemplate the systematic gassing of small children was to feel a cold hand clapped to one's mouth, and one understood to some small degree why the Germans could not think about it. But the righteous stupidity of that guard who expected to better his case by declaring his hatred of Italians remained most vividly in my head; this man had had the power to order thousands of people about, even to kill them—people of talent, perhaps of genius, doctors, artists, fine artisans, philosophers, or just ordinary lovers.

On second thought, maybe the problem with identifying the universals in the Nazi condition was precisely that power and stupidity were so commonly joined in the world that there was something unremarkable about it, something lacking in explosive illumination.

It was after returning from Germany that I began to feel committed to the new play, possibly because its theme—the paradox of denial—seemed so eminently the theme of Germany, and Germany's idealistically denied brutality emblematic of the human dilemma in our time. The theme's most poignant manifestation was in Lorraine, the character from the unfinished pharmaceuticals company play, in whom I saw symbolized a far more general irony. For she appeared so trusting in her candor, and as strong and nonjudgmental as a fine animal, while within she felt painfully illicit, a kind of freak whose very candor brought her little but disguised contempt in the serious opinion of the world. And so, bewildered and overwhelmed, she secretly came to side against herself, taking the world's part as its cynicism toward her ground down her brittle self-regard, until denial finally began its work, leaving her all but totally innocent of insight into her own collaboration as well as her blind blows of retaliation. She felt besieged, could trust nothing anymore. The complex process of denial in the great world thus reflected in an individual seemed a wonderfully illuminating thematic center, and so completely did it overtake my imagination that, as Robert Whitehead remarked later, I was totally surprised to hear him say that everyone would of course reduce Lorraine, renamed Maggie, to a portrait, purely and simply, of Marilyn. I was sure that the play would be seen as an attempt to embrace a world of political and ethical dilemmas, with Maggie's agony perhaps the most symbolically apparent but hardly the play's *raison d'être*. The play was about how we—nations and individuals—destroy ourselves by denying that this is precisely what we are doing. Indeed, if Maggie was any reflection of Marilyn, who had many other dimensions, the character's agony was a tribute to her, for in life, as far as the public was concerned, Marilyn was practically barred from any conceivable connection with suffering; she was the "golden girl," the forever young goddess of sexuality, beyond pain and anxiety, a mythically anesthetized creature outside the reach of ordinary mortality, and hence of real sympathy. But of course she had unwittingly worked to create this myth, which seemed her triumph once it was established.

Looking back, I could see that in disconnecting the fictional character from any real person I was blinding myself to the obvious, but blame was certainly no part of the play; the very point of it all was that Maggie might be saved if she could cease to blame, either herself or others, and begin to see that like everyone else she had essentially made her own life, an awesome fact toward which one had to feel humility and wonder rather than such total remorse as was implied in her denial of any decisive part in her calamity. In this sense, innocence kills. But as I would shortly discover, it reigns, as it doubtless will forever.

I had not begun with the idea that Maggie would die but that she and Quentin would part, a stronger ending in that it would prevent the audience from disposing of the tale with comforting death. But as the character formed, she seemed more inescapably fated, and I could feel the bending of that arc toward death. And this also separated her in my mind from Marilyn, who as far as I knew was busy making films again, had bought herself a house, and was probably leading as good a working life as the movie business would permit.

Buying a paper at a New York newsstand one afternoon, I happened to see a photo of her—it may have been in *Life*—that showed her in a swimming pool, her nude body stretched out in the water and her face turned up to the camera. The accompanying copy said that she had insisted on not faking the nudity in *Something's Got to Give,* a comedy she was starting to shoot with Dean Martin. It seemed to me that she had a grin of willed insouciance quite different from the genuine joy with which she had shown off her glorious body years before. It was hard to down the feeling that she should not be doing this anymore, that she was past the need to rely so patently on her body; were all her years of travail for this naked swim in a pool? That photograph, meant to celebrate the return of the old carefree Marilyn, was overcast with a kind of doomed coolness for me, as though she had given up trying to cease being the immemorial prey.

An item in the paper said that *Something's Got to Give* had been canceled because Marilyn had been consistently late for shooting. An ad in *Variety* signed by the grips and other workers on the picture sarcastically thanked her for having self-indulgently cost them their jobs in a difficult time. Nothing could have wounded her more terribly.

I knew her analyst cared deeply for her and had allowed her practically to make herself one of his children, to visit with the family and hang around the house like one of his daughters. But after this latest shock I hoped he would move in strongly with special precautions, because it was just the situation to send her searching for the relief of unconsciousness. In Hollywood during another film I had been driven to call in the head of the University of California Medical School to persuade her to break her barbiturate addiction; all the other doctors had gone along with her demands for new and stronger sleeping pills even though they knew perfectly well how dangerous this was. Her very name and power conspired to attack her life. She had reached the point of toxicity, and the professor had swept all the bottles off her night table. His firmness had impressed her enough to keep her clear of pills for some days, but to continue she would have had to face down a lethal combination of ideas that chained her to the conviction that she was meant to be a sacrifice and a victim. In a quiet moment the professor seemed to have almost convinced her that it was she who was poisoning herself, but his authority could not overcome her lifelong self-image. Besides, there were always new doctors willing to help her into oblivion.

One day Bob Whitehead came to the Chelsea with exciting news. He had been appointed head of a new repertory theatre to be installed in the Lincoln Center complex then under construction above Columbus Circle, due for completion about two years hence. Bob had co-produced *A View from the Bridge* and *A Memory of Two Mondays* with Kermit Bloomgarden and was the most artistically ambitious producer on Broadway. As successful as he had been, his real desire was for a permanent theatre, like the National or the Old Vic in England, where American artists—writers, actors, designers, directors—could develop in a coherent way, spared the instant disbanding of commercial productions at the end of a run. To do his Lincoln Center job he would give up producing on Broadway, a financial sacrifice that indicated his dedication to the project.

Would I write a play to open this theatre? The question he wanted to put to me right off was whether I thought I could work with Kazan, who would be the artistic director, along with Harold Clurman, dramaturge and general adviser, and Bobby Lewis, who would head an acting school as well as direct some of the productions. Obviously, it was the old Group Theatre resurgent two decades after its demise, but this time with public financing and a permanent home. It was a thrilling prospect.

As for Kazan, I would have to define my feelings. I did not know if we could, in fact, work together; for my part, I had not changed my opinion that his testimony before the Un-American Activities Committee had disserved both himself and the cause of freedom, and I had no doubt that he still thought himself justified. In the intervening years, of course, the whole Communist issue had gone cold, and a new generation hardly understood what it had all been about. What it came down to now was whether his political stance and even moral defection, if one liked, should permanently bar him from working in the theatre, especially this particular kind of publicly supported theatre. As for morals, perhaps it was just as well not to cast too wide a net; for one thing, how many who knew by now that they had been supporting a paranoid and murderous Stalinist regime had really confronted their abetting of it? If I still felt a certain distaste for Kazan's renouncing his past under duress, I was not at all sure that he should be excluded from a position for which he was superbly qualified by his talent and his invaluable experience with the Group. Nor could I be sure that I was not merely rationalizing my belief that he was the best director for this complex play; but to reject him, I thought, was to reject the hope for a national theatre in this time.

My more immediate concern at that moment was whether I could finish the play in time to open Lincoln Center. I was still swimming through a couple of hundred pages of dialogue with no sight of the farther shore. And as a practical matter, I could hardly afford to give a play to a repertory theatre that would only perform it a limited number of times a month; since it always took me years to come up with a play and I was barely making it financially, I was in no position to be generous. But after some weeks and a lot of talking with an increasingly enthusiastic Clurman and Whitehead, and several conferences with Kazan about his production concepts, I finally agreed to go ahead. In short, with all the weightier factors pointing me toward the exit, I followed my enthusiasm and opted for joining up.

I had no position in the new theatre except that of a contributing playwright, and no interest in the interior politics of its administration. I wish I could say that too much has been written about its controversial history to call for more now, but the truth is that with all the tonnage of theatrical journalism in New York and elsewhere, a just and accurate account of what happened to the Lincoln Center Repertory Theatre under Whitehead and Kazan remains to be written.

It is beyond the scope of this book to tell that important story in its entirety; I can only touch on what I knew at the time and learned at second hand afterwards, which is by no means the whole of it. It is important for more than the personalities concerned that the facts be known, if only because immense amounts of public money were involved, not to speak of the hopes of artists and audiences who deserved better than they received. Finally, if this country is ever to create a national theatre worthy of the name, we shall have to learn the buried lessons of this lost attempt to build such an institution.

In a nutshell, the board of Lincoln Center was made up largely of bankers who had raised the money for the buildings. They accepted that opera and ballet and a symphony orchestra would show operating deficits each year, but—for reasons peculiar to the

American culture of which they were part—they assumed that
theatre should return a profit or at least not lose money. Over
months of discussions and statistical demonstrations, Whitehead, a
man of enormous patience and sympathy with such types, explained the paradox that the more successful such a theatre was the
more money it had to lose. This made absolutely no business sense
to the board; after all, Whitehead had made money on Broadway
producing Robinson Jeffers, Carson McCullers, Friedrich Dürrenmatt, and Robert Bolt, so why not here? But on Broadway a producer was not paying to store the sets of two, three, or more
productions waiting to take their places in a repertory company's
always changing program; or supporting a whole troupe of actors,
many of whom were idle for days, weeks, or even longer; or making and storing costumes for more than one production, and so on.
That the highly successful Old Vic and lately the National Theatre
of Great Britain were always running enormous deficits failed to
take root in these bankers' psyches. The chairman, George Woods,
then president of the World Bank, was especially impervious to so
seemingly uncomplicated a situation.

But at the time I knew nothing of all this. As I was coming to the
end of the writing of *After the Fall,* the horrifying news came that
Marilyn had died, apparently of an overdose of sleeping pills.

There are people so vivid in life that they seem not to disappear
when they die, and for many weeks I found myself having to come
about and force myself to encounter the fact that Marilyn had
ended. I realized that I still, even then, expected to meet her once
more, somewhere, sometime, and maybe talk sensibly about all the
foolishness we had been through—in which case I would probably
have fallen in love with her again. And the iron logic of her death
did not help much: I could still see her coming across the lawn, or
touching something, or laughing, at the same time that I confronted the end of her as one might stand watching the sinking sun.
When a reporter called asking if I would be attending her funeral
in California, the very idea of a burial was outlandish, and stunned
as I was, I answered without thinking, "She won't be there." I could
hear his astonishment, but I could only hang up, it was beyond
explaining. In any case, to join what I knew would be a circus of
cameras and shouts and luridness was beyond my strength. I had
done all that was in me to do, and to me it was meaningless to stand
for photographs at a stone. For some reason what I had said to her
long ago kept returning—"You're the saddest girl I've ever
known." And she had replied, "Nobody ever said that to me!" and

laughed with an inward-looking surprise that reminded me of my own as a boy when the salesman with the artificial leg suddenly remarked, "You've gotten serious," and made me see myself differently. It was so strange that she had never really had the right to her own sadness.

And now, naturally, the press gathered to chorus its laments, the same press that had sneered at her for so long, whose praise and condescension, if not contempt for her as an actress, she had taken too seriously. To have survived, she would have had to be either more cynical or even further from reality than she was. Instead, she was a poet on a street corner trying to recite to a crowd pulling at her clothes.

Coming out of the forties and fifties, she was proof that sexuality and seriousness could not coexist in America's psyche, were hostile, mutually rejecting opposites, in fact. At the end she had had to give way and go back to swimming naked in a pool in order to make a picture.

Years later, her life would be taken up by a writer whose stock-in-trade was the joining of sexuality and the serious, but avowedly desperate for money to pay his several alimonies, he could only describe what was fundamentally a merry young whore given to surprising bursts of classy wit. If one looked closely, she was himself in drag, acting out his own Hollywood fantasies of fame and sex unlimited and power. Pain of any kind would have unnecessarily soiled the picture even though he was describing a woman on the knife edge of self-destruction all her adult life.

I had to wonder if her fate at the great author's hands would have been better had she agreed back in the fifties to my suggestion that we invite him for dinner some evening. I had heard that Norman Mailer had bought a house in Roxbury, and from what everyone knew of him, he would have rushed to meet her. Though I remembered our short conversation long ago in front of the Brooklyn Heights brownstone where we both lived—when, astonishingly, he had announced that he could write a play like *All My Sons* anytime and presumably would when he got around to it—I dismissed it as a youthful overflowing of envy, which every writer feels and does well to outgrow. Now, some ten years later, he might make good company for an evening. I thought then that we were too much alone and more visitors might ease her distrust of strangers. But she rejected the idea of inviting Mailer, saying she "knew those types" and wanted to put them behind her in this new life she hoped to create among civilians who were not obsessed with images, their own or other people's. Reading his volume, with its grinning vengefulness toward both of us—skillfully hidden under a magisterial aplomb—I wondered if it would have existed at all had we fed him one evening and allowed him time to confront her humanity, not merely her publicity.

And so as the subject of his novel-that-was-not-fiction and at the same time his non-novel-that-was-not-actually-true, she would emerge precisely as she hated to appear, as a kind of joke taking herself seriously; but it was a picture that allowed the reader to condescend to be charmed. The basics of her career were supplied by that disinterested witness Milton Greene, who had been prized out of her financial life by main legal force, while her beloved supporters—her analyst, Dr. Ralph Greenson, who had fought for her life to the end, and her nurse-companion, an elderly woman—were caricatured as almost frivolous about her welfare. Indeed, questioned on television by Mike Wallace as to why he had alleged the nurse's possibly lethal carelessness on the fatal evening, badly damaging her professional reputation and her honor, when it would have been easy to check her movements in the final hours, the author replied that he could not get in touch with the lady; and when a surprised Wallace said that he had had no trouble finding her through the Los Angeles telephone book, the author resumed his literary excursus on the ancient license of the fictionalist, finding it convenient at this particular point that his "Marilyn" not be quite a real person surrounded by real persons, although on other occasions he would of course desire her to be taken as such, as when a prospective reader looking for the real goods picked up his book in a store and considered buying it with real money. Indeed, asked by Wallace why he had written the book at all, he candidly replied that he needed the money.

She had been right in the first place, and I had been far too trusting, often witlessly and irritatingly so; I wasn't used to the ocean of great fame seething with sharks—but I unwillingly watched them attack again and again, to the point where the whole fame game became an institutionalized paranoia that stunned the soul and made one dead. But to live day after day in the fog of unrelieved suspicion had seemed pointless and, as it turned out, was finally impossible for her as well.

Coming so soon after Marilyn's death, *After the Fall* had to fail. With a few stubborn exceptions the reviews were about a scandal, not a play, with barely a mention of any theme, dramatic intention, or style, as though it were simply an attack on a dead woman. Altogether ignored was the fact that the counterattack on me was supplied by practically paraphrasing Quentin's acknowledgment of his own failings—by the play itself; it was as though the critics had witnessed an actual domestic quarrel and been challenged to come to Maggie's rescue.

I could not help thinking that this gleeful and all but total blindness to the play's theme and its implications was one more proof that they could not be faced, that it was impossible to seriously consider innocence lethal. It was this kind of denial that had brought about the play's tragic ending. I was soon widely hated, but the play had spoken its truth as, after all, it was obliged to do, and if the truth was clothed in pain, perhaps it was important for the audience to confront it uncomfortably and even in the anger of denial. In time, and with much difficulty, I saw the justification for the hostility toward me, for I had indeed brought very bad news.

But *After the Fall*'s reception was not as uniformly negative as I imagined in the heat of the moment. When I looked back, it was obvious that aside from *Death of a Salesman* every one of my plays had originally met with a majority of bad, indifferent, or sneering notices. Except for Brooks Atkinson at the beginning, and later Harold Clurman, I exist as a playwright without a major reviewer in my corner. It has been primarily actors and directors who have kept my work before the public, which indeed has reciprocated with its support. Only abroad and in some American places outside New York has criticism embraced my plays. I have often rescued a sense of reality by recalling Chekhov's remark: "If I had listened to the critics I'd have died drunk in the gutter."

An old friend looked down at year-old Rebecca in her stroller. We were the same age, nearing our fifties, had married in our twenties after leaving college, and had had our children at about the same time. Now here I was, the owner of a stroller again. After smiling at her, he turned to me and said, "Didn't we do this already?"

Rediscovering fatherhood a second time, I was finding that like youth, it is wasted on the young. A child underfoot in middle age was a steady remonstrance against the prevailing pessimistic view of life in the warring sixties, for there is some absurdity in an older man as a new father, an unnaturalness through which he sees a small child's movingly imperious demand that life return life to her clear, primordial gaze. I found in myself a certain protectiveness toward whatever around me seemed hopeful, and a suspicion of all easy negativism. I was not sure what the source of this feeling was, but I dreaded that life was very easy to kill. It may simply have come from knowing that I was growing old.

But I also knew times had changed when neither Bob nor Jane showed any interest in going to college, which seemed irrelevant to them. I recalled that in my last couple of years as a student I had been impatient to go out into the far more interesting world and had stayed in school mainly because there was no choice, what with jobs so hard to find. Though they seemed to be in danger of cutting themselves off from the culture of the past by this total rejection of academic work, I lacked conviction in opposing them, unsure that I understood their vision of the real. Even before the Vietnam War had taken its toll on their generation's belief in America, they seemed to have lost something of the success drive that I had more than once lamented as a distorting pressure on my generation. And now I was worrying that they had turned their backs on it! But one dared not say this openly anymore. I relied on my faith in them. What would be would be.

Marcello Mastroianni came down to the Chelsea one afternoon to talk about his doing Quentin in Franco Zeffirelli's production of *After the Fall*. A more unprepossessing human never lived; he really seemed to see himself with the same ironic humor he applied to everyone else, as though life in general was a nearly total misunderstanding. His first part had been as Biff in *Salesman* years before. I thought he would be wonderful as Quentin because he seemed to be trying to puzzle out what was happening to him while still regarding himself from a certain distance. I was curious about his attitude toward the play, which I suspected might seem rather strange to him, given what I had heard of his experiences with women.

"How do you connect with Quentin? Can you sympathize with what he does in the play?"

"Of course. The same thing happens to all of us one time or another."

"So you understand him?"

"Oh, yes."

I sensed some reservation and pressed him to let me have it.

"But so much trouble over a woman?"

"Why? What would you do?"

"I would"—he flipped out his hand to indicate a long distance—"take a walk."

In fact, the American notion of having to relate one's own personality so closely to a part was a strange idea. He was on his way home to talk to Fellini, who wanted him for a film, which he would of course accept sight unseen (and which would prevent him from playing Quentin for Zeffirelli). It turned out to be *8½*. He had no idea of the story and was content to be handed the script on the first day of shooting. "An actor is first of all an animal; if he hasn't that, he has nothing. I am happy to be so." It was somehow a relief just talking to him, as though a weight had been lifted from the whole idea of performing.

The attacks on me for *After the Fall* were not easy to accept, but I found some small solace in recalling the incomprehensible hostility that the very announcement of a Lincoln Center repertory company aroused even before a program had been chosen. I confess I am not sure I understand this yet. I thought it exciting that successful and talented people like Whitehead, Kazan, Bobby Lewis, and Harold Clurman should be lending their prestige and idealism to an untried enterprise. After all, most of their generation had left the theatre for TV and films, and they were among a very few who might hand on an American theatrical tradition. But the press, especially certain academic commentators in the more literate journals, was perplexingly and bitterly hostile, quite as though something underhanded were being plotted, while the professional theatrical writers stood aside, at best neutral if not mildly cynical toward this attempt at a new noncommercial theatre. So damaging was this negativism-in-advance that Clurman had received few scripts for consideration as future productions. I went to several schools to encourage young writers to send in their plays, but the propaganda was as successful as it was incredible.

With Jason Robards as Quentin and Barbara Loden as Maggie, Kazan created a production of great control and truthful feeling, surely one of the best things he had ever done. I had not made it easy for him; with stream-of-consciousness evocations of characters, abrupt disappearances, and transformations of time and place, the play often verged on montage. He never tried to simplify his job by thinning out the material, and he faithfully sought to bring out the play's intentions. The audiences that packed the temporary theatre on West Fourth Street seemed deeply moved, despite all the surrounding antagonism. My one great regret was my failure to stop Loden from wearing a blonde wig, which seemed to invite identification with Marilyn. Later I had to ask myself if this blindness was my own form of denial, but as usual I was buried in the play's structure, and the characters' resemblance to real models was far from the center of my attention.

Whatever its failings, Lincoln Center was conceived as a theatre that would reach out to the general public. By confronting the unconverted rather than a congenial cultural clique, playwrights and actors would be called on to stretch and deepen their art. But the "revolutionary" critics and avant-garde establishment scorned the whole project as a creation of bankers and old theatre "pros." Actually the real battle inside this theatre was between a banker, George Woods, and the old pros Whitehead-Kazan-Clurman, but it went entirely unreported, a matter of no interest to journalists and academics out to establish their own chic credentials; nor, it must be said, would Whitehead break ranks and go to the press with the facts, hoping instead to win a new theatre as a gentleman among gentlemen.

But he got his first real whiff of Chairman Woods's angry opposition to the very theatre he was supposed to be leading when, rather than wait a year or two for the Vivian Beaumont Theatre to be finished, Whitehead asked the chancellor of New York University to lend, for a dollar a year, the land on which to construct a temporary theatre on West Fourth Street. Completed almost overnight by builders who specialized in steel industrial warehouses, this inexpensive structure had incredibly good acoustics and a bare concrete ambience that quite accidentally expressed the actual poverty of this maligned and ultimately doomed attempt at a public New York theatre. The metal roof would leak on opening night, and on that afternoon of the *After the Fall* premiere, Whitehead and I went out on Sixth Avenue to buy a pair of screwdrivers and screwed about six rows of seats into their brackets.

The fury against the whole attempt destroyed it finally, especially when the Lincoln Center board had no firm principles with which to resist criticism that was mindless enough to include the allegedly rotten choice of actors for the company. That the roster featured Jason Robards, Jr., the still unknown Faye Dunaway,

David Wayne, Joseph Wiseman, Salome Jens, and the young Hal
Holbrook did nothing to mute the abuse. Mistakes were certainly
made, some of them bad ones in the selection of plays that were
not right for the company, but probably the worst miscalculation
was to give the appearance of making grandiose plans when in fact
it was all an experiment that should have proceeded as quietly and
privately as possible until the company had found its voice and
some degree of self-assurance.

Despite everything, *After the Fall* continued to play to very
high attendance. A beleaguered Whitehead and Clurman were
soon knocking on my door for another play, and with my weakness
for solidarity, as well as the tempting availability of what I knew
was a superior acting company, I began *Incident at Vichy* and
completed it in a short time. This, like the inception of *A View from
the Bridge* in Marty Ritt's invitation, seemed to indicate that had
I been fortunate enough to live in a period when a high-level
repertory or art theatre existed, I would certainly have written
more plays than I had. The very prospect of struggling through the
difficulties of casting and production in the commercial theatre,
and the often frivolous junking of years of work after a single
thoughtless review, have cast a pall of futility over the enterprise
of writing plays, at least for me. And I am sure I am not alone in
this.

The root of *Vichy* came from my friend and former psychoana-
lyst Dr. Rudolph Loewenstein, who had hidden out in Vichy
France during the war, before the Nazis openly occupied the country. But all I recalled was the bare outline of his story: a Jewish
analyst picked up with false papers and saved by a man he had
never seen before. This unknown man, a gentile, had substituted
himself in a line of suspects waiting to have their papers and pe-
nises inspected in a hunt for Jews posing as Frenchmen.

There was a second root in an old friend of Inge's, Prince Josef
von Schwarzenberg, senior surviving member of a very ancient
Austrian noble line, who had "declined" to cooperate with the
Nazis and had suffered for it during the war. He was a source for
Von Berg, the prince in my play who steps in to take the place of
a condemned analyst. It was not altogether a romantic idealization,
for in some absurd yet logical way Josef von Schwarzenberg embodied an elemental resistance to the fascist spirit, which is fundamentally one of enforced vulgarity in all its forms. An elegantly tall
bachelor allowed by the postwar Austrian government one wing of
the Schwarzenberg palais in which to live out his life, Josef could

look out his window and muse upon the massive five-story marble Soviet monument to the Russian soldier while hopelessly scolding his last remaining servant, who padded through the halls wearing white gloves as he served inedible spaghetti. Between subsidizing string quartets and scrounging gas money for his Peugeot, he managed to create an image of cultural integrity that seemed a moving proof against subornation by every kind of power. Schwarzenberg's breath came faster and his hand shook excitedly as he listened to a Mozart sonata on his old record player or read a verse from some new poet's work. He would rush off to mass with his papal decoration, the Golden Fleece, hanging from his neck, and then to Inge's mother's for a bowl of rice as he believed only she could cook it, then to a séance of mystical contemplation with Arnold Keyserling, about whose ideas he had immense curiosity, but as a Catholic, no belief. Having denied the Nazi movement the glory of his name, he never considered any other course; there had simply been no choice, and he could not imagine deserving the remotest sort of credit for his dangerous refusal. That he had spent much of the war doing menial work in France he hardly regarded as a punishment. What I found fascinating in Josef was a mixture of worldly discernment and a naive, almost thoughtlessly pure moral code that perhaps only one so protected in youth could possess, and that measured the corruption the world took for granted.

Inge and I had decided on one of our visits to her family in Austria to go to Radomizl, the Polish village near Kraków from which all my grandparents had emigrated. Inge's father eagerly got out his military maps and under his magnifying glass found a Radomizl in the Ukraine. Soon after, the Polish ambassador to Austria, a theatre buff, invited us for lunch to rave about what he thought a fabulous production of *After the Fall* in Warsaw, and happily invited us to visit a Radomizl in western Poland, nowhere near Kraków. Now Josef showed up to announce that in a Bohemian province once owned by the Schwarzenbergs was a Radomizl that he remembered well from his youth, and that he insisted was the town of my origins. "But I'm sure it wasn't in Bohemia," I said. "But you can't be sure," he laughed, "so you have to choose your Radomizls, and you must choose mine! For all you know, we are related!"

We never made the trip to what now seemed an arbitrary hometown, a nowhere. And besides, if by chance I did hit on the right Radomizl, my relatives were not likely to have survived the Nazi conquest. All the Radomizls, and all the towns like them, were now *judenfrei.*

Harold Clurman's production of *Incident at Vichy* in Boris Aronson's almost mythic police station was quite beautiful, but such was the ongoing contempt for the Repertory Theatre of Lincoln Center for the Performing Arts that it was given an unexcited if respectful welcome. Within a year the London West End production by Peter Wood, with Alec Guinness playing the prince, fared far better. I found it necessary, incidentally, to explain to the British actors—hardly twenty years after a war that had come closer to destroying England than any calamity in a thousand years—what the Nazi SS had been and what it had done. The past has simply ceased in our time, maybe because too much is changing too fast.

The play would have a curious history. The first of my works to be banned in the Soviet Union, during one of its anti-Jewish convulsions in the late sixties, it was optioned in France by three different producers, each of whom decided to relinquish the rights for fear of resentment at the implication of French collaboration with Nazi anti-Semitism. Finally, in the early eighties, Pierre Cardin produced it in Paris, but the defensive bitterness of the reviews was unmistakable. Norman Lloyd's production on national public television, directed by Stacy Keach, is probably the most expressive one I have seen.

It was not until 1987 and the Gorbachev liberalization that *Vichy* finally made it onto a Soviet stage, produced by the same Galina Volchek whose 1968 Maly Theatre production had been shut down the night before the premiere, after six vastly successful previews. This time, a *Moscow News* reporter phoned me and in an excitedly happy voice asked such questions as "What do you think is the significance of this play being produced in Moscow after twenty years? What is the message of the play?" And finally, "We wish to assure you that your answers will be published unedited verbatim thank you very much." And indeed they were.

I often learned something about the state of the world's mind through the various receptions of my plays, and new perspectives about our theatre have come from the past thirty years of travel. In 1965, Laurence Olivier listened incredulously as I reported the Lincoln Center Repertory debacle. "But you'd hardly begun! We were seven years in Chichester building our company before we ever opened in London. And got roasted fully twenty-five percent of the time. And no one thought to suggest the whole thing ought to be scrapped. It's incomprehensible!" But he reckoned without American instant culture.

Olivier was doing *The Crucible* in London, and for two months now we had been in correspondence about a dialect for the characters. His production, with Colin Blakely as Proctor and Joyce Redman as Elizabeth, had a nobility that was at once moving and austere. The actor playing the octogenarian Giles Corey made me wonder how such an aged man could still possess such energy, but he turned out to be in his twenties. What I would not forget was a long silence at the beginning of the second act when Proctor enters his farmhouse and washes up and sits down for dinner. It must have lasted many minutes as Elizabeth served him and then went about her chores, the absence of speech itself the proof of their hurt pride, their anger with one another, and somehow their mutual regard, too; and at the same time it drew the mounting fear of what was happening in Salem Town into this house. From such exactness, what passion!

On the plane going over I read in the *Times* that Vincent Riccio, a member of the New York State Legislature, had been indicted for keeping on his payroll a woman who had never done any work. A prison sentence was possible.

It was now more than ten years since Riccio and I had spent nights together in the Bay Ridge streets. I had read about his election to the legislature a while ago, and I thought there was something anomalous in the only Republican social worker I had ever heard of becoming a regular politician. He had always angrily condemned personal ambition in the social work hierarchy; was it because he had some of it himself?

Now I thought of him sitting on a car fender in the purple light of a Bay Ridge evening, a gutsy former navy boxer with slick black hair and overlarge dentures replacing his own knocked-out teeth; in between teaching the hoodlums how to block punches, he had tried with a finesse I envied at the time to lead them out of their forest ways to live among peaceful people. His accurate analyses of the social workers' moral hypocrisies passed before me as I stared at the newspaper. Poor brain! How helplessly it dissolves when willing eyes meet and the nose warms to those old jungle scents.

Soon there was a short paragraph reporting him convicted and jailed. Then another, some months later, that he had died, cause unstated. I wondered if it was all the confusion brought on by too many options. Who would have thought that back in the fifties, working the Bay Ridge streets to head off another mindless gang war, he was actually living his best of times?

* * *

You know you have reached a certain age when irony dominates whatever you see. When I spoke and wrote against the Vietnam War, it felt like a rerun of the Spanish Civil War with new actors, a movie of defeat that I'd seen before. In the militancy of the sixties, the black awakening, the thrilling alienation of the times, I saw the seeds of a coming new disillusionment. Once again we were looking almost completely outside ourselves for salvation from ourselves; in the absolutely right and necessary rebellion was only a speck of room for worrying about personal ethics and our own egoism. At fifty and counting, I tried to block out the echoes of past crusades, but it was impossible.

The Price was in part an exorcism of this paralyzing vision of repetition. Two brothers, one a policeman, the other a successful surgeon, meet again after an angry breakup many years before; the time has come to divide the family's possessions after the father's death. Grown men now, they think they have achieved the indifference to the betrayals of the past that maturity confers. But it all comes back; the old angry symbols evoke the old emotions of injustice, and they part unreconciled. Neither can accept that the world needs both of them—the dutiful man of order and the ambitious, selfish creator who invents new cures.

Despite my wishes I could not tamper with something the play and life seemed to be telling me: that we were doomed to perpetuate our illusions because truth was too costly to face. At the end of the play Gregory Solomon, the eighty-nine-year-old used furniture dealer, is left with the family's possessions, which he has purchased from the brothers; he finds an old laughing record and, listening to it, starts laughing uncontrollably, nostalgically, brutally, having come closest to acceptance rather than denial of the deforming betrayals of time.

There are scenes in *The Price* that I especially love for the memories they bring back of David Burns, an inspired lunatic with an oblique sense of the ridiculous that threw all life into a long perspective. It was a troubled production, and rehearsal threatened to disintegrate one afternoon when Arthur Kennedy, Kate Reid, and Pat Hingle—three-quarters of the cast—got into an angry argument with the director, Ulu Grosbard. Suddenly Davey appeared onstage above the others, who were in the auditorium; he was wearing his hat, jacket, and tie, but his trousers were draped over one arm, and he was looking with alarm at his wristwatch.

"My God, I forgot," he called out to no one in particular, "I've got a baby in an incubator in Philadelphia!" and rushed off the stage like the White Rabbit. The argument ended then and there, swamped by this marvelously sculpted ridicule of man's foolishness.

In Philadelphia, I had to take over the direction myself, the growing differences having become irreconcilable. In New York, finally, with opening night forty-eight hours away, I was sitting in the front row rehearsing Pat Hingle and Kate Reid. It was about seven fifteen, and the preview audience could be heard out in the lobby. Arthur Kennedy came up behind me, leaned over, and whispered, "Davey's been taken to the hospital with a kinked colon. He's going to be operated on tonight."

I asked the stage manager if the understudy knew the part, and was assured he was ready and getting into costume. I nodded to Kennedy, stared up at Hingle and Reid working on the stage, and fell deeply and satisfyingly asleep. When I awoke, refreshed, the audience was already filing into the theatre and the curtain was coming down and Hingle and Reid had gone to their dressing rooms. The understudy, Harold Gary, was amazingly good; he had understudied Davey for twenty years, and this was his first chance to take over a role.

Even close to death, Davey couldn't resist comedy. Whitehead and I had rushed to the hospital and found him on a stretcher awaiting emergency surgery, his skin already turning a deathly white. Seeing us, he whispered, "Sorry, fellas," and we reassured him that the part was his whenever he was able to return.

An attendant came over to him and said, "We're taking you upstairs now."

Davey drew his brows together as though he had to consider this proposal, waited a few inconclusive seconds, and finally nodded to the attendant. "I'll go."

He recovered and in a little while was starring in *70 Girls 70* with Mildred Natwick. In a gale of laughter from the audience at one of his finely honed deliveries, he collapsed and died, applause ringing in his ears. No great note was taken of his passing, but along with some others I have often thought that in another time and place he would have had the attention of writers and intellectuals who treasured the sublime.

The Price ran a season and has played everywhere in Europe with some fine actors, especially in Solomon's role. The most recent incarnation, with Raf Vallone, was a long Italian tour from Sardinia to Milan. A play is bread cast on the waters, this one especially; Lev Kopelev, the Russian dissident author, told me that during the Moscow production, Solzhenitsyn came repeatedly to watch and give his notes to the actors, evidently fascinated with some element in the play, precisely which I never learned.

I thought the woman on the phone was kidding: "We've nominated you as delegate to the convention . . ."

Some days later, the Roxbury Democrats, fifty or so people of whom only a handful were known to me, sat listening expressionlessly in the tiny wooden town hall as I explained that since I had no parliamentary experience they would be much better served by electing my neighbor, a dairy farmer named Birchall, a party regular with whom I was in a dead tie. I did not think by this time that my participation was really going to slow the war, but they had another ballot, and I won by one vote. It pleased me to think I had bred such confidence in the town, for I rarely left my land to mix into its affairs.

Chicago, 1968, buried the Democratic Party and the nearly forty years of what was euphemistically called its philosophy. The images of that week in Chicago would remain forever.

At two o'clock in the morning in front of the Hilton Hotel, I was standing around with Douglas Kiker of NBC. We were chatting aimlessly, like two Americans in a foreign country. Helmeted troops stood with rifles in a long line facing Grant Park across Michigan Avenue, where in the darkness one could make out a camping mass of the young, quiet now after the day's beatings and arrests.

A jeep moved slowly along the avenue. A wooden frame mounted on its front bumper supported a mass of barbed wire with which to ram a crowd. Kiker and I stopped talking at the sight of the slow pace of that jeep, which could turn at any moment and chase us down the street and tear into our flesh. Kiker said, "I was in Berlin during the uprising in 1953 and in Budapest when the Russians came in, but this is the most frightening violence I have ever witnessed."

I had never seen such whitened faces as on those Chicago police. The blood seemed to have drained into their clublike fists. Earlier, a hundred or more delegates had marched past the line of battle-ready troops, each of us carrying a lighted candle and wearing a convention badge, but the rigid, blanched faces of the police, staring at us relentlessly as we passed, warned us that we were not immune to their fury.

The Connecticut delegation had been seated beside the Illinois people on the convention floor. In the center of some hundred of his men, just below the podium, sat Mayor Richard Daley of Chicago. The Illinois delegates looked like a football squad, the men bursting out of their shirts, and their faces too were white with anger, and their heavy feet stretched the leather of their pointy dress shoes.

Senator Abraham Ribicoff, former governor of Connecticut, came to the podium and began to speak. I had in my hand a sheet of paper slipped to me by an usher, on it a wild scrawl: "They are killing us in the streets, they are murdering us out here . . ." I had been going from leader to leader with it, trying to get permission to use a microphone, and now at last Ribicoff, with all his importance to the party, was actually looking down at Daley over the rim of the podium and calling what was happening in the streets outside the hall "Gestapo tactics." I looked at Daley, seated in his overcoat no more than twenty feet from me, flanked by his immense team, who kept scanning the periphery of their massed delegation with Doberman stares, as though for a cue to attack whoever might move in their direction. It was hard to meet the ferocity of their gazes. Then I saw Daley, glaring up at the podium, draw his index finger broadly across his throat, and I clearly heard him yell at Ribicoff, "Jew! Jew!" Daley seemed literally to writhe, but Ribicoff went on speaking anyway. My ears went deaf then, I suppose because everything I had feared in my life was dropping on my head like a load of coal.

Despite rumors that he would land on the roof of the convention hall in a helicopter, the president of the United States had not dared to attend his party's convention.

In a second of silence in that immense gathering of people a strangely soft sound drew my attention to the visitors' gallery high above it all. There stood Allen Ginsberg, unmistakable with his thick wiry beard and bald head and eyeglasses, his arms outstretched in a gesture of blessing, his baritone issuing a long humming *ommmm* to invoke the voice of God and peace. But it didn't help much as the bricks of the edifice tumbled all around us.

I had never had much hope that the convention would really allow the peace people to separate the party from support of the Vietnam War, but when it became obvious that Humphrey would be the presidential nominee, and without really promising to end the war, I thought the time had come to unify the Robert Kennedy and Eugene McCarthy factions; the resulting strength of the challenge to Humphrey might at least create some leverage on future policy. I drafted a statement freeing the many delegates pledged to Gene McCarthy to vote as they wished. This meant that some might go over to the camp of the late Robert Kennedy, who had scrambled aboard the antiwar movement and declared his candidacy only after McCarthy had proved it had a future; it was widely hoped that Teddy would volunteer to take his brother's place now. McCarthy said with some indignation that he would release his people to vote for George McGovern but never Ted Kennedy.

I felt totally defeated by the absence of any spoken word commemorating the long fight to end the war, and by the abdication of the men who had led the struggle within the Democratic Party and were now allowing it to vanish like this, unmourned and unsung. What a moment for a great leader to rise and nail the flag of right reason to the pole! But no one did, and it all went away into nothingness.

But in the sixties everything one thought one knew was up for grabs. Robert Lowell, his wife, Elizabeth Hardwick, and their eleven-year-old daughter came by for a few hours with our neighbors, Henry and Olga Carlisle, longtime friends of theirs. It was a gray November day, all the leaves were down. Still in the car, he feigned not to see me emerging from the house and kept fussing with his daughter as she got out. Finally we shook hands. His thinning hair was wetted down crossways on his scalp. He was quick to say that my speech at the Bled, Yugoslavia, International PEN Congress had moved him—I had praised his refusal, in protest against the war, of President Johnson's invitation to a festival of the arts at the White House.

He asked about the varieties of trees I was raising, and I got on the tractor to show him how I pruned the roots with a device I had fashioned and attached to the cultivator bar. He leaned far down to his daughter and gently said, "You can't imagine me pruning tree roots, can you?" The girl barely shook her head, her expression uncomfortable.

We walked down toward the pond side by side, he turning when I turned and halting when I did. He hardly paused in his talking.

"I like Kazan, he has enormous charisma, but I wouldn't let him put on my Greek trilogy; *The Changeling* is a masterpiece, and he ruined it for years to come."

"I'm not sure it's a masterpiece."

"It is. Eliot said so."

I would have liked to argue T. S. Eliot's theatrical credentials, but Lowell was forging ahead and would not have listened, could not. Everything Chinese was astonishing, even perfect. He had considered attending the White House function, falling to his knees at the appropriate moment, and praying for America's mercy upon Vietnam. Roosevelt was a fraud and a liar; Kennedy read a lot.

"Roosevelt," I said, "regretted not having helped Spain, you know."

"He did?" This was the first thing that stopped him, and he looked eager and happy to hear it. "Why do you say that?"

"It's in Harold Ickes's diary. He told Ickes it was one of the greatest mistakes of his life not to have supported the Loyalists against Franco."

Lowell brightened. He loved gossip, concealed facts, and I think he rather liked the idea of Roosevelt feeling a stab of remorse. Then he was off again, quite calmly referring to "my manic phase at the time"—presumably of the White House affair. He must be brave, I thought, to be able to endure the wreckage of his attention like this. It was as though uninterrupted talking kept reality both together and at bay.

It was painful to think what would have happened had his courageous pacifist view prevailed and kept us from entering the war against Hitler, during which he had gone to prison as a conscientious objector. As I sat on the grass with him looking at the pond, trying to follow his rush of barely connected unequivocal ideas, he seemed to symbolize our time, its immensities, its free-floating streams of aspiration and its murdered rationality. It suddenly occurred to me that we resembled one another—we were about the same age and about the same height, wore the same tortoiseshell glasses, and were balding in the same way—but I had no demon in me that was so careless about surviving. His views, however they functioned in his work, were so absolute as to be pretty useless in reality, while I could not long commit myself to anything I did not consider somehow useful in living one's life. He flew high toward his visions, I felt bound to persuade an audience equipped with nothing but common sense at best. Despite everything, I still thought writing had to try to save America, and that meant grabbing people and shaking them by the back of the neck.

* * *

The undeclared war began to seem, as in Orwell's *1984,* a permanent television show, but secretly it throttled, choked, numbed. And it changed the dramatic problem oddly: in former time you had to bring the unconscious to the surface by the end of the third act, but we were already *in* the third act. I had seriously begun to question whether a play that gradually unveiled a submerged theme could ever be written again. If not, we were really moving into a new kind of culture. The fact was, we were too conscious, too aware that we were lying to ourselves in the matter of this war, knew we were bartering away reality itself rather than face our national self-deception. What was left to reveal, except the lack of courage to stop the lies?

I kept being reminded of my former friend Sid Franks, the policeman: "I can't read fiction because I keep asking myself how the author can know what the characters are going to do. Anybody can do anything, and I'm talking about *anybody* and *anything.* And as far as plays—why is it that whenever it gets really interesting they pull the curtain down?" He had been ahead of his time; "serious" plays were all but nonexistent now, and the ruling style was one of ironic surprise—anybody was indeed shown to be capable of anything, the mere suggestion of improbability being in itself an invitation to portray just that and nothing more. It was the cop's chuckling aesthetic, common in every precinct station in the world.

I dallied with a comic Oedipus: a contemporary man discovers that his wife is his mother, but instead of tearing out his eyes he sits down and complains, "Jesus, what a situation. We'd better ask the doctor if it's going to affect the children." Where the sublime has been stripped from the violated order of things, there can be nothing but anecdotal plays, for the pressure to transcend and steal a glimpse of God is no more.

I was really surprised, on seeing *Hair,* to find that it was a protest against the Vietnam War, nothing in the reviews and publicity having prepared me for this. Of course, the war was what shaved off the guru's flowing hair and symbolized anti-life, but it was so submerged in the seeming chaos of the production—people masturbating, copulating, and singing and dancing with avowedly mawkish amateurishness—that war became desublimated and ridiculous and lost its killing power. But every style of art pays a price for being what it is; the audience happily enjoyed the uninhibited mockery of the sacred—the flag and other psychic props of war—all done in delightful high spirits rather than hatred.

I wondered if *Hair*'s appeal did not stop at the belly without rising to the brain; on the other hand, when since the failure of *Lysistrata* to do so had theatrical propaganda really slowed let alone stopped a war?

Some local students phoned one evening asking if I would donate a tree to be planted on the lawn of their high school as a "peace tree." The caller's voice was hushed, nearly conspiratorial. I agreed, provided they came and helped me dig one from my tree farm, and even though I suspected that most people would be sympathetic, if silent, I knew that I would now be open to attack. A day later the caller rang again and said that a peace tree on the lawn of another area school had been sawed down during the night, and the students now feared that planting mine would further arouse the local patriots, who in the press reports would appear to outnumber the cowed majority. I was sorry and slightly relieved at the same time.

It was hard to know where the majority really stood. A friend in nearby Torrington, who was in charge of labor relations for a large metalworking company, appeared at the plant one morning wearing a black armband as part of the nationwide campaign for a pause in our bombing of Vietnam, the so-called Moratorium. Workers on the shop floor solemnly asked him who had died, and he explained. When he returned the next morning, every machine on the floor had an American flag defiantly draped over it. Still, I continued to believe that there must be a way to enlighten such workers, whose sons were the ones doing the fighting.

A boy from down the road who as a child used to come and sit watching in silence while my family and guests talked, swam, or played ball, and whom I later helped to get into the Neighborhood Playhouse acting school, one day poured gasoline over himself in his backyard and set himself afire and died. Of course there was more to it than protest against the war: he had once confided that his father's values were exactly like Willy Loman's. But Biff loves his father enough to fight him and his lethal beliefs. The boy's acting teachers had told me that he had a big talent.

Another boy I had known since his babyhood, the nineteen-year-old son of a local merchant, would appear stoned at my door late at night and offer "to write a poem on any subject" on the spot. He was draft age, not in school, with no excuse for staying out of the war he hated. Within the year he was dead of an overdose. He had become a great salesman, having invented a business retailing local rocks to collectors, and his car trunk was always weighted down with valuable samples he found hidden in the woods of his rosy-cheeked country boyhood.

But everyone, it seemed to me, knew perfectly well that such things were happening. What could a play or fiction add? The country's unconscious really had been overleaped, its guilt canceled as we learned to harden ourselves by a most elaborate routine of denial. It was all so conscious that even the usual accompaniment of every war, the celebration of the veteran, was reversed, and he was expected to slink back into civilian invisibility. It was strange and sinister to me, and inevitably I had to recall the people working the hillside below Mauthausen, who did not look up as we drove past them toward that killing camp.

Still another young man, the son of an old friend, returned from Vietnam, got on his motorcycle, and headed toward a town six hundred miles away to locate and kill a guy from his outfit who had screamed and drawn Vietcong fire on them. But the guy was not home, and my friend's son came back. He began investing on the stock market and soon made a bundle but continued hinting darkly that certain vets, buddies of his, were prepared to "clean up" society.

The surreal danced on. One day I spoke against the war on the New Haven green—where I had the luck to meet William Sloane Coffin, Jr., the Yale chaplain, who would become a close friend—and a few days later to several hundred plebes at West Point. I had been invited by a colonel in the English department, and at first I responded that he must have intended a different Miller, since I was opposed to the war. "We know who you are, and that's why you've been invited," he said. It was impossible to refuse him then.

West Point—how I had ached as a teenager to be admitted there!—was an hour-and-a-half drive from Roxbury. The large lecture hall was packed, and standing along the back wall, a dozen faculty looked on, decorated officers watching me expressionlessly as I talked about the Vietnam War, and particularly about the certainty of our defeat. I figured I might as well be eaten whole as in small pieces.

Our bombing of Cambodia had just begun. Inge, Rebecca, and

I had returned from a trip there only two weeks before; Inge had wanted to photograph Angkor Wat and its fabulously carved temples and sculptures. There was a sublime *rootedness* in the god statues, as though they had grown in place centuries before. And in portaled little kiosks here and there stood the lingams, upright stone phalluses, shiny from women sitting on them to bring on pregnancy—or so I'd theorized. A dozen or so fey young monks in saffron robes and shaven heads wafted from quiet niche to niche begging alms and looking very flesh-bound to my jaded eyes.

But my news to the cadets was unaesthetic. I said that I doubted we had six people in our government who could read and understand Cambodian; that Mr. Nixon's bombing the place would hardly endear us to an agricultural people who, as I had seen, loved to stand around in front of their stilted houses staring at their water buffalo or bathing and fondling their children, their lives bounded by the immemorial flooding and draining of their rice fields. I assumed that the profundity of my ignorance of the Cambodian people must be shared by our leaders, who had decided to bomb the hell out of them because they had made a deal allowing the North Vietnamese to use a corridor down one side of the country to supply guerrillas in the south, something Cambodia's Prince Sihanouk could not have prevented anyway.

For color I told how Rebecca, then nine, had come to us after breakfast one morning to report that the hotel swimming pool was half drained and full of soapsuds and that the hotel was being evacuated; and how the management had denied this, saying they were only cleaning the pool, and I had phoned our embassy in Phnom Penh and been reassured that nothing was happening and we should continue our holiday. At that very moment, of course, we were installing Lon Nol and overthrowing Prince Sihanouk, and Cambodia had entered the war and all the airports were shut down. To get out of Angkor we and a British couple, the Foxtons, who had a daughter Rebecca's age, practically had to buy a bus that would drive the four hours over roads of broken rock to the Thai border, and of course Angkor was all but destroyed in short order, gods or no gods. But the gist of my remarks was that we could hardly hope to have the Cambodians on our side when we didn't know them, had no interest in them, and didn't really give a goddam for them anyway, and that a people had a way of catching on to this sooner or later, just as the Vietnamese had long since done.

A cadet with a size seventeen neck—I later learned he was the son of the Teamster boss in Chicago—was the first to raise his hand in the question period. He said he was outraged that I should be allowed to make this kind of defeatist propaganda at the Military Academy. I braced for the onslaught. A bald colonel with a bright red Guard's mustache, his chest covered with decorations, now raised his hand from the back of the room. During my speech a certain glaring ferocity in his straight bearing had attracted my worried attention.

"I . . ."—his first vocalization, in a commanding basso, sent a chill up my back here in the heart of the war—"was military attaché in Phnom Penh for twelve years." A pause for effect. A bit of an actor, a ham, in fact, considering the mustache. Here it comes, I thought, I am dead. "And I want to tell you that everything Mr. Miller has said is the truth." With which he turned and left the room.

Through the evening until two o'clock next morning, in the home of a young colonel who insisted I have dinner with him and his wife, surrounded by half a dozen of his fellow officers, I now heard the other side of the catastrophe, that of these tormented young soldiers. The army, they were saying, each in his different way, had had nothing to do with starting this war. They had known from the beginning that it was unwinnable on the battlefield, that it was a political and not a military problem. They were now having to get into civilian clothes to go down to New York City; people were blaming them, insulting and sometimes even attacking them in the streets. They had all fought in Vietnam, all had many decorations, and with a tense lostness in their eyes they were asking me to tell the country what they could not: to stop the war. They had an austerity—yes, and a kind of purity—reminiscent of young priests. And all of them were due to return to action, some within weeks, to lead yet more men into deaths they knew were useless and could never be redeemed.

But in time Ronald Reagan would invent a redemption, would cook it up like a new movie script out of the longings of the audience. What had once been common tragic knowledge at West Point was carefully, assiduously rewritten by experts in denial who gave us in myth the victory that had eluded us in reality. The pain was apparently too great to bear if untempered by the merest meaning, and so the doors were thrown open to an orgy of sentimental self-appreciation, and we were "standing tall again" on the same quicksand of unreality as ever. The monumentalized dead were mourned, but avoidance was the survivors' lot. It was as though the people had witnessed something in Vietnam so repulsive, so inexplicable for Americans to have done, that they could not acknowledge the casting away of fifty-eight thousand of their countrymen and finally found solace in a show business presidency with its incandescent reassurances of greatness reborn.

The sixties was a time of stalemate for me, perhaps because I had lost the last belief in any social prophecy, whether the common expectation that America was now being revolutionized by the youth and black movements or the pretensions of the orthodox to a democratic crusade in Vietnam. I could find no refreshing current of history such as I had imagined touching in the thirties and forties, only a moral stagnation that mocked creation itself. In a two-hour play, what could I hope to reveal that would compare with Lyndon Johnson facing a regiment of troops on some Pacific island and happily calling out, in reference to the Vietnamese, "Nail those coonskins to the wall, boys!" We had not descended to such vileness even against the Nazis, but it seemed to fill the entire canvas, leaving nothing to be said about it that it was not already saying itself. And yet it was an evasion to enjoy declaring the death of all values. In American side streets they still wanted better lives for their kids, wished marriages could last, clung to a certain biological decency. I could not forget that. But they had no place in art except as boringly sentimentalized wish figures.

The fashion—I hesitate to call it a ruling idea—was to let it all hang out, to acknowledge oneself utterly. But I no longer believed that "truthfulness" was merely a matter of social undress and defiance of norms. There were naked liars too.

The Truth Drug, a film scenario, was one of a score of abortive attempts to grasp my feelings about the sixties. Hogy, a young researcher at Columbia who is also a jazz flutist and a fencer and falls in love with a new girl every few weeks, stumbles on a chemical that transforms a wolverine, one of the most aggressive of animals, into a loving beast that fairly weeps with tenderness. The mixture apparently stimulates a part of the brain involved not so much in sex as in empathic identification, for the wolverine is not trying to mount everything in sight, only to offer affection.

On his way to visit a girlfriend one night, Hogy is mugged by an addict couple, and after drinking a bottle of the mixture they promptly dissolve into sympathy for him, for one another, and for the children they have neglected. The chemical finally finds its way into the hands of Hock and Stutz, manufacturers of pharmaceuticals, and is marketed under the trade name Love. It sweeps the country, since it is inevitably rumored to be an aphrodisiac.

Love transforms hateful people into friendlier folk, but there are quick complications. Professional football collapses as players instead of tackling the ball carrier run beside him trying to persuade him to stop. The subway system grinds to a halt as passengers lovingly decline to push their way into crowded cars, leaving thousands stranded on platforms. Most dangerous of all, the armed forces begin swallowing Love, and submarines are discovered surfacing so that the men can lie on deck sunbathing, exposing their positions to the Russians, while air force crews flee into jungles to escape having to bomb anybody. The crusty chief of the Hock and Stutz ad agency tries a glassful and, instead of rudely breaking into American TV programs with the company's commercials, falls in love with his Rolls-Royce and goes to bed with two hubcaps. Without its aggression the society begins to totter, and in desperation Washington bombs the Russians with kilotons of Love in the hope that it will immobilize them as badly as it has us. Soon both societies have all but ceased to operate, and everyone is passively lying around raising an occasional tomato—everyone, that is, but the true believers of all faiths, who have of course forbidden their followers to drink what they are sure is a sex-enhancing drug. Orthodox Jews join with pious Catholics, Protestants, and Moslems all over the world in a new International devoted to the rooting out and destruction of Love, a manifestation of the Devil in his age-old campaign to make man love himself with no need of God.

But I broke off the script before the end. The compelling desire to address people, let alone entertain and enlighten them, was somehow no longer with me. And maybe, too, the violent rejection of *After the Fall* had helped to burn it away.

In the late fall of 1973 a reprint of an article in *New Times* magazine arrived in the mail, sent by its author, journalist Joan Barthel. It contained parts of a Connecticut state police interrogation of an eighteen-year-old boy, Peter Reilly, in which he confessed to brutally murdering his mother, Barbara Gibbons. It had been a fiendish knife attack; her throat had been cut, her vagina forced with a bottle. The boy had been tried and convicted, but some of the local people in this rather remote northern Connecticut community had raised bail, many of them by putting up savings account books or even mortgaging their homes, such was their belief in his innocence. Along with a lot of others I was now being asked to help with money that might get him a new trial.

Peter was not black or Hispanic, Jewish or radical; he was pure victim. Knowing nothing whatever about the murder's circumstances, I was initially drawn into the case by reading the interrogator's horrifyingly cool and perfectly cynical misuse of Freudian psychology. To me it screamed of fraud. After twenty-four hours without counsel and ten hours of questioning, Peter, who had never known a father, was reduced to asking if his warmly paternal interrogator was sure he had murdered his mother, because he still felt only a loving sadness at the thought of her death. Wherewith the cop blithely confided that the Oedipus complex was quite universal in men, and considering his mother's practice throughout his childhood of having sex with innumerable strangers right there in the lower level of the double-decker bed while Peter slept in the upper one, the laws of psychology practically demanded that he conceive a monstrous fury against her, which had at last erupted. Naturally, Sergeant Kelly assured him, this hostility was all unconscious—but a hip boy like Peter must certainly know about the unconscious, and so the best thing to do was to "get it off your chest." Exhausted beyond exhaustion, Peter finally signed a confession, which he retracted after a night's rest. But it was too late.

As appalling as any other part of this nightmare was the acceptance of the "confession" by a judge, and the muting, once the court had spoken, of any real criticism of the proceedings by the local or national press, despite the crude brainwashing that glared out of it.

I ended by spending days and then weeks at a time over the next five years trying to help solve this case and extricate Peter. Only by the dogged efforts of two men—James Conway, a private investigator working most of the time with no pay and little gratitude, and T. F. Gilroy Daly, a lawyer I located with the help of the same law firm that had been representing me since the late forties—was it finally proved that Peter had been five miles from his home at the very moment his mother was murdered. Moreover, the eyewitnesses who had seen him were a local policeman and his wife. Their affidavit, of which the state police had to have been aware, was discovered in the files of the prosecutor after he suddenly died of a heart attack. The new prosecutor, presenting it in court, blew the case apart, and Peter was completely exonerated.

In short, with full knowledge of Peter's innocence a prosecutor had gone ahead and convicted him, and the state police had sewn it all up. Incredibly, even after the exculpatory evidence had been revealed, the state police department would try to rescue honor by presenting yet another stupefying "theory" that was so absurd as to be simply thrown out of court. In the end, State Police Chief Fussenich, retired by then, would take himself over to Peter's house to apologize, admitting that mistakes had been made.

The Oedipus complex may or may not operate universally, but the sheer animal reflex of bureaucracy in stonewalling against embarrassing truths surely does, and no less so here than in Russia or China or anywhere else. The vital difference is our right of appeal from its decisions, but appeals are expensive and depend too often on sheer good luck. There is a lawyer in almost all my plays, perhaps because man is what man is, nature's denial machine. In the course of the Reilly case I grew to treasure the law as our last defense against ourselves.

Peter's story was a moving one, but I found it impossible to write about despite having been closer to its center than anyone except Conway and Daly. I was uneasy with the idea of using this attempt to right a wrong to my own advantage and possibly adding to Peter's suffering. But in time I sensed another reason for my absence of creative enthusiasm. It is still difficult to describe with any precision, but I think I was oppressed by a certain brute repetitiveness in the spectacle of the Reilly prosecution. It was simple enough to understand that the police, once locked onto Peter, could not relent lest they endanger their professional reputations. Quickly the question changed from who murdered Barbara Gibbons and might still be walking around loose to who was impugning the state police. But as simple as the explanation was, it offered a vision of man so appallingly unredeemable as to dry up the pen. Except for the intervention of private citizens, a young man, physically slight and in many ways still psychologically a boy, would have been tossed to the wolves in the state penitentiary and eaten alive. The very absence of any racist motive helped to push the mind beyond sociology; indeed, Peter had from childhood idolized the police and was thus set up to believe a state policeman telling him that he had murdered his mom even though he had no memory of doing so.

The mystery was not how it had happened but that the motives for so grand an injustice should be so paltry. Who would have objected if the state police had admitted a mistake after Peter's arrest? It all seemed to bespeak an evil transcending any commensurate gain or motive, as one understands gain and motive, and I could not escape the feeling that I was watching a shadow play of mindless men dumbly miming roles of very ancient authorship, rather than a spontaneously new and real event. It was not an honest mistake but a dishonest one, and it was the labor of Hercules to break through the armor of a bureaucracy that extended right into the office of the liberal governor Ella Grasso, who for too long was loath to take action against her own officers. It was the mystery of all the senseless and profitless conflicts I had known, and to write about yet another was beyond me.

If the long months of the Reilly case left a darkened picture of man, it was no less perplexing for being accompanied by the most unlikely examples of courage and goodness, of people rising to the occasion when there was little reason to expect they would.

Once I had become involved in Peter's defense, I was soon convinced that he would need a new lawyer. There was an unforgettable interview with T. F. Gilroy Daly in the dining room of an elegant Connecticut country club. On first sight I felt uncertain that he was the right man for the task ahead, but he seemed interested despite my warning that there would be little money in it. In short, I persuaded both of us that he should take the case.

My doubts about Daly sprang from a belief that Peter's first lawyer had been too high-minded a civil liberties type when it was a tough criminal attorney who was needed here. Daly had had some experience as a young staff member of the New York federal prosecutor's office, but my initial impression was of a fashionable, very tall, blue-eyed horseman in a tweed jacket, a suburban lawyer who seemed restless and unhappy with himself; it even crossed my mind that he might not be overwhelmed with work at the moment. Out of Yale and the culture of toleration and wealth, he struck me as an unlikely gutter fighter—and I sensed that the gutter was where this case was going to be fought out in the end. With no idea that the proof of Peter's innocence was already in the prosecutor's safe, I knew that a new attorney would have to butt heads with some hard types in and out of uniform before it was all over.

I watched Daly grow remarkably during the largely unpaid months and years of the case. His patina of horsey-set sophistication fell away; there built up in him a cold personal outrage at what had been done to justice in his state, a gutsy shrewdness sharpened his mind, and his spirit took joy in an enlivening, almost palpable focus upon a loving task. He won brilliantly and in the process, I think, changed his own life, for he became a federal judge of great distinction.

Daly, Jim Conway, and I spent many evenings together at my place or around the Gibbons house, a former roadside hamburger stand turned into a grungy little home, the three of us trying to piece together what had happened on the fatal night. I got the aged Dr. Milton Helpern, perhaps the greatest criminal pathologist in the country, to examine the evidence, from which he concluded that Peter could not have done this murder and come away without a spot of blood on his clothes or his body, as even the police admitted he had. I located a New York physician, Dr. Herbert Spiegel, a noted specialist in hypnosis, who examined Peter and gave testimony in the second trial that helped mightily in clinching the acquittal. I also managed to bring the *New York Times* up to watch the formerly ignored court proceedings, which put the judge and prosecution on their mettle. But it was Daly and Conway's incredibly subtle reconstruction of the night of the murder, along with Daly's concentrated outwitting of the prosecution, that finally freed Peter Reilly.

I should have exulted in this victory and I did, but the truer voice was sounded in a play completed during the struggle to free Peter, *The Creation of the World and Other Business*. Like *The Price*, written in the sixties during the war, *Creation*, reconsidering Genesis, is essentially the fratricidal enigma, but seen now as a given of man's nature. In the setting of the original family, shorn of societal influence, the play seeks in fratricide, the first dilemma and the Bible's opening event, for a sign of hope for man. The fundamental competition between brothers for a mother's—and therefore God's—love is discovered with amazed perplexity for the first time. The purely loving and practical Adam and Eve, looking down in disbelief at the murdered Abel and the unrepentant Cain, can only fear for their lives under a God who not only permits such monstrous acts but has apparently designed mankind so as to perpetuate them. In this play the catastrophe is built into man's primal nature; in his very brotherhood he first tastes the murder of his own kind. Against that ticking bomb within us the defense, if there is a defense, is hardly more than Adam's imprecation to his wife and remaining son—to an Eve filled with hatred for a defiant Cain: "Ask her pardon! Cain, we are surrounded by the beasts! And God's not coming anymore! Boy, we are all that's left responsible—ask her pardon!" Cain, smiling and justified, walks adamantly away into his exile, leaving his father to call after him on his darkening desert, "Mercy!" But Adam's outcry is also integral to man.

It was only in college that I discovered the Bible, but as a man-made collection of fascinating literatures by different authors. I asked wise-guy questions in the margins, like: Where'd the folks come from to whose company Cain was exiled? Was this a slip? Had the author of Genesis forgotten there were not yet supposed to be other people besides Adam and Eve in Paradise? Or was "God" so old when he "wrote" the Bible that his mind wandered?

Slowly, however, it began to matter less that humans had authored the Bible, for what remained was hypnotic. I wondered why. The stories are told with the spareness of electrical diagrams, perhaps that's part of the fascination—you are left to fill things in, to create what has been omitted. Over the years the question of whether God *exists* gave way to another mystery—why are men, generation after generation, pressed to invent Him again? I more or less settled for the idea that God certainly is *always about to exist,* and this gives a legitimacy to jumping the gun somewhat and saying He already does. He may show up tomorrow, for all we know. Meantime, people have a ready vessel into which to pour their longings for the sacred, for transcendence, for oversight by a good guardian, for a reprimander and cautionary voice, and at best, for the concept of their having the obligation to make choices against evildoing, which is what helps keep the good alive. For the inventor of God, He is as animate as for the believer, maybe even more so, because he can never tear his invention out of his heart and set Him in stone, where He can be evaded if need be. It was the imperishability of this procedure that went into *The Creation of the World and Other Business,* a play that asks, among other questions, what sort of psychological situation must have given rise to the creation of God in the first place. And in the second place, right now.

The ironies would roll on through the seventies and right down to the present moment. In 1986, along with fifteen other writers and scientists from America and Europe and Africa, I found myself standing in the offices of the Central Committee of the Communist Party of the Soviet Union, looking down into the witty eyes of Mikhail Gorbachev as he shook my hand and said, "I know all your plays."

I was tempted to say, "Not all," for it was now eighteen years since I had been blacklisted on Soviet stages, for one thing because violent exception had been taken to *In Russia,* the first of three books Inge and I had jointly produced (her photographs, my text). One picture, of Comrade Ekaterina Furtseva, then minister of culture, had offended that lady, what with the deep lines of worry and exhaustion on her face, impossible to conceal short of airbrushing. (She had had a hard life; ousted as Khrushchev's favorite some years before, she had cut her wrists.) But more than her vanity was involved; at about the same time, as international president of PEN, the writers' organization, I had begun annoying the Soviets with protests against their treatment of writers and of course their anti-Semitism. To all this they had responded by closing down Galina Volchek's production of *Incident at Vichy.* I was sure it was not coincidental that the play dealt with the Nazi roundups of Jews during the war. And it probably didn't help that one of the characters is a Communist quite as deluded about the rationality of Marxism as the bourgeois victims are about their own ideologies.

I had traveled a long and twisting road to this moment at the very apex of Soviet power, and the changes in direction had left me not so much disillusioned as smiling, painfully sometimes. For the political world, I have come to believe, is fundamentally beyond anyone's control, yet we all go on as though it were a kind of vehicle that only needs a change of drivers in order to steer it away from its frequent hair-raising visits to the edge of the cliff. The immediate circumstances behind the meeting with Gorbachev were especially curious yet somehow logical in terms of my life.

Almost a year earlier I had gone with the greatest reluctance to a meeting of American and Soviet writers in Vilnius, Lithuania, at the vigorous urging of my good friend Harrison Salisbury, a co-leader of our delegation, who has a vast knowledge of the Soviet Union. Our group was varied, including Louis Auchincloss, Allen Ginsberg, William Gaddis, William Gass, and Charles Fuller. These periodic conferences among intellectuals from both sides were nearly all that was left of the promise of of détente. If such seminars had ever been politically significant, I had regretfully come to regard them as routine and finally got thoroughly fed up with being a sitting duck for Soviet attacks while having to observe the constraints of American politeness. In Vilnius, in 1985, I had blown the cork when, conforming to the agreed-on plan, the Americans around the table talked about their lives and work only to find the Soviets, most of whom were critics, journalists, and officials of the Writers Union rather than creative writers, picking off the American Black Problem, the American Indian Problem, Pornography in American Literature, and so on. We had traveled too far to be set up like this; irritated by the futility of it all, I pulled out a PEN dossier on the persecution of the poet Irina Ratushinskaya, ill at the time and in prison for some poems she had written, and read it off.

As I had expected, the Soviets fumed at this "interference in their internal affairs," but I concluded by pleading for candor from both sides, something impossible when to all our questions about Soviet life we received the same canned answers and could hardly tell one Soviet writer from another.

Further outraged, they blew up like birds under a beaten drum, but surprisingly one of them quietly and seriously proposed that I might be correct. This was Chingiz Aitmatov, a stocky man in his late fifties, at the moment possibly the most renowned novelist and playwright in his country. He was also an elected member of the Supreme Soviet from Kirghizia and would have the honor of addressing that body a day later, just before Gorbachev himself, a most prestigious spot on the program. He had written works that required some courage, confronting the deformations Stalinism had forced upon the Kirghiz minority, still a delicate subject regardless of the pro forma condemnations of the dead dictator in the press.

Nearly a year later, Aitmatov phoned from his native Kirghizia to invite me there for what he assured me would be an independent meeting, not under the wing of the Writers Union or any other governmental arm but purely his own invention and responsibility. The idea was to discuss how the world was to get safely into the third millennium, and he had asked Fellini to come, and Dürrenmatt, and they were interested. "Let us talk freely about the future," he said, and reeled off the names of others who had accepted: Peter Ustinov of England, the American Alvin Toffler and his wife, Heidi, the French Nobel laureate novelist Claude Simon. James Baldwin had also promised to attend, which indeed he did, along with scientists and artists from Italy, India, Ethiopia, Cuba, Turkey, and Spain. That our expenses and fare would be paid could only mean that the government was somehow behind it, but given Aitmatov's unprecedented stand at Vilnius and his assurances now of a really open gathering—plus Inge's eagerness to photograph in sequestered Kirghizia—I accepted. If Soviet intellectuals were ever to join the world community—from which, largely because of their own government's paranoid supervision, they stood apart as strangers—one owed them what help one could give.

It was in the final hour of our third and last day of discussions in a comfortable health resort on Lake Issyk-kul in Kirghizia that the invitation to meet with Gorbachev was announced. I assumed it would be a ten-minute hello, but it lasted two hours and forty minutes.

Unlike his predecessors, Gorbachev did not look baggy and bloated with drink; he wore a brown suit and beige shirt and striped tie, and had an eager grin and a certain contemporary wit in his eyes. An air of haste about him reminded me of John Kennedy, who also wanted writers to like him (so did Moshe Dayan, whom I had met years before).

His welcoming handshakes completed, he led the way from an outer office into a conference room with a long table that might seat thirty. He sat at the head with no advisers or assistants or notes. Several interpreters sat along the walls wearing earphones connected to microphones in the tabletop. As I had noticed on entering this modern office building, which fronted cobblestoned Red Square and the ancient Kremlin, its finish was remarkably fine by Soviet standards, and an acoustical hush emphasized its solidity. Here was the heart of darkness or beacon of light and hope, as one chose, and Gorbachev's sheer human ordinariness merely added to the mystery of power, for I sensed some personal need speaking from within him, beneath the command of authority.

Confessing with an ironic grin that he himself had never been in Kirghizia, he asked what we had been talking about way out there on the lake, and each of us in turn made a brief and rather inadequate comment on the discussions. The truth was that they had not been very profound, though there was one potentially important aspect: for the first time, at least in my experience, the Soviets were not defensive toward Westerners. In fact, they were clearly disciplining themselves against this old and bad habit. Otero of Cuba was no doubt a Marxist novelist, and Afework, a lofty Ethiopian, worked at his painting under a new and raw Marxist military junta that was filled with uneasily suspicious men, but neither they nor Aitmatov nor his two assistants sought at any time to put their Marxist loyalties on record. We could speak about planetary pollution or anomie, about technological unemployment in both East and West, about Chernobyl or anything else, and the result was nothing worse than the suppressed friction in an ecumenical conference among Catholics, Protestants, and Jews. Which is to say that the issue of converting one another was no more, there were only the common problems. For me, the lifting of the usual paranoid fog was almost palpable. How long it would last I could not know, but that it had been tried was, I thought, a tremendously hopeful thing.

In his comments, Gorbachev stressed the "new thinking" that he said was rapidly spreading in Russia—a transideological if still nominally Marxist pragmatism instead of an outmoded dogmatism. Pointedly, he kept returning to Lenin rather than Stalin for inspiration. "Politics needs to be nourished by the intellectual in each country because he is more likely to keep the human being at the center of his examination. Any other concentration is immoral. I read and reread Lenin," he said at one point, "and in 1916 he wrote, 'There must be a priority given to the general interest of humanity, even above that of the proletariat.' " He paused then and grinned. "And I wish 'the other world' would also realize this." He seemed to be hinting that the general welfare should even come before the needs of the Party. If he was indeed saying this aloud in public, he had to be taken seriously as a remarkable new force, for to question the absolute priority of Party interest had always been sacrilege. But when I returned home and wrote an account of the meeting, which contained information new at the time, I could not find a newspaper or national magazine that would print it, so total was the editorial cynicism toward any possibility of change in the Soviet world. Nor was my authorship the issue; Alvin Toffler, author of *Future Shock* and other probes into the technological world to come, met with the same press blackout. In the end, *Newsweek* published a boiled-down version on its "My Say" page of purely personal opinion. It was not only the Soviets who ought to be hearing what they preferred not to. Denial was in the saddle, as ever.

In my turn I repeated to Gorbachev what I had been saying at Issyk-kul, that our sacred ideologies were keeping us from irreverent facts. Marx ruled Russia, and Adam Smith the American administration, one philosophy a century old and the other two, and neither had dreamed of the computerized, televised, half-starved and half-luxuriating world we had now, a world with a shrinking proletariat and a burgeoning middle class (despite Marx), and a growing mass of the starving or the merely hungry and deranged wandering the cities of capitalism (despite Adam Smith). If only it were possible to allow the facts of life to rule rather than to serve what each side wished to prove ideologically . . .

Our history is the baggage of our brains, and I was carrying a lot of it in my head as I watched the chairman; it went all the way back to the handball game on East Fourth Street, Brooklyn, when that college boy first whispered to me about Marxism. By this time— having just spent my seventy-first birthday in Kirghizia, and already nearly twenty-five years married to Inge—I bore an old man's skepticism toward genuine changes of heart as I listened to

Mikhail Gorbachev impressing us Westerners with the liberality of his mind. But I thought I knew what he wanted, and it was encouraging because there had to be more than his personality behind this new toleration; the leadership must have realized that technological advancement was impossible under a government with a paranoid fear and suspicion of its own people as well as foreigners. My real question was not whether he wished to liberalize the regime but whether it was possible without legalizing a genuine opposition, be it inside the Communist Party or without. I judged that he had before him the Chinese dilemma—which I had seen in operation in two visits there, especially during my two months of directing *Salesman* in Beijing three years earlier—namely, how to unleash a nation's ingenuity and still keep it under one-party control.

But I had also had the personal experience of dealing with other Soviets who "wanted to change," and I had learned some hard lessons in the process. In that room with the chairman, my thoughts went back and forward and back again to 1967 and a Moscow hotel room where I had come to negotiate the entry of Soviet writers into International PEN.

It all began in 1965 with a call on the crackling French telephone in Inge's apartment in Paris, where we had come for the Luchino Visconti production of *After the Fall* with Annie Girardot. I had found it unfocused. His acutely thought-out movies notwithstanding, Visconti seemed to have missed the verb of the play, regarding it as a sort of exposé of primitive American sexual perplexities. There would be a far more incisive production, directed by Franco Zeffirelli, a year later in Rome, with Monica Vitti and Giorgio Albertazzi. Zeffirelli was not afraid to allow Quentin the full anguish of a man not at all trying to explain himself but searching for himself, a different attitude entirely, and one I thought moving and persuasive. His set was a series of six or eight concentric steel rectangles growing progressively smaller upstage—it was like looking through the back of a bellows camera toward the lens in the far distance—and the black velour between each square allowed actors to enter and exit up the whole of the very deep stage while silent lifts in the floor raised and lowered pieces of furniture to create and erase the locations in Quentin's mind almost instantaneously, as in a dream or reverie. The production toured the main Italian cities, and its reception confirmed the play for me.

On Inge's phone, I was having a hard time making out that it was "Keith calling from London" and that he had to see me tomorrow and would fly to Paris with someone named Carver, who would explain everything. Keith Botsford, a novelist and teacher, had been one of the editors—along with Saul Bellow and Aaron Asher, who by this time was my editor at Viking—of *The Noble Savage*, a lively but short-lived periodical to which I had contributed two short stories a few years earlier. Now he was saying something about "PEN," of which I had only vaguely heard.

Next day Keith, with whom I had only a passing acquaintance, arrived at Inge's apartment on the rue de la Chaise with an immense Englishman in tow: David Carver, a Sidney Greenstreet without the asthma. In fact, as I soon learned, he had been an opera baritone of some note until the Second World War, when he became the Duke of Windsor's aide and suffered through the war with his royal charge in the Bahamas.

Inge's apartment was in a house that had been the Spanish embassy in the sixteenth century. The walls were thick, the ceilings very high, and the windows overlooking the ancient little two-block-long street were immaculately polished by her longtime Basque maid, Florina, who served us our coffee with a formality fit for three barons in a palaver about the spice trade. Florina's black eyes were charged with the pleasure of having something important to do at last, after months of waiting for her adored mistress to return from America for a visit.

Keith quickly gave the floor to Carver, a man of rounded diction, apt usage, and sudden descents into the raw street-level observations of a realistic theatre pro. He had served as secretary general of PEN for many years now and had obviously given much of his hope and time to it, "but I must candidly tell you, Mr. Miller, we are now at such a point that if you do not accept the presidency, PEN will be no more."

The presidency of PEN? I hardly knew what the organization did beyond the haziest impression that it was some sort of literary discussion club.

PEN, Carver explained, was established after the war—the First War—by such people as John Galsworthy, Bernard Shaw, G. K. Chesterton, H. G. Wells, John Masefield, Arnold Bennett, Henri Barbusse, and a number of like-minded others in England and Europe who thought that an international writers' organization might help prevent another war by combating censorship and nationalist pressures on writers. Of course it didn't stop the Second

War, but in the thirties it helped draw the world's attention to the menace of Nazism by expelling the German delegation, which had refused to condemn Hitler's censorship and brutality toward writers. But the point now was that they had come to the end of the string.

"Why me?" I asked. I had no connection with PEN and no desire to run any organization. I frankly wasn't sure I even believed in organizations for writers anymore.

Despite its valuable work, PEN had not made a bridge to the generation now in its twenties and thirties and had come to be regarded as tame and largely irrelevant. It had also been a victim of the Cold War, which had damaged if not destroyed its credit in smaller countries that were not entirely enlisted on the side of the West. The recent détente policy called for new attempts to tolerate East-West differences, which PEN had not yet gained the experience to do. A fresh start was needed now, and it was me.

Carver snapped open his gold cigarette case. Certain as I was that I wanted nothing to do with this new diversion from writing, there was no way of cutting short this great figure of a Briton, blond of hair, blue of eye, with silky skin as white as the inside of a grapefruit rind, two jolly pink rosettes on his cheeks, and shoulders as broad as the back of a wagon.

"We are trying to save some lives. We've managed to now and then. Not enough, but a few."

"Lives?" This was still the mid-sixties, well before human rights concerns had surfaced in the West through such politically impartial organizations as Amnesty International, founded only a few years earlier. At this point the politicalization of human rights was complete, the Communist side erupting only when its partisans in the West were harassed, while the West made noises only when Eastern regimes clamped down on *their* dissidents. Carver was opening up an entirely new vista of a depoliticized human ground on which to stand and defend everybody at the same time, and thus perhaps to speak to the sterility of two decades of Cold War. It was an attractive if not quite credible position.

PEN had been able, Carver said by way of example, to convince the Hungarian government to let some imprisoned writers leave after the Russians invaded in '56. They still had centers in Poland and Czechoslovakia (later to be dissolved or crippled) that collected information and publicized cases of oppression from time to time. "It's very irregular," he confessed, "and doesn't always do much good, but it does often enough to make it a pity to have to go out of business now."

But what was PEN's leverage? Why should anyone pay any attention to it?

"They dislike bad publicity in the East quite as much if not more than we in the West. In fact, they are eager to be seen as modern, up-to-date societies and not tyrannies at all," he said, raising his eyebrows and trying not to smile.

"Why must you go out of business?"

One could almost see him put on his diplomatic black homburg. They had been unable in recent years to attract sufficient writers of note, of international standing. I could draw in people of that kind, he thought.

"I couldn't possibly run a . . ."

"I run everything. You need only appear for the international congresses that come up periodically, perhaps once a year. I assure you it will not mean much time at all."

"You want a figurehead."

"Not at all. The president has real power if he chooses to take command of it."

But I had a suspicion of being used and wondered suddenly whether our State Department or CIA or equivalent British hands might be stirring this particular stew. I decided to flush them out. "What if I wanted to invite Soviet writers to join PEN?"

Carver's mouth dropped open. "Why, that would be wonderful! Of course! Yes! In fact, you see, we are always in danger of splitting apart altogether, our East bloc centers are always rather on the edge; and you would be most persuasive to the Eastern people."

". . . Because if the point is to help prevent war, the presence of Soviet writers would be . . ."

"Absolutely, yes. It would be stupendous if we and the Soviet writers could all join together in a single organization. Will you take it on?"

I stalled, said I'd think about it for a bit. But he had to know in the next few days, "before the invitations go out for the Bled Congress."

"Bled? Where is Bled?"

"In Yugoslavia."

"There's a center in Yugoslavia?"

"Oh, yes, a very good one. And they need us very much. It will be our first congress in Yugoslavia."

After a couple of days, reluctantly but snagged by curiosity, I consented, but I was left with the mystery of why I had been chosen. I could only suspect what two decades later I learned was probably the truth. Among the entries in my dossier, which I was finally able to wheedle out of the FBI in 1986, was a 1965 cable to Washington from the U.S. embassy in Moscow describing my reception there, two short weeks before this visit of Carver's, as "semi-official" and warm; in fact, Botsford had phoned the day we returned to Paris from the East. The British press may have reported my welcome at the train station by a quite large delegation from the Soviet Writers Union, but it was also possible that Carver had other sources of information about my current favor with the Soviets. In any case, he knew that I was acceptable to both East and West, the perfect PEN president now that the organization's very existence was in grave question. PEN stood stuck in the concrete of what I would soon learn were its traditional Cold War anti-Soviet positions, but like the Western governments at this point, it was now trying to bend and acknowledge Eastern Europe as a stable group of societies whose writers might well be permitted new contacts with the West, from which they had for so long been cut off. Thus, after some forty years, PEN's original peace-preserving impulse might have a chance to exert itself in the real world. Willy-nilly, I was pitched into the still indeterminate tangle of détente politics to begin a new and totally unexpected stage of my learning life.

For Inge, to see a valise was to start packing. With her genius for languages she had learned Russian before the trip began. She could also speak English, French, Spanish, and Italian fluently, and Rumanian with some residual difficulty, because she had studied it early in the war years and had not used it since. After two weeks in Greece, I suddenly realized on one of our last evenings there that she was now speaking that language, which she had never studied at all. I would gradually learn to turn to her in any foreign country for interpretation of what the local barbarians were trying to tell me, and it usually worked. This capacity for concentration, and at the same time a romantic playfulness of spirit, had a way of disarming men of power. In the late forties, after she interviewed and photographed German chancellor Konrad Adenauer, he insisted she become his chief secretary. In China one lunchtime in the eighties, she found herself between a German-speaking Chinese official, a Russian-speaking Chinese writer, and an English-speaking Chinese tourist guide. These men rarely got a chance to speak their second languages, so they happily tried them on Inge, and at one point she was translating three European languages into and out of Chinese. I thought I saw smoke coming out of her ears as she grew paler and paler, but she refused to give up until everyone realized what was happening and broke down in laughter.

We had gone by train to Moscow from Düsseldorf, two nights and nearly two days across an ocean of January snow, an expanse without limit or definition. It made one realize all over again that the human race most adores its leaders who are most mad; that Napoleon could put an army to marching, let alone fighting, through such chest-high drifts, and that Hitler could repeat the attempt, had to prove that these were insane men leading credulous hordes of devotees into their final frozen dream. The train moves at a good clip, and you have your breakfast looking out the window at the snow and then your lunch looking out the window at the snow and then your dinner looking out the window at the snow, and then you sleep dreaming of the window and the snow and wake next morning to look out the window at the snow, and there is nothing else for two and a half days.

My plays had been on the Soviet stage for nearly twenty years, and the affection of the audiences for my work ran deep, as I shortly discovered. Because the press was so tightly controlled and fiction writers had to battle for each paragraph and even word of candor, it was in the theatre that people found the most ample room for their spontaneous, unhampered insights and emotions. It was not that plays with unorthodox themes could be produced but that irony could be introduced by a raised eyebrow, a gesture, and the sheer human presence of the actor. The tactile vividness of live performances even of classic plays somehow energized the audience, and Russians treasured the theatre's relative freedom of feeling and imagination.

In 1965 it happened that *A View from the Bridge* was being played, and of course we had to see it. The large theatre was packed, and at the end I took ten minutes of applause, but I learned several contradictory things in short order.

I knew no Russian, but I thought that at least in the first scene the text had been altered, and my interpreter confirmed my suspicion. In *View* the feelings of the longshoreman Eddie Carbone for his niece, Catherine, prompt him to betray his illegal immigrant relatives to the authorities in order to get rid of the young man Catherine wishes to marry; his unacknowledged love, illicit as it is in his eyes—he has raised Catherine as a daughter—is gradually pressed out of him by circumstances. But on the Soviet stage, hardly had the young girl walked past him for the first time when

Eddie, with an obvious sensual inflection, said to Beatrice, his wife, "I love her." It was almost like Oedipus turning to Jocasta in the first moments of the play and saying, "It's no good being married to you, Mother . . ."

After the performance I complained about this foolish tampering to Oleg Efremov, director of the Sobremenik Theatre and later head of the Moscow Art Theatre. What struck me was not his remarkable defense of the change—"We are not interested in all that *psychology*"—but his underlying easy disdain, amounting to a contempt for an author's right to his own work. Not that I had always been spared such arrogance elsewhere, including New York. But in combination with the elaborate adulation that was heaped on me, it seemed a mockery and somehow added a sinister color to our welcome, quite as though what had been given by one hand was being crushed by the other.

I learned in future years that while it was fairly common practice in the Soviet Union to laud and publish writers like Twain and Hemingway, the translations excluded politically or "morally" inconvenient passages and even added more convenient new ones, especially such as would underline criticism of American society. I was glad to know that *Death of a Salesman* had been produced, but my pleasure was greatly diminished by the news that it had been severely changed: Willy had been caricatured as a total fool, and Charley, who offers him financial help, was rewritten and acted as a clownish idiot, since as a businessman he could not possibly be even slightly altruistic or have a shred of sincerity.

At the same time, there was the theatre audience and its almost prayerful attention, the power of its concentration on the happenings on the stage, and its openhearted joy in greeting me. Between that audience's innocent generosity and a luncheon given by the head of the Writers Union, Alexei Surkov, I first began to glimpse the coil of the Russian paradox.

Surkov's reputation rested on some very popular war poems, but his ruthlessness in carrying out Stalinist repression of writers was by now the source of his renown. A gray-haired, grandfatherly man, he affected that big-chested country heartiness which tends to freeze the soul, and at the large luncheon in my honor at the Writers Union he lost no time in laying on the subtle two-ton hand. To get things going with a non–Russian speaker, the weather was the inevitable opening topic, and I said that it seemed terribly cold to me. Someone at the end of the long and crowded table opined in a gently polite tone that it had been even colder this time last year, and someone else disagreed, recalling it was warmer. There were several variations on both positions until Surkov leaned back and roared, "You see, Miller—we writers can never agree on anything!" The whole company howled approval, heavily nodding right down to the tablecloth at this instantaneous disintegration of any compulsory Party line in a writer's life.

The heart sickened at the childishness of this organized naiveté, but what interested me was that at least in a foreigner's presence liberty was still the standard. Why could it not simply be acknowledged that they believed a writer should carry out a predigested Party line in his work? Why shouldn't writers agree with the all-seeing Party if it helped the human race to progress? But they persisted in nodding toward liberty, and I chose to see something perversely heartening in this.

But then there was the stroll through the snowy street past the Kremlin with our guide-interpreter, a young and serious fellow. When I glanced up toward the windows of what I was told had been Stalin's apartment and wryly said, "There must have been some goings-on up there the night he died, right?" he returned a look of blank surprise.

"Why?" he asked.

"Well, all those other guys rushing around trying to decide who would succeed him."

"It is not our business what goes on in there."

This was a stern rebuke; who ruled them and how was not rightfully within the bounds of their curiosity. In fact, my prying seemed slightly unholy. How to understand this?

Yet within hours we sat watching a Yuri Lyubimov production of an adaptation of *Ten Days That Shook the World,* and hope soared again, for it was so subtle, so tasteful, so expertly conceived and acted, as to raise it above almost any other theatre I could recall. Surely we must share a common humanity! A couple of decades later, of course, Lyubimov would be in self-exile in Italy, having given up trying to work under the attacks and strictures of the Party. Russia would not cease the lavish waste of her talents.

Through our two weeks there, we received the warmest welcoming embraces from Russian artists: Maya Plisetskaya in *Don Quixote* at the Bolshoi performing a special cadenza in my honor, her eyes lifted to our box as she danced; the novelist Konstantin Simonov in his country house offering us the respect of candor about the terrible past; Ilya Ehrenburg describing his discovery, upon his return from reporting the Spanish Civil War, that every

Soviet journalist who had come back from Spain before him had been shot for fear of contamination by the West, though he had somehow survived not only this but also the general purge of the time, what he called "the lottery."

There seemed no single, simple thing to be said about Russia by the time we were back in Paris, except possibly what I did say to David Carver, that if PEN could penetrate Soviet isolation it could only be to the good. Entering the country by train had helped me to understand something of the littleness a Russian writer must feel as he tries to speak his unique truth to that awful immensity, which at the same time enfolds him in a primitive smothering warmth.

In my head too, as I watched Gorbachev in 1986, was our trip to Czechoslovakia in 1969. Not yet plastered over were the bullet holes made by the guns of Soviet tanks in the building facades of Prague, and the teenager Jan Palach had only recently burned himself to death in protest against the Soviet occupation that destroyed the Prague Spring, the Czechs' attempt at "socialism with a human face."

The enormity of it all was naked in Prague, and probably more immediate because we were moving around the city with anxious playwrights, with Václav Havel and Pavel Kohout, the first not yet in prison, and the latter still not driven to escape to Vienna after the police attacked his actress wife and nearly broke her leg in a viciously slammed car door.

At dinner at a novelist's home his child peeked around a drape calling, "Papa?" and pointing down to a car across the street in which the police sat waiting, a maneuver to warn us all that we were not alone. I would learn how to accept this surveillance as they did, by numbing my fears and informing my brains.

In the shabby offices of the literary magazine *Listy,* facing a couple of dozen writers, I sat for an interview that turned out to be the last before the magazine was shut down forever. It had not dawned on me until then that Prague was not "East" but a European city west of Vienna and quite simply, as was clear from up close, the prize of straightforward aggression, for just out of town hundreds of Soviet tanks were parked in ranks. But I was perversely thankful for my onetime attraction to Moscow since it gave me some understanding of Prague writers who had also looked to the East for liberation during the war, infatuating themselves with conflictless "socialism" and the redemption of mankind they had seen in it. I knew all about that, and it was part of the same surreal pastiche for me as it was for them, and I was glad of it.

Some eight years later I would write *The Archbishop's Ceiling* out of this maze of relationships I found in Prague, but true to form, it took a decade more to establish itself, in the 1986 Royal Shakespeare Company production at the Barbican. It is a play of shaded meanings and splintered implications, of double and triple repercussions not altogether unknown in the political rooms of Washington, Paris, and London but more blatantly and brutally evident among writers the farther east one moves. It was basically my own bad revisions that crushed the first production, at the Kennedy Center in Washington. I mistakenly allowed myself to be persuaded that the play would not be clear enough to naive Americans in its original form. But that was the form in which it succeeded in London and in an earlier Bristol Old Vic production. Time also helped, for by 1986 people could see that the play was not about "the East" alone; we were all secretly talking to power, to the bugged ceiling of the mind, whether knowingly or not in the West; even unconsciously we had forgone the notion of a person totally free of deforming inner obeisances to power or shibboleth. It was more and more difficult to imagine in the last quarter of the century the naked selfness of a free human being speaking with no unacknowledged interest except his own truth.

I was still not sure why I had accepted the presidency of PEN even when I sat on the Belgrade-bound plane from Paris, but there is an instinct that decides such things, if not always for the better. The man who took the seat next to mine that June afternoon in 1965 looked familiar, although I knew we had never actually met. "Norman Podhoretz," he said, offering a handshake. I was surprised that the editor of *Commentary* magazine should dignify enemy territory by his presence in Yugoslavia, but in a few moments I was finding him warm and rather funny about literary people and the New York scene. Still, if he was going to Bled to see what this PEN thing was all about, I had to assume it was with some skepticism if not outright suspicion. As for myself, I hadn't the slightest idea what to expect of this, my first congress, whose president I incredibly was. I was glad that Podhoretz, a broadly educated essayist, thought there was some point in the organization, but at the same time his presence beside me clarified at least one of my reasons for having accepted the presidency: PEN seemed to promise an awak-

ening of humanist solidarity at a time when the opposing creed of
untrammeled individualism and private success was beginning its
most recent sweep of the American political landscape.

After a thankfully short flight the plane landed on a runway at
the border of a field just then being plowed. Podhoretz, whose
face normally had the surprised look of a suddenly awakened
baby, was even more wide-eyed as he eagerly tried to see past
me through the window. Here was his first sight of a Communist
state, a broken-off piece of what years later his favorite American
president would call the Evil Empire. As the plane turned
around to taxi to the airport, two tractors appeared in the field.
"They have tractors!" he exclaimed; thinking he was kidding, I
turned to see his mixed look of excited confusion. The plane
stopped and the tractors drew closer. He pressed toward the window to stare at them. What a roiling mixture of feelings in him!
And what an ideology that it could leave him, with all his learning, so surprised at their having tractors in Yugoslavia.

The machines were now only yards away, and I could read the
Cyrillic letters cast into their radiator frames. "I think they make
them here," I said with a straight face, pointing the lettering out
to him. When he looked absolutely appalled, I let him off easy. "But
they're more likely Russian."

"Probably from American designs."

"Well, no, ours are better, I understand. These are kind of clunky
and hard to maneuver."

Now he seemed to feel some relief.

"But I hear they last."

He caught on and unwillingly had to laugh. Having been in
Russia, I was pretty sure he'd find plenty here to exercise all his
feelings, from condescension to fear.

Hardly had I unpacked in the Belgrade hotel when there was a
knock on the door and there he was, the commentator-critic-editor
craning to see what accommodations I had been given. Actually,
I had the vast suite used by Tito when he came to town, five or six
bedrooms and baths reeking of power and gloom, a full kitchen,
and a conference-living room containing three couches and a huge
dining table with a cut-glass vase and three welcoming roses on its
gleaming surface.

"How the hell do you rate this? I've got a lousy little room!"

"I'm the president, Jack, and I may have to make a speech out
there to an enormous crowd, too." I took him to a corner window
opening onto a balcony from which, one story above the great
square, Tito had probably given some speeches. Norman laughed,

but not heartily. He had not yet published his book *Making It,* but looking back on this day, I would wonder if he wasn't already working on it there in the Croatian capital. As a competitor myself, I recognized the symptoms, and he had them really bad, as he was all but admitting to me himself.

Bled is in high mountains, and the restaurant near midnight was cold. The woman on the tiny stage up front was apparently going to take off her clothes despite the fact that of the thirty or so tables only ours and five or six others were occupied. Earlier, I had hooked up with a Yugoslavian newspaperman named Bogdan, and two other journalists had attached themselves to us after one of the PEN round table discussions in the hotel that faced the lake on the other end of town. Now we all sat staring at the stripper, who was unhooking her skirt and undulating to the bumpy jazz of a small, cold band. At a table nearby a couple of stumpy local women in thick sweaters were sipping vodka with their men, stolidly watching the tiny stage as Yugoslavia went modern, no matter what.

The PEN Congress had been going for two days, long enough for me to fear that I was out of my depth in this job, too hopelessly ignorant of writers who were not out of New York, London, Paris, or more recently Latin America. For all I knew, there were writers here who might well be world figures had their works been written in one of the major languages. What provincials we all were, not only the Americans but also the British and French.

Nevertheless, the majority of the hundred and fifty or so delegates were really academics or journalists, like my table companions, not creators at all. And up to this point PEN seemed little more than an intricate exercise in diplomacy leavened only by a rare moment or two of frankness. I could see no great victory in the fact that French, British, and West German writers were sitting in the same room as East Germans, Bulgarians, Hungarians, and Poles, not when the deep moral and political conflicts between them were rarely allowed to surface. Nobody wanted the same kind of logjam in PEN that they had in the United Nations, but we seemed to be indulging in vacuous discussion instead. I was starting to be sorry I had accepted the presidency. I was not looking for trouble, but it was hard to see how we were doing much bridging of hostile cultures here. Yet Bogdan kept insisting PEN was vital and that to Yugoslavs it was important that I be president, especially since I was an American.

"In the first place, I am not an 'American.' My government

doesn't like me, never did. I don't represent the American people either."

"Yes, we know," he would say, and leave it cryptically at that. The simple and nearly absurd fact was that with an American as president, they thought their cultural independence from the Sovietized East more safely confirmed. We were in a world of pure symbolism here, to the point where I wondered if all of life was this same sort of dream.

The stripper dropped her blouse, revealing a pair of anticlimactic surprises, but I saw she had good legs now that they were bared, and I asked my new friends if they could tell from looking at her what her ethnicity was. Bogdan was Croatian, the two journalists were Slovenian and Serb, and now each began trying to foist her off on the others—she was too short for a Slovenian or too fair for a Serb and so on. When her act was finished she came down past us in a blue woolen bathrobe, carrying her clothes over her arm, and I reached out and stopped her to ask where she was from.

"Düsseldorf," she said, and went on out with no pause.

The men suppressed an explosive laugh and even wiped off their smiles in deference to the holy and lethal divisions in the country, which were no laughing matter—unless you thought about them for a minute. And now I remembered wondering, way back there in the Brooklyn of the Marxist-materialist thirties, who would be left to bury the Jewish dead and support the synagogues once my parents' generation was gone, since it was perfectly obvious that the age of religion and small pesky nationalities was finished forever. Ah, yes.

The irreality of my life was not improving here in Yugoslavia. The mood was symbolized a few days hence when I climbed out of the Adriatic off Dubrovnik and sat on a rock beside my friend Bogdan, who only then informed me that these waters were full of sharks but that he had not wished to spoil my swim by telling me in advance. Up in Bled, I kept trying to identify delegates and was given meaningless names of editors of unknown newspapers and magazines and professors at colleges I had never heard of, and the depressing futility of so voluble yet powerless a gathering of people all but convinced me that I had been had.

Slowly, however, matters improved. I found Stephen Spender, who made a speech strongly suggesting that the poets present should read their poems to whoever was interested, and this simple but amazing idea banished the prevailing dustiness for a while. I noticed that Ignazio Silone, the fiercely anti-Communist novelist, was able to sit quietly talking to Pablo Neruda, the Chilean Communist poet. And some hard searching turned up other creators: Rosamond Lehmann, Richard Hughes, Charles Olson, Robie Macauley, Roger Shattuck, and Susan Sontag among the writers in English, and Yugoslavia's Nobel laureate Ivo Andrič. It turned out that we were all equally skeptical of any reality here but all secretly hoping to see something come of this largely gestural meeting. Almost despite myself I began feeling a certain enthusiasm for the idea of international solidarity among writers, feeble as its present expression still seemed.

I learned that A. den Doolaard, a burly, mustached member of the Dutch Center, had been making clandestine trips into Poland for years now to distribute PEN money to destitute families of imprisoned writers. As a result of the Bled congress Mihajlo Mihajlov, whose *Moscow Summer 1964* had earned him a nine-month jail sentence, was freed (although not totally cleared), and even the Yugoslav bureaucrats present openly expressed their relief. Carver, I discovered, had quietly negotiated his release with Matej Bor, chief of the PEN Slovene Center.

It was not lost on me, as I moved among the Westerners and shared their guarded conversations with writers from the East bloc, that American PEN had been silent when my passport was taken from me in the fifties. But the past was the past, and now perhaps there was a chance to rise to the same indignation no matter what the quarter from which repression spoke. With Carver I became the advocate of a new birth of PEN's influence in America, and also in Africa and Asia. We must have a congress soon in Africa, I thought (and indeed the Ivory Coast hosted the 1967 congress).

The common enemy was our terrifying provincialism. I thought of Lillian Hellman's 1948 dinner with the two pleading Yugoslav UN delegates and felt embarrassment now at how abstractly we had talked around her sparkling table, as though it were simply an ideological dispute! But the Yugoslavs had torn their country away from the Germans, and in Belgrade Bogdan had pointed out apartment buildings with concrete firing slits cut discreetly into their upper stories to take on the expected Soviet invasion after Tito had defied Stalin. "The slits are facing east," he had said. The two young UN delegates were no doubt thinking of those slits.

The big news at Bled was the appearance of seven Soviet "observers," plus the fact that they did not huddle together, as their delegations normally did, but attended round table discussions separately and without supervision. With the exception of the novelist Leonid Leonov they were dutiful members of the apparatus, but that was less important, I thought, than their uniform efforts to show me, the new president, a kindly face—PEN was clearly no longer the suspicious instrument of the Western secret services in official eyes.

At the closing party of the congress in the old Bled castle-fort, whose battlements were romantically floodlit for the gala night, I sat with Alexei Surkov and his accompanying Soviets, who were comparing their vodka with the slivovitz of some Yugoslav writers, all of them awash and being heavily Slav and singing old Partisan songs, and what with the eastward-facing firing slits in Belgrade, PEN seemed to assume a relevance, or at least a promising irony.

In fact, by this time I knew that PEN could be far more than a mere gesture of goodwill; whatever their talents, the writers here had unquestionably responded with an instinctual self-preserving attention when in my main speech to the whole congress I said that we must indeed maintain our apolitical standards of free expression but this did not mean that we had to stay out of politics when repression was a political fact. If we wished to become universal, we had to confront the political impediments to our universality. "As with all things, you never do any good," I concluded, "unless you get into some trouble. I am not sure people who write will not be getting into trouble in America again, and we may need your assistance. We must look at every culture with the same eyes." It was fine to see our American delegation applauding heartily along with the Russians, for I realized that the fate of the world—as this congress certainly saw it—was in the hands of both our giant countries.

But PEN was still far from sufficient for its universalizing task, as we all understood perfectly well. As very serious waiters hastened over ancient stone floors bearing strong white wine for delegates who were getting drunker and drunker, the company seemed a band of survivors of two European civil wars. Maybe my very remoteness as an American was my value here, since as someone out of Radomizl and Brooklyn, I was a stranger to their old feuds. They were first to grasp this, but I caught on at last, and in threatening moments of unresolvable ideological tension, I took to declaring lunch, which at eleven or eleven thirty in the morning rather astonished them; but they soon got the idea, and whenever words got too hot cries of "Lunch!" would fly up from the ranks, even from the round Bulgarian lady who had not been noted for a sense of the ludicrous, able as she was, two or three times a day, to repeat word for word her ardent invitation to visit Sofia, where she would show me the fields of roses that produced their main export, the attar.

So this was my function: to be fair, to keep the peace, and to persist in apolitically advancing the political concepts of liberty of expression and the independent author. The great thing was that these were the unspoken longings of most of those present, no matter where they came from.

But at times you could get exhausted trying to figure out why they were telling you something. One of the Hungarians—who during the sessions would rise to defend passionately his government's treatment of writers, as well as to proclaim its civilized behavior in general—had privately buttonholed me: "The new prime minister called in the former prime minister, the Stalinist who had previously been his boss—this was after the death of Stalin, of course—and the new prime minister climbed up on his desk and commanded the former prime minister to stand under him with his mouth open, and then the new prime minister pissed into the former prime minister's mouth." (And, I thought, they were both Marxists, of course.) Was he being hip, or was this an authentic urge to square himself with American-British liberalism, which despite everything they all still regarded as the ultimate civilized standard?

And now, totally unexpectedly, Surkov, head of the Soviet Writers Union, swaying slightly from his drinks and as big-chested as his worshiped Steinbeck and Hemingway, informed me in a most solemn if not belligerent tone, "We want to join PEN, we are ready to negotiate. We would have to have a few changes in the rules and the constitution, but we can discuss all that. When I get home we will arrange an invitation for you to come."

We shook hands; I was proud of myself; on one corner of the world's field of battle a sort of truce was apparently about to be made.

When I reported to Carver, who flushed red with excitement at this proof of PEN's relevance so soon after it had seemed moribund, we decided that Surkov's "changes" must involve the voting procedures, which he had indeed mentioned to Carver as a problem. The Soviet Union had a great number of literatures in different languages, and the question was how many votes they might demand; in the UN, of course, the USSR had its representative, and the Ukraine and Belorussia had their own delegates. If worse came to worst, we could match them with separate votes for the Los Angeles and Chicago PEN centers, but one way or another we would have to avoid being swamped with legions of Soviet writers outvoting the rest of us. In any case, though there were problems to be smoothed out, we had moved PEN closer to its original peace-preserving purpose. With no modesty left me, I believed that it was the persuasiveness of my plays on stages on both sides of the ideological battle line that had made this bridge building possible for me. If indeed that was what had been begun here.

It took more than a year to get to Moscow; I was by now a proper lawyer for my emotions, for I had been sending what seemed an endless stream of wires and letters to Surkov protesting arrests of writers not alone in Russia but also in Lithuania and Estonia, occasionally succeeding in getting people exit visas, and pressing as well for a letup on the repression of Jews. So that by the time he lumbered into my Moscow hotel room in 1967 with his broad smile, I had resolved to be certain that when and if they entered PEN we were all of one mind about what they were doing there.

From my friendships with the less contented Soviet writers I knew what the score was for them: PEN was an exciting window on the West with some very practical advantages in view, such as better possibilities of translation into European languages, which was only fitfully done now, and the protection of solidarity with Western writers, which would widen freedom of expression—once the USSR was in PEN, it would be harder to make a Soviet writer disappear. For Surkov and the regime, membership in PEN promised prestige in the West, possibly the most needful thing of all to the Russians. But whatever his reasons, surely Surkov was sophisticated enough to see that PEN would not be deflected from its basic purposes, and if he still wanted to become part of it, no one could object. Now I would finally learn what "changes" he had cryptically referred to in Bled.

With Surkov came a large blond linguistics professor with the size and mien of an overweight Viking, an authentic Russ bonecracker out of the bear cave, and jolly too. I have forgotten his name, but in my mind he was always Nat. He and Surkov had a few vodkas and sprawled in their chairs, and for a few minutes we were back on the weather again, talking relative mean temperatures from Novosibirsk to Philadelphia. At last Surkov said flatly, "Soviet writers want to join PEN." It sounded final.

Was I dreaming? Was the time at hand when in Moscow or

Leningrad or Yalta writers from over sixty nations would move freely among their Soviet counterparts? The very image was bursting with possibilities of smashing the moral and political stalemate institutionalized by our time, to the impoverishment of everyone everywhere. Might the day have arrived when our *real* horrors on both sides would be allowed to surface freely—and we humbly resolve to go back and start all over again trying to figure out how to live with incessant change and lethal progress, to put man in his fragile environment on top again, not last, where he was now?

"I couldn't be happier," I said. "We would all welcome you in PEN." The writing community would at last be a light unto the nations.

"We have one problem," Surkov said, "but it can be resolved easily."

"What is the problem?"

"The PEN constitution. There would have to be some changes in it. But they could easily be accomplished."

Nat interpreted with great speed, and I almost forgot he was there, despite his size. Earlier, during our weather warm-up conversation, he had complained to me that young nothing-writers like Yevtushenko and Voznesensky flipped off a few dumb lines and were celebrated coast to coast and around the world and got to fly everywhere free while hardworking professors who had put lifetimes into mastering their fields were unknown and never got to travel anywhere—all this when I asked if he had ever visited America. It was the same worm that bored holes in the academic heart everywhere, one more universality that I hoped PEN might uncover, thereby enhancing our identifications with one another, and our sense of humor too. In that time of détente I was determined to find the good in everything. Vietnam was blasting away, we were killing ourselves there, and I needed all the hopefulness I could find.

"What changes do you have in mind?" I asked, assuming he meant the voting problem. But it was something else, he said, and looked at the carpet. My illusions began to curl up like paper in a fire. My recollection of the PEN constitution was of a total of four brief articles, each a variation on the same theme—that the writer was to be protected in his right to say what he wished, without governmental or other censorship; also, that he was bound by his membership in PEN to oppose such censorship in his own country as well as abroad. What could Surkov want to change in this crystal litany?

"But let us not worry about that now," the burly ex–wartime

tanker said. "We will come to the next congress and talk further there."

"Wait, now," I broke in, trying to keep smiling. Incredibly, his manner insinuated some kind of collaboration on my part that would end with me acting as his instrument. Why else—in a cynic's estimate, it suddenly occurred to me—would I have bothered inviting them? Surely it could not have been a desire to weaken Soviet censorship! My hopes all but totally gone, I asked now out of pure curiosity, "What kind of changes are you thinking of?"

"We can discuss these things at the congress next time."

"Very well, but you must understand that before the constitution can be changed we would . . ."

"Oh, now, Miller, you can change it." He leaned toward me over the arm of his chair with a worldly wink that clattered shut like a guillotine.

"Me?"

"If you wanted it they would do it. It is up to you."

"Well, that's very flattering, but you don't get the idea—they'll have to vote on any changes."

"Not if you tell them, Miller. If you tell them what you want them to do . . ."

"You will have to be specific. What changes are we talking about?"

"There are certain things that Soviet writers can't accept. It would be impossible."

Of course. It was all quite simple: they would never agree to mitigate censorship in Russia, much less protest it; I was as unquestionably in dictatorial control of PEN as any such leader of a Soviet organization would normally be, and they had approached me in the belief that I would help to gut the constitution and its libertarian aims. What they were after was merely the prestige of membership in a Western organization whose newly rewritten rules would no doubt continue to espouse freedom while being transformed into another justification, an international one this time, for the disciplining of their own writers.

This whole scene came back to me when, in the eighties, UNESCO introduced a new press "charter" under which governments could not be criticized and offending journalists could lose a "license" to operate. Of course I could not foretell such a horror back in the sixties, but my senses told me that Surkov was offering Soviet membership in PEN in return for its emasculation.

"I don't want you to walk into a scandal," I now warned. I felt dried up and angry and simply wanted him gone. His grandpa's smile sank away. "It will be a big step backwards if you propose what you seem to have in mind." He did not ask me what I thought that was, so it was obvious. "Better leave things as they are than blow up a new conflict between us. Maybe sometime in the future we can get together on terms we can all support, but I like the constitution as it stands, and I don't want you imagining I would help change it."

The pudding thickened then and cooled quickly. When the door had closed behind them and I stood alone again, paranoia hit me full force. Did they mean to replace PEN's charter with some code of "responsibility"—I could just see it—"of the writer to peace-loving forces," absent which said writer could be read out of PEN? I could not help going even further—was Surkov thinking to drive a wedge of Soviet "discipline" into the West, spreading the age-old Russian sludge of state control of authors into the lands of the Renaissance and the Enlightenment? In short, was their wish to join PEN a mere campaign of a disguised aggression?

Surkov had taught me a lot in a few minutes. The pity of it all was that I knew Soviet writers who despite my every doubt had pressed me to continue this kind of negotiation, hoping for a miraculous change in policy that they insisted I must encourage, no matter what the odds against it.

But anxiety dissolved as I realized that the world, in effect, was against Surkov. The wish for freedom was built into human nature, and his kind had to lose.

And once these reassurances were digested I began worrying again, but not only about Russians. The barbed questioning of the Un-American Activities Committee resurfaced. Of course they could be voted out of office, as their like in Soviet society could not be, but how could American democracy keep producing people who saw nothing illegitimate in using their tremendous powers to make outcasts of political dissidents?

Was this battle never, never to end?

The miraculous rationalism of the American Bill of Rights suddenly seemed incredible, coming as it did from man's mendacious mind. America moved me all over again—it was an amazing place, the idea of it astounding.

I have mentioned that there is a lawyer in almost all my plays—a fact of which I was not aware until a scholar wrote me and pointed it out. In the four years of my presidency of International PEN, and then over the long months of the Reilly case, I began to see that to me the idea of the law was the ultimate social reality, in the sense that physical principles are the scientist's ground—the final appeal to order, to reason, and to justice. In some primal layer Law is God's thought.

But the power this idea had in my deepest consciousness was dramatized for me most clearly long after I had finished my term as president, when I went with Inge to China for the first time in 1978. One of the first people we met there was an expatriate left-wing American lawyer who had spent more than twenty-five years as a translator in Beijing and now, faced with the recent passing of Mao and the Cultural Revolution, was trying to orient himself not only to the mysterious present and unknown future but, of necessity, to the past with its almost total destruction of the very notion of law itself.

I had thought myself reasonably informed about China by the American press and American sympathizers until it dawned on me that we had been meeting writer after writer who replied with virtually the same line whenever I asked what he was working on now: "I am not ready to start writing again—it has been so long." Why had it been so long, and why for all of them? It was perplexing.

Of course my angle on China had been laid down in the late thirties by Edgar Snow's account of the Long March and the heroism of the revolution, and so the real life of the later era had never entered my dreamworld. It was a hard shock to learn that every one of the two dozen or more writers, stage and film directors, actors, and artists we met in the first week of our stay had been either imprisoned or exiled to some distant province to feed pigs or plant rice, for as long as twelve years in some cases. Many had lost spouses to torture in those years, and they were a mere handful out of thousands.

It was all succinctly put by an English-speaking Chinese who happened to sit beside us on a train, a man who got caught in Connecticut by the outbreak of the revolution in 1949 and had been forbidden by the State Department to return until now, nearly thirty years later. A physics professor, he had come back with the resolve to reorganize the department at Beijing University.

We could not believe that there was no physics department at Beijing University, but so it was.

"The Red Guards dispersed the staff ten years ago," he said sadly.

"I am traveling around to find some of the older men who were demoted to various low-grade positions and see whether I can gather them so that they can begin to form a department." But there were hardly two hundred and fifty thousand university students left in the whole country now—fewer than on Manhattan Island, probably—and it would take some time to get things started again. "And of course the physics they know here is very much out of date. China in some fields is ten, twenty, thirty years behind the times . . ."

It was still very bad form for Westerners to report the Maoist catastrophe, but in *Chinese Encounters* I described a talk with the American lawyer in his Beijing home. I asked whether any new legal measures were contemplated to guarantee against future explosions of self-righteous (and ambitious) fanaticism masking itself as militant revolution. He did not think that necessary, although he did look a bit uneasy when he said, "The Party knows what it must do and is going to prevent it ever happening again."

But had there been a legal system independent of the Party, a nonpolitical court of appeal—might it not have saved China these decades of lost development?

I felt a mixture of compassion and disgust with him in his situation. We all protect our spiritual investments, and he had put a lifetime into a China where classes had supposedly been abolished and level equality reigned, and he could only say now—even now—"A so-called independent judiciary implies that the Party can perpetrate injustices; this implies that it is a separate ruling class imposing its will on the people. But the Party *is* the people and cannot oppress itself, and therefore there is no need for lawyers or the Western idea of a separate body of professionals to protect the innocent."

A rationalist, Marxist materialist, he was intoning a hymn of denial poetry nearly incredible now after millions of Chinese had been displaced, "put down," murdered, or jailed with almost total arbitrariness by the very Party he was ready to rely on to insure that such insanity would not recur. What ideology, I wondered, was not based on a principled denial of the facts?

Back in China again in 1983 to stage *Salesman* at the Beijing Peoples' Art Theatre, I stood in the courtyard of the building with actor-director Ying Ruocheng, my Willy, who pointed out the place where one day, more than a decade earlier, a troop of Red Guards had lined up all the dozens of actors in the company to watch as they began hectoring sixty-year-old Lao She, the famed author of many plays and novels (including one, *Rickshaw Boy,* that had been a success in America back in the early forties); cuffing him and calling him a bourgeois counterrevolutionary, they looked as though they were about to beat him severely then and there, when a passing policeman intervened, pretended to put the vile writer under arrest, took him around the corner, and let him loose. Next morning Lao She was found at the edge of a shallow pond. In his widow's opinion, they had held his head under, for his shoes were dry, but others believed he had ended his own life in total despair.

Memory keeps folding in upon itself like geologic layers of rock, the deeper strata sometimes appearing on top before they slope downward into the depths again.

Inge and I left the Gorbachev meeting for London to see two of my plays, the Royal Shakespeare Company production of *The Archbishop's Ceiling* at the Barbican Pit, and Peter Wood's of *The American Clock* at the National Theatre's Cottesloe. Despite Margaret Thatcher's budget cuts, these subsidized theatres were alive with a spirit of artistic engagement and adventure refreshingly different from the tense semi-hysteria of New York's cash-blighted fear of every shadow. *The American Clock* at the National had a live jazz band and a real crowd onstage when they were needed (already half a million dollars in costs on Broadway), and with scheduled limited runs, the whole success-flop terror was muted, lending artists psychic room to imagine and stretch before the broad British public rather than a narrow cult of initiates. As always when actors are free, the audience was swept up and into the fantasies of the play. And it didn't hurt their aesthetic pleasure that they were able to afford their tickets.

It was already over a decade since I had written *Clock,* and seeing Wood's version, I felt the happy sadness of knowing that my original impulse had been correct in this work; but as had happened more than once before, in the American production I had not had the luck to fall in with people sufficiently at ease with psychopolitical themes to set them in a theatrical style, a challenge more often tackled in the British theatre. I had described the play as a "mural" of American society in the Depression crisis, but the very word *society* is death on Broadway, and as with *The Archbishop's Ceiling,* I had hopelessly given way and reshaped a play for what I had come to think of as the Frightened Theatre. In the end, as always, I would only blame myself, but I had felt despairingly alone then and was persuaded to personalize what should have been allowed its original epic impulse, its concentration on the collapse of a society.

Both plays in England were done in their early, uncontaminated versions, more or less fresh from my desk. Both were hard-minded attempts to grasp what I felt life in the seventies had all but lost—a unified concept of human beings, the intimate psychological side joined with the social-political. To put it another way, I wanted to set us in our history by revealing a line to measure from. In *Clock* it was the objective facts of the social collapse; in *Archbishop,* the bedrock circumstances of real liberty. For what seemed to pervade almost all the arts then was a scattered, amusing, antic, taunting surrealism, but with its original post–World War I rebelliousness tamed and made chic, a form of gay naturalistic reportage of life's crazed surfaces, with no moral center. In short, it was a style of mere escape from a confrontation with our destiny, which is always tragic but always waiting to fall into pathos when shorn of social context. We had come to prize and celebrate in our art disconnection for its own sake, but this was not at all the same as tearing apart the givens of experience in order to recreate a fresh unity that would inform us newly about our lives. Our surrealism was naturalism disguised, and as incapable of projecting alternatives to what we were doing and why as naturalism had always been.

But the unity I had in mind is suspect in our theatre, where, when it does appear, it is more likely to be credited as artistic the more exotic its sources. Athol Fugard's fiercely partisan imagination and social commitment, for example, would hardly have been as welcome as it was on Broadway if his scene had been black Newark or Philadelphia or Harlem; then, lacking the romance of distance, it would have dangerously flashed the menace of its racial anger—a message that Americans, like most other people, are far more able to admire comfortably from afar than up close.

Peter Wood, who as a very young man had directed *Incident at Vichy* in London nearly twenty years before, now had his own acting group within the National, artists with whom he had a very intimate directorial connection. And rather than plunging blindly into *The American Clock,* he first asked me my feelings about how to treat this script, which after all had failed on Broadway. (More precisely, it had closed to nearly full houses a few days after opening, when the producer did not have a cent left with which to advertise its existence, such was the brutal inanity of Broadway.)

Wood's question threw me back to my initial vision of the play. What I had been after, I told him, was an epic style, like a mural. In painting, I thought of the mural as a profusion of individual images woven around a broad social or religious theme—Picasso's *Guernica*, and Rivera's work or Orozco's, or more subjectively Hieronymus Bosch's, as well as innumerable religious paintings. These often compress into one scene the Virgin, Christ, and a few saints, intermixed with the faces of the artist's patron or of his friends and enemies, and sometimes his own, all of it organized around some sublime theme of resurrection or salvation. From up close you can make out individual portraits, but they are subordinated to or swept along by the major doctrinal statement, which is overt and undisguised. In acting terms, the play should have the swift panache of vaudeville, a smiling and extroverted style, in itself an ireny when the thematic question was whether America, like all civilizations, had a clock running on it, an approaching time of weakening and death. This, of course, was the question the Great Depression raised until the Second World War solved the unemployment-consumption problem at a stroke.

"At the play's end," I said, "we should feel, along with the textures of a massive social and human tragedy, a renewed awareness of the American's improvisational strength, his almost subliminal faith that things can and must be made to work out. In a word, the feel of the energy of a democracy. But the question of ultimate survival must remain hanging unanswered in the air."

Here were two plays of mine that at home had been branded null and void; but the London theatres were packed—*The American Clock* had to be moved to the Olivier, the largest of the three National Theatres, and was nominated for the Olivier Award as best play of the season. It was significant that though the reviews had not been uniform at all, no one critic in Britain was powerful enough to lower the curtain on a show and keep it down. Within a few months the National Theatre would produce *A View from the Bridge*, directed by Alan Ayckbourn, with Michael Gambon as Eddie Carbone (it later moved to the West End), and that made three of my plays on at the same time in London, all of them originally either condemned or shrugged off in New York over the previous thirty years.

Perhaps interviewers would now stop asking what I had been doing through the seventies and start looking into whether a significant number of worthwhile American plays had been chewed up and spat out by that lethal New York combination of a single all-powerful newspaper and a visionless if not irresponsible theatre management, some sectors of which had, yes, profiteered to the point where the whole theatrical enterprise was gasping for air and near death while a handful of men grew very rich indeed.

In the sense that we lack any real awareness of a continuity with the past, we are, I think, a country without a theatre culture. I—as only one example—have gone through years when my plays were being performed in half a dozen countries but not in New York. Thus, when George Scott did *Salesman* in New York and Tony LoBianco *A View from the Bridge* on Broadway and then Dustin Hoffman *Salesman* again and Richard Kiley *All My Sons,* and a score of other major productions of my plays were mounted in and around the big cities, I seemed to have been "revived" when in fact I had only been invisible in my own land.

There are occasional painful reminders of our condition. To play Adrian, one of four fairly equal roles in the 1986 Royal Shakespeare Company production of *The Archbishop's Ceiling,* Roger Allam gave up the leading role as Javert in the monster hit *Les Misérables* because he had done it over sixty times and thought my play more challenging for him at that moment of his career. Nor did he consider his decision a particularly courageous one. This is part of what a theatre culture means, and it is something few New York actors would have the sense of security even to dream of doing. Perhaps an analogy lies in the medical culture, in which scores of researchers and practitioners simultaneously work on various lines of investigation, competing for excellence and fertilizing one another's ideas. That most of their results will not be commercially viable goes without saying, but it is equally obvious that the few great breakthroughs are all but impossible without a surrounding yeast of inquiry and false starts. The problem is not that the American theatre has no place for great plays but rather that it doesn't support good ones, the ground from which the extraordinary spring.

It seems to me now that I have always been caught between two theatres, the one that exists and the one that does not. In the early eighties, working at a long play, two one-acts for the second, ideal theatre emerged. *Elegy for a Lady* intrigued me as an attempt to write a play with multiple points of view—one for each of the characters, plus a third, that of the play—in a sense a work without the first-person angle, like the neutrality of experience itself. A man enters a boutique looking for a gift for his dying lover. The proprietress of the store is moved by his inability to decide what would be appropriate; he feels that every object she shows him will either painfully remind his lover of her coming demise or cast blame on him for not having acknowledged her and their relationship. At moments the proprietress seems actually to be the dying lover herself. A play of shadows under the tree of death. I thought it was like an Escher drawing in which water runs uphill, defying the eye's effort to trace the ordinary pull of gravity, a reminder of how our brains have created the "objective" physics of our lives.

I directed *Elegy* in a tiny space at the Long Wharf Theatre in New Haven on a double bill with *Some Kind of Love Story*, about an aging private investigator in a small town, inveigled into a case by a woman who seems both idealistically dedicated to clearing an innocent man and possibly implicated in his having been condemned. She is part whore and part challenge to his moral commitment to justice, and of course the reviver of his moribund sexuality. In both plays the objective world grows dim and distant as reality seems to consist wholly or partly of what the characters' needs require it to be, leaving them with the anguish of having to make decisions that they know are based on illusion and the power of desire.

Over the next years I would become more and more deeply absorbed by a kind of imploding of time—moments when a buried layer of experience suddenly surges upward to become the new surface of one's attention and flashes news from below. I tried to explore this process in *Danger: Memory!*, two one-act plays of the later eighties, especially in the one called *Clara*. A violent shock—Albert Kroll's discovery of his murdered daughter's body in her New York apartment-office—disarms him before the questioning of a detective investigating the case. Unavoidably, her character becomes an issue as clues to the killer's identity are sought. Kroll finds himself having to confront her idealism, which looms now as the path to her death since she persisted in working with ex–prison inmates to save them for useful lives. The likelihood is that the killer is one of these men, particularly one with whom Kroll knows she had fallen in love—a relationship he had failed to oppose despite Clara's having told him that the man had served time for murdering a former girlfriend.

Kroll, it now appears, had handed Clara some of his own early idealism as she grew up. He had lived a decent life, even a courageous one, with a certain instinct for being useful to others. He was what Whitman might have thought of as one of his "Democratic men." But in the past twenty years Kroll has changed, become like others, and as a minor executive in a construction company has had to deny to himself the shadiness of the operation. Not that he has become a bad man but simply that the ideal has flown, along with his youthful hopes for himself and his faith in people.

But in this bloodied room where his daughter died he is confronted with that ideal again. Must he disown it, suffer guilt and remorse for having misled his child? Or, despite everything, confirm the validity of the ideal and his former trust in mankind, in effect keeping faith with the best in himself, accepting the tragedy of her sacrifice to what he once again sees was and is worth everything? The play ends on his affirmation; in her catastrophe he has rediscovered himself and glimpsed the tragic collapse of values that he finally cannot bring himself to renounce.

Albert Kroll, not surprisingly to me after more than four decades of playwriting in and around New York, was understood by no one but some of the so-called second-string critics, a few television critics, three British reviewers for London papers, and the audiences that continued to pack the Lincoln Center Mitzi Newhouse Theatre despite the main critics' incomprehension of even the bare facts of the story. That Kroll might be bringing onto the stage a slice of our historical experience over the past decades since World War II was not to be noticed, apparently. Nevertheless, *Clara* evoked an unprecedented number of letters from younger playwrights; the play had indeed landed, if on a field largely unknown to the New York press. Never before had this kind of excitement been expressed to me, and it justified the whole effort. These writers understood that I had cast off absolutely every instrumentality of drama except the two essential voices of the interrogating detective and Kroll—the voice of realism and the flesh against the immortal spirit that transcends gain and loss; the death-in-life, and the life-in-death.

Down deep in His heart God is a comedian who loves to make us laugh.

In 1978, knowing I was in Paris, Jacques Huismans, head of the Belgian National Theatre, insisted I come up to Brussels for the twenty-fifth anniversary production of *The Crucible,* since it was his theatre that had been the first in Europe to put it on. Nearing the French-Belgian-border, I realized that I had left my passport in Paris but was allowed across by a forgiving douanier who loved theatre. Inge, like any good European, could not conceive how I could leave a passport behind, and I was struck by the contrast between my latterday easiness about documents and the very different emotions of twenty-five years before, when I had been forbidden by the State Department to leave my country.

At the reception in my honor, given by the consul general of our embassy, he naturally offered to be of any service during our stay in Belgium, and I asked if he could possibly issue a new passport in a day since we were planning to leave for Germany the following night. He was happy to do the favor and thought it could be ready the very next morning, an extraordinarily short time for that procedure.

When I walked through the door into his reception area the following day, the dozen or so men and women working at their desks turned and applauded. Amazed, I almost burst out laughing and thanked them, but it was the bending of time that had tickled me, for in that instant I could see myself and Monty Clift in 1954, on the day he accompanied me downtown for the passport renewal so that I could come to this selfsame Brussels for *The Crucible's* European premiere. I recalled the refusal I had been given at the end of that week by Mrs. Ruth Shipley, head of the Passport Bureau. Where was Mrs. Shipley now? Well, I was certainly here, and these embassy Americans were applauding, and *The Crucible* was alive and kicking.

The consul general came out and asked if we could talk in his office for a few minutes; with an expectant grin on his face, he said he wanted to explain his special effort in getting me the passport so quickly. A tall man in his fifties, he sat at a wide desk with the flag behind him and the gray Belgian light coming through the broad, curtained window, and told his tale.

In the McCarthy time he had also had some problems with the State Department. In fact, he had been fired from it and had had to sue to get his job back, an expensive legal proceeding that had forced him to mortgage his family home and scratch around for a living for six years, so tough had it been to land a responsible position after being canned by the government.

Refused any explanation for his separation from the Foreign Service, he had finally forced a departmental hearing and there learned the reason. His first post in the service had been Cairo, and as a young unmarried man he had shared an apartment with another young Foreign Service officer who turned out to be a homosexual. This meant that he, the consul general, must also have been homosexual. The fact that the department itself had given him the list of apartments available for sharing did not count at all, not while Joe McCarthy and Roy Cohn, himself a closet homosexual, of course, were baying at the moon against "perversion" in the State Department.

The hearing officer was Graham Martin, a tough right-wing character who would later become our last ambassador to South Vietnam, supervisor of the frantic evacuation of the Saigon embassy. He had turned to Scott McLeod, the man in charge of security in the department and the consul general's chief nemesis, and asked him if that was the extent of his evidence of unreliability. McLeod confidently replied that it was. Martin then and there ordered the consul general restored to his rank with back pay plus interest.

The consul general grinned with pleasure as we shook hands and parted. "I just thought you'd like to know why I was especially pleased to hurry your passport," he said. I felt good to have lived this long.

Glamour is a youth's form of blindness that lets in light, incoherent color, but nothing defined. Like the rainbow, it is a once uplifting vision that moves away the closer you come to it.

My father, on the other hand, got more glamour-struck the older he became. He loved to stand in front of a theatre where a play of mine was on and every once in a while stroll in to chat with the box office men about business. "How do you know they're giving you the right count?" he would ask me. Indeed, how did I?

In 1962, after our divorce, Marilyn took him as her escort to John Kennedy's birthday party in Madison Square Garden and introduced him to the president. My father would treasure a news photographer's picture of the occasion: Marilyn stands laughing with her head thrown back while Kennedy shakes hands with him, laughing with spontaneous, innocent enjoyment at what I am sure must have been one of my father's surprising remarks. I was not aware that for the rest of his life, which lasted some four more years, he spent considerable time on the lookout for his name in the gossip columns and entertainment news, until one day he gravely asked me—he was about eighty then—"Do you look like me or do I look like you?"

This was serious. "I guess I look like you," I said. He seemed to like that answer.

How strange it was—not only had I competed with him but he with me. And the fact that this vaguely disappointed me signaled that even now I saw him partly shrouded in his myth.

He was an American and saw all things competitively. Once our old basset, Hugo, an immense dog whose incontinence was matched only by his lassitude, rose like a senator from one of his naps and unaccountably attacked a rag doll, throwing it up in the air and growling menacingly at it and charging at it again and again until he settled down once more into his habitual torpor with one ear covering his eyes. My father had watched in surprise all this uncustomary activity and then said, "Well . . . everybody has to be better than somebody."

In his last years my father would sit on the porch of the Long Island nursing home wearing a crumpled white linen cap and looking out on the sea, and between long silences he would speak. "You know, sometimes I see a little dot way out there, and then it gets bigger and bigger and finally turns into a ship." I explained that the earth was a sphere and so forth. In his eighty years he had never had time to sit and watch the sea. He had employed hundreds of people and made tens of thousands of coats and shipped them to towns and cities all over the States, and now at the end he looked out over the sea and said with happy surprise, "Oh. So it's round!"

He died the day I was to make the opening speech at the 1966 New York PEN Congress. My mother had died five years before, and I had only felt the shock of grief for her when suddenly, looking up at the coffin and hearing the voice of Rabbi Miller—no relation, an old, bent man whom I had known in my youth but had not seen since some other funeral two decades ago—I was surprised by the simple, lucid tenderness of his voice, his nearly cheerful calm as he seemed really to believe he was sending her off. Unexpected tears moved up into my eyes as I imagined her a young woman in that casket—a life of expectations and pride in her children, but not in herself. I wished I had felt freer to acknowledge my love for her, but I was so much the incarnation of her own thwarted ambitions that the knowledge cramped any open flow of feeling. Our relation was unfinished, and her death too soon.

Despite my father's death I decided to go ahead with my PEN speech, and it surprised me, in a remote way, that I could do this. But I felt uplifted by what was clearly a new life being born around me in this congress, here in one of the most perfect spring weeks I had ever seen in New York. It was not only that many of the greatest writers in the world had come but that they showed such a serious desire to confront real issues, primarily the defense of culture. For the first time in my experience it was no longer a simple question of left and right. The Cold War was far from being over, but with amazing unanimity writers of the most conflicting political commitments refused to reduce to polemics what turned out to be really informative discussions about the conditions of writers and publishing in every kind of society.

The novelist Valery Tarsis, who had not long before left Russia after being psychologically tortured in an institution, stood on the platform, declared the Cold War ineffective, and demanded the atom bombing of the Soviet Union. The audience was stunned at first, but when as chair I condemned the speech as outrageous, both in content and as a violation of PEN's purposes, there was heartening applause from all sides, and the anti-Communist Writers-in-Exile Center itself quickly and strongly disowned the speech. The step I had once vaguely hoped for, way back in my first talk with Carver in Inge's apartment, had been taken, and real life rather than sterile ideological combat was on the agenda.

I thought the most encouraging and useful session was the unprogrammed one among the Latin American writers. I had noticed that they were gathering in knots in corridors and at the backs of the rooms during formal sessions, to whisper excitedly in Spanish and embrace like newfound friends. Many of them lived a few hundred miles from each other but had never had the money to travel, and here in New York they were meeting for the first time, by virtue of funds especially raised for this purpose by the American Center.

Lewis Galantière, a translator, and Jules Isaacs, a lawyer who gave PEN much of his time simply out of a bemused enjoyment of writers' insanities, had managed to get the State Department to lower its ban (which did not yet include ex-Nazis) on "political undesirables" entering the country, and a genuine cross section of Latin American writers was present (except for the Cubans, who pretended that their invitation had arrived too late for them to attend, an awkward fabrication that nevertheless allowed them to condemn Neruda later as a sellout to imperialism—an attack upon his honor that, as his memoirs attest, he never forgave them).

I suggested that we open a special Latin American mini-congress to be held on the spot, and they quickly and excitedly gathered in one of the public rooms of the Gramercy Park Hotel. The great explosion of Latin American novel writing had not yet detonated over the American and European consciousness, but one could sense among them a kind of ravening appetite for the oncoming future that each of them, albeit from different countries of varying social conditions, seemed to anticipate they would all share. From Peruvian Mario Vargas Llosa in the middle to Argentine Victoria Ocampo on the right and Carlos Fuentes of Mexico on the left, the panorama opened out upon a literary viewpoint that to me, since I had always believed in it for myself, seemed coherent and vital and promising. In a word, literature had to speak to the present condition of man's life and thus would implicitly have to stand against injustice as the destroyer of life. The congress's theme, "The Writer as Independent Spirit," naturally raised the question of the "pure" versus the "committed" writer, or, as Fuentes put it, Mallarmé or Dickens. But this was a meaningless distinction in Latin America (I thought it was in the United States, too), because a Neruda or a Borges, a Carpentier or an Asturias, an Octavio Paz or a Cortázar, all contributed to the same defense through their commitment to the life of the spirit and its free evolution. Two days before, in my speech opening the congress, I had inadvertently stumbled upon a different version of the same thought: that the basis of our mutual toleration lay "in the knowledge that men in one country are in a different situation than men in another country," and therefore one had to ask deeper and broader questions of writers and literature than any political formulas could ever supply. As an example, I repeated an idea I had broached in London for an annual international day to remind ourselves of the hundreds of writers in prisons all over the world.

For by this time I was certain that PEN had to be the conscience of the world writing community. In fact, I had to suppress the pride I felt now that it was the American writers who had seized the idea and with our far greater solvency and incurable idealism might be the ones capable of putting it on the map. If PEN had ever been an inconsequential literary club, it wasn't one anymore.

The very presence here in the same meeting of such a variety of opinions was already creating new illuminations. Neruda, the great tree of Latin American poetry, who had been my introduction to Latin American writing back in the thirties, had arrived with a certain defensiveness, knowing that we had had to arrange a special permission for his entry into the country. But he was quickly swamped with invitations to read, and did so twice at the Ninety-second Street Y, and made a commercial recording besides. In Dauber and Pine's bookshop on lower Fifth Avenue he spent hours buying up all they had by and about Whitman, and also Shakespeare's sonnets. When he opened a book to read, his eyebrows rose and he looked like a jungle bird, an immense, roundheaded parrot. His warmth toward New York and America, despite his opposition to our Latin American policies, was palpable.

Roaming the Village with him and Inge, I was baffled now more than ever how a man of such all-embracing spirit could continue to countenance Stalinism. I could only think that once again the depth of alienation from bourgeois society had locked a man into a misconceived, nearly religious loyalty to the dream Russia of the believing thirties, a country whose sheer human reality he felt it dishonorable to acknowledge. But of course it was also that American foreign policy was so systematically defending right-wing dictatorships as to leave all but the most timid local reformers with no models and no support but the Soviet ones.

By the time of the congress I had received many a telegram like the one from London saying that a Wole Soyinka, a Nigerian writer whose name I barely knew, was in danger of execution. Apparently he had taken it on himself to carry communications between breakaway Biafrans and people within the Nigerian government who were trying to negotiate a peaceful settlement of the dreadful civil war. Would I quickly send some sort of message to General Gowon, who headed the soon-to-be-victorious army of the Nigerian government, asking mercy for Soyinka?

David Carver in London knew a British businessman named Davies who was just leaving for Nigeria and could get my message to the general. Gowon, on seeing my name, asked Davies with some incredulity whether I was the writer who had been married to Marilyn Monroe and, assured that this was so, ordered Soyinka released. How Marilyn would have enjoyed that one!

Another writer, Fernando Arrabal, a Spaniard living in Paris in exile from Franco Spain, had returned to Madrid to see one of his plays and made the mistake of signing one of his books with a dirty pun on Franco's name. When, incredibly enough, he was about to be sentenced to several years in jail for this affront to El Caudillo, his friends cabled me that the judge was an aficionado of the theatre and might be influenced by a message from me. *Death of a Salesman*, for one, had played a long time in Madrid. My cable assured his honor that Arrabal was a playwright of the first importance and an old favorite of mine, wherewith the judge allowed that as a man of such noteworthy talent Arrabal could get out of Spain forthwith on his promise never to return.

And so I began using what credit I had won for such purposes—in Lithuania, South Africa, Czechoslovakia, Latin American countries, the Soviet Union, Korea, and on more than one censoring school board closer to home, in Illinois and Texas and other states. PEN was now the good right arm its founders had dreamed it might one day become.

For three days we went out and climbed the hillside, planting the hundreds of seedlings out of the pail, and finally, with some help, six thousand of them. Inge, pregnant then but hardly showing it—she would be photographing from a high crane in the Brooklyn Navy Yard four hours before the labor pains began—carefully set roots in the slits I was cutting with a flat spade. From the middle of Europe she has brought this reverence for the consecration of such moments in life when the consciousness of time's flow is supreme. And twenty-five years later our ankle-high seedlings are dense sixty-foot trees with stems thicker than telephone poles, and Rebecca is a young woman, a painter and actress, and her brother Robert is working in film in California, and her sister Jane is a weaver and busy sculptor's wife, and I have heard the word "Grandpa!" from a girl of three, a boy of ten, and a girl of fifteen, Bob's kids.

There was no denying the resistance to that word—my God, I had hardly begun! What are these small persons doing on my lap lovingly repeating that terrible accusation with all its finality? How confidently they imagine I am Grandpa. And this makes me wonder who I imagine I am.

And then the pleasure of growing accustomed to it and even getting to where I can call it into a phone—"Hello? This is Grandpa!"—as though I am not an impersonator trying to show some kind of fatuous procreative accomplishment.

The shocks are there but feel more distant. At a recent town meeting in the high school on the nuclear freeze issue, people standing up to make their comments had stated their names and the number of years they had lived here: "John Smith; I've lived here seven years," as though this gave their opinions more authority. The longest period of residence was around twelve years, except for one young woman whose family had settled here in 1680. I felt a slight unwillingness to announce that I had lived here forty years. Heads turned. I was the old man. Okay, but who was I?

I have lived more than half my life in the Connecticut country-side, all the time expecting to get some play or book finished so I can spend more time in the city, where everything is happening. There is something about this forty-year temporary residence that strikes me funny now. If only we could stop murdering one another we could be a wonderfully humorous species. My contentment discontents me when I know that little happens here that I don't make happen, except the sun coming up and going down and the leaves emerging and dropping off and an occasional surprise like the recent appearance of coyotes in the woods. There is more unbroken forest from Canada down to here than there was even in Lincoln's youth, the farms having gradually vanished, and there is even the odd bear, they say, a wanderer down from the north, and now these coyotes. I have seen them. They have a fixed smug grin, as though they just stole something. And they cannot be mistaken for dogs, whom they otherwise resemble, because of their eyes, which look at you with a blue guilt but no conscience, a mixture of calculation and defensive distrust that domestication cured in dogs thousands of years ago.

And so the coyotes are out there earnestly trying to arrange their lives to make more coyotes possible, not knowing that it is my forest, of course. And I am in this room from which I can sometimes look out at dusk and see them warily moving through the barren winter trees, and I am, I suppose, doing what they are doing, making myself possible and those who come after me. At such moments I do not know whose land this is that I own, or whose bed I sleep in. In the darkness out there they see my light and pause, muzzles lifted, wondering who I am and what I am doing here in this cabin under my light. I am a mystery to them until they tire of it and move on, but the truth, the first truth, probably, is that we are all connected, watching one another. Even the trees.

INDEX